D1317873

The Diaries of a Cabinet Minister

also by Richard Crossman

PLATO TODAY
SOCRATES
GOVERNMENT AND THE GOVERNED
HOW WE ARE GOVERNED
PALESTINE MISSION
THE GOD THAT FAILED (editor)
NEW FABIAN ESSAYS (editor)
THE CHARM OF POLITICS
A NATION REBORN
PLANNING FOR FREEDOM
INSIDE VIEW: Three Lectures on Prime Ministerial Government
THE DIARIES OF A CABINET MINISTER
(Volume I: Minister of Housing 1964–1966)
(Volume II: Lord President of the Council and Leader of the House of Commons 1966–1968)

RICHARD CROSSMAN

THE DIARIES OF A CABINET MINISTER

Volume Three

Secretary of State for Social Services
1968–70

HAMISH HAMILTON
and
JONATHAN CAPE

FIRST PUBLISHED 1977

HAMISH HAMILTON LTD, 90 GREAT RUSSELL STREET, LONDON WC1
JONATHAN CAPE LTD, 30 BEDFORD SQUARE, LONDON WC1

BRITISH LIBRARY CATALOGUING IN PUBLICATION DATA
CROSSMAN, RICHARD HOWARD STAFFORD
THE DIARIES OF A CABINET MINISTER
VOL. 3. SECRETARY OF STATE FOR SOCIAL SERVICES, 1968–70
1. GREAT BRITAIN — HISTORY — 20TH CENTURY
2. GREAT BRITAIN — POLITICS AND GOVERNMENT — 1964
941.085'6'0924 DA 592
ISBN 0-241-89482-4
ISBN 0-224-01492-7

SET IN 10 PT. TIMES NEW ROMAN 2 PTS. LEADED
PRINTED IN GREAT BRITAIN
BY EBENEZER BAYLIS AND SON LTD
THE TRINITY PRESS, WORCESTER, AND LONDON

Contents

Illustrations

Editor's Note

This third and last volume of Richard Crossman's *Diaries of a Cabinet Minister* is in an important respect different from the first two. In Volume I, which runs from October 1964 to August 1966, the period that he spent as Minister of Housing and Local Government, and Volume II, August 1966 to April 1968, describing his time as Lord President and Leader of the House of Commons, Crossman was himself responsible for rearranging and revising his original dictated text. In the last weeks before his death, on April 5th 1974, Crossman began work on Volume III but he prepared only a first draft for the months April to October 1968. I have finished this task.

Crossman explained in his Introduction to Volume I that his original tape-recorded diary was 'dictated very much *ad lib* and often for two or three hours on end . . . when transcribed it was hardly readable.' He decided to redictate 'this whole first transcript in plain intelligible English', with, as his criteria, clarity and relevance. He also edited passages that seemed libellous or in bad taste. But, as he himself declared, much of the special historical value of the Diaries derives from their being 'dictated while the memory was still hot and uncorrupted by "improvements" ' and he sought to reassure his readers that the text which he had prepared for publication, though entirely redictated, nevertheless remained faithful to the unrehearsed account which he had set down between 1964 and 1970. I was therefore asked to check the revised draft against the original transcription, to ensure that the content, mood and balance of the original were accurately preserved. Thus for Volumes I and II I was a referee. But in this last volume the responsibility for selecting, rearranging and, often, interpreting the original material has fallen to me. The referee now doubles as a player and for this reason it is important to explain the methods I have used and the principles I have followed in preparing this text.

I found manifold problems, of which the most immediate were of three main types: chronological, technical and stylistic. More fundamental and difficult questions of interpretation also arose. First, chronology. The Diaries were dictated at weekly intervals and an entry generally begins with a reflective passage, surveying trends or summarizing the events of the past week, before the diarist settles down to describe each ministerial day. The account does not always fall in strict chronological order – a story that begins early in the week is, for instance, frequently taken to its conclusion some days later, or, contrariwise, another story may involve flashbacks to episodes that have been omitted hitherto. Other passages repeat accounts from previous weeks.

A dictated diary presents technical problems too and in this case both the original diary and my own second draft were tape-recorded and then transcribed. The typist who is responsible for turning the spoken into the written word may find it hard to distinguish words and phrases, 'fifteen' for 'fifty', for example, or 'Crosland' for 'Crossman', and less familiar expressions and names may give even greater difficulty. Usually a brave attempt has been made at deciphering; elsewhere there are gaps and occasionally the dictation machine has broken down altogether. Moreover, as the account passes through its successive forms, human error intervenes. Diarist or transcriber may inadvertently insert an extra 'not'; a superfluous zero, inappropriately placed quotation marks or other misleading punctuation may intrude. Nor can a typed transcript, however accurate, convey the tone of voice, emphasis, inflection or nuance of the original spoken word. Some of these difficulties can be resolved by listening to the actual tapes; fortunately the recordings for the period covered by this volume survive.

Stylistic problems came as no surprise. The original diary is a raw draft and, while Crossman wrote and argued brilliantly, even he did not dictate finished sentences into the microphone. In his own preface he drew attention to this. For instance, searching for the right adjective or phrase, he would try a number of alternatives; anxious to press on with the narrative, he would leave tantalizing loose constructions and sometimes he was just tired and, consequently, verbose. In his most interesting, relaxed moments the material he produced is very much a 'stream of consciousness'.

I discovered that in solving such problems intuition and common sense were as useful as academic study, particularly since I wished to edit Crossman's material as he would have done himself. Questions of chronology were the most straightforward. I have followed Crossman's own method of rearranging the Diaries, as he instructed me to do. Each weekly chunk has been unravelled to make a day by day account of events; the reflective passages have been restored to the Saturday or Sunday at the end of the week, when Crossman originally formulated them. Like Crossman, I have not only put each entry in daily order; I have unstitched the entire text. Crossman redrafted Volumes I and II by fitting together entire paragraphs, single sentences and phrases from his original account, cutting out superfluous or repetitive material and supplying omissions. I followed his practice.

Technical error was harder to deal with, largely because it is not always evident. I have been able to discover and alter many mistranscriptions of words that sound alike or nearly alike, to sort out obvious confusions and fill in some brief gaps. Where I remain baffled, a footnote tells the reader.

Crossman's style was personal and inimitable and I felt that his editor should intervene as inconspicuously as possible. Where Crossman tried out successive words and phrases I have pruned what appeared to be his bosh shots. I have also completed sentences, disentangled metaphors and corrected the grammar so that the account reads smoothly but retains the appropriate colloquialisms. Of course in some places major textual surgery has been essential. National superannuation and health service reform, for example, are complex subjects, which Crossman knew extremely well but his readers may not. It would have been clumsy to use footnotes to expand his allusions and elucidate his points and the reader might find this tedious. In such cases I have made substantial clarifications.

Finally, interpretation. This was the most challenging aspect of the editorial exercise. I have not tried to interpret every ambiguity in the original draft. Here and there Crossman was himself unclear about the details of policy or the arguments for it, while at other times he was deliberately vague. The interest and value of the Diaries comes partly from the fact that they reflect the blur as well as the lucidity of a mind at work and I would not wish to tidy Crossman's text so thoroughly that we lose this sense of eavesdropping as he thinks aloud. I have often edited the text to reveal Crossman's meaning but I have tried to indicate where he is puzzled himself, either because he misunderstands or has been misled.

It is not easy to describe these editorial difficulties nor the process and method of their solution. Readers who are interested in close textual comparison will in due course find the full, unedited version of Crossman's Diaries at the University of Warwick. The original diary is very long; the editing process which I have described has considerably reduced its length, and to roughly the same proportion of the original as the two volumes which preceded this one. A few unimportant happenings have been omitted, for reasons of space, but otherwise every incident which Crossman recorded figures here. This book is certainly massive, but so it must be if, as Crossman wished, it is to be an unexpurgated source, to convey 'a daily picture of how a Minister in the Wilson Government spent his time' and to demonstrate, perhaps at the cost of some reiteration, what his preoccupations were.

The editorial method which Crossman and I adopted had its disadvantages, but it has allowed us to fulfil the diarist's wish to publish as soon as possible, 'so that controversy could take place while memories are still green' and to provide, quickly, material for public enlightenment and academic debate. For this reason, too, and because Crossman wanted the Diaries to present an unvarnished picture of facts, personalities and opinions as he perceived them at the time, I have not sought to correct all factual slips and inaccuracies in his text. These are bound to occur in a diary, especially one that is dictated at weekly intervals, and a definitive check of his recollection of every meeting and every encounter would have taken many more years. Moreover, the necessary documentary evidence is not always available. Official papers, including Cabinet minutes, are closed to historians for a period of thirty years after the events they record. As a former Minister, Crossman was permitted to consult the documents concerning his own period of office and the text of Volume I was checked against Cabinet minutes, just before his death. Volumes II and III must remain unchecked until the years 1998 and 2000, as the Cabinet Office refused to extend this access to his editor.

Again, we agreed that annotation should be kept to a minimum. The asterisked notes are Crossman's; I am responsible for the other footnotes and the bridging passages. An appendix gives brief biographies of persons who were important to Crossman during the period covered by this volume; where necessary, other people are identified in notes at the foot of the page where they are first mentioned.

There may be drawbacks to the way in which we have chosen to revise and present Richard Crossman's Diaries. The overwhelming advantage, however, of preparing these volumes as we have done is that, as Crossman hoped, we have been able to publish within a reasonable time a lucid and intricate account of a Cabinet Minister's daily life and his part in contemporary politics.

JANET MORGAN

1968

In the three and a half years since their victory at the 1964 General Election the Labour Government had struggled to keep to their programme of socialist measures, a commitment that was exceptionally difficult when national economic growth was feeble, productivity low, exports poor, industrial strikes and stoppages frequent and the strength of the pound doubtful. Some had believed that devaluation of sterling and drastic cuts in Britain's overseas defence commitments would alleviate these troubles and, eventually, those remedies were tried in late 1967. On November 18th, 1967, after speculative rumours had caused a massive loss to the reserves, the Chancellor of the Exchequer, James Callaghan, announced that sterling had been devalued by 14·3 per cent, from $2·80 to $2·40 to the pound.

On November 30th Mr Callaghan moved to the Home Office, and Roy Jenkins, who had been Home Secretary, became Chancellor.[1] *After a fundamental review of Government expenditure, a programme of post-devaluation cuts was announced by the Prime Minister on January 2nd, 1968. Defence spending was reduced by £110 million for 1969/70 and between £210 and £260 million by 1972/3, and the proposed savings included the withdrawal by the end of 1971 of all British forces in the Persian Gulf and the Far East, except for Hong Kong, the phasing out after 1971 of the Royal Navy's aircraft carriers, and the saving over the next nine years of a further £400 million by the cancellation of an order for fifty American F-111 strike aircraft.*

The domestic cuts included reductions of the road and housing programmes, increased weekly national insurance contributions, the deferment of the raising of the school-leaving age, and the introduction of higher dental charges and charges for N.H.S. prescriptions, with a system of exemptions for certain special categories. In all, Government expenditure was to be cut by £716 million over the next two years.

Sterling strengthened at first but by February the visible trade deficit had increased from £35 million in January to £70 million, with imports at record level of £664 million, and in early March a speculative rush into gold had a major effect on the dollar and on sterling. The Governors of the Central Banks of the United States, Britain and five West European countries were determined to keep the official gold price at $35 an ounce and, while at their request the British Government closed the London Gold Market from March 15th to April 1st, the international bankers made arrangements to safeguard the international monetary system. These included further support for sterling against speculation and the standby credits available to Britain were increased to $4,000 million (£1,666 million). These events, as well as devaluation, dominated the budget which Mr Jenkins presented on March 19th. He announced increased taxation of more than £923 million, all of it indirect, except for a special levy on personal investment incomes of £2,000 a year or more. The Chancellor intended to establish an eventual balance-of-payments surplus of £500 million a year,

[1] For the full Cabinet list see p. 955.

and the necessary structural changes in the economy would, he said, require 'two years of hard slog'.

Britain's difficulties had also brought the Government to a more favourable attitude towards membership of the European Economic Community, and in the autumn of 1967 she submitted to the European Commission her application to join the other six members. On November 27th General de Gaulle announced in Paris that France was not prepared to begin a negotiation with Britain, whose unstable economy would put the Community at risk. Although the other five members unanimously supported the British application, they did not wish to jeopardize the Community by challenging France, so, in mid-December 1967, the British attempt once more foundered on the opposition of de Gaulle. The Government announced that talks would be held with the other five E.E.C. countries and, possibly, agreements made, but meanwhile it was to domestic measures that Britain must look for recovery.

These included prices and incomes legislation, and on April 3rd the Government published a White Paper outlining the measure that was to replace the 1967 Prices and Incomes Act when it expired in August. The new Bill extended the Government's power to delay price or wage increases from seven to twelve months and gave the Government power to limit rent and dividend increases and to order price reductions recommended by the National Board for Prices and Incomes. A 3½ per cent ceiling was imposed on wage and salary increases but this could be exceeded where there had been a genuine rise in productivity. The Government's powers were to last until December 31st, 1969, and, as in the 1967 Act, they sought from both sides of industry voluntary obedience to the policy, with the compulsory powers held in reserve.

Responsibility for administering the policy fell upon Barbara Castle, Secretary of State for Employment and Productivity and Michael Stewart's successor as First Secretary of State. (Mr Stewart had replaced George Brown at the Foreign Office, after Mr Brown had resigned the Foreign Secretaryship, but not the elected office of Deputy Leader of the Party, on March 16th, during the gold crisis.) Mrs Castle's new appointment was announced on April 5th as part of a Cabinet reshuffle. Ray Gunter, her predecessor at the Ministry of Labour, became Minister of Power, replacing Richard Marsh, who succeeded Mrs Castle as Minister of Transport. Patrick Gordon Walker resigned from the Government and Edward Short replaced him at the Ministry of Education. George Thomas became Secretary of State for Wales, succeeding Cledwyn Hughes, who was moved to Agriculture. Fred Peart, Mr Hughes's predecessor, took Richard Crossman's place as Leader of the House of Commons, while Mr Crossman remained Lord President of the Council.

Mr Crossman's new duties were to co-ordinate the Ministries of Health and Social Security, which were to be reorganized and merged into one giant Department. He also undertook to complete the work on a national superannuation scheme which he had begun in 1957 and to introduce the necessary legislation. In addition, Mr Crossman remained a member of the Inter-Party

Conference which had been meeting since November 1967 to devise an agreed scheme for the reform of the House of Lords. He also retained the room he had furnished and it was from this base in the Privy Council Office that he set out to co-ordinate two separate Departments, the Ministry of Social Security at the Adelphi and the Ministry of Health at the Elephant and Castle.

Monday, April 22nd

I made my first visit to the collection of huge modern glass blocks that was custom-built for the Ministry of Health at the Elephant and Castle. It is on a ghastly site and Kenneth Robinson told me they chose it for its cheapness. It cost only half as much as normal sites for government buildings but a great deal of the money they saved is now being spent on air-conditioning and double-glazing because the building stands right on top of an underground railway which makes the most dreadful din. It's also appallingly inconvenient because, though it's only three-quarters of a mile from Westminster and though from his room at the top of the twelve-storey block the Minister can see the House of Commons, he may take anything from three to twenty minutes to get there through the traffic. It was hoped that one effect of planking the building down there would be to improve the area and attract other government buildings. It hasn't happened and the Ministry stands isolated and terrible.

I had a quiet talk with Kenneth, Sir Clifford Jarrett, his Permanent Secretary, and one or two other officials. Whatever they think of the merger, the civil servants were not unfriendly and I had little to complain of in this first contact. I had one or two questions about the exemption scheme for prescription charges, which are now certain to come into force on June 10th.[1] The other big political problem is that the doctors have been turned down in their demand for an increase of pay by the Kindersley Committee,[2] but this is a crisis I shall certainly leave to Mr Robinson.

[1] The principle of a free National Health Service had always been important to the Labour Party: in April 1951, Aneurin Bevan, former Minister of Health, Harold Wilson and John Freeman had resigned from the Government over the proposal of Hugh Gaitskell, Chancellor of the Exchequer, to introduce a charge for teeth and spectacles. These charges were retained and a prescription charge of 2*s*. was introduced by the 1951–5 Conservative Government, to be doubled in 1961, despite vehement attacks from the Labour Opposition. As soon as Labour came to power in October 1964, prescription charges were abolished in the November budget, but, to the horror of the left wing, the cuts in Government expenditure announced by the Prime Minister in January 1968 included the proposal for a charge of 2*s*. per item for N.H.S. prescriptions (as well as a rise in dental charges from £1 to £1 10*s*.). Kenneth Robinson had been struggling to devise a system of exemptions for the chronic sick, children, pensioners and expectant mothers. See Vol. II, p. 637 ff.

[2] Lord Kindersley, who had succeeded to his father's barony in 1954, was the Chairman of the official Review Body on Doctors' and Dentists' Remuneration from 1962 to 1970. He was a director of the Bank of England 1947–67, Managing Director of Lazard Brothers & Co. Ltd 1927–64 (Chairman 1953–64) and a director 1965–71, and then Chairman of Rolls-Royce Ltd 1956–68, and of Guardian Royal Exchange Assurance Ltd 1968–9. He died in 1976.

In their evidence to the Review Body, the representatives of the G.P.s had claimed an

The children were up in London for a few days of the Easter holiday and I had agreed to spend the afternoon at the Zoo. It was a miserable day of drizzle but we got through three hours fairly satisfactorily. We saw the new polar bear baby and the world's tiniest deer, more like a beetle, and then slogged round the other compounds in trying thundery weather before we finally returned home and got down to our reading aloud. Just when I'd started I was told that I had to be at No. 10 at 7 o'clock.

When I got there I found myself ushered in for a drink with the P.M. in Marcia's little room,[1] and there was Harold with Fred Peart, who was off in high spirits to a farewell dinner at the N.F.U. When Peart had gone, Harold waited a minute or two and then said to me, 'I want to ask you a question, Dick. Did you give Auberon Waugh the material for his article in the *Spectator*?'[2] I had only glanced at the article, the usual kind of political gossip, and had noticed that it ended with a description of Roy Jenkins, Barbara Castle and me getting together. Of course I've talked to one or two people about our new collaboration and I've said that the only sensible way to make things work is for we three to get together as the nucleus of the P.M.'s inner Cabinet. It might well include Michael Stewart. So I told Harold that I had only glanced at the article and, though I strongly support some of the views in it, I hadn't given the material to Auberon Waugh. On one occasion Waugh had accused me of being leaky and I hadn't spoken to him since. 'I wish you hadn't told me this,' Harold said, 'because if you didn't give it to him there is only one other person who did, in view of what you told me the other night about your talks with Roy Jenkins.' I think I've reported in this diary that I told Harold that Roy, Barbara and I thought it would be useful to dine together.[3] Did he mean that my statement convicted Roy of this leak? It seemed to me utterly depressing that the Prime Minister was more concerned with looking for leaks than with organizing his Cabinet and that he'd felt it important enough to call me specially over for a drink and a talk about it.

Then I asked him if I could bring the children in. Patrick had said he was being laughed at at school because he had never seen the Prime Minister so I had told the children to come along with Anne. In they came but there is nothing really to see in No. 10 and Harold found it curiously difficult to talk to them. So I took them off to the Private Secretaries' room next door where there's more to see, including lights which switch on and off and clocks timed for Washington and Moscow, and left Anne alone with Harold.

---

increase of 8 per cent in net remuneration, including a minimum 10 per cent increase in practice expenses. In their Report, Cmnd 3600, published in May 1968, the Kindersley Committee were to recommend that there should be no general increase, only an increase in basic and supplementary practice allowances of £1,100 and £220 per annum respectively.

[1] Marcia Williams.

[2] Political Correspondent of the *Spectator* 1967–70 and since 1976.

[3] See Vol. II, p. 787.

Apparently he talked to her entirely about the vitally important job I was to do in my new Department and what a wonderful assignment I'd got. We got out after about forty minutes and had a splendid dinner in a fish restaurant at Charing Cross.

Tuesday, April 23rd

I spent the first part of the morning with Burke Trend, preparing my work as co-ordinating Minister, and listing all the Cabinet Committees I have to chair or to serve on. Burke said he'd never known Harold more difficult, uncommunicative and wrapped up in himself than he is now; or more suspicious of his colleagues, I added. I went on to tell Burke very frankly my ideas for an inner group and the hopelessness of getting Harold to allow it, and if Harold wouldn't do it, I said, we must do it ourselves so I am arranging an evening with Roy and Barbara this week. I was aware that this would be passed on to Harold and I thought that would be a good thing.

Back in my office I spent the rest of the morning discussing our new co-ordinating staff with dear Paul Odgers. All round me now there's the sense of a new office growing up. Odgers is a very professional civil servant, who's tremendously skilled at swelling the size of our staff, and he's also busily acquiring office accommodation all around the Privy Council. I've already referred in this diary to the trouble it takes to go the 120 yards from my office through the back passages into No. 10. First my Secretary has to provide the key which unlocks the back door of the Privy Council and lets me in to the Cabinet Office. Then a senior official of the Cabinet Office has to be fetched with the key to open the next door at the head of the staircase down to No. 10. I have constantly complained to Burke that this double barrier is an infernal waste of quite important people's time and asked him how many thousand pounds a week it costs to have this endless dislocation every time a Minister passes through. Civil servants are allowed keys; I'm not. It shows you how Whitehall is run for the convenience of civil servants and not for the Ministers who are supposed to be in command, but Paul Odgers has now pierced through the barred doors.

I went into the House to listen to the Prime Minister's Questions, where the Tories were prising out of him the admission that he had abandoned his control of D.E.A.[1] Harold had announced this by means of a Written Answer, and when Peyton nudged him he repeated testily that he didn't advertise that kind of thing.[2] He loses a lot of credit by this kind of deviousness. It would

[1] On August 29th, 1967, Peter Shore had succeeded Michael Stewart at the D.E.A., with the Prime Minister assuming overall responsibility for the Department, but in April 1968 Peter Shore was given sole charge of the portfolio. The Department was henceforth to concentrate on the general allocation of real resources, investment, export policy and import replacement, and on co-ordinating the work of the industrial departments.

[2] John Peyton, Conservative M.P. for Yeovil since 1951. He was Parliamentary Secretary at the Ministry of Power 1962–4, Minister of Transport June–October 1970, and Minister for Transport Industries at the D.O.E. 1970–4.

have been far wiser to announce the change candidly rather than have it extracted from him.

Wedgy Benn made a much more cheerful impression when he announced our abandonment of ELDO [European Launcher Development Organization] and ESRO [European Space Research Organization] and those other futile space projects.[1] The announcement went like clockwork, and none of the difficulties anticipated by the Foreign Office materialized. This is a really successful action for which unfortunately we shan't get full credit, thanks to the F.O.

After that we came to the big debate on the Second Reading of the Race Relations Bill.[2] The first part of Jim's[3] speech, where he outlined his philosophy, was done in a decent, unassuming way, which was very successful precisely because it was straightforward and completely bipartisan. Then up rose Quintin Hogg and made one of the most statesmanlike speeches I've ever heard, transforming the whole party situation. If he hadn't made this speech and we'd just been left with the attitude adopted towards Enoch Powell by Heath and Maudling,[4] bipartisanship might well have broken down

[1] The Minister of Technology announced that there was no justification for further financial contribution to the development of the ELDO launcher, beyond Britain's original commitment of support until 1971. She would support an average increase of no more than 6 per cent in the 1968 ESRO budget of 250 million francs. Crossman suspected that the Government's alternative proposal for a European Centre for Technology was stimulated by Foreign Office eagerness for British participation in the E.E.C.

[2] The Bill made it unlawful to discriminate, on grounds of colour, race, ethnic or national origin, in the provision of goods, facilities, housing accommodation or land, or to publish discriminatory advertisements. Breaches would constitute civil offences with the right of action in special county courts for damages where loss could be proved. The legislation was to be administered by a Race Relations Board which would establish local conciliation committees.

The number of Commonwealth immigrants, largely coloured, who had been granted work permits had fallen from 30,000 in 1963 to less than 5,000 in 1967 although, in the same period, there had been a rise from 26,000 to 52,800 in the number of dependants entering Britain.

On April 20th, in Birmingham, Enoch Powell made a speech in which he charged that the Bill would 'risk throwing a match into gunpowder', encouraging immigrant communities who were already making Britons into 'strangers in their own country'. He added that he was filled with foreboding: 'Like the Roman, I seem to see the River Tiber foaming with much blood.' On April 21st Mr Powell was dismissed from his Shadow Cabinet post of spokesman on defence policy, on the grounds that his speech had been racialist in tone and liable to exacerbate racial tensions.

In the Commons discussions of the Conservatives' reasoned amendment, declining 'to give a Second Reading to a Bill which, on balance, will not in its practical application contribute to the achievement of racial harmony', Quintin Hogg reminded Members that their duty was 'not to create a false unity . . . or to paper over real differences, but to create a pattern in which controversy can take place in a civilized way . . .' (*House of Commons Debates*, Vol. 763, cols 67–81.)

[3] James Callaghan.

[4] Conservative M.P. for Barnet since 1950, Parliamentary Secretary to the Ministry of Civil Aviation 1952, Economic Secretary to the Treasury 1955–7, Paymaster-General 1957–9, President of the Board of Trade 1959–61, Secretary of State for the Colonies 1961–2 and Chancellor of the Exchequer 1962–4. He was an unsuccessful candidate for the leadership of the Conservative Party in 1965. In 1970 he became Home Secretary, resigning that office in 1972.

and the Tory Party lurched nearer to Enoch. There sat Powell in the third row back, glowering, with everybody eyeing him and only Gerald Nabarro up in the front giving him overt support.[1] I suppose there are a number of active supporters of Enoch Powell among the back benchers but the vast majority obviously feel he's behaved very badly and that they must support their front bench in order to avoid a split.

Unfortunately I had to go out to my office for the first of a series of interviews with high officials of my new Ministry, this time to give me a picture of the work of the Social Security side. It's a huge affair of some 62–63,000 people, with 10,500 of them in the central filing Department in Newcastle, and another 2,000 or so at Blackpool doing war pensions. As well as these, 47,500 are out in the social security regional offices. Of these 63,000, precisely 78 are of the rank of Principal or above. The Ministry I have to deal with consists of these 78 in the Adelphi.[2] I am beginning to realize what Titmuss and Abel-Smith meant when they warned me about the differences between the two Ministries we are merging.

I had a little supper at home with Anne and the children before I went back to the House to hear David Ennals make a pretty good wind-up speech and see us get a lowish vote.[3] I am told some fifteen Tories ostentatiously abstained but there's no major crisis. The two big parties, thanks to Quintin Hogg, have held together in supporting the bipartisan policy.

After the debate I went round to Ronnie Grierson's[4] house, where I found Carrington and Jellicoe, as well as Christopher and Mary Soames.[5] It was fun talking to Christopher about what he'll be doing at the French Embassy but the most important thing for me was to hear what Carrington and Jellicoe had to say. Carrington was in rather a serious mood. He repeated that he couldn't give me any promise that he could change his colleagues' opinion about the date of the implementation of Lords' reform.[6] Even if we pass the

[1] Sir Gerald Nabarro (Kt 1963), Conservative M.P. for Kidderminster 1950–64 and for Worcestershire South from 1966 until his death in 1973.

[2] There were 2,500 staff in the London headquarters.

[3] The Conservative amendment was defeated by 313 votes to 209 and the Bill was given a Second Reading.

[4] Executive Director of S. G. Warburg & Co. 1958–68, Deputy Chairman and Managing Director of the Industrial Reorganization Corporation 1966–7, Chairman of Orion Bank 1971–3, Director of Davy-Ashmore 1970–3, Director-General of Industrial and Technological Affairs at the E.E.C. 1973–4 and Senior Partner of Panmure, Gordon & Co. 1974–6. Since 1968 he has also been a director of the General Electric company and since 1974 of International Computers (Holdings).

[5] Sir Christopher Soames, Conservative M.P. for Bedford 1950–66; P.P.S. to the Prime Minister 1952–5; Parliamentary Under-Secretary of State at the Air Ministry December 1955–January 1957; Parliamentary and Financial Secretary at the Admiralty 1957–8; Secretary of State for War 1958–60, Minister of Agriculture, Fisheries and Food 1960–4. He was Ambassador to France 1968–72 and a Vice-President of the Commission of the E.E.C. 1973–6. His wife, Mary, was the youngest daughter of Sir Winston Churchill.

[6] In their earlier negotiations, the Inter-Party Conference had failed to agree on the timing of the implementation of the Lords' reform scheme. Iain Macleod had maintained that reform should wait until the new Parliament but those who wished to see the scheme implemented in the session following the passing of the measure maintained that a delay,

Bill in the next session the Tories might insist that it doesn't come into force until the next Parliament. I said I would explain all this to our side and that personally I saw no disadvantage in producing an agreed White Paper which made this point very clearly but which also made it clear that it was the Tories who were insisting on it. Maybe when the White Paper is published the Tory peers will insist on a change of view but Carrington is doubtful about another aspect of Lords' reform. He is anxious lest the Tories in the Commons should ask themselves why a Government which has no credit should be shored up by the Opposition in a bipartisan agreement. I very much share this feeling and I also doubt whether this reform will look to the general public like the kind of thing a Labour Government should put forward. I'm not sure it won't seem an appallingly humdrum attempt to buttress an ancient monument which really wants rebuilding. The general public will ask why we don't have a proper reform and why we are being so intensely conservative and inward-looking. I am also sure we're going to have terrible trouble with the Labour Party, yet I know this is a very sensible and solid proposal which will be of enormous assistance in the second stage of my parliamentary reforms.

Wednesday, April 24th

The morning papers show it's Hogg's day. He's got a tremendous press for his speech and his is the only name which stands up against Enoch's. It's clear that Powell now has enormous public support behind him and for the first time, I'd say, he's appealing to mass opinion right over Parliament and his party leadership. The movement he is arousing has no respect for Parliament and for our institutions and it detests the bloody things that so-called educated people in the Establishment are doing to ordinary, decent mortals. That's the feeling Enoch has let loose and that's what Hogg's speech has, to some extent, stemmed.

My first job was to see Seebohm of the Seebohm Committee.[1] He's a tall

of perhaps three years, would be dangerous. It would mean that in the last year of the expiring Parliament the Conservative peers would retain powers to obstruct Labour legislation and the momentum of the agreed scheme might be lost. Were a Conservative Government returned to power the scheme might be dropped altogether. Those who wanted speedy implementation also argued that a three-year transition period would permit the gradual evolution of the new House of Lords from the old. See Vol. II, pp. 737–57.

[1] Sir Frederic Seebohm, Chairman of Barclays Bank International Ltd 1965–72, and, since 1974, of Finance Corporation for Industry, of Finance for Industry and of the Industrial and Commercial Finance Corporation. He is a member of the Seebohm Rowntree family of Quaker philanthropists and Chairman of the Joseph Rowntree Memorial Trust. In 1972 he became a life peer. He was Chairman of the Committee on Local Authority and Allied Personal Services, whose Report, Cmnd 3703, published on July 23rd, 1968, recommended that major local authorities should each create a single, unified social service department, with a central government Department assuming responsibility for overall planning. In the Committee's view, some social groups, particularly the very old, the under-fives and the physically and mentally handicapped, were inadequately provided for by existing social services.

man with a reddish moustache, and I found him nervy and depressed. He was worried about the publication of his Report and I gave him an absolute assurance that directly the text was delivered I would personally look after publication and press relations and make sure we got as much coverage as possible. I think he was a little disconcerted by these assurances since he'd come to complain. I was the fourth Minister he'd had to deal with and that was really one or two too many for him. After he calmed down he told me in great secrecy what was to be the central recommendation of the Report. I didn't particularly want to know but he informed me that it was going to be a demand for a reorganization of social services, cutting across local authority boundaries, and he was anxious to get his Report out before my Ministry of Health Green Paper which is to be published fairly soon.[1]

In the afternoon I took the children to the Transport Museum in Clapham to see old buses and engines; everything fine except that you can't get inside a bus. Perhaps we ought to have telephoned in advance and seen that we were given a special conducted tour. The Imperial War Museum, where we went next, turned out to be surprisingly good, with masses of marvellous guns and torpedoes which we all enjoyed.

Meanwhile there'd been a very important Statement in the House on Rhodesia.[2] Apparently we ourselves are putting up a motion at the United Nations demanding completely comprehensive mandatory sanctions, including all the pinpricks I wanted to avoid. The interesting thing is that all this has been done without a Cabinet, without an O.P.D. [Defence and Overseas Policy Committee] and, it seems, without a meeting of the Rhodesia Committee, which, indeed, has ceased to exist. With Michael Stewart's help, Harold has quietly pushed all the objectors aside and got his way. As Prime Minister he's perfectly entitled to do this, just as he was perfectly entitled to make Michael his Foreign Secretary because he knows that this gets him his way on Rhodesia and the Common Market.

This was the evening that I had arranged to have Roy and Barbara to dinner. Roy and I sat waiting for Barbara and he told me how jittery and unstable is the state of the economy and how little we have achieved so far. He is a very worried man. The unemployment figures remain very bad and

[1] Kenneth Robinson had announced on November 6th, 1967, that his Ministry would inquire into the structure of the N.H.S. and his Green Paper, *The Administrative Structure of the Medical and Related Services in England and Wales*, was published in July 1968. Crossman's Green Paper, *The Future Structure of the National Health Service*, was published in 1970.

[2] The Foreign Secretary told the House that Lord Caradon, Britain's Permanent Representative at the United Nations, had presented to the Security Council a draft Resolution requiring all member states to place prohibitions on trade with Rhodesia, including imports 'in transit' or to so-called 'free ports', similar to the sanctions Britain already applied. It also required members to apply sanctions through the exchange control system and to deny entry not only to known sanctions breakers and active supporters of the illegal regime, but also to persons relying on a Rhodesian passport.

the import figures not much better.[1] 'We aren't making much headway,' he said, 'and the money which should have been sucked back to London still isn't coming in.' I remembered that he had told me that everything depended on getting the money back after the budget, so this was an admission that so far he's failed in the budget's major objective and we are still teetering on the edge, in a position where we could be knocked off by any twist of the gold crisis. On the other hand, as Roy also pointed out, the immediate threat to the pound has vanished. Our friends seem to have given us a chance to make good and I suppose that is the first stage of getting money back into the reserve. The Americans have accepted our new reduced status, shorn of our overseas commitments and with our new home policy. We have been given a chance and the heat is now off but we've only achieved half of what we need since we're not getting the money back. When Roy had finished, I told him about the P.M. sending for me to ask the question about Auberon Waugh. Roy said he was in the same predicament because he hadn't seen the young man for years either. Altogether Roy was as cool and collected as ever but a bit world-weary, passively accepting the international difficulties and wondering aloud whether we can overcome them.

Finally Barbara came along and we found ourselves entirely concerned with the speech she was to make to the A.E.U. tomorrow.[2] Roy and I contributed a great many good ideas towards it and that was the only real discussion we had. On prices and incomes it's clear that Barbara's prepared to be as good as her word, to stand loyally by Roy and get the Bill through in its present form by stressing the need for higher productivity, exactly as she said she would. They must get the Bill through before the old legislation slackens off because the policy is required to maintain the credibility of the pound.

Thursday, April 25th

The most interesting thing in the papers was that three polls, Gallup, N.O.P. and the O.R.C., were all saying that a clear majority of the public were in favour of the Race Relations Bill. When you look carefully it isn't quite as good as it sounds because you find that those who are in favour of the Bill seem to be against all its provisions. They don't want it to deal with housing, for example, or employment. Nevertheless it does indicate that with strong bipartisan leadership the vast majority of the people in this country, though emotionally open to Powellism, are prepared to adopt a sensible and stable attitude.

My first conference was with Judith Hart and her Permanent Secretary,

[1] In the first quarter of 1968, unemployment stood at 510,000 (2·2 per cent of the total number of employees) and imports at £1,793 million. There was a deficit of £83 million on the balance of payments.

[2] The A.E.U. National Committee, led by Hugh Scanlon, were discussing their tactics for a major wage claim. Mrs Castle had succeeded in inducing the Committee to invite her to their meeting at Brighton.

Clifford Jarrett. I have recorded her unsatisfactory deal with the Chancellor, whereby she had exchanged for the second-round increase of 3*s*. in family allowances, a saving of £15 million on the money paid out on the three 'waiting days' of the first ten days of sickness.[1] This had caused consternation in the Parliamentary Party, but as I very much feared, Jarrett wholly confirmed my view that Judith's next idea of getting out of her difficulties by transferring the first week, or even month, of sickness benefit to the employer is absolutely unrealistic. I now see that I must get her off the hook by persuading Roy Jenkins not to expect the £15 million this year because there's no chance of her realizing it.

Harold had called a special Cabinet Committee at 11. a.m., which turned out to be the famous Parliamentary Committee.[2] There are eight members: the Prime Minister, the Foreign Secretary, the Lord Chancellor, the Secretary of State for Defence, the Chancellor of the Exchequer, the Lord President of the Council, the Lord Privy Seal and the First Secretary. Also present at the first meeting were Peter Shore and Tony Crosland for the first three items, Willie Ross and George Thomas, the Secretaries of State for Scotland and Wales, in a waiting capacity, and the Minister of Housing for items four and five. There was also the Deputy Leader of the House of Commons, as John Silkin is now called,[3] David Ennals from the Home Office and the full Cabinet Secretariat.

We started by discussing next week's Parliamentary business until we realized that the poor Cabinet Ministers who weren't present would have to hear it all over again. We went on to discuss next Sunday's big meeting between Cabinet and the National Executive Committee and finally we got on to race relations. This was a perfectly sensible and extremely useful discussion which did justify the existence of the Committee. It was the kind of discussion we would never normally have in Cabinet and which we ought to have regularly.

To my surprise the next item on the agenda was council house rents. I'd had a fearful tiff with Tony Greenwood the other day when I discovered he was going to put down a Written Answer saying that the Prices and Incomes Board Report on council house rents had been published and the Government was going to introduce legislation to forbid councils to raise rents this year

[1] An employee who was sick for at least ten days received benefit for the full period, including the first three 'waiting days'. The Minister sought to save £15 million by abolishing payment for these three initial days but the Treasury argued that since the payment was ultimately financed by the employers' contribution to the national insurance fund this was not a real saving. The Minister then proposed that employers should be responsible for financing the whole of the first month of sickness benefit, so saving £150 million. See Vol. II, pp. 745 and 747.

[2] The small 'inner Cabinet' that the Prime Minister had promised at the time of the Cabinet reshuffle on April 5th. See Vol. II.

[3] The Chief Whip's official title was Parliamentary Secretary to the Treasury (or Patronage Secretary) and by tradition he did not speak from the Floor of the House of Commons. John Silkin wished to be given the new title of Deputy Leader of the House of Commons and to be allowed to speak in the House. See Vol. II, pp. 761, 770–1.

by more than 7*s*. 6*d*. I told him this was an enormously important statement which should be given maximum publicity but he said he didn't want the councils to get upset and he felt a Written Answer was the right thing. I had been so angry that I had gone to Fred Peart and put the fear of God into him and he had shoved it on to the agenda of this Committee. The result was instantaneous. Mr Greenwood was ordered to make a full Statement to the House and submit it for approval to the Publicity Committee. In a way, I suppose, this item also justifies the existence of the Parliamentary Committee. At last we have got something though not quite an Inner Cabinet.

In the Commons this afternoon Tony Greenwood had an excellent response on rents. His trouble is that he has no guts and is no good at policy or running a Department but he's excellent as a presenter of other people's ideas. Then we had David Ennals on immigration officers. David Winnick had asked a Private Notice Question about a report that thirty-nine immigration officers had been giving support to Enoch Powell.[1] What shook me was that in a supplementary question Maudling tried to some extent to indicate support for the officers' line and to justify their action. David Ennals said very properly that he wasn't going to express an opinion until the results of an inquiry were available.

This evening Tam[2] had arranged a dinner for me in the Members' Dining Room with John Mackintosh, David Owen and David Marquand,[3] three of our ablest young right-wing intellectuals. At least they were pleased about the creation of the merged Ministries of Health and Social Security, which they themselves had suggested. Mainly though, they were browned off by Harold's complete failure to give promotion where it is most needed, to vigorous persons like themselves, and I was also uneasily aware that they thought I had something to do with the selection. It was an ineffective evening but I certainly learnt something more about the cynicism that has set into the Commons.

Friday, April 26th

I have tried to keep the details of Lords' reform away from Harold but this morning I had to go across and discuss one vitally important question with him and Eddie Shackleton. This is how in future the life peers shall be selected and, in particular, whether the role of the Prime Minister should remain the same. If all the effective power in the Lords is taken out of the

[1] David Winnick was Labour M.P. for Croydon South 1966–70.

[2] Tam Dalyell.

[3] John Mackintosh, Labour M.P. for Berwick and East Lothian 1966–February 1974 and since October 1974, was Professor of Politics at the University of Strathclyde 1965–6, Visiting Professor at Birkbeck College, London 1972–6 and since 1977 Professor of Politics, University of Edinburgh. He is the author of several books on British government, including *The British Cabinet* (London: Methuen, 1972). David Marquand was Labour M.P. for Ashfield 1966–77, when he became adviser to Roy Jenkins in the office of the President of the European Commission. He was Lecturer in Politics at the University of Sussex 1964–6 and is the author of *Ramsay MacDonald* (London: Cape, 1977).

hands of hereditary peers and put into the hands of life peers in effect the whole patronage of the House of Lords will be in the Prime Minister's hands. This is only theoretical, of course, because, to take our own example, Harold nominates the Labour life peers, but he nominates Conservative life peers on the advice of the Conservative Leader and Liberals on the advice of the Liberal Leader.[1] In our reformed House perhaps the most important issue will be the composition of the cross-bench peers for they may well exert an absolutely decisive balancing role.[2] Should the Prime Minister appoint the cross-bench peers or should he only act on the advice of a committee, and if so, who should be on it? I told him there were those who wanted to reduce the P.M.'s patronage by creating a committee to advise him and, as I had guessed, Harold was extremely opposed to this idea. He said he wouldn't mind a committee which discussed the party balance of the Lords after each of his batch of appointments but they weren't to advise him on the appointments themselves. From his point of view he's right because his position would be undermined. He certainly showed himself extraordinarily alert to the problems of patronage, taking it all very seriously. What's so staggering about it is that nevertheless he does select such extraordinarily conservative and reactionary people.

I was lunching at Courtaulds with Ronald Kerr-Muir,[3] who is the Chairman of the Social Services Sub-Committee of the C.B.I. and a director of Courtaulds, to whom Jack Butterworth first introduced me at Warwick University.[4] I found him and his fellow directors terribly upset because this morning the news had leaked from New York that George Brown is joining the Board. They've certainly got a constellation of politicians, Rab Butler, David Eccles, Douglas Jay and now George Brown.[5] We had a thoroughly

[1] The Crown creates life peers, on the nomination of the Prime Minister. He asks the leaders of the other major parties for their lists of names but decides himself how many nominees each party will have. The final list is also submitted to a Political Honours Scrutiny Committee of three peers, one from each of the major parties, but their approval is usually formal.

[2] Cross-bench peers are those who take no party whip. They sit on benches placed across the Chamber, facing the Throne, overflowing only if there is a shortage of places on to the benches occupied by the Conservative, Labour and Liberal peers.

[3] He had been with Courtaulds Ltd since 1946 and was a director 1958–71. He was a member of the Council of the University of Warwick from 1961 and its Treasurer from 1965 until his death in 1974, and was Deputy Chairman of the Meat and Livestock Commission 1973–4.

[4] Vice-Chancellor of the University of Warwick since 1963.

[5] R. A. Butler, Conservative M.P. for Saffron Walden 1929–65, was Under-Secretary of State at the India Office 1932–7, Parliamentary Secretary at the Ministry of Labour 1937–8, Under-Secretary of State for Foreign Affairs 1938–41, Minister of Education 1941–5, Minister of Labour June–July 1945, Chancellor of the Exchequer 1951–5, Lord Privy Seal 1955–9 and Leader of the House of Commons 1955–61, Home Secretary 1957–62, First Secretary of State July 1962–October 1963, Minister in Charge of the Central African Office 1962–October 1963, Secretary of State for Foreign Affairs 1963–4 and Chairman of the Conservative Party Research Department and of the Conservative Party Organization 1959–61. Created a life peer in 1965, he has since that year been Master of Trinity College, Cambridge. He had married into the Courtauld family. David Eccles, Conservative M.P.

good talk about national superannuation and I was able to say to Kerr-Muir, as I had said to Harold Collison,[1] that the C.B.I. shall have every detail of our pension plan in advance and that I intend to have no secrets whatsoever reserved for the Bill. In my experience as a Minister so far, telling the truth and trusting people always pays if you want to get them on your side.

I had to get back to my office quickly to prepare my speech for Brian Parkyn's constituency at Bedford.[2] He is a curious, mild-looking man with a beard, whom I had thought rather feeble and left wing, but in Bedfordshire politics he obviously counts for a great deal since he is one of those passionate local politicians who defeated Christopher Soames in 1966 entirely because he stood as a local man and a dedicated left-wing socialist. He was waiting at the station with his wife and a large Bentley and we went on to a really encouraging meeting in the Technical College, with two or three hundred people of all ages. He made an excellent speech and I made a good, thorough speech entirely on the race issue. A good atmosphere, a good press, and I got home at midnight feeling I'd done an interesting week's work.

Saturday, April 27th

There's no doubt how last week has got to be described. It was Powell week and we are still absolutely dominated by the effect of his Birmingham speech. I've known for some time that Powell has strong views about race. He's a curious contradiction, an ultra-liberal in economics who requires an absolute state ban on coloured immigrants. The significance of his Birmingham speech, as David Watt pointed out in the best piece on all this,[3] is that he has successfully appealed to the mass of the people over the heads of the Parliamentary leaders for the first time since Oswald Mosley,[4] and in doing

---

for Chippenham 1943–62, was Minister of Works 1951–4, Minister of Education 1954–7, President of the Board of Trade 1957–9, Minister of Education October 1959–July 1962 and Paymaster-General, with special responsibility for the Arts 1970–2. He became a viscount in 1964. He was a director of Courtaulds 1962–70 and since 1973 he has been Chairman of the British Library Board. Douglas Jay, Labour M.P. for Battersea North July 1946–74 and since 1974 for Wandsworth, Battersea North, was Economic Secretary to the Treasury 1947–50. Financial Secretary to the Treasury 1950–1 and President of the Board of Trade 1964–7. A notable anti-Marketeer, he has been Chairman of the Common Market Safeguards Campaign since 1970. He was a director of Courtaulds 1967–70.

[1] A Gloucestershire farmworker 1934–53, he had served in the National Union of Agricultural Workers since 1944, becoming its General Secretary and a member of the T.U.C. General Council 1953–69. He was Chairman of the Supplementary Benefits Commission 1969–75 and in 1964 he became a life peer.

[2] Labour M.P. for Bedford 1966–70 and since 1953 a director of a chemical manufacturing company.

[3] Washington Correspondent of the *Financial Times* from 1964 until 1967, when he became Political Editor.

[4] Sir Oswald Mosley, who succeeded to his father's baronetcy in 1928, was Conservative Unionist M.P. for Harrow December 1918–22. He then sat as an Independent for the same constituency 1922–4 and as a Labour M.P. in 1924. He represented Smethwick 1926–31 and was Chancellor of the Duchy of Lancaster 1929–30. In 1932 he founded the British Union of Fascists.

so he's stirred up the nearest thing to a mass movement since the 1930s. Aldermaston was not a mass movement but a collection of liberal individuals and families drooling along the road[1] while Enoch is stimulating the real revolt of the masses. There he is with his 40–50,000 letters streaming in, the marches from the docks and from Smithfield, all part of a mass response to a very simple appeal, 'No more bloody immigrants in this country'.

I ought to get the political background quite clear while I remember it. Powell took part in the Shadow Cabinet discussion which resulted in the Opposition front bench putting forward a reasoned amendment to the Race Relations Bill. He actually made one or two amendments to the draft and then fully agreed to it, yet when Heath sacked him from the Shadow Cabinet Powell replied that he was stating Conservative policy whereas the rest of them were playing it down. Now that, he must know, is not true. Conservative policy was defined in the reasoned amendment and it was a deliberate compromise to hold together on the one side Enoch, who really wants to make an issue of race, and on the other Edward Boyle and Quintin Hogg,[2] who want a bipartisan Race Relations Bill to prevent the revolt of the masses which Enoch has let loose. I haven't spoken to anybody who has talked to Enoch since his sacking. Apart from coming into the House and sitting glooming in the third row from the back he hasn't been in the Commons and now he's gone abroad. I suspect he made the Birmingham speech with the calculation that if Heath didn't want the resignation of Boyle and Hogg he would have to sack him and so split the Party. I should guess he miscalculated the extent of the popular appeal and has been slightly appalled by it. He isn't a fascist but a fanatic, a bizarre conservative extremist with violent views on this subject.

However he has changed the whole shape of politics overnight. There have been amazing demonstrations outside while, inside, the Palace of Westminster is filled with awareness of this mass movement. Talk about plebiscitary democracy! Here it is in action, making its impression direct on the Government. We have had the amazing phenomenon of Ian Mikardo being howled down by his dockers and denounced and he denouncing them.[3] It has been the real Labour core, the illiterate industrial proletariat who have turned up in strength and revolted against the literate.

[1] In 1958 the Campaign for Nuclear Disarmament began an annual Easter march to London from the Atomic Weapons Research Establishment at Aldermaston, Berkshire.

[2] Sir Edward Boyle, Conservative M.P. for Birmingham, Handsworth, 1950–70, was Parliamentary Secretary to the Ministry of Supply 1954–April 1955, Economic Secretary to the Treasury 1955–6, Parliamentary Secretary to the Ministry of Education 1957–9, Financial Secretary to the Treasury October 1959–July 1962, Minister of Education 1962–4 and Minister of State, D.E.S. April–October 1964. He became a life peer in 1970. Since 1970 he has been Vice-Chancellor of the University of Leeds and since 1971 Chairman of the Top Salaries Review Body.

[3] Labour M.P. for Reading 1945–59, for Poplar 1964–74 and since 1974 for Tower Hamlets, Bethnal Green and Bow. He was Chairman of the Select Committee on the Nationalized Industries 1966–70 and Chairman of the Parliamentary Labour Party March–November 1974.

There are, of course, a few literate racialists but the vast majority of well-informed public opinion supports bipartisanship and the Bill and, in so far as it does so, the respectable public has disregarded the views of the masses. It's the same problem we've had with the abolition of capital punishment, the repeal of laws against homosexuality and all the other liberal causes where a minority of the well-informed public has leapt well ahead and dragged mass opinion resentfully behind it.[1] Now we have the leaders of the Transport and General Workers and the A.E.U. saying that these demonstrations are outrageous but it's their own mass rank and file, the same people who've been supporting them against the Government's prices and incomes policy, who are supporting Enoch Powell against the Government's race relations policy.

It has also provided the first great test of Heath's leadership and he's handled it, rather as Gaitskell would have done, by first dismissing Powell and then desperately trying to hold a middle course.[2] Harold Wilson's contempt for Heath is on this occasion largely justified. He has been rushing into print with letters to the *Express* and special I.T.V. interviews and now he's going round the Midlands, to Rugby and Dudley. He's going to have a rough time. Of course he will get the official Conservative hierarchy on his side but there is no doubt that in the Midlands a vast majority of those who vote Conservative and, indeed, of those who vote Labour will say 'No more immigration. Pay them to go home'.

It's in these crises, as David Watt rightly says, that the British constitution is like a rock against which the wave of popular emotion breaks, and one hopes that after a time the tide will go down and the rock stand untouched. This is the strength of our system, that, though in one sense we have plebiscitary democracy, actually the leadership is insulated from the masses by the existence of Parliament. Parliament is the buffer which enables our leadership to avoid saying yes or no to the electorate in the hope that, given time, the situation can be eased away.

In narrow terms of party politics the Powell speech has been an advantage to the Government. It has made it almost certain that when the Bill has had its Report Stage, the Third Reading will be supported by all three parties. Though Heath may come out of it with strengthened moral fibre, I don't

[1] In December Sydney Silverman introduced his Murder (Abolition of the Death Penalty) Bill as a Private Member's Bill. The Cabinet resolved to provide time for the measure to be debated every Wednesday morning and it was passed in July 1965. The Commons carried a Conservative amendment that, unless both Houses carried motions for permanent abolition, the measure should automatically lapse after an experimental period of five years. Such motions were carried in December 1969. See Vol. I, p. 226 and n., and below, pp. 751 and n., 760 and n. The Earl of Arran's Sexual Offences Bill was passed in the Lords in October 1965 and June 1966 but was twice defeated in the Commons. With the support of the Government's business managers, it was re-introduced as a Commons' Private Member's Bill and in July 1967 became law. See Vol. II.

[2] Hugh Gaitskell was Labour M.P. for South Leeds from 1945 until his death in 1963. He was Chancellor of the Exchequer 1950–1 and Leader of the Labour Party 1955–63, at a time when the party was severely split.

think it will do the Tory Party much good since it will cause a split within their ranks, whereas on our side it will have revived the relationship between idealistic socialists and the Government. We have been hopelessly down and out recently because we have lost the respect of our own idealistic rank and file, especially in the schools and universities. We've looked like a humdrum Government which is just utterly and hopelessly Establishment. Here, in contrast to the Kenya Asians Bill, is a cause where we have got a rapport and where we are standing for a principle our enthusiastic followers believe in.

In February and March 1968 the Kenya government began to refuse work permits to non-citizens, who were mainly of Indian and Pakistani origin, and who, under the terms of the 1963 Kenya Independence Agreement, could hold British passports and were exempt from restrictions on entry to Britain. There was a flood of immigration into Britain and on February 22nd the Home Secretary announced that the Government had decided to introduce emergency legislation to establish a new category of 1,000 vouchers for the Kenya Asians, bringing them and their dependants under the same restrictions as other Commonwealth citizens. The Bill received a majority of 372 to 62 on Second Reading on February 27th and it was passed with much controversy on March 1st.[1]

In the evening Anne and I motored over to Coventry for a dinner organized by my agent, Winnie Lakin.[2] After tremendous effort she had got together some eighty people, forty or so from the constituency, the rest from outside. I suppose one must reckon this an excellent turnout but in constituency terms it was pretty disastrous since nearly everyone came from Betty Healey's ward at Willenhall and from the other wards there were only ones and twos and threes.[3] I tried to cheer them up with a talk on the Government's decision to keep council house rent increases down to 7*s.* 6*d.* a week, which will mean halving the increases introduced by the Coventry Tories. They liked what I said but they were still terribly uncertain and unhappy. They all seemed to be saying, 'We must be loyal despite the hopelessness of our Government. We are the gallant few who are standing staunchly by it.' Were they anti Harold Wilson? No. Were they anti me? Not at all. They just felt we had totally failed as a Government and nothing I said would alter their view that after three years there had been no real improvement in their standard of living, only a series of crises which showed we weren't in control. I accept this criticism but it's only half the story and I do agree with what Peregrine Worsthorne in last week's *Sunday Telegraph* described as doing 'Socialism by

[1] See Vol. II.
[2] Winnie Lakin was a member of Coventry City Council 1955–67, and was elected again in 1972.
[3] Betty Healey was Secretary of Binley Ward in the Coventry East constituency.

stealth'.[1] We've had our flops, like the Land Commission,[2] but we've had our successes, like leasehold enfranchisement, social security policies and re-nationalization of steel. We've done most of the things we were supposed to do but they don't match our central failure to control the economy.

When the dinner was over I went into the Council House to pick up Eddie Shackleton, who was the guest speaker at the St George's Day dinner. I waited for a very long time and then heard that the Bishop was still to make a great speech and there were others after him.[3] Eventually the new Deputy Lord Mayor turned up but he couldn't unlock the drinks' cupboard in the Lord Mayor's Parlour or do anything for us. When I heard that the dinner had finished I insisted that Eddie Shackleton be fetched so that I could drive him home. I suppose I was angry that the Lord President had been left sitting in the Council House while they, in their white ties, were boozing away and perhaps I secretly thought I should have been the guest of honour. I don't often admit it to myself but I was thoroughly rude and I may have to pay for it later this year because the Deputy Lord Mayor is the Tory Lord Mayor for 1968/9.[4]

Sunday, April 28th

We spent the whole of today on the meeting between the Cabinet and the N.E.C. in Downing Street. There was only one word to describe it, flat. There was flatness on the part of the Prime Minister and flatness on the part of the critics, the latter largely resulting from the absence of Jack Jones,[5] who is now on the T.U.C. General Council and has been replaced by Harry Nicholas, a complete time-server.[6] The morning was mostly devoted to an uncompromising but muted trade union attack on our new prices and incomes policy. It was led by Frank Allaun, Willie Simpson, Joe Gormless [*sic*] and Frank Chapple.[7] They detested the new powers in the Bill but they listened

[1] Deputy Editor of the *Sunday Telegraph* since 1960.

[2] In accordance with a promise in the party manifesto the Land Commission was set up in 1966, to acquire land for State ownership and to collect 'betterment levy' on land sold for development. The Commission was established by the Ministry of Land and Natural Resources, founded in October 1964 and abolished in February 1967. See Vols I and II.

[3] The Rt Reverend Cuthbert Bardsley, Bishop of Coventry 1956–76.

[4] Alderman Leonard Lamb, J.P.

[5] James Larkin Jones, a member of the T.U.C. General Council since 1968, Assistant Executive Secretary of the T.G.W.U. 1963–9 and General Secretary 1969–78, has been Deputy Chairman of the National Ports Council since 1967. As Midlands Regional Secretary of the T.G.W.U. 1955–63 and a Coventry City Magistrate 1950–63, he came to know Crossman well.

[6] Assistant General Secretary of the T.G.W.U. 1956–68 (Acting General Secretary October 1964–July 1966), a member of the T.U.C. General Council 1964–7, of the N.E.C. 1956–64 and since 1967 and General Secretary of the Labour Party 1968–72. He was knighted in 1970. See below pp. 117, 119, 155.

[7] Frank Allaun has been Labour M.P. for East Salford since 1955 and a member of the N.E.C. since 1967. Willie Simpson, General Secretary of the A.U.E.W. 1967–75 and a member of the N.E.C. since 1962, has been Chairman of the Health and Safety Commission since 1974. Joe Gormley, General Secretary of the N.W. Area of the National Union of Miners 1961–71, became President of the N.U.M. in 1971. He has been a member of the

to Barbara when she seized her chance at the end of the morning, speaking, I thought, absolutely brilliantly. She put herself across as a singer singing the same tune but in a totally different style. She had to be loyal to the policy and yet completely different and she did it. She deserved the cheers before she went off in her helicopter to address a big trade union conference later this afternoon.

Lunch was arranged by the Government Hospitality Fund and paid for by Transport House.[1] It cost 54*s*. a head for a dreary cold collation. The after-lunch session was on social services and the difference was remarkable. In the morning there had been a sense of deadlock, exasperated but quiet and resigned. Now we were discussing problems where we are completely agreed on our basic long-term aim and where, if mistakes have been made, we all want to see them cleared up. There was a short speech by our new Education Secretary, Ted Short, who has replaced Gordon Walker and who seems to know what he wants. He is a handsome, decisive schoolmaster, whose main point was that there must be a stop to all this nonsense that education should be child-directed and community-directed. He was going to see that the child was made to feel its place in the community. His speech impressed everybody. Even more surprising was the ease with which I was able to deal with prescription charges. Here the real complaint of the N.E.C. was that we should ever have promised to abolish them and we were urged not to make such precise promises again. The final session was supposed to discuss the relationship between Party and Government. Harold should have given a speech about the role of the new General Secretary but the N.E.C., having wrongly decided that even for the rest of this Parliament the new man won't be allowed to remain in the Commons, has knocked out either Merlyn Rees,[2] Jim Callaghan's candidate, or Tony Greenwood, whom Harold is said to want, and no one can really talk about the relationship of Party and Government unless Len Williams is replaced by someone of real political importance.[3] We know this isn't going to happen so the last session was a complete flop.

Monday, April 29th

I started the morning with a long talk with John Diamond about the three

T.U.C. General Council 1973. Frank Chapple, General Secretary of the Electrical, Electronic, Telecommunication and Plumbing Union since September 1966, has been a member of the T.U.C. General Council since 1971.

[1] The Labour Party headquarters.

[2] Labour M.P. for South Leeds since June 1963. He had been Callaghan's P.P.S. at the Treasury in 1964. He was Parliamentary Under-Secretary of State for the Army at the Ministry of Defence 1965–6, for the R.A.F. 1966–8, and at the Home Office 1968–70. He was Secretary of State for Northern Ireland 1974–6 and since 1976 has been Home Secretary.

[3] Len Williams, an official of the National Union of Railwaymen and of the Labour Party since 1920, was National Agent of the Labour Party 1951–9 and General Secretary 1962–8. He became Governor-General of Mauritius in 1968 and received a knighthood. He died in December 1972.

waiting days and Judith's wish to transfer the responsibility for payment of sickness benefit for the first month from the Government to the employers. Ray Gunter and I have both said that this is impossible and when she opened negotiations with the employers and the trade unions she got exactly what I expected, a statement that they couldn't possibly consider it seriously until they saw the scheme. It is clear that I could do this as part of a long-term scheme coming in two or three years' time but if I try to force the pace I won't get what I want. I'd have to impose it by legislation and meanwhile I'd upset my negotiations with the unions and the employers on the long-term scheme.

Judith has gone off to Israel and I said that in her absence I would try to sort things out. Diamond confirms that, as I feared, the Chancellor is determined not to let her off. The Ministry of Social Security must make its £15 million contribution come what may. He also confirmed that both the Treasury and the Ministry would like to see payment for the three waiting days abandoned because they think it a waste of money. I'm afraid that Judith's officials are determined to force their views on her and perhaps we shall have after all to accept a fearful row in the Party, and force the clause abolishing it through the House of Commons. It's perfectly possible to do it.

Freddie Warren and Freddy Ward came into the office for a drink. I had sent for them and said I wanted to talk to them seriously. For weeks I have been asking the Chief[1] for a paper on the possibility of moving certain deliberative sittings of the Scottish Grand Committee to Edinburgh and possibly the Welsh Grand Committee to Cardiff.[2] This is all part of my scheme of controlled devolution to meet the separatist nationalist propaganda.[3] The Chief has been very obstructive about this and his paper was absolutely hopeless.

I told the two Freddies I wasn't concerned with their convenience but with the political decision. I had been thinking I'd been quite wrong in taking the Committee away on Mondays and Fridays but why shouldn't we do this for a week in the recess or two periods of three days, one in the Christmas recess and one in the Whitsun recess? Well, this changed the whole situation. It was a practicable proposal and we got it out of a drink and discussion by ourselves without the Chief and the Leader of the House.

After this I had an office lunch with Odgers and Co. to discuss our plans for expansion. Already new staff are arriving so fast that I hardly know them

[1] The Chief Whip, John Silkin.

[2] The two Grand Committees contain respectively Members from all Scottish and Welsh constituencies and they may debate not just the estimates and principles of Bills on Scottish and Welsh matters, but also subjects of general concern to their respective countries.

[3] In Scotland support was growing for the Scottish National Party, which had won the formerly safe Labour seat of Hamilton at a by-election in November 1967. In Wales the separatist party Plaid Cymru was recruiting followers and in January 1968 Lord Wade, a Liberal peer, had introduced a Bill asking for devolution of powers for Welsh self-government in internal affairs.

by name. In the Private Office I've managed to keep Janet Newman,[1] and have got another lovely blonde coming in. This increase is partly because we have kept control of the Home Publicity Committee and because we must also have the staff to plan the merger. I was able to report that after a talk with Richard Titmuss I thought Brian Abel-Smith would be able to work for us, part-time at least, and this will be very important for our organization of the Intelligence side. I have also got out of Titmuss a list of the important social welfare people I should know.

This afternoon I had the delicate task of meeting for the first time the party Health sub-group. I knew there might be difficulties because the merger had been proposed by a number of back benchers but not by this group, which is run by Laurie Pavitt, an old Ministry of Health employee, and Shirley Summerskill, daughter of the famous Dr Edith.[2] Sure enough, the group turned out to be a lobby for the Ministry of Health, just as the Social Security Group is a lobby for its Ministry. I think I managed to placate them but it was a dicey job and showed that we don't have much support in the Parliamentary Party for the new Department we propose to create.

In the House this evening John Silkin was playing his new role as Deputy Leader. There was a long discussion going on about whether there should be a second Scottish Standing Committee or a Select Specialist Committee for Scotland and in the end John simply said he thought the Select Committee on Procedure would discuss all these problems. Aha, aha, I noted, that's what he and Peart are up to. They are anti-devolutionists and when I get my paper for the Devolution Sub-Committee put to Cabinet they will propose that it should all be referred to the Select Committee on Procedure. In that case nothing will be done before the election and if we make any changes the Government won't get the credit. The balloon I launched so successfully will have been nicely punctured by my colleagues.

Tuesday, April 30th

At the Lords' consultations today we broached the ticklish item of the powers to be given to speaking peers. The issue is between Eddie Shackleton and Jellicoe on the one side and me on the other. They think the new House won't function unless the speaking peers have the right to vote in committee whereas

[1] Janet Gates (as she was before her marriage) had joined Crossman at the Ministry of Housing and Local Government in August 1966 and remained his secretary in the Lord President's Office, at D.H.S.S. and at the *New Statesman*, until she left to have a baby. See Vol. I, p. 613 and n. and Vol. II.

[2] Laurie Pavitt, Labour M.P. for Willesden West October 1959–74 and for Brent South since 1974, had been National Organizer for the Medical Practitioners' Union 1956–9 and Chairman of the party Health sub-group since 1964. Dr Shirley Summerskill, a medical practitioner since 1960 and since 1964 Labour M.P. for Halifax, became Parliamentary Under-Secretary of State at the Home Office in 1974. She was Vice-Chairman of the party Health sub-group 1964–9 and Chairman 1969–70. Her mother, Baroness Summerskill, had qualified as a doctor in 1924 and had been Labour M.P. for West Fulham 1938–55 and for Warrington 1955–61. She was Parliamentary Secretary at the Ministry of Food, 1945–50 and Minister of National Insurance 1950–1. In 1961 she became a life peer.

I am obsessed by the need to stick to the single principle that a voting peer must vote and a speaking peer must only speak. Eddie said, 'You won't get it through. It will be a breaking point for the other side', but to my great surprise Maudling supported me on this and Jellicoe was slapped down. We established that we would have speaking peers only to speak but that we would look favourably on the possibility of their being allowed to move motions and amendments and so on.

The second question concerned the Prime Minister's patronage and we reported exactly what he had said to Eddie and me last Friday. He had accepted that at the start of the reformed House there should be a committee to select which cross benchers should have voting rights because that would be a once-only occasion but after that the P.M. couldn't have any advisory committee hanging round his neck. We were asked to refer back to him the possibility that the Inter-Party Conference might remain in being and at least see his list of nominees before he finally announced it. I said I doubted if he would accept that but we would try. Altogether, the meeting was surprisingly successful and now we have got over those hurdles we are on the way to getting the White Paper written.

Tony Crosland and I dined together. I wanted to ask him about Harold Wilson's astonishing allegation that Tony had been conspiring with George Brown in the Foreign Office and that a tape-recording had been placed on Lord Thomson's file.[1] He wanted to discuss the same subject. Roy had cautiously approached Tony about it and he replied that it was a complete and absolute invention and that he didn't know how such nonsense could be spread. When we came to discuss the new balance of power in Cabinet I told Tony quite candidly that I had been against his being Chancellor of the Exchequer and had insisted on Roy. Tony replied that Roy would prove much more difficult to Harold than he would have been himself. I said, 'Exactly. Roy is a more formidable enemy and therefore it was right to buy him in.' That is still my view.

The last thing I did this evening was to look in on the radio broadcasting experiment in the House of Commons.[2] A little box has been built in at the back where the officials sit and here we have a man from the B.B.C. and one of our door keepers to tell him the names of the people who are up. The B.B.C. are now experimenting with half-hour and quarter-hour programmes using the actual words of the M.P.s. I find it doesn't add very much but you do get the noise and the atmosphere of the House. I think the fact that it is being taped for radio is bound to influence Members and a lot of the silly noise and interruptions during Question Time will be discouraged, and a

[1] Roy Thomson was Chairman of the Thomson Organization Ltd, which included among its subsidiaries *The Times* and the *Sunday Times*. He became a peer in 1964 and died in 1976. For the 'astonishing allegation' see Vol. II, pp. 772, 779.

[2] Just before Easter, the House had agreed to a recommendation of the Services Committee that the B.B.C. should experiment in making a radio recording, for internal broadcasting only, of its proceedings. The history of this decision is set out in Vol. II.

good thing too. Indeed, I am greatly encouraged. Of all the reforms I've introduced this is the one I'd like to see pushed through, since it would change the House more than anything else if people outside could hear the misbehaviour which now goes on.

Wednesday, May 1st

May Day. I was in the chair for the first meeting of the Electoral Reform Committee, finishing off our paper for Cabinet on this year's proposals. We had three things, the first a sensible proposal from Jim Callaghan that the Government positively ought to support the proposal for votes at eighteen. It will be impossible not to support it now that we have announced our support for the Latey Committee's recommendation for reducing the age of consent from twenty-one to eighteen.[1] I entirely agree with Jim. The only difficulty is that in Scotland and Wales the young people will vote nationalist, and next year this will be disastrous.

The second change we recommend is an hour's extension in the time of polling in elections. Harold and I are both keen to see the polling stations close not at 9.0, but at 10.0. The returning officers, i.e. the town clerks' departments, are making every kind of objection, and threatening that they might have to do all the counting the following day. There was at one point a danger of a compromise of 9.30 p.m. but I was able to persuade the Committee that we should either keep it at 9.0 or go right forward to 10.0.

Thirdly there is the problem of party labels. I am very pleased because I not only managed to persuade the Committee to negotiate with the Opposition about the printing of party labels on ballot papers but also to tell the public of the constitutional reason for the change. Our constitution now gives us two-party government and people can vote for this party or that party irrespective of the name and the quality of the candidate put forward in a particular constituency. This change would require parties to be officially registered and that would be a very good thing because we would knock out bogus parties and also the obsolete anachronism that members are primarily individual constituency M.P.s and not party members at all. I would be delighted if I could get all this. At least I've got most of it into the paper for Cabinet.

My next meeting was in Committee Room A on Sachsenhausen.[2] We were

[1] A Committee chaired by Mr Justice Latey (Kt 1965), a judge in the High Court of Justice Family Division since 1965, who had recommended in a Report (Cmnd 3342) published in July 1967 that the age of majority should be lowered from twenty-one to eighteen, thus enabling young people to marry without parental consent, to own land, obtain mortgages, make contracts and bring and defend legal actions. See Vol. II, pp. 538 and n., and 548–9. The Speaker's Conference had recommended twenty as the appropriate voting age. Crossman's references to the 'age of consent' are hereafter corrected to the 'age of majority'.

[2] The office of the Parliamentary Commissioner, or Ombudsman, had been established in 1967. The duties of Sir Edmund Compton, the first holder of the office, were to investigate administrative delays, errors and injustices, or complaints, referred to him by M.P.s. The

back on the old problem, which would have been settled but for George Brown's disastrous personal statement, which inevitably led to a second investigation by a Select Committee. In the course of this reinvestigation Airey Neave gave the name of a junior Foreign Office official who, he said, had been chiefly responsible for this case of maladministration.[1] Sir Edmund Compton's report had shown that though the Foreign Office collectively were to blame,[2] no official, in his view, bore any personal responsibility, so that if the Committee had adopted Airey Neave's evidence it would have constituted itself a Court of Appeal over the Ombudsman despite the fact that he has access to information which none of us, not even the Minister, can see. I was able to argue that if all this information were to be hawked out again by the Select Committee it would violate the intentions of the Act and we briefed Elwyn Jones, the Attorney-General, to persuade the Committee to delete all reference to the official. So this particular crisis is over but we must still resolve the whole issue of what Governments are to do when reports from the Parliamentary Commissioner find cases of maladministration and whether they can be rejected.

At the Immigration Committee Jim Callaghan produced a tentative paper on the numbers of immigrants to be allowed into the country. He said we shouldn't consider the vouchers for work permits, but look at the total quotas, including dependants, and ask ourselves if, say, 50–60,000 a year is too high. He also thought we should run a system of granting entry certificates from the country of origin and not from the aerodrome when they arrive here. Far better to do as the Americans do and arrange that you can't come in without a document from your own passport office saying you are suitable. It would cost a lot of money, but solve a lot of problems.

The discussion once again confirmed the astonishing lack of information. We have quite adequate information on those who enter the country each year but once they are here they disappear into the population. That is why we are trying to get a little more information at the next census on what people do when they get here. On the other hand, nobody knows anything about

---

case which Airey Neave (himself a former prisoner-of-war) brought to the Ombudsman's attention concerned twelve former prisoners-of-war at the Sachsenhausen concentration camp, who had been denied the right to compensation from the £1 million fund provided by the West German government for Nazi victims. The Ombudsman's report found against the Foreign Office but the Foreign Secretary, George Brown, protested vehemently and a Select Committee was appointed to inquire into the dispute. See Vol. II.

[1] Airey Neave, Conservative M.P. for Abingdon since July 1953, was Joint Parliamentary Secretary at the Ministry of Transport and Civil Aviation 1957–9 and Parliamentary Under-Secretary of State for Air 1959. A Member of the Select Committee on Science and Technology 1965–75 (Chairman 1970–4), he has been Head of the Private Office of the Leader of the Opposition since 1975.

[2] Sir Edmund Compton entered the Civil Service in 1929 and spent the greater part of his career in the Treasury. He was Comptroller and Auditor General 1958–66, Parliamentary Commissioner for Administration 1967–71 and Parliamentary Commissioner in Northern Ireland 1969–71. Since 1971 he has been Chairman of the English Local Government Boundary Commission.

emigration. Since no one fills in a form when he or she leaves the country there are only total figures for those going out each week without any breakdown into the numbers on holiday and the numbers who are genuinely emigrating. Here everything is guesswork and government departments are frivolous in their attitude to facts. I noticed recently in a statement on Commonwealth immigration that the cost to the social services of assisting these immigrants is no more than that for the indigenous population. I found this difficult to believe in view of schooling costs and asked for the source. I have just discovered that it's a document that was produced in 1961 by an independent economic bureau, before the first Immigration Act.[1] Since then, this so-called fact has never once been checked but is still being used by the Home Office.

I got back to my office in the Privy Council to find Michael Adeane and Godfrey Agnew waiting to talk about revising the procedure for calling a meeting of the Privy Council.[2] Michael assured me that the Queen wants to use these occasions for getting to know her Ministers, but in fact she hardly sees her Ministers because most of them stand there without saying a word, the Privy Council is over in three minutes and then we withdraw after two minutes' strained conversation. It is maddening, especially in the recess, for busy Ministers to be made to go to Balmoral or Sandringham for a futile ceremony of this kind.

I thought we should have two reforms. First of all to have, say, six carefully chosen meetings a year, with one at Sandringham, one at Balmoral and one at Windsor, where she actually had a discussion with people, with lunch at least, and then all the other meetings cut down to the merest formality, with as little bother as possible. I would have a pool of long-standing Privy Councillors so I wouldn't have to bother present Ministers. I have been putting this scheme forward in conversation for months but this was the first official meeting and Michael Adeane promised to put it to her at Buckingham Palace next week.

[1] The first Commonwealth Immigration Act had been passed in July 1962, providing that, for a five-year trial period, Commonwealth citizens should apply to the Ministry of Labour for vouchers, entitling them to enter the country. There was violent opposition to the measure, particularly from the Labour leadership. In August 1965, however, the Labour Government brought out a White Paper, recommending that entry from the Commonwealth should be restricted to 7,500 permits a year for professional and skilled workers only. Between 1963 and 1967 the number of work permits issued had dropped from 30,000 to 5,000 per annum but the number of dependants who had joined those already in Britain had risen from 26,200 to 52,000 p.a.

[2] Sir Godfrey Agnew, a senior Clerk in the Privy Council Office 1946–51 and Clerk of the Privy Council 1953–74, was a Deputy Secretary in the Cabinet Office from 1972 until his retirement in 1974. Sir Michael Adeane was Private Secretary to the Queen and Keeper of H.M. Archives 1953–72. In 1972 he became a life peer and was appointed Chairman of the Royal Commission on Historical Monuments. As Lord President of the Council 1966–8, Crossman had been obliged to attend the Queen, with other Ministers, for meetings of the Privy Council. He describes these occasions and his intention to reform the procedure in Vol. II.

On the front bench this afternoon I heard Barbara, who's been in the news every day, making a big speech on rising prices. She's been at it eighteen hours a day, often until three in the morning, rushing from one trade union conference to another. This afternoon she was defending herself on a vote of censure and I found her speech a flop for a very interesting reason. At a meeting with the A.E.U. she'd been unwisely driven into making a vague pledge about dealing with prices. But when you've devalued you can't reduce prices. Devaluation should cause an increase of domestic prices and that indeed is what the Government wants as part of the process. She should have made a speech on rents and wages as well but by concentrating on prices she made it sound phoney. When she sat down, she knew she hadn't done too well, but she's a tough girl and I predict she'll come back with a bang when she answers tomorrow's debate on intervention in industry.

Thursday, May 2nd

Harold tried the experiment of preceding Cabinet by a meeting of the Parliamentary Committee, where we dealt with prices and incomes and then with race. On prices and incomes we have the practical problem of getting the Bill through the House. The Chief Whip reported that the situation is much worse than last year. We may have up to 65 abstentions and we only have a majority of 72 so it's clear that we have to reduce the number of abstentions by at least 20, which means getting every P.P.S. fully committed to vote and bringing home to the Party that abstention could bring the Government down. I think if John works hard he will get it down to 40 but it will need a tremendous amount of thought and activity to achieve this. We also had to consider whether there are any parts of the draft Bill which can be made more palatable to our back benchers. It is clear, for instance, that we're going to have one very difficult new clause which applies the policy not, as before, to wages but to earnings and therefore reopens every issue of principle. It was a good discussion because we did at least face up to our appalling parliamentary difficulties even though some of us who don't believe in the policy know that the Bill has got to be forced through anyway without concession.

The debate on race was very half-hearted because there are deep but unexpressed disagreements here. Jim reported on the work of the Cabinet Committee and then there was a pause when no one had anything to say, so I piped up, saying I thought it was essential to get back to a bipartisan policy, and that I wanted the Prime Minister to try this in his speech at Birmingham.[1] He should invite the Leaders of the two other Parties to consultations, both on the total number of immigrants and on the general character of the Race Relations Bill. I was at once smacked down, and quite rightly, because the others were able to point out that we can't concede on the principles of the

[1] The Prime Minister was to speak on May 5th at Birmingham, where Enoch Powell had made his charges on April 20th.

Bill in order to get Quintin Hogg's agreement.* At least I got agreement, however, that we could invite the other side to talks on the total quota of immigrants.

At Cabinet we started with yet another discussion about leaks. Wedgy Benn, who had obviously consulted with the Prime Minister, expressed alarm about articles in the *Spectator*, the *Financial Times* and the *Sunday Telegraph*, one of which was a bitter attack on Peter Shore. A lot of feeling was worked up and I suspect the aim was to direct suspicion at John Harris and Roy Jenkins. What worries me is that the Prime Minister should seem to be encouraging this obsession. The Lord Chancellor's Committee was once again instructed to discuss it.

Michael Stewart made a long report on foreign affairs, at the end of which I raised the problem of the Permanent Secretary at the Foreign Office. The whole of this week there's been a great stunt organized by the Sherlock Holmes Society. Paul Gore-Booth travelled to Switzerland and was photographed in fancy dress with Adrian Conan Doyle at the Reichenbach Falls,[1] where the struggle with Professor Moriarty and the death of Sherlock Holmes took place. I asked about these antics and was severely rebuked by Michael Stewart, who said he had given permission for this and told me I ought to have a sense of humour. Having made my point I shut up and I noticed that there's not a word in the Cabinet minutes about my intervention. But I have filed a little letter to the Prime Minister saying how shocked I am and Whitehall will hear that this has been discussed.

At 3.30 Fred Peart had his real test on the Business Statement and did extremely well.[2] He's developing a line of his own which couldn't be more different from that of the arrogant, high-handed, intellectual Dick Crossman. Fred is an easy-going, pleasant, non-progressive, sensible man. There are terrible ructions going on about the conditions in the committee room upstairs, where the Finance Bill is being taken, but all the odium,[3] thank

* Since his great speech Quintin has been careful to widen his approach in such a way as to mollify Enoch Powell's attacks on the Tory Party and he's made it quite clear that there will be an ordinary party disagreement about the Bill.

[1] Sir Paul Gore-Booth (K.C.M.G. 1957) joined the Foreign Service in 1933. He was Permanent Under-Secretary of State 1965–9 and Head of H.M. Diplomatic Service 1968–9. In 1969 he retired and became a life peer. He was President of the Sherlock Holmes Society in 1967. In 1968 the Society made an expedition to Switzerland where Adrian Conan Doyle, the son of Sir Arthur, entertained them at his castle near Lausanne. He and Sir Paul, both attired in deerstalker and Inverness cape, posed for a photograph by the Reichenbach Falls where, as Conan Doyle describes in 'The Final Problem' in *The Memoirs of Sherlock Holmes* (London: Murray/Cape, 1974 edn) Sherlock Holmes appeared to fall to his death.

[2] On Thursday afternoons the Leader of the House tells Parliament the business for the following week.

[3] The Finance Bill contains the taxation proposals which the Chancellor has introduced in his budget and until 1968 all its Commons' stages were taken on the Floor of the House, with the Committee Stage taken in Committee of the whole House. After the 1965 Finance Bill, an exceptionally complicated one which required sixteen days of scarce parliamentary time, there was support for an experiment to take the Finance Bill Committee Stage

heavens, is falling on me. The Tories are now all complaining about the physical accommodation in Room 10, although they insisted on moving out of the much bigger Room 14 when I offered it to them on the grounds that the 1922 Committee has always met there.[1] Fred fended them off very well but I think he's going to be a tremendous reactionary about parliamentary reform. However that will be all right until the new House of Lords and the second big bulk of reforms of the Commons come into action and by that time there'll be another Leader of the House to carry them through.

Barbara, as I expected, made a tremendous come-back after her flop. Unfortunately I didn't hear her speech on the setting up of the new D.E.P. because I was downstairs dealing with details of the pension scheme and then with prices and incomes. You see what my life is. I am now a senior Cabinet Minister on almost every Cabinet Committee.

This evening I found myself taking over from Roy in the chair at the beginning of the Prices and Incomes Committee because he had to be away. As soon as he came back I slipped out because I wanted to go to the Israeli Embassy for their Independence Day celebration. At Cabinet this morning Michael Stewart had said very stiffly that in view of their marching through Jerusalem he was refusing to attend.[2] There was a tremendous crush but the presence of the Lord President was duly registered and I thanked God that they had done their march through East Jerusalem without incident and shown their strength. I'm on their side and I'm not going to disguise it. I fought my way out of the party because, at Tam's suggestion, I was giving dinner to Brian Walden.[3] He's a tight-faced, ambitious, clever little man whom I got to know in the Midlands. He's now one of the ablest Birmingham M.P.s, a fanatical, independent-minded right-winger. His manners are a little odd, he insisted on ordering the expensive 14*s.* 6*d.* dinner but then eating none of it and on entertaining me to an expensive bottle of wine. I

---

upstairs. After 1969 a compromise was devised by which those clauses dealing with taxes of wide application are taken on the Floor and the rest sent to a Standing Committee. See Vol. II, pp. 96, 680.

[1] All Conservative back benchers belong to this Committee, which originated in a meeting of Conservatives at the Carlton Club in October 1922, which led to the fall of the Lloyd George Coalition and to the premiership of Bonar Law. The Committee can influence but not formulate policy.

[2] As a result of the Six-Day War, from June 5th–10th 1967, Israel now occupied all Palestine west of the Jordan, including the Gaza Strip, most of the Sinai peninsula and the Golan Heights in Syria. Israeli forces had captured the old walled city of Jerusalem and the Holy Place of the Wailing Wall. For the first time since 1947 the Arab city and the Jewish city to the west and south were unified and the city of Jerusalem administered as a single municipality. Since December 1967, Dr Gunnar Jarring, a Swedish diplomat, specially appointed by the U.N. Secretary-General, had been attempting to find a basis for negotiations between Israel and the Arabs but Israel's coalition Government continued to demand that the Arabs themselves negotiate terms for peace.

[3] Labour M.P. for Birmingham, All Saints, 1964–74 and since 1974 for Birmingham, Ladywood. He was P.P.S. to the Chief Secretary and to the Financial Secretary to the Treasury 1964–6.

rather like someone who so insists on being on equal terms and on showing that he's got plenty of money. Then he tested me on the subject of Harold Wilson. He's obviously determined to get a new Leader and I was equally determined not to give an iota. When he said, 'You never would on any condition?' I replied, 'No, on no condition whatsoever'. It doesn't happen to be true but if I had given one inch it would have been all around the Party that Dick Crossman was prepared to consider replacing Harold by someone else.

Friday, May 3rd

Barbara's big speech yesterday announcing that the D.E.P. was to be an interventionist Ministry dominated the headlines and created a good deal of disturbance. I thought it pretty good.

First of all I was back with the Prime Minister, Eddie Shackleton and the Lord Chancellor discussing once again prime ministerial patronage in nominating peers. As I expected, Harold refused to allow any kind of committee. 'If a committee came in and saw my list they would make difficulties about my choice of Tommy Balogh, for example, or on the other hand about some person whom they had never heard of. If I am to get anybody unusual into the Lords,' he said, 'I don't want a committee checking on me.' How sensible and right.*

When we had finished I stayed behind, because Tommy Balogh had insisted that I should talk to Harold about a particularly odious article in last week's *New Statesman*. I've mentioned the Cabinet row about the articles in the *Spectator*, the *Sunday Telegraph* and the *Financial Times*. I had had nothing to do with these but directly I read the *New Statesman* article I recognized that it was based on talks someone had had with me. One of my difficulties is that when I am in form I talk well and sooner or later formulations which I make at the lunch table get into the press. Part of this article was based on things I had said about the new balance of power in the Cabinet and the role of Roy and Barbara and myself. However, Alan Watkins had managed to add some extremely unpleasant remarks about my row with Harold,[1] asserting that I had broken with him and ceased to be Leader of the House because I didn't like to be accused of leaking. This happens to be true but it's not something I want to see in print.

But Harold wasn't particularly concerned and didn't accuse me of this leak. I think he's now obsessed by his suspicions of Roy Jenkins and John Harris. It's a very great worry to me that this should be his main preoccupation and I tried to make him realize that the best way of driving out this kind of gossip is to give the journalists better news of what we are doing. If they're kept short, they pick up a bit of gossip or, even worse, they read a

* But I wish he would get a few more unusual people in!

[1] Alan Watkins was Political Columnist of the *Spectator* before moving to the *New Statesman*. He later wrote for the *Observer*.

story in one paper and then embellish it in their own. This is what happens when we're an unsuccessful and uninteresting Government.

I then went across to the meeting of the Home Affairs Committee and there Denis Howell and I celebrated a great triumph on Aintree.[1] Denis and George Wigg had worked very hard and it's now clear that Liverpool can buy the site, put a sports centre in the middle and open it up to the public, while the Horserace Betting Levy Board will carry the whole cost of the building and the racing. Throughout this battle we were opposed by the Ministry although Tony Greenwood himself hadn't come to the meeting. He had sent his deputy, Jim MacColl,[2] who claimed that the money shouldn't come from Housing but from the Treasury. What balls! If there's one thing the Ministry of Housing wants it's open space and sports centres for cities like Liverpool. Here was a good example of a Cabinet Committee overruling a Minister and doing the right thing, provided, that is, that the Levy Board coughs up the cash and Liverpool remains sensible about the purchase.

This afternoon I was off to Warwick University where I was due to address an academic society, the Politics Society, about race. Looking back over my life I realize how many of my formative moments have been those which have dealt with the impact of nationalism and racialism on politics. I take a much tougher view, which shocks the liberal progressives as well as the Communist International. I believe that the differences which divide mankind are as strong as the universal principles which unite us. These differences are of course matters of race and culture which are, emotionally at least, as important as economics and self-interest—probably more important. Liberal progressives and Communists share the view that there is such a thing as a universal human being who can be united by universal rational principles, and they believe that differences of colour and culture and history are incidental and superficial compared to the unifying principles of mankind. I believe that our main effort must be to control racial and cultural passions. We must be prepared to admit that our country has a very severe limit to its capacity for racial assimilation.

Because I believe that we must not exceed our racial limits and we must cut back immigration quotas to the necessary level I was against Gaitskell and Brown when they opposed the Immigration Bill in 1962, strongly in favour of the 1965 White Paper and the new Bill in 1968 and I'm for further quotas now because I believe that as a nation we have the right to decide a

[1] It had been feared that if Mrs Topham, the owner of the racecourse, should die before arrangements could be made about the future of the course, the land would be sold to the highest bidder. See Vol. II, p. 730. Denis Howell, Labour M.P. for Birmingham, All Saints, 1955–September 1959 and for Birmingham, Small Heath, since 1961, was Joint Parliamentary Under-Secretary of State at the Department of Education and Science, with special responsibility for Sport 1964–9, Minister of State at the M.H.L.G. 1969–70. He has been Minister of State (Sport) at the Department of the Environment since 1974.

[2] A member of the L.C.C. since 1936 and Mayor of Paddington 1947–9. He was Labour M.P. for Widnes from 1950 until his death in 1972 and Joint Parliamentary Secretary at the M.H.L.G. 1964–9.

great issue for ourselves. Should we become a multi-racial community which has large amounts of Indians and Africans from abroad mixed into it or should we remain predominantly a white community which permits small foreign communities to come and live here and become full citizens? I expounded this theory to the students at some length and found they were surprised by it and in some ways impressed.

Sunday, May 5th

Another lovely sunny day at Prescote, the rain having greened us all up all over the farm. The grass is now growing fast and so are the weeds on my island. We're really having a splendid year. I don't remember ever having as much sunshine throughout winter and spring. In the spring, though, we've had our share of cold winds which held back the growth and the buds and now, after a long period of cold and drought, we've got this April weather in May, plenty of rain mixed with sunshine and warmth. There ought to be a pretty good harvest this year.

While I'm discussing the farm I ought to mention that during the week Mr Paisner, Mr Pritchett and Mr Proctor met me in London for the first meeting of the trustees of Prescote Manor.[1] We've now made all the legal arrangements to ensure that our 500 acres will be farmed as a whole for the foreseeable future. There's a pretty high rate of annual profit, the herd is steadily going up in value and we're beginning to breed our own bulls and sell our heifers at a high price by private contract. There's no doubt whatsoever that Pritchett's a very good manager and if he could manage people as well as he does machines and animals he would be superb.

I've considered more than once in this diary what effect Prescote has on me. I've no doubt that the business experience I gain here is of practical value to a Labour politician. Of course I have nothing to do with the day-to-day running of the farm but for something like fifteen years I've been looking at its business and tax side and getting some idea of what growth and profit really mean in a business of this size. I can't help thinking that it'll be of some use to me now that, among my many other chairmanships, I'm Chairman of the Cabinet Committee on Agriculture. But does our wealth blunt our socialism? The answer, I'm afraid, is that of course it does. It means that we look at things from on top and this stratospheric approach is accentuated in my case by the little attention I have to pay to my constituency. I have a cast-iron majority and because my local party is extremely weak I see far less of Coventry and far less of Coventry people than I used to.[2] So I'm receding from the common touch in Coventry at the same time as I'm getting thoroughly used to Whitehall on the one side and on the other this highly affluent style of living at Prescote Manor. But I suppose it's fair to say that

[1] Crossman's solicitors, Leslie Paisner and G. F. L. Proctor, and his farm manager, Dennis Pritchett.

[2] In the 1966 General Election Crossman had a majority of 18,696 at Coventry East.

this might have occurred even if we hadn't had Prescote and I'd just bought a cottage in the country and at my age begun to get out of touch with life.[1]

Today Anne and I motored over to see Barbara at her new house near Ibstone. She'd been living a few miles nearer High Wycombe when a great by-pass plonked itself down just at the bottom of her garden so she had to sell up. She found this old farmhouse hanging on the edge of one of those steep, wooded, Chiltern valleys with some pasture on one side and, on the other, beechwoods and flowering *Prunus* and cherry. We motored there in a most wonderful pellucid evening, so beautiful that we climbed to the top of Brill Hill to see the whole land shining around us and the pale greens and blues of central England. The cooling towers at Didcot looked like an Arabian Nights' palace and even the radio mast at Watlington acquired a romantic glow.

We found Barbara sitting on the steep lawn with, behind her, an orchard which must be over 100 years old. There was a nice housekeeper looking after her, with Ted looking like a distinguished old country squire. Jennie and Chris Hall were our fellow-guests and Barbara took us all over the house. Here she is after her first three weeks as Secretary of State for Productivity and Employment. She has rushed full tilt into the job and taken everything on with the maximum blare of publicity. It's not the way I would have handled a new Ministry. I would have come in quietly, avoiding the publicity at the beginning and above all avoiding making decisions too quickly. But her technique has made the biggest impact of any Minister in any Department since George Brown arrived on the first day of the D.E.A. I'm sure she has frightened the C.B.I. with her threats of an interventionist policy but I'm equally sure that she's impressed them and, even more, impressed the trade unions. Some people call her a neurotic and self-centred politician. Sometimes she is, but in the atmosphere of home she's lovely. She knows how to enjoy home and how to make it enjoyable. She's got very ordinary middle-class taste in furniture and pictures and books and in none of these ways is she high-falutin'. She and Ted are the nicest kind of people and she's one of the few good things in our Cabinet.

Monday, May 6th

We tried this weekend to persuade every Minister to make a May Day speech on the subject of race and the newspapers showed that our marathon has had its impact. Here was Denis Healey marching and speaking at Glasgow, there was Jim Callaghan at Hull and Roy Jenkins at Swansea dolling up his ex-Home Secretary's liberal image, getting headlines by his annihilating personal attack on Enoch Powell. Above all, there was Harold's big speech at Birmingham yesterday. With the agreement of the Parliamentary Committee, he had gone in for an appeal for a bipartisan Select Committee to control and supervise the execution of immigration policy but he had added

[1] He was born in December 1907.

to this a great piece on the Tory policy in Rhodesia and removed any appearance of bipartisanship. Obviously he scored a very great success.

So we'd used May Day pretty well. But there were some glaring weaknesses. At the London Labour demonstration in Hyde Park apparently only two or three people had marched behind the Labour banners, while a couple of thousand young people had joined in the Trotskyite-anarchist rally. Poor Judith Hart had the job of addressing this tiny gathering in Trafalgar Square.

There's one other story in the Monday papers I feel bound to mention. Poor Jack Ashley was a quite successful B.B.C. fellow who came over to us and was looking forward to a lifetime of politics. He was one of those solid, loyalist, working-class right-wingers who was bound to do well. Despite his semi-working-class accent, he was a university person and a thoroughly typical loyalist. Suddenly now a virus strikes him stone deaf and he has to retire from Parliament.[1]

My first job in London was to see Burke Trend, Eddie Shackleton and the Lord Chancellor about the draft White Paper on Lords' reform. The Chancellor wanted to put down a skeleton outline of our proposals in the shortest and simplest language possible. At first I thought this a good idea but it was pointed out to me that if we just planked before the public, especially before the Parliamentary Party, detailed proposals for a two-tier chamber of voting and speaking peers, they might well be greeted with derision. In six months' committee work we have developed a scheme which really is the next stage in the evolution of the Second Chamber. It fits today's circumstances exactly and it's designed to secure the abolition of the hereditary principle with the minimum of trouble. But the scheme is so closely fitting and so expertly made and it depends on such inside knowledge that to the outside world it will look fussy and unimportant.

David Faulkner and Wheeler-Booth had provided a draft of the brief skeleton analysis but they had preceded it with a lengthy introduction.[2] This seemed to all of us to fall between two stools. We argued at length and finally it was suggested that I should take the draft away to see what I could

[1] Labour M.P. for Stoke-on-Trent since 1966. He had been a B.B.C. radio producer 1951–7 and a senior television producer 1957–66. He did not in fact retire from Parliament but learned to lip-read and from the back benches campaigned successfully on behalf of the deaf and disabled.

[2] David Faulkner, then a Principal at the Home Office, had been seconded to serve with Michael Wheeler-Booth, then Principal Private Secretary to the Leader of the House of Lords, as Secretaries to the Inter-Party Conference. Together with Lancelot Errington they were responsible for much of the work on the Lords' reform scheme. Michael Wheeler-Booth, a Clerk in the Parliament Office at the House of Lords 1960–5, Secretary to the Leader of the House and the Chief Whip 1965–7, was seconded from 1967–9 as Special Assistant to the Leader of the House, to work on the scheme for Lords' reform. He was Clerk in the Committee Office, 1969–70, Clerk of the Journals 1970–4 and since 1972 has been Clerk of the Overseas and European Office. Lancelot Errington, Under-Secretary of State at the Cabinet Office 1965–8 and at the Ministry of Social Security 1968, was Assistant Under-Secretary of State at the D.H.S.S. 1968–71, Deputy Under-Secretary of State at the D.H.S.S. 1971–3 and has been Second Permanent Secretary there since 1973.

do with it. I said I would go away on Thursday and see if I couldn't draft the first part in two and a half days, so I went back to the office and made arrangements to leave at lunchtime on Thursday and have the whole of Thursday afternoon, Friday and Saturday writing at home.

I had intended to sit in the House this afternoon to do something very unusual, listen to the Second Reading of the Social Work (Scotland) Bill.[1] This had started in the House of Lords, and it's very important, because the reports on which it is based were published long before we got our Seebohm Committee going, so on this issue the Scots are a good year ahead. It seemed to me natural that I should want to hear about the Scottish solution and I thought I would go and sit on the front bench along with Judith, who had been the Parliamentary Under-Secretary for Scotland when the Bill was prepared. Just as we were going in we realized that the Scots would suspect some poisonous English conspiracy so we would have to keep out, come what may. I quote this to show how deep is the separation which already exists between England and Scotland. Willie Ross and his friends accuse the Scot. Nats of separatism but what Willie Ross himself actually likes is to keep Scottish business absolutely privy from English business. I am not sure this system isn't one that gets the worst of both worlds which is why I'm in favour of a Scottish parliament.

Poor Anne had to stay in the country with Virginia, who has german measles, so she couldn't come to her cousin Jane's twenty-first birthday party in Fulham. I had to represent her and I was just preparing to go off in my black saloon car with Molly when I suddenly had an urgent message that the Prime Minister wanted to see me in No. 10.[2] I went with some foreboding because I knew he was worried about leaks, but not at all. He wanted to talk about Tommy Balogh's future. Now, ever since this Government began, Tommy has been a consultant with an office in No. 10. Oxford finally said they wouldn't give him any more leave unless he went back to regular teaching but of course he has tried to have the best of both worlds and has kept his office here and his staff. The university have written him a horrid letter saying they want evidence that he really is just a part-time consultant. I put it to Tommy that the simplest thing would be to become a life peer quickly and then they couldn't question his right to come to London. I had also put it to Harold and for fifty minutes this evening we talked round and

[1] The Bill provided for the reorganization of the welfare, probation and other personal and community services in Scotland. Its proposals were based on the recommendations made in 1964 by the Kilbrandon Committee on Children and Young Persons, Scotland (set up in 1961) and on the White Paper *Social Work and the Community*, published in October 1966. Charles Kilbrandon became a life peer in 1971, had been a Senator of the College of Justice in Scotland and was Lord of Session 1959–71 and Chairman of the Scottish Law Commission 1965–71. Since 1971 he has been a Lord of Appeal in Ordinary. In addition to chairing the Committee on Children and Young Persons, he was later a member, and on the death of Lord Crowther, Chairman, of the Royal Commission on the Constitution, 1969–73.

[2] Molly Crawford, Crossman's driver.

round Tommy's personal problems. There's no one in the world who takes more trouble about his friends than Harold Wilson. It was quite like old times and I heard later that Harold felt that the rift between us had been removed.

Then I rushed to Fulham through driving rain with the presents.

Tuesday, May 7th

Today's Gallup poll shows that Powell has suddenly jumped from having 1 per cent of Tories thinking him the best alternative to Heath to having 24 per cent. He is now far more popular than Maudling and nearly as popular as Heath. This is the result of the three-week sensation following his Birmingham speech. The other astonishing figure in the poll was that 72 per cent of the population think that on race there's no difference between the Tory and the Labour Party. They all think that Powell is different, not the two official party organizations. This is enormously helpful to us but on the other hand it also widens the gap between Westminster and the public outside. Ordinary people feel that the Establishment and the two party machines are working together, disregarding public demand and fixing everything in defiance of the will of the people. That's what irritates them and makes them reach out for Powell as a leader.

At Legislation Committee this morning we had the Hovercraft Bill back again.[1] The Board of Trade had wanted simple enabling legislation to deal with it. While I appreciate that it's difficult to introduce new safety regulations for a machine which is neither an aeroplane, a ship nor a land vehicle nevertheless, as Leader of the House, I had felt it outrageous to permit an enabling Bill which simply gave civil servants power to devise regulations and legislate by Order in Council. I had sent the Bill back to the Board of Trade but it had come back almost unchanged. Once again the Minister was asking for the Second Reading Committee procedure which has only been invented for completely non-contentious Bills.[2] So I objected again, whereat Fred Peart, who's now in the chair, remarked that we couldn't go on like this for ever because very soon we're going to have hovercraft crossing the Channel and we must have some safety legislation. I said I couldn't help that, we'd got to see the procedure correctly applied. At least it will have to go through the ordinary proceedings in the House. (In fact all they needed to do was

[1] The hovercraft, a British invention, was a cross between a boat and an aeroplane. Jet engines inside and jet propellers at the rear drove it forward a few feet above the sea on a cushion of air. The Hovercraft Bill had its second Reading on May 16th and received the Royal Assent on July 26th. The first cross-Channel hovercraft service, operated by British Rail, was inaugurated on July 31st, 1968, and the journey time of forty minutes compared well with the boat service of one and a half hours.

[2] Proceedings on some Bills may be accelerated by taking their Second Reading stage upstairs in Committee. The Report Stage can be similarly remitted. As objection by a specified number of Members keeps the Bill on the Floor for these stages, the device is in practice only used for non-contentious Bills.

temporarily to classify it as marine and apply the marine regulations until they thought of something better.)

At S.E.P. [the Steering Committee on Strategic Economic Policy] we had Roy Jenkins reporting on the state of public expenditure. Despite all our efforts it is due to rise by 5 per cent next year and 7 per cent the year after. I put up my idea of a social service budget and other group budgets and Roy was grateful because this if it works could be a very big change. What I'm trying to achieve is a scheme where all the social services expenditure is expressed as a single block sum so that we can get decisions on priorities. My first meeting on this takes place next Tuesday.

I was surprised when afterwards Gunter came up and asked me to take him back to my office for a talk. He wanted to publish a White Paper on the siting of nuclear power stations near big cities. His predecessor had announced that this was now a safe policy and cheaper than putting them in the wilds. I warned him that a White Paper would be used by Alf Robens in his campaign to discredit nuclear energy,[1] although I was the only Minister who expressed any doubts. Everyone else had agreed with Gunter. I told him that a White Paper would not remove fears but probably increase them.

At this point I gave him a drink and he looked at me and said, 'My heart is not in this job any more. I feel inclined to go.' I told him he couldn't do this now. The time to go had been when Harold was doing his reshuffle. Gunter replied that he had been so flabbergasted that he hadn't realized what was happening to him. He'd never thought it possible that he would be moved from the Ministry of Labour until he had carried out his one political ambition, to introduce legislation based on the Report of the Donovan Commission.[2] Suddenly Harold had sent for him and started accusing him of leaks and disloyalties and such absurdities. After a pause, Gunter said that he was now being approached to become General Secretary of the party. I replied that if his heart wasn't in it he shouldn't do it and that on no account should he take this on at his age and in his state of health. 'You and I, Ray, are in the same age group,' I said. 'We've each got only one more job before we retire.'

This is the first time I've talked to Gunter. He has always been a great puzzle to me, a huge, squat, bullfrog of a man, with a great Welsh voice and with the less attractive qualities of the Welsh as well. We sat together on the N.E.C. for years and he's always treated me as a crafty, disloyal intellectual

[1] Labour M.P. for Wansbeck 1945–50 and for Blyth 1950–60. He was Parliamentary Secretary at the Ministry of Fuel and Power 1947–51, Minister of Labour and National Service April–October 1951 and Chairman of the National Coal Board 1961–71. He became a life peer in 1961 and since 1971 has been Chairman of Vickers Ltd.

[2] Appointed in April 1965, under the chairmanship of Lord Donovan, to examine Trade Unions and Employers' Associations. The Royal Commission was to publish its Report, Cmnd 3623, on June 13th. See below, p. 141. Terence Donovan (Kt 1950) was Labour M.P. for East Leicester 1945–50 and for North-East Leicester February–July 1950. A judge of the King's Bench Division in the High Court of Justice 1950–60 and a Lord Justice of Appeal 1960–63, he became a life peer in 1964.

and I suppose I've always responded in kind. I never trusted him a yard, but I listened with fascination because I felt he was talking from the bottom of his heart.

At the Lords' reform consultations this afternoon we at last dealt with the Macleod objection that though we could put our scheme into law this session we couldn't set up the new House of Lords until the next Parliament.[1] I replied that this was quite all right and that we would write it into the White Paper. Macleod then began to argue that this was impossible because his objection was so basic that he couldn't sign an agreed White Paper if at the same time there was to be disagreement about the timing of the implementation of our scheme. By saying this he infuriated Carrington and Jellicoe, who want to have a reformed House as soon as possible. But Macleod had got the decision of the Shadow Cabinet behind him and he was now pushing it a good deal further. Maudling protested vigorously and said that of course we could publish an agreed White Paper while disagreeing about the timing. I managed to keep my temper and said on behalf of our people that we'd get on with drafting the White Paper and ask the Conservatives to state their disagreement in a paragraph at the end. I also suggested we should put, finally, to a free vote of both Houses,[2] the question of the date of implementation. Macleod grunted a lot of opposition on the ground that a free vote wouldn't be fair.

I am aware that if we seem to be rushing and skedaddling we might lose everything and the White Paper might go off at half-cock. So we turned to the timing of our programme and decided after a lot of to-ing and fro-ing to get the White Paper through Cabinet before we break off for the Whitsun recess and then to let it go to the Shadow Cabinet first thing after the recess, with the debate soon after that. I was quite pleased when at the end of the meeting Jim Callaghan said to me, 'You will have nothing to blame yourself for if you don't get this reform. I think you have conducted the negotiations, if I may say so, perfectly.' One of the things that has annoyed me about Harold, the great negotiator, is that I have been excluded from all negotiations whether domestic or international but on the House of Lords we haven't done too badly.

Wednesday, May 8th

The newspapers were full of the Scot. Nat. victories in the local elections but Tam came downstairs to tell me that in his part of the country we actually

[1] Iain Macleod, Conservative M.P. for Enfield from 1950 until his sudden death in July 1970, had joined the Conservative Research Department in 1948. He was Minister of Health 1952–5, Minister of Labour 1955–9, Secretary of State for the Colonies 1959–61 and Chancellor of the Duchy of Lancaster and Leader of the House of Commons 1961–3. From 1961 to 1963 he was Joint Chairman and Chairman of the Conservative Party Organization, and when the Conservatives returned to office 1970 he served as Chancellor of the Exchequer for one month.

[2] I.e. with no party whip instructing back benchers how to vote.

won back a seat from the Nationalists and I'm sure that hard-working Labour parties have been able to hold their own.[1] It's also worth noticing that despite the tremendous victories in Scotland there was no increase in the Welsh nationalist vote. Scottish nationalism is clearly different in kind from Welsh nationalism and one shouldn't generalize about the two.

This morning's Party meeting was the first of two to be held on prices and incomes. We decided to have one general discussion and then next Wednesday a debate, all leading up to the crucial Second Reading debate on May 21st when, unless we get a majority, the Government will collapse. Today Barbara made a very long speech, nearly fifty minutes. I felt she was enormously tired. She wasn't only measuring her words, they were coming out slowly because she was exhausted. But she had prepared with enormous care and as Gunter, Stewart, Brown and Wilson never did, she presented the Party with a really reasoned case for the prices and incomes policy, seen first historically and then in terms of the practical situation. I had to go out to a Privy Council before Shinwell's famous outburst when he said he was going to vote for the Party against the Government.[2]

This was the morning for the Privy Council after which the Queen would discuss my suggestions for reform. As usual the Privy Council only took a minute or two and after it was over I stayed behind to talk to her alone. I explained to her my idea of having the normal Privy Council with only one or two people present and with the minimum of fuss and then, since she had expressed a desire to get to know her Ministers, perhaps five or six times a year a Privy Council after which she might entertain her Ministers to drinks. She listened to me very attentively. I became convinced that I could have gone much further and proposed the abolition of the whole thing. However, I had made a little advance and I must now inform Harold and clear up the details with Godfrey Agnew and Michael Adeane.

After this I had a meeting with the social security officials to discuss at last how the new pensions are to be composed. In our original plan it was to be a graded benefit on top of a flat-rate element. Now we had decided that it should be a graded benefit, a percentage of earnings, all the way up, but that would mean the lower income groups would get too little. So the Ministry had thought up the idea of having an earnings-related scheme with two bands. On 25 per cent of your earnings you would get 60 per cent, whereas on the rest of your earnings you would get only 25 per cent. I must say I was worried at this further complication and also at the discrepancy between the officials' and Judith Hart's views. She is always trying to make the scheme more

[1] In the local elections held on May 7th the S.N.P. won 105 seats. It held the balance of power in Glasgow where, as in Aberdeen, the Progressives won control.

[2] Emanuel Shinwell, Labour M.P. for Linlithgow 1922–4 and 1928–31, for Seaham 1935–50 and Easington 1950–70, was Financial Secretary at the War Office 1929–30, Parliamentary Secretary to the Department of Mines 1924 and 1930–1, Minister of Fuel and Power 1945–7, Secretary of State for War 1947–50, Minister of Defence 1950–1 and Chairman of the P.L.P. 1964–7. He became a life peer in 1970.

redistributive, i.e. to get more money for the bottom of the income scale, whereas I realize that a superannuation scheme has to give value for money all the way through.

The meeting turned into a very rough discussion. I told them I sometimes felt it would be better to scrap this appallingly elaborate scheme and have some perfectly simple flat-rate pensions formula as part of our national insurance scheme. I doubt if these calculations of everybody's income for life and precise assessment of pensions varied according to life earnings are really worth it. Finally we decided to call in the circus, Brian, Richard, Tommy and Nicky, to think together about it before we commit ourselves.[1]

This evening I had dinner with Tam to talk over the Scottish elections. Meanwhile it was clear that the Finance Bill was running into trouble, and was going to have its first all-night sitting. Tom Bradley, Roy's P.P.S., came into the dining room almost neurotic about the strain, discomfort and misery they were suffering.[2] This is my responsibility because as Leader of the House I had decided to put the Finance Bill upstairs. I had very carefully calculated that to make this work we should have to impose a voluntary time-table from the very start and it had been agreed with Callaghan and John Diamond. But a new Chancellor had plumped in front of Macleod a very expensive Finance Bill, raising a record sum of money, and Macleod had refused to collaborate at all. Roy could have clamped on a time-table before they started the sittings. He would have been far better off if he had done that, but now the Tories have begun to sabotage the Committee and complain about the room, and there is a general feeling of failure.

I tried to explain all this to Bradley but I knew that my name was mud, not only with the Tories but also with our own people.

Then Michael Foot came across and we discussed the mood of the Party. We are in a new situation, dramatized by Manny's threat yesterday. I think there is a simple reason for this change. As long as the majority of the Parliamentary Party thought there was a good chance of winning the election or at least holding their own seats they were bound to the Government by a sense of loyalty. Now that a large number of them think there's no chance of survival and that they have no future in the House, they start saying to themselves, 'I may as well stand up and be defeated for my principles rather than be defeated for supporting a Government which is sacrificing them.'

Then there are other people in the Party like Brian Walden or Michael Foot who ask what shall be left if we go on supporting the Government and Harold. Shouldn't we at least ensure that when the Party goes into Opposition it still retains some principles, some fight, some spunk? You are castrating

[1] The 'Pensions circus' of Brian Abel-Smith, Richard Titmuss, Thomas Balogh and, occasionally, Nicholas Kaldor.

[2] Labour M.P. for Leicester North-East 1962–74 and for Leicester East since 1974. He had been a member of the N.E.C. since 1966 and Roy Jenkins's P.P.S. since 1964.

and destroying the Party before it gets there. That's the other part of the mood and it's equally difficult to manage.

Thursday, May 9th

The day of the borough elections, which everyone knew were going to be disastrous. My first job was to go round the corner with Tam and to register my vote before going to the Legislation Committee.

Here we were faced with the text of that damned Prices and Incomes Bill. Barbara had done her work well but, alas, she has had to make one major concession. We had hoped to rely on the Expiring Laws Continuance Bill to enable us to continue after the first eighteen months,[1] whatever parts of the Prices and Incomes Bill were still necessary, but now it is clear that when she goes to talk to the trade union group on Monday before the Bill is published on Tuesday she will have to appease them by sacrificing this.

At Parliamentary Committee we cleared our whole programme of electoral reform. The Committee accepted all our recommendations—that we should now support votes at eighteen and accept a free vote on this in the House, that polling should be extended until 10 p.m., that we should not have a second electoral register and, above all, that in future not only the name of the candidate but the party label should appear on the ballot paper. Personally I think it a scandal that this should be approved by the Parliamentary Committee and not by Cabinet. But it's not for me to complain and it's some credit to Jim Callaghan and me that we've got our package through intact.

I spent most of the rest of today on devolution, redrafting my paper as a final Cabinet paper for initial presentation to the Devolution Committee. It was ironical that I should be doing this two days after the nationalist victories in Scotland. The more I look at our proposals for a measure of administrative devolution the graver are my doubts whether they're not completely out of date. We've put together a thoroughly sensible package which two years ago might have done a great deal to appease nationalist sentiment. Now we've waited too long. However, one has to wind up a job of this kind and I shall be amused to see what actually happens.

Meanwhile quite interesting things were happening on the front bench. Neil Marten extracted from Harold the admission that if he is to be away he will nominate Michael Stewart to take his place,[2] thus acknowledging that Michael is virtually Deputy Prime Minister. Very characteristic of Harold that this had to be extracted in the same way as his admission that he was no longer in charge of D.E.A.

I got in just when Harold was answering yet another question about my de-

[1] An annual bill for continuing a number of statutes (many dating from wartime) which only have annual effect. Since 1970 it has no longer been in use.

[2] Neil Marten has been Conservative M.P. for Banbury since 1959 and was Parliamentary Secretary at the Ministry of Aviation 1962–4.

valuation speech, this time from Knox Cunningham.[1] As usual the P.M. did it very effectively. The moment he sat down he turned to me and said, 'I spent the morning after our meeting, Dick, giving evidence to the Lord Chancellor, Fred Peart and Willie Ross about those three articles.[2] I explained to them how absolutely I believed in you.' What am I to make of that? He knows those articles reflect a view which I hold strongly but that I didn't give them to the press. Yet he can't leave them alone, because, I suspect, he wants to prove that Roy was really responsible for the leak.

Then came Fred Peart's Business Statement. He's going down very well with the Tories, as you will see from one question put to him by Peyton. Peyton is a particularly toady, Tadpoly Taperish Tory who stands up there with his head on one side and tries to be offensive. He has always hated me from the bottom of his heart. 'Is the Leader of the House aware,' he asked, 'how very appreciative many of us are of his good nature, helpfulness and courtesy, particularly as we have been quite unaccustomed to receive such things from the previous Leader of the House?' There wasn't a great cheer but only an awkward silence, as though the House didn't quite like it but all the same recognized an element of truth in it. Certainly the whole unpopularity of the Finance Bill and the pressure of the work in the Standing Committees is now coming back upon me. Anthony Kershaw,[3] Heath's P.P.S., said to me as we left the Chamber, 'What a mess you've made of it, driving us all upstairs into those endless committees.' I replied that I didn't think we should always spend all our time on the Floor and he spat out, 'I knew you were a shit but I didn't know you were a deliberate shit.' That is the mood of a good many Tories. After the division on the Public Service and Armed Forces Pensions Bill I made Molly drive me down to Prescote in order to do my job on the draft of the Lords' reform White Paper.

Friday, May 10th

I woke up early and went downstairs to hear the election results on the radio.[4] Listening to the national results I assumed we were done for in Coventry. 'My God,' I thought, 'that means Peter Lister will have lost in Binley along with another eight or nine defeats.' However I rang up Albert and found that, whereas in Birmingham every ward had been lost, in Coventry

[1] Sir Knox Cunningham, Q.C., heavyweight boxing champion, Cambridge University, 1931, was Ulster Unionist M.P. for South Antrim 1955–70 and P.P.S. to the Prime Minister 1959–63. He became a baronet in 1963 and died in 1976. Crossman's speech in Birmingham on January 28th had described devaluation and the subsequent measures as part of the Labour Government's giant strides to socialism. The Prime Minister expressed his delight at Knox Cunningham's obsession with the Lord President's speeches.

[2] See above, p. 41.

[3] Conservative M.P. for Stroud since 1955, Parliamentary Secretary at the Ministry of Public Building and Works June–October 1970, Parliamentary Under-Secretary of State at the F.C.O. 1970–3 and for Defence (R.A.F.) 1973–4.

[4] The Conservatives made a net gain of 535 seats to Labour's net loss of 596 and won 27 out of 32 London boroughs.

we had lost two, won one and had no change in the others.[1] It's astonishing how one's local results influence one's general political views. The London defeat, losing control of Islington and Hackney, for example, was really devastating. So was the loss of the Labour majority at Sheffield. But the draw we had achieved at Coventry was what really interested me.

When the *Coventry Evening Telegraph* rang up, I said at once that I hadn't seen the detailed election results and the voice replied, 'We don't want to talk to you about that but about Mr Cecil King.'[2] That was the first I heard of the demand in the *Mirror* that Harold Wilson should go, the revelation of a grave financial crisis concealed by the Treasury and the Bank of England and, finally, the resignation of Cecil King himself as a director of the Bank. I told the *Telegraph* I had nothing to say and sat down in my study to draft the Lords' White Paper.

Heavens, it was hard work. I hate redrafting from somebody's old half-done manuscript. I slogged, slithered and wasted the morning and then I said to myself, 'I'd better do a press release for my speech tonight.' I'd been asked to address a new dining club organized jointly by the Northampton, North Oxon., South Oxon. and Banbury constituency parties. Just as I was starting this I was rung up by Roy, who told me he was in some trouble because Barbara was insisting that he should repudiate Cecil King and assert his belief in Harold Wilson's leadership. 'If I do this', said Roy, 'there are great difficulties. I can't afford to get into an argument about the financial situation because there's a run on the pound today and, as for reasserting my faith in Harold, I shall be accused of doing it precisely because I am conspiring against him.' I thought for a moment and then said, 'I tell you what. I'll ring up Barbara and tell her I'm the man to make the speech.' Barbara appreciated that I could speak as an ex-*Daily Mirror* journalist as well as a member of the Government. I went back to my study and wrote a short, sharp press release reminding the country that Cecil King was the nephew of Lord Rothermere and Lord Northcliffe, the two megalomaniac press lords who tried to dictate to Prime Ministers.[3] I made sure that Transport House would put it out for 8.30 p.m.

[1] Peter Lister had been a member of Coventry City Council since 1957 and subsequently became Chairman of Coventry South-East Constituency Labour Party. Albert Rose was Secretary of Coventry East Constituency Labour Party 1955–71.

[2] Chairman of *Daily Mirror* Newspapers Ltd and *Sunday Pictorial* Newspapers Ltd 1951–63 and of the International Publishing Corporation 1963–8 and the Newspaper Proprietors' Association 1961–8. He was a part-time member of the NationalCoal Board 1966–9 and since 1965 had been a director of the Bank of England. He resigned from the latter post on May 9th, the day before his article, 'Enough is Enough', appeared in the *Daily Mirror*, which, like the other main Labour paper, the *Sun*, was owned by I.P.C. Mr King alleged that Britain was 'threatened by the greatest financial crisis in our history. It is not to be removed by lies about our reserves but by a fresh start under a new leader'. See *The Cecil King Diary 1965–70* (London: Cape, 1972).

[3] Lloyd George, Prime Minister 1916–22 and Leader of the Liberal Party 1926–31, had courted and had been courted by Viscount Northcliffe, owner of the *Daily Mail* and, later, of *The Times*, and in 1919 Prime Minister and press proprietor had attacked one

I slogged away at the White Paper all afternoon and at the evening meeting I was able to deliver my piece on Cecil King before turning to the problems of the party. I particularly discussed with them the thing which worries me most, that what is turning the electorate and the party against us is not the things we've done wrong but the things we've done right. Our own people are turning away from us because we won't go along with Enoch Powell, because we insist on using family allowances to protect the lowest-paid workers against the effects of devaluation, and because we must have a prices and incomes policy if we're not going to have mass unemployment. These are essential policies for any socialist government and are the very things our staunchest Labour supporters are blaming us for.

By the end of the speech I'd forgotten all about the press release but when we got home the telephone was ringing. It was our Mrs Marriott who had been with us at the dinner and who had just got home to find that her Harry had seen a report of the speech on the television before I had delivered it. She wanted to know how this was possible. This illustrates that a press release which interests the press gets a quick circulation.

Saturday, May 11th

I woke up to find my speech was the main B.B.C. news story and it was apparently a lead story in many of the papers, even the *Telegraph*. Harold rang through delightedly and told me what an effect the speech was having. He asked me about other Ministers. I explained Roy's difficulties and Harold finally agreed that Roy was right not to make a speech.

Let me sum up my reflections at the end of this astonishing week. The vote in the local elections is not the most depressing feature. It's the financial and economic situation which is really depressing, the appalling impact on the P.L.P. of our intentions for prices and incomes and the lack of success of the interventionist policies of Peter Shore and Tony Wedgwood Benn, young men who with carefree arrogance think they can enter the business world and help it to be more efficient. It's the amateurishness of Harold and his bright young men which gets me down.

Could Roy take his place? Well, quite certainly Michael Stewart and I could not and Barbara could not because she's a woman. So Roy is really the only possibility. But is he a serious possibility? Can this elegant, patrician, easy-going, tennis-playing, aloof, detached dilettante be a Labour Prime Minister who could get a grip on the situation and restore public confidence? I have my doubts. But it may well be true that within six months any change will be better than no change. And if so a change will take place. My job this week has not been to prevent change taking place but to tell the press

---

another over the terms of the peace with Germany. Northcliffe's brother, Lord Rothermere, had, as his successor at the *Mail*, attacked Baldwin's tariff policy and in 1931 his leadership. It was in this context that Baldwin had spoken of the press proprietors aiming at 'power without responsibility—the prerogative of the harlot throughout the ages'.

to keep their bloody nose out of our affairs so that we can make our own decisions about our leadership.

I don't dispute for a moment that Cecil King's attack has temporarily strengthened Harold's position a great deal. Nevertheless I have no doubt that this week has seen another move in the direction of a new leadership. I think the party will sooner or later insist that whether it's going to win the next election or at least lose it honourably (which is the least we can hope) it will have to have a new Leader, unless Harold can show a power of retiring into the background and letting leadership headed by Roy and Barbara give the inspiration which he can't give. I think all that will happen but it can't happen just when our press lords start ordering the party about.

Monday, May 13th

I went into the House to hear Roy Jenkins reply to a Private Notice Question from James Dickens about Cecil King.[1] It was a superb performance. He withered him up, dealing with King with an olympian detachment. As a result the miners whom Alf Robens had invited to the annual party of the National Coal Board walked out when they saw Cecil King on the other side of the room and more than 150 Labour M.P.s have now signed an Early Day Motion saying that King must be sacked from the N.C.B.[2] It's gone far enough, as Harold remarked to me.

What a stroke of luck Cecil King has been to Harold. As one Tory put it, he was the only flaw in a perfect day of Tory victory news last Friday. At once he provided the positive factor required for rebuilding Harold's reputation. This was confirmed to me when Alma Birk rang me up in the greatest distress to tell me how terrible life had been,[3] that the directors were now all working together to try to get rid of Cecil King, that her husband, Ellis, who had been in Paris was now considering whether he should resign from the *Mirror* board and that she had persuaded him to stay on and fight the King influence. She also told me that 98 per cent of the letters which the *Daily Mirror* and the *Sun* had received were pro-Harold and only 2 per cent pro-King. She was terribly shocked that Sydney Jacobson and Hugh Cudlipp had both accepted the Cecil King line and failed to foresee and warn him of the consequences.[4] Indeed, they'd all celebrated with King at a great dinner

[1] James Dickens was Labour M.P. for West Lewisham 1966–70 and since 1970 has been Assistant Director of Manpower at the National Freight Corporation.

[2] Early Day Motions were motions which M.P.s put on the Order Paper for debate on an unspecified 'early day'. Other Members could append their names in support and thus the motion became a device to show back-bench attitudes to topical or critical propositions.

[3] Leader of the Labour group on Finchley Borough Council 1950–3 and an unsuccessful parliamentary candidate 1950–5. She became a life peer in 1967 and was a Baroness-in-Waiting March–October 1974. Since 1974 she has been Parliamentary Under-Secretary of State at the Privy Council Office. She was Associate Editor of *Nova* 1965–9 and Chairman of the Health Education Council 1969–72. Her husband, Ellis, was lawyer to the *Mirror* group.

[4] Sydney Jacobson, Political Editor of the *Daily Mirror* 1952–62, Editor of the *Daily Herald* 1962–4 and of the *Sun* 1964–5, was Chairman of Odhams Newspapers 1968,

on Friday night. Despite this, she added, I must understand that there were no enemies of the party at the *Daily Mirror*. Alma's terrified female social agony about the clanger King had dropped was a tremendous revelation. The one thing the *Mirror* doesn't like is failure or being made to look silly and this is what King had done for them over the weekend.

My first job when I got to London this morning was to meet Roy in his room at the Treasury. It's the same room in which Jim Callaghan worked but Roy's made it look totally different. He's put the table crosswise instead of lengthwise, stripped the room of some rather dull landscapes and got some pretty good, severe eighteenth-century portraits and a nice Canaletto. At the far end, where you enter, he has left a sort of easy-chair corner though he's quick to tell you that these were ordered by Jim Callaghan, not by Jennifer.[1]

I was there with Judith to plead her case for the three waiting days. I expected to have a terrible time, with the Chancellor insisting that she must find the £15 million for this herself. That is what the Treasury officials had told ours would happen. We sat facing Roy across the middle of the table and he asked, 'Do you want to say anything?' I stopped Judith from making a speech and let him have his say. 'It's a very difficult situation indeed,' he said. 'I can't see how we can force this clause through Parliament but I can't see any alternative.' Then he turned to Jack Diamond who was sitting beside him and said, 'Have you got a proposal, Jack?' He replied that we could save a little money by saying that any employer with a sickness scheme should not claim sickness benefit for his workers. 'But you can't say that,' I replied, 'because it means that every decent employer is denied Government assistance while every bad employer has his employees' sickness paid for him.' That was the end of the Treasury proposal and then, after a little bit of a chat, there was no more discussion.

I went out bewildered. I'd never before known a Chancellor give away £15 million in that haphazard way. The Ministry of Social Security officials couldn't believe their ears and indeed they began to wonder what magic qualities the Lord President of the Council possessed. It was not a question of any magical qualities, just that Roy had made a singularly weak misjudgment. He had apparently been bluffed by us (possibly also by the

---

Editorial Director of I.P.C. 1968–74 and its Deputy Chairman 1973–4. He became a life peer in 1975. Hugh Cudlipp was Editor of the *Sunday Pictorial* 1937–40 and 1946–9, Managing Editor of the *Sunday Express* 1950–2 and Editorial Director of the *Daily Mirror* and of the *Sunday Pictorial* 1952–63. He was Joint Managing Director 1959–63, then Chairman of Odhams Press Ltd 1961–3 and of *Daily Mirror* Newspapers Ltd 1963–8, becoming Deputy Chairman of I.P.C. 1964–8 and Chairman 1968–73. He was knighted in 1973 and became a life peer in 1974.

[1] Mrs Jenkins, Chairman of the Consumers' Association since 1965 and of the Historic Buildings Council for England since 1975, had been a member of the Council of the Consumers' Association since 1958 and was a member from 1970 to 1973 of the Executive Board of the British Standards Institution and from 1971 to 1974 of the Design Council.

Prime Minister) into thinking it would be really difficult to push the clause through Parliament. Actually with determination it could have been done. So he gave way when he needn't have done and told us to find the £15 million from other social services. It will be a nice chore for me in the next two or three months, visiting various Ministers and getting them to pay for Judith's mistakes.

This afternoon I had rather an interesting meeting with Kenneth Robinson. Our Minister of Health has cooled down a bit since his threats of resignation when I took over and is really rather pally with me. He came along with a very stuffy-looking, dapper little man to discuss the publicity for explaining the prescription charges exemption scheme. The official said, 'We are going to spend £60,000 on advertising and here is the text of the advert.' He pushed across three pages of foolscap. I said, 'But you're not going to print all that, are you? What you had better do, surely, is to have an advertising campaign in the first week saying "Are you entitled to exemption? Are you an old age pensioner, chronically sick, a nursing mother?" and hadn't you better have another simple advertisement telling them to go to the post office?' 'Oh, you can't just tell them to go to the post office,' said the official. 'On the other hand,' I replied, 'they can't read an advert that length.' 'But their reading it is not the important thing,' he replied. 'If my Minister puts everything in, my Minister is not to blame for their not having read it.' So I said, 'But that is £60,000 down the drain.' They then pointed out that the Ministry of Health never gets its fair share, that the Ministry of Transport has just got £1 million for a breathalyser campaign,[1] and that £3 million a year is spent on advertising for recruitment to the armed forces. I said, 'Well, you won't get your fair share if you and your press officer behave in this ridiculous way.'

This is not the first time I've noticed this ghastly small type-kind of Government advertising. The truth is that a great deal of it is printed not to induce people to take up their claims or to explain Government policy, but simply to ensure that the civil servants won't be criticized for not having informed the public of the details.

This evening I had got Tam to arrange a dinner for me with two of the brighter younger M.P.s. Paul Rose, who used to be Barbara Castle's P.P.S., and Ben Ford, another keen young man, were both glad to tell me what was wrong with the Government,[2] but most of our conversation actually concerned the revolutionary students in Paris and at Essex University.[3] The

[1] Since October 1967 police had been empowered to ask motorists involved in an accident or suspected of an offence to blow into a plastic bag. If crystals in a connected tube turned green this was *prima facie* evidence of excessive alcohol in the system and the motorist was then required to take a blood or urine test. After the introduction of the 'breathalyser' the number of road accidents fell dramatically.

[2] Paul Rose has been Labour M.P. for Manchester, Blackley, since 1964; Ben Ford has been Labour M.P. for Bradford North since 1964.

[3] On May 3rd students from all the faculties of the University of Paris, led by Daniel Cohn-Bendit, a German studying in Paris, began a lengthy protest against inadequate facilities and the arbitrary imposition of discipline by the French university authorities.

Paris events are wildly exciting. Not since the 1840s have we had such revolutionary incidents in Paris as these, 2 million strikers all over France and the students fighting back at the barricades, with marches and counter-marches. Simultaneously we are having at Colchester our own tiny student row, with the whole University of Essex paralysed because the students tried to prevent a lecture by an expert from Porton Down where they do research into germ warfare. Instead of hearing and heckling him as students should, they tried to stop him altogether and the Vice-Chancellor then suspended three of them. We are lucky that our disturbances in this country are so small-scale. The stock truth is that, like everybody else, students are growing up much earlier now and the requirements of a young man of twenty-one or even eighteen are more like those of a young man of twenty-five twenty years ago. Student self-government is something which goes with student marriage and the whole early maturity of boys and girls. One also has to consider the sheer increase in the number of the students. They've become quite a formidable pressure group in the community and have a group will of their own. During dinner I said I couldn't really understand the student mentality. They are completely out of my ken. Paul Rose said, 'They're as much out of my ken as out of yours. There's an absolute barrier now between those who are over twenty-eight, who are absolutely out, and those who are under twenty-eight. We have no feeling or contact with these modern students at all.'[1]

The longer I spent with these two young M.P.s the more I thought Paul Rose was right. They had quite a lot to say about what was wrong with the Government and wrong with Parliament but it was the self-same analysis which I myself have not only made but published. They had nothing new to tell me whatsoever and I went to bed reflecting that the main value of the dinner was probably to show me that there's no alternative policy available in the Parliamentary Party.

Tuesday, May 14th

I had the second meeting of the Social Service Ministers and their Permanent Secretaries. This time they did not all turn up as they had done before but sent mostly their number twos—and I didn't blame them.[2] We had a very

---

Student grievances were linked to demands for an end to the Vietnam war and, encouraged by dedicated and efficient Maoist, Trotskyist and Communist groups, to protests against the class struggle and capitalist repression. French students occupied the Sorbonne, which was closed on May 6th, and at barricades of paving stones fought the riot police. For a short time they attracted the sympathy of the workers, including those from the Renault factory. British students were in comparison subdued and, save for an outburst at the London School of Economics in 1967, had hitherto been restrained. During 1968, however, nearly every British university had demonstrations of some kind and a high point was reached on March 17th when an international crowd, many of whom were students and former students, packed Grosvenor Square and attempted to storm the American Embassy, in protest against the Vietnam war.

[1] Paul Rose was thirty-three and Ben Ford forty-three.

[2] See Vol. II, pp. 749–52.

technical meeting, with Ken Berrill describing the more sophisticated methods of cost analysis, how, for instance, one can cost against each other old age pensions, increased school meals and building programmes.[1] I soon got the feeling that the meeting was tired and impatient so I put a series of questions to the Treasury about whether they regard national insurance contributions as savings or as expenditure. But I'd known the meeting was a flop since the beginning when they started by complaining that they'd only got the papers yesterday and we learnt that the Treasury had only sent them round to us last Friday evening. The truth is that neither the Ministers nor the officials wanted the meeting and there was a strong sense of suspicion that I was up to no good. I had to bring it to a halt as soon as possible.

After lunch Burke Trend came across to the House to see me. I wondered what this could be about; was it another crisis in my relationship with Harold? But he said, 'I have come to see you about the Cabinet Committee on Industrial Building. You said you wanted it wound up but the Prime Minister said he thought it ought to go on just a bit longer. I wonder who you want on it?' Well, this was interesting. Here is one of the most powerful and busy civil servants coming across to the House from the Cabinet Office to ask me a question which takes two minutes to answer. What a man Burke Trend is, younger than me by several years but with this shock of greying hair and an untidy, donnish manner. I find him nice. I know he's upright and feels himself loyal in all he does. He has tremendous grasp, but is immersed in detail. Everything comes to his office. He makes notes on everything but never are the notes of any interest and he finds himself always so busy doing things that he is doing nothing at all.

We settled down for a chat and agreed that physically Harold is back at the best of his form and that the Parliamentary Committee is going better than we expected. We both consider ourselves loyal friends of Harold though we know his limitations and we have not very much expectation of great success.

At this afternoon's meeting of the Transport House Small Committee there was a better turnout than usual and we had an intelligent discussion of the local government results. The patchwork I had noted in the Midlands with the astonishing contrast between Birmingham and Coventry has, I gather, been found in many other parts of the country. Some areas had been much less bad than others. Someone quoted *The Economist*'s remark that Blackburn and Coventry possibly had two of the least bad results 'because an aura of success still hangs round Barbara Castle and Dick Crossman'. This is absolute rubbish. Local government elections aren't decided by such factors. I suggested that all this evidence should be carefully analysed by the

[1] Kenneth Berrill, Fellow and first Bursar of King's College, Cambridge, 1962–9, was Special Adviser to H.M. Treasury 1967–9, Chairman of the University Grants Committee 1969–73 and of the Council for Scientific Policy 1969–72. He was Head of the Government Economic Service and Chief Economic Adviser to the Treasury 1973–4 and has been Head of the Central Policy Review Staff since 1974. He was knighted in 1971.

Research Department so that we could draw some conclusions. Once again I noticed an extraordinary lack of enthusiasm from the Transport House staff. Nothing will happen. I have had some success today, though, because after many weeks I've persuaded the Prime Minister that the Parliamentary Committee should have a strategy discussion based upon the monthly reports of the opinion polls.

This evening I'd been invited to a buffet supper by the Commonwealth Parliamentary Association. I was never a great believer either in the C.P.A. or the I.P.U. [Inter-Parliamentary Union] but I was especially asked to come because there were some twelve Speakers or Deputy Speakers from various Parliaments abroad who were anxious to meet a few of us. There was a perfectly pleasant atmosphere and we sat around chatting in the usual feeble way. Why are the British so bad at running political parties? In America when a guest like myself is asked to a party he's put through it. They all cross-question him or even make him start with a little speech but all this is thought much too serious in Britain and though I knew that most of these people would have liked to ask me questions we did nothing of the sort.

After an hour and a half I went back to the House where I found a debate going on on the report of the Specialist Committee on Agriculture. This Committee is one of my own creations and I thought it decent to sit and listen,[1] but as I did so I began to wonder how effective these investigating committees really are. Is Henry Fairlie right when he says that an investigatory committee dominated by the Whips is a contradiction in terms?[2] I must say that what I heard tonight somewhat strengthened that view.

Wednesday, May 15th

At the Party meeting this morning we continued last Wednesday's discussion on prices and incomes. It had been preceded by a meeting between Barbara and the Prime Minister and the trade union group last Monday night when, as we had agreed at Cabinet, the concession had been made that we should not be legally entitled to extend the Act by the Expiring Laws Continuance Bill. Instead we will have to pass a brand-new Act of Parliament. This concession hasn't made a great impact but it may give an excuse to support us to a number of thoughtful people who realize we must if possible get a majority of 40 on Second Reading next week.

It was one of the best Party meetings I have ever attended. At last the argument for the Government was being put not simply in terms of the prices and incomes policy but on the basis that since the Government is deeply committed to it the Party must see it through. Early on, Roy made an excellent intervention, very tough and precise, though it didn't add anything new. I thought the two best back-bench speeches were by Edwin Brooks and

[1] See Vol. II.

[2] Political commentator and freelance journalist, formerly with the *Spectator*. Author of *The Life of Politics* (London: Methuen, 1968).

Ray Fletcher.[1] Edwin spoke as someone who had opposed the prices and incomes policy but now felt the situation so grave that, however reluctantly, he had to give the Government his vote. Ray Fletcher made an interesting cross-bench speech, saying something I have mentioned more than once, that this Government is being mercilessly flayed not for the abandonment of its pledges but for carrying them out.

Barbara intervened brilliantly with concrete instances of productivity agreements and price reductions that had been achieved. After this splendid debate, up stands Harold Wilson and there is a deadly silence as he gathers together a good thick wodge of No. 10 writing paper and starts reading aloud a carefully prepared oration. I was sitting just behind him with George Brown next to me and when Harold said, 'I must say I haven't lost my nerve,' George said, *sotto voce*, 'One doesn't have to say that unless one has.' It was the most contrived performance, I thought, cold, uninspired rhetoric. I was surprised when later this evening Anne said she had heard on the car radio about the marvellous speech with which the Prime Minister had defeated the rebels. I realized what had happened. We had an astounding vote at the meeting, 202 votes to 42, far better than we had expected, and that result coupled with the Prime Minister's speech allowed people outside to conclude that it was the speech that got the result. I don't think a single vote was changed by Harold, only by the general line of the debate where the Government had the better argument.

This evening I went to Pam Berry's for a dinner in honour of Arthur Schlesinger Jr.[2] There we had the usual gang, the American Ambassador and his beautiful wife Evangeline,[3] Tommy and Pen Balogh, Noël and Gabriele Annan.[4] Arthur was very cautious but in the end he revealed his presidential preferences – pro-Robert Kennedy, anti-Humphrey, anti-Eugene McCarthy.[5]

[1] Edwin Brooks, Labour M.P. for Bebington 1966–70, has been Senior Lecturer in the Department of Geography at the University of Liverpool since 1972. Raymond Fletcher has been Labour M.P. for Ilkeston since 1964.

[2] Pamela Berry (Lady Hartwell) has been President of the Incorporated Society of London Fashion Designers since 1954. Arthur Schlesinger Jr, Professor of History at Harvard University 1954–61, was Special Assistant to Presidents Kennedy and Johnson 1961–4 and since 1966 has been Schweitzer Professor of the Humanities, City University of New York.

[3] David Bruce had been U.S. Ambassador to France 1949–52, American Under-Secretary of State 1952–3, Special Representative to the European High Authority for Coal and Steel 1953–4, U.S. Ambassador to the Federal Republic of Germany 1957–9 and to the U.K. 1961–9. He was U.S. Representative at the Vietnam Peace Talks in Paris 1970–1, Chief of the U.S. Mission to the People's Republic of China 1973–4 and U.S. Ambassador to N.A.T.O. 1974–6.

[4] Noël Annan was a Fellow of King's College, Cambridge 1944–56 and Provost 1956–1966, when he became Provost of University College, London. He was made a life peer in 1965.

[5] On March 31st the incumbent President, Lyndon Baines Johnson, had announced that he would not seek another term of office. The chief rivals for the Democratic nomination were therefore Senator Robert Kennedy, brother of the late President and until recently Attorney-General, Vice-President Hubert Humphrey and Senator Eugene McCarthy, who

I didn't get much out of the dinner except great enjoyment at being in Pam's lovely house and having the sort of conversation over good food and drink which one always gets at her table.

Thursday, May 16th

Cabinet. The only matter which vitally concerned me was Roy's report on Judith Hart's three waiting days. When he said he had agreed that the clause must be dropped and that Social Security could not find the money there was a deadly silence. Obviously Judith and I didn't want to add a single word. With the rest of the Cabinet looking highly embarrassed and Roy saying the £15 million had got to be found somewhere else, we put our heads down and said nothing. Cabinet had to agree. It can hardly tell Chancellors not to be too generous on the rare occasions when they are.

The big thing was votes at eighteen. When the Parliamentary Committee's report was submitted I'm glad to say that Richard Marsh raised the whole issue and said it was a zany thing to give young people the vote. Quite an interesting discussion followed. Peter Shore gave the obvious reply that the modern Labour Party has for years been committed to votes at eighteen and we had put the case for this to the Speaker's Conference. It would look very strange for us, having approved the Latey Report, to deny the vote to eighteen-year-olds. Michael Stewart repeated his admirable argument that people aren't granted rights, they grow into them, and the group rights of youth have changed in the last ten years just as the group rights of women changed in the 1920s. Wedgy Benn made it clear he wouldn't stay a member of the Cabinet unless the eighteen-year-olds got justice.

Marsh was supported by an odd collection, including Cledwyn Hughes, whose grounds were that in Wales and Scotland the Nats would gain since young people tend to vote nationalist. Gunter was worried that schoolboys and schoolgirls voting at the age of eighteen would be unduly influenced by their teachers. Barbara Castle, in her new position as a woman of power, wondered if it was really wise to do this, while Roy sat there careful, canny and saying nothing. We have left it open and it will be considered again.

In the House this afternoon we had to deal with the immense sensation of Ronan Point, where a block of flats had collapsed as the result of a gas explosion.[1] Tony Greenwood was away in Poland. (I wasn't allowed to go to Poland when I was Minister of Housing in case of adverse criticism but when Tony is away nobody notices.) In his absence Jim Callaghan, as

had declared his candidacy in 1967 as a challenge to the Administration's Vietnam policy. Humphrey had declared his candidacy on April 27th, too late to enter the primary elections where, by May, Kennedy and McCarthy were running close.

[1] Four people were killed and eleven injured when a leaking gas main caused an explosion in a twenty-three-storey block of flats, Ronan Point, at Custom House, Canning Town, in East London. The flats were largely pre-fabricated, and their collapse caused anxiety about their method of construction. The Home Secretary announced that there would be an immediate and full inquiry.

Chairman of the Emergency Committee, was asked to take responsibility and make the Statement, which he did extremely well.

This was followed by an immense row on the Business Statement. Peart was attacked from our own side for giving only one day for the Prices and Incomes Bill Second Reading, having denied a day for the White Paper. At the same time there were objections from the Tory side about the Finance Bill guillotine.[1] He was extremely lucky that the two sides cancelled each other out so conveniently. He handled the situation well as usual but people are already beginning to find that though they may like him better than me he doesn't treat them any better.

I went to the 5.30 P.L.P. meeting. I haven't attended since I ceased to be Leader of the House but Judith and I wanted to hear the reaction to the three waiting days. She quietly told them and there was no comment whatsoever.* As this was a really sensational climb-down by the Treasury, we were very lucky indeed. I suppose we got away with it simply because a lot of other news was coming in.

I rushed back to the Privy Council Office for a meeting of my Pensions circus – Titmuss, Brian Abel-Smith, the Ministers and their two Permanent Secretaries, Clifford Jarrett and Arnold France, and my staff. I wanted to have the circus without the Permanent Secretaries. They could come if they insisted but I didn't think they would want to insist because they had been complaining that they had too many committees. I thought it was outrageous that I had to have these people who always want to come to scotch good ideas but I knew I had to behave properly. From the Treasury we had Dick Taverne and an excellent new man called Moss.[2] New personalities at the Treasury made an enormous difference. At this first meeting a real policy

[1] The obstruction and exploitation of Commons' procedures by the Irish members in the 1880s had led to the introduction in 1881 of 'the guillotine', a motion that, at a given hour, all outstanding questions should be put to the vote. Standing Orders now provide for two kinds of guillotine, one being an Allocation of Time Order, agreed upon by a 'Business Committee' of all-party spokesmen whose decision is put to the House to be accepted or rejected without debate. The other more recent form presupposes the Government's attempt to negotiate with the Opposition on an allocation of time between various parts of the Bill. If this fails a guillotine motion is proposed, providing that each stage of the Bill should be completed by a particular date. This motion must be decided by the House after two hours' debate. The Business Committee then decides, within the established dates, how much debating time shall be given to each part and stage of the Bill. No Finance Bill had been guillotined since 1931. The Leader of the House reminded the Opposition that they had refused to discuss a voluntary timetable.

* Even in the next day's papers there were only two tiny little paragraphs.

[2] Dick Taverne was Labour M.P. for Lincoln from March 1962 until his resignation from the Labour Party in October 1972 and Democratic Labour M.P. for Lincoln from March 1973 until his defeat in the General Election of October 1974. He was Parliamentary Under-Secretary of State at the Home Office 1966–8, Minister of State at the Treasury 1968–9 and Financial Secretary to the Treasury 1969–70. He has been Director of the Institute of Fiscal Studies since 1970. N. Jordan Moss was the Under-Secretary in charge of the Social Services division of the Civil Public Sector of the Treasury. From 1971–6 he was a Deputy Under-Secretary of State, D.H.S.S., and since 1976 he has been a Deputy Secretary at the Treasury.

began to emerge. We were able to get the Treasury to define its attitude to savings, contributions and benefits and we also got the Titmuss people to be surprisingly affirmative to the Ministry's version of national superannuation.

Friday, May 17th

This morning we found ourselves in yet another financial crisis. Once again it was the American Congress who caused it by refusing the President his 10 per cent tax surcharge.[1] A sudden scurry of gold-buying drove the pound desperately low and both Tommy and Nicky rang me to tell me how bad things were.

My mind was mostly full of national superannuation. Down at the Ministry I had a great meeting on contracting out to which Judith and I contributed a completely new idea. The Ministry's attitude to private superannuation schemes and to life assurance companies has always been extremely hostile. I am determined to show that we're not really opposed to private schemes at all. If we're not going to close them down altogether we ought to try to make them collaborate with us while simultaneously imposing transferability on them. At this first meeting I found all the officials wholly adverse and the Inland Revenue representatives almost impossible. Still, it was an initial bash and I'm going to raise it again.

After that I went down to the House to lunch with John Silkin and his deputy, Brian O'Malley. My relationship with the Whips is very delicate at present. They're having very great difficulties and it seems to me that Brian is steadily growing in stature whereas John seems to be losing the prestige he acquired in the Party. Maybe it's a good thing I'm out of the way.

This evening I took the train to Cambridge to address the Democratic Socialist Club and stay the night with Nicky Kaldor. I got to the station at the right time and found no undergraduate there to meet me. When I'd waited fifteen minutes I took a taxi to Nicky's house and there had supper with Clarissa and his daughter Penelope. All the Kaldor women are terribly nice and hospitable and we had a lovely time together and I didn't fuss about these damned Democratic Socialists who still hadn't turned up. But finally Clarissa said, 'Maybe we ought to find out', and she motored me round to the zoology labs where I found a couple of the young men. They took me through a dark tunnel and through a whole series of underground passages, saying this was necessary to avoid the demonstrations which might be staged by either of the two other socialist societies. (The Labour Club, I learnt, is now split into three groups of which I was to speak to the least attractive, the one, for instance, which neither Judith Hart's son nor Tommy Balogh's son goes to.) When I finally got to a very bleak lecture hall there were thirty

[1] The President had requested a 10 per cent tax surcharge as a means of controlling the United States' inflationary rate of economic expansion but the Chairman of the House of Representatives' Ways and Means Committee, Wilbur Mills, would only agree to the measure in return for large cuts in government spending. After long delay, cuts of some $4,000 million were granted and the Bill was finally passed in June.

or forty rather bored students patiently waiting for me. I lectured them on the Marxist question, whether an elected Labour Government can ever, through parliamentary democratic means, persuade a country to make the sacrifices required for the socialist revolution. I pointed out to them that it's our socialist measures which are causing our unpopularity.

The discussion afterwards was pretty flat until one fellow said, 'The fact is that what is wrong with you is that you're defeated on whatever you stand for. You fight for three years against withdrawing from Suez and then withdraw. You fight for three years against devaluation and then devalue.' It was unanswerable because it is true.

When I got home to Clarissa, Nicky was already there and eager to fill me in on the gloom of the situation. He reinforced my feeling that everything is going wrong and that we're failing to get on top of the crisis.

Saturday, May 18th

I took an early train back to London and there picked up Wayland Young and his family and we all motored down to Prescote.[1] In the driving rain the children all miraculously got together. The two they'd brought are nine and ten compared to our eight and ten and within a matter of minutes were chattering together. This evening Wayland, Elizabeth, Anne and I all had a terrible argument about children's schooling. They had sent their children to primary and comprehensive schools in London but now they're sick of it because the children don't do well. They'd taken the boy out and sent him to a fee-paying school where he's learning Latin at the age of ten. One of their girls was taken out and sent to a grammar school where she could try for Cambridge. They have much more experience with comprehensive schools than us because their children are older and I'm sure we shall find many of the same kind of difficulties. But I couldn't help saying that Labour Ministers have a special responsibility. Wayland disagreed and suddenly we were in that eternal argument about what we socialists should do with our children. They took the broad Balogh view that the children come first and one must find out what is best for them and do it. I said, 'That may be true of other people but if you're a Labour Minister you can't, or you shouldn't.' Then, because I hate sounding self-righteous I got bad-tempered and we had a filthy row that got worse when it spread over on to Vietnam.

Sunday, May 19th

Yesterday we had Ted Heath's big speech saying that there should be a Scottish Assembly though, characteristically, it should not be independent of Parliament but just a bloody compromise of the kind which I have been

[1] Lord Kennet succeeded to his father's barony in 1960. An author, he was Parliamentary Secretary at the M.H.L.G. 1966–70, Chairman of the Advisory Committee on Oil Pollution of the Sea 1970–4 and of the Council for the Protection of Rural England 1971–2 and Director of Europe Plus Thirty. His wife, Elizabeth, was a writer on arms control and disarmament.

sniffing at and attacking through the months on my Devolution Committee.[1] But it is a Conservative concession to nationalism and it is cunning that he has managed to get it in before the Government.

Let's look at the history of devolution. It was eighteen months ago that I went to Harold and over a year before I got agreement to have a committee to look at a proposal for some positive and constructive response to nationalism. Harold himself had been swaying to and fro and it was his journey up to Scotland a few weeks ago that imbued him with the conviction that Willie Ross was a tremendously good Secretary of State and we ought to have no appeasement of separatism. Hence Harold's readiness to sack Cledwyn Hughes from Wales and replace him with George Thomas, an avowed U.K. man. This completely upset the balance of my Devolution Committee as well and he also put Victor Stonham in the Home Office,[2] instead of Dick Taverne, who is sensible, and added Peart, who is virulently opposed to any concession on nationalism.

There is tremendous natural inhibition in the Party against home rule and against constitutional innovation of any kind and if I had put devolutionary measures forward in Cabinet there would have been strong opposition from a whole group of people, like Dick Marsh, headed by Callaghan. There would have been very little support except for purely opportunist reasons.

Last week, when I knew this move of Heath's was coming up, I had felt that our efforts were a waste of time but we've ploughed ahead with proposals for visible concessions, like moving some of the Grand Committee sessions to Edinburgh and Cardiff and possibly televising them, together with a conscious policy of transferring large sections of U.K. Ministries to Scotland and Wales. The last meeting of the Committee will consider my draft this week and then we shall bring the thing to Cabinet and see what happens.

Monday, May 20th

Another meeting on Stansted airport, this time of the Cabinet Committee appointed to study the terms of reference for the new Inquiry.[3] Ten Ministers

[1] In a speech to a rally of Scottish Tories at Perth the Leader of the Opposition urged the establishment by the Government of a constitutional committee on the reorganization of government in Scotland and said that the Tories would recommend the creation of an elected Scottish Assembly. The proposals were the result of an interim report by a Conservative policy group. On May 25th the General Assembly of the Church of Scotland asked for an early Royal Commission on Scottish self-government.

[2] Victor Collins, Labour M.P. for Taunton 1945–50 and for Shoreditch and Finsbury 1954–8, was Joint Parliamentary Under-Secretary of State at the Home Office 1964–7 and Minister of State 1967–9. He had become a life peer in 1958, taking the title of Lord Stonham. He died in 1973.

[3] In 1954 the decision had been taken in principle that Stansted, in Essex, should be the site of a third London airport. This was announced in 1966 and provoked angry criticism and a public inquiry. The Inspector's report, published in May 1966, recommended that the Government should review the whole question of a third airport, but in May 1967 a White Paper, Cmnd 3251, announced that the Stansted site had been finally approved. In the face of bitter protest and the likelihood of the Stansted Order's being defeated in the House

attended this very solemn affair. We all sat round for an hour until right at the end I said, 'What about a Statement?' Whereat Mr Crosland produced a draft Statement from the back of his folder and said that he thought it should be made this afternoon at 3.30. This kind of *post facto* committee is the mumbo-jumbo of Cabinet government. But thank heavens Stansted is now removed from politics for a couple of years.

This afternoon Fred Peart held a meeting of his Future Legislation Committee. All my efforts to reorganize the planning of future legislation have been blown to the winds. Once again we simply had a fight between various Ministers, who all want their Bills as soon as possible. Here was Dick Marsh saying he must have Nationalization of the Docks in the next session even though the Bill isn't ready. Here was Kenneth Robinson with his Bill for banning coupons in cigarette packets, a Bill which he had already touted unsuccessfully round the Private Members.

The big unknown quantity is the Trade Union Bill which we are pledged to base on the Report of the Donovan Commission. There seems to be hopeless dissension on the kind of Bill it should be but it is clear that the next session we shall have three major constitutional measures – the Trade Union Bill, a Representation of the People Bill to give votes at eighteen and Lords' reform.

I went across to No. 10 to talk to Harold about the Privy Council. I told him about our little idea of making it more interesting and he accepted it all in a not very interested way. There he was with his weekly meetings with the Queen, just a little bit jealous of the Lord President for nipping in with his meetings as well. I tried to move on to my own and the question of the merger of the two Departments but he isn't with me this week. It is clear that the balance of power in Cabinet has shifted a bit, with Jim Callaghan right back in front, leaping in to the emergency of the Ronan Point tower block. It is extraordinary how in politics you can't kill a man. Back he bobs into power and influence and to some extent popularity. I walked the Prime Minister over to the boardroom of the Treasury for a party of statisticians and economists and then I disappeared to Covent Garden for Visconti's production of *La Traviata*. The settings were an imitation of Aubrey Beardsley, with the whole thing turned into a decadent, late nineteenth-century show. I saw one can really go to a dud performance of an opera.

Tuesday, May 21st

I spent most of the day in the Prices and Incomes Bill Second Reading

---

of Lords, the Government decided in May 1968 to hold another inquiry. The Roskill Commission, reporting in mid-December 1969, suggested four possible sites and excluded Stansted and in April 1970 a series of public hearings began. In April 1971 the Conservative Government announced that the airport would be built at Foulness on the Thames estuary but further controversy over the costs, environmental and financial, of a third airport caused the project to be abandoned in July 1974.

debate. Poor Barbara had a tooth out at 9 o'clock last night and when I rang her early this morning she was obviously not in very good form. She seemed like a plaintive schoolmistress and she then made what I think is her cardinal mistake of committing herself to price control and saying very little about incomes control, a view which unseated George Brown and will unseat her. Fortunately she was followed by Robert Carr, a very dull, plodding Tory.[1] I had to go out to a committee so I missed George Brown's come-back speech from the back benches in which he chided the Government for giving up the power to continue the Act under the Expiring Laws Continuance Bill. This is the same George Brown who in 1966 nearly resigned because the Government was trying to make prices and incomes a permanent policy. Mind you, I don't blame George. We are all deeply schizophrenic on this Bill, hate the interference, hate the break with the trade unions, yet we can see that without it there must be a higher level of unemployment than we can tolerate.

In the evening I came in to hear Roy Hattersley wind up.[2] We had agreed he should do it rather than a stock senior Minister like Fred Peart or me but he was hopeless. The left wing hate him too much and there was Ann Kerr talking loudly as he spoke and describing him as a contemptible coward.[3] He just ploughed ahead against a background of conversation, bullied and stabbed at from behind. It was painful.[4]

What a change when we came to the Finance Bill guillotine debate. It was started by Fred Peart with an excellent speech written by Freddy Ward. Then came Edward du Cann,[5] ex-Chairman of the Tory Party, speaking for the back benchers as a businessman, then Boyd-Carpenter and finally Iain Macleod and Roy.[6] Macleod was curiously short, ineffective and uncomfort-

[1] Conservative M.P. for Mitcham 1950–74 and for Sutton Carshalton 1974–6. Parliamentary Secretary at the Ministry of Labour and National Service 1955–8, Secretary for Technical Co-operation 1963–4, Secretary of State for Employment 1970–2, Lord President of the Council and Leader of the House of Commons April–November 1972, Home Secretary 1972–4. He became a life peer in 1975.

[2] Labour M.P. for Birmingham, Sparkbrook, since 1964. He was Joint Parliamentary Secretary at the D.E.P. 1967–9, Minister of Defence for Administration 1969–70, Minister of State at the F.C.O. 1974–6 and since 1976 Secretary of State for Prices and Consumer Protection.

[3] Labour M.P. for Rochester and Chatham 1964–70. She died in July 1973.

[4] The Bill was given a Second Reading by 290 votes to 255.

[5] Conservative M.P. for Taunton since February 1956. He was Economic Secretary to the Treasury 1962–3, Minister of State at the Board of Trade 1963–4, Chairman of the Select Committee on Public Expenditure 1971–2, of the Public Accounts Committee, and later of the Expenditure Committee, since 1974, and since 1972 of the 1922 Committee. Chairman of the Conservative Party Organization 1965–7, he was also Chairman of Barclays Unicorn Ltd and associated companies 1957–72 and of Keyser Ullman Holdings Ltd 1970–5.

[6] John Boyd-Carpenter was Conservative M.P. for Kingston-upon-Thames 1945–72, Financial Secretary to the Treasury 1951–4, Minister of Transport and Civil Aviation 1954–December 1955, Minister of Pensions and National Insurance December 1955–July 1962, Chief Secretary to the Treasury and Paymaster-General 1962–4 and Chairman of the Public Accounts Committee 1964–70. In 1972 he became a life peer and Chairman of the Civil Aviation Authority.

able. Roy gave himself twenty minutes to demolish him. I'd watched him beforehand, scribbling away at his notes, thoroughly uncomfortable, but he does his homework and had put a lot of power and thought into this speech. It was effective because it centred on the single point that Macleod was a hypocrite because he was opposing the guillotine after refusing from the start to have any agreement on the timetable. That is perfectly true and Jenkins put it with enormous effectiveness although he himself was hardly an enthusiast for the guillotine.[1]

Wednesday, May 22nd

I had one enormously important meeting, as I imagined, where we were to present our draft White Paper on Lords' reform to the Cabinet Committee. It showed how things are going that Fred Peart, the Leader of the House, turned up without having read the draft and Jim Callaghan, whom I met just outside the door, wasn't even bothering to attend though his Department is responsible for the Bill. From their point of view Lords' reform is a lost cause. They won't knife it, kill it; they'll let it go on until it dies or collapses ignominiously.

This evening the Home Policy Committee of the Party gave a dinner at the St Ermin's Hotel. While we were sitting on the front bench together Harold had mentioned that he had forgotten to invite me and that he wanted me to take Jim Callaghan's place. When I arrived George Brown had just bashed in and insulted Roy and when Roy said he would have to be going on to another dinner George added 'Oh, we can't spare you. We want the Chancellor here to knock him about.' It was all a bit testy and uneasy until Harold came in and sat down at the other end of the table. I wondered what on earth the dinner was for until George Brown got up and said, 'We all want one Cabinet Minister to liaise with the N.E.C. about all home policy affairs and I think it should be Dick Crossman.' Good old George Brown. One day he hates my guts and wants to throw me out, the next he wants to put me in sole charge – but only now I have finally resigned from the Executive.[2]

I think the explanation of the meeting is that the Home Policy Committee is overawed by the catastrophe that the party has suffered and is anxious to rebuild bridges with Westminster. But what odd views you hear expressed at Labour dinners. Sara Barker,[3] who had scarcely said a word, looked across the table at me very severely and said, 'I'll tell you what really matters now, all those scroungers getting more social benefits than they deserve.' It made me realize the difficulties I shall find as Secretary of State for the Social

[1] The Government secured a guillotine motion, at 12.27 a.m., by 303 votes to 245.

[2] In 1967 Crossman decided not to stand for election to the N.E.C., of which he had been a member for fifteen years. See Vol. II.

[3] Dame Sara Barker (D.B.E. 1970), Women's Organizer of the Yorkshire Labour Party 1942–52, Assistant National Agent of the Labour Party 1952–62 and National Agent, with her headquarters at Transport House, 1962–9. She died in 1973.

Services. The Labour Party wants to be the great liberal party which expends the social services but it also wants at all costs to avoid the unpopularity of being accused of giving money to scroungers.

Thursday, May 23rd

We started with a meeting of the Parliamentary Committee. I was livelier than some because last night I'd been able to pair before going to the dinner but other people had been at an all-night sitting on the Town and Country Planning Bill until 7 o'clock this morning.[1] We started with an interesting discussion of the Finance Bill and how the experiment upstairs was going. Roy said he doubted whether we could repeat it next year because it meant so much more work not only for Ministers but also for our own back benchers, who now have to play a much more active role in the proceedings. 'Do you mean', I said 'that the Bill is much more thoroughly handled in Committee upstairs than on the Floor of the House?' 'Yes,' he said 'without any doubt. On the Floor we can get away with murder in the course of the night because nobody's there but in a Committee of fifty they attend.'

In a way that conversation sums up the whole difficulty of carrying through a Parliamentary reform. I want to increase Parliamentary control of the Executive by making sure that the Finance Bill is really thoroughly discussed but the Executive want less effective control and so the Ministers want to leave it downstairs.

The discussion switched to the methods which were being employed to force the Transport Bill, chunk by chunk, through the Commons. Fred Peart and I had discussed this on Monday morning. He agreed that it was intolerable to impose a guillotine and then put in a whole series of brand new Government clauses on brand new subjects, for instance the Channel Tunnel.[2] Fred put the point to the Parliamentary Committee and I blew up and said, 'This isn't only a question of outraging Parliament. It's an outrage of Cabinet Government because these subjects like the Channel Tunnel and the nationalization of shipping have never been discussed either in Cabinet or in Cabinet Committee.'

[1] The Whips would excuse an M.P. from attending the House to support his party if he could 'pair' with a Member from the other side who also agreed to be absent. An informal system had developed by which individual M.P.s had regular pairing arrangements.

[2] The Transport Bill had been given its Second Reading on December 20th, 1967. The measure, prepared while Barbara Castle was Minister of Transport, included proposals to reorganize the railways, to create a state-owned National Freight Corporation, a National Bus Company and new urban passenger transport authorities, and to give increased powers to nationalized transport undertakings to diversify in other fields. It had 191¼ hours in Standing Committee in the Commons and 245 hours' Commons' stages. Proposals to build a Channel Tunnel had first been made in 1895 but it was not until November 20th, 1973, after a treaty had been negotiated between Edward Heath and President Pompidou of France, that a Bill for the construction and operation of the tunnel was introduced in the Commons. On January 20th, 1975, Anthony Crosland, Secretary of State for the Environment, announced that, as the Government could not meet the timetable required by the two Channel Tunnel companies, the project was to be abandoned.

By now everybody was thoroughly tired and bad-tempered and we decided to summon Dick Marsh immediately. He sidled in, sheepish, brash and arrogant in rather an attractive kind of way, and said that he couldn't deny that the Department had put the Channel Tunnel clauses in without Stephen Swingler's knowledge. He went on to say that he didn't like the behaviour of the Department and felt he had taken over a pretty awful show. At this point he took a look at Barbara, who sat there with her head down. He was sorry about it, the whole of this should not have happened and no more new clauses would be inserted.

Then the Prime Minister said, 'We must have you withdrawing.' Marsh said, 'Well, I can do it quietly.' I said it was no good having a sacrificial lamb unless there was a good advertisement for it. The Leader of the House must order him to withdraw it and he must do it this afternoon. Marsh said this was a terrible climb-down and he threatened to resign and went out after a great commotion.

This afternoon, three days late, the clause was withdrawn but we had to suffer the carefully prepared demonstration of Dame Irene Ward.[1] She stood there in front of the Mace and stood and stood and stood until she was successfully named and was able to say that she had made her protest as a demonstration against the Labour Government's dictatorship to Parliament. The press loved every moment.

The worst mess above all today was the Party meeting at 6.30. It was in the Grand Committee Room in Westminster Hall which has as fatal an atmosphere for Party meetings as the P.M.'s room in the Commons has for Cabinet meetings. Some sixty or seventy members of the Party were scattered over that huge space, with Douglas Houghton, John Silkin and Fred Peart on the platform. A storm blew up about the debate on Laurie Pavitt's Prayer to annul prescription charges, which as long ago as February John Silkin and Fred Peart had planned to have on the last day before the Whitsun recess. The idea was that by then many people would have gone home so the debate would have less publicity.

In order to make assurance doubly sure John had put in front of this Prayer some quite important business, the Lords' amendments on the Industrial Expansion Bill, which would go on for two or three hours so that the debate on charges could start late and finish at 11.30. This plan had been seen through immediately and the whole Party was infuriated. The 3:1 majority for accepting the charges which we had arranged with such tremendous care was blown away in this storm of hatred, sourness and indignation.

[1] Conservative M.P. for Wallsend 1931–45, and for Tynemouth 1950–February 1974. She became a D.B.E. in 1955 and a life peer in 1974. At 4.30 p.m. on May 23rd she stood before the Table, interrupting proceedings and refusing to obey the Speaker's request to return to her place on the benches. The Speaker called for order and 'named' Dame Irene Ward, at which the Leader of the House moved that she be suspended from its service. She protested that Parliamentary dictatorship prevented her from protecting her constituents' interests and then the Serjeant-at-Arms escorted her from the Chamber.

I had to listen to George Lawson (John's old deputy Chief Whip who let him down so badly by being disloyal) get up and say 'We're just a mob now, not a Party' and face the fact that most people there know there is a certain amount of truth in the remark.[1]

I felt utterly dejected as I went across to No. 11 where in those stiff, rigid rooms Roy was giving his first At Home. He was bending from the waist in a chivalrous way with Jennifer, looking a little tense, going the rounds. All the right people had turned up, from Hugh Cudlipp and Pam Berry and Ann Fleming to Dick Crossman (my Anne should have been there but wasn't) and Ted and Barbara Castle.[2] It was a very good and select party that went on until well after midnight when I walked home, having drunk a great deal of champagne, sick at heart.

Friday, May 24th

A ghastly press, with Irene Ward the heroine of the day. I had drunk too much champagne on an empty stomach and I felt even worse because at 9.0 I had to see Shackleton and Carrington who both felt that in the present situation it was hopeless to think of Lords' reform. We are proposing a thoroughly sensible consensus reform at the precise moment when the Tories were going to start using the Lords in a real anti-Labour way for saying no to this insensate Government which is trying to rush business through in a ridiculous fashion. A successful Government could have afforded to be evolutionary on Lords' reform but if we can't master our back benchers on prescription charges, we shan't be able to master them on this.

Saturday, May 25th

I went down to Prescote last night and today drove across to Wilton Park with Anne to see Heinz Koeppler and give an address on Parliamentary reform.[3] They seemed quite impressed and afterwards, while they went off for a tour, Anne and I had a lovely walk with Heinz over the downs above Chanctonbury Ring where the air was freeing itself a bit after the rain.

Sunday, May 26th

This morning we had a walk in the park in sweltering heat after the rain. At

[1] Labour M.P. for Motherwell, April 1954–February 1974 and for Motherwell and Wishaw from February 1974 until his retirement in October that year. He was a Government Whip in 1964 and Deputy Chief Government Whip 1966–7. See Vol. II, pp. 233, 259.

[2] Ann Fleming, widow of the 3rd Baron O'Neill, was the former wife of the 2nd Viscount Rothermere and widow of Ian Fleming, the author of the James Bond series of thrillers, who died in 1964. Edward Castle was Assistant Editor of the *Daily Mirror* 1943, Assistant Editor of *Picture Post* 1944–50 and Editor of *Picture Post* 1951–2. He was an Alderman on the G.L.C. 1964–70 and has been an Alderman of Islington Council since 1971. He became a life peer in 1974.

[3] Born in Germany, Heinz Koeppler was a history don at Oxford 1937–9 and in 1940 joined the Political Intelligence Department of the Foreign Office. Since 1946 he had been Warden of Wilton Park, Sussex, a discussion centre for members of the Atlantic Community, and since 1972 Warden of the European Discussion Centre. He was knighted in 1977.

last I had a sense of release and when we had motored back home and I had finished reading *Greenmantle* to the children and had my talk with Pritchett about the farm and the new swimming bath I felt less despondent but only a trifle less.

One sign of my despondency is that early this morning I got what Elizabeth Longford first described to me as 'morning panic'.[1] It's something which grows on you with age but which I've scarcely had since I became a Minister. You wake up at 4.0 or 5.0 a.m. and see the whole of your life's problems with a kind of strange, nightmare clarity. So my mind brooded over last Thursday's events when Irene Ward was being named to the cheers of the Tories and then over that terrible Party meeting and I reflected that the very same afternoon the pound hit a record low since devaluation, stimulated largely by the international situation and the refusal of the American Congress to vote the tax surcharge. As if that wasn't enough, yesterday morning the National Institute of Economic and Social Research published a report saying that our deficit is now running at £300 million and may well remain at that figure for the rest of the year. So the hopes with which we started the year are slipping away and we're still teetering on the edge of the precipice, without any reserves and with the I.M.F. bankers sitting in the offices of the Bank of England watching us.

Then I began to brood about my tummy being too fat and on the fact that this diary which I thought of as being enormously important to future historians will probably be regarded as the rather dull detailed history of the last days of the British *ancien régime*. Nor shall I be able to follow it up with a book on how Parliament works because nobody's going to care about this Parliament which is going to be swept away. Isn't it true that we're now in a revolution which may actually succeed? I'd always thought it would have been very exciting to have lived through 1848 and now I find we're living through the most momentous year that I can remember since the war. It's been the year of the Czech anti-Stalinite revolution,[2] the year of the American defeat in Vietnam,[3] the year of the students' uprising in Western Germany

[1] The Countess of Longford, wife of Frank Longford, whose books include *Victoria R. I.* (London: Weidenfeld & Nicolson, 1964), *Wellington: Years of the Sword* (London: Weidenfeld & Nicolson, 1969) and *Wellington: Pillar of State* (London: Weidenfeld & Nicolson, 1972).

[2] In January Antonin Novotny had resigned as First Secretary of the Central Committee of the Czech Communist Party and he had been succeeded by Alexander Dubček, for five years First Secretary of the Slovak Communist Party. Novotny remained President until March, when General Svoboda was elected in his place. The 'Prague Spring' saw the abandonment of press censorship and the rehabilitation of many important people. The party's Action Programme, approved on April 5th, promised that travel abroad, freedom of the press and freedom of assembly would be guaranteed and that press conferences, public opinion polls, better housing and a more active European policy would be introduced.

[3] When President Johnson had declared on March 31st that he would not seek a further term of office he had also announced that there would be a partial halt in American bombing raids on North Vietnam. On May 10th North Vietnamese negotiators met American representatives in Paris to begin peace talks.

and in Paris.[1] East and West of the Iron Curtain, establishments are being challenged by new forces from below which have little care for the concept of parliamentary democracy as we know it. They're in revolt against a parliamentary democracy which was an ideal in 1848 but is now part of an established oligarchy, part of the Establishment in the West just as Communism is part of the Establishment in the East. These uprisings this year are in both cases anti-Establishment. Strangely, when I think about this some of my depression goes away. It's a great relief to feel that what we're suffering here is part of a world phenomenon and that we're not the only government that's totally incompetent, unable to cope. I like to feel that in America L.B.J. is failing as abjectly as Harold is here.

I see two factors which make 1968 quite different from 1848. First of all we are faced by individual alienation from government, a protest against the remoteness of government, whether the government is Communist or Western democratic. Secondly, this is going on in a world of relative affluence. It is not the result of the elemental forces of poverty, desperation and penury coming up from below. On the contrary, these movements are powerful because all over the world living standards have been attained from which one can criticize governments not merely in terms of economic need but in terms of freedom and alienation.

Yet however much I make allowances for our situation being affected by world problems, I can't get away from my depression at our failure to tackle even our narrow economic problems. We have made very little progress, the pound is still teetering and what is disappointing is that so far Roy's Chancellorship has not made as much difference as I had hoped.

Apart from Roy the other big personal factor is Barbara Castle. She has made a new and exhilarating impact but she's also made a fatal mistake by committing herself to price reductions in a period when we need price rises. As a result we're now committed to a new prices and incomes policy in which no one, except possibly Barbara, still believes. Roy, I know, doesn't believe in it although he doesn't believe that we can sweep it away either. It is not good for a Government to be fixed on a procrustean bed of a government-controlled prices and incomes policy which it doesn't itself believe in, especially as this involves us splitting the Government from the Parliamentary Party and the trade unions while we force the Bill through. I suspect that in the short run Barbara may gain a little by believing in state intervention and rushing about pretending to control prices. But in the medium term the situation will not be improved in this way. Indeed this year may well end in another devaluation and what we must pray for is that the devaluation of

[1] In West Berlin on April 11th there was an attempt to assassinate Rudi Dütschke, left-wing leader of the militant Socialist Students' League (S.D.S.). It had been followed by violent student demonstrations throughout Germany, mainly against the publishing house of the right-wing Springer press, and all political parties took up the issue of public order.

the pound will coincide with that of the dollar and the franc and be excused on those grounds.

As for the Government itself, I am now convinced that one of Harold's greatest mistakes is his constant reshuffling. Too many job changes in three years means a tremendous decline in the power of the politician over the Civil Service machine and a tremendous growth in the power of the Whitehall Departments, both to thwart central Cabinet control and to thwart departmental Ministers' individual control. The truth is that a Minister needs eighteen months to get real control of his Department. I had just about got it when I was moved from Housing and therefore I was deprived of the third and fourth year when I could really have achieved something. Harold has appointed Denis Healey for a five-year period and he probably has done a great deal to change the detailed running of Defence. But look at Transport where Barbara, having just got control of the Department and launched her Bill, was ripped out to go to Productivity and an unenthusiastic Dick Marsh was sent in. The Department takes over and does exactly what it likes. It's the constant fiddling with Ministers and shifting them round which has undermined the central strategy of this Government. Thank God it's nearly the Whitsun recess. It's months since we started planning our holiday in Cyprus. We decided to go to Cyprus again partly because it's not as severe and austere an island as Crete and it's better for the children, but mainly because it's part of the sterling area. We've expended £400 on a B.E.A. package flight which includes the cost of the air tickets as well as six days at a first-rate hotel in Famagusta, two days up in the mountains and then six days at the hotel where we stayed last year in Kyrenia.

While we're away our new swimming bath in the walled garden may be started. How come that I, a Labour Minister, should be spending well over £400 on a family holiday, nearly £4,000 on a swimming bath and nearly £300 on a garnet necklace as a birthday present for my wife? It's because we're joining in the movement out of money into things which has been prevalent in this country during the last six months. I now know that if I want to save, the right policy is to buy things which are valuable and not hoard money or shares.

I expect this last week before the recess to be absolutely ghastly. I've described in my previous slab of diary the sense of rout in the Party meeting and this week we face an infinitely more formidable programme. We are to start on Monday, Tuesday and Wednesday with the Finance Bill, from 3.30 on Monday until 1 a.m. on Tuesday: resuming at 10 a.m. on Tuesday and carrying on until 1 p.m., then breaking off until 2.30 and starting again to go on until 12.30 a.m. on Wednesday. The same process is to be repeated on Wednesday and Thursday. That is Fred Peart's plan and simultaneously the Committee on the Finance Bill will be sweating its way upstairs in Committee Room 10, with the Race Relations Bill and the Prices and Incomes Bill going on near by. So the Commons will be humming with activity upstairs and members will be chasing to and fro to vote simultaneously on the Floor and in Committee.

Out of this the Tories have created a tremendous protest, alleging that we have permitted Parliament to degenerate into chaos. There was Irene Ward's great scene and there has also been enormous pressure in the press, with every Sunday paper this morning full of the incompetence and mismanagement of a Government which is destroying real parliamentary discussion. The truth is that in his determination to recess before the end of July, come what may, Fred Peart has piled a tremendous burden of work on both Houses. The pressure which culminates this week will ease off in the Commons for the rest of June and July but the log-jam will move up into the Lords and possibly produce a crisis between the two Houses.

How far is the grievance genuine? I think it's largely pi-jaw since a vast number of M.P.s never think of attending the Report Stage of a Bill on the Floor of the House and if they want to attend for a particular clause they can get away from their Committee upstairs and come down to speak and vote. So this overlap is quite normal. However, as a result of my reforms, we have as well as Standing Committees more Select Committees meeting than ever before and we also have the Finance Bill being taken in Committee upstairs.[1] Nevertheless I think Ronald Butt is talking nonsense in the *Sunday Times*,[2] when he implies that I am to blame for using the new reforms to ram through vast amounts of Government legislation and so destroying democracy. It is a theme which has been re-echoed in a good many papers and also by Mr Emanuel Shinwell, who once again blew his top on the subject of my incompetence.

Of course, because up to two months ago I was Leader of the House, I have been careful not to say a word in criticism of Fred Peart. The judgment I have kept to myself is not that he's been overloading the House in these ten days before the recess but that the ten days' parliamentary time we have gained by putting the Finance Bill upstairs has not been used for general debates as we intended but merely for the Report Stage of Government Bills. This really is a great pity. Apart from that the criticism has been artificially worked up and we shall survive it without difficulty.

Monday, May 27th

The morning papers are full of Wedgy Benn's speech on Saturday at the Welsh Labour Party's annual beano in Llandudno. He has hit the headlines

[1] Eight or nine Standing Committees, titled alphabetically, are appointed each session to debate the clauses and amendments to Bills. This is the 'Committee Stage'. Their size is regulated by Standing Order and their members are nominated by a Committee of Selection, which ensures that party strengths on the Committee reflect those in the whole House. When a Committee has reported a Bill to the Floor of the House it is disbanded and before considering the next Bill is set up afresh.

[2] Assistant Editor and Political Columnist on the *Sunday Times* since 1967, and Political Columnist on *The Times* since 1969. He is the author of *The Power of Parliament* (London: Constable, 1967).

with a great account of what is wrong with the democratic system of government and how if it's not put right we might even share the experience of de Gaulle and Czechoslovakia. He attacks the mass communication system for alienating public opinion and his one concrete suggestion is that we should have government by electronic referendum. This is characteristic of Wedgy because he doesn't seem to realize that two of the countries which employ the referendum are Australia and Switzerland, which are without doubt among the most reactionary democracies in the West. As Duncan Sandys once pointed out,[1] a referendum on capital punishment, homosexuality, prices and incomes or Rhodesia would be quite sure to bring a defeat of the Government. The real problem about Wedgy is that his presentation is brilliant but what he says is normally second-rate and sometimes disastrously stupid. This was one of the occasions when the presentation was alpha and the content gamma minus.

At S.E.P. where we started with a socialist classic – the problem of Short Bros, the aircraft works in Belfast, which Cripps nationalized during the Second World War and which since then has become a white elephant that has managed to lose more money by producing, or not producing, than any other aircraft factory in the world.[2] It has also managed to absorb more injections of capital to less effect. Yet Wedgy solemnly proposed that Cabinet should allocate £3¼ million extra capital to keep Short's going and give the new manager he had appointed a chance. He was answered by the Chief Secretary, Jack Diamond, a neat little Jewish accountant who's built himself up into quite a formidable Cabinet character first under Jim and now under Roy. He said that he'd privately checked, since the civil servants don't have the time to check on these things, and he reckoned that another £3 million would just go down the drain. It would all be exhausted by next September when Wedgy would be back asking for another £4–5 million to keep the firm going. Jack then gave figures to prove that it would be far cheaper for us to pay wages to totally unemployed workers than to go on producing aircraft at the present staggering rate of loss. Harold said that it was very serious that no less than four government Departments were concerned in this and none of them was responsible for assessing profit and loss. There must be an independent inquiry into Short's but meanwhile the £3¼ million would be paid. Well, that was that. It was very characteristic of our Government. Just carrying on.

Bristol Docks, our second subject, I found fascinating. When Barbara was

[1] Conservative M.P. for Norwood 1935–45 and for Streatham 1950–February 1974. He was Minister of Works 1944–5, Minister of Supply October 1951–4, Minister of Housing and Local Government 1954–January 1957, Minister of Defence January 1957–October 1959, Minister of Aviation October 1959–July 1960 and Secretary of State for Commonwealth Relations July 1960–October 1964. In 1974 he became a life peer, taking the title of Lord Duncan-Sandys.

[2] Sir Stafford Cripps, Labour M.P. for East Bristol 1931–50 and for South-East Bristol 1950, was Minister of Aircraft Production 1942–5, President of the Board of Trade 1945–7, Minister for Economic Affairs 1947 and Chancellor of the Exchequer 1947–50.

Minister of Transport she had put forward a paper suggesting nationalization of the docks by means of a central national docks board which would be responsible for policy planning but which would leave the actual administration to nine regional dock authorities. It was not unlike her urban passenger transport authorities in the Transport Bill. She was determined to prevent centralization of control in London since she said it would be fatal to labour relations. Cabinet gave her permission to negotiate with the various interests but before the report came in she had been moved to D.E.P. Here was Dick Marsh saying that after consultation he had decided Barbara's scheme was utterly wrong and that we ought to have a highly centralized dock board to own and run all the docks from London.

Dick is a tall, willowy young man with thin silk suits and mauve ties. He has a trade union background but has got on very well with Lord Melchett and such people in the swing.[1] He mixes very naturally with the wealthy and the successful and he has a contempt for sentimentality and failure. I regard him as young and brash and devoid of any settled convictions, and he can be attracted very easily by the aristocratic or wealthy embrace. I think he was in the case of the Steel Board. However I don't think that's happened here. He has simply taken the Department's brief, swallowed it hook, line and sinker and decided to scrap all Barbara's ideas. Where he came unstuck today was in insisting on a quick decision to give him time to complete the policy ready for a Bill next session. It couldn't possibly be ready until January but he hoped it could then be forced through so that we could start implementing our nationalization pledge in 1969/70, before the election.

I had read all this on the way up to London. I always retain massive departmental papers for reading in the train as I find it concentrates my mind wonderfully to have to read them at the last moment. Here I had very soon grasped what was going on and I regarded it as a nightmare. First we must face a tremendous row between Barbara and Dick. Secondly, we must rush through nationalization so we could start closing down about half the total area of docks in the country and creating major redundancies. Our Mr Marsh is a great closer of coal mines.[2] Now he wants to be famous as a closer of docks as well.

Fortunately Cabinet took against him. Roy started by saying that on no account should we have this Bill at all, least of all in the run-up to an election. Tony Crosland joined in to say the same thing and I found myself merely

[1] Julian Melchett succeeded to his father's barony in 1949. A banker and industrialist and a member of the Mond steel-making family, he became first Chairman of the British Steel Corporation in 1967. He died in 1973. For his appointment, see Vol. II.

[2] During Richard Marsh's tenure at the Ministry of Power, the Government had published in November 1967 the White Paper *Fuel Policy* (Cmnd 3438), forecasting a drop in the demand for coal, as natural gas and nuclear and hydro-electric power took its place. The Ministry of Power had decided that nuclear-generated electricity would be the cheapest source of power and Lord Robens, Chairman of the N.C.B., alleged that this policy would lead to a fall from 387,000 jobs in 1967 to 65,000 by 1980, with an end to mining in traditional areas like Scotland, Northumberland, Durham and South Wales.

echoing my colleagues. Only Barbara lashed out and said that it would be a major disaster to postpone the vesting day of the National Docks Board until after the election. 'The Party is firmly committed,' she said, just as she herself was personally, and the National Executive and the dock workers would be deeply upset if we failed to begin nationalization under this Government. I must say that for once Ray Gunter, who sits for Southwark, talked common sense. He said it wasn't his impression that any of his voters were going to go on strike against the failure to nationalize. They would quite like a couple of years of quiet life after the upsets of the de-casualization scheme.[1]

I think if Dick had come to us with Barbara's scheme unchanged and they had stood shoulder to shoulder they might easily have got their way, but we opponents were strengthened by the split between Marshite and Castle-ite expositors of the true spirit of the party and of British socialism. Roy continued to say he wanted the whole thing dropped but very sensibly Cabinet decided not to have a Bill this session and to let Dick have a year to work out a new scheme in consultation with Barbara.

This afternoon I answered my first two Parliamentary Questions as co-ordinator of the Social Services.[2] They were quite simple and took a matter of seconds. It reminds me that if you look in Hansard I've said nothing in the last six weeks. I'm neither a departmental Minister nor Leader of the House. I sit about on the front bench quite a lot but I don't do anything there and I won't do it until I get control of my new Ministry.

Then I took the chair for another meeting of our Devolution Committee. I'm aware that all the little devices I've put together in this paper and which could have been effective two years ago are now totally inadequate to meet the tremendous rushing tide of nationalist feeling in Scotland. It may well lose us half the Scottish seats in the next election but none of this seemed to worry the Committee. Fred Peart continues to want us to go on as if the Scot. and Welsh Nats didn't exist and at the other extreme I have Cledwyn Hughes, the Welsh Secretary of State, twittering and manoeuvring and wanting somehow to create a Welsh National Council which is neither truly national nor part of local government. He wants to wamble his way through. There are one or two on the Committee who try to see the problem on its merits, Peter Shore, Shirley Williams and Dick Taverne, for example, but most of them have been removed in shuffles or have become disillusioned. On this occasion I had a typical result of a reshuffle. Instead of Edmund Dell,[3]

[1] In a Report (Cmnd 3104) published on August 5th, 1965, a Committee chaired by Lord Devlin had recommended drastic changes in the labour structure of the docks. The Docks and Harbours Act 1966 had introduced a partial de-casualization scheme.

[2] On the probable publication date of the Seebohm Report and on the likely date of the merger of the Ministries of Health and Social Security and the consequent structural changes.

[3] Edmund Dell, Labour M.P. for Birkenhead since 1964, was Parliamentary Secretary at the Ministry of Technology 1966–7, Joint Parliamentary Under-Secretary of State at the D.E.A. 1967–8, Minister of State at the Board of Trade 1968–9 and at the D.E.P. 1969–70. He was Chairman of the Public Accounts Committee 1973–4, Paymaster-General 1974–6 and since 1976 he has been Secretary of State for Trade.

a fanatical unionist, Peter Shore himself attended. He thinks we haven't considered the case for self-government seriously enough and said he would have to vote against the paper because it is inadequate. I had to say to him, 'It's very nice, Secretary of State, to see you here today but for the last eight meetings you sent somebody who opposed any concession to nationalism.' He smiled quite sweetly. Suddenly, after a great deal of railroading, I managed to get a draft to go up to Cabinet. It's a pretty hopeless document and I intend to attach my own Lord President's saying that the obvious tactic is to outdo Mr Heath by offering a Royal Commission on self-government and nominating to it people who look as though they will be serious about it. This might really stem the tide—but how much better if we'd done it a year ago.

Waiting upstairs was a vast collection of top brass brought together to consider the merger of my two Ministries. I sat as Chairman, the first work I'd done on the merger. We had Sir Arnold France, a very characteristic Treasury figure, tall, long-faced and pale, with Kenneth Robinson, his neat little bureaucrat twin. They represented the Ministry of Health and I must say that, looking at them, I felt they were the right people to speak for a Ministry over at the Elephant and Castle, utterly cut off from reality. Then we had Judith and her Permanent Secretary, Sir Clifford Jarrett, who was Permanent Secretary at the Admiralty before he became an expert on pensions four years ago. Willie Armstrong has told me that Arnold France is soon to leave and go back to the Inland Revenue but that I can have Jarrett as head of my merged Ministry. He's a good rough tough man and I said to Judith, 'Once he's on my side he'll be useful but he'll be a bloody nuisance as long as he's not.' Further round the table we had Sir William Armstrong and Sir Louis Petch as well as the Secretary of State for Scotland and Sir Douglas Haddow.[1]

It was important that sufficient formal business should be provided to last an hour and this had been done by producing a paper listing three possible ways of doing the merger. In fact there was nothing to discuss because there was only one possibility. If I wanted a merger quickly I had to become Secretary of State for Health and Social Security and then by affirmative order a single Ministry of Health and Social Security should be created. The announcement would alter nothing but it would put me in charge of both. The only snag is that this procedure requires me to become Secretary of State and at the moment there isn't a Secretary of Stateship to spare because I surrendered the job of First Secretary to Barbara Castle. I shall have to sit it out until a space is created.

[1] Sir Louis Petch joined the Civil Service in 1937, becoming Second Secretary to the Treasury in 1966. From 1968 to 1969 he was Second Permanent Secretary at the Civil Service Department, and from 1969 to 1973 Chairman of the Board of Customs and Excise; since 1974 he has been Chairman of the Parole Board. He was knighted in 1968. Sir Douglas Haddow joined the Department of Health for Scotland in 1935 and from 1965 to 1973 was Permanent Under-Secretary of State at the Scottish Office. Since 1973 he has been Chairman of the North of Scotland Hydro-Electric Board. He was knighted in 1966.

I solemnly went through the two non-existent possibilities but, as everyone knew, the P.M. backed me on this so the action had to be taken. Both Ministries obviously detested it but nobody said a word until I asked about timing and mentioned that I hoped to have the merger by July. Sir Arnold France suddenly observed, 'Something must be said for my civil servants and doctors whose morale is disintegrating.' I saw my chance. 'If you want something quickly, Permanent Secretary,' I said, 'I'm afraid it can only be the merger described in possibility number one. So let's agree to forget long-term reconstruction and get on with it quickly.' Out of Sir Arnold's one remark I got what I wanted, a minuted agreement by all the Departments that I am to be made Secretary of State. I shall be able to say to the P.M., 'Everything's ready now. You give the word', and it will all be over after one and a half hour's debate in the House of Commons on the affirmative order. They went out gnashing their teeth and I at once got off my minute to Harold. Meanwhile the Report Stage of the Transport Bill, begun at 3.30, was pounding its way through and it pounded right along until 1.30 a.m. when I left the House and walked home with Tam.

Tuesday, May 28th

Up to the P.M.'s room to discuss the B.B.C. licence fee, which we've already been discussing for two weary years. Wedgy Benn, Ted Short and I have all been convinced that the B.B.C. must go over to advertising, at least in part.[1] This has always been opposed by Harold, the Methodist, and by Michael Stewart, the atheist, on the grounds that it's immoral to permit a virtuous organization such as the B.B.C. to be in any way related to commercial profit.

This time we had an even more ridiculous proposal than ever from the Postmaster-General. Instead of raising the licence fee by £1, as the B.B.C. have been insisting for the last eighteen months, to prevent them running into the red, he proposed that we should raise each £1 by getting 15*s.* from the increased licence fee and 5*s.* from permitting advertising on Radio One. Everyone in Cabinet thought this pretty futile. The whole subject could have been settled in five minutes because after we'd turned down that proposal there was really no doubt that we had to give the B.B.C. their £1 rise. But no! The P.M. chose to indulge in one of his tirades. He'd been listening to Radio One and noticed how some of the disc-jockeys bring in news items with an anti-Labour slant. He insisted that a special study must be made with the

[1] In 1966 Mr Wedgwood Benn, then Postmaster-General, floated a proposal to establish a new public broadcasting corporation with one wavelength financed by advertising revenue. After six months' discussion, Mr Short, Mr Benn's successor, published in December 1966 a White Paper on Broadcasting Finance, Cmnd 3169, declaring that the B.B.C. would continue in its present form, as a public corporation deriving its revenue from the licence fees, paid by the public to the Post Office and voted, as a matching sum, by Parliament. In 1969 the licence fee was £6 p.a. for radio and black-and-white television receivers and £12 for colour.

Lord President in charge. He supported this decision with an extraordinary outburst about the wicked political bias of the B.B.C. contrasted with the honesty of commercial television under Charles Hill in the old days,[1] and now under the virtuous Bert Bowden.[2] Every now and again someone would quietly say, 'But Prime Minister, look, fine, but shouldn't we have the £1 licence increase?' And finally, of course, we got it.

Then we turned to the fascinating subject of Bristol docks. About two years ago Bristol had decided to rival Southampton by having a port big enough for the great transatlantic liners. Partly owing to the jealousy of Newport and the other Welsh ports and partly because, quite frankly, there was really no chance of Bristol getting this amount of trade out of the hands of Southampton and Liverpool, Bristol had been turned down but told that they would be allowed to put a secondary scheme for a more modest port. They were themselves going to raise the money, some £50,000, to rebuild the West Dock and this scheme had been studied and passionately supported by the Regional Economic Council we had established.[3]

What the Council wants for the South-West is a spine road through Devonshire and down through Cornwall, with Plymouth classed as a Development Area, and a dock for Bristol. We had turned them down on the spine road, we had turned them down on a Bristol–Plymouth road and today the paper before us said we must turn them down on the dock because national port planning requires Bristol to cease to be a port in the next five years.

The Ministry of Transport's experts had done a cost analysis which showed that £50 million worth of port facilities at Bristol wouldn't be as valuable as £50 million worth in many other parts of the country. I couldn't help remembering that when we were discussing Stansted no one demanded we should prove that we would get 5 per cent profit from it.

Before any of the critics could speak Dick Marsh unwisely remarked that we needn't waste much time on this because there was really no serious opposition to the paper. Denis chimed in on rather similar lines and Barbara

[1] A doctor, Secretary of the B.M.A. 1944–50, and Conservative M.P. for Luton 1950–63. His offices included those of Postmaster-General 1955–7, Chancellor of the Duchy of Lancaster 1957–61 and Minister of Housing and Local Government October 1961–July 1962. In 1963 he became a life peer and from 1963–7 he was Chairman of the I.T.A. In 1967 not uncontroversially, he was appointed Chairman of the Board of Governors of the B.B.C. He retired in 1972.

[2] Labour M.P. for Leicester 1945–67, an Opposition Whip and Chief Whip 1951–64, Lord President of the Council and Leader of the House of Commons 1964–6, Secretary of State for Commonwealth Affairs 1966–7. In 1967 he became a life peer, taking the title of Lord Aylestone, and from 1967 to 1975 he was Chairman of the I.T.A. (subsequently, the I.B.A.).

[3] In February 1965 the Government had appointed Regional Economic Planning Boards and Regional Economic Planning Councils for the eight regions of England, together with national boards for Scotland and Wales. The Boards, chaired by the D.E.A. with representation from all departments, served the Planning Councils, which consisted of nominated members drawn from local government, both sides of industry, the universities and other regional interests.

Castle and Peter Shore, our transport economists, gave their support to Marsh. Tony Wedgwood Benn made his constituency case and then I said, 'I am a simple-minded man and I just want to know why Bristol should be forbidden to use its own money to build itself a port because gentlemen in Westminster and Whitehall know better. Planning requires political judgment.'

I went on to say that it was impossible to tell a famous 500-year-old port like Bristol that we have decided they should be a port no longer. This shook Harold, who knew there were five Labour constituencies in Bristol,[1] and I added that people all over the country would be affected by the attitude which the decision implied. We're just treating a Regional Economic Council like dirt. At this point the Chancellor of the Exchequer, an acute, canny character who had remained absolutely silent, looked across at me and said, 'I am prepared to have another look at this.' He kicked me under the table and whispered, 'That should be good enough for you, Dick.' So I went out and had a jolly good lunch, feeling that Cabinet meetings are sometimes worth while.

I went on to my own Social Services Committee to deal with a draft White Paper from the Ministry of Health, this odious institution that has been trying to get ahead of the Seebohm Committee with its own proposals for reorganizing the Health Service. The Ministry's White Paper showed that the only sensible way to reorganize the Health and Welfare Services was to take all services away from the local authorities and put them either under independent Boards or under the Ministry of Health and the doctors. A very simple view of life. As soon as I'd got a glimpse of this draft I had sent for Kenneth Robinson and said, 'It wouldn't be wise for you to put this out before the Seebohm Report is published. Four other Ministries are concerned, Housing, Social Security, Home Office and Education, and they would all think that you were jockeying for position. However,' I added, 'I don't mind your trying your draft out on the Social Services Committee.' Today we had the tryout and as a strictly impartial Chairman I had a splendid time. In an hour and a half every single Minister round the table had registered a string of serious objections so that after the amendments little would be left of the paper. It was quite a successful manoeuvre.

We then turned to the much more delicate problem of public expenditure. It's got to be cut this year as usual and the social services may well be asked to hack another £100 million out of next year's estimates as well. How are we going to face this? The Chancellor usually acts bilaterally, sending for each Minister and doing a lone deal. I had tried the experiment of getting the five Ministers together on a Saturday to see whether we could form a common front, but how can one persuade a Minister of Education to sacrifice money allocated to school meals in order to improve social security?[2] Or how can

[1] At the 1966 General Election Labour's majority in one of the six Bristol constituencies had been only 669. The Conservatives held Bristol West.

[2] For the meeting on March 30th, 1968, see Vol. II, pp. 749–52.

I get the Minister of Health to accept hospital charges because they will provide the money for the school building programme? The Saturday discussion had been a total failure. When I had said so, Ted Short had remarked, 'They'll have to take the cuts out of defence. That's all there is to it.'

Nevertheless at today's Committee we very gingerly approached the problem again. I shall have a separate talk with each Minister but even someone more tactful than I am would find it impossible to persuade five independent Ministers to work out a common policy obliging each of them to accept departmental cuts to help someone else. That was the real reason why I wanted to merge Social Security and Health – so that I can make my own priorities inside the unit I control. As long as I'm trying to co-ordinate unmerged Ministries each will go on working on its own.

This afternoon I went along to the Lords to finish redrafting the Reform White Paper. We worked for two hours and got final agreement but at the end I said to Peter Carrington, 'You know, the chances of getting it through now are zero.' He agreed and said, 'We've missed the quiet time.[1] Now I'm having to make noises about the House of Lords standing up to the Commons in order to appease my back benchers who are anyway pretty uncontrollable. What's the chance of your back benchers doing what you want?' he said, turning to me. 'None,' I said, 'they're going to be infuriated by the proposals. If we put the baby into the bathwater at this temperature it will die. I'd better see Harold and tell him that the best thing to do is for him to find some excuse for delay. We need to go into purdah for a couple of months.' It was a depressing conversation but it's pleasant that we could talk about it with such complete freedom. Eddie and I, Peter and George have really become quite a band of brothers.

After this I went over the river to the Festival Hall to a concert by the Israeli Philharmonic Orchestra. The music wasn't up to much, a Chopin piano concerto and Mahler's First Symphony, but the soloist, Arthur Rubinstein, aged eighty, played as an encore a polonaise which was worth the rest of the concert put together. But I shall remember best what happened in the interval. I had seen Cecil King having a hearty talk with Denis Healey and had carefully avoided going near them. A wealthy friend of the orchestra suddenly rushed up and buttoned me to say that Hambro's Bank had given £10,000 to the Conservative Party. 'I'm going to give £10,000 today and every other industrialist will give £10,000 so they'll get £10 million in five months.' 'What are they going to use it for?' I asked. 'For the education of the public,' he replied. 'To show them that you have destroyed everything of value in the country and that we must get rid of this Government.' He was frenetic and

[1] Major and contentious measures, like the Transport Bill, were now going to the Upper House for their Lords' stages. Moreover, Conservative peers felt that in the second half of the five-year Parliament they could justifiably oppose the Government's programme more vigorously.

this shows how difficult it is for the pound to remain stable if people like these have this view of the Government.

Wednesday, May 29th

Directly I got into the office Paul Odgers and Harry Salter said they must see me about an important Cabinet paper.[1] A Cabinet Committee had given me an instruction to organize an educational campaign on the facts of immigration. 'We submitted a draft,' said Odgers, 'and you've written at the bottom "No good".' 'Yes,' I said, 'that's my view.' 'But it's a Cabinet decision,' he replied, 'and we've summoned a meeting of the Cabinet Committee to discuss the paper.' 'But there's nothing we can do,' I said. 'Do you deny that if we call the Ministers together they'll just waste their time?' 'No, of course I know they can't do anything,' he said, 'but we have to follow Cabinet instructions and submit a paper.' 'I don't send in under my name papers which have nothing in them,' I said. 'How on earth can you have an educational campaign about race before you've got a policy? We haven't fixed the number of immigrants or the quota or agreed on any principles, so I don't want any education done at all.' It took a full half-hour to persuade my two civil servants that the meeting had to be cancelled. It seems an interesting example of how time is wasted in Whitehall.

Some notes on a characteristic O.P.D. meeting. The first item was Hong Kong. As a result of withdrawing from Singapore we are putting two more battalions into Hong Kong as well as fighters and frigates and minelayers, a bloody fleet, because Hong Kong must now have its own defences. 'That may be a justifiable short-term policy,' I said, 'but what about our long-term policy for withdrawal?' Michael Stewart replied, 'There's a special Hong Kong Committee at work on this.' Once again something really important is being discussed not at O.P.D. but in a special committee which I know nothing about.

The second subject was minor dependencies. What on earth are we to do about Ascension Island, Easter Island, the Falkland Islands, the Seychelles, Gibraltar, etc.? The paper submitted went right through the list, providing us with excellent reasons for staying in each one and increasing the amounts of troops available. Not a single recommendation to wind up.

The next paper was on the need to maintain forces for the evacuation of British personnel. At present we still accept the commitment to have forces available for evacuating any largish group of British citizens living abroad. The paper noted that most of the countries of Europe had no forces for this purpose and that, if they need to evacuate, they pay someone else to do the job. We, however, as the third world power, have always maintained this

[1] Harold Salter had been an Assistant Secretary at the Ministry of Health since 1963. He was an Under-Secretary at the D.H.S.S. 1971–3 and since 1973 has been Director of Own Resources and Accounts, Directorate-General of the Budget, Commission of the E.E.C.

commitment. I said, 'Look, we've just ceased to be a world power and are becoming part of Europe. Wouldn't it be possible to find out what they do?' A withering look from Harold. 'But they wouldn't tell you.' 'I didn't mean to *ask* them. I thought you had other means of obtaining information.' Michael Stewart primly replied, 'One can hardly waste money on finding out that kind of thing.' I accepted the point and then asked whether we couldn't ask a couple of reliable journalists to give us a report. This was very bad form but Denis Healey did agree that it really would be sensible if we gave up this kind of contingency planning and that I was on to something. It's great fun behaving in this way but it's not much good. All I contribute to O.P.D. is a macabre joke.

I had to stay behind because one of those great anti-Israel rows was blowing up. At a party last Thursday I'd run into Hugh Thomas,[1] who said he was doing a serious programme on Ernest Bevin.[2] He asked me to make some critical comments, sent me a letter and I told my Private Office to fix it up, but David Williams, my new Private Secretary, rather an innocent man from the Colonial Office, had looked at the protocol and observed that Ministers must always apply to No. 10 for consent to broadcast. He had formally applied and No. 10, without telling Harold, had gone to the Foreign Office, which had said no. I had written to Michael Stewart saying there must be some mistake and had received a two-page letter forbidding me to do the broadcast because of the damage it would do to our relations with the Arabs. I had sent a little note back to him saying that the broadcast couldn't possibly do any harm and that his attitude stimulated me all the more.

So this morning I told Michael Stewart that it would be perfectly O.K. 'It's twenty-year-old history,' I said. I would discuss Ernest's mistake in seeing Judaism as a creed about a religion rather than a nation and I would describe how he was deceived about the military aspect of the question and how he hadn't understood the Americans' view of George III. They all got quite interested. I finished by asking, 'How can that harm your relations with the Arabs?' Michael replied, 'You must appreciate why I feel so strongly. I detest the situation where those poor Israelis are sitting there encircled by Arabs who refuse to recognize them but I can't express a word of what I feel and I don't see why you should.' 'Thank you for telling me,' I said, 'but in that case I'll do the broadcast. It's been laid on for 5 o'clock this afternoon. I'll

[1] From 1966–76 Professor of History and from 1973–6 Chairman of the Graduate School of Contemporary European Studies at the University of Reading. His books include *The Spanish Civil War* (London: Eyre & Spottiswoode, 1961; rev. edn Hamish Hamilton, 1977), *The Suez Affair* (London: Weidenfeld & Nicolson, 1967) and, as editor, *Crisis in the Civil Service* (London: Blond, 1968).

[2] General Secretary of the T.G.W.U. 1921–40, Labour M.P. for Central Wandsworth 1940–50 and for East Woolwich 1950–1. He was Minister of Labour and National Service 1940–5, Foreign Secretary 1945–51, and Lord Privy Seal March 1951 until his death in April. As Foreign Secretary he had appointed Crossman to the Anglo-American Palestine Commission in 1945 and, when it reported, Crossman unexpectedly took the American view that Israel must become a national home for the Jewish race.

send the script round to you and you will discover that nothing whatsoever will happen.' Hours of time wasted, fussing about a two-and-a-half-minute broadcast when more important things were going on.*

I stayed behind to discuss with the P.M. Mr Callaghan's notorious speech to the Firemen's Union. This had been causing a tremendous sensation. He had apparently told them without any qualification that there would be no more legislation on incomes and prices. Harold said, 'That fellow's getting above himself. We must teach him a lesson. I will do so after Cabinet tomorrow.' 'Fine, Prime Minister,' I said, 'and we'll all support you,' and we had a nice drink together.

The Party meeting this morning gave me a chance to assess back-bench morale. It is clear that the House has settled down to the appalling routine imposed upon it this week. Despite all the talk of chaos the Bills are churning their way through and what pleases me most is the marvellous success of the device we invented to allow us to stop business at 11.30 p.m. and start it again at 10.0 o'clock next morning.[1] This is working like clockwork.

After the Party meeting I went into the smoking room where I spotted Mr Callaghan and after a minute or two he came across and we had a drink together. 'I think I'd better tell you frankly,' I said, 'that there's a bit of trouble between you and the P.M. He's taking a bit rough what you said to the Firemen's Union and especially that you treated Barbara in that way. After all, she's the Minister in charge.' I added, rather maliciously, 'This is the electioneering season, of course, for the seats on the National Executive. Last year in order to get the trade union vote you knifed Michael Stewart in the back when he was trying to do the prices and incomes policy at D.E.A. Now you seem to be knifing Barbara in the back.' Jim was quite cool and collected. He said, 'But I don't want their votes next year,' and I replied, 'Quite right. It's not trade union votes you want, it's their money. As Party Treasurer you've got to collect the funds for the next General Election campaign and you're going round the trade unions telling them that if they give us a good donation you can give them the assurance that there won't be any more prices and incomes legislation.[2] It's been very clever of you, Jim, and you've forced the P.M.'s hand. But you mustn't expect to be loved by him. Anyway, he'll talk to you about it himself.'

At this point his temper began to rise: 'How often did you or Barbara knife

* And on Friday Michael told me that he'd heard the broadcast and that it was very satisfactory.

[1] After the difficulties over morning sittings (see Vol. II) a Sessional Resolution was passed to provide that a sitting of the House could be suspended at night and resumed at 10 o'clock next morning. A motion to this effect could be introduced any time after 10.0 p.m. and had to be put forthwith. On November 12th, 1968, the Resolution was embodied and passed in Standing Order No. 2 but the procedure was used only eight times in the 1968/9 session and has never been used since.

[2] Mr Callaghan had been elected Treasurer of the Labour Party (and thus an *ex officio* member of the N.E.C.) in 1967. He held this post until he became Prime Minister in 1976. See Vol. II.

me in the back in those three years when I was Chancellor? I've never forgotten how time after time you went behind my back to the Prime Minister and tried to destroy me. You got your own way against me. Why shouldn't I get my own way now?' We had a nice drink together for forty minutes or so and eventually Jim said, 'You're one of the few people I can talk to frankly, Dick. All I care about is the party.' And I said, 'Well, that's fine, Jim. I feel you're right back on top of your form and playing for the highest stakes again. You're obviously feeling the better for the change to the Home Office.'

Then I went in for a quiet lunch with Michael Foot and told him what Jim had said.

This evening I was to dine with the Chancellor, who had been saying to me for some days that he had to talk to me alone, and would take me out to Brooks's. So we drove off in his great big Daimler, unloaded ourselves halfway up St James's Street and went into the club. Upstairs is the gaming table with the slice cut out to give room for Charles James Fox's tummy.[1] At the bar down below were Mark Bonham Carter and other willowy young men.[2] It's a classy club, not at all like the Garrick, and after we'd had a drink we went into the dining-room and had claret and gulls' eggs and were gentlemen together. We had a good talk about Callaghan and Barbara Castle. Roy and I are both worried about her health as well as about the line she's taking on prices, which really looks as though it can't be sustained.

Then we got on to Harold's future. What are the alternatives? Roy thinks Michael Stewart is hopeless. Barbara? Splendid but a girl. Callaghan? We would fight to the death to stop him. 'Well,' I said, 'there's no alternative,' and Roy said, 'There is you, Dick. I would support you as successor to Harold without hesitation.' I was taken by surprise and replied, 'Well, it's lucky for Harold that it's me.' Roy passed on to the next part of the conversation but I'm sure this was the point of the meeting.

At 9.0 p.m. we retired from Brooks's to the House of Commons, where I found a deadly hush because everyone was watching the European Cup match on T.V. Harold was at Wembley and when he came back later in the evening he asked me what I thought of it. 'What match?' I said. 'I think it's such a waste of time and I stopped poor Tam from using my T.V. upstairs because I was working.' Harold clearly felt this attitude makes me incapable of being a great political leader because the mark of a leader is to be a man who sees football or at least watches it on television.

[1] Secretary of State for Foreign Affairs 1782, partner in the Fox–North Coalition February–December 1783 and Secretary of State for Foreign Affairs 1806. The table was more probably cut away to make a place for the croupier at the bank.

[2] Liberal M.P. for Torrington March 1958–9, first Chairman of the Race Relations Board 1966–8 and Chairman of the Community Relations Commission 1971–6. Since 1976 he has been Chairman of the Outer Circle Policy Unit and since 1975 Vice-Chairman and a Governor of the B.B.C.

Thursday, May 30th

I briefed Barbara on Callaghan before we went into the Parliamentary Committee. We all waited for the great moment when we were to have the P.M. on Callaghan and nothing happened. We had a little bit about the B.B.C. and party political broadcasts and then at 10.30 Cabinet was called in.

Finally the P.M. got himself together and said, 'There is, of course, Home Secretary, your speech.' The Home Secretary said, 'I've got absolutely nothing to apologize for at all. There's nothing inconsistent there.' But the P.M. said, 'I think there was something a little bit inconsistent, wasn't there really?' and Jim blazoned it out and then there was a mild interjection from Barbara and a much stronger one from Michael Stewart. 'Well,' the P.M. said, 'I think we can move on now.' I said, 'But we can't move on, Prime Minister. Has the Cabinet disowned Mr Callaghan or not?' Callaghan said, 'Not at all, nothing to disown.' From that point we spent twenty minutes fencing round this business, all done on the issue of what we should tell Fred Peart to say at his weekly press conference this afternoon. I insisted that Cabinet should disown Callaghan and indeed the whole Cabinet insisted.*

The only other item on the agenda was votes at eighteen. I had to manage this because Callaghan had now disappeared to a Committee upstairs. At the Cabinet Committee we had unanimously held the view that Cabinet would be wise to accept the Speaker's Conference decision to reduce the age from twenty-one not to eighteen, but to twenty since this would make the danger of the young Scottish and Welsh nationalist vote less grave.

We had just been on the point of reporting this to Cabinet when Gerald Gardiner, in one of his liberal moods, insisted on making an announcement that we had accepted all the Latey Commission's recommendations on the age of majority being reduced to eighteen. It was obvious that if you reduced the age for everything else it was impossible to keep voting at twenty so our Committee had to come back to Cabinet and say that despite our previous view, owing to the Lord Chancellor's precipitate announcement, we now had to recommend votes at eighteen.

A fortnight ago Cabinet had said it wanted more information on this, Gallup polls and so on. There wasn't very much material but we got it all together for them. This morning was one of the occasions when Harold Wilson asked for individual votes. Michael Stewart, who's often very good on this sort of thing, looked across at Harold and said, 'You can't *give* votes to young people. They're taken from you. The young are insisting on their rights and you'd be mad to resist now. Of course you must give way.' The fanatical supporters were Wedgy Benn, Peter Shore, Michael Stewart, Gerald Gardiner, and the fanatical opponents the Welsh Secretary and Dick Marsh, our youngest Cabinet Minister, as well as Eddie Shackleton who is always

* But in the next day's press there wasn't a single newspaper reference to Callaghan. He had in fact called the P.M.'s bluff and clearly Harold had carefully given instructions that the Home Secretary was not to be disowned.

cautious and corky. I think Barbara would have been against if she'd been there. The unenthusiastic supporters, by the way, were headed by Tony Crosland and myself. However, we are now, by this peculiar form of argument, committed to votes at eighteen.

I dropped in on the front bench to hear Harold Wilson conducting a quiet and good-humoured Question Time and Fred Peart handling what could have been a very awkward incident when he was furiously attacked by Ted Heath about the chaos of the timetable. His reply was innocent but artful: 'I hope the Rt Honourable Gentleman ... will not exaggerate. He should approach these matters in a more relaxed fashion.' If I had said this it would have been regarded as insulting and arrogant but Fred can say it with charm and sincerity.

This evening we had the debate on prescription charges at a time when Fred hoped most people would have already left for the recess. Kenneth Robinson ought either to have resigned on this issue or fought, but he did neither and just sat about being feeble. Three Tories were present on the other side. At the end there were 52 votes against the charges to about 129 for and there was a terrible sense of dreariness in the House but also of relief that soon we would be safely out of the place.

Friday, May 31st

I rang up Harold to say goodbye and he told me that things had been looking up for the last fortnight and he smelt success in the air. I thought, 'Holy God, I hope it isn't the kind of success which hit us last November.'[1] I believe we face another disastrous batch of by-elections. However, it's nice that Harold is optimistic.

The big news of the day was the sacking of Cecil King by the *Mirror* Board of Directors. Alma Birk had told me weeks ago they were planning to do this but I hadn't believed a word of it. What was really cheering was that this could actually happen in Fleet Street. Here is the Chairman of the I.P.C. overthrown successfully by a *coup d'état* in the same way as he overthrew Guy Bartholomew and made himself king.[2] I rang up Hugh Cudlipp, his successor, and without thinking said over the phone, 'It's marvellous to think it possible.' I heard a great laugh at the other end of the phone and I said, 'You must draw no conclusions from that, Hugh.'

While I'm away on holiday there'll be some changes in my Private Office. Anne Ridoutt is going back to the Ministry of Housing and says it makes her extremely happy.[3] I gather she's going into Tony Greenwood's office and that will suit both of them down to the ground since she's heartily glad to get rid of

[1] When the pound was devalued. The by-elections were at Oldham West, Sheffield Brightside, and Nelson and Colne.

[2] Guy Bartholomew was Editorial Director of *Daily Mirror* Newspapers Ltd from 1934 to 1944, when he became Chairman. In 1951 he resigned and was replaced by Cecil King. He died in 1962.

[3] Mrs A. S. Ridoutt, an Assistant Secretary.

such a rough customer as I am. So with her out of the way I've got my beautiful Janet Newman promoted with a large salary increase and she is to do the work of Jennie Hall as well.[1] My Private Office grows steadily in size and on the whole decreases in competence. But that can't be helped because a Minister without a Department will always have inferior civil servants.

Odgers is a great deal better than I thought at first and he's backed by Mr Salter who's a mild little official, quite clever, and David Williams. Each of them has a secretary as well and in addition to all this I have Molly, my driver, and Janet to look after me.

One other little story to illustrate my life with the Civil Service. This morning I had a very troublesome problem about supplementary benefit. I decided that it was important enough to inform both the P.M. and the Chancellor. When I got into the office there was Paul with a frightful effusion so I shaped and sharpened the letter up and said, 'Right, clear that and I will sign it this morning.'[2] Just as I was leaving the office I remembered I hadn't signed it. I went in to the outer office and found Paul closeted with a bespectacled man. 'Who are you?' I said. 'Oh, I'm over from Social Security,' he replied. 'We're finding it very difficult to get the formulation of your letter right.' I discovered that they had completely rewritten it, adding more and more relative clauses and conditions and removing any value it had. I lost my temper and said, 'It's my private letter to Harold and to Roy. What on earth are you doing mucking about with it? I didn't tell you to bring this chap over from Social Security.' 'We had to clear it,' Paul replied, 'otherwise the Treasury would have caught us out.'

I got up and walked out, but I wasn't all that successful because I then found that I hadn't collected from the office the tickets for the cinema to which I was taking the children. I had to telephone to have them sent. Characteristically, the senior officials had all gone off on holiday so the unfortunate porter was left to hang about outside the cinema for an hour and a half waiting for me. I went away on my holiday with a bad taste about officials in my mouth.

Talking to Anne last night, I reflected once again on that strange conversation with Roy and his quite consciously expressed willingness to serve under me. No doubt if I were physically capable and had the mental energy to do it I could make a better job of it than Harold for the remaining life of this Government. I certainly don't have any desire to do it, I really genuinely don't. Is that a good reason for doing it? Possibly it is, as Plato said about philosopher kings, but it is really only interesting in that Roy is prepared for it and if Roy is prepared others are too. And this remains the reserve position with which I close this diary and go off to Cyprus.

[1] Crossman's former secretary.
[2] Paul Odgers.

Sunday, June 16th

We got back from our fortnight's family holiday in Cyprus today. I didn't see a newspaper while I was away and took care not to see one until we were on the plane back, so we only heard from somebody in the hotel about the murder of Robert Kennedy.[1] I must admit that even if this meant the end of the Kennedy clan I wouldn't be profoundly sorry since I've never fallen for the Kennedy cult. But it was striking to see the Cypriot flags flying at half-mast. For whom else in the world would this be so except for Archbishop Makarios or a member of the Kennedy family?[2]

The other fact which we rather vaguely gathered was that the near revolution in France had collapsed, things had settled down and that de Gaulle had promised an election and would probably get a great Gaullist majority because of the fear of the communists.

General de Gaulle had been visiting Roumania from May 14th to May 18th, and on his return on the 24th he found some 9–10 million workers still on strike, the Communist Party demanding 'Action Committees' and the Gaullists a 'Committee for the Defence of the Republic'. He announced that further measures of industrial participation would be introduced and a referendum held and then disappeared from Paris, leaving the electorate uncertain whether he would resign if defeated in the referendum. He returned to make a second broadcast on May 30th, postponing the referendum and announcing the General Election. In the first ballot on June 24th 142 Gaullists were elected outright and after the second on June 30th they and their affiliates had won 353 seats (including 61 Independent Republicans), the Centre Party 33, the Democratic and Socialist Left 57, the Communists 34 and non-aligned deputies 10. Instead of a minority of 3 the Government parties now had a majority of 109 and the Gaullist party, renamed the Union des Démocrates pour la République (U.D.R.) could, with 291 members, form a Government on its own.

As soon as we arrived we found big political news. Apparently Roy Jenkins made a big speech in Birmingham yesterday, threatening that the all-party talks on Lords' reform might break up if the Tories voted against the Rhodesia Sanctions Order.[3] This was given tremendous prominence and I

[1] Robert Kennedy had been campaigning in the California primary, where on June 4th he won 46 per cent of the vote. On the following day he was shot in the head at close range as he addressed supporters in the Ambassador Hotel in Los Angeles. A Jordanian Arab, Sirhan Bishara Sirhan, was arrested and charged with murder.

[2] Archbishop and Ethnarch in Cyprus since October 1950 and a supporter of the revolutionary struggle led by EOKA 1955–9. Elected President of Cyprus in 1959 and taking up his official duties when Cyprus became a Republic in 1960, he was re-elected in 1968 and 1973.

[3] On May 29th the United Nations Security Council had unanimously accepted a resolution imposing heavy sanctions against the rebel Rhodesian regime. Regulations implementing this resolution and renewing existing sanctions set out in the 1966 Order were embodied in the S. Rhodesia (U.N. Sanctions) Order, to be debated by the Commons on June 17th and by the Lords on June 17th and 18th. The 1947 Parliament Act had

was a bit surprised at Roy because his speech was unlikely to help the all-party talks to survive.

Monday, June 17th

When I got to the station this morning I read in the papers that a firm decision had been taken by the Tory Shadow Cabinet that the Tory peers would be whipped and would vote against the Rhodesia Order when it is taken tomorrow. Apparently there's to be a one-day debate in the Commons today with a Commons decision this evening and a two-day debate in the Lords with a vote at 5 p.m. tomorrow.

This morning Tommy Balogh came urgently along to tell me what had happened to him. Apparently he was given his life peerage on a Saturday and when he had come into his office in No. 10 on the Monday he was told to be out by midday. In those two hours everything was closed down, his security pass handed in and his cupboards emptied. Finally he unsigned himself from the Official Secrets Act.[1] So at midday he was out on his ear, leaving Burke and the rest of the civil servants rejoicing. The description sounds fantastic but it is exactly what had happened. Harold had agreed that once Tommy became a peer he would have a political platform and wouldn't be a civil servant or an adviser. I told Paul Odgers that I want to take Tommy on as a part-time economic adviser, shared with Barbara, along with Brian Abel-Smith. Odgers said, 'I don't think it will be allowed. I don't think they are going to allow Tommy to have access to secret papers again.'

My main job this morning was to chair the meeting of the Social Services Committee. I'd been warned about this when I was on holiday and told that together the Chancellor and the Prime Minister were proposing cuts in the social services. When I got back to Prescote I found the usual secret document which I had been studying over the weekend to see what Harold and Roy had been up to. Paul told me there was a great deal of waiting about last Friday because the Chancellor had suddenly changed his plans and persuaded the Prime Minister not to make one single big cut of £113 million but a series of cuts, spread over all Departments so that they could be brought in imperceptibly. It was a nice idea, but directly I heard it I realized it would be difficult to fulfil.

As soon as my meeting started Ted Short complained that he'd only just received the document and that it had been impossible to study it. Everybody was blowing up, saying they hadn't got the documents, and Dick Taverne

---

limited the peers' delaying powers on Bills but had not limited their authority to reject Orders passed by the Commons. The Conservative Party was now split over the Rhodesian question and it was feared that Conservative peers would use their overwhelming 'backwoods' majority to defeat the Order and deal a blow to a Government whose authority and credit had declined. Such action would jeopardize the all-party agreement on Lords' reform and revive the traditional hostility to the powers of the Upper House.

[1] On taking office Civil Servants sign the Official Secrets Act and, on leaving office, a reminder.

said that of course they had, that every precaution had been taken to ensure that they went out last Friday. Mine had certainly arrived on the Friday.*

I had assumed the meeting would go perfectly easily and had reassured Roy but it was obvious that the Ministers were not inclined to do any business today. So I told them I would advise Roy that S.E.P. must be postponed for a week. After an hour of a kind of protest meeting the Ministers went away, leaving the civil servants round the table looking very white and worried, particularly Miss Nunn,[1] who felt that she and I were personally to blame.

Immediately after this I went across to No. 10 for a drink and within a minute Harold had plunged in on the subject of Roy's speech. 'Now there can be no question of any more talks. We must break them off and force through a Bill taking away the powers of the Lords.' I said, 'For God's sake, Harold, are you mad?' and he replied, 'That speech of Roy's in Birmingham was deliberately intended to put me in my place. I must show that I am stronger than him.' We were in the middle of a party, with the butler standing beside me. Harold was excited, suffused with a jealousy which shocked me. Somehow I began to get just as emotional, probably because I was angry and personally injured that behind my back he had thrown away, as I always suspected he might, our negotiated settlement on Lords' reform. Now he was careering along on his old-fashioned, radical high horse, determined to outbid Roy in capturing the radical Left.

I was supposed to go on to the Queen's birthday dinner at Lancaster House. London was hot and stuffy and I didn't feel like putting on a dinner jacket. Anyway there was no point in going without Anne, so I'd agreed to take Michael Posner and Thomas Balogh to dinner at the Athenaeum and let them fill me in.[2] They explained that Whitehall was in no sense responsible for spreading the cuts evenly over the Departments and that the economic advisers had recommended a cut of £80 million in the investment allowances which, if a bit was taken off the Land Commission, would clear the whole thing. They agreed that a tiny slice off education, off health, off pensions, was ridiculous.

I had to go back for the 10 o'clock vote on the Rhodesia Order and ran into Roy who asked me back into his room.[3] I described the meeting of the Social Services Sub. 'If you present my Committee', I said, 'with this *fait accompli* and try to make them take it as it stands there'll be a rebellion.'

* I made some careful inquiries towards the end of the week and found that the Ministers were correct. None of them had got the document before midday on Monday and Ted Short only after he'd had a talk with the Chancellor. This had left no time for them to be briefed by their Permanent Secretaries.

[1] Miss Jean Nunn was a Deputy Secretary in the Cabinet Office 1966–70.

[2] Michael Posner, Fellow and Director of Studies in Economics, Pembroke College, Cambridge since 1960, was Director of Economics at the Ministry of Power 1966–7, Economic Adviser to the Treasury 1967–9, Economic Consultant to the Treasury 1969–71, Energy Adviser to NEDO 1973–4, and Economic Adviser to the Department of Energy 1974–5. He was Deputy Chief Economic Adviser to the Treasury 1975–6.

[3] The Order was approved by 319 votes to 246.

Roy first spent a lot of time disbelieving that the papers had only arrived on Monday. When I said, 'I can't persuade them to do it,' he replied, 'I must have the £113 million. Don't talk to me like that.' He twice tried to get out of his own room saying, 'I'll resign if I can't get it.' I said, 'Look, two can play the resignation game, Roy. I'm as good a resigner as you,' and I dragged him back into the room and made him discuss it all over again. I finally said that the best thing would be a week's postponement to give me time to reason with the Ministers. Meanwhile he should send round a further paper giving the second-year programme as well as the first so we could judge the two together.

I smoothed him down but then he had another major complaint. While I was away Harold had apparently circulated a paper recommending that we immediately accept the main recommendations of the Fulton Committee.[1] This included making a considerable section of the Treasury into an independent Department to deal with the civil service, something which obviously affected the Chancellor, but Harold had come to his decision without saying a word to Roy. 'That's very tough,' I replied. 'But tell me, Roy, did you discuss your Birmingham speech with Harold before you delivered it?' When he said he hadn't, I told him that Harold was furious and convinced that Roy is competing for the radical vote. Roy said, 'But on the way up to Birmingham I was making some notes and I took the line of the No. 10 briefing in the press. I can't be blamed for taking the Prime Minister's own briefing.' Clearly a thoroughly bad mood has grown up between these men and while I was in Cyprus it has got a great deal worse. I was just leaving the room when Roy said, 'Now, Dick, let's be practical. If I agree with you about postponing the decision on Social Service cuts for a week will you give me your full support on Fulton?' 'Yes,' I said, 'if you will support me on Lords' reform as well.' And that, roughly speaking, was the deal we came to.

Tuesday, June 18th

Because it was dealing with the annual cuts S.E.P. was a very big affair. The first part of the meeting was limited to the permanent members and we had a long discussion about the control of finance. How can it be that within three months our estimates are running too high? Tommy and Posner had both pointed out to me that the £113 million is only 0·007 of the total estimates and anyway part is due to increased prices, £31 million to the farm price review, which took place after the January cuts, and £40 million to a grotesque mistake in Housing's estimate of the return from councils on mortgage payments. They also reminded me that one of the deficiencies of the January

[1] Lord Fulton, Vice-Chancellor of the University of Wales 1952–4 and 1958–9 and of the University of Sussex, 1959–67 was Chairman of the Arts Council 1968–71. The Committee on the Civil Service, which he chaired, was to publish its Report, Cmnd 3638, on June 26th, 1968. Its recommendations included the establishment of a Civil Service Department and of a Civil Service College and the abolition of 'grading' between administrative, executive and clerical appointments.

package was that there was no contingency fund to deal with this sort of situation. So at the meeting this morning we discussed the importance of having a contingency fund and of trying to find out accounting errors and put them straight and that was as far as we got in the inner group.

As soon as the Ministers came in there was the usual row but the meeting didn't go on for long because Roy kept his promise and said he would postpone the decision for a week.

In the Commons this afternoon we had another Question to the Prime Minister on the Home Secretary's speech to the Firemen's Union. Harold mildly disowned Jim and that was that. Meanwhile the Lords were finishing their debate on the Rhodesia Order and, to everybody's amazement, the Government was only defeated by nine votes.[1] I am told that 166 of the 300 odd Tories on the Tory whip turned up to vote against the Order, along with a few cross-benchers. The Government supporters consisted of 90 per cent of the Labour peers, all the Liberals, 18 bishops and some 30 cross-benchers. The built-in Tory majority had nearly been defeated by the new House of Lords which has been gradually growing up since life peerages were introduced.[2]

I went along the corridor to celebrate in champagne with Eddie and Michael Wheeler-Booth and then Alma Birk came in and I brought them all back to the Strangers' dining-room. Sitting at the next table was the Chief Whip with his Whips and Gerald Kaufman.[3] I strongly suspected they were up to no good but they were very discreet until Freddie Warren came over. 'How's life?' I said, and I discussed our triumph in the House of Lords. 'What do you think is going to happen?' 'One alternative,' he said, 'is a Bill to end the powers of the Lords.' 'That's absurd,' I said, 'they couldn't possibly do it.' 'Couldn't?' he said. 'It's all fixed. We've prepared the Bill already.' Now whether the Bill was really prepared and printed I didn't know but Freddie Warren had alerted me about what the Chief, Fred Peart and Harold were up to. No doubt it had finally been clinched in Harold's mind by his furious reaction to Roy Jenkins's speech and indeed he had hinted this to me yesterday. All round me was rising a tide of popular indignation against the House of Lords which had now finally proved itself a reactionary body, worthy only of total abolition. Not a very bright prospect for our reform.

[1] The Order was defeated by 193 votes to 184. It was reintroduced and passed on July 18th.

[2] Peerages for life had been introduced in 1958. Simultaneously the hereditary peerage was being steadily depleted.

[3] A member of the political staff of the *Daily Mirror* 1955–64, Political Correspondent of the *New Statesman* 1964–5 and Parliamentary Press Liaison Officer for the Labour Party 1965–70, Gerald Kaufman was a member of Mr Wilson's inner circle at No. 10 (see Vols I and II). He has been Labour M.P. for Ardwick since 1970, and was Parliamentary Under-Secretary at the D.O.E. 1974–5, when he moved to the Department of Industry. Since 1975 he has been Minister of State at the Department of Industry.

Wednesday, June 19th

The first thing I did when I woke up was to ring the Chief Whip. I briefly asked him his view and he told me there could now be no question of carrying through the agreed scheme. It must be scrapped and we must take radical action to reduce the Lords' powers. 'You can't believe that, John,' I said. 'You've been in all our consultations and you know you can't destroy powers unless you deal with composition.' 'Well,' he said obstinately, 'that's my view today.' I said, 'Okay,' and slammed down the phone. Of course from Harold's point of view today's press was wonderful, lambasting the Lords for their idiocy in putting themselves in the wrong. Apparently this was the first time they had rejected a piece of subordinate legislation and, moreover, this particular Order in Council empowered the Government to carry out a unanimous recommendation of the U.N. Security Council. So the Lords had blurbed in every way.

What should I do next? Directly I got to London on Monday I'd filed a request for an appointment with Harold. As I expected, he had in fact avoided seeing me alone and I knew that behind my back something was up. Still, a meeting had been fixed for this morning and I had asked that it should be attended only by the Lord Chancellor, myself, Eddie Shackleton and Frank Beswick.[1] When we arrived I found outside the door the Chief Whip and Fred Peart so it was obvious that we were in for a slogging match in which the Prime Minister was going to defeat us if he possibly could.

Harold's attitude at the beginning of the meeting is described pretty fairly in the Cabinet Minutes:

> The Government supporters in the House of Commons will undoubtedly press for drastic retaliatory action. And it was for consideration whether the Government should forthwith introduce in the light of the requirements of the Parliament Act a Bill to curtail the powers of the House of Lords on the lines which had been provisionally agreed in the confidential inter-Party discussions on the reform of the Upper House.

I started very angrily and said abruptly that this just wouldn't work and it was impossible to accept it.

Harold replied that I'd been living in a cosy world of my own during our all-party conversations. 'You've lost contact with reality, Dick,' he said. 'Outside, things have been changing and since then you've been away on your holiday in Cyprus and we've had to take decisions in your absence. Anyhow we are not going to tolerate for a moment the composition and

[1] Frank Beswick, Labour and Co-operative M.P. for Uxbridge 1945–October 1959, was Parliamentary Secretary at the Ministry of Civil Aviation 1950–October 1951, a Lord-in-Waiting 1965, Parliamentary Under-Secretary of State at the Commonwealth Office 1965–7, Government Chief Whip in the House of Lords 1967–70, Chief Opposition Whip 1970–4, Minister of State for Industry and Deputy Leader of the House of Lords 1974–5. He became a life peer in 1964. Since 1975 he has been Chairman of the Organizing Committee for British Aerospace.

powers which you agreed with the Conservatives and the Liberals. We shall deal with the powers first and possibly with composition later.' 'You've got it wrong, my dear Prime Minister,' I replied. 'We *have* to deal with composition and powers together. The so-called delaying powers don't obstruct us much. It's a fact that at any time they can use their Tory majority to filibuster, to work to rule, look at every Bill, hold our programme up. Composition *is* their power and if you try to pass a Bill destroying their powers, while you are passing it they will do everything possible to sabotage our programme. It would take us the best part of a year to get a Bill of this kind through both Houses. What are you going to do and what are they going to do during that period? If you launch the Bill this session their reprisal will be to stop the Prices and Incomes Bill which has to be through on July 11th and to hold up the Transport Bill, where anyway our case is very weak. And if you postpone until next session the Bill to abolish their powers that whole session will be dominated by the Lords' filibuster. Is it really worth provoking that? One of the main reasons why I wanted an agreed solution was to take this dangerous power out of the Tory peers' hands for the crucial period between now and the Election.'

The debate went to and fro. Gerald Gardiner was good and loyal, Eddie was sound and even Frank Beswick was in form. In opposition we had the Prime Minister arguing mainly against me, Fred Peart virtually silent and out of his depth and John Silkin occasionally coming in rather feebly from the side. The P.M. got rattier and rattier, accusing me of appeasement and at one point asking why he should try to get my agreed solution through at the cost of opposition from our own back benchers. Nevertheless at the end of an hour and a half it was clear that we had licked them. The moment of defeat came when Fred Peart finally said, 'I do agree with the Lord President that we shouldn't close all avenues. We can't just break off the talks. We should leave it open either to resume them or not, as we think fit.' I had won at least this particular round.

As we went out I asked Eddie what he thought of the morning's work and he said, 'It seemed to me to consist of an hour and a half's argument between you and the Prime Minister and as such it was quite interesting hearing.' Throughout the proceedings Burke looked on very contentedly.

After lunch I found at the office William Armstrong, Sir Laurence Helsby's successor as head of the Civil Service.[1] He had come to discuss Arnold France's successor as Permanent Secretary to the Ministry of Health. I am apparently going to have Clifford Jarrett from Social Security as Chief Permanent Secretary and then France's successor as number two. William's suggestion sounded all right and I said I would have a look at him. Then William got on to the Fulton Report where of course he knew of the tension

[1] Sir Laurence Helsby, Permanent Secretary at the Ministry of Labour 1959–62, was Joint Permanent Secretary to the Treasury and Head of the Civil Service 1963–8. He became a life peer in 1968.

between the Chancellor and the Prime Minister. He told me it was very unpopular in Whitehall but that although he had informed the Prime Minister he didn't think the information would be passed on to me. Armstrong is a very good man but he is worn, exhausted, and he wasn't going to inject himself into a battle between the Chancellor and the Prime Minister.

I had received a message that Peter Carrington wanted to meet me on secret ground in Michael Wheeler-Booth's room in the House of Lords. It was a puzzling talk. I said I had heard from Harold Wilson this morning that in the Prime Minister's view Heath had deliberately seized this opportunity, confident that he could force a General Election by inflicting a humiliating defeat on the Government. 'That is quite untrue,' said Peter Carrington. 'In fact I made up my own mind.' He said he had a meeting with the Lords and offered them two alternatives, a vote of censure without a vote on the Order and, when they turned that down, a vote at once on the Order, strictly in conformity with the proposed reform, where the reformed House would retain the right to vote down any Order so that the Government could think again but with the limitation that the Government could reinsert it into the following day's business. 'I made it very clear that they could only do it on this one occasion.'

When he'd finished I said, 'But if you appease your back benchers in that way we have to appease ours and the Commons will get out of control.' He replied, 'I had to decide either to ride the storm or be thrown out of the Leadership and Heath rather reluctantly allowed me to ride the storm.' On the whole I believe this story but I had to reply that he'd set off something tremendous because there is now overwhelming pressure not only from the Labour back benchers in the Commons but from inside the Cabinet for an immediate Bill to remove the Lords' powers. 'It's going to Cabinet tomorrow,' I said, 'and I can't be sure what they will decide. As far as I can see, Roy is still on my side but there will be tremendous pressure from all the abolitionists. But whatever happens in Cabinet, my dear Carrington, I don't now see our agreement being ratified by either side. The talks are bound to be suspended for the time being and I'm not sure they can ever be resumed again.'

That concluded our conversation. We were both perfectly friendly and I believe I was wise to be completely candid. Several times he said, 'I may have been wrong in the position I took and if so I'm sorry.' He certainly saw he had put me in a difficulty by doing what his back benchers wanted and then relying on me to stop any back-bench reaction from our side. When he'd finished I felt I'd had enough work and took Anne to see *The Charge of the Light Brigade*, a very nice colour film with quite realistic acting but which somehow wasn't terribly interesting.

Thursday, June 20th

Practically every newspaper confidently anticipated that the Prime Minister would announce in the House this afternoon a Bill to limit the Lords' powers.

At Cabinet the House of Lords came up as item one and Harold was quite fair and put to the Cabinet exactly what we had agreed. He pointed out that we should denounce Heath strongly for an outrageous action which failed to correspond with the spirit of the inter-party talks. The talks clearly cannot be continued and Harold would, as Prime Minister, retain freedom of action to carry out a comprehensive and radical reform of the Lords.

Barbara Castle keenly welcomed this initial statement and nothing was said by Gerald Gardiner, Eddie or me. Barbara then made it clear that she wanted to go back on the agreed solution and simply abolish the House of Lords as such so I then had to go all over again into the arguments about the importance of composition rather than powers. Surprisingly, the traditional opponents, Ted Short, Gunter and Greenwood, didn't speak. Michael Stewart was the one man who said we ought to resume the talks straightaway since we need the agreed solution more than the Tories but no one else supported him. Roy Jenkins was discreet but on our side, Healey pretty well on our side and Tony Benn against us because he had his own idea of how to end titles. Certainly there was no kind of a majority for continuing the talks. Though we won the argument, my God, we didn't win the battle because from the beginning of the meeting it was clear that Harold had jettisoned the talks and during last weekend committed himself to a radical reform. The fact that I made him back-pedal at the last moment hadn't won me any liking.

We still had what was for the Prime Minister the main item on the agenda, the Fulton Committee report. I haven't asked him but I'm pretty sure that the reason he has committed himself to this report so early and so personally is partly because he has a strong liking for Fulton and even more for Norman Hunt and partly because he thinks this way he can improve his image as a great modernizer.[1] He put his case for immediately accepting the main recommendations of the report, including the creation of a Civil Service Department. Then the Chancellor put his case against what he described as precipitate action. Denis Healey, Michael Stewart and I supported Roy and all the support Harold got was from Wedgy Benn and Peter Shore, his two hirelings. He was so upset that at this point he stopped the meeting and asked that it should be resumed later.

In the afternoon I went down to hear Harold. I had denied him the triumph he really wanted but he was able to reassert his authority over the House and over our own party and to the exterior world there was nothing wrong at all. He got cheers from our side. If they are uneasily aware of the, from their point of view, disappointing ambiguity in the Statement they don't care.[2]

[1] A Fellow and Lecturer in Politics at Exeter College, Oxford, since 1952, Norman Hunt was a member of the Fulton Committee and, later, of the Royal Commission on the Constitution. He was Constitutional Adviser to the Government March–October 1974 and Minister of State at the D.E.S. 1974–6 and the Privy Council Office 1976. He became a life peer in 1973, taking the title of Lord Crowther-Hunt.

[2] The Statement ended: '. . . there can be no question of these all-party talks in these new circumstances continuing. Although the time has not been wasted, and valuable

As Carrington said, no one else on the Tory side but him and no one in the Lower House but me cares a fig about Lords' reform or knows anything about it.

At the Social Services Committee this afternoon we began our reconsideration of the cuts. This time we'd had, well in advance, Roy's paper on the second year's policy. It made a great difference since we'd been able to prepare ourselves and we could see how the minor cuts suggested for this year fit into the big programme. We could also see a number of big policy decisions we could take which would make the minor cuts unnecessary. We could abolish family allowances and substitute a housing allowance or begin switching from agricultural deficiency payments to levies, putting the price on the consumer rather than the taxpayer. We could cut back the whole system of government help to industry, whether by investment grants, the Regional Employment Premium or the rest of them. Or push on to the employers the responsibility for the first three weeks of sickness. There were any number of things we could do in the second year to enable us to keep our expenditure down to the required level. But they didn't help us at all with this confounded £113 million for 1968. The Committee were adamant. They all followed Ted Short's example and said they wouldn't move an inch so now I've got to go back to Roy and say that though I've tried hard the Committee just won't do it.

As I was leaving the House tonight the *Daily Telegraph* number two lobby man met me in the street and said they'd got a story that there had been a Cabinet split and that Eddie Shackleton and I had managed to stop the Prime Minister from legislating to remove the Lords' powers. 'Well, I don't know where they got that from,' I replied, hiding how disconcerted I was.

Friday, June 21st

I was much more disconcerted when I read the papers. There wasn't much in *The Times* or the *Guardian* but David Watt, whom I'd briefed at lunch last Monday, had an extremely good article in the *Financial Times* and the story was in the *Telegraph* and the *Express*. I don't believe this was a leak from our side and indeed the only explanation I can give is that after I filled Carrington in he must have told the Shadow Cabinet some of what I had said about Peart and Silkin's attitude and one of the Tories, probably Willie Whitelaw, had gone to the press. This shows that the intimate relations and mutual confidence we've had for months must stop. Even though Carrington had talked to me with such freedom about exactly what had happened and who had taken the decisions on his side I shouldn't have talked to him so freely

---

proposals have been put forward about the powers and composition of another place, I must tell the House that it is the intention of Her Majesty's Government, at an early date of the Government's choosing, to introduce comprehensive and radical legislation . . .' (*House of Commons Debates*, Vol. 766, cols 1314–6.)

about our goings-on. I think there'll be a good row about this and I shall have to tell my colleagues what I think happened.

I spent the day in Wolverhampton renewing acquaintance with a number of local authority people I met when I was Minister of Housing. Then I went down to their social security office for a talk with some of the staff who decide on the amounts that are paid out and who also do the actual visiting. I was surprised by the tone of the office, lower middle class and anti-intellectual. When I said to one young man, 'Why not take a diploma in social studies?' he answered, 'Why? I do quite well in this job anyway.' If they were properly trained these people would be superb. I found myself lunching in the very room where I lunched as Minister of Housing and they presented me with a magnificent so-called baptismal jar, rather like a gay pottery platter.[1] After the official opening of an old-people's home and an official tour of a children's reception centre I was off, motoring through Worcestershire to Prescote, where I found the whole family concentrating on preparing the tombola for the village fête tomorrow.

Saturday, June 22nd

The rainiest day we've had for weeks and weeks. It drenched, it stormed, it blew, yet over 100 cars had turned up on the field beyond the Donners' house in time for the official opening at 3 p.m. Thank God they'd selected me as the official opener. Anne and the children had to go on struggling at the tombola but after wandering round I could escape to work for three hours clearing up the weeds on my island to save it from being overgrown again.

Thomas and Pen turned up to see our new heated swimming bath in the walled garden and we had a very nice evening together, with Thomas telling us about the financial situation. We've drawn all we possibly can from the I.M.F., who are now carefully watching us. They will see us through provided we behave thoroughly respectably for the next two or three months. 'That,' says Thomas, 'is why the Chancellor had to be so fussy about cuts.' But we do possess one weapon. We know that if the cuts fail and we devalue again we shall immediately have a controlled economy, clap on import and capital controls and refuse to float the pound wide open to the world. It's the knowledge that Roy is prepared to go to those extremes that may put the international bankers on our side.

Of course Thomas no longer has access to secret documents but the accounts he gives are just as vivid. He told me that the last thing Harold said to him was that Roy would never allow Barbara and me to take him on as a part-time adviser, just as Burke told me earlier this week. Oh dear, what a queer character Harold is. Loyal to Thomas and me for three to four years, then suddenly everything is changed and Thomas is out.

[1] See Vol. I, p. 286.

Monday, June 24th

To my surprise Roy asked me to see him this afternoon about the cuts. He told me that no real cuts could be imposed on the Social Services and Housing would have to take the brunt. So for the second time I've won against the new Chancellor. In this case I've been greatly helped by the bloody-mindedness of the new Minister of Education, Ted Short. Patrick Gordon Walker had agreed to the postponement of the raising of the school-leaving age because his Permanent Secretary, Sir Herbert Andrew,[1] had assured him that this would save the rest of the school-building programme. Short issued a paper showing that this was completely untrue and that there has been a disastrous effect on primary as well as comprehensive school-building. We went on to discuss the second year and Roy was quite enthusiastic about substituting housing allowances for family allowances and about the idea of starting the move from deficiency payments to import levies.

Finally I told him about Harold and the Lords' leak, and explained exactly how it happened. I said I thought Harold would be very angry and Roy agreed, though he said he hadn't seen Harold at all.

At the meeting of the Parliamentary Committee today, though, the Lords' subject wasn't discussed. We considered a strange, sad, melancholy paper by Willie Ross, saying how awful life is in Scotland and how Scotland is penalized in comparison with other regions. He is mainly complaining about the loss of the Edinburgh–Carlisle railway and the closing down of a brand-new pit at Dumfries. But the whole of the country is suffering and the North of England has a higher rate of unemployment. The fact is that the Scots' peculiar problem is one of nationalism and Willie Ross is in these difficulties only because he is determined to treat nationalism as a mere emotional attitude which can be cured by economic policies alone.

So we came to the second paper, my paper on devolution, a cold, calculated paper, and, as Harold pointed out, not very inspiring. But, as I said, it was the lowest common denominator of consensus and that was because of the changes in personnel of the Devolution Committee. All we had to offer were these minor suggestions about bashing the nationalists and fiddling with Grand Committee meetings. Harold said that a more warm-hearted attitude might be got if the Lord President sat down with the two Secretaries of State. I thought this was too silly and told him so.

Tuesday, June 25th

A special Cabinet had been called to come to a decision about the Fulton Report but it started with a statement from Harold about the leak. He complained that, unlike the disagreement about the Fulton Commission where the

[1] The Reverend Sir Herbert Andrew (K.C.M.G. 1963), Deputy Secretary at the Ministry of Education 1963, Permanent Secretary 1963–4 and Permanent Under-Secretary of State at the D.E.S. 1964–70. Since 1974 he has been Assistant Curate of Kirkbymoorside, Gillamoor, Bransdale and Farndale.

confidence he specially asked for had been kept, in the case of Lords' reform there'd been an appalling and deliberate breach of loyalty. Five of Friday's papers had come out with a detailed and accurate account of a Cabinet split. He then indicated in the smallest detail the Ministers who could have known about various parts of the leak. There was no question, he said, that this was an example of a systematic briefing of five newspapers by one or two of the people sitting round the Cabinet table. He knew that it was one of a very small number because there was at least one thing in the leak which only he and one other person knew. Then he glared at us and stopped.

There was no discussion and Harold started on the Fulton Report, where we gave him a very easy time. It's a second-rate Report written in a very poor style by Norman Hunt. He and Harold are tremendous buddies who live in the same world of uninspired commonsense. The Report is perfectly sensible but, oh dear, it lacks distinction. However it's been a success with the press and the public. Harold needed a success for himself and Cabinet consented to his getting it with a Statement tomorrow.

Thomas had invited me to a lunch in the Lords before his introduction into the House. It was a small party, with Jock and Phyllis Campbell and Gavin Faringdon.[1] Thomas was looking very spruce and neat and Penny seemed uncomfortable. Thomas's introduction to the Lords was intended as a farewell to No. 10 but Harold has made it a clean cut.

This afternoon Harold had summoned me to No. 10 so I knew the fight was on. I started by asking whether I could employ Tommy Balogh as a consultant in the Ministry, along with Brian Abel-Smith. 'Would he be an official?' said Harold. 'No, he'd be a consultant but he would have to be able to read all the papers.' 'But he could read Brian Abel-Smith's papers,' Harold said. 'I don't want him to have access to Cabinet papers now he's a member of Parliament.' I said, 'Don't be absurd. You can have a peer working as an official.' 'Yes,' said Harold, 'but I don't want to, so make sure that Tommy only has access to Abel-Smith's papers. We don't want anybody to think he's come back to Whitehall. Why don't you take Theo Cooper,[2] the girl from Oxford, who is still in Tommy's room at No. 10? She is first-rate. Tommy can see her papers just as well.' As I wasn't getting much out of the discussion I turned to the main subject and said to Harold, 'Why have you

[1] Sir Jock Campbell was Chairman of Booker, McConnell Ltd 1952–66 and has been its President since 1967. In that year he also became Chairman of the *New Statesman and Nation* Publishing Co. Ltd and of Milton Keynes Development Corporation. In addition, he has been Director of the Commonwealth Development Corporation since 1965 and Chairman of the New Towns Association since 1975. A member of the Community Relations Commission since 1968, he was the Commission's Deputy Chairman 1968–71. He was knighted in 1957 and became a life peer in 1966. Lord Faringdon succeeded to his grandfather's barony in 1934 and had since the 1930s been associated with left-wing causes. He was a member of Labour's Parliamentary Committee 1957–60 and of the Fabian Society's Executive Committee 1942–66. He died in February 1977. His socialist friends were invited for discussions and rest to his house at Buscot Park, Faringdon, Oxfordshire.

[2] Fellow and Tutor in Economics, St Hugh's College, Oxford, since 1963. She was seconded to the Cabinet Office 1965–9.

infuriated Roy by virtually accusing him of the Friday leaks? In your speech you said this was like the South African arms struggle and that there was no doubt that there are people in the Cabinet who are trying to throw you out of your job.[1] You added that they could have your job because it doesn't provide much pleasure to anybody. That's all outrageous,' I said. 'There is absolutely no conspiracy in Cabinet. There is no attempt to get rid of you and I happen to know it because on this occasion I know how the story got into the press.' I then told him in detail. 'You mean you talked to Carrington?' he said. 'I wouldn't have thought it possible.' 'Well, you haven't got a very wide knowledge of human nature, Harold,' I replied. 'My relations with Peter Carrington have been extremely intimate for four or five months and we have been talking completely freely to each other.'

I explained how Carrington had given me every detail of what went on at the Shadow Cabinet meetings, the role Heath and Quintin, Macleod and Maudling each played, and how Carrington had always utterly disparaged the futility of them all. I also told him it was completely untrue that Heath ordered Carrington to whip the Lords into the Division Lobby on the Sanctions Order. It was Carrington's own decision on an issue about which he desperately cared and where he felt he might possibly have been wrong. When I'd finished, I said to Harold, 'I haven't said a word in Cabinet about these talks with Carrington because it was all in confidence but now my confidence has been let down by this leak so I'm telling you the truth.' 'If you talk to the enemy,' said Harold, 'if you have that kind of bedwetting mania for compulsory communication you get what you deserve.' 'If you have such loathsome thoughts about me the less we see of each other the better,' I replied. 'Anyway, what you've got to realize is that at Cabinet this morning you made a false accusation because you jumped to the wrong conclusion. This is the first time I've been able to catch you out and give you positive facts to prove how ridiculous you are to expect a conspiracy.' 'I'm not wrong to expect a conspiracy,' he said, 'I've had them in the past. It just happens not to be so in this case but it's given me the opportunity to dress the Cabinet down.' 'No it hasn't, Harold,' I said. 'It's given you the opportunity to reveal once again to Cabinet your persecution mania and how obsessed you are by these suspicions of an inner conspiracy. Instead of assuming that it came from the Opposition you always assume it came from your closest friends.' 'Of course,' he said. 'Who else could it have come from? What you've told me is utterly incredible. I still can't understand it.'

[1] Since November 1964 the Government had banned the sale of arms to South Africa, a policy which had been questioned by some members of the Cabinet in December 1967. Alarmed by rumours of a Cabinet split, some 140 Labour back benchers had signed a motion demanding the retention of the embargo and after several Cabinet meetings a statement was issued on December 18th, announcing that the ban would continue. See Vol. II, pp. 597–610 and pp. 596–603 of Harold Wilson, *The Labour Government 1964–70: A Personal Record* (London: Weidenfeld & Nicolson and Michael Joseph, 1971) hereafter cited as *Wilson*.

He then said that Roy had stayed behind after Cabinet for a long talk, in which Roy had insisted on a full explanation. 'Don't do that,' I said, 'because the only other person who's been talking freely to the other side about Lords' reform is Freddie Warren.' I told Harold the whole story of Freddie's behaviour last week at dinner and how he'd revealed the existence of the Prime Minister's secret Bill. 'Now,' I said, 'that's a piece of information which almost certainly went to Willie Whitelaw from Warren. Anyway the whole House of Commons expected you and Silkin to announce a Bill on powers and every newspaper predicted it on Thursday morning.' 'It didn't come from me,' he said and I replied, 'Of course not. It came from John Silkin and Fred Peart, doing their job and feeding the press. I'm not blaming anybody, Harold, but trying to make you see facts.' We had a fairly rough row.

Wednesday, June 26th

This evening there was a big rally of London Labour Party key workers with Bob Mellish in the chair.[1] By golly, it was a terrible meeting. It started fairly quietly with delegates describing the whole series of disastrous electoral defeats they had suffered and how they had lost the G.L.C. last year and the boroughs this year. It gradually warmed up into a tremendous attack on the prices and incomes legislation, first and foremost on Aubrey Jones's Board for saying that 7*s*. 6*d*. should be the maximum increase in council house rents.[2] Judging from Coventry, I would have thought this was enormously helpful but in Camden they found it terrible. But what they were really concerned about was the very principle of prices and incomes policy which is, in their view, the root of all evil. Bob very wisely left me only twelve minutes to reply and I went out desperately depressed, just in time for yet another talk with the Prime Minister.

It happened this way. On the front bench this afternoon Harold sat down beside me and at once started telling me of a wonderful talk he'd had with Roy in which the two men had completely restored their trust in each other and now understood each other completely. 'This row has cleared the air,' he said. 'Has it?' I replied, and he said, 'Come and see me after the Party meeting.' I went to his room and he repeated all the wonderful things which had happened and all the assurances Roy had given him that John Harris would be kept to his last. He then was kind enough to add that he accepted my story and would just report the affair to Cabinet, explaining that he was

[1] Labour M.P. for Bermondsey Rotherhithe, 1946–50, and since 1950 for Bermondsey. He was Joint Parliamentary Secretary at the M.H.L.G. 1964–7, Minister of Public Building and Works 1967–9, Government Chief Whip 1969–70, Opposition Chief Whip 1970–4 and Government Chief Whip 1974–6.

[2] Aubrey Jones, Conservative M.P. for Birmingham, Hall Green, 1950–65, was Minister of Fuel and Power December 1955–January 1957, Minister of Supply 1957–October 1959. He was Director of Guest, Keen & Nettlefolds Steel Co. Ltd 1960–65, and of Courtaulds Ltd 1960–63 and was Chairman of the National Board for Prices and Incomes 1965–70. Since 1970 he has been an economic consultant and a director of various companies.

satisfied that a Minister had been indiscreet, making it clear that the Minister wasn't Eddie Shackleton and assuring me that he wouldn't of course point a finger at anyone else. He looked at me and said, 'All the same, it was an intolerable thing for you to do,' and we went all over the ground once again, with my trying to persuade him that my personal relationship with Carrington during the talks was no more intimate than the perfectly usual relationship between Willie Whitelaw and John Silkin.[1] I added however that, by breaking off the talks without consulting me, Harold had given the Tories the excuse for behaving in a grossly improper way and using what I had told Carrington to damage the P.M. in the press. I concluded, though, that it wasn't all that important and only a person as obsessive as Harold would really notice it. He keenly resented this remark. 'I am not obsessive,' he said, 'and anyway I don't know what to do about you and Roy. Everything I say to you seems to get passed on to him.' 'Quite right,' I said. 'I told you months ago that when you talk to me you should know that anything you say may be passed on to Roy, just as Roy should know that anything he says to me can be passed on to Harold Wilson. There's no other relationship I can have with you both in which I can hope to do any good. I have not conspired with Roy against you and I shall not conspire with you against Roy.' 'But don't you sometimes feel,' he said, 'that you think only what Roy thinks?' 'Well, Harold,' I said. 'Now you're saying that I don't express my own personal opinions. Frankly, Roy doesn't express enough opinions to keep me going for a morning. I need my own and I express far more of them to Roy than he does to me because he's a canny, aloof man.'

After this second conversation I was aware that we'd reached a point of finality. I had really ended our period of mutual confidence when I ceased to be Leader of the House and had finally broken with Harold because I felt he never could trust me again and I never could trust him again. If only he had filled me in on what had happened when I got back from Cyprus. But, as I told him now, 'You didn't say a word to me about what you were up to or about your new plans for abolishing the Lords' powers.' 'Well,' he said, 'I didn't want you at that meeting because I thought if you were there the press would get to know of it but you insisted on coming.' 'Do you really mean that you thought you could have that discussion last Wednesday without me?' 'Yes,' he said. 'I intended to.' That taught me a great deal about Harold's relationship even with people he regards as his closest friends. He intended to take all the decisions behind my back last Wednesday and then let me try to fight it out in Cabinet. I told him that if he had done so he would have bitterly regretted it because then we would have had the row there instead.

[1] The Government and Opposition Chief Whips must enjoy a close and confidential relationship if the 'usual channels' are to work successfully for the arrangement of parliamentary business. Vol. II of the *Diaries* describes this phenomenon.

Thursday, June 27th

In Cabinet Harold made his statement about the Lords leak and carefully avoided saying anything indiscreet or referring to me at all. He just said he was completely satisfied that the information had gone to the Opposition through the actions of one member of the Cabinet who was perfectly sincere and who had discussed it with an Opposition peer. Fred Peart tried to discuss the principle of this but he was smacked down and we turned to our big discussion of public expenditure. After what Roy had told me there were no surprises when I listened to his account. Having tried and failed to win ministerial co-operation for spreading the cuts equally across the board Roy realized that he had to decide on one or two big victims, investment allowances and the I.R.C. on the one side and house-building on the other side.[1]

As usual there were endless protests about the P.E.S.C. method of accounting. What depressed us all was that we should be having another of these ridiculous affairs only six months after the January package. But there is one serious financial crisis which Judith and I have discovered. There's a real danger of the national insurance fund running into the red because of the unexpectedly heavy expenditures on unemployment benefit following on the very heavy sickness payments last winter and spring. It may be necessary to rely on the £1,000 million reserve fund but, to do that, the Minister has to get an affirmative order out of the House of Commons and the Government's equity holdings have to be sold. The public would therefore see that we are selling £260 million government stock in order to get £200 million of available capital. An appalling situation.

Friday, June 28th

The papers announced the result of the by-election at Nelson and Colne.[2] It was much worse than we had feared. We had an 11 per cent swing against us on a high poll. Of course it has been a terrible week with a railway strike and the threat of a machinists' strike at Ford's and I think myself that to have

[1] In October 1967 the Royal Assent was given to the Act establishing the Industrial Reorganization Corporation, empowered to borrow up to £150 million from the Treasury to enable it to set up new companies, and buy, hold shares in and advise existing ones. The first Managing Director was Ronald Grierson and its Chairman Sir Frank (later, Lord) Kearton.

[2] On June 13th polling took place in a by-election at Oldham West, caused by the resignation through ill-health of Leslie Hale, who had represented Oldham from 1945–50 and Oldham West since 1950. There was a swing of 17·7 per cent to the Conservatives, whose candidate, Bruce Campbell, took the seat with a majority of 3,311. In Sheffield Brightside, where Richard Winterbottom, the Labour M.P. had died on February 9th, polling on the same day resulted in the election of the Labour candidate, Edward Griffiths, with a majority of 5,248. The swing to the Conservatives was again 17·7. Polling on June 27th in Nelson and Colne, which Sidney Silverman had held for Labour from 1935 until his death on February 9th, resulted in a Conservative gain. David Waddington took the seat with a 3,522 majority, on a swing to the Conservatives of 11·4 per cent.

got the swing down from 18 per cent to 11 per cent was very satisfactory for this time of year.[1]

We spent the whole morning in O.P.D. on the Defence White Paper. It's an interesting document because Denis Healey has been trying to raise morale by saying that we are going to have Europe's most powerful armed forces—the biggest navy, the biggest air force and an army second to none. The more he tries to pep up the morale of the soldiers, sailors and airmen, the more likely he is to infuriate the left wing. I was interested to observe the difference between his O.P.D. White Paper on the real situation and the draft White Paper for publication.[2] The original document was extremely reactionary, reeking of cold war and implying that we ought to base all our strategy on the need to maintain conventional forces against the first part of a Russian attack. Everything of any real interest, including the estimates of de Gaulle and the analysis of the Eastern European situation, had been removed in the public version which we waded through.

Sunday, June 30th

Home to Prescote for two lovely quiet days. I treasure my weekends more and more. Yesterday we went over to Oxford to attend the marriage of my niece Ann Woodhouse, Charles and Mary's only child, and then I sweated on my island while Patrick went out on his bicycle. The new swimming bath is getting done fast. Life at home couldn't be better. The farm is looking splendid now despite all the rain we've had. Gosh, what a contrast with that dreary Government which I have to deal with during the week.

Last week was another dominated by Barbara Castle but so far I have to record that she hasn't been very successful. Her interventionism is upsetting business and it's certainly disturbing the trade unions. She has had the rail strike though she has been lucky about the threatened Ford strike where she got stuck with twenty-eight women sewing-machinists fighting for equal pay and jeopardizing the whole of Ford's exports. Instead of doing nothing, she got the women alone, had a cup of tea with them and announced this evening that the strike had been called off. This, by the way, in the same news bulletin where Ray Gunter announces his retirement from the Government. He is a

[1] On June 7th the Railway Staffs National Tribunal had rejected the N.U.R. claim for general pay increases of up to 9 per cent, irrespective of any later productivity agreement. Successive offers by the Railways Board were also rejected as insufficient. On June 24th the N.U.R., and on June 25th ASLEF, ran a work-to-rule and a ban on overtime, Sunday and rest-day working. Services were severely disrupted and from 10.0 p.m. on Saturday, June 29th, to 6.0 a.m. on Monday, July 1st, they were cancelled altogether. Richard Marsh told the Commons on June 25th that the Government would not intervene.

[2] The *Supplementary Statement on Defence Policy, 1968* (Cmnd 3701) was to be published on July 11th. It announced the Government's new European-based policy and the withdrawal by the end of 1971 of all forces from the Persian Gulf and the Far East, except for Hong Kong. The armed forces would be reduced by 17 major units by April 1970, and by a further 9 by September 1972. Twenty R.A.F. stations would be closed by the mid-1970s. Defence expenditure was estimated at £2,254 million for 1969/70, and with these and other economies would be reduced by £126 million by 1972/3.

coldblooded tactician and has been thinking for weeks of how he can resign with maximum damage to Harold. Now he's gone, simply declaring that he can't stick working in a Cabinet with Harold Wilson.[1]

Monday, July 1st

The morning papers show that Harold had been quick and decisive in handling the Gunter crisis. Roy Mason has taken his place at Power, the fourth change in a key Ministry.[2] I gather there were three possibilities, Reg Prentice, Roy Mason and Bob Mellish.[3] Personally I would have preferred Mellish as I have never thought very highly of Mason but I've no doubt that the decisive factor was that Harold wanted to put in a miner to placate the miners.

I started with a Pensions Committee this morning. I don't record all these meetings in the diary as they're too detailed and technical but this was interesting because there was a big paper on the transferability of pension rights between jobs. It had been suggested that this subject should be postponed and the necessary legislation left until we had done national superannuation. I went to the meeting gloomily certain that my colleagues would accept this. I found to my delight that Roy Hattersley, for Barbara's Ministry, and Dick Taverne, for the Treasury, were saying that all the legislation should be simultaneous and that even if we couldn't legislate for transferability we could legislate for the preservation of pension rights.

Then we turned to an enormous paper on unemployment benefit. Barbara had made it clear that she was not interested in D.E.P. operating this so the paper was prepared by the Ministry of Social Security. It concluded that earnings-related unemployment benefit should last only for six months and after that everybody should go straight on to what used to be called national assistance and is now supplementary benefit. This was the officials' idea but of course it is politically impossible. I had made sure the politicians had brought along their Parliamentary Secretaries, Norman Pentland, Charlie Loughlin and Ernie Fernyhough,[4] who all happen to be trade unionists. They

[1] See *Wilson*, pp. 541–2.

[2] From October 1964 to April 1966 the Minister was Fred Lee and from April 1966 to April 1968 Richard Marsh, whom Ray Gunter had succeeded. Roy Mason's place as Postmaster-General was taken by John Stonehouse, formerly Minister of State in charge of the aviation industry at MinTech. J. P. W. Mallalieu succeeded him, moving from the Board of Trade, where William Rodgers took his place as Minister of State. David Owen became Under-Secretary of State (R.N.) at the Ministry of Defence.

[3] Reg Prentice was Labour M.P. for East Ham North 1957–74 and has been M.P. for Newham North-East since 1974. He was a member of the staff of the T.G.W.U. 1950–7, Minister of State at the D.E.S. 1964–6, Minister of Public Building and Works 1966–7, Minister of Overseas Development 1967–9, Secretary of State for Education and Science 1974–5 and Minister for Overseas Development 1975–6.

[4] Norman Pentland was Labour M.P. for Chester-le-Street from September 1956 until his death in October 1972. He was Joint Parliamentary Secretary at the Ministry of Pensions and National Insurance 1964–6 and at the Ministry of Social Security 1966–8, Joint

thundered and said there must be a second six-month period of unemployment benefit which can if necessary be flat-rate. I've no doubt they'll get their way. It will be scandalous but it's necessary for political reasons.

I went next to Gerald Gardiner's room, for the first meeting of the new Cabinet Committee Harold had established to consider what radical reform of the House of Lords the party wanted. We had managed to include the Foreign Secretary, to counterbalance Wedgy Benn and Ted Short who are both against us. Characteristically, the Home Secretary didn't turn up and the Leader of the House was very late but we did have the Foreign Secretary, me, Wedgy Benn and Eddie Shackleton. We supporters of the scheme all stayed quiet and waited for Wedgy to outline his plans. He said he had read the draft White Paper and it was unacceptable because it was far too appeasing. I asked him, 'Did you think the powers were wrong?' to which he replied, 'No, the powers were roughly right. What was wrong was the preservation of the peerage.' He wanted the peers transformed into Privy Councillors. This is merely a change of title and I said I wouldn't mind changing the title for one moment but that I was interested to hear his criticisms on the central issues of powers and composition. He had no criticisms.

After a longish discussion we agreed to put up a paper to Cabinet saying that our colleagues must tell us what they wish. Do they wish to force through a new comprehensive radical reform or do they basically wish to revert to the old scheme, with minor amendment so that it can be put forward either as an agreed measure or as a party measure? While Cabinet chews that one over we must get to work on some of our new colleagues. I'm having both Short and Benn to private dinners with Eddie Shackleton next week to try to clarify their minds. But it's already clear that the crisis, if there ever was one, is over. Harold's instant politics put us on the hook but we can unhook him fairly successfully.

Tuesday, July 2nd

In *The Times* there is an extraordinarily inane proposal that, to test his popularity, Harold Wilson should stand for re-election as Leader of the party. I was much more disturbed by another story that Tony Greenwood had said that he would be prepared to stand for the secretaryship of the party.

Parliamentary Under-Secretary of State (Social Security) at the D.H.S.S. 1968–9, and Parliamentary Secretary at the Ministry of Posts and Telecommunications 1969–70. Charles Loughlin was Area Organizer of USDAW 1945–74 and Labour M.P. for Gloucestershire West 1959–October 1974. He was Parliamentary Secretary at the Ministry of Health 1965–7, Joint Parliamentary Secretary at the Ministry of Social Security 1967–8 and Parliamentary Secretary at the M.P.B.W. 1968–70. Ernest Fernyhough was an official of USDAW and has been Labour M.P. for Jarrow since 1947. He was Joint Parliamentary Under-Secretary at the D.E.P. 1967–9.

For weeks there have been rumours that Harold is determined to fix this key appointment and this has provided the evidence everybody wanted.[1]

In the House this afternoon Denis Howell made a statement on Aintree.[2] It will be bought by Liverpool Corporation and the racing side will be put under the Levy Board and the open space developed to the advantage of the city. Thank God for that. Four years' work has come to fruition. It's a job for which we ought to have got more credit.

I had another very awkward meeting when my Home Publicity Committee met to consider the huge entitlement campaign which Judith Hart will launch in mid-July. She will distribute 70 million leaflets of a can-I-help-you type, listing all the things one can get from the social services. In normal times I'd be keen on this but, coming in this month of financial difficulty when we have a rise in public denunciation of scroungers, it seemed to me to be timed all wrong. But Judith was relentless. She had already got her authorization from the Treasury but at the last moment Dick Taverne pointed out that the Secretary of State for Education may decide to drop the free school meal for the fourth child and in that case the pamphlets will be out of date within a matter of weeks. What we finally decided was to postpone the national campaign and to replace exclusive distribution in urban areas with three or four areas of urban population mixed with surrounding rural areas, carefully selected. In this way we could test the entitlement campaign, see how it works, have some proper market research and then launch it. I was pleased with this because at last I've got the beginning of what I've spent two years trying to work for. Ministers don't realize that it isn't just a question of the Minister of Education giving away his free school meals, the Minister of Health giving away his free milk and the Minister of Housing giving his option mortgages. These are all services which people regard as given by a single government and which need most carefully concerted publicity, as well as carefully concerted policies behind them.

After dinner I went back to my room to watch Gunter performing on '24 Hours'. He certainly has blanketed the media today, with a talk on the 'World At One', programmes on B.B.C. 2, B.B.C. 1 and I.T.N., and in every single one he has spent ten minutes or a quarter of an hour attacking intellectuals, attacking the Prime Minister's leadership and in particular making it clear that he regards poor Tony Greenwood as an intellectual who is totally unsuitable to be General Secretary.[3] As I watched him I thought, what a tremendous performer he is. He was never a normal Minister because all he

[1] Len Williams was about to become Governor-General of Mauritius and there had been rumours that Anthony Greenwood would succeed him at Transport House as General Secretary of the party.

[2] See p. 44.

[3] Apparently Mr Gunter's name had been put forward for this post but he was ruled out by the two trade-union members of the special N.E.C. committee set up to consider the nominations. It has been suggested that Mr Gunter thought that the Prime Minister blocked his nomination. See *Wilson*, pp. 541, 548–9.

did at the Ministry of Labour was to conduct the negotiations with the unions and the relationships with the press and the media. Nevertheless it was obvious tonight that he had in fact ruined his own plan. How much wiser George Brown was to hold back and make a quiet resignation Statement in the House. By blanketing the media, Gunter had discredited himself and ended his influence within the week. He overdid it and destroyed himself by revealing his motives too grossly.

Wednesday, July 3rd

Gunter's broadcast may have excited people, but even more extraordinary was yesterday's announcement of the appointment of young David Owen, the doctor and M.P. for Plymouth. It's quite true that he was on Roy Jenkins's list but Roy hadn't been consulted on this at all and nor had the Chief Whip. David Owen is an arrogant young fellow, a close friend of David Marquand and John Mackintosh, who are senior to him, far abler and more deserving of promotion if you want somebody from that section of the Party. Why did Harold take him? Apparently he said he had to have somebody whom Denis Healey would accept but everybody at Westminster knows that only three weeks ago Dr Owen was telling his constituency party he wouldn't work under Harold Wilson. This will cause a great deal of trouble.

I rang Roy this morning and found that the whole Gunter crisis had been conducted in high Harold style. When Harold had made his decision he rang Roy and even then didn't suggest that he should motor over the forty minutes from East Hendred to Chequers, nor did he suggest that Barbara or I should motor over to discuss it with him. No, he sat in Chequers and operated entirely on the 'phone, with the instant politics he likes.

I spent the morning at a P.L.P. meeting which was debating Lords' reform. Seventeen peers turned up but there were never more than twenty-four members of the Lower House there. So much for the idea that there's a great demand for radical reform. I listened to Willie Hamilton demanding total abolition in a minority of one.[1] Then there was a good speech by Denis Coe leading the moderate line,[2] and comments by a number of peers warning our people not to get silly ideas of how reform can be carried out. Fred Peart gave a fatuous but amiable wind-up and it's clear that the excitement, if it ever existed, has faded out altogether. There is no clear demand from the Party to be much more radical than our scheme though it's perfectly clear that the Party won't accept any agreed scheme precisely because it is agreed.

I had lunch at the Savoy with nine American correspondents who were solely concerned with the Gunter affair, the leadership crisis and the rumours of who was to replace Harold. I tried very hard to make them realize how

[1] Labour M.P. for Fife West 1950–74 and since 1974 for Fife Central. He was Chairman of the House of Commons Estimates Committee 1964–70 and since 1966 has been Vice-Chairman of the P.L.P. He is noted for his republican opinions.

[2] Labour M.P. for Middleton and Prestwich 1966–70, Dean of Students at N.E. London Polytechnic 1970–4 and Assistant Director at Middlesex Polytechnic since 1974.

futile it is for us in the Government even to consider the possibility of a change of leadership this summer. The credibility of the Government and of the pound is undermined. How can we now suggest that we should undermine credibility still further by a *coup d'état* against the leader? I needn't go through it all over again in this diary but I went through it with the correspondents as clearly and as candidly as is possible in a purely off-the-record briefing.

This evening I went off to see *Measure for Measure* at Polesden Lacey, a lovely house on the Downs where my stepdaughter-in-law, Dorothy Baker,[1] was acting the part of Mariana. I had never seen *Measure for Measure* before and it was curious to see it with *Così fan tutte* coming tomorrow because there is a strange resemblance between them, the extraordinary formalization of emotions in comedy. Though *Measure for Measure* is supposed to be dealing with bawdiness and terrible crises in a brothel one doesn't believe in it for a moment because it is more like an Iris Murdoch novel or a ballet and one must therefore look at it in a rather cynical detached way.[2] I thought the actors did it very well though it was a bit midgy and a bit cold sitting out in the open-air arena.

Thursday, July 4th

As Chairman of the Cabinet Housing Committee, I'd had a bad conscience about Tony Greenwood and had asked him to set up a meeting and to provide a paper. He had got massacred in the last P.E.S.C. cuts by having no friends and going along alone.[3] I asked him to give us full details of his situation and he had circulated a most miserable paper, though this was no worse than his behaviour under cross-examination. Poor Tony. He's a weak stick, accomplished in certain ways but cowardly. At present he's suffering under an odious press campaign. There was a horrible story in yesterday's *Times* about his refusing to become General Secretary unless the salary was raised to £6,000 a year. As we were going out of the room he said to me, 'I couldn't put my mind to this meeting, I was so upset by all that's happening about the General Secretaryship. I never wanted it, I never asked for it. I was asked a question at a press conference and I didn't know how to avoid saying what I did and then suddenly it blew up into a front page story.' I am sure this is the precise truth.

Cabinet. We had already discussed the Bristol Dock at S.E.P. last Tuesday but this was the day for the final decision.[4] We had been able to strengthen our case slightly by pointing out that as well as the Regional Economic

[1] Wife of Gilbert Baker, son of Crossman's second wife Zita.

[2] The novelist and philosopher Iris Murdoch has been a Fellow of St Anne's College, Oxford, since 1948. Among her many books are *The Bell* (London: Chatto & Windus, 1958), *A Severed Head* (London: Chatto & Windus, 1961) and *The Nice and the Good* (London: Chatto & Windus, 1968).

[3] See Vol. II.

[4] See p. 85.

Council the Central Port Authority had come out in favour of the Bristol Dock. So it really was the man in Whitehall against the people in the region. What made it particularly unpleasant is that when the subject comes before the House next Monday John Silkin has decided to put on a three-line whip, something we don't often do to defeat a Private Bill. We shall be ordering our own Bristol M.P.s to destroy Bristol's future and maybe to jeopardize their own futures. I would like to think there'll be a blazing row. Cabinet today was warned of the possible consequences of its actions by Fred Peart and by the P.M. But when it came to the vote we were overwhelmed by a solid alliance of D.E.A., the Ministry of Transport, D.E.P. and the Board of Trade, but what really tipped the scale was the Welsh block. Callaghan barged in as Home Secretary and also as Member for Cardiff saying we couldn't have a port at Bristol because Newport and Cardiff wouldn't like it. So Callaghan, Cledwyn Hughes and George Thomas provided the weight to defeat the Bristol scheme. This is politics at its worst. I don't think any of them were thinking of this in terms of Government policy or politics but purely in terms of Welsh regional self-interest. What made the defeat even more painful was that when the Welsh had voted Roy Jenkins tipped off the fence and voted against us and Tony Crosland followed suit.

After that I had another failure with my Social Services Committee over Roy's new paper on cuts in 1968/9. The spirit of rebellion was as strong as ever. We decided that when we next meet S.E.P. we shall tell them that if there are to be any cuts they must be made by major changes of policy. The Chancellor must break himself of the habit of paring programmes away every six months.

Then I got into my dinner jacket and went off with Anne to the Banqueting Hall in Whitehall, the room with the magnificent Rubens painted ceiling, for the formal party for the twentieth anniversary of the Health Service. A conference had been going on the whole week and I said I would attend whatever Kenneth Robinson wished. He only wanted me to come to this single show for 1,500 people. He did have the courtesy to introduce me to the Secretary of the B.M.A. and one or two other bigwigs.[1] When I get into my new job I shall find myself in a completely new world, nothing like local government. Nobody knows me by sight and I don't know them. What's worse, they all know that I'm working Kenneth Robinson out of a job and by all their tests he is an excellent Minister. I wish I could keep him and use him as a full Minister but Whitehall has told me it's impossible.

From there we went on to Covent Garden. Unfortunately the vote on the Third Reading of the Finance Bill was coming at 10.0 and I had to go back to the Commons after the first act.[2] Then the vote was postponed till 10.15. I met Harold hanging about in the division lobby and he took me into his

[1] Derek Stevenson, Secretary of the B.M.A. and of the Joint Consultants' Committee 1958–76.

[2] The Bill was given a Third Reading by 295 votes to 243.

room. He had told me yesterday at Cabinet that he'd been trying to get me for an informal chat on life in general, nothing in particular. 'I just want to talk to you,' he said. But now he discovered I was at *Measure for Measure* yesterday and *Così fan tutte* tonight. Was I doing any work? I replied that I was doing some work but had plenty of time to spare.

I asked him about a minute on devolution I had sent over ten days ago but apparently he hadn't read it yet so I tried to switch him over to discuss the merger and the need to get Judith another job before the autumn. 'Oh,' he said, 'I can't guarantee that. We may have to wait some months to find her something else.' The merger is one of the least of his concerns. I mustn't push him too hard but on the other hand I must make sure it takes place in the autumn, at the same time as the Commonwealth Relations Office/Foreign Office merger.[1] I must be in charge by then because I didn't give up being Leader of the House in order to be totally unemployed.

His next topic was Anthony Greenwood and he gave me his version of the facts. The National Executive saw the short-list and thought none of the candidates good enough. So it set up a committee of eight, including the P.M. and George Brown, to look at two possible candidates, Alf Allen and Tony Greenwood, and they were both approached to see whether either of them would do it.[2] This elicited the fact that Allen is most unlikely to do it so the issue now seems to be whether, despite the vile press campaign and all the nauseating things Gunter has said, Greenwood can become General Secretary. I think it's true that Harold wants Tony for the job but it's not true that Greenwood wants the job or was formally approached or did anything about it. Indeed, from his point of view, it's a miserable affair and the sooner ended the better.

This long conversation took place in a very friendly atmosphere over brandy. Harold was obviously mending his fences with me. Though I got nothing out of him about the merger, I did get a great deal about the House of Lords, where he's back on the lines laid down for him before he skedaddled.

I returned to hear the last half-hour of *Così fan tutte* and then we drove to a gala party George Weidenfeld was giving. I've never seen such wonderful lighting of gardens or bourgeois grandeur of living. The only thing which fell below standard was the sit-down supper served at 12.30. As Anne said, it would have been much better if we'd had a buffet we could get at a bit earlier.

Friday, July 5th

I motored down to Leamington to see the Royal Agricultural Show at its new permanent site at Stoneleigh Abbey. As a Minister I had to lunch in the

[1] The merger took place on October 17th, 1968.

[2] Alfred Allen, General Secretary of USDAW since 1962, is a member of the T.U.C. General Council (Chairman 1973–4). He has been a Crown Estates Commissioner since 1965 and became a life peer in 1974.

Royal Box and be received by the top brass—but what top brass? Junior country brass of a pretty vulgar kind which I detest. Afterwards I went round with Pritchett and we concentrated on weedkillers and wheats before rushing via home to Nuffield College, where David Butler had invited me to an informal discussion on the role of television in the next election.[1]

He had collected a good gang. Peart and I had come for the Government, the Tories were represented by Willie Whitelaw and Anthony Barber and the Liberals by Grimond.[2] Then there were David Butler, Bob McKenzie and, representing the B.B.C., John Grist and Oliver Whitley, with various representatives of I.T.V.[3] We started with a long wrangle about the B.B.C.'s paternalist attitude to party political broadcasts. On this the politicians won hands down, saying unanimously that it was outrageous of the B.B.C. to say that politicians should run their own party politicals and then to constantly interfere to prevent them doing what they want. If we want regional broadcasts we should be allowed to do them. Anybody who doesn't know how bloody-minded the B.B.C. is would have learnt a great deal by listening to this conversation.

At last David turned us to the lessons of the last election and he obviously wanted us to agree that there should be more of the companies' own programmes and fewer party politicals. I wanted the same number of party politicals and fewer B.B.C. and I.T.V. programmes. I also wanted the programme companies to face the fact that their method of inserting extracts from politicians' speeches into their news bulletins created an appallingly trivial impression. Every evening we have two minutes of Wilson, two minutes of Heath, one minute of Grimond, or four of Wilson, four of Heath, two of Grimond, just snippets without any serious account. Then we had an interesting discussion about heckling and about the Scottish nationalists and whether or not they should have their own programme. Oh, what tension there is between the politicians and the broadcasting authorities. It was a bad-tempered meeting.

[1] A Fellow of Nuffield College, Oxford since 1954, his books include studies of the General Elections of 1951–74 (London: Macmillan, 1952–75) and *Political Change in Britain* (London: Macmillan, 1969).

[2] Anthony Barber was Conservative M.P. for Doncaster 1951–64 and for Altrincham and Sale February 1965–September 1974. A Conservative Whip 1957–8, Economic Secretary to the Treasury 1959–62 and Financial Secretary to the Treasury 1962–3, he was Minister of Health 1963–4, Chancellor of the Duchy of Lancaster June–July 1970 and Chancellor of the Exchequer 1970–4. On his retirement from the Commons in 1974 he became a life peer and since 1974 he has been Chairman of the Standard and Chartered Banking Group. Jo Grimond, Liberal M.P. for Orkney and Shetland since 1950, was Leader of the Liberal Party 1956–67 and May–July 1976.

[3] Robert McKenzie, the broadcaster, has been Professor of Sociology, with special reference to Politics, at the London School of Economics since 1964. His books include *British Political Parties* (London: Heinemann, 1955; rev. edn 1964). John Grist, Controller of the B.B.C. T.V. Talks and Current Affairs Group 1957–72, is Editor of 'Gallery' and 'Panorama' and has been Controller of the English Regions at the B.B.C. since 1972. Oliver Whitley was Chief Assistant to the Director-General of the B.B.C. 1964–8 and was Managing Director of External Broadcasting from 1969 until his retirement in 1972.

Sunday, July 7th

I thought the weather was breaking up yesterday, but the heatwave seems to be back. It began last Monday when the temperature rose to 90° in the shade. When I walked out of my office, Whitehall hit me with hot air as though I was on the sand at Famagusta. Since then we've had spanking hot weather for Wimbledon and the Royal Show and it's given the farm the further break it really needed.

The great thing we're talking about here is whether Mr P. can win the farm management prize this year. A great deal will depend on the herd, one of his greatest achievements. We are moving slowly from a serviceable commercial herd to a pedigree herd, without buying in, upgrading it animal by animal. Prescote heifers are selling extremely well, this year for 140 guineas and next year they should be up to 160 guineas. We're nearly always first or second in the county for the most efficient milk production but that's thanks not only to Pritchett's planning, but to our wonderful cowman, Joe Osborne, who has been here seven years.

Neither Anne nor I have anything to do with the detailed management of Prescote, though I am responsible for going through the accounts with Mr Pritchett and for discussing each year's cropping plan and capital expenditure. Over the years that teaches me quite a lot but what we really care about is living on the land. Anne and the farm are the two most intense pleasures of my life. I adore walking over Prescote and sweating myself pink clearing the undergrowth from my island. Why do I do it? Because I'm trying to make some little part of Prescote my own, and that's why I work on my island and we put in the swimming bath and plant poplars along the front drive. All this is a pleasure I could only dream of when I was young, of living in a lovely house with water running through the garden and even then I never dreamt there might be children in the house. Next Friday I am going to give the prizes at the village school. Despite all her doubts about whether I would last the pace and keep the children there, Miss Samuels has finally settled down to accepting us as unintelligible people. I've been very discontented with her this year and thought she was spending too much time on her religious exercises, but nevertheless the net effect on the children of the Cropredy primary school has been good. True, Patrick has vegetated most of this year in Miss Samuels's form but he's been growing up at home, reading a lot of books for himself, and what matters to him is his relationship with the other children in the village and particularly with the Pritchett family. When I met Charles and Mary Woodhouse last week at the wedding, I didn't feel in the remotest degree ashamed or sinful because I had done the wrong thing by the children. I'm not sure I've done the right thing but I'm certainly not sure that I've done the wrong thing, though the state way has its dangers and the second stage, at Banbury School, may not go as well as the first. Up till now the life on the farm has justified itself, and justified my pressing it on Anne.

Monday, July 8th

Harold certainly made a great big success of his speech at Newtown and got a tremendous press for it.[1] He was back at the top of his form and full of his old self-confidence. This comeback is partly because he had information that the trade figures this week were going to be good and some hope that the bankers in Basle were beginning to organize the funding of the sterling balances.[2] In addition he had the pleasure of the N.O.P. going slightly in our favour.[3]

The other surprise news today may not turn out so well. Suddenly we are told the railway go-slow has been stopped. Len Neal went down to Penzance and announced quite unexpectedly a settlement which, ironically, is worse for the lower-paid men than the Board's original offer.[4] I think Barbara may be in trouble for being too soft, just as she was to the lady machinists at Ford's.

When I got to London today I soon discovered that my interview with William Hardcastle on 'The World This Weekend' yesterday had been almost as successful as Harold's speech.[5] The whole period from 1 p.m. to 2 p.m. is now full of nothing but news, talks and discussions. It's interminably lengthy, but it's certainly built up a very big audience and what one says on it matters not only because of that but also because it provides the news for the Monday papers. I wasn't at all clear what I'd said to Hardcastle, who'd come to me during one of my rushes last Thursday. Indeed I was so anxious about it that I sat outside on the terrace in the sunshine yesterday having a gin and tonic listening to our little transistor. I soon knew it was okay. It chimed well with Harold's Newtown speech. I had knocked the anti-Harold movement on the head by being quiet and sensible about it and yet being

[1] On Saturday, July 6th the Prime Minister addressed the all-Wales Party rally at Newtown, Montgomeryshire. His theme was 'change' and an attack on the 'Establishment'. See *Wilson*, pp. 543–5.

[2] On July 12th in Basle the Governors of the twelve Central Banks undertook to provide a credit of $2,000 million (£832 million) for ten years, to guarantee sterling against speculation. The agreement was signed on September 12th and, according to the Governor of the Bank of England, it marked a change in the role of sterling as a reserve currency.

[3] The National Opinion Poll showed a fall in the Conservative lead over Labour from 19·7 per cent in May to 19 per cent in June.

[4] Sir Leonard Neal, Labour Relations Adviser to Esso Europe Inc. 1967–71, was a member of the British Railways Board 1967–71, Chairman of the Commission on Industrial Relations 1971–4 and since 1970 Professor of Industrial Relations at the Institute of Science and Technology, University of Manchester. He was knighted in 1974. On July 2nd the British Railways Board had offered increases for some 120,000 men but this had been rejected by both ASLEF and the N.U.R. However, at their Annual Conference at Penzance on July 5th the N.U.R. had decided by 71 votes to 5 to accept the Board's most recent offer of 3–4½ per cent increases, to be paid immediately and to be absorbed in the current talks on pay and productivity. On July 6th the ASLEF executive also accepted the offer. The Minister of Transport admitted to the Commons on July 8th that the original offer of June 22nd had been redistributed and 'some of the money which would have gone to the lower-paid workers has gone to the higher-paid workers'. (*House of Commons Debates*, Vol. 786, cols 44–8.)

[5] Journalist and broadcaster. He died in 1976.

completely frank about the grave situation facing the Government. You can do this kind of interview on your head if you're prepared to be relatively candid. It's what I can do and what Harold can't and he normally resents it when I bring it off.

When I came into S.E.P. this morning I congratulated him on his speech and he replied, 'It was you who made the speech of the weekend.' Indeed from today's papers you might have imagined I had made a speech. They gave me extensive quotation and treated my remarks as finally ending the Gunter incident in a victory for Harold. So here I was right back in his good books and for once emerging from complete obscurity.

At S.E.P. we were in quite cheerful mood as Roy gave us his analysis of the trade figures but we were soon quarrelling fiercely about the I.R.C. When the I.R.C. was founded it had been allocated £40 million in this year's estimates and £40 million in 1969. This morning Peter Shore demanded that he must be given a free hand to spend more if required, while the Chancellor was saying that the I.R.C. must realize that the very maximum they can spend this year is £50 million. Peter said this would wreck a new and creative organization. We'd just established the I.R.C., given the directors the idea that whatever they wanted to do they must do quickly and decisively and up till now they'd been extremely successful in positively intervening to help useful mergers. 'How can we hold them back now?' asked Peter, 'the very people who are creating the economic basis for recovery and growth.' Following the Chancellor's lead, I was as implacable as always. 'The rules of the P.E.S.C. game,' I said, 'apply to Mr Shore just as much as they apply to the rest of us. Even though they are absolutely idiotic rules that make nonsense of any serious attempt to cost our social services and have ruinous results, my Departments are made to obey them. The I.R.C. is included in total public expenditure this year and its figure is listed as £40 million. That is the maximum which can be allowed.'

It was a raging argument and Harold tried hard to help Peter Shore. Finally we settled on £10 million extra in 1969. I'm hoping this incident will force the Chancellor to revise the P.E.S.C. rules. We very nearly got a change out of the old Chancellor last year because we had educated him with some pretty rough treatment and to some extent we had educated William Armstrong, his Permanent Secretary.[1] But Callaghan is now Home Secretary and William Armstrong the new head of the Civil Service Department, so we have a new Chancellor with a new Permanent Secretary and all the fantastic abracadabra of rules and regulations is still enforced upon us.[2]

Towards the end Dick Marsh made a very good point. He said that we had all been urged to read the Report that the Brookings Institution has just

[1] See Vol. II.

[2] The Permanent Secretary was Sir Douglas Allen (K.C.B. 1967), Deputy Under-Secretary of State at the D.E.A. 1964–6 and Permanent Under-Secretary 1966–8. He was Permanent Secretary to the Treasury 1968–74. Since 1974 he has been Head of the Home Civil Service and Permanent Secretary at the Civil Service Department.

published on Britain, which concludes that the really big economies we ought to make are in the capital investment programme of the Central Electricity Generating Board. Brookings believes we've grossly over-invested there as well as in the nuclear programme, just as we've grossly overdone the pit-closure policy. Even a fractional slowing-down of these programmes could save us hundreds of millions of pounds and avoid any cuts in the social services.

We reached an even higher level of fantasy when a little later in this very long meeting the Chancellor solemnly proposed that we should scrap the rail subsidy which is being granted under the new Transport Bill. The central aim of Barbara's Bill was to put the railways on a business footing but to make it clear that where a railway is kept open for social need the Government will pay the deficit. By proposing to cut this away Roy would destroy the Bill and we should have decided to abandon our new socialist transport policy before it is on the Statute Book. How can a Chancellor make such a proposal? The answer, I'm afraid, is because it is there in his Treasury brief and the officials who draw up that brief are often quite extraordinarily ignorant about the working of the economy. Well, that's as far as we got this morning. It was exhausting but we managed to stop a good deal of nonsense.

In the Commons this afternoon there were no less than six Statements, first Michael Stewart on a Ministerial Meeting of NATO,[1] then Fred Mulley on the Non-Proliferation Treaty,[2] George Thomson on Nigeria,[3] Dick Marsh on the railways settlement, Roy on the Basle agreement and finally Cledwyn Hughes on the deep-sea fishing industry.[4] I had hoped the Government would get a little credit for the trawler Statement but it was of course killed by being made at 4.15. I had gradually learned that the job of the Leader of the House is that of a stage-manager of parliamentary occasions. Fred hasn't yet.

By coincidence this was the Tory Supply Day and they had chosen the I.R.C. as the object of attack.[5] The main interest of the debate was a bouncing

[1] Which had issued a declaration on mutual and balanced force reductions between the NATO countries and the Warsaw Pact Powers.

[2] On the implications of Britain's acceding to the terms of the N.P.T.

[3] On the discussions, channelled through the International Red Cross, about an emergency airlift of food into the famine-stricken areas of Nigeria, notably Biafra, and the alleged objections of the Federal authorities to R.A.F. aeroplanes bringing such relief.

[4] On the Government's decision to continue the trawler subsidy for a further period of at least five years and to introduce on August 1st, 1968, for three years, a new form of operating subsidy.

[5] The House of Commons must annually debate and pass three Consolidated Fund Bills, authorizing the issue of the supply of funds to cover the civil and defence estimates and supplementary estimates. However the voting of supply takes place formally on only three days of the twenty-nine 'supply days' each year, before or after the main debate. On the remaining twenty-six days, spaced throughout the session, the Opposition may choose to discuss not the estimate of a particular sum of money for a particular purpose, but either a motion expressing criticism of Government policy or administration or a neutral adjournment motion covering a discussion of Government action. The Conservatives' attack, led by Sir Keith Joseph, concerned the bid by two companies, Kent and the Rank Organization,

intervention by George Brown, speaking on behalf of Frank Kearton,[1] who is Chairman of the I.R.C. and also a director of Courtaulds where George is now an employee. It's curious how George Brown has diminished. He exemplifies the fatality of resignation. No resignation under this Government has affected anything, neither his nor Peggy Herbison's nor Ray Gunter's.[2]

Later this evening we had the debate on the Bristol Dock. I've described my own feelings about this affair and my alarm and despondency. But none of my dire predictions has been fulfilled. There's been distress and alarm in the local Bristol press but no great fuss. There's been a sense of victory in South Wales and tonight the Bill was crushed by a low turnout and disappeared from view without a serious struggle.[3] Dick Marsh and Barbara made brilliant speeches and the case for poor Bristol went by default.

Tuesday, July 9th

At this afternoon's Social Services Committee we had a quite unprecedented paper from the Home Office. Nothing like the normal Civil Service brief outlining a new idea but a philosophical paper on a project developed by a man called Derek Morrell who had been an enormously important and dynamic factor at Education and was now being transferred to the Home Office,[4] where he is fighting the battle to make the Home Office the central pivotal office of social welfare. He is by no means a normal civil servant. He's a red-faced explosive man with an enormously inflated public-school sense of morality and it's he who has put Jim Callaghan up to this proposal which breaks every law and precedent. It asks that we, that's to say the Social Services Committee, should select twelve blackspots, each in a local authority area where social crisis and tension are at their highest. Having selected these, there should be sent into each an inter-service team, consisting of representatives of the children's department, the treasury department, the health department, and the housing department of the local authority, to assess the problem of how such a community can pull itself up by its own bootstraps. Having made the assessment, the team must then get down to the

---

for the Cambridge Instruments Company. After market intervention by the I.R.C. Kent was the successful bidder. There were 233 votes for the Conservatives' Motion of Censure and 307 against.

[1] Sir Frank Kearton (Kt 1966) was Deputy Chairman of Courtaulds Ltd 1961–4 and Chairman 1964–75. He was Chairman of the Industrial Reorganization Corporation 1966–8 and in 1976 became Chairman of the British National Oil Corporation. He was made a life peer in 1970.

[2] Miss Margaret Herbison, Labour M.P. for North Lanark 1945–70, was Joint Parliamentary Under-Secretary of State at the Scottish Office 1950–51, Minister of Pensions and National Insurance 1964–6 and Minister of Social Security from 1966 until her resignation in 1967. From 1970–1 she was Lord High Commissioner to the General Assembly of the Church of Scotland.

[3] The Bristol Corporation Bill failed to get a Second Reading by 166 votes to 63.

[4] Formerly an Assistant Secretary at the D.E.S. and Joint Secretary to the Schools Council. He was an Assistant Under-Secretary of State in the Children's Department of the Home Office from 1967 until his death in 1970.

job of seeing that the community tackles it itself. The work of the twelve local 'community development schemes' would be co-ordinated by a group of civil servants at the Home Office.

I noticed once again the strangeness of departmental briefings. Every one of my colleagues was perfectly prepared to bless the Home Office scheme and let it go through, presumably because Mr Morrell had squared all the officials on the official committee. I had to point out that there were quite formidable political difficulties. I was highly dubious about a team consisting exclusively of local government officials going into an area controlled by their superior officers and being free to tackle the job themselves. I just don't see how constitutionally that is going to work. Morrell is coming to see us next week so we can cross-examine him.

Then I had a most satisfactory meeting. As soon as I took over my Social Service job I had told the T.U.C. and the C.B.I. that I wanted to consult them throughout the preparation of the big Superannuation Bill and I had given them a whole series of questions in writing. Here were Harry Collison and his colleagues coming back for a talk. I had asked them to start on the retirement rule, which deducts from the old age pension so much for each pound that a pensioner might earn. I had wanted to see our national superannuation, like any private scheme, entirely devoid of a retirement rule but the T.U.C. disliked this as much as the civil servants and I lost. Then, to my delight, they came up with a whole series of interesting and constructive points and we had a wonderful two hours before we had to break off.

I went down to the House to see how the Report Stage and Third Reading of the Race Relations Bill was getting on. On this the Tories have split. They decided to oppose the Second Reading with a reasoned amendment and just after that, of course, Powell made his speech, saying he wanted extreme measures. With Powell out, the Shadow Cabinet decided not to oppose the Third Reading. It was completely inconsistent because they had said they were deeply dissatisfied and wanted major changes. We had given them only minor changes and yet now they were saying they didn't want to oppose, so forty-five Tory M.P.s had rebelled and put down a reasoned amendment and we all knew that the row tonight wasn't going to be on our side for a change.

I should like to know how this Tory change-back has happened, since three weeks ago I was talking to Quintin Hogg who said there was no question of his voting for the Bill and that indeed it would be difficult not to vote against it. I suspect that he and his colleagues now feel that they don't want to make the mistake we Labour people made with the 1962 Commonwealth Immigration Act when we were in Opposition. The moment the news broke that the Tories were not opposing the Third Reading, the pressure in the constituencies mounted because there Powell is supported by 90 per cent of Tories.

The debate went on till 4.30 a.m. I didn't stay all night but there were tremendous scenes with Quintin being jeered and attacked by the forces behind him. Meanwhile I had slipped home to bed and left Tam to represent 9 Vincent Square.

Wednesday, July 10th

I was sitting up in bed working when Tam came back to tell me with great excitement of the scenes he had just witnessed. I wondered whether the B.B.C. would carry them and, to do them justice, they did make a tremendous lot of this news. In their 8 o'clock and 9 o'clock programmes they carried a detailed report, which was a tremendous tonic for us. The attack on Quintin won all the headlines this morning and provided a welcome relief for an exhausted Government.[1]

Today had been accepted as the day for the Party meeting at which the twenty-three rebels on our side were to be rebuked. I decided to absent myself because I couldn't vote for this when Gunter was to be allowed to say what he liked about Harold and get away with it. Anyhow my main concern was to deal with the troubles of Tony Greenwood.

I had insisted that he must come to see me about his housing problems and I'd asked him to attend a Cabinet Housing Committee but he had refused. Finally he said that he and his officials would see me privately in my room this morning so that at 9 o'clock in filed Tony himself, along with Ronald Brain and Mr Beddoe and two or three of the other old lags I know.[2] I suppose he felt he'd be happier with his officials there. I'm not sure he was because they all know me much too well and within half an hour I had got out of them the essential facts which had been blurred and disguised before. Finally I asked, 'Well, gentlemen, without damaging your programme, is it practicable for you to cut back 2,000 houses this year and 4,000 next?' They agreed that there was no difficulty at all this year and they thought that 4,000 next year would be possible, though there would then be a risk of the annual total falling below 400,000.

I moved into the Parliamentary Committee where for the second time in a week I received an enormous douche of Barbara Castle. I'm in two minds about her now. Her public image is very good indeed. She's a sporting character, lively and good-humoured, especially considering the strain she's under, but in private she gives the impression of indecisiveness and unhappiness. I think that at the back of her mind she's probably worried that both the Ford settlement and the railway settlement may be too soft. On these occasions she and the P.M. monopolize the discussion. He loves discussing the details of a negotiation with her and chips in with little

[1] The Bill was given a Third Reading by 182 votes to 44.

[2] Ronald Brain was Deputy Secretary at the M.H.L.G. (later the D.O.E.) 1966–74. Jack Eglinton Beddoe, Under-Secretary at the M.H.L.G. 1961–5 and 1966–74 and Assistant Under-Secretary at the D.E.A. 1965–6, was Chairman of the South-East Planning Board during 1966 and has been Chief Executive of the Severn Trent Water Authority since 1974.

constructive suggestions, whereas the rest of us are inclined to say, 'Tell us, for heaven's sake, what it's all about.'

The next subject was our Lords' reform paper. I tried to force the Committee to a clear decision but I didn't have much success, partly owing to Barbara, who pleaded that the whole reform should be postponed until next session and that meanwhile we should set up a working party with the Parliamentary Party. (I didn't say that if we'd had a working party with the Parliamentary Party on prices and incomes we wouldn't have had much of a result). Harold was cool and collected and tried to help me – he has a thoroughly bad conscience – and finally I managed to get an agreement despite Barbara and Fred Peart who kept on saying that nothing could be got through the Parliamentary Party and that we should publish our White Paper after Parliament had gone into recess. I told the Committee quite frankly that I would hope to spin out the time over the recess and wait for action until the winter.

Meanwhile outside the door Cabinet was stamping and baying as it always does now because it hates the Parliamentary Committee. Gunter said one of the reasons for his resignation was that he didn't like the fact that he was just a member of the outer and not of the inner Cabinet. I know Wedgy Benn feels the same and I certainly would as well.

At Cabinet we had to listen to a repetition of Barbara on prices and incomes before we got down to some new business – the Ministry of Health draft Green Paper on the reform of the Health Service. I had forced Kenneth to submit his draft to all the other Ministries concerned and it had been greatly watered down. Even so it was resolutely opposed by Jim Callaghan in a brief prepared by Derek Morrell. The paper was got through by each of us agreeing the others' amendments and producing a final result so washy that it was completely useless.

On his own initiative Burke came to see me this afternoon and we had the most interesting talk we've ever had. He said straightaway, 'As for your merger, we must have it by October or November. That's already decided in Whitehall, even if it means formally carrying on with Kenneth Robinson and Judith Hart as Ministers.' I said I was delighted to hear this and then Burke got down to his main point. 'Apart from the merger,' he said, 'can you give me an assurance that once you've got your huge new Ministry, you will keep your co-ordinating job?' I said I would try and he said, 'Well, at least you must keep your room here in the Cabinet Office. You can't co-ordinate the social services from across the river at Elephant and Castle or from that cosy little Ministry in the Adelphi. You can only co-ordinate from the central point of power where people come to be co-ordinated, the Cabinet Office.[1] You see the point, Dick, of your keeping an authority here

[1] During the two years that he had served as Lord President of the Council and Leader of the House of Commons, Crossman had become very attached to the beautiful room which he had furnished. When Mr Peart became Leader of the House on April 6th, 1968,

which otherwise you'll lose when you go out there to Elephant and Castle? Why not keep the title of Lord President and your co-ordinating staff under Paul Odgers? You can run them here in addition to running your merged Ministry. What none of you politicians realize,' he said, 'is that being promoted from departmental Minister to co-ordinating minister is a promotion to real and more effective power. Of course you're doing a job when you're Minister of Housing or Minister of Health but you're doing an even more important job when you're getting the basis of block budgeting for the social services worked out. I want you to go on with that job. It could make more difference to the Government than anything you achieve inside a merged Ministry of Health and Social Security where you'll get immersed in the details of negotiations with the doctors.' I said I would think it over and that I'd have a talk to Harold about it.

But Burke was really thinking of his own peculiar co-ordinating powers. It's ludicrous to say that I have more power in my present job than I did at Housing.

Right at the end I asked him about the paper on devolution I sent to Harold weeks ago. I said I was disappointed that the P.M. hadn't read the follow-up letter I sent over a fortnight ago in which I'd commented on the comments from Willie Ross and George Thomas. Burke replied, 'When his box is piled up now he doesn't read through it.' He made it very clear that he thought Harold wasn't working as hard as he had before. I said, 'Yes, that's right and of course the truth is that he is becoming a wee bit of an Asquith and he's in nothing like the physical condition to go through his boxes late at night that he was eighteen months ago.' Heaven knows, no one can blame him for that in view of the strain to which he has been subjected. But I never expected to find myself discussing it with Burke.

This afternoon we had another good and original Committee meeting under Jim Callaghan to deal with the so-called urban programme, for improving community relations, especially on race. The truth is that when the P.M. needed to make his great speech at Birmingham on immigration he thought up the idea of a new urban programme which was going to help the areas of social need without being a burden on their budget.[1] The difficulty since then has been to make any practical sense of this idea. However, the officials had done pretty well. They came up today with an enormous thick paper dealing first with the method of selecting the half-dozen areas in which the programme would be concentrated. They proposed that Whitehall officials should decide in what part of each town the programme would be carried out. In that case, I said, there must be 100 per cent grants because the local authorities wouldn't accept this under any

---

Crossman remained Lord President and was able to retain this room in the Privy Council Office. He was obliged to relinquish it on October 18th, 1968, when Mr Peart assumed the office of Lord President of the Council.

[1] See p. 46.

other terms. We all agreed that we must find out from S.E.P. how much money will be available and make sure that the Chancellor knows that this is extra money which is not to be found by any Department or local authority.

I had to go to Coventry tonight for a special meeting on race relations. Since my first meeting in London tomorrow is at 9.0 in the morning, Molly took me down the motorway in very heavy rain and I sweated away on my brief on the Race Relations Bill. Inside the Herbert Museum we found about 20 people and I suppose that by the end of the meeting about 50 had turned up, of whom 30 were immigrants and 20 white. Bill Wilson,[1] who'd been up all night on the Race Relations Bill, made a really splendid impression. He's a lawyer and knows the Bill from A to Z. Jack and Doris Butterworth were also there but, as usual in Coventry, you organize a big meeting and have everybody down for it and then the public don't come.

We started back at 11.0 in drenching rain, returning to London through the biggest thunderstorm I'd ever experienced with sheets of lightning over the road and the M1 a lake of water. That day Rugby had three inches of rain and even at Prescote we had an inch and a half. When Molly got me back at 1.0 in the morning I had a curious sense of anti-climax. I'd turned up dutifully, made my speech, yet I knew that I needn't have taken all this trouble. Coventry had responded very poorly.

Thursday, July 11th

S.E.P. this morning was really a kind of Cabinet again, a monster meeting to consider the cuts. Of the twenty-four members of Cabinet twenty-one turned up, which makes fair nonsense of calling it a Cabinet Committee, quite apart from annoying the three who are excluded. The first item which caught my attention was the Chancellor's proposal to knock £5 million off external publicity. One of our few successes in January was to get a minute recorded that as our defence expenditure is reduced we must steadily increase the importance we give to overseas aid and foreign publicity to counter-balance our loss of military power. Michael Stewart was quite good and so was Tony Crosland and we managed to have the Chancellor's proposal held up. Strangely enough, there's no Cabinet Committee to deal with foreign publicity and once again it struck me how curiously ignorant are the briefs on which the Chancellor relies on such occasions.

When we got to the Research Councils you could see what happens when there is a group working together. They asked for a £2 million cut in addition to the £1 million cut imposed only last January. Since their four-year programme had already been mauled, this, I pointed out, would destroy it altogether. Shirley Williams and Ted Short and I had discussed this in our Social Services Committee and now we managed to get the £2 million cut reduced to £1 million, a major change.

On housing everything I'd agreed with Tony went smoothly until he said

[1] Labour M.P. for Coventry South 1964–74 and for Coventry South East since 1974.

that the 4,000 cut next year might bring the annual target below 400,000. Peter Shore, who doesn't have much success in Cabinet discussions, quite rightly pointed out the enormous political importance of avoiding this fall. He didn't say why instead of cutting the building of public sector housing we shouldn't simply abolish local authority lending altogether and so save £130 million. I had to say that for various technical reasons I didn't think this possible but that perhaps we could take £65 million instead of £50 million off local authority lending, which would give us the extra £15 million to cut by 2,000 houses in 1969 instead of 4,000. Nevertheless we've agreed to have an early meeting to see whether we can abolish local authority lending altogether.

I must have spent more than three hours at the meeting of my Pensions Committee this afternoon. It's now meeting incessantly and I don't bother to record all the details of our discussion in the diary because they're highly technical. The trouble is that I'm supposed to be the impartial Chairman but more and more I find myself running a seminar and expounding the theory of my new scheme to a class who are in a sense like students arguing with a professor. On this occasion Richard Titmuss had brought along his friend Professor Morris who said to me afterwards, 'I never thought I'd be given a lesson on how to run seminars by a politician.'[1] Perhaps the proper solution is for there to be an independent chairman of the Committee – but what member of the Cabinet could do it?

Friday, July 12th

At O.P.D. this morning the first item was Greece. I had read a newspaper story that as a result of the P.M.'s reference to the 'bestialities' of the Greek regime, the Colonels had threatened to cancel all British contracts and I'd asked for the matter to be raised.

The military junta which had deposed King Constantine and assumed power on April 21st, 1967, survived the King's attempted counter-coup in December of that year. Although the Papadopoulos regime was overthrown on November 25th, 1973, it was not until July 23rd, 1974, that the military junta was overthrown and the former Premier, Constantine Karamanlis, was recalled to Athens to form a new democratic administration.

In answering a Question on June 25th the Prime Minister had referred to the 'bestialities' perpetrated by the Greek dictatorship. According to his own account (Wilson, p. 542) *and a Statement made by Anthony Crosland, President of the Board of Trade on July 3rd, the Prime Minister had intended to use the phrase 'barbarous methods'. The offensive phrase having been withdrawn, the regime apparently issued no further threats to British trade.*[2]

[1] Professor J. P. Morris of the London School of Hygiene and Tropical Medicine, an expert on preventive medicine.

[2] *House of Commons Debates*, Vol. 767, cols 1499–503.

Michael Stewart had circulated one of his long, dry papers which I had read early this morning. Since I had requested this item, Harold said, 'You asked for it, Dick, you start.' I was a little abashed and said cautiously, 'I see a certain contradiction between the strong line you took on the barbarities in Greece and the fact that the Foreign Secretary is simultaneously urging that if possible we should conclude a frigate deal with the present regime.' Michael Stewart gave a long, conscientious reply, saying there was no comparison with South Africa where we were bound by a United Nation decision.[1] I was opposed to any such frigate deal, I said, and Barbara and Eddie Shackleton took the same view. The P.M. was uncomfortable when it was pointed out how awkward it would be if it ever came to light that this deal was being pursued at the same time as he was being given credit for opposing the bestial atrocities of the Colonels. Then the Lord Chancellor turned up quite a useful report of the International Red Cross which is going to be discussed judicially by the Commission of Human Rights.[2] He'd discovered that the Foreign Office hadn't even bothered to get it translated. However O.P.D. meetings can go in any direction. Suddenly it was discovered that after all the frigate deal was not an immediate prospect but a vague idea, so we left it with Michael Stewart assuring us that there was every sign that the regime would honour its word and switch over to democracy in the course of the summer.

At midday I had to shoot off to Buckingham Palace for the first of our new-style Privy Councils. The Queen had agreed that after the formalities we should withdraw to the Caernarvon Room next door and have drinks with her. For the first of these festive occasions I had gathered Jennie Lee, Roy Mason, Dick Marsh and Kenneth Robinson and then there was myself and Michael Adeane.[3] The Queen was in tremendous form. After the Council when the drinks were circulating, she began to describe to me a television programme she had seen yesterday of a wrestling match, at which Philip had been present. An all-in wrestler had been thrown out over the ropes, landed on his feet, and after writhing in agony had suddenly shot back into the ring, seized his opponent and forced him to resign. She said what tremendous fun that kind of all-in wrestling was. 'Do you want a Royal Charter for them?' I asked, and she said, 'No, not yet.' It was interesting to hear what a vivid description she gave of the whole scene, writhing herself, twisting and turning, completely relaxed. It was quite an eye-opener

[1] See above, p. 108.

[2] In Strasbourg on April 3rd, 1970, the Committee of Ministers of the Council of Europe considered the Report of the Commission of Human Rights and decided that Greece had violated several Articles of the Convention.

[3] Jennie Lee was the widow of Aneurin Bevan and herself Labour M.P. for North Lanark 1929–31 and for Cannock 1945–70. She was Parliamentary Secretary at the Ministry of Public Building and Works 1964–5, Parliamentary Under-Secretary of State at the Department of Education and Science, 1965–7 and Minister of State 1967–70. In 1970 she became a life peer, with the title of Baroness Lee of Asheridge.

to see how she enjoyed it. Afterwards each of the Ministers had a good long talk with her alone before we all slipped off.

I got back to Prescote in time to walk down to the school prize-giving. The schoolroom was packed with parents and children and Miss Samuels started the proceedings by addressing the children for well over half an hour. Then she called upon me to give the prizes. All my good intentions crumpled. I just couldn't make the kind of parent's thank-you speech required and so this was one of my few quite clear flops in public speaking.

Sunday, July 14th

Yesterday, for the first time, our swimming bath was full of water. Indeed it's over-full owing to the flood we had on Wednesday and Thursday night. Pritchett and I decided we'd have to put a five-foot fence all round it with a wicker gate, to stop people tramping dirt in when they come to bathe. We also think it looks very large indeed. Thank goodness it's inside the garden where it can scarcely be seen but it is a tremendous success with the children who are dashing in and out. Nicholas and Olga Davenport came over with David Butler and his dear wife Marilyn and they all stared at this magnificent great bath in our garden.

I was on my island again for most of today, continuing the clearance. After the floods it has been completely overwhelmed with water. In last week's storm we had higher floods than ever before, with the water three foot above the little humped bridge at Upper Prescote, and I hear from the people who live at Fisherman's Cottage on the canal that immense floods poured over the island. It has, temporarily at least, got rid of all our nettles, though it looked pretty awful afterwards. Once again I've had a quiet weekend with the children. I started reading John Buchan's *Midwinter* to them, but at Patrick's request we broke off today to read Macaulay's 'How Horatius Kept the Bridge', which he thought was a suitable poem to celebrate the opening of the swimming bath.

I've reported already on the good news from the economic front but we've had a good week in Parliament as well. That is because the end of term is coming. An M.P. is like a schoolboy in the summer term, counting and ticking off the days on the calendar until July 26th. The Government has managed to keep to its legislative timetable although it looked impossible just before the Whitsun recess and even a month ago we were being accused of breaking Parliament with the weight of business. Everything has now settled down. The Prices and Incomes Bill got through the Lords on the day appointed and they're now settling quite easily to the Transport Bill.[1] They're taking an extra week in August after we've gone down and they're coming back without a murmur for an extra week for the session's overspill in October or November. All this has helped the Government's morale and

[1] The Prices and Incomes Bill received its Third Reading on July 8th.

also given it a real chance of survival. But not more than survival; its chance of recovery is still highly dubious.

This week we had a series of industrial mishaps, beginning last Sunday with the sudden stopping of the railway strike, about which Barbara knew nothing at all. She's very nervous about dangerous repercussions and a sudden lunge forward on the wages front and Cabinet have been discussing how she should handle the municipal busmen, to urge the postponement of their wage claim. Prices and incomes have been the disturbing underlying factor together with the knowledge that we shall be starting the autumn on a higher plateau of unemployment than at any time since the war.[1] These two factors are the black side of an otherwise encouraging week for the Government and, by the way, a bad week of open turmoil for the Opposition.

I'll just add one small item which didn't fit in to the daily diary. I was approached some weeks ago by Kenneth Robinson about a thing he called Scientology. He told me he now wanted to publish a White Paper to expose it and asked me to have a look at it, because the Home Secretary, who'd backed him at first, has now pulled out. I took a look at this draft White Paper and it tells an extraordinary story. Scientology is an American cult with headquarters at East Grinstead. I must admit that, after asking to be shown all the evidence upon which the White Paper is based, I find it almost incredible that a Minister and his civil servants should be so reckless as to publish a White Paper and to seek mercilessly to expose the Scientologists. It will certainly advertise them even more widely and give them the fame they want. I fear it will help more than it will injure them and anyway Governments really shouldn't publish White Papers on insufficient evidence. That's my personal view. My examination of Kenneth Robinson reinforces my view of the limited value of civil servants as political advisers. He's much too much in their hands. Last year a Mrs Barbara Robb published a book which made most grave allegations against half a dozen long-stay hospitals for old people.[2] In retaliation Kenneth ordered committees of inquiry to investigate all six hospitals and he is publishing their Reports. I feel he has done nothing whatsoever to silence Mrs Robb because the bare picture is not terribly convincing. Now he wants to charge into trouble again by mounting a battle against the Scientologists. Of one thing I'm sure. The public relations of the Ministry of Health are terrible. It has an appallingly bad press office and really faulty relations with the general public.

My publicity problem with Judith Hart continues to develop along very different lines. I've mentioned her anxiety to launch her gigantic entitlement

[1] The unemployment figures for July were 514,605 (2·2 per cent). They were to be 561,382 (2·4 per cent) in August and 547,383 (2·3 per cent) in September.

[2] On July 9th the Minister had told the House that the Report of the six independent committees of inquiry had found most of the allegations in *Sans Everything* (London: Nelson, 1967) to be 'totally unfounded and grossly exaggerated'.

campaign and the skill with which I've diverted her into a trial run in six areas. Simultaneously she wants to run a campaign against the abuse of social security provisions, which I accepted on the one condition that it should take place in areas of high employment and be forbidden in areas of high unemployment. What's certain is how obviously unaware she is of the danger that a too well-advertised entitlement campaign may actually excite public agitation against scrounging. Nor does she understand that a well-advertised anti-abuse campaign can do nothing in an area of high unemployment. Judith is far more professional than Kenneth Robinson and I think their main trouble is mainly the quality of the staff in their Departments. But certainly they also need a Home Publicity Committee with a senior Minister as chairman, such as I am supposed to be and am not. I've been thinking about Burke Trend's passionate appeal that I should continue my co-ordination work when I take over my new super-ministry and I think it's probably largely impractical. It's certainly impossible for me to retain the chairmanship of Home Publicity as well and even now I haven't been doing it keenly enough to do it really well. All I know is that where publicity is concerned we're a lamentably deficient Government and that deficiency is largely due to a curious ministerial blindness to how badly they are advised by their officials.

Monday, July 15th

This confounded S.E.P. We've had six meetings on public expenditure and today and tomorrow there are two more.* I had to come up early from Prescote to meet the Housing Committee before S.E.P. in order to see if Housing could contribute a big cut in local authority mortgage money. We couldn't abolish the local authority mortgage altogether because obviously local authorities would need to make loans to council house tenants moving out of their houses or to immigrants or to people whom the local building societies might regard as a bad risk. Anyway, if we closed down local authority lending, with no competition the building societies would get stiffer and revert to their bad old practices.

I had to explain all this at S.E.P. when I offered to increase the cuts elsewhere from £65 to £75 million, thus providing about half the total saving achieved on the social services. However, I did try to extort conditions. I said the money would not be available unless Roy would abandon any attempt to raise £5 million by increasing the charges on school transport and £5 million by increasing the cost of dentures and spectacle lenses. Thus I avoided a major row in Parliament and two politically most unpopular measures.

Next Education, where Short made his first full assessment of the damage

* For convenience I'm running Monday's and Tuesday's S.E.P. meetings into one entry since my notes have got mixed.

caused by Gordon Walker's decision to postpone the raising of the school-leaving age.[1] You can see the effect in Coventry, which is one of twenty-seven authorities devastated by the cuts. Coventry's programme comes down from over £1 million to £300,000. Yet Roy was proposing to go further this time and to cut the minor works programme and make the other cuts deeper. Fortunately this was stopped by the Committee but only at the cost of conceding increases in the charges on further education – literature, knitting, industrial training courses – and cuts in the university building programme.

In consenting to these cuts we were able to enforce the condition that, before we start considering in the autumn the £250 million cuts Roy's going to demand in the 1971 estimates, we shall consider a paper on a reconstruction of P.E.S.C. accounting, to be prepared by a group of Ministers including (I hear from Tommy Balogh) myself. This is a real achievement but we ought to admit that meanwhile we've done colossal damage to ourselves. There'll be a major row about the further education savings and of course we shall get no credit for the disasters we have saved the public from.

Looking back on these eight meetings, what conclusions can I draw? First, the obvious fact that by standing alone and refusing to come in with the rest of the social services the Minister of Housing permitted himself to be massacred. I've had to make sure that he was massacred in a relatively civilized way.

Secondly, there's been a tremendous shift in Barbara Castle's attitude. Her view now is that we're over-committed to expenditure on social services and must be prepared to cut back in the next three years. There really is a tremendous conflict between the production Ministers who say we must spend our money on I.R.C. and investment grants and the social service Ministers who say that there's no evidence that we're over-committed on the social services and that if we now cut them back we shall be cutting their essential roots.

Roy is emerging as an extremely doctrinaire Chancellor. One day when I was talking outside the Cabinet room Jim Callaghan said to me, 'Roy's getting support which I never got from you people.' 'That's perfectly true, Jim,' I said. 'I remember organizing the attack on you, getting the P.M. to undermine your position by insisting on more and more housing.' Roy, coming in after devaluation, has behaved like a faultless Robespierre, cold-bloodedly cutting back public expenditure and allowing unemployment to reach higher levels than we have ever known. All this is required by the I.M.F. because he must convince them that he is reducing not only public expenditure but also the State borrowing requirement. I am alarmed at all this Treasury activity because I know my national superannuation is going

[1] In January 1968 the raising of the school-leaving age to sixteen had been postponed from 1971 until 1973, thus saving some £33 million in 1968/9 and £48 million in 1969/70. Lord Longford had resigned over the issue.

to pre-empt a much larger amount of social investment for the old, and as their number will increase over the next ten years, the cost will be very considerable. Roy believes we simply can't afford this. I've already seen the draft paper on the economics of the pensions plan which Dick Taverne is to present to the Social Services Committee and it will argue the case that the scheme is impracticable because it pre-empts far too much. I am working out a reply to show that if you look at the amount spent on old-age pensioners over the last fifteen years you will see that a very large increase has been extracted from the Treasury by the worst kind of political pressure. What the national superannuation plan does is to ensure that instead of surrendering year by year to political pressure we have an escalator to carry the old-age pensioner up at a speed fixed in relation to the increase in national wages. We shall proclaim this as a great social advance but I know very well that John Boyd-Carpenter will be able to prove that the escalator will not be moving any faster than it has done by the jerks and jumps with which pensions have been upped in the last fifteen years. My pension plan is not in fact wildly extravagant but unfortunately we dare not say so.

This afternoon I had an informal talk with Carrington. He assured me that after his talk with Heath the Tories were prepared to resume the all-party talks without qualification but that there is no chance of their permitting us to publish the draft as an agreed White Paper when in fact it was not agreed and the talks were broken off.

Another danger I foresee is that the Lords may turn nasty and reject the Transport Bill. If they do that, an agreed reform will indeed be impossible. I made it clear to Carrington that I still hadn't given up hope of persuading our extreme colleagues to let us resume the talks and get the reform according to the agreed scheme.

Next I visited the Social Security group of the Parliamentary Party. I'd offered them pre-legislation discussion, just as I'm having with the C.B.I. and the T.U.C., if they were prepared to turn up regularly and do the work. We had only seven or eight people there. This gives a nice picture of the attitude of a Parliamentary Labour Party which has pensions as one of its major issues in the General Election. When Ministers offer to have completely confidential discussions with them they simply don't turn up, not because they don't know about the meeting but because they don't want the trouble. It's a grim thing to say but the real truth about the House of Commons is that it loves complaining about itself but basically it likes itself as it is, doing very little work, having most of the debates on the floor and resenting the hard work of the Standing Committees. It certainly doesn't want any more work and it certainly hasn't got any ambition to control the Executive.

This evening I gave a little dinner for Doug Garnett to meet John Silkin.[1] Doug is a typical East Anglian, solid, slow, ultra-right-wing, ultra-loyal and

[1] Douglas Garnett was the Labour Party Organizer in East Anglia.

deeply shocked by our liberalization of Party discipline in the Commons.[1] He'd been telling me of the damage it has done in the constituencies and I told him he should have it out with John Silkin. John told Doug that of course he realized the damage which back-bench rebels do by attacking the Government. On the other hand, would it not have been far more damaging to remove the whip and split the Party from top to bottom? We're now at the end of a second session during which we've got through a most difficult time without really effective discipline being imposed but also without a Party split. Gradually we're making the Labour Party accept the Tories' idea of how to run discipline. They have never relied on expulsion or the withdrawal of the whip, as we've seen in their recent passionate disagreements about race, and so they've had to develop other kinds of more subtle discipline, internal personal and social pressures, for example. We haven't got as far as that yet but we have got the Labour Party out of its belief that you can use the threat of expulsion to bully left-wingers to obey. When I next see Doug, I shall be interested to discover whether John made the faintest impression on him.

While I was talking to Doug, Tam was having a tremendous row about the disbandment of the Argyll and Sutherland Highlanders.[2] This had caused great local consternation and the Tories had put down a vote of censure on a three-line Whip. Tam had come in to speak for the Government and chose this moment to launch a tremendous attack on the colonel of the Argylls battalion,[3] who had recaptured the Crater district of Aden during the 1967 disturbances and got himself nicknamed Mad Mitch and acclaimed a popular hero. Tam now accused him of disobeying orders. Oh dear, I remember how I once made a mild joke about the Highland Light Infantry in a debate on Cyprus. I nearly got my trousers removed. Apparently Mad Mitchell has already resigned from the army and is preparing to get a safe Scottish constituency so that Tam's attack may quite possibly be a useful spoiling operation against the Tories.*

Tuesday, July 16th

After we'd finished public expenditure at S.E.P. we went on to discuss the Home Office paper on departmental co-ordination on urban community relations. Jim is delighted with this job since it strengthens his departmental

[1] As Leader of the House of Commons from 1966 to 1968 Crossman and his Chief Whip, John Silkin, had relaxed the Party's disciplinary rules so that withdrawal of the party Whip was no longer the automatic penalty for abstention or even for voting against the Government.

[2] In the reorganization of the army into new divisions, announced in Cmnd 3701 at the beginning of 1967, the Highland Brigade was to lose one battalion, the first battalion of the Argyll and Sutherland Highlanders. The motion deploring the decision to abolish Scottish units was defeated by 299 votes to 250.

[3] Lt-Colonel Colin Mitchell had joined the Argyll and Sutherland Highlanders in 1944. He retired in 1968 and was Conservative M.P. for West Aberdeenshire 1970–February 1974.

* Next day Tam got tremendous headlines and some real sympathy as well.

position in the battle against me for control of this part of the urban social services. He put the problems extremely tactfully to the P.M., showing all the way through how helpful he was trying to be and, indeed, giving way to Harold's wishes on everything. Then came the problem of timing and it was proposed that the plan should be launched straightaway. I said it was ludicrous to rush into this before we'd even discussed it with the local authorities and that I would like to have it postponed until the autumn, particularly as the amount of money required for this year is £1 million for the whole of the United Kingdom and if that figure comes out we shall look ridiculous. However Harold insisted on an immediate launching and this very afternoon he hinted at an announcement in the Commons.

Today we had a little scene in the House. Jack Ashley introduced a little Ten-Minute Rule Bill proposing a Disablement Income Commission, just to show he wasn't defeated by his deafness. He'd already made far too long a speech at the Party meeting and I still think it will be terrible to have a man who's stone-deaf in the House of Commons. But I've no doubt it is giving enormous encouragement to other deaf people and Harold believes passionately in it. He's delightfully soft-hearted about this kind of thing.

At Social Services Committee we had another discussion of this extraordinary community experiment idea the Home Office has put forward, drafted by Derek Morrell. He made a curiously Buchmanite kind of religious speech about action changing lives and I suddenly heard him saying, 'There must be a second revolution in the welfare state, a second revolution.'[1] I was more amazed than ever that the official paper had been accepted without a word of criticism from any other Department, though it's an astonishing mix-up of sociology and mystical religion. Then came a very dramatic moment. Jim suddenly said, 'We must stop all this bloody religious nonsense.' Had the Home Office put this idea forward without taking him into their confidence? No, I fancy he had liked the paper when he first read it and it wasn't until he heard Morrell's mystical explanation that he was a smart enough politician to see that this wouldn't go down in that form, or help him in his battle between the Home Office and social services Departments. Jim said he would produce a paper of his own and I gather that his intention is to keep Morrell out of it as far as he can.

This evening I had a meeting of my own brains trust headed by Brian Abel-Smith and Richard Titmuss, to discuss a Fabian pamphlet on housing allowances as an alternative to family allowances. This had been produced by their colleague, Della Nevitt.[2] I'd already had a proposal from the Ministry of Social Security for a housing allowance as a way of reaching really poor people, using a more civilized kind of means test, but the trouble

[1] Frank Buchman had been the founder of the Moral Re-Armament movement which flourished in Oxford in the 1930s.

[2] An expert on housing finance and since October 1976 a Professor of Social Administration at the London School of Economics.

is that precisely because it would be related to rents it wouldn't cover the poor who live in low-rent areas. So I was anxious to have Miss Nevitt's pamphlet analysed. It was one of those awkward evenings. Within ten minutes one of my officials shot it down in flames and poor Miss Nevitt never really recovered during the next hour and a half. From this I learnt a very hard lesson. We have nothing to substitute for 'claw-back' next year and if I put something on top of it there may be extra complications.[1] If the Chancellor deepens the 'claw-back' it may well bite right into working-class incomes but nevertheless we must now make the best of what we've done, accept the fact of 'claw-back' and popularize it as far as we can as part of our campaign to sell our social security system this winter. We've introduced these wonderful new earnings-related sickness and unemployment benefits on top of an improved flat rate. We've abolished the National Assistance Board and have brought in an enormously more humane system of supplementary allowances but we seem to have been almost ashamed of these tremendous social reforms, partly because of the continuous criticism of the Child Poverty Action Group on the one hand, and on the other the continual attacks of the general public that we are tolerating scroungers. Frankly, we've been panicked and can't make up our minds whether the scheme is too lavish and should be tightened or whether it is a major reform which for the first time does provide something like security in unemployment and sickness for millions of people for at least the first six months. Then there are family allowances. At the by-elections we've been ashamed to claim that we have increased them because we're afraid of losing votes. I think that before we launch our National Superannuation White Paper in the autumn we have to decide whether we will stand absolutely firm on what we've done so far and demonstrate that national superannuation is merely the apex of a great scheme of social reform. If we are undecided and timorous there will be a tremendous campaign inside Whitehall to cut back the scheme and destroy it.

Afterwards we all went to my room to see a big programme on B.B.C.2 about the Health Service. I presume it was put on in response to the protest Kenneth and I had made about the twentieth anniversary programme on the N.H.S. a few weeks ago. Anyhow, it was strongly biased in favour of the hospitals and it cut the critics down to size. Even so, the section on long-stay geriatric hospitals had a macabre effect on me. We were shown an evening in the Cowley Road Hospital at Oxford with the young sisters giving the old things their tea, putting them on their commodes and then into bed. It was all meant to look splendid and hopeful but it suddenly reminded me of my mother sitting there in that dark room in that private nursing home. Heavens, it was disgusting. I could almost smell that same stale smell again and feel how odious it is to grow old and die in a hospital.

[1] For the development of the system of 'clawing-back' from income the revenue to pay for allowances and supplements to family income, see Vol. II.

Wednesday, July 17th

We had agreed to devote the Wednesday Party meeting to discussing the Donovan Report on the trade unions. In the House yesterday the Tories had given their Supply Day to this and it had been a complete flop, but not as much a flop as today's effort by the P.L.P. to discuss what is their most central and important problem.

The report of the Royal Commission on Trade Unions and Employers' Associations (Cmnd 3623), chaired by Lord Donovan, had been published on June 13th. It attributed the great number of unofficial strikes (some 95 per cent of industrial disputes) to poor wage structures, inadequate procedures for industrial negotiations and unsatisfactory trade union communications. It advised institutional reform and recommended that wage bargaining be moved from national agreements towards agreements between individual companies and the unions. It also recommended that factory agreements covering 5,000 or more workers be statutorily registered with the D.E.P. and that an independent Industrial Relations Commission be established, with a system of Labour Tribunals. Immunities from legal penalties for certain offences, which would be actionable if done in the ordinary way by an individual but were not actionable so long as they were part of a trade dispute, were in future to apply only to registered trade unions and employers' associations. Thus the leaders of 'unofficial' strikes and disputes would no longer be immune from penalties. Although the report recognized the need for more union mergers and improved organization it rejected either legal enforcement of collective agreements or criminal proceedings against unofficial strikers.[1]

When I arrived I counted thirteen people present on the floor plus three on the platform, myself, Barbara and Roy Hattersley. The Chancellor came in for a few minutes and the Chief Whip came to sit beside me, with Fred Peart and Willie Ross. But down on the floor there were never much more than thirteen people, of whom five or six were trade unionists. Barbara's trade union legislation is going to be one of the most important parts of our pre-election legislative programme and it is vital to get a picture of how serious trade unionists and serious non-trade-union socialists react to this long complex report. The answer is that if they do react they don't say so in public. There was no disagreement today because the Party is anxious to get away for the summer and has got over its feuding for the moment. It is relieved that the Tories are quarrelling about race whereas we are not quarrelling; anyway, our people feel that there are plenty of good reasons for not coming to the Party meeting.

This afternoon Tommy Balogh made his first speech in the Lords on the Finance Bill. He had written it all out and sent it to me last night and this morning I rang him up and said it was a bit dull and I wondered whether he couldn't jig up the last two paragraphs. But I added it was probably a

[1] See also the discussion of the 'Shonfield alternative', p. 306 and n.

good thing to have a quiet maiden speech which slipped into the House of Lords without a great deal of fuss. I told him not to be unduly disappointed if nobody noticed it.*

This evening Harold was having another of his No. 10 parties (I think it was for an organization of the blind) and I wouldn't have bothered to go if I hadn't heard at 6.30 that the Seebohm Report is on the Cabinet agenda and that he has made four Ministers prepare their proposals about it and is hoping to bring the matter to a head tomorrow. In due course I got him to the end of the room. He was floppy, airy, pleased with himself, with perhaps a little bit of drink in him, and when he had shuffled all the people out of the way he said in his own Harold fashion, 'Well, you ought to get what you want but we can't push it too hard and maybe I shall have to do the job for you myself. But I'm not sure whether you're in the right.' 'Well, if unifying the social services isn't in the right what on earth am I at a merged Ministry for?' I replied very indignantly. 'Of course you're in the right in that sense,' he replied, 'but you don't know what pressure Callaghan is putting on me. He sees enormous Home Office prestige at stake and feels that he's fighting for his life.' I got nothing out of him except a vague sloppy support and I was fairly unhappy.

I was so upset that I decided to relax by taking Anne to see *Dr Zhivago*. Until we walked in I forgot I'd already seen the second half of the film and enjoyed it a great deal. Actually the first half is a good deal better. It's a pretty film, with very attractive acting, though somehow it diminutizes [*sic*] Boris Pasternak's novel and there is nothing great in it. It's a kind of not even bourgeois Western version of the Russian novel, and I can see how furious the Russians are. But it kept me awake and didn't bore me as much as many other things do.

Thursday, July 18th

I had to get into my office very early to have a row about the draft pension paper which was in my box last night. The draftsman is a dry little man from the Cabinet Office who was lent to us for House of Lords' reform and is from my point of view hopeless. Only Wheeler-Booth's skill saved us on Lords' reform. Now this man had put together an absolutely unintelligible piece of crabbed officialese, with no order, no sense, not even a list of the things on which decisions must be taken. So there with Paul Odgers and Peter Oglesby I spent half an hour sweating it out.[1] I had to lay down exactly how it must be written and I got very angry because however hard I tried the paper was angled in such a way that we were bound to be defeated.

* Once again I was utterly wrong in my estimate. The speech was dull but he struck the front page of *The Times* and the *Guardian* and a prominent page of the *Telegraph*. This is tremendously important for Tommy since he must make his way as a politician in the Lords if he's ever going to cut the umbilical cord which keeps him hanging on to No. 10.

[1] Peter Oglesby was Crossman's Assistant Secretary in the Office of the Secretary of State.

The Treasury view stuck out a mile and there was no attempt to present our departmental or political case.

In Cabinet we started with a neat little Stewart lecture on Czechoslovakia where all this week a ghastly crisis has been blowing up.[1] There's no doubt that Czechoslovakia is now threatened by the Russians with exactly the same crudity as Hitler threatened it with in 1938 and yet there is hardly a shimmer of indignation in this country. No one marches up Whitehall saying 'Stand by the Czechs,' not even 100 people. In 1968 people here can work themselves up about Biafra and Vietnam but Eastern Europe is written off to the Russians, just as we wrote off Hungary in 1956. All our indignation has run into the sand and Europe to us just means Western Europe.

So we had the Foreign Secretary with his tidy little report and when it was over he asked for questions. Nobody round the table had a question to ask so I asked one: 'Have the Czechs approached us in any way or approached any Western country?' I was told there had been no approach. 'All right,' I said. 'Then I would like to know one further thing. If the Russians do march in and the Czechs ask for aid, what will happen?' Immediately Denis Healey and Stewart said there would be no response whatsoever and that they must fend for themselves. It makes me shiver a bit. At least when Neville Chamberlain said of the Czechoslovakian crisis in 1938 that it was 'a quarrel in a far-away country between people of whom we know nothing', most of us were deeply shocked. Now we all know about Czechoslovakia but we avert our eyes from just as brutal a tragedy as that earlier one. So no more was said and I was made to look rather an old fool.

Next the P.M. loyally pushed through the unpopular conclusion the Parliamentary Committee reached about Lords' reform. We are now empowered to go ahead and prepare a Bill on the lines of the agreed solution and we will wait to see what happens in the autumn. Barbara Castle opposed outright and Dick Marsh was by no means enthusiastic. Frankly, I was extremely surprised that we got away with it so easily, though I was also surprised that Harold felt it necessary to submit it to Cabinet. Alas, Cabinet was not nearly over. Once again we had Barbara on prices and incomes, this time weeping her heart out about the problem of the municipal busmen. She feels she could have made a settlement with Frank Cousins but Roy forbade her to allow an exception and now, however, he isn't backing her sufficiently.[2] She's in an uncomfortable position at the moment. She

[1] Since May there had been an intensified campaign in other East European communist countries against 'revisionism' in Czechoslovakia, and Warsaw Pact troops which had finished exercises in Czechoslovakia on July 2nd had not yet been withdrawn. In a letter to Czech leaders, issued after a meeting in Warsaw on July 14th, Soviet, Bulgarian, East German, Polish and Hungarian leaders demanded the end to the activities of political organizations outside the National Front, the restoration of democratic centralism and control of the mass media.

[2] Frank Cousins, General Secretary of the T.G.W.U. 1956–69 (seconded as Minister of Technology October 1964–July 1966), was Labour M.P. for Nuneaton January 1965–December 1966. He was Chairman of the Community Relations Commission 1968–70.

complains that behind the scenes Roy insists she should be tough as hell about the wages freeze and yet lets her down publicly. I've no doubt she's still an absolutely first-rate Minister but was it really wise to transfer prices and incomes from what used to be the conciliatory Ministry to a new Ministry which in part represents the employers? The price we have paid for Roy vetoing Barbara's appointment to D.E.A. is the creation of a new D.E.P. in which the Minister of Labour has ceased to be a conciliator and is very much a protagonist in the struggle. From this point of view Ray Gunter's criticism is justified.

Well, this morning she spoke for forty or fifty minutes. We listened attentively and once again approved what she said. Trade union negotiations are brought to Cabinet time after time and we spend many hours discussing them but the discussion consists of the rest of us sitting bored and disconsolate while Barbara and Harold chat together across the table with the Chancellor occasionally intervening. In the previous dispensation it was the same: there were George Brown, Callaghan, the P.M. and Gunter chatting together and the rest of us twiddling our thumbs. I suppose what Harold is really doing during these hours of wasted time is getting Cabinet backing in the event of things turning sour.

This afternoon I had another meeting with the Minister of Health about Scientology. He was determined to publish his White Paper though I warned him that the logical procedure was to set up a Committee of Inquiry first and have a White Paper afterwards. I finally persuaded Kenneth that the proper thing was either, as I would have liked, to hand all the material over to the *Sunday Mirror*, or, as he wished to do, to refuse these people work permits in England and to use all his administrative powers to deter them. Secondly, he should set up a full inquiry into the file he had collected.

Down to Prime Minister's Question Time, and, blow me, if No. 3 was not from Tam, who was battling all last week about Mad Mitch. Tam is now busy attacking the P.M. on the microbiological research establishment at Porton. This is an awkward issue for Tam, who is already up before the Privileges Committee for a breach of confidence in handing over an early copy of the Science and Technology Select Committee Report to the *Observer*. An extraordinary fellow, Tam, but although he's my P.P.S. I'm fortunately not taken to be in control of him. He's regarded as a wild, foot-loose, mad, goofy fellow and this week he carried it a very long way.

Later this evening I had to go across to No. 10 because I suddenly heard that Harold was now prepared to deal with my letter to him about devolution and had got Willie Ross and George Thomas in attendance as well as William Armstrong, Jean Nunn and Burke Trend. When we'd all sat down he turned to me and said, 'Well, it's your subject. You start.' I paused for a moment and then I realized that though the papers had been there for three weeks he probably hadn't read them so I had to begin. The result was well over an hour's discussion, in which he agreed that all the recommendations I had collected were perfectly sensible.

Indeed, he became quite interested, and started to improve them with the usual resource and ingenuity he has once he's gripped on to a thing, but what he really wanted was to hitch these ideas on to some kind of regional council. William Armstrong finally had to say, 'These proposals can be carried out by the Secretary of State but they can't be considered as part of regional government until after the Maud Report.'[1] So we decided to have Plan A, to do what we can now to create a good atmosphere, and Plan B after the Maud Report, so that we can put in the manifesto.

Although Harold was complimentary enough I knew that the whole of my paper was completely useless, two years too late. Ironically, today was the day of the Caerphilly by-election.[2] As I was chatting to George Thomas before this meeting, he told me that he'd just come back from there. Last night, he said, he had gone into the Central Committee Rooms after his eve-of-poll meeting and found there Emrys Jones, the Regional Organizer, sitting alone. That's an eye-opener. When one thinks of the bustle, the cups of tea and everybody saying, 'My God, this is a marvellous campaign' and the people pouring in and out of the room which is normal in any well-organized by-election and then thinks of this one person sitting alone it's terrifying. Certainly George Thomas was terrified and he told me that we weren't going to win. Three times this evening when we were talking about devolution the P.M. turned to me and said, 'We'd better write off Caerphilly. I'm afraid we've lost it.' I knew he was arranging some psychological insurance against defeat, acclimatizing himself to the disaster before it hit him. My mind was on devolution and the more I thought about the major onslaught which is going to overwhelm us the less adequate my proposals seemed to be.

Friday, July 19th

The Caerphilly majority has slumped from 21,000 to under 2,000 and though the Tories lost their deposit their vote hasn't gone down quite as badly as ours.[3] This was a disaster, yet it was a relief that we had won.

[1] The Royal Commission on Local Government in England had been set up under the chairmanship of Lord Redcliffe-Maud in May 1966 (see Vol. I). It was not to report until May 1969. John Maud (K.C.B. 1946) was Permanent Secretary at the Ministry of Education 1945–62, a member of the Economic Planning Board 1952–8 and Permanent Secretary at the Ministry of Fuel and Power 1952–9. He was British Ambassador to South Africa 1961–3 (High Commissioner 1959–61) and High Commissioner to Basutoland, the Bechuanaland Protectorate and Swaziland 1959–63. From 1963 to 1976 he was Master of University College, Oxford. When he became a life peer in 1967 he took the title Lord Redcliffe-Maud. He chaired the Commission until 1969.

[2] Caused by the death on May 3rd, at the age of seventy-one, of Ness Edwards, who had held the seat for Labour since 1939.

[3] Alfred Evans held the seat for Labour; the majority fell from 21,148 to 1,874. The Welsh nationalist candidate secured 14,274 votes for Plaid Cymru, which had gained 3,949 votes in 1966, and the Conservatives fell from second to third place with a vote that was cut to 3,687 from 5,182 in 1966.

Indeed, just imagine if we'd lost? Then all Harold's troubles would have been back and the divisions in Cabinet would have started again.

There was another item in today's *Times* which caught my attention. It occurred in *The Times* Diary and ran:

> James Callaghan is still fighting inside the Cabinet to keep his Home Office empire intact, in spite of all the arguments of Mr Wilson and Mr Crossman that a chunk of it should be detached and built into the merged Social Security and Health Departments in the autumn.
>
> When he constructed his Mark Two Cabinet in April, with Mr Crossman designated as the overlord for all the social services, Mr Wilson planned to wrench responsibility for children's welfare out of the Home Office. The first Mr Callaghan heard of the proposal was when he read it in the papers.
>
> His initial spasm of annoyance has been succeeded by a shrewd rationalization of the case for leaving child welfare with the Home Office. He insists that it is important for the morale of the Home Office that they should not be stripped of creative social responsibilities and left simply with the regulatory responsibilities which now and then are bound to bring them into a harsh glare of controversy.
>
> It makes a very respectable argument and a portent that it may prove to be the winning argument will come next week in the Commons when Mr Callaghan, not the Minister for Housing and Local Government, will make the Statement on the help the Government are going to give the urban authorities whose social and financial problems have been bedevilled by a high density of immigrants. In other words, the Home Office has become the co-ordinator of Ministers and Departments who are involved in helping local authorities to improve community relationships, the kind of overlordship the Home Secretary wants.
>
> Mr Callaghan may have lost his place on the Cabinet economic committee since he ceased to be Chancellor, but the signs are unmistakable that he is quickly re-establishing his influence in the Cabinet and the Labour Party. The elder-statesman role of the Chancellor who has lived through it all before suits him, and now that he is fully recovered from the two or three months of exhaustion which followed his three years at the Treasury, he is putting a lot of energy into consolidating Cabinet and Party unity.
>
> Long before the next General Election comes he is likely again to be a force to be reckoned with.

That had obviously been inserted into *The Times* by Jim's excellent Public Relations Officer. It came as a shock and a warning to me because it's very sensible and because the threat is a very serious one. Jim does regard me as his rival and he has begun the battle of the Departments. Moreover he backs winning causes whereas I back losing causes like devolution.

This morning there was the usual meeting of the Home Affairs Committee, a vast affair attended almost exclusively by number twos and Ministers interested in a particular item. Sure enough, round the great table in the great ministerial committee room about twenty Departments were represented. The only item which interested me was Kenneth Robinson's old proposal to forbid cigarette advertisers to use coupons. At an earlier meeting I'd been a lone voice saying it was a mistake to give him permission to make a statement vaguely announcing legislation.[1] At Legislation Committee I'd made sure the Bill was not included in next year's programme and this was ratified by Cabinet, which instructed us to reconsider the matter at Home Affairs. So here we were, discussing the same old thing. Kenneth was quite brief and then the Lord Chancellor turned to me. I was unprepared and simply blurted out that this was another of those Bills which we simply couldn't afford to pass when we were running up to an election because bans of this sort made us intensely unpopular, particularly with children and families. If you're going to deal with the cigarette-smoking problem you should not try this kind of frivolous but intensely unpopular method. There was a tremendously violent reaction with everyone saying that here we must stand on moral principle. I heard it from Eirene White,[2] Dick Taverne, and Edmund Dell, representing the Board of Trade which has switched its Junior Ministers round, and, indeed, I only had two or three people on my side. However I'm still just powerful enough to hold the thing up and finally I suggested that instead of forbidding coupons we should ration the amount of money to be spent on advertising and leave it to the cigarette manufacturers to decide how they should spend their money. I found this infinitely preferable. Harmony achieved. Kenneth Robinson is submitting another draft Bill and meanwhile I'm pretty sure it will be too late for the election.

I went back to my room to find the indefatigable Callaghan had sent me a letter saying he thought it unfair for me to preside at the Press Conference Seebohm would give on his Report. I rang the P.M. who had seen *The Times* piece and understood the battle that is going on. He was friendly but pretty detached and in this case he clearly wasn't prepared to defend me. Indeed, he made it quite clear that he thought I was, in his language, 'doing a fast one' and should not take the chair. So I had lost this round and had to write and admit it to Callaghan. I was surprised at the reaction of my Private Office. Janet Newman, my beautiful secretary, was appalled when I dictated the draft and said that she'd never known me surrender in a letter such as this. Well, she hasn't known me defeated before and I have a deep sense of having been driven into a corner this week. Callaghan has been able to

[1] See Vol. II, pp. 532, 556.

[2] Labour M.P. for East Flint 1950–70, Parliamentary Secretary at the Colonial Office 1964–6, Minister of State for Foreign Affairs 1966–7 and at the Welsh Office 1967–70. She became a life peer in 1970 and 1972–6 was Deputy-Chairman of the Metrication Board, since 1974 a member of the Royal Commission on Environmental Pollution and of the British Waterways Board and since 1975 Chairman of the Land Authority for Wales.

demonstrate the power and authority of the Home Secretary against me, a mere co-ordinating shadow. I resigned the Leadership of the House in order to regain the power of a big departmental Minister but here I am an impotent co-ordinator licked by a cool and calculating Home Secretary. Of course I need my new merged Ministry but will a new merged Ministry be able to stand up to the Home Office? Will I from that little Ministry in John Adam Street and that horrible place in Elephant and Castle be able to challenge the revered power of the Home Secretary, second only to the Chancellor in Whitehall prestige? Well, it's an open question, but if I have the energy and heart for departmental battles I had two years ago I can do it. I'm not sure I have it still.

Kenneth Robinson came in to see me this afternoon. I had asked him to report on how the prescription charges and exemptions were going. He told me we had only had one press story since the Order came into force and that was a complaint from the chemists. When I asked him what the customers were feeling he said the Ministry had no way of knowing. I told him I would lay on a social survey to study the effects and that the first figures would be ready by the end of this month. It's true, there is a total absence of news and even the Ministry are not getting letters of complaint. The public has accepted it with extraordinary acquiescence. Some people may resent it or be angry but they've accepted it without bothering to write either to the Ministry or to their M.P.s. But what about the working of the exemptions scheme? Here again Robinson expressed bland ignorance. The Ministry knew nothing.

After this I had two fascinating visitors. A young executive officer who'd worked for a few weeks in my Private Office had previously been in a social security district office and these were two of his friends from Croydon. They are both managers now, very self-assured, very alert. I sat them down on the sofa, gave them a strong drink and we had a really informed chat. First of all, I asked whether they thought there should be some kind of training for the people who did the counter work and visiting the old people on supplementary benefit. I told them this was a vital issue for me. Both were convinced that training is fatal. It doesn't matter what training you've got —sociology, or social welfare—it makes you take too long over your job. For their job training means knowing how to ask the right questions quickly, how to make a quick judgment on whether someone is a scrounger or not and then giving the right decision on the entitlement. They said you don't want university education for this, it's a positive hindrance. A university graduate couldn't do the job quickly and reliably in a business-like way. I enticed them on and it soon became clear that both felt Peggy Herbison's 1966 Social Security Act had had a disastrous effect.[1] The atmosphere now is soft, based on the assumption that everybody must be given the maximum

[1] The concept of national assistance was replaced by that of supplementary benefit. See Vol. 1, pp. 410–11, 421, 435, 533.

possible benefit, and the campaign for entitlement is breaking the heart of good officials up and down the country. Under these conditions it is impossible to stop scrounging, larger and larger numbers of people are sitting back and enjoying their benefit and most of the stories about this are true.

Since Judith has just launched an anti-abuse campaign to go with her entitlement campaign I asked them about the letter she had just sent out. They said it meant absolutely nothing. She may want the officials to be firm now but they won't because they feel that if they do they'll be let down by the politicians. The staff believe that an applicant has only got to write to his M.P. to get an improved benefit. They don't dare to stand up and say no to an applicant because they think the M.P. will make a complaint and they'll be in the soup. These two then told me a whole string of stories of how they had been discouraged from doing their proper investigating job. The stock example they took was the bogus deserted wife, a case which can only be demonstrated by spying at night when the husband comes back for his dinner and his bed. 'Under the new dispensation', one of them said, 'if you are caught doing this your own manager may tell you "Don't interfere, it's not for us to interfere, we must take people at their word".' I must say I was impressed by the conversation and felt it raised a problem for me. Should I regard these two quiet, assured young men as the product of the old National Assistance Board and therefore of the attitude we want to eliminate? Or should I take them as they appeared to be, keen young members of the staff, realistic and sensible, warning me of the dangers of excessive benevolence? It certainly made me feel the necessity for regular meetings so that this kind of person can come up and talk in an open and fresh way to the people who make policy.

Tonight we went to the first night of the revival of Benjamin Britten's *Billy Budd*, which I'd first seen almost by accident in 1951. I had walked into the second night and had never in all my life been more exhilarated by a new opera. We'd also seen it on television here at Prescote and liked it very much. This time I must admit I found the production dim and unnautical. Though John Piper was doing the scenery you never felt you were on a ship as you did in the first production. You didn't feel that the scenes below deck were in a narrow, dark enclosure because the whole damned, huge Covent Garden stage was there. Nevertheless the music was as good as ever. After it we motored all the way down to Prescote through the night and got home at 1.0 in the morning.

Sunday, July 21st

Our swimming bath is now properly heated. Pam Berry cut the tape and Eleanor made a splendid speech at the official opening. She's a very solemn child and she was being bullied by her mother. Then our children plunged in for sixpences thrown by Pam. Suddenly I noticed Virginia was holding onto the edge and bursting into tears. This was because when Patrick brought the sixpences back he was told to keep them and when Virginia brought hers back she was not. This is a little revealing about Virginia but more about Pam, who is rather male-oriented.

I started the day with twenty-five lengths in the bath and I am going to try another thirty this evening before supper. Today we went over to see Edward and Virginia Ford,[1] who run a farm about the same size as ours at Eydon, 7 or 8 miles away in Northamptonshire. There I met Frank Roberts,[2] whom I've always found one of the most intelligent professional diplomatists we have. We talked about Czechoslovakia and he confirmed that our policy is that they must fend for themselves.

The Sunday papers carried a number of stories about the departmental battle which is proceeding in Whitehall between Callaghan and me. Since I have not seen a journalist all the briefing's been provided from the Home Office side and the stories all commit me to making a bid to capture the children's service from Jim as soon as I take over in the autumn. This clash has come as a complete surprise to me. It happens in my life. I drift along for weeks and everything seems fine and then suddenly I see a danger I haven't seen before and the clash is on me before I know it. This time it has left me full of doubts, largely because of a talk with Burke. He says that running a huge merged Department, even if Kenneth Robinson and Judith stay as Ministers under me, is going to be a cumbersome and burdensome job which will stop me doing the co-ordinating work which I do so well and which is so desperately important to the Government. He says that if I'm to be a fair-minded chairman I shouldn't simultaneously be the Minister fighting for the new merged Department and he wants the merger postponed at least until after the crucial decisions on the Seebohm Report have been taken.

But what future have I got as a pure co-ordinator? Is it right to say that in the next six months this co-ordinating work is more important than getting myself back the power of a departmental Minister? If I stay a co-ordinator I shan't be able to appear more than very seldom in Parliament or to be effective on the public platform and Callaghan will take over more and more of the big shows which get publicity. On that *The Times* Diary was quite right.

What complicates matters is the character of Jim Callaghan. He's not merely a schemer, he's also got a very nice side to him and I like him because he can't resist talking to me. His feelings about me are very much divided. He's attracted by my ability and probably knows that ultimately I'm not nearly as thrusting and ambitious as he is and that unlike him I am

[1] Sir Edward Ford (K.C.V.O. 1957; K.C.B. 1967), Assistant Private Secretary to King George VI 1946–52 and to the Queen 1952–67, was Secretary to the Pilgrim Trust 1967–75 and Secretary and Registrar to the Order of Merit since 1975.

[2] Sir Frank Roberts (K.C.M.G. 1953) was Ambassador to the U.S.S.R. 1960–2 and to the Federal Republic of Germany 1963–8.

intellectually honest. So he talks to me in the friendliest way possible and fights me ruthlessly behind my back. It's not an attractive combination but in politics it's sometimes inevitable.

Monday, July 22nd

Over the weekend I had been deeply concerned by a Treasury memorandum I found in my red box. Dick Taverne and I had agreed that we would each prepare a paper on the pension scheme, with the main decisions we had reached over eighteen months, I on the mechanism and he on the economics. But when I saw the Treasury paper, well, we were back to square one. He and Jack Diamond before him had sat in for eighteen months on the Pensions Committee, agreeing step by step all the papers we had prepared, and now he has suddenly produced a paper which proves that the whole scheme is ludicrously too expensive. Having added up all the items and found it far beyond our capacity, he concludes by saying that if we have to have a scheme at all a number of features should be dropped. The scheme should, first, be without any Exchequer contribution, secondly, it should be devoid of any pre-award dynamism[1] and, thirdly, the post-award dynamism which we had wanted to link to the increase in national average earnings should be on a cost-of-living basis. It was this paper he proposed to put to the Social Services Committee I had arranged for Thursday. So I shall find myself putting in a paper on national superannuation and the Treasury putting in a paper repudiating it as too costly. I was still angry about this when I arrived in the office this morning and got through to Taverne on the phone. 'Honestly,' he said, 'I haven't had time to look at the paper.' I then found out that the Treasury official in whom he had had such confidence was away on leave and that the paper had been drafted by a brand-new young man.

I decided at once to cancel the Thursday meeting and to see Dick and Judith tomorrow. Then I poured out the vials of my wrath to Paul Odgers and Peter Oglesby. Paul said, to soothe me down, 'You know, this often happens to departmental Ministers. It's normal Treasury behaviour. One has got to understand it.' When I told Burke the story he said just the same. 'That's what you must expect from the Treasury.' But why should one expect the Treasury to behave in a way that no decent respectable Department would behave? And why should they put young men on to write papers of this kind who know absolutely nothing about pensions? Well, Burke smiled his polite Civil Service smile and that was that.

At S.E.P. there were the P.M. and Barbara, who had been at the Durham Miners' Gala yesterday. There had been heavy rain but Barbara had attracted

[1] 'Pre-award dynamism' would allow the pension bought by contributions made during a person's working life to be inflation-proofed so that entitlement would be increased in relation to the increase in national average earnings. It appears that the Treasury wished to avoid this and also to establish that 'post-award dynamism' (i.e. post-retirement inflation-proofing) should be linked not to the increase in national average earnings, as Crossman wished, but to the increase in the cost-of-living, that is, in prices.

all the spectators round her rostrum, leaving only some thirty to forty people for poor Dick Marsh, with Tony Wedgwood Benn addressing an empty field on the other side. She told me how enthusiastic people had been and that the press had been entirely wrong in describing everyone as hostile. At least there wasn't a repetition of what happened last year when the P.M. and Callaghan were subjected to such a pummelling that they made major concessions about the speed of pit closures, from which it has taken us months to extricate ourselves.

At last we got down to an examination of the regular monthly report which confirmed once again the record high level of unemployment for July and the inevitability that figures will begin to rise steeply during September, October and November. Peter Shore made his usual noises about the need for a winter campaign to combat unemployment and Roy made his usual negative comments. It seems to me almost certain now that the Brookings Report is correct and that we have overdone the pit closure campaign which anyway is working faster than we anticipated. In general, as Tony Crosland pointed out, we're in the most appalling mess. For instance, having forced the roads cuts back on Dick Marsh in May we shall probably be launching an emergency road-building programme in September and October. We made all those mistakes last year and now we seem to be repeating them once again.

After that we turned our attention to the joint plan for a European airbus which is being built to beat the American airbus.[1] Again there seemed to be a repetition of past mistakes. The price was escalating once again, particularly of the air frame. Tony Crosland made the very modest suggestion that we should defer a final decision for five months and go on paying till then. The Chancellor wanted to cut the project now and it was fairly obvious that he was mainly concerned that if we postpone the decision on this we shall find it more difficult to cancel Concorde in December.[2] But I've got a feeling the French won't allow us to cancel Concorde anyway and we must be content to cancel the airbus by itself.

This afternoon Jim Callaghan made two first-rate Statements, the first on another demonstration in the West End and then one announcing the urban programme.[3] The whole House could feel the strength of his tremendous comeback. However I didn't have to sit there feeling the pangs of envy because I was busy with Mr Anthony Greenwood. He was due to make his last speech as Minister of Housing before the N.E.C.'s meeting to consider

[1] On July 25th, 1967, France, Britain and West Germany had agreed to build a 250–300-seat airbus, with Britain being responsible for design leadership of the engine and France of the air frame. Both would contribute 37½ per cent of the estimated £190 million cost and West Germany 25 per cent.

[2] It was estimated that Concorde, the Anglo-French supersonic aeroplane, would now come into service in 1971.

[3] Three to four thousand demonstrators had assembled in Trafalgar Square to protest against the Vietnam war. They marched to Speaker's Corner and as they passed through Grosvenor Square some 500 remained behind and stormed the American Embassy.

the General Secretaryship on Wednesday and he came along to see me because I'd heard that he was stopping the sale of council houses.[1] He explained the reason with great candour. The decision to save £75 million on local authority mortgages was extremely unpopular and, to cover it up, he was going to announce the ban on the sale of council houses so that the popularity of the second cancelled out the unpopularity of the first. I said that the general public would detest what he had done and it would seem to put him against owner-occupation, but nothing would budge him. He is determined to have a farewell speech which pleases our own back benchers.

Tuesday, July 23rd

I was in a pessimistic mood when I went into the office this morning, partly because the P.M. had allowed Callaghan to win his series of successes in the war of the Departments, partly because neither Burke Trend nor William Armstrong believe at all in the new Ministry, and partly because whatever happened I felt the P.M. wouldn't give me enough backing. So I sat down and wrote him a discreet memo saying that I'd been talking to Burke and Armstrong and describing their points of view. Of course, I said, there was nothing I wanted more than to go back to running a Ministry and I knew I could do it. But if he felt my co-ordinating job would be imperilled by it I would be prepared to see the merger postponed, provided he made me the sole and really effective co-ordinator over the whole home front. I drafted this more than once, putting it in a slightly more dynamic form because I felt it was too passive. I sent it off before lunch.

In the afternoon I had the row about the Treasury document. I had selected for the meeting Dick Taverne and Judith Hart with Sir Clifford Jarrett and two men from the Treasury. My own staff were also present. It was a fairly tough discussion. I started by telling Taverne that I couldn't understand what had happened. We had worked together for eighteen months and suddenly the Treasury had gone back on all its agreements and was apparently planning to take me to the Social Services Committee and there use the Ministers of Health, Housing, Education and the other spending Ministers against me by telling them that the pension plan is far too extravagant. 'If that's your plan,' I said, 'I shan't tolerate it. I am Chairman of the Social Services Committee and there won't be a meeting with this item on the agenda unless we have agreed it together first.'

There was a great row. Taverne said primly that I couldn't insist on prior agreement. I responded, 'Well, I can have a jolly good try,' and we got down to the substance of the disagreement. To my mind, national superannuation is a system of deferred pay and the essential thing is to convince the working class that this is a genuine pension plan and not another Tory swindle. 'If it's simply a pay-as-you-go scheme,' I said, 'where each year you're just collecting enough money to pay out again that's another version

[1] It was not, after all, to be his last speech. See below, p. 155.

of the Tory swindle and it's ridiculous to use thousands of officials for such a bogus pretence of a pensions scheme.'[1] Judith joined in and sided with me against Dick Taverne and then Mr Phelps made it quite clear that to the Treasury the whole thing was a pay-as-you-go scheme.[2] But I got my way. We have cancelled the Social Services Committee on Thursday and, more important, the Treasury agreed to my paper on the mechanics of the scheme. The whole economic issue is to be omitted and postponed until we come back in September. At the end I was still surprised that such a thing could happen and shocked that, after agreeing to write the paper on the economics of the scheme, Taverne hadn't even looked at the Treasury draft, because, as he told me, he was too busy.

Wednesday, July 24th

My press office had made the most careful arrangements that there should be plenty of room in the press for accounts of Kenneth Robinson's N.H.S. Green Paper and of the Seebohm Report, which were both published yesterday afternoon. But the best laid plans . . . The headlines were taken by Tony Greenwood's ban on council house sales,[3] and by Tam's appearance today before the Commons Privileges Committee.[4]

I spent most of the morning in Downing Street at a meeting of the Supplementary Benefits Commission, which has taken the place of the National Assistance Board and is an independent commission loosely connected with the Ministry of Social Security. I had already met the

[1] Crossman intended the national superannuation scheme to be a mixture of a pay-as-you-go scheme, where contributions by today's workers are paid out to today's pensioners, and a funded scheme where contributions accumulate interest. The 'Tory swindle' was the scheme introduced in 1960, providing an earnings-related pension that was neither funded nor inflation-proofed.

[2] Anthony Phelps was an Under-Secretary at the Treasury and since 1973 has been Deputy Chairman of the Board of Customs and Excise.

[3] In his reply to a Conservative Motion of Censure moved on July 23rd by Geoffrey Rippon, the Minister announced that, in order to maintain an adequate supply of rented accommodation, sales of council houses in the four conurbations of Greater London, the West Midlands, South-East Lancashire and Merseyside should be limited to 1 per cent of total housing stock in any one year.

[4] Premature disclosure of Select Committee proceedings conducted in private was a breach of privilege. The Select Committee on Science and Technology had on May 16th taken evidence in private from Ministry of Defence witnesses at the Biological and Chemical Warfare Establishment at Porton Down, on condition that, subject to the final discretion of the Committee, the witness might subsequently mark certain passages for omission from the published record. A report in the *Observer* on May 26th appeared to derive from the confidential proof of the Committee's proceedings and on June 19th Tam Dalyell appeared, at his own request, before the Committee of Privileges and stated that he had handed a copy of the proof to an *Observer* journalist, with the understanding that, subject to its being checked against D-notices on embargoed material, it might be used as source material. Mr Dalyell had admitted responsibility and apologized for the premature disclosure. The Committee recommended no further action in the case of the *Observer* editor and reporter, whom they found in contempt of the House, but they recommended that Mr Dalyell be reprimanded by the Speaker for breach of privilege and a gross contempt of the House.

Chairman and quite liked him.[1] His deputy is Richard Titmuss. Then there was Catherine Carmichael,[2] the wife of Neil Carmichael, now Parliamentary Secretary at the Ministry of Transport, and Professor David Marsh,[3] with a professional welfare officer and a professional from Prison Aid.

We started by discussing a lengthy report on immigration collected by their managers, which showed that immigrants are law-abiding, decent people unless and until they are corrupted by the Irish, to put it crudely. Next they dealt with the problem of supplementary benefit paid out during strikes and for this item they had in three of their managers, one each from Oxford, Liverpool and London. I had assumed that the families of lower-paid workers would all apply for supplementary benefit but I couldn't have been more wrong. Even at the time of the Liverpool dock strike in the autumn of 1967 only some 35 per cent of the strikers applied, although the strike lasted six weeks.[4] How did they avoid it? Partly because of the income tax rebates for strikers but, even more important I suspect, they take odd jobs. It's certainly true that when a strike is on in Coventry everybody's windows get cleaned and for three or four weeks there are 10,000 jobbing gardeners about. I found the whole thing fascinating and took them back to the Privy Council Office for a quick lunch before they returned to their work.

Meanwhile at Transport House the famous N.E.C. meeting had been going on, when against all expectation Harry Nicholas was selected as the new General Secretary by 14 votes to 12 instead of Tony Greenwood. Poor Tony, from the beginning he hadn't been in the least keen to stand but had been persuaded to seek the post and, having finally warmed himself up to it, was now publicly repudiated. I was sitting beside Callaghan on the front bench this afternoon while he was making another of his great Statements, this time about electoral reform, votes at eighteen and party labels.[5] He gave me his version of what happened and on the whole I must say I thought Harry Nicholas a far better choice. To take a failed politician and shove him into Transport House is an insult both to the unions and to the party workers. Harry will be quite an efficient administrator though he can't be

[1] Sir Richard Hayward, a former Post Office boy messenger who became Deputy General Secretary of the Union of Post Office Workers in 1951. He was Chairman of Supplementary Benefits Commission 1966–9 and of the N.H.S. Staff Commission 1972–5.

[2] Senior Lecturer in Social Work and Social Administration at the University of Glasgow since 1974. Her husband was Labour M.P. for Glasgow, Woodside, 1962–74 and since 1974 for Glasgow, Kelvingrove. He was Joint Parliamentary Secretary at the Ministry of Transport 1967–9, Parliamentary Secretary at MinTech 1969–70, Parliamentary Under-Secretary of State at the D.O.E. 1974–5 and the Department of Industry 1975–6.

[3] Professor of Applied Social Service, University of Nottingham since 1954.

[4] See Vol. II, p. 519.

[5] In a White Paper (Cmnd 3717) published that afternoon, the Government accepted all but four of the conclusions of the Speaker's Conference on Electoral Reform. They recommended, however, that the voting age be reduced to eighteen, not twenty, that polling hours be extended to 10 p.m. and that party labels should be allowed on nomination and ballot papers. A ban on public opinion polls and betting odds on the outcome of an election, 72 hours before polling, was considered impracticable.

the second focus of power which we recommended in the Advisory Commission's Report last year.[1] The fact is that Tony would have been the P.M.'s stooge and that's why he lost. It's my considered view that Callaghan, Brown and Alice Bacon,[2] who organized the anti-Greenwood coup, may say what they like about the P.M.'s supporting Tony but he would probably have preferred the old trade unionist, Alf Allen. Tony was the P.M.'s number two choice but, alas, Harold played his hand very unskilfully and has subjected himself to a gratuitous defeat.

James and I discussed all this as we sat on the front bench listening to Tony Crosland making a hesitating, unconvincing Statement about those confounded aluminium smelters.[3] Tony is far abler than James but what a contrast there is between their performance on the front bench. Callaghan's our best Parliamentarian, as everyone felt when they heard him today. Tony is still an intellectual. Edmund Dell, his Parliamentary Secretary, told me afterwards that for four months he's done virtually nothing about the smelters and that's why he sounded so unconvincing.

Then came the miserable debate on the report of the Committee of Privileges. Tam had made a terrible muck-up by giving the proofs of the Science and Technology Committee's proceedings to an *Observer* journalist. What made him do it? One thing undoubtedly was that Kathleen was having a baby that very day and Tam was overwrought. But he's also full of publicity mania and a kind of Christian martyr's complex which made him feel he must expose the secrets of Porton Down and all this produced a great confusion in his mind and made him an appallingly bad witness to the Privileges Committee. It was also clear that when he appeared before them most of the members resented his behaviour during this inquiry into the Ministry of Defence. Tam has been trying to use the Committee as it should be used, in proper American style, for the prosecution of a dangerous Minister and the exposure of a Department. It's clear that most of the members of the Committee resented this as much as Denis himself so Tam laid himself wide open.

The actual debate should have been very short but it went on for nearly four hours. It started with a very decent statement by Fred Peart but when discussion should have stopped Willie Hamilton got up to move an amendment recommending that no further action be taken, but during which he attacked Tam in a disastrously mixed-up and bitchy speech. I've seen a good deal of Willie on the Liaison Committee. He's a curiously egotistical, way-

[1] See Vol. II.

[2] Labour M.P. for North-East Leeds 1945–55 and for South-East Leeds 1955–70, Minister of State at the Home Office 1964–7 and at the D.E.S. 1967–70. A member of the N.E.C. 1941–70, she became a life peer in 1970.

[3] The arrangements for planning permission and for loans, granted under the Industrial Expansion Act, for a smelter to be constructed by the British Aluminium Co. at Invergordon and by Rio Tinto Zinc at Holyhead. Alcan Aluminium (U.K.) Ltd was already proceeding with a smelter in Northumberland.

ward character, unreliable, publicity-seeking, bloody-minded, a Geordie sitting for Fife, one of the few men in the House I really dislike. I disliked him all the more for ruining Tam's position and extending the debate. It would have been far better if the whole thing had ended with an acceptance of Tam's apology, but, no, the Speaker had to put on his three-cornered black hat and condemn Tam like a criminal receiving a sentence of capital punishment. However, this may have done some good by turning people against the procedure. The vote certainly showed good-will for Tam. There were 242 votes for the reprimand and 52 against. Practically everybody in Cabinet abstained and though I don't often defend abstention on this occasion I was among them.

I didn't hear much of the debate because William Armstrong had come to see me about the memorandum I sent on Tuesday. Harold had acknowledged it with an invitation to see him next week. William made it clear that he himself was against the merger, that he wanted me as a co-ordinator and disliked the confrontation between the Home Secretary and the new Secretary of State for the Social Services. He made it clear that he and Burke would do everything possible to persuade the P.M. to give me the extra power which would make me a supreme co-ordinator on the home front.

Back in my office Peter Carrington came to see me. The conversation didn't add very much to my knowledge and was clearly a mere introduction. Just as we were saying goodbye I told him what had happened about the Lords' reform leak. He apologized and admitted straightaway that he had talked to Heath.

Thursday, July 25th

The papers were terrible. The big news was how the P.M.'s nominee had been defeated at Transport House and there was an account of the Callaghan/Brown/Bacon plot, and of how Eirene White changed sides. Everything was in full detail with tremendous headlines and then Tam was a second lead story, plus rather gloomy Gallup and National Opinion Polls, showing no real improvement and the Tories ahead again.[1] Yes, it was a bad press.

I suddenly had a message to see the P.M. at 11 a.m. He led me in and said he was very surprised by my minute; had I lost heart? It seemed a resigned, sad minute. Did I not want to be a Minister? 'God, no,' I said. 'I merely wanted to give you the choice in an increasingly awkward situation. I would prefer you to bulldoze it through but it will take some bulldozing.' He said, 'I do want to bulldoze it.' And suddenly I realized that the Callaghan plot yesterday had completely changed Harold's mind. This morning he was now willing to back me 100 per cent against Jim in a way that he certainly wasn't twelve hours ago. The evidence is quite clear. I had, as I've mentioned already, got an acknowledgment of my memo with an unenthusiastic

[1] The Gallup Poll still showed a $19\frac{1}{2}$ per cent lead for the Conservatives over Labour and the N.O.P. a 14·3 per cent lead.

statement that he would see me next week. Now he sees me today although he is due to make a farewell holiday speech at the P.L.P. meeting.

I found it very difficult to get any words in. 'If you want me to be the new Secretary of State,' I said, 'I'll take the job on, but you've got to support me and that means not giving Callaghan any more responsibilities like the urban programme.' Harold knew what I was talking about. I then said we'd got to deal with William Armstrong and Burke, both of whom are very strongly against the merger. 'Oh, Burke,' he said, 'he's always wrong,' and the fact that Burke opposed the Ministry was actually in my favour. 'What about Armstrong?' I said. 'I know he's against it,' Harold replied. 'But how will you get rid of the obstruction?' I asked. 'Will you set a timetable and will you give an instruction that my merger will be completed at the same time as the Commonwealth/Foreign Office merger in October? At present Whitehall is full of uncertainty about my future. You must clarify it now and give me full backing.'

On such occasions Prime Ministerial decisions really do count. I've now no doubt that before he goes away to the Scillies he will have given all the necessary instructions, everybody will know the timetable and be prepared to do what they're told.

Off Harold went to the Party meeting where Callaghan was speaking on Parliamentary reform. I didn't feel like going. I'd lost interest in the Party so I went back to my office and then on to the British Museum where I'd arranged to show the children (they're up for the weekend) the Assyrian Room and the Egyptian mummies. Then we went to lunch at Bertorelli's where I haven't been for years.

When I got back I went to the House and sat beside the Prime Minister for Question Time. He was at the top of his form. This was the third week running that he was scoring a rip-roaring success, taking points off Nabarro and quietly making himself the master of the House.

When he had finished I went straight to the Cabinet Office to tell Burke what had happened. He accepted the situation straightaway and only asked whether I could stay as Lord President. 'I want you to continue your co-ordination work,' he said. 'I can co-ordinate the social services from my new position,' I replied, 'but I doubt whether I can do very much else.'

This was the evening for the long-delayed dinner I was to give the Chancellor and Dick Taverne so we could discuss pensions. I put my case quietly but firmly and then Dick put the Treasury case quite fairly. During all this we had a jolly good dinner with a bottle of white burgundy and two bottles of claret. At the end, Roy, who'd been very silent, said, 'I'm relieved that there don't seem to be issues of principle between you. It seems to me that we ought to be able to reconcile your views.' 'All right,' I said, 'I'll prepare the paper during August and September and put it forward ready for Cabinet in late September.' Roy had said nothing which committed him nor had he revealed any interest in the pension problem.

Friday, July 26th

At the O.P.D. we had an utterly futile paper on non-military methods of preserving our influence east of Suez. I found it a kind of schoolboy essay on diplomatic relations and made the great mistake of saying so. Michael Stewart looked very nettled and I realized that he himself had drafted this masterpiece. After the meeting Burke said, 'You're naughty and you shouldn't behave like that. Nevertheless it was a terrible piece.'

In the afternoon Sir George Godber came to see me and I took his advice straightaway on how to handle my new position. 'Will it pay me,' I asked him, 'if Kenneth stays on for some time with me as Minister and I become a super-Minister?' He was commendably frank. 'No,' he said, 'it would be impossible for you because there would be unfavourable comparisons between you and him. The break must be complete and it's fortunate for you that it will be all the more complete because at the same time Arnold France is going to the Inland Revenue.' Godber said that in Jarrett I'd got the best man available but the break would be difficult to manage.

I went home and saw the children at Vincent Square and then this evening we had a little party in my Privy Council palace for all my friends and relatives and also for my Private Office staff. There were thirteen or fourteen people in that lovely room and I think they mildly enjoyed themselves. I took them on expeditions to see the Cabinet Office and what is left of Henry VIII's tennis court behind No. 10 and it turned out a pleasant enough evening with the children staying up till after midnight.

Sunday, July 28th

Yesterday Patrick and I went to see *Space Odyssey 2001* for the second time. I must say I found it more interesting and also more beautiful than ever before, and I'm deeply impressed by it.

In the evening I took the train to Dorking to stay the night at the Labour Party School at Pasture Wood. I gave my lecture this morning and then strolled through the woods with Sara Barker. 'Oh dear,' she said, 'it's a tragedy your not being on the N.E.C. We missed you on the drafting of the Manifesto and we missed you in all this Greenwood business. You know, I didn't realize you were retiring until the last moment otherwise I would have made you postpone it. Can't you get yourself nominated to stand again? It would be wonderful to have you back.' What she said was all pretty good nonsense but it slightly warmed my heart and I had to agree that if I had been there (though I would have voted for Nicholas, not Greenwood) I think I could have prevented Harold from even appearing to commit himself to Tony. As for my resignation from the N.E.C., I know now that it was a great political mistake. I intended to set an example but it has not been followed and all I have done is to remove myself at a moment when my influence as an independent character could have been extremely important.

After lunch Anne brought the car and we motored right through Surrey, Bagshot, Bracknell New Town, Henley, past Jennie Hall's cottage in the Chilterns and back to our swimming bath. In it I went and did my thirty lengths. Heavens, how wonderful it is to have a swimming bath at home.

Monday, July 29th

Parliament in recess and the most important engagement for me today was that after lunch I had the first meeting of our Committee to deal with the Seebohm Report. It consists of the four Ministers concerned – the Home Secretary, Social Security, Health and Housing. I tried to discuss the best approach we could make to the local authorities but found them all extraordinarily gingerly and nervous as they know they're involved in a Whitehall battle. Since we weren't getting very far, I said I had another awkward problem to discuss, the Community Development Project put forward by the Home Office.[1] Callaghan, I knew, wanted Morrell as the Director responsible, reporting personally to him. 'That,' I said, 'is impossible. The four Ministers must be responsible and I will be in the chair as the co-ordinating Minister.' To my surprise, that was agreed to straightaway but I suspect I shall get into difficulties later.

At Social Services Committee we discussed an interesting idea of Ted Short's, that there should be one school-leaving age in the summer each year instead of the present system of having two school-leaving ages, one in the spring and the other in September. Many schools prefer the present situation on the ground that the less intelligent child has a better chance of finding a job if he leaves school in the spring rather than staying on for the last term. Ted said he wanted this small reform now so that, when we finally raise the school-leaving age three years from now, school-leaving would generally be postponed not for one year but for eighteen months. When he'd finished I waited. There was absolute silence. Not one of the other Ministers present had anything to say, yet this was an addition which will cost an extra £1 million in family allowances, an extra £1 million on school budgets, and may also be for many children far too big a jump, taking them to nearly seventeen before they are permitted to leave. When I made this objection Ted replied that he was going to arrange that the last year could be done at a technical college, and not necessarily at a secondary school. 'In that case,' I said, 'put the whole thing forward as a constructive plan

[1] The Community Development Project, long-planned, was to become part of the 'urban programme' which the Prime Minister had unexpectedly announced in his Birmingham speech on May 5th, 1968. The Project itself was announced in July 1969 and between January 1970 and October 1972 twelve local project teams were established in Coventry, Liverpool, Southwark, Glyncorrwg (Glamorgan), Canning Town (Newham), Batley (in the West Riding of Yorkshire), Paisley, Newcastle, Cleaton Moor (Cumberland), Birmingham, Tynemouth and Oldham. The teams' tasks were to identify needs, promote co-ordination of local social services and to encourage the community and citizens to involve themselves in the problems of their area.

which includes the possibility of further education in a tech. in the last year rather than staying on at the secondary school. That's an attractive programme.' I told him to come back with it.

The next item was Judith's presentation of the big paper on national superannuation, the one which had caused me so much trouble with the Treasury. Though it was in my name I was in the chair, so Judith moved it. She did extremely well, though she had some apprehension lest the Treasury Ministers present would fail to keep their word. But they remained mum and most of the objections were complaints that the better-off worker would be paying more in contributions than his pension was worth. I was also asked why the employer's contribution was equal to that of the employee instead of much bigger and why I hadn't greatly increased the Exchequer contribution. There was a series of extremely intelligent questions from Callaghan, who had seen a lot of this scheme as Chancellor. He was skilfully and quietly stimulating criticism of a worried but not of a bitchy sort. He saw the point of the scheme in a way that nobody else did and he certainly gave no sign of supporting the Treasury view.

I got the Committee to agree to the mechanism of the scheme and to leave Judith and me to present a series of papers in September on the major issues. It had been a very long meeting and right at the end we slipped in an item on the Seebohm Report. This decreed that I should be the Chairman of the Ministerial Cabinet Committee and that there should be a Home Office co-ordinator of the Official Committee slotted into the Home Office staff. This compromise between Callaghan and me was quickly agreed and out we came.

I spent the evening with Andrew and Mary Meake, the lady who used to look after us at Vincent Square until her husband's Post Office work was moved to Glasgow. Molly went round to fetch them and in they came for a very enjoyable time in my office. The sun was shining across the Horse Guards and St James's Park was looking lovely. They'd never seen such a wonderful room and I had never seen such magnificent sunlight on the Teniers. There they sat and had a drink and told us how happy they were in Scotland. Mrs Meake revealed how 9 Vincent Square had been the house which was everything to her. She recalled all the exciting times we had with the Bevanites (she didn't like Harold Wilson because he never thanked Anne for lunch) and gave me some most vivid portraits of the impression they made on her. For her this little house with the nice furniture and the middle-class standard of living had been liberation from her slavery to a large family and an L.C.C. flat.

Late in the evening Peter Shore came in to talk to me about S.E.P. tomorrow morning. I told him I had been very upset to find that Tommy Balogh had disappeared to France, leaving me in the lurch and depriving me of economic advice before a very important meeting. So I told Peter he must now brief me and he went through the situation as he saw it. I was able to ask him about the monthly trade figures,[1] which again are extremely gloomy. He also told me that though prices have been rising slightly, earnings have been rising much faster, and in the first six months of the year have gone up by 8 per cent. So we really haven't been imposing a prices and incomes policy, and it looks as though we shall be lucky if this whole elaborate apparatus makes 1 per cent difference. Quite likely it won't give us even that. Peter was worried that at the I.M.F. meeting this weekend Roy might permit even tighter borrowing conditions to be imposed upon us, because public expenditure is regarded as too high. He asked me whether we couldn't raise this at S.E.P. I said I would help all I could and we came to a rough kind of arrangement under which he would help me on one or two of my causes. His briefing was enormously valuable.

Tuesday, July 30th

At S.E.P. we considered a big paper on investment in nationalized industries. Although we have spent weary hours slashing public expenditure this is the first time we have ever touched public investment. One interesting point came up straightaway. The Post Office has nearly doubled the size of its investment programme in telephones in two years because they make money on this and if they can make money then the Treasury feels they're entitled to unlimited investment. Indeed, the paper made a very interesting contrast between the profitable parts of the public sector and those like health or education whose benefits to the consumer can't be priced and so aren't comparable. I said it was absurd to ration investment to the social services and leave the enormously larger investments of the nationalized industries completely uncontrolled.

We then turned to one particular example of such investment, the new nuclear power station at Seaton Carew in the heart of the Durham coalfield. We've had this problem before us very frequently and at one time it got muddled up with the problem of the aluminium smelters. We are so deeply convinced that, despite heavier capital costs, its running costs would be vastly less than a coal-fired station that we've insisted on building it on top of a coalfield and creating unemployment among the miners. Once again it was asked whether this was wise. I noticed that Roy Mason is already firmly against more coal-fired stations. It's astonishing how quickly these working-class boys get taken over by the civil servants. Maybe he is right. I've no way of knowing but I don't believe they have the evidence from which to draw such expensive conclusions. However we were pretty firm. We decided to have the extra station provided it was nuclear-powered. This was a thoroughly good discussion and I agreed with Roy and Sir William Armstrong that it was a real sign of the beginning of economic planning.

[1] The balance of trade deficit had risen sharply from £50 million in June to £81 million in July.

Next we had the problem of Cheddar cheese. Some weeks ago the Warwickshire N.F.U. came to see me about the danger of European cheese being dumped here as the result of the Common Market milk surplus. There's a crisis now because our stocks of hard cheese have trebled (we produce 45 per cent here and 55 per cent is imported, mainly from New Zealand and Denmark). Prices had been tumbling and the arrangements with New Zealand were breaking down, all because the French are selling the cheese in our market far below the Common Market price. The N.F.U. pleaded with me to act. My first job was to find out the facts and I'm afraid they were exactly as they described them.

After five weeks Cledwyn Hughes came to warn me that there was no chance of any help for our farmers because the Board of Trade and the Treasury wouldn't do anything. They say that if cheese is really cheap let's buy it cheap and benefit the balance of payments. Roy Jenkins, Denis Healey and the P.M. were solidly together on this. Cledwyn put our case, saying very sensibly that the New Zealanders would be ruined and that we should ask for some voluntary restraint on the price of cheese, while over the summer the Agricultural Committee investigates and reports on controlled prices for cheese and eggs. This was such a moderate proposal that I was staggered by the resistance it aroused. Tony Crosland said it was quite impossible to consider seriously and he was strongly supported by Barbara. On our side all we had was the food lobby: Cledwyn, George Thomas for Wales, Willie Ross for Scotland, Victor Stonham for Northern Ireland. Fred Peart also weighed in as ex-Minister of Agriculture. I thought we were bound to lose but then George Thomson and Michael Stewart spoke up for the Commonwealth and I was able to point out that it really was a bit undignified for us to say that we were going to cash in on cheese dumped by France far below cost price despite our relations with New Zealand and the protests of our own farmers. The P.M. started summing up and he said we were very evenly balanced, but Roy Jenkins then suggested that he ought to ask the opinion of the other members of the Committee. So the P.M. looked up and asked Dick Marsh who replied, 'I am for our cheese.' Then he asked Roy Mason who said, 'I'm for our cheese too.' We had won by a single vote. There'll be voluntary restraint on prices until next winter.

From Cheddar cheese to Cumberland and another fascinating piece of politics. As I've mentioned before,[1] Harold Wilson has been trying to persuade Donald Stokes of British Leyland to build a huge bus production unit up on the Cumberland coast,[2] to relieve the desperate plight of Whitehaven and Maryport and the little industrial area north of Barrow-in-Furness.

[1] See Vol. II, p. 775.

[2] The merger between Leyland Motors and the British Motor Corporation, announced in mid-January 1968, had created a £400 million company, the world's sixth largest motor manufacturer. Donald Stokes was Chairman and Managing Director of British Leyland Motor Corporation Ltd 1968–75 and President of British Leyland Ltd 1975–6. He was a member of the I.R.C. 1966–71 (Deputy Chairman 1969) and became a life peer in 1969.

Although Donald Stokes said he could only guarantee 650 jobs, Tony Crosland recommended that he be given for this full Government assistance, millions of pounds, roughly £20,000 a man. In addition we were to build a West Cumberland motor highway at enormous expense. Dick Marsh said he wouldn't pay for this as part of his normal roads programme.

However one doesn't beat the P.M. when he's in a Yorkshire terrier mood. I argued that there must be a limit to what the Government pays out to penalize genuine growth areas and create artificial employment in dying areas but Harold's reply was simple. He couldn't let Cumberland go. It had been one of his earliest causes when he was at the Board of Trade and he'd been up there recently. That film which he had seen on the telly nine months ago had burnt into his soul.[1] 'It's all very well, Dick, but you can't admit that an area is doomed. You've got to try to save it.' The Chancellor took the other view and so did Dick Marsh but after half an hour we gave way to the P.M.'s pleading and Tony Crosland's pressure. Harold won.

The fact that this had gone on the whole morning made Peter Shore lucky. He had a paper on his new revised national plan, which Roy detests since he thinks publication in the autumn will be terribly dangerous and make us look fools. But as we wanted our lunch Peter was allowed to assume publication and go ahead. It was now some time after 1 o'clock, when it had been arranged that I should see the P.M. and Burke to discuss the merger. However we felt bound to push Harold into a decision. 'All I need to know before the end of this week,' I said, 'is whether you have given the go-ahead. Can you do that or not?' 'Yes,' said Harold 'I can,' and, though I had a mass of other things I wanted to talk about, at that point I decided to slip away.

Wednesday, July 31st

In order to have a long-postponed lunch with Roy I had to cancel lunch at the *Sunday Times*. My main object was to clear in my own mind his view about the economics of the pension scheme. What I got clear was that there was very little about it in his mind. He repeated that he saw no difficulty in reconciling the position of Dick Taverne with mine (though in fact they are irreconcilable) and he promised that directly Dick was back from holiday he would be given as his first job the preparation of the Treasury paper. At one point I said that he and Harold ought to realize that they must take an active interest in national superannuation because it affects the whole strategy of the Government and I suggested that we should have two or three meetings together on it in September.

Then George Brown's name came up and we were suddenly discussing

[1] On September 25th, 1967, the Prime Minister had appeared on the B.B.C. 'Panorama' programme. The interview had been preceded by a film about unemployment in West Cumberland. See Vol. II, p. 493.

something which really interested him. There's a great deal of talk now of Fred Peart replacing George as Deputy Leader of the Party and I hold the view that it will be a great pity to have an election.[1] 'If there were,' I explained to Roy, 'there would be you and Barbara and Jim and Fred all fighting each other and wooing the Parliamentary Party. Far better to let it lie.' That wasn't Roy. 'I'd go for it if I knew I could win it,' was the remark he made and it summed him up. I didn't get as much out of him as I'd hoped, but then you never do. He never tells you more than the minimum that is necessary for courtesy on any particular occasion.

Rather thoughtlessly the Prime Minister had set up a new Cabinet Committee on the finances of the B.B.C. and it had its first meeting this afternoon. I asked straightaway whether anyone there thought we still had a chance to go for advertising. John Stonehouse who's the new P.M.G. and Roy Mason, the old one, both said they were against it. But I told them that if nobody wanted advertising what this Committee had better do would be to try to improve the system of licensing. That's what we agreed and so under my chairmanship a major Cabinet controversy finally spluttered out.

Later this afternoon Paul Odgers had set up in my office a very solemn meeting about the merger. William Armstrong was there with the two new Permanent Secretaries, Jarrett and Marre, the old Permanent Secretary of Health, Arnold France, and Miss Nunn from the Cabinet Office. Paul had prepared exactly the kind of paper they like. Burke at once raised the problem of whether I should be allowed a small co-ordinating unit in the Cabinet Office or whether my whole headquarters, including my outside advisers, should be moved to John Adam Street. Should I have two lots of civil servants, one lot as co-ordinating Minister and one as super-Minister? Everyone except Burke was against separating the co-ordinator's office. As I also thought it was quite unrealistic, I said I would as co-ordinator only retain the Lord Privy Seal's present suite of rooms for myself when Fred Peart moves into my Privy Council palace. What will be the name of the Ministry? It was agreed that in the first instance it should be called the Department of Health and Social Security, so as not to claim control over the other social services too imperiously. We agreed that I should sit in John Adam Street and that this should be the headquarters of the merged Ministry for the meantime, until we could get a decent new building for the merged Department. The only staff to be merged are the press relations people and I immediately said I'd try to get Peter Brown back from Housing.[2] He will be taking over two very incompetent press relations divisions and will have a tremendous job to raise the standard.

Towards the end of the meeting my mind began to wander because I was

[1] See p. 16.

[2] The most able press officer in Whitehall, according to Crossman, whom he had joined at the M.H.L.G. in 1964. See Vols I and II.

looking forward to entertaining Alfred Gollin,[1] the political historian who wrote an excellent book on Garvin and the *Observer* as well as a biography of Milner. He's now writing on Baldwin and he came to see me the other day so that I could show him the House of Commons. He's a shy young man with a treble voice that is hardly broken and that day he was suffering from a terrible cold. I had also offered to show him No. 10 and he was duly thrilled. However, just as we were leaving today who should walk into the hall of No. 10 but the P.M. and John Freeman.[2] John used to be a rather willowy, elegant young man with wonderful wavy hair but he's thickened out and his actual complexion has roughened so that he looks like an extremely tough colonel of a polo-playing regiment just back from India – big and bluff. Beside him was little Harold, relaxed and gay, having undoubtedly been drinking with John. Harold was full of interest when he heard who Gollin was and immediately offered to show him the busts in the passage from the front door, the photographs of his predecessors on the stairs and all the rest of the Prime Minister's standard display. This he did with stories about everybody since Pitt, genial, well-balanced and humorous. When Gollin's tour was over Harold suddenly turned to me and said, 'How dangerous it is to be a Christian. Look what happened to me with Callaghan. I showed a perfectly Christian mood. I did nothing whatsoever. I didn't react at all when they appointed Harry Nicholas but, by God, the time will come when I'll dig Jim's entrails out for what he did to me. By the way,' he said, turning to me, 'you've been a bit of a Christian this week too, haven't you? You had a moment when your courage failed and you were just going to give up.' 'I didn't know how much backing I was going to get from you, Harold,' I replied, 'and I shall be very glad if it's really all right. But I'm not yet sure.' I suppose the whole incident lasted twenty minutes. It was Harold at his most relaxed and happy and I felt relaxed too because I'm not so close to him any more. Instead of me he's got Fred Peart, an excellent boon companion who, though he hardly has a policy-making mind, fortunately knows it.

Thursday, August 1st

At O.P.D. Michael Stewart was back with another request that we should

[1] Professor of History at the University of Santa Barbara since 1967. He is the author of *The Observer and J. L. Garvin 1908–14* (London: Oxford University Press, 1960); *Proconsul in Politics: a Study of Lord Milner* (London: Blond, 1964) and *Balfour's Burden* (London: Blond, 1965).

[2] Labour M.P. for Watford, Herts, 1945–50 and for Borough of Watford 1950–5, he was Financial Secretary at the War Office 1946, Parliamentary Under-Secretary of State for War April 1947, leader of the U.K. Mission to Burma 1947 and Parliamentary Secretary at the Ministry of Supply from 1947 until his resignation in 1951. He was Assistant Editor of the *New Statesman* 1951–8, Deputy Editor 1958–60 and Editor 1961–5. He was British High Commissioner in India 1965–8 and British Ambassador in Washington 1969–71, and then Chairman and Chief Executive of London Weekend Television from 1971 until 1976, when he became President of the organization.

review our policy towards the Greek Colonels. He's hoping for a big British contract to supply them with frigates and patrol boats. At the previous meeting we had agreed that since there was no urgency we had until the autumn to make up our minds but now we were told that it would be impossible to wait because the contract might be signed at any moment and he didn't want to tell the company concerned to withdraw or show any second thoughts. It was perfectly clear that ever since last March the F.O. has been encouraging the company to try to get this £18 million contract and has seen nothing incompatible between doing this and talking publicly about replacing the Colonels by a constitutional Government. The only thing wrong here is the hypocrisy and I rather prefer the attitude of Denis Healey and Roy Jenkins who seem to be saying that beggars simply can't afford to be choosers and that we've got to get the contract come what may. In that case we musn't go on pretending that we care about Greek democracy and what Harold described as the bestialities of the Colonel's regime.

In Cabinet itself we had another rather futile discussion on Czechoslovakia. We had already known that whatever the Russians did in Czechoslovakia we should not intervene.[1] All we learnt this morning was that on his own initiative the Russian Ambassador had come to ask Michael Stewart to join an inter-Sputnik organization of a singularly unimportant kind and then, just when he was leaving the room, had said, 'I want to talk to you about Czechoslovakia.' I found out later that the Russians had given their Ambassadors in every capital instructions to make an identical approach in order to test Western reactions. I hope Michael gave ours.

When I got back to my room at lunch-time there was the P.M.'s famous minute giving the go-ahead for my merger in mid-October. Apparently he had summoned William Armstrong this morning and with his help had drafted the minute required. No doubt he'd taken his decision earlier and the moment he acted it becomes a *fait accompli*. Things go ahead and the new chapter opens. From this moment all the wheels in Whitehall began to turn the way I want them to turn. That shows you the power of a P.M. It is his word in writing which settles an issue.

Two hours later Callaghan rang me up. He wanted his man, Morrell, to be the Chairman of the Official Committee on the Community Development Project instead of my man, Paul Odgers. 'Be reasonable,' I said. 'If I'm in the chair of the Ministerial Committee, my man must chair the Official Committee. You've already got your man as director of the whole operation. To have the chairmanship of the Official Committee as well would be too much for anybody.' Jim replied with these remarkable words: 'You're going

[1] In late July the Soviet Politburo had invited the Praesidium of the Czechoslovak Communist Party to bilateral talks on Soviet territory. The Praesidium had preferred the meeting to take place in Czechoslovakia, and it was held at Cierna-Nad-Tisou from July 29th to August 1st. A short communiqué said that there had been a 'broad comradely exchange of views', and that on August 2nd, in Bratislava, the Czechoslovak leaders would meet the signatories of the Warsaw letter of July 14th.

to win anyway, Dick. You'll get the Children's Department out of me. Why not be generous in this small thing and make a few friends?' What this meant of course was that Callaghan had seen the P.M.'s minute. Well, I called his bluff and refused to do what he wanted. I can now comfortably afford to do so.

I was off to Newcastle this evening on the 6 o'clock express which does the 240 miles in three hours and forty minutes. With me I had Lewin,[1] the brain behind the whole pensions plan. He dined with me and I learnt how he had fought in the war after doing one year of P.P.E.[2] and then did one year afterwards. He's a real intellectual, a potential Fellow of All Souls, and he's also a passionate musician. He had been at the concert last night at the Albert Hall where he'd heard the Russian State Orchestra and Rostropovich, the famous Russian cellist, playing the Dvorak Cello Concerto and getting the most wonderful reception. After chatting about that we settled down to the details of the pension plan.

I was met at Newcastle and put into Harold Wilson's suite at the Station Hotel where I was just able to see on the 10 o'clock news programme a wonderful film they had brought out of Czechoslovakia. After that I started reading my enormous brief for tomorrow when I am going to spend the morning with the 10,500 workers of the Ministry of Social Security and the afternoon with the staff of the Newcastle hospital system.

Friday, August 2nd

I had breakfast with the Labour Party regional organizer, Alderman Andrew Cunningham,[3] and the Chairman of the local Regional Executive. All they wanted to talk to me about was the level of unemployment which this morning's papers had announced had gone up for the first time in six months, to a record high level of 4·6 per cent in the North-East.

After breakfast in came Mr Lewin and I was taken to quite a modest site on the outskirts of Newcastle where there's a small town of prefab buildings in which the whole of the records department of the Ministry of Social Security has been stored ever since Jim Griffiths launched National Insurance.[4] I thought it was going to be rather boring but I was delighted because on the one side you see thousands of civil servants pushing pens in the old style, doing the pension and contribution records of each person by hand. Then in the other half of the compound they are computerizing the whole process. Moreover they're starting by computerizing the records

[1] Herbert Lewin, Assistant Secretary at the D.H.S.S. He died in November 1970.

[2] The Politics, Philosophy and Economics degree course at Oxford University.

[3] In 1972 Andrew Cunningham was found guilty of corruption charges relating to the architect John Poulson and was sentenced to five years' imprisonment. His sentence was reduced on appeal, to four years and he was released in 1976.

[4] James Griffiths, Labour M.P. for Llanelly 1936–70, was Minister of National Insurance 1945–50, Secretary of State for the Colonies 1950–1 and Secretary of State for Wales 1964–6. He was a member of the N.E.C. 1936–59. He died in 1974.

of the earnings-related element which I have always nicknamed the Boyd-Carpenter Tory swindle. They explained to me that if it weren't computerized 1,500 extra staff would have been required to record every week this miserable little graded element. The man who took me round controls the whole affair and he's the only member of the whole staff in Newcastle who is a civil servant of the administrative class. Everybody else is an executive or a clerical officer. The girls like being here because with their wages they're much better off in Newcastle than they would be in London. I had an awful lunch in the canteen but it was very friendly and pleasant as I got to know these people. And as I know the pension scheme backwards I was able to discuss it with them and test its practical possibilities. I was relaxed and felt really at home and they told me afterwards that they'd never had such a time for ten years at least. It was marvellous to have a Minister down but to have a Minister who knew all about the scheme and who could talk over the blower to all these people sitting in their offices was too good to be true.

In the afternoon I motored out with a Ministry of Health man to an old-fashioned maternity hospital and then went on to the Newcastle Infirmary. Suddenly I was plunged into a world of doctors, health officers, Regional Hospital Board secretaries. How different. Social Security was something I could understand but here were doctors, manoeuvring, knocking each other and, in the course of showing me round, always trying to get their own oar in somehow. I realized by the end of the day that in claiming both Health and Social Security I've certainly taken on a challenge because it means mastering two completely different worlds.

At the airport I was on the plane punctually to fly down over thick white cloud to London, where it cleared a bit. After waiting half an hour we got down and I was put into a Ministry car and driven to Prescote. Suki came running out and the driver brought out his photograph of his alsatian, which is taller than himself. He and Patrick then had a great chat about dogs and I was happy to be home again. During the drive I'd been listening on the radio to the news of the Czech crisis.[1] The more I hear, the more unsure of myself I feel as the Cabinet Minister selected to speak at the mass demonstration this weekend. I'm no good at mass demonstrations but I've got to be competent and so I got to bed early this evening.

Saturday, August 3rd

I rang up Harold and we chatted about the background to the news and the impossibility of my giving a press release. Immediately he said resourcefully, 'Give a press conference just before you make your speech. They'll go away and write it up and not listen to what you say and you'll get a good press.' So I've made arrangements with Percy Clark and hope the idea works.[2]

[1] See pp. 76, 143, 167, 172–3.

[2] Publications Officer of the Labour Party 1947–57, Regional Publicity Director 1957–60, Deputy Director of Information 1960–4 and since 1964 Director of Information.

Nicolai and Georgie, the two boys who came to Polzeath with us on holiday last year, have just arrived this afternoon and have been bathing. Now they're coming pea-picking in the fields by the two top spinneys while Pritchett cuts the timothy grass in the field next door.

Sunday, August 4th

The day started gloomy, windy and wet, not actually raining but looking as if it might turn sour. I worked away at my speech from 7.0 in the morning and felt less and less enthusiastic about myself as a mob orator, standing in a coal cart in Hyde Park with 10,000 people round me. At 10.0 I gave the B.B.C. a longish interview for their 1 o'clock news programme and at 12.0 we started for London. I was in a real sweat trying to get my pages sorted out and the statement for the press ready. As we drove up the Chiltern escarpment the weather changed, as so often happens, and on the London side it was brilliant and warm and balmy. When we got to Kilburn we looked for somewhere to take our sandwiches and have a glass of beer and found a nice little pub where we could sit in the open among friendly Londoners. I felt life was a bit better.

Then we drove up and parked in the underground car park at Marble Arch and I found my way to our big coal-dray, which was surrounded by a whole mass of red banners, on one side Trotskyites and Biafran supporters and on the other anti-Vietnam demonstrators. The only Czech supporters seemed to be Trotskyites, right-wing extremists and totalitarians. It was a terrible mess. Next to arrive were Jennie Lee and Eirene White in a big car, and soon George Brown turned up, looking as sweaty as myself, along with Fred Hayday.[1] I asked George why on earth we couldn't have had the meeting indoors in the hall we'd booked at St Pancras and he said, 'You may well ask that question. So do I.' Apparently since Trafalgar Square had been booked by the Apostolic Church, we had to take Hyde Park if it was available. In one sense it was available but our meeting coincided with a day long-planned for a major Biafran demonstration and all the Africans who had turned up were infuriated and had the impression that we were talking about Czechoslovakia in order to divert attention from their cause.

When Jennie got up to introduce us there was steady booing (not heckling, as the B.B.C. said later), mainly from the right and centre and from 4–500 people who were immediately in front of the microphones. There were 10–12,000 people in the crowd but even those who were standing further away could hear us quite well because the loudspeakers were good. The plan was that I should speak for twenty-five minutes, and George for half an hour, with ten minutes each for the others. But with that pressure of shouting people round us, the blazing heat of the sun, the wild gesticulations of the Negroes on the one side and the Trotskyites on the other and the television cameras going round to televise not the speakers but the interrupters it was

[1] National Industrial Officer of the N.U.G.M.W. 1946–71. He was knighted in 1969.

clear that we were playing a very minor part in this modern St Bartholomew's Fair. When my turn came I made my difficult case. I said we were supporting communists in Czechoslovakia who were trying to liberalize the regime and that we weren't going to intervene from the West whatever the Red Army did. The interrupters shouted quite effectively, asking why, if we objected to the Russian intervention in Czechoslovakia, we didn't object to the Americans in Vietnam? I couldn't say what I really felt about that.

Immediately I'd done my piece I slipped away to find Anne who'd got the car round the corner and we drove straight home, listening to the radio news all the way down. They quoted one sentence from my speech, unfortunately quite wrongly. I came back pretty well convinced that it doesn't pay us to organize Labour Party demonstrations in this way. The right way to mobilize public opinion is not to put George Brown, myself and Jennie Lee on a coal-cart in Hyde Park to compete with African demonstrators as well as the whole of Speakers' Corner. In fact we were doing it for completely old-fashioned reasons, not because we're skilled at it but because we think it's the right thing for a Labour Party to do. After four years of Government we do it clumsily and obsoletely.

Directly we got back to Prescote we saw the two combines working on the big bank, each looking like something between a prehistoric monster and a moving house, with the blue tanker in between and Pritchett's Land-Rover darting to and fro. The boys and I took Suki and got on to the combine to stand beside Pritchett and see how much of the wheat had been laid in this field and how the potatoes were growing through it. It looked a terrible mess to me but he told me we should get 36 hundredweight but not the 2 tons we'd have got with decent weather. Then we moved over to Upper Prescote to see the grass dryer at work before strolling back down to the Manor, letting Suki chase hares across the field, in a cool breeze and brilliant sunshine.

Now I've had time to reflect on the day's events I've realized that this was my first speech on foreign policy for a very long time. I found it immensely stimulating to switch back to foreign policy again, to a subject I know very well, a country I know quite well, a part of the world I've been thinking about for years. It all comes back with a bang when one starts speaking again and I should now do rather more public speaking on foreign affairs than I've done in the past.

But there's very little a member of the British Labour Government can say at such a mass meeting or with which he is likely to impress the audience. All we can do is to show an understanding of what Dubček wants of us, show our friendship with the Czechs and give them a message of encouragement. But that's not very much and as well as our own Labour Party difficulties we have the Foreign Office, which only wants to keep in with the Americans, already throwing great doubt on Dubček's power to resist and anxious to accept a Russian-imposed *fait accompli*. At last week's

Cabinet meeting that was the impression I got of Michael Stewart and Denis Healey. They rule out the possibility of real Czech resistance and they assume the rapid creation of a Russian-controlled puppet government which we shall on no account exclude ourselves from recognizing. And at this point all the departmental Ministers intervene on the side of prudence. The Board of Trade, of course, is concerned to get the ban on strategic materials reduced and to see that there are no upsets in our improved trade relations with the U.S.S.R. Wedgy Benn is almost entirely concerned with the sale of computers to the Russians. All my colleagues have their departmental interest in economic relations with Russia and that takes the edge off any conviction that we are really in any sense prepared to stand by the Czechs.

The other thing I might just note in this diary is the effect of the television coverage. It's the first time that a major crisis of this kind – the invasion of a country – has been transmitted so immediately and so fluently with reels and reels of television tape being smuggled out by experts. The Czechs are Westerners, skilled in this kind of job, first-rate radio and television technicians and natural liberal journalists. So we've had absolutely superb television coverage of the whole crisis. In the B.B.C. 'Review of the Week' I heard someone saying that this has been the week in which the press must have learnt its place and known that it could do nothing compared with radio and television.

In a superficial sense that's true but it's not true immediately one stops considering only the news coverage. All you get on the television are minute details of the view in a street, of a boy kicking a tank or a Russian saying '*Niet*'. As for analysis, all you get are endless conversations between experts chatting away in the studio. I felt as I opened the Sunday papers and saw the analysis by the serious commentators that anybody who wanted to understand the Czech crisis couldn't really have learnt much from television alone. I don't pretend that the discussions on television were any worse than usual because they're always on a fairly low level but once again it seemed to me that the need for the written word, the serious article in the daily or Sunday paper, or weekly periodical, has been proved more clearly than ever by the Czech crisis.

On the night of August 20th Czechoslovakia was invaded by Warsaw Pact forces, at the request, it was alleged, of unnamed Czechoslovak officials, and several prominent members of the Czechoslovak Praesidium and Secretariat, including Smrkovsky and Dubček, were arrested by the Russians. Riots, strikes and demonstrations broke out against the invading troops, over 500,000 soldiers, with 500 tanks in Prague alone, and protests were broadcast from secret radio and television transmitters. President Svoboda flew to Moscow on August 23rd and secured the release of his colleagues, and a communiqué issued on his return on August 27th announced that the troops would not interfere with internal affairs and would be withdrawn as soon as the situation became 'normal'. The invasion was condemned by Yugoslavia and Roumania and by nearly all the West European communist parties.

In Britain the Prime Minister and Foreign Secretary had immediately returned to London on August 21st and in a statement issued from No. 10 Downing Street the British Government condemned 'a flagrant violation of the United Nations Charter and of all accepted standards of international behaviour.' Britain had joined six other Western countries in tabling the resolution at the U.N. Security Council, calling for a withdrawal of all the Warsaw Pact forces from Czechoslovakia and for a declaration that the sovereignty and independence of Czechoslovakia would be respected. Parliament was recalled for a two-day emergency sitting on August 26th and the Prime Minister proposed that the crisis in Czechoslovakia should be debated on the first day and on the second the Nigerian civil war.[1] *On August 31st a new Praesidium had been announced but, although the progressives retained the balance of control in both the Government and the party, censorship was reimposed, recruitment to the Democratic National Front abandoned and the Club of Committed Non-Party People and Club K231 (established to promote rehabilitation of those who had suffered in the 1950s) were dissolved. The press and radio of the invading countries and occupying forces continued to attack Czechoslovak leaders and the troops remained.*

Monday, August 26th

House recalled. I had lunch on the train and went straight to the Commons where the carpets hadn't even been laid and everything was being spring-cleaned. I went in through Speaker's Yard and wandered round before coming back to Harold's room while Prayers were still on in the Chamber. He was just getting his speech ready. Then it was time for us to go in and there was horrible nasty pushing and shoving because there was no Question Time during which Members could slowly drift in to take their places. If anybody wanted a decent place he had to do some fighting with his arms and shoulders. I saw just ahead of me Roy going round the corner into the Division Lobby, determined to get the place he wanted. I nipped in and just got the last seat on the gangway, the Chief Whip's seat. Fred Peart wasn't yet there but there was a fight when John Silkin arrived, back from Montreux, and he just got his big bottom on to the edge beside me. Fred Peart then squeezed in beside him and the P.M., Michael Stewart and Roy Jenkins, all tight as sardines on that front bench but trying to sit back and look important. The P.M. made a perfectly decent speech but one thing tickled me. I had started my speech at Hyde Park by saying that anyone who compared the crisis in Czechoslovakia today with the Munich crisis in 1938 wanted his head examined. Harold started his speech by saying

[1] See *Wilson*, pp. 551–61.

history repeats itself. He then took the superficial F.O. line about the situation. There was even the passage about the Czechs' love of democracy whereas our concern is that the Czech Communists should be allowed to liberalize a regime which is in no sense democratic. Harold doesn't take to philosophy. Indeed he has one of the most un-philosophical minds in the world and when he claims that he never got past page one of *Das Kapital* it's probably true. Still, the speech was perfectly decent and Heath followed him with an equally pedestrian oration. Later on George Brown was on his feet for an excellent little speech, very much on my line, urging us not to abandon our cultural contacts.*

It was certainly a big occasion. The floor and galleries were packed, some 300 M.P.s had come back from their holidays and for these two days they had nothing else to do except crowd into the Chamber. It was obviously right to recall Parliament but these historic occasions are anyway a bit depressing, and this one was more so than usual because everyone now knows that Britain can do nothing to help the Czechs. I suppose that with President Johnson and de Gaulle both opting out Britain had a chance to count for something if Harold could have spoken for the uncommitted nations and said something really striking. But he couldn't and so he didn't. And perhaps that's the feeling which made us specially depressed.

I slipped out during the debate to have a talk with Roy who is back from a holiday in Cyprus, as detached and as quiet as ever. We agreed that our families must meet and he's going to come across and bathe in our pool. Then I said to him, 'Lucky for you that this Czech crisis covered up the disastrous July trade figures. A second lot of figures as bad as that and we should be for it.' He replied, 'I can assure you that there will be action if the next figures are equally bad.' So I presume that a plan for slapping on import quotas has been prepared.

I then had Kenneth Robinson to see me, about Scientology again. The papers have carried the story, there has been a tremendous build-up and the Scientologists have got advertisement. Kenneth had agreed in July to have a short statement and a public inquiry. Now he wanted a complete reversal back to a White Paper. 'Not on your life,' I said. 'I won't ever allow a White Paper because there isn't enough evidence to make it stand up. The only chance of a White Paper is after a public inquiry.' He seemed quite surprised that I still held this view and that I obviously resented his coming back to me in this way. Finally I had to tell him that in a few months I should be the responsible Minister of the new merged Ministry and therefore it is essential that whatever decision he takes now must be in line with what I shall want to do in October.

Tuesday, August 27th

I went in early for an important meeting with Roy Hattersley and Dick

* He was rebuked by *The Times* the next day for making a weak speech!

Taverne and a whole mass of officials on a very complicated issue which could be political dynamite. Ages ago, before the 1966 election, we had suggested a Bill to end the worst anomalies of unemployment benefit, including the payment of flat-rate benefit to workers who are being stood off by employers but not made redundant. It's an open scandal that in the Midlands motor-car employers can make millions by arranging to pay the wages for half the week and for the other half of the week to lay off their employees, who then receive flat-rate benefit. We wanted to stop this and we said the employer should be responsible for paying men he laid off temporarily. This morning we had an unexpected comeback from the Ministry of Labour. They said there was one area where the employer should on no account be made responsible for a lay-off, the case of men laid off not by a strike in their own works but by a strike in somebody else's works which indirectly affected their employment. If the employer was made to pay that bill he would weaken the hands of the other employers. (It was interesting that this Government's concern is mainly to back the employers against the men. It's one of the things that should worry Barbara.) In such cases the Ministry of Labour proposed that there should be payments from the redundancy fund and not from the Exchequer. The Treasury took the contrary view and said that both were evil but the lesser evil was to keep flat-rate unemployment benefits. By the end of the morning I was convinced that the Treasury was right. But what made up my mind was not the remarks of the Ministers at the meeting but the procedural case the officials presented. Proof again that on important issues Cabinet Committees work far better when officials as well as Ministers attend.

This afternoon my most important job was to talk to my new Permanent Secretary, Jarrett, about the siting of the headquarters of the merged Ministry. I had assumed that we would have the Ministers and the senior staff in John Adam Street, which is just off the Strand and which you can reach in three or four minutes, and that we'd let the mass of the officials live at Elephant and Castle. But Jarrett had discovered that John Adam Street isn't big enough to handle five Ministers and their offices and in addition all the Permanent Secretaries, Deputy Secretaries and Under-Secretaries. The choice before us was either to have a tiny headquarters staff in John Adam Street or, after all, to settle in the Elephant and Castle. I made Molly spend a couple of days measuring how long it takes at various times of the day to get from Vincent Square and from No. 10 to each of the two buildings. As I rather feared, the difference is only two or three minutes so I can't use the excuse of the time it takes to get from Elephant and Castle to a Cabinet meeting to defend having John Adam Street as our headquarters. It looks as though it's got to be Elephant and Castle.

Another vital issue we discussed was the timing of the pension plan. After my visit to Newcastle I'd insisted that we could save a whole year by speeding up the building of the computers. But they haven't even begun to construct the computers yet and anyway they're not sure that the machines can actually do all the complex tasks we are setting for them. So we're taking a very big risk in assuming they'll be ready, but meanwhile we agreed we would go ahead on the assumption that they'll be ready in 1971.

There was just time for the T.U.C. to file in. They were coming back for consultation about the position of the present pensioners when the new plan is introduced. The truth is, if you introduce a new and much better pension scheme for which everyone pays much more and from which therefore everybody draws a better pension, the people who rely on the old national insurance scheme are bound to do worse. The T.U.C. think this a fatal defect. I argued that it was unavoidable. This was the first occasion when we really did defeat the T.U.C. in argument but we didn't destroy the political effectiveness of their objection. Indeed, they demonstrated that there will be millions of present pensioners anxious to prove they're being cheated under the new national superannuation scheme and we've got to do something effective to meet that argument.[1] In the course of all these consultations I have found (it's a sad thing to have to admit) that my own personal position has been fatally undermined. I am fighting both the Ministry and the Treasury in support of a properly funded scheme. Alas, the unanswerable Treasury argument is that if we piled up millions in the fund it would only be appropriated for the existing pensioners. We must therefore really accept pay-as-you-go.[2] This is a tremendous blow to me since I must have spent twelve hours arguing with the officials and now I've been beaten by them. If my funded scheme is out I've got to find some way of making national superannuation not merely a swindle. Suddenly I realized that I need to draft the economic paper which I said that Dick Taverne should write and I therefore decided to have a quick meeting tomorrow morning with Jarrett, Lewin and the other officials at which the outline of our paper should be fixed.

Thursday, August 29th

I was down at Prescote yesterday with Janet because I had promised to complete the revision of the last chapter of *Government and the Governed*,[3] which is needed for the new edition. I am rather proud of this dear old

[1] The national superannuation scheme would require substantial increases in contributions in order to build up a fund from which future pensioners, who had built up their entitlement, could draw benefits. Existing pensioners would not be entitled to increased benefits.

[2] In real terms any pension scheme is 'pay-as-you-go'. When a funded scheme is first introduced, however, no benefits are paid to those who have not contributed to it throughout their working lives, and this affects the way in which, for example, the national debt is calculated. Mr Crossman does not make it clear whether the 'Treasury argument' concerns the public presentation of the scheme or the assessment of the appropriate rate of contributions in the early years of the new scheme. He may not have entirely appreciated the Treasury's economic argument.

[3] London: Chatto & Windus, 1938; rev. edn 1969.

school book, which I produced in 1938 and to which I've added three last chapters. The final one, closely related to the Czech crisis, is pretty good.

Then I went up to London for the big meeting with Jarrett and Lewin. It went excellently and I was able to catch the train to Preston with a good conscience. I shouldn't have caught it unless I had checked the arrangements made by my dear, silly Private Secretary, David Williams. He had booked us on a train without a restaurant car and we only got re-booked in the nick of time. We had just started dinner on the train when David told me that a friend of his, the Assistant Secretary dealing with prescription charges, was also in the restaurant car. Could she join us? She did and we had three hours of very lively discussion about all the mess on prescription charges and the exemption scheme. I said I thought it was mainly owing to the friction between the Ministry of Social Security and the Ministry of Health and the last-moment decision to alter the forms. She said this couldn't be true since she saw her opposite number every day and they exchanged all their information. 'The real thing,' she said, 'was that you people at the top changed your mind at the last moment about the refund. The Department had always assumed that the people who were exempted would have to pay their prescription charges and then get a refund and all its plans were based on this supposition.' 'But you must have known from the start that we wouldn't tolerate that?' I said. 'No,' she said. 'It was many weeks later when the instruction came down from the Ministry.' This is something else Kenneth Robinson has to answer for.

The Assistant Secretary was a very nice-looking woman, married to a Q.C., with a house in the country outside Preston. She works in London and comes to Preston for weekends (I suppose they have no children) on the Friday evening train, going back by the Sunday sleeper. Her husband does it because it's his home and he loves it. She does it because she adores being in the country. I told her about our life at Prescote and she said, 'You must make sure you live where you want to live and then shape things to suit it.' She was a lively woman, who put me off at first by blinking all the time, but she warmed up on a bit of claret and I learned a lot from her.

I won't describe my Lancashire tour in detail but I will just mention the long journey we made after lunch down to Greaves Hall Hospital, Southport, through most lovely countryside of woods and harvest fields. At the hospital there were some 700 or 800 patients, nearly all of them deeply subnormal aged from eight or nine to seventy or eighty. The doctor who took me round didn't believe in research or that anything was going to be gained by undertaking it. 'One just has to be kind to these people,' he said. 'There is really no hope of their getting any better.' So there are fifty trained nurses looking after these human wrecks whose recovery has been ruled out by the medical profession.

From there we went on to a very different place – a huge hospital built in 1837, a Dickensian public assistance institution of great red-brick blocks running up a hill. A dynamic little Jewish doctor showed me what he was doing in the geriatric ward of this ghastly old place. It used to house fifty a room. In his part they've got them down to twenty-four and what miracles they were doing in trying to make these ghastly buildings into homes. The main thing I noticed was the high quality and the shortage of the staff. They are wonderful but you can't recruit them. On one ward I asked, 'How many of you are there?' and got the reply, 'For the weekend there's me and one other for three wards.'

This evening I did my stint for the Labour Party by driving down to Manchester and doing a meeting on local government in the big art gallery. Unfortunately the council group had fixed their meeting for the same evening so that none of them could turn up. Then back to London on the night train.

Sunday, September 1st

Prescote. The ten days of fine weather are over and we're now back to the foul squally days we had at the end of July and we can begin to assess the damage it has done to the harvest this year. Though on the milk side we've got our first prize once again for the herd as well as the first prize for the best-managed farm, we're not going to make much of a profit. The farm price review gave us a 1½d. extra for milk but this has been completely cancelled out by the glut of cheese caused by the French imports.

On Amos ground, the field nearest to the village, we've got twenty-six Young Socialists camping. Coming back last night from dinner with Harry Judge,[1] the headmaster at Patrick's school, we saw the great bonfire they've made with wood off my island and they're spending this afternoon in our garden, using the swimming bath. After that they're going to have a discussion with me and I shall be interested to see what Young Socialists can make of cross-examining a Minister. Anne tells me some of them have been out to East Berlin, hiking right across Germany, and they have been telling her about the plight of the Social Democrats in Germany and how like the plight of the Labour Party it is. Of course West German politics with its multi-party system is very different from ours. The S.P.D. are required to join the grand coalition with their fiercest enemies, the C.D.U., but directly they start using power in this pragmatic way, they begin to lose the support of the Left and of the youth. I was reading this weekend a Foreign Office Green Paper which described the situation of the German Social Democrats and emphasized the sense of alienation among young people. I felt I was reading through what has happened to us. It isn't that the Left hate the Social Democrats or the Labour Government now; they've written us off. So we have the Democratic administration in the U.S.A., the Labour Government here and the Grand Coalition in Germany all written off as no longer a radical force. We have utterly disappointed those who wanted

[1] Principal of Banbury School 1967–73 and now Director of the Oxford University Department of Educational Studies.

the application of principle to politics. We have shown ourselves competent politicians, administering the country, introducing what social justice we can but not undertaking radical change. I suppose the French students and progressive workers are just as disillusioned by the events of May. On top of all this comes the collapse of liberal communism in Czechoslovakia. I've never been particularly fond of the Russians or in any way pro-communist and when I look back at the old diaries of my trips to China and Russia I realize how I hated the intellectual brutality and narrowness of the people who conducted my tours. Yet somehow I had persuaded myself over the last three or four years that a change was setting in and that with the policy of peaceful co-existence the Russians would grow more civilized. But they're exactly as bad as they ever were. True, Khrushchev did denounce Stalin in 1956 but Khrushchev himself shared all Uncle Joe's values and standards of utter contempt for the intelligentsia and genuine parliamentary democracy.

I suppose I must be thankful for small mercies. None of our speakers at the Hyde Park Rally fell into a paroxysm of anti-communist crusading, or, alternatively, pro-communist lack of criticism. We showed just about the proper balance but we did it without any élan or imagination. The attitude of the Government has shaken me, broken my heart in certain ways, and only very recently have I learnt with relief that other intelligent people share my view and my diagnosis.

Wednesday, September 4th

I heard the P.M. was back from his holidays so I sent a message asking whether he would like to see me after lunch. Sure enough, he was there waiting for me at 3 o'clock when I went through to No. 10, after a long chat with Odgers. I was taken not into the Cabinet Room but into Harold's brand-new study. I didn't much like the bare boards or the panelling but I admired his Lowry painting very much as well as his new chair and table and above all I liked the sense of his having a study where he could think alone. 'This is good,' I said. 'Yes,' he said, 'I can work here.' 'Well, why didn't you have it before? It was Churchill's room, wasn't it?' Harold said that as soon as he came into No. 10 in 1964 he gave up this study because he thought he could do all his work and his writing down in the Cabinet Room. As a result he hadn't done any writing and it's taken him four years to learn this lesson.

He asked me what I'd been doing and I said I'd been writing the revised chapters of my textbook and was really happy. He looked at me quizzically and said, 'You like writing, don't you, Dick?' I knew he was thinking that I wouldn't mind retiring and that my attention is not wholly on my job. Then we switched to the T.U.C. All this week at their Conference they've been bashing the Government,[1] defeating the prices and incomes policy by an overwhelming 7 : 1. 'Do you think we have to worry about Congress

[1] The Trades Union Congress met at Blackpool from September 2nd to September 6th.

this year?' he asked. 'You can take a detached view.' When I didn't answer straightaway, he went on, 'I think we can safely disregard them. The Government's standing with the public won't be affected by T.U.C. hostility, will it, Dick?' He wanted my support and on the whole I felt it was better to give it. But I realized for the first time that he doesn't feel himself representing the Labour movement, really caring about the trade union leaders or feeling great loyalty to the party. He cares about being P.M., about politics, about power. He has become de-partied to a great extent, an occupant of Downing Street who adores running things well, an occupant who has had his leftist loyalties battered by the roughness of relations within the party.

Very soon he got round to the subject of Callaghan. Harold's now building me up consciously as the big Minister of the Social Services who will teach Callaghan a lesson at the Home Office. Once again he told me that Callaghan was intriguing against him and trying to create a position favourable to his succession to the leadership. 'He's inordinately ambitious and inordinately weak,' said Harold. 'So weak that as Chancellor he used to weep on my shoulder and then go away and intrigue against me. That's a pretty fair analysis.' Then he turned to Tony Crosland, about whom he expressed a great deal of disappointment. 'In Cabinet,' he said, 'he very often contributes an idea but never a policy or a decision.' I found that a shrewd judgment and remarked, 'What a contrast with Roy.' 'Yes,' he said, 'but neither runs his own Department. Tony is run by the Department and if Roy isn't too it's because he has a cabal to run it for him. But at least when Roy's made a decision he sticks to it and that's why I'm thankful we've had him since devaluation. Right at the beginning,' he went on, 'I had decided in favour of Roy.' It's obvious that Harold's imagination is now rewriting history to show that he made the decision alone and no one else had any influence on him.[1]

Finally we turned to my own Ministry and I said I would like the merger to coincide with that of the Foreign and Commonwealth Office on October 17th. 'That would be O.K.,' he said, 'if Roy for some reason doesn't oppose this timing and insist on January 1st.' 'Well,' I said, 'it's much better to put the big change before Parliament when it is in session.' He liked that idea and then we went on to the name. He would like it to be called the Ministry of Social Services because Burke Trend and William Armstrong have obviously sold to him the importance of my co-ordinating function in the Cabinet Office. 'You must have your co-ordinating brains trust over here,' he said 'and spend a lot of time with it. I must arrange with Burke and Armstrong that you have a real team, including Tommy.'

It was a pretty solid discussion and it meant his relations with me were established and sensible. Not terribly intimate but on the level. He was liking having me there. He kept on saying, 'Can't you stay to tea?' and I

[1] See Vol. II.

had to say that I had to catch a train to Bristol to look at a health centre and a supplementary benefit office.

Friday, September 6th

I came up to Bristol last night, where the doctors gave me a dinner as delicious as the one I got from the doctors at Liverpool last week. It took place at Fosters, that delicious, old-fashioned place in the Archways, where Mr Clark, who is the Grand Master of the Bristol and Merchant Adventurers, had organized it with the Regional Hospital Board. At 11 o'clock we were turned out of the vaults and I went back to the Grand Hotel before making an early start this morning towards home.

Saturday, September 7th

We had Peter Shore, Barbara, Ted and Tommy all down for dinner and to stay the night and we bathed in the pool last night and before breakfast. Ted and Barbara were as charming as they always are. Barbara is a super guest for children. Tommy was back in great form and even though Peter is uneasy and lanky and unsure of himself he was all the better for his holiday in Cornwall. We sat down to a tremendous pow-wow and what came out as a central theme was Barbara's repetition that she wasn't going to run both her Department and the prices and incomes policy and incur the appalling unpopularity which went with it all if we didn't have a strategy to give us the chance of winning the election. She felt we had no chance with the present strategy and she went on to say that though the French had been through a terrible crisis they were using the strategy originally outlined by Frank Cousins, leaping ahead on expanded production, whereas we were just continuously deflating. The best answer the rest of us could give was that it isn't the strategy which is wrong but the timing. We certainly ought to look very carefully at whether there's a reasonable chance of the present strategy providing sufficient recovery to win the next election and we decided this should be our line at S.E.P. next week.

Sunday, September 8th

This afternoon Roy and Jennifer arrived with Ronnie McIntosh,[1] who had obviously been staying with Roy over the weekend. It was pleasant – nice and hot with the combines roaring away. Last night I had been able to take Barbara and Ted up to watch the combines, the trailer and the truck all clocking in together at precisely the right time. But the machines finished at exactly 1 p.m. today, so that by the time I got Roy out on to the fields I could only show him the machinery. During our walk I put to him the main

[1] Under-Secretary at the Board of Trade 1963–4 and at the D.E.A. 1964–6, Deputy Under-Secretary of State at the D.E.A. 1966–8 and Deputy Secretary at the Cabinet Office 1968–70, Deputy Under-Secretary of State at the D.E.P. 1970–2 and at the Treasury 1972–3; he has been Director-General of the National Economic Development Office since 1973. He was knighted in 1975.

points from last night's discussion. 'Of course one has a chance of winning the next election,' he said, 'and all the better because Ted Heath is so hopeless. But it's fully possible that we shan't be able to win it and anyway one's first aim must be not to get a strategy for winning the election but to get the economy straight.' He was very aloof and very negative on all this.

I learnt quite a lot about him by watching the Jenkins family's behaviour round the swimming bath. Directly they got into the walled garden, they took things over and organized competitions among themselves on speed records and underwater swimming. I realized that Roy is one of the most competitive men in the world, setting himself trials and trying to win everything. In this sense he is a caricature of a public school boy, and he loses his attraction unless he is fully clothed. But the main thing I noticed was the difference between the casual easiness and rightness of my relations with Barbara, Ted, Peter and Tommy and the stiffness of my relations with Roy. His is a life of social ambition and tremendous ambition for himself. He doesn't believe in working hard and indeed he's obviously indolent. He told me that he does do six hours' work on Saturday and Sunday but very little on his red boxes throughout the week. One feels that his career has been made by knowing the right people. My conclusion as they drove away is that we have no common life and I don't think his life at East Hendred and ours at Prescote cross over a great deal.

Monday, September 9th

A mildly naughty feeling because I've stayed here instead of going to London. It's been a delicious September day. I got up at 7.15 and it was still grey and cloudy but by the time I'd done my forty lengths in the bath the sunshine was breaking through. Patrick and Virginia went to school, a real schoolboy and a real schoolgirl, Patrick in his blue blazer and blue and white striped tie, vainly trying to look tidy, and Virginia beautifully neat with her satchel.

Today I had to deal with the row which has burst out about Crossman's clanger about scroungers. When I visited Bristol last Thursday I had a press conference and as there was really nothing to give the journalists I found myself discussing voluntary unemployment. Next day the *Daily Mail* had a great front-page story, saying that I had claimed that a man who was content to idle about on his state benefit was behaving perfectly justifiably. There was also a little story in the *Telegraph*, borrowed from the *Mail*, and one in the *Sun* which was quite fair to me. I had some talk on Friday with Peter Oglesby and we decided to leave well alone. I'm not sure we were wise because on Saturday there was a leading article in the *Telegraph* and the *Mail* was still gunning. Yesterday there came a tremendous front-page story in the *Sunday Telegraph* about Judith Hart's hostile reaction to my remarks. Fortunately I'd been rung up on Saturday by the B.B.C. and I very cordially agreed to do an interview for Sunday lunchtime to clear the matter up.

Today the press campaign is still going on. The *Mail* has an article on Crossman's clanger and *The Times* makes me the second half of a big story. This evening Judith Hart rang me up from Stoke-on-Trent. The *Sunday Telegraph* story was, as I guessed, a complete invention. The Harts had arrived home a day early because they'd driven so fast across Europe and they'd spent Saturday unpacking and relaxing at home. On the Sunday morning Tony had brought Judith in a cup of tea and the *Sunday Telegraph* and she saw this outrageous headline. Although she had made no contact with any journalist all this had been attributed to her. Anne says we should appeal to the Press Council but I am more tempted to write a letter to Michael Berry.[1] In fact I shall do nothing at all, the incident is over. A Minister has been assaulted and in a flat season slightly damaged but I think we regained most of the lost ground by yesterday's B.B.C. interview. There's one other advantage too – the idea of the social danger of the narrow gap between low wages and social security payments has had a jolly good airing.

The other story in today's papers is the news from Basle that the sterling balances and sterling creditors are in future to be helped by a special fund, supplied for the next ten years by our fellow I.M.F. members.[2] Alas, it means that we're in the hands of the bankers more than ever before but it also means that we've started winding up the sterling area. We can add this positive advance to the scrapping of the T.S.R.2, the abolition of the F-111, the destruction of our position east of Suez – all things which Roy and I have believed in from the start but which Harold, George and Jim have steadily fought against.

I was able to look at the press cuttings in the other papers. Not a single paper, apart from the *Mail*, printed anything to support the *Sunday Telegraph* story but just one journalist, choosing the right moment, can still stick something on a Minister. It makes no difference that eight other stories give a fair account of what I said. Only the dramatic, unfair account hits the headlines and is remembered. It's something every Minister must bear in mind and it's no good complaining; it's bound to happen sometimes. I have also noticed that the weekly periodicals, the *New Statesman*, *New Society*, *Tribune*, all come out on my side. Nevertheless 95 per cent of the public will now think how terrible it was that I should have said such a monstrous thing.

Tuesday, September 10th

My main job was to prepare the big paper we are drawing up for our confrontation with the Treasury on the economic background to our pensions scheme. There were the usual gang in my room, Brian Abel-Smith, who has

[1] Chairman and Editor-in-Chief of the *Daily Telegraph* and the *Sunday Telegraph*. He was Chairman of Amalgamated Press Ltd 1954–9 and became a life peer in 1968, taking the title of Lord Hartwell.

[2] The agreement, reached by the Governors of the twelve Central Banks on July 8th, was formally signed on September 9th. See above, p. 122.

now got a room in John Adam Street and is very happy there, Theo, Tommy's assistant, Thomas himself and Nicky Kaldor, breezing in from his holiday – a retinue of economic advisers plus the officials in charge. Before this big paper goes up to Cabinet via the Social Services Cabinet Committee I have to sell it privately to the Chancellor and the P.M. I hope to God I shall be able to pull it off.

I had a visit late in the afternoon from William Armstrong about the progress on the merger. He had of course heard about my talk with the P.M. and told me that Harold had said no instructions should be issued until I had talked to Armstrong. They had both agreed that my title should be Secretary of State for the Social Services. The Ministry is to be called the Department of Health and Social Security, so I shall have one title as Secretary and another as departmental Minister. The merger will take place on October 16th or 17th and the debate on the Affirmative Order creating the new Department on the 22nd. But the P.M. had once again emphasized that he wouldn't make the announcement on the 16th or 17th and William Armstrong is pretty sure he'll make it during the Tory Party Conference week.[1] 'Oh, God,' I said, 'that's the week I'm due to go to Sweden to study their pension scheme.' So we are moving ahead under the careful control of the P.M. who has also agreed that we must have the headquarters at Elephant and Castle, but that I must also have a suite of offices in the Cabinet Office for co-ordination purposes and a brains trust. There's no doubt that the Government and Whitehall are deeply committed to the merger and after this talk with William today I knew I could sit back for an easy life of relaxation before the strain of the enormous new job I shall be doing.

Wednesday, September 11th

For weeks we have done nothing about House of Lords' reform but over the weekend Eddie Shackleton sent me another redraft of the White Paper in preparation for a meeting with him and Gerald Gardiner this morning. The truth, if I admit it, is that I have lost interest in this. I find it frightfully difficult to concentrate on things unless I am personally doing something about them. I am sorry to say that I hardly glanced at the draft White Paper at Prescote, though I noticed that it had been drastically changed and that even more of my draft had been omitted. What does that matter? Mine was an early draft and conditions change. However, what Eddie and Gerald wanted to discuss was tactics. Fortunately, when he was lunching with me this week Roy said that he now hoped we could get on with Lords' reform quietly and resume the talks, so I knew he was solidly on our side. I know that Michael Stewart is still solidly for our tactic, and I know the P.M. is still with us. The real opposition is from a combination of two very disparate but powerful forces, Fred Peart and Barbara Castle. Not John Silkin, though he is against the reform, because when the P.M. cracks the whip he can be

[1] To be held in Blackpool October 9th–12th.

relied on to do what he's told, despite the opposition of Freddie Warren. Strangely, Freddie is fanatically against the plan, maybe because he wasn't consulted. Fred Peart is against it because he dislikes all reform as he dislikes all devolution and most progressive things, and Barbara's against it because she's a fanatical socialist who has always been opposed to second chambers.

At this meeting we worked out three tactical possibilities. One: we could go ahead on a new plan of our own, changing the scheme to our satisfaction. Two: we could resume the all-party talks in the hope of getting the plan agreed. Three: we could push the agreed scheme through without resuming the talks. We all knew that if the Tory peers were to try to oppose the Transport Bill these options would no longer be open and we would have to go back to a new scheme of our own.

The timing is also very awkward because whatever happens a statement has got to go into the Queen's Speech so the decision has to be taken in a matter of days. I made the point that we must talk to Harold and the P.M. responded to the idea very speedily. At 3.30 we were ushered into his little upstairs study. In the few hours since our meeting this morning he must have read the papers over lunch and grasped every detail, as well as reviving his interest and making up his mind. On tactics our Prime Minister is always alert, quick, decisive. He decided on the third course, which none of us had much liked, of going ahead without resuming talks and within ten minutes he had convinced me that tactically this was correct. 'If you ask Cabinet's permission to resume the talks, you will split it wide open,' he said, 'and give a handle to Fred Peart and Barbara Castle and also to John Silkin, who will report on the appalling divisions in the Parliamentary Party. No, don't resume talks and don't try to have a new Bill with new ideas. We must have the agreed plan and present it as our own.'

I think he believes he has found a device for resuming talks without officially having a Cabinet decision. He wants us to prepare the White Paper and the Bill and then at the critical moment to summon the Tories and show them what we have done and say that we would have liked to talk to them but we couldn't. Then if they should say, 'Let's talk about these documents,' I've no doubt he would let us. If that is his tactic he didn't say so but it's most ingenious and I have recorded this in full to show one of his main qualities as a politician. It isn't deviousness, just a clever understanding of how to get something through Cabinet with the minimum trouble.

Ironically a meeting had been laid on this afternoon between Barbara and me on the subject of the abuse of social security benefits on which I had gaffed at Bristol. I found it a bit awkward. Barbara took advantage of my plight in a friendly way and said it wasn't a subject we wanted to air. This is a very characteristic difference between us. When a subject interests me I want to air it (I am an old don in that sense) but she will say, 'Don't talk about it just for the sake of airing it. Talk about it when you are ready to do something.' So she said firmly, 'No speeches', and then went on to outline what she would say if she were driven to make a speech on the topic. I came to the conclusion that what she was telling me was that this was something she could handle if the right moment occurred at Conference. It is my kind of topic, she was saying. You, Dick, would handle it just wrong. I suspect she was quite right.

It was nice to have my economic advisers, Abel-Smith and Tommy, at the meeting. I think they are beginning to enjoy themselves. Brian, I know, was anxious whether there would be enough for him to do. He has suddenly found that there is plenty on his plate, and Thomas and Theo also have a lot to get on with.

This evening Anne and I went to *Rheingold* where we were in *The Times* box again. I would have liked to see the whole cycle through and particularly the *Valkyrie* which is coming tomorrow. I was sitting right above the stage, facing across to the woodwind which were all massed on the left of the conductor, and I had a magnificent view. I found the production very stiff indeed and the libretto, which I had studied beforehand, unintelligible. Yet you have to read it because the music and the words are so wonderfully fitted together. It ended early and I was able to get home at a reasonable time.

Thursday, September 12th

An enormous S.E.P. with a vast agenda of which we only got through the first half, three items of great political importance. First of all, Millom. I have described the battle about the placing of the Leyland bus factory in Cumberland but I haven't mentioned that while we were on holiday this summer at Loweswater a delegation from West Cumberland came to talk to me about the closure of the iron ore works near by, which will knock the little town of Millom clean out. When I first heard this I thought that government help could possibly come from Donald Stokes's concern but Millom is too far away from Barrow-in-Furness for this. We had a long debate on whether we should declare it a special development area but many of us felt that this wasn't really appropriate. Roy Mason pointed out that the proper cure for Millom is to move the ironworkers down to Corby or Scunthorpe where there are hundreds of jobs. Of course people won't leave their owner-occupied houses if there are rumours of work being brought to Millom. It was the usual line-up, Roy Jenkins, Tony Crosland, Roy Mason and myself on one side and everybody else backing Harold and Fred Peart on the other.

Item two was the General Electric Company/English Electric merger, which has suddenly been announced. Tony Crosland warned us that we should sanction it without reference to the Monopolies Commission, arguing that any reference would take six months and hold up development at a critical stage. He concluded that the merger would certainly have to be approved in the end. It sounds convincing; nevertheless, by failing to refer it we make nonsense of the Monopolies Commission, which was established in 1948, as some people forgot when they made their remarks, by a young

President of the Board of Trade called Harold Wilson.[1] Tony Benn brought out the real objection when he said that in the announcement the firms were making they had given the Government a very minor role, merely asking for our opinion. What made it even worse was that the I.R.C., our own creation, had taken a quick look and given it full support. In this instance the Government was pushed aside in the creation of a vast concentration of power which will enable these industrialists to free themselves from accountability to the public.

Barbara was the only person who provided constructive opposition. She said that if we are to make nonsense of the Monopolies Commission then we should at all costs have a continuing reference to the Prices and Incomes Board. That would be an extension of the P.I.B.'s powers but at least it's our creation and our instrument and unless we have some instrument for continuous review of these industries we are surrendering power to an irresponsible financial oligarchy. I had been rung up by Tommy in high concern early this morning and I supported Barbara as strongly as I could. But it was really no good. The P.M., Roy Jenkins, Tony Crosland and Wedgy Benn were all determined to let this go through without even the pretence of a fight.

The third political item was Short's of Belfast. Since we last discussed it we had asked a commercial consultancy to advise us on the problem and they had come to the conclusion that for social and political reasons more subsidies had to be given. Thank God the P.M. said straightaway that we hadn't asked this firm of accountants to advise us on our social and political duties but on the strictly commercial side, where they admit that the firm has no future. Why should we pay vast sums to a firm in Belfast? What good do we get out of the twelve Ulster M.P.s? What social results do we achieve by pouring into Belfast money which we deny to Millom or the North-East coast? Then (he was in great form) Harold evolved an ingenious scheme under which we would say to the Government of Northern Ireland, 'We're going to stop the subsidies to Short's and you can take the firm over.' At once it was pointed out that if we did this they would still get the subsidies from us because of the way Northern Irish finances relate to U.K. finances. At this point I said, 'I am an ignoramus; may I be told what is the exact financial arrangement?' Nobody could say. Neither Jack Diamond nor the Chancellor knew the formula according to which the Northern Ireland Government gets its money. In all these years it has never been revealed to the politicians and I am longing to see whether now we shall get to the bottom of this very large, expensive secret.

This afternoon I set out for Sheffield where a group of G.P.s had asked me to dinner, before I start an official tour tomorrow. It was a very hot day up there – they are always getting better weather than we get in the South.

[1] Harold Wilson was President of the Board of Trade 1947–51. The Monopolies and Restrictive Practices Commission (as it was called until 1956) was established in 1948.

On arrival I was driven off in an enormous Austin Princess to our headquarters at Nottingham. My destination was the new Hallam Tower Hotel, a skyscraper standing on top of one of the hills outside Sheffield with a magnificent view over the great new housing estates. From the hillside, now that a smokeless zone has been created in the centre of the city, Sheffield really is worth seeing, and the hotel was splendid. As a nation we don't recognize our genuine achievements like the reconstruction of Sheffield. It's something we ought to be proud of, something which would get us out of the inferiority complex and defeatism which is now the prevailing mood of this country.

Friday, September 13th

This morning I had to visit mentally deficient children in hospital, a thing I seem to do every weekend. I saw ghastly wards where the children have no communication with the outside world and nothing can be done for them but keep their bodies alive. Here I saw a lot of other mental deficients, mongols for example, who can be taught a very great deal and enabled to live at home and have a useful life. It's wonderful work but it still depresses me to see it in action.

At midday I had a long talk with the administrators of the Regional Hospital Board. In 1946 we set up a vast new Civil Service consisting largely of untrained amateurs mostly derived from the voluntary hospitals, where the former Secretary as often as not became the Secretary of the Hospital Management Committee or even of the Regional Hospital Board. Since each R.H.B. has £20 or £30 million a year to spend it is important to get really efficient administration, and they are struggling to do so, against a great deal of opposition from the consultants who are suspicious of the professional administrator and who fear that he will deny them the freedom they enjoy at present. Doctors seem to me very difficult mavericks. They behave a bit like dons at universities (though dons are a good deal more cunning). They will take some dealing with when I really get to grips with the reorganization of the Health Service.

In Sheffield the Labour majority has been ended after forty years and I went to the Town Hall to visit the Labour Mayor who survives in the Tory administration. We had a pleasant chat together before they popped me off in my own official car down the M1 to get me home in two and a quarter hours. It was a beautiful evening and what did I see behind the island? A huge fire burning, and I knew they were burning the stubble. Patrick and I rushed out there to see it. It was just sunset and there was time to run with a burning torch from stubble line to stubble line, catching each alight and setting it aflame. For some reason our poodle Suki, who is terrified of water, isn't afraid of fire. Patrick and I stayed on after the Pritchetts had gone home and we stirred the fire with our torches in a most exciting way. I kept on thinking, 'I would have loved this as a boy, and this is Patrick's home life.'

Saturday, September 14th

I had a job to do for the farm today. The *Farmer and Stockbreeder*, one of the better agricultural papers, wanted an illustrated story about Prescote and two men duly turned up, one from a new independent agency at Banbury and the other a London photographer. Within a minute or two it was clear that they wanted a story about how I breeze down on Saturday, live in a lovely house and do nothing about the farm. It was pretty important to kill that so I took them round the farm for two hours and then got Pritchett in to discuss what we had done in the thirteen years since he arrived here. If they would only tell the true story it would be all right.

Monday, September 16th

I had decided to take it easy and go up by the afternoon train. This morning, though, I came in for my first serious tiff with Albert Rose, the Secretary of my constituency party. He is a retiring person, who doesn't make life easy for his colleagues in the constituency, but he has always been absolutely loyal to me and I was very surprised when he rang me up, wild with indignation. Could I explain how Tony Greenwood, after seeing a delegation from the Coventry Council last week, had come to give the Tories an extra month before they had to reduce their rents?

I hadn't heard about the incident, but to Albert this was the last straw in his relations with the Labour Government. He just couldn't take something which made nonsense of the whole Labour movement. He finally said, 'The Government is betraying us and you must come and explain yourself to a meeting of the G.M.C. this week.' He has never suggested this before, even when I have had the gravest disagreements with the Party, and he wasn't in the faintest degree interested in my difficulties with my remark about scroungers. What mattered was the postponement by a month of the lowering of Coventry's council rents. I couldn't help feeling that he had got the affair out of all proportion and I was as sharp with him as he was sharp with me. But there are limits to what a Cabinet Minister can do about a local housing problem when somebody else is Minister of Housing. I expect that Greenwood gave the month's delay to the Coventry delegation without any thought at all. They no doubt complained that they wouldn't have time to get the agenda through the Housing Committee in time for the October meeting (which I am sure wasn't true) and so he humoured them in a way which infuriated his own side.

The tiff with Albert greatly disturbed me but it didn't counterbalance my cheerfulness about an article in yesterday's *Sunday Times* about my clanger. I had accepted an invitation to lunch from Harold Evans last week and I had discussed my problems in great detail in a pretty lighthearted way, without abusing the press too much.[1] Little did I know that as a result Harold Evans would send down to Bristol, discover that a transcript of the press

[1] Editor of the *Sunday Times* since 1967.

conference existed and check that I was right in my account of what I had said and the *Daily Mail* was wrong. So yesterday I had the pleasure of seeing a prominent article stating that I had been grossly misrepresented.

I went up to London today only because I had gathered my whole working party of officials and experts to make our final decisions on the paper we will present to the Chancellor and the P.M., before putting it through the usual Whitehall mill. The trouble about the draft was that at the last moment it had suddenly been changed by our economic advisers and I certainly hadn't grasped the difference between edition one and edition two. Indeed, this only came out when, on quite a minor point, Brian admitted that while drafting they had come upon a Treasury paper, based on statements of the Government Actuary,[1] giving the impact of the plan upon private pension schemes. The Actuary's calculation was that the plan would cause a closure of 25 per cent of the private schemes and that each year we would be cutting them back still further. We were floored. So I said, 'Get hold of this fellow, whoever he is. Bring him back on Wednesday. We must find out what's wrong.' Nicky Kaldor was there and was very helpful. Afterwards Nicky, Tommy, Judith and I stayed behind drinking, and then I took Nicky off for a good dinner at the Garrick. As a Treasury adviser he is from the enemy camp and his influence there can be decisive.

Tuesday, September 17th

At our first Defence Committee since the holidays we were back on the old topic of aid to Greece. In addition to the talk about hooking a big arms contract (which was still purely talk) we were told that we were going to continue to give £1 million of aid from the Overseas Development Fund. Reg Prentice, a rather prim young man from the T.&.G., came along to say that his Ministry didn't think we ought to give the Greek dictators aid and he wanted the money to be lent to them as a commercial transaction, to which Michael Stewart replied that this would be quite impossible because it would be regarded as extremely offensive. In came the President of the Board of Trade and revealed that the Colonels had been promised this aid two months ago. Once again I barged in with remarks about Foreign Office hypocrisy but Jim Callaghan did better than me and said he didn't see why it should be done in the form of aid and asked what was wrong with a loan. The Foreign Secretary couldn't explain, but of course the Wilson/Jenkins/Crosland side won.

The only other item was Nigeria where the Federal forces may have nearly won the war and we face the possibility of having to contribute to a Commonwealth peace-keeping force.[2] Whatever happens we must in my view be ready

[1] Sir Herbert Tetley (K.B.E. 1975), Government Actuary 1958–73 and Chairman of the Civil Service Insurance Society 1961–73.

[1] The Federal forces had made substantial gains, capturing Port Harcourt on May 19th, and Aba and Owerri on September 4th and 16th. Though the Biafrans had now lost some 80 per cent of their territory they continued to resist, and their leader, Colonel Ojukwu,

to supply aid to Nigeria on a big scale. But Jenkins took a tough line. 'There may have to be aid,' he said, 'but it can't come out of my budget; it must come out of the budget of Overseas Development or Commonwealth Affairs.' We spent half an hour arguing how it should be paid for in Whitehall. This is the degree to which the I.M.F. and the bankers dominate our thinking. We have to satisfy them by cutting back public expenditure and seeing that if there is any extra expenditure the money is made available by a cut in a departmental budget.

This evening off I went with Anne to see *Fiddler on the Roof* at Her Majesty's Theatre, a musical comedy about Jewish life in the Russian pale before the pogroms. A strange subject for a musical comedy but wonderfully acted. Everybody on the stage was a character. By the end you personally knew the butcher, the rabbi, the cobbler, the tailor and each of the three daughters of our dear friend the milkman. I felt a little soporific in the first part but it was a wonderful evening, which we ended as we sometimes do with a dinner at Prunier a few streets away. Madame Prunier still loves me because I left my documents there.[1]

Wednesday, September 18th

This afternoon I personally conducted the cross-examination of the Government Actuary. I really put him through it and finally drove him to admit that there was no firm basis for calculating the effect of a government scheme upon private pensions, and that no expert ought ever to say more than that the estimate he makes is 'a guess which shouldn't be dignified with the name of a calculation'. Having admitted this, he knew very well that he would have to provide some figures so the main thing is to get the figures agreed between him and the Treasury and approved by my bunch of experts.

No one has dared to use this paper again in our discussions, yet it's interesting that it had become sacred law because the figures had been incorporated in a paper handed over to the Treasury. Like other officials, the Treasury men aren't really interested in factual analysis but in getting facts and calculations which can be used in argument. Once a so-called fact gets into the system it's almost impossible to prove that it's wrong or out of date and should be dropped.

---

still attempted to seek international assistance for his ill-equipped forces and starving people. In June the French Government had banned arms sales to either side but many claimed that France was involved in the arms deliveries that, in late September, helped to stiffen Biafran resistance. Meanwhile at the September summit of the Organization of African Unity Nigeria was offered more arms. On the initiative of the Commonwealth Secretariat, talks were held in London, Uganda, Niger and Ethiopia but they all foundered on the incompatibility of the Biafrans' wish for self-determination with the Federalists' plan for twelve Nigerian states. The Nigerians would not allow the introduction of a peace-keeping force that might protect the secessionists and both sides were suspicious of international attempts to bring in airlifts of food and supplies.

[1] See Vol. I, pp. 216–18, 223, 226.

All this week I have spent my time rallying round me my unusual gang of experts, some in the Treasury, some in my own and some in the Actuary's Department, some dons at university, getting them to work together as a team. It will be a tremendous achievement if we can get an agreed paper by Friday.

After this we had the usual committee of high-level Ministers to approve the Prorogation speech and consider the draft Queen's Speech for the next session.[1] I mentioned that when I saw the Queen just after her last Speech she told me how physically difficult it was to give any sense to some of the phrases concocted by civil servants for her to read aloud. I suggested that this time we should make an effort to write the Speech in such a way that it could be read aloud and sound reasonably sensible. There is no mention of this, of course, in the minutes but I think what I said had quite an effect. Certainly all the Ministers want to help as much as they can but the civil servants get the last word because they can insist on the vital importance of the right legal phraseology.

From there to the Parliamentary Committee. The first item concerned the response which should be made to an invitation from M. Monnet that we should join his European Action Committee, which consists of leading Europeans like Willy Brandt.[2] They would like Harold Wilson and Michael Stewart from England, and Michael proposed that we should join as a Government and then tell the Parliamentary Party and ask for its approval. Fred Peart blew his top. He saw a Common Market plot, and indeed there was one, to get a little extra pressure in favour of the Market. But the meeting soon relapsed into another of our interminable discussions about the party constitution. If the invitation were given to the Parliamentary Party it must go to Douglas Houghton and it was by no means certain that the Parliamentary Party would recommend the Foreign Secretary or the Prime Minister as our representatives. On the other hand the invitation might go to the N.E.C., which might appoint two trade union members to the Committee. It sounds fantastic but it's uncertain whether the N.E.C. or the Parliamentary Party would select either Harold Wilson or Stewart as its representative on such a body. Harold finally said the invitation had better come to him and he would then put it to the N.E.C. because the P.L.P. should be kept out of it.

As the meeting was breaking up there was a discussion about Conference at Blackpool and Fred Peart asked me when I was going.[3] I replied, 'I'm not going at all. I'm off the N.E.C. now and I have no obligation to be there.'

[1] The House was to meet on October 25th to hear the Queen's Speech reviewing the session of Parliament that had opened on October 31st, 1967, and proroguing Parliament until the new session opened on October 30th.

[2] Jean Monnet was President of the European Coal and Steel Community 1952–5 and, as Chairman of the Action Committee for the United States of Europe 1956–75, the virtual founder of the E.E.C. Willy Brandt was Governing Mayor of West Berlin 1957–66, Chairman of the Social Democratic Party (S.P.D.) of the Federal Republic of Germany 1964–74, Vice-Chancellor and Foreign Minister 1966–9 and Chancellor 1969–74.

[3] The Labour Party Conference met from September 30th to October 4th.

'But,' he said, 'we all go.' I said, 'Do you think, after fourteen years of sitting on the platform and speaking for the Executive, I am going to sit about on the floor and have no part to play?' I turned to Harold and said, 'Do you think I must go?' He looked a bit embarrassed. 'I think you ought to put in an appearance,' he said. I am going to Manchester anyway to see hospitals there so I shall go up by the night train, spend Thursday at Blackpool, and get off in the late afternoon to Manchester.

This afternoon Terry Pitt came to see me about devolution.[1] He had got all his ideas from Callaghan, the Party Treasurer, who is now going to make the Conference speech on the machinery of government which I would naturally have made if I had been on the Executive, and who wants to recommend a Royal Commission on Home Rule. That's the stalest idea one can think of. We have had Royal Commissions on devolution *ad nauseam*. I spent a lot of time trying to persuade Terry and now I suppose I must try to persuade Jim that this isn't really good enough. The whole attempt to get moving on devolution has been a ghastly failure because Harold has no sureness of touch. He doesn't understand either devolution or nationalism because he is basically an economist and a manager who sees things in terms of economic problems and for whom anything non-economic is either foreign policy, nuclear weapons, etc., but not nationalist movements among people in this country.

Thursday, September 19th

Things are looking up this week. Good trade figures have been followed by surprisingly good unemployment figures.[2] This means that the secret emergency plans for import controls have been postponed again. We have squeezed through the danger months of August and September and we now have the Basle Agreement to sustain the pound. True, poor Barbara is faced with absolute chaos in the motor-car industry, a rash of unofficial strikes and manufacturers bitterly complaining of the loss of some £70 million of exports but this other news is a great deal better.

At S.E.P. we continued the subjects from last week. We agreed on the Prime Minister's initiative to give Millom the title of a Special Development Area and having got the symbol, he conceded that the main cure was to remove people to Scunthorpe and Corby, as there was no future for the area. So we got that problem out of the way.

On Short Bros Roy had taken tremendous trouble. He had a special paper on the relation between British and Northern Irish finances and on the basis of this he made a very ingenious proposal that the Northern Ireland government should be persuaded to allocate £2 million, from a reserve fund for

[1] Terry Pitt, Head of the Labour Party Research Department 1965–74, was Special Adviser to the Lord President of the Council 1974.

[2] The (seasonally adjusted) trade deficit fell from £81 million in July to £28 million in August, rising again in September to £33 million. In August unemployment stood at 561,382 (2·4 per cent) and by early September it had fallen to 547,383 (2·3 per cent).

industrial development, to paying Short's latest deficit. Meanwhile secret negotiations should go on to try to get them to take greater responsibility for this firm. It was a perfectly sensible practical solution. When Roy wants to he takes trouble. This morning he was really briefed from top to bottom and got exactly what he wanted.

His paper argued that there was parity in the help given to social services in this country and in Northern Ireland. But there were cases where money was given to make up the leeway, for example on roads. I said this was not parity. If you say that Northern Ireland is a Development Area, treated like any Development Area in the United Kingdom, that's one thing. But if Northern Ireland is getting better than parity in roads it's getting something better than Cumberland and Durham. Why? I was able to insist that we should have a paper showing the areas where something better than parity is conceded to the Province.

After S.E.P. I had to spend a lot of money on a lunch over which Eddie Shackleton and I were to sell to Fred Peart our tactic on Lords' reform. It is quite easy to butter him up and he seemed to agree that we should complete the work on the White Paper and the Bill and then wait to see whether the Tory peers behave properly on the Transport Bill. If they do, we can show them our finished product, ask them what they think of it and, if they want talks, engage in discussions at that point. I put to Fred this version of Harold's proposal, as I had put it yesterday to John Silkin, who had already heard it from the P.M. and accepted it equally easily.

This afternoon I had a splendid meeting of my Pensions Committee, with two hours of highly technical argument about the details of the transition period. Then I had to get back to my own office where Alan Marre was due to see me. I had been told that he wanted to retain this year the traditional Christmas cocktail party for fifty people from the Health Service and fifty from the Ministry. I said I didn't want it done this way because I want to demonstrate that the two departments are merged. I thought he had better come along and talk to me about it. He is a very attractive, amiable man and we didn't take long to reach a sensible compromise. He would ask ten extra guests, including Judith and me and our spouses. He would ask Jarrett and the head of the Supplementary Benefits Commission, so we would spread the party over both sides of the Ministry. We will precede it by a general entertainment for the merged Ministry which I will give at the end of November.

I started talking to him about the merger and our plans for the timetable and I suddenly realized that there is an express injunction by the P.M. and Armstrong that Jarrett and Marre should not be told. Luckily Marre is still at the D.E.P. where there is nobody for him to talk to. With this kind of secrecy, it is difficult to remember who knows and who doesn't.

Friday, September 20th

I spent the day in Oxford on an official tour of inspection. My first visit was to the main social security office, where I was surprised to learn that the most interesting effect of the University had been to increase drug addiction. 'It is brought in by the women who come down from the North to consort with these young men,' I was told. 'They are a strange lot; if they marry as students and can't get a wife's allowance from their own local authority they come to us for supplementary benefit and for their children as well.' Oxford has changed a good deal since I was a councillor.[1]

Then another change, this time a good one. I went across to Littlemore. God, I remember Littlemore. I went there once when I was a councillor. It was a Dickensian nightmare of huge great shadowy halls, with about 150 people in each. As you came in they crowded round you, women with their grey hair in disorder and long nails. It was a kind of nightmare madhouse. Now all that's gone. They told me that all the padded cells have disappeared and they have also removed the terrible haunting sense by giving these long rooms new paint and curtains and by partitioning them as far as possible. They have also removed the great wall which surrounded the asylum and the inmates are allowed to go to the pub at Littlemore, with, I should guess, some resistance from the local inhabitants. This revolution has been carried out in the last twelve years by a European Jew called Dr Mandelbrote. One finds these adventurous things in modern medicine and it strikes me how reckless doctors are allowed to be and what enormous risks they are allowed to take. Walking round with the Chairman of the R.H.B., the great Dame Isabel,[2] I asked whether Mandelbrote does all this on his own. 'No, it's with our full sanction,' she said, but I knew very well that he had got a team together and they had driven ahead and I wasn't the least surprised to learn that what he was doing at Littlemore had already produced intense opposition from most of the doctors. Mandelbrote is in a minority but he is able to make these tremendous changes.

Later in the day I went to the geriatric hospital at Cowley, which had been attacked so savagely in Mrs Robb's book *Sans Everything* and defended in a rather half-hearted way in Kenneth Robinson's White Paper. There I met another tremendously energetic, dynamic Central European doctor, who is convinced that the thing to do with old people is to get them out of bed and keep them moving. He has stimulated the nurses to shove the old people and only let the acute cases stay in bed. Everybody else must be outside. It's a fine idea but it obviously requires much higher quality staff than most of these huge old geriatric hospitals possess. If you take second-rate nurses and encourage them to push the old people around there will be slappings and cruelties as well, and some of this had apparently happened here. I went round with the woman who is in charge of staff problems, who told me that

[1] Crossman was leader of the Labour Group on Oxford City Council 1934–40.

[2] Dame Isabel Graham Bryce, Vice-Chairman of the Association of Hospital Management Committees 1953–5, was Chairman of the Oxford Regional Hospital Board 1963–72 and of the National Nursing Staff Committee 1969–75.

the staff in both these hospitals hate the doctors because they make the work infinitely more difficult. It is much easier to have old people lying quietly, dying in bed. If they are all freely wandering around there is far more anxiety to the work of caring for them. Is it possible ever to get staff capable of carrying out the new ideas, the revolution in geriatric care? That's what was worrying me as I left.

Sunday, September 22nd

Yesterday the wind blew in the right direction so that the leaves of the white poplars along the Cherwell turned to silver in the sun and all day there was a brilliant blue sky. We pulled the cover off the top of the bath and the heat steamed up out of it. It was magnificent. Christopher and Venice Barry came over with two of their children and the Pritchetts came down to bathe as well.[1] It was a splendid party. Meanwhile I was talking to Chris about my Granada lecture on 'Television and Politics'. I have got my ideas pretty clear but I want to check with the literature. If Chris is right there are only about two really useful books. I went over to see David Butler in the evening and he admitted that there was practically nothing on the subject. So I shall be able to go ahead and produce quite a controversial, striking lecture without making a fool of myself.

Today we are expecting Pen and Tommy for lunch, and after that John Nicholson,[2] the economist from the old Ministry of Social Security. Then Canon Verney from Coventry is arriving with a Greek patriot and finally Charity Loveday brings her daughter Claire to supper from Williamscot.[3] Quite a day! Anne does have tremendous work at the weekend. Things aren't so bad mid-week because both Patrick and Virginia have settled down to lunching at school but it's difficult to limit the weekend entertainment and Anne is so conscientious that she does all the cooking completely on her own and finds it difficult to get helpers for the washing up. So entertaining is becoming quite a chore, but an enjoyable chore.

Monday, September 23rd

We started with a big S.E.P. on the Winter Relief Programme. Last winter we spent about £32 million on relief works, mostly road building, to try to mop up unemployment, at a cost of about £6,000 a job. It was proposed that we should have another programme this winter and we were offered three possibilities, the cheapest £10 million, the second £21 million and the third £32 million. Peter told me afterwards that the assumption was that the middle programme would be accepted. These programmes are the most total waste

[1] Venice Barry was Crossman's stepdaughter, Christopher her husband.

[2] Chief Economic Adviser to the D.H.S.S. since 1968 and 1972–4 Associate Professor of Quantitative Economics at Brunel University.

[3] Canon Stephen Verney, Vicar of Leamington Hastings and Diocesan Missioner of the Diocese of Coventry 1958–64, was a Canon Residentiary of Coventry Cathedral 1964–70 and since 1970 has been a Canon of Windsor.

of money. We spend weeks in the summer cutting our essential social service programmes, including roads and school-building, and two months later we put back £21 million into inessential roads and minor works in the schools in order to stop the unemployment which we created by cutting back. It's too silly for words and it was clear today that Roy thought so too. What was fascinating was that nobody dared say so. Sheer fear of unemployment rising to 2·5 during the course of the winter was enough to drive people like Tony Crosland to O.K. this nonsense. Of course it was also supported by the Secretaries of State for Wales and Scotland and, as far as he possibly could, by Harold Wilson.

But fortunately two things happened. We had taken the Winter Relief Programme in conjunction with the enormous Post Office capital investment programme for the next three years. Mr Stonehouse put forward his departmental paper indicating that the proposed cut in the Post Office telephone programme would have a disastrous influence on employment prospects, expecially in the Development Areas where many of the new telephones are being provided. He made his point and the cut was abandoned.

Next came Wedgy Benn with the proposition that we should build the next nuclear-powered submarine at Barrow-in-Furness, thereby creating 1,400 jobs in the North-West at far smaller cost than the Winter Relief Programme would require. That turned the scale. Everyone round the table knew that we should have to let him have the money for this proposal, and we couldn't afford both the Barrow-in-Furness scheme and the £32 million. So at this point it was assumed that this winter we should do Barrow and the £21 million programme. Then I weighed in and said, 'This is an absolute nonsense. These Winter Programmes are pure politics and this winter is not the time when we win or lose the election. We ought to have a strategy worked out from now until the election in October 1970 and we shouldn't just pump out money and appease our own guilt feelings by Winter Programmes which won't help in any way to win the election next autumn.' Harold replied, rather primly, 'Of course we don't accept the philosophy of Dick's argument but there's something in what he says. We certainly oughtn't to mention the election!' So I got my way and the programme was cut back to the basic £10 million which is, in fact, not worth announcing.

In this way we have launched the proposition which Peter, Barbara, Tommy and I have been discussing—for a political strategy from now until 1970. When I had first put it to Roy he didn't like it but he took it like a lamb this morning and even Harold was forced to take it. Quite a nice triumph.

This afternoon we presented our tactical plan to a meeting of the Cabinet Committee on Lords' reform. I have described how this was worked out first with Harold, Eddie and Gerald Gardiner and then approved in turn by Michael Stewart, John Silkin, Fred Peart and Wedgy Benn. The key man we now had to win to our side was Callaghan and I had no idea how he would react. He couldn't have been more helpful. 'We'd better face it that this is the right thing to do,' he said. 'We must be firm and show that we're prepared to go ahead but we must also be ready when we have made up our own minds, written our own White Paper, and prepared our own Bill to show it before publication to the Tories and then, if they choose, to resume talks with them.' So there was no serious opposition. Even Wedgy Benn was easy on this occasion and, as for Ted Short, he was away so we didn't have to bother about him.

Tuesday, September 24th

My first task was to call on Callaghan in his room at the Home Office. I had asked him at yesterday afternoon's Cabinet Committee whether he would mind having a chat about devolution and though he seemed surprised he agreed. After a few words about the progress of our Community Development Project I told him that when I take over the merged Ministry I wouldn't have time for things like devolution. 'As you know, I have spent a tremendous lot of time on this during the last twelve months,' I said. He didn't seem to know that I was the Chairman of the Cabinet Committee on Devolution, but he said he had been talking to Harold and had his ideas about this. I told him I had heard from Terry Pitt that he proposed that we should set up a Royal Commission and that I thought that this would make us a laughing-stock. 'Well,' he said, 'I'm not so sure. I have some thoughts about how the Commission should be manned and two possibilities for Chairman have occurred to me, Rab Butler or Lester Pearson.'[1] Both of them were in their time very active politicians but Lester Pearson is finished and Butler is now the head of a Cambridge college and a bit decrepit. I suggested that either of those would make the Commission seem rather musty and old-fashioned and then I said, 'I am giving this whole thing up. Why not take Devolution over?' 'As a swop for the Children's Department?' he asked. I know that he and his whole Department are anxious to keep the Children's Department as part of the Home Office and not see it mopped up in my new Ministry and I have always realized that as long as Callaghan is Home Secretary I can't take the Children's Department out of his hands. It could only happen under a new Home Secretary who would come into the Home Office on condition that he accepted the transfer. So I said straightaway, 'I'm not hoping to grab this from you, Jim. I promise you I shan't.' 'Is that a deal?' he asked. 'Well,' I said, 'it's not a deal. I am just telling you what my attitude is.' So that's the way Jim's mind works.

We walked across to Cabinet together. The whole press had been full of the doings of a Colonial Office official who had been sent on a secret mission to Rhodesia. When the news leaked he had been flown back this morning

[1] A member of the Canadian Liberal Party, Foreign Minister 1948–57, when he was awarded the Nobel Peace Prize, and Leader of the Opposition 1957–63, Lester Pearson was Leader of the Liberal Party 1963–7 and Prime Minister 1963–8. He died in December 1972, at the age of seventy-five.

and Barbara asked what was going to happen. The question was not unreasonable. Everybody knew he had been sent out by the P.M. and George Thomson without consulting anybody except a small inner group. Everybody knew he had come back and that papers were being prepared without consultation either with Cabinet or O.P.D. Does this show the reassertion of the P.M.'s authority? No, I think it merely indicates that Cabinet now has a more settled centre. We members say, 'Don't let's hold him back all the time, don't let's insist on sitting in committee on everything the P.M. does. Let him go ahead and present us with a solution for our approval.'

The last item was North Sea Gas.[1] It arose out of a proposal put forward by an N.E.C. working party that we should have a nationalized Hydrocarbon Board which would own and develop the chequers in the North Sea which are not at present allocated. Instead of selling the rest off by auction, this corporation should hold them for the nation. I thought the proposal made very good sense and Tommy is fanatically keen on it but once again the Ministry of Power was adamant. Dick Marsh was in the hands of his officials and now Mason is getting under their control too. He tried to persuade the Cabinet to give him the right to slap down the National Executive at Conference. This was fortunate because it turned most of the Cabinet against him. He was told that the statement will be made by a member of the Executive, not by him, and the final decision has been postponed for further consideration.

This evening I went down to Coventry to give the annual presidential lecture to the Fabians. It was an excellent turnout and a first-rate meeting. I talked about the notion of participation – the feeling that the Labour Party has been left out by a Labour Government which is utterly remote from it and the question of whether the Party Conference has any point if its decisions are completely disregarded. In talking about participation I tried out one section of my Granada lecture. It was one of my more successful appearances in Coventry.

Wednesday, September 25th

At O.P.D. we had a first paper on what our defence reactions should be to the Russian coup in Czechoslovakia. It was better than the usual run of papers, cautiously indicating that we might respond by a British initiative showing a readiness to take a great part in the defence of Western Europe. Harold at once said that he didn't think it was a question of a military initiative but of a political initiative, which would apparently consist in continuing our efforts to enter the Common Market. Denis Healey then said that we would be missing a great chance on the military side since the

[1] During 1967 the Gas Council had been negotiating with the companies that had acquired concessions to exploit the reserves of natural gas in the North Sea, mapped in squares for the purpose. The Gas Council and the Ministry of Power wanted the gas price to be 2½*d.* per therm whereas the companies wished to put it at 5*d.* per therm, based on the world market price. In 1968 negotiations were still going on.

strengthening of NATO was something which could not be denied after the Russian behaviour in Czechoslovakia and this was something we could do despite the French.[1] The P.M. would have nothing to do with this and he was supported by Michael Stewart and George Thomson.

I was thinking afterwards about this division between Harold and the Foreign Office on the one side and the Defence Ministry on the other. I believe that the Anglo-American connection, particularly on nuclear weapons, is the key. That's the connection we must keep if we want to have our own nuclear deterrent. But if we are going to be really Anglo-American we can't consider helping to build a European defence community. Of course this is all pure guesswork on my part, since we haven't discussed nuclear weapons in O.P.D. during the two years I have served on it. I once asked for a discussion but it never materialized. It's only when there is some disagreement that has to be brought to O.P.D. that discussions come to the surface.

The second item was Guatemala, where the Foreign Office suggested that in fulfilment of our treaty obligations we should sweeten the Guatemalans by building a road to link their country with Honduras and make them so amiable that we could then persuade the Honduras government not to incommode us by asking for a defence treaty when they become independent.

I noticed that Harold threw a note across to Fred Peart, who isn't usually very bright on such subjects. Fred barged in and said, 'If you build the road you will strengthen the Guatemalans and enable them to invade Honduras. So why on earth build the road which will only make it more difficult for us to avoid coming to the rescue of Honduras?' There really was no answer to this. The F.O. paper was just riddled with holes. This is worth noticing since our friend George Thomson, who is supposed to be such a remarkable fellow, whispered to me that it was the best they could manage and then just sat back and went along with the whole thing. However it was withdrawn – the second time in one day that the Foreign Office had mucked it up.

Back I went to my own office for the last big meeting on the pension plan before we discuss it with the Chancellor. I had given the economic experts, the Government actuaries and the Treasury two or three days to get together and iron out the scheme. This evening the draft turned up and I soon discovered that it had gone to the Treasury in a totally and incredibly inept form. Apparently it had been written by John Nicholson because Tommy has really slipped back into No. 10. Nicky Kaldor has somehow been excluded and so Nicholson has been forced to do the work. I said the draft simply wasn't good enough and that I was outraged that they had sent it to

[1] President de Gaulle had announced on February 21st, 1966, that he intended 'progressively to modify' the link between France and NATO. In a series of Notes sent on March 11th and 29th to the other signatories of the North Atlantic Treaty he stated that French troops would be withdrawn from the Allied Command in Europe on July 1st, 1966, and that the NATO Defence College, the Supreme H.Q. of the Allied Powers Europe and the Headquarters of the Allied Forces Central Europe must be removed from French territory by April 1st, 1967.

the Treasury without my leave. The thing would have to be decently rewritten and I would ask Brian Abel-Smith to do it for me. It's the first time I have been really rough. However it wasn't a wholly wasted meeting. Nicky arrived late though Tommy didn't come and I think in the time available he will establish the real statistics on which we can base our calculations of the impact of our scheme.

Nicky had asked me to go in later for a spot of dinner. Meanwhile he had gone out to two parties while Clarissa and I sat and waited for him. When he came in he fell asleep twice on the sofa and I went home to bed. Nicky is a great sleeper, the only man I know who can fall asleep at High Table in the middle of a King's College Feast. I love him for it and don't begrudge it a bit.

Thursday, September 26th

All the papers had the announcement of Nicky's withdrawal to King's. He and Tommy have been withdrawing to Oxford and Cambridge for at least twelve months. But Nicky is still retained as consultant by Roy Jenkins and Tommy by me, though in the last ten days Tommy has been back with Harold and up to Blackpool, writing his speeches because Harold simply can't do without him. It's fascinating to see how those two men need each other. Tommy is profoundly loyal to the Prime Minister, dedicated to him and to keeping him in power. It's curious that this tight, competent Yorkshire politician can't be without this difficult, awkward, brilliant, sensitive Hungarian. Without Thomas Harold has no spark, without Harold Thomas's spark has no proper outlet. They're a wonderful pair.

In the Ministry of Social Security there was terrible turmoil. Poor Judith has just discovered that the Attorney General has made a ruling that for the last twenty years the law has been flouted when tax refunds made during a strike are disregarded in the assessment of supplementary-benefit. For twenty years now strikers have been able for the first fortnight at least to rely on £2 or £3 a week of tax refunds, and since they could get that and their wives and children could draw supplementary benefit in addition, life was relatively easy and the strike could carry on. Judith says that a working party is going to report to her any day now and that the Attorney General is talking about the present practice as outrageous and illegal.

I thought the issue such dynamite that I rang up Harold and asked for a meeting in his room but he finally told me to have our own meeting. So this afternoon in breezed the Attorney General (Barbara couldn't be there) and he and I and Judith had a talk. Judith said, 'Surely it's all a question of what is reasonable? Can one really discount that for twenty years all the officials have paid out these sums? Doesn't this indicate that it was reasonable and shouldn't you consult the Department?' I found that he hadn't asked the Department about this and as he left he promised to do so. However I didn't believe him and sure enough that promise has fallen to the ground and he has reverted to his position of total opposition. I knew this would be so unless the meeting took place in Harold's room. Attorney Generals aren't impressed by Lord Presidents!

William Armstrong came in to report on the progress of the merger. Burke, unfortunately, had come back from a three weeks' holiday and immediately retired with a bad throat. This means that until he recovers the exact placing of my co-ordination unit will remain in doubt but it's clear from what Armstrong and the P.M. have said to me that I shan't be able to keep the Lord Presidency and I shall therefore have to let Fred take my offices and move into his Lord Privy Seal's office, which is a pleasant suite at the corner of Downing Street. Armstrong is a curious man. Though he had no more business he chatted to me for half an hour about nothing in particular. I suspect civil servants like taking the measure of the men around the P.M., judging their quality, discovering what they are up to, and I like to do the same with him. I like to keep in contact with him, in step with him and Burke, because this puts me in an infinitely stronger position.

This evening Anne was in London and I took her to Albert Finney's first film production, *Charlie Bubbles*. He wrote it and took the principal part. There was nothing to it but it was wonderfully produced and acted. We were walking home, looking out for a taxi, and we kept on reaching a bus stop just as the bus was going off. The third time I turned to Anne and said, 'Dash it, why can't you keep up?' She was furious with me and walked home on her own while I walked home on my own. When we got in we just went to bed and didn't say anything about it. We haven't said anything about it since but the fact that these things happen so rarely shows how happy we are together. It was a tiff to remind us that we usually don't have them.

Friday, September 27th

By now all the others had gone off to Blackpool on the Thursday train. I stayed behind and Harold has refused to go to Blackpool till Sunday and is having a dinner tonight for the Swedish Prime Minister, Tage Erlander.[1] This morning we had a meeting of the Home Affairs Committee and once again cigarette legislation came up. Last Friday I was told that a paper was going before the Cabinet this week recommending once again Kenneth Robinson's Bill outlawing gift schemes for cigarettes. This was an outrage because Kenneth should have submitted the paper to me before sending it in to the Cabinet Secretariat. But when I rang him up this morning he said that he thought the whole thing was perfectly in order and had no idea that I wanted to see it beforehand. There was nothing I could do but to ring up the Lord Chancellor and he agreed that the item must be removed from the agenda, which it duly was. When I told the story to Harold he said that

[1] Social Democratic Prime Minister of Sweden for twenty-two years. In the General Election on September 15th, 1968, his party had won an absolute majority for the first time since 1940 and on September 16th he had announced that before the 1970 General Election he would retire from political life.

Robinson might be trying to get a cause for resignation but I don't think this is true. No, it's the bloody-mindedness of a man isolated out there at Elephant and Castle and sore at being thrown out of his Ministry in order to give place to me. I am more and more aware that if he is left out of the Government when I take over it will be very bad for me since he has built up a very high reputation in his four years as Minister of Health. If I seem to chuck him out in order to take his job it won't do me any good in the National Health Service. On the other hand, everything he is doing now is making it very difficult to avoid just that.

I went off to get ready for the big confrontation with Roy for which we have been preparing for so many weeks. At last the day had come when the Lord President, the Minister of Social Security and Miss Riddelsdell, were to present our pension plan to the Chancellor, his Minister of State and his assembled Treasury officials.

The three of us gathered in my room and chatted nervously. Then I said we should walk because it was a lovely sunny autumn day, so we walked through to No. 10, on through the Foreign Office courtyard and up to the Treasury, getting there two minutes late because we'd underestimated the time. We entered Roy's long room, he stood up behind his wide table and we settled down. I had very carefully prepared a short speech. From the very beginning Roy made it obvious that he was impatient. Then he started and said that we were not legislating for a few years but perhaps for the rest of the century and what we did was enormously important. It was better to do little now than to go forward too far and find ourselves unable to reverse. By this time I thought, 'Oh God, what is coming?' Roy said he was going to choose five of the points he wanted to raise. He then went through these five points and I calculated that he had given us four and a half.

Most of them were highly technical but one was not. I had conceded that the pension should be adjusted not according to the movement in average wages but according to the cost-of-living index, a great concession to the Chancellor. In return, I suggested, he should let me have an annual instead of a biennial review but this he firmly refused. 'If you will agree with me on the biennial review,' he said, 'I won't query any financial issues on the rest of the scheme.' It was clear that after thirty-five minutes he wanted to get out of the meeting. There had been no discussion, no cross-examination on any point. The scheme had apparently been accepted and we felt a sense of anti-climax because we had been briefed and thrilled at the idea of a couple of hours of really arduous defence of our position. No, we weren't going to be given it. The whole thing had been accepted apart from the major point of the annual review.

Right at the end I said that one of the things he hadn't mentioned was the impact of our scheme on private pensions schemes, which is absolutely vital. Roy replied, 'I haven't thought much about that, I'm afraid.' Why did he do it? I don't know. With Callaghan and his officials we would have had a really gruelling time. However we went back to the Ministry and later I rang up Judith to ask her to a celebration lunch at Locket's, and we had a jolly good one.

This evening was the big dinner for Erlander. The P.M. normally goes to Conference on Thursday with the rest of the Executive, to be at the N.E.C. meetings on Friday and Saturday. But this year, making an excuse of Erlander, Harold is only arriving early on Sunday morning. I happen to know that he only asked Erlander a week ago. The dinner took place in No. 10 at the horseshoe table with too many people and in terrible heat. (Macmillan spent over £2 million restoring No. 10 and left it without air conditioning or adequate ventilation.)[1] At the dinner I sat next to Mrs George Thomson and started talking to her about the ghastly position of politicians' wives who have to attend these ceremonial occasions, telling her how Anne and I had never gone to anything at the Palace and how we managed to get out of most of the formalities. She told me she loved all these things and even adored living in Government accommodation in one of the flats in Admiralty House. She finds the Foreign Office life perfect. 'Doesn't George want a change?' I asked her. 'No,' she said, 'neither George nor I would like to move.'

So anybody who thinks they're going to make themselves popular with George Thomson by making him Secretary of State for Scotland instead of Willie Ross is in for a surprise. Mr and Mrs Thomson are the perfect, professional External Affairs Minister and wife, because they are absolutely inoffensive. I have never heard him take a personal line at Cabinet or O.P.D. He has an excellent presence in Parliament and I am sure that when he goes abroad he is excellent at negotiations, just carrying out his instructions. Since Michael Stewart is also totally ineffective this pretty well explains what's happened to Labour's foreign policy. After the Erlander dinner Anne motored me straight down to Prescote where we prepared for what must surely be the last weekend of summer.

Sunday, September 29th

But summer this year went out with a whimper. Indeed, there was a real soak today when we went for a walk at Weston Park with Lord Kennet's daughter who was staying with Virginia, her first invitation to a friend to stay. I wasn't particularly cheerful because I was reflecting on Blackpool. There was a terrible press there, of course, with the P.M.'s failure to go up and Erlander's unfortunate admission that he had only been invited last week and was delighted to come at the last moment. He had said this in an impromptu speech at the No. 10 dinner and it had got to the journalists, showing that Harold had invited him in deliberate contempt for the Executive. As a result there was a tremendous row at Conference. Harold is becoming

[1] Harold Macmillan, Conservative M.P. for Stockton-on-Tees 1924–9, 1931–45, and for Bromley November 1945–September 1964, was Prime Minister January 1957–October 1963.

more and more a Lloyd George figure,[1] detached from his party, feeling not much loyalty or affection for the organization but resenting the bloody nuisance it causes him. And yet he can afford to have these views because whenever necessary he pulls it off.

Monday, September 30th

This morning I went over to see Ron Hill who runs the Labour Exchange at Coventry. He is one of the most interesting men there, a classicist by education, five or six years younger than me, very keen and dynamic and he has chosen to stay in Coventry because he finds it an interesting city. I felt rather bad because I hadn't been to see him for a couple of years and there I was being entertained in his very bleak office to an excellent lunch with a bottle of white wine. The first thing I put to him was an idea which has been coursing through Barbara Castle's head for a long time, that the payment of unemployment benefit should be transferred from the Ministry of Labour to Social Security or, as we should say now, from the Department of Employment and Productivity to the Department of Health and Social Services.

At first it does seem a fairly obvious suggestion because the Ministry of Labour want their labour exchanges to compete with private employment agencies, whereas our Ministry really knows how to handle the payment of benefit to every different kind of person. Ron said straightaway, 'A lot of my staff would agree with Barbara. I don't. I don't think we want to turn our office in Coventry into a dolled-up employment agency cut off from the whole problem of poverty. Look, there's a queue outside here. Some people don't like it, they want the place to have lovely flowers in the rooms and to forget poverty and unemployment. Well, it doesn't do them any harm and anyway we couldn't possibly allow the separation because we need to know both those who come to get a job and those who come to draw benefit. Indeed we need to know the second group better than the first because it's more difficult to find them jobs.' I thought this was a pretty sensible answer and I was more impressed than ever by Ron. There he sits in his humble little office, a bare room with brick walls and girders in the ceiling, and somehow his life and vitality suffuses the Labour Exchange. He has a sharp nose and grey eyes and he is a shrewd operator, although sometimes when he writes to me he is so full of Greek and Latin quotations that he sounds gaga. I want to see more of him.

I got off to London in time for a big meeting in John Adam Street to discuss the results of my meeting with the Chancellor. I found we were all agreed on the type of paper we must now put forward through the usual channels. I also had time to go through the minutes of the meeting with the Treasury. I must be a little careful before I crow because what the Chancellor has really

[1] After 1924 Lloyd George became increasingly a lone voice in his party.

done is to remain neutral on every issue except the annual review. On everything else he has left it up to Cabinet to react and if Cabinet are hostile he has given no assurance that he will be on my side.

This evening we had a big dinner at the Swedish Embassy. Before dinner I had a long talk with Erlander about pensions and I begin to realize how lucky the Swedes were to get on to national superannuation early. They didn't have to tell the electors any details of their scheme or its costing. (Indeed every penny is paid for by the employers.) Their system bears no relation to ours mainly because we have so many more private superannuation schemes. But most interesting was Erlander's confirmation that if you can get the pension issue right it's an enormous electoral help. In the last election he had been challenged by the Liberals and Conservatives for being too ambitious and he had won. After dinner Alun Chalfont and I had another long talk with him,[1] this time about the E.E.C., and I explained how strongly opposed from the defence point of view Harold and Michael were to the idea of going into Europe. This is something the Swedes very much wanted to hear. Just before I left I received another invitation to visit Sweden and I have now agreed to go in the second week of December.

Tuesday, October 1st

All the papers are full of the crushing 5:1 defeat which Barbara suffered at Blackpool on her prices and incomes policy.[2] The first two days of the Conference – on Sunday a split in the Executive and yesterday this major defeat – have been as bad as we expected. On the other hand this probably means, as Harold calculates, that the worst will be over before he arrives.

This morning I found myself invited, as Lord President, to the Lord Chancellor's annual reception. This is a very curious occasion on which the Lord Chancellor receives in the Royal Gallery behind the House of Lords all the judges down to the rank of recorder, all the Q.C.s and a select number of junior counsel. I walked in from the Lords and saw a queue hundreds of yards long winding up the stairs to shake hands with the Chancellor, so I got the servants of the House to take me round the back and push me through the catering tables to an open space. There I found the judges standing about in full fig, their regalia of black, gold or red, and white ermine. They vary enormously in looks. There is a small thin-looking drunken minority but most of them are judges cherubic and all of them are marked with the judicial glare. It struck me once again how separate we keep ourselves in Britain. There is the legal world, the doctors' world, the artistic world, the dramatic

[1] Alun Gwynne Jones, Defence Correspondent of *The Times* 1961–4, became a life peer in 1964, taking the title of Lord Chalfont, and was Minister of State at the Foreign Office, with special responsibility for Disarmament, 1964–70.

[2] At their meeting on Sunday the N.E.C. had agreed to support the Government's prices and incomes policy only by a casting vote, and on Monday a motion moved by Frank Cousins demanding repeal of the policy was carried by 5,098,000 votes to 1,124,000.

world, the political world. We are tremendously separate and here was one world having its annual get-together on beer and sausages.

I spent the rest of the day on my Granada lecture. I got a book list from the Commons library and found that there were actually four or five books worth reading. I had also read a lecture David Butler had delivered while he was in Australia and now I was actually drafting in a way that drives secretaries frantic, not because I dictate too fast or too slow but because there are so many stages in the process and so many drafts and redrafts and redrafts of the redrafts. I had to stop fairly early because at 5.45 Anne and I were to be in the Royal Box at Covent Garden with the Mosers[1], to hear the *Valkyrie*. Last Saturday evening I had been with Stanley and Adèle Sadie to hear *Götterdämmerung*.[2] I hadn't relaxed my attention for a moment and I never felt like nodding off in those four and three quarter hours because from beginning to end I had been thrilled with Solti's tigerish conducting. I had studied the text pretty carefully so I was able to enjoy the fact that in *Götterdämmerung* Wagner manages to combine a slab of grand opera with slices of music drama. With *Valkyrie* we were back in the purest of dramatic music and though I enjoyed the first act very much I found much of the rest interminably long. Anne wasn't exactly bored but she found the words even worse in English than they are in German. Altogether she didn't find quite enough shape in the music and I found it nothing like as exciting as *Götterdämmerung* had been.

Wednesday, October 2nd

I lay in bed, read the papers and heard the wireless and delighted in Harold's triumphant speech yesterday morning. Even the Tory papers couldn't refrain from slightly spiteful cheering. For example, David Wood, Political Editor of *The Times*, said it was one of those Conference speeches which succeed because they are shamelessly bad and that Mr Wilson had all but a few of the Labour delegates standing to acclaim him for about ninety seconds. David Watt of the *Financial Times*, whom I admire, commented:

> 'magnificent balderdash' was how one member of the Government privately described his Leader's speech to the Labour Party Conference today—and one really cannot do better than that...Technically Mr Wilson is a terrible speaker, he gabbles his words half the time as if he himself were bored by them. He builds cliché on statistic on cliché in mountainous sandwiches of tedium; he has no gestures to speak of and

[1] Sir Claus Moser (K.C.B. 1973), Professor of Social Statistics at the London School of Economics 1961–70, has been Director of the Central Statistical Office and Head of the Government Statistical Service since 1967. He is a member (and since 1974 Chairman) of the Board of Directors of the Royal Opera House, Covent Garden.

[2] Stanley Sadie is the Editor of the *New Grove Dictionary of Music and Musicians* (London: Macmillan, 20 vols, to be published 1979) and has been music critic on the staff of *The Times* since 1964.

very little variety of inflection. Yet in front of this familiar audience...he was in complete command. One feels, as one felt with Harold Macmillan and the Tory conference that there is no ultimate rapport. No deep warmth, but, as with Macmillan, there is the artful understanding of a musician for a well-worn instrument which he can play with his eyes shut and never miss a note.

Harold won't like that kind of discriminating praise but it's worth a great deal more than the uproarious backslapping which the popular press have given him.

By first refusing to come until Sunday and then by making this kind of speech he has shown his disdain for the Executive's intrigues and I think this has probably been good for his public image and his T.V. persona. Now he is in a position to sack any Minister he wants and the only thing I am doubtful about is whether once again he will fail to use his power.

Nicholas Davenport gave me lunch at the Athenaeum to meet Mr Lyon of the Life Assurance Offices.[1] I happened to read one or two of his articles in the *Actuaries Journal* which seemed to show a complete inside knowledge of everything I am doing and also a great deal of sympathy for it. In real life he is as nice and understanding as he is on paper. I think he is on our side and if he heads the delegation from the Life Offices when the consultations begin we shall reach agreement. Just as important, I think he will help us to get the sympathetic press we very much need.

The only meeting I had today was on prescription charges. Once again I was bothered about the advertising policy of the Ministry. They are anxious to popularize the new 'season ticket', which enables you for quite a small sum to obtain as many prescriptions as you need for six months. But they have made this one of four subjects jammed together in a single newspaper advertisement. I have discovered that the advertising agency hadn't even been given a chance to air its ideas but was only given the copy and instructed to lay it out. This was absolutely hopeless and I told the officials so but, as they know perfectly well, I shall just have to wait until I take over.

Then I caught the night train to Preston, where I changed to a slow train for Blackpool.

Thursday, October 3rd

After breakfasting with Judith and Tony Hart, we walked down to the Conference. They gave me their impressions and Judith emphasized that despite the 5:1 defeat on the prices and incomes policy, there had been no applause for the speeches against Barbara. But Judith was mainly excited by a splendid dinner she had last night with Harold, Beattie Plummer and

[1] C. S. S. (Stewart) Lyon, Actuary for the Legal and General Assurance Society Ltd and a leading member of the Disablement Income Group.

Marcia.[1] She has clearly been tipped that she may become Paymaster-General or Chancellor of the Duchy of Lancaster.

I blew into the old Imperial, the N.E.C. hotel, and as I walked up the steps there was Robin Day coming down.[2] 'I hear you're writing terrible nonsense in the lecture you're preparing for Granada,' he said. 'Is it true that you're going to contrast radio as a good medium with television as a bad medium and lecture us on the failure of the visual side? Please don't make a fool of yourself.' That set me off and we had a talk for about one and a half hours, walking through the rain on the promenade, with people watching us curiously as we shouted at each other. Finally we stood outside the Winter Garden arguing away. It did me a lot of good because my mind does tend to get into a groove and run logically along it inside. I need to be told, 'You have only looked at it from one point of view. Shift your vision.' I had forgotten in my thinking to give credit for the current affairs breakthrough when the B.B.C. monopoly ended. I had been comparing T.V. to radio and forgetting that under Reith radio was a monopoly,[3] with no current affairs, no controversy, no vitality in news treatment. I must get the thing in balance and if I do it will be partly owing to Robin Day.

I got into the Conference Hall about 11.30 and at once ran into Harold being photographed holding some magazine in his hand. We had a few words. He was glad to see me; how long was I staying? I prevaricated a bit because I was actually going off to Manchester this evening for a dinner with the Regional Hospital Board. Behind the platform sitting on a hard chair I found Mary Wilson, who told me that she was trying to listen from there because it was too hot on the platform itself. She was as nice and sweet as ever. I always get on extremely well with her. We chatted away until the stewards around us looked rather shocked, so we drifted off. I ran into James Callaghan and asked him about Harold's speech. He said, 'The real thing it has done is to devalue Conference. People now know that Conference decisions don't matter.' It is true that Harold was very careful to insist that Conference can warn but can't give instructions to the Government, so I think there is something in what Callaghan said. Maybe it's a good thing it has happened, that people realize that under a Labour Government Conference cannot make the decisions. That fact has to be accepted if the delegates are to have any contact with reality. But one result of this knowledge is that the

[1] Beatrice Plummer, widow of Sir Leslie Plummer, Labour M.P. for Deptford from 1951 until his death in 1963, became a life peer in 1965. She died in 1972.

[2] A television journalist, with a reputation for incisive interviewing. He was a newscaster and Parliamentary Correspondent for Independent Television News from 1955 to 1959, when he joined B.B.C. television's current affairs programme 'Panorama', which he introduced from 1967 to 1972.

[3] John Reith became the first General Manager of the B.B.C. in 1922, Managing Director in 1923 and Director-General 1927–38. He was the first Chairman of B.O.A.C. 1939–40, Minister of Information 1940, Minister of Transport 1940 and first Minister of Works 1940–2. He was elected as National M.P. for Southampton in 1940, but later that year, was created a baron. He died in 1971.

speeches become even more extreme and remote from reality than before. There was a discussion on NATO going on this afternoon, and I heard solemn speeches announcing that spheres of influence shouldn't exist and that we should in no sense strengthen NATO as our reaction to the Czech crisis. The speeches on Rhodesia were just as unrealistic. These speeches, of course, are normally a mere background to conversation. Under the enormous arc lights the usual chat continues. You wander round the Hall, people come up for autographs and you meet more and more people who claim to be old friends and of whose identity you haven't the vaguest idea. I thought I could stand this for a day but if this is all I have to do, wandering round the hall having chats or sitting in the Executive hotel having tea with the ladies, it's not the place for me.

I had arranged to meet my stepson, Gilbert Baker, who is the candidate for Carshalton, and we went out for a walk, proceeding slowly along the rainy, dreary, awful Blackpool promenade. Apparently it has been like this the whole week with never a gleam of sunshine. Back in the hotel we sat down with Joe Haines and Gordon Brook-Shepherd,[1] the Diplomatic Correspondent of the *Sunday Telegraph*, and chatted with Marcia. She probed me: 'Where are you staying? You oughtn't to be away tonight. I shall have to see you're looked after.' 'Very good,' I said and within a minute or two a message came that I was to go to a cocktail party for the press at 7.0 p.m. I was just too timid to say in Marcia's presence that I couldn't go. I listened to the chat and said nothing.

John Silkin was the only person whom I told I would be going off at 8.15. He and Rosie had an excellent lunch with Gilbert and me in the Regency Bar, or whatever it's called, where we sat till after three. If you're not on the Executive all you can do is to sit about after lunch. John and I had a long discussion of a problem that had suddenly become very real when we learnt from the newspapers last Sunday that a P.R. firm representing the Greek government had claimed to have an M.P. working for it behind the scenes.[2] For years everyone has known that this kind of thing goes on. As well as the Greek government there are the Israeli and East German governments, which both systematically dole out free holidays to M.P.s and sometimes quite a lot of pocket money too. Of course there's no open influencing of their minds. The bogeymen we talked about all the time in the 1930s were the merchants of death; now I believe it's the public relations firms and it struck me this afternoon that this is an ideal topic for investigation by a Select Committee. It may be much easier to start with a Select Committee and then let the Commons recommend legislation than for the Government to legislate on its

[1] Joe Haines, Political Correspondent of the *Sun* 1964–8, was Deputy Press Secretary January–June 1969 and Chief Press Secretary to the Prime Minister 1969–70 and 1974–6 and Press Secretary to the Leader of the Opposition 1970–4. He has given his account of his period in No. 10 in *The Politics of Power* (London: Cape, 1977).

[2] See below, p. 406.

own. John promised he would sell the idea to the press and I will do my share before next weekend.

Conference had got on to the subject of Biafra, I think, when I got into my taxi and went off to the station. Here I was officially received by the stationmaster, the regional head of the Ministry of Health and the regional head of the Social Security Information Service, because I had now changed from my party into my official hat. When we got to Manchester I was wafted into a magnificent suite in the Midland Hotel in time for a quick bath before getting down to the new offices of the Regional Hospital Board.

Among the members of the Board and the officials there seemed to be a number of quite outstanding men and women. Very early in our talk I asked them, 'Which services in your experience are better run, those controlled by elected councillors in local government, like education or housing, or those controlled by ministerial appointees, as in the Regional Hospital Boards?' There was no doubt what people thought. Even those who are now with the local authorities said the R.H.B.s are better run, mainly because there are no party political divisions amongst the members. There are special reasons why a lot of the Labour people in Manchester should feel so bitterly anti-political. Many of them have been knocked out by the electoral landslide after twenty or thirty years of experience as local councillors. I don't think the Tories ever believed as much in the application of party politics to local government as we did. Now, I admit, I have been shaken and I am asking whether it has really justified itself. How can one defend a system of administering local services which every three or four years sweeps out of office everyone with experience? Of course, where there's no two-party system, as in the R.H.B.s, you get the evils of a self-perpetuating oligarchy but you don't have the appalling evil of the substitution of one lot of machine politicians for another.

Friday, October 4th

I was enormously stimulated by my dinner last night and was up bright and early for my tour. My first port of call was a supplementary benefit office in the roughest part of Manchester. Quite a large group of managers were there to see me and I put to them the point that I had put to Ron Hill in Coventry —why not transfer to D.H.S.S. the distribution of unemployment benefit from the Ministry of Labour? They said unanimously that this would be an intolerable reform. 'If the whole job were shoved on to us,' they said, 'we would be overwhelmed by the queue of callers and quite unable to strike a decent balance between the work at the desk and the visits to our customers which are an equally important part of our task.' When I went round the office I saw what they meant. Young people don't join social security offices unless they are keen on welfare work, on helping old and sick people. They certainly don't join in order to stand at the counter and be bullied and hit by toughs demanding that they should be properly looked after. I watched them at work and then went out and joined the queue. It was composed of two quite different elements. First, the element which had been too proud to claim entitlement before 1966, but who had been induced to come by Peggy Herbison—quiet old ladies, some young men and women who obviously hated the idea of coming but felt that now they were entitled to their benefit as a right. Oh God, but they must have been disgusted by the atmosphere. The seats had been slashed to pieces by the toughs and there was a smell of the slum. Our change in the law has stimulated the two opposing types, those who previously were too proud to accept government help and those who will take any bloody thing they can get from the state. By the end of my visit I was quite clear that if the staff at these offices are to be obliged to spend all their time at the counter, with no visiting of the sick and the elderly, recruitment will dry up altogether.

At lunch at Withington, which has been turned into a teaching hospital, I sat next to the Dean,[1] tall, thin, alert, who took me in hand and lectured me brilliantly. He pointed out that a whole thick slice of Commonwealth doctors is being inserted into our medical hierarchy so that in ten years' time there won't be any room at the top of the profession for home-grown doctors. It will be entirely dominated by foreigners and this means that we shall get no recruits from England. This, he said, is the result of the voucher system under which we only allow in Commonwealth people who are fully trained professionals and keep the unskilled and unprofessional out. I expressed my shock because Cabinet has a bad conscience about the way we are sucking the best skills out of the Commonwealth and keeping them here because it is in our interest to do so. The Dean taught me that it is not only not in our interest, it is utterly disastrous. Once we have trained the Commonwealth doctors they should go back to their countries straightaway so that we can let our own young men come forward and have a decent chance of promotion. This was one of those eye-opening conversations which I so often have on these official tours. I went away from lunch sobered and thoughtful.

One of the institutions I visited this afternoon was a so-called Children's Centre, run by the Children's Department and responsible to the Home Office. This is Jim Callaghan's dominion and I thought I might be in for trouble. But I was shown in with no difficulty to a great big middle-class house, a reception centre where some forty or fifty children can be kept under observation before it's decided whether to send them to foster parents, a remand home or whatever. These are all the most difficult children, truants from school, problem children from problem homes. On the other side of the yard was a school where I was puzzled to find five or six schoolmasters, all from the Department of Education. What on earth could six well-trained

[1] Professor A. C. P. Campbell, Dean of the Faculty of Medicine and Pro-Vice-Chancellor of Manchester University. He was Professor of Pathology and Pathological Anatomy at the University of Manchester 1950–73 and is now Professor Emeritus. He has been Director of Studies at the Royal College of Pathologists since 1973.

schoolmasters do with this collection of psychotic problem children? The explanation of their presence was that the Department of Education was running the school and the Home Office the boarding establishments. This split was utterly destroying the place. Over a cup of tea, I asked the Chairman of the local committee why it was allowed to go on. 'Oh, it's been going on for years,' he replied, 'and it's too late to change it now.' The officials of both sides want a change but neither committee will move, so that's that.

My last visit was to a magnificent block in Deansgate, where a whole floor had been taken by the National Health Service for blood donation. At first I wondered how the R.H.B. could be so extravagant and then I realized that the British system, which is by far the best in the world, is entirely supported by voluntary donors and if you want volunteers you've got to make them not only proud of themselves but comfortable, so it is probably a good investment to rent this convenient and splendid suite. There I had another cup of tea and checked over my impressions before David Williams put me on the last train for Rugby. Anne picked me up and I was home shortly after midnight.

Saturday, October 5th

I noticed in the morning papers that Harold has had a terrible quarrel with the B.B.C. and that at the end of Conference he appeared on I.T.V. but refused to appear on the B.B.C. He has also made it clear that he disapproves of David Wood of *The Times*. This being the case, he will certainly have noticed that I failed to turn up at his party for the press yesterday evening. But what's the good? I find the way he handles the press and above all the B.B.C. absolutely lunatic and I wish he would leave press relations to other people. Meanwhile all these rows may possibly make the lecture I am delivering in a fortnight's time into quite a political event. Now that so much is being written about the relations between politics and broadcasting I shall have to be far more careful and balanced in what I say. There's a lot of work to be done on the draft.

Today is Patrick's birthday, and for the first time Anne and I are going to be able to be home for his birthday tea on the proper day. Every other year Conference has prevented this but now I am a free man. He had chosen as his birthday present tickets for *The Mikado* at the New Theatre in Oxford and we luckily managed to get six for the Saturday matinée. We were also lucky in managing to persuade Patrick's godfather, Michael Howard,[1] to join us for the second act. The theatre seemed to be full of children who hadn't an idea what *The Mikado* was about and were far too young to appreciate it. But it was just right for Patrick, and Virginia liked it too.

[1] Professor of War Studies at King's College, London, 1963–8, Fellow of All Souls' College, Oxford since 1968 and since 1977 Chichele Professor of the History of War in the University of Oxford.

Monday, October 7th

The final draft of my Granada lecture was pretty well completed this weekend and it is now ready for Harold, who wrote to me expressing a desire to see it. It's becoming quite an important little event. There was a full article on the front page of the *Sunday Times* last week about how Harold and I wanted to prevent the B.B.C. from doing anything more than publish straight extracts from our speeches, a version, I suppose, of what I said to Robin Day during our argument in the rain at Blackpool. Another bit of news is that on October 16th at 3.30 Harold will announce the merger of the Foreign Office and the Commonwealth Relations Office, the merger of the Social Security and Health Ministries and the creation of a new Civil Service Department, with Eddie Shackleton as its Minister. I think that at the same time he will announce my new title of Secretary of State for the Social Services, though my official takeover has now been postponed until November 1st.

As I looked at the papers in the train this morning, it was clear that Silkin and I had been successful in placing our story about the Government's determination to deal with public relations firms acting for foreign governments. Indeed some of the stories were blown up in such a way that I shall have to keep myself clear of this for a few days.

The first meeting this morning was the Cabinet Committee on immigration which Jim Callaghan chairs. I got in two minutes late because my train was half an hour late at Paddington and as I pushed through the door I saw them all sitting waiting. 'Ah!' Jim said, 'we were just going to start without you, Lord President,' and I realized that I am now a sufficiently senior member of the Cabinet to be waited for by a Committee of fifteen or sixteen people. Or was it merely that Mr Callaghan was recording his thanks for my promise not to steal his Children's Department?

The great issue this morning was whether we should have compulsory entry certificates for immigrants, something which David Ennals had strongly recommended last July.[1] Now we had a paper signed by officials strongly opposing it. Callaghan started with a thoroughly reasoned statement of the arguments for not doing it, David Ennals made an extremely powerful case for doing it and then everybody round the table, looking at their departmental briefs, said that if the Home Office didn't want certificates their Department didn't want them either. I then said, 'I am sure I am not the only one in the room this morning who is by no means certain that we shouldn't have them. I notice that this is one of the things Heath is demanding with Hogg's support. Should we turn them down flat? Shouldn't we wait until we hear what the Tory case is? Isn't bipartisanship worth something? Surely if the Tories want compulsory entry certificates and with the issue of race looming hugely over the election, we should be careful before turning this down.'

Nobody gave an inch and finally I said, 'Are you quite sure that between now and the election we shan't have to introduce quotas? If you are going to

[1] See above, p. 38.

refuse compulsory entry certificates and then concede on quotas you will get the worst of both worlds. I propose that this should be referred to the Parliamentary Committee.' Sure enough, it was.

Afterwards Fred Peart said he wanted to talk to me about the Cabinet reshuffle, so I ran through my ideas with him. I told him that I wanted either Roy Hattersley or Stephen Swingler as my Minister of State for Health and Fred Peart said, 'We don't want Roy Hattersley, he's a right-wing bastard; better give Stephen a chance.' That was fine by me. Then he agreed that Julian Snow and Charlie Loughlin should be dropped and that these two should be replaced by bright young men, one of whom might possibly be Brian Walden. I was solely concerned to represent my interests since I knew Fred was talking to Harold this afternoon.

Then he said to me, 'Of course you know where Harold will be going this week?' I was slow-witted and I should have guessed it was Rhodesia but frankly I did not know and I felt a little nettled.[1] Nevertheless I have no complaint if Harold doesn't discuss Rhodesia with me. By the afternoon it was in all the evening papers.

Tuesday, October 8th

Cabinet, and of course the T.V. cameras were outside No. 10 with all the usual excitement you get when the Prime Minister announces he's off to secret talks with Smith. I went from my own office along the passage, staying inside the building to avoid the cameras, and as I came down the steps into the ante-room in came Harold, plump, round and bouncing as ever. Before I could say a word, he started 'No, I didn't do it in order to spike the Tories' guns at their Conference.[2] Why, I wanted them to have all the press they possibly could to advertise their split. I decided on this date months ago.' He was perfectly friendly and merely anxious to disabuse me of the obvious idea that for the third year running he was making news in Tory Conference week. The real truth, as William Armstrong remarked to me, was that this was the one week when the P.M. could go away without there being a major hiatus. There won't be another chance until August and it just happens to be the week of the Tory Conference as well.

Directly we sat down in Cabinet Harold began his lengthy and laboured explanation of why he had decided on the Gibraltar talks without consulting Cabinet or O.P.D. He explained that it was best to have a working party composed of those most keenly interested and so during Conference week he

[1] There had been rumours that the Government was considering further negotiations with the Smith regime and the Party Conference had carried a resolution opposing this. Nevertheless from October 9th to 13th the Prime Minister held thirty hours of talks with Ian Smith on H.M.S. *Fearless*, anchored off Gibraltar. Before he left London the Prime Minister declared that any agreement must include guarantees that there would be unimpeded progress to majority rule and that no independent Rhodesian Government would introduce retrogressive amendments to the constitution.

[2] The Conservatives met at Blackpool from October 9th to October 12th.

had consulted Gerald Gardiner, Elwyn Jones, Fred Peart, Eddie Shackleton, Michael Stewart, George Thomson, Denis Healey and Tony Crosland. He had also got Jenkins's consent before Roy flew off to Washington. That's an interesting list of names, since every one of them was committed in advance to Harold's going if he wanted to go. It's worth noticing that at the time when this meeting was taking place there were available at Blackpool Barbara Castle, Tony Greenwood, Wedgy Benn and Jim Callaghan but none of them was asked or even briefed about the idea because all of them would have been against the journey.

This is a good example of how a Prime Minister can get his way against the clear wishes of the Cabinet and O.P.D. It is worth noticing, as William Armstrong pointed out to me, that it wouldn't have been so easy if Harold hadn't had a completely compliant Commonwealth Secretary. For instance, when Douglas Jay was President of the Board of Trade, a vital Ministry in all Common Market matters, Harold was terribly inhibited by the need to consult him throughout. George Thomson, in contrast, provided no difficulty as he's a perfectly pliable person. However Cabinet made a fair amount of fuss and Harold took a tremendous amount of trouble to ascertain our views. Every single person had to express his point of view in turn round the table. This went quite well until the P.M. asked Jim Callaghan his opinion and Jim said, 'I get a bit sick of being asked for my view when the T.V. cameras are outside and everybody knows you're going. I will wish you good luck and say no more.' I was the next to speak and said I would rather Harold didn't go because I didn't like the feeling that a British Prime Minister was having an annual stunt meeting with Smith at which I saw not the remotest chance of success. Denis Healey, I went on, had said there was a 15 per cent chance. I thought that much too high an estimate. I added that if we were to have negotiations with Smith Harold should send somebody dispensable and not somebody indispensable. Why not send George Thomson or even me, people who could be got rid of without any effect on the strength of the Cabinet? Harold took this up very quickly and said he wouldn't dream of sending anybody else. This was a Prime Ministerial problem he'd inherited and if he didn't tackle it himself he would be failing to give the necessary leadership.

By the way, it is clear from what was said at this long Cabinet meeting, and this is made clear in the Minutes as well, that the result of the Goodman and Aitken probes on the one side and the probe by Bottomley on the other,[1] was to extract not a single concession from Smith.[2] Yet Harold is determined

[1] Sir James Bottomley (K.C.M.G. 1973) was Deputy High Commissioner in Kuala Lumpur 1963–7, Assistant Under-Secretary of State at the Commonwealth (later the Foreign and Commonwealth) Office 1967–70, Deputy Under-Secretary of State 1970–72 and Ambassador to South Africa 1973–6. Since 1976 he has been H.M. Diplomatic Service Permanent Representative to the United Nations and other International Organizations at Geneva.

[2] Prompted by Mr Wilson, Lord Goodman and Sir Max Aitken, Director and Chairman of Beaverbrook Newspapers Ltd, had a secret meeting in August with Ian Smith, to establish whether the Rhodesian leader would respond to an invitation to discuss a settlement with

on the action and once again he is in his 'finest hour', thrilled, longing to be off, loving having the press all around him, loving being the centre of world attention, feeling that at last he must win when he faces Smith eyeball to eyeball. So he gave us a good long lecture on how Smith needed a solution much more than we did, how economic sanctions had reached their maximum, how the South Africans wanted a settlement and how there was every reason why Smith should finally come to heel.

It's my impression that this lecture didn't convince a single member of Cabinet. In fact the only result was that Harold got a practically unanimous warning that he couldn't diverge one iota beyond the *Tiger* agreement.[1]

This afternoon I had to chair the committee on B.B.C. finance, knowing in advance that there was no chance of supplementing the licence fee by a degree of advertising. The fee has to go up by at least £1 and Harold hates to do this for fear of electoral unpopularity, although we pay less in Britain than in any other country in Europe for by far the best radio and television service. Harold is still looking for other methods. The other day he asked my committee to consider a method of purchase tax on T.V. and radio sets so we duly considered it and found it made no sense whatever to try to finance the B.B.C. this way. I had to find a way of politely turning him down. Our other problem was that Charles Hill, the new Chairman of the Governors of the B.B.C., had responded to pressure and publicly suggested that we should try to help old age pensioners and the sick by relieving them of the burden of their licence fees. This is much easier said than done but you can't give a blank negative to Charles Hill.

This afternoon the Social Services Committee met under my Chairmanship and my complete pension plan went through without any serious questioning except from James Callaghan, who after being Chancellor knew a great deal about it. The rest of the Ministers spent nearly all their time asking about the effect of the scheme on the pensions of the Civil Service. It's mainly because Ministers get so ministerial that we have such appallingly ineffective discussion of great social issues. No one looked at the main economic impact of the scheme, its social impact or its effect on women or its effect on trade unions. All that was left to the Ministry in charge.

---

the British Prime Minister. Mr Smith's determination to have no further negotiations except 'person to person' and the urgent need for a meeting were confirmed by an official meeting between Sir James Bottomley, the Governor and Mr Smith himself. See *Wilson*, pp. 565–70.

[1] From December 1st to 3rd, 1966, the Prime Minister had met Ian Smith for talks on board H.M.S. *Tiger*, cruising in the Mediterranean. Agreement was reached on a constitution that envisaged the eventual possibility of majority rule within ten to fifteen years and on terms for a return to legality, with the resignation of the Smith Government to be followed by an interim period of direct British rule by the Governor until a new Government had been elected. The Rhodesian Cabinet refused to agree to this process.

Wednesday, October 9th

Harold has flown away. He went off last night and we have a week almost empty of business. Everything is dominated by Rhodesia and the Gallup Poll shows the Tory lead has fallen by another 3 per cent.[1] So we have now been gaining slowly and steadily for nearly two months.

I had my first interview on this topic with Miss Nunn, who, with Burke on sick leave, is in charge of the Cabinet Secretariat. Burke apparently has virus pneumonia and will require another week at least before he can come back. Anyway Miss Nunn is in charge. She is a Bath girl, whom I first met at May Cowper's[2] beautiful flat in Cavendish Crescent. Miss Nunn is a very prim woman, with whom I usually get into difficulties although I keep trying to get on with her. For years she has been in charge of Social Services and on this occasion she had been sent to talk to me about devolution because once again this damned subject is at the top of the Prime Minister's mind and before going away he gave instructions that he wanted another paper from me on what could be done.

I explained to her in detail that nothing could now be done this session. The only thing I could suggest was that the paper, which was originally to be in two parts, A (what could be done now) and B (what must be done after Maud), should be run into one. I pointed out for the ninth time that as all our proposals on what could be done now had turned into chicken-feed, they should be discarded, so only a single paper was required. She drew herself up and said, 'I'm afraid it's part of the directive from the Prime Minister. We must have a paper and present it to all the Ministers concerned, at a meeting under his chairmanship.' 'Holy God,' I said. 'This is the kind of meeting I must try to spare him,' and we soon got into a real little row. She is a martinet; she had her instructions and was bound to carry them out or make me carry them out. It was no good my saying that I know what Harold wants and that it's my job to let him take the big decisions and keep the others out of his way, so I finally said she could have a go at drafting the paper.

This evening we went to one of the magnificent Weidenfeld dinners. What a marvellous host he is. I said to him as we came in, 'There ought to be an organization called "The Friends of George Weidenfeld" and one day the two or three hundred of us who come to your lovely parties will give a party in your honour with you as our only guest.' I certainly meant it and I think he was touched.

Thursday, October 10th

Harold is in Gibraltar and the talks are obviously bogging down, as they were bound to do. Meanwhile the Tories are settling down to a very successful Conference. I never shared Harold's view that this Conference was going to be terribly embarrassing for Heath. On the contrary Enoch Powell is a

[1] The Conservatives' lead over Labour had fallen from 10 per cent to 7 per cent.

[2] Anne Crossman's aunt.

positive advantage to him and clearly the Powell threat has, as threats often do, strengthened the Leader's position and developed his personality.

The Procedure Committee of the Cabinet, now chaired by Fred Peart as Leader of the House, held an important meeting this afternoon. We had to tell the Chief Whip what specialist committees we wanted and this enabled members of the Committee to vent their usual outbursts of complaints. Only Wedgy Benn had a word to say for specialist committees. He found them useful and the subjects they discussed helped him as Minister provided he handled matters right. But, broadly speaking, Ministers reflected the view of their Departments, which are still ferociously opposed and say that the committees are imposing a burden of work on civil servants at the same time as we are holding down staff numbers. At the end there was a great discussion on whether we couldn't abolish the abominable Agriculture Committee. It was agreed that we couldn't do so because there would be such an outcry in Parliament. Parliament, I was told, would insist that the Agriculture Committee should become permanent. This seemed sheer nonsense. We have given it the two-year run we promised, and Education should have a two-year run too, and then I can't see why we shouldn't switch to covering another Department.

But the most important problem we discussed was my new idea of pre-legislation committees. Now there were two candidates for the sort of measure we could discuss in this way. The Lord Chancellor wanted a committee on the law of privacy – bugging, invasion of privacy by mass media, telephones, etc. The other subject is that of public relations firms working for foreign governments. I thought the second far more interesting and fruitful than the first but I knew that owing to the excitement there had been about it in the press my name had become associated with this and it would be fatal for me to say a word. So I allowed the Lord Chancellor to make his case for a committee on privacy and to win a great deal of support for the idea. When he'd finished I was asked my opinion and I simply said that the Home Office was bound to note that the terms of reference would have to exclude all invasions of privacy by central or local government, by the army or by the police, and Parliament might well feel this a ridiculous frustration. Indeed I suspected that a committee could be prevented by its term of reference from considering particular areas which the P.M. and the Home Secretary didn't want invaded. I said this in such a way that I knew it would be in the Committee minutes and the moment the Home Secretary and the P.M. see it they will veto the affair and then I can run my own candidate.

This afternoon I caught a train to Winchester, to spend the evening at the hospital at the top of the hill above the castle. I met John Revans and Miss Gundry,[1] head of their nursing section, and a very able Secretary. This is a

[1] Dr John Revans, Assistant Senior Administrative Medical Officer to the South-West Metropolitan Regional Hospital Board 1948–51, Deputy SAMO 1951–9, and SAMO to the Wessex R.H.B. 1959–74. From 1974 until his retirement in 1976 he was Medical Officer to

tremendously lively group with extremely independent ideas. They took me upstairs after dinner to discuss new techniques of hospital building and I also put to them the problems of the N.H.S. Green Paper. Once again I got a very clear picture of what the Regional Hospital Boards want. If I go in for a reorganization in which there is integrated control of the hospitals and, with some modifications, G.P. services broadly administered through the present regions, I'll get a great deal of support.

Friday, October 11th

Drenching rain all day. My first appointment was to see an experiment in gipsy settlement outside Romsey in the New Forest. It was successful because a few people really cared about it, starting with the Chairman of the Welfare Committee and an excellent local government official who is number three in the Hampshire County Council. They had found the right young man for warden, bought a few old pre-fabs and planked down eighteen families of gipsies on the site and told them to make their homes there. They are gradually breaking their vagrancy and turning them into settled citizens. Something worth seeing. Then on to a geriatric hospital, the third I have seen. Again the R.H.B. is enormously proud of it. It is headed by a Catholic who is getting marvellous work out of his nurses. Here I found the doctor in charge adored by all the nurses, who were content to work under the most appalling physical conditions so they could serve under him. The patients were under far worse conditions than any I'd seen anywhere else. There were far too many beds crammed into a room, so crowded in fact that my last picture was of old men sitting by their beds having their dinner because there was no room in the living room.

When we had been round I specially kept back Revans and his staff and tried to clarify matters. The difference between the people here and the people in Oxford is in their attitude to the number of patients. At Oxford they say they will only have in hospital the number of people they can really look after with their new techniques, so twenty beds have been closed down. Here in Hampshire the wards are packed but there is plenty of staff because this hospital is so popular. The difference is that this doctor believes in letting all the old people who need it come into hospital, even if it means overcrowding. The Oxford people would say that true humanity requires you to harden your heart and refuse to overcrowd your hospital. The Hampshire humanity says that an overcrowded hospital with plenty of happy staff is the best thing you can hope for.

Saturday, October 12th

Last night I drove back from Southampton, reaching Prescote just before

---

the Wessex Regional Health Authority. He was knighted in 1977. Miss Freda Gundry, Chief Nursing Officer at the Wessex R.H.B. 1959–73, has been Regional Medical Officer at the Wessex R.H.A. since 1973.

midnight. Today we had a lovely day motoring across the Wantage hills, down into the Lambourne valley, where Michael Howard has his country cottage. On the way home we got out and walked along the Ridgeway in a beautiful evening. After a beastly summer we seem to have alternate days of ghastly driving rain and days of magnificent sunshine. This has been a lovely weekend, the last I suppose of my easy-going five months when I have been only three-quarters occupied but possibly serving quite a useful role in Cabinet. Soon I shall be back at the old departmental grind but this time everybody will be gunning for me and delighted to see me the fall guy.

Monday, October 14th

The return of Parliament but not in the sense of the start of a new term since we have a tag-end of a fortnight's overspill. We have come back to discuss the Lords' amendments to the Transport Bill and get it on the Statute Book. The Lord Chancellor, Eddie Shackleton and I had a great discussion this morning about the tactics for Lords' reform and the exact moment when we are to present our White Paper to the Tories. It will be drafted as a Government, not an all-party, White Paper and presented to Carrington and Jellicoe over the weekend, with a request that they make sure we have faithfully carried out the plans laid down during the all-party conference. Officially there will be no resumption of talks because, as Harold has seen with his brilliant sagacity, the Tories themselves don't want this, nor to take responsibility for the White Paper or the Bill. They are content to let it go ahead as a Government measure and they will be willing to let it be known that we are carrying out what was basically agreed at the talks. In this way we shall satisfy the extremists in both the Tory and the Labour Parties who detest the all-party discussions.

Tuesday, October 15th

At Cabinet the Prime Minister reported back from Gibraltar. He had flown in yesterday and got quite a good press this morning, though I still doubted whether he had achieved very much.[1] But by this morning I was pretty clear

[1] Before leaving for the talks on board H.M.S. *Fearless*, the Prime Minister had said that any agreement must include guarantees of unimpeded progress to majority rule and of a veto on any subsequent retroactive amendments to the Constitution. When the talks ended Mr Smith announced that his Cabinet in Salisbury would consider the British proposals but that 'disagreement on fundamental issues' remained.

In the White Paper (Cmnd 3793) published on October 15th it appeared that Mr Wilson had to a substantial extent conceded to the Smith regime on the terms for a return to legality, the point on which the *Tiger* talks had allegedly foundered. It was now proposed that Mr Smith should form a broad-based administration as soon as possible, including Africans. This would remain in office until the new constitution was introduced, elections held under it and a new parliament convened. There was to be an elected Legislative Assembly and Senate, with a guaranteed 'blocking quarter' of African elected members to prevent amendment of the constitution's 'entrenched clauses'. During the fifteen years envisaged as the period required to achieve majority rule, appeals might be made to the Judicial Committee of the Privy Council in London against proposed constitutional

that I had been wrong to oppose his going. By staying till Smith got sick of it and walked out he had created a situation where nobody could say that the British had not tried to make peace.

Harold was bouncy and full of energy; he had enormously enjoyed it but the new factor was his attitude to Smith. He admitted to me that their thirty hours' debate was the most exhausting experience of his life. Harold said Smith was the quickest-witted debater he had ever been up against and it was amazing that this former flight-lieutenant, with no real political background, had such ability and drive. I said to him, 'Yes, and isn't there something else amazing, Harold?' and I pointed out the article by Colin Legum in Sunday's *Observer*,[1] which asked why, after all, if Smith was a crook, the Rhodesians didn't at any rate sign on the dotted line, get their independence and then double-cross us.

'No,' Harold said. 'Quite right, Smith wouldn't do that. He wouldn't like to sign if he didn't mean to carry it out. In that sense he is basically an honest man.' It's clear that Harold has come back not despising Smith as he used to but admiring his qualities and this has made a very big difference.

Then we turned to the Queen's Speech and here you will find an interesting point in the Cabinet Minutes. Old Fred Peart said, 'This time we are trying to make the speech more readable for the Queen.' There was a hearty laugh all round, as though Fred Peart had really scored off that literary Crossman. As a matter of fact it was I who had first put this up and who had had the whole thing looked at because after last year's Queen's Speech I had learnt this from the Queen herself and had passed it on to Fred Peart. I hope it will mean that for the first time the Queen's Speech will be more than a mere rigmarole of Civil Service phraseology.

Afterwards Harold asked me to stay behind and we had a very short talk about the situation. He simply said, 'Look, this may be a very great disappointment to you but I am afraid you are not going to be able to keep Judith. I shall want her in the Cabinet.' I said immediately, 'I've always told Judith that if she is to get into the Cabinet she will have to leave me. That's absolutely clear but it's a great loss.' 'Yes,' he said, 'but doesn't that mean that you will need to keep Kenneth Robinson?' 'I'm afraid I can't,' I said, 'because I don't think he'll stay under me but I will have a try. The important thing, Harold, is to see that he gets another job and, as I told you before, he ought to take Niall MacDermot's place.'[2] 'Yes,' said Harold, 'but I don't want these changes to be a Cabinet reshuffle. I want to close them off

amendments that seemed discriminatory. The British Government also undertook to provide for ten years an annual matching grant of up to £5 million for an African education programme.

[1] The *Observer*'s Correspondent on African Affairs.

[2] Labour M.P. for Lewisham North February 1957–9 and for Derby 1962–70. He was Financial Secretary to the Treasury 1964–7 and Minister of State at M.H.L.G. 1967–8, and since 1970 has been Secretary-General of the International Commission of Jurists.

and just deal with the two mergers, with no other changes until I have had time to reflect. I haven't had time because of the Rhodesian talks.' 'Well,' I said, 'shall I go back to Kenneth straightaway and ask him to consider whether if Judith goes he will now stay or whether he will go and, if so, would he take Niall MacDermot's place?' I was given the authority to do it that way.

I rushed back to my room and immediately assumed that the decision must have been taken to sack Willie Ross and put Judith in for Scotland, because there didn't seem to be any other possible place. So I got hold of Kenneth Robinson and he came rattling round. He is a curious man. Once again he had been desperately hoping for a place in Cabinet. He had been told there was no chance but that makes no difference to Kenneth. He said to me, 'I'm a fighter, you know.' But he is not a fighter, he hangs on in the hope of something turning up. I said, 'It's not for you,' and I made it worse by saying, 'Judith is going to the Cabinet so you will be the only person here. Will you stay and work with me?' Fortunately we had the sense to say to each other that it wouldn't work because the doctors would be coming to him behind my back, which wouldn't be fair on either of us. 'In that case,' I said, 'why not take Niall MacDermot's job?' 'That's a step down, a mere Minister of State,' he said. 'On the contrary, Niall has been virtually running the Ministry of Housing. Poor old Tony can't do without him unless he gets a substitute. You would be infinitely better, my dear Kenneth, than anyone I could possibly imagine,' and then, warming to it, I said, 'and also you would get the responsibility for the Maud Commission and we could increase the salary and make it a special responsibility.' 'Ah,' he said, 'with a different title?'[1] 'Yes, a different title,' I said. 'Now please go away and think about it and talk to the P.M. Please do, because you will make all the difference.'

I had to rush off to the Ritz for a little lunch with George Weidenfeld who wanted to offer me the chairmanship of some board to run an international publishing venture in political studies. What a pretty place the Ritz is and how pleased I am that while I was at Housing I got it listed as one of the buildings worth preserving. There is that elegant corridor where you see on the left the sort of indoor terrace for drinks and then in this lovely garden room atmosphere you have the restaurant looking out on the park, light and airy with room between the tables – and old George Weidenfeld smooth and elegant. We had a most enjoyable time.

At 3.30 Harold made his Statement on Rhodesia. It was a triumph. I think this is the first time since devaluation that the P.M. has carried both sides of the Commons with him. This afternoon he convinced the Tories that he had been prime ministerial, that he had done an honest job and had genuinely tried to do what they asked him, while on our side there was the sense that there had not been a sell-out. The sense was still strong because

[1] He became Minister of Planning and Land.

people hadn't had time to study the terms and because they were themselves moved by the mood of the House.

Then I had to give the news to Judith. She swallowed a bit, because she had become unpopular in Scotland when she replaced Peggy Herbison at Social Security and now she realized that she would be unpopular because she is English. Yet of course she wanted to be in the Cabinet and here was the offer. Poor girl, she didn't sleep all night because with the best of faith I had given her the wrong information. At least I had said I was willing to give her up to give her a chance of promotion and, fortunately, I had been able to get her ideas for a replacement. I had mentioned the possibility that I should get Ivor Richard[1] (Denis Healey's P.P.S., an extremely able, fat lawyer, who batted very well against Callaghan on immigration). 'Oh no,' said Judith, 'he is too tough. You need someone with a heart. Why don't you have David Ennals?' I tried this out on the P.M. and he liked it straightaway, not, I've no doubt, just because David needed promotion but also because it would mean taking someone away from Jim Callaghan. So I decided to have Ennals and Stephen Swingler and cleared it with Harold before going round to Lockets, where I was to give a little dinner to Tommy, Peter Shore and Barbara.

This dinner was important in two ways. First of all we four, and possibly Wedgy Benn, have been trying to work out some kind of long-term policy for S.E.P. and the Cabinet on which we can keep together and tonight we made some progress. More important, I was asked about the shuffle and explained straightaway to Barbara how Judith was probably coming into the Cabinet,[2] how I thought Kenneth should go to Housing and that I wanted David Ennals and Stephen Swingler. Barbara fired off. 'That would be outrageous. You will be wrecking the Ministry of Transport. It's only because of Swingler that anything of what I fought for remains. I shall go to Harold straightaway and try to stop you.' And she did. She told Harold it was outrageous, that the Ministry of Transport couldn't do without Stephen and that she couldn't allow Dick to wreck her Ministry and her ideas. I think she went so far as to say that Harold ought to remove Dick

[1] Labour M.P. for Barons Court 1964–February 1974, he was Parliamentary Under-Secretary (Army) at the Ministry of Defence 1969–70, and has been U.K. Representative at the United Nations since 1974. He was Chairman of the December 1976 General Conference on Rhodesia.

[2] In a small Cabinet reshuffle on October 18th, Judith Hart took Lord Shackleton's place as Paymaster-General. He became Lord Privy Seal, succeeding Fred Peart, who was appointed Lord President of the Council. The mergers were announced between the Foreign and Commonwealth Offices and, taking effect on November 1st, between the Departments of Health and Social Security. From that date two new Ministers of State were to join Lady Serota at the D.H.S.S.: Stephen Swingler, who had been Minister of State at the Ministry of Transport, and David Ennals, who had been Under-Secretary of State at the Home Office. Norman Pentland, Charles Loughlin and Julian Snow were to be Under-Secretaries of State at the D.H.S.S. Niall MacDermot left the Ministry of Housing and Local Government on September 28th and from November 1st Kenneth Robinson was to be Minister for Planning and Land.

and, as a matter of fact, I am not sure that Dick now isn't in danger – but there it is.

Wednesday, October 16th

At O.P.D. we had a paper on Europe. This was another of M. Harmel's initiatives and Michael Stewart was seeking authority to welcome it.[1] There was a slight revolt from Denis Healey who said he felt these political initiatives never came to anything. We couldn't say no but we shouldn't set any great stock by it. We ought to get down to more practical things for Europe, like strengthening the military side. 'Ah,' said Roy, 'as long as it doesn't cost anything.' Then came the usual line-up. I tend to be with Denis, saying, 'Let's go into Europe in a practical way on the defence and NATO side. Let's stop this stately minuet between the rest of the Six and ourselves because, frankly, the Foreign Office is under a complete illusion to think we could possibly get in while General de Gaulle is President of France or even shortly afterwards. Our main job is just to go it alone, whether we like it or not. We are outside Europe and to be pleading and endlessly talking and manoeuvring is surely a mistake.' That's what Fred Peart, Denis and I feel, but of course the F.O. and, to do them justice, Harold Wilson too, can't take their hands off the effort to get into Europe.

But the time had come for me to go to the Palace for a Privy Council, my last time as Lord President. Next time it will be Fred Peart, whose appointment is to be announced tomorrow night. I had a little talk with the Queen, who knew that this afternoon I was to be appointed Secretary of State for Social Services and she asked where I was going to be. I said, 'The Elephant and Castle.' 'Oh,' she said, 'what a with-it address.' A funny remark, showing how completely out of touch she is, because of all the places which are not exactly with-it that dreary part of South London is the worst, brand new and yet unpopular and unmodish. However perhaps she meant to be nice to me.

In the afternoon we had the Statement on the mergers, quietly and with no excitement. I sat beside the P.M. while he announced them and I couldn't help remembering that it was exactly what he had offered me. I should stay Minister for co-ordinating the Social Services, with the title of Secretary of State, but under me I should have the Department of Health and Social Security, a narrower realm. My departmental responsibilities are far narrower than my Secretary of State responsibilities, which means that if

[1] In January France had refused to agree to the reopening of negotiations towards British membership of the E.E.C. France's partners in the E.E.C. still hoped that Britain would continue to seek to join the Six and during the autumn they offered further initiatives. On October 21st and 22nd a meeting of the Council of the Western European Union in Rome discussed proposals of M. Pierre Harmel, the Belgian Foreign Minister, to expand and strengthen the W.E.U. in the fields of foreign policy, defence and technological co-operation. All the Foreign Ministers of the member Governments except France received the proposals with interest and agreed to consider them at an informal meeting in Brussels in November during the NATO ministerial meeting.

I am successful I can, not control, but have a considerable influence upon the whole block. Harold is awfully good in these ways. In the end he does with great conscientiousness deliver an offer he has made.

This afternoon Judith came up and said, 'You were wrong. I can't tell you what it is.' She had just heard from Harold what she had been offered. In the evening Anne came up for dinner. We had to stay in the House as it was a three-line whip on the Lords' amendments to the Transport Bill and we were dining together at one table and Judith and her Tony at another near by. She was happy and gay because she had got her Cabinet job and Tony was delighted. Afterwards we had drinks with them. Everybody was curious about Judith's job. I racked my brains, I couldn't see what it could be and didn't guess that Harold was going to make her a female George Wigg and put her into his old room at No. 10 as Paymaster-General.

Thursday, October 17th

The announcement of the mergers had an excellent press. Michael Stewart and I received a great deal of attention and it had been a good day for the Government.

At Cabinet we had the European thing again. The doubts expressed in O.P.D. about the value of all these manoeuvres were much more strongly expressed all round the table and Harold and Michael were really rather alone in battling against them. Denis and I were very strong and the others backed us up.

We got Lords' reform through in eight minutes, the tactic and the whole White Paper. It was curious, a whole elaborate piece of reform agreed when they have never really read it. It's something that happens in our Labour Cabinet. I had been reflecting on how to handle all this and when I talked at length to Eddie Shackleton we agreed that Callaghan must be brought in to take over the Bill. At the meeting of the Cabinet Committee on Lords' reform where the White Paper was presented, Jim had been in a dangerous mood, saying it wasn't popular enough and that we must now angle it towards our own supporters and not go on praising the House of Lords. So we had deleted a great many passages mentioning qualities the House of Lords possesses. I have been fascinated by the absolute arrogance of our Commons Members, led by Jim, who say about the Lords, 'They've got no more distinction than the House of Commons.' The fact is that the Commons is an absurd place. But no one ever goes up from the Commons to the Lords to see what is going on there and M.P.s feel it is a place they have to retire to and are insulted when someone suggests that it has any merits. On this I really am a minority in Cabinet. Carrington said ages ago and Gardiner said again today, 'You are the only member of the House of Commons, Dick, who has seen enough of us to appreciate us.' And I think they are right.

Next we turned to the big pension plan. We had forty-five minutes for it and I decided to concentrate on the two issues of how to get our state scheme working alongside the private scheme and what terms of contracting-out we should allow the private schemes and, secondly, the annual review. Roy and I had a fairly elevated discussion and afterwards the P.M. said to me, 'I couldn't read the papers and I only began to understand it when you and Roy discussed it.' We shall resume this next week and before then I must see Roy and try to settle things with him.

Prime Minister's Questions this afternoon were very dull. I had to catch Harold afterwards between 3.30 and 4.0 and he told me at length about Judith and her new job and made it quite clear that he missed George Wigg and wanted someone to play that kind of role as his confidant and adviser. It struck me immediately that Judith would be very good at this. 'Would I,' he asked tactfully, 'let her take over the Small Committee?' My God, that bloody Small Committee at Transport House. I was delighted to let it go and I said I'd let her have the Home Publicity Committee as well, but that I would like to keep the Cabinet Committee on Agriculture. All that went very easily. He was able to report that Barbara's intervention about Stephen Swingler had been ineffective and that Dick Marsh had decided not to appoint anybody in Stephen's place but would be content with just two Parliamentary Secretaries. Why? Because he wants to get rid of Stephen, Barbara's legacy, and to have his own Ministry. There's arrogance for you, combined with incompetence to a point which makes me feel he is heading for a disaster.

Harold also told me that Kenneth Robinson had come to see him and accepted MacDermot's job. This pleased me enormously because yesterday I had discussed the whole thing with Niall. He is going to leave Parliament to go and earn his living in Geneva so it is an enormous relief to hear that Kenneth has accepted. I had a feeling the whole thing was pretty well lined up and Harold told me that he would be announcing it this evening and that Fred Peart would be taking over from me as Lord President, while I would take over Fred's rooms in the Privy Council Office. Harold was extremely pleased with the press this morning and elated as a result of his Rhodesian success. There is always the danger with him that directly he gets any success the whiff goes to his nostrils and he over-inflates his importance and what he can actually do.

So off I went to King's Lynn on the easy-going East Anglian train, getting down there in time for a quick change and a drink with Douglas Garnett, before we went to their splendid Town Hall, a huge great gilded room with a lovely plaster ceiling. There were some sixty or seventy people, including Derek Page, the young Member,[1] an enterprising Chairman of a small chemical company of his own, with a forceful wife. He quarrels with me

[1] Labour M.P. for King's Lynn 1964–70 and unsuccessful Labour candidate for Norfolk North West in February 1974. Since 1962 he has been Director of Cambridge Chemical Co. Ltd, and since 1970 of Buckmaster & Page Ltd.

pretty often, he is an awkward cuss on the specialist Agricultural Committee and he fought me on the tied cottage,[1] but he really is a splendid local Member.

Friday, October 18th

This proved to be a very interesting day and I began to realize that, with its desperately low wages and dwindling population, with the young people pouring out and old people coming in, Norfolk needs industrial development at least as much as many parts of the South-West, Wales, Scotland or Northumberland. It isn't getting it. All the way round Norfolk I found little towns like Swaffham and Dereham that are dying.

The Norwich Labour Party had just spent £50,000 on an enormous magnificent new hall and we had a kind of procession, acted by the Ipswich Women's Section, to celebrate the fiftieth anniversary of women's suffrage. We also celebrated on Judith's behalf and I was asked what I thought about women in politics. I said that I thought the qualities required for a Prime Minister are more often held by women than by men and it made a little news item for them.

On I went, right across the fen lands, dreary, flat country, to a great dinner at Wisbech and then down to the huge railway sidings of March, a dwindling area with again a dwindling party. The Chairman of the Council said March wants overspill from Peterborough, eighteen miles away. It was fascinating to think that Peterborough was booming and here was March in the atmosphere of Norfolk and the Isle of Ely, dying on its feet. That was my lesson. I was motored all the way home and got here at 1 a.m.

Saturday, October 19th

The first thing I heard on the B.B.C. news was that Tony Wedgwood Benn had addressed some thirty people in a church hall in his constituency and made a tremendous declaration of war against the B.B.C. for lack of objectivity and failure to do its duty in reporting current politics. I did remember that when the boxes arrived for me yesterday morning at King's Lynn they had contained a press release of a speech of his and I am afraid that though it looked mildly interesting I hadn't had time to read it. Even if I had, I couldn't have done anything about it because by then it had been issued to the press. The speech covered the whole area that I am going to discuss in my Guildhall speech. I don't think I can have any doubt that Tony knew about this lecture. Everyone has known that it is coming on, it has been discussed in the newspapers for months and I think I have discussed

[1] Farm workers living in tied cottages were particularly vulnerable to eviction and this issue had always been politically contentious, especially as the N.U.A.W. spokesman on the N.E.C. came from East Anglia, where agricultural labour was highly organized. Crossman had inserted in his 1964 Protection from Eviction Act a change requiring a six-month delay before farmers could legally evict their tenants, during which the magistrates' court would assess the balance of interests. See Vol. I, p. 62n.

some of my thoughts with Tony. Now he has bashed in his speech without a word to me. After working away for a fortnight on my lecture it is now finished and I have just sent a script over to Granada. My whole aim has been to create a new atmosphere between the B.B.C., the Independent Television companies and ourselves, by showing that there is one member of the Government who understands the problems of the press, radio and T.V., is sympathetic about them and is expounding fairly objectively the problems of co-operation between the Government and the T.V. authorities. There is a long tradition of bickering between the Labour Government and the B.B.C. and what Tony expressed is much more what the Prime Minister feels. Tony has muddied the waters and whatever happens I shall have to speak in the atmosphere his speech has created.

I was really pretty angry. I rang up No. 10 and talked to Henry James,[1] who was very helpful, and then I got on to Harold and checked that he hadn't known about this speech until Thursday night and that though he had approved the tone of the speech, he was angry with Tony for making it. There is a certain doubleness here, because though the P.M. was truly indignant and sympathetic it really isn't to be denied that he agrees with Tony and feels it is unwise for him to make a broad frontal attack on the B.B.C. himself. There wasn't much to be done. Our friend Henry James said he would make sure the press was briefed.

Sunday, October 20th

As far as I can see Henry James only spoke to Jimmy Margach because he hasn't dealt at all adequately with the other papers.[2] Tony, though, has hit the headlines in an astonishing way and now I am told that Ray Gunter has made a great speech attacking Tony for his attack on the B.B.C. Tony Crosland rang up today to sympathize, saying he supposed I didn't love Tony very much. The only issue now is whether my speech will fall flat and be regarded as pure milk and water compared with Benn's thunder and lightning, or whether the contrast will be noted and approved. I am pretty satisfied with what I have done and I can't do it any better now. It's completely finalized and circulated and I've just got to wait until I deliver it.

John and Catherine Freeman are staying here. He is just back from being High Commissioner to India and is on his way to be Ambassador to America. I am godfather to his son Matthew, and John's boys and our children have got on wonderfully. It has been an extremely enjoyable weekend, with the added touch of good fortune that while I have been worrying and fuming over the row about T.V. and broadcasting I have had on the whole issue

[1] Chief Press Officer at the Ministry of Education 1963–4, Deputy Public Relations Adviser to the Prime Minister 1964, Deputy Press Secretary to the Prime Minister 1964–8, Chief Information Officer at the M.H.L.G. 1969–70, Press Secretary at No. 10 Downing St 1970–1 and Director of Information, D.O.E. 1971–4. Since 1974 he has been Director-General of the Central Office of Information.

[2] James Margach was the Political Columnist of the *Sunday Times*. He retired in 1976.

such a quiet, reliable, steady, sensible adviser as John and such a lively adviser as Catherine.[1]

Monday, October 21st

I went up by train to a busy morning, starting with the House of Lords. This week Eddie Shackleton, the Lord Chancellor and I have to face the problem of whether to make contact with the Tories or not. Everything still depends on the Transport Bill but it was pretty clear by today that the Tory peers were going to climb down and that the Bill would go through.[2] We went in to advise the P.M. on the line we wanted to take and to check over all the arrangements. We explained the idea of Jim Callaghan's being the Minister in charge and the P.M. saw this straightaway. Jim is a magnificent Parliamentarian but untrustworthy on the Bill and might easily suddenly surrender to a pressure group, so we need to give him a small committee. We suggested for this our delegation to the all-party talks. 'No,' the Prime Minister said, 'let's have a reconstituted committee, a Cabinet Committee called Parliamentary Reform (Lords).' Sure enough, after our talk, this was all redictated by him in a minute.

I lunched in a corner of the dining room with David Ennals and Stephen Swingler, whom I found keen and excited at their new prospects. I cleared in their minds the division of labour. I wanted Stephen to take over from Judith at John Adam Street with charge of all Social Security except the Pension Plan. David Ennals has to accept the fact that I am bound to pay more attention to Health in the first six months and that I will be more on top of him at the Elephant and Castle. This is quite natural because Stephen is a Minister of State already while David has only just earned his promotion. All that went very easily and we really had no difficulty.

At 5.30 I got home to the children. Anne has brought them up for their half-term holiday and I found them being got ready for bed and our reading aloud. After a last-minute look at my lecture, Anne and I climbed into the car and Molly drove us off to the Guildhall. There was an excellent dinner beforehand but I was a bit edgy and excited because there had been an immense build-up for the lecture and all 900 seats had been taken. Hugh Greene introduced me very formally and I realized that although I had hoped just to read the lecture quietly,[3] this huge audience would have been bored stiff so I would have to perform. I put it over with as much dynamism, expression, movement as I could, standing up, bending down, I really let

[1] Catherine Dove had been a television producer.

[2] On October 23rd the Lords considered the Commons' Amendments to the Lords' Amendments, the Commons' Reasons and the Commons' consequential and other Amendments. The Bill received the Royal Assent on October 25th.

[3] Sir Hugh Carleton Greene joined the B.B.C. in 1940 as Head of the German Service. He was Director of News and Current Affairs 1958–9, Director-General 1960–9 and a Governor 1969–71. Since 1969 he has been Chairman of the Bodley Head and since 1971 Chairman of Greene, King & Sons Ltd. During the war he and Crossman had worked together on propaganda methods and psychological warfare.

myself go. I had to stand up again at the end and bow before Hugh Greene got up to comment.

Now at table Hugh Cudlipp had been telling Hugh Greene that he must attack Wedgy Benn and I think he overdid it. He attacked him four times, praising me and making the contrast between Benn's speech and my constructive suggestions and committing himself wholly to the idea that I had said what was right. Then he offered me an open-ended programme on Thursday evening. I didn't have the quickness of wit to say, 'I'll come on if you do.' The whole atmosphere was one of congratulation and I was enormously exhilarated. After weeks and weeks of work I had pulled the damned thing off. I knew I had gone across with a bang but as I rushed home to see Tommy, who wanted to prepare me for S.E.P. tomorrow morning, I wasn't sure how the press would treat me.

Tuesday, October 22nd

I have never had a speech so fully and adequately covered. I got an overwhelming press. The whole of *The Times* centre page was beautifully laid out, the *Telegraph* gave a very full account and even the *Guardian* mentioned Hugh Greene's offer. At 8.45 I was down in the sitting-room being interviewed by William Hardcastle for 'The World At One' and then off I went with Patrick for our haircut. His hair is cut every three months now so that Mr Large can do it. Haircuts are getting American. We just had a haircut and shampoo and I had a manicure and between us it cost 38*s*. It would have cost £1 at most, perhaps 18*s*., before.

Because of this I was late at S.E.P. and I found that no new places had been arranged to take account of the Cabinet shuffle. Denis Healey had come in late and taken my place next to Roy Jenkins so I found myself sitting at the far end of the table up amongst the Cabinet Secretariat. It made me realize how difficult it is for a Minister at the end of the table on the same side as the P.M. to get an oar in. In Cabinet the talk goes on between the P.M. and the Chancellor on the one side and between the Foreign Secretary, the Home Secretary and the Defence Secretary on the other. Those at the middle talk to each other and those at the ends of the table have to shout to be heard. There I was up beyond Burke Trend, where I used to sit as Minister of Housing and where Roy Mason sits today. Quite an interesting experience. I had to lean right back to catch Harold's eye behind people's heads before I could get in.

It was an extremely important meeting because we had the first paper on the reform of P.E.S.C. I have often talked about this. For the whole of our four years we have been on a procrustean bed as a result of always assessing the amount of public expenditure by what has to be cut. We are now trying to see whether we can work out a method of classifying expenditure according to various other criteria: (1) according to the amount of resources it absorbs; (2) according to the amount of borrowing we have to do to pay for it; and (3) according to the amount of taxation that has to be raised. A brilliant paper had been produced which did all this. I'm not absolutely sure of the net result because, as someone rightly pointed out, how much you have as the total still doesn't depend on how you've broken it down into component parts.

The really critical paper this morning was on the planned expenditure for 1970/1, the last year of this Labour Government. The Chancellor said he must ask us now to agree firmly to a further £250 million cut in public expenditure, to bring ourselves within the borrowing requirement we've agreed with the I.M.F. No doubt about it, as a result of handing ourselves over to the international bankers, we are tied hand and foot. Certainly Tommy, Barbara and I felt that in this winter of 1968 it would be an absolute tragedy to commit ourselves to cuts for 1970/1 because this really is surrendering long before we get there. Roy's case was simple enough. We had agreed to put the balance of payments as top priority, and this demands that the borrowing requirement be kept down and that we sacrifice everything to this, including the election. Further cuts of £250 million will probably mean charging for hospital beds or at least abolishing free school milk, putting up the price of school meals again and another round of that kind of thing. Tony Crosland said very vigorously, as he always does, that he didn't want to assume in advance that it was preferable to cut £250 million from expenditure rather than to raise it in tax. He was strongly supported by Barbara and me, Fred Peart too. Indeed, the Chancellor got very little support except resolutely from the Prime Minister. Roy then tried saying, 'We won't make it absolute but we will say that we will make the cuts and if things get better later on we can revise it nearer the date.' We know very well that if cuts are made and Whitehall Departments know the decision three years ahead revision becomes infinitely easier. It's true that it's easier to revise up than revise down. On the other hand, Whitehall being as it is and the Chancellor's influence being what it is, it is also true that the chance of the Chancellor revising up is very small, once the cuts have been written in, the decision taken and a certain amount of information produced. So we resisted. Before anything is done we must have the meeting I have been asking for for so long, on the strategy for the run-up to the election and what we are trying to achieve in our last two years. Here we can discuss the balance of advantage between absolutely committing ourselves to cuts in expenditure or leaving the possibilities open.

Afterwards I got back to the Privy Council office where Patrick and Virginia were waiting. All this week I have been loving that big office with the National Gallery pictures melting into the walls, that beautiful little outer hall, the loveliest place I have ever had to work or indeed to live in. I shall miss it desperately.

Sir Godfrey Agnew had made all the arrangements for our afternoon. I took the children across to the Commons for lunch and then we went off to the Palace, where they were allowed to come in. They were taken to see the gardens and a little of the Palace while I went in for the transfer of my authority to Fred Peart. We had the tiny little Privy Council, Fred first, Shackleton second, Michael Adeane third, and me, as the new Secretary of State, fourth. My seals of office were rather ridiculous because they were really the seals of the Commonwealth Office with sticky tape over them to change their character.

The Queen was rather careful, examining the boxes in a friendly way to see we all had the right seals, and then she had a jolly talk with Fred and Eddie. I felt she was very much more at ease with them than she was with me. She thanked me very much for what I had done, said goodbye and I was out. I found the children in the garden and we had a walk round the Palace and saw a few of the rooms before we drove back to the House of Commons. Interesting, the effect on them. They are usually bouncing and ebullient but Virginia said, 'I shan't tell anybody at school about this.' She is clever and wise, because she would be laughed at. Strangely enough, I think the children really were impressed. It looked and felt like the kind of palace they had dreamed of and they were a bit solemn inside.

A mysterious message was waiting that Lord Carrington wanted to see me. He didn't want to see Eddie, he wanted to see me. I found Carrington looking rather uncomfortable. He explained he wanted to see me alone because although he liked Eddie he had been appallingly upset by a story he thought had been planted in the *Sunday Telegraph* saying the Government had decided that if the peers opposed the Transport Bill the whole reform deal would be off and we would have to have a radical reform.*

However when Carrington had got off his complaint, I told him exactly what I wanted. He said, 'It's no good talking to me, you should go personally to Heath and explain it all to him.' I spelt out to Carrington exactly what we required. In a nutshell, we are going to ask for a release from the pledge of confidentiality so that we can publish the results of the all-party talks. We want an assurance that the scheme we are propounding faithfully conserves the principles agreed in the talks and we need an assurance that the Tories will operate the scheme if it becomes law. 'Can you arrange', said Carrington, 'to go to Heath with Eddie? He will have me there.' So I got on to the Lord Chancellor, we had another talk this evening and we are to have the meeting on Thursday.

Barbara had called a dinner together in her flat. She had invited an odd collection, Gerald Gardiner, Wedgy Benn, Judith, Tommy and Peter too. Meeting Wedgy was awkward for me. He tried to apologize and I think I was reasonably courteous but Barbara told me afterwards I wasn't. In the course of our short talk he said that by the time he had talked to me about

* I am almost certain that Eddie did put this in, though he denied it later on, but it was very effective. The Lords let us have the Bill without a murmur and Eddie was wise to give them a reminder.

the Granada speech last Tuesday his constituency meeting was already fixed and that he couldn't possibly go back on the promise he had made to deliver that very day this particular one in his series of important speeches. I had forgotten about our Tuesday talk. It completely confirmed my suspicions that he did know about the contents of my Guildhall lecture and deliberately got ahead of me. He felt very sore about being treated so badly, misquoted and abused and I felt angry at what he had done to me.

However we moved on to the central issue of this morning's S.E.P. We were determined that, as well as Tony Crosland, Barbara, as First Secretary should write a paper and put it in so we should have two papers on the alternatives to what you might call Roy Jenkins's policy of acceptance of catastrophe. Roy may want to have a record of upright Chancellorship for his survival. He will still be a young man in the next Government or in the next Government but one. For all I know there may be a break up of the two-party system. But it seemed clear to us that it would be a disaster to accept the policy of cuts in 70/1 now without any resistance. I have a feeling we are by no means out of the wood here with the Chancellor and we are in great difficulty about the possibility of high rates of unemployment in 1969 and again in 1970/1. Our main case will be the madness of cutting public expenditure at a time when we fear we may find ourselves with unused resources and unemployment.

It was really an exciting and useful evening and in the middle some of us decided to stay on. It was the day of the vote on the Adjournment Motion on the *Fearless* terms. Our own people didn't need us there and anyway I am sure Judith and Barbara didn't much want to vote on that issue. But Wedgy said he had to rush back and as he went he threw a piece of paper at Judith and said, 'I hear you have now become the censor of our speeches. Here's mine.' Judith and I read the speech he is to deliver tomorrow, the second of his great series, an interminable fourteen-page philosophical homily about participation. The real trouble about Wedgy is that philosophically he is, not second-rate, but non-existent. Curiously, he has got this great public relations sense but he is no serious thinker. He is furious with Judith having become Paymaster-General and he had also learnt that Harold had issued an absolutely stinging directive, with sly references to the 'guru of Wolverhampton', saying we shouldn't have any guru, implying that Wedgy was trying to be a Powellist kind of party prophet and that cobblers should stick to their lasts.

Wednesday, October 23rd

The papers were full of the Labour Party revolt on Rhodesia, something like fifty instead of thirty rebels.[1] During the week feeling against a settle-

[1] The motion was carried by 177 votes to 66 but 49 Labour M.P.s voted against the Government and at least 100 abstained. In Salisbury the Chairman of the Rhodesian Front, Mr Smith's own party, had attacked the terms as 'total and abject surrender'.

ment on the basis of the *Fearless* discussions has been steadily growing. It looks as though Smith has also ratted on his side of the world, so once again the two men were brought together, tried very hard because they really want a settlement and were then torn apart by their own supporters. However this time I think the Prime Minister has greatly strengthened his position *vis-à-vis* the Tories, indeed probably *vis-à-vis* his own supporters, by going as far as he could and then showing he won't go over the edge.

At 6 a.m. I started on the draft White Paper on National Superannuation and at 8 o'clock Brian Abel-Smith came and, as we often do, we breakfasted together until 10 o'clock when back he had to go to L.S.E. (which, by the way is now in revolution). We have had a great struggle with this White Paper and, my God, I hope we get it right because we ought to have a draft ready for the end of next week. I know that Brian's part, the first part, really won't do and I know that other parts of the draft are devastatingly dull. I dread reading them and though I musn't put it off any longer I funk it. The White Paper is important and if I get one that flops, as it does at present, I may really have to postpone publication until after Christmas.

After Home Affairs Committee we had a new meeting on the eternal problem of devolution. Last week the Prime Minister had called a special meeting because we had to decide quickly whether or not to announce in the Queen's Speech the establishment of a constitutional commission. I had put in a paper, saying, 'For heaven's sake don't rush it. We may be driven to a Royal Commission but let's try everything else first. We really shouldn't take any decision until after we have seen the Maud Report.' This morning I found the cards had been stacked against me. The P.M. was scrupulously nice and to every point I made he replied, 'That is very important,' but he and Callaghan had made up their minds and Callaghan had submitted a paper, signed by Willie Ross and George Thomas recommending a commission. Those two have been bought over very easily, because they are anti-nationalist and this is a way of doing nothing. The Home Secretary plus two Secretaries of State against a mere one voice, me, were bound to win and they did. They had fixed it with the P.M. and I could do nothing about it.

Thursday, October 24th

At Cabinet we started on devolution. Right at the beginning, when we were discussing parliamentary business for next week, the P.M. tried to slip in that there would have to be a reference to devolution in the Queen's Speech, because the Committee had met and agreed on what he then called a Constitutional Committee. As you might expect, there was an explosion. Poor Peter Shore was outraged, as D.E.A. is vitally affected by questions of regional government, and our friend Judith was pretty upset, though she couldn't complain because she had been asked to the meeting. The man most insulted of all was the Minister of Housing and Local Government and for once old Tony fired off. Quite clearly Harold couldn't just push this through so now we are to have another paper next Monday, to be discussed at a large meeting of Ministers, including Housing and D.E.A., chaired by the Prime Minister. It will be extremely interesting.

Next we had Gerald Gardiner making a great protest on Biafra. As usual he was completely ineffective and was quietly demolished by the Foreign Secretary and George Thomson, the old Commonwealth Secretary, who said, 'Look, every African State is with us. They are supporting Nigeria against Biafra.[1] Don't be so ridiculous.' Then we had the P.M. on Vietnam,[2] which had been raised, I think, by Barbara, with pleas that we should change our policy. The Prime Minister and George Brown had decided long ago to play their role as mediators for peace and standing close to the Americans is the price. I am convinced that this is the central issue. The P.M. passionately thinks we have been effective and can still be important. Denis Healey and I feel we really can't play any part in peace-making precisely because we have not been able to denounce the Americans. Denis put it very clearly. He would like to see us behaving more like Europeans, more like the Germans, and we should dispense with postures of this sort. This is the opposite of what people like Barbara, Peter Shore and Tony Benn want. They all believe that this country still can be great, and they don't see that if we are going to cease to be a great power and withdraw from east of Suez and go into Europe then the peculiar Anglo-Saxon lecturing will have to go.

After all this at about noon we got to the pensions policy where the discussion was totally inadequate because the P.M. had to drop out half-way. This is something to note about Cabinet – if you have an important issue, don't let it come up to number three, or, even worse, number three in two Cabinets running, as has happened to pensions. The central economic issues are still undecided and Roy and I both want them settled. I also had some difficulties about whether the Paper is to be White or Green. We have a White Paper when it's Government policy and a Green Paper if we are trying things out, and I rather rashly said in Cabinet it should be Green. Later, though, I got the Cabinet minutes rewritten because the Secretariat is wholly in sympathy on this particular item. Instead we shall have 'a White Paper with a greenish tinge', something I certainly didn't say in Cabinet.

[1] As the Nigerian civil war continued the eastern state of Biafra sought diplomatic recognition. Only four states, Gabon, Ivory Coast, Tanzania and Zambia, were prepared to grant this. In September it appeared that France was contemplating recognition and not only did she give Biafra increasing diplomatic support but, despite her ban on arms sales to either side in the war, arms continued to flow into Biafra through the two former French colonies of Gabon and the Ivory Coast. Meanwhile Nigeria continued to receive Soviet and British weapons.

[2] On March 31st President Johnson had announced that the bombing of North Vietnam would be limited and in May the Americans and the North Vietnamese had their first talks in Paris. It seemed that some understanding was reached and from November 1st the bombing of North Vietnam was completely halted, although the war between North and South continued to rage.

Back to my room for a quick plate of meat and to think for a tiny bit, if I could, about this damned T.V. evening ahead. I was interrupted all the time and then I had to rush round to the House of Commons to see Ted Heath. There I found Reggie Maudling, who had just come from the Escargot, where he had eaten a great many snails and said he smelt of garlic. What he smelt of was having had too much to drink for lunch. He was unable to follow what we were saying, but Ted Heath was very dignified and statesmanlike. I delivered the message, gave him a copy of the White Paper and left.

After P.M.'s Questions I had to make my little speech on the Merger Order and then sit through two hours of debate. It seemed interminable. I wound up with a pleasant little reply and my new Private Secretary, Ron Matthews, an extremely efficient young man, who was watching me with great care, turned and said to Paul Odgers who was in the box with him, 'By jove, he is surprisingly relaxed, your fellow.' It's true that compared with the tightly-buttoned attitude of Kenneth Robinson my general method of informality and candour is quite different.

When I had finished there was time to go across to the Privy Council Office to think out what I was to do tonight. John Grist had told me that the B.B.C. was going to try to get twelve people to take part. 'Too many,' I said. 'Four is the number you want.' I wanted a cross-examination and I suspected more and more that this was becoming an 'on trial'. I said, 'I'm awfully sorry but the Director-General has asked me to expound on an open-ended broadcast and if I am to expound my views I must do it in the order I want and with the balance I want.' I had spent forty-five minutes hammering and bullying him, because he is an obstinate cuss, and by saying I wasn't going to come unless we got it right I forced the thing through.

There was no real difficulty at all. Huw Wheldon and Robin Day seemed friendly.[1] 'Of course,' they said, 'you've done enormous good already.' I found Hugh Greene sitting about looking rather sheepish. The only man who didn't talk to me at all was the strange, anodyne, colourless chairman, Robin McNeil,[2] who had been specially flown back from covering the Presidential elections in America. I should perhaps have noticed him more before we got on the air. It was scrappy but it wasn't so bad and the main thing was that we covered the ground in the order I wanted. Though we

[1] Huw Wheldon was Head of Music and Documentary Programmes for B.B.C. T.V. 1963–5 and Controller of Programmes 1965–8. He was Managing Director, Television, at the B.B.C., 1969–75. In 1975 he became Chairman of the Court of Governor of the London School of Economics. He was knighted in 1976.

[2] A Canadian (known in North America as Robert MacNeil), he had worked for Reuters in London 1950–60 and joined the National Broadcasting Company of Canada in 1960. From 1967 to 1974 he worked for B.B.C. T.V., mostly for 'Panorama', and since 1974 he has presented his own programme 'The MacNeil Report' on the American Public Broadcasting Service. He was the author of a book about the influence of television on American politics, *The People Machine* (New York: Harper & Row, 1968).

had eight people instead of four it was a great advantage to me because they were all running over each other trying to get their piece in.

Right at the end, and this was the fascinating thing, the chairman said, 'Excuse me, just before we close can I raise a point? From the way that your speech and Mr Benn's were reported in the press there seems to be a general impression in the country that your Government is trying to intimidate the television industry, eighteen months or so before you might be going into an election. I am just wondering if you would address yourself to that just before we close.' I must say that seemed staggering, 'just before we close', and so I argued back. McNeil said again, 'Would you deny that there is any connection between the crisis in communication that your Government suffers from at the moment and the coincidence that within a few days of each other two Ministers of the Government suddenly come out with very stringent criticisms of the B.B.C.?'

This made it clear that the chairman was my most hostile opponent. He was putting charges which during the course of the hour nobody else had made and maybe I lost my temper, I don't know, probably not. I think that the B.B.C. hoped there would be a sensational flare-up and that this would continue for another twenty-five minutes, but it didn't. We managed to cut it down and right at the end I turned to McNeil and said, 'You dirty bastard, what did you do that for? You're supposed to be a chairman and you behaved like a bleeding member of the prosecution.' He took affront and walked away. As we went out I said the same to John Grist, who objected to being called a bastard in the presence of all his junior staff. I said, 'I'm delighted your staff should hear it because I think you are. It's an outrage. Chairmen are there to be impartial. You had eight people there to raise things. If they weren't capable of it why should the chairman drag them in?' This went on over drinks downstairs. I never saw Robin McNeil again but I had a long talk to the others. People were very congratulatory and as Hugh Greene saw me out he said, 'Well, it was an event, anyhow.' And it was.

Friday, October 25th

I got to bed at 1 a.m. and I was up at 8.0 to breakfast in the House of Lords with Eddie and Michael Wheeler-Booth. They had the draft letter to Heath confirming our conversation yesterday and at 10.30 I had to go into the Prorogation with the P.M. to talk to him about it. I found him in his room with Fred Peart. In the Commons Fred and I, the two atheists, stood for prayers on the Government side and then the House filled up a bit while we waited for the Lords to finish. We had the usual performance, the march across to the Lords, standing, hearing the interminable list of all the Acts which have been passed. Second came the Transport Act. I said 'Hear, hear,' and the P.M. looked round, shocked because for him it was the middle of divine service. He looked the most respectable man, standing there with his head in the air, in his black coat with his grey hair. He was due to go to Princess Marina's memorial service and enjoy that as well.[1] Oh, dear, I really am an irreverent, independent old boy compared with our Establishment Prime Minister.

Saturday, October 26th

Michael Bessie, my American publisher,[2] and his wife Cornelia are staying with us and last night he and I and Jack Butterworth had a great talk about tomorrow's protest against the Vietnam war. Yesterday we had the capture of L.S.E. by the students, making it a harbour of refuge during this demonstration. On Thursday Cabinet discussed the Home Secretary's refusal to have troops even standing by behind the scenes, because the police think they can manage it. The police plan to let the students sit down in Whitehall and go on sitting there for ever. What does this demonstration represent? Is it, as Jack Butterworth was asking last night, that a small hard core of revolutionary, so-called Che Guevarists are organizing and stimulating anarchy and violence?[3] Or is it really rooted in student discontent with authority, or in protest against Western democracy? All I know is that if I had to choose between being a Minister in a Labour Government, however unpopular, and a university vice-chancellor, it would be a far more anxious job now to be a vice-chancellor.

Whatever we say about the particular reasons for the student thing I am sure it is centred in a hard core of professional troublemakers. There is no question, though, that in a sense it is part of a broader issue, the crisis of democracy, the subject I was raising in my Granada speech and in the television round table on Thursday. Television can make or mar. It doesn't only report but it has a great influence on events and my argument is that trivialization on television has created indifference, cynicism and, by the wrong coverage of things like heckling and disturbances, has actually caused violence. Television can bring the whole of politics and Parliament into contempt. This was my theme and it was fiercely repudiated by the television people, the B.B.C. and in fact by all the press, who have joined in. I did it pretty well but the net effect of the Benn–Crossman row has been that Benn is on top because he is the one they want to remember, and, though I have reduced the damage Benn did, he has prevented the kind of new and more rational approach which I had hoped my lecture would provoke.

Monday, October 28th

The press is full of the rumbles of the Crossman–Benn controversy. I have already had some of the viewers' letters, a surprising number of approvals

[1] Princess Marina, the widow of Prince George, Duke of Kent, the youngest brother of King George VI, had died on August 27th at the age of sixty-one.

[2] Michael Bessie works at Athenaeum, who published Crossman's *Politics of Socialism in the U.S.A.* (London: Hamish Hamilton, 1965).

[3] Admirers of the Bolivian guerilla leader Ernesto (Che) Guevara, killed in 1967.

but many quite definitely complaining that I bit off the Chairman's head at the end. One shouldn't lose one's temper. Apart from that I think the whole affair has not come out too badly, though, because of Benn, it is now lined up just as the old Government–B.B.C. squabble. The other news is the Prime Minister's recovery. There are some friendly articles showing he has completely reasserted his position in the country, largely owing to Rhodesia. The papers also talk about the coming test of Bassetlaw and the general view that we should just scrape home.[1]

At S.E.P. we again struggled with the Chancellor on the cuts. We were firmly asked to agree because if we didn't do so now the negotiators on the rate support grant would not be able to substantiate the 5 per cent limitation on the increase permitted up to 1970/1.* Today the Chancellor said that if we want to have the gap discussed we have to tell the local authorities what economies to make. He and Tony Greenwood had really agreed on this as another ingenious device to force us to concede the cuts in advance. Roy very kindly said to start with that of course if the economy got a great deal better the cuts would be reversed and the policy changed but we must have firm decisions now. But I said, and nobody else had thought of this, 'That isn't the way I see it working at all. Why on earth should we take on ourselves the job of telling these Tory local authorities to cut school milk? Why reveal all our plans on these minor adjustments? If we say all this now we shall get the odium for it whereas if we say nothing they may well make the cuts themselves.' Waxing to my theme, I said, 'Our whole idea has been to leave more discretion to the local authorities, not less. This would only be doing exactly what the Tories told us not to do. It is interfering in detail and we shall damage ourselves as well.'

It's surprising, but nobody else round that table, including the Chancellor and the Minister of Housing, could reply because nobody else knows the facts. Neither of these two men have more than the vaguest conception of how the grants work so on this one I was able to have the whole thing referred immediately to a committee. I simply said, 'Let's meet Matthew Stevenson,[2] see all those concerned and see if I'm right to say that it's not necessary for us to make these decisions on the 70/1 cuts in order to give the right material to our negotiator.'

Then we turned to the future. Roy said we must have our strategic dis-

[1] The by-election, to be held on October 31st, had been caused by the death on May 11th of Fred Bellenger, who had represented the constituency since 1935 and had held it in the 1966 General Election with a majority of 27,623.

* Each Ministry negotiates every two years with the local authorities about the amount we spend on education, housing, health and so on. Then you see how big a gap there is between what the minimum local authorities say they need and the maximum rate support grant we say we will give them, and you argue about that.

[2] Sir Matthew Stevenson (K.C.B. 1966), Permanent Secretary at the Ministry of Power 1965–6 and at the M.H.L.G. 1966–70. He was Deputy Chairman of Mersey Docks and Harbours Board 1970–1 and was a member of the British Steel Corporation 1971–6. See Vols I and II.

cussion before we took our final decisions. Tony Crosland strongly supported this, and then Barbara Castle talked, as she always does, about expansion and growth. I once again pointed out that there were some strategic issues I wanted clear in my mind before I agreed to any further cuts. If we could take one big decision that would save us £100 million or £150 million, possibly on investment grants, on oil or on agricultural imports, we should be saved all this cheese-paring. The Chancellor was a bit disconcerted and nettled and said these were all big issues, nothing to do with it. Still we won. We are to have our debate and Barbara is to produce her counter-paper for what will be an important discussion.

This evening Anne and I went to a splendid buffet supper party given by Harold Lever and Diane, who looked like a delicious toy princess. Will she not disappear one day? She can't have produced three children and still look so beautiful. There was Mary Wilson. It was a distinguished gathering, the beginning of a mixed salon of a sort that is most useful in politics. I had my first real talk with William Rees-Mogg,[1] and found this goggle-eyed intellectual rather sardonic and amusing. He is a Catholic, the kind who in the 1920s would have been an aesthete. He is essentially more of a political amateur than people take him for, more slap-dash if you like, and that's the quality his whole newspaper has. He is nice, he likes being liked and talking to clever people and I think it was useful for me to meet him.

Tuesday, October 29th

Cabinet. The first thing was to congratulate Jim Callaghan on what had happened on Sunday.[2] There had been weeks of build-up for the great revolutionary demonstration, the march through Trafalgar Square and along the Embankment, with the Trotskyists and revolutionaries intending to break off and rush to Grosvenor Square for a confrontation. Five thousand or so turned up and the police held successfully. Callaghan was there to congratulate them afterwards. Jim's real strength was that he wasn't rattled and that he took police advice not to have troops in readiness. There were American Marines inside the Embassy but no troops of ours. He deserved our congratulations because he would have got all the curses if after all the demonstration had turned violent. No doubt it has added even more to his strength, building him up as the only alternative to Harold Wilson.

After this we had a sudden announcement by the Prime Minister that the Chancellor had a surprise statement to make. He wanted to add just a

[1] Assistant Editor of the *Financial Times* 1957–60, City Editor of the *Sunday Times* 1960–1, Political and Economic Editor 1961–3, Deputy Editor 1964–7, and Editor of *The Times* since 1967. He was an unsuccessful Conservative candidate for Chester-le-Street in the 1956 by-election and the 1959 General Election.

[2] Some 30,000 people took part in what was largely an unprovocative march, ending with a rally in Hyde Park. The 5,000 who filled Grosvenor Square spent five hours trying to storm the American Embassy but they were firmly and calmly restrained by the police.

touch of the whip and impose higher hire-purchase terms on cars and certain other things. He wished it to be announced tomorrow afternoon, the day of the Queen's Speech, otherwise he would be accused of waiting until after the Bassetlaw by-election on Thursday.[1] It emerged at Cabinet that a small Committee of Ministers had been working on the plan. This was, so Barbara told me, the committee which had been set up to prepare all the contingency plans for another devaluation and so forth. Let me just remind myself who is on this: the Chancellor of the Exchequer, the First Secretary, the Secretary of State for Economic Affairs, the President of the Board of Trade and the Foreign Secretary, and on this occasion also Tony Wedgwood Benn, for the motor-car industry. It is really the inner strategic committee which I asked for. S.E.P. has become a demi-Cabinet, too big to be effective, and so another effective group has been devised which hasn't even got a name and whose minutes are certainly not circulated to anybody else.

We had a long discussion. One or two of us, I particularly, made the point that it does seem very puzzling that if before the Budget we can only do one thing it should be this minor thing. What are we to do if it doesn't work? Roy immediately replied, 'No, I must make it clear. It is not one thing only. If this doesn't work more will be in store.' That, from my point of view, settled it for me.[2]

How did the rest of Cabinet react? It was clear that Barbara had been against it in the inner group and so had Tony Crosland, but when they spoke it was to put different objections. Tony thought the measures too early and too little. He wanted to wait another month and then, if the likelihood of a worse inflation was substantiated, to put on much heavier measures using the regulator.[3] Barbara opposed because she didn't want any measures at all. She has completely taken George Brown's place as the uncritical expansionist, never prepared to make any concessions to the Chancellor. This is quite a useful function because someone has to stand up for industry against finance. We all said it was crazy to announce this on the same day as the Bassetlaw by-election, whether it had any effect or not. If we were to lose Bassetlaw we should never be forgiven. We decided to postpone the announcement till the following Tuesday, and put it in the Chancellor's contribution to the Queen's Speech debate.

We went on to report on the little Devolution Committee meeting yesterday, which the excluded Ministers – Peter Shore, Tony Greenwood and Judith

[1] The 'touch on the tiller' was announced by Anthony Crosland on Friday, November 1st, the day after the Bassetlaw by-election. See below, p. 248, and *Wilson*, p. 572.

[2] In this passage Crossman does not make it clear whether he supported or opposed the Chancellor's proposal but the entry for Friday, November 22nd, suggests that he was against the introduction of higher hire-purchase terms and, since the Chancellor had other measures in store, preferred Crosland's alternative of using the regulator. See below, p. 269.

[3] The Chancellor's power to vary the rate of purchase tax (subsequently, V.A.T.) by 10 per cent up or down was known as 'the regulator'.

Hart – had attended. They had all come in breathing fire and slaughter, determined to postpone the announcement of a Constitutional Commission, but they were all persuaded that there really was no choice, as the P.M. and Jim were convinced of this and had carried us along.

It happened again this morning at Cabinet, where it was felt that if the inner group chaired by the P.M. had decided Cabinet could only accede. Here we see another interesting constitutional development, the setting-up of these inner groups. The first two that I went for, S.E.P. and the Parliamentary Committee, were attempts at an inner Cabinet that, because they were official Committees, rapidly extended themselves to include more than half the Cabinet. So we moved back to the old situation where there are small groups of Ministers close to Harold, groups that are not even given names. It is 'the Ministers most closely affected have been meeting'. There are four of these: a little group who meet about the economic situation, certainly an inner defence group smaller than O.P.D., the informal group on Rhodesia, which is now never discussed, as it used to be, at the special O.P.D. committee but is dealt with by the P.M. and his closest friends and then presented as a *fait accompli* to Cabinet, and now this inner group on the constitution.

During our discussion on devolution Michael Stewart made a speech about the danger that the terms of reference of the Committee might permit consideration of a written constitution. He really is admirable on these things and he spelt out how appallingly reactionary this would be. Out of this came a thought which impressed us all. This constitutional commission could be an excuse for delaying the reform of the House of Lords, as it could be for delaying everything else.

This afternoon I got an urgent message that Eddie Shackleton and I were to see Heath after the Shadow Cabinet had met and discussed Lords' reform. Eddie came over to talk to me beforehand. We were both very gloomy and felt sure the Tories would now take the opportunity of using the constitutional commission to postpone House of Lords' reform. We went along to the Leader of the Opposition's room and stood outside his little office where we used to stand waiting for Gaitskell and subsequently, and even more, waiting for Harold Wilson, chatted with the girls and thought how crowded and mean it was. Then we were in with Peter Carrington and Ted Heath. Heath gave me a very reasonable letter which went much further than I expected. He said the Tories agree in principle that they would like to have talks about the conventions for the new House. It looked therefore as though he was clearly saying to us that if we could get the Bill through the Tories would operate it. That seemed to me encouraging and I went away quite excited. I rushed across to No. 10 where Harold was having the annual party for all the Ministers who had come to hear the contents of the Queen's Speech. I got in first and told him what had happened. He said, 'We must publish the Lords' White Paper on Friday and you must get the whole thing done in time. There will be a leak if we don't and there have been enough leaks in Nora Beloff's *Observer* column already.'[1] We had hoped to have three days to deal with the amendments which Ted Heath and the Liberals wanted but Harold said no, so now I am busy on this.

Wednesday, October 30th

Queen's Speech day was wet and spongy with pools of water. I remembered all the fuss and bother I had last year as Lord President. Now I am free of all this so I spent the morning with Michael Wheeler-Booth tidying up the White Paper. I also had to write a little party political broadcast on the Queen's Speech for radio this evening. This took me most of the morning until I drove off to lunch with the B.M.A. at their magnificent place in Russell Square.

Molly, by the way, is leaving me. I have had her for four years and we get each other down. I now have a new kind of Austin which she hates. However I am getting a new driver now, a man, who will be at Paddington when I arrive on Monday morning. A driver is important to a Minister because he is the person with whom you are together more than anyone, except perhaps your Private Secretary. Somebody once said in a very biting leading article that Harold Wilson can't nominate peers because the only person he knows intimately is his driver. There is something in this. You do get to know him or her extremely well and you chat together. Well, Molly couldn't love me, compared with Keith Joseph whom she could mother. I was rough and I shocked her in almost every way because of my attitude to royalty, to the Privy Council, and so on. I am only relieved that the change has taken place with the change of office, although for all I know the young man may actually be unbearable.*

Lunch with the B.M.A. was amazing – expensive, rather bad and absolutely tasteless. I went back to the House to hear Heath who made a lightweight, gad-about speech. Harold was very boring, as he said he would be, and he did it quite well, starting the whole thing off on the lowest possible key. The Queen's Speech used to be a great debate, but now it's another of those institutions which has run down-hill. There is no queue for speaking and hardly more than a handful of people were in the House.

This evening the phone rang and the Prime Minister said, 'This is really urgent. Would you come over straightaway?' I trotted round to find him sitting in his study with Roy Jenkins. Mr Short had resigned. He had sent a letter saying that the Prime Minister must make some sense of the education cuts that he had been asked to accept. If the Chancellor insisted on the £10

[1] Nora Beloff was the *Observer*'s Political Correspondent.

* As a last request, by the way, I asked Molly to buy a bottle of the bay rum lotion for my hair. This lotion is nice and cheap and old-fashioned and I can only get it from a shop in St James's Street. She gave it to the Private Office to put in the box, though I didn't want it down here at Prescote but up in London. It smashed, rather as if it was a farewell time-bomb.

million increase in further education fees Mr Short would go. The P.M. said, 'This is really serious. It could be disastrous for the Government.' It was true. Ted Short, an ex-Chief Whip from the centre-right of the Party—if he resigned and spilt the beans on the educational cuts it could create a kind of Bevanite revolt.[1] I saw this immediately. The Chancellor on the other hand wasn't willing to give an inch, so I said to the P.M., 'Look, it's quite simple. The first thing to do is play it off. Thank your lucky stars for what I said about the rate support grant. We needn't have all these announcements of cuts and we can postpone the issue. Play it out, Roy. You can still get your cuts but at least let us stop him resigning this week. The reason he has given for resigning now is that he is compelled to make a Statement announcing the £10 million increase on Thursday evening, the day before he goes off for two days in the North. You defuse this by merely saying, "You needn't make a Statement".' 'Is that really true?' asked the Prime Minister and Roy was very dubious. Finally we agreed to meet at 10 p.m. and that I should bring Matthew Stevenson with me for a proper discussion. Roy couldn't possibly be there so we would have Fred Peart instead.

I gave dinner to Alastair Hetherington and at 10 p.m. I went back again with Matthew Stevenson.[2] Ted Short was there and we spent till 12.30 a.m. convincing him, not with drink because he is a teetotaller. What did I give him in exchange? I first got Steve to say, as head of the negotiators for the rate support grant, that they didn't need the announcement and indeed it would be slightly convenient for them not to have it. Steve loyally supported everything I said because I had had a long discussion with him beforehand, cleared it up and got it in writing. He couldn't have been better on this occasion. He was in on high politics and excited that he was doing it well. We gave this to Ted Short, who swallowed it hook, line and sinker. Fred Peart said to me later, 'He wasn't going to resign, it was all bluff.' Bluff or not, it took two and a half hours of the Prime Minister, Fred and I, steadily drinking whisky, as Mr Short sat silent but got more and more human. That was Wednesday evening and I think the job was done decently and well.

Thursday, October 31st

This was the day I took over my new office, the day Kenneth Robinson went to Housing and Judith to the Paymaster's Office and I became Minister in charge at the Elephant and Castle.

[1] Aneurin Bevan was Labour M.P. for Ebbw Vale from 1929 until his death in 1960. He was Minister of Health 1945–51 and, in 1951, Minister of Labour and National Service. Crossman had been a leading member of the Bevanite group. The Bevanites, critics of the Labour Leader Hugh Gaitskell, met at Crossman's house in Vincent Square during the 1950s and 1960s. They constituted a small party within the Parliamentary Labour Party itself.

[2] Alastair Hetherington was Editor of the *Manchester Guardian* (subsequently the *Guardian*) 1956–75 and since 1975 has been Controller of B.B.C. Scotland.

But my first job was O.P.D. NATO defence after the Czechoslovakian invasion was the topic and what we could do to strengthen European defence without it costing us anything. Michael Stewart made a rather tentative suggestion that we might allow the German air force to come here as a sign of our good-will and the end of our resentment against Germany. I almost instinctively gave a kind of derisory laugh and then felt thoroughly ashamed. He put it out in such a cautious way. Fred Peart smacked in and said how unpopular it would be, so then I did intervene to say, 'Nobody hates this more than I do but I am sixty, we are out of date. Nothing would appeal to the younger generation more than a dramatic action to set aside the old feud against the Germans. I believe that by doing this for Willy Brandt you will do more towards getting the Germans to help you into Europe than by any other single action.' The moment I said it, in came Denis Healey. 'The Germans don't want this militarily,' he said, and he made every kind of technical difficulty. Oh, dear, here we have a problem.

Just before Cabinet Roy Jenkins caught me and said that as a result of a leak in the *Sketch* about 'the touch on the tiller' we could not wait as we had intended until Monday or Tuesday next week for the announcement but we must make it either tonight or tomorrow morning. 'God forbid tonight,' I said, 'tomorrow it must be.' He said he agreed, would I back him? It's scandalous to do it just before Bassetlaw, but we couldn't possibly have it tonight without chaos in the House. It was not too difficult to get agreement and we will have it tomorrow morning.

There was a tremendous row in Cabinet about this leak, though, and a great deal of suspicion, with leak inquiries to be set in train by the Lord Chancellor. Samuel Brittan wrote a brilliant article in last week's *Financial Times* on the whole danger and the need for some minor deflationary measures.[1] The logical next step was a touch of the whip and it was in the air that this action was inevitable. The *Sketch* picked it up and once you had one paper everyone else could guess. I have no doubt that Sam Brittan's Treasury briefing and his writing such a good article was the basis for these stories, which could explain why Roy looked a little embarrassed.

After the leaks discussion I had to report on the Lords and we had no difficulty there. I reported how unexpectedly favourable the Tories had been and how the White Paper will be out this week and they all took it quite quietly. Then we came to my pension scheme, late on the agenda for the third week running. It was now 12.10 and I won because it was so late. Roy and I had agreed on this last night. I had said, 'Supposing you win, as you will, on biennial rather than annual review, give me the rest,' and he said, 'Yes, I'll give you everything else in exchange.' That was our deal. At

[1] Economics Editor of the *Observer* 1961–4 and Principal Economic Commentator of the *Financial Times* since 1966. He was an Adviser at the D.E.A. in 1965 and is the author of, among other books, *Steering the Economy* (London: Secker & Warburg, 1969).

Cabinet I formally put my case as strongly as I could for an annual review, warning of the difficulties. I was overruled (it was clear I would never have won it), I was given the rest rapidly and the thing was over.

For the rest of the day I did House of Lords briefing. I had seen Alastair Hetherington last night and now I saw Rees-Mogg, Maurice Green of the *Telegraph*,[1] Harold Hutchinson, Political Correspondent of the *Sun*, surprisingly friendly, and Jimmy Margach of the *Sunday Times*. I did my duty on this all day but I felt more and more anxious about the press reaction. This evening the Lord Chancellor gave a dinner for Tommy, Peter, Tony Benn, Barbara and me, where we went on working towards Barbara's paper on the cuts. I don't think we got very much further. I notice that she is becoming more and more a departmental Minister and less and less interested in general policy and I suppose that in about three or four weeks that will also be true of me. I shall become immersed in the Social Services block and find myself less and less able to lead any kind of internal opposition. Nor do I really want to do so against Roy.

Friday, November 1st

Bassetlaw.[2] We scraped home by less than 800 votes. We had hoped perhaps for 1,500 but this was an enormous relief. Frankly, 800 fewer and a defeat by however small a number would have been a deadly blow to the Government's recovery. The result showed we are infinitely better off than at Acton, Dudley and Meriden seven months ago.[3] We haven't made a great recovery but the swing against us has ebbed. The Tories haven't gained at all, everyone now knows we have a chance, and that, plus the internal situation in Parliament, has given us a good feeling.

I sat on the front bench this afternoon alongside the P.M. and Tony Crosland to hear Harold on Rhodesia.[4] To my dismay I heard from the Lord Chancellor at last night's dinner that the P.M. really was hoping for a settlement. Well, I think if George Thomson really has been sent to make a settlement, he is a weak man and we are in trouble because we will have a revolt of a 100 to 150 Labour M.P.s, a major portion, far more serious than on any disagreement about the House of Lords.

Anyhow the P.M. got away with the announcement but he had an icy reception and there was no good-will at all. He slipped out after that. He doesn't often do this but he said, 'I don't want to face the music about the

[1] Maurice Green had been Financial and Industrial Editor of *The Times* 1938–9 and 1944–53 and Assistant Editor 1953–61. He was Deputy Editor of the *Daily Telegraph* 1961–4 and Editor 1964–74.

[2] Joseph Ashton held the seat for Labour but with a majority of only 740 votes. There was a swing of 10·8 per cent to the Conservatives.

[3] Labour had lost all three seats to the Conservatives on an average swing of 18 per cent.

[4] The Prime Minister announced that George Thomson had left for Salisbury for further discussions on the proposals that had been made aboard H.M.S. *Fearless*.

hire-purchase announcements.'[1] Tony Crosland got up and it was first-rate. After three or four minutes of uproar about Bassetlaw and how intolerable it was, the discussion settled down to the significance of the measures. Thank heavens we hadn't had this difficult thing yesterday because if we had happened to lose Bassetlaw we should never have been forgiven. As it was, the whole thing was a bit dud because when the Tories tried to say this was a scandal we could remind them of the occasion in 1956 when, as Chancellor, Macmillan followed three by-elections by a genuine economic freeze. They all looked a bit silly. The Tories are men of the world and they tried to lather up a bit on this but, quite rightly, their emphasis is not now on this breach of faith but on the measures. Even here they can't be very convincing, because everybody knows that a touch of restraint is what we need and the mistake we made before, as Roy said, was always to do too little too late. It's better to do a little early and be able to do more next time. On the whole I think we shall be all right.

Meanwhile in my room there was a meeting of my Ministers of State and Parliamentary Secretaries to sort out Questions. As well as everything else, we have not only had a day on social affairs in the Queen's Speech debate but, much more seriously, we are first in P.Q.s next Monday. We have to deal with 100 to 150 Questions deciding who should answer them and what answers should be prepared. I have some sixteen or seventeen Questions to answer on policies on both the Health and Social Services side and it will be our first test as a team. Perhaps it is a good thing to get everything over at once.

Off to a farewell party at the Privy Council Office, with nice little speeches by Godfrey Agnew and myself. We have had a love-hate relationship. I said goodbye to Mr Pickersgill, a splendid man who looked after our silver, took people round and helped with my parties at night. He reached the apogee of kindness when I wanted to get a pencil torch to read the libretto of *Götterdämmerung* and he borrowed his daughter's. He is a marvellous type of old-fashioned butler and we said a very fond farewell.

After that, I had a long and difficult struggle over the White Paper with Lewin and Brian, before Lewin and I caught the train to Oxford, where I was to address the Oxford Democratic Socialist Club. Would there be a riot? They couldn't have been nicer or more eager to listen. It was a splendid quiet, old-fashioned Oxford evening. How can one guess what's going to happen? One of them said to me, 'They will probably lay on a row next time for Healey.' Then Anne picked me up and brought me home in the rain.

[1] For cars the new minimum deposit was to be raised from 33⅓ per cent to 40 per cent and the maximum period of repayment reduced from 27 months to 2 years. For most other consumer durables the new minimum deposit would be 33⅓ per cent and the maximum repayment period 2 years, and for furniture the new rates were to be 20 rather than 15 per cent and 2 years rather than 30 months. Corresponding changes were made in rental regulations.

Saturday, November 2nd

Here I am, Secretary of State for Social Services, and the terrible problem has been what to call me. S.S.S.S.? Impossible! So in Cabinet they are now saying Social Secretary, which has a slightly comic ring and was invented by old Jim Callaghan. This use of titles still goes on in Cabinet and, though it has its convenience, with so many Secretaries of State and so many odd titles it is getting more and more difficult. I noticed another small thing when the boxes came down this morning. True, the hair lotion had smashed in one of them and had covered all the Cabinet papers with a wonderful scent of bay rum, but the boxes were very fine. The civil servants had been determined that on the first day as the new S.S. for S.S. I should have brand-new boxes with a beautiful new gold name across them. This is what they adore. To do them justice, all this weekend they are working away on the transfer of my files from the Privy Council to the Elephant and Castle. The danger is that out there in exile I might become detached unless I very consciously try to make good the deficiency. I have lost my nearness to Burke Trend, being able to ring him up at a moment's notice and go round, and the nearness to the P.M. I must struggle and the civil servants have been struggling. In Ron Matthews I have obviously got a really conscientious nice, efficient man, who will establish continuity and is obviously going to be a first-rate Private Secretary. My staff are dividing up but Janet Newman is heroically coming with me into exile. I am leaving Paul Odgers behind in my co-ordinating office in Fred Peart's old rooms, quite a decent office where I shall have to go after Cabinet and where I shall have to be a great deal. One of my difficulties will be to spend sufficient time over at Elephant and Castle.

Monday, November 4th

Today we took over Alexander Fleming House, the great skyscraper at the Elephant and Castle. I have a long room in a suite of offices on the seventh floor with magnificent but not very pretty views of modern skyscrapers. Still, it is exhilarating up there and when the door from my Private Office is shut and I sit alone I am totally insulated. That's the first thing I notice. I'm not in an ivory tower but a steel tower miles away from Westminster and Whitehall, with double glazing to give a sense of absolute silence, so far up above the world that nothing seems to be relating to me. I got there this morning at the right time, 9.30. I was photographed coming in with David Ennals and Stephen Swingler, and the B.B.C. interviewed me for 'The World At One'. Then I had to get across to the other side of the river for a big S.E.P. meeting to ratify last week's decisions on the rate support grant. Ted Short is to be permitted to submit a paper to Cabinet on the crisis in education and it will come to our Social Services Committee in a fortnight or so. I am very doubtful whether we can do anything about it and whether by playing for time we can prevent his resignation.

Tuesday, November 5th

This afternoon we had the final day of the Queen's Speech debate. This time it has all been duller than usual, including the Tories' attempt yesterday to work up a debate on the fivepenny post.[1] This had really conked out. Today we had the big economic vote of censure.[2] We had discussed at length how to handle this and when Iain Macleod got up we were a bit apprehensive. He made a terribly fustian, old-fashioned kind of speech and then Roy replied. It wasn't his fault but I think he over-gunned a bit. The Tories couldn't take the Bassetlaw thing very seriously because they knew they would have done the same thing themselves and there had been no heart in their attacks, but Roy pulverized them with example after example of what *they* had done and of their hypocrisy, and as a result of all this he had to say there was no question of a freeze yet, making a rather more optimistic speech than he intended or than Tommy or I liked. It was in a way a perfectly successful afternoon but we were back in the old mud and the old boring trudge along the way and it was disappointing.

In the evening I was up in my skyscraper dictating a book review for David Astor,[3] when I saw a series of fire-balls going up all round me. I wondered vaguely what they were and of course it was Guy Fawkes Night.

Wednesday, November 6th

I found myself invited to one of a series of C.B.I. dinners at No. 10, I suppose as part of my new job. There were about six or seven of them there sitting round with the P.M. and for two hours after dinner we were entirely concerned with methods by which the Government could have pre-legislation discussion with the C.B.I. John Davies kept on saying that everything would be all right if you had the same kind of consultation as the Lord President had about the pensions scheme,[4] so I was quite pleased. On the whole, though, I was rather bored with the whole thing because little was being achieved except that they weren't rowing. I was struck when Harold said afterwards, 'We've never had such a successful C.B.I. dinner, more con-

[1] The Post Office had introduced in October 1968 a two-tier system of letter delivery. 'First-class' letters, now charged at 5*d*., would be given priority and 'second-class' letters, at the old charge of 4*d*., would normally be delivered on the second day after posting. The rate for postcards rose from 3*d*. to 4*d*. It was alleged that the two-tier system was a device for masking an increase in postal rates, that mail was delayed and that the first-class delivery failed to materialize, despite the Postmaster-General's claim that 94 per cent of first-class mail was delivered the day after posting. There was a reduction in the number of letters posted and estimates of the significant revenue from the increased charges had to be substantially revised.

[2] The motion criticizing the Government's handling of the economic situation was defeated by 310 votes to 247.

[3] The Hon. David Astor, son of the 2nd Viscount Astor, was Foreign Editor of the *Observer* 1946–8 and its Editor 1948–75.

[4] John Davies, Director-General of the C.B.I. 1965–9 and a member of N.E.D.C. 1964–72, has been Conservative M.P. for Knutsford since 1970. He was Minister of Technology July–October 1970, Secretary of State for Trade and Industry and President of the Board of Trade 1970–2 and Chancellor of the Duchy of Lancaster 1972–4.

structive and useful than ever before.' I thought, my God, what must the others have been like.

Thursday, November 7th

A remarkable Defence Committee meeting on the issue of selling Chieftain tanks to the Israelis. Negotiations about this have been going on for months and months and we had sent the Israelis two prototypes about a year ago. If you sell Israel tanks they are likely to be used. They buy the best available and they have been buying our Centurion tanks for years. Now they have asked for 200 Chieftains to replace the Centurions in 70/1. They said they were out-tanked four or five to one now that the Russians have rearmed the Egyptians after their losses in the Six-Day War.[1] I had managed to read the papers beforehand and it was quite clear that to sell the Israelis Chieftains would give an extra turn to the armaments spiral in the Middle East. Giving the Israelis military ascendancy was quite ridiculous.

This was Michael Stewart's argument advising us not to sell. His paper was a real F.O. paper, indicating that by selling to the Israelis we should be jeopardizing our sales to the Arab world and, secondly and much more important, politically we had to keep on the good side of the Arabs and this would end our neutrality between the Arabs and the Jews. Luckily, as often happens, the F.O. apparently hadn't concerted with the Ministry of Defence. Denis Healey said he couldn't quite accept the military estimate of the situation as it didn't seem to be in line with the Joint Intelligence Committee estimate, an annexe to the paper. A general was called in and asked to speak and we then had an hour of fierce discussion. Fred Peart and I are fairly solid Israeli men, saying, 'Don't make the same mistakes all over again,' but there was Michael putting forward exactly the same F.O. argument which no doubt had been put to Ernest Bevin in 1948. Nothing may have changed in the F.O. but something has changed outside. We managed to hold the situation by asking for further information.

When I got into the Department poor Ron Matthews was nearly breaking down. He said, 'I'm terribly sorry, Secretary of State, it's complete chaos. I'll try to get it right.' It's true that the service has been deplorable. At first the Office couldn't get the Cabinet papers to the two Ministers of State, they couldn't get the telephones right, nothing went right. They couldn't even type and circulate my speeches for next week. But I said, 'What you haven't understood is that none of us could have got it right immediately. This is the difference between a senior Minister's Private Office and the Private Office of a non-Cabinet Minister.' It's quite clear that Kenneth Robinson really lived inside his Ministry and the whole tempo of his life was the tempo of his Ministry. The papers came up and he dealt with them. He had tremendously detailed administrative control but he didn't have to work faster than his Ministry wanted to. With a senior member of the

[1] See Vol. II.

Cabinet the whole Private Office is different now. Its work is centred on Cabinet, on Whitehall, with pressure coming from there on one side and on the other from John Adam Street and Alexander Fleming House. I think, and Ron agrees, that we need about double the staff in the Private Office and a completely different layout. 'Above all,' says Ron Matthews, 'the pace of work is faster. Decisions have to be taken and arrangements made at a faster rate.' The Ministry's work has now to be fitted to my life and it is this galvanic struggle that has been going on.

Friday, November 8th

Last night I travelled up to Scotland on a sleeper with Tam. I had agreed to do a weekend school for the Scottish Fabians at Perth, and today I fitted in a look at social security offices in Scotland. We had the usual talks about the strain in interviewing and the appalling weight of the ½ million extra claimants brought by the establishment of the Supplementary Benefits Commission. Managers are as splendid as ever, visitors as keen. In one office they had a 60 per cent increase in the number of deserted wives in the last two years. It's perfectly clear what the reason is: money. People now know that they can walk out on the wife and that she won't be on her beam ends because she can go on the Friday to the S.B.C. and draw for herself and children. There was some of the usual bogus desertion but mostly, I suppose, the working-class have now got the middle-class economic security that enables you to get away from the wife if you don't love her. It made me think pretty hard.

The Scottish Fabians were a jolly good collection, mostly professional people, ambitious young lawyers, their wives, representatives of local authorities and social security workers. I gave them a little speech and then we had long discussions. More than ever did I find that people do want to have a realistic account of what goes on in the Cabinet. When you give it they say, 'Oh, how utterly shocking, how appalling,' and I say, 'What hypocrites you are, you know perfectly well that it's true. You know it would be true if you were there; why do you say it's shocking?' We live by hypocrisy.

I spent Friday night with Tam at The Binns and had a lovely moonlight walk with his father-in-law, John Wheatley.[1] We discussed the role of his Royal Commission, the Scottish equivalent of Maud, and the publication of his Report. I told him of the significance of the Constitutional Commission which Harold has set up, without of course even asking John Wheatley's advice.

[1] Labour M.P. for East Edinburgh 1947–54, Solicitor-General for Scotland March–October 1947 and Lord Advocate 1947–51. He has been a Senator of the Royal College of Justice in Scotland since 1954 and Lord Justice-Clerk since 1972. He became a life peer in 1970. He was Chairman of the Royal Commission on Local Government in Scotland, appointed in May 1966 at the same time as the Maud Commission. His Report, Cmnd 4150, was published in September 1969.

Sunday, November 10th

This evening I motored into Edinburgh with Tam for dinner with Michael Swann and his wife Tess in their magnificent old Victorian mansion,[1] dazzlingly decorated inside. They gave a splendid party for me to meet the historian Steven Watson and his wife, Heba, the Deans of the Faculty of Medicine and Rosalind and Murdoch Mitchison, Naomi's professor son.[2]

Unfortunately Michael Swann was in bed with 'flu so we didn't have much discussion about medical things but out of the conversation did come the following curious item. At Perth one of the Fabians had asked me to clear up the murky story of merit awards. I'd never heard of them before but I had my N.H.S. notes and looked them up quickly. They gave a perfectly clear account. A consultant can get one of three classes of award, A, B, and C, in addition to his salary and they are given by a most respectable committee, of which Lord Platt is Chairman.[3] So I had answered, 'Don't be upset, there is nothing hugger-mugger about this,' but the questioner had said, 'Well, we find even the Chairman of the Finance Committee of the R.H.B. is not entitled to know the names of the people who get merit awards.'

I raised this after dinner tonight, and the Dean said, 'I am about the only person I know who had a merit award and gave it up when I went back to academic life. But all that is true.' They gathered round and told me all about merit awards. This was the way Nye Bevan got the consultants to back him, so that he could stand out against the B.M.A. when the N.H.S. was originally founded. The promise of merit awards bought them, with the condition that though the total sums and the subjects are published the names are not. It has been a kind of old boy arrangement for consultants and has caused the keenest resentment from both the G.P.s and the young consultants. I came down to London full of the idea that we should either end the system or publish the names but it seems crystal clear that, though this is the right thing to do, I will only do it after a row royal with the Colleges, and many of the leading consultants. It is the kind of quarrel one ought not to go into without careful calculation.

[1] Professor of Natural History, University of Edinburgh 1952–65 and Principal and Vice-Chancellor 1965–73. He has been Chairman of the B.B.C. since 1973 and was knighted in 1972.

[2] Steven Watson has been the Principal of the University of St Andrews since 1966. The Deans of the Faculty of Medicine were K. W. Donald and A. S. Duncan. Murdoch Mitchison is Professor of Zoology at the University of Edinburgh, a post he has held since 1963. His mother, the writer, is the widow of Gilbert Mitchison, Labour M.P. for Kettering from 1945 to 1964, when he became a life peer; he was Joint Parliamentary Secretary at the Ministry of Land and Natural Resources 1964–6 and died in February 1970. Of their other two sons one became in 1971 Professor of Bacteriology at the Royal Postgraduate Medical School and the other Jodrell Professor of Zoology and Comparative Anatomy at University College, London, in 1970.

[3] Professor of Medicine at Manchester University and Consultant Physician at the Royal Infirmary, Manchester 1945–65. He was President of the Royal College of Physicians 1957–62 and became a baronet in 1959 and a life peer in 1967.

Monday, November 11th

Today the office had intended to issue to the press my address to the National Council for Social Services tomorrow, but the draft was so frightful and so dull that I said it couldn't possibly be sent out. I would give the speech first and they could make a draft for the press release afterwards. I spent much of the day going through the speech and found two passages, one an assurance to the doctors about the Green Paper, another a rather dull passage about pensions, and then I thought to myself that I would put in a really interesting piece about family allowances. I rapidly wrote it, with another about staff at the Ministry of Social Security and by 4 o'clock they were typed.

Tuesday, November 12th

Cabinet today was chiefly about the Report on Ronan Point[1] which shows that the flats collapsed as the result of a structural fault permitted by our revised building regulations, so the Ministry is involved. The main issue has been what Tony Greenwood should do with this Report when we got it and I heard a lot about it from Peter Brown last week. Apparently the Ministry had got everything ready and the Report clear in their minds when the experts suddenly said, 'Look, you must have new standards for the flats you build in the future but you can't impose it on existing flats. You will simply have to go along with two different standards.' Quite rightly Stevenson and Brown had said, 'That's impossible. We can't put that to the Minister, he can't survive on that,' and they have been fighting to get a satisfactory form of words. Then David Frost got hold of the Report,[2] said that people in the existing flats would be in danger and summoned the Minister to go on his television programme. Tony had refused, all the press had attacked him for refusing and he had then attacked television for irresponsibly inventing dangers.

We started Cabinet with Harold saying, 'You see what happens, Tony is in a terrible difficulty because he has refused to go on television. But other Ministers, Dick Marsh and Jim Callaghan, have been on the "Frost Programme". Oughtn't we to have some kind of a rule?' Now two years ago we had a self-denying ordinance that we shouldn't go on David Frost's

[1] On May 16th four people died when one corner of a 23-storey block of flats collapsed, after a gas explosion on the eighteenth floor (see above p. 65 and n). In August all large-panel system-built blocks over six storeys high were appraised and an inquiry into the disaster was set up. The Report of the tribunal emphasized the inadequacy of present regulations and codes of practice for constructing high buildings. Gas supplies were to be cut off until tall buildings liable to collapse could be strengthened.

[2] David Paradine Frost (O.B.E. 1970), Joint Founder of London Weekend Television, has been Chairman and Chief Executive of David Paradine Ltd since 1966. He was the central figure and, in some cases, producer, of such satirical and current affairs television programmes as, for B.B.C., 'That Was The Week That Was' 1962/3 and 'The Frost Report' 1966/7, and, for I.T.V., the 'Frost Programme' 1966/7, 1967/8 and 'Frost on Friday', 1968/9, 1969/70. He was a friend of Harold Wilson.

programme, until George Brown broke it and had an hour of Frost buttering him up with a most successful interview. Since then Ministers have felt they could do well on it. Denis Healey had a bleeding row but on the whole felt he had done satisfactorily, more recently we had Callaghan and I am told Dick Marsh was quite good, though I think poor Wedgy Benn was not. However Harold not only mentioned David Frost but said we had got to review the whole thing, because it was not only the 'Frost Programme', 'The World This Weekend' was particularly bad. I held my breath because I think this is the most useful current affairs programme and I said so. Indeed, in my television broadcast I had paid a special compliment to 'The World At One' and said that a radio programme really was valuable because a politician could say more in five minutes than he could in ten minutes on television. Out of all this discussion came the fact that Ministers have such different ways of handling situations and that it all depends on their Press Officers. The second fact that emerged was how violently the Prime Minister is prejudiced.

I then went off to make my speech to the National Council for Social Services, but in my absence the decision on the Chieftain tanks was sustained against the Foreign Office. Starting in 1970/1 Chieftains will be sold, with secrecy maintained up to that point, and it will pay the Israelis to keep it secret. Meanwhile I delivered my speech, ad libbing a good deal, presenting it with talent, vivacity and amusement. There was a lot of grinning. Well, it was a bit of play-acting but it went down like hot cakes and I had a wonderful ovation at the end.

This afternoon we had our first ministerial task in our new Department, the question of the appointments to the Regional Hospital Boards. The Hospital Management Committees (H.M.C.s) are all appointed by the Regional Hospital Boards (R.H.B.s) which are in turn all appointed by the Minister. He does it in rotation over three years, one-third every year. After twenty years it has virtually come about that the chairman and secretary of an R.H.B. first go through all the names suggested by the people allowed to put them forward, the T.U.C., the Nursing Council, a whole lot of official organizations. Each time very few of the new names put forward get on because overwhelmingly the Boards reappoint themselves. They are self-perpetuating oligarchies who like to retain people for two or three terms so there is a very slow turnover. This work is apparently left entirely to the chairmen of the R.H.B.s and the Regional Officers of the Ministry of Health who together fix up a complete list and present it to the Minister saying, 'Here it is.' At this point the Minister is allowed to suggest any names he wishes but of course it is practically impossible for him to make any changes.

First I cleared with the officials that in fact most R.H.B. members are merely there for reasons of balance and presentation. The real work is done by three or four people and, unless you are chairman of a sub-committee, you really have no authority or power at all. We then asked the officials to withdraw and the Ministers had a short discussion together, where we quickly evolved a proposal that in future David Ennals should ask each R.H.B. to come to see him about the appointments, so that the names could be discussed before the finished list was prepared. I went in to David a little later on to make sure he was carrying this out and he was. He said, 'Now I'll write to each of our Labour Party Regional Offices and get them to give a list.' 'You jolly well won't write,' I said, 'You'll have them up secretly to Transport House and talk to them. There musn't be a single thing on Ministry paper.' 'Oh, yes,' he said, 'I'll put it on House of Commons paper.' 'No you won't,' I said. 'No House of Commons paper, no writing at all. We can't let it be known we have had consultations with our people. We'll just have a private talk at Transport House, they'll put their names up to the T.U.C. and secretly let us have a copy.' So this was our first little change. I hope it will help us a bit. There has been constant disgruntlement at the sense that most R.H.B.s seem to be 80 per cent non-Labour, or, to put it mildly, 65 per cent Tory or Establishment in outlook.

Wednesday, November 13th

This morning at 11.30 we had the big debate at the Party Meeting to discuss the White Paper on Lords' reform. We had agreed in Cabinet that Callaghan should start and I should wind up and we should reverse the order when we debated the White Paper on the Floor of the House. We published the White Paper twelve days ago and it was striking how little had happened.[1] Eddie and I had worked hard with the press but there had been no flurry of excitement or any real stirring of indignation from our own back benchers. The whole thing had fallen flat, thank God, in the sense that people had remarkably felt resigned acquiescence.

The White Paper recommended a two-tier system of voting peers, with a right to speak and vote, and non-voting peers with a right to speak. Succession to a hereditary peerage should no longer carry the right to a seat in the House of Lords but existing peers by succession should have the right to sit as non-voting peers for their lifetime. Voting peers would be exclusively created peers but some peers by succession would be created life peers. The voting House would initially consist of about 230 peers, distributed between the parties in a way which would give the Government a small majority (of some 10 per cent) over the Opposition parties but not a majority of the House as a whole when those without party allegiance were included. All serving Law Lords, the Archbishops of Canterbury and York and the Bishops of London, Durham and Winchester would continue as ex-officio *voting peers: the remaining 21 bishops would be re-appointed members of the House on the basis of one new bishop to every two retirements until the number was reduced to 16. Voting peers*

[1] *House of Lords Reform*, Cmnd 3799.

would be required to attend at least one-third of the sittings of the House, they would be paid some remuneration and would be subject to an age of retirement (of seventy-five during the transitional period until the new Parliament, thereafter of seventy-two). A committee with a chairman of 'national standing' would be established to review periodically the composition of the reformed House.

The reformed House should be able to impose a six-month delay, which should be capable of running into a new session or a new Parliament, on the passage of an ordinary public Bill sent up from the Commons and it should then be possible to submit the Bill for Royal Assent, provided that a Resolution to that effect had been passed in the Commons. The reformed House should be able to require the Commons to reconsider an Affirmative Order or to consider a Negative Order but the power of final rejection should be removed. All peers should in future be qualified to vote in Parliamentary elections.

What was to happen when the Party got together? When we started about thirty-five people were there, over half of them members of the Lords. It had grown to about eighty by the time I got up to speak at 12.30. First of all Jim made a very careful, friendly, deliberately muffled speech, saying, 'I'm not an expert on this at all. Dick must take all the credit for it.' He was followed by Manny Shinwell at his most wild, saying it was dreary rubbish and that the least we must go for is abolishing all peerages by succession and then Michael Foot whipped himself up. The striking thing was that the opponents, and nearly all of them were opponents, were oldish people, Charlie Pannell,[1] Michael Foot, Manny Shinwell, Willie Hamilton. After nine speeches I had to reply. I managed to explain how the Party had given us our instructions to go in and get the terms, the advantage of getting an agreed solution passed in this Parliament if we could, and the importance of Macleod's denial of our right to bring in the reformed House in this Parliament. It went pretty well, but Douglas Houghton showed that he has now got into a very nasty mood. As Fred Peart said, 'He's a maverick, you know. He's gone wild now and is against us on everything.' So we've got the Chairman of the P.L.P. agin the Government.

Thursday, November 14th

In the evening we had been told to sit in readiness for a crucial meeting of the Prices and Incomes Committee. One after the other the wage claims have been pouring in, the building trade operatives, the bank employees, I.C.I. We sat trying to work out what we could do and how we could help Barbara, who was to come to report on her day of negotiation. There we waited in Cabinet Committee Room A, a beautiful room with a Nollekens bust over the mantelpiece, and great portraits of our seventeenth-century

[1] Labour M.P. for Leeds West from 1947 to 1974, when he became a life peer. He was Minister of Public Buildings and Works 1964–6.

predecessors around the walls. We kicked our heels and I talked desultorily to Roy. In came Barbara, looking very delicate in a great big blue overcoat, with a frilly embroidered shirt underneath, clean and dimity and nice. She had come back to report on her deal with the Building Trade Operatives that they should take a gamble and that both sides should accept the findings of the Prices and Incomes Board. Of course she knows what the findings are going to be and what we can afford to pay. Interesting that to this extent she is limited in what she can do. In this case she clearly had to get our authority and she got it without any difficulty.

When we had finished Roy and I walked through from the Cabinet Office to his room, for a gin and tonic. 'We had a bad day today', he said, 'as a result of the trade figures.[1] It doesn't seem to get any better, does it?' I realized that ever since he became Chancellor we have been on the tightrope. Devaluation gave us no relief. We had a devalued pound but also an unstable pound, a pound people don't believe in at home, a pound people get out of into real estate, goods or pictures. Roy says we are obsessed by the nightmare of the monthly trade figures. We can't get away from them. He said that three months ago we were getting a fairly good three-monthly average and with a good fourth month we would have been getting away from our obsession. But no, this month is bad and today we already see the effect on the pound.

Friday, November 15th

The pound got infinitely worse today because of the events in France and I am sure Nicholas Davenport wasn't exaggerating when he told me we were in a new crisis.[2] This could mean a second devaluation at a time when there are no reserves at all, along with the franc. It would not be as disastrous for the Government, I suppose, since we couldn't be blamed as much but it would mean that all our calculations on public expenditure and all our efforts to keep in the black would be upset. Above all, of course, there would be the feeling that in the fifth year of this Government we are still not on top of the financial situation and we could really say goodbye to any hope of regaining public confidence in time to win an election.

The big news for me today was that the draft White Paper on National Superannuation was finally through Cabinet and is now going round Whitehall. We have had great difficulties with the Treasury. For instance, at the last moment they couldn't provide any information about the public

[1] The visible trade deficit for October was £68 million.

[2] In spite of exchange controls and a number of highly unpopular tax measures introduced in the 1968 Budget, on September 3rd there had been persistent speculation against the franc, exacerbated by rumours of an impending revaluation of the Mark. By mid-November France was facing a major financial crisis and on November 17th representatives of the twelve Central Banks met at Basle to consider the situation. On November 18th the French Government announced that there would be no devaluation. There was heavy speculation against both the franc and the pound and the sterling balances fell to their lowest point since July.

service scheme for school teachers and policemen and the key issue of how to fit them in with the occupational pensions schemes. The Treasury were not going to put anything down on paper about these because it would weaken their bargaining position. This is wholly characteristic. What is one law for the other Departments is another for the Treasury. The other difficulty was to get them to provide any chapter on financing the scheme. We have had no less than three Treasury experts, one after the other, in the two years I have been working on this scheme so the fact is that nobody at the Treasury knows as much about it as I do and none of the experts is capable of dealing with the subject. The Treasury is overworked now and undermanned, its morale broken, and it is incompetent in many ways. These days it is an inefficient Ministry, with on top of it a Chancellor who doesn't do his homework. He doesn't know about pensions and the P.M. admitted to me yesterday, 'He doesn't know his muttons in the job.' But when I look at the White Paper my main worry is to sell it. I may find that it is on this, which is supposed to be the Government's biggest reform, that my reputation will stand or fall and it looks as if we may be in very great trouble next January. The question is, whether I can soften the shock in any way and give an antidote by warning people in advance what the measure will deal with and what it won't.

Sunday, November 17th

When I woke at 6.50 I lay in bed with one of my morning panics about pensions. I also thought there must be a mistake in the time, that it must be an hour earlier because it was so pitch-dark, but when I crept downstairs there was a light on in the dairy with the milking still going on and it was 7.30. We are now beginning to feel the result of keeping Summer Time all through the year.[1] I noticed it in Scotland last weekend and it is even bad down here in the Midlands. The real disadvantage is that we will have two months of real early-morning darkness for the children to go to school in but it's one of those things which Roy Jenkins did as Home Secretary. It's one of those reforms we gaily accepted in Cabinet in half an hour, against the mutterings of Willie Ross who said it would be deeply unpopular in Scotland, one of those proposals which we accepted when we thought we were a Government of change, of not keeping to the old-established methods.

[1] On February 18th the annual practice ended of putting the clocks back for an hour for the winter months and in the summer forward again to take full advantage of the hours of daylight. For an experimental period of three years British Standard Time was introduced, one hour ahead of Greenwich Mean Time, and British clocks were permanently advanced by one hour and brought into line with the rest of Europe. Although this meant that winter evenings remained light for longer, mornings stayed darker until an hour as late as 10 a.m. in the North of Scotland and 8 a.m. in the South of England. It was alleged that road accidents increased and on December 1st the Home Secretary announced that the experiment would be reviewed at the end of the winter, as well as in 1971. British Standard Time was abandoned on October 31st, 1971.

Nicholas Davenport rang me up yesterday and said, 'In the City there is another major crisis and talk about another devaluation in a matter of days.' It's all grown up gradually, starting perhaps with the sudden decision of the inner group to propose a slight increase of hire-purchase charges, the touch of the whip. That was mucked about because of leaks, and by announcing it on the day after Bassetlaw we destroyed its effectiveness and made it look like a political device. It was followed by last week's terribly bad trade figures, which toppled the pound a bit. That, and this is the important thing, was followed by the convulsions of the flight from the franc into the Mark, a flight of such dimensions that it began to affect the dollar and the pound, with the pound as the weakest currency taking the knock.

For the past fortnight a whole succession of wage claims has been hanging over us as well. Barbara has been in the headlines every day. The Gallup Poll, by the way, shows that personally she is growing more and more popular because people see she is working hard but despite this she is wearing herself out in a frantic effort to plug the holes in the dam and prevent the wage increases rushing through in an overwhelming torrent. By the end of the week she had just managed to get the building trade operatives to refer their claim to the Prices and Incomes Board but she still has the bank clerks wanting 7½ per cent. She is going to give them 3½ per cent and looming ahead is a crisis with I.C.I. These awards can't be held back and as a result the whole prices and incomes policy will collapse. The terrible thing here is really that it *has* collapsed. Public opinion and the unions have won. We know that by the end of 1969 we shan't replace the powers we've got. They are already figments, myths. People know we are licked and Barbara just struggles, struggles to hold on and to try to operate a policy which is detested, which has riven us from our own supporters, separated us from the unions and is creating the biggest split inside the P.L.P. and inside the Labour Party.

So much of the Government's energy is concentrated on keeping this completely unreal, unworkable policy going. We relaxed our grip after devaluation and, having done so, we then tried to reimpose it in the stringent post-devaluation conditions. The one thing you can't do is to reimpose a prices and incomes policy once you have relaxed it. It's only fair to say that Roy never believed in the policy but he realized that he couldn't at that moment take the lid off the pressure-cooker because the mere removal of the lid is in itself dangerous. As Chancellor Roy couldn't afford to do this, so we had to keep the policy going and now Barbara is rushing from hole to hole valiantly damming them up. Tremendous courage that girl shows. Though she gets terribly excited, on each of these negotiations she is in a sense intellectually and personally cool. The further complication is that she is not only in George Brown's D.E.A. position but she is also Minister of Labour, and the creation of D.E.P., by which Harold squared Roy, who didn't want to see Barbara taking George Brown's place and creating tension between D.E.A. and the Treasury, has now put the Treasury in supreme control. The conciliating role of the Minister of Labour has been undermined because the conciliator is also the person in charge of the policy and we have also lost a good deal by that arrangement. The policy has fallen to pieces.

The third thing that has been going this past fortnight has been Rhodesia. I know no more than is in the newspapers because we haven't had any discussion in Cabinet. The six ministers concerned with Rhodesia have been meeting from time to time to give George Thomson instructions of which I know nothing.[1] In fact I know less than the press, as I discovered when Jimmy Margach came to see me on Friday. He told me that his Foreign Editor, Frank Giles, had been at a party at the American Embassy for John Freeman, and Frank had sat at the same table as Harold Wilson. Harold emphatically told Frank Giles we were going to get agreement. Giles said, 'Surely that will be a great jolt for your party?' Harold, talking coolly, was confident that he was going to get an agreement, that public opinion wanted it, the Labour Party would have to swallow it and that he would take whatever resignations were necessary. The whole of the press came out at the beginning of last week with a tremendous story that agreement was on the way. I think it came partly from Arthur Bottomley,[2] partly from the Foreign and Commonwealth Office and largely from No. 10. But what was it based on? Certainly not on any decision that George Thomson would sell out. His directive was not to move one iota from the *Fearless* terms. The story was therefore based on a delusion of Harold's that Smith would finally come to heel. This estimate of Smith is the result of Harold's knowing him much better than I do, yet I think it is complete self-deception. Now it looks as if George Thomson has come home with the gap just as wide as it was before.

The other big item on the news this morning was that Enoch Powell has made another big speech demanding a government-financed scheme of voluntary repatriation to get rid of the blacks. Powellism is a popular violent force. I was looking yesterday at a fascinating computerized study in *The Times* of the policies which would win a large electoral majority and the electorate's main attitudes are that Britain is still a great power, Britain

[1] The Minister without Portfolio visited Salisbury from November 2nd to 16th for more talks with Mr Smith. He also spent four days in Kenya, Tanzania, Uganda and Zambia. No settlement was reached, for although the Rhodesian regime claimed that it was prepared to accept the principle of ultimate majority rule, it objected to the British Government's requirement of the right of appeal to the Privy Council against constitutional amendment, asserting that this infringed Rhodesian independence.

[2] Labour M.P. for Chatham 1945–50, Rochester and Chatham 1950–59, Middlesbrough East 1962–74 and since 1974 for Teesside, Middlesbrough. He was Parliamentary Under-Secretary of State for the Dominions 1946–7, Secretary for Overseas Trade 1947–51, Secretary of State for Commonwealth Affairs 1964–6 and Minister of Overseas Development 1966–7.

shouldn't pay a penny more of overseas aid, Britain should reduce her taxes. There it is, just what Nye Bevan said would happen if we cut the empire and became unimportant. We are getting a kind of unpleasantness and evil in our political atmosphere and Powell is taking full advantage of it. It will certainly result in a terrific swing to the right which Harold can do nothing to stop.

Monday, November 18th

I was in the chair at the meeting of the Social Services Committee and the first item was my new Ministry's proposal that we should postpone the introduction of embossed cards for prescription charges. As a part of the initial proposition Kenneth Robinson had put it forward that we should have embossed cards rather like Barclaycards which people should be able to take to the chemist as proof of exemption. Our short-term system has been to make people sign their names on the back of the prescription form and of course this is wide open to abuse since only a tiny sample can be checked. On the other hand, the introduction of embossed cards would cost us £2 million and the opposition of the chemists and the doctors. The fact is that prescription charges are now an albatross round our necks.

The other item came from Ted Short who had at my request submitted the paper he had taken to Cabinet on the state of the school system as a result of the cuts. His paper dealt with the system right across the board, describing how more money was needed for schools, universities and further education systems, just saying that everything wanted more money and nothing could be cut. Everyone was sympathetic. They quite like Ted Short, though he is no longer over-estimated and is seen to be a very limited headmaster, erratic and emotional. We said, 'Ted, you must have some priorities. If you want to save your comprehensive education, which we are all deeply committed to in the party, you must say that is what you want.' Of course there was argument. Some agreed with him that we should make a great effort to launch nursery classes now and get a little more money for comprehensive education by postponing the raising of the school-leaving age. Others, and I was one of them, thought that £1 million for nursery schools would merely whet the appetite and would be unwise. I think we can safely say that we are unlikely to give much away to Ted after this and we are still faced with his threat of resignation.

After this I went to Judith's room for informal drinks with Tony Wedgwood Benn, Barbara, Tommy Balogh and Peter Shore, because we couldn't get a dinner party together. It was a profoundly depressing meeting. Barbara, as a member of the inner group, was already consulting about a second bout of economy measures and she just sat making a long speech, saying we must have more production. I realized she was talking about proposed restrictions of which we know nothing and which she can't mention. One of the reasons why it is so difficult to have any coherent Left inside the Cabinet is that each of us is now privy to different things. It was a horrible day. I greatly admire Barbara and she is cool and collected, but her speech totally disregarded the failure of the prices and incomes policy, the fact that she had been over-successful in keeping prices down and had completely failed to keep wages down and that therefore consumption had somehow to be cut back. All this she completely failed to see. It made me realize that the job and the situation make the person. She never has the time or the occasion to reflect on basic economic problems, she has no advisers and therefore she gets kicked by the Treasury even more than George Brown because she is not even at D.E.A. but sidetracked into the D.E.P.

This afternoon I settled down to prepare my speech on Lords' reform. It was a great problem to know how to introduce the White Paper. I know it is going to be difficult with our own side but I can't anticipate how difficult it will be with the Tories. I worked away with Janet and Ron Matthews and the invaluable Michael Wheeler-Booth and David Faulkner, who rallied round, as they have done with all the other speeches. We sweated away again after supper in 70 Whitehall until 11.30 or so, when I sent them all home.

Tuesday, November 19th

In the morning we tidied up the speech ready for 3.30. First there were P.M.'s Questions, then a Statement by Willie Ross about a warehouse in Glasgow which caught fire yesterday and caused twenty-two deaths, a ghastly thing. The Scots wallowed in it and it was also bad for me because all the Scots then left and I began in an empty Chamber.* After this awkwardness I got going. I had cut out about a fifth of our final draft and, looking back, I delivered it too fast and too self-confidently. My greatest mistake was that when I was interrupted, which was a great deal, I replied cleverly, intellectually, superiorly, and the more I was questioned from behind the more clearly I showed what fools they were to put things to me in that way. So, though the back benchers didn't dislike me, by the end I had done nothing whatsoever to persuade them. My speech was followed by Dingle Foot,[1] Enoch Powell and Willie Hamilton. I heard those three before I had to leave. The second and third speeches were ribald and dangerous, with Powell fanatically proving the case that no change could be made, Hamilton fanatically proving the case that the whole House of

* The Commons' debate on the White Paper took place over two whole days, November 19th and 20th, with three whole days in the Lords, and during that period Tam and I counted pretty carefully. There were never more than 70 people in the House. I had 70 when I sat down and after that there were usually 30 or 40. Of our back benchers about 40 attended some part of the first debate, so I reckoned that we were lucky if 150 M.P.s out of the 630 heard anything of the debate before coming in and voting.

[1] Michael Foot's elder brother. He was Liberal M.P. for Dundee 1931–45, Parliamentary Secretary for Economic Warfare 1940–5, Labour M.P. for Ipswich 1957–70, Solicitor-General 1964–7 and Chairman of the *Observer* Trust 1953–5. He was knighted in 1964.

Lords must be abolished. Then came Maurice Edelman,[1] mostly about placemen, portraying Harold like another Robert Walpole,[2] and then David Marquand, whose speech I really recommend as by far the most revealing.

It was this, when I read it later, that made me suddenly realize something I had completely failed to anticipate. I had always known we would have great difficulty with our scheme and that it would be extremely difficult to get people in the House of Commons to accept it, and we knew that the point about remuneration and nomination had not been understood at the Party meeting. What I hadn't realized was the inferiority complex, the deep suspicion that if at the other end of the passage on those red carpets we set up a nominated House of Lords with a real, nice, tidy, neat job at £2,000 a year, it would be far more attractive to be a peer than to be a commoner, sitting on the green benches.[3] M.P.s cannot tolerate the idea of giving the Lords a sensible job in the best club in the world. There really is something in this.

I felt this very strongly when I went along to the Lords and sat on the steps of the Throne and had a drink with Eddie in their bar, a magnificent room, a club room. There were Beattie Plummer and Patricia Llewelyn-Davies and Ted Heath talking to St Aldwyn,[4] Eddie, Malcolm Shepherd and me.[5] It was frankly a far more civilized, clubby atmosphere. I must admit that though people laugh and say 'Lord Crossman of Banbury' there is a great deal of truth in it because I would be wholly at home in the reformed House of Lords I have been creating, and I think back benchers have a point when they feel that we on the front bench are creating a better hole for ourselves.

Wednesday, November 20th

The debate continued and Elwyn Jones, who had exactly the same brief,

[1] Labour M.P. for Coventry North 1950–74 and for Coventry North-West from 1974 until his death in 1975. He was the author of several political novels, including *Who Goes Home?* (London: Hamish Hamilton, 1953), and *Disraeli in Love* (London: Collins, 1972).

[2] Sir Robert Walpole, First Lord of the Treasury and Chancellor of the Exchequer 1715–17 and 1721–42, first 'sole and prime minister', renowned for his skilful distribution of patronage and honours.

[3] At the junction of the corridors of the House of Commons and the House of Lords the colour of the carpets changes from green to red. The benches in the Commons Chamber are of green plush and in the Lords of red.

[4] Patricia Llewelyn-Davies was Chairman of the Board of Governors of Great Ormond St Hospital for Sick Children 1967–9 and Director of the Africa Educational Trust 1960–9. She became a life peer in 1967 and was a Government Whip 1969–70, Deputy Opposition Chief Whip 1972–3, Opposition Chief Whip 1973–4. She became Captain of the Gentlemen at Arms (Government Chief Whip in the Lords) in 1974. Michael Hicks Beach, Earl St Aldwyn, succeeded to his grandfather's earldom in 1916. He was Parliamentary Secretary at the Minister of Agriculture and Fisheries 1954–8, Captain of the Gentlemen at Arms 1958–64 and 1970–4 and Opposition Chief Whip 1964–70 and since 1974.

[5] Malcolm Shepherd succeeded to his father's barony in 1954 and was Opposition Chief Whip in the Lords 1964, Captain of the Gentlemen at Arms 1964–7, Minister of State at the F.C.O. 1967–70, Deputy Leader of the House of Lords 1968–70, Deputy Opposition Leader 1970–4, Lord Privy Seal and Leader of the House of Lords 1974–6.

couldn't have been more different from me, in the canoodling, soft, diffident way he pressed things, just as Macleod, who came after him, couldn't have been more different from Maudling, who had followed me with a kind of bumbling. Maudling wasn't actually letting us down yesterday or failing to admit his own and the Tories' support for the scheme, but he didn't really commit his party in any clear way. Macleod, on the other hand, today committed himself fully and resolutely to the scheme, differing only about the timing. Then the back benchers resumed their emotional, ribald attack on the front-bench mafia, as they called us, who were putting over this iniquitous extension of prime ministerial power.

We were able to dispose quite effectively of this, by arguing that there was no serious extension of prime ministerial patronage and that a salary or remuneration of £2,000 a year is far better for poor people than an expenses allowance which mainly helps the wealthy. What we couldn't beat was the thinking behind the arguments of the really intelligent critics, the Foots, the Edelmans, the Marquands. The whole Tory opposition was quite different. There we had Establishment figures in the Tory Party, the 110 hereditary baronets, the Tory knights, the characteristic solid Tories who also dislike the extension of patronage, also hate their front bench, and, I suspect, also feel, 'Well, it would be jolly nice to be along there as a voting peer but I mightn't get in. Why should we give the Prime Minister the power to get it?'

In his winding-up speech, Jim was at last able to make the basic point. He is not known to be an enthusiast for the scheme, so for that very reason he was convincing, and he told our back benchers that whether they liked it or not they must support us in order to eliminate the Lords' threat to the last two years of this Government. But I very much doubt whether it made the faintest difference. I saw Michael Foot in the gallery and he said, 'I'm afraid you've had a very bad day.' I said, 'Not I, Michael, you, because if you defeat our scheme your nationalization of the docks will not get through in this Parliament and you will be sorry. You will give the Tories the power to have it defeated in the House of Lords.' He said, 'We can't determine the constitution for tactical reasons.'

There were two other reasons why we had peculiar difficulties in this debate. First was the astonishing fact that, though the two front benches had agreed to have a two-day debate, 'taking note of the White Paper', i.e. without a division, at the last minute the Speaker permitted Willie Hamilton to move an amendment to reject the White Paper. It suddenly meant that instead of my introducing a general discussion on the reform the debate became quite a different thing, a defence of the reform against back benchers who would organize all their effort to get an adverse vote. This meant that the speeches were much more ferocious and violent, and as Bagehot says in *The English Constitution*, debates are a waste of time unless they end in a decision. My God, this debate became different, full of edge and passion, precisely because suddenly and unexpectedly we were to have a vote.[1] As it turned out we managed to win by a substantial majority, with only 47 of our people against us and 40 abstentions. We had most of the Tories against us in the lobbies.* Nevertheless, the Speaker's obvious prejudice against the scheme (I believe that is true) did have a deep effect on the debate. The other factor, of course, was the international economic situation. People were saying, 'What the hell are we doing discussing the House of Lords when the whole international monetary system is breaking up, with the Chancellor of the Exchequer flying to Bonn to try and patch up the pieces?' That told against us a good deal.

Speculation against the franc and £ continued and on November 19th Western Finance Ministers were asked to attend a hastily convened meeting in Bonn on the following day. Although the Prime Minister and the Chancellor felt that to call such a meeting was unwise and would lead to further loss of confidence they agreed that the Chancellor should attend. Meanwhile the German Ambassador was asked to come to Downing Street,[2] where the Prime Minister, the Chancellor and the Foreign Secretary explained the British Government's distress at the creation of further uncertainty and the hope that the Germans would now revalue the Mark, an episode that considerably upset the German government.

At the Bonn meeting, November 20th/21st, the Ministers agreed to back the franc with a substantial credit, and some $200 million of support from the Group of Ten was arranged. It was assumed that the French had agreed to devalue by 11·11 per cent but on November 23rd it became known that General de Gaulle had rejected this. On November 24th France introduced austerity measures, including expenditure cuts of some 6 milliard francs and a reimposition of severe exchange controls on foreign currency. In a broadcast on November 27th, General de Gaulle categorically rejected any devaluation. The Chancellor of the Exchequer returned to London from Bonn on November 22nd, in time to see the P.M. and show him the draft of a Statement to be made to the Commons before the Friday adjournment at 4.30 p.m. Mr Jenkins's emergency Statement was intended both to reinforce sterling against speculation and to dampen internal demand. The measures were designed to raise an

[1] The motion to reject the White Paper was defeated by 270 votes to 159. There were 47 Labour M.P.s against the scheme, 40 who abstained and 233 who gave their approval. All 8 Liberals voted against the White Paper and, of the Conservatives, only 47 voted for the scheme, 50 abstained and 104 voted for rejection. In the Lords' division on November 21st the White Paper was approved by 251 votes to 56. All 72 Labour peers who voted, 13 Liberals and 108 Conservatives approved the scheme, together with 58 cross-bench peers, bishops and law lords. Only 3 Liberals, 43 Conservatives and 10 cross-benchers, bishops and law lords opposed the scheme.

* Twenty or thirty Tories would almost certainly have voted differently had they known what the Lords' own result would be next day.

[2] Herbert Blankenhorn, German Ambassador to London 1965–70, an old friend of Crossman's.

additional £250 million a year in taxation. Indirect taxes were raised by 5d. on a gallon of petrol, 5d. on a packet of twenty cigarettes and 4s. on a bottle of spirits. All rates of purchase tax were increased by 10 per cent, bank credits were to be severely restricted and a new scheme of import deposits was introduced, requiring traders to deposit for six months 50 per cent of the value of a large number of imports before the goods were released by Customs. Imports and consumer demand had continued at a high level, undermining the export growth that had followed devaluation.

The announcement was received with shock. Rumours continued and the position of sterling reflected the uneasiness of the political and economic situation. When the measures were debated in the Commons on November 25th the Government defeated an Opposition motion of No Confidence by 328 votes to 251 votes. The Import Deposits Bill was given a Second Reading on November 28th by a majority of 61 votes but on the same evening the Order itself, authorizing the increases in purchase tax and excise duties, was approved by only 282 votes to 242.[1]

Thursday, November 21st

I must say I had been jolly angry with the Whips yesterday because the Chief Whip had done absolutely nothing and he never attended the two-day debate at all. The fact is that his father was today making a passionate attack on the scheme in the House of Lords and John has tremendous loyalty to his father.[2] He knows the P.M. is a bit ambivalent and so, with one thing and another, we had a most unreliable Chief Whip from my point of view. Nevertheless, he did send out a three-line whip on the first day, and, looking back, it undoubtedly saved the situation because nobody was really listening to the debate. This morning Fred Peart, the Chief and I had a chat with the Prime Minister and when we came to discuss it at the Parliamentary Committee it was clear that the Chief would have his way. Harold said we must postpone the Second Reading until after Christmas. It sounded worse than it was since they had originally fixed it for December 19th which was too near the recess anyway. What was sinister was that the P.M. said, 'If we find things too difficult on the economic front and that our back benchers are really difficult to carry, we may have to drop the whole thing because we can't get it through Committee.'

By now the whole House of Lords issue had been submerged by the economic crisis and by the usual press rumours of a new Jenkins squeeze. We had been expecting a Cabinet but instead a Parliamentary Committee was called, as Harold had told me yesterday, to deal with the squeeze proposals in a smaller, more leak-proof group than full Cabinet.

After an endless discussion about British methods of centrifuge production

[1] See *Wilson*, pp. 580–6.

[2] Lewis Silkin, Labour M.P. for Peckham 1936–50 and Minister of Town and County Planning 1945–50. He became a life peer in 1950 and died in May 1972.

we finally came to the package. Roy was in Bonn and the P.M. explained that we were going to have import deposits. That was all right, nobody contradicted. Then there was to be a credit squeeze, bank credit tightening, all that. Then there came – yes – the full 10 per cent of the regulator, including purchase tax on cars and consumer durables. Discussion centred almost entirely on this last point, because Wedgy Benn and I heard it for the first time and Barbara was against the whole thing. It was too restrictionist, too anti-expansionist, and, after all, it is only three weeks since we announced hire-purchase restrictions to hit the car industry. I said that what bewildered me was that three weeks ago we had asked if it was really wise just to have hire-purchase increases. Why, I asked, should we suddenly do this now? The answer was that we had to make a presentational case to the world. It was clear that the aim was to use this opportunity to make our necessary changes on the home front and cover them up with the international crisis. Jenkins had in fact been thinking of these measures before the Bonn meeting. Another very awkward thing was Barbara's behaviour at the Bassetlaw by-election meeting where she had said this was not a freeze but only a touch on the tiller. Here is a whole new batch of measures which by no stretch of the imagination can be called a touch on the tiller, extremely vigorous measures, a freeze or a squeeze or whatever you like. We were either caught saying we had thought of them before Bassetlaw or we had to justify them as the British contribution to the measures for dealing with the international crisis. The second alternative was wholly unconvincing because the passage which the Chancellor was dictating from Bonn had nothing to do with the international situation but a great deal to do with the internal situation. Nor could we discuss it with him. It was intolerable. However, Harold was specifically asked, in view of the h.p. increases we already had on the car industry and consumer durables, whether the purchase tax part should not be dropped altogether. Anyway it couldn't affect things before the Christmas shopping boom, except adversely by stimulating the boom and, if so, was it really wise to have purchase tax measures? We would leave only the 10 per cent on hydrocarbons, i.e. petrol, on drinks and on cigarettes. That was our recommendation. We ended that meeting with me profoundly depressed by what I had heard, and Callaghan also depressed, I think. Both of us are now the sort of old men of the Cabinet, I feel, nuisancy old men, deeply doubtful whether what was being proposed would work.

In the afternoon we had the debate on the Fulton Report going on in the House and our postponed Cabinet meeting took place at 7 o'clock. It went on for one and a half hours and it was clear that nothing had yet been decided at Bonn. We still didn't know whether the French were going to devalue or what the Germans were going to do about revaluation. Then another thing came up. Nobody really knew how tough the British measures would have to be because we didn't know what would be the effect on the balance of payments. It was a fantastic situation. We broke off without any further information.

Friday, November 22nd

At 9.0 o'clock we met again in the P.M.'s room at the House of Commons, not in No. 10 because that creates so much notice. Cabinets in the P.M.'s room in the House are nearly always failures. It's a bad shape, there's not enough room round the table and somehow it inhibits, cramps. We crouch there not as Cabinet Ministers but more like American Cabinets, more hopeless and impotent. We had an interminable four-hour meeting, from 9.0 till 1.0 since we met in Parliamentary Committee first and then in Cabinet. This morning there was still no communiqué and when at last a telegram came from Roy describing what was happening, this was the first intimation Cabinet had received since he left for Bonn yesterday. He had been carrying on on his own without any briefing or any consultation, trying to force the hand of his colleagues. Barbara said that we must make it clear that last month the imposition of the regulator had not been regarded as an alternative to the increased hire-purchase charges. When we had discussed this before, she said, there had been no question of a second batch of measures. She had spoken the truth at Bassetlaw. I had to correct her.[1] 'On the contrary,' I said, 'she would recall that when it was suggested that the hire-purchase restrictions were an alternative to the regulator, I had said that in that case I was against it.' Tony Crosland, Jim and I had all said that we thought the hire-purchase terms totally ineffective and we would have preferred tougher measures then, or, alternatively, to wait and have them all together a bit later. We had been overwhelmed by the alliance of Roy and Barbara.

When Cabinet joined us at 9.45 we went on with a great attack about briefing. We knew nothing except what was in the newspapers but they contained everything about the international conference. We heard that Roy had been bitterly complaining about the Germans. 'Well,' said Jim, 'the briefer outbriefed.' He said it *sotto voce* but the whole Cabinet laughed grimly, because we also suspected that all last week Roy had been briefing the British press in order to bounce the Cabinet. Roy and John Harris had been madly determined to see to it that the right atmosphere was prepared for the Chancellor's policy and that we should unavoidably accept his will. Although the Prime Minister firmly denied this and said he had gone into two instances and had discovered that one of them had come from the joint stock banks and he didn't think the Chancellor of the Exchequer was guilty, on the whole there was a universal conviction in that room that John Harris had become Roy's evil genius and that Roy was sitting in an ivory tower with John Harris and David Dowler, cut off from the rest of the world, planning Roy's political future.

[1] See p. 242 and n.

The meeting went on and on. A lot of it was repetition because many members of Cabinet had not heard any of this before. Ted Short, Dick Marsh and Roy Mason had to be brought in. Cabinet said again that the raising of purchase tax would stimulate the boom the Chancellor was trying to stop but we were overriden by the experts, who were determined to do it. Another thing that Tony Wedgwood Benn pointed out very strongly was the absolute essential need for our package to be timed simultaneously with the French package. If they didn't devalue we shouldn't put our package out. This was put time and time again but always turned down. Perhaps the most remarkable thing was that when we asked about the details and machinery of the import deposits scheme no one knew. Tony Crosland was in Vienna, the P.M. didn't know, neither did Jack Diamond nor Barbara. The inner group of six who had prepared the package didn't know what goods were covered by the scheme. Three-quarters of an hour later a note was brought into the room and we learnt that the list of goods would be the same for the import deposits as it was for the import surcharge,[1] with two or three minor exceptions. I threw a note across the table to Jim saying that if they are going to have these crises (this is the seventh time, I think, we've sat around impotently discussing a plan with the three or four people who have known of it beforehand but couldn't answer our criticisms effectively because they knew none of the facts), if they are going to consult Cabinet at the last moment like this, the only possible way to make sense of it is for us to bring along our senior civil servants so that we have some departmental expertise, and to have people from the Treasury and the Inland Revenue too, so that politicians don't discuss these things and make last-minute decisions in almost total ignorance. It is fantastic that in this particular case there was no bit of paper giving the package or the reasons for it. It was all told us verbally and we have serious doubts whether a clear-cut plan had ever been worked out. The most depressing fact about the whole of yesterday's and today's meetings was that there has been no change from the original 1965 July meeting, the 1966 meeting or the 1967 devaluation meeting. All the way through we have had the same phenomenon of a small group suddenly saying to Cabinet, 'This is it. Take it or leave it. It's too late to do anything else.' If a Cabinet meeting is based on adequate paper preparation the absence of the Departmental civil servants may be defended but where Cabinet works without papers the absence of officials is devastating because it leads to the most appalling mistakes.

Well, that was Friday. Most of our time was spent on the question of the timing of the Statement and whether Jenkins should make it if he got back

[1] An import surcharge of 15 per cent had been announced on October 26th, 1964. It was reduced to 10 per cent on April 27th and finally abolished on November 30th, 1966 (see Vol. I, p. 165, and Vol. II, pp. 39–40). The exceptions to the import deposit scheme were to be on basic foods, feeding stuffs, fuel and raw materials and some categories of goods, largely imported from developing countries. The scheme would therefore apply to about a third of Britain's total imports, worth some £3,000 million a year.

from Bonn in time. I said anyway the P.M. should do it because Jenkins would not be in tune with the Cabinet and wouldn't have been apprised of our doubts. It was clear that the P.M. didn't dare to deny Jenkins the Chancellor's right to introduce his measures in his own way and he certainly wasn't going to deny him the right to put his interpretation on the whys and the wherefores of the measures. That was actually what happened this afternoon at 3.50. Meanwhile I had gone off to Hammersmith for my first visit to a London postgraduate teaching hospital, where I had a really thrilling time before I caught the train down to Banbury for Patrick's school concert.

Saturday, November 23rd

I had to go off to Leicester for a conference on local government and when I got there I found the press and photographers and all the television apparatus in the hall, with some fifty people waiting rather anxiously. I did have the sense to say what was necessary about the economic situation and I brought in my simple point that we had hit the consumer because consumption had gone up. We hadn't hit Government expenditure because that has been brought under control and I was able to make this point effectively whether Jenkins liked it or not. But at the actual conference people were utterly heartbroken. They said they were disillusioned. Finally I was stimulated by somebody who said, 'With what the Government is doing how do you think we can get a majority at the next election?' I answered, 'That depends on you. It depends on whether we shall ever get the electorate to allow a Government to cut the standard of living because if we don't cut back and spend more on improving the economy we can't get out of our difficulties. We are living beyond our means. We are all refusing to hold back and the terrible thing now is that if you give a turn of the screw it has less and less effect and people become more and more mutinous.'

I felt this depression extremely strongly as I came specially up to London this evening for a dinner at Tommy's with Barbara, Peter, Tony Wedgwood Benn and Judith Hart. Almost for the first time I showed myself really despondent. I said I didn't see how we were going to avoid a second devaluation. No one really showed any confidence. Barbara goes on being bright and able but is terribly sore because she feels she is not being supported by Roy. Peter is rather enigmatic but more on Roy's side now and trying to survive in his own way. I am completely isolated and I am out of all these discussions.

Monday, November 25th

I had to go down to Cambridge for a Union debate against Lord Beeching on a motion 'That Parliamentary democracy in its present form inhibits the solution to Britain's problems'.[1] That's a dicey thing to argue against because it's pretty obviously true. However I was right to reckon on Lord Beeching, who was supercilious, boring, patronizing and incredibly bigoted in his anti-socialist doctrinairism. He had written notes which he read aloud hopelessly at the dispatch box. I had prepared something fairly carefully on the way down but I had the wisdom to tear it up and make most of my speech impromptu, wrapping up Lord Beeching and then turning to give the undergraduates what they wanted to hear, my recognition of the need for participation. I pointed out that there was plenty to reform in Parliamentary democracy but that the one thing that is right with it, which is what Beeching thought was wrong, is its sense of participation, its refusal to think managerial efficiency the only thing worth having. All this was being televised and the heat was terrific and the cameras terrible. On the whole I thought Beeching was pretty awful and that I was so-so. The young men were quite good. I motored back to London thinking I hadn't done too badly.

Tuesday, November 26th

A rather sinister meeting of S.E.P. on poor Peter Shore's revised National Plan. The National Plan totally collapsed after George Brown left D.E.A. in 1966 and Peter has been trying to recast a new plan to discuss with NEDO and the first draft he had put forward was absolutely dreadful. This morning a redraft was being put to us and we were told to treat it only as an official paper, not a Ministerial paper, so that he could circulate it to NEDO in four days' time. This is the kind of pressure the P.M. uses when he wants to get a thing through which he knows is unpopular. 'We shall be bankrupt of planners', said Peter Shore, 'unless you let me put this thing forward, though I really don't defend the drafting and I will call it only an officials' working document.' Roy Jenkins and Tony Crosland were absolutely united on postponing this at all costs until after the budget and, when challenged, Roy said, 'Actually I don't really want it postponed, I'd like to get it out of the way altogether.' Peter was known to have the P.M.'s full support and it was striking that virtually no one in the Cabinet supported Roy and Tony. Everyone round that table knew we could hardly say we didn't believe in having a plan so we all spent our time making suggestions as to how to make it more palatable. We felt that chapters should be published seriatim as working documents, that the regional chapters and the public sector chapters should be omitted. All of us, including Fred Peart, Dick Marsh and me, said that however awkward it might be we really must have it. Owing to the violence of their negativeness, as often happens, Roy and Tony were fairly easily routed.

[1] Lord Beeching, Deputy Chairman of I.C.I. 1966–8, was Chairman of the British Transport Commission 1961–3, and of the British Railways Board 1963–5, when he carried out a programme of drastic cuts in the railway network. In 1965 he became a life peer.

Then we were lectured again on the eternal subject of leaks because the fact that there had been a row between Roy, Tony and Peter Shore about this draft National Plan had all come out in the *Financial Times*. I must say we have had a whole series of leaks designed to promote one group of Ministers against another. No doubt about it, these are Treasury-motivated leaks against D.E.A. It's disappointing because I thought that the removal of George Brown and Ray Gunter would end the Cabinet leaks but perhaps the Wilson Cabinet is inherently leaky. There is constant talk and nothing is secret, which undermines things a great deal. Harold uses this leakiness more and more as an excuse for not telling anybody anything and for dividing us all up into our little groups and fractions.

Off we went to Cabinet from 12.0 to 1.0 for a discussion of the French decision not to devalue. I suppose we can say Roy felt fairly relieved but really all I was concerned about was the astonishing story of last Tuesday night when the Prime Minister had summoned the German Ambassador in the middle of the night to Downing Street and the Chancellor and the Foreign Secretary had dressed him down. When we had had an extraordinarily uneventful discussion of what had happened in Bonn I finally asked whether we could be told about this affair. Harold didn't like being asked but said, 'Well, it wasn't late at night, it was only 12.30 and he came along in evening dress from a party. Of course he wasn't threatened but merely told that if things came to the worst, if there was another major crisis, we shouldn't be able to maintain our troops in Germany.' So really Harold confirmed this story though he said the episode only lasted half an hour. He was careful to say that it had been followed by Roy Jenkins and Michael Stewart talking even more strongly than he had done.[1]

The P.M. then had to go off to the Palace and left Roy in charge of Cabinet. I asked Roy afterwards what actually had happened and he said, 'I have to take full blame. Though I was doubtful about it, I agreed to the summoning of the Ambassador and I took part. But it was a terrible mistake, a disaster, and I bitterly regret having agreed to it.' Of course it was. It was one of the most ludicrous pieces of misjudgment and of insular self-deception. Who are we to threaten the Germans for refusing to come to our rescue by revaluing the Mark? What role did we think we were playing? Above all, if we are seeking to get into Europe, to placate the Germans and win them to our side against the French, why play into the French hands and let poor Roy Jenkins arrive in Bonn with a black mark against him? It was an episode of gross mismanagement.

The other thing I learnt this morning was that no plans had been made to stop the outflow of nearly £200 million of capital to Australia. Harold said, 'This is so secret we can't even discuss it.' This is the kind of ridiculous situation we get into in our Cabinet so I said, 'Look, I'm not going to discuss it. All I'm going to say is that at each crisis, and I think this is the

[1] See *Wilson*, p. 583.

fifth I've been in, all I can do is to register the fact that I'm disappointed that, despite asking for it, nothing is ever done in between this discussion and the last one.' Then Harold said, 'But nothing has to be done. It's a perfectly simple thing, it doesn't need a lot of complications.' This discussion did make me feel pretty despondent and as I was going up to my room I said to Wedgy Benn, 'When can we expect the next devaluation?' Wedgy said, 'Oh, you shouldn't talk like that here.' Of course I shouldn't.*

This evening I dined with the General Medical Council and then went in to the House to see a vote on the Committee Stage of the Representation of the People Bill. The vote was 275 for, 121 against. Characteristically, again we had a free vote on an important issue and really only about half the House bothered to vote and the rest avoided it. I was paired but I wouldn't have paired if I had known this particular division was on votes at eighteen.

John suggested I should come upstairs to see the B.B.C. programme of the Cambridge Union debate. Really I was amazed, because I didn't remember what I had said and it was so much an outside broadcast, with shots of the young men listening, that I forgot who it was that I was. I was quite interested in what I was saying, thought what a lively, interesting debate it was and realized I had done quite well. More and more people have congratulated me on this. Once again one sees that if the B.B.C. do politics as straight coverage of an outside event they get a larger and more appreciative audience, far less critical of the medium than it would otherwise be.

Wednesday, November 27th

Monday, Tuesday and the whole of this morning I have spent with Clifford Jarrett going through the Superannuation White Paper paragraph by paragraph. I have treated the Department worse than ever before, pushing, bullying, tugging, shoving. I said, 'I will bloody well drag you into this, because in journalism we have to take decisions quickly.' They all went out of the room about every hour and a half staggering with the pummelling they received and they all apparently said they thanked God for a Minister who knew how to handle a White Paper. They knew that some time or other the thing had to be finished. 'When can I have a new draft of the first part?' I asked, and Jarrett said, 'Tomorrow at 12.0.' I said, 'Today, at 4.0.' It came at 4.0 and asking for it today when I was offered it tomorrow saved our bacon. There wasn't a breakdown and it turned out good and sharp because they didn't have time to criticize or dilute it. So though the draft White Paper is not finalized it is in a form which has been able to go

* It was wholly characteristic that two days later when we were discussing security, Wedgy Benn, Barbara and I, he said, 'After all, who was it, Dick, who said in the open gallery and was overheard "When shall we have another devaluation?"' Of course I wasn't overheard. Wedgy Benn invented it.

to the printer. This will then be circulated to the Social Services Committee and then it will go to Cabinet in galley and be ready for publication in January.

Thursday, November 28th

At the Parliamentary Committee we had our friend Ted Short with his great paper trying to show us that the cuts in the educational programme are all fatal. We had given him an excuse not to resign and now we had to see what could be done. There had been universal agreement at the Social Services Committee that the money had to go to comprehensive reorganization. This I reported but the P.M. knew better. He wanted to have a higher amount of money per child spread over the country as a whole and he was obviously affected by Ted Short's arguments that all the good schools had gone to the new areas of the South and all the slum schools were left in the North. Harold was also deeply shocked when I said we really should start cutting down the number of students admitted to universities and expanding other sorts of further education instead. Every really radical solution makes Harold shiver, especially in the educational field, where I know he feels, 'Thank God I didn't put Dick Crossman in.'[1] However, perhaps the biggest thing which came out of this was a decision for comparable papers to be done for health, social security and for housing, so that the Social Services Committee can carefully compare the four. I promised to get these done and have them discussed and I went back and worked out the timetable. If I can get these comparable studies done and can see which areas really have suffered and where the cuts are biting, I shouldn't be surprised if the damage does prove to be deepest in education and least deep in housing. We may be able to move forward a little in getting our priorities right.

After this I had an evening of studying hospitals. I find these visits enormously exhilarating but I am beginning to reach the conclusion that, by jove, the set-up is oligarchical. The patient is completely unrepresented and the public completely excluded. It is all controlled by the doctors and the men who work with them, the Chairmen of the boards of governors, professional men, remote, detached, confident and absolutely undemocratic.

Friday, November 29th

I had a message today that the Prime Minister has scrapped the timetable for the Social Services Committee discussion on health, social security, housing and education, and insists that the whole thing should be put on a week earlier. This would mean that I couldn't go to Sweden next week and I asked Paul Odgers if Harold knew this. 'Yes,' said Paul. 'I think he and Burke mean you to cancel the Swedish visit.' Just on the off chance, I

[1] In 1963 Crossman had become Shadow Minister of Education and Science and when Labour won the 1964 General Election he was surprised to be offered, not that portfolio, but the Ministry of Housing and Local Government.

wrote an urgent memo to the P.M. saying that this would mean cancelling the visit altogether, because I have postponed it once already even though it is at Mr Erlander's personal invitation. I got an urgent message back saying he did not want me to cancel the visit and that I really ought to go, so I don't know how I'm going to fit everything in next week. What is more, I have been developing the most appalling cold in the head and I had the greatest difficulty in getting through Wednesday and Thursday. It was almost intolerable by the time I saw Cudlipp this morning to discuss the popular version of the White Paper. He couldn't have been nicer. He came at 9.30 with Mark Abrams[1] and John Harris, and he started by saying, 'I've read the White Paper and understood it reasonably well, and, frankly, with a thing like pensions it is far too dicey to have a popular version. What I can do is study the White Paper, take sentences out of it and string them together with a lot of illustrations and tables. But you mustn't alter a word.' That is the kind of brilliance which is very simple and which shows a tremendous understanding. We discussed the popular and the unpopular parts of it and, as I knew he would, Hugh backed my view and said, 'We've got to sell this as the only fair and decent thing and make people feel bad about being too selfish about it.' So we will first of all prepare a simplified form for the press conference and then challenge the B.B.C. to let me have an hour in depth on it with all the experts. I am going to have fun getting hold of all this and putting it over. Then there will be a series of regional Labour Party conferences. Am I exaggerating? No, because this is a scheme which for four years has been really carefully worked out in detail, and, much more important, where we have consulted the vested interests beforehand, briefed them before legislation, brought them right in – the T.U.C., the C.B.I., above all, the Institute of Actuaries and the Life Association people. On the whole, the concentrated work on this scheme has kept me going in this very depressing and defeatist week.

Then I had an interesting meeting on Scientology. I had discussed this at a meeting in the Ministry and every single person except George Godber had been resolutely against my proposal to substitute a public inquiry for measures against the Scientologists. So I had sent a short message to those colleagues who were vitally affected, the Home Secretary, the Secretary of State for Scotland and the Attorney General, saying that I wanted to have a public inquiry and asking them to come and talk to me about it. I found they were all opposed too, the Home Secretary for curious reasons. He explained that he was only acting for my predecessor. He hadn't much liked what Kenneth Robinson had done but now he just wanted to get on with it as fast as he could. Every kind of reason was put up against the

[1] Like Crossman a member of the Psychological Warfare Executive 1941–6, Mark Abrams was Managing Director and later Chairman of Research Services Ltd 1946–70. He has been Director of the Survey Research Unit at the Social Science Research Council since 1970.

inquiry, questions about immigration, about the effect on other religious and quasi-religious orders and so forth, so I switched my line and finally found they all agreed that Kenneth Robinson had made a mistake. We all agreed we ought to get out of it but the others thought the best way was to play it down quietly and that a public inquiry would be an embarrassment. I had to change my line despite the fact that I had already discussed the possibility of an inquiry with Iain Macleod, who had made out an excellent case to me, pointing out the unfairness of our attitude to Scientology, and asking why we were harassing these particular people. I find his argument completely unanswerable. I have been disappointed on this but not too disappointed.

Off on the 2.15 train to Birmingham to address a meeting of high-powered local government officers, who are on a four-month postgraduate course at Birmingham University. I got a frantic message that I wasn't to go to the campus as the students have seized the Vice-Chancellor's office in order to extract his agreement to their demands. We were to meet at an hotel in town instead. There I found deputy treasurers, deputy town clerks, deputy engineers, the number twos, who have been sitting here week after week, going home each weekend to their wives, thinking about what is wrong with local government and how to put it right managerially and philosophically. I was able to let my hair down and tell them all my doubts and feelings about local government and about the efficiency of locally elected councillors. It was excellent and healthy for me because they were able to put the other case and ask, 'But aren't your Regional Hospital Boards totally unrepresentative? They have all the vices of self-perpetuating oligarchies?' Yes, if we call local government an oligarchy, at least it is one with a mythology of contact with the ordinary citizen and the councillor does feel responsible to ordinary citizens in a way that a member of an R.H.B. doesn't. We had a splendid and thrilling discussion, which somehow continued this evening when I went to address the Birmingham Socialist Dining Club, crowded into the Good Earth restaurant. I gave the 200 people there an account of my new pensions plan, outlining it in great detail. Four women came up, new Labour members of the R.H.B., to tell me how the Board crushes you, how they don't want you to see patients or visit hospitals, how they flatten you into being a mere presentational piece. I am sure all this is true that there is a very big difference between the local government atmosphere and the atmosphere of the élitist R.H.B.s. I must bear this contrast in mind.

Sunday, December 1st

The end of the week. The children have been watching 'The Saint', their favourite programme.* I have been reading Henty to them and finding it

* A television series with Roger Moore as The Saint, based on thrillers written by Leslie Charteris.

first-rate – the book called *Through Russian Snows*, greatly enjoyable, excellently told. We have just got back from Coventry, where we had quite a sensible meeting with the Executive of Coventry East and then a meeting with the Executive of the Council Tenants' Federation. There is an atmosphere of quiet resignation and utter defeatism in the party. One feels it everywhere, a growing sense that whatever happens there is no time before the election to get into a boom, even to get any distance away from failure, and no time to be a successful Government. We still have the interminable self-defeating optimism of Harold Wilson, backed now by the straight, formidable, but limited abilities of Roy Jenkins. How conventional he is, how little on top of his Department, how much a creature of John Harris and Dowler, forcing his image all the time, not really a master of affairs. I should add something to this. I switched on the wireless when I got back from Coventry and heard that Jim Callaghan had made a speech in Scotland telling people we will review British Standard Time at the end of the summer. After three weeks of this our mornings are growing darker and darker and we don't really notice the advantage that our evenings are not. There has been a growing storm of agitation, and now here is Callaghan not bothering to come to Cabinet, just announcing that we will review it after a year. I remember when we discussed this I said there should be a free vote and I was turned down. Now we've made the change and it's ludicrous, after three weeks, to start querying it. The lesson is that everything goes wrong for a Government which is going wrong, and B.S.T. added to everything else has increased our unpopularity. I can't help wondering how my pensions plan is going to be affected by all this.

By jove, we are in a bad way now, there's no doubt about it. I feel that what we are hated for is not what we have done wrong but what we have done right, like our trying to hold back consumption and put more money into investment and actually taking measures to enforce this through the prices and incomes policy and now through the regulator. These, the realistic things, are what we are not forgiven for. We have done them not like the Tories in a class-biased way but with every possible arrangement for looking after the nurses, public servants, the unemployed, the sick, the workers with large families. We have done them in a decent way and got nothing but curses and kicks from our own side. There are people going round saying they'll never vote for Labour again. Why? Because we've done what Nye Bevan told us to do, we have tried to make a democracy voluntarily vote for the unpleasant necessities of its existence. Of course that is only half of it. The real trouble is that we have never done things in time. Every decision has visibly been extracted from us. Instead of deciding to devalue, we were driven to it; instead of deciding to get out of east of Suez, we were driven from there; instead of deciding on import controls six months ago, we are seeking them at the very last moment in an international crisis. It is the terrible timing of Harold Wilson, the inability to move, the constant gimmicky effort to leave things till the last moment, this disastrous leadership, which has caused the catastrophic disintegration of morale, and at this moment the P.L.P. is loyal to us only because it can't do anything else. It feels left out, it feels it's too late to do anything but coast along.

Monday, December 2nd

Our new Ministry was first in Parliamentary Questions. They had all been sent down to me by special dispatch rider at the weekend. Parliamentary clerks in the Department had worked all through Saturday to get them ready. We met at 1 o'clock today for lunch in my room at 70 Whitehall, Stephen Swingler, David Ennals and Julian Snow, with Ron Matthews to help us as well. We got down to it very late and the Questions were not clicked into their books until 1.30. What had struck me, as I read them at Prescote, in the train and in the half-hour I had before 1 o'clock, was the appalling amount of work which had been put in, huge great briefs prepared on every Question. And then you consider the ease with which they were disposed of! We got through some forty-five Questions and no one was really troubled because on a Monday afternoon very few people are there. I have had a special note sent round telling the Department to cut the thing back and shorten their notes unless we specially ask for briefs. Unless it's some Private Notice Question or Questions regularly asked of a Prime Minister or Lord President, Question Time is not a formidable test for any capable bunch of Ministers and, whatever else, we are quite a capable bunch at the new Department. Indeed the only Question which tested me at all was the one on Scientology, where I could only say I was carrying on for the time being. Inevitably I was pressed because Robin Balneil knew I had talked to Macleod about the idea of a public inquiry. I wasn't sorry since it has enabled me to go back to the Home Secretary and say, 'After this I've got to get the Inquiry.'

This afternoon we had the second of our big new seminars at the Ministry of Health and Social Security on medical manpower, in preparation for our reaction to the Report of the Todd Committee on Medical Education.[1] Once again I tried to get them to explain the method of assessing manpower numbers and the first thing which emerged is that nobody knows to within thousands how many doctors are at work in this country because the B.M.A. just registers doctors, whether they are working in this country, are retired or are working abroad. As for the N.H.S., we know how many are working there but not what proportion are part-time and the whole-time private practices simply aren't registered at all so the whole of our medical manpower figures are unsound. When I said, 'When was the last time the Minister asked you about the private sector?' there was an uneasy silence. It looks

[1] Established in June 1975 under the chairmanship of Lord Todd, Professor of Organic Chemistry at the University of Cambridge 1944–71. Their Report, Cmnd 3569, had been published in March 1968.

as though this is a subject my predecessors just neglected. I was very glad about the other thing which came out. I have described how in Manchester the Dean of the Medical School had told me about the immigrant doctors who come here to get their M.D. and then stay on as registrars for up to seven years because they are barred higher promotion, with the result that a block forms in the middle of the scale and a regular log-jam develops for our own young men.

When somebody mentioned immigrant doctors I asked about this, and received the blandest denial that it mattered at all. Gradually I dragged all this out of the Committee and it was reluctantly admitted that, even if we carried out all the Todd recommendations, hogging the immigrant doctors and reducing the short-run shortage, we might possibly pile up the most appalling trouble for ourselves in the future. When poor David Ennals, who had dealt with immigration at the Home Office, heard this, he said, 'But you people egged me on to the voucher scheme, to knock out all unskilled workers and allow in 3–4,000 more doctors. Now I hear that it is not only doing desperate damage to the Commonwealth and to the developing countries but is not really an advantage to us.' This shows the effect of this narrow-minded policy. The Ministry of Health apparently failed to foresee this and they wouldn't have said a word to me about it if I hadn't picked it up on one of my journeys.

This evening I had to go to the Pilgrim Trust dinner for John Freeman, the Ambassador-designate to Washington. David Harlech was in the chair and had asked me to come along and give the toast,[1] a ten- to twelve-minute speech. When I was brooding over it earlier today I suddenly had an idea. I would make an entirely personal speech and describe John and his three careers as politician, as journalist and as diplomat. As a politician he had tremendous success and then saw through it, was bored and tried a new career in journalism, where he took my place on the *New Statesman* and immediately succeeded as an editor. Then he saw through that and became the B.B.C.'s most brilliant profiler, saw through that and said to himself, 'Let me find a career so chilly and austere that I can never see through it or be bored by success.' He chose diplomacy and went to India and now naturally has been sent to the toughest assignment of all, Washington. I would say that, John being John, I didn't expect that he would be able to give up and say, 'I have succeeded'.

David Harlech made a nice ribbing speech with a lot about me as Dean of New College. Then I made my cheeky address. I even got as far as

[1] David Ormsby-Gore, Conservative M.P. for Oswestry 1950–61, Parliamentary Under-Secretary of State for Foreign Affairs November 1956–January 1957, Minister of State for Foreign Affairs 1957–61 and British Ambassador to Washington 1961–5. He succeeded his father as the 5th Baron Harlech in 1964 and was Deputy Leader of the Opposition in the House of Lords 1966–7. He has been President of the British Board of Film Censors and of The Pilgrim Trust since 1965, and is Chairman of Harlech Television and 1969–75 of the European Movement.

suggesting that John was glad Nixon was President so that he was really obliged to start at square one.[1] Up got John, solid, enormously pontifical, to read aloud a very slow and serious speech.

Certainly it was risky because what I said was very near the bone because it was true. It was light, elegant, gay, not at all what the Pilgrim Trust expected, and David and I were slightly embarrassed when 'Peterborough' pointed out in the *Telegraph* that our two witty speeches made John himself sound a trifle boring. As for John himself, well I wonder. I don't know how he really felt about it. He sent me a letter telling me that my speech was 'brilliant in more ways than one' and I expect he meant that the second way was as a diagnosis of his character and motives.

Tuesday, December 3rd

This afternoon George Godber had arranged that after many weeks, I should see Lord Platt, the Chairman of the Merit Awards Committee. I think Godber had expected that this conversation would finish the discussion for Platt was quite firm that one couldn't possibly publish the results of the merit awards and he gave all the normal reasons for not doing so. I then said, 'But look, Lord Platt, in the course of saying this to me you have said that the scandal is not the system of merit awards or how many wrong people have them, but how many right people don't have them. All right, how many more awards would you require to give them to all the people who deserve them – 30 per cent, 40 per cent? Why not put that up to me? I might then say to you, "Let's have an adequate number and publish." Let's consider this again.' He went away to think it over and we will wait for the next round.

Off I went with Anne to a dinner that Phil and Hannah Kaiser were giving in my honour.[2] The guests had been beautifully selected – Paul and Marigold Johnson,[3] Nicholas and Olga Davenport, Harold and Diane Lever, and Charles Curran and his wife.[4] Curran is taking over the Director-Generalship of the B.B.C. next April and when the men got round their brandy and cigars we asked him about the astonishing B.B.C. concentration on Enoch Powell that we have had this past weekend. He was on 'Any Questions' last Friday, 'The World This Weekend' on Sunday and yesterday he had a

[1] On November 5th the former Republican Vice-President Richard Nixon won the presidential election, with a clear majority of electoral college votes, 302 to Hubert Humphrey's 191 and George Wallace's 45, although both Nixon and Humphrey each took 43 per cent of the popular vote.

[2] Philip Kaiser was Minister at the American Embassy, London, 1964–9 and Chairman and Managing Director of *Encyclopaedia Britannica* International Ltd, London, 1970–5. In 1975 he became a director of Guinness Mahon Holdings Ltd and in 1977 U.S. Ambassador to Hungary.

[3] Paul Johnson had been a member of the staff of the *New Statesman* since 1955 and was its Editor 1965–70.

[4] Charles Curran was Producer of Home Talks at the B.B.C. 1947–50, Assistant Editor of *Fishing News* 1950–1, Director of External Broadcasting at the B.B.C. 1967–9 and Director-General of the Corporation 1969–77. He was knighted in 1974.

fifty-minute profile on 'Panorama'. 'Frankly,' said Charles Curran, 'it was because there was nobody in control at the centre.' I suspect that the central control of the B.B.C. has disappeared.

I sat next to Curran's wife at dinner and we had a long talk. Poor woman, she is obviously a nice little thing but she is terrified of the new weight of responsibility for her husband. Indeed, he is obviously aware that he is a very small man for this and though it's conceivable that this pair will grow into it and he will become a great Director-General, I rather guess he won't. I bet our friend Mr Curran has been selected by Charlie Hill as an anonymous, anodyne character who will run the B.B.C. under his direction and that will be a thoroughly bad thing.

Wednesday, December 4th

We began with a big S.E.P. meeting for a long discussion about economic prospects, forecasting and what we could do. These bloody quarterly economic forecasts – this one was coolly telling us that, as a result of the measures imposed by the Chancellor, we would now get £1,000 million turnover next year in the balance of payments and that next year we would be able to get a surplus. All they have done is to move on their predictions for one year and then predict blithely and optimistically that they will achieve this. I asked if it wasn't important for us to have an analysis by our economic pundits. Might they not be asked to explain how they go wrong each time? As Ronald Butt said in an extremely powerful leading article in the *Sunday Times*, hadn't the Government better sack its pundits? The Treasury and the economic experts are consistently wrong because they try to analyse in terms that are utterly remote from reality. Several of us made a very important point to Roy: 'You always talk about cutting consumption but what you are cutting is not consumption. You are trying to hack at buying but people are buying not to consume but to get out of holding money. That's the really dangerous thing.' Roy admitted there was something in this but not so very much and said a little about how he would try to do something about saving, for presentational reasons. We went on to discuss what could be done, and Roy again made his demand that we commit ourselves now to £250 million cuts in the 1970/1 programme. Tony Crosland and the rest of us resisted and on Friday we shall have our big Social Services Committee to consider the programme all over again with full analyses. It's pretty clear to me that instead of Roy's fiddly cuts here and there we should have one major change of policy and in my view defence and investment allowances are the likely ones to go.

Thursday, December 5th

We had two subjects of excitement at Cabinet, first Biafra and then the House of Lords. I have been reluctantly supporting the Government in its policy of support for the Federal Government of Nigeria. We did not cancel the supply of arms to the Federal Government but we have unsuccessfully tried to make peace between them and Biafra. Now we are being blamed because there is a danger of mass starvation in what is left of Biafra, which the French are supplying with arms. It is clear that we have utterly failed in our attempt to put over to the British public the fact that the Russians are supplying arms to the Federal Government and the French to the Biafrans. The Gallup Poll shows that 70–80 per cent of the public are in favour of our sending help to Biafra, an emotional but intelligible view. However Cabinet did revolt on this. A lot of people felt that we can't go on like this. We've got 150 people filing a resolution and if we have a debate in the House we will be defeated. As I said, we may have to face it that unless Harold can get what he hoped for, ourselves, the French and the Russians all working together to stop the supply of arms, it is probably impossible to stop the war. We ourselves might have to take the initiative in giving up the sale of arms. Frankly, I said, this is something we have to do for public opinion, though in a sense there is no justification for it.

Then we turned to the House of Lords. I was aware that there was no enthusiasm in Cabinet for this and I wasn't expecting an easy time. I was also aware that Harold Wilson had been nearly persuaded by the Chief Whip not merely to defer consideration of the Bill but to drop it. On the other hand, I was confident that Harold would be very reluctant to drop a Bill which was in his election manifesto and to which he had committed himself anew last June, in a statement that he was going to push the Bill through. How did it go? The Lord Chancellor was asked to begin and he did it very badly. He started by taking two dreary secondary issues, of Scottish peers and their rights under the Act of Union of 1707, and then remuneration. I knew how dicey this second one was and I thought the best thing was to say we would set up Committees to consider the remuneration of both Houses in the next Parliament. Harold and the Chancellor would have none of this, the increase of M.P.s' salaries could not be mentioned, so very reluctantly I agreed that the only thing to do was to maintain for the time being the present system of 4½ guineas expenses.[1] Then we found, ironically, that the people most against Lords' reform, Willie Ross, Jim Callaghan, Tony Crosland, said that they wouldn't take this, it was very unjust. However we got it through but Cabinet was already in a thoroughly bad mood for the third point, the timing of the Second Reading. The Lord Chancellor said he wanted it before Christmas and then Callaghan said, 'Before we do anything about this, I think we ought to abandon the Bill altogether.' He then launched into a fantastic, wild, flailing attack on the whole concept of Lords' reform and of the two-tier House. He said it was

[1] Payment of travelling expenses depended on frequency of attendance, but after 1957 peers were entitled to claim, in addition, for every day that they attended the House, reimbursement of up to 3 guineas a day, untaxed. In November 1964 this sum was raised to 4½ guineas a day and in December 1969 to £6 10s.

nonsense, that we should break down with attacks from the right and the left, that it was a hopeless, silly, futile reform which he had gone along with but, as he had made clear all the way through, this was what he really felt. I have never heard such an outburst. Callaghan was hysterical once or twice before, as Chancellor, when he was overpowered, and Harold has always told me how he does break down and his whole funkiness comes out. I am sure he is overwrought by the tremendously heavy burden of legislation in the last five or six weeks when three or four of his Bills have been going through the House. Actually he gave it to us. We would never have got the firm decision to go ahead with the Bill if it hadn't been for this embarrassing outburst. Fred Peart came in and though, as I know very well, he doesn't like this Bill and has never liked it, he is a man of honour and as Leader of the House he stood by it. He roundly turned on Callaghan and said it was quite untrue, the Home Secretary had never disclosed this kind of attitude before. However as we went round Cabinet it was clear that there was no support for this measure. Tony Crosland didn't want the Bill and I can't think of anybody there who did, except for Peter Shore, the P.M., the Lord Chancellor, Shackleton, myself, Peart now and of course Tony Wedgwood Benn, who also said we couldn't go back on it. Michael Stewart was away. Most of the others reluctantly said that they detested the Bill as a difficult nuisance but they didn't see how we could go back on it. Fred Peart and I made the most of the point that a Government which abandoned a Bill of this sort when there were only 47 left-wingers against it, fewer than were against Prices and Incomes, would find it very difficult to rally the Party to other things. So we decided to publish the Bill before Christmas, and have a Second Reading in January.[1] The fight has been won for the time being.

Friday, December 6th

The first thing was the meeting of the Social Services Committee, with the comparative papers of the allocations to the four Departments. What they really showed was that, in terms of total bulk of money, education has done pretty well, because the Tories started educational expansion in 1963 and it has continued ever since. Education, social security and roads burst ahead in 1963, whereas health was launched later and housing later still. It also showed that social security will take a very big cut in 1969, whereas education has been relatively spared, and that all these services are suffering terribly because if you cut back their increase too much you spoil their quality, especially in the light of the steady increase during this period in the number of old people and of children. In order to stand still you have to move forward relatively fast. Out of this meeting came one very useful thing. I made an offer, saying we would postpone by one month to November the implementation of the pension uprating next year. That will save us £19 million for the year and with that we can at least give the Minister of

[1] In fact the Second Reading did not take place until February 3rd, 1969.

Education a year's grace and avoid the two things he dislikes most of all, the raising of further education charges and the cutting back of teaching. I hope this will be a help when we come to our meeting tomorrow.

Saturday, December 7th

I woke up to another morning panic occasioned by the whole sense of depression at the situation closing in around us. The new measures aren't working and here was the morning news bulletin with the pound exposed again to rumours of German revaluation. I fear sterling will go again and there will be another devaluation while the franc manages to survive. I was rung up tonight by William Hardcastle of 'The World This Weekend'. Would I deny the rumours that Roy Jenkins and Harold Wilson were resigning, ludicrous rumours which have been sweeping round yesterday and today? I rang up Harold and O.K.'d it and a young man has been over from Oxford for the interview. I did a first version and then a second and I hope to God he only sent one to London because there will be trouble if he tries to mix the two bits together.

The November figures for the gold and dollar reserves published on December 3rd showed a fall of £82 million and the lack of confidence in Labour's management of economic policy, coupled with a lack of political acuteness in the City, was reflected in a tide of rumours, including stories that the Prime Minister was about to resign, that another devaluation was imminent, a coalition Government about to be formed and even that the Queen was about to abdicate. (*The Prime Minister had left London for Cornwall but to visit his sick father.*) *There were heavy sales of gilt-edged securities and of sterling, bringing a temporary loss on Friday, December 6th, of some $100 million from the reserves. Labour Members who might otherwise have been hostile backed the Government and when on December 9th a leading article in* The Times *called for the formation of a coalition Government both Government and Opposition brushed it aside. The publication on December 12th of the improved trade figures for November* (*the visible trade deficit fell from £68 million to £16 million*) *completed the dismissal of the rumours and in a speech to a rally at Dunstable on Friday, December 13th, the Prime Minister attacked the irresponsibility of the rumour-mongers and the way the story had been seized upon.*[1]

Sunday, December 8th

The weather has been awful, grey overhanging clouds and the whole sky dripping down. I walked right up past Williamscot, along the top to Wardington and down to the old mill where Anne and I got ourselves engaged in the ruin fourteen years ago. I came back over the hill past Cox's Farm and through Upper Prescote. The lights were on in the nursery and I knew the

[1] See *Wilson*, pp. 586–8

family had come home from the Coventry Bazaar. I didn't have to go to this because I was supposed to be in Sweden but S.E.P. has been reorganized for tomorrow morning and I have cancelled one day of the Swedish visit because the Cabinet Office and the P.M. insist on my attendance. In preparation I am going up to London tonight to have a talk with Barbara, Tony and Peter.

Sunday, December 15th[1]

While I was in Sweden the trade figures came out showing a gap reduced from £68 to £16 million, a substantial improvement which enabled Harold to hold a Party Meeting and rally support. Morale really has improved a bit. As Stephen Swingler said when he blew in yesterday, 'When things are as bad as this, with a 20 per cent Tory lead, everybody in the party is in the same boat.'[2] So things have been pulled round.

All day today a Chequers conference has been going on with the little Neddies.[3] I would normally have expected to have been invited but just as all the economic decisions are being made by the inner group so this meeting has taken place without me. I have become aware that I am, not out in the cold, but out on the sidelines again. Strictly speaking, I have no complaints because I insisted I wanted to have a great Department and as it's not the Foreign Office or the Exchequer I can't expect to be central but I do feel my exclusion rather strongly.

Monday, December 16th

I have to be in 70 Whitehall this week for endless discussions about the Superannuation White Paper, all with Social Security at John Adam Street. I got Peter Brown over from Elephant and Castle for a drink to meet Stephen Swingler and David Ennals and left him to talk to Stephen because Peter's first job is to launch the White Paper. He is being a bit of a problem to me because he is slightly neurotic about the Ronan Point episode and now I find him after only three days in the Ministry dashing round talking about resignation. He has been having difficulties with the information department and I think that after leaving the safety of a big organization in Housing and finding things here splayed between two buildings, with no staff, facing a great test in the production of the White Paper, he is on the point of collapse. He also had a bad throat (there are all sorts of bad throats and 'flu going about) and he has lost his nerve. I had to summon him later and read the riot act because Stephen was saying it just wouldn't do.

On to an important meeting with the Chancellor from whom I had an

[1] From Monday, December 9th, to Friday, December 13th, Crossman was visiting Sweden to study the working of their social services and pension scheme.

[2] According to the Gallup Poll, the Conservatives increased their lead over Labour from 15½ per cent in November to 20 per cent in December. The National Opinion Poll showed a Conservative increase from 12·4 per cent to 21·2 per cent.

[3] Small economic development councils for various industries.

ominous letter over the weekend to say he must again remind me that there could be no certainty about launching the pension scheme on January 9th, the day I had chosen. Jarrett and I went in at 4.30 to see him. There he was, his black table placed across the room (Callaghan used to have it lengthwise). He rose from behind the table to greet me and I sat down expecting the worst. I said that we could postpone it till the 21st if that would give him time. We found out that on January 8th he would know precisely how the trade figures were going and by January 10th we would be able to have a firm decision. Would I therefore make it January 21st, the day after we come back from recess, on condition that the trade figures are known to be good? I said that was O.K. because, clearly, if the trade figures were disastrously bad we couldn't do it and in this way maximum pressure is put on him to think them good. Indeed, I can't risk having the White Paper presented to the public in the middle of an economic crisis because it would make the whole scheme incredible.

After this we had another meeting of the Immigration Committee under Callaghan. This was interesting because we were given a report from William Whitlock[1] that we were going to have trouble from Africa, which might expel 30,000 Asians. There was general awkwardness around the table because both Jim and I made it perfectly clear that in our view it would be intolerable even to consider accepting them and we would have to decide what measures could be used to stop them if this threat were to materialize. The most important thing was that it should be known outside that we were determined to stop them coming in. This required a Cabinet decision so we duly recommended that there should be a Cabinet policy on this matter ready for presentation to the Commonwealth Conference late in January.

A lot seems to have happened today. I also turned up at a meeting of the Communications group of the Parliamentary Party. Hugh Jenkins was in the chair and there were about four people there.[2] This just shows you our problem of P.L.P. morale. Virtually half our back benchers came in for the first time in 1964 and they have nearly all found jobs and second lives outside Parliament. The smaller their chances of retaining their seats the less interest they take in the life of the House. I suspect an awful lot of people in the P.L.P. now subconsciously rule themselves out as M.P.s in the next Parliament and are just turning up for three-line whips. The old Left turns up religiously at Party meetings, the forty or fifty bloody obstreperous people who are always voting against us are to be found in the tea room, but the new Centre, the people who are for parliamentary reform, who believe in

[1] Labour M.P. for Nottingham North since October 1959, a Whip 1962–7, Deputy Chief Whip March–July 1967, Under-Secretary of State for Commonwealth Affairs 1967–8 and Parliamentary Under-Secretary of State at the F.C.O. 1968–9.

[2] Labour M.P. for Putney 1964–74 and for Wandsworth, Putney since 1974. He was Assistant General Secretary of British Actors' Equity Association 1957–64 and Minister for the Arts at the D.E.S. 1974–6.

communication, the wonderful new faces from the techs, are no longer active members of the House. I think it is also due to the impression they have had of life in Parliament. It has not attracted them. Their first reaction was to demand reform but now they have lost interest.

After I had talked to this group for forty minutes or so, I went along the passage to the Parliamentary Reform group for a meeting about the House of Lords. In view of the dislike of the reform expressed in the Commons' debate, I wondered how many people would turn up. There were sixteen, plus the Lord Chancellor, Eddie Shackleton and myself. Of course some of them were prominent able people, but it was mostly the usual gang, people like Charlie Pannell, Robert Sheldon and Joel Barnett.[1] I have heard their speeches three, four, five times now and here we were round the table arguing it again. Sixteen people even on an issue which was supposed to be of mass interest. We've now got a Cabinet decision to go ahead and publish the Bill on Friday. It is quite clear that even if we can get the help of the Whips the difficulties in Committee Stage will still be very formidable indeed.

Tuesday, December 17th

At Cabinet a most illuminating little altercation occurred between the Prime Minister and Michael Stewart. The P.M. said across the table, 'I hope you won't forbid me to send a Christmas card to the Russian Ambassador,' and Michael Stewart said, 'It's a personal decision. I should send one but I have decided not to this year.' This is fascinating because here is a man with a clear, rational mind who can see as clearly as anybody I know the issues involved and, in particular, the principles involved in a course of action, yet, when it comes to the point, the action Michael Stewart takes never seems to match up to the principles he enunciated before he took it. The Prime Minister obviously felt peeved because he hadn't been told about Michael's decision and felt himself half bound by it. The rest of the Cabinet exploded and there was raucous laughter from Dick Marsh at the other end of the table. 'Quite right,' everybody said. 'If you were deciding to send Christmas cards for the first time that's one thing but if you are going to make it a decision not to send them this year as a mark of your disapproval it's absolutely ridiculous.'

Wednesday, December 18th

Today I had Scientology. I got my officials together again because I can't afford another Question Time without a decision on the Public Inquiry. We had quite a good discussion and I put to them the idea of having John

[1] Robert Sheldon has been Labour M.P. for Ashton-under-Lyne since 1964. He was Minister of State at the Civil Service Department March–October 1974, and at H.M. Treasury October 1974–June 1975. He has been Financial Secretary to the Treasury since June 1975. Joel Barnett has been Labour M.P. for Heywood and Royton since 1964 and Chief Secretary to the Treasury since 1974. In 1977 he was given Cabinet rank.

1 Richard Crossman as Secretary of State for Social Services.

2 An official Labour Party rally in Hyde Park in August 1968 expresses condemnation of the Soviet invasion of Czechoslovakia which ended the liberalizing administration of Premier Dubček. In the centre on the platform are George Brown (the deputy leader of the Labour Party), Jennie Lee and Richard Crossman.

3 On October 10, 1968, aboard the British warship *Fearless*, Harold Wilson (left) begins talks with the Rhodesian Prime Minister, Ian Smith (right), aimed at a settlement of the Rhodesian crisis.

Foster as Chairman of the Committee.[1] Davey[2] had given me lists of active Q.C.s and pointed out that it was difficult to get them so it really must be John Foster unless I am willing to take some kind of colonial Governor. I shall have to talk to the Lord Chancellor about it.

O.P.D. I couldn't help remembering yesterday's little scene about the Christmas card when an infinitely more important issue came up, what we should do about the strategic embargo on Soviet goods in the light of the invasion of Czechoslovakia last August. There has been every kind of pressure from the Prime Minister and Tony Wedgwood Benn that though we should register our disapproval of the invasion of Czechoslovakia it should not be allowed to affect our economic connections or our trade. For Tony Wedgwood Benn trade, in this instance, means selling computers to Eastern Europe. For months there has been an argument about this behind the scenes between us and the Americans. There has also been tension between MinTech and the Ministry of Defence. After the invasion of Prague the one thing we can't do is to loosen the embargo and Denis Healey has been against our pressing to relax it.

I went to the meeting today determined to raise all this but in fact we heard an agreed statement from the Foreign Secretary announcing that MinTech has surrendered. We must allow the officials to seek agreement with the Americans in what is really an effort to climb down, based on the fact that we can't afford to break with the Americans. If we try to sell British computers to Russia against the Americans' wishes our computer production may stop altogether because there are quite a number of processes in their manufacture for which we are dependent on America; particularly in digital computers (whatever that may mean).[3]

It all seemed to me characteristic of our Cabinet and, probably, of all British governments. We sedulously avoid drawing any conclusions about the Russian invasion of Prague. Why do we not face the consequences for our future foreign policy? Partly for the reason I have given, partly because we desperately want trade, partly because Harold still feels himself to be an essential link between Washington and Moscow. For four years he pretended to himself that he was an important mediator in the Vietnam discussions and now he feels the same about this. He says all the time that we mustn't

[1] Sir John Foster (K.B.E. 1964; Q.C. 1950), Conservative M.P. for Northwich 1945–February 1974, was Parliamentary Under-Secretary of State at the C.R.O. 1951–October 1954. He has been a Fellow of All Souls' College, Oxford, since 1924.

[2] K. A. T. Davey, the Principal Assistant Solicitor at the D.H.S.S.

[3] Computers in science are predominantly used to make mathematical simulations of real systems; the calculations these require are performed either by analogue computers, in which physical variables represented by electrical variables are manipulated, or by digital computers, which manipulate numbers representing the real variables. Digital computers are nowadays regarded as the more versatile of the two and are also useful for 'book-keeping' purposes (e.g. keeping payrolls, telephone bills). In the late 1960s the semi-conductor components used in British computers were either imported from America or fabricated from materials produced by America.

lead the way in making anti-Russian noises and he wants a special position both in the White House and in the Kremlin. Here lies the whole idiocy of the Christmas card episode. If Harold is working for that special position it is quite illogical and irrational to use such pin-pricking tactics as refusing to send Christmas cards. If on the other hand he feels so strongly that he must withdraw his card, he really can't be in a minority of one in the West trying to urge what would be virtually the end of the British strategic embargo against the U.S.S.R. I have the impression from reading the daily papers, though I don't get a word of this from the Defence papers, that the Russians are rapidly catching up now. I think the situation is very ugly indeed and that the chances of détente between Russia and America under Nixon are possible but a great deal smaller since last August. There is another side to this because we know that the Americans are also self-interested. They don't really care about the Russian enslavement of Eastern Europe. What they want is peace. On the other hand, if the Russians are rearming fast you can see why the Americans want us to stiffen the strategic embargo and slow up the arms race. I record all this in some detail because it seems to me an extremely interesting example of the total ineffectiveness of Michael Stewart as Foreign Secretary and of the extent to which Harold Wilson's so-called foreign policy is based on his image of himself as a maker of world policy.

This afternoon Tam told me that Eric Moonman wanted to see me.[1] I was vaguely aware that Eric had been fussing about so-called Mao 'flu but what I didn't know was that he had refused to see David Ennals. Tam told me this at the last moment and though I thought it was pretty cool I said I would talk to him. He came into my room and got out of his pocket a long list of complaints, saying I was mishandling this whole thing completely. I said, 'You know, we may have a policy in our Ministry that we oughtn't to work up anxiety about Mao 'flu. This is a very mild form of 'flu, no different from any other just because it has a Chinese name. We are doing all we can to meet it and anyway I'm not running this, Eric. I've left all the details to David. Please go and see him and don't condemn us before you have heard what he has to say. We shouldn't work up propaganda about this. If an epidemic is coming, it's coming, and nothing can be done to prevent it.[2] Of course we will get some of the blame but our job is to make sure we have taken all adequate precautions.' He went straight out of my room, got hold of the *Guardian*, *The Times* and the *Telegraph*, told them he was deeply dissatisfied with his interview and tried to work up agitation on Mao 'flu. It infuriates me but it also did a bit of good because I immediately set in motion a meeting with David Ennals. The *Daily Express* this morning

[1] Labour M.P. for Billericay 1966–70 and for Basildon since 1974. He was Chairman of the All-party Parliamentary Mental Health Information Unit 1968–70.

[2] The influenza epidemic of the so-called Hong Kong A-2 '68 virus lasted from January to March 1969.

had a whole front page on the 'flu 'sweeping across the Atlantic', which had already paralysed the Americans and was coming to us. We had a full-scale conference in the Ministry and the facts as they emerged reflected on us very well. The virus had only been detected in August but three of our firms were already working on a special vaccine. I realized we had a pretty good case and keen young David had a speech and a press release ready for Dover on Friday.

This evening we had the endless continuing stages of the Representation of the People Bill. We had now reached Report Stage and Callaghan has made a concession on party labels which I think will cost us dear. Instead of registering the big parties, as I want to, he is letting anybody put any name they like on the ballot form. I think this will produce chaos and very little advantage. After my absence in Sweden I am being virtuous and am in the House a good deal. I decided to ask Tam to assemble a number of back benchers to have dinner with me last night and tonight. He collected a very interesting gang tonight, five solid, decent, youngish people, all interested in pensions, people whom I wanted to have on my side when the White Paper comes out. They were enormously receptive and it strikes me once again how much people appreciate being consulted beforehand, how different they feel when a Minister says, 'I want your help,' and fills them in. We were just settling down to dinner when Michael Foot came rolling past from the Smoking Room and said, 'Ah, there is Dick in his new incarnation as Father Christmas, bestowing Christmas presents on the boys,' implying I was just giving them all dinner to please them. Well, there was a certain truth in it.

Thursday, December 19th

Today was the last day in Parliament. The whole of these last few days before Christmas have seen the Home Secretary's endless Bills going through. I didn't get down in time to see Harold Wilson operating his last Question Time but this evening I did go in to the No. 10 Christmas party for the Lobby. I went partly because something had happened to me which has never happened before. I had asked to see Harold tomorrow but he simply said he couldn't manage it. He asked, 'Will you be in the Department on Monday?' 'Yes,' I said. 'Oh,' said he, 'I've lots of time then,' so I decided I would go up to London with the children and visit No. 10. I think it is not insignificant that Harold just didn't have time tomorrow. I didn't want him for anything in particular but just to say goodbye, nevertheless there is a certain chilliness which needs to be met. I also ran into Mary. I had just answered a letter of hers about the X-ray apparatus in the hospital in the Scilly Isles and I said, 'Look, come back to the charge, Mary. Don't take no for an answer. I have only sent you the official reply.' She gave me a really good grin. By the way, Harold and Mary sent us this year a Christmas card of such ineffable awfulness that I said to Anne, 'Really, I believe that each one of them must have deliberately chosen the photograph of the other which was the most unattractive.'

After that I went back to Elephant and Castle to the annual party that Alan Marre was giving. He turned out to be a splendid host and our caterers were excellent. Normally it is a wholly Health party with the R.H.B.s but this time everybody was there. I felt cheered because the Christmas parties this year have been a good mix. This one, the First Division party on December 3rd when the Social Security administrative class invited some twenty or thirty from the Health side, and my own Secretary of State's party on December 4th were all for once not a sheer waste of time but have brought people together in a really constructive way.

Friday, December 20th

David did a very effective job on the 'flu. He got interviews on I.T.V., B.B.C., all the radio programmes and an excellent press. By waiting until many people would have thought it too late, until the storm had been worked up, we were undoubtedly much more effective in producing the counter-action than if we had poured out information earlier. It may be that the 'flu epidemic will spread and in that case we shall get some of the blame but I am certain that we have applied the effective propaganda at the right time.

I ran into Michael Foot the other day and asked him whether he was going to have mercy on Lords' reform. 'No, no,' he said. 'This is a great chance to continue our campaign against Callaghan.' I said, 'You'll not only be against him but against Fred Peart and me who will be sharing the responsibility.' Michael's face fell. 'Oh,' he said, 'Oh, no, Dick. We don't want you mixed up with it.' 'But I shall be,' I said. I am very much aware that Callaghan on his own would have a terrible time with this Bill. Callaghan backed by Fred Peart and me will be a far more powerful combination and we should be able to make a substantial difference to the ferocity of the resistance from our own back benchers.

Over to the House of Lords in the afternoon, where Eddie Shackleton had started his press conference on the publication of the Bill. He and I thought it would be a good thing to have a little publicity although we had been told not to and it had been recorded in the Cabinet minutes. How right we were, because we found that Fred Peart had fully briefed the press yesterday and included the idea that remuneration might be dropped. I came along to make sure Eddie didn't overdo it. There were some twelve journalists there and we worked quite hard. This will at least kill the rumour that we are not going to fight the Bill through. Then I had a drink with Eddie before going back to the Department for a long and difficult meeting about various aspects of the superannuation scheme. I finally said goodbye and caught the 4.15 because I wanted to get back to our farm dinner.

I thoroughly enjoyed this. We had lots of drinks up at Prescote and then went down to the Red Lion, where they put on a splendid meal for us. The dinner lasted from 8.30 until midnight and as the evening went on and people had drunk their excellent red and white wine, round the table they began to bring out all their frustrations and anxieties. I suddenly realized that this was just like the rest of the British public, who want a bit more, not for more work but for the same amount of work, because they see other people having a jolly good time. It was all healthy, good-humoured and boisterous, and, let's be clear, very democratic. Nobody had any fears or doubts, they were talking to Mr Pritchett face to face. They were in the presence of their master, they felt they could argue good-naturedly and still like us. It was splendid.

Saturday, December 21st

A foul day. We have had these extraordinary alternations of brilliant sunshine and appalling downpours of rain but it happened to be a perfect night, the roads were dry and we decided to go across to Barbara and Ted Castle's party at Hell Corner Farm. Judith Hart and Tony suddenly had 'flu so they couldn't come. Curly Mallalieu and his wife Harriet and daughter Anne were there but the guests were mostly local people,[1] Mia Connor[2] and a friend of hers, a young guitar player who sang some brilliant and amusing songs, after a buffet supper with magnificent food and drink. Denis Barnes,[3] a youngish-looking man, was there and they were all full of the problem of Aubrey Jones and the university dons.[4] The P.I.B. has produced a very anti-don report advising a very small increase of salary and adding for good measure that maybe dons' efficiency should be tested by seeking student reactions to their teaching. This has suddenly caught on in the press and created a sensation and the Vice-Chancellor of Liverpool University has resigned.[5] Barbara told me that the P.M. had been ringing up from Chequers insisting on a withdrawal but she didn't want this at all.*

[1] J. P. W. Mallalieu, Labour M.P. for Huddersfield 1945–50 and for Huddersfield East since 1950, was Minister of Food 1946–9, Under-Secretary of State for Defence (R.N.) 1964–6, Minister of Defence (R.N.) 1966–7, Minister of State at the Board of Trade 1967–8 and at the Ministry of Technology 1968–9.

[2] Mia Connor is the widow of Sir William Connor, the *Daily Mirror* columnist who wrote under the name of Cassandra.

[3] Sir Denis Barnes (K.C.B. 1967) joined the Ministry of Labour in 1937. He was Permanent Secretary 1966–8, Permanent Secretary at the D.E.P. 1968–73 and from 1974 to 1976 Chairman of the Manpower Services Commission.

[4] The First Report of the National Board for Prices and Incomes (Cmnd 3866), published on December 18th, 1968. It recommended that university teachers' productivity might be assessed in some way and suggested that students might be asked to submit reports on the efficiency of those who taught them.

[5] Winston Barnes, Professor of Philosophy at the University of Durham 1945–59, Professor of Moral Philosophy at the University of Edinburgh 1959–63, was Vice-Chancellor of the University of Liverpool 1963–9. He was Visiting Professor of Philosophy at the University of Auckland, New Zealand 1970 and Sir Samuel Hall Professor of Philosophy Manchester University 1970–3. He is Professor Emeritus of the Universities of Manchester and Liverpool.

* The P.M. did eventually snub Aubrey Jones despite Barbara's objections.

We decided to move away about eleven along with Jock Campbell but we found our car battery was flat. Is there anything more ignominious than saying goodbye when you are leaving a party rather early and then having to come back? We had to ring the A.A. and to my amazement it wasn't more than half an hour before a man came along from Reading with a couple of leads to boost the battery. It only took ten seconds before we were able to drive home.

Sunday, December 22nd

John Foster rang me up this morning about the Scientology inquiry. I had seen the Lord Chancellor last Thursday and he had been a bit shocked at the idea of a one-man inquiry, remembering the Denning Inquiry into the Profumo affair,[1] but he began to like the idea and when I suggested John Foster he liked that too. On Friday I got John Foster to see me in my room at the House and he agreed to my invitation straightaway. I said, 'I suppose you want time to decide.' He replied, 'No, no time to decide,' and it sounded as though he liked the idea, particularly when I said, 'You are always complaining about our Parliamentary investigatory methods. Now I want you to do a bit of investigating yourself.' However I agreed that he had better check it with Ted Heath and today he told me that Heath strongly objects to his doing it on the grounds that he shouldn't help the Government to get off the hook. Foster had said, 'I think the Government has given me absolute freedom. I am invited to say they are quite wrong if I wish.' I said that was fine and I let him write his own letter of invitation. I have just confirmed it with Harold, who is quite pleased. I said, 'Do you think there will be an objection from our back benchers?' and he said, 'Well, we've never known Foster give an orthodox Conservative report.' Scientology, one hopes, has been cleared up for the moment.

A wonderful Sunday, brilliant sunshine again, a splendid day for a walk. Up to London tomorrow for the children to go to the pantomime with their mother and for me to see the Prime Minister in the evening.

Monday, December 23rd

The children went off to the pantomime and I did my Christmas shopping, looking after presents for Peter Smithson, my driver, Janet and Anne. At 4.30 I went along to Downing Street and found Harold in his study, comfortable and easy, a little careful with me. I filled him in on the difficulties of reorganizing my Ministry. I said I was rather remote now, something that had been brought home to me on Thursday when Gerald

[1] In 1963, Lord Denning (a life peer since 1957), Master of the Rolls since 1962, conducted the inquiry into the resignation of J. D. Profumo, Secretary of State for War, who had lied to the House of Commons about his association with a call girl who had connections with an attaché at the Russian Embassy. The Report, Cmnd 2152, published in September 1963, cleared Mr Profumo of any breach of security.

Gardiner had said that he had to go off to No. 10 for talks about the Donovan Report and assumed that I was coming too.[1] I must say I had expected to be on the inner group which decided that, but I'm not. Harold told me a little, rather reluctantly, about Barbara's White Paper and how it had been decided, in one meeting, to put it on the Cabinet agenda a fortnight before mine.[2] I also got him to talk about the dangers arising from Russian rearmament and also from reactionary forces in West Germany. We agreed that the world is becoming very gloomy but there doesn't seem to be any policy that we can easily pursue. He successfully evaded the issue of computer sales, simply saying, 'Well, it depends what computers we sell,' gazing at me with that look in his eye of cleverness and complacency which shows when he is not prepared to talk. This computer thing is yet another example of the complete departmentalism of our Cabinet. He has got it all nicely in a corner with Tony Wedgwood Benn, Denis Healey and Tony Crosland, just as I have my whole corner without interference. Well, there are worse ways of running a Government but it does destroy the effectiveness of collective Cabinet responsibility. It looks as though he has had enough of that for some time.

I got a little bit of talk about the Cabinet and the future of George Thomson, who, poor man, has been chucked out because Michael Stewart insisted on it.[3] Diplomacy was the one area where he was first-rate, he was the perfect Commonwealth Secretary and now there he is sitting in Cabinet at £8,500 a year with absolutely nothing to do. Harold said, 'He might be given something in a reshuffle but would he be any good on the home front?' 'Why not make him Home Secretary?' I said, and Harold looked at me and said, 'That's a job I can't take away from Mr Callaghan at the moment.' I was assured that there would not be a shuffle until after the Commonwealth Prime Ministers' Conference, which is absorbing all the P.M.'s thoughts. He was perfectly easy with me but there was a certain distance. He was watching me, realizing I was accepting my position outside the charmed circle. For instance, I suddenly realized that I have hardly seen or talked to Marcia for six months. I got a printed Christmas card from her. I hardly ever see Gerald Kaufman. Fred Peart has fully taken my place and Harold is delighted to have him there because although Fred hasn't any great intelligence he has a kind of shrewdness. Harold praised him highly. I said, 'Yes, Fred Peart is in our Labour Cabinet what the Duke of Omnium is in a Trollope Cabinet,[4] a man of natural breeding, nobility and decency who

[1] The Donovan Report was published on June 13th. See above, p. 141.

[2] The First Secretary's proposals for the reform of industrial relations were to be set out in the White Paper *In Place of Strife* (Cmnd 3888), published on January 17th, 1969. Crossman's White Paper, *National Superannuation and Social Insurance, Proposals for Earnings-Related Social Security* (Cmnd 3883), was published on January 28th, 1969.

[3] When the Department of Commonwealth Affairs was merged with the Foreign Office on October 17th, 1968, George Thomson ceased to be Minister of Commonwealth Affairs and became Minister without Portfolio.

[4] See Anthony Trollope's six novels of nineteenth-century political life, especially *The*

speaks with a kind of commonsensical wisdom.' We talked rather guardedly about Roy and the difficulties of the Treasury. No, Harold wasn't giving much away to me and I wasn't giving him anything, but I think my going along was useful. In due course, after forty-five minutes, in came Michael Halls and Trevor Lloyd-Hughes, off I went and Harold left for Chequers to have Christmas laid on for him by the Wrens.[1]

Tuesday, December 24th–Friday, December 27th

At Prescote we had an unexpected white Christmas for the first time for many years, clear, dry weather, with cold, grey clouds reaching down to the earth and then a tremendous fall of sleet. On Christmas Eve I walked right up the canal and back by Claydon village in sleet which was scarcely holding on the grass and I assumed that by Christmas Day it would be all gone. In the morning it was still there, slushy wet snow, and it gradually got colder so that we had the most lovely two or three days after Christmas, with brilliant blue skies by day and starry skies at night, the floods on Amos meadow freezing over into perfect sliding ice with a little snow falling on top. It was beautiful. I had some splendid walks in the snow, and we had a lot of guests.

This was the astronaut Christmas and,[2] bluntly, the fact that we had them appearing on our television all the time wasn't a great success. I wanted the children to listen and tried hard to persuade Patrick that it was exciting, in view of his interest in space, but nothing would induce them to watch. Patrick repeated to me, 'After all, Pop, *Space Odyssey 2001* is real.' What he meant was that these factual news bulletins about the three astronauts in Apollo 8 circling the moon seemed to him less real than his science fiction. Of course we aren't at all representative as a family in finding the whole thing boring and a waste of money. Many people we know, like Nicholas Davenport who rang us up on Boxing Day, have found the astronauts exciting but it could all have been done better by machines and then the men wouldn't have taken up so much room in the space craft. All they have

---

Prime Minister (London: Chapman & Hall, first published in eight monthly parts between November 1875 and June 1876).

[1] Trevor Lloyd-Hughes was Political Correspondent of the *Liverpool Echo* 1950 and of the *Liverpool Daily Post* 1951, Press Secretary to the Prime Minister 1964–9 and Chief Information Adviser to the Government 1969–70. He has been Chairman of Lloyd-Hughes Associates Ltd, Government and Parliamentary Consultants, since 1970 and was knighted in 1970. Michael Halls was an old friend of Harold Wilson, whom he knew from their days as civil servants at the Board of Trade. He became the Prime Minister's Private Secretary at No. 10 in April 1966 and served until his sudden death in April 1970.

[2] The Apollo 8 space craft, with three men on board, was launched from Cape Kennedy on December 21st and television pictures showed the 240,000-mile flight to the moon and, as the craft performed its ten orbits on December 24th and 25th, pictures of the moon's surface and of a moon's-eye view of the earth. On December 27th Apollo re-entered the earth's atmosphere at a speed of 25,000 m.p.h. and splashed safely into the Pacific, in a perfect landing only 6,000 yards from the recovery ship. It was an encouraging step in the Americans' preparations to land a man on the moon in 1969.

done is to prove they can send three men round the moon in preparation for landing on it and it is all part of a gigantic competitive effort between the Americans and the Russians. I suppose we can only defend it on the grounds that if one has to have Russian–American tension it's better to have them competing in space than in atom bombs. They gain something militarily on both sides from their explorations in moon-craftery but presumably it deflects some attention and may possibly reduce the tension between the two. That's really my reaction to the whole thing. I can't help feeling it's a waste of money. If they concentrated on underwater exploration, the kind of thing we now see on our wonderful B.B.C. 2 colour television we have been trying this Christmas, how different it would be.

During the Christmas holiday I had time to reflect a little on my own feelings at the end of 1968 and the beginning of 1969. This has been a curiously important year in my life and the longest of my four years as Minister. It seems to have stretched out interminably since devaluation in November 1967 and during that period I seem to have grown a good deal older and I have certainly grown fatter. Until the end of October I did manage my forty lengths each morning before breakfast in the swimming pool and kept myself wonderfully fit but now the swimming bath is just silting up with a lot of damp leaves underneath where we let the covering blow off. My tummy is sticking out and in my sixty-first year I am getting much more conscious than ever before of physically growing older. My memory is not as good as it was, I now tend to forget the things I read and my reading speed is reduced.

Yes, in all intellectual ways which are so useful for my writing, my other work, I seem to be running down but as a Minister I don't find any signs of my being less good. I am as vigorous in my inspections and as active and much more experienced in my handling of the Department. There I seem to be keeping up to scratch but I am definitely losing political zest, looking and feeling more detached, with less zoom, watching, not believing in things, not as enthusiastic or inspired.

That may be due to what has happened during this year. I have to remember that this has been a year of devastating disappointment for the Government. When we started, twelve months ago, those days and days of discussion about devaluation and cuts I still believed that, if we did it right, devaluation could have an enormous effect and I managed to retain some of this belief in a new start for the Government up until the summer. I can't say I was very strong on it through the summer (it can be traced in this diary) but the time it got its awful knock was in November when Roy first came along with his hire-purchase restrictions. That was all right but then three weeks later we had the regulator, clamping down on everything all over again. That was a tremendous knock because it showed that devaluation had not worked, that we were still just on a knife-edge and the entire year was revealed in realistic perspective.

The whole year has been one of too little too late. Some of us, I remember, wanted to cut consumption in January and do the whole job then without waiting for the budget. Well, we didn't. We came to the budget. Roy made a very successful speech and we did all we could but it didn't really halt home consumption and the imports poured in, far higher than we expected. We had only dealt with consumption and we left imports right until the end of the year, by which time we had again piled up a record deficit, almost equal to the deficit of 1967.[1]

It's been a terribly depressing year. Inside Cabinet we have got closer together but we have also realized that further shuffles will make no real difference now. George Brown walked out, yes, and Ray Gunter, two of the big trade unionists, but I don't think their departure even intensified the lack of credibility in the Government. But it did point up the fact that we have lost the confidence of the trade union movement in a way we never expected and now we are faced with Barbara Castle's proposals for trade union reform. I find the new team, Barbara and Roy, infinitely superior to George and Jim, but I have to admit that the objective effect of what they are doing is not so different. Then we have another troika, Harold, Barbara, Roy. Barbara chases round the country with the water pouring through the dam, patching it up, trying to stop this leak and that leak, dealing with the builders, busmen, agricultural workers. Really, of course, she is only effective in stopping price increases and not wage increases. For the fourth year running real wages have gone up, the very year when we wanted the opportunities that a fall would give.

All I can say is that the world outside hasn't been much more cheerful than our world at home. It's been astonishing. I've often compared 1968 with 1848, the Year of Revolution, as I call it. On reflection, 1848 was the year of failed revolution, when all over Europe crowned heads were tumbling, republican regimes seemed to be succeeding and yet, by the end, virtually nothing had happened. The Establishment had been shaken but it had survived.

It was the same in 1968. There was the tremendous May uprising in Paris, followed by de Gaulle's re-election with a vaster majority. Although it is clear that the French regime is terribly unstable, because after the devaluation threat in November de Gaulle went back on all the concessions he had made in May, nevertheless, he has succeeded in smashing the Left. The Left has shown itself imbecile in its anarchism and bogus leftism. How terribly depressing is the student movement all over the Western world, these curious student revolutionaries in America, France, and West Germany and of course, to a lesser extent, in Britain. The students have been the

[1] In November 1967 there had been a record deficit of £158 million and the overall figures for the whole of 1967 showed a deficit of £514 million on the current account, with £136 million surplus on invisible trade. Overall figures for 1968 showed a deficit of £419 million on current account, with a surplus of £377 million on invisibles.

spearhead of the anarchist, Maoist, Che Guevarist revolutions, all infantile.

It's been a year of failure all over the world. We have it in England with the nationwide acclaim of Enoch Powell as the great unspoken leader in the nation's revulsion against what has happened, first of all under Macmillan's Tory regime and now under Wilson and our regime. That is to say, racialism is a protest against the decline of Britain as a world power, and this semi-fascist reaction has been accompanied by a general lack of credibility in the whole establishment. Our reputation has been shattered and broken by what we have done but it hasn't accrued to the benefit of the Conservative Party. The whole structure has fallen in esteem.

It's been a terrible year, terrible at home, terrible abroad and throughout the period there has also been the threat to the whole international monetary system of the Western world. This has seemed to be a crazy makeshift, shored up by the world bankers, and we in Britain are completely at its mercy, with no reserves and no strength left. This is the situation in the world at the end of 1968, the year in which I was a leading Cabinet Minister. Not a very cheerful picture with which to enter 1969.

Tuesday, December 31st

The family came up to London for the rest of this week. We had an excellent London expedition to the film of Lionel Bart's musical of *Oliver Twist*, and to a rather tatty performance of *Gulliver's Travels* at the Mermaid, with a tea-party afterwards with Helga and Stuart Connolly and all the Baker children.[1] I gradually got back to work and my first job was to deal with the popular version of the White Paper. Hugh Cudlipp had sent John Beavan and Alan Fairclough, the *Mirror* leader-writer, down to Brighton and locked them in an hotel with some stenographers and it was clear when we sat down together this morning that they had turned out a first-rate version.[2] We hardly had to change a word before it went to press.

This afternoon I had to see the Chancellor and clear with him and the Treasury the cost and the giving of top priority to this popular version. I also had to meet a major crisis in my own life which is still hanging over me. It concerns Barbara Castle's White Paper on trade union reform and the timing of its release. As I have already reported in this diary, I had discovered from Harold that Cabinet was to meet on January 3rd to discuss Barbara's White Paper, which is to be published on January 9th. Harold had let the cat out of the bag. He realized it would upset the trade unions and the Labour Party but felt that didn't really matter because this was going to be a great popular success. This had shaken me quite a lot and I brooded over it during Christmas. I realized that as Secretary of State for the Social

[1] Helga Connolly was Crossman's literary agent and the former wife of Hugh Carleton Greene.

[2] John Beavan was Editor, *Daily Herald* 1960–2 and Political Adviser to the *Daily Mirror* Group from 1962 to 1976. He became a life peer in 1970, taking the title of Lord Ardwick.

Services I should have been consulted so last Friday I finally gave instructions that at all costs I must see the Chancellor today and Barbara tomorrow to discuss the situation. I didn't want to break with her or have a row about it in Cabinet without prior discussion, but I was alarmed at this effort to railroad Cabinet.

When I went to see the Chancellor today I cleared the whole future of my White Paper with him relatively easily and then I turned to the other subject. He said, 'Yes, it's true. I have been supporting Barbara on this but we only had one meeting of this Miscellaneous Committee just before Christmas and after Christmas another brief meeting.' This was the meeting which I've mentioned in this diary, to which the Lord Chancellor went, the Law Officers, the Chancellor of the Exchequer and the Leader of the House. But that was about all, because Peter Shore, who was supposed to be there from D.E.A., was ill with bronchitis and suspected embolism of the heart. 'Frankly,' said Roy, 'I just went along at the last moment and I don't know very much about it. I had given Barbara my approval.' I warned Roy, saying, 'Won't she be in some trouble in Cabinet?' and we went through the people who are liable to react. I said, 'Dick Marsh is a friend of yours, Roy, shouldn't you get hold of him quietly? In the same way I will try to quieten other people and I will talk to Barbara about it.' I was aware that if you suddenly summon Ministers and say, 'Here's a draft White Paper for publication next week,' and it's revealed that there's been no meeting of Ministers to go over the policy and no preliminary work, even our tame Cabinet might blow up. Roy seemed to understand this and I left feeling I had at least done something.

1969

Wednesday, January 1st

The first thing I did today was to visit the Harperbury sub-normal hospital and when I got back I saw Barbara for an hour and a half, with one of her personal advisers, a highly political young man. It took me some time to make her realize what I was saying. 'I haven't come', I said, 'to see you about the content of the White Paper as I'm not an expert on that and I can't judge. I have come about the row you are going to have because even this Cabinet isn't going to have this railroaded through in one afternoon.'

'Oh,' she said, 'there will be plenty of room for Cabinet to change its mind on Friday. It will be open to reverse me on any point; I have made arrangements for the White Paper to be published on Thursday, 9th, even if we only get the corrected version on Monday, 6th. Even if we give it in that late I've got top priority at the Stationery Office.' However, as she said, things would get rather more complicated because she had agreed to see the T.U.C. General Council again on Tuesday, 7th, and perhaps it would look a bit odd to publish within two days of that and might seem to be an insult to the Council. She explained what had happened. 'It seemed to me,' she said, 'that we had to do this because of Jim Callaghan. We planned to have a Ministerial Committee reporting to S.E.P., and S.E.P. or even the Parliamentary Committee reporting to Cabinet in the normal way. But when I went to see Harold he suddenly said, "Let's foreshorten all this. You bring it to a special small meeting of Ministers. That's the only safe way to do it and we will clear it there." ' 'Barbara,' I said, 'that was a pretty reckless thing to do.' 'It was the least dangerous thing to do,' she said. 'Remember that on all previous prices and incomes policies we've always done it.' 'Nonsense,' I said, 'we haven't. You can't give me a single instance where Cabinet hasn't authorized you or your predecessor to negotiate with the T.U.C. and the C.B.I., but you have always had to come to Cabinet first to get the broad line of policy agreed. Then you have to negotiate on that basis and then come back to us. We've permitted you to make changes in between but this is something absolutely unprecedented.' Well, she admitted all this but she said it was something she had to do.

I then spent the rest of a very, very long hour with her, saying, 'Has anybody spoken to Michael Stewart?' 'No.' 'Well, shouldn't Harold speak to him? He is a prickly, difficult man. You really have to persuade him that this is a reasonable course of action.' I said that meanwhile I would talk to Judith and see that she was cleared. I hope that Roy will square Crosland and Denis Healey. Denis will be O.K., I think, but Tony might be a bit difficult.

I presume that Tony Wedgwood Benn and Peter Shore have been pretty well squared by the P.M. The more we talked round it, the more aware I became of how determined she was. 'Frankly, Dick,' she said, 'you don't know much about this, any more than I know about pensions. If I back you on pensions, you back me on this. It will be popular, there will be no real opposition in the Party and, though I am having difficulties with the T.U.C.,

George Woodcock says he isn't really basically opposed to me.'[1] She and Harold have got themselves into the mood of saying that if they can get this through Cabinet on Friday there will be no difficulty in handling it but I have the gravest doubts, I must admit, and they are only somewhat allayed by what she said to me today.

Thursday, January 2nd

I have been struggling at my own merged Ministry and becoming more and more convinced of the appalling difficulties caused by the physical division of the two Departments, the Elephant and Castle south of the river and John Adam Street north of it. This may well determine our Ministry's failure. Though I have two excellent and technically quite competent Ministers in Stephen and David I am not very cheerful about the future or my success in getting on top of the Department. This week I have one of my co-ordinating jobs to do. I have to get hold of the Secretary of State for Education, to whom I had offered one month's delay in the introduction of our Social Security uprating this October so there will be £19 million with which he could postpone the increase of further education fees. I hadn't got much thanks from him for it. With Paul Odgers's help I then worked out a small programme by which we could offer him another £2 million, this time from Health, to allow him to have a discriminating programme of assistance for comprehensive education, politically one of the most important things we have to do. The £2 million might well be needed to implement the training part of the Todd Report but I am doing it on the gamble that by increasing the N.H.S. part of the employers' national insurance contribution in 1969/70 I might be able to get the money for these purposes and persuade the Treasury that they count as Health Service revenue. I have asked Ted Short to come down specially from Newcastle to agree this and he is coming tomorrow.

Meanwhile I did what briefing I could for tomorrow's Cabinet. I had a word with Fred Peart, who was loyal but not enthusiastic and I found that John Silkin was unbriefed. I saw Judith, who was very unsympathetic indeed, and, as a result of talking to her at lunch, another thing struck me. We can't possibly have both prices and incomes legislation and anti-trade union legislation next autumn, so at the very least Roy will have to give up his prices and incomes legislation in order to get Barbara's Bill through.

Friday, January 3rd

A six-hour Cabinet, from 10.0 to 1.0 and again from 3.0 to 6.0. Barbara and Harold started on their explanation, which was taken relatively well, and then, to my surprise Jim Callaghan said he had no objection to what she had done and the order in which she had briefed people. It was clear that when

[1] George Woodcock was Assistant General Secretary of the T.U.C. 1947–60, General Secretary 1960–9 and Chairman of the Industrial Relations Commission 1969–71.

she saw him yesterday at least she had succeeded in squaring him too. (However, as we saw later on, it didn't give her much advantage.) I tried to support Barbara by remaining totally silent. It was also noteworthy that, just as we expected, Barbara got tacit support from Roy, fanatical support from Harold Wilson and strong support from Roy Mason, our trade unionist Minister of Power. There was scepticism and considerable opposition from Marsh but Cabinet was pretty well silent, most of them doubtful but the middle ready to be swung into support. Tony Crosland led the middle-of-the-road group but not really standing by it and I bided my time. That was the morning. We accepted the explanation she and the Prime Minister gave and then we allowed her to present her case.

Barbara made her first mistake by speaking for forty-five minutes, after she had said she would simply give a shortish Second Reading account, and as it got on towards midday it became clearer and clearer that she wasn't all that conversant with the details of her scheme. She is able and driving but like all the rest of us she is an amateur, quite new to trade union law and legislation, a tremendously complex subject. Here she was trying to give us her explanation of the relationship between trade unions and the law and her proposals for a package to deal with it.[1] It all seemed perfectly sensible. She wanted the setting up of a statutory Commission, with all sorts of positive things to help the unions, and two negative things: powers to enforce a ballot before an official strike and powers, backed by the threat of a fine, to order unofficial strikers back to work whenever she felt inclined. These were the two key controversial themes.

Callaghan then led for the other side. He didn't deny, he said, that he had been talking to members of the T.U.C. General Council. 'They're all old friends of mine,' he said. 'I'm Treasurer of the Party, we are bound to discuss it. Frankly I think it is absolutely wrong and unnecessary to do this. I think what you ought to do is to set up the Commission, put the trade unions on their honour and do what you can.' Harold and Barbara then made it clear that there would be a horse-laugh from the general public and that the Government must take action to control strikes. Dick Marsh opposed. He was extremely dubious about these proposals and as upset as I was by the unconstitutional nature of trying to do it all in one go. Tony Crosland, who

[1] The Secretary of State proposed the establishment of a permanent Industrial Relations Commission to advise both sides of industry on ways to improve industrial relations and negotiating machinery, and that a register of collective agreements reached by firms of more than 5,000 employees should be kept by the D.E.P., though the White Paper rejected the principle of making collective agreements enforceable. There were to be a number of reforms to strengthen the bargaining position of trade unions, to establish the legal right of a worker to join a union and to give statutory protection against unfair dismissal. Financial assistance was to be given to smaller unions that wished to merge, and to help the unions to become more efficient. The White Paper proposed that the Minister should have discretionary powers to order trade unions to hold a ballot of their members before calling an official strike and to impose a 28-day delay, the 'conciliation pause', on workers threatening an unofficial strike. An Industrial Board would be empowered to impose penalties for failure to follow the Minister's orders.

had broken his elbow just before Christmas and is going away to convalesce on a tour of D.E.A. installations, very sensibly said he had read the Donovan Report and, though he was an amateur, he thought there was an alternative to the sanctions which were implied by the powers it proposed for the Government. That was to rely on the Shonfield proposal for strengthening the Commission itself and this ought to be looked at.[1]

Mr Andrew Shonfield, one of the members of the Commission, had argued that in a modern society trade unions should no longer be 'exempt from all but the most rudimentary legal obligations'. He recommended the establishment of a much more autonomous Industrial Relations Commission than that proposed in the main Donovan Report, with powers of investigation independent of the Secretary of State's orders, 'wherever there was evidence of serious friction in industrial relations or inefficiencies in the employment of manpower'. The Industrial Relations Commission should have, he believed, a section exercising 'independent judicial authority in certain matters concerned with the conduct of collective bargaining', including disputes between unions and employers about recognition, the range of subject matter to be covered in collective agreements liable to compulsory registration, and restrictive practices. If conciliation in industrial disputes should fail, the C.I.R. should proceed to impose a reasonable monetary penalty, with a maximum of some £500, on one or both of the parties judged to be responsible for refusing to bargain.

By the time we broke off it was clear that Barbara had failed to get Cabinet to agree. We came back at 2.45 and finished at 5.45. I weighed in, mostly emphasizing the procedural problems and insisting that there must be a further meeting, with the Ministerial Committee in between, and that the Prime Minister couldn't rush us like this. He needed a Cabinet consensus. Adopting the Shonfield alternative of strengthening the Commission and dropping the penal clauses would meet the objections of the trade unions and the Party. 'We haven't had time to look at this and we must before Cabinet sees it again.' Harold said, 'All right, but Cabinet shall meet next Wednesday morning, after Barbara has had a report from the General Council, and we will see where we are.' So that is the proposal. Harold intends to railroad it through Cabinet. It's clear that at present he has got only one serious opponent in Jim Callaghan, with a number of doubters, including Tony Crosland (who won't be there next week), myself and Judith Hart. I am entirely doubtful. I made it clear to Barbara, to Roy Jenkins and also to John Harris that if we could railroad the Bill through, get the penal sanctions this year and then enter 1970 with the difficulties behind us, I could tolerate it but I find it difficult to see how we can go into an election year,

[1] Andrew Shonfield was Director of Studies at the Royal Institute of International Affairs 1961–8, a Research Fellow at the Institute 1969–71, and its Director 1972–7. He is the author of *Modern Capitalism* (London: Oxford University Press, 1965).

1969/70, with the legislative burden of a White Paper launched this month, followed by legislation next November. It sounds to me tactically disastrous because it leaves almost a whole year for gnawing at the bone, with possible defeat in the autumn at the Trade Union Congress and at Party Conference. Then to try in November to order the Parliamentary Party to carry a Bill after such a defeat seems an intolerable burden for us to impose on ourselves. I am not so much objecting to the Bill itself. Probably it would be quite popular with the public and I daresay the powers wouldn't actually be used but I am extremely doubtful about our taking, once again, symbolic powers giving the state ultimate sanctions and the right of discretionary intervention to the Minister, even though she promises not to use it. We have tried it in prices and incomes and it hasn't really worked. I am afraid the same thing will happen here. Either we will have to use these powers against unofficial strikers and fine them tremendously or in fact the whole system won't work at all.

That wouldn't matter so much if it wasn't for the crisis of our relations with the Party and the unions and I just think that if we are to have any chance of avoiding absolute disaster in the election we must spend time between now and then recovering their confidence. We can't do it if we have a Bill of this sort ahead of us in the autumn and spring.

I made this point very strongly and got Roy to do so too. We must either have the Bill immediately as Barbara wants or have a much weaker version next autumn. Towards the end there was a great speech by the Prime Minister, saying that on no account must Barbara be embarrassed by any press leaks. Callaghan said, 'We can't prevent leaks but we'll all do our best.' I said, 'When Barbara goes back to the General Council on Tuesday, it's her scheme she is taking. Let's be perfectly clear that Cabinet has not approved it.'

Saturday, January 4th

But this morning all the newspapers said Barbara's scheme had been approved by Cabinet. I rang up Harold at Chequers and said it was impossible. I suspect he had already been rung up by Callaghan. Of course he denied doing any briefing himself from No. 10. Probably he thought Barbara hadn't done it either and that it had been some rather ebullient junior person. I pointed out that the stories even said the White Paper would be published in January, something which Cabinet explicitly said was impossible if there was to be genuine consideration of the Shonfield alternative. All the newspapers were saying Barbara had won. 'I quite agree it's impossible,' said Harold. 'Can you do a counter-briefing,' I asked, 'through Trevor Lloyd-Hughes, for the Sunday papers?' Harold said yes and rang back an hour later to tell me he had given these instructions. It shows what a bad conscience he had.* I also rang Roy and said, 'You are aware of the fact, are you, that to have both prices and incomes and this Bill together is impossible? Are you prepared to

* But the Sunday papers had very little about it.

have a package agreement and drop your prices and incomes?' 'Oh, no,' he said. 'We can't possibly drop it now. Perhaps we won't have legislation next autumn but we couldn't announce that now.' 'Well,' I said, 'you may be faced with the necessity of announcing it because I don't think you are going to get Barbara's Bill through except by conceding on prices and incomes.' He said, 'I shan't be present next Wednesday,' and I replied, 'You had better make sure you are.'

I must say I am more depressed than ever before by this whole episode because it is absolutely characteristic of Harold and, to a lesser extent, of Barbara to try to carry their colleagues without any proper Ministerial Committee, without an official Committee, without either the Ministers or the officials getting together and pooling their knowledge. It seems utterly ludicrous after the experience of the last four years, reckless too, and it's impossible for us to do anything about it without wrecking Cabinet. It's so characteristic of Wilson to say that they would short-circuit everything and rush it through Cabinet and then, when he is in difficulties in the Cabinet, to back-pedal, put himself into another jam and then try to have the press briefed to give the victory to Barbara. I have no doubt that next Wednesday he will make every effort to get this half-boiled thing through by fair means or foul and I also have a feeling I shall be the only person who will be independent enough to say no and delay him. I can't ask my Coventry people to approve another anti-labour measure, another beating of the trade unions with no beating of the employers. We haven't the authority to do so and I shall fight very strongly against it. But I don't know – I've got no alternative to propose. There is no time to think of one. I may well be forced to toe the line and see us tearing ourselves to pieces all over again.

Sunday, January 5th

Another lovely quiet weekend down here. Not enough work to do from the office, which proves I'm not getting control. We have had Wayland and Elizabeth Young and their daughter Louisa, and though Virginia has got mild 'flu the two girls get on together sitting in bed. Patrick and I are struggling along because when he goes back to school Miss Spencer is going to make him spell properly, so we are starting on that. There we are, with our lovely family life here. All that is wrong is the world and the Labour Government.

Monday, January 6th

Much the most amusing thing I found when I got to Alexander Fleming House was a meeting to discuss the desirability of my addressing the Annual Conference of Public Health Inspectors. When I had received the invitation I had minuted that I would quite like to do it but the Department had told me it was undesirable because it wasn't worthy of a Minister. I remembered that as Minister of Housing I had accepted but failed to go, so I simply said,

'Look, is there really no precedent for it?' No less than five civil servants were lined up outside my room this morning, ready to advise me, armed with a file of three or four pages of written consideration of this knotty problem. The argument was quite clear. The Conference would take place next October and as we should not have clarified our position on Seebohm and the Green Paper by then, we might be unable to tell the public health inspectors what their future would be. I said, 'Of course we wouldn't, but I don't have to make a speech about that. They will be gratified to get the new Secretary of State and they will be content to hear whatever I want to say.' The officials looked a bit surprised and said, 'But we thought it would be dangerous for you to go there and we would advise you against it.' It took me half an hour to get it into their heads that when I decide to go to a Conference it's not to say what the audience expect to hear. I am free to make a speech on any subject I like and they can't really complain. Ron Matthews said to me as they all filed out, 'Well, of course, Secretary of State, if you insist. We have a tradition of nursing our Ministers here, Secretary of State. They are not used to the new kind of Minister.' I think that's a fair comment. It looks as though Kenneth Robinson did what he was told. The Department selected what they thought was suitable for him and he would make a speech according to the text provided. I have found very little evidence of his ever challenging the Department in any serious way. In a sense he was a member of it and he didn't challenge it any more than a Permanent Secretary would, possibly less.

Next we had the delayed meeting of S.E.P. I announced my savings of £19 million on the uprating and the £2 million cut in the Health estimates, to make our little contribution to Education. I think it impressed the Committee that the co-ordinating Chairman was using his position not to get advantages for his own Department but to squeeze it just a little. There's no doubt that Ted Short's shouting and unbearable mulishness has succeeded. The trouble is that I was convinced that he was bloodyminded and right, because Patrick Gordon Walker, his predecessor, had given away too much.

The real excitement of the meeting came after the Prime Minister had gone off to the Commonwealth Conference,[1] when we settled down to a strange little paper born of the Central Advisory Committee for Science and Technology, which had put forward saying that the whole of defence R. & D. was based on an out-of-date wartime balance and there was room for

[1] The Commonwealth Conference was held in London on January 7th–15th and representatives from twenty-eight nations discussed an agenda that included the international economic situation and Rhodesia, where Britain found herself in a minority. Mr Wilson rejected demands from Zambia and other African Commonwealth countries to withdraw the *Fearless* terms and to use force to bring down the Smith regime. The Nigerian civil war was not on the official agenda, as the Nigerian representative opposed this and it was regarded as an internal matter, but in informal talks the British and other Prime Ministers tried to play a peacemaking role.

substantial savings. Solly Zuckerman,[1] who chairs this Committee, had launched a definite attack and gave some very telling figures. Denis Healey stormed against Fred Peart, who he said had been exploited, and in the rudest possible way poured contempt on Solly, who was sitting next to him. It was illiterate, stupid, he said. I have never heard such an outrageous attack. It was very silly, because, as often happens in such cases, it lined up the whole of S.E.P. on Solly's side, particularly as we are prepared to believe it is possible to save money on defence. The Report made only a modest demand for £25 million to be saved in defence R. & D. starting in 1971/2. Pathetic, after fours years of Labour Government, and it shows how powerful is the enclave that Denis has built up in his four years at Defence.

All our election commitments were to reorientate the whole balance of R. & D. away from defence to civil affairs. We haven't done it. Instead, Denis has managed to say that if we make major cuts in overseas military commitments we must maintain a predominant position for R. & D. and have the best even for our limited, new, European-based defences. If our equipment is reduced it must, he maintains, be of the best and if we are going to buy British it means that the R. & D. can't be cut back in proportion to the cut in foreign commitments. This came out very clearly in what Denis said at the end of this three-hour meeting. He was supported by the Foreign Secretary and, mildly, by George Thomson but everybody else laughed and supported Fred Peart – who maintained his position with imperturbable good temper, making Denis look not a fool but a bully – and the Lord Chancellor, who summed up decisively against Denis. Still, Denis had won before the thing started because for four years he has prevented this major change. He should have been implementing it himself.

I then said I had to go out to dinner and John Silkin and I went round to the Garrick, where we haven't been for a long time. It is a wonderful club, with the best food and drink in London, fairly expensive but really splendid. John and I nearly always go to a guests' table, but tonight we were at the members' centre table, talking over prices and incomes. John was squashy and sympathetic and kept on saying, 'You and I always agree with each other.' I kept on saying, 'You agree with me.'

John agreed with the estimate that there would be more than the usual forty to sixty of the P.L.P. in opposition. He thought the party outside would be in a desperate plight and I said, 'If you feel that, you ought to go to see Harold. Have you talked to him yet?' 'No,' John said, 'I haven't actually.' He promised to see Harold about it and throughout the evening he kept on saying to me, 'We always see eye to eye.' John, however, is completely in

[1] Professor Emeritus of the Universities of Birmingham and East Anglia and Fellow of University College, London. He was Deputy Chairman of the Advisory Council on Scientific Policy 1948–64, Chief Scientific Adviser to the Secretary of State for Defence 1960–66, Chief Scientific Adviser to H. M. Government 1964–71 and Chairman of the Central Advisory Committee for Science and Technology 1965–70. He became a life peer in 1971.

Harold's hands and he wasn't going to move against him or play any role whatsoever.

Half an hour after we went in to dinner Jim and Audrey Callaghan came in with their host, the future Ambassador to the Congo,[1] and his wife. We went over for a drink with them and John had his chat with Jim, who explained that he wasn't doing anything and that there was no real crisis.

Wednesday, January 8th

Yesterday I spent visiting the Great Ormond Street Hospital for Sick Children but by this morning I had begun to organize the battle for this evening's Cabinet. John Silkin told me that, as he promised, he had seen Harold, who had said, 'Is Dick hard or soft?' John had answered, 'Dick is hard.' Harold had seemed to be very relieved. All he really wanted to know was whether I was threatening resignation.

Judith and I had been working away at getting what information we could about the conciliation pause. She had been a member of the Ministerial Committee to which, after last week's Cabinet, the White Paper had been referred and she has been keeping me abreast of what has been going on. She is a competent, efficient woman, not tremendously creative in mind, lacking many good ideas and a bit slapdash, but she is dashing, courageous, with a good political instinct for being on the right side.

However I first had to go down to Coventry today. Albert Rose had invited me to a lunch which is held once a month in Foleshill Community Centre for all the people in social work in the area, primary and secondary schoolmasters, doctors, health workers, psychiatric social workers, officers of the children's department, the housing department, the whole lot. I found myself before nearly 100 people, a marvellous gathering. I gave them a talk about the abolition of poverty and the difficulties that arise when, for instance, the low-wage earner with a large family is better off when he is sick or unemployed than when he is at work, and I explained that if you are to prevent that you must increase his family allowances. I submitted myself to questions for an hour during the meeting and for another one and a half hours afterwards, when more than half of them stayed on. It was tremendously invigorating and I shall follow it up by writing to the Coventry Town Clerk to ask for a similar conference for field workers and heads of departments, using Coventry as a kind of pilot study.

I got the train back and went straight to 70 Whitehall, where I found Judith, who reported to me in full while we waited for Barbara to turn up. Barbara had said she wanted to see both of us before Cabinet because Judith

[1] Paul Wright had been British Minister (Information) in Washington 1965–8 and Director-General of British Information Services, New York, 1964–8. He was Ambassador to the Congo (Kinshasa) and to the Republic of Burundi 1969–71 and British Ambassador to the Lebanon from 1971 until his retirement in 1975, when he became Special Representative to the Secretary of State for Foreign and Commonwealth Affairs. He was knighted in 1975.

had now circulated the one constructive alternative paper we had, a good paper which she had largely written herself. Barbara had just been to see the T.U.C. who had given her a 28-paragraph letter blankly rejecting all her plans. She was in a way contemptuous, saying how silly they were, and also very guarded and extraordinarily careful with us, as if she didn't want to antagonize us and only wanted to tell us everything was O.K. But already Judith had done enough work, and I had confirmed it, to know that Barbara's proposals in the first draft of the White Paper were half-baked. She hadn't really worked out the conciliation pause or its exact machinery or at what point the Industrial Commission would come in to fine strikers, or what it was to fine them for, or how far it was to investigate the causes of the strike all over again. Nor had she considered what was to be the relationship between the Commission and her own conciliation officers, the role of the trade union heads among its members, what was to happen when the fines were paid, or what exactly was to be the Supplementary Benefit entitlement of somebody who had been fined and thrown out of a job or of someone who refused to go back to work and was still being fined so much a day. None of these questions, nor half a dozen others, had been adequately considered and the more we pressed, the more Barbara, who is very shrewd and quick, was having to fill in. In fact we were doing the work of a Ministerial Committee after she had already published her plans to the T.U.C. and the C.B.I. The discussion was a little tense. She was then summoned to see Harold at No. 10.

Cabinet began at 6.30, an interesting meeting that went fairly well for the opposition. Callaghan opted out for the first hour or two, remaining silent. Dick Marsh tried a bit, and then I took the lead in asking about procedure, really to get the meeting on to the subjects I wanted. First, timing. How were we going to fill in the year? Had we faced the full results of having a Bill after we had been defeated at Congress and Party Conference? What was to be the effect on the local parties and on the P.L.P. of airing all this, especially the impracticability of the conciliation pause, for a whole year? I concentrated the discussion on that one section.

It became clear that on our side were Judith, myself, Dick Marsh, Tony Crosland, who was away but who had sent a little letter, Roy Mason, surprisingly, who had come out strongly in favour of strike ballots and equally strongly talked of the impracticality of the 28-day cooling-off period, and we had Tony Greenwood, rather courageously, and Callaghan. We seven were pretty resolutely opposed, on the grounds that the broad tactic of slapping this on the table and rushing ahead, getting into a point-blank conflict with the T.U.C. and the party in this particular year, was crazy and doomed to defeat. We had a long, arduous, free discussion which mostly consisted of us critics making our point at length, with very short statements of support for Harold from the other side. I think (as Jim Callaghan has now said on two occasions) I was pretty effective because I was dealing with the political and not the practical issue, talking not as an expert on trade unions but as an experienced member of the party and also as someone who is able to read and discuss a White Paper. By the time we finished at 9.15 it was clear that Barbara wasn't going to get what she wanted today because we were holding out successfully, and it was also clear that Harold would have to put me on the Industrial Committee. He can't have me conducting all the opposition in full Cabinet if he is to get anything like an agreed document.

Thursday, January 9th

Harold's plan had been, I suppose, to finish the White Paper and get it out before the Commonwealth Conference began but I had entirely defeated this ludicrously optimistic idea. The Conference is now in full swing and Harold is having to deal with this in the middle of it all, so today we began Cabinet at 9.0 a.m. The discussion was chiefly about procedure. All last night and early this morning I was thinking of an idea and, right at the beginning of the meeting, I said, 'The key thing is, why should the cooling-off period be something to which we are irrevocably committed? Why can't it be drafted in such a way that we put it to the unions and clinch it that we want them to consult their members?' It had suddenly become clear to me that the real difference is one of our attitude during this coming year. If we have to have a whole year on this, through Conference right up to the Commons' discussion of the Bill, we must spend it negotiating not quarrelling with the T.U.C. To achieve this, we should draft the White Paper in such a way that, willy-nilly, whether they want it or not, they should be induced into negotiations to keep them quiet. This was the tactic I wanted to evolve. It was pretty hostilely received by Harold, who didn't at all like the idea of climbing down or of giving the impression that there was no clear-cut smack of firm government. Barbara didn't like it either but most of the others did. It was on this that I worked, the idea of making the White Paper as Green as possible as it relates to these particular critical problems.

After Cabinet those of us on the Industrial Committee stayed behind. I have now been put on this by Harold, who has realized he had made a great mistake in taking me off it.[1] We agreed to meet twice on Friday and once next Monday before Cabinet on Tuesday, in a frantic effort by Barbara to get her White Paper passed and approved, printed and published next week. I am still not clear what the desperate hurry is but I said, 'All right, we'll have a try.' In fact I am pretty sure this will actually happen.

I rushed back to Alexander Fleming House to a meeting on 'flu. We had confirmation that the Mao virus had been located in Birmingham and Wolverhampton and here was David Ennals with his draft communiqué, ready to announce the epidemic on the B.B.C. at midday. He is a tremendous man for publicity, David. He does it quite well although on this occasion I had again to say to him, 'Not *my* doctors advise me, David, *our* doctors have advised us in the Ministry.' Sure enough, at 1 o'clock there was his voice and

[1] When Crossman had become Secretary of State for Social Services.

I was able to say to him this evening, 'We have launched our first 'flu epidemic successfully. Well done. We cannot say we have an inactive Ministry.'

After that over to the *New Statesman* for lunch with Paul Johnson and Marigold, who cooks for them, Francis Hope, his new literary editor[1], and Alan Watkins. We lunched upstairs in the boardroom, which used to be my dining room, and I remembered how when Zita and I had just moved in and furnished the whole top floor we went away for the weekend during the Blitz and when we came back it was just catching fire.[2] I found a tired fireman and said, 'Do put it out or it will burn down,' and he said, 'My nozzle doesn't fit. I've come from Reading.'

At 4.45 I was to see Roy to learn whether on the first indications of the trade figures we should be able to launch the superannuation White Paper on Tuesday, January 21st, as we were planning. I went in with a pretty sure feeling and he took me aside almost like a doctor giving bad news, saying, 'I'm awfully sorry, old boy, I'm afraid I shan't be able to tell you. I've had a good look at the figures and though they're not very bad they are bad. We have a £55 million deficit for December. It's largely owing to vast unnecessary expenditure on some foreign ship but there it is, it's very dicey now and we must look carefully.' 'How long must we postpone it?' I asked. 'Until the 28th?' 'Yes,' he said, 'but you might want to postpone it until March.' I said, 'No, I think we'd better have the 28th because, after all, if we can't get it then, when can we do it?' He was obviously apologetic and unhappy at the idea that the position was so unstable that he was scared at launching even a pensions plan, which is in a sense a savings plan, just because of one month's unsatisfactory trade figures. On the other hand, he also knew very well that Barbara's White Paper was coming out and he argued, not unreasonably, that I might want to separate mine from hers by a certain distance. She hopes hers will come out on the 15th. Would there be anyone at all listening to mine on the 21st after the row there will be about hers? I think this may be true but nevertheless I told him that I would go back quickly and advise my people. I went out feeling thoroughly depressed, not so much about the week's delay till the 28th but at the instability of the Government which it revealed.

I went home and found Anne changing for the Commonwealth Prime Ministers' Dinner at No. 10. I found I was sitting between Harry Lee and Julius Nyerere.[3] I found Harry Lee as unbearable as ever, constantly saying how sad it was that the British no longer knew how to work, making the sort of remarks that the most intolerant or reactionary British or American

[1] Francis Hope, a former Fellow of All Souls' College, Oxford, became Assistant Literary Editor of the *New Statesman* in 1962, later becoming Diplomatic Correspondent of the paper. He was killed in the D.C. 10 Paris air crash in 1974.

[2] While Crossman was assistant editor at the *New Statesman* he and his second wife Zita Baker lived for a time over the newspaper's offices.

[3] Lee Kuan Yew, Prime Minister of Singapore since 1959. See Vol. II. Julius Nyerere was Prime Minister of Tanganyika 1961–2 and President of the Tanganyika Republic 1962–4 and has been President of the United Republic of Tanzania since 1964.

capitalist makes. I was much more interested in Julius Nyerere on the other side, whom I asked about the main problem which is worrying me in regard to the Commonwealth, the threat of an Asian exodus from Kenya reinforced by one from Uganda.[1] Nyerere said he had his own 80,000 Asians in Tanzania and they are being left as they are because he doesn't approve of racialism. He approved of stopping exploitation and he strongly disapproved of his African colleagues for behaving in the way that they were. It was a normal Harold evening, with perhaps rather shorter speeches than usual but the usual standing about afterwards. There was Jim Callaghan, who was Shadow Commonwealth Secretary,[2] full of knowledge of all these people, whom he also got to know as Chancellor. I feel very much out on a limb because I have been excluded from all these foreign affairs jaunts and I have also excluded myself by refusing to go to dinner parties. I stood about there with Anne feeling a bit embarrassed, talking a little bit to Makarios, having a word with the Indian High Commissioner,[3] but on the whole disconsolate and regarding it as a fair waste of time. I did talk to Marcia, who said she had heard I had been difficult and that Harold had said I was perhaps over-tired and therefore behaving in a strange way. I tried to make her see why it is and that there is nothing of a conspiracy against Harold. It is Judith and I and Tony Greenwood, after all, his best friends, who are warning him against the tactic he is committed to. I didn't get very far and I realized how long it was since I had talked to her. After that we all had to go round to Lancaster House to an enormous reception for 700–800 people and there I had a little chat with Patricia and Richard Llewelyn-Davies and Jock and Phyllis Campbell.[4] Anne and I escaped pretty rapidly and I got home to my boxes.

Friday, January 10th

Back at Barbara's Committee, we started on the policy, beginning with my corner of it, supplementary benefits for strikers, and then we got on to the main issue, the presentation and drafting of proposals for consultation rather than for an already decided Bill. Barbara stressed once again that this was a purely jurisdictional matter. The conciliation pause would only be ordered when there was an unconstitutional, i.e. unofficial strike. That was about the end of the morning.

We resumed at 2 p.m., having just got a huge bunch of amendments, to

[1] See above, p. 287.

[2] James Callaghan was the Labour Party spokesman on Colonial Affairs 1956–61 and Shadow Foreign Secretary 1972–4.

[3] Shanti Swarup Dhavan was Indian High Commissioner in London 1968–9 and Governor of West Bengal 1969–72. Since 1972 he has been a member of the Law Commission of India.

[4] Richard Llewelyn-Davies, Senior Partner of Llewelyn-Davies, Weeks, Forestier-Walker & Bor, was Professor of Architecture at University College, London, 1960–9, Professor of Urban Planning 1969–75 and subsequently Emeritus Professor. He has been Chairman of the Centre for Environmental Studies since 1967 and became a life peer in 1963. He was married to Patricia Llewelyn-Davies.

find that over lunchtime Barbara herself had completely redrafted the section on the conciliation pause. It was now quite different. The new section described the cases where she would be able to order people back to work not only when a strike was unconstitutional, but even in official strikes when there were no clear-cut procedures for conciliation she would order them back and produce her own procedures. We had a long wrangle and I said, 'In that case you have misled Cabinet because you told us that official strikes are perfectly O.K., and that what is really wicked is neglecting official procedures. Now you are saying that you want to intervene even in the very many cases where there is no clear-cut procedure because you have large numbers of unorganized workers or badly run managements. You can't call this an unconstitutional strike. You must say, "all strikes except those which are run by strictly official procedures". I can't see that the men are to blame if there is no constitutional procedure for them to be breaking.'

At this Denis Barnes said, 'They are not to blame for the strike, only for disobeying the First Secretary. That's the only crime they have committed and they must go back when she orders them.' I said, 'That really is dictatorship. You are saying that she can order them back under any terms she likes and she isn't even limited where strikes are constitutional.' The truth is, if we look back in the Cabinet minutes we see this idea in the original draft. It is submerged there but you can see it in the draft if you know it's there. It looks as though her civil servants had put it in, she had not explained it to us clearly, and now in her new draft she was spelling it out.

We had a long and arduous struggle and she thought I was just sabotaging and filibustering. To some extent I think it's fair to say I was. (Judith told me that when she got into the room she overheard Barbara saying to the others, 'My God, a colleague rewriting a White Paper for another colleague. By jove, when he has another White Paper, what won't I do to him.' What Barbara forgets is that in the case of my White Paper every word of the policy has been approved after long consultations with Roy Hattersley, her own Parliamentary Secretary, whom she sent to represent her. There is no aspect of the policy which hasn't received his approval.)

Barbara got pretty hysterical in the course of the afternoon and the Committee got more and more angry with me, saying I was unreasonable, until slowly it at last began to dawn on them that they had been misled. I challenged the Solicitor General,[1] saying, 'Wasn't it your view that it was only when the strike is unconstitutional that she has the right to intervene?' 'Certainly,' he said. 'That was my impression but she has made it very clear now that there are these other cases.' 'But,' I said, 'it makes a great deal of difference to the argument, and I think there is going to be quite a row when this is disclosed

[1] Sir Arthur Irvine (Kt 1967), Liberal candidate for Kincardine and West Aberdeenshire 1935 and 1939 (by-election), Labour candidate for Twickenham 1945 and South Aberdeen (by-election) 1946, has been Labour M.P. for Liverpool Edge Hill, since 1947. He was called to the Bar in 1935 and took silk in 1958. He was Solicitor-General 1967–70.

to Cabinet on Tuesday.' We went on until 5 o'clock when we agreed to break off and that we would all work on our drafts over the weekend and come back on Monday morning at 10.15.

Saturday, January 11th

There was a thick fog this morning. I must admit I'm still profoundly depressed. This afternoon Stephen Swingler rang me up from his cottage near Ilmington. He has been having bronchitis so he's stayed away from the office all this week. He asked me how things were going and is obviously as concerned as I am. John Ellis had come over specially from Bristol to talk to him about the madness of what is going on,[1] Eric Heffer[2] has written to me, and Tam has rung me up from Scotland. What's come out during the week as really controversial is the idea of fining strikers who won't obey and whom Barbara has ordered to return to work under the conciliation clause. Meanwhile the T.U.C. has replied formally in a unanimously signed letter, objecting far more strongly to the right to impose strike ballots before an official strike than to the clauses about the cooling-off period and the fining of trade unionists who don't return to work. They regard the first as outrageous and the second as merely impracticable and unrealistic. I think this is because the first weakens the position of the trade union leader, and possibly strengthens the hand of the strikers, whereas the second is so remote and so difficult that they think it's unworkable and are not so alarmed by it. But it doesn't necessarily mean that when we come to the crunch we shall find the second easy. On the contrary, the really sensational innovation is giving her the power to intervene whenever she likes, to order a pause or order the strikers back to work and fine them for each day they stay away. I think this will cause trouble.

I have been studying Barbara's proposals all weekend and very late tonight, as I was just going to bed, there came a ring at the bell and there was a dispatch rider from the Ministry of Works bringing the revised text of the White Paper. It was sent to press at the same time so that if it is approved next Tuesday evening in Cabinet Barbara can go ahead and publish. She is determined on this rush, which also struck Stephen Swingler as odd, and then, apparently, after it has been rushed out she will wait till next November for the Second Reading of the Bill. This time-tabling also disturbs me.

Monday, January 13th

I found a big banner headline in the *Guardian*, where Ian Aitken had a very accurate story that Barbara and I are at loggerheads and that I am pleading

[1] Labour M.P. for Bristol North-West 1966–70 and for Brigg and Scunthorpe since February 1974. He became an Assistant Government Whip in 1974.

[2] Eric Heffer has been Labour M.P. for Liverpool (Walton) since 1964 and was Minister of State at the Department of Industry from 1974 until his resignation, after breaching Cabinet guidelines on speeches concerning E.E.C. membership.

for green edges to her White Paper.[1] This was interesting because for once I knew precisely how the leak had come about. On Saturday John Bourne of the *Financial Times* had rung me up and I had given him a very good briefing on the strict understanding that my name shouldn't be used and that there should be nothing personal in his story.[2] The *Financial Times* printed this faithfully this morning but it's quite clear that Ian Aitken got it from John Bourne and added all the personal stress between Barbara and myself. This is a concrete example of how these two work together.

I wondered uneasily whether this would have upset Barbara and certainly she was very cross this morning when we settled down at 10.15 to continue the Committee work on her White Paper. In Cabinet I had said, half-jokingly, that if she didn't have a Ministerial Committee before the White Paper she should jolly well have one after it and this was what she was getting. It was our third meeting and she was still ferociously angry at the idea that any Cabinet colleague should submit her to this indignity. However here we were. The copy which had come down to me at Prescote had already gone to the printers but she bustled in and took out of her bag yet another whole mass of redrafts which she had been preparing herself during the weekend. It soon became pretty clear that there was still one major issue, and only one, worth fighting. This was for green edges, that is, to get a White Paper framed in consultative form, which didn't close our options but if necessary permitted us without loss of face to drop either the strike ballot or the conciliation pause. This was what I wanted and I wanted to see how she took it. When I had gone through the White Paper at the weekend I had noticed that all the amendments I had proposed, including those she had ferociously opposed, had been wisely accepted by her officials in their redrafts and this had tickled me a good deal.

However, all that really mattered was Clause 18 (I think it was) on the conciliation pause and there she drew out a new draft and said, 'I have a much better draft to propose.' She had toughened up sentences in the redraft of the White Paper, having decided, I expect with Harold's backing, to move the other way. She had removed any suggestion of conciliation altogether and now it said that if the trade unions were to propose positive recommendations it would reduce the need to use her powers to intervene. It is clear that she is determined to take these powers, and she is going to tell the unions without qualification, 'Right, I'll take them and then I won't have to use them.' She had obviously decided this over the weekend. At this point I cut the Committee short, saying 'Look, this must go to Cabinet,' and after a bit of discussion she said, 'I'll report it to Cabinet.' 'No,' I said, 'I think the Paymaster and I would prefer to put it in a paper.' Barbara obviously didn't like this but when Judith and I left the meeting we immediately got on to Sandy

[1] Ian Aitken was Political Editor of the *Guardian*.
[2] John Bourne was the Lobby Editor of the *Financial Times*.

Isserlis,[1] a very good man who was with me at Housing and who is now at the Cabinet Office, but working full time for Judith. Over lunch and this afternoon he produced a very decent draft, which I changed once again in time for it to be circulated in this evening's boxes so that Ministers will get our paper and Barbara's simultaneously.

The other thing I managed today was to get Jim Callaghan and the rest of them to agree to work out the details of my announcement that John Foster was going to undertake an inquiry into Scientology. They were surprised that I had got somebody as good as him, and there was a little bit of alarm that John might be too independent, but I think they felt it was sensible. Indeed, they have every right to be a little alarmed, because it is clear that he is going to enjoy himself enormously.

Tuesday, January 14th

An interesting meeting with the Registrar-General and Claus Moser, Chief Statistician and chief inviter of me to Covent Garden.[2] Tommy Balogh was there too. There had been a great fuss at Home Affairs Committee about framing the questions for the 1970 census and only by a narrow majority did it squeak through Cabinet that questions on income and race should be asked in the small pre-test. Now we have had the results, which show that the question on race, which we had all feared most, got through perfectly easily, while the question on income got a very bad response. People had greatly objected, particularly to the fact that householders were asked the income of inmates of the house. We had to consider whether to redraft the questionnaire, or whether, as the Registrar-General and Claus Moser proposed, to put in the same question but with other arrangements for people who did not necessarily wish to answer it through the householder. Brian Abel-Smith had said to me, 'Look, the Americans have had all this before. When they first had these questions in 1940, people were just as suspicious and they couldn't put the question in its full form, to get exactly the information they wanted, right at the beginning. They had to break it down and lead people gently towards this kind of questioning. One of their methods was to have a cut-off and say, "If you are earning more than £30 a week, put 'over £30' ". The cut-off was put at this point because it is on the whole the wealthy who are most afraid of disclosing their income.' The officials said this morning that the feeling in Britain came not particularly from the wealthy, that it's not 1940 but 1969, and it's the skilled workers, the people who are cheating on double time, who

[1] Assistant Secretary at the M.H.L.G. 1963–9, Under-Secretary at the Cabinet Office 1969 and at the M.H.L.G. 1969–70, Principal Private Secretary to the Prime Minister 1970 and Assistant Under-Secretary at the Home Office from 1970 to 1972, when he became Director of the Centre for Studies in Social Policy.

[2] Michael Reed, Under-Secretary at the Ministry of Health 1956–8, at the Cabinet Office 1958–61 and at the Ministry of Health 1961–3, was Registrar-General from 1963 and Director of the Office of Population Censuses and Surveys from 1970 until his retirement to South Africa in 1972.

now feel that their income is something to be kept jealously concealed from the Inland Revenue because everybody now is a potential tax defrauder – these, I was told, are the people who fear this sort of question. There's a lot in that. However it also became clear to me that these questions are prepared by going to each Department, asking what they want, and, then, out of all these requests, phrasing the census to cover these endless requirements.

It seemed obvious to me that if you frame appalling questions you get appalling results and, sure enough, when I looked at the question on income the way it was put was enough to terrify anybody. I said, 'Does anybody submit these questions to social scientists who are skilled in social surveys?' 'No, we do them ourselves.' Claus Moser said, 'If you are not concerned with social science or propaganda or education, no wonder your questions are repugnant and you get bad answers. Have you, for instance, studied whether you should try a kind of question where you have to tick answers rather than one where you have to state things?' No, they hadn't bothered, it wouldn't make any difference. I found Claus Moser was almost as bad as the Registrar but I think I may have had some effect on them. The trouble lies in the Whitehall system of trying to reach a decision by asking everybody what their requirements are and then trying to collate them. In this particular case you got an obviously impossible result because the kind of question which is asked is not the kind of question which is likely to overcome prejudice and fear.

The next and rather unexpected thing was doctors' pay. Last week I was told that the Kindersley Committee had submitted a letter to the Prime Minister recommending an 8 per cent increase.[1] I had a copy of the letter to study, and the Ministry assured me that this was just within the $3\frac{1}{2}$ per cent ceiling,[2] since 8 per cent could just about squeeze through on the grounds that the level of doctors' and dentists' remuneration had fallen seriously out of line. I didn't like the look of this at all. Moreover the recommendation was based on comparability and I remembered that the P.I.B. had just turned down the university teachers' claim based on comparability.[3] Aubrey Jones had made a great attack on the whole principle, saying it was a major cause of inflation, and now the Kindersley Committee was telling the Government to give a comparability award to a not dissimilar profession. The moment I saw this I didn't think the Ministry was taking it seriously enough. I was even more alarmed when I found the lead story in this morning's *Daily Express*, based on an obvious briefing from a D.E.P. official, saying that the doctors' award

[1] In the Tenth Report (Cmnd 3884) of the Review Body, published in February 1969, the Kindersley Committee justified a general increase in doctors' and dentists' remuneration on the grounds of comparability with wage and salary movements of groups with equivalent professional qualifications and stated that such an increase would be consistent with the present application of incomes policy and would be in the national interest.

[2] Prescribed for all wage and salary settlements in the White Paper, *Productivity, Prices and Incomes Policy in 1968 and 1969* (Cmnd 3590), published on April 4th, 1968.

[3] See above, p. 293 and n.

4 At their new offices in Alexander Fleming House, Elephant and Castle, November 1968, the three ministers in the team that takes charge of the new Department of Health and Social Security get down to work. Left to right: Stephen Swingler, Minister of State responsible for Social Security; Richard Crossman, in overall charge as Secretary of State; David Ennals, Minister of State responsible for Health and Welfare.

5 The Secretary of State visits the Great Ormond Street Children's Hospital in January 1969.

6 Richard Crossman listens to nurses putting their grievances to him on the steps of the Ministry in April 1969.

7 & 8 Arriving to address the Labour Society at the London School of Economics in May 1969, Crossman finds the front of the building heavily picketed by protesting students but eventually enters by a door at the rear.

would be decided at the same time as the teachers' award and that one could hardly turn down the teachers' claim of 6¼ per cent and allow the doctors' claim of 8 per cent since both were based on comparability. This story could only have come from Barbara and here I was at 5 o'clock faced with the Prices and Incomes Committee.

It was a very tense meeting because although the teachers' claim came before the doctors' on the agenda, Barbara insisted that the two should be taken together. Actually they had nothing to do with each other but it soon became quite clear that she was gunning for me and for the doctors. I'm not going to say for a moment that this was purely personal but there is no doubt that I have infuriated her by refusing to support her White Paper and making her spend all this time on it. I suppose she wasn't sorry to see the possibility of counter-attacking me, and she did it viciously, saying that of course the doctors' award should be submitted to the Prices and Incomes Board. My Ministry had thought that impossible and that no one would even claim that it should be referred.[1] The Department told me that the Treasury officials had briefed the Chancellor to support the award and that Eddie Shackleton's new Civil Service Department had briefed him to support it, so that with these two I ought to be able to get it through.

However it was clear that I was in a very small minority because doctors are hated. Barbara was able to say, 'How can we get industrial workers to show restraint when professional people, great surgeons who get £400 a year extra, are given these enormous increases?' All this is complete hooey. During 1968 industrial workers got 6½–7 per cent increases in real wages, far more than the teachers and doctors were asking for. Nevertheless this *ad hominem* argument had a great effect on the Committee. Ted Short sat by and saw his Barbara batting for him, saying, 'I can't turn the schoolteachers down.' This was pretty crude because the schoolteachers' claim was outside the ceiling and mine was within it. Moreover, the Kindersley Committee was set up in 1962 to make a direct recommendation to the P.M. and no one had ever rejected their reports before or subjected them to the Prices and Incomes Board. Moreover, last time the Committee had given a nil award, which the doctors had accepted, and now they were being given a modest award within the ceiling, so to object to this was quite unjust.[2] I pointed out that to reject the recommendation would quite clearly be considered a breach of faith and that it would make my relations with the doctors impossible. It was soon evident that we were going to reach no kind of an agreement and that the matter would have to go to Cabinet.

[1] In an Addendum to their Report, the Kindersley Committee stated that they were fully conscious of the situation to which the P.I.B. had drawn attention, in Cmnd 3866, 'wherein we make recommendations upon the remuneration of doctors and dentists while the pay of academic staff had been referred to the Board'. They felt it improper either to comment on this or to revise, or be thought to revise, their own conclusions, independently attained, by reference to those of any other body (Cmnd 3884, p. 13).

[2] See above, p. 17 and n.

We were to have a pretty exhausting evening. As the morning had been taken up by the Commonwealth Conference, Cabinet took place at 6.30 and we moved from the Prices and Incomes Committee in Cabinet Room A to No. 10. The Prime Minister proposed to take Barbara's White Paper clause by clause. 'Surely not,' I said. 'We should take the main issue first because it colours the whole attitude to the White Paper. Whether the White Paper should have green edges or not will determine the consequential amendments.' Harold gave way and we then had something like a two-hour debate on my amendment and Barbara's reply. I needn't rehash all the arguments here. They are not unfairly expressed in the Cabinet minutes, except of course for the really powerful argument on my side, the argument about politics. As I wound up, I made this point even more strongly, simply saying that whatever the desirability and popularity of what she was doing and the rather doubtful fact as to whether it would work there was the other question of its impact on the Labour Party and the Labour Movement. If, instead of going through in a rush now, the Bill is to be fought over throughout the spring and summer, voted upon at Congress and the Labour Party Conference and only put into Parliament in November, maybe finishing next March or May, we could just imagine what a preface to an election campaign that would be.

Right at the end I said there was something else I wanted to add. At the previous Cabinet I hadn't had clear answers about the relationship between this Bill and the Prices and Incomes Bill. Surely it was clear to everybody that we couldn't have both of them in the new session next autumn? That had been the case for rushing this Bill through this session and having the Prices and Incomes Bill next session but since it had been decided not to rush this Bill through presumably there would be no Prices and Incomes legislation. When knowledge of this got about it might produce a grave crisis in the autumn. Supposing the Chancellor needed stronger prices and incomes measures to save the pound and was inhibited from introducing them? It might force an autumn election. One or two people had strongly advised me against saying this but I dropped it in. Roy immediately intervened. He couldn't accept any of this and at this point he cut the discussion on his Prices and Incomes Bill. I had noticed that on the Cabinet agenda there was a second item after Barbara's, the timing of legislation, and my suspicions had been aroused. Roy was clearly siding with Barbara, but I could do nothing apart from making my initial speech.

It was rather a formal Cabinet. Harold wasn't there at the beginning, and the Foreign Secretary had started it from the Chair but now the P.M. was back he took the greatest trouble to commit everybody on this. Four people were away, paired, on our side Tony Crosland and Tony Greenwood and I have forgotten who the two were on the other side. Each person was asked for an opinion and it was fairly predictable, 6 : 6. We had all known that George Thomas would be for Barbara and George Thomson for the Prime Minister, the Establishment side, but then there were the critical votes. The surprising ones were Ted Short, who came out for Barbara in a short speech, and Wedgy Benn, who had ended the previous Cabinet by saying how important it was to have consultation but who had obviously now been brought into line behind the scenes. Our only surprising convert was Peter Shore and on this hangs a comic story. He had been away with a suspected coronary embolism so this was his first Cabinet on this issue. He has a lackadaisical voice and, so Roy Jenkins told me afterwards, directly he began, the Prime Minister, who was making a list, put him down firmly for Barbara. After talking for three or four minutes in a very ambiguous way Peter suddenly said, 'I agree wholeheartedly with Barbara about her policy but if the only issue is consultation and whether we should give an impression of willingness to consult between now and the Bill, well, of course, I favour consultation.' The P.M. was chatting with Roy so he didn't hear what Peter was saying and later on he had to be told to correct his list because he hadn't heard his Secretary of State for Economic Affairs. Willie Ross came down on our side for the same sort of reasons as mine. We therefore had as solid allies the three trade union members, Callaghan, Mason and Marsh, all against Barbara, as every other trade unionist would have been too, I think, if they had been there to hear the argument. She had got what you might call the normal Establishment characters, Michael Stewart, Gerald Gardiner, Eddie Shackleton, Fred Peart (despite all his worries) but, as everybody had really known would happen, the result was a predictable 10 : 6 and Harold Wilson would have been the eleventh if he had been asked to cast his vote.

I had known that however reasonable I was and however obviously I was right, it would be impossible to win as Barbara had Roy and Harold on her side. The whole drama of the meeting, therefore, came after this. Barbara wasn't allowed to wind up. I did and I think everybody felt it was a pretty devastating repetition of all the political difficulties involved and of the reasonableness of consultation. I said, 'You have got six major issues in the White Paper on which you promise consultation. Why not talk about it on the other two issues as well?' Roy Jenkins leant across and said, 'By jove, that winding-up has nearly persuaded me that you are right.'

The Prime Minister came in immediately for fear Barbara would upset people, and she wasn't allowed to reply. He called on Roy to introduce the second item on the agenda, the timing. To my astonishment, Roy said that there really was grave danger next autumn and he now said himself all the things I had referred to in my speech which he had refused to accept before, the possible need for a severe Prices and Incomes Bill and the impossibility of dropping that. He *said* all these things and it was obvious that people were shaken by what seemed to be a carefully contrived conspiracy between Roy, the Prime Minister and Barbara. Having given her the White Paper, Roy was now going to say, 'Yes, but you must give me the precautions I need to get a Prices and Incomes Bill as well. My Bill came before this demand for her early legislation. Her package ought to go through this session.' But technically, both in terms of parliamentary drafting and parliamentary time, and in terms of Barbara's own machine, it is quite impossible to rush her Bill through. She still has only the vaguest statements of policy. Pages and pages of half-baked White Paper had been redrafted, stiffened and improved but she is nowhere near the preparation of a Bill and endless consultations have to take place before her policy is developed. She couldn't give Roy his point but we were all uneasily aware in this case we might well be faced with a major crisis next autumn. It might well turn out that the whole prices and incomes policy and the future of the pound have been jeopardized by railroading Barbara's Bill through Cabinet. Once Barbara has got her Bill approved in Cabinet, who will say in the autumn that it should be postponed in favour of a severe Prices and Incomes Bill? Indeed, it is quite clear that both Barbara and the Prime Minister are gambling on being able to avoid new prices and incomes legislation altogether. This was the drama at the end of the meeting and, as Eddie Shackleton said on the telephone later on, 'You know, if Roy had spoken before the decision was taken I would have voted for you. Most of us were only very marginally in favour of Barbara on that issue you put and many of us thought you made a very strong case. Roy has made a very bad impression on his colleagues by doing this.' By jove, that was certainly true.

Wednesday, January 15th

I lunched at the Athenaeum with Nicholas Davenport and in came Callaghan with his Parliamentary Secretary, Victor Stonham. I went across later and asked Jim, 'What did you think of Cabinet yesterday?' and he said, 'The plot thickens. Roy has been thinking of an autumn election.' Jim had come to the same conclusion as me as a result of Roy's intervention. I said, 'I don't think it would be fair to say they have made up their minds but it does look as though Roy and Harold must be saying to themselves that in the last resort we can have an election this October.' Certainly on three or four occasions in our discussions Harold had said that we might not have to implement Barbara's Bill. Maybe he really is thinking of using it as a White Paper to win popularity and then never implementing it at all, and this would explain his willingness to face the possibility of forging ahead at the autumn Conferences.

My suspicion was confirmed by a conversation I had with Roy later today. I had to see him again about the timing of my own White Paper and in the course of this I took the liberty of saying that I thought he had made a great mistake yesterday evening and done himself no good, and I quoted what Eddie Shackleton had said. 'Well,' Roy replied, 'I may well have been wrong. The truth is, I was convinced completely by your arguments but I promised my support to Barbara and I couldn't let her down. That's why I did it.' I said, 'How did that happen?' 'I think it was on December 10th or 12th,' he said, 'when the Prime Minister, Barbara and I discussed the tactic of pushing her Bill through. I didn't know anything about it and I still don't know much but, whether it was right or wrong I gave her my support.' 'Surely,' I said, 'you realized that by doing that you were possibly prejudicing the survival of the prices and incomes policy, certainly prejudicing your new legislation and finally knocking it on the head?' 'I realize it now,' he said, 'and that's why I am so insistent on early legislation for her Bill.' 'You won't get it,' I said. 'I'm not beaten,' he said. 'In a month's time we shall see the situation more clearly, when we know what the impact of her Bill is. Perhaps it's not as controversial as we think. I shall have to come back to Cabinet if the situation is serious and say I can't survive without a Prices and Incomes Bill. I may have to say that Cabinet can face the choice, either to rush a short Industrial Relations Bill through this session after all or to postpone it for a Prices and Incomes Bill which must be rushed through before Christmas.' This conversation confirmed that, at least in Roy's mind, there is now a possibility of an autumn election.

I also spoke to Roy about the doctors' pay award, saying I was disappointed he hadn't been able to support me on this as his officials wanted him to. 'It is very difficult,' he said. He thought the award would go through, but he wondered whether we shouldn't just postpone it for three months. This means taking 25 per cent off the value of the award which I said would be intolerable. It would be preferable to limit it altogether. I pointed out that the right thing to do was to let the award go through this time but to announce that we were going to reconsider the whole structure under which we deal with awards. Some are referred to the Prices and Incomes Board and two to independent Commissions, the Plowden Committee for senior civil servants and the Kindersley Commission for doctors.[1] We might announce that all three will be put together and not necessarily submitted to the P.I.B. Roy seemed to listen quite attentively and to be helpful but I am still extremely worried.

However the real reason he had asked me to see him was to give me his final decision on whether we could publish our White Paper on January 21st. He hadn't quite made up his mind. His officials said it was O.K. but he wouldn't feel sure until Friday evening. Could I give him until then? I said, 'No, I can't. I have to have the thing completely turned up, we have to send out 600 letters, to organize parties, press conferences. That's impossible.' He said, 'Couldn't you postpone it for a week?' I said, 'No, we've got to do it on the 21st. Can you make up your mind?' 'Can you give me until Thursday at 5.30?' he said. We had a long argument. There was no sign of the pound being unsound. I gather from those who know that the Treasury thought all this absolute hooey. Although the trade figures were lamentable, a £55 million deficit, in fact the outside world has not been alarmed because its view of the British position has greatly improved. It was Roy's own disappointment at

[1] Sir Edwin Plowden, Chairman of Tube Investments Ltd 1963–76 and a life peer since 1959, was the Chairman of the Standing Advisory Committee on the Pay of the Higher Civil Service. The Committee was established in 1968 but in 1971 its functions were given to the newly created Top Salaries Review Body.

the trade figures that had coloured his judgment on what the outside world would think. Roy, nervous, anxious, couldn't keep his fingers off them, and finally I said, 'All right, I'll go away and let you know tomorrow morning.'

I discussed with Judith my talk with Roy and I went to see Fred Peart to explain that we have the prospect of being forced to go to the country as a result of a secret deal, if it is true, between these three people, Harold, Barbara and Roy. I told Fred, who was extremely worried, what Roy had said and that we must talk to the Prime Minister about it, because a really serious and dangerous situation is developing behind the scenes.

Thursday, January 16th

A second Cabinet where Harold prosed on for nearly two hours on the Commonwealth Conference. An enormous, absolutely unreadable, pompous communiqué has been published. There is no doubt, though, that he has handled it quite skilfully and got through far better than he anticipated. The people who came to curse had gone away blessing. Trudeau had been a flop but Harold was a success.[1] It is clear that he is at his best chairing a Commonwealth Conference, where nothing much is happening and all that is required is skill, tenacity, agility, subtlety at keeping the thing going and no great imagination or strategy. He had surpassed himself on this occasion and wanted some commendation from Cabinet. I am afraid everybody sat around, rather bored, and didn't give it because their minds were either on Barbara's policy or on the following item on the agenda, immigration. Callaghan was to report on this. Now though Harold has been pretty good at chairing the Conference the man whose personality has dominated the British press has been Mr Callaghan. There he was standing up for Britain against the Africans, saying, 'No more bloody immigrants whatever happens. We won't increase the immigration quota, and if the Kenyan Asians have to come it will be at the cost of other voucher-holders from Pakistan and India.'[2] He has had tremendous coverage for his presentation of the British line and Harold was very much aware of it.

Here came Callaghan, asking in a modest, quiet way for Cabinet approval. No, he didn't ask for it. Barbara raised the question and Jim gave an answer. Barbara said, 'We must have the papers first and the decision afterwards.' I had completely forgotten this. I had thought that we had already given a decision but we hadn't. Jim had taken the liberty of announcing a policy firmly and clearly and coming to Cabinet afterwards. He is now doing this more frequently and more successfully and there is no doubt he is building up his position in the public eye. He did it as the only person who stood up against Barbara's Industrial Relations Bill, apart from Dick Marsh. On

[1] Pierre Elliott Trudeau, Prime Minister and Leader of the Liberal Party of Canada since April 1968.

[2] See pp. 287, 315 and n.

immigration, on everything you see, there is Jim Callaghan, sensible, constructive, sturdy, thoroughly English, doing his job, a big man who could keep the movement going even when it is defeated and gets rid of Harold Wilson. That is what he achieved even at the Commonwealth Conference, to Harold's great annoyance.

The other little episode today was a meeting of the Lords' Reform Committee to tidy up the legislation. My God, it's going to be awful to get this Bill because it's going to be so unpopular, and it will be even worse now with the I.R. Bill and the Superannuation Bill in the offing. Gerald Gardiner had taken the precaution of seeing Harold to ask whether he still wanted to speak in the Second Reading debate and the P.M. had replied, 'I will if the Committee wants me to.' Gerald put this to us, and immediately Fred Peart said, 'Oh, no. I don't think we would want to engage the Prime Minister in this.' That was the general view of several other people there, a dangerous view that we had to stop very quickly. 'Look,' I said, 'if the Prime Minister is prepared to speak, who on this Committee says that it wouldn't help the Bill through the Commons and who will say that his absence wouldn't be noted as further proof of our half-heartedness?' So we got it.

I dined with Tommy and Pen Balogh at the Little French Club, to try to resume relations. At Christmas he suddenly popped off to somewhere in Khartoum, at this critical period, and he has not really got down to working with me in my new job. I told him a little about the crisis in Cabinet and he said, 'Ah, I have seen the first paper put in by the Treasury officials, who are criticizing D.E.P. and urging much stronger measures in a new Prices and Incomes Bill. *They're* certainly not relaxing the demand for a new Bill.' I asked if he could get me a copy and he said, 'Oh, yes.' It is to come to me at the end of the week.

Friday, January 17th

The Times has a poll showing a 20 per cent lead for the Tories, with a new popularity rating specially designed so that Ted Heath can be ahead of Harold Wilson, and a splendid letter from Michael Foot about the Marplan popularity index for the Prime Minister.[1] It's a really revolting arrangement to test, in the crudest way, the likeability and popularity of Prime Ministers. Michael's letter points out that the qualities mainly required are courage, integrity and a sense of history, which the poll completely disregards, rating instead the worst qualities.

Barbara has launched her scheme and by doing it on the Friday before people come back to Parliament she has got a tremendous Press. On the whole the coverage is pretty good. Some people say it is weak and indecisive, but everybody thinks it's a first step forward. The conservative papers tend to

[1] On January 22nd *The Times* published a second letter from Mr Foot on what he called the Marplan Mediocrity Index.

say this will prepare the way for adequate Tory legislation later on and more friendly papers that it is a bold and courageous thing to do.[1]

There will be nothing like this stir for my Pensions White Paper. There was that outrageous leak in the *Guardian*,[2] and today David Watt has done a much better-informed piece in the *Financial Times*. He came to see me twice and what could I do. He had collected all the bits and pieces from different places, put them together and got a very accurate picture of the figures, but so concise that fortunately I think we will still have enough that is new to make an impact when the Paper is released. The fact that Barbara's scheme was leaked hasn't done any harm to her coverage when the actual text was published and I don't think premature release will harm mine. There may be a great effort to call it an anti-climax, a dud, a bomb which hasn't gone off because it has been oversold, but that is because my Bill is a solid thing which over a period of time will gain us support because we are carrying out the policy we promised in a competent and efficient way. My reforms – the Rent Act, House of Lords Reform – are not popular because they are too sensible and are unradical ways of dealing with problems by taking them out of politics. That is what the pensions reform is designed to do and why it is so embarrassing that Harold should have been selling it all the time. I do not wish to seem to be competing with Barbara and, as Hugh Cudlipp, John Beavan and Alan Fairclough said when we met for dinner this week, we must have at least a week between Barbara's White Paper and mine. Hugh and Stephen Swingler had no doubt that even if the Chancellor permitted it we should not release it on the 21st, next Tuesday. Barbara's White Paper is the sole topic of conversation. No. 10 is very much in favour of our keeping Tuesday, 21st because they hope we will smother discontent against her White Paper but this is exactly what we want to avoid, so we have plumped for the following Tuesday. Nothing could be more different from her proposals than our pensions scheme.

I spent the whole day chairing a big Conference of the Regional Hospital Board chairmen and officials on the N.H.S. Green Paper. David and I sat up on the platform with some 100 people, five from each of the regions, in a kind of V-shape below us. The seminar went better than anybody expected. In

[1] In 1971 the Conservatives did pass an Industrial Relations Act, which established new legal rights for the individual employee in matters of trade union membership and activity, protection from unfair dismissal, information about his employment and improved terms of notice. A new concept of 'unfair industrial practice' was introduced and a National Industrial Relations Commission established, together with industrial tribunals, to maintain standards by hearing complaints and determining rights and liabilities. The Act also provided for a new system of registration, with legal immunities restricted to registered trade unions, for new methods of settling disputes over trade union recognition to be administered by a Commission on Industrial Relations and for new powers (the 'cooling-off period' and strike ballots) to be exercised in emergency situations by the Secretary of State. The 1971 Conservative Act was repealed in 1974 by the Labour Government's Trade Unions and Labour Relations Act, except for the provisions on unfair dismissal. The National Industrial Relations Court and the Commission on Industrial Relations were abolished.

[2] See above, p. 318.

the first session we discussed the Green Paper that Kenneth Robinson had put out, indicating, as I now know the Department really wanted, that the Health Service should be reorganized into some twenty huge areas run by sixteen oligarchs responsible to London. It was the most astonishing piece of misjudgment of public opinion to think that such a recommendation could go through. Before lunch we discussed whether we should have two-tier or one-tier planning, whether we should have sixteen oligarchs or, alternatively, a Regional Planning Board at the top and the effective management done by much smaller units down below, grouped round district hospitals. From the very start person after person spoke for the two-tier system, which David and I had both told the Department was the only possible solution. After a time I said, 'There have been so many speeches on one side, can I now please have a speech in favour of the one-tier system, in favour of the Green Paper?' There was silence. I said, 'Not one? Can I give you half a minute for meditation and then decide that this is an expression of opinion?' There was a murmur of relief. My civil servants were sitting behind me as I ruled out the Green Paper in one stroke. If that is the view of the Regional Hospital Boards, just imagine what the doctors' Executive Council or the local authorities will say. These R.H.B.s were the only people who could have supported the Robinson plan and they had rejected it. It was amazing that the Ministry should have put it up.

After lunch we dealt with the problem of representation on the Boards and all the speeches were in favour of selection rather than election. We also discussed complaints where they were also incredibly stuffy. The third topic was their relations with the local authorities. They were quite clear that each new Area Board should incorporate all the health services which are now under the local authorities, not only the health centres but the health visitors, the old people's homes, home helps and so on. I had to disillusion them and say this was quite unrealistic. I then talked to them about representation saying, 'Regional Boards were and are remote, hospitals are frightening things anyway, and hospitals run by Regional Boards are even remoter. You must consciously cultivate your relations with the community, particularly if you don't want election.' This was my first real intervention on this question and I am not sure how it succeeded but I certainly put something very positive to them.

Until late in the evening I cleared up the third draft of the Cabinet paper on the doctors' pay award. A further thing which has alarmed me is that I thought there had been a Statement either by Kenneth Robinson or by the Chancellor of the Exchequer that the Kindersley Committee should report direct to the Prime Minister and that its report should not be referred to the Prices and Incomes Board, but this is by no means true. Not only has such a Statement not been made but it has been suggested on at least one occasion that a submission should be made so it is more difficult for me to show a clear breach of faith. It is, however, true that the proposal for a submission was then withdrawn and that George Brown had made a statement saying that such a thing would not be done without consultation with the Commission, so I can plead that it cannot be done without my first consulting the doctors. The P.I.B. are going to have a very, very tough time on this. Why is it so important to me? Because, when I took over as the new Minister of Health and Social Security, I told the doctors that their only advantage was having me in the Cabinet. If on the first test I am unable to defend them it will have a disastrous effect on my relationship with the whole of the Health Service, the most ignominious thing which could happen to me. I must say that for the first time I am reflecting on the possibility that I shan't be in Cabinet for ever. I am heartily sick at the way Barbara's trade union legislation was railroaded through and if she railroads this over me I shall feel very inclined to go to Harold and say, 'I don't want to cause a crisis, I don't want a sudden break, but by Easter I think I should get out into retirement. I am getting too old for this kind of game.' I shall warn him before Cabinet next week and we will see how he responds.

Saturday, January 18th

I had to go to Birmingham for a big Labour Party conference on health and social security. There were 180 delegates, some of whom said they wanted to talk about Barbara's White Paper so I thought I should give them half an hour on this at the end.

I spoke for about forty minutes with the press present and then we had about two hours of discussion. There was tremendous enthusiasm and it was really successful. In the extra half-hour at the end of the conference only two people rose to ask questions. They hadn't had time to read the White Paper and I had to explain briefly what Barbara had done. I said, 'For heaven's sake, don't turn this down overnight. There will be plenty of time for consultation. This is a White Paper full of good things. Let's look at it very carefully and, I beg you, give it the same kind of considered, constructive criticism which you are going to give to our pension Paper.' I got away with it without the faintest difficulty. This was however only a test of party delegates and I think in places like Birmingham or Coventry people will be passionately opposed to her initiatives about unofficial strikes and strike ballots.

Sunday, January 19th

George Hodgkinson confirmed this to me this morning on the telephone.[1] He said, 'All the people I've talked to, my old trade union friends, ask why she keeps lambasting us, why she puts into her Bill these anti-trade union things she doesn't need?' I said, 'But, you see, she needs to because she mustn't be said to shirk the issue. If she is going to protect the trade unions

[1] An old friend and colleague of Crossman. He was the agent of Coventry Borough Labour Party 1923–58 and, from 1928 to 1967 was Councillor and then Alderman of Coventry Council. He was re-elected as an Alderman in 1972.

from re-inclusion within the law she has to have something as a substitute.' George said, 'Yes, but she doesn't have to do *those* things,' and I know of course that she doesn't. At least, she needn't have proposed them. She could have said, 'These are possibilities I may have to consider if we can't find constructive alternatives.' I have really no doubt that Donovan and Castle are both making a great mistake. The right thing would be to put the trade unions under the law, to require them to have the same penalties for breaking solemnly contracted obligations which other people have. I am sure that if the Conservatives win the election they will introduce this and Barbara is making it easier for them by producing her substitute of personal ministerial intervention. I think it's a fairly bad policy, probably unworkable and that it will only breach the wall of trade union privilege and let the Tories in next time. And what is it doing inside the Labour Movement? She has launched her scheme and she sent telegrams to 137 members of the Trade Union group, of whom only 27 turned up at the meeting, so I don't think one can judge much from that.

I am worried, though, about what is happening behind the scenes. The papers Thomas sent down this weekend confirm exactly what he said. The Treasury officials are working on the assumption that there must be an urgent Prices and Incomes Bill next October, to retain our present powers and possibly even add to them. It is out of the secret consultation between Harold, Barbara and Roy on December 12th and their decision to force things through, Roy's failure to see how it affected him, his attempt to recover his position by asking for an early I.R. Bill and his possible failure to do so, from all these added together, that disaster could come. If Harold goes to the country in the autumn it would be a combination of 1931 and 1951, the break-up of Ramsay MacDonald and the running away from responsibility of Attlee.[1] There is no chance whatsoever of our winning this autumn. In the Gallup Poll the Tories are 17 points ahead and in *The Times* Marplan Poll 20 points ahead, an overwhelming Tory majority. Forcing us to the country in the autumn would be suicidal. This is probably the most serious threat to the Government which I have known in a pretty tumultuous four and a half years.

Monday, January 20th

I had an illustrative meeting in the Department on local authority building. We have cut back the capital investment in this side of our work very heavily. Health and Welfare build old people's homes, psychiatric hospitals and so

[1] Ramsay MacDonald, Leader of the Labour Party 1922–31, was Prime Minister and Foreign Secretary 1924, Prime Minister 1929–31 and Prime Minister of the National Government 1931–5. Clement Attlee was Leader of the Labour party 1935–55 and Prime Minister 1945–51. The formation of the National Government in 1931 was held by many to be a betrayal of the Labour party, which had been elected in 1929 with an overall majority of 28, and, similarly, some felt that Attlee should have struggled on with the small Labour majority of 5, elected in 1950, rather than going to the country in 1951.

on and the Department had put forward a perfectly sensible allocation dividing up the total into lump sums for various kinds of activities, health centres and so on. This seemed perfectly all right and when I asked, 'After this, what happens?' they said, 'That is the end of it for you. Ministers now leave the rest to the officials. The actual decisions of what authorities shall do what things are entirely made by the Ministry.' 'Well,' I said, 'it won't be done like that in future.' I recalled that at the Ministry of Housing I had Bob Mellish doing nothing else except allocations of money to individual authorities,[1] while here this highly political job of deciding whether one gave a contract or whether one allowed Manchester or Liverpool their requests was being left entirely to the officials. That was how it was done before we came along.

This evening Anne and I went to see *Così fan tutte* again. We had been to the gala first night, and now we were seeing it from the Royal Box with Claus and Mary Moser and Jean Floud.[2] All the horse-play which had rather marred it at the gala show had been knocked out and the theory that *Così fan tutte* has to be broadened for Covent Garden was shown to be utterly wrong. Played properly, discreetly, for its music, its rhythm, its humour and also for its pathos, played straight it was magnificent and exhilarating and I doubt whether anywhere in the world you could get a better performance.

Tuesday, January 21st

The big news was Harold Wilson's return to television on 'Panorama' last night.[3] This time he had more cautious chairmen and obviously had a good time being the tough, strong Prime Minister.[4] I know it all by heart now. Apparently he pleased himself and the audience thought he was back in form. Certainly it made him much more cheerful and self-confident at S.E.P. this morning. I came to this for the last time as Chairman of the Agricultural Committee, having been made to hand over my duties to George Thomson who had been literally unemployed. I shall miss it because I was a good Chairman of the Committee but clearly it was felt that there was something undesirable in my both doing this and being a departmental Minister. When I asked Burke whether I could stay on the Committee I knew from the back of his head that he was going to say no. Sure enough he did.

An item about the abolition of the Egg Marketing Board took forty-five minutes and then right at the end Roy said, 'Some serious business is coming up. I am worried about this year's Vote on Account.'[5] This is the adding up

[1] See Vol. I, pp. 332 and n., 333, 421.

[2] Sociologist and Fellow of Nuffield College, Oxford, from 1963 to 1972, when she became Principal of Newnham College, Cambridge.

[3] See Vol. II, p. 493.

[4] Robin Day, David Dimbleby and Robin McNeil all interviewed the Prime Minister.

[5] In January the House of Commons is presented with the Civil Vote on Account, a lump sum comprising four-twelfths of the total civil expenditure proposed for the forthcoming financial year beginning in April, roughly representing the needs of the first four months, April to July, and providing some credit on account. The balance is voted in July, by which time, during the twenty-nine days of Supply, the House has completed its criticism of

of all the estimates, which is most misleading as it always shows a great increase. Public expenditure for the coming year has been kept within the 3½ per cent, yet it will show an 8 per cent increase, and Roy is worried stiff about the effect on the pound. He wants to give assurances to the bankers, which is all right for 69/70, but he wants to go ahead, he says, on 70/1, our very last year, and tell them that we won't increase our expenditure by more than 2½ per cent. As this is absolutely brand new, I raised my eyebrows pretty vocally and so did Tony Crosland and Judith. We are obviously going to have a serious problem because Roy is rattled about the pound and about his position and anxious not only about the Vote on Account but also the budget. He wants to tie things tight in a form which seems to me quite ridiculous. This may be a test of strength at S.E.P. and recently Roy has not been very skilful at winning battles.

All day I was worrying at the Department and in the evening the news was about that the admirable, fair and detailed paper which the officials have prepared on doctors' and dentists' pay had been drastically cut by the Chancellor, who had taken out two of our vital passages. I thought, 'My God, this must mean that Roy, Barbara and Harold are together determined to force the reference of the doctors' award to the P.I.B.' I felt really anxious and I had a long discussion first with Ron Matthews, who I think understood why I felt I couldn't stay on as Secretary of State, and then with Tam. Poor Tam took a lot of persuading but gradually he began to see that while Kenneth Robinson, as a Minister outside the Cabinet, could go round saying to the doctors, 'They ordered me to put on prescription charges, it wasn't my fault,' I, as a senior Cabinet Minister, can't behave in this way. I have to take full responsibility. I simply can't do this without destroying all the doctors' confidence in me, and making it absolutely impossible to get any co-operation in the reorganization of the Health Service.

This evening we had in Judith's room a curious first meeting of the new Joint Cabinet/N.E.C. Committee which is to meet monthly to try to sort out policy. Six Cabinet Ministers were there and seven members of the N.E.C. It seems ages ago since I left the N.E.C. and I feel quite remote from it. I sat in an armchair rather ostentatiously while they all sat around the table, and listened. Although George Brown was Chairman and in charge he characteristically came in late and suddenly walked out before the end. The Chancellor hadn't been able to come but Michael Stewart was there. He had been sent six subjects by Harry Nicholas who is very much better, firmer, more efficient and more confident a General Secretary than Len Williams. Michael made little speeches of ten to twelve minutes on the E.E.C., on NATO, on the Commonwealth Conference, classic Michael Stewart demonstrations, perfect sixth-form analyses reeking with virtue and correctness, precision, decency

---

Government policy and administration. In February the main estimates, civil and defence, for the new financial year, are presented to the House and the defence Vote on Account is laid, the balance being voted, likewise, in July.

and utter unreality. Oh, dear, it was depressing. It was pretty clear that the N.E.C. is wildly angry and as upset and bewildered as I am by the course which Harold and Barbara have taken, although they have decided to postpone the discussion of her White Paper for a month.

Wednesday, January 22nd

The P.L.P. had insisted on a second meeting on Lords' reform directly we came back, so here we were at 5.30. Callaghan had said he probably wouldn't be able to come, and I had said that I would only have a watching brief. But I got in there and found myself sitting at the end of the row next to Callaghan, who had Harold beyond him. On the far side of Douglas Houghton were Eddie and Gerald Gardiner, and down on the floor some thirty or forty people. I saw Michael Foot, Denis Coe and Eric Heffer, the usual gang. When I arrived Douglas was saying, 'Come along now, who is going to speak?' and nobody spoke. This fantastic situation went on for about ten minutes, until some middle-of-the-road M.P. made a speech against the scheme and Denis Coe a speech for the scheme. The others sat tight. They wouldn't take part in the debate they themselves had demanded. Harold and I left the meeting at 6.45 and Harold said, 'Well, that's that.' 'We will get a very bad press,' I said, 'because Douglas Houghton will make the worst of it.' 'That's all right,' said Harold, 'we shall have no difficulty with them. They don't really care either way.' It's also true that they are all waiting for next week's P.L.P. meeting, when we shall be discussing Barbara's White Paper, which is the one the Left really wants to fight. They didn't want to speak this time and risk not being called next week. I also feel that Lords' reform is different. Though they don't like it it is in the party manifesto. They haven't got a passionate objection to it, unlike their attitude to the trade union legislation.

After this came my critical meeting with Harold, the first time I had really had a talk with him since the recess. I had put in a request to see him after the Committee on the Kindersley Report but last week he found he had no time. I had put in an urgent request for this week and he didn't suggest Monday or yesterday but he did offer me tonight at 6.45. I was well aware that it was a sign of displeasure or aloofness that we should have spent a whole week since Parliament came back without having a chat. We went down to his room from the Party meeting, earlier than I might have expected, and had forty-five minutes together. I started straightaway on the subject of the doctors. I had spent a great deal of time during the last two days making sure at official level that everybody knew I was making this a test issue. I knew the Cabinet Office, No. 10, D.E.P. and the Treasury knew that this was a test of strength. I had ensured that our case was being mustered and the brief I finally got was like a Cabinet dossier. Harold said he had heard there was something the matter though he himself, he said, hadn't read the papers for a very long time. He tried to indicate that he really knew nothing about this issue and that he was a little bewildered. Who was it who was being difficult? I explained that it was Barbara. I could quite see, I said in passing, that she was angry with me, but I did realize how difficult this case was for her. I explained how the Kindersley review body had based its reward on comparability, which Aubrey Jones had disavowed in the case of the university teachers. We would have to publish Kindersley, which was already difficult but didn't invalidate my point that the doctors' award was within the pay ceiling and within the present practice of comparability with regard to civil servants' and to doctors' pay. For half an hour Harold gradually let himself be filled in. I am pretty sure he knew all about it already because he was pretty well-informed. I dropped it to him that I had just left George Godber, who had made it clear that if this was rejected or referred to the Prices and Incomes Board he would have to resign and the fact that perhaps one of the most prominent civil servants would go duly registered with the P.M. After half an hour it became clear that, unless Harold was deceiving me, he would back me. I mentioned Roy Jenkins's compromise that we should accept the award with a three-month postponement, and pointed out that this meant a 25 per cent cut. Harold said, 'That makes no sense whatsoever. If you accept the principle of comparability applied in the Report, how can you deny them the full award, provided it's within the ceiling? That's a silly suggestion.' 'Well,' I said, 'it's the Chancellor's suggestion.' He left it at that. He didn't seem to be all that friendly to Roy but he was loyal to Barbara and also somewhat anti-Aubrey Jones. I then brought out my trump card. I had discovered that Aubrey Jones had sent a letter not to the Prime Minister or to me, the two people he might have written to, but to the Chancellor, telling him that if he didn't disallow the Kindersley award he would be striking a blow at the whole prices and incomes policy and destroying all the work the Board was doing to tumble down the general theory of comparability. I said, 'It really is megalomania for him to think he can circulate letters ordering the Chancellor to do this,' and I threw in the thought that probably Tommy Balogh, who had done the teachers' award, was behind him. I am sorry to say that somehow the Prime Minister quite cosily took my complaining about Thomas and we had a good long chivver about how impossible he was. Right at the end Harold said, 'What about the *Financial Times*?' With his message agreeing to see me Harold had sent a short memo on David Watt's front-page article on the pension scheme and had asked me for any comments. I said I didn't think that it was very important. 'David Watt has paid attention to the published stuff and done his homework. There has been no specific leak and he certainly hasn't had access to the White Paper.' Harold asked, 'What about the passage in which he said that publication had been postponed for a week because of the diceyness of the international situation? If that comes out it's as good as publishing.' The honest fact was that I hadn't noticed this and I thought, heavens, has Roy been complaining to the Prime Minister? But, as I discovered when I asked Roy about it, he hadn't noticed it either till the

Prime Minister mentioned it and this had been the P.M.'s private little anxiety. I think he had never regarded the doctors as important at all and it was the article that he had wanted to talk about.

I immediately went back to 70 Whitehall to see a fully fledged delegation of eight members of the Department to discuss the Kindersley brief. We had good news because Alan Marre said that through his D.E.P. contacts he knew that the officials there would be providing a brief advising Barbara that the award was undoubtedly in conformity with the incomes policy and strongly recommending her not even to press for a Statement by the Prime Minister that the whole structure of comparability had been discussed. We might decide to reconsider it but nothing should be put in the Statement. This was amazing. 'Well,' I said, 'that's very good news.' 'Yes,' said Marre. 'Whitehall thinks that a great effort is being made to stop the attack on the doctors.' I have no doubt of the reason for this. The senior civil servants have a similar review body under Edwin Plowden and an attack on the doctors' review body and on comparability would be an attack on them. The Civil Service has rallied. I went to bed a great deal more relieved.

Thursday, January 23rd

I woke up at 6.0 and sweated through the Defence White Paper.[1] There is always one thing which Denis writes for himself and in this case it was a very good passage on the impact of the Czechoslovakian invasion on Russian rearmament and the proper reaction of NATO. It was all extremely well-argued, a powerful White Paper, and at 9.30 we got down to it at O.P.D. One or two other people had noted this passage which the Prime Minister immediately said was far too long and needed revising. He didn't challenge its correctness; he just said it was too emphatic and that the Parliamentary Party would have an instinctive feeling that we were sticking our necks out, and would resent it. Roy and I defended Denis against the Prime Minister but the passage was watered down and emasculated in the hour and a half before Cabinet.

All through Cabinet I was waiting for my item. We started with a piece of parliamentary business and then came the doctors and teachers. Roy had seated himself beside me and said, 'I daresay you'll be able to get your doctors through but we had better do them separately from the teachers. I can let you have your way on the doctors but I must have mine on the teachers. You understand that? I can't let both awards go through.' I sort of nodded and said I understood. The Prime Minister had arranged business so we would have my speech first, then Ted Short's, and after we two had spoken we would take the issues separately. I could see that Harold and Roy were making quite sure that the vote on the doctors would take place before that on the teachers and, having got the first award safely through, Harold would let Roy try to persuade Cabinet to vote against the second.

[1] Cmnd 3927, published on February 20th. See below, pp. 393 and 397.

Roy spoke briefly in a very negative and detached sort of way, by no means especially against the doctors. Then I was allowed to speak. I marshalled the case in a fairly quiet way, asking for no special terms but simply giving the case that the doctors' award was in conformity with the incomes policy as at present practised. I added that the doctors weren't even like the university teachers, who had a 10 per cent increase last year, that there was no sign of a shortage there whereas doctors were emigrating, and that to refuse this award would have a disastrous effect.

I then read aloud the passage from Aubrey Jones's letter, saying that it was quite impossible. I didn't of course mention George Godber or give any threat but I said my position would be intolerable and any sort of reconstruction of the Health Service would be out of the question. I left it at that and then Ted Short made a powerful and most ingenious case, saying that he wanted to accept the $6\frac{1}{4}$ per cent which the Burnham Committee was offering the teachers, and to add 1 per cent for restructuring. If the civil servants were allowed to have regular increases and add on a bit for restructuring, the teachers should as well. The restructuring he was concerned with was the removal of the discrimination between primary and secondary education. As somebody pointed out, how did they know it would cost 1 per cent? Surely this was just a trick for giving more than the award and getting agreement with the teachers? But before we decided on the teachers my case was taken and Barbara said that late last night she had received a brief from her officials advising her to accept the Kindersley award and saying that it would be unwise to announce that the Government was reconstructing the whole award system and challenging the issue of comparability. She was reading aloud a brief the same as mine. It is quite interesting to see how far Whitehall can go to influence a decision when it has really got something at stake. She caved in completely and gave me my case and the whole Cabinet felt completely let down. They had come expecting a real battle between us, they had read the papers, but suddenly Barbara was saying, 'No, I have surrendered the whole thing.' Callaghan threw up his hands and everybody round the table asked what on earth all the row had been about and why it had come to Cabinet at all. The answer is that it came to Cabinet because she had forced the issue of prices and incomes but this time she had thought better of it. After that there wasn't any fight left. Tony Crosland made a feeble effort, and a number of people objected to the doctors getting the award but they were completely nonplussed by her surrender.

Then we turned to the teachers and it was quite clear that Cabinet were not going to give the doctors their award and leave the teachers out. Roy spoke very strongly, saying that there could be no question of conceding this and that it was very dubious that the 1 per cent extra for restructuring was anything more than a trick. But as the P.M. began to go round the room it became clear that hardly anybody was on Roy's side. The Prime Minister took the first ten or twelve voices and I sat quiet because I was in a hell of a jam. Roy had told me he would back the doctors on the clear understanding that he was going to get the teachers. What was I to say? The Prime Minister suddenly turned and asked me. 'Frankly,' I said, 'I am too embarrassed and in too prejudiced a position to give judgment.' There was a general smile and finally I did say that if I wasn't in this prejudiced position I would have to say one thing to the Cabinet, that in strict terms all Ted Short was asking was for the teachers to be treated like the doctors and that in the case of the doctors, as I had confirmed before Cabinet, we don't reckon restructuring costs as part of the claim. That really is one of the clinching points. As Harold Wilson said, it was clear that we were prepared to give the teachers their case.

I have never seen Roy more upset. He had lost phenomenally and had been outwitted, but he had lost, too, because he has no psychological understanding. I suppose, just as he had backed me and found himself put in a fix, so he had backed Barbara and found himself put in a fix about prices and incomes. He clapped the books together and walked out of the room in great dismay. It was a desperate moment; a real blow for him, two major awards in which the professional classes were getting what the public would regard as far too much and which would stimulate the workers to put in even higher claims. For Roy the whole issue is the bank rate, the bankers, the Vote on Account, the lead-up to the budget and he is terribly worried and was terribly upset at what happened this morning. For me it has been the most exciting fight for a long time, the most crucial issue I have ever had. As Minister of Housing I sometimes had issues on which I didn't expect to win and then did win but I have never had an attack made on my Department which it was vital for me to survive. I went out pretty relieved and rushed back to 70 Whitehall to let Alan Marre and George Godber know what had happened.

Back in my room after lunch Roy rang up to say, 'There is a Prices and Incomes Committee on the postal workers this afternoon.[1] You will be all right on this?' I said yes and then turned to read the papers for it. This is the strike of the post-office cable operators, who have refused arbitration and are insisting on 5 per cent without productivity agreements, a violation of the policy. John Stonehouse is asking for our authority to make an offer largely conceding their demands. There he was at the meeting. Since, of course, he hadn't been at Cabinet this morning, he didn't know that concessions have been made to the doctors and teachers. Everybody round the table said that to concede to the postal workers was impossible and certainly I thought we couldn't deny this to Roy. We all played up. Stonehouse had, I think, ten people round the table telling him, 'No, you can't do this. You have got to tell them that if they threaten to continue the strike we must fight them. The Government can't afford to relax on it.'

[1] From January 20th to February 1st, 3,900 overseas telegraphists withdrew their services over a pay and productivity dispute. On January 31st 72,000 other staff held a ban on overtime and a one-day token stoppage in support.

He is a strange fellow, Stonehouse, a tall, dark rather sleek young man, with a great long back. I often see him from behind as I sit there on the front bench and his coat and the whole proportion of his back to his legs is long. He has this rather insolent, handsome face, and when he is nervous an incipient stutter. I have always had the profoundest suspicion of his moral reliability. I met him first in Kampala in 1954 when I was reporting on the Mau Mau. He was Secretary of the Uganda Producers' Co-operative, which closed down in a great stink and he had to fly the land. I wouldn't have taken that seriously at all if it hadn't been for the fact that when his name next turned up in 1957 as the man who had slipped in as the Member for Wednesbury George Wigg had some stories about him. He certainly used pretty rough tactics in 1962 when he got himself made President of the London Co-operative, which is a Society seething with politics. He is an experienced tough politician, very unreliable in his personal veracity. When Harold gave me the job of investigating that great scandal at the Ministry of Technology,[1] I found that there was no doubt that John Stonehouse had behaved in the most extraordinary way and that his relationships with the Secretary were very bad.[2] I had written a report for Harold which was very critical of the Permanent Secretary and mildly critical of John Stonehouse but I know what a violent, fierce, implacable, unscrupulous young man he is. I have watched him in every job – for some reason he always gets advancement – and I think he is a kind of dangerous crook, overwhelmingly ambitious but above all untrustworthy. Well, this time he had to face the Prices and Incomes Committee and he lost. He was finally slapped down from the chair by Roy Jenkins, who simply got a majority of the Committee, all of whom knew the background, to disregard Stonehouse's warnings and say that he must postpone any settlement.

Friday, January 24th

A good deal of my day was spent tidying up matters of timing. The Department wanted the doctors' award to be announced in a Written Answer on Monday or Tuesday next week but Barbara had sent me an urgent message saying that she wanted it delayed until after the announcement about the agricultural workers,[3] and after she has got rid of the cable operators. I could quite see her point. If the teachers' and doctors' awards are published now there really will be trouble and I shall have to be as helpful to her as I can. I shall ring her up tomorrow morning and see the Chancellor about the timing.

[1] See Vol. II.

[2] Sir Ronald Melville (K.C.B. 1964). He was Second Permanent Under-Secretary of State at the Ministry of Defence 1963–6, Permanent Secretary at the Ministry of Aviation 1966–7, Secretary (Aviation) at MinTech. 1967–70, Permanent Secretary at the Ministry of Aviation Supply 1970–1 and Permanent Secretary attached to the Civil Service Department 1971–2. Since 1972 he has been Director of the Electronic Components Board.

[3] Following the publication on January 30th of a report by the Prices and Incomes Board, on February 2nd an increase of 17*s.* in the weekly minimum wage rate of £11 11*s.* was awarded to farm workers.

Now I have got the doctors' award and they have been privately informed we can certainly wait for a fortnight before the announcement is made.

Sunday, January 26th

Although I had a lot of work this weekend with Questions on Monday, the White Paper coming on Tuesday, and six boxes as a result, I found time for a good walk over the farm. This afternoon Patrick and I got back to work on the island, where there has been an awful lot of flooding and my poor bulbs aren't doing too well. I began some nettle-clearing, and persuaded Patrick to start working with a pick and an axe at the roots of the trees. It was a great thing, this chopping and splitting of wood, and we have had a splendid weekend. It's also been an exciting week, when I have personally established myself, and I am now looking forward to seeing what will happen with the White Paper. We've only had a quiet build-up and although I gave a story to Jimmy Margach there has been nothing in the Sunday papers. They are full of Heath's tremendous pronouncement on race.[1] He went to Walsall yesterday, made a great declaration in favour of a complete quota system for immigration. In a nutshell, the Commonwealth citizen will be treated exactly like a German or a Frenchman and of course if we are going into Europe that is natural enough and perfectly practicable. In my view it is quite a sensible policy, one which I have indeed suggested on two recent occasions at Jim Callaghan's Cabinet Committee on Immigration. I expressed the hope that we shouldn't get ourselves jockeyed by the Tories into putting this thing forward and now the Tories have done so themselves I think it will be very, very popular indeed. This insistence on doing something about immigration and doing it quickly is a very potent political force which will realign the Tory Party and stop the rift. I think the Tories' fear of a split Party is much greater than their desire to get more votes to defeat us. I think this is a speech of the greatest importance, not as the Tories' attempt to endear themselves to the electorate but as a defensive effort to create a basis for Heath's remaining Leader of the Party.

One or two papers have inevitably got a story about Barbara and me. Alan Watkins, with whom I am pretty friendly, and whom I talked to about it, must have talked to her or someone near her as well, because in the *New Statesman* he has rather a malicious story about how her White Paper had

[1] The Leader of the Opposition called for a Bill, to be passed before August, that would allay 'the fears and anxieties' of all classes, by strictly controlling the entry of all Commonwealth citizens, who would be put on a par with aliens. Entry should be permitted only for a limited period and for a specific place and job, there should be annual review of permits and eligibility for permanent residence should be admitted only after four years' residence and for British citizenship after five. New entrants would no longer be permitted to bring in dependants. Mr Heath stressed that immigrants already in Britain must be treated without discrimination and, obviously alluding to Mr Powell's proposals for repatriation, said that he would not countenance any harassment, still less any compulsion, to force immigrants to leave, but he advocated generous government financial assistance to encourage immigrants to leave Britain voluntarily.

scooped mine and how I was personally sore and bitter about it. How much truth is there in that? Well, certainly I was angry when I found out that Harold had fixed the whole thing and that my announcement was to be jammed in this way and postponed for a week. All that did seem to me infuriating although, to be fair, Roy Jenkins's attitude made the postponement inevitable anyway. But I don't really think that was much of the motivation for the conflict Barbara and I had in Cabinet and I think both of us have realized the importance of getting together and removing any justification for such stories, which can do both of us quite a lot of harm.

I am getting excited about the coming week. My own feeling is that the fact that my pensions plan is a workable scheme will impress people. I shall get a blast from the Left, but not a very effective blast, because we've got a complete answer to it. The test, though, will not be what is said in the first twenty-four hours but how it revives the Party and how the public take it. It's the next six weeks and the organization of our campaign which will decide the scheme's success or failure.

Monday, January 27th

I have decided to do the Diary in rather a different way, keeping to the main stories of the week and just rounding up the other bits and pieces. This will give a less precise account of the balance of my daily work but I am very much aware that the Diary has sometimes been dull. In future I shall not account for every hour of the day but deal mainly with the chief features of the week.

There is no doubt about it that the main feature of this week, apart from my own pension scheme, has been what has gone on behind the scenes of the postal workers' strike. After he was slapped down at Thursday's Prices and Incomes Committee John Stonehouse talked to the newspapers, saying that he had wanted to make the concession but had been overruled. Over the weekend, Friday, Saturday and Sunday, the press built up sympathetic stories describing Stonehouse as the innocent Postmaster being forced by a Cabinet Committee, headed by Roy and Barbara, to be tough to the postmen. I am sure that, formally, Stonehouse took the line that he was in agreement with Cabinet but he gave out the story in such a way as to make it perfectly clear that he was acting under orders and against his own sentiments. With his connivance, the postal workers, headed by Mr Jackson,[1] built up this picture in the press. It did not need any active briefing from Stonehouse himself because it is that Department's traditional tactic to isolate the Postmaster from the rest of Cabinet.

When we got to our Parliamentary Committee Harold insisted that before we did anything else we must deal with the Post Office. He summoned Stonehouse and gave him the nearest thing to a rebuke that anybody could have. Harold said it was intolerable that these leaks should have occurred and that

[1] Thomas Jackson, General Secretary of the Union of Post Office Workers since 1967.

Ministers should be loyal to Cabinet decisions. Roy and Barbara also lectured Stonehouse and dressed him down but he is a tough chap and he held on. He had to put himself against the full ferocity of Roy and Barbara, both uneasily aware that they were getting into a terrible fix. By now it was already clear that the strike, which some people, including Eddie Shackleton, had written off as unlikely to spread to all postal workers, seemed as if it was going to be much more effective and the union much more powerful in calling people out than anybody expected. Things looked bleak. It now involved the honour and prestige of the P. and I. Committee and of Barbara and Roy, and Eddie was to be told that as Minister in charge of the Civil Service he must take an active part in all future negotiations. Roy Hattersley would also be there and the Postmaster would bloody well be made to behave himself. Stonehouse was extremely tough, saying this was utterly impracticable and futile and that he knew he was right. It was a rough, unpleasant meeting.

We were first in Questions this afternoon and from 2.30 to 3.30 we had to mop up 100 questions, dealing with them in our usual competent team style without any difficulty. I also got a good reception for the announcement of the inquiry into Scientology under John Foster's chairmanship. I spent most of the day briefing individual journalists, Geoffrey Smith of *The Times*, David Watt of the *Financial Times*, and Stephen and I had an ordinary Lobby Conference for the others. I took it for granted that they had read the releases and as they are people who always assume they know everything I didn't make much of a speech to them but just answered questions for an hour and a half. I got quite a decent, friendly reception, like the old days when I was Leader of the House.

After a whole busy day of this I went back to my room where Marre was waiting. I had found in my box this morning a draft statement of Harold's Written Answer on the Kindersley award. Marre had written in it that we had accepted the award because it was within the ceiling and in accord with the prices and incomes policy.

I also found another note recommending that there should be no statement and not even an announcement that a statement might be coming that we were considering comparability, because this might come to nothing. I realized that the Civil Service were extracting their last ounce of victory over Barbara. She was not even to get the announcement that the Government would grapple with this problem of trying to relate public service pay and doctors' pay to other norms like productivity. I was angry but I knew I could do nothing except perhaps deal with one point. I minuted back that we would not say that it was in accord with prices and incomes policy, only that it was within the $3\frac{1}{2}$ per cent ceiling, because if we said it was in accord with the policy we were blatantly accepting Kindersley on doctors with comparability, and Aubrey Jones on university teachers without comparability, which was absurd. Here was Marre who had turned all this down. It was impossible, he said. If we didn't put it in that this was in accord with incomes policy where would we be? I was tired and I blew my top, saying, 'You civil servants, I have never met anything like it. Talk about ministerial responsibility. You are determined to get your way whatever happens because you are looking after your own interests. All right. But I am a Minister; how do you think we are going to get on?' I talked and I talked. I was violent, I got all steamed up. Marre looked more and more injured and slipped away.

I went off to the Athenaeum for a dinner party with the journalists. I had Nigel Lawson and Norman Macrae sitting at my end of the table,[1] and Alastair Hetherington, Nicholas Davenport and David Watt at the other with Clifford Jarrett. I think it was useful but we shall see when their pieces appear at the end of the week. Meanwhile a half-day debate on the Post Office was going on in the House.[2] The Tories were working it up and I went in to hear John Stonehouse at the end. He stood loyally by the Government but in a most skilful way, letting it be seen that he thought the whole thing was a disaster and that he was a hero being forced to do what was wrong-headed.

Tuesday, January 28th

We had a most interesting discussion at S.E.P. When people couldn't get wage rates up they started to work longer hours or to do additional jobs and real earnings have been rising faster than ever. Productivity has been rising and exports have been doing well but unemployment has not gone down as fast as it should and Roy is desperately anxious that we may be in another inflationary spiral. If real earnings and consumption rise at the same time we are heading for inflation but to hold back consumption we need increased taxes and that means a more penal budget than ever. Not a pleasant prospect —and that is the problem.

In over two hours of discussion the prevailing thought was the future of the prices and incomes policy. As we all know, some months, even a few weeks, ago Roy was determined to get a new Prices and Incomes Bill next autumn, with legislation reaffirming the Government's powers. But what difference does our having these powers actually make? Is it worth having Roy, Barbara and Harold endlessly intervening, holding this one back, stopping that one, making a mess of things with the Post Office, saying no to the agricultural workers and then seeing the policy give way? Is it worth the Government's constantly taking responsibility for the wage rates and then seeing them run away? It certainly makes an appalling difference to our relations not only with the general public but, above all, with the trade unions and our own party. In terms of the economy isn't it really a better gamble to

[1] Nigel Lawson was City Editor of the *Sunday Telegraph* 1961–3. Special Assistant to the Prime Minister 1963–4, he was a columnist on the *Financial Times* 1965, Editor of the *Spectator* 1966–70 and Special Political Adviser at Conservative Party Headquarters 1973–4 and has been Conservative M.P. for Blaby since February 1974. Norman Macrae has been Deputy Editor of *The Economist* since 1965.

[2] The motion regretting the deteriorating services provided by the Post Office was defeated by 191 votes to 155.

get out of this ghastly responsibility for wages and be content to take powers to stop a strike occasionally? Roy must be asking himself whether he shouldn't scrap Prices and Incomes altogether and only have the Industrial Relations Bill, which is of course what Barbara and Harold want. Well, I think to leave one lot of powers off and to take another on is ludicrous because there are all the same objections to Barbara intervening in an unofficial strike as to her intervening in a wage claim. It's this occasional, arbitrary poking our noses in, taking powers we don't intend to use much and using them spasmodically and erratically which is the curse of this Government.

Here I am in complete agreement with Callaghan, who took the lead in this morning's discussion. We were all very, very gentle about this but it was interesting to see how feeling had moved. Roy, who sat beside me, said, 'That was a really good discussion. I take a lot from it; it's a valuable thing to happen to me,' and he was clearly thinking hard. As you can see, I have begun to be interested in Prices and Incomes in a practical way. Dealing with the doctors has made me think about it in general, and to see prices and incomes and trade union legislation as our central problems, on the solution of which our fortunes will largely depend at the next election.

From S.E.P. I went on to my own room at 70 Whitehall to see the financial correspondents, who had come in specially for a drink. I had long talks to the *Sunday Times* and *Financial Times* men and I shall be interested to see if this has any effect. After a rapid lunch I went on to the Royal Commonwealth Society to do two television programmes, news items for I.T.N. and the B.B.C., and then I had my press conference. The White Paper was published at 3 o'clock and my conference was at 4.30.[1] I made a big speech to 180 people, followed by questions. Half the audience were from the Press and half from all the social service and welfare organizations in England – a good idea of Peter Brown's. I am convinced that the more the public understand the scheme the more impressed they will be, and it will pay me to have the greatest elucidation of it.

I then rushed round to Kingsway for a television feature programme on Thames Television, the 'Éamonn Andrews Show'.[2] I found myself sitting with a very smooth and totally ignorant Chairman and on my right on a sofa an

[1] The White Paper, *National Superannuation and Social Insurance, Proposals for Earnings-Related Social Security* (Cmnd 3883), proposed that contributions and pensions should be related to income and should be sufficient to live on without other means; that there should be regular reviews to take account of price rises and changes in the national standard of living; and that women should be brought fully into the scheme on the same terms as men. The scheme would start in 1972 and would be based on a twenty-year period of contributions so that its full benefits would not appear until 1992. The employee's contribution would be 6¾ per cent of his earnings up to £33 per week, and the employer's 6¾ per cent of the total pay-roll. The low-paid would contribute less to the new scheme than to the existing flat-rate scheme and their pensions would be higher. Those who already subscribed to private superannuation schemes would have a limited right to contract out.

[2] Television compère, broadcaster and writer. He joined the B.B.C. in 1950 and was Chairman of the Radio Eireann Statutory Authority 1960–6. In 1964 he joined A.B.C. Television, moving to Thames Television in 1968.

incredibly stupid Tory called Brandon Rhys Williams,[1] with his own made-up ideas. I had allowed him to come on if he would only ask questions but I knew he would break the pledge and he lectured us all, me and three so-called members of the general public. It was my first test and I managed to keep my temper reasonably well. Meanwhile Stephen Swingler had gone to Edinburgh for a press and a television conference, and Eirene White to Cardiff.

Back to the House for dinner with Jack Mendelson,[2] who was very upset because at 3.30 Iain Macleod had made a personal attack on me for not giving a Statement to the House. This had been quite an issue. The obvious thing to do was to go the House at 3.30 and say that the White Paper was published today and submit myself to half an hour of questioning. However I knew that either we would have had nothing except points about the leaks, which have been quite numerous, or we would have had a lot of totally illiterate questions because the House would not have had time to read the White Paper. John Mackintosh, who was dining with us, was on my side. He agreed in a quiet way that we do not reduce the standing of the House by discussing a White Paper on television before going to the House. The standing of the House is not maintained by publishing an enormously complicated White Paper at 3.30 and answering questions at 3.31 from people who have never seen it. Nevertheless something good did come out of this because I realized I must be careful. If I was doing television presentation I must be merely a Minister explaining the scheme, not arguing it. I must not anticipate the Commons by debating with politicians. The Tory front bench had clearly been careful. Balneil had refused to come on '24 Hours' with me this evening and wanted to reserve his comments. (Mr Brandon Rhys Williams didn't matter. He could just be treated as the equivalent of a journalist.) I must merely answer questions as factually as possible and that is what I tried to do on '24 Hours'. The B.B.C. had given me the whole of the programme with four people, Mrs Megan du Boisson of the Disablement Income Group, Mr Ralph Harris,[3] Mr Bayley and Peter Townsend. It was carefully organized. Michael Barratt was in the chair,[4] and I was perched up on one side of the room, high up on a platform, about as severe and uncomfortable and

[1] Sir Brandon Rhys Williams (he succeeded to his father's baronetcy in 1955) was Conservative M.P. for Kensington South March 1968–74 and since 1974 has been M.P. for Kensington. He had written on *The New Social Contract* (London: Conservative Political Centre, 1967).

[2] Labour M.P. for Penistone since June 1959.

[3] Since 1957 Ralph Harris has been General Director of the privately sponsored Institute of Economic Affairs. Gordon Bayley, Actuary for the National Provident Institution. In 1971, he became Chairman of the National Pensions Joint Committee of the Life Offices Association and the Associated Scottish Life Offices. He later became a member of the Occupational Pensions Board, serving until 1974. Professor Peter Townsend has been Professor of Sociology at the University of Essex since 1963 and Pro-Vice-Chancellor since 1975. He has been Chairman of the Child Poverty Action Group since 1969, of the Social Policy Committee of the Fabian Society since 1970 and of Disability Allowance since 1974.

[4] A reporter on the B.B.C.'s 'Panorama' programme in 1963, he was presenter of '24 Hours' 1965–9, and has presented 'Nationwide' since 1969.

remote as possible, with these people at four desks high up on the other side. This gave me an enormous advantage. We didn't have a shouting match or an argument and I was able to answer their questions politely and to give the image of a reasonable man who was prepared to listen to their points. The programme was an immense success and I motored home thoroughly content.

Wednesday, January 29th

I shot off to Liverpool. It had been thought at one time that I ought to stay behind but, as I said to Peter Brown, that would be absolutely crazy. We couldn't possibly get any more publicity. If we had all that television we simply couldn't get any more and anyway the Docks White Paper was due to come out at 3.30 today.[1] It was clear as we surveyed the press over breakfast on the train on the way up and also from the reaction of all the people I met at Liverpool that the thing had really got across and our White Paper was successfully launched. It was clear too that there was going to be a tremendous Tory effort to call it a fiasco, as one saw in the *Daily Express*, the *Daily Sketch* and *Daily Mail*, and even to some extent in *The Times*. But as I found at the Blood Transfusion Centre at Liverpool (which I was opening) and at lunch afterwards with the Regional Hospital Board, people really had begun to understand it and as I came back in the train I felt that it was a reasonably successful show.

I arrived back in London at 7.15 and as I had nothing else to do Anne and I got dropped at Soho and took a little walk there before we went to the Jardin des Gourmets for a superb dinner at £2 5*s*. each. It wasn't so much more expensive than anywhere else, dining is expensive now. We strolled home with a delicious sense of relaxation.

Thursday, January 30th

O.P.D. Greece came up and a recommendation that we should go ahead with arms sales, apart from small arms, which might be used to suppress domestic insurrection. There was an awkward silence, really, I suppose, because nobody wanted a row.

Despite the Greek Government's proclaimed intention to restore democratic processes, power continued to lie in the hands of the junta of army officers, exercised through the civilian Government headed by George Papadopoulos, and some 1,600 political prisoners remained in detention. In 1968 Norway, Sweden, Denmark and the Netherlands had laid allegations of torture against the Greek regime and in January 1968 the Assembly of the Council of Europe had voted to expel Greece if Parliamentary democracy was not restored by the

[1] The White Paper proposed the establishment of a National Port Authority to take over all ports and harbours handling over 5 million tons a year in 1967, whether owned privately, by local authorities or already nationalized (as in the case of docks formerly owned by railway companies).

spring of 1969. The allegations were heard before the Commission on Human Rights in December and in 1969 hearings were continued in Greece.

Tony Crosland, who had been so anxious about the arms sales as retarding our effort to overthrow the dictatorship,[1] said nothing, because trade is now what matters to him. Roy has always been clear that he wanted the trade, and the balance of payments is what matters to him. Here was the Prime Minister, wriggling to try to make the issues compatible, and here was Michael Stewart, that virtuous little prig, saying there was no incompatibility in declaring that our first interest was to promote the rapid restoration of democracy in Greece and that we must pin up NATO in the Eastern Mediterranean by strengthening the Greek army, navy and air force against the Russians. The other complication is that all this is now being discussed at the Commission of Human Rights in Strasbourg. It was a tortuous meeting and I came out with another of my explosions, which Cabinet really expect from me, saying, 'Now, look, don't we get into the greatest difficulties by pretending it is one of our major aims to restore democracy in Greece? Shouldn't we say that our major aim is to strengthen NATO in the Eastern Mediterranean, our second aim to sell goods abroad for our balance of trade, including arms, our third to look after British nationals and our fourth, as far as possible, to help Greek democracy to be restored, and that they come in this order, with the last the one we can do least about? If we get that clear in Cabinet we can be as hypocritical outside as we like. Our hypocrisy is another name for diplomacy, but why do we need to deceive ourselves in Cabinet?' It was fascinating. Most of the people around me agreed, Roy, of course, and George Thomson. I could see Tony Crosland and Fred Peart nodding their heads but opposite me Michael Stewart and Harold sat wriggling with anger and discomfort because they had managed to contrive this combination of high-minded principle and arms sales. They don't feel the contradiction. They are smug people who combine, as Gladstone did I dare say, high moral principle with highly expedient practice. That is their strength as statesmen and also, if I may say so, their weakness because an increasing number of people find it unbearable. I had to go out to prepare my item on pensions for Cabinet while the Parliamentary committee was on but I came back for Cabinet.

We had another long discussion with our friend John Stonehouse present. By now it was clear that Cabinet was careering downhill into a disastrous situation where all postal services would be utterly disrupted. There had been a one-day strike which showed the tremendous willingness of the ordinary postal workers to come out for the overseas operators. True, only half the telephone ladies had been on strike but, still, the thing was gathering force and we had to get out with the minimum loss of face. It was a very beastly Cabinet. First we had the report of last night's Prices and Incomes Committee, which Stephen Swingler had attended for me while I was in Liverpool. At this

[1] See above, pp. 131, 132.

meeting, we were told, it had suddenly been revealed that the earnings of the overseas operators, the workers concerned, would be substantially reduced as a result of the reintroduction of the mechanized process which was at the centre of the dispute. John Stonehouse now fiercely said that the Ministers had known this all along, the officials knew it and anybody competent knew it. Certainly Barbara hadn't, Roy hadn't and Eddie hadn't, but then they didn't really know anything about the background to the strike, and the fact that they didn't know this relevant point and that Stonehouse hadn't mentioned it to them did not seem to me impossible. Here, however, was a way of escaping from the difficulty. We could say that since Stonehouse did not give us the relevant information, now we have discovered it we can negotiate with the union and treat them more gently. Once again Stonehouse fought back. He wouldn't concede an inch from his stand that he had been right on this matter and that the others were wrong and that it was their interference that had stopped him doing what he wanted. I was observing him. He wasn't even sitting at the table but behind at the window yet from that disadvantageous spot he fought and fought and fought. If there was to be a concession now he would insist that the Postmaster-General should do the job. Roy was caught out. Despite all his fine words and postures, as usual he knew nothing about it, although he had been Chairman of the Prices and Incomes Committee. Barbara was very badly briefed, because she had simply sent Roy Hattersley instead, and Eddie, the great, competent, efficient Minister, came out pretty badly because, though he had taken charge in one sense, he and his Ministry didn't really seem to have briefed themselves very well on the whole affair. Cabinet gave us the power to seek a formula for negotiation to put before the Prices and Incomes Committee on Friday and this is to be agreed by Eddie, Barbara, Roy and Stonehouse.

We also had an interesting discussion on specialist committees, something that had been mentioned, in my absence, at the Parliamentary Committee. The Prime Minister reported that we would be announcing the end of the experiment on specialist committees and leaving it to the next Parliament to decide whether to keep them permanently. This took my breath away. The end of the experiment, as though we had written it off as a failure. In fact, I think Harold has. He started this Parliament keen on the whole idea of parliamentary reform and specialist committees but now they are getting going and standing up to the executive he has had nothing but complaints from Whitehall about the extra work it has caused and he has surrendered to the insistence that we should cut them back. Tony Crosland, Tony Wedgwood Benn and I are old supporters and we were able to persuade Cabinet to decide that this would all go to a small Committee which will then report back. There must be no question of announcing the end of the experiment until the Committee has had time to look at it.

Right at the end of Cabinet the P.M. suddenly said, 'The Chancellor has something to announce because it needs a change of decision.' Roy said, 'We have come to the conclusion that after the Written Answer on the Kindersley award there shouldn't be a Statement announcing that we are going to look at comparability because we might not get any result and such an announcement would create anxiety among the Civil Service.' Cabinet sort of nodded its head and that was that. Roy and Barbara had surrendered to Harold and victory had been given to the Civil Service.

In the House yesterday Dick Marsh made his Statement on the docks and this episode answered the back benchers and Jack Mendelson who had been so angry with me for not allowing myself to be questioned on Tuesday. After Dick Marsh had spoken, Keith Joseph attacked him straightaway and all our back benchers therefore thought it must be a jolly good White Paper and praised it. They found to their horror that if they had had time to read it they would have had a very different reaction so very soon nobody was questioning my wisdom any more.

I had been called to the P.L.P. social security group to expound the scheme. Being modest, I had said to Tam, 'I suppose I won't get many people, they will all have gone home. Perhaps we will get thirty.' Four people were there when I came into the room and eight were there in total. It didn't mean that people were against me. I found that I had got Left, Right and Centre thinking the pensions scheme a good job and people were proud that it is being presented in this way; but, still, only eight people turned up.

The same thing happened when the P.L.P. were summoned to discuss the notorious Castle White Paper *In Place of Strife*. Only fifty people turned up at the beginning and at most 100 people looked in for part of the time. The P.L.P. is the most non-participatory party in the world. It could have enormous influence but it is so browned off now that it has lost the will to try.

Friday, January 31st

I got a little note from Marre. He had done what I told him and he said, 'You will be happy to hear that your amendment has been confirmed, and that all the other Departments say it would be better to leave the reference to Prices and Incomes out of the Written Answer and just say that the Kindersley award is in accord with the 3½ per cent ceiling.' So I have had my way and saved a tiny little piece out of the capitulation. By the way, Ron Matthews had said to me, 'You must be careful. You know, if you are too rough with people, if you always talk to civil servants as if they are agin you, they won't do their best for you.' I knew he was talking about Alan Marre so I have been pretty nice to him today and have taken care to make amends. I have said things to him which it is all right to say to somebody you can trust not to pass it on but I don't want Marre going round the Department repeating what I say, even though there is profound truth in it.

This morning we had the Prices and Incomes Committee and here we were, with Roy in the chair, sitting round the table in the big Cabinet committee room under the portraits and the bust by Nollekens, to look at the formula as agreed by Eddie, Barbara and Roy. First of all Stonehouse raised the issue of timing, saying, 'It is really essential to start negotiations now,' whereupon Eddie said, 'I don't think we ought to hurry into that. We shall seem as though we are surrendering. We ought to wait till Monday or Tuesday.' At this both Fred Peart and I said, 'For God's sake, we are losing so fast, let's get into negotiations and settle it today.' This was the only issue on which outsiders like ourselves could really be useful. Barbara felt the same. The situation was lost and we had to get out. However, they started discussing it and it was clear that John Stonehouse had a pretty good conceit not only of himself but of his control of the situation. He was explaining how he would modify it this way and that. In the end I left them. They talked for six hours and worked out a formula. The dispute was settled this evening with a palpable capitulation by the Government because the central issue, our refusal to pay twice in productivity deals for the introduction of a new process, was conceded to the union.

So that was the story of the postal workers. It has two aspects. One is the internal aspect, the role of Mr Stonehouse. He has made mortal enemies of Eddie Shackleton, Roy and Barbara, whom he has made to look fools. He has fought by a very skilful use of press relations, a very unusual thing for a junior Minister to do. I can't remember a case in the last five years of a Minister successfully defying the Prime Minister, the Chancellor and the First Secretary, and proving himself completely right by always getting his role right in the newspapers. I don't think it will take him much further in the Government but he certainly won't be sacked as he might have been had he been weak and relented. Both sides played for high stakes, he for much higher and riskier stakes, and he won.

The second thing which strikes me is the hopelessness of a Government's trying to manage a strike in this way. You either trust your Postmaster-General or you don't. It all goes back to the fact that the First Secretary had never bothered about this but left it to Hattersley. She and Roy Jenkins simply wanted Stonehouse slapped down because they knew, as nobody else knew, the concessions they had made to the doctors and to the teachers. The treatment of this particular negotiation with the postal workers was fundamentally upset by the fact that it was dictated by Roy and Barbara for reasons that had nothing to do with the merits of the postal dispute but which had a great deal to do with surrender on two other issues. If the Postmaster-General had been trusted, he would have gone in and settled it but of course settled it in a way which would have upset the First Secretary. In this particular case too, Barbara was badly informed because her Ministry couldn't intervene or seek to conciliate for the curious constitutional reason that the Post Office is still a government Department and one government Department can't intervene in the industrial relations of another. This will change after this session when the Post Office becomes a public corporation in July and the Chairman of the Board will have his own industrial relations. The Postmaster-General won't, unlike John Stonehouse, be doing the negotiations and Barbara will not be excluded from conciliation. Despite these special reasons, however, this episode is another demonstration of the absolute futility of the Prices and Incomes Committee, three powerful Ministers and the other tiddlers taking over and just knocking a junior Minister about without due thought and background knowledge. In this case the junior Minister won.

After this I had Clifford Jarrett, whom I hadn't seen since my press conference on Tuesday. We talked things over and he told me that the managers of all our local social security offices will be available to explain the scheme to any Rotary Club or Women's Institute who want it. This is good. We are getting to work with Stephen Swingler and Peter Brown on the next stage, the organization and public discussion of the scheme, something to which I attach very great importance because I really want the public to understand it.

Last of all I went to Greenwich to see the new hospital being built by the Ministry. Tremendously exciting. A fellow called Howard Goodman,[1] a fat little man, is the architect in charge of a team which is making a tremendous revolution, halving the price, rationalizing hospital building. It was thrilling to see them at work and I had a wonderful two hours in between my briefings and other organizations for the pensions scheme.

In the evening I went down on the train to Charlbury. I travelled with John Maud, who, before he got off at Oxford gave me the full details of how his Royal Commission on Local Government is going. At Charlbury fifteen of us got out, including Paul Johnson, John Grigg and Eric James and we got into a bus to go to Ditchley Park for a conference of British and American legislators.[2] I have always said that Ditchley is one of the most beautiful houses in the world, this lovely estate in the Cotswolds which was Churchill's hideout during the war. It has been taken over by a foundation supported by Wills money to make something so wealthy and comfortable that Americans can be taken there and feel that it is pukkah. (We took a Polish delegation there and they were suitably impressed, as communists always will be by good living.)

We got in, changed for dinner, and after a very slap-up dinner in that magnificent dining room with all the silver we sat round an enormous table in the library and Paul Johnson began the discussion. By God, it was worse than I imagined. It was supposed to be about new political ideas and it was dominated by the thoughts of what has been happening all this week at the London School of Economics, where a couple of hundred revolutionary

[1] Assistant Chief Architect at the Ministry of Health (later the D.H.S.S.) 1966–71 and since 1971 Chief Architect.

[2] John Grigg, journalist and author, was a columnist for the *Guardian* 1960–7. He succeeded to his father's barony in 1955 but disclaimed the title in July 1963. Sir Eric James was Vice-Chancellor of the University of York 1962–73. He became a life peer in 1959. Ditchley Park, an eighteenth-century house in Oxfordshire, was used during the Second World War by Winston Churchill as a refuge from London when 'the moon was high' and German bombing likely. In 1958 the house was given by Mr David Wills to the Ditchley Foundation.

students have closed the place down.[1] Paul made not a bad six- or eight-minute start and then an American Senator talked for half an hour. I remembered that American legislators are professional talkers about the role of ideas in politics. They can just talk and talk. It isn't a filibuster, just that they know how to say nothing in a professionally statesmanlike way. The only spark of life came when George Kennan,[2] who is staying at All Souls' for six months, barged in with a tough statement on the Negro situation, saying he thought the Negroes had to have an independent state or something of that sort and that black power was a reality. I supported him, saying that it wasn't until the Jews got their state that they were ever satisfied or that other people began to treat them as equals. I wonder if there isn't something equally true about the American Negroes. I don't know but it is a thought. I must say both George Kennan and I shook them a bit before we both departed, he for Oxford, I for Prescote, under a brilliant full moon, leaving them to the most boring conference you could imagine.

Sunday, February 2nd

Last night I went over to a Feast at Brasenose College, to which I had been invited by Vernon Bogdanor,[3] the young don who helped me with my book. There I found John Freeman a guest of honour and after dinner I went up to High Table to sit and drink Madeira next to Noël Hall, who is now the most appallingly effete head of a college.[4] Oxford colleges are not very different, lots of dons looking very neat, lots of young, vigorous dons very much introverted, but Oxford has the advantage, unlike L.S.E., of being broken up into colleges. It can discipline its undergraduates and know what is going on much better than the Governors of the students at L.S.E. The events there have been hanging over us all this week. Ted Short has been talking about student hooligans, backing Walter Adams and Lord Robbins and the Governors who I think are a pretty dicey lot who really haven't greatly helped.[5] Once again we have had a sense of the cracking of order. I happen to think it's all

[1] A series of strikes and demonstrations by the students, dissatisfied by the running of the School and inspired by left-wing and anarchist movements, culminated in the smashing of the gates. On January 24th the Governors decided to close the School and it remained closed till mid-February.

[2] A member of the U.S. Foreign Service 1926–52, he was U.S. Ambassador to the U.S.S.R. 1952–3 and to Yugoslavia 1961–3. From 1956 to 1974 he was a professor at the Institute of Advanced Study at Princeton.

[3] Fellow and Tutor in Politics at Brasenose College, Oxford, since October 1966. He helped Crossman with the new edition of *Government and the Governed.*

[4] Principal of Brasenose College, Oxford, 1960–73. He was knighted in 1957.

[5] Walter Adams, Principal of the University College of Rhodesia and Nyasaland 1955–67, Director of the London School of Economics from October 1967 until his death in 1975. He was knighted in 1970. Lionel Robbins was Professor of Economics in the University of London at the London School of Economics 1929–61, Chairman of the *Financial Times* 1961–70 and Chairman of the Court of Governors of the London School of Economics 1968–74. He chaired the Committee on Higher Education 1961–4 and was made a life peer in 1959.

phoney. The real fact of the modern world is the enormous power behind the Establishment and the feebleness and ridiculous abstractness of the revolutionaries. In 1968–9 as in 1848–9 the Establishments have been warned and they will almost certainly strengthen themselves and then make concessions from a position of power.

I have been looking at the weekend press and I think my dinner party for the journalists was pretty important. *The Economist* is hostile but in an intelligent and reasonable way and it admits the soundness of the scheme. Nigel Lawson has written absolute tripe on the front page of the *Spectator* but this was compensated for by Nicholas Davenport at the other end, who made an admirable summary. To my great surprise, I have got the *Tribune* strongly supporting me and, as for the *New Statesman*, where I already had some support on the front page last week, 'Taurus', their city editor, has also helped by saying that this is a practical scheme. The only paper which has really supported me is the *Financial Times*. *The Times* just said miserably that we ought to substitute for my scheme one of compulsory insurance in private occupational schemes, a wholly impractical solution which is picked up by *The Economist* and the *Spectator*. This is one thing which won't work and if the Tories put it forward it will be perfectly easy for me to demolish them altogether. On the whole this has been a fairly successful week for the launching.

Monday, February 3rd

We began with a meeting on the Community Development Project. After a good deal of sparring, in which I insisted on chairing the Executive Committee supervising the Morrell scheme, I am the Chairman of this Sub-Committee of the Social Services Committee. The official Committee has been left in the hands of Morrell but they are responsible to me. I have been very much aware that the Home Office are hedging because they want to get the credit for the scheme as a Home Office device. Today we were discussing in particular which were to be the first four pilot areas and I noticed that Callaghan was a bit edgy. We were talking about how we would handle this with the local councillors and who should be the local executive committee and the team leaders. Callaghan talked about his children's officers and I said, 'We can't have more than one children's officer because it will make it look as if this is being bossed about by the Home Office.' He gave way. I shall have to send Callaghan a letter about all this because it is obvious that he is making a bid for it. Callaghan's political ambition and subtlety and Morrell's fanaticism combine to make the Home Office determined to put a spoke in. It is an example of pure departmental imperialism.

We went straight on to a meeting of the House of Lords Committee, where we were discussing a number of erudite subjects and cleaning up the Bill. We also considered what conclusions we should draw from the P.L.P. meeting and, first on the agenda, the speech which Harold had prepared for the

Second Reading debate this afternoon. At last Monday's Committee he had read aloud a very dull, routine speech, flat as a pancake, though I had noticed an extraordinary passage in which we seemed to be giving away the main issue of the timing of implementation. This passage said, in effect, that this was a Committee point on which we would have consideration. When we got to Callaghan's draft speech, I had noticed this again and he had emphasized it even more strongly, saying, 'This is just a Committee point which we can consider later.' I had thought, 'That is a peculiar thing,' and as I went up to Greenwich last Friday, I had read over Harold's draft and observed it again.

So this morning I said, 'I thought, Home Secretary, that new passage you and the Prime Minister cooked up was very interesting.' Callaghan said, 'That wasn't something I cooked up with the Prime Minister. I saw it in the brief and I read it out.' I asked Gerald Gardiner and Eddie Shackleton. No, they'd not seen it before. I said I hadn't seen it either. The draft of the Prime Minister's speech had been circulated by the Secretaries, David Faulkner and Michael Wheeler-Booth, to each member of the Committee for our comments and we hadn't commented. We left the matter there but I suspect that each of us thought the others had talked it over with the Prime Minister. I thought that Gerald Gardiner or Callaghan had, they thought I had, and on our somehow tacit assumption that this was something that Harold had fixed, we let this major announcement of policy go through. This does reveal something about the Committee's attitude. Instead of raising the matter last Monday or ringing up the Prime Minister or the Secretariat, we all thought, 'Well, that's that. It's probably been fixed and we won't discuss it.'

The American Senators and Congressmen who had been at Ditchley came up this afternoon to London and this evening we gave a dinner party for them. They told me how bitterly cold Ditchley had proved to be and this surprised me because it means that even the Wills millions can't make an old house warm. Prescote had been piping hot and lovely during the weekend and there was Ditchley perishing cold. I found myself sitting opposite William Whitelaw. We discussed with the Americans the difference between their constitution and ours, and I described how, except for some twenty or thirty real back benchers like Michael Foot, professional Parliamentarians who care about the House itself, virtually everybody else sees the House of Commons not merely as a forum for debate where the front bench predominate, but as a place where reputations are made and ministerial status is established. You can't get into Government or into office except through the House, so that everybody regards life on the back benches as, in a sense, a second-best. Think how different it is if you are an American legislator. You work full-time in the House of Representatives or the Senate, you absorb its standards of success and failure and its ambitions, you acquire a life's devotion to the job, with no prospect of promotion to being a member of Government in our sense, unless you stand for President like Kennedy or are hooked out of the Senate to join the Executive.[1] Legislation, as distinct from government, is a whole-time job for a politician. I was describing how in the House of Commons one had tremendous ambition to be a Minister and how marvellous it was if one succeeded, and the American opposite me said, 'We have something of the same thing, you know. I waited fifteen years before I became the Vice-Chairman of a Committee and got the real power which that brings.'[2] I thought, 'I have proved my point.' It struck me more and more this evening that they didn't really understand what I was saying and they couldn't make the comparison because their lives are lived inside legislation. Willie Whitelaw then tried to describe our special committees and how he had tried to start them under my Leadership. He was quite blunt about how they had been frustrated by the Whips, who nominated their members, and he said, 'Frankly, in one sense the experiment has failed. It's not suited our system and now we can see that Government can frustrate our specialist committees in a way it cannot possibly do in America.'

After dinner, as I went upstairs to hear the final hour of the debate on Lords' reform, this conversation made me realize what a difference I might have made. I had rushed into the Leadership of the House and left it too early after fourteen or fifteen months.[3] I should have stayed on two or three years to make my mark and go through all the tough times. How much of that reform I would have kept going! I could have continued the experiment in radio broadcasting of proceedings, leading up to televising Parliament. I could have kept going the specialist committees and the drive to get the House controlling the executive and pressing for more private business. Yes, as Leader one's personality counts an enormous lot and just when mine was beginning to count I walked out on it. Fred Peart took over and his complete lack of interest in encouraging parliamentary criticism of the executive, his complete loyalty to the Government and complete opposition to my ideas about broadcasting have all made a difference. He counts as much as I did.

Thinking about this as I went along, I got on to the front bench in time to hear Alec Douglas Home making an absolutely charming speech.[4] Alec,

[1] John F. Kennedy was Democratic Senator for Massachusetts 1953–60 and became President of the United States in 1960. He was assassinated in November 1963.

[2] In both Houses of Congress permanent committees, many of which are set up by law, are nominated at the beginning of each Congress. They consider all Bills and Resolutions, including financial appropriations, and their members, especially the chairmen, have great power. Select and special investigative committees may also be set up for a particular purpose and a limited amount of time.

[3] It was, in fact, twenty months.

[4] Unionist M.P. for South Lanark 1931–45 and Conservative M.P. for the Lanark division of Lanarkshire 1950–1. He was Joint Parliamentary Under-Secretary to the Foreign Office May–July 1945. In 1951 he succeeded his father as the 14th Earl of Home and from 1951–April 1955 he was Minister of State at the Scottish Office, and from 1955 to 1960 Secretary of State for Commonwealth Relations. He was Deputy Leader of the House of Lords 1956–7, Leader of the House of Lords and Lord President of the Council 1957–60, and Secretary of State for Foreign Affairs 1960–3. In October 1963 he resigned his peerage for life and became Prime Minister, sitting as Conservative M.P. for Kinross

who was in the Commons, then in the Lords, and then back in the Commons, a man of unrivalled experience of both sides, made the only good and original speech, trying to persuade the Tories that our reform was a good thing. After him Jim Callaghan was a very poor second. One shouldn't fuss, but all this time we were fussing because we thought we might possibly lose. Tam had rushed up to me and said, 'I can tell you the report from the back benches is very bad. We shall only just scrape through. There will be a mass abstention and an increased number of people intend to vote against.' By the time we came to the actual vote there was real nervousness. Harold turned to me and said, 'Now look, if we lose this, Dick, and if we lose it because the Tories defeat the Bill, tomorrow we will put in a short Bill to deal with powers without composition.' Good old Harold! He is back where he was last May,[1] when he and Freddie Warren concocted a short Bill of this kind. He does hang on to his ideas. He was saying to himself, 'We'll get something out of it if the Tories defeat us today.' I shall always remember this, his thinking that it was the Tories who would defeat us. Well, they didn't. We had a huge majority, 100 more than we expected.[2] Very many fewer of our people voted against the Bill than we expected and the number of abstentions was rather smaller. Alec Home had rallied the Tories but on our side the Government managed to get more acquiescence than we had hoped.

Tuesday, February 4th

The only thing to remember today is a little row I had with Alan Marre. It is already clear that these two Permanent Secretaries are a bloody nuisance. Marre is an effective head of the Health side, whereas poor Clifford Jarrett is neither an effective head of the Social Security side nor the head of both. Nor am I really, that's the trouble. I *am* the effective political co-ordinator of Social Security but I find it very difficult to get any kind of control over Health and it's not made easier by David Ennals's ambition and drive. I don't resent it a bit but he is determined to run things for himself and it makes difficulties. Well, David was away with 'flu today and I summoned Marre because I had been reading a minute on rural dispensing he had sent me. David and Marre had recommended to me that we should re-enforce a so-called agreement we had reached with the B.M.A. in 1966, a decree that dispensing by rural doctors must now be curbed. Dispensing by doctors, by the

and West Perthshire November 1963–September 1974. He was Leader of the Opposition October 1964–July 1965 and Secretary of State for Foreign Affairs 1970–4. In 1974 he became a life peer, taking the title of Lord Home of the Hirsel.

[1] See above, pp. 100–3.

[2] There were 285 votes for and 135 against the Second Reading of the Parliamentary No. 2 Bill (so entitled because earlier in the session Lord Mitchison had introduced a Private Members' Bill in the Lords, which made no progress after First Reading). Of the Labour M.P.s, on a two-line whip, 226 voted in favour of the Bill and 25 against and on the Conservative side, with a free vote, 58 supported the measure with 105 against. The Liberals were divided 3:3, with one abstention, and a Welsh and a Scottish Nationalist both voted against the Bill.

way, is enormously popular with the public in rural areas, but we are told that the doctors are taking away the trade of the pharmacists. The doctors had repudiated the agreement in 1967 and we were being asked to reimpose these regulations. I am not sure whether I would have entered into the agreement three years ago or whether it is popular or wise, and anyway I am not bound by it, so I said, 'Let's look at our whole strategy of dealing with the B.M.A. before you ask me to pick a row with them about this,' and I gave instructions for a paper to be brought up.

After the day's work I went off to change before going to Covent Garden to hear their production of *Die Meistersinger*. I found Susan Crosland was my fellow-guest in the Directors' box, and she looked very beautiful with her skirts far above her knees and her dress right down on her breasts. Anne had refused to come because she thought four and a half hours too long and so had Tony and it was very nice just to have Susan and myself. The Sadler's Wells production I saw a few months ago was nice and melodiously musical but this one was dramatic and dynamic. We went out enormously exhilarated, not feeling the performance a moment too long. Susan said she wanted to pick up Tony from Ann Fleming's and as I was curious to see what the famous hostess was like, as I am a Pam Berry person, I said I would go round to Victoria Square and drop Susan in. There I found Arnold Goodman looking, I thought, like Bottom in *A Midsummer Night's Dream*, a great big man dumped down on a very small chair, surrounded by fairies and fays and elegant people, among them the director of the Victoria and Albert Museum,[1] who lent me a clock for my Lord President's room. There was Elizabeth Bowen,[2] the novelist, who had quite forgotten me. We had a long talk about Oxford and schools and children together. And there was Ann Fleming herself. Her house was full of a kind of smartness and cultural elegance, quite different from Pam's hard-boiled, political, journalistic atmosphere and I found it interesting at the end of a longish evening.

Wednesday, February 5th

I gave dinner to Nicky and Clarissa Kaldor, and asked Peter and Liz Shore along.[3] I hadn't known that Liz is a doctor in my own Ministry. Peter has been ill and rather sore that I haven't been after him. We had a pleasant dinner but the fact is that he is almost as much out of things as I am. As a senior Minister of Health and Social Security I am probably even further away from the centre than I was as Minister of Housing. I am not consulted about the setting up of Select Committees, which I do know about, and certainly not

[1] Sir John Pope-Hennessy, Director and Secretary of the Victoria and Albert Museum 1967–73 and Director of the British Museum 1974–6. See Vol. II.

[2] She had once lived at Headington, Oxford, where she had come to know Crossman. Her novels included *The Death of the Heart* (London: Cape, 1948) and *The Heat of the Day* (London: Cape, 1949). She died in 1973.

[3] Dr Elizabeth Shore joined the Medical Civil Service in 1962 and in 1972 became a Senior Principal Medical Officer at the D.H.S.S.

consulted about the general state of the economy. We are now in one of those curious states where the Chancellor is incommunicado because he is preparing the budget, which, I suspect, may be brought on earlier. Obviously Roy is terribly worried about the I.M.F., about the trade figures this year and about his budget. He and the Prime Minister have the whole thing in their own hands and, though perhaps Harold is talking to Barbara as well, once again Cabinet has been squeezed out of any collective responsibility for the economy. Although I am going to see Roy next week to discuss the whole uprating of pensions with him, the increase of contributions next autumn and the impact on the economy, I don't expect him to show any kind of candour or to have any kind of consultation with me.

Thursday, February 6th

The morning was spent on the so-called Parliamentary Committee and then at Cabinet. This Parliamentary Committee was started when Harold produced his Mark II Cabinet, and it's not too bad, but its membership is very arbitrary. We have a little less than half the Cabinet, just as at S.E.P. and O.P.D. I am sure Harold has dozens of these miscellaneous committees because he is more and more inclined to solve a problem by setting up a new committee where he can select who deals with what. This morning we considered the issue of party political broadcasting during elections. While I was in Sweden the Parliamentary Committee had almost decided that we should accept a B.B.C./I.T.V. proposal for a reduction of at least a quarter of our party political broadcasts. When this was put forward Harold Wilson, thank heaven, had shown a little doubt, and said that at least we should postpone it until the B.B.C.'s new Director-General had taken up his post. I pointed out that I hoped there would be no question of getting rid of party politicals. We were going to face a totally different situation from the last General Election. In 1966 we were bound to win and it didn't matter what propaganda we did, good, bad or indifferent. Next time we shall want above all to communicate with our old rank and file, to raise and hold their morale, and for this our party politicals are absolutely indispensable. People may be said to resent being a captive audience but we know our own people listen to them in very large numbers. How can we dispense with them? The very fact that the Conservatives say they can should make us suspicious because they reckon to have the press on their side and they can afford to dispense with a captive audience in a way which we can't. It was an effective intervention and I can claim I changed their minds. Callaghan said later that was clearly what had happened. We held the item up for further consideration and I think that on this kind of thing my view really does count for something.

We went straight on to Cabinet and perhaps the most important thing came up when we discussed Parliamentary business. I learnt that I had no hope of a debate on the White Paper this week. They were planning my debate for me on March 21st, nearly seven weeks ahead, and a debate on Barbara's

White Paper in the same week.[1] They had pushed me right back. I pleaded that this was futile. Here we had something to sell. Until I had authorization from the Commons I couldn't get into full swing on my campaign of public education and discussion, and I would have a disastrous hiatus between the launching and the follow-up. I said this very briefly and there was a silence. 'Well,' said Peart, 'everybody wants their own White Paper and the Minister of Social Services must be patient.' It came out that the Tories had been saying 'Why debate Dick's White Paper before Barbara's, when Barbara's was published first?' The Tories know that Barbara's is embarrassing and mine isn't. I looked around the room and realized that there was no collective feeling to back me. Judith was the only person who spoke up for me and she is head of publicity. She did her duty and so did the Prime Minister and I think I may get forward a bit on this. But Cabinets are selfish things and, though they all know that this is one of the few things we have that has gone down well, they won't actually help a fellow Minister to get his own White Paper a bit of publicity.

Friday, February 7th

The story of the Kindersley award finally came to an end yesterday afternoon, when the evening papers published banner headlines 'Big Awards for the Doctors'. We were lucky this morning though, as there were a lot of other sensational stories and only one paper, the *Financial Times*, fully understood the significance of the conflict between Aubrey Jones on the university teachers' award and Kindersley on the doctors' award, and the contradiction in the Government's accepting both. No one leaked, not me on our side nor Roy and Barbara on the other, so we squeezed through. This is a very interesting example of the lack of understanding by political journalists. Here is a *post hoc* which is actually *propter hoc* and at last gives the explanation of the Government's extraordinary behaviour towards the postal workers. No journalist spotted that the fact that the postal workers' claim was considered after the doctors' was the determining factor in making Roy and Barbara lose their heads for a moment and say we have to hit the postal workers in view of all the concessions to the doctors (just as few people saw that it was our anticipation of a defeat in the Lords if we moved the Stansted Order which made us reverse our views on that).[2]

At eleven o'clock, after one more meeting at 70 Whitehall, I went over to the front bench for a big Parliamentary day. I had decided to take charge of the opposition to young Maurice Macmillan's Private Member's Bill on contributory pensions for the over-eighties.[3] This Bill had immense appeal in

[1] The debate on the National Superannuation White Paper was eventually held on March 6th and that on *In Place of Strife* on March 3rd.

[2] See above, p. 69 and n.

[3] Conservative M.P. for Halifax 1955–64 and for Farnham since 1966. He was Economic Secretary to the Treasury October 1963–64, Chief Secretary to the Treasury 1970–2, Secretary of State for Employment 1972–3 and Paymaster-General 1973–4.

1964 and we jolly nearly got defeated on it and this was the fourth occasion on which it had been brought up.[1] During this week I have been working on and off on a brief the Department were preparing for me and I had had a brief distributed to everybody at the P.L.P. meeting, because I knew it was quite formidable. You can read it all in Hansard. Macmillan didn't make a very good speech and, unluckily for him, he had assumed that the statistic of 125,000 deserving cases was relevant whereas in fact the figure includes everybody who is not entitled to a pension for good, bad and indifferent reasons. There were only seven or eight people present at the start of the debate, and as we slowly moved along the Tories worked up their rather artificial passion against the outrage. I had in reserve a really annihilating reply but my main anxiety was about the voting. On the last occasion the Tories has mustered 150 votes and we needed over 160 to win. It seemed very clear that we just hadn't got them and messages about this came in throughout the day. At 3.15 I finally got up and made a perfectly adequate reply, which I think pleased everybody because it showed competence plus a certain amount of humanity. Just before the vote, John Silkin came in and said, 'If by any chance you lose remember to sit tight, because Fred Peart will get up and say that in a matter of such great importance we can make no statement now, and we will have a considered Statement on Monday.' I said, 'Balls! "Matter of such importance" for Private Members' Bills, John! Why, say the opposite. Say, as the Private Member's Bill has been carried on Second Reading, we will consider it when it comes to Committee.' He said, 'Oh, Dick, thank you so much. Of course that's right.' It shows you how jumpy John Silkin has become and that he knew he hadn't got enough people there. Actually we won by 61 votes, not because we had enough but because the Tories only had 96.[2]

I went up to my room and I was feeling pleased with myself, drinking a glass of whisky with Ron Matthews, when down came a blanket of scurrying snow. I got into the car and just caught the 5.48, and we got into Banbury only about twenty-five minutes late. I found that Anne had been delayed for nearly twenty-five minutes in coming to meet me but we were lucky because we had to creep past a car stuck on Williamscot Hill and if it had been a foot further out in the road we would have had to stop behind, blocking the whole road. Once you stopped you couldn't get going again over the quickly caked, powdered snow. When we got home Prescote was a cube of warmth. Oh, the comfort of the place.

Sunday, February 9th

Two absolutely cloudless days of sunshine, with a brilliant moon at night. Yesterday we made a lovely expedition over the snow with Patrick delightedly

[1] See Vol. I, p. 188, Vol. II, pp. 671, 686. Similar bills had been introduced in 1965, 1967 and 1968.

[2] The National Insurance Bill was defeated by 157 votes to 96.

floundering up to his waist in the drifts and Suki gambolling over it. Anne and I went out to dinner with Brian Lillywhite, who has been looking after the farm while the Pritchetts are away in the Canaries, out beyond Claydon on a remote road. We went across two humped bridges and on the way back we stuck on the second one and it took us four goes to get the car slithering up over the top. If we had been caught between the two humps that would have been that. We have had ten to fifteen degrees of frost, with the swimming bath freezing over, and here we have enjoyed it enormously. I don't want to go back to London. I would be perfectly content to stay here for the rest of time.

Monday, February 10th

At 11.30 I went for a little talk with Roy about a number of things, uprating, the need to raise contributions by 3*s*., the best way of doing it and so on. I also told him of another evil which we have now discovered. As Stephen Swingler told me last week at lunch, the number of letters being sent by M.P.s to local offices has doubled since 1964. In my view, M.P.s have found that social security is a real pork-barrel for their constituents. The person who goes to his M.P. gets something, the person who doesn't gets a worse deal from social security. When it is known that you get better treatment through M.P.s and Ministers, we are in for trouble. I told Roy I thought we ought to stop this and also that we ought to stop the increase in children's allowances. This is something which could be political and dicey and I asked if he wanted me to help and obviously he did. I shall try to do it for him, build on from there and finally say, 'Well, in exchange I want a constant attendance allowance for the sick and disabled, which won't cost you anything because I will really save you a lot of money by tightening up on supplementary benefits.' It is costing us vast sums and abuses are now bringing us into disrepute. In this area I must try to combine humanity with an efficient severity.

Roy, though detached, seemed as friendly, or as little and as much friendly as before. Harold, on the other hand, is very averse and remote from me now. He sat himself down beside me today on the front bench and for a long time stayed completely removed from me. After a time we slowly began to talk. The House was discussing the Nabarro affair, which started on February 2nd when Nabarro shouted on the B.B.C. that he knew that the road fund licence tax on motor vehicles was going to be put up to £35 a year. Since then he has been forced to climb down and say that perhaps he just heard trivial gossip. Equally suddenly, the Prime Minister, Roy and Fred Peart agreed to put a Motion to the House for a Select Committee of Inquiry, headed by George Strauss.[1] I did think this was using a hammer to smash a nut and I was even more surprised because I thought we had got it clear in our minds that Select

[1] Labour M.P. for North Lambeth 1929–31 and 1934–50 and for Vauxhall since 1950. He was Parliamentary Secretary at the Ministry of Transport 1945–7 and Minister of Supply 1947–51. As one of the longest-serving Members he was considered an appropriate Chairman for such an inquiry.

Committees should be on more important subjects and should not be used for purely party reasons. Well, I had no doubt that Nabarro would be pulverized by it but today when the Motion was put it gave him a tremendous chance to make the most vulgar, arrogant, interminable speech, withdrawing nothing. I learnt from Roy this morning, however, that this was Roy and the Attorney General's alternative to the Prime Minister's suggestion for an old-fashioned Tribunal of Inquiry, which, heaven knows, in one sense would have been worse and far too grandiose an affair, though I must say within the judicial atmosphere of such a Tribunal Nabarro wouldn't have had a chance to misbehave in the way he did this afternoon. My own feeling is that the whole thing should have been dealt with by the Prime Minister asking Heath to come and see him and saying, 'My dear Ted, you know, if a back bencher feels he can at any time get on his hind legs and rush to the B.B.C. saying he's got documentary evidence of a budget leak without providing any evidence for it or being rebuked afterwards the House would go into chaos. Don't you agree we must together rebuke Nabarro, in the interest of my Government and your future Government?' But the answer is that Harold Wilson can't put those things to Ted Heath because he is this kind of man and Ted Heath is that kind of man and they hate each other and won't work together at all. Anyhow, at least the Nabarro affair took the heat off Barbara Castle's labour troubles.[1]

Tommy Balogh had asked me to dinner tonight and I had been screwing myself up to tell him that he couldn't come back to be my economic adviser. I am certainly concerned to get good research and intelligence for my big new Department but I am concerned with what from his point of view are endless minor details of social services and I really want the kind of person like Brian Abel-Smith or Nicky Kaldor, who is magnificent at inventing devices for improving contributions or arranging the uprating more skilfully, things which Tommy doesn't care about at all. I am afraid Tommy chiefly wants to come back in order to get at the Cabinet papers, to advise me on things which would enable him to see all the secrets of the state, but now I am on the sidelines and out of that kind of thing.

Anyhow, thanks to a talk which Anne had with Pen Balogh, we had found out how Tommy felt and I was finally able to have things out with him this evening. I think I have nearly persuaded him that he should bow himself out, not of my life but of my departmental life. I am not at all good at getting rid of people but I think in this case I managed to do so and I thank God for it.

Tuesday, February 11th

Cabinet, and to our amazement the Prime Minister said first of all that there was a statement he wanted to make about the negotiations which had been suggested with the Opposition with regard to the Parliament Bill. Everybody looked a bit surprised. When Gerald Gardiner was asked to speak he looked

[1] A strike was threatened at Ford's. See below, pp. 417, 423.

completely bewildered and asked Harold what he meant. 'Well,' said Harold, 'I gathered last Friday from my talk with the Chief Whip and the Leader of the House that the P.L. Cabinet Committee had met and discussed negotiations. I think those negotiations should be brought to the attention of Cabinet.' In fact almost the opposite had happened. As I have described, we had all agreed that we were surprised that, as we thought, the Prime Minister and Callaghan had cooked up this overture to the Opposition. We had found out at the Committee that each one of us thought someone else had fixed it with the Prime Minister. We had said to ourselves, 'No doubt the Chief will be discussing with the Opposition Whips through the usual channels how to conduct the Committee Stage of the Bill,' and we had thought in the course of this they would raise the issue with the Prime Minister as we wanted it raised. But, apparently, at Harold's Friday morning prayers Silkin and Peart had complained bitterly that Gerald, Eddie Shackleton, Callaghan and I had been talking about negotiations behind the scenes and leaving them out. It was a totally imaginary idea, a clear misunderstanding, and the rest of Cabinet sat around bewildered while this talk went on. It became more and more abstruse and I finally said, 'I feel I had really better tell you the whole story of what happened at the Committee. So far from our conspiring, we thought you had fixed it with one of us and now we have found that none of us did it and all that happened was that young Michael Wheeler-Booth had written a speech for you which you read aloud. It is Michael Wheeler-Booth who is the conspirator.' This produced a pretty good laugh in Cabinet and everybody who wants to see how little Cabinet minutes reflect what actually happened can look this item up. Harold sat there plump and grinning but he looked rather sheepish and uncomfortable.

Wednesday, February 12th

Fred Peart had been busy on the annual farm price review and wasn't able to come in for the first go on the Committee Stage of the Parliament Bill today. Callaghan, Fred and I roughly divided the clauses up between us. Clause 1 was mine and Peart's so I sat there in a fury for five hours by myself on the front bench. I was worried because my briefing notes were very short, nothing like the notes we had on the Rent Bill,[1] when every Clause had pages and pages of briefing. This time I just had a few lines on what I should say in answer to a mass of amendments dealing with the principle of the ending of the hereditary system. It was interminable. Forty-five minutes on a point of order at the beginning, endless speeches. The House of Commons was at its most drearily boring and they all thought they were funny. They weren't quite filibustering because a lot of the speeches were perfectly serious and highminded on the whole idea of the Bill. Admittedly the Speaker isn't keen and nor were any of the chairmen of Standing Committees and we had a kind of Second Reading debate that went on and on and on.

[1] See Vol. I.

At 8 o'clock we got the first vote on which only forty-five of our side voted. Then, while I gave Anne a quick dinner, Fred took the second group of Clauses from 8.0 to 11.30. There was a brilliant speech by Michael Foot and a dirty, brilliant speech by Nigel Birch and I wondered whether once they'd got their speeches off their chests they would repeat them time after time.[1] In America of course they would filibuster to destruction but there isn't a great deal of life in this Opposition, just a vast mass of people acquiescing and turning up to vote. We shall see how it goes on. We've got two more days, Tuesday and Wednesday next week, with probably one all-night sitting, and we shall have to try to move it along. So far the Tory front bench haven't spoken at all and the Tory Whips are hardly operating, so it is just our front bench pushing the Bill through, with the tacit support of the Opposition front bench and very little other positive support in the House. Frankly, all those people who support the Bill are doing so because they want to be life peers sooner or later. If it goes on like this we're going to take at least sixteen days over it.

Thursday, February 13th

Nabarro has been pushed out of the papers by the trade figures, the best we have had for months.[2] However, it is by no means absolutely certain that the Chancellor has now made up his mind and is preparing for a stiff budget with increased taxes. From my talk with Roy on Monday it was obvious that he hadn't taken a final decision about the amount of money he would have to raise but here and there once or twice this week, in Cabinet on Tuesday and in other places, he has made it only too clear that he is under tremendous pressure from the banks and, despite the good trade figures, that he is terrified that he may have to increase taxation because he can't cut public expenditure enough. He is still dreading the Vote on Account and the admission that this year the Estimates have gone up by 8 per cent.

I took this morning off to write speeches, one for the Harrogate Labour Party Local Government Conference and one for Coventry announcing the Callaghan–Morrell Community Development Project. Meanwhile Stephen Swingler was to take the chair for me at a key meeting on the new plans for a White Paper on short-term sickness and unemployment benefit, but at the beginning he collapsed and was rushed to Charing Cross Hospital, where they thought he had a coronary thrombosis. Apparently, though, he has been trying to stand out against an appallingly severe virus for ages, and now his heart has collapsed on him. It isn't too much to run that bit of the Depart-

[1] Nigel Birch was Conservative M.P. for Flintshire 1945–50 and for West Flint 1950–70. Parliamentary Under-Secretary of State at the Air Ministry 1951–2 and at the Ministry of Works 1952–4, he was Minister of Works 1954–5, Secretary of State for Air 1955–7 and Economic Secretary to the Treasury from 1957 until his resignation, over economic policy, in 1970. He became a life peer in 1958, taking the title of Lord Rhyl.

[2] The deficit on visible trade had fallen from £55 million in December 1968 to £10 million in January 1969.

ment and I can do it in his absence, but it has stopped me getting on with much of my own work.

This afternoon Harold came in to answer Questions and sat down beside me on the front bench. He didn't come into conversation straightaway, but ostentatiously sat there side by side for three or four minutes without saying a word. I think neither Jim nor I now dream of trying to unseat him. There is no chance of that whatsoever. Indeed, from now to the election his tactical short-term skills and his energy and leadership will be far more suitable. We are now moving more into a 1964 situation, where there can't be long-term strategy but only short-term calculations of electoral benefit. It's what really suits him and he is stronger than ever now. What are the chances of such short-term skills being successful? There is no doubt that the party is in better heart. It has recovered from the shock of the November crisis, the November flick of the whip that was followed by yet more slashing increases in indirect taxation.

This afternoon we were having a three-line whip on the Tory Vote of censure on Barbara's policy.[1] At the end of her speech Barbara again stated that we hadn't excluded the possibility of another statutory prices and incomes policy next session. Really what she was doing was plaintively, tenuously holding on to this possibility, though everybody inside the Cabinet really knows that the chances are almost zero. However everybody outside will get it wrong and take it that we have reasserted the threat.

After this I rushed round to Charing Cross Hospital where I found Anne Swingler, who had been brought down after lunch and had waited for three and a half hours while Stephen, blue in the face, was having his lungs inflated and adrenalin poured into his heart. He apparently nearly passed out this afternoon and he is only just maintaining his position.

Friday, February 14th

I started with a forty-minute meeting on short-term benefits and then was forty minutes late for the next meeting. This was David Ennals's meeting on cigarette-smoking and the measures we could take against it. I have been very clear that I will not have legislation on this and I suppose I had a guilty conscience for keeping them waiting. I started by saying, 'You know I'm not keen on this and it was a Freudian delay.' After that I gave way a certain amount. This year we are going to work hard to see whether we can't have differential taxation in favour of cigars and pipe tobacco and we are going to look hard at the possibility of a Bill to compel people to attach to cigarettes every kind of publicity, saying they are poisonous and cancerous.

Next was a meeting of the P.L. Committee to discuss the terms of any offer we could make to the Tories on Lords' reform. Of three possible courses we finally decided the only thing we could really go for was to say that we might

[1] The motion criticizing the Government's statutory powers was defeated by 289 votes to 230.

postpone the actual operation of the Bill until the next Parliament, if we got as near as possible to an absolute assurance that the Conservatives wouldn't use the Lords to sabotage our legislative programme for the remainder of this one. It is certainly not a bit absurd to hope for this from Jellicoe and Carrington in the Lords, but I don't know if the Commons could deliver such an assurance. It would help us a great deal in the Commons if an agreement of this sort could be made in the next week or ten days. The negotiations are going to start on Monday evening and if we do get the assurance in return for postponing the implementation of the Act, on that basis the opposition in the House might not peter out and we might get the latter Clauses of the Bill relatively fast.

After this a meeting with Dr Cameron,[1] who is head of the G.P. section of the B.M.A. I said to him, 'Tell me what are these things we are fighting about? For instance, is rural dispensing a great issue?' He looked very surprised. 'No,' he said. I had been told it was going to be so I went through the issues with him and talked a little about the Kindersley Report and I find that the Ministry's view of our relations with the doctors is very odd. The Department have steamed me up into the idea that I have got a terrible series of difficulties here and when I get the doctors there don't seem to be any difficulties at all. I think David and I can make direct contact with them, and it was a rather cheerful and relieving meeting.

Off from there on the train to Coventry to make my speech on the community development project. It was really a lecture at the opening of a series on adult education and not one Labour councillor turned up. I gave them a very lively lecture on the difficulties of devising priorities, and then, as I had arranged, I made the announcement that Coventry had agreed to be one of the four pilot areas for the project. After that, back to stay at a bleak and tattered hotel out on the London Road, where Peter Lister is to pick me up tomorrow.

Saturday, February 15th

Peter Lister and I set off in his little two-seater, right up the M1 to Sheffield and on to the A1 up to Harrogate. Thank heavens it was Saturday morning because there were only two cleared channels along the M1, and, thank heavens too, the snow had stopped last night. When we got into Harrogate the streets were being cleared. It was a splendid, vigorous, perfectly sunny morning and in the course of the drive I had a long talk to Peter. He is one of the ablest Councillors surviving in Coventry, leading the Labour Group in Opposition, and he's the candidate for Meriden as well. We talked about the state of the party. There is no doubt about it that the party in Coventry is a great deal better and really beginning to operate as an Opposition party. The key point is that, instead of being merely anti-Government, railing at us

[1] Dr James Cameron, Chairman of the General Medical Services Committee of the B.M.A., and since 1976 Chairman of the Council of the B.M.A.

for our prices and incomes policy and our attack on the trade unions, the local party is beginning to move into supporting the Government in the way that they are bound to do sooner or later. If this is sustained, we may see sufficient recovery to hold the election. This was also my impression from the Harrogate conference. At these annual Labour Party local government conferences last year and the year before there has been a frightful atmosphere, with councillors showing nothing but bitterness and disillusionment at being the few surviving fragments of the great Council groups which used to dominate in all the big cities. Today I found them much more cheerful, much more willing to accept one as a leader.

We arrived about twenty minutes before they finished their morning session, and there was no reception committee, no one to greet me or look after me, so I stood about. There was no one to give me a drink, take me into lunch or even to show me where the meeting of the health and welfare group was afterwards. Typical Labour. I was just left to fend for myself. It isn't coldness, but merely the party behaving in its normal way. I ran into Harry Nicholas, our new General Secretary, and said hallo. I saw Terry Pitt, the head of the research department, sitting having a drink. He didn't even get up to greet me but just waved a hand. They're quite glad to see you and although you feel a bit browned off at being so cavalierly treated you shouldn't misinterpret it. It is a sign of the party being in good health. The whole show was pretty encouraging and pretty sensible. They didn't spend their time complaining about prescription charges and they are not going to assault Barbara. They just think she is crazy, that her package has been excellent but that it was a pity to spoil it with the two bits on the strike ballot and the conciliation pause. But they want her leadership. There are signs that we shall go into the next election fairly united and fairly determined to win and, as Peter and I agreed on the way up, all this is possible unless we are hit by an international crisis. Our longer-term strategy must be to stick together and whether we win or lose now will depend on whether we can fight and profit by luck or go down with misfortune if it should come.

Sunday, February 16th

Patrick and Peter Pritchett have been practising with their air guns on the terrace and we have had wonderful Louisa Kennet staying here with Virginia. I took a walk and it was so cold that I could hardly breathe as I went with Suki along the river in a bitter cold wind and sharp frost. We've had very little snow and brilliant sunshine here and the land is iron-frosted, something we have been waiting for for two years. Pritchett and I were discussing our contract and I found it at least cheerful compared with the losses we have sustained on the farm this year.

It has, though, been a relatively good week for the Government, with the Nabarro affair taking the heat off Barbara, and the trade figures on Thursday making us seem economically successful. But in my general review of the week I have to note that Cabinet is more flat than ever and we shall go on like this until after the election.

We have gone right back to Harold as the spider in the centre of the web. I am pretty sure he and Roy are working extremely closely together on the budget and this has given the Prime Minister another excuse to avoid any strategic discussion of general policy. Even a number of Cabinet Committees have fallen off and will remain off until the budget is through. You have got Harold and Roy on the budget, Harold and Michael Stewart, with George Brown on the sidelines, working away on foreign policy and plans to try to get into Europe again, and on defence Harold, Michael and Denis Healey working away on nuclear weapons.

Nor is there really any inner coherence. You have this feeling that the Prime Minister is suppressing general discussion, very clearly in the case of Rhodesia. The Rhodesia Committee simply disappeared, just as the Committee on Industrial Relations disappeared when we got to the planning of Barbara's White Paper. True, on political issues we now have the Parliamentary Committee, but honestly whom Harold calls in seems to be purely arbitrary. We haven't got any inner circle there and the real old-fashioned, cosy group of friends of Harold we had in 1966 is all split up. Peter Shore has been pushed to one side more or less, Judith Hart, who was brought in as a confidante, seems to have quarrelled with Harold on almost everything and is really more my confidante now. Harold lives a very lonely life with Marcia, Gerald Kaufman and Trevor Lloyd-Hughes, his little group of satellites in No. 10. There are the Chief Whip and Fred Peart, but the Chief is not as much in favour as he was and Fred is such a dear old idiot that his presence at the centre is really proof of the vacuum there.

Jim and I really are excluded now. Jim sits on the sidelines, a kind of wise old man, friendly with the trade unions, blunt, bluff, sensible about being anti drugs and not too strong on colour, very much a man of the middle, powerful because as Treasurer of the Party he stands closer to the N.E.C. than anyone else. And I? I have pushed myself on to the sidelines too. Harold doesn't want to discuss things with me. We have no strategic discussion now and therefore no strategy. We are simply carrying on from day to day, from month to month, hoping to avoid a crisis, hoping that somehow we will get through and things will begin to turn. We have asked, time after time for years, for a discussion of the strategy leading up to the election, the planning of the moment when we shall move into a real election mood, but it's not going to be planned. We just have the Prime Minister's characteristic day-to-day moving for tactical advantage, calling us in when it's convenient.

Monday, February 17th

Today I had a huge conference at an hotel in Kensington, that place on the corner of Millionaires' Row. The B.B.C. and I.T.V. were there to cover it and some 1,100 people turned up from the occupational pension funds for a whole day's discussion. I began in the morning and we had Balniel in the afternoon. I took a lot of trouble with this and I have no doubt that it was a major success.

In the evening the C.B.I. came to see me, John Davies, Kerr-Muir and the pensions staff, to begin the negotiations and our formal consultations. They had been delighted by the reception of the scheme this morning and couldn't have been more helpful later.

I have been talking this evening about another important task for the Ministry, which had been impressed upon me by the case of the Shelton fire. A year ago there was a terrible fire in a Midlands hospital, when twenty-one old people were burnt alive. It was a great scandal because an inquiry found there had been no fire practice and now the Department were being told that the Regional Hospital Board, to whom this had been reported by the Hospital Management Committee, wanted to advise us that it was too late to take disciplinary action against any of the staff, the fire officer or the engineer. I had read all the papers and so had David Ennals and neither of us doubted for a moment that we would have to tell the R.H.B. that on no account should they shelter the H.M.C. They must carry out the investigation and the discipline. One of the things which strikes me about the hospital service is how bad they are at not disciplining and dismissing. A man could have had no training when he started in 1948 and be there twenty years later, mucking things up, but never be sacked because of the Whitley Council or some other objection. I have got to shove all these disciplinary activities forward.

I really did try to impress this on the R.H.B. chairmen when I was their host tonight at a most expensive and elegant dinner. I insisted on having Desmond Bonham-Carter on one side of me,[1] and Dame Isabel Graham Bryce on the other and, as I had been saying to David, I told them that the chairmen really must come to us, the Minister or the Secretary of State. Only secretaries go to officials. When they heard this one or two of the chairmen actually said they couldn't believe it. This was a new dispensation, to get action and leadership in the organization.

Tuesday, February 18th

A fortnight ago I found in my box a request for a draft press release of an important memorandum on the re-recruitment of women doctors, who had been lost to the profession by marriage. There are some 3,500 of them. It was an uninspired but perfectly sensible memorandum but I didn't know whether the policy had been agreed. So I waded through a terrible file (the Ministry of Health files are exasperating because the documents are divided in such a way that you can't read consecutively through) and discovered that at no point had Kenneth Robinson or David Ennals agreed on the policy. It was

[1] Chairman of the Board of Governors of University College Hospital 1963–74 and of the South-West Metropolitan Regional Hospital Board 1968–74. He was a Director of Unilever Ltd and was knighted in 1969.

just being processed through. 'This won't do,' I said, and I had a row with Marre. But it didn't really matter much. Anyhow, compared with the very expensive scheme we discussed three weeks ago for getting thirty to forty doctors back from America it will need very much less money to get some of these 3,500 married women back and we ought to be able to do it if I write to each of them personally.

Today I found myself in collision with a woman doctor. Peter Shore's wife was in charge of this and I had a difficult time with her. She is an obstinate woman, who said, 'It's no good, we are doing everything perfectly all right. There is no more we can possibly do. Publicity and administrative memoranda don't have any effect. We have to do it through our personal relations between the doctors in the Ministry and the doctors in the regions but most of the regions will do nothing because they don't pay attention to us.' I finally said, 'You know, what you are really saying is that our job of advising the regions doesn't have any influence,' and she said, 'I don't deny that.' She is a courageous woman, a curious mixture of ability, shrewdness and bloody obstinacy, and it was a queer little talk.

After this I went along to No. 10 for an S.E.P. on transport. Dick Marsh put forward a Green Paper on the highway system. He wanted to launch a great map of Britain, showing the first 1,000 and the next 1,000 miles of motorway. In my view the map was absolutely half-baked. It either showed too much or too little and the text was terrible. It was obvious that we would have to break it up into seven or eight regional maps and to treat roads not merely as means of transport but as infrastructure for economic growth.

Lots of suggestions were made and it became clear that Marsh had been to Harold with the slapdash proposal and they had decided to issue it in four weeks. Just like Barbara's White Paper, another thing fixed between the P.M. and the Minister, rushed through unprepared without enough homework. This is another instance of Harold's bloody awfulness as a leader. He either dallies and is indecisive or he rushes into a thing. He likes gimmicks and prefers a half-baked to a deeply worked-out idea.

True, he always praises me for the work I have done on national superannuation in the last four years but he doesn't realize what a difference all the preparation has made. We have looked all round it and are forewarned and forearmed against the dangers. It's getting excited about an idea, like Barbara's *In Place of Strife* or this damned transport thing, and never doing enough work on it that makes our Government look so amateur, silly and childish.

Another disastrous day on the Parliament Bill from 3.30 to 11.30. I settled down to do the amendment on Clause 1 today and Bob Sheldon got up and spoke for two hours and twenty minutes. There were a few minutes' more debate, then the amendment was put and he didn't even say yes to it, i.e. there was no division and what he was doing was pure filibustering. I managed to do one more amendment today before Fred took over while I went out to dinner and when I came back I found him in a terrible mess because the back benchers had been challenging the nature of the Preamble to the Bill. I had known this would cause trouble and, sure enough, there were another three hours' debate until it was adjourned until tomorrow morning. It's now clear that we are in really serious difficulty with this. We've always known that back benchers can hold up almost indefinitely a Bill for which you can't get a closure unless there is tremendous provocation,[1] and with a constitutional Bill of this sort it is easy for every Member to speak and to make a very long speech. I shall have to see Callaghan about it tomorrow.

Wednesday, February 19th

When I came in for a meeting in my office at lunchtime, I was told that Stephen Swingler died quite suddenly last night. I had given Anne Swingler lunch yesterday and she seemed definitely more cheerful. In the evening she and Judith had dinner together, so we looked after her all day, and she said the viral pneumonia seemed to have cleared up, and the only area of danger was his bronchial tubes. At the hospital in the evening they sent her away saying it was all right and she could relax but when her back was turned his heart failed and he died. It has been a great shock. He was not a wonderful administrator but he had other superb qualities.

When he was Parliamentary Secretary to the Ministry of Transport he did more adjournment debates than anybody else. When Barbara was translated to D.E.P. in April last year and Dick Marsh was brought in at the last moment in place of John Morris who was moved to Defence,[2] there was a fiasco because there was nobody there to run the Transport Bill. Dick Marsh was against it and sulky and wouldn't do any work. Stephen, who was promoted to Minister of State, took command and apparently ran the Committee Stage absolutely magnificently. He showed himself an able, resolute parliamentarian. It wasn't that he was very creative in policy-making but he was an admirable front-bench politician. When I got him over to John Adam Street and gave him complete charge he showed powers of getting on with people and they liked him, though he never came up to me with an original idea. At Christmas he was ill and I got him to stay away for an extra week and, as I look back, he never has been well and I rather suspect that I never saw the best of him. There it is, a tremendous blow.

This morning from 10.0 to 1.0 we had the postponed session of yesterday's

[1] The guillotine is 'the extreme limit to which procedure goes in affirming the right of the majority at the expense of the minorities of the House', and as such its use to assist the passage of a controversial and constitutional measure like the Parliament No. 2 Bill would probably have been unacceptable even to many of those who supported the Bill itself.

[2] Labour M.P. for Aberavon since October 1959. He was Parliamentary Secretary at the Ministry of Power 1964–6, Joint Parliamentary Secretary at the Ministry of Transport 1966–8 and at the Ministry of Defence (Equipment) 1968–70 and since 1974 has been Secretary of State for Wales.

Committee Stage of the Parliament Bill, and Mr Callaghan, who had been away the whole of the first day and practically the whole of the second, put in an appearance, made a ferocious speech attacking the Opposition front bench for breaking their part of the compact and threatened to use the guillotine. This afternoon he took me into a near-by room and said, 'I made a great speech this morning. I have shown our line. I think the tactic is to just plough the Bill through in eighteen days. Either we plough it through or drop it altogether, or we can try making a deal with the Opposition, but the one thing we mustn't have is a defeat. Both you and I have got to be tough and we must have no truck with them. I am the leader and this afternoon I am going to show them how I will lead.' I thought this was fine. However, I was sitting in my room upstairs when suddenly the telephone rang. It was Jim's Private Office saying he had to be away at 7.0 for dinner and asking if I could take over, a request that went to Fred Peart's office as well. The fact is that Jim is absolutely split-minded. He doesn't want the Bill, he has predicted it will fail, he wants it to fail and to be destroyed by the House of Commons, and yet he doesn't want himself to be injured in the process. He wants it to be known that he was gallantly trying to get the Bill through and that it wasn't his fault if it didn't, so he is being both very tough and yet is prepared for tactics which are bound to provoke the maximum irritation. It's obvious that people on our side can stand seeing me and Fred pushing the Bill through because we genuinely want it but they can't stand the dishonesty of Callaghan and nor can the other side.

This evening began the political story of finding Stephen Swingler's successor. Harold rang me up to say that he thought that the right man was Reg Freeson, Reg Freeson, that little wet Jew from Willesden who should never have been promoted to Parliamentary Secretary in the Ministry of Power and who has been a deeply unpopular flop there.[1] I was to have him made Minister of State, the worst appointment since Tom Urwin,[2] who himself was the worst since Caligula's horse. I blew up, and when I was asked whom I wanted I said, 'Roy Hattersley, of course.' Harold said, 'You can't have him, partly because Barbara can't do without him and partly because he is disloyal and belongs to the wrong side. I must have the political balance kept. We must have another left-winger, and Reg Freeson is on the Left.' 'Well,' I said, 'I must consider competence and Roy Hattersley and Dick Taverne, both of whom I know are C.D.S., are the only two.'[3] Harold said, 'Oh, do be serious,

[1] Labour M.P. for Willesden East 1964–74 and for Brent East since 1974. He was Parliamentary Secretary, at the Ministry of Power 1967–9 and at the M.H.L.G. 1969–70; he has been Minister for Housing and Construction at the D.O.E. since 1974.

[2] Labour M.P. for Houghton-le-Spring since 1964, he was Minister of State at the D.E.A. 1968–9 and Minister of State for regional policy, with special responsibility for the northern region, October 1969–June 1970.

[3] The Campaign for Democratic Socialism was born after the Labour Party's 1960 Scarborough conference decided in favour of unilateral nuclear disarmament. It organized in the unions and constituencies with a view to reversing that decision. It dissolved itself on the return of a Labour Government in 1964.

that's impossible. I think Freeson is the man for you.' 'We'd better think it over,' I said, 'and I will ring you tomorrow morning.'

At the end of another evening of the Parliament Bill I was sick to death and I started to walk back through the heavy deluge of snow that fell today. As I was wading through the slush a little Mini stopped in front of me and there was Marcia Williams, whom I hadn't seen for weeks and weeks. She said, 'Get in. I'll be your chauffeur.' As she drove me to Vincent Square, I said, 'Heavens, Marcia, save me from Reg Freeson.' She said, 'What?' I must say, to Marcia's credit, after she tipped me out in Vincent Square she drove straight back to talk to Harold about it.

Thursday, February 20th

When I rang Harold this morning there was no more talk of Freeson. That had been knocked out and I was told I could meet him with new ideas just before Parliamentary Committee at 10.15. I went in at 10.10 and this time he did say, 'We'll see if we can fix Hattersley with Barbara.' He called Barbara in and alluded to it and then we moved to Parliamentary Committee and on to Cabinet.

The main incident at Cabinet was the de Gaulle explosion. I had vaguely noticed in our telegrams an account by the Ambassador, Christopher Soames, of an interview he had had before a luncheon with de Gaulle. This morning, in the course of a report by Harold Wilson on his visit to Bonn and by Michael Stewart on his visit to the Western European Union and the manoeuvres there, they both referred to this conversation. It became clear that Harold had felt compelled to tell Kiesinger in Bonn of the astonishing proposals de Gaulle had made to Soames. It would prove Harold a good boy and a loyal NATO and E.E.C. man if he passed on what de Gaulle had suggested about the breakup of the E.E.C. and NATO and the need to formulate new ideas.

Since the breakdown of the negotiations for British entry to the E.E.C. President de Gaulle had made no contact with Sir Christopher Soames, the United Kingdom's Ambassador in Paris, but on February 4th he had invited him to luncheon, and outlined his views on the future of Europe. The General's plan included the virtual end of the existing Common Market and of the European commitment to NATO, and its replacement by an enlarged European Association, led by a small inner council of Britain, France, West Germany and Italy. Mr Wilson was to visit Bonn from February 12th to 14th and President Nixon was coming to Europe in late February so the British Government suspected that the General's remarks might be a device to compromise Britain in the eyes of her European allies and of the United States. Accordingly, the Prime Minister told Dr Kiesinger, the West German Chancellor, of the conversation and then disclosed the General's remarks to the press. On February 24th the French Government made a formal protest to Britain, alleging that the President's remarks had been distorted and diplomatic channels and the press improperly used.

I must admit that I hardly listened to this item. As Michael Stewart had not suggested that the de Gaulle subject was particularly important and had preceded it with four other items, with his boringly dull voice drilling through your head, on and on for half an hour, I didn't really notice. Harold Wilson did of course discuss it more and then Fred Peart made some observations on whether it was really important for us to make ourselves examine this proposition for something beyond the Common Market but he was hardly listened to.

I had a lunch-time engagement at the Café Royal with the Industrial Society. Never have so many people turned up for one of their conferences. Seven hundred sat down to lunch and listened to me giving a fifteen-minute speech followed by ten minutes of questions. This time we had taken the precaution of having a little press release issued beforehand but here again, as on Monday, there was virtually nothing in the press or on T.V.

Today was a pretty good pension day for me because I also had a meeting with some twenty M.P.s who were ready to be trained to go out to the constituencies as prophets and apostles preaching the doctrine. Stephen had got a fine group of people together and they were pretty keen. From that I went on to the P.L.P. Meeting, where first we had a terrible row about the Parliament Bill. A right-wing, muddle-headed man called Richard Mitchell said,[1] 'I'm not against this Bill, but why the hell are we wasting all our time on it when we have important things like the Merchant Shipping Bill?[2] We should either give it up or fight it through, I don't mind which.' There was a furious outburst. The tremendous discontent which is boiling up in the Party is being fomented by Callaghan who both leads and doesn't lead. It's, in a sense, politically the most difficult and dangerous parliamentary situation I have ever seen. When we got on to my pensions scheme there was no difficulty. Woodrow Wyatt asked me questions about funding and I didn't have much difficulty in fending them off because they came from him.[3] It is obvious we have got a solid support for the scheme in the Party. It is workable, relatively popular and something they can sell.

This evening Anne came up to London in a tremendous snowfall and we had four young relations to a gay dinner in the House. There were only Private Bills going on, and I had an enormously lively time. I do enjoy relaxing and talking in the company of young people.

Later this evening Harold rang me up again. There were great difficulties

[1] Labour M.P. for Southampton, Test, 1966–70 and since May 1971 for Southampton, Itchen.

[2] The Bill to modernize the law on Merchant Shipping failed to pass in the 1968–9 session but it was reintroduced in the following session and became law in 1970.

[3] Labour M.P. for Birmingham, Aston, 1945–55, and for Bosworth 1955–70. He was Parliamentary Under-Secretary of State and Financial Secretary at the War Office May–October 1951 and since 1976 he has been Chairman of the Horserace Totalisator Board.

about my Minister of State. He had had further reports. Roy Hattersley had made three disloyal remarks recently and we couldn't really promote him. What about other people? 'Well,' I said, 'do the few remarks matter?' We cast round and I suggested Dick Taverne. He said, 'Have you lost all your political antennae that you fail to remember what our loyalties are? Dick Taverne, he is a silken, treacherous member of the C.D.S. group, he is most unpopular in the Parliamentary Party. If you have him it will be a betrayal of all we stand for. I am amazed at your forgetting.' I said, 'It's not I who have forgotten, Harold. I think these young men have forgotten their past. I know Roy Hattersley is no more loyal to Roy Jenkins than he is to you. He is just an able young man on the way up and I think Dick Taverne has rather more loyalty and decency about him. He is a loyal Jenkins supporter but he is not going to be disloyal to you in his job for me.' Then Harold said, 'It's out of the question.' 'Look,' I said, 'can I perhaps move David Ennals to Health?' 'Yes,' said Harold, 'you can, and put somebody else into Social Security in his place. What about Shirley Williams?' I said, 'Shirley Williams is much more C.D.S. than Roy Hattersley or Dick Taverne.' 'But she is a woman, it would suit you. Shirley Williams, that's a good idea.' I don't know what to think.

Friday, February 21st

I rang Harold again because I didn't want to discuss this at Stephen's funeral, and said, 'Shirley won't do.' 'Yes,' he said, 'I agree with you. What about Bea Serota?' 'She won't do for Social Security,' I said, 'she's in the Lords, but she might do for Health.' Yes, this was a possibility. Bea Serota, ex-Chairman of the Children's Committee of the L.C.C., a very powerful woman, now one of the Whips in the House of Lords. I tried this out on Clifford Jarrett and Marre later on during the day and asked them to try it out this afternoon.

At lunchtime I went to Stephen's funeral at Golders Green crematorium. When I rang up yesterday his brother Humphrey had said he would fix the funeral for Saturday afternoon. I got that changed, saying, 'Look, it will cost each Labour M.P. £10 to stay in London on Friday and Saturday night. Do have it on Friday if you possibly can.' So there we were at 12.30. A big snowfall was melting away and there was snow mist all around us, green grass with yellow crocuses growing through and pale sunlight, all desperately forlorn. Nearly all our civil servants from Social Security turned up and there were our two Permanent Secretaries. They had been fond of him in the Ministry. There was a good round-up of left-wing M.P.s, and Barbara Castle, in the front row Harold and Mary Wilson and up in the chancel Harold and Mrs Davies and Michael Foot.[1] There wasn't a service, just the coffin waiting to slide down into the fire and a chap playing the organ. Michael got up and said

[1] Harold Davies, Labour M.P. for Leek 1945–70, was Joint Parliamentary Secretary at the Ministry of Pensions and National Insurance 1965–6 and at the Ministry of Social Security 1966–7. He became a life peer in 1970.

a quiet obituary, then Harold Davies, more florid but curiously touching. I thought, 'My God, I'd rather have a bit of ritual at a funeral. It's too desperately heartbreaking for the wife and the kids when it's all addressed to them as human being to human being and though God may not exist there is something to be said for him to stop everybody from mopping their eyes as we are all doing.' We walked out through the back of the chancel into the sunshine on to the lawn and saw the flowers and each other and couldn't say much.

I came back with John Ellis and gave him a lot of drink at lunch. We talked about the draft of the motion for the order paper for the debate on Barbara's White Paper and on mine. The dates have now been moved to March 3rd for hers and March 6th for mine. We wanted identical wording and tried to formulate the proper phrase. We had thought we would have 'The House gives approval to the general principles of the White Paper', which seemed to me too vague, and Barbara had thought 'the principles and proposals', which I thought too specific. I said, 'structures' but that was too specific and now John Ellis said to me, 'Why not "This House approves the White Paper as a basis for legislation and invites her Majesty's Government to continue consultations with a view to preparing legislation".' So this afternoon I had a meeting with Barbara and Fred Peart and this is what we shall propose as a basis for our two debates the week after next.

It became clear that during the course of the day a major decision had been taken on the Soames affair. The Foreign Office would formally announce that the Soames–de Gaulle conversations had taken place and give their version of them but this produced a major Anglo-French crisis, because this decision by the British Foreign Secretary to announce a top-secret conversation is quite distinct from Harold Wilson's decision, on going to Bonn, to tell Kiesinger about it. I quite understand that Harold should feel that, if he hadn't told Kiesinger and the French had, our whole position would be undermined. This was the trap de Gaulle had laid for him. I don't so much blame Harold for that but I was very interested as to why on earth this decision had been taken this afternoon, though no suggestion had been made to Cabinet that the conversations should be published, and I thought I would ask Harold about it at the weekend.

Saturday, February 22nd

We drove over in the fog to Jock Campbell's house for lunch today and Jock was saying what a good piece John Freeman had done in the *Statesman* this week about Kingsley Martin.[1] Kingsley had died in Egypt and, as he would have wished, his body has been handed over to an Egyptian hospital by his companion Dorothy Woodman. Four or five papers rang me up, desperately asking me to do an obituary, but I had the sense not to do a single line because my feelings are too prejudiced, too sore if you like, to be fair about him.

[1] Kingsley Martin was Editor of the *New Statesman* 1931–60.

There were some pretty good obituaries. Our old friend Francis Williams did one in the *Guardian* and Denis Brogan did a very sympathetic and kind one in the *Spectator*.[1]

Then there was John Freeman, to whom I can't help feeling an increasing hostility. He celebrated his departure to his non-partisan position as Ambassador in the States with a curiously detached piece about Kingsley, saying what a marvellous editor he was, how unbearably untidy, how unfair, but he didn't say a word about his influence and I found myself arguing about this with Jock. I said, 'I know you are Chairman of the directors of the *Statesman*, that it has been made the most influential paper in the world, and you are pleased that John said it had been made so by Kingsley, but what has happened since then? Since Kingsley left it has declined in importance and the one thing John Freeman didn't show is why it was so influential under Kingsley. It wasn't just because of his so-called genius as an editor, it was because of his ideas. They enormously influenced Nehru in India,[2] they influenced the chief people in Burma just after the war and the Laski–Martin ideology was an ideology which half the leaders of the colonial revolution had imbibed.[3] It made them not passionately anti-British and pro-communist but liberalistic and pro-British. I won't forget a visit to New York when I asked to see U Thant and he gave me an interview within an hour.[4] Why? Not because I was a Minister, not because I was a prominent journalist, but because I was a friend of Kingsley and we were fellow readers of the *Statesman*. Kingley's ideas, like Laski's, were bogus, phoney, sentimental, but they were important, and the two of them were marvellous teachers who appealed enormously to the foreigner. They were hopeless at influencing British politics, where they alienated people and where they only appealed to non-political people in universities.' In the end Jock said, 'You ought to be writing a second article.' I said, 'God forbid, I don't write articles on Kingsley.' But I think it's true that people haven't seen the real role that he played.

I also met at the Campbells' an Oxford professor of obstetrics, who is appalled at the present situation in London of the private exploitation of the abortion law. Fortunately I am well briefed, because George Godber has been keeping me fully informed. It is perfectly true that many more private nursing homes have been set up in London, while in the National Health Service the numbers haven't increased very remarkably. The Act is being implemented by doctors for money in a very odious way and there is little

[1] Francis Williams, Editor of the *Daily Herald* 1936–40, was Controller of News and Censorship at the Ministry of Information 1941–5 and Adviser on Public Relations to the Prime Minister 1945–7. He became a life peer in 1962 and died in 1970. Sir Denis Brogan was Professor of Political Science at the University of Cambridge 1939–68. He died in 1974.

[2] Shri Jawaharlal Nehru was Prime Minister of India and Indian Minister for External Affairs from 1947 until his death in May 1964.

[3] Harold Laski was Professor of Political Science at the University of London from 1926 until his death in 1950. He was a member of the Labour Party's N.E.C. 1936–49 and an early contributor to the *Nation*.

[4] Secretary-General to the United Nations 1961–71. He died in 1974.

we can do except tighten our control of the private nursing homes. This is the price we pay. The professor and I discussed it at length with Thomas and Pen Balogh, sitting round in the new house which Jock has provided for them, a lovely place 100 yards from their own, in the wood. It was extremely pleasant, and we and the children had a nice time there with them all.

Sunday, February 23rd

I rang up Harold this morning and told him Bea Serota was O.K. Late on Friday afternoon my Permanent Secretaries came to me and said 'first-rate'. Philip Allen had given her a tremendous write-up and there had been nothing but praise for her.[1] I put in one other fact. When I had seen Barbara and Fred Peart on Friday afternoon and discussed it with them, Fred had rather confirmed Harold's view about Roy Hattersley and even more about Dick Taverne. Barbara, on the other hand, said quite openly, 'Poor Roy Hattersley, there will be a terrible row in the office if he doesn't get the job this time. He would have got it if Stephen Swingler hadn't been there.' She thought he ought to be given the job and that John Ellis ought to come to her. John Ellis was Stephen's P.P.S. at Transport, a left-wing engineer from Bristol, very nice but very inexperienced, and no match for Roy Hattersley in the job of fighting at the dispatch box, so this is rather a sentimental view of Barbara's. Although, no doubt, I could have got Roy Hattersley, I had come to the conclusion that Bea Serota, who is so thoroughly competent and who was a Home Office nominee to the Seebohm Commission, would do me a world of good by coming to our side in the battle against the Home Office on the implementation of the Seebohm Report. Nevertheless, looking back on it, Fred, Barbara, the Chief Whip and I all agreed about the hopelessness of the Prime Minister. (The Chief Whip, by the way, wanted me to take Brian O'Malley, his number two, and the P.M. said, 'He's always trying to get rid of his number two.') Harold had not consulted Barbara, apart from one obscure reference on Thursday, and he hadn't consulted the Chief Whip or Fred at all. Here he is, once again, packing his Cabinet and balancing his administration in terms of the loyalties of 1963 when people were voting between him and Gaitskell. It is strange and almost unbelievable that a man can be four years a Prime Minister and still be so obsessed with party ideological irrelevancies.

I also took the opportunity of asking Harold about the Soames affair and he said, 'Well, when we got back into London at about 1.30 from Stephen's funeral, just before I went off to Ipswich I got a proposal from the Foreign Office that in view of the French leaks we should publish. Of course I didn't want to lay a trap for de Gaulle but maybe I was wrong.' I said, 'My God, do you mean that is how it was fixed?' 'Yes,' he said. 'I gave my consent

[1] Sir Philip Allen (K.C.B. 1964) was Permanent Under-Secretary of State at the Home Office 1966–72. He has been Chairman of the Occupational Pensions Board since 1973 and a member of the Security Commission since 1973. He became a life peer in 1976.

then. I am not so sure it was wise.' 'What will Christopher Soames do about it? He's coming back today.' Harold said, 'He will be in a terrible fury because he will think his honour has been impugned.' Then Harold explained how he had told Kiesinger before Soames had got permission from the French Foreign Office, although the plan had been for Soames to go to the Quai d'Orsay the evening before Harold talked to Kiesinger. It didn't work that way because Soames's meeting was postponed until the next morning and so technically we had put ourselves in the wrong by telling the Germans before we had got the leave of the French. This had been followed up by the Foreign Office announcement of the content of the conversations. No wonder the French talk about a crisis. I suddenly became interested in foreign affairs again. For ages I have been saying to Tommy that I wasn't really interested in anything but my own Department but here I am aroused once more and aware that I was slack in Cabinet on Thursday morning. I rang up Roy and tested him and he said that he knew all about this episode as he had been in Paris, but he was as surprised as I had been about the publication of the General's remarks and he suspected that it was that infantile Foreign Office again.

I rang up Barbara too, who told me that the half-baked motorway map of Britain hadn't even arrived in her box this weekend. It came down in one of my red boxes today with some minor changes in the text and concessions on the road maps but I have written a tough letter back saying, 'This is really insulting. We are told we must give our approval by next Thursday, and it has only just arrived.' When I asked her about the de Gaulle episode she admitted that, like me, she had found Michael very boring on Thursday morning and as she had been busy waiting for her items on the two big strikes, she hadn't paid adequate attention. As she said, Michael has the power of making everything equally unimportant and boring. She saw enormous dangers to us in this overture of de Gaulle's, the danger of being trapped, particularly when de Gaulle said that Harold, not de Gaulle himself, should take the initiative and, unlike me, she thought that Harold shouldn't have said anything to Kiesinger. We both agreed, however, that this was a terrible thing. She emphasized, of course, the futility of our trying to get into the Common Market with £600 million shortfall on our balance of payments and the humiliation of trying to get in and failing, so she said that if this episode stopped that, it would be a good thing. We both agreed that the real trouble was the infantilism of Harold and Michael Stewart, priggish children who showed moral disapproval of the de Gaulle overture. They threw up their hands and averted themselves from it in horror. They didn't see it as possibly permitting a breakthrough in Anglo-French relations, but instead they created a situation in which we have managed to come out as villains of the piece. It's an extraordinary story, another proof of Harold's ineptitude in foreign and external affairs, the area where he prides himself so much. Harold, Michael, George Brown and Jim Callaghan really know nothing about Europe, nothing compared to myself or Barbara, who have studied Europe for twenty years, but we have stood aside, letting them get away with laying down the law. Denis Healey has had a role to play as Minister of Defence but he has been on the sidelines, sulking in a corner most of the time. He has just given a lecture at Munich about nuclear retaliation, with a very wild interview in *Der Spiegel*, no doubt hoping that the German would not be translated into English but it has appeared in the *Observer* in full. His line is that we must build up our entry into Europe via defence, something which is not at all incompatible with the de Gaulle overture and no doubt he will feel as angry as Barbara and I do about this. As for Roy, once again he has shown himself as a man who is in on everything and yet doesn't have any influence. For four years now I have said to myself, 'I must leave foreign affairs to them, they know all about it,' but they know nothing about it and I am beginning to feel something growing in me which I have long suppressed.

Monday, February 24th

Bea Serota saw the Prime Minister this morning and I have got her as my new Minister of State. At 10.30 David Ennals went round to hear the news that he had been transferred. He rang me up last night very sad and of course it is sad. He had been doing extremely well on the Health side, which suited him and gave him plenty of publicity and T.V. appearances. Now he has to go to a very different, tight little group of people, a rather monastic collection of inward-looking experts working on the incredibly complicated subject of social security. I had realized that Bea's appointment would be unpopular among our M.P.s because it denies them a job, but what I hadn't perhaps calculated was that both Norman Pentland and Julian Snow would regard themselves as outraged because they hadn't been considered. Julian actually came to see me. He was terribly upset but he is on the edge of retirement and not likely to be in the next Parliament and I told him this and tried to soothe him down. The real difference between him and Norman Pentland is that I think Julian Snow is worth keeping on for the next two years, whereas Norman Pentland is certainly worth the sack. By and large the Parliamentary Party is irritated that a good job has gone to a peeress. London M.P.s, who know Bea and how good she is, have congratulated me but they are very few and the provinces thought fairly badly of it. It has added to their irritation with my association with House of Lords reform.

The de Gaulle affair has gone on just about as I expected. This afternoon Michael Stewart answered questions and he put up the best possible defence of his and the Foreign Office's rather prissy, self-righteous line. He didn't give a very convincing account of the thinnest point in his argument, that Harold had been sent off to talk to Kiesinger before de Gaulle was informed and why all this had been given out to the press on Friday, but he is always extremely good in Parliament and he did it well and with conviction. But surprisingly the Speaker permitted a discussion for tomorrow under Standing

Order No. 9 and the effect will be to postpone the starting of our next two days on the Parliament Bill.

Tuesday, February 25th

This morning's papers had the results of the Ulster elections. We have been very excited about this General Election, where Terence O'Neill,[1] the Progressive, was testing the strength of his hold over the Unionist Party and his ability to defeat the old-fashioned Orangemen. O'Neill was the man we were relying on in Northern Ireland to do our job of dragging Ulster out of its eighteenth-century Catholic–Protestant conflict. I have been reading with the children the story in *Gullivers' Travels* about the dispute between the Big Enders and the Little Enders among the Lilliputian aristocracy. The children have been enjoying it enormously because now they can appreciate the sardonic jokes about politics as well as the excellence and the comedy of the story. Well, this is just like Ireland.

O'Neill called the election and I had great hopes that he would bring it off, that he would fragment the opposition, smash the old-fashioned people and enable Ulster to go forward.

Since October 1968, there had been increasing clashes in Northern Ireland between Protestant extremists and Civil Rights demonstrators, mainly Roman Catholic, and there was also growing disunity in the governing Unionist Party. Although Northern Ireland had been a self-governing province since the partition of Ireland in 1922 ultimate responsibility for its Constitution and for law and order rested with Westminster, where the situation was observed with concern. The Unionist Party, led by Captain Terence O'Neill, was politically linked with the Conservative Party in Britain rather than with Labour but nevertheless Prime Minister O'Neill had over the past few years sought to ease tensions between Northern Ireland and the Republic of Ireland and between Protestants and Catholics in the province. In an effort to rally and assert the dominance of moderate Unionists, on February 3rd Captain O'Neill had called a General Election. Polling took place on February 24th and though, as parties at Westminster hoped and expected, the Unionists were victorious there was little comfort in the results. The Ulster Unionists were returned with a majority of only 20, in a number of formerly safe Unionist constituencies their vote was split, and the Reverend Ian Paisley, who stood against Captain O'Neill, lost by only 1,414 votes in a total 16,400.[2]

[1] Unionist M.P. for Bannside, Parliament of Northern Ireland, 1946–70, Parliamentary Secretary at the Ministry of Health 1948, Deputy Speaker and Chairman of Ways and Means 1953, Joint Parliamentary Secretary for Home Affairs and Health 1955, Minister of Home Affairs 1956, and of Finance 1956. Prime Minister of Northern Ireland 1963–9. In 1970 he became a life peer, taking the title of Lord O'Neill of the Maine.

[2] See *Wilson*, pp. 670–5.

If he doesn't we shall have to do something about it and Callaghan told me some weeks ago in the greatest secrecy that as Home Secretary he was having to work out plans in case the Northern Ireland Government collapsed. I had hoped that this was a remote possibility but today we see that O'Neill's effort to get a kind of liberalizing mandate has totally failed. He himself has only just held his own against the Reverend Ian Paisley,[1] leader of the reactionary Orangemen. Despite my vague hope we are not in an age when liberalism will win. O'Neill played a bold stroke for the best of reasons but he has failed and I doubt whether he will last very long.

At Alexander Fleming House Julian Snow was waiting for me. I had him in for a drink last night with Alan Marre, Clifford Jarrett and David Ennals to meet Bea Serota but today he was saying that he must write to the Prime Minister to ask for a transfer. His work would be too heavy with no Minister of State in the Commons to deal with all the adjournment debates and Questions. This was really the result of his reflecting on my terrible remark that I had not considered him for the job. It has hurt him to the core. He is very slow-minded, though he is conscientious and perfectly capable as a Parliamentary Secretary, and totally impossible for any promotion. But he begged me and I said, 'Well, if it's too much work, old boy, I could certainly try to get another Parliamentary Secretary. When I next see Harold I'll talk to him about it.'

Off to lunch with Pam Berry. I haven't been to her for ages and I found her recovering from bronchitis. Her dark eyes are as bright as ever, her cheeks as clean as ever, but she is beginning to look her age. There we were, with Paul and Marigold Johnson, Hugh Massingham[2] and Tommy Balogh. Paul Johnson was fanatically supporting the Foreign Office and Michael Stewart on the de Gaulle affair, saying they were absolutely right. I didn't bother to go in for the Standing Order No. 9 debate this afternoon but Michael triumphed once again as the number of Tories who voted against him was negligible.[3] He had got out of this extremely well.

But I did go to Harold's room in the House this afternoon and mentioned that I had been asked about a second Parliamentary Secretary and that there was feeling in the Party that we now had one fewer job for commoners. 'You might make yourself popular,' I said, 'by making an extra Parliamen-

[1] The Reverend Ian Paisley, minister of the Martyrs Memorial Free Presbyterian Church, Belfast, since 1946, was Protestant Unionist M.P. for Bannside in the Northern Ireland Parliament, 1970–2, Democratic Unionist Member for North Antrim in the Northern Ireland Assembly, 1973–5 and United Ulster Unionist Coalition Member for North Antrim in the Northern Ireland Constitutional Convention, May 1975–6. From 1970–4 he was Protestant Unionist M.P. and from 1974 United Ulster Unionist Coalition M.P. for North Antrim at Westminster.

[2] The son of H. W. Massingham, Editor of the *Nation* 1907–23 and himself a novelist and journalist. He was the *Observer*'s Political Columnist from the end of the Second World War until 1961, when he moved to the *Sunday Telegraph*, where he remained until his death in December 1971.

[3] In the debate on Anglo-French Relations the Government's policy was approved by 270 votes to 33.

tary Secretary for Health.' Harold looked at me and said, 'Popular with one man who gets the job, unpopular with the thirty-five who feel they ought to have got it. No, my boy, for the moment you'll carry on as you were. You told me only a few weeks ago that you could manage.' 'Yes,' I said, 'that was a bit different. Now that I have a Minister of State in the Lords, in the Commons I shall be short.' But he said, 'It will be good for you. You can manage perfectly well.' I went back and told Julian that I had talked to Harold and he seemed pleased and relieved. But I shall have to pamper him all through the week.

I went across to the House at 7 o'clock. No progress had been made on the Parliament Bill, we were struggling with Clause 2 and there, as we sat on the front bench, we realized the utter futility of the filibuster that is now going on. Michael Foot on the one side, in his most brilliant, demagogic, amusing form, and Enoch Powell on the other, in his most brilliant historical form, were supported by a whole series of people like John Boyd-Carpenter and Robin Turton on their side and on our side Bob Sheldon, [1] and a lot of absolute rag, tag and bobtail like Arthur Lewis and that terrible fellow from Portsmouth.[2] Every single amendment was being discussed and the chair was getting more and more scared. There is the alliance between twenty to thirty distinguished, reactionary fundamentalists on both sides and the fundamentalists who want total revolution of the Second Chamber, and they are enjoying themselves with no whips on. It was a terribly depressing performance which I watched until 7.30 when I popped off in my little dinner jacket to the Guildhall. There was the Builders' Association in full regalia and I found myself sitting next to the Dean of St Paul's, a very earnest, worthy New Zealander.[3] How different from Dean Inge or the intellectuals of the past.[4] We had a long talk about immortality and I was able to tell him what it felt like to be an agnostic and he listened with great interest. He couldn't really see anything against it. One of the Sheriffs made a very brilliant, funny speech and the Lord Mayor quite a funny speech and then I moved a toast to the

[1] Robert Turton was Conservative M.P. for Thirsk and Malton 1929–February 1974. He was Parliamentary Secretary at the Ministry of National Insurance 1951–3, Minister of Pensions 1953–4, Joint Parliamentary Under-Secretary of State for Foreign Affairs October 1954–December 1955, and Minister of Health December 1955–January 1957. Chairman of the Select Committee on Procedure 1970–4, he was knighted in 1971 and in 1974 became a life peer, taking the title of Lord Tranmire.

[2] Arthur Lewis was Labour M.P. for Upton, West Ham, 1945–50 and for West Ham North 1950–74 and since 1974 for Newham North-West. The 'terrible fellow' was Frank Judd, Labour M.P. for Portsmouth West 1966–74 and since 1974 for Portsmouth North. He was Parliamentary Under-Secretary of State for Defence (R.N.) 1974–6 and became Parliamentary Under-Secretary of State at the Ministry of Overseas Development in 1976.

[3] The Very Reverend Martin Sullivan, former Dean and Vicar-General of Christchurch, New Zealand, Archdeacon of London and Canon Residentiary of St Paul's Cathedral 1963–7, has been Dean of St Paul's since 1967.

[4] Fellow and Tutor of Hertford College, Oxford, 1888–96, Lady Margaret's Professor of Divinity and Fellow of Jesus College, Cambridge, 1907–11, was Dean of St Paul's from 1911 until his retirement in 1934. He was a popular journalist and a figure of some controversy, as well as a religious thinker of stature. He died in 1954.

Builders, which I did competently but not outrageously well.[1] I had to rush away because before I could get back to the House of Commons I had been instructed to go into No. 10 for Nixon.[2]

He is due to leave tomorrow morning and this evening there was a dinner party for him at No. 10, to which a select number of the Cabinet had been invited, Barbara, the Lord Chancellor and the Chancellor of the Exchequer. Fred Peart, Jim Callaghan and I were excluded. Interesting to see who was there and who was not. Those of us who had not been invited had been told to get back to No. 10 at 9.45 so that Nixon could have a sort of short Cabinet Meeting with us. I needn't have rushed back from the Guildhall because it was 10.15 before they got out of the dinner, which had obviously been very boring. After a bit of standing about in the drawing room upstairs we went down for Harold's pseudo-Cabinet and there Burke Trend sat himself away from the table and Nixon beside the Prime Minister, with Roy, myself and all the others in their usual seats around the table. It was a sort of ghastly parody of a Cabinet. We started with Nixon being asked to talk, as Harold said, about the problems of youth and race and he gave us a perfectly competent address on the need for a new religion and idealism.

There was absolutely nothing extra or new in it, (why should there be?) but already I saw that he was different from his television image, fresher, more vigorous, in contrast to Hubert Humphrey who, when I last saw him at dinner, had given me a long, ideological, democratic lecture for forty-five minutes about the need to support L.B.J. in Vietnam. Nixon was altogether nicer than he used to be, with a certain charm, a man, as Harold had said to me earlier this afternoon, without the doctrinaire ideology of the anti-communist crusading democrats, Dean Acheson,[3] Walt Rostow,[4] Hubert Humphrey or L.B.J. There was clearly a great change in Harold's attitude and he was finding Nixon's pragmatism and lack of doctrinaireness a positive relief. This struck me too.

Harold then called on us, starting with the Home Secretary and going on to Ted Short. Messages were passed round; each of us was made to do our little piece. I noticed that those like Barbara who had been at the dinner were a bit left out and the others brought in. We put on quite a decent show and finally I got a message that after the youngest member of the Cabinet had spoken the senior member would make a philosophical wind-up, so I found myself having to finish off these proceedings. I started by describing how everybody talked about youth and revolution and how we had to find a

[1] Sir Charles Trinder (Kt 1966), Consultant to Trinder, Anderson & Co. Ltd, Chairman of the Australian Steam Shipping Co. Ltd and of the Bideford Shipyard Ltd, was Alderman of Aldgate 1959, Sheriff of the City of London 1964 and Lord Mayor of London 1968–9.

[2] Richard Nixon visited London from February 24th to 26th. He had been elected President of the United States in November 1968 and was re-elected in November 1972 but resigned, rather than face impeachment, in August 1974.

[3] American Secretary of State 1949–53.

[4] Special Assistant to the President 1966–9, Professor of Economics and of History at the University of Austin, Texas, since 1969.

philosophy to satisfy youth, but that I very much doubted this because the numbers of youth in revolt were a tiny minority of university students, with no philosophy, just an anti-philosophy. The significant fact is that they are sentimentalists with no understanding of power and this is how they differ from all their predecessors, who at least understood Marx and that politics is about power. These don't. They think it is about protest and it makes them so hopeless. I made my observation about 1968 being like 1848, the year of unsuccessful revolutions, when the tottering Establishments hit back. I said, 'It was the crushing of Czechoslovakian modern liberal communism which was the really characteristic event of 1968 and, equally, de Gaulle's crushing of liberalism in France while in America the Establishment rose up and you took over.' I had got up enough momentum to carry me along without this being thought rude and it was not too bad. I went on to say that even in our countries, America and England, the great problem of the day was the difficulty of combining the general growth of liberty with the authority and efficiency of the executive, how we were trying to do this ourselves in Parliament and how our specialist committees were all turning against us. There were great cries of protest and excitement and laughter and we ended in a bit of a chaos. Nixon said, 'I'll swap our Professor Marcuse any day if you will give me your Professor Crossman', so that was all right.[1] I suppose I had put on a turn to serve the Prime Minister and given a certain intellectual cachet to some fairly dreary proceedings. Then it was over and there were all the dispatch riders outside waiting to escort Nixon back to the Embassy and off to his plane tomorrow morning.

Wednesday, February 26th

After the Nixon Cabinet last night I went back to the House and sat there on the front bench in my evening dress to listen to the interminable discussion on the Parliament Bill. It showed only too well what happens when you try to run the House of Commons without the usual channels. The House only functions because of the agreement on timetabling between the Government and the Opposition Whips and now our front-bench machine was trying to run it without the co-operation of their front bench. We were paying the price for breaking off the talks. That had given the Opposition the let out. Their own back benchers hate them for having agreed to this measure and now they are evading the responsibility for it, something that became clearer and clearer throughout the night.

I went back to my room, did my work and came down again, to find Callaghan in an extraordinarily bad temper, wanting to crush the people who are wasting his time and at the same time agreeing that the Bill is no good.

[1] Herbert Marcuse, Professor of Philosophy at the University of California at San Diego, whose books, including *One-Dimensional Man* (Boston: Beacon Books, 1964; London: Routledge & Kegan Paul, 1964) and *Eros and Civilization* (Boston: Beacon Books, 1966; London: Sphere Books, 1969), had attracted a large following.

He is in the most appallingly divided mood. At 3.0 a.m. we both went across to his room and talked to the Chief and Fred Peart about the tactics to be pursued. We all agreed that we must go ahead and that our best chance is perhaps to get a guillotine. If we lose it that's that but it's the best thing to go for. Then I was sent home to bed.

I walked home, read a bit, went to sleep and at 5.45 the Whips rang up to ask if I would come back as they couldn't get 100 votes for the closure.[1] The Labour back benchers had packed it in and disappeared. I got dressed, walked back again and there I waited for two hours. We got the closure, but only by two votes, and Clause 2 was finished. I left them at it and they said they would run through the morning. In fact they didn't. They dug themselves into most of Clause 3 but when they finally broke off in the middle of the morning they still seemed to be far away from Clause 4.

I went off for a tour of Westminster Hospital this morning and finally got back to the front bench this afternoon at 3.30. I hung about and then Anne came to dinner and it was only at 9.0 p.m. that we started on Clause 4. There I sat discussing the age of retirement for voting peers. The back benchers kept on and on, Robert Sheldon bitterly complaining that we had given no information about the facts and figures on which we had based our calculation of the age of retirement and the number of sessions which a peer must attend in order to be a voting member. I said that we had all the figures and I would give them but this produced another forty-five-minute debate and I was reminded that Callaghan had, quite rightly, said, 'For heaven's sake, don't speak a word. Don't ever give them any encouragement.' I had done it because I really want this Bill and when they see me on the front bench they know it. They know he doesn't want it but frankly it doesn't make any difference now, because they just sabotage and delay and so they did all evening.

Thursday, February 27th

All last night the back benchers were saying, 'This bloody Government, we don't want this bloody House of Lords Bill, we don't really blame people for filibustering against it. Why don't the Government get a guillotine or drop the Bill? Something must be done to stop this intolerable business of staying up night after night on this boring, second-rate measure.' All this is directed at me because the Tories spent the night saying that nobody else apart from me really wanted the Bill. This morning I saw in *The Times* a long account of how the back benchers are demanding that the big Bill should be dropped in favour of a Bill on powers. Obviously this is utterly ridiculous. We have done sixty-one hours on the big Bill and got the three most difficult clauses

[1] Any Member may rise during a debate and claim to move 'That the Question be Now Put' and the Speaker or Chairman must instantly decide whether the closure is justified. If he does, the House immediately proceeds to a vote on this but there must be a majority of at least 100 Members voting in support of a closure for the motion to be effective. If so the House then votes on the question which was under debate when the motion was moved.

through. If we were to drop this and go for a Bill on powers we should have the whole Tory Party against us and their front bench in open opposition. It would take seven or eight days to get through and then we would have the House of Lords fighting it line by line, something that would be far worse. I assumed that Callaghan had put this in *The Times* and that we should have a tremendous row in Cabinet.

But before I got to Cabinet I had a long fierce row with Tam, who said, 'You must drop this Bill and give us the small Bill, or you must force it through. You won't be able to get a guillotine, you'll not have enough people. If you try for a guillotine there'll be not only the forty-five who are now inveterately against the Bill but another seventeen to twenty who will vote against you just because you ought not to guillotine a constitutional measure. You must drop this Bill and put in a short Bill.' I said this was nonsense and we had to plough ahead. It isn't just the fact that this is the Lords' Reform Bill because we could be in exactly the same trouble if we tried to do a Finance Bill without the informal collaboration of the Chancellor and the Shadow Chancellor going behind the Speaker's chair to decide on timetabling and each of them going to discipline their own back benchers, saying, 'Look, boys, freedom is a very good thing but we must get on a bit'. People would be just as bored and angry at a Finance Bill after fifteen or sixteen days. I got ready to say this at Cabinet.

Right at the beginning Harold allowed Dick Marsh to make a bitter complaint about a vicious little story which had appeared in the *Guardian* and the *Financial Times*, recounting how he had put forward his Green Paper on the highway system and Cabinet had forced him to rewrite it. The story had mentioned a particular road in the South-West which Marsh had been forced to reconsider. Of course it was absolutely outrageous that this story should have appeared and it showed that Ian Aitken and John Bourne had once again been getting gossip. Thank heavens I had never been near either of them. It makes me curious who does these things. I suppose it might be Peter Shore or Barbara or somebody close to her. Again, it might be our friend John Harris. I suspect that Harold always suspects Roy Jenkins and John Harris of these things. He said it was a terrible thing, but he has now given up trying to stop it.

The conversation moved from there to an attack by Harold on the B.B.C. because young David Dimbleby had made a flippant commentary on the Nixon arrival.[1] Harold had made a formal complaint to the B.B.C. via the Chief Whip and demanded the text of Dimbleby's remarks. The net result, as Harold himself frankly admitted, was that he had made this the major story in the Tuesday press and entirely eclipsed the story he wanted of the historic Cabinet the night before. He is obsessed with the B.B.C., and this

[1] Elder son of the famous broadcaster Richard Dimbleby (who had died in 1966). He was a reporter for B.B.C.'s 'Panorama' programme 1967–9 and has been its presenter since 1974. From 1969 to 1972 he was presenter of '24 Hours'.

and his obsession with leaks are his most outstanding weaknesses as a leader.

Harold then asked Fred for a report on Lords' reform. After Fred, Callaghan came in. I was expecting him to launch into a speech saying we ought to give up the Bill, but no, he was far cannier than that. He said things were very, very difficult and we had our own side against us. He thought we ought to soldier on, knowing that this would take not five days but more like the fifteen or sixteen that the Social Secretary had prophesied. Then I made my speech about the lack of collaboration between the usual channels and said that it seemed to me that we had got to face sitting on perhaps into the Whitsun recess or well into August. We had to remember that Arthur Balfour got his 1902 Education Act through by sacrificing everything else,[1] sitting until the middle of August and then getting Royal Assent in December. These things did take time and the important thing was that our own back benchers shouldn't believe that we were going to drop it. Once they knew we were going to soldier on life would be very different. Nothing really happened. Harold was careful and he also seemed to think we should soldier on. Michael Stewart took the same view and nobody dared say 'Drop the Bill'. I know why this is. If we dropped it at this stage because thirty or forty people are making a nuisance of themselves, it would be only too easy to apply the same argument to the Prices and Incomes or the Industrial Relations Bill. I think this was the basic thing which kept the Cabinet so uneasily quiet. We decided to soldier on but this is something we can't do. Maybe it is true that we can't get a guillotine yet, although Eddie Shackleton tells me that the Opposition aren't absolutely against it. Maybe we must hang on for another week or two but I am pretty sure we shan't be able to get through this unless we really work all through August or unless we can reconstitute the relationships between the two front benches. It is a major parliamentary problem and we left it unresolved.

We next had a long talk about the future of Black Arrow, the only one of our space projects which survives, and a general discussion on General de Gaulle and foreign affairs. Then we turned to Barbara's terrible problem at Ford's.[2] A new progressive pay deal had been fully agreed between the union representatives at Ford's and the new management and then had been rejected

[1] Arthur Balfour, Conservative M.P. for Hertford 1874–85, for Manchester East 1885–1906 and for the City of London 1906–22, P.P.S. to Lord Salisbury 1878–80, President of the Local Government Board 1885, Secretary for Scotland 1886, Chief Secretary for Ireland 1887–91, Leader of the House of Commons and First Lord of the Treasury 1891–2 and 1895–1902 and Prime Minister 1902–5. He was Leader of the Conservative Party 1902–11, First Lord of the Admiralty 1915–16, Foreign Secretary 1916–19 and Lord President of the Council 1912–22 and 1925–9. He became the 1st Earl of Balfour in 1922. He died in 1930.

[2] The management at Ford's had worked out a pay and productivity plan giving substantial wage increases, including the loss of bonuses for workers on unofficial strike. Most of the union officials accepted the plan but it was subsequently rejected by some employees, who began an unofficial strike in protest. On February 28th the T.G.W.U. and A.U.E.F.W. declared the strike official. The dispute ended on March 18th, after three and a half weeks, which cost the company and the country £1 million a day in lost exports.

by a combination of shop stewards in the factory and, much more sinister, the top level of the T.&G. and of the A.E.U. In one sense this plays into Barbara's hands, because if the union leaders can repudiate their own negotiators in this way, and if Jack Jones from the T.&G. and Scanlon from the Engineers can override the union representatives,[1] it makes a nonsense of any form of contracting and completely bears out those who say that the unions deserve nothing better than to be made subject to the law. Industrial troubles have harmed this Government more than anything except its own prices and incomes policy and the Ford example is a crucial one.

Right at the end Roy announced that the bank rate was to go up.[2] It was altogether an interminable chatty Cabinet and afterwards I went off for a briefing and a drink with some fifteen or sixteen London journalists at an informal press conference on the revision of my N.H.S. Green Paper. Bea Serota was there and this evening, over a quiet dinner together, she told me a pleasant story. We have a nice, plump deputy driver called Joy, who had said to her as they came across from the Elephant and Castle, 'Lady Serota, may I say something to you? Everybody says that the Secretary of State is an ogre but he is really perfectly all right if you stand up to him.' Bea told me this with a twinkle in those cool grey eyes of hers and was obviously as enormously pleased with it as I was.

Friday, February 28th

We had arranged a big programme at Norwich and Lowestoft. I got to Norwich at 11.30, breezed in to the social security offices and then gave a press conference at the Bethel Hospital. We got good coverage but another week of inaction on pensions has done us no good. When I asked at the social security offices how the scheme had been received they said, 'Splendid impact on the first day but no queries since.' The impetus seems to have petered out and, as I feared, starting off with a bang and then doing absolutely nothing for three weeks has given us a very bad start.

We stayed at the Bethel Hospital for an excellent lunch, well-served, with very good food and drink. Then I found that the patients there are kept on £7 a week, half the average cost of keeping patients in psychiatric hospitals, which, God knows, is low enough. Out of these funds we were being served this slap-up lunch, dinner for the Guardians, just as in a Dickensian workhouse. Here in a beautiful eighteenth-century building was a real old-fashioned lunatic asylum, with virtually no trained staff, one part-time consultant and 120 psychiatric patients.

What a contrast with Lowestoft and the special accommodation for the elderly that I saw there in the afternoon. It was a kind of cloister, built round

[1] Hugh Scanlon, President of the Amalgamated Union of Engineering Workers since 1968, has been a member of the T.U.C. General Council since 1968.

[2] The rise, from 7 to 8 per cent, was in response to previous increases in earlier rates and it was also hoped that banks would find it easier to keep their advances under control.

a square of grass, twenty-eight delightful little flats with a sitting room, curtained-off bed, separate bathroom and lavatory and separate kitchen, exactly right for old people. I then moved on to Lowestoft District Hospital for a seminar on geriatric services.

I had asked for some twelve to fourteen people, a few G.P.s, consultants, local authority welfare and children's officers, Regional Hospital Board and H.M.C. members, to come and discuss the Green Paper. I sat in the middle and got them to talk and we had a most interesting discussion on where the line should be drawn between local authorities and the Health Service. On from there to a magnificent luxury holiday camp, where I sat down to dinner with 590 Labour Party members from the Lowestoft party. We had a splendid dinner and I made a fighting speech afterwards, with quite a good speech by the candidate, only to hear later that this party, one of the wealthiest and best-organized in the country, with £14,000 in the kitty, is split from top to bottom by a searing row between the candidate and the agent on some dreary subject of organization. It only shows that you can have all the money in the world and all the organization but personal rivalries still tell. But there was a far better spirit there than I expected. I sat and talked with the East Anglia party organizer before Douglas Garnett finally motored me back to Ipswich, where I got to bed at 1.30 in the morning. I had started out from home at 9 a.m. after an all-night sitting and a pretty tough week and I was pleased that I had lasted well enough, particularly as I had heard when I got to Lowestoft that Julian Snow had been carted into the Westminster with a slight stroke. So here I am with another member of the Department on the sick list.

Saturday, March 1st

Up in the morning to get the 8.37 to Liverpool Street and then on to Coventry where I gave lunch at the Chace to Albert Rose and Winnie Lakin. She is very down and seedy and really frustrated by the fact that she is no longer a councillor. We discussed the meeting this afternoon, a day school for the trade unions on pensions, and agreed that we would be lucky to have a dozen people because the trade unionists wouldn't turn up. But they did, some sixty to seventy people at the A.E.U. hall in Corporation Street, including a number of trade union leaders, and we had an excellent meeting. It's curious, once you have got people there pensions are an absorbing subject. In an hour and a half's discussion, on a day when the Ford strike was on everybody's mind, not a single question was asked about anything but pensions. We had an interesting afternoon just like the old days. I can always tell how I stand with them in Coventry. By the end of the afternoon they were getting up and saying, 'Now, Dick, about this,' or 'Now, Dick, about that, would you tell us, Dick,' absolutely familiarly, treating me as their adviser and counsellor. This was probably the best meeting I have had with trade unionists for the last two or three years. Twenty copies of our popular version went like hot cakes. It did me a power of good but it reminded me that none of this is going on up and down the country. Neither Transport House nor the Ministry has launched a campaign to get the scheme across. It is not my fault. We have been made to wait for the White Paper debate so we can have it in the same week as Barbara but afterwards I must make every possible effort.

Sunday, March 2nd

Today we just had Miss Spencer, Patrick's class teacher, to lunch with us. She is a rather tough young woman, who shows an extraordinary personal interest in him. He has started writing and spelling much better and he is making enormous advances. It was nice to have her here. We discussed the whole future of her comprehensive school and she said she would know by the end of this year whether it was a success or not. She has got four different streamed groups and a fifth group of backward children. She certainly wonders whether Patrick is being wasted there and, as she says, one can see that he comes from a totally different background. In a funny way she confirms the view of the people who say he ought to have gone to the Dragon and on to Winchester, but I don't agree with her. I think that on the whole the kind of mixed life he is getting there, the knockabout, the travelling in the school bus, the mix-up on the football ground, is good for him and, so far, I am content.

It's been a dreary week and I have been rather grimly reflecting that the Government haven't picked up yet. We are struggling along on the bottom and the February National Opinion Poll that came out this week showed us four points down and Heath several points up.[1] We are scraping along with a 21½ per cent gap between us and the Tories. Although the morale of the party outside is somehow improving and Labour is settling down to the job of Opposition in the councils, inside Parliament there seems to be a real hardening of the ranks. People are soured. They will vote against us not only on the Parliament Bill but on a three-line whip on the Industrial Relations White Paper and they are threatening opposition on a three-line whip on the Defence White Paper next week.[2] This will be heightened by the raising of bank rate this week.

Life is made even more difficult by the Ford strike, which has dominated the whole of this week. The firm has now, very unusually, taken out an injunction against the union, which will be tried in the courts tomorrow afternoon. We will see whether it pays a big firm like Ford's to take a union to law but all it seems to have done so far is to unify the men somewhat behind their

[1] Labour's percentage had fallen from 35·9 in January to 31·4 and the Conservatives' had risen from 46·0 to 52·7.

[2] The Defence White Paper (Cmnd 3927), published on February 20th, set the 1969/70 defence budget at £2,266 million, £5 million less than the previous year (and in real terms a good deal less). The White Paper emphasized the Russian threat to the stability of Europe, illustrated by the Czechoslovak invasion in 1968, and the increasing air and sea activity of Soviet forces in the Mediterranean and the North Sea. A strengthening of Britain's contribution to NATO forces, particularly in the Mediterranean, was announced.

shop stewards and Jones and Scanlon. Meanwhile Barbara's Industrial Relations Bill has been trundling along inside the Labour Party. There is no doubt that the majority of M.P.s are prepared to back it and also that a minority are passionately against it. This is more than the forty-five solid left-wingers; it extends to the right wing of the Party too. Despite all our skill at drafting the resolution, it doesn't seem to have placated the critics, who are in a very resentful mood. I just don't see how we are going to have both this Bill of Barbara's and the Prices and Incomes Bill next session and, anyhow, it's possibly the prices and incomes powers we have already taken that have set off this vindictive reaction from those who believe in collective bargaining against socialist state intervention. That may be behind the industrial troubles which are doing us such enormous harm.

We were discussing this at the new small Prices and Incomes Bill Committee which met for the first time this week. There are only six of us, Roy, Tony Crosland, Fred Peart, Barbara, myself and Jim Callaghan and we were trying to hammer out the awkward choice between trying to get a new Bill this autumn to extend state powers or dropping the idea and returning to a voluntary system. In assessing this we saw very clearly how crucial the Ford example is. As Roy and Barbara say, it is essential to have state sanctions because the trade unions and the T.U.C. just won't do a damn thing to keep increases in earnings related to productivity increases unless the state takes an active role behind the scenes. On the other hand, Jim, Tony Crosland and I are arguing the opposite case, saying, 'Look, even you yourselves admit that at most the prices and incomes policy has only made a 1 per cent difference each year. Are you sure that this 1 per cent hasn't been accompanied by such animosity, such fierce hatred of the Government and such a general desire to hit back that it may have done more harm than good?' On the whole I am inclined to hold the second view. The Government is becoming more and more unpopular with the unions and the raising of bank rate will make it unpopular with the owner-occupier. It has not been an encouraging week and I don't see any likelihood of the future being less discouraging.

Monday, March 3rd

Eddie summoned me across to the House of Lords where I found George Jellicoe. Just like last year Carrington has gone off to Australia at a critical moment and George wanted to talk to me about the Bill. We discussed things quite amiably until I finally said, 'But you see, George, we shall only get it through if you face the fact that your people are absolutely failing to help. It's like running a Finance Bill without a voluntary timetable. We only have our Whips there, yours aren't functioning at all and though it is making life virtually impossible we are going to jolly well slog ahead.' George had asked if there was any chance of a deal. I said, 'There's no chance of a deal because there is nothing we can get out of it. We have nothing to deal with because your people say they are incapable of leading your party and so they've bloody well got to face it, we're going to plough on even if it means their losing their Whitsun holiday.'

We were first in Questions this afternoon. Bea Serota came from the Lords to lunch with the rest of us beforehand but really David and I handled them, with a few being done by Norman Pentland, and we had no earthly trouble with the 100 that were down.

I went into the Westminster Hospital this evening to see Julian Snow, a huge great fellow, six foot six inches tall, partly paralysed in one leg. I found him looking much better but scared stiff that he might not be able to come back to work, so I shall see him every now and again this week and cheer him up, as a Minister has to do. My other visit was to the farewell party for David and Evangeline Bruce. I have known Evangeline for years as a fellow-guest at lunch with Pam Berry. She's a tall, woodland creature, jolly nice and interested in progressive things, and David is a very stiff, reactionary New England banker. As I went in to say how do you do to him he took me aside and said, 'You are the most popular man in the Cabinet with Nixon. He could talk of nothing except you and what you said at that famous Cabinet. I do congratulate you on it. You have an entrée to the White House whenever you want.' I don't know whether it is true or not but he said this before I could pass on. I also ran into Denis Healey. He and Edna were as gratified as ever, and I congratulated them on a really good piece from David Wood in *The Times* today. The article portrayed Denis as an Irish navvy,[1] always tough, brave, resolute and reckless, a good write-up in preparation for his White Paper debate tomorrow and the day after. He remains inscrutable to me. He has this sort of bloodshot, rough complexion, bushy eyebrows, an Irish blackguard look about him, with the ability, crudeness and ambition of the Irish, but I think his affinities are wholly Anglo-American, wholly with McNamara,[2] and I am pretty sure that he has sold himself completely to our chiefs of staff as their great protector. He has managed to see that while our commitments are cut the quality of the materiel and the number of generals' salaries have been maintained, so the forces have survived pretty well. We've managed to lop our commitments without cutting the defence budget or defence status nearly enough.

Tuesday, March 4th

The papers are full of the result of the vote on Barbara's White Paper yesterday.[3] Ninety-five people, including four P.P.S.s, had voted against,

[1] The article spoke of Mr Healey's 'letting the Irish ancestry in him come to the top and asking for a rough-house'.

[2] Robert McNamara, President of the Ford Motor Co. 1960–1, was American Secretary of State for Defence 1961–8. He has been President of the International Bank for Reconstruction and Development since 1968.

[3] The motion approving the White Paper was carried by 224 votes to 62. The Conservatives and some 39 Labour M.P.s abstained and 53 Labour M.P.s and 9 Liberals voted against the motion.

among them John Ellis, who had been obliged to resign. Not only that, but three members of the Liaison Committee, Douglas Houghton, Willie Hamilton and Joyce Butler,[1] had also refused to vote for it. This really was something like a vote of no confidence, and, combined with the Ford strike, the threat of a steel strike and of a bank strike, made things pretty gloomy.

We sat down at a meeting of the Ministers concerned with the House of Lords affair. It wasn't a meeting of the P.L. Committee but Callaghan was in the chair with Fred Peart, John Silkin, Eddie Shackleton and me. We discussed tactics. It was obvious that Jim was going to go for a guillotine and he railroaded through the view that this is what we must have. We all knew what the choices were. One, to soldier on, trying to get the Bill through and taking about ten to fifteen days over it, which he ruled out on the ground that the Party wouldn't take it. Two, he ruled out abandoning it. He didn't mention the short Bill which I know is his real desire so we were left with three, the guillotine, and he got the Committee to agree. I said, 'A guillotine is no good. What matters with a guillotine is getting some chance of success. You won't have a chance of carrying a guillotine unless you show determination to carry on. In fact, you won't be able to shorten the proceedings unless you really are prepared to get the Bill even with long proceedings.' I was pushed aside but it was obvious that though Jim was shoving hard neither the Chief Whip nor Fred Peart were convinced that a guillotine was really possible.

At S.E.P. we discussed the reform of the organization of the P.E.S.C. presentation. There is no doubt that there has been an enormous improvement. When we started trying to cut public expenditure it was impossible to do it fairly because it was presented in such a ridiculous form with, for instance, nationalized industries left out and with transfer payments counting for as much as straight expenditure. After four years' work, with a great deal of outside pressure from Tommy Balogh, all this has finally been ironed out but at a time when I have lost interest in it. There was general congratulation all round for Roy Jenkins and Jack Diamond who took the credit, though it was of course wholly an official paper. Suddenly, at the end, the Prime Minister asked John Diamond to speak and John said that the right thing now was to have an annual White Paper in the autumn presented to a special parliamentary committee. This took my breath away as it was an official recommendation that had been blithely accepted by Roy, who seemed to think this was a foregone conclusion to which we should agree. Now, only three or four weeks ago, we were told at a meeting of the Parliamentary Committee that we should wind up these experimental committees because they were such a nuisance in Whitehall but here we now were lunging into an enormous new commitment. I objected two or three times but the Prime Minister simply said that people just notice the difficulties in this kind of

[1] Joyce Butler was Labour and Co-op. M.P. for Wood Green 1955–74 and since 1974 has been M.P. for Haringey and Wood Green. The Liaison Committee served as a link between the P.L.P. and the Cabinet.

thing and I realized that his mind was wholly fixed on the electoral advantage next autumn of planning to present a rolling three-year plan and a new White Paper to a new finance committee. Whether he is planning this for a spring election or an election in the following autumn, who can say, but this was pretty hard evidence of his intention.[1]

I lunched at the Athenaeum with Nicholas Davenport. Harold Lever was our joint guest. I learnt quite a lot because I asked Harold Lever point-blank what he thought of Roy's decision to put up bank rate. Harold Lever said he thought it was an insane idea with no advantage at all. It was pushed on Roy by the Treasury and was certainly unnecessary in international terms and probably damaging to business and our economic prospects at home. I said, 'But weren't you asked for advice, Harold?' and he said, 'No. In this kind of thing they never ask my advice.' In Harold Lever Roy has a man who knows more about the reactions of the City of London and the business community as a whole than any other member of the Government, yet, because he is Financial Secretary to the Treasury, his advice is not asked on a thing like bank rate. This is one of the mysteries of the insularity of departmental Ministers.

In the afternoon the Prime Minister sent for the House of Lords Committee. I was in the middle of a meeting but the others reported to him that we were going for a guillotine. The Chief was to inquire carefully what was possible and our representatives were to talk to the Opposition front bench about the likelihood of their supporting us. I got hold of Harold afterwards and we had an interesting half-hour. I said, 'Well, there's no doubt about it now, Jim wants the guillotine even if we are defeated on it. After the election, when we are in Opposition, his chances will be better if it's been defeated. You have got to face it, Harold, he is playing for high stakes.' We discussed this a bit and then I said, 'But you know, the real truth is that if we have a guillotine we shall have to carry on.' 'Oh,' he said straightaway, 'I don't think we will. It's what I thought last summer and I've come back to it again. We ought to do just the Bill on powers if we can't get the other one.' I then said, 'You've forgotten the argument I gave you. I keep telling you it and after five minutes you interrupt me.' He said, 'I remember, Dick, but I warn you that at present I am thinking in terms of the short Bill.' Although he didn't agree with me he trusted me, and I was able to say, 'Well, I'll spell it all out for you at Cabinet on Thursday.' We were sitting in his room in the House, drinking whisky, and in half an hour we got through quite a lot and into a very friendly state together, so I was able to say this to him.

[1] The first Expenditure Committee, replacing the Estimates Committee, was appointed by the House of Commons in the 1970/1 session. Its forty-nine members worked through a steering sub-committee and six functional sub-committees, on general public expenditure in defence and external affairs; trade and industry; education and the arts; unemployment and social services; environment; and Home Office. Besides the estimates the Committee considered the assumptions underlying the Government's Capital Expenditure White Paper, which sets out the forecasts of capital and current expenditure over the next five years.

Meanwhile, although our Committee had agreed that our three, Callaghan, Peart and Silkin, should meet the Tory three, Maudling, Whitelaw and Jellicoe, the meeting wasn't organized because Callaghan didn't want it. He merely talked to Maudling, who said there could be no question of the Tories helping us and that they would have a three-line whip against the guillotine. There was no life left in the Tory Party for this Bill and least of all would they support a guillotine on a constitutional issue. When I met Willie Whitelaw in the Lobby this evening he took me aside and repeated this. He said, 'I don't often have a chance to talk to you, Dick, but I just want to make sure that you know there can be no question of this. I know John Silkin isn't always believed but we really are going to have a three-line whip on this. I may think it right or wrong, I am one of the few who wants your Bill but this is really it.' This was completely at variance with what we had thought yesterday when we had vaguely talked about the hope of getting some twenty or thirty Tories to abstain on the guillotine motion. It was now clear from what Whitelaw was saying that their lists would be carefully examined, that nobody would be able to stay away and there would be a real Tory vote. So we know before Thursday's Cabinet that the guillotine will end in a Government defeat by about thirty votes.

Wednesday, March 5th

I spent the morning in consultations with the B.M.A. on the N.H.S. Green Paper. I went with Tam and Bea and within ten minutes it was clear that the B.M.A. were responding to my treatment and we had two hours of nothing but sweetness and light. They were obviously delighted to be consulted. Afterwards I took Alan Marre upstairs for a drink and asked him how it had gone. He said, 'Wonderfully. I've heard five Ministers since Nye Bevan talking to the B.M.A. and nobody has talked to them like you. You don't hide anything from them.' I said, 'Well, why not?' He said, 'You know, it might be awkward for some of your colleagues.' But it occurred to me that the advantage of being a senior Cabinet Minister in charge of all the social services is that I can be far more authoritative and informal than a mere departmental Minister like Kenneth Robinson, who must speak strictly for and within the departmental brief. Because I have authority I can just risk the expression of a personal view and risk thinking aloud.

This evening Anne and I went with the Sadies to *Fidelio*. I had made a tremendous effort on Monday and Tuesday to get the draft of my speech done for tomorrow, working up to 10.0 and 11.30 at night, so Anne was able to pick me up at 7.0 for a drink and to go on to Covent Garden, where Otto Klemperer came tottering in, supported by two attendants.[1] He sat down and raised his baton, the great long fingers of his left hand quivering. It was an astonishing, statuesque performance. Often he stopped conducting altogether. It was a very non-dramatic musical production but then *Fidelio*

[1] He died in July 1973 at the age of eighty-eight.

is a very non-dramatic musical opera. It was nothing like as good as *Così fan tutte* but it was interesting to watch this terrific classical figure, just alive, almost playing with the score, letting it run along under his control.

I had to leave at 9.50, just after the second act had started, to vote in the three-line whip on the Defence White Paper. When I got there I heard that there was going to be a second division but I thought this must be a formal division on the Tory amendment, and, as I was determined to get back and hear the second act, I went through the first division and pretended not to have heard about the second one. I got back just in time to hear the 'Leonora III' played and to hear the last scene. Then Anne and I went to Lockets for dinner and drove home. When we got back Tam said there had been great excitement because I hadn't attended the second division and the lists had now gone to press and the B.B.C. were ringing up to ask why I hadn't voted.[1] Tam had had the sense to say that I was busy preparing my speech so that was how it appeared in the press.

Thursday, March 6th

This morning I found myself on the front page of the *Telegraph*, the *Guardian* and *The Times*. It was lucky that they didn't say I was at *Fidelio* because I think the Party might have been upset. Still, it might have improved my image, that of the person who eats alone at Prunier and leaves secret Cabinet papers under his chair, and who absentmindedly goes to the second act of *Fidelio* and forgets a crucial division. It was a key division, because the bloody left wing voted against the Defence White Paper, so all the papers were full of it.

At Cabinet we first of all discussed the Parliament Bill and already the Ministerial Committee's proposition for a guillotine was out of date, unless we were prepared either to challenge John Silkin's figures or to accept a defeat. In a sense Jim Callaghan tried to do both and we saw that he didn't mind the Government's losing and Fred Peart or John Silkin's authority being undermined. He revealed himself far too openly and it knocked out his views. The notion of a guillotine was defeated not only because we thought we might lose it but also because to use it would almost certainly make the Lords also vote the Bill down.

But when we came to an alternative things weren't so clear. Harold Wilson duly put up the notion of the short Bill and I am glad to say it was defeated, not only by me. Four or five people almost immediately said, 'For heaven's sake, don't let's think of short Bills as all that easy.' Another proposal was to have a timetable for a Committee of fifty upstairs but this was also seen to be practically impossible because there we would have an even smaller majority and even more difficulty in getting it through. It was felt that we should try to get the Bill through on the Floor of the House without a guillotine

[1] In the second division on the main question the White Paper was approved by 279 votes to 232.

just as we are trying to do, and the first requisite is for the Party to know that we intend to do it. This is where the difficulty comes in because so long as Callaghan is in charge of the Bill no one's going to believe that this is our intention because he goes round saying it isn't. We are in a circular trap. Roy Mason then spoke extremely well and started up a new train of thought. It wasn't merely a question of the Parliament Bill, he said, or the difficulty we have on a measure which our own supporters don't care about and the Tories hate. People are being difficult about this Bill because they are being difficult about our legislative programme as a whole. The Party's discipline is being undermined and the chronic opposition, the thirty Labour M.P.s opposing the Defence Estimates, the bloody-mindedness on *In Place of Strife*, the difficulty on almost every subject we touch, is all part of the same thing. 'If we lose the Parliament Bill,' he said, 'we lose Barbara Castle's Industrial Relations Bill.' Barbara saw this absolutely clearly and again Jim Callaghan miscalculated and lost because it brought every member of Cabinet who wanted any legislative programme to realize that we must not only soldier on but take active dynamic steps to get the P.L.P. to fight the bloody Bill through. If we were prepared to fight without a guillotine we could conceivably get enough of our people to vote for a guillotine, and that is roughly speaking where we got to.

The other big thing was the farm price review, continuing a debate of a fortnight ago. Cledwyn Hughes had come back to say that he couldn't possibly settle for £30 million and wanted £40 million. I can't really blame Roy for saying that this was only repeating earlier arguments. Cabinet had decided on £30 million and that was that. The only thing we could add in support was the bank rate increase, which, I pointed out, had been clapped on and meant about £2 million extra interest charges to the farmers. Roy was able to reply that bank rate had been lowered after the last farm price review and nobody had said that should affect the award.

However it did affect things psychologically. I pointed out that it would be difficult to persuade any farmer that the £30 million we offered them would sustain the agricultural expansion programme and I wanted it upped to £35 million. Roy turned to the Prime Minister, who was just beside me, and I heard him say, 'We can't let Dick have this.' The Chancellor made a passionate speech against me, really rather ridiculously saying, 'But, after all, the farm price review is just like school meals and has to be paid for.' He was effectively answered by Cledwyn Hughes who said that the farm price review isn't money which will necessarily be spent but a kind of limit to your drawing account at the bank. Last year it had been underspent by £35 million and over the last ten years by £225 million, therefore it is rather ridiculous of Chancellors to take this the way they do. By now there was a blatant split between the economic Ministers, led by Roy, Tony Crosland and Barbara, and the agricultural Ministers. The Prime Minister had been got at fairly effectively and finally he settled on £34 million. After that I left.

I went back to my room for a quick lunch and to prepare my speech for the debate this afternoon. I had wondered whether I shouldn't just make a speech from notes but I knocked it all together and made it compact and balanced, with a special new beginning and end. That is the only advantage of writing these speeches out. Before I got up to speak we had Prime Minister's Questions. They were entirely on Europe until Bromley-Davenport got up,[1] a big lumbering fellow who is a comic card. He made a point of protest on one of those issues which the House of Commons likes to laugh about, and in ten minutes we were in a tremendous uproar, with people from all sides bombarding poor old Fred about a debate on Biafra. Biafra is in a kind of way this Cabinet's small-scale Vietnam and poor Fred Peart was up against it and had to concede a debate. It was only after all this buffoonery that I was able to start.

It was a goodish speech and indeed the whole debate was a great relief. This was the first White Paper debate of the week in which we got the whole of the Party on our side. The only surprise for me was the ferocity of the Tory opposition. When our White Paper had first come out, Balneil had written a very cautious article in the *Sunday Times* and even the Tories' reasoned amendment was still cautious in the sense that it said they couldn't support us until they knew the details of the contracting-out arrangements. However Balneil's speech was far more violent, saying all our policies were a bogus pipe-dream. The Tories were trying to discredit the whole idea, treating it as electioneering policy, but all through Balneil, Boyd-Carpenter and Worsley were caught out because they didn't make themselves clear or reveal anything about their intentions or alternatives.[2] The afternoon was not unsuccessful and David Ennals made a brilliant, precise winding-up speech. Within a fortnight he has made himself competent in Social Security matters. It is his fourth job in three years and he is doing it all extremely well. Afterwards Anne and I were able to have a drink together and to enjoy ourselves, feeling that though it is a pity that this has become an issue of party warfare nevertheless it is one on which we are not doing too badly.[3]

Friday, March 7th

Although our pensions debate was extensively quoted, actually the most interesting news item last night was the O.R.C. Poll, which is published in the *Evening Standard.* It showed the Tories with a 25 per cent lead, although Bob Carvel, their Political Editor, very fairly pointed out that while they have a lead on three or four of the most important issues, unemployment, prosperity, individual satisfaction, there has been a big shift in favour of the Govern-

[1] Lieutenant-Colonel Sir Walter Bromley-Davenport (Kt 1961) was Conservative M.P. for Knutsford 1945–70. He was a Conservative Whip 1948–51.

[2] Sir Marcus Worsley was Conservative M.P. for Keighley 1959–64 and for Chelsea 1966–September 1974.

[3] The White Paper was approved by 289 votes to 232.

ment and it may be that we are on the edge of finding ourselves doing rather better.

After lunch with Tony Howard at the Escargot I had a meeting on immigrant doctors.[1] This has really become a very dicey problem. We have ahead of us what was intended to be an uncontroversial Second Reading Bill for a new kind of registration. Responsibility will fall on the General Medical Council, as the Todd Report had recommended, for registering doctors in England but just before he left Health David Ennals had suddenly asked whether we shouldn't now write into the Bill a new Clause requiring the G.M.C. to register and test the qualifications of immigrant doctors. The papers had come to me to say that the Department had looked into this and found no necessity for it and they wanted the non-controversial Bill to go to the Legislation Committee at once. I insisted on a meeting today and it was quite clear that there was no difficulty in our legislating to require the G.M.C. to test the knowledge of colloquial English of any alien doctor coming to practise in this country. If the G.M.C. said they couldn't do it, they could get somebody else but it had to be done. I said that was one alternative, or on the other hand we could make it compulsory for an immigrant doctor to be temporarily attached to a consultant or a G.P. The only difficulty with that is that we need so many immigrant doctors each year that there aren't enough consultants to give them the month's attachment, so both proposals were fraught with difficulty. All I said was that we had to insist on one or the other, even if it meant transforming the non-controversial Second Reading Committee Bill into a controversial Bill. The Department thought I was a bit rough but I have got it done and we are having it again next week.

At 7.35, after looking in on Julian Snow, I took the train to Prescote, where there was a magnificent starlit night.

Sunday, March 9th

We have been having the most wonderful spring weather, sharp, thick, white hoarfrost, cloudless skies night and day, brilliant moonlight and brilliant sunshine all day yesterday and again today. Spring comes, just as it often does, late but in the nick of time. I have been pruning our willow tree today and cutting off its top to make it a real weeping willow once more. Wonderful weather for our walks, good food and good drink in our lovely warm house. Anne and I are dreading the arrival of the new furniture, two great new sofas and magnificent new chairs, on which we have spent the vast sum of £800, for fear they are going to spoil the drawing room. Last time we dreaded it and now we have got used to our splendid new table. Patrick said to me at breakfast today, just before we started our last reading from *Gulliver's Travels*,

[1] Anthony Howard was Political Correspondent of the *New Statesman* 1961–4, Whitehall Correspondent of the *Sunday Times* 1965, Washington Correspondent of the *Observer* 1966–9 and Political Columnist 1971–2, Assistant Editor of the *New Statesman* 1970–2 and Editor since 1972.

the part about the Yahoos, 'Why doesn't home ever occur in your diary?' and I said, 'I think it does quite a lot, it's always there in the background.' Perhaps it doesn't appear enough to make a real picture of my life and perhaps I ought to put more in about the role of the family to show how important it is to a politician but I am not sure really that I wouldn't then be writing creative fiction rather than the sort of diary I want.

Here at Prescote I am reflecting on the week. Once again it's been dominated by the Ford strike. The Company's seeking an injunction to stop the union's breaking the contract caused an almost universal strike, then the Company lost its case and now the situation is worse than ever. Do Jones and Scanlon want to smash the Company and get a huge wage rise without promising any productivity or accepting any discipline? We have to face it that the unions are getting more and more out of control and difficult to manage than ever before.

The second thing we have to face is the crisis over the House of Lords. We are now getting to a situation where the Government might find itself in such a fix that it might have to go for an autumn election because we have disintegrated. I have already described in this diary what a mess we got into over Barbara's White Paper *In Place of Strife* because of Roy Jenkins's extraordinary lackadaisical agreement to rush through her package. By agreeing to this, Roy has lost his incomes policy legislation; that is obvious now, nobody even discusses it any more. The Government is clearly not going to have another Prices and Incomes Bill, and Callaghan has won *de facto*. We always assumed that in its place we would have Barbara's trade union reforms as our main policy and we thought that this was a more constructive, more suitable electoral theme, but now slowly, slowly over a period of weeks, the inner crisis about Lords' reform is deeply affecting all our legislative plans. Callaghan is schizophrenic on the Parliament Bill, which has been one of the major factors making it easier for the Tory front bench to opt out of any responsibilities they had. The Committee Stage is at a standstill and we are not doing anything about it next week. Perhaps we can be excused by saying that this is the period to get the Defence White Paper through but it is obvious that unless we can finish the Lords' Bill before the end of April we shall be in a first-rate crisis.

This brings me to something which I was reflecting on this morning at 7.15 when I came down to my study and got my tea. I have been trying to compare the Cabinet of today with the Cabinet we first had in 1964 and the Mark II version in 1966. Harold said to me yesterday week that he found Cabinet so much easier to manage now. Well, that's certainly true. He has the whole of foreign affairs, including Rhodesia and entry into Europe, completely under his control, along with his old buddies Michael Stewart and Denis Healey. Then he has the economic side tightly tied up, with discipline entirely under Fred Peart and John Silkin and very little consultation about that. It's true we have Parliamentary Committee, where we discuss political problems a bit, but S.E.P. has now become two-thirds of the Cabinet, doing just the kind of stuff we used to do in Cabinet itself. O.P.D. hardly meets and when it does it's on secondary issues and whenever Harold arbitrarily chooses to call it rather than because it's got a regular job of work. So Cabinet as a Cabinet is meeting less and is less effectively controlling policy than ever before but, as I have said, it really matters less because there is less policy to control. As usual the budget has all been tied up absolutely secretly and no doubt the main post-budgetary decisions will already have been taken. The main thing is that there is nothing much to be done since we are now set on course and we can't move off it. Somehow, then, we have a lightweight talented Cabinet and one that is no longer a team. Nixon apparently said after he had been to our Cabinet that it was one of outstanding ability and calibre and variety. This is true; it isn't simply that we have six Oxford Firsts (seven before we lost Frank Pakenham), it is that we are still quite an interesting gang of people.

However there are two big contrasts between our Cabinet now and our Cabinet of '64, one being loss and one gain. The gain in my view is that the economic group – Barbara Castle, Roy Jenkins and Tony Crosland, buttressed by Peter Shore and Tony Wedgwood Benn – are infinitely superior to the collection we had running the economy in 1964 – James Callaghan, George Brown and Douglas Jay. There is no doubt that if we had had this group at the beginning we would probably have made far fewer economic mistakes. On the other hand, Cabinet is now terribly unbalanced on its class and its trade union side and this is directly related to our present disastrous relationship with the trade union movement. George Brown and Ray Gunter may not be very big fish in the trade union pond but in our world they were. Although I think Roy Mason is one of the most promising new Members and one of the ablest, infinitely superior, for example, to Dick Marsh, one can't really say that Mason and Marsh make up for the loss of Brown and Gunter and Frank Cousins.

Let's just spell the Cabinet round. There is Harold in the middle, facing out towards Horse Guards Parade, next to him now sits Roy Jenkins, then me, Willie Ross, George Thomson, George Thomas, that lickspittle from Wales. Next the Chief Whip, Tony Wedgwood Benn, Ted Short, Peter Shore, Jim Callaghan, Michael Stewart, Gerald Gardiner, Tony Crosland and then comes Dick Marsh. We are now on the far right, along the Horse Guards side. We find on Harold's right Jack Diamond, Roy Mason, Tony Greenwood and Burke Trend. Now I think what Nixon said is true – quite a talented gang, but politically lightweight. The fact that there are so many people who don't weigh at all in Cabinet is extremely expensive.

The third thing is the sameness of the Cabinet bloc. In the centre of the Cabinet is Denis Healey, still running defence like a tight little monopoly and trying to stray into foreign affairs fields. We have Willie Ross, conscientious, hard-working, with that terrible braying voice, almost as bad as Alice Bacon's, but decent, honest and still miraculously surviving all the changes. Gerald Gardiner, the Lord Chancellor, is as utterly remote from the reality of politics as ever, and ineffective, though he could be a great influence from that position. He is as Quakerish and high-minded as ever but also Quakerish and ruthless in his determination to get his way. Then we have John Diamond, who wasn't in Cabinet before, but here he is now with just the same accountant's mind, and then Michael Stewart, to and fro either in Education or D.E.A. or the Foreign Office, absolutely dull but a brilliant debater, an important, doctrinaire right-winger at the dead centre.

That group is all exactly the same, so I turn to what has happened at the other levels. What about the make-weights, the people who are there just because Harold wants them in? Tony Greenwood has stayed the pace throughout, holding an important office extremely badly, and he is there as a vote for Harold. We have three other complete cyphers – Cledwyn Hughes, George Thomas and George Thomson not doing a stroke – all Harold's henchmen. I mentioned Benn and Shore as members of the economic team and they have of course a great role. They are not as close to the Prime Minister as they were because each of them has settled down and established himself in his own job. Benn has enormously improved at MinTech. after a ghastly start as Postmaster-General. He has obviously put himself over to British industry, a very easy thing to do because he has gone for only that research which is going to be commercially beneficial. He and Shore represent the interventionist side of Harold's mind, his belief in the I.R.C. and in investment grants.

Let me turn now to mavericks. There are always some of these. In the first Cabinet we had Frank Pakenham and now we really have two odd characters. There is Ted Short, who began with a brilliant press as a wonderful chap, but he is just a martinet headmaster, bleating for what he can get, with no wisdom and giving very little to the Cabinet. There is Dick Marsh, our Minister of Transport, brash, erratic, invariably swallowing the departmental line, preaching it, and otherwise expressing as the youngest member of the Cabinet the most reactionary views on things like votes at eighteen or the attitude to students. They really add very little.

I haven't yet mentioned Eddie Shackleton. Cabinet is greatly strengthened by having Frank Pakenham out and Eddie in. He is now the Minister of the new Civil Service Department, an addition to some extent to the economic side and to the solid Centre. I have also left out of account discipline, which is enormously important. The Bowden–Silkin regime of 1964 did extremely well in the first Parliament when things were relatively easy and there was a majority of three. Then came the second liberalizing regime of myself and Silkin, the reforming period that ended very abruptly when I quarrelled with Harold and demanded to get out. I was replaced by Fred Peart, who as Minister of Agriculture had been quite a force in his own right, a loyal Harold Wilson supporter, an anti-European, standing for a lot, right in the middle of the Cabinet. As I have said before, he is like the Duke of Omnium, a solid representative of the Labour establishment, charming, nice, decent; I am fond of him. He hasn't got the intellectual substance which I had but he's a great deal more popular in the House and I think in the Party. Here his ineffectiveness is almost an advantage because they allow him to get away with the business of the week more easily. But he lacks authority on a thing like the Parliament Bill and the new crisis of discipline which is now threatening the Party. I don't think the Government can hold together for the rest of this Parliament with Peart and Silkin in charge of discipline, Peart because he lacks authority, Silkin because he has not developed a yard. He is still the Prime Minister's lap-dog. When he took over from Ted Short in the summer of 1966 he was very young, having only been in power four or five years. He is a squashy, fat Silkin, anxious to please, and he does not assert any authority over the Prime Minister. John changes his mind whenever Harold's mind changes, to and fro he goes, talking differently to different people.

What about Barbara? She is the great new axis of strength. She has jumped from the bottom of the Cabinet to the top and she is really, though not the Deputy Prime Minister in title, the effective number two. She is the only person of Prime Ministerial timber in the Cabinet. She is very unpopular now and though the job she is doing is terrific it is unsuccessful. A dynamic prices and incomes policy attached to the person of the First Secretary is, I think, terribly damaging to the Party. But she is as nice as ever and as effective. She is a real politician. Barbara has risen and expanded as a person, whereas Roy Jenkins, after an early rise to fame, has settled down to being a rather narrow, conventional Establishment Chancellor, not much coming out of his shell, and being defeated when he tries to.

I must say the only other person who is in any way of the same stature as the Prime Minister or Barbara is, in my view, Jim Callaghan. He and I in a funny way are the two odd men out in the Cabinet. As Chancellor Jim was for some months psychologically out, clearly exhausted, nearly physically broken, and when he recovered he did an enormous take-over of the Home Office, building up his position as a plain-style man of the people who will have no nonsense. With great skill he has established himself quite consciously over the past nine months as the only man who is known to be opposed to Harold, known to have no particular support for this Government in its present form or for the prices and incomes policy, speaking out on behalf of the trade unions or anything else he likes, setting himself up fairly openly as an alternative to Harold Wilson. Not, of course, the alternative now but the other axis of attraction. There he sits, and there he knows perfectly well, as I do, that right up to the election there is no future for Jim beyond the place he occupies. It's after the election, leading the rump in Opposition, that he sees his chance will come. He is also a tremendous intriguer, a politician in the Daltonian sense, except that Dalton couldn't keep his secrets and his Machiavellianism to himself.[1] Jim can be two-faced, but his fault is perhaps that he does far too much talking for a really successful Machiavellian politician, round the smoking room, round the tea room, dashing away with all the boys. He is a tremendous chatterer with the press, especially the *Guardian* 'Miscellany' column, and he is as compulsive a communicator with the press as I am and a great deal more leaky. Most of what I chat about is stuff they don't want to print but I suspect that Jim is now a major source of embarrassing material.

What about me? Last of all, we come to the Social Services Secretary. I am still rated, and rightly, as an absolutely solid Harold man, never dreaming of challenging his authority. I am very free in my outspoken, objective criticism of him, which is not all that elevated, but saying quite clearly that whatever his deficiencies he is the only thing we've got and we will keep on having him. What else am I in Cabinet? Having given up my central position to Fred Peart, where I might have stayed as a general authority in Cabinet and in the House, I have now got right away to one side, on to the back of a huge Department in the Elephant and Castle where I rule my own roost. It is as big as Defence and in a way much nearer to public opinion. Then in the Cabinet I have my very downright, outspoken, utterly independent position as the one man who can really stand up to Harold because his loyalty is not in dispute. So here we have Jim, the one man who stands up to the Prime Minister because his loyalty is in dispute, I the one whose loyalty is not in question, the two big old men, so to speak. That is roughly what we are.

Monday, March 10th

We had a Parliamentary Committee in the morning on a whole series of political problems. The Parliamentary Committee is beginning to function now its permanent membership is quite small. If it wasn't for the fact that Harold has allowed the Secretary of State for Wales and the Secretary of State for Scotland to be included it would be quite an effective inner Cabinet. The eight of us are Harold Wilson, Michael Stewart, Gerald Gardiner, Barbara Castle, Fred Peart, Jim Callaghan, Richard Crossman, Roy Jenkins. This matches the inner group on the economic situation which consists of Wilson, Jenkins, Crosland, Shore, Wedgy Benn, Barbara Castle and John Diamond. This morning we were joined by Peter Shore, Shackleton, Judith Hart, John Silkin and Elwyn Jones, and our meeting was very characteristic. First of all we discussed the pros and cons of having a half-day debate on Nigeria on Thursday or a whole-day debate the following Monday.[2] We

[1] Hugh Dalton, Labour M.P. for Camberwell 1924–9 and for Bishop Auckland 1929–31 and 1935–59, was Minister of Economic Warfare 1940–2, President of the B.O.T. 1942–5, Chancellor of the Exchequer 1945–7, Chancellor of the Duchy of Lancaster 1948–50, Minister of Town and Country Planning 1950–1 and Minister of Local Government and Planning 1951. He became a life peer in 1960 and died in 1962.

[2] The British Government continued to sympathize with the Federal Government of Nigeria, rather than the Biafran regime, but reports of mass starvation in Biafra and the

finally managed to get a whole day on Thursday by persuading the Chairman of Committees to knock out his private business at 7.0 p.m.

Then we had a repetition of all the arguments on the Parliament No. 2 Bill and once again Jim Callaghan tried first for a guillotine, although the Chief Whip said we'd be down by 30, and then for slogging it out. We now have to go on day by day and it may be ten or fifteen days, possibly running through the Whitsun recess or even part of August. This has now been accepted and also that the P.L.P. must be made to feel disciplined because what is at stake is not the reform of the House of Lords but the discipline of the Party in carrying out the Government's major legislation. If we give up on this Barbara doesn't stand a chance on her Bill.

Then we had a new scandal. It had been known since last October that Gordon Bagier was being paid by a P.R. firm to popularize the Greek Government and on a very dramatic programme last night he admitted this.[1] He had denied it before and now he's in a pretty awkward situation. When I had looked into this question as Lord President I felt that it was not a subject on which the Government could act alone because it would infringe parliamentary privilege and would be unpopular.

I was persuaded of this by Burke and so I had written a minute to the P.M. recommending that the whole issue of public relations firms working for foreign powers and of Members of Parliament declaring an interest if they worked for such firms should be submitted to a special Select Committee to advise the Government on whether legislation was required. Nobody knows quite what happened to this minute. A copy was found in my file but not at No. 10. I think what happened was that when we found there was such a queue of people, the Scots and the Welsh, wanting new Specialist Committees my idea of pushing this on would have stood no chance at the Procedure Committee of the Cabinet, especially if I were not going to be there to see it through.

So here it came again. The Prime Minister was tremendously excited and had already virtually committed himself to submitting to a Parliamentary Select Committee on Procedure the redefinition of the doctrine of Members' interests and of subsequently producing a Bill on the lines I had recommended. But Callaghan and Marsh said not unreasonably, 'What do we get out of this? All we shall do is to expose the two or three other Labour M.P.s who may well have been working for P.R. firms. If we set up a committee of Inquiry into this, don't we merely damage the Government at this stage?' We discussed it at length and there was an interesting division of opinion. The Prime Minister wanted to go ahead with the Select Committee and the Bill

---

indiscriminate bombing by the Federalists led the Prime Minister to send Sir Denis Greenhill, Permanent Under-Secretary at the Foreign and Commonwealth Office, to Lagos on March 10th, to warn the Federal Government about feeling in Britain and to explore ways of ending the war.

[1] Labour M.P. for Sunderland South since 1964, he was P.P.S. to the Home Secretary.

as fast as possible and all the newspapers have been full of our intention to do so. He has clearly let himself and Judith Hart, who was acting as his agent, brief the press beforehand. That is really as far as we got this morning.

Then we had a number of other things, an item on Members' constituencies, on Parliamentary Labour Party meetings and on the relations of the N.E.C. A good bunch to indicate the kind of work that this particular Committee does.

This afternoon I looked in at a party which Lord Kennet was holding to celebrate the new Town and Country Planning Act and the section dealing with historic buildings and the centres of historic cities. As I had initiated this when I was Minister of Housing I thought I ought to go along.[1] There in the Royal Gallery in the House of Lords was the longest buffet table I have ever seen. It seemed to stretch for forty yards along one side and there were about 100 people, among them half a dozen Wedgy Benn and Kennet children looking charming and dashing about. There was a very nice collection of people from York and Bath, cities I had been trying to help, and most of the nicer and more interesting members of the Government. I ran into Patricia Llewelyn-Davies and while I was talking to her Harold breezed in. We were soon surrounded. She told me afterwards that he had blurted out in a loud voice congratulations on her appointment as a Whip in place of Norah Phillips.[2] This news was still top secret but in consequence it rapidly leaked out. He is absolutely unaware that he is one of the major sources of leaks in this Government because he doesn't understand that talking in this cheerful and friendly way gives out new information.

Meanwhile our beautiful weather had turned to heavy rain and it was drenching when I was dropped at a magnificent swimming baths in Putney where there was a very nice hall. We had some seventy people, a very good turnout in the rain. I found it difficult to talk there but again I was staggered on the subject of pensions. For an hour and a half there were a whole series of highly intelligent, well-informed questions asked by people who were getting away from the pure partisan point of view and really studying the subject. Pensions is a marvellous theme if you can only get people into a room to discuss it. I was motored back by Hugh Jenkins and his nice jolly wife, for whom I remember opening the election campaign in 1966 along with Vanessa

[1] The 1962 Act had been replaced by an Act that received the Royal Assent in October 1968. The new legislation established a two-part scheme for broad structure plans, to be submitted to the Minister, and detailed local plans for local adoption by local authorities. Part V of the Act simplified the procedure for controlling works to listed buildings by putting a blanket building preservation order on all buildings of architectural or historic interest and Clause 48 deterred owners of listed buildings from allowing them to fall into disrepair. Lord Kennet had been Chairman of the Preservation Policy Group from whose thinking much of the proposals derived. The Act had first been introduced in May 1965, when Crossman was Minister of Housing and Local Government. See Vol. I.

[2] Widow of Morgan Phillips, former General Secretary of the Labour Party. She became a life peer in 1964 and was a Government Whip in the Lords 1965–70.

Redgrave, the actress. I gave them a drink of whisky and we had a very pleasant evening together.

This evening I had a great deal of reading to do. One of my three boxes last night was entirely devoted to the Ely Hospital near Cardiff. Brian Abel-Smith had reminded me that in October I had been told that I would soon have this appalling problem. Geoffrey Howe,[1] one of the ablest of the young Tory lawyers, had been Chairman of an Inquiry into an outrageous newspaper story that there had been cruelty and pilfering in the Ely Mental Hospital. Kenneth Robinson had established the inquiry in September 1967, and it had taken more than a year, submitting its report in September 1968, before I took over. The report had been 83,000 words long and straightaway the Ministry had said that there must be a confidential report in full for the Department and a shortened version for publication. 'Not on your life,' Geoffrey Howe had said, 'I must get out the essential facts.' For three months the Department and Howe had fought about the character of the report. We had three drafts, the full, unabridged 83,000 words, a much shorter version of some 20,000 words and a medium version omitting only one-twelfth of the original stuff. I was suddenly told that I had to agree this because it was necessary to publish the report of the Inquiry before March 31st, the date on which I hand over control of Health in Wales to the Secretary of State for Wales. I was furious because it was outrageous to bring it to my notice on Monday night, giving me two days to agree with it when I could have seen it at any time in the last three months.

Tuesday, March 11th

This morning I summoned Miss Hedley,[2] the head of the Hospital Section, and Dr Yellowlees and said,[3] 'What the devil is this? I can't possibly decide it overnight.' I told them I would read it all tonight because time was really pressing. We would have a special meeting tomorrow morning and I would meet George Thomas on Thursday. I think I put the fear of God into them and I also warned them that I would then make the decision whether to publish in full or not but that in my view of the situation there was no alternative to publishing the full, unabridged 83,000 words. If I published any less Geoffrey Howe would be entitled to go on television and talk about suppression.

So tonight I went to bed and read and read and it seemed clearer than ever

[1] Conservative M.P. for Bebington 1964–6, for Reigate 1970–4 and for Surrey East since 1974. He was Opposition front-bench spokesman on health and social security matters. He was defeated at the 1966 General Election and on his return to Parliament in 1970 became Solicitor-General, moving to the D.T.I. in 1972 to become Minister of Trade and Consumer Affairs and serving in that capacity until 1974. He was knighted in 1970.

[2] Under-Secretary at the D.H.S.S. 1967–75, she had been Secretary to the Royal Commission on the Law Relating to Mental Illness and Mental Deficiency 1954–7.

[3] Sir Henry Yellowlees (K.C.B. 1975) was Deputy Chief Medical Officer at the D.H.S.S. 1967–72, Second Chief Medical Officer 1972–3, and since 1973 Chief Medical Officer at the D.H.S.S., the D.E.S. and the Home Office.

that the whole thing had to be published. The report completely substantiated the *News of the World* story and I might as well make the best of it by outright publication. But I was also clear in my own mind that I could only publish and survive politically if in the course of my Statement I announced necessary changes in policy including the adoption by the Ministry and the R.H.B.s of a system of inspectorates, central and regional, such as there are in almost every other Ministry and such as the Health Service has never yet permitted itself.

Wednesday, March 12th

At Cabinet all the issues we had conveniently sorted out at Parliamentary Committee had to be gone through again. On Nigeria there was something new. Greenhill,[1] the new Head of the Foreign Office, who had been sent out on a forty-eight-hour mission, was due back this evening and Harold said very carefully that until then we couldn't really make up our minds on the exact line which the Foreign Secretary should take. Nevertheless Michael Stewart had produced a paper on Nigeria, one of those implacably moralistic Foreign Office papers which you will also find, I am sure, on the Palestine troubles, and we did have a full-length policy debate.

The paper was written with the deep assumption that there was only one case, that because it would damage Britain's interests for Nigeria to disintegrate, we should support a united Nigeria. Denis Healey and I put the point that, whether we liked it or not, Biafra had broken away and would survive in some sense as an independent people, very much like Palestine or Ulster. If the Biafrans had really proved their case by fighting, it was no good saying we would back the Federal Government to force them into a Federal Nigeria that had fallen in pieces. We had to recognize the new situation *de facto*. Of course most of the Cabinet were not concerned with this at all but with the indignation aroused by the daily bombing of villages in Biafra, and the fact that we have been supplying arms to a Federal air force which is killing civilians. All that argument seemed to me weak and ineffective and merely the result of pro-Biafran propaganda by an American firm in Geneva. There was a difference between the *Realpolitik* of myself and Denis Healey and the moral objections of people like Judith, Tony Greenwood, Dick Marsh and Harold. I think this division is nothing new (I suspect it occurs in all left-wing governments) and it's a division between Left and Right. The really striking thing was that in the course of this Cabinet Harold never gave any kind of indication that the reason that Denis Greenhill had gone out was to prepare the way for a Prime Ministerial visit to Lagos.[2]

[1] Sir Denis Greenhill (K.C.M.G. 1967) was Deputy Under-Secretary of State at the Foreign Office 1966–9 and Permanent Under-Secretary of State 1969–73. He has been H.M. Government Director of the British Petroleum Co. Ltd since 1973, a member of the Security Commission since 1973 and a Governor of the B.B.C. since 1973, and, since 1975, H.M. Government Director of British Leyland Ltd. He became a life peer in 1974.

[2] The visit, announced during the debate on March 13th, took place from March 27th to

The other item which came up again was the question of Gordon Bagier. Harold has got this on his mind and was trying to force it through Cabinet. At last he had seen that the Committee on Privileges should deal with the matter but he still wanted us to announce our intention to legislate. I told him again that the thing to do was not to rush into legislation. 'For heaven's sake,' I said, 'let's get the House of Commons to have a special look at public relations firms acting for foreign governments. Let's have an exposure of this American public relations firm in Geneva and what they're actually up to, not an inquiry about the Members.' I must say that for once I got the whole Cabinet to realize that I was right. I very much hope that this is what we shall actually do.

At 12.30 this afternoon we had the critical meeting on Ely in my room at Alexander Fleming House with about twelve people round the table. Bea Serota came. She has been extremely good and forced this issue through directly she took over from David Ennals, who had done nothing about it for two months. There we were with the retinue of officials. I started by saying that we had better face it that this report was not only a tremendous indictment of the Ely Hospital but of the Hospital Management Committee, which had failed to be aware of what was going on, and of the Regional Hospital Board and of ourselves, because we as a Ministry are responsible for our agents down there in the Health Service. Ghastly things had gone on for years at Ely. We hadn't known, for example, that two nurses had been dismissed because they had tried to expose the scandals. The officials were on the defensive and I discovered that they intended me simply to publish the report with a Statement deploring it. I said, 'Not on your life. If I do that there will be a whole series of investigations into hospitals all over the country' – because I had found during this week that there are no less than 250,000 people in long-stay, sub-normal, psychiatric or geriatric hospitals, cooped up in these old public assistance buildings with no adequate inspectorate – 'and the inquiries might be able to find in many of the other ones equally scandalous things. It is a first-rate crisis for the Service.' This produced some consternation. They said my idea was quite impracticable. An inspectorate would have all kinds of difficulties. The doctors would demand that their affairs should only be inspected by doctors and anyway this decision couldn't possibly be taken between now and the publication of the White Paper.

Then we had a long, long argument about which version should be published and on that I simply won. At the end one or two of the officials said, 'Frankly, there doesn't seem to be any difference between the twelve-twelfths and the eleven-twelfths.' I pointed out that either we took the credit of publishing the whole thing or we would be at the mercy of one of the cleverest

31st. Mr Wilson talked to the Federal Prime Minister, General Gowon, but his offer to meet the Biafran leader, Colonel Ojukwu, as a conciliator was rebuffed. Mr Wilson then went on to Addis Ababa for discussions with Emperor Haile Selassie and the Secretary-General of the Organization of African Unity. See *Wilson*, pp. 623–39.

Conservative lawyers. One of the most dramatic moments of this meeting was when I referred to our not knowing anything about it and Bea said, 'Didn't we? You ask the Chief Nurse what she knows about it.'[1] Dame Kathleen said, 'Oh, yes. We used to have people going down there, regularly visiting.' I said, 'Did they report?' 'Yes.' 'When was the last report?' 'Three or four years ago.' 'Have you got it?' Bea had arranged to have it and she threw it across the table to me. It was a deplorable report, admitting scandalous conditions, bad nursing, the basis of all the *News of the World* revelations that Geoffrey Howe had confirmed. I asked what had happened to this when it came in and the answer was that it had gone on file. So the Ministry did in fact know and I am pretty sure they have a shrewd idea that there are a great number of unspecified long-stay hospitals with conditions not very different from those at Ely. I have to be careful of course, because the badness of the ghastly old buildings I have visited doesn't necessarily mean there is pilfering, torture and cruelty. That is a matter of staffing. Nevertheless staff do get utterly demoralized by bad buildings, bad pay, staff shortages, lack of domestic help and the two things are linked together. It was a tremendous meeting and I simply told them, 'I am going to see the Welsh Secretary tomorrow. I shall get his leave to publish. Not what you propose, just putting a copy of this in the Library and giving it to the press, but publishing a White Paper. We will bring it right out into the open and I want a draft Statement to be submitted to the Social Services Committee. Incidentally, I have talked to the Prime Minister already about it and he agrees.' This produced real movement.

In the evening Anne and I went to see the film *Isadora* with Vanessa Redgrave in the title role. It's an amazing film in lovely colour, beautifully produced, but of course Isadora Duncan is such an absolute idiot that she is almost impossible to swallow despite the brilliance of the acting, and somehow she became sillier and sillier all through. Nevertheless it was thoroughly worth seeing. I found myself suddenly looking at the Town Hall at Paignton, the little town between Brixham and Torquay, which I visited when I was creating the Torbay area.[2] It shows you that being Minister of Housing gives subsidiary bonuses on the way.

Thursday, March 13th

At 9.45, before Future Legislation Committee, I had Peter Brown in. He is settling down and gradually getting the Department into shape but the fact remains that things go terribly slowly because people are in two separate buildings. We still have six girls cutting newspapers at John Adam Street, another eight cutting newspapers at Alexander Fleming House, and we can't

[1] Dame Kathleen Raven (D.B.E. 1968) was Matron of the General Infirmary, Leeds 1949–57 and Deputy Chief Nursing Officer 1957–8 and Chief Nursing Officer at the D.H.S.S. 1958–72.

[2] See Vol. I, pp. 175–6.

sack half of them until we actually put the offices together. It is more and more clear that it's on the information, Intelligence and policy-planning side that the real advantage of the merger comes and below that level there won't be very much merger between these extraordinarily different Departments. If we can establish a departmental policy for information, policy planning and financial priorities in Social Services it will be an enormous advance. Peter is quite decent at this work, the best man I could have had, and after a bit of anxiety I feel he hasn't let me down.

Tommy Balogh, looking very gay and dapper with his little bow-tie and his neat little self, also bustled in to tell me how disastrous the trade figures were.[1]

The pound and the Government have had a bad week, and the public has had a bad week in terms of increased interest rates. The home mortgage rate has gone up to 8½ per cent after the increase in bank rate, so the crisis is brought home to ordinary people at the same time as it is brought home to the bankers by the badness of the trade figures. Once again we are teetering along on the edge of the precipice, with the budget coming on in a month's time. I said to Tommy, 'Ah, well, it can't be helped. I'm busy on something else,' but Tommy is my conscience. He is saying I must remain a *Cabinet* Minister and continue to take an active part in all current main policy issues. I am saying, 'No, it's not worth it. I'm not in Harold's confidence any more, I can't,' and in a way Tommy doesn't disagree with me. Now he's off to America to lecture and make money. He is really, thank heavens, throwing his hand in and breaking the umbilical cord which still half ties him to No. 10.

Then I had an interesting meeting with Godber and Henry Cohen,[2] about immigrant doctors. I had been told that the G.M.C. would object if I laid upon them the obligation to see that the doctors are qualified. We have now discovered that this legislation is the easiest thing possible, needing only a tiny little minor amendment of the present Act. I don't think Cohen made any great difficulties about it. Once again one of the major obstacles put up by the Department had been dissipated by the simple technique of summoning the person and asking if he actually objected, calling the officials' bluff. As with abortion and Ely, I am hoping to advance on immigrant doctors by forcing the Department into action which they are reluctant to undertake, if only because they are really a deeply inactive, reflective, advisory Ministry.

Today I was able to see George Thomas and his staff about the Ely report. Our choice is whether to publish on March 31st, the day before he takes over the Welsh Health Services, or whether we should put publication back to March 27th. I would much prefer to do it on the 31st but George Thomas said, no, we couldn't do this because he was having a two-day tour of Welsh

[1] The deficit on visible trade had risen from £10 million in January to £59 million in February.

[2] Sir Henry Cohen has been Consulting Physician, at the Royal Infirmary, Liverpool, since 1924. He was Professor of Medicine at the University of Liverpool 1934–65 and President of the General Medical Council 1961–3. He became a baron in 1956.

hospitals before taking them over and it would spoil this to publish in the middle of it. I said, 'It will spoil it a great deal more if we announce it three days earlier and blanket the press. Still, it's up to you, George. You choose. Don't let it be said I forced you.' He tried to argue but I said, 'Don't try to convince me. I will do what you wish. If you wish it on the Thursday, I will do it on the Thursday but it's a bad day of the week. It gives the Sunday press publicity.' He said, 'Right.' I made him instruct me to do it and I have now agreed to publish on Thursday, March 27th. I was busy having the 83,000 words of the White Paper printed at double-quick speed. The Department has been shoved into line, and as a result of this crisis they have conceded the setting up of what is tantamount to a system of visiting inspectors. On the other hand they seem to feel that by conceding this they can now get a lot of extra money out of the Chancellor. I have told them that there is no chance and that we have to shift the priorities within our present very large budget. Here will be the real crunch because when one thinks that the cost per inmate of our long-stay institutions is, say, £12 to £14 a week whereas the cost in a district hospital is between £40 and £80 a week, it is clear that more money simply has to be taken from other current and capital expenditure.

The psychiatric and geriatric sections have been scandalously pushed down and this is a puzzle, because one of Kenneth Robinson's first intentions was to give these services a fair share. What has happened is that though in the brand new hospital palaces there are 200 beds for this and 200 for that the real problem is to help those who are in the old slum hospitals. We really want to force the local authorities to do their duty and not decant unwanted defectives from the old hospitals into the new palaces. We shall have to tell our hospital service to be far tougher in insisting they won't take in more than the number they can adequately nurse. These 250,000 people are said to require hospital care but the only people who should be in hospital are those who are genuinely ill and need curing. The vast majority of these unfortunate people are not ill in that sense, merely sub-normal or old, and what they need is to live at home or in hostels or old people's homes and for this we need far better local authority services.

All this has been exhilarating and exciting for me. I have got a cause at heart and a job I can really do. Above all, this is the first instance in which I have been able to get a moral authority over officials who without doubt are some of the most old-fashioned kind of highly intelligent civil servants. Of course, they were headed before by Arnold France, a wonderfully old-style civil servant, and Kenneth Robinson, a very old-style traditional member of an R.H.B. This Ministry of mine has all these pen-pushers in it living within the Ministry. The only thing which corresponds to them in British history is, I should think, the old Colonial Office which used to run the Empire from within the Ministry, or the old India Office, which ran India in the same way. The people who really knew about things were the I.C.S. and the Colonial Service, who were always exasperated by the remote abstractness and paper-working of the officials in Whitehall. This is my first great opportunity and I have got to break through whatever happens.

This afternoon was the day of the Nigerian debate but at Question Time Harold was awkwardly caught by Heath, who for once was effective and in the Business Statement challenged Fred Peart about the P.M.'s intention to go to Nigeria. Heath had caught Harold out on a leak in the *Financial Times*. The result was that the Opposition could provoke him with it before the debate even started. They exploded his gimmick and what was supposed to be the dramatic climax petered out. Michael Stewart really had nothing to announce. As Harold was walking out he fell over my knees and said bitchily, 'Well, they boxed me up owing to that confounded leak from Lagos,' and I felt like saying, 'You would have done better to trust your colleagues, who would have advised you against the idea.'

The fact is that if Harold had put this to us the whole Cabinet would have advised against his going, but he never learns. One of the abiding facts about Harold's foreign policy is that he always sees himself as being able to help. He wants to run a foreign policy that enables him to shine as a negotiator, to intervene, to make Britain active on the job. He kept on supporting the American side in Vietnam because he wanted to be able to intervene in the negotiations. Giving us a chance of doing something is his major preoccupation. But in this particular world of ours there's not much point in getting a chance of doing something or constantly sacrificing principle and popularity for the sake of doing something when we are hardly in a position to be useful at all.

As it turned out the debate was totally unlike what had been expected. There had been a tremendous build-up in the press about the Labour revolt and the crisis in the Government and I don't think our Whips knew much more than the newspapers. I got in for the last hour and heard the wind-up by the two sides. The place was half-empty. I am told that the remarkable thing was a very powerful speech by Alec Douglas Home, who once again came out as a statesman speaking above party lines, pleading that we were not able to alter our policy of supplying arms to the Federal Government and criticizing us for not trying to secure an international embargo on arms supplies to all sides. As so often happens, he did our work for us.

Throughout Michael Stewart's speech nobody seemed really to be desperately concerned about the vote and when the result was finally announced we had only sixty-two people voting against us.[1] Of those the usual thirty-five were ours but still there had been no atmosphere of crisis. This has its interest and good political correspondents are beginning to notice the fundamental fact that in this Parliament the Labour Party's moralistic discipline has gone and what John and I tried to do in our year has worked out. The Labour

[1] The vote was 232 votes to 62, with the Conservatives officially abstaining. Those opposing the Government's policy comprised 20 Conservatives, 34 Labour, 6 Liberals, 1 Independent Conservative and 1 Scottish Nationalist.

Party has learnt to tolerate thirty or forty people constantly voting against us whenever they like. Outside the House it has not produced any ill-effects. Inside it has produced terrible ill-will but the atmosphere is also extraordinarily indifferent and this was once again proved this evening.

Friday, March 14th

O.P.D., specially summoned to deal with the subject of Anguilla.[1] This little island was part of the St Kitts group and had been given a relationship of association with Britain, independent in home affairs but with their external relations dependent on us. Two years ago Anguilla had come more and more to dislike the Government of Mr Bradshaw, the Premier of St Kitts, and had chased away his policemen. Then Mr Webster, the leader of what you might call the Independence Group of Anguilla, was taken over by a group of American gangsters. This little island, fifteen miles long and three and a half wide, with 6,000 inhabitants, really consists of nothing but coral beaches and the gangsters wanted to turn it into a gambling resort, a casino, and make it independent of Britain. In view of all this, Whitlock had arranged a conference in London with Webster and Bradshaw to try to sort it out, but it hadn't been successful so Whitlock had been sent to Anguilla on a frigate. He had asked the people on the frigate whether it would be wise to assume there would be armed resistance, and to take with him a naval or a marine guard. 'Oh,' they had said, 'it would be a great mistake to have a display of force,' so he had gone in peacefully, landed from a little aeroplane and was making a speech to some 500 people on the airstrip, when he was chased off the island by armed thugs. Here was Mr Whitlock, very bronzed, giving us as the result of his half-hour on the island his assessment of the situation.

We had discussed this earlier in the week and hoped it wouldn't get into the papers – a vain hope it was – and this morning we had to decide what to do about it. Well, this meeting was like an Evelyn Waugh farce. There we were sitting round discussing how to enforce British authority on an island where perhaps some thirty or forty people with a few guns were defying the whole power of the British Raj. Michael Stewart made a long, detailed, boring speech, indicating the need to restore law and order and to impose Mr Lee as the British Commissioner.[2] We had had a request from Bradshaw in St

[1] Anguilla, in the Caribbean, had in May 1967 'seceded' from the Associated States of St Kitts–Nevis–Anguilla. Mr Ronald Webster, the self-styled 'President of the Republic of Anguilla', demanded complete independence and, after talks in London failed, William Whitlock, Parliamentary Under-Secretary of State at the Foreign and Commonwealth Office, had attempted to visit the island on March 12th and had been forced off at gun-point.

[2] Under the terms of an interim settlement between the St Kitts and Anguilla leaders, negotiated by the British representatives in January 1968, Mr A. C. W. Lee (Senior British Official in Anguilla from January 8th, 1968 to January 9th, 1969, and from March 19th to April 20th, 1969, when he went on leave and was succeeded by Mr John Comber) was appointed to advise on the administration of Anguilla for a period of twelve months. After the failure of the talks held in October 1968 in London between Mr Bradshaw and Mr

Kitts to do this and the argument was that the rest of the West Indies would welcome this assertion of force because otherwise the federal grouping might disintegrate and island after island might establish itself as an independent gangster base. Michael had a very powerful argument and we all assented. Then Denis Healey said, 'Wait a bit. Where's our intelligence on the strength of the island? We might need a battalion of troops and once we'd got there how would we get off again? What authority would we have and would we be hauled before the United Nations for an act of aggression?' He even got in a mention of Suez and Rhodesia and we solemnly sat round with the Chiefs of Staff discussing this comic opera situation. Callaghan said bluffly, 'Whatever you may say, Defence Secretary, we've got to go in. We can't have our nose twisted. I'll give you twenty policemen to keep peace on the island once you have restored law and order.' I thought it was pretty absurd but it did seem to me as the discussion went on that this was quite an important issue. It's true that all these islands strung out across the Caribbean are miles away from here and that Britain has no great authority any more, but there is de Gaulle occupying part of the next-door island. One saw the instability of world politics when great powers cease to be great and a partial vacuum of power brings instability and uncertainty. Finally, I merely said, 'For God's sake, if we do it, do it quickly. Don't let's delay for the sake of another week's intelligence, summoning all the people back. Take a risk. If the Chiefs of Staff say, as they do, that we can occupy the island within fifty hours of giving the word, let's for heaven's sake do so.' So at the very last moment the whole situation was changed. Instead of bringing Mr Lee and the rest of them back we decided to send the colonel in charge of the Marine landings out there and to get a landing on the spot done quickly.

I had just got back to my office in 70 Whitehall when a message was telephoned through. Ron Matthews came to me grinning and said, 'The Prime Minister has just been telephoning round all the Private Offices to say would we please remember that the subject discussed this morning is top secret.' Just reflect on that. Here is a man who, four and a half years after he has taken over in No. 10, doesn't understand that such a message will tip off every Private Office that the paper we discussed and which they had read had ended in a decision to take action. In his effort to maintain security he had from the best of motives given an official leak. I often wonder about Harold. I sometimes say that in certain ways he is naïve and innocent and I think he is. Innocent in having that message telephoned round, innocent in deciding to fly off to Nigeria. Last night before I went to bed I read an astonishing interview he gave to the B.B.C.'s religious programme last Sunday on his attitude to religion and God. He hasn't got any doctrinal beliefs, I don't

---

Webster, Mr Lee was withdrawn on December 30th but it was arranged for him to pay periodic visits to the island. When Mr Whitlock visited Anguilla on March 11th he had proposed that Mr Lee be established there as H.M. Commissioner while a long-term solution to the island's problems was worked out.

think he really believes in God, but he has the structure of moral behaviour of a Nonconformist Boy Scout. This is what differentiates him so profoundly from, say, Denis, Roy or myself, and gives him something in common with such different people as Barbara, who has something of the Girl Guide in her still, Judith, an old-fashioned, sentimental left-winger and Michael Stewart, an old-fashioned, doctrinaire social democrat. They all have this right-and-wrong attitude to life, this prissy rigour combined with an extraordinary power of self-deception.

Sunday, March 16th

Dreary weather here at Prescote, the sky drooping down yesterday when Richard and Patricia Llewelyn-Davies came over to see whether they were interested in a site on the Wardington side of the river. I took Richard down to Major Donner's place, where he keeps his bees on the other side of the ruined mill, but what was the good of looking at the view through thick mist? We haven't had Richard and Patricia here for six or seven years, which shows how time passes. Patricia has just been promoted to being a Whip in place of Norah Phillips, who took umbrage because Bea Serota had been promoted over her head. It gave us our chance to give Patricia a place in the Government and she was pleased with that, though she has got to give up her chairmanship of the Governors of the Great Ormond Street Hospital, and we had to discuss who should take her place. Richard is full of interest about our hospital building schemes and we may bring in him and his firm to check on the efficiency of our 'best buy' hospitals at Bury St Edmunds and Frimley. It was a very pleasant day.

Today was colder and bleaker. We spent part of it with a very nice fellow discussing what we are going to do with our desert of a garden to make a civilized place round the new swimming bath. Should we fill in the moat—but we haven't enough earth? Should we drain it or have the water running through? It was fun discussing this but we are anxious because we are so reluctant now to spend any money.

At least our minds were off the problems of the week and of the Government, which really are pretty desperate. If last week was an indeterminate week this week was disastrous. The Ford strike continues and I haven't even dared to listen to the wireless today to hear whether Barbara has got some sense into these people. There is a real danger now that Ford's will move all their European activity to their French and German factories. We feel totally impotent and of course the unspoken thought is that Jones and Scanlon are organizing a political strike against Barbara's *In Place of Strife* and trying to break this Government. Harold Wilson made a great speech in his constituency on Friday, trying to appeal to the rank and file over the heads of their union leaders. I don't know whether he was successful or not. Barbara has been busy all weekend but the situation is desperate because this defiance of the Government could destroy us altogether.

As if that wasn't enough we have had the disastrous trade figures on Thursday and the increase of the mortgage rate. Was this depressing picture relieved at all by Harold Wilson's announcement that he is going to fly out to Nigeria? Well, that gimmick was exploded even before he had intended to announce it and of course all today's papers are full of Anguilla, tipping us off that *Fearless* is being moved from the Mediterranean in order to make the landing. I am a bit surprised about this because I think myself that although they say the operation will only take fifty hours it will take the *Fearless* longer than that to get across the Atlantic. *Fearless* is probably being prepared for the Prime Minister to go to Nigeria but there are plenty of rumours now about the action in Anguilla so the Prime Minister's security blanket had the opposite effect to what he intended. On the whole I should say this is a week in which we are back on the edge of disaster.

Monday, March 17th

This morning I had a big meeting on Ely for all the big-wigs in the Ministry, who were still struggling hard to prevent my setting up the inspectorate. I was quite prepared to give up the main inspectorate and have a scrutiny or advisory service but the key to it in my mind is that it should be an organization completely separate from the policy-making and administrative set-up in the Ministry. It should be an independent group of people inspecting and reporting to me. We have painfully to fight all this out but, as the Secretary of State fully backed by Bea Serota, I have got the whip hand because the Ely Report is an exposure of the Department's failure as well as that of the Regional Hospital Board. I also told them that I was bound to warn the R.H.B. chairmen, whom I happen to have a meeting with tomorrow, that I couldn't tell them in advance about the White Paper.

I spent the morning at St Thomas's, looking at the treatment of people with mental diseases and having lunch with the Governors. I find myself really getting a curious kind of expertise on the details of London hospital reorganization.

Tuesday, March 18th

We started with Anguilla. Yesterday Robert Carvel had a pretty detailed story of how the landing was to be made and in particular of how forty-one London policemen had been put on standby. I ought perhaps to add that I have no evidence that Harold's telephone calls did anything more than generally tip off people in Fleet Street to the idea that there was some action going on. Anyhow, we started the meeting in some anger about the security leak because by this morning the whole world had been alerted just as the troops were landing close by on Antigua.

Yesterday the Foreign Secretary had pretty successfully escaped having a question on this but now the whole world was waiting for the British invasion. Harold said that he had practically traced the leak to a police officer so for once Cabinet was acquitted. Very little else was discussed this morning because as usual O.P.D. had trusted the actual detailed supervision of the operation to an inner group of three, the Prime Minister, the Foreign Secretary and the Defence Secretary.

I ran across to Alexander Fleming House and found the R.H.B. chairmen just finishing their meeting. I suddenly woke up this morning and thought, 'Why on earth shouldn't I tell them about the Ely White Paper? It might pay me to get them on my side,' so I gave them a really bracing talk, telling them what a ghastly report it was and why I had decided to publish. I told them they must themselves take the responsibility for failures in their own regions, just as I must take responsibility for mine. In fact I am primarily responsible, but therefore I must have eyes and ears and a change of priorities. I must get justice for this underprivileged section of the Health Service and I told them I wanted to fight this shoulder to shoulder with them. If this were to be just another report admitting these things are true and doing nothing about them the morale of the Service would collapse but if we were to have a real policy we should survive. I felt I made some advance there.

Meanwhile the tragi-comedy of the Parliament Bill continues. For some extraordinary reason it had been decided to resume this afternoon. So at 4 o'clock they began with points of order and Motions for Progress. I wasn't there at the beginning because I had insisted on going to see Roy on the crucial issue of the Todd Report. I wanted to ask him to overrule Jack Diamond and permit me to announce that the Government had decided to accept Todd's minimum of 3,700 places in medical schools by 1975. Diamond had wanted to pare this down to 3,500 and I had said for the sake of 200 places it was ridiculous to get the discredit for disowning Todd. A great file, inches thick, had gone endlessly to and fro and now with the help of George Godber, I finally got the Chancellor to agree in half an hour. This shows what an appalling waste of time Treasury tactics really are, especially when there is a surrender.

When I got back into the Chamber the whole thing was out of control because that miserable little fellow Harry Gourlay,[1] who had been put into one of the chairmen's jobs in order to get him out of the Whips' Office, had weakly let the back benchers have points of order entirely on the question of the attendance figures which I was supposed to have promised them about the House of Lords. They now had a new story of a document available in the House of Lords' library giving the voting record of all the peers for fifty years back. Robert Sheldon was making a tremendous issue of how this document ought not to be confidential and this discussion went on and on. I said I would certainly be prepared to try to get their Lordships to release it, which produced another lot of points of order. After four and a half hours

[1] Labour M.P. for Kirkcaldy Burghs October 1959–74 and for Kirkcaldy since 1974. He was Chairman of the Scottish Parliamentary Party Labour group 1963–4, Government Whip 1964–8, and Deputy Chairman of Ways and Means 1968–70.

we got on to the first amendment. I kept my temper fairly well but I realized that the document story was a concerted plot between Sheldon, Michael Foot and Eric Heffer on the one side and Boyd-Carpenter, Enoch Powell and his gang on the other. The first group of amendments was successfully carried in four votes at 11.30 and we got to bed at midnight.

Wednesday, March 19th

S.E.P., and meanwhile at 10 o'clock the Commons started again on the Parliament Bill. No points of order for a full hour until the second amendment was carried at 1.30. Fred Peart had failed to turn up, Callaghan was in America and the only person I had with me was Elystan Morgan,[1] whom I had thought of as a rather dismal Minister of State from central Wales. I now found him to be excellent and simply left things to him. He handled it superbly. I stayed at the S.E.P., which was meeting in the Prime Minister's room at the end of the passage, for the very simple reason that if I had gone into the Chamber this morning it would have started another storm of protest.

I worked out the Ely policy this morning and got the committee set up with Brian Abel-Smith, Frank Mottishead and Henry Yellowlees, two keen young men who are on my side against Miss Hedley, all working together.[2] I am trying to get them to face it that our priorities are wrong and that too much is given to new modern hospitals and too little to this particular depressed segment.

Lunch at the Royal College of Physicians in their strange ultra-modern Denys Lasdun building on the right-hand side of Regent's Park,[3] a huge picture gallery, library, banqueting hall, all empty, all expensively useless like those of many other London livery companies. Then I went back to the House of Commons to hear Michael Stewart making a Statement on Anguilla. By now the troops were installed. In the course of Friday's O.P.D. I had urged more than once that the success of the whole operation depended on the way it was done and that in view of our rather dicey situation we needed to work out an elaborate psychological warfare plan. We were only in charge of the external affairs of these islands and we would have to demonstrate that we were not invading but going in in terms of our external association. I had strongly urged that the forces should be there for the landing but that they shouldn't necessarily be used. In the first instance the frigate should sail up to the island and then the Commissioner or whoever it was should go ashore for a peaceful landing with two or three armed Marines. Force should only be used if the peaceful landing met with armed resistance. Of course the very opposite had happened and a tremendous military performance was put on

[1] Labour M.P. for Cardiganshire 1966–February 1974. He was Parliamentary Under-Secretary of State at the Home Office 1968–70.

[2] Frank Mottishead was Deputy Secretary at the D.H.S.S. 1965–71.

[3] The architect, whose work includes the design for the National Theatre on the South Bank. He was knighted in 1976.

with parachutists and the rest of them. Instead of producing law and order it's produced a crisis, a kind of bogus Suez, and we have made a complete fool of ourselves in the world. Michael Stewart made a good Statement and it became clear that if it was simply in the House of Commons that we were being judged we would be all right. It was perhaps ominous that George Brown, an ex-Foreign Secretary, got up and told us that he didn't believe in gunboat diplomacy but by and large Stewart succeeded by his coolness and rationality.

In the evening I rushed in to a farewell party for one of our doorkeepers at the Ministry of Housing, who used to look after me and bring me a few eggs and flowers. He had been given the B.E.M. and a party was being held in his honour. There was Henry Brooke and Matthew Stevenson.[1] This man is the kind of reverent public servant whom senior civil servants love, the man who is really respectful, and I felt slightly sick at joining in the billing and cooing. I wondered how much the fuss we make about people right at the bottom is because it lets us condescend to them.

From there I went to a Committee Room in the House of Commons where Eric Lubbock,[2] the Liberal Chief Whip, tall and angular, looking rather like an unpopular public school boy, was holding his first meeting of the Fluoridisation Society. This is a campaign to answer the powerful lobby of the Anti-fluoridisation Society and I had to persuade them that the work of propaganda must go on before we can legislate. After that a quick three-line whip on mortgages.[3] Thank God I voted twice this time as I should. Then to the opera for a splendid evening with the Sadies hearing Berlioz's *Benvenuto Cellini*, not a very dramatic opera, but with lovely music and lovely arias. You can see the difference between the work of a talented genius who wasn't a dramaturgist and the work of Wagner.

Thursday, March 20th

Cabinet. There was a good deal of protest from people who hadn't been to O.P.D. on Friday and who had heard for the first time from the press what had happened in Anguilla. Tony Crosland and a good many other people said last Thursday's Cabinet hadn't been consulted. The only person who didn't complain was Dick Marsh, who pointed out that he had left Cabinet convinced that we were going to use military force and he was puzzled why anybody else should have been in doubt. Cabinet had been given a broad strategic outline and all that happened on Friday was that O.P.D. officially

[1] Henry Brooke was Conservative M.P. for West Lewisham 1938–45 and for Hampstead 1950–66. He was Financial Secretary to the Treasury 1954–7, Minister of Housing and Local Government and for Welsh Affairs 1957–61, Chief Secretary to the Treasury and Paymaster-General 1961–2 and Home Secretary 1962–4. He became a life peer in 1966.

[2] Liberal M.P. for Orpington from 1962 until he lost his seat in 1970, and Liberal Whip 1963–70. In 1971 he succeeded to his cousin's barony and became Lord Avebury.

[3] The mortgage rate had been raised to 8½ per cent. The Government amendment was approved by 269 votes to 215 and the Government's policy on home ownership was approved by 255 votes to 215.

sanctioned the plan to use force. However Harold made it very clear, and this was put in the minutes, that it was O.P.D. which had been responsible for the actual expedition. This isn't true. All fifteen people couldn't arrange the actual details of the landing and of the psychological warfare, and O.P.D. did not take responsibility for this, merely for the decision not to delay the operation. Once again it was the little inner group, the three I have mentioned, who did the job. I can now see two characteristic reasons why this went wrong. First of all, there was the terrible no-risk attitude. This is Michael Stewart's greatest fault, a complete psychological misjudgment, plus the desire to make assurance doubly sure. If we send in troops we mustn't risk a man's life. No doubt the idea of sending in Lee or Whitlock in a pinnace with three armed Marines to see if they could make a peaceful landing was dismissed because it would endanger their lives but, after all, that is what one is for on these occasions.

Because we preferred to put the military force in the foreground and the civil commission in the background, we managed to antagonize not only the islanders but a large number of the governments in the West Indies who had previously backed us and we annoyed the United Nations as well.

The other basic mistake was, as usual, the failure to check the information supplied by the Foreign Office. I can confirm from what I said in the diary last week that after half an hour on the island Whitlock gave us a lot of information about a mafia and the serious chance that Anguilla might be turned into a gambling hell. Now it seems that British correspondents there are saying all this is sheer gossip. The island is a perfectly peaceful, religious, primitive place, which simply wants to be independent of St Kitts, and the mafia talk is all invention. Certainly it has been confirmed that there are no arms. Only one rifle was found on the island and that was voluntarily handed in. If the people did have a lot of arms they successfully concealed them. The absence of any take-over threat by American gangsters removes the main justification for our sailing very near the wind in using military force to intervene in Anguilla's internal affairs, where after all we are no longer responsible for anything except the external situation. We now look complete fools in the papers and the cartoons. This is 'Wilson's Suez'. This is our kind of invasion. We wouldn't invade Rhodesia but we indulge in this sort of posturing.

The trouble is that it all fits extremely well with the critical picture of Wilson which is building up in the public mind and it fits, I am afraid, with my picture of him, for it is my view, confirmed once again by this affair, that the failures of the Government are not peripheral failures, not on the whole failures of Departments, but failures of central direction, of the Prime Minister and his personal relations with his inner group. It is reflected particularly in foreign policy, which the Prime Minister has retained completely in his own hands. It is here that our failure as a Government has been most abysmal, second only to the failure in economic control, where the Prime Minister has always worked hand-in-glove with the Chancellor and where once again he has personal responsibility. So that is Anguilla, yet another idiotic fiasco like the fiasco with de Gaulle, the fiasco with the Common Market, the fiasco with Rhodesia, the fiasco we are likely to have with Nigeria when the Prime Minister flies out next Tuesday. They are all expressions of Wilson's naïveté, indecisiveness, posturing, his failure to make strategic decisions. Failure on the foreign field, failure on the economic front is what is bringing this Government down.

After the row about Anguilla Cabinet returned to the Parliament Bill where we had a puzzling little incident. I agreed with those who asked why it was that we did an odd day here and an odd day there and why we didn't have a real go at it. 'Well,' said Fred Peart, 'we intend to have a go at it on Monday, Tuesday and Wednesday before the Easter recess,' and Willie Ross said shrewdly, 'That's damn silly. Unless you have a three-line whip on the Thursday, nobody will be here on Tuesday and Wednesday,' to which of course John Silkin replied that we didn't need many people there if they were adequately paired and we really must have a good crack at it. I couldn't make out why we weren't having anything next week but the Prime Minister said that we must have these three days and then we would review the situation. I replied tartly that the thought that we should be reviewing the situation after three days is exactly what causes the trouble. We've got to face it that there is no alternative to ploughing ahead and until we do we shall have an opposition holding out successfully against us. The Prime Minister said, 'I didn't mean that we should say so outside, but I can say it here, surely,' and I said, 'But here is the area of greatest weakness.' I don't think we got much further this morning and I shall be very surprised if our three solid days bring us much progress the week after next.

After that we had Barbara Castle on the Ford strike. She had been obliged to make some pretty big concessions to the men last Tuesday but, still, the strike was off and she was congratulated on it. Then she brought in a paper on the salaries of the heads of the nationalized industries.[1] This had been referred ages ago to the Prices and Incomes Board, who have recommended a salary structure to compete with private industry and a plan for implementing the increases in three stages. We looked back to my Cabinet paper of 1966 or perhaps 1967, when this was thought to be totally incompatible with incomes policy, so at least three years have taught us something. Barbara led the way and she was supported by Tony Crosland and Dick Marsh and indeed by Harold himself. However I have no doubt that there will be another storm from the P.L.P. and if we do this it will be another nail in the coffin of the prices and incomes policy. We just had time to begin a brief discussion on Concorde, which will be the main item in Cabinet next week.

[1] With the exception of the Chairman of the recently established British Steel Corporation, who was paid £16,000 a year, the salaries of the Chairmen and Deputy Chairmen of the nationalized industries ranged only from £9,500 to £12,500 a year. The P.I.B. recommended that they should be increased by up to £7,500 a year.

This evening there was a memorial ceremony for Kingsley Martin at the Friends' Meeting House in Euston Road. Rather reluctantly I had accepted Paul Johnson's invitation to speak and I found that Barbara had also accepted. I thought it was a great mistake to have two Labour Ministers speaking. He should have had a bishop or somebody from the arts, but V. S. Pritchett was ill so there was just Barbara and me, Norman MacKenzie and C. H. Rolph, with Jock Campbell in the chair.[1] I had thought very hard and read the obituaries in bed on Wednesday and Thursday morning after *Benvenuto Cellini* while Anne lay asleep beside me, and then I worked away in Cabinet to prepare details of the speech, with Barbara doing the same. I set off from 70 Whitehall, got into a traffic jam and only arrived by running round the back of the Friends' Meeting House at five past seven to find Michael Foot looking out for me outside and Barbara looking bad-tempered inside. The meeting was fairly satisfactory. Jock Campbell read aloud rather badly the speech which V. S. Pritchett had prepared and then I spoke second, giving what Jock described to me later as the most brilliant and moving performance he had ever heard. As I sat down he gripped me and said, 'Oh, if only I could speak like that.' I won't go into my speech. I just described Kingsley as I knew him and how I, the renegade Oxford don who wanted to be defrocked, found a place at the *New Statesman* where I disagreed with him on everything and on every policy. We did agree though in our belief in the 'bump of irreverence', which made us always assume a theory or a government action wrong unless it could be proved right and, above all, that a Labour Government must always be assumed to be wrong because the more people are your friends the more awkward you must be to them. I brought out all my old paradoxes and said these were right for the *New Statesman*. C. H. Rolph told a marvellous story and Norman MacKenzie gave a very quiet, studied, good description. Then Barbara got up and made, I thought, a terrible mistake. She spoke a great deal about me and a great deal about herself, until Jock Campbell whispered, 'I hope she is going to mention Kingsley'. Finally she did, only to say that he had said to her just before he died, 'One can't blame Harold about Rhodesia'. This was perhaps not the happiest thing to say to the huge, nice, old-fashioned, *New Statesman* audience.

I rushed away from there to the Westminster Hospital to see Julian Snow, who was going home this evening. He was better, speaking faster, desperately anxious to know whether he would lose his job if he stayed away until the beginning of May. 'No,' I said. 'I think you can stay away until then.' It has been good for Bea and me to get ourselves well into the Health Service side and I told him we would be able to manage.

[1] V. S. Pritchett, the author and critic, was a director of the *New Statesman and Nation*. He was knighted in 1975. Norman MacKenzie was the former Assistant Editor of the *New Statesman*, Cecil Rolph Hewitt, author (under the name of C. H. Rolph) and a member of the *New Statesman* editorial staff since 1947, has been a director of the *New Statesman and Nation* Publishing Co. Ltd since 1965.

Friday, March 21st

I went for the day to Cambridge. I was annoyed to find I was being made to go to King's Cross on a train without a breakfast car which stopped all the way down and I was even more annoyed when I got to King's Cross to find that there were two people from the Health Service side and nobody from Social Security, although I was due, I thought, to make a speech in the afternoon to the chairmen of the East Anglian war pensioners' committees and I knew nothing about the subject. I was even angrier because my brief simply said Speech, with two little notes and nothing on it. There we were, but it went a bit better than I expected and I learnt a great deal by sitting there this afternoon, before being motored back to Prescote in just over two hours to settle down to a delicious family weekend.

Sunday, March 23rd

When I got my boxes yesterday I found at last a file on Ely, a businesslike action plan and a better draft, more like what I wanted. At last I'd got a concession that the inspectorate will be independent and reporting to me, so I won on that one. Altogether it was a serviceable job and I worked over the draft trying to sharpen it up. I rang up the editor of the *News of the World*, the paper whose sensational disclosures had started the whole thing off, and warned him what was happening, saying that I would give him an exclusive article. Wilfred Sendall, Political Correspondent of the *Daily Express*, who had scented something, rang up and wanted to know where the place was. I wouldn't tell him or give him anything about it except that there was a sensational report coming and I would be making a Statement next week. I have already seen George Thomas and shown him my draft paper and we've had an interesting discussion about linking things up with his office.

For the rest of the day Charles and Mary Woodhouse, my favourite sister and brother-in-law, came over from Oxford, and Charles spent the whole afternoon playing games with Patrick and Virginia, who adore him, while I took Mary and Anne for a walk in the bleak east wind, the sort of weather we always seem to have here in March. This is a bitterly cold month in North Oxfordshire. Our grass never seems to grow and there is always a shortage of food for the cattle and an anxiety about how we shall keep them going. When it hasn't been snowing it's been raining and flooding and the farm is really down. However, everything was fine for the children and we have now to make arrangements for the pool to be heated on Good Friday, ready for our Easter holidays, so that I can have at least a week of daily swimming whatever the cold outside. Life at home is as good as ever.

Monday, March 24th

I was able to have a special meeting of the Social Services Committee to report on my draft on post-Ely policy and formally get their consent. It is part of our Cabinet machinery that it is wise to get your Committee behind you and as I was introducing a new service and inspectorate which would require manpower and money, though of a limited amount, it was wise to do this. The Ministry are now calling the inspectorate a policy advisory service and in the draft it is clearly stated that the Director of the new service should be directly responsible to me. It was a very sympathetic meeting. Everybody seemed to admit frankly that they knew the whole treatment of mental health was inadequate. It was one of those occasions when each person could chip in as a human being, not as a Minister, for, except for the Treasury, there was virtually no departmental briefing. After this I cleared the redraft of the Statement with George Thomas. We had agreed that I would first announce this and take upon myself the responsibility of the scandal (which has taken place not only in a Welsh hospital but in his own constituency area of Cardiff). He has been tricky and jumpy but I have managed to carry him along.

All this went fairly smoothly and this evening I finally had Geoffrey Howe to see me. He turned up at Alexander Fleming House at 6.15. From his photographs I thought he was plump and rather fleshy, but he is an elegant young man, good-looking, sharp and keen, an enormously ambitious Tory lawyer. He was defeated in the last election but now he is a candidate for a fairly safe constituency and is bound to get in next time. It was a surprising meeting. I had really called it to suggest to him that we should both go on '24 Hours' together on Thursday and discuss the whole thing man-to-man, he as Chairman of the Committee, I as Minister. To my amazement he refused, on the grounds that he wanted to maintain his position as the Chairman of an impartial Committee and didn't want to find himself compromising its Report in any way by making political statements. That in a sense was the whole tone of his attitude. He was not a young Tory seeking to make party capital but interested in the Committee and what the inquiry would do, good or bad, to his career. He told me that he had certainly taken a great risk because undoubtedly he would make himself unpopular in legal circles which determine what kind of inquiries and jobs of this kind Q.C.s get. The Lord Chancellor's Office had more than once emphasized how important it was for Q.C.s to keep this kind of inquiry narrow but he had felt very strongly about this episode and so had two members of his Committee. They had all believed that they really ought to widen their responsibilities and carry the inquiry outside Ely up to the H.M.C., up to the R.H.B., really up to the Ministry, so that the Report was not only a Report on Ely but one which illustrated a defect in the structure of the Health Service. We discussed publication. He was very surprised but very pleased that I was publishing the full version; surprised, because three months had been spent trying to get shorter versions. I think he was relieved that he had got a Minister who was going to go all out to accept his recommendations and really make his report worthwhile. I wondered whether he would be resentful at my taking the kudos from him and that my immediate action would take the searchlight off his Report and his Committee. No, and, to be fair, I think he was relieved and pleased that this had happened. I am going to get him to come and talk to me about improvements in our methods of inquiry. It was a pleasant, informal interview over glasses of dry sherry, with all the appurtenances of old-fashioned parliamentary life.

After that I gave dinner to Godfrey Nicholson,[1] from the Nicholson's gin family, wealthy, at school with me, much older than me, who strongly disapproved of me at first but now finds me quite reputable. He is the Chairman of a group of six hospitals in South Oxfordshire, with sub-normal and psychiatric patients, and he hates the Regional Hospital Board and thinks that Dame Isabel is a mere stooge. He has a strong character and couldn't have been more delighted when he found out what I was doing about mental hospitals and about the notion of an inspectorate. It was a most useful evening.

Tuesday, March 25th

I reported on our meeting at Social Services Committee and Cabinet was pretty aghast. They thought, 'My God, another bloody scandal,' but really the interest to the Prime Minister lay in the fact that it was being announced on Thursday, the day of three by-elections.[2] It appalled him that I should have forgotten this and it was even worse when it was discovered that Fred Peart, who had given me written leave to make my Statement, had forgotten it as well. Harold wondered how it was possible that one should ruin the chances of people voting Labour by having this terrible story blurted out on the 6 o'clock news that very evening. It is quite true that neither Fred nor I had remembered the by-elections when we fixed the date. We had wanted to have a Monday for it and we had put it back to the Thursday for the convenience of the Secretary of State for Wales. Nor would it have occurred to me that this could do us electoral harm. Indeed it was my deep conviction that it could do us only electoral good to be seen to be acting courageously, but that was not Harold's view and he sat and fretted until I finally made it clear that all the arrangements had been made and we couldn't go back on them. Anyway he was due to fly to Lagos on Wednesday night and I suppose he went away feeling, 'There's Dick, out of touch again.' Otherwise the

[1] Conservative M.P. for Morpeth 1931–5 and for Farnham, Surrey, 1937–66. He became a baronet in 1958 and was Chairman of the St Birinus group of hospitals 1966–74.

[2] The by-election at Walthamstow East was caused by the death in October 1968 of Walter Robinson, who had taken the seat from the Conservatives at the 1966 General Election. On March 27th Michael McNair-Wilson regained the seat for the Conservatives with a majority of 5,479 on a 15·9 per cent swing from Labour. In the by-election at Brighton Pavilion, caused by the retirement through ill-health of Sir William Teeling, Julian Amery held the seat for the Conservatives with a 12,982 majority and a 17·9 per cent swing from Labour. At Weston-super-Mare, where David Webster had died in January 1969, Alfred Wiggin held the seat for the Conservatives with a 20,472 majority on a 13·9 swing from Labour.

colleagues were chiefly anxious about the blame which would attach to the Government and anxious that we should put it back on the Tories, so after Cabinet I did take some trouble to get out the records. First of all I dug up the papers from Kenneth Robinson's time and found to my amazement that the Ministry had been concealing from me the very great improvement we had had in the staffing and capital investment in mental hospitals since 1964. We had a much better record than I had realized and I am grateful to Cabinet for prompting me to investigate.

Wednesday, March 26th

As I was away in Paignton all day at the Labour Party Women's Annual Conference I wasn't able to touch the Ely job at all but I did manage to read the Report all through as I returned to London in a fast train from Torquay. I soaked myself in the brief and I noticed something interesting. In the supplementaries describing the nature of the new advisory service there was no mention made of the Director being directly responsible to me. I rang up Brian Abel-Smith. 'Ah,' he said, 'that is very interesting. I was present at the meeting and Miss Hedley said that in view of what you had said to the R.H.B. chairmen she thought your enthusiasm for a Director responsible to you had waned and we could put the emphasis back in the regions where it belonged.' This shows the way civil servants work. She still had hopes of blunting the edge of what I was doing.

Thursday, March 27th

The actual day of my Report – and the whole of the morning from 9.0 to 12.0 I had a series of meetings. I started the briefing preparations at 11.45 with Miss Hedley, and I said, 'There is some mistake here.' 'Oh, yes,' she said, 'a little mistake. Just wrongly phrased and wrongly emphasized.' I said, 'Let me assure you that when I answer supplementaries on that the key point will be the Director's responsibility to me and the fact that this is an independent service, not mixed up with administration, whether at national or regional level.' Then I had a whole series of interviews, the first with the Editor of the *Nursing Mirror*,[1] a lady who had been running an excellent campaign about the difficulty of getting the truth out of hospitals and how nurses won't speak up for fear of victimization. I also talked to the *Lancet*, the *B.M.J.* and the *Nursing Times* because I had to carry them all with me and tell them that this sensational Report was going to show that the Minister was on their side.

After a quick lunch with Tam I went back at 2.45 for another big meeting with overseas doctors, this time in the larger ministerial conference room. I am quite sure that the Department put this in out of fury with me at going away to Paignton all day yesterday, giving me this meeting in the few minutes when I should have been collecting my thoughts before the Statement itself.

In the House of Commons Michael Stewart was answering Questions for

[1] Mrs Yvonne Cross.

Harold, who had set off for Lagos. I had a considerable time to wait because my Office had slipped up. In order to speak before the Business Statement I would have had to answer a Private Notice Question but, as the Office hadn't put one on at the end of the list of Questions, my Statement on the White Paper had to follow the Business Statement. After Michael Stewart's Questions, therefore, we had half an hour of the real heavy, idiotic House of Commons' humour that there is from 3.30 to 4 o'clock on Thursdays, ribbing the Lord President of the Council about the Parliament (No. 2) Bill, about Nabarro and everything else. The House got sillier and sillier and I felt a bit bleak and wondered whether I could switch their mood in the way I needed.

At last we got to the Statement. This must have been the ninth or tenth draft and I felt a great frog in my throat when I started because I really do care and feel righteously indignant about this. I launched in and in thirty seconds I knew I had gripped the House by admitting the truth of the allegations, the excellence of the Report and the need for remedial action. Tam had done well and briefed three or four Labour M.P.s so we managed to have questions from which all the points I needed were made thoroughly and effectively, about the preliminary clean-up which has taken place at Ely, the need for professional support on the Advisory Service, the need to get our priorities right within the N.H.S., not just to get extra money for mental hospitals but to get our balance right between these and ordinary hospitals. Nearly all of it came right and all the way through Ted Heath, Quintin Hogg and Iain Macleod sat on the Opposition front bench and approved. Although it had come after the Business Statement they stuck it out for the next half-hour. I sat down knowing I had brought off a success.

After that things moved fast. I did five interviews at John Adam Street for the B.B.C. and I.T.V. and after that I went back to the House for a Party meeting. People were all excited about the story which broke yesterday on the P.I.B. proposal for huge increases in the salaries of the chairmen of the nationalized industries, something Barbara and Dick Marsh had been rooting for for ages. We hadn't intended it to get out but through bad luck it had leaked. Although Barbara was only eighth in Questions yesterday they had reached this one and Harold Walker had to answer it,[1] so the fat was in the fire and now she had to take a definite line. People were crowding in and I thought she did very well, simply quoting the Nationalized Industries Committee Report of Ian Mikardo and other left-wingers urging higher salaries. It was an uneasy atmosphere but I also sensed that I was in quite decent esteem.

Back from there to John Adam Street to celebrate the publication of the White Paper on pensions. The party had been postponed partly because of Stephen's death and partly because Lewin, the foster-parent of the scheme,

[1] Labour M.P. for Doncaster since 1964, Assistant Government Whip 1967–8, Joint Parliamentary Under-Secretary of State at the D.E.P. 1968–70, Parliamentary Under-Secretary of State 1974–6 and Minister of State since 1976.

had been away on leave. There were thirty or forty people there. Clifford Jarrett made a speech, I made a speech and there was Titmuss and Brian Abel-Smith. It was a delicious, cosy party in that cosy Ministry. How different it is from the huge, vague, professional Ministry of Health. The compact group of policy-making officials in John Adam Street know what they want and are cohesive, like a small, tight Oxford college. It was a pleasant meeting from which I went straight home and then off with Anne to dinner with a delegation of health experts from Yugoslavia.

I had been afraid I might have to rush away from dinner to do '24 Hours' which Peter Brown had hoped to get, but the B.B.C. now felt that with three by-elections there wasn't time for me. I really suspect that they had failed to get Kenneth Robinson on the air to embarrass me, but I was well out of it because I had already had huge news publicity on both channels and a tremendous evening press.

Friday, March 28th

Despite the by-elections, despite Anguilla, I got a really good display for my Statement and for the Committee's Report. Poor old Dick Marsh, who chose yesterday to publish his Green Paper on Highways, was utterly swamped. Enoch Powell was on 'Any Questions' and the first one was on Ely. He said quite frankly that all of us, as the Ministers in charge, have to share the blame. It obviously shocked him that though when he was Minister of Health he had spent time and more trouble, as he put it, on mental hospitals than on anything else, so little change had obviously been achieved in the years since then. That is the story of Ely and it has meant a great deal to me.

During the week before Easter the Government's difficulties on the Committee Stage of the Parliament Bill came to a head as back benchers continued to filibuster. The party and the Government also continued to be deeply divided over the industrial relations policy. On March 26th the N.E.C. had voted against the First Secretary's plans by 16 votes to 5, the first occasion on which they had formally rejected a Government proposal since the 1964 General Election. James Callaghan, the Party Treasurer, appeared to be one of those opposing Mrs Castle's policy.

According to Mr Wilson's own account, while he was returning to London from Ethiopia he received en route, *on April 2nd, a telegram from Barbara Castle about the Chancellor's proposal for a short interim Industrial Relations Bill, to be announced together with the dropping of further prices and incomes legislation in the Budget speech. The First Secretary saw some advantage in this course but stated that she had received advice that such a short Bill could not be prepared in time. On his return to London and after making a Statement to the House on his Nigerian visit the Prime Minister had a late meeting with Barbara Castle and Roy Jenkins and, to his surprise, the First Secretary 'was now confident that the Bill could be got ready'.*

On April 3rd the Cabinet met and the Prime Minister began by making it clear to Mr Callaghan and any other critics of the proposed trade union reform that they were free to resign. Cabinet unanimously reaffirmed both the decision to introduce an Industrial Relations Bill and also the obligations implied by collective responsibility. The Chancellor's proposal for the package was put to Cabinet and approved.[1]

Friday, April 4th–Monday, April 7th[2]

This is a kind of part work, part holiday, pre-budget diary. The first thing to mention about Easter is the weather, which turned good last Wednesday. I came down yesterday evening and now we are having absolutely perfect cloudless days. There was a cold east wind at the beginning but the temperature is creeping up into the sixties and seventies and spring is slowly coming out of winter. When I got back, Anne Swingler had come over from Ilmington to take a few days off and to escape from a tiny cottage and a lot of relatives. I should have been more sympathetic to her when I arrived but I came in somehow keyed up. I was sure the swimming bath would be ready and heated but the *En Tout Cas* company haven't turned up from Leicester and there I was with my greatest anticipation frustrated. It made me more downcast than it should. Perhaps I was overwrought, perhaps I had had a long time in Parliament, but, oh dear, I felt that my Anne and Pritchett had let me down.

I have spent quite a lot of time on my island and quite a lot of money planting bulbs. I had been in despair because time after time they were flooded in this drenching winter but now there are scillas and young irises and daffodils. It's only a tiny beginning but the little patches of flowers on my island are my pleasure. By the end of the weekend my bad temper had quite disappeared.

Tuesday, April 8th

Over the Easter weekend I rang Roy and Barbara and we agreed to meet at Roy's this afternoon at 6.0. It was convenient for me because I had arranged to spend the day looking at the group of mental hospitals of which Godfrey Nicholson is Chairman. There had been a tremendous commotion when he had rung up Dame Isabel to say that I would be going without the R.H.B. She turned up with the Secretary and, heaven knows, we had full representation from the Board. I went round with something like ten people.

In the evening I motored back to Wantage and along to East Hendred

[1] According to Mr Wilson's own history the proposal was also put to Cabinet on April 14th. See *Wilson*, pp. 642, 626–7, 639–40.

[2] The entries for the next two weeks are difficult to place. There appear to be no entries between Friday, March 28th, where one magnetic tape finishes, and Friday, April 4th, where another begins, perhaps because Crossman thought he had dictated the missing week before he changed the reel. In a retrospective diary dictated on Friday, April 11th, days but not dates are given. It seems from internal evidence that Crossman is setting down the events of Easter week beginning on Good Friday, April 4th, to Monday, April 7th, and the appropriate dates have been supplied.

and there in the garden just as the sun was setting I found Roy with Barbara, who had arrived at 5 o'clock in time for tea and a long talk with Roy. We got down to business and began to discuss what our political strategy should be. I outlined my idea that we should drop the Parliament Bill in exchange for an immediate short Industrial Relations Bill this session. 'Well,' said Roy, 'we have been thinking rather differently. Barbara has proposed that in my budget speech I should announce that we are not reviving the 1968 prices and incomes legislation when it lapses at the end of the year and then some weeks later, just before the Whitsun recess, Barbara will announce her immediate short-term I.R. Bill. She would like us to do it in these two stages. She is reluctant to depart in any way from her principle of full consultation with the T.U.C. and she sees every kind of difficulty, but if she has to do it she would like to do it this way. I think we should do it all in one. I can't just announce the end of prices and incomes. I ought to announce in the budget speech both that and the immediate I.R. Bill at the same time as part of a single strategy.'

I immediately agreed with Roy, and said it had always been my view that the fatal flaw in Barbara's strategy was to have a White Paper in January and then ten months of bickering and so-called consultation before the Bill could be got ready. As a result she would have to make far more concessions than she wanted and I just didn't think it was practical politics. I then said, 'It is a bit difficult to know about this unless we know what is in the budget speech,' whereupon Roy pulled himself together and said, 'Let's go indoors and have a drink in my study and I'll tell you about the budget.'

Then he filled me in on the main proposals of the budget, what you might call the socialist proposal to make bank overdrafts no longer free of tax, the clauses removing the injustices of the Land Commission and on the taking of £¼ million out of consumption by relatively mild methods, including the increase of S.E.T.[1] We all agreed it would be the making of this humdrum budget to have a broad statement of our policy with regard to prices and incomes and trade union legislation. All this would therefore have to be said on the budget Tuesday, and at the party meeting on the Wednesday morning Harold would announce the dropping of the Parliament Bill in favour of the immediate short-term Industrial Relations Bill and the Merchant Shipping Bill. Barbara didn't like the idea, and was insistent at first, but she finally understood that the only way to get her Bill in the form she wanted was to shove it through this session, so that next September the Trade Union Congress will be presented with a *fait accompli*. Barbara said she and the Prime Minister were seeing the T.U.C. and that she would no doubt be told by them not to have a Bill. We told her that in that case it was most important to keep things open.

We discussed what we should say to Harold. We agreed to fill him in on the telephone tomorrow and we decided to meet again the day after tomorrow

[1] Selective Employment Tax was a payroll tax paid by employers, with some rebate for industrial enterprises.

and ask Harold to see us. We then talked about the problem of the inner Cabinet and finally agreed that to be sensible it should have seven members; that is, Harold, Michael Stewart, Roy, Barbara, myself, Fred Peart and Denis. If we brought in any more we would have to have ten or twelve. Now of these seven, Fred is in Israel and Denis and Michael are both in Washington for NATO, so really only Harold, Roy, Barbara and I can meet on Thursday. At first we thought we would ask for a Prices and Incomes Committee on the Thursday to ratify the decision there, and then an Industrial Relations Committee on Friday but we left it that we would see what happened and how we would fit it all together, assuming, though, that we would be seeing Harold on Thursday evening. After supper I drove away.

Wednesday, April 9th

It was my last full extra day of holiday, a beautiful day. We had got the bath going and I spent the afternoon trying to clean it with our underwater Hoover and bathing in it. Now I can have my regular swim of 500 yards each day before breakfast and another 500 yards before supper. Heavens, the difference it makes to my general health and sense of strength and well-being. In the evening I motored with Anne to Coventry to talk to the Cathedral Association about the welfare state. We had a little supper in the refectory and I gave a pretty moving explanation to 150 people of what social security meant in my life, growing up before 1914 in a middle-class family, and how I wanted to transform that privilege into a right. I spoke of how the problem was twofold, the moral shock of ordinary people when you give social security to everybody, in the fullest sense, and secondly the practical question of how to pay for it, with the conclusion that we can only afford it if we have an enormous amount of community and voluntary organization. I found as I came home that I had developed a satisfactory philosophy.

Thursday, April 10th

Harold was coming back from the Scillies this afternoon, travelling up by train from Penzance to arrive in London at 4 o'clock, so this morning I took the 12.30 train up to London, the only one which would get me there in time to see Roy before Harold arrived. I went in and had tea with Roy and then Barbara arrived and we checked things over. The new fact was that in preparation for the meeting with the T.U.C. General Council tomorrow, Vic Feather had last night sent Harold a very friendly letter,[1] simply saying 'Let's settle this amicably in tripartite discussions with the C.B.I.' It was quite different from the threatening tone that, according to the morning papers, he was supposed to have adopted. This was however much more difficult to handle because it was so much more reasonable and at first sight it seemed

[1] Assistant General Secretary of the T.U.C. 1960–9 and General Secretary 1969–73. He became a life peer in 1974 and was Vice-Chairman of the British Waterways Board from 1974 until his death in 1976.

that it would knock out the idea of an early Bill to be announced in the budget. How could Harold and Barbara meet the T.U.C. on Friday and blankly listen to them, knowing at the back of their minds that the following Tuesday we were going to announce the immediate Bill which they don't want?[1] But the more we reflected, the more we realized that the T.U.C. letter was chiefly tactical and that if we accepted it we would go on talking till kingdom come and there would be no Bill. What we had to do was to use Friday's meeting to warn them that we couldn't exclude the possibility of legislation and this was something we had to bring home to Harold.

We went from Roy's room through to No. 10 so the press outside didn't know we were there and found Harold, fat and bronzed, coming into his study, anxious to talk to us as though nothing had happened. He was full of fitness and life and he simply turned to Roy and said, 'Come on.' Roy, who had already explained it all to him on the telephone, started with a few sentences and then turned it over to Barbara. She is a curious girl when she talks, unwinding her skein of long, slow sentences, repetitious and rather trying to listen to, and to my surprise the package we had agreed on was not what she was describing. She started by saying that if it hadn't been for the letter we had received and the need to talk to the T.U.C. tomorrow she would have advised us to let Roy announce the Prices and Incomes Bill, then to make her own announcement three or four weeks later. She said, 'It would be less of an affront to the T.U.C. and would give them more time for consultations. Since they are now going to directly question us tomorrow, I think this is what we have got to do.' She had found herself a complicated new reason for lining up.[2] Harold listened and then jumped in before I could have a word, making it clear that he wanted the whole shoot right at the beginning. He immediately saw the case for instant politics and that instant it must be. I interrupted and said, 'Look, the most powerful reason for a package is the Parliament Bill. If Barbara has her way and we take this in two stages, we shall have another four weeks of the Parliament Bill. Now, either we push that Bill or we drop it and as we can't drop it without a good reason, what we need is a package with Roy making his announcement as we have planned, next Tuesday, and Harold making his announcement on dropping the Parliament Bill the day after.' 'Yes,' said Harold, thinking of something new. 'I can do it at 3.30 on Wednesday and put the blame on the Tories for breaking the all-party arrangement. This makes the whole difference, Dick's quite right.

[1] The meeting was originally to take place on the morning of budget day, April 15th, but the Prime Minister felt that, since that meeting would be concerned with the Chancellor's announcement of the package in the budget speech, there should be an earlier meeting 'for them to make their formal representations on the White Paper'. A meeting was accordingly arranged for Friday, April 11th. See *Wilson*, p. 641.

[2] From Crossman's ambiguous account of the First Secretary's remarks it is impossible to tell whether she is saying that she still wished to 'line up' the two announcements in the same package or to separate them by three to four weeks. It seems from Crossman's account of the conversation on April 18th and his own arguments on April 10th (below) that the First Secretary favoured the second, longer drawn-out course.

This is what is really important.' Then he was off again for a good half-hour's discussion with Barbara on his idea of how to get round the difficulty of fining unofficial strikers, cooking up the most elaborate alternative of a special levy on industry, and so on. The difficulty with Harold is that, time after time, he shows how anxious he is to get off the central issue and goes off on to side lines, gimmicks, interesting ideas, anything except the central strategy.

However we did agree that after the budget Cabinet next Monday morning there should be a meeting of the I.R. Committee where we would clear Barbara on her short Bill. There should then be another Cabinet in the afternoon at which, having dealt with the budget only in the morning, we would deal with the sensational new things. We would have Roy's budget speech on Tuesday and on Wednesday at 3.30 Harold's announcement about the Parliament Bill, unless he decided to make it, as I would prefer, at Wednesday morning's Party meeting. Though I don't think we imposed this on Harold on the other hand I am not sure what would have happened if we three hadn't thought it out last Tuesday. It is the first time I have ever been in on the presentation of a plan to Harold by his senior colleagues. Incidentally he insisted that Fred Peart should be brought in and if Fred hadn't been away I would have agreed. Indeed, I would have liked to have got all seven members of the inner Cabinet together to agree on this before we went in to Harold but Denis and Michael Stewart happened to be away.

We then had a very interesting time listening to Harold discuss the reactions of the rest of Cabinet. Should the Chief Whip be told? Well, not too soon, he is fairly secure, but he talks. What about Denis? Roy said that he had already told Denis on the telephone to Washington. What about Tony Crosland? Roy had talked to him too and he was mainly concerned not about the merits of the plan, which seemed to him fairly sound, but about the procedures and the possibility that the inner group would be blamed for not consulting Cabinet in advance. Should Judith be told? 'She is a talker,' said the Prime Minister and we agreed that I should speak to her on Monday just before Cabinet. Tony Greenwood? 'He'll cut up rough but he's ineffective.' Short? 'Absolutely unpredictable and doesn't matter.' Willie Ross? 'He's all right,' said the Prime Minister. 'Cledwyn Hughes is bound to be all right and so is George Thomson.' Nobody mentioned Peter Shore or Gerald Gardiner, I realized afterwards; they didn't count in our calculations. Dick Marsh is unpredictable and he'll sprawl but he'll come down on our side and Mason will be loyal. I said finally, 'What about Jim Callaghan? Do we plan for his resignation? I think if we have this package and wrap it up tight, after the terrible press Jim has got he may be compelled to resign, not for reasons of courage but for reasons of cowardice. I wouldn't rate it as probable,' and I added something Roy had said to me minutes before, 'but highly possible. I'd rate the chance of his resigning as 40 per cent.' Harold said, 'I don't mind if he does.' We all agreed that it would be infinitely less damaging if he resigned now that we had taken the initiative than if he had resigned on the Thursday before Easter. All this had taken from 5 o'clock until just before 7 o'clock, when I strolled out across the park.

Friday, April 11th

I could have caught the 7.35 back to Banbury last night if I had known how long we would take, but I had allowed the office to arrange meetings for me today and it was useful to be in London because I had a lot of work to do. After a haircut I went in to start work on the post-Ely policy, PEP as Bea likes to call it. We havered and hovered a great deal about the list of possible external members of our working party and we finally decided to have only Peter Townsend and Geoffrey Howe, giving a party balance, the Chief Nurse from the Maudsley Hospital,[1] and my Dr O'Gorman from Borocourt.[2] In all this Bea was enormously helpful. The other big thing which came up today was South Ockendon, where we may have another scandal on our hands.[3] We have already had complaints from three or four M.P.s, headed by Arthur Lewis, and I had rather snubbed poor Norman Atkinson when he had asked a Question on this as I made my Statement on Ely.[4] During the recess things had got worse and an R.H.B. committee, together with one of my own doctors, had gone down to investigate. This man came to discuss it with me and reported appalling overcrowding and staff shortage. One mustn't be surprised that if one takes the lid off other evil spirits appear and we should have known that after Ely we were bound to have more trouble. But this has come pretty quickly and in a hospital that has just had £1 million spent on it and where there is a young and vigorous staff. We had an interesting talk about this and I said the obvious lesson was that we must immediately suspend all further recruitment of patients and cut the numbers down to 100. George Godber strenuously replied that you can't deny hospitals the right to take a patient in even though it does mean overcrowding. No doctor can deny a patient a place. I said, 'This isn't an acute hospital where you can put a bed up for three to five weeks. This is for life. If it is residential you must give yourselves the power to refuse entry and say to the local authorities that the problem has to be solved.' This is one difference between George and me, the other being that I am determined to take money from other parts of the Health Service, whereas he wants to see us just getting more money from outside.

[1] Miss Eileen Skellern, Superintendent of Nursing at the Royal Bethlem and Maudsley Hospital.

[2] Dr Gerald O'Gorman was Physician Superintendent at Borocourt Hospital, near Reading, which Crossman had visited on Easter Tuesday.

[3] On February 22nd a young boy had died at the South Ockendon mental hospital, allegedly as the result of violence. In answer to a Private Notice Question from Arthur Lewis, the Secretary of State announced that a preliminary inquiry had been held into conditions at the hospital and that remedial action was under way.

[4] Norman Atkinson was Labour M.P. for Tottenham 1964–74 and since 1974 for Haringey, Tottenham. He has been Treasurer of the Labour Party since April 1976.

Well, it's a quarter to twelve on Friday evening and I've got through the day. Life is good for me at the moment, good at home, good in the office, where I am getting a grip, and even not too bad in No. 10, where we have begun to form the nucleus of central leadership. But we must see how it all works out next week.

Monday, April 14th

The budget Cabinet went quite quietly. Roy explained his ingenious contraption at some length. It showed what you could do with a no-change budget.[1] We were carrying on the strategy exactly as before and only raising the minimum amount to see us through. He has added £340 million on taxation, out of S.E.T. and little bits on estate duty, wine and purchase tax, so ingeniously disposed that it won't hurt too much and will only increase the cost of living by ½ per cent. A masterly minor performance again, each item beautifully prepared by Roy and beautifully rehearsed. He has prepared his budget speech as carefully as I prepared my Ely announcement but it only marks the contrast with the flaccid, indecisive bungling of Harold's central direction.

I don't think we had any serious discussion of the speech and it all went through relatively quietly because we made it clear that the really controversial issue was to be discussed this afternoon at 4 o'clock.

From there I went at midday to the Industrial Relations Committee, where Barbara put before us the package she proposed for the short Bill. The Committee changed it tremendously. We firmly recommended the substitution of a section on inter-union disputes for the section on compulsory strike ballots and we also thought that attachment of wages was out as well and that Barbara should think of something else. We thought we had done pretty well and after that Barbara and I rushed off, ironically, to the Café Royal, right up to the top to a delicious flat where Charles Forte now lives.[2] He not only has a string of cheap restaurants including the motorway ones where Patrick and Virginia love to eat baked beans, sausages and chips, but he now owns the Café Royal and he has made it into a slap-up restaurant. He is a

[1] In what was the third heaviest imposition on the taxpayer of any post-war budget the Chancellor raised the tax on petrol by 3*d*. a gallon, increased taxes on gaming and table wine, raised corporation tax by 2½ per cent to 45 per cent of net company profits, removed tax relief for interest payments on loans and bank overdrafts and raised from 37*s*. 6*d*. to 48*s*. a week the Selective Employment Tax paid by employers in the service industries for each adult male worker they employed. The only concession was an increase in income tax allowances, which abolished income tax for about 1 million of the lowest paid and reduced it for a further 600,000. The Chancellor also announced that in the autumn there would be an uprating of social security benefits, so that from November the basic pension for a single person would rise by 10*s*. to £5 a week and for a married couple by 16*s*. to £8 2*s*. a week. The increase would cost the National Insurance Fund an extra £250 million and substantial extra provision would also have to be made. This would be 'distributed as fairly as possible among contributors' and a Bill would be worked out to do so. No further details were given, a fact that was to cause Crossman much anguish later in the year. See below, pp. 484, 488 and n., 491 and n.–493, 502.

[2] Deputy Chairman of Trust Houses Forte Ltd since 1970, Chief Executive 1971–5 and Joint Chief Executive since 1975. He was knighted in 1970.

tiny, clever man, with a big voice and a long head, who has proposed that we should borrow his motor-yacht and crew at Whitsun. We decided to cruise from Rome down to Naples and we've booked out flights to Rome for four Crossmans and the two Castles. But will this be possible? The Parliament Bill is out of the way and so the main parliamentary obstacle to a full fortnight recess at Whitsun has been removed but will Barbara and I still be on the same side? I don't know.

I had to get back to the House because I was first in Questions and this time it was a tremendous success. I had taken great trouble with the South Ockendon Question and warned the local M.P.s, Arthur Lewis, Hugh Delargy,[1] Tom Driberg and Norman Atkinson to be there.[2] It got virtually no notice and I didn't get a second sensation about a second hospital because I had deliberately worked up a tough answer on abortion. I simply said I was very worried about the private sector but not about the public sector. Afterwards I rapidly did a television interview to go out on the news at 5.50. I did it against the strong advice of Peter Brown and George Godber but it worked like magic. I said I didn't want to see abortion just on demand but that I wanted us to be a country of family planning and I think I got it about right, though the pro-abortion lobby was upset that I was seeming to play into the hands of the opponents.

I went straight from the House into Cabinet and the question of the short Industrial Relations Bill. There was a good deal of complaint and not only from our old friend James Callaghan. Roy Mason, Dick Marsh and Tony Crosland were all upset at the sudden change of plan. Why should the Cabinet be rushed, why shouldn't we work out a package which the trade union movement as a whole could accept? On the other hand there was a deep feeling that a short Bill was the only practical thing and Tony Crosland was certainly influenced by the thought, although this wasn't allowed to be mentioned, that the dropping of the Parliament Bill was some compensation for this. Strangely enough, the thing which excited most alarm was the dropping of the Prices and Incomes Bill. There was a feeling that Part II of the present legislation was not sufficient, that we were shifting about and obviously being harried from pillar to post and that this would give a tremendous sense of weakness and disillusionment in the country outside. I am afraid that all this is true and that the situation is desperate, and Cabinet think this as well. I feel that in giving up the Prices and Incomes Bill now, and saying so in his budget Statement, Roy is asking for trouble because from now until the end of the year everybody will forge ahead with their wage claims while we are indulging in a fight with the unions about industrial relations which will almost provoke them into increasing wages if they possibly

[1] Hugh Delargy was Labour M.P. for Manchester (Platting) 1945–50 and represented the Thurrock division of Essex from 1950 until his death in 1976.

[2] Tom Driberg was M.P. for Maldon, Essex (as an Independent 1942–5, for Labour 1945–55) and Labour M.P. for Barking 1959–February 1974. He became a life peer in 1976, taking the title of Lord Bradwell, and he died in the same year.

can. This point was well put by Peter Shore and also by Tony Wedgwood Benn, who was gravely anxious about the whole strategy. What about Mr Callaghan? When I had discussed this with the Prime Minister and Roy beforehand, they were quite certain he wouldn't resign, though I myself felt rather the opposite. I couldn't have been more wrong. His whole attitude at Cabinet was that his presence was essential to retain the unity of the unions and if he thought he saw, as I thought I saw, that we had dropped the idea of a compulsory strike ballot and were going to modify the clauses on attachment of wages he clearly felt that this justified him in staying and in adopting the line he was going to take. So he made a long speech about how we must now work together and how pleased he was at the decision. I got a little note from the Prime Minister, which I have kept, saying 'the most salubrious part of Cardiff will in future be called Paper Tiger Bay.'* It showed that Harold was still capable of a skilled wisecrack and I was delighted, as indeed I was on the whole delighted by the entire meeting.

Immediately afterwards came another Industrial Relations Committee. I only went to the beginning because I had to keep going out to the last divisions of the Parliament Bill that was still tottering along, but I am told things got worse, and that Barbara floundered and floundered. It is obvious that she has no available solution to the problems of attachment and of the conciliation pause and more and more clear that she is no longer in control.

I escaped from the Parliament Bill to the party Olga Davenport was having for her private view, with a little supper afterwards at her house. It was relaxing to get away from the House of Commons to good food and good drink. I came back home at 11.0 to hear that in the final fiasco of the Parliament Bill the Government had been unable to get 100 people for the closure. It was a good preparation for our announcement tomorrow and on Wednesday.

Tuesday, April 15th

I started the morning with a meeting on the most appallingly difficult subject, contracting out in my pensions scheme. I am not numerate, only literate, and I had never really understood the negotiations between the Ministry and the Life Assurance Offices. I had read and reread their paper and it seemed to be absolutely unintelligible. Well, after an hour of being at my most unbearable and stupid, I did come to understand it. To get a fair deal between the state scheme and private superannuation schemes we have to build up a picture of how private superannuation schemes are devised. Then we can compare the two to see how much pension entitlement in the state scheme must be sacrificed if you are to allow entitlement to pensions in the private schemes. Having got this clear, we can then work out the contributions. I was at my most bloody and most awkward but I think it was one of the cases where I was justified and we really made an advance.

* A reference to the fact that the very insalubrious dockland area of Tiger Bay is part of Jim Callaghan's constituency.

I rushed off to the P.L. Committee, with Gerald Gardiner in the chair. Callaghan said, perfectly rightly, that the choice was now between guillotining the Parliament Bill and giving it up and it was quite clear that the Prime Minister wouldn't go to the Party and say to them, 'If you don't vote for a guillotine the authority of the Government will crumble and I shall order an election'. We couldn't fight an election on that. The other choice was to give it up. I agreed with Callaghan and said bluntly to Shackleton and Gardiner, whose position in the Lords will be enormously undermined by giving up this Bill half-way through, 'Look, it's my child which is being murdered but, frankly, without the co-operation of the usual channels or real backing in Cabinet, we are simply not in a position to shove this through. I agree with Callaghan that we should put the choice to the Prime Minister and Cabinet tomorrow morning.'

I got to the House in time to hear Prime Minister's Questions. The House was quite good-tempered, not very full, and it was a pleasant, easy atmosphere. Then Roy made his budget speech. I didn't pay much attention to the first half but he did it extremely well. He had obviously prepared and rehearsed the speech, because he had said it would last for two hours and twenty minutes and in fact it lasted exactly two hours and twenty-three. A man can only know that if he has read it aloud beforehand. He dealt with Nabarro with perfect skill,[1] and that, too, was something he had obviously practised in front of a mirror and got absolutely right. I had a free evening because the Chief Whip, who had agreed weeks before to dine with Eddie and me, had in some strange way forgotten the engagement. When in doubt the Chief evades an important meeting (that at least he has in common with Harold) and I suspect he really funked having dinner with us because of the murder of the Parliament Bill. John's position has been particularly ambivalent on this Bill, because his father, who has been opposing the Bill in the House of Lords, is still the dominating factor in his life.

I decided to take Michael Foot round to the Athenaeum. He made it very clear that he didn't think the dropping of the Parliament Bill would make any difference. The Left has completely broken with Harold. I knew from Tam that the Tribune Group had met and said I was the only possible person to take Harold's place but Michael was careful not to mention this to me, nor I to him. He made it clear that though the concessions on the compulsory strike ballot and the attachment of wages that I thought I had got on the Industrial Relations Bill might help to some extent, still the battle must go on. In his view, the time has now come when we must face even the break-up of the Government rather than have this legislation gratuitously imposed.

I found it extraordinarily difficult to talk to him because most of the

[1] The Chancellor proposed no increase in the motor-vehicle licence duty and 'knew from the start' that claims that a leak had taken place 'must be, shall we say, colloquialisms'. See pp. 361–2.

arguments he was using were the arguments I had used to Harold and Barbara last January. He said, 'When the Donovan Commission, by miraculous good luck for the Government, did not adopt the Tory line and gave its reasons for rejecting this policy for bringing the unions within the law, why on earth didn't we just content ourselves with a weak Bill based on this weak Report? We would have got a certain amount of contempt from the Tories and yet on the basis of that we could have united with the trade unions in putting forward the Donovan Bill and the Crossman Pension Bill as the two major unifying forces to bring the movement together in the year before the election.' There was no answer to this. He had it clear in his mind. I went away liking him more than ever before, he liking me, and both of us knowing we are in for tremendous and appalling difficulties.

Wednesday, April 16th

Eddie Shackleton and Michael Wheeler-Booth were round at Vincent Square at 8.45 this morning to discuss further possibilities. They made the solemn proposal that, having got seven clauses of the Bill, we might be content with that and leave out the clauses on powers. I pointed out that this was a ridiculous proposal, since the Labour Party wanted reform of powers and not composition, and I only mention it to show what extraordinary and extravagant notions people get in desperation. The fact is that Eddie is deeply upset by the failure of his personal leadership in the Lords. He is a hard-working, tough, pertinacious man, disliked, I find, in the House of Commons. I like him but he is reactionary and cautious. I then had to go and see the Chief about some minor issue of a speech I was going to make and we had a short chat about the Parliament Bill. The Chief loves saying that he and I never disagree on a major issue and we can always talk together. Then he feels he is getting on well with you.

So we came to the Cabinet discussion on the Parliament Bill. I decided that today I would put my whole weight on the side of saying the Bill had to be dropped. It was unrealistic to say we should impose a guillotine because we wouldn't be able to get it and we shouldn't be able to force the Party into a General Election on this account. Nor could we afford to have our bluff called. There was pretty strong opposition. Tony Wedgwood Benn, who had never helped us at all up to this point, now felt an affection for the Bill because he thought that by dropping it we should weaken our authority with the Party, a view which was held by two or three other people and very strongly by Michael Stewart. Stewart and Benn and a number of others also showed great anxiety about tactics. They felt that if we were to do this the Prime Minister's authority could not be re-established. As a result of their argument it became quite clear that we had to put the whole thing in a package, and the Prime Minister's Statement had to say that the Parliament Bill was being dropped for more important things, such as the Industrial Relations Bill and the Merchant Shipping Bill. This was in striking contrast to the assurance given on Monday that the two issues would be considered in absolute separation from each other. As the meeting went on, the Prime Minister kept saying, 'We shall have to get this through because I want to get the statement ready to make to the Party this morning.' He intended to go across to the Party meeting and make a short statement right at the end. It was quite clear to me by now that this proposal, which I had made last week, was wrong. He should first make a Statement to the House this evening and then make the statement to the Party tomorrow. Again we noticed that the Prime Minister's decision had been taken and the Statement drafted hugger-mugger in his own little band of satellites, with nobody else's advice. However, Cabinet overruled him and, rather nettled, he went over to the Party meeting, where Roy dealt with the budget in a relatively non-controversial atmosphere.

Thursday, April 17th

I missed Barbara's speech in the budget debate as I was addressing the annual conference of the National Union of Insurance Workers at Hastings but her speech apparently cancelled out all the good effects of Roy's. The accounts in this morning's press weren't too bad but it looked as though she was making major concessions, particularly on the strike ballot, and indeed there were plenty of reports saying that Callaghan was taking credit for this. It seemed to me that we would be able to get a basis for negotiations with the trade unions and the Party but I learnt later in the day that she had apparently produced an appallingly governessy speech. She had first made the great mistake of spending thirty-five minutes trying to answer Macleod, who had opened the debate. She had spoken for some eighty-five minutes altogether and when she got to her own proposals on the Industrial Relations Bill she was flaccid and uncertain of what she meant. On the absolutely critical question of attachment of wages and whether an unofficial striker would go to jail if he didn't pay a fine she had made it plain that she had no adequate solutions.[1]

Parliamentary Committee had been summoned first thing. There we were, the usual eight, Wilson, Stewart, Gardiner, Jenkins, Callaghan, Crossman, Healey and Peart, plus the extras, Ross, Thomas, Shackleton, Silkin. Twelve members of Cabinet out of twenty-two. You never know what is coming up at any of these damned committees. We had a whole series of reports by Michael Stewart on the NATO meeting in Washington, on Western European

[1] The First Secretary also got into difficulties over the part of the speech dealing with the enforcement of penalties for unofficial strikers who refused to obey an order to return to work. Imprisonment, or the threat of it, for non-payment of fines had never been considered but the Government had by now realized how repellent to the Labour Party and the unions was the sanction originally proposed, that of recovering fines through the attachment of wages. Mrs Castle suggested that fines could be recovered by normal debt-collecting processes and that the penalties might be paid into a special fund for the benefit of workers as a whole, for instance to finance research into industrial health or safety. The suggestion was received with exasperated ridicule.

Union, his first interview with Michel Debré on the Soames affair,[1] his first interview with the Dutch since the refusal to give them Hong Kong air-landing rights, the coming visit of the Italian President,[2] the four-power talks in the Middle East, Anguilla, the Council of Europe's discussions on Greece, Nigeria, an hour and a half or so of that interminable voice grinding away. Roy leant across to me and said, 'Do you find it as difficult as I do to know what on earth Michael Stewart has said?' and I said, 'Yes, I can't listen to it. That is why he gets away with it, by being so boring.' The second reason why he gets away with it is because he is merely reporting and even if we do ask questions there is no way of changing policy, unless we are prepared to have a formidable row and insist that an issue be taken separately. This is what concentrates power in the Foreign Secretary's hands.

At 11.30 came S.E.P. At our Parliamentary Committee we had mentioned the report of the Hunt Committee,[3] which Michael Stewart appointed when he was at D.E.A. to deal with complaints about our policy for the Development Areas. The R.E.P. and discriminatory grants and permission for new factories have really done something to stimulate a revival of industry in Scotland, the North-West and parts of Wales and Merseyside but in the course of reviving the Development Areas we have aroused keen objections from the people on their boundaries. The Hunt Committee had been, typically, set up to see if there was anything to be said for creating intermediate areas or adding further Development Areas and after sitting for two years it had produced a huge slab of a Report with no very clear philosophy. It proposes to widen the areas a great deal and introduce the whole of the North-West, Yorkshire and Humberside, all costing some £5 million, far more than we can now possibly afford. There was however a good appendix by Professor Brown.[4]

The whole thing had been planked on our plate months ago and Peter Shore was asked to put it together. He has done quite a lot of work but he has made it terribly complicated, disowning some of the Hunt areas and putting other places in, and we thought, quite rightly, that this was something which would cause endless political trouble. At a previous meeting before Easter,[5] the Prime Minister had started by saying that Merseyside,

[1] Michel Debré has been the Deputy from La Réunion in the French National Assembly since 1963. He was Prime Minister 1959–62, Minister for Economic Affairs and Finances 1966–8, Minister of Foreign Affairs 1968–9 and Minister for National Defence 1969–73.

[2] On April 22nd President Saragat was to pay an eight-day state visit.

[3] The Report on Intermediate Areas (Cmnd 3998) was published on April 24th. The Committee had been set up in 1967, under the chairmanship of Sir Joseph Hunt (Kt 1966), Chairman of the West Midlands Economic Planning Council 1965–7, General Manager of the Hymatic Engineering Co. Ltd 1938–65 and Chairman since 1960. See *Wilson*, pp. 667–9.

[4] Professor Arthur Brown, Professor of Economics at the University of Leeds since 1947, had written a dissenting note that expressed anxiety about the effects of certain proposed measures on the Development and the Intermediate Areas and his doubt as to the readiness of Merseyside for the loss of Development Area status.

[5] On March 18th.

which the report suggested should be taken out of the Development Areas, should stay in.

This morning he began again by saying that this was a highly political subject, elections were coming up and we must look at this with open political eyes. 'That's fine,' I said. 'Let's remember, as our first political fact, that there are at least as many marginal seats in the South-West, the South-East and the West Midlands and the South as there are in either the grey areas or the Development Areas. We have unemployment at Greenwich, which is Dick Marsh's constituency, in Coventry, mine, and we know that this is being deliberately allowed if not created, to enable people to have better work conditions elsewhere. This is fine in theory but it is not a thing which people like.' Dick Marsh pointed out extremely ably that if we confined our development policy to places with clear-cut unemployment it would be possible to defend this principle in Coventry or in Greenwich but if we were going to spread this to grey areas as well it would be impossible. I chimed in that we must get a little flexibility in the allocation of I.D.C.s otherwise we would make nonsense of our New Town policy in the Midlands and South-East. When I asked for this last time, I said, it was not even minuted and I wanted it minuted now. After I had finished the Prime Minister said, 'That shows you what kind of politics we are having.' He had wanted politics of a very different kind, not a blunt reminder that the whole policy is probably extremely unpopular. 'The frank truth,' as Tony Wedgwood Benn said, (he has been pretty sensible in the last Cabinet or two) 'is that if you try to look at this politically you will come unstuck because there are no political advantages in the policy. The only thing to do is to give help where it is needed.' Time after time, however, people pointed out the real difficulty that the total amount of money we could allocate was only about £20 million and we couldn't find any more for the grey areas without taking it away from the Development Areas. That is the trouble about doing this kind of job out of a dwindling budget. Both Roy and I agreed that the best thing to do was simply to say that Hunt was impracticable and that we didn't intend to do anything but carry on with our Development Area policy. But we were pushed aside because according to our colleagues so many promises have been made in Blackburn or Humberside, in Yorkshire, in Derbyshire and Plymouth that all kinds of expectations have been built up. So here we have yet another example of a Committee being set up by this Government without any proper consideration of its implications and coming down on us in the end. The final decision will be taken next week and it will be a decision which, as we universally agreed today, can do us nothing but harm.

We got through Questions and the Prime Minister's Statement fairly all right this afternoon but then we came to the Party meeting, which was held under the shadow of Barbara's speech last night. Harold was a complete flop. He started by reading aloud a short, fairly strong Statement which had been typed out. It was all right as a beginning to a debate, simply stating the situation and what we were going to do, and that this had to be a vote of confidence. But there was no attempt whatsoever to give people a vision of our policy or to indicate our new line in terms of a broad strategy. He just plunged in, saying, 'You will bloody well have an Industrial Relations Act.'

Then came the discussion, with practically everybody against, and a powerful speech by Eric Heffer and a speech by Michael Foot, every word of which I agreed with. It was painful to sit beside Harold, trying to console him and listening to these speeches. Half-way through, I turned to him and said, 'For God's sake, let's have somebody move the adjournment because we are going to have another meeting on this and you needn't speak again today.' 'Oh,' he said, 'I've got to answer them. I must deal with this,' and he obviously felt he must reassert his authority. Sure enough, Manny Shinwell got up and to help Harold suggested an adjournment but it was refused. Harold made a disastrous wind-up, a bumbling, fumbling, argumentative reply, devastating in its failure. It gave no creative leadership, no setting of the Party on a new course; it was just a flop. The policy has been launched but Harold's leadership has not re-emerged. On the contrary, it has sunk to a record low level. When the meeting was obviously going wrong, I said to him, 'Surely the Chief Whip prepared this and got a couple of speakers organized, or didn't he?' and Harold said, 'I fear he didn't.' It's crazy to go into a Party meeting without any preliminary organization of support for the Leader. We now have complete failure, not of discipline as Denis Healey is always saying but constructive work by the Whips to build up the Prime Minister. The centre isn't holding; there is no centre.

I went off to *Don Giovanni* in an absolute desperate temper, but I couldn't keep my mind on it. I sat there in the Royal Box with Jack and Frankie Donaldson[1] and their daughter and her pleasant young man, and Susan Crosland, but I couldn't concentrate. I gave the two young things a lift home and then went back to Vincent Square to hear from Tam how he had heard from all sides of the Party what a disastrous evening the Prime Minister had had. It didn't just come from the left-wing but from people as far to the right as Micky Barnes and Terry Boston.[2] They all feel that a gratuitous blow has been imposed on them and that we have picked a quarrel in order to push a gimmick. Even the newspapers are laying the blame for the failures of the Government on the Prime Minister himself. Tam and I discussed all this long into the night. He is a tremendously faithful Sancho Panza, a person of real qualities, although he is sometimes funny, ingenuous, a blurter-outer. He has

[1] A former farmer, John Donaldson was Chairman of the Consumer Council 1968–71. He became a life peer in 1967, was Parliamentary Under-Secretary of State at the Northern Ireland Office 1974–6 and since 1976 Minister for the Arts at the Department of Education and Science. His wife Frances, daughter of the playwright Frederick Lonsdale, is herself an author, whose books include *The Marconi Scandal* (London: Hart-Davis, 1962) and *Edward VII* (London: Weidenfeld & Nicolson, 1974).

[2] Michael Barnes was Labour M.P. for Brentford and Chiswick 1966–February 1974. Terry Boston, Labour M.P. for Faversham June 1964–70, was an Assistant Government Whip 1969–70. In 1976 he became a life peer.

got ears for the Party and he can listen and he brought back to me a tale of disillusionment with Harold Wilson, disillusionment which I think we can only cope with now, if we can at all, by the establishment of our inner Cabinet to confine him, to try to give us something like collective leadership to steer us through the appalling months that lie ahead.

Friday, April 18th

A lovely light interlude away from London. I caught the 9.15 from Euston to Coventry, where I was transported to the Leamington social security headquarters which are in a great big mansion standing on a hill. Why is it that social security staff are so nice? They like the job, they find it interesting, they are not routine civil servants and are splendid people. From these palatial new offices I went on to a really dud second-class government office building, headquarters of the executive council in Leamington, where I found a splendid man, the extremely intelligent M.O.H. for Warwickshire.[1] We had a whole series of things to see there, occupational workshops and so on, before I went on to two old people's homes. This was a fascinating contrast. First the Arden House at Stratford where, although miracles have been done, people sit round as though they were still in the old workhouse. Five minutes away there is a new home, light and middle-classy. What a difference. This was putting into practice the philosophy of supplementary benefit, that people are entitled to a decent old age. What is striking is that it costs more to maintain the old workhouse than the new home. I was exhilarated by all I saw.

Before I knew it I was taken on to a cocktail party at the offices of the Shakespeare Memorial Theatre. The party was the final event of what is a kind of Ministry of Social Security Annual Eisteddfod. It seems to be different each year, one year for sport, this year for drama and culture. There had been singing, concerts and dramatic productions from voluntary teams of the Ministry and now eighty of us gathered to have dinner and to see *The Merry Wives of Windsor*. We sat at little round tables so I didn't talk to anybody except the Clifford Jarretts and the Ennalses. There was no ill-will at all and we all had a splendid evening. I think we have really made advances out of my bloodymindedness earlier this week. Then we had the performance of that ghastly play but marvellously produced, so that when we finally got to the scene of Falstaff getting into the laundry basket it was worth the dreary hours of waiting. The whole thing was done with terrific spirit and vitality, more like a ballet or an opera. Afterwards we had drinks with the cast and the actress who played Mistress Page and who happened to come from Coventry, said, 'We are all socialists in this company, Falstaff as well.' What a lovely evening. If only I could be a decent departmental Minister and keep my nose to the grindstone of the job I would be entirely happy. But it can't and mustn't be done. I have to do what I can to save this Government, a backbreaking, dispiriting, unsuccessful business.

[1] G. H. Taylor.

Sunday, April 20th

I was really cheerful earlier this week because I thought we were launching the new policy with reasonable success and that at least we had cleaned out the compulsory strike ballot and made one major, clear-cut concession to the trade unions. Now I find that in a speech in Scotland on Friday Barbara has announced that we haven't dropped the strike ballot but merely postponed it to the big Bill in the next session.[1] When I look back at Wednesday's Cabinet minutes, sure enough, I see that it has only been postponed for discussion till this coming week. Again, on the attachment of wages we have still found no way of not sending strikers to jail. This has all been mucked up, nothing is clear and we have come totally unstuck. What happened? At Easter we three met and after that Harold and Barbara saw the T.U.C. for two hours on the Friday and again on the Monday and nobody knows what they said. Tony Crosland thinks we understand one thing and they decided another. There is no inner coherence and we are blundering ahead with Barbara and the Prime Minister just as much a two-man show as ever they were. They launched this thing in December, pushed it through Cabinet by extremely unscrupulous means in January and, when we learnt what they were doing, got Cabinet to accept the Bill. They refused to give it green edges, decided to go ahead on the long-term plan and then, when it failed, as we predicted it would because they couldn't sustain consultations, we put on a short-term plan. Now we have agreed on this, we haven't any inner body to plan exactly how to put it through and what will be the form of our discussions with the trade unions, the N.E.C. and the Parliamentary Party. It now sticks out a mile that we are having a quarrel on a phoney issue.

If only we were tackling the real problem of how to bring the trade unions within the law. Instead, as I predicted last January, we are having a gratuitous head-on collision with them. We are floundering deeper and deeper, with an uneasy feeling that though brilliantly presented the budget is inadequate and that once again we shall be in trouble before the autumn unless some miracle intervenes. Frightful though it is to think of this Government surviving to drag on through the terrible year which looms ahead, another economic crisis is an even more dreadful prospect. The Government is obviously bungling, exterior credibility is failing and in that case we should be hounded out of office next September. I hear on the wireless this morning that in the *News of the World* Desmond Donnelly is writing about an autumn election and if it seems that it would otherwise be forced upon us the demand for a new leadership to save us from it will get stronger and stronger as the summer goes on.[2]

I talked to Roy about the leadership yesterday on the telephone and we

[1] Mrs Castle was addressing the Annual Conference of the Scottish T.U.C., who were meeting at Rothesay.

[2] Desmond Donnelly was Labour M.P. for Pembroke 1950–70. He resigned the Labour whip on the issue of defence cuts east of Suez and from 1968–70 acted as an Independent. In 1971 he joined the Conservative Party but was unable to find a seat. He died in 1974.

feel that we must now get Harold to have at least a little strategy group to plan for next year. Between our talk to him that Thursday evening after Easter and the implementation of our scheme nothing has been done about this. Harold has no chief of staff, no executive, and with Burke Trend away ill he just has his Marcia, his Gerald Kaufman and his new fellow Eric Varley.[1]

Harold lives in his lonely little place and doesn't do anything. We have got to get an inner Cabinet to restrain him and to see whether with that we can steer the Party through the terrible year that is coming. Harold has not reasserted himself. Indeed, something very strange, macabre and tragi-comic is now happening in the Parliamentary Party. The disillusionment of the Left, which has now broken for ever with Harold, has taken the form of a new cult of Crossman. Crossman, who took a reasonable line last January and has been relatively successful in the last two or three weeks, is being spoken of as the only person who can get us out of our difficulties. Tam is picking up this remark from all kinds of people and though I have told him from the start that it is sheer nonsense and that there is nothing to it whatsoever, when Tommy Balogh came back from Paris this week he said the rumour there was that Crossman was the man. Well, it wasn't Paris but what he picked up when he got home to Hampstead and had a gossip there. If it's true that this is being said in the Parliamentary Party, if only as a reaction against Harold, it is totally impractical for three reasons. One is that I don't want it and haven't the energy or the belief to do it. Secondly, it is far too late to do anything but pull the Party together a bit and prepare it for a less disgraceful election defeat. Thirdly, and most important, unless Harold falls down dead it won't happen. He will fight until his dying day and if he heard or suspected for a moment that I was countenancing anything of this sort it would do nothing but damage. It would turn him in on himself and make him even more conspiratorial, even more persecuted and even more devastatingly isolated.

Monday, April 21st

I went back to London depressed by Albert Rose, who had rung me up to say that he couldn't get more than twenty-five people to attend the constituency annual dinner and so we must call it off. I told this to Roy outside the Cabinet room before S.E.P. and he laughed and said, 'That has often happened to me in the last five years at Stechford. We don't take it too seriously.' Nevertheless Albert's news had cast me down.

Most of the morning S.E.P. discussed the Hunt Report and we finally worked out a solution. We got on with the pork barrel, sorting it out and sweating it round, with Peter Shore on the whole losing and Tony Crosland

[1] Eric Varley, Labour M.P. for Chesterfield since 1964, was Assistant Government Whip 1967–8, P.P.S. to the Prime Minister 1968–9, Minister of State at MinTech. 1969–70 and Secretary of State for Energy 1974–5. He has been Secretary of State for Industry since 1975.

gaining. Part of the solution was a decision to build the Humber bridge ten years earlier than the traffic requirements justify. This was something Barbara and I had promised in order to win the Hull by-election in March 1966 and, ironically, the money was found by deducting it from the Development Areas, to the fury of Willie Ross. We will submit this to the full Cabinet on Thursday.

The only interesting thing today was a party given by Hugh Thomas at a big house in Ladbroke Grove. There we were, with three tiny children rushing in and out between our legs, and as I said to Mrs Thomas, the daughter of Gladwyn Jebb,[1] it was one of those parties where everyone you ask comes. Everybody was there. There I was, old at sixty-one, in a gathering of a lot of girls and young men with beards. I ran into Robin Blackburn, whom I had read all about this morning as one of the people sacked by the Governors of L.S.E., and we had a short talk about this fascinating incident.[2] I have been talking about the appalling row at L.S.E. with my dear Brian and it seems that the only grounds for throwing Blackburn out were that he had come out in favour of the students. This seems to be the kind of typical, self-defeating lunacy of establishments all over the world, vice-chancellors and governors in particular. It is only really in the last five years that the social order has been challenged and undermined and this is what makes the life we live interesting and also makes me feel less disconsolate about the failures of the Government.

This evening we were having the five votes on the budget and I had to stay right on to the end to deal with the adjournment. On S.E.T. we had a huge abstention and vote against us.[3] As Barbara quite rightly said to Roy, the really shocking thing was that when the budget was presented to Cabinet in the usual way we did not consider its impact on the Co-operative Party or its fissile effect on the Parliamentary Party and we have got enough battles going on without gratuitously seeking more. Tonight the Co-operative Members united with the left wing and voted against the Government. Why did we not anticipate this? We had just forgotten it. This is where we should have had an inner Cabinet, slightly more able to see things politically in the round. Without one, Harold has constantly made these astonishing psychological blunders and omissions of thinking. It is for this which she and I must plead when we go to see him, as we hope to do in a week's time.

[1] The Liberal peer Hubert Miles Gladwyn Jebb (K.C.M.G. 1949) was Permanent Representative of the U.K. to the United Nations 1950–4 and British Ambassador to France 1954–60. In 1960 he was created 1st Baron Gladwyn. Since November 1975 he has been Vice-Chairman of the European Movement.

[2] The London School of Economics had been re-opened in mid-February and on April 19th the Governors had dismissed two lecturers for their part in the January disturbances. On April 29th there was a one-day protest strike by lecturers but on May 7th the staff voted in support of the Governors' action.

[3] The vote was 282 to 255 in favour of the increase. Some Labour and Co-operative M.P.s were uneasy about the measure. See below, p. 469 and n.

Tuesday, April 22nd

The first thing I had was a demonstration outside the Elephant and Castle by a body of militant nurses led by Sister Veale, who had about a couple of hundred girls out there with her. They were demonstrating about a problem which might turn into serious trouble.[1] In the new pay deal it had been agreed that instead of having the costs of meals lumped in with their salaries nurses would be treated as adult people and have £106 a year added to their salary with which to pay for their meals themselves. I had said that this wasn't sufficient for a student nurse and that they had quite a legitimate complaint. I went out and talked to them in front of the television cameras and apparently I made a perfectly good impression. It was quite clear that Sister Veale was refusing to let me have the microphone and I seemed friendly, though harassed and unhappy about it all, as we stood shouting in the cold April wind. I had to leave them but Bea brought eight or ten of them inside, gave them cups of tea and spent half an hour discussing things, so that they went away rather quietened down. We are working away at this but the papers are gunning for me and working up agitation. This is not helped by the weakness of the Government and the crisis of confidence, which really does make it increasingly difficult to maintain authority. It affects the pound, it affects our ability to get the trade unions to accept Barbara's package and it is going to become more and more difficult to rule.

Off to a lunch at W. H. Smith in High Holborn, where I found myself talking to the Chairman and the Secretary about the future of their pensions scheme.[2] We had an extraordinarily interesting and lively discussion. This is the only thing I really can handle and I promised that if they would write to me I would make their scheme a kind of test case, trying out our theories on it and seeing how they actually worked. I got back to the House in time for the Standing Order No. 9 debate on Northern Ireland and to hear Bernadette Devlin, who within an hour of entering the House was making her maiden speech.[3] I am glad I didn't miss the occasion. I stood behind the

[1] On January 1st nurses' salaries had been increased from 9 to 14 per cent and the training allowance for student nurses under twenty-five from £395 to £480 a year. The P.I.B. had recommended (Cmnd 3585) that the current rates should last until March 1970. There were many protests, inside and outside Parliament, against the 'pay-as-you-eat' scheme and the Secretary of State assured the Commons on April 28th that the matter had been referred to the National Whitley Council, who would meet on May 13th.

[2] The Hon. David Smith, Chairman of W. H. Smith & Son (Holdings) Ltd 1949–72. He was Lord Lieutenant of Berkshire 1959–75. He died in 1976.

[3] Miss Bernadette Devlin, a twenty-one-year-old student, had won the Mid-Ulster by-election on April 17th, defeating the Ulster Unionist candidate by 4,211 votes. She had stood as an Independent Civil Rights candidate, uniting Catholic Nationalist Republican and Protestant Labour supporters. On the following weekend there were riots and marches in Londonderry and in Belfast, where a water main was destroyed and supplies cut off. In response to a request from the Northern Ireland Government, on April 20th the Ministry of Defence announced that British troops would be sent to Ulster to guard key public utilities, although there would be no question of the troops being used to quell demonstrations or maintain public order. The Commons held an emergency debate on April 22nd, during which Bernadette Devlin, departing from the tradition that a maiden speech should

Speaker's chair and watched this black, dark, tiny thing standing up in the third row back. The crowded House was spellbound by a tremendous performance. She was ruthless. Everything was barred – the English were hopeless, the Unionists were hopeless, the Orange regime and the O'Neill concessions were hopeless, the Southern Irish Government and the English Government were hopeless. Everything would lead to disaster and everybody was to blame for the situation in Ireland. She spent her time building the barricades for a class war. The left-wing Labour back benchers cheered, all the Members falling over themselves to congratulate her as actors congratulate one another. I suppose that in a few days' time they will realize the significance of what she has said.

This evening there was a meeting of this extraordinary P.C.C., the Committee linking the National Executive and the Cabinet, which was set up a few months ago to meet once a month on Tuesdays, the day before the N.E.C. meeting (a very silly time to meet, by the way). We were going to be in Judith Hart's room as usual, but the meeting was switched to the Prime Minister's room in the House. I got there at 7 o'clock, and found the Prime Minister and a few people standing about over some food and drink. It was soon clear that, except for George Brown, all the trade union members of the Executive had refused to turn up, which really made a nonsense of the whole thing. However for three and a half hours we sat listening to George discuss with the Prime Minister the kind of programme we should have, the kind of relationship there should be between the Cabinet and the Executive, and the committees we should set up to prepare our policy. The substance of it was quite sensible and George was perfectly sensible too, but the thing which fascinated me was that, while our strong, powerful Prime Minister was supposed to be reasserting his influence, it was in fact George who was much more positive and creative and much more the leader. There was Harold sitting puffing his pipe and drinking his brandy with no sense of what was required of him. George harangued and shouted, Walter Padley got drunker and drunker and the thing drooled on and on with repetitions *ad nauseam.*[1] What was so terrible was the lack of authority, central drive, or inspiration, and at 10.20 I had had enough of it and went away profoundly depressed.

Wednesday, April 23rd

A departmental meeting about abortion. We had quite a good and successful bout on this at Question Time a week ago and we have made quite a good impression on the public. But now we have to make a further Statement

---

be non-controversial, violently attacked the Northern Ireland Unionists and the failure of the British House of Commons and successive British Governments to relieve the grievances of 'the ordinary people'.

[1] Labour M.P. for Ogmore since 1950, Minister of State for Foreign Affairs 1964–7 and a member of the N.E.C. since 1956. He was Chairman of the Labour Party's Overseas Committee 1963–71.

because, after visiting and inspecting all the nursing homes, we had made a decision that the seven in the West End which really specialize in abortion and are doing a high proportion of the total number should only have two-month licences, on much more severe and stringent conditions. Bea Serota has had a terrible time with Godber and the Department, who don't want to be tough on these homes, and say that they are businesses and we can't really intervene. This is a good example of the Department's congenital timidity. Today we had our lawyer, Davey, saying we would be sailing near the wind if we went an inch beyond laying down requirements for the physical conditions of the homes. If we were to do anything to interfere with the doctors we would be transgressing the terms of the Act.[1] I finally said, 'But are they going to challenge us?' and he said this was most unlikely. 'Well,' I said, 'in that case we can call their bluff. I don't mind being shown for once to be going slightly beyond the Act because then there would be a good case for amending it.'

This afternoon I had to tell the chemists that I had decided against them in their battle with the doctors over rural dispensing. I decided, against the wishes of the Department, that there was no great rural demand for more chemists' shops and that I would abide by my strict legal position and say I would keep the *status quo*. I have said one or two unpopular things to the doctors and on this there is no reason to make myself unpopular again, so I am not going to fall into the trap of imposing a solution. I put it to the chemists, who threatened me with dire penalties, and I shall wait and see what happens.

Meanwhile the Anguilla debate was going on in the House and the Foreign Office survived.[2]

Thursday, April 24th

Cabinet. We dealt with the Hunt Report and suddenly Tony Crosland came up with a paper saying that the whole method of financing our solution by reducing the differential investment allowance from 40 per cent to 35 per cent to produce £20 million a year would be appallingly difficult, partly because it would mean repudiating the written agreement with three aluminium companies for smelters (about which this diary has said enough in the past). Here was the Board of Trade, a leading protagonist in the discussions we have had for weeks on end, suddenly saying on the very last day that the basis of our solution is unworkable. But he was right and we were left with the appalling job of patching up a Statement for Peter Shore so he could say that the whole cost of the new help to the grey areas would be financed out of

[1] The Medical Termination of Pregnancy (No. 2) Act 1966, originally introduced as a Lords Private Member's Bill by Lord Silkin in November 1965, and eventually successfully steered through as a Commons Private Member's Bill by David Steel, Liberal M.P. for Roxburgh, Selkirk and Peebles.

[2] The motion, deploring the Government's 'inept handling' of the situation in Anguilla, was defeated by 286 votes to 239.

the existing funds being spent on regional development, but not exactly how. This is the second time we have to announce a solution without being able to produce the money. Roy Jenkins had already insisted on giving a 10*s*. pension increase and had announced it in the budget without being able to say how the money was going to be raised in contributions. Although my Department had fought like hell and my Permanent Secretary had actually written to the Treasury warning them of the dangers of doing this, Roy was determined to have it as a feather in his cap in the budget. Anyhow this time there was an absolute schemozzle. For once Harold Wilson was as tough as a Prime Minister should be.

When we had finished this Harold turned to the Home Secretary and asked him to make a short report on Northern Ireland,[1] but said, 'I don't think we can discuss it.' It was very odd, so nevertheless I insisted (and I can do that to Harold) on ten or twelve minutes' discussion. I had already been angered by the constant references to the Northern Ireland Committee and I asked five or six key questions. Harold had said that under the constitution we were legally bound to send in troops to preserve law and order and in the last resort to sustain it. I asked what law and order meant. Does it mean whatever the Royal Ulster Constabulary, who are Protestant Orangemen, define as law and order? If so, are we in time to do it? It was pointed out that our aim would be to put pressure on the Irish Prime Minister to make concessions to create a unified community. I said, 'But it's because he has been doing so that his party is disintegrating and the whole of the Establishment breaking up and law and order being destroyed. Where do we come in?' The answer was that, as things are going now, we shall be dragged in to support the Orangemen with British troops, so then I asked what the attitude of the Opposition was. On everything I got prevaricating answers. Harold did not want this to come to Cabinet. It would come up in due course when the constitutional issue was raised. His attitude really infuriated me and Barbara and made us realize that nothing has changed. He is determined to run things in his own peculiar divide-and-rule fashion.

This afternoon we had a strange meeting of the Immigration Committee with Callaghan in the chair. He proposed to impose a requirement that in future any immigrant should bring with him an entry certificate that he had obtained in his own country. Nobody but I had bothered to go back to the earlier papers but when we discussed this idea last October Callaghan had put forth a paper stating that the officials thought the disadvantages of such a policy very greatly outweighed the advantages. I had been the only member of the Committee who had seen its advantages and who had pointed out that the Tories were demanding the same thing. I had said that we would have to do this some time and for God's sake we should do it quickly. There was nothing racialist in requiring entry certificates. It would be very sensible and would stop the appalling business of people arriving at Heathrow and having

[1] On April 25th a further 550 British troops were sent to Ulster.

to hang about in corridors for days on end while their *bona fides* were looked into. At today's meeting nobody except Judith, who was against the change, saw the difference between the official attitude last October and the attitude now. All the Ministers were briefed by the officials to accept the change, including David Ennals, who I had thought might possibly join Judith. At the end of the meeting I asked Jim Callaghan what had made the difference and I learnt that when the chief immigration man at the Home Office had been shifted there had been a change of policy and something which Callaghan had not been able to get past his Department before had got past them now. To be fair, there was also the fact that this amendment could be tacked on to an Immigrant Appeals Bill, and of course with a system of appeal the requirement is far more justifiable. But it is one of those cases where one sees that when the officials are all against a policy it is difficult to get it through and when they switch the change can take place.

After this I caught the train to Cambridge for a Union Debate that had been booked months before.[1] Young Hugh Anderson, who had spoken with me last year in that tremendous T.V. debate against Beeching, had got Des Wilson, the twenty-eight-year-old New Zealander, a toothy, fair-haired, sprawling young man who has been organizing *Shelter* and raised £1 million for the homeless.[2] They were quite determined to lick me with this motion and there were tremendously moving speeches about the wickedness of poverty and the tyranny of the majority. The fascinating thing is that both the speakers on the other side maintained that in this country we are now an affluent society, with the wealthy majority living off the backs of a poor minority, the classic account of American poverty in a capitalist society applied quite simply to Britain. At the end of Des Wilson's speech he had a standing ovation for two minutes. Well, I was able to batter them by the simple thought that I was older than they were and could remember the times before the First World War and right up to 1945 when the majority were poor and the minority rich. I reminded them of the astonishing achievement of this country in transforming itself into a place where the majority are well off and the minority are poor. If we can do that in thirty years, in the next thirty we can get rid of poverty among the minority. I pointed out what we were actually doing with supplementary benefit and how we were grappling with poverty. It was wrong to say that Britain was a country whose greatest evil was poverty. Our greatest evil was oligarchy, monopoly power, class snobbery. It was not a bad speech and they gave me a pretty good ovation too, before I slipped out to be driven back to London by Peter Smithson. In a way it was an achievement. They were exploiting every kind of self-righteous

[1] The motion was 'That poverty in Britain is self-perpetuating and meant to be so'.

[2] Hugh Anderson, President of the Cambridge Union Michaelmas 1969, was the organizer of Students for a Labour Victory, at the 1970 General Election. He died of leukaemia in August 1970. Des Wilson, Director of *Shelter* 1967–71, Head of Public Affairs at the Royal Shakespeare Company 1974–6 and since 1976 Editor of *Social Work Today*. In 1973 and 1974 he was Liberal candidate for Hove.

emotion and trying to get morality on their side. I bludgeoned them with logic and fact and debunked them and I felt glad that I hadn't lost my skill.

Friday, April 25th

All week I had been working on an address to the golden jubilee of the Matrons' Association. Peter Smithson drew up at the Department at 9.50 and at 9.55 I set out, but I was angry that nobody from the Private Office came in the car with me and even angrier because they hadn't supplied the brief of David Ennals's speech on the adjournment debate in the House last night, so that I didn't really know what he had said about the 'pay-as-you-eat' system. We got to Church House and were directed to the wrong entrance, so I sent the car away, wandered about and finally got inside flushed, hostile and bothered. Then I found the speech the Private Office had given me had no end to it. However, it went pretty well. Five hundred matrons were there and I humoured them along. I was furious with the Private Office. They are nice people, but at this kind of thing dear, dear Ron Matthews and dear Janet aren't up to scratch and are nothing like as good as my Private Office in the Ministry of Housing.

Back to lunch with Godber and Pauline Morris,[1] a neat, bright, precise, dark-haired woman in navy-blue, extraordinarily competent and sensible, the author of the book about sub-normal hospitals. Just before lunch I had received a memo from the C.M.O. telling me I couldn't possibly put to the Regional Hospital Boards the need to shift priorities to the sub-normal area without upsetting the consultants and having a blow-up in the medical service, so I now instructed Pauline Morris to give me a whole number of things which we could do to ease the position of sub-normal hospitals. These things, costing hardly any money, are what we shall have to concentrate on in the first year.

After that I went off to Hampstead to look at the supplementary benefit offices in Ben Whitaker's constituency,[2] right at the top of Hampstead Hill. He is a curious, elegant, dilettante young man, likeable, silly, difficult, with a certain amount of charm and a charming wife. I went round the office and it was clear that it was a badly managed, horrible place and, as Ben Whitaker had proved by timing it with a stop-watch, it was an hour before you could get a form to fill in and two hours before you could get any satisfaction. What they needed, it was quite clear, was decent management and this was demonstrated when we drove to the other office in Kilburn, which was excellently managed and in a decent building. By then however our friend Whitaker had gone back to the Commons. He hadn't visited this place or ever seen the

[1] A lecturer at the South Bank Polytechnic and the author of *Put Away: A Sociological Study of Institutions for the Mentally Retarded* (London: Routledge & Kegan Paul, 1969).

[2] Labour M.P. for Hampstead 1966–70 and Parliamentary Secretary at the Ministry of Overseas Development 1969–70. Since 1971 he has been Director of the Minority Rights Group.

manager even though it was in his constituency as well. Nevertheless he has a genuine grievance and I may be in trouble with him.

I wanted to catch the 5.38 train, but when I got back to 70 Whitehall I found an urgent message that Godber and Marre wanted to see me. They warned me once again of the danger of antagonizing the medical staff by insisting on a $1\frac{1}{4}$ per cent shift in financial priorities to sub-normal hospitals. Brian Abel-Smith has produced a brilliant paper, giving for the first time a statistical analysis of the difference between the way the regions are spending their money and suggesting how we might make good our pledge to clear up the derelict areas of the Health Service. I listened and told them that I would work this out, thanks very much, and then, just as I was going, Marre said, 'There is something else we want to talk to you about,' and pulled out a letter, dated April 16th, which I had dictated to Tony Crosland. Tony had written me a short letter endorsing a resolution passed by the Labour Group on the Grimsby City Council recommending that the Health Service be put under democratic control by the local authority and he had very reasonably asked me for a statement of our case. I had been given a flatulent answer by the Department, which I had re-dictated to explain how we were genuinely trying to get a much more community-related Health Service and how I had thrown out Kenneth Robinson's Green Paper outline of a highly autocratic, centralized structure. I had added that the obvious reason why we couldn't transfer things to local government was that the doctors objected and also that there were difficulties in financing it. I also told him that anyway the tripartite system was working badly, everybody agreed on that.[1]

I read the letter through again and asked what on earth was wrong. The C.M.O. said, 'First of all you seem to imply that Kenneth Robinson's working party is to be blamed. It would injure the Department a great deal if that were published.' 'I am sorry,' I said, 'but I really think that is pretty far-fetched. However I'll bear it in mind. What about the second point?' He said, 'On your second page you say the tripartite system is working badly and many people will assume that this is an attack on the professions.' It was obvious that Marre and Godber, solemn, busy men who had come across to rebuke me, were warning me that I was stirring up a hornets' nest. It's true that Serota and I have made it pretty clear that we are baffled and bewildered at what these 4,000 people in the Department can be doing and that we think previous Ministers have just been carried along with the Department, whereas we want to get a hold and have a policy. The Department is warning me, 'Take care. We will ditch you if you are a trouble. We will see to it that you have two or three stumbles and we have registered that we disapprove of you.'

I missed my train and had to catch the 6.14, getting home on a lovely

[1] The N.H.S. tripartite system consisted of (i) hospitals, run by Regional Hospital Boards and Hospital Management Committees; (ii) Executive Council Services (general practitioner, dental, pharmaceutical and ophthalmic services); and (iii) local authority health services. These three parts were brought together when the N.H.S. was reorganized.

evening. We have at last had a little bit of rain, everything has started growing, even the grass, and there was my lovely swimming bath too.

Sunday, April 27th

Albert Rose rang up Anne yesterday to say that the moment he had cancelled the constituency annual dinner the applications began to pour in but this doesn't really satisfy me. I know that in a place like Coventry the industrial relations issue is terribly serious. It has been mounting up all this week. The whole trade union machine is going into action with conferences one after another, the calling of a special Congress and the possibility of a May Day demonstration with a maximum number of strikes.[1] Although public opinion is still vaguely but quite warmly on our side, a lot of the people who think there ought to be legislation are going to vote Tory anyway and the minority who think there oughtn't are the people whose votes and whose work we desperately need. There is a further difficulty that people in the movement have a deep suspicion that the Government is anti-trade union. It's likely, as Tony Crosland said, that around the country nobody has read *In Place of Strife*, and they just think that Wilson has got a massive trade union bug in him and that Barbara has gone bonkers. However hard Barbara tries, she won't sell her package as a pro-trade-union law and they will just think a Labour Government hasn't the right to do this to them. I fear that if we introduce the law in its proposed form the general public will gradually get less enthusiastic and more sceptical, as has happened in the case of prices and incomes. It is increasingly difficult to try to go on governing in this period, with such a despicable Gallup Poll rating, every fortnight recording the up and down, mostly down, of the Government's reputation, and therefore of the decline in its authority. I think we may well have to face the fact that by next autumn there will be a unique kind of political crisis, a situation where a Government with a majority of 100 and backed by a relatively united party has, however, lost so much authority that it is justified in demanding a dissolution, yet cannot go to the country for fear of a débâcle.

I think this is linked with the muddle-headed incompetence of the central direction of the party. The thing which worries me most of all is the failure of Barbara, Roy and me to get an inner Cabinet going. How often Harold has said he is agreeable to having an inner Cabinet and how often, the moment he has said it, he evades and sidesteps. This is what he has been doing all this week. We agreed that Roy should have a word with him on Friday and that Barbara and I should try to see him at Chequers this weekend, but the Italian President, Saragat,[2] is at Chequers today and the P.M. made it clear that he hadn't even got an hour for us. After a long talk with Barbara on the

[1] The special Congress was to be held at Croydon on June 5th.

[2] Giuseppe Saragat, founder of the Italian Workers Socialist Party (later called the Social Democratic Party) 1947 and a Member of Parliament 1948–64, was Minister of Foreign Affairs 1963–4 and President of the Italian Republic 1964–71.

telephone this morning, I put in a very urgent request for a meeting with him late tomorrow night, if Barbara is free, when we can frankly put our preoccupations to him.

And what are they? Quite simply, of course, that there is no inner strategy. We are lurching along with lunging leaps into Rhodesia, into the European fiasco, into this Industrial Relations Bill, into Anguilla, and now I am desperately worried that we are going to leap into another disaster in Northern Ireland. Here we are on the edge of civil war, with the O'Neill Government tottering, and Bernadette Devlin announcing a policy of suicidal class war and destruction. We are being dragged closer and closer to the precipice of protecting the Orangemen in Ireland and, according to Jim Callaghan, here is the Prime Minister only concerned to get over to Ulster. He has as much passion to get there as soon as possible as he had to get to Nigeria three weeks ago or to get to Moscow. He has a passion for being on the spot, being in the news. Perhaps that isn't fair. It is, rather, that he sees himself influencing events personally. He wants to be active in international affairs rather in the way that he has stopped one or two strikes at home. Just as he waited for the chance to intervene in Rhodesia with the *Tiger* or the *Fearless* talks, so he is now trying another such adventure and that is all the leadership he is giving us.

On Northern Ireland he has operated with his usual functional separatism. He has what he calls his Northern Ireland Cabinet Committee, consisting of himself, the Foreign Secretary, the Home Secretary and the Minister of Defence. Barbara and I are both left out. Another sinister little thing I have to mention is his Cabinet minutes. Now there are times, quite rightly, when the minutes are so secret that they are not circulated to all Private Offices. I noticed that the minutes of the Cabinet and O.P.D. meetings about Anguilla had not been generally circulated and I also noticed that, though in this week's Cabinet we discussed Northern Ireland for a short time, that particular piece has not been circulated. My Private Office sent me a note saying they think the Anguilla one will be circulated when it has been O.K.'d but that the Northern Ireland one will not be circulated without the Prime Minister's personal permission. This was news to me. I had never heard it suggested before that members of the Cabinet should be denied access to minutes of their own meetings. It means that the Prime Minister doesn't want to have the minutes of Anguilla circulated until he makes sure that the minutes are tolerable for the historical record. So you will see why it is important that I describe in this diary what happens in Cabinet.

Barbara and I feel completely frustrated at the conduct of affairs. Anguilla, the budget, industrial relations – on each thing Harold works bilaterally with the key Minister and a group of cypher Ministers who can be reckoned on to be compliant. This is the traditional Harold bilateralism of the last five years and it has grown not better but worse. 'He is in danger of total disintegration,' Barbara said to me on the telephone today. It is a word that I have dared to use myself more than once in the last three weeks. Total disintegration! There is nothing left of him as a leader and a Leftist. He is just a figure posturing there in the middle without any drive except to stay Prime Minister as long as he can. The other thing which I suspect has now begun to happen, beginning perhaps in the Scillies at Easter, is that he assumes that we can't win the next election. I noticed that in Cabinet this week he twice spoke on the assumption that the Tories would be taking over in the 1970s, whereas he has been scrupulously careful to avoid such talk in the past. He must therefore be facing the evidence of the polls. Marplan, in *The Times*, shows a 26 per cent Tory lead, at the very time when we are supposed to be moving into an election period. The loss of confidence in the country is steadily increasing and it is linked with Harold's own leadership more than with any other single thing. This affects the whole of the conduct of the Government and means that everything the Government does is under question. It is more difficult to get anything sensible through and, equally, any weakness in a Ministry is mercilessly attacked. Barbara and I don't have any great hope of succeeding very far in our talk to him but we are prepared to go a long way towards saying that, frankly, we are not prepared to go on working under these conditions.

Monday, April 28th

On the B.B.C. this morning was the news that de Gaulle had lost and that he was out.[1] I met Neil Marten on Banbury platform and we agreed that this was the beginning of a new epoch in international relations. The last of the wartime leaders, except, I suppose for Mao Tse-Tung,[2] has gone. The situation has changed, suddenly there is a real chance of Britain negotiating an entry into the Common Market and, as happens at the end of an epoch, we felt a bit scared. Can France go on without de Gaulle?

At S.E.P. we had an interesting item, which provides an extremely illuminating anecdote about Whitehall. For some months we have had the Report of the Northumberland Committee,[3] which came to the rather drastic conclusion

[1] In March President de Gaulle published his plan to reform the French Senate and to establish Regional Councils in each of the twenty-two planning regions. Despite warnings from his Ministers, the President insisted on submitting the plans to a referendum in April, with both issues as a single question. There was widespread criticism of this insistence on a single question and on the resort to constitutional amendment by referendum and only de Gaulle's own party supported him. On April 10th the President made it clear that if defeated in the referendum he would resign. In the poll on April 27th 46·8 per cent voted yes and 53·2 per cent no. At 12.11 a.m. on April 28th de Gaulle announced that at midday his resignation would take effect.

[2] Mao Tse-Tung, born in 1893, was Chairman of the Central People's Government of the Republic of China from 1949–54 and in 1954 became Chairman of the People's Republic of China. He died in 1976.

[3] After the 1967/8 outbreak of foot-and-mouth disease, during which some 352,300 animals had been slaughtered and a temporary ban placed on meat imports from countries where the disease was endemic, a Committee was set up in February 1968, under the Duke of Northumberland's chairmanship, to inquire into the means of preventing and minimizing

that we would run least risk if we banned the import of all meat from countries where foot-and-mouth is endemic – that is, South America, the Argentine, Uruguay, Chile, and Germany too – though we could import meat, whether on or off the bone, from countries free of foot-and-mouth – Ireland, Australia, New Zealand. However the Committee rather thought this was too much for the Government and recommended that if there wasn't to be a total ban there should be a ban on everything except boned meat, which could be allowed in as long as the offal, bones and lymph glands were excluded, because these (I still don't know what lymph glands are, by the way) carry the virus and the real risk of disease. The Report came to me with a whole mass of folders and unanimous official advice that the Northumberland Committee's second recommendation should be accepted. Then I had a note from my Department saying that if you take the lymph glands out you may remove the danger to animals but you greatly increase the risk of human disease. The lymph glands are a kind of barometer of infection and if they are removed before the meat is exported tuberculosis and other human diseases may possibly be reintroduced into this country. I was asked to put in a mild protest along these lines. I looked at all this, sent for the civil servant concerned and asked why the devil our officials had originally agreed that we should take the second recommendation of the Northumberland Committee. It was obvious to me that if the Minister of Health could accept the meat neither with nor without the lymph glands, there must be a total ban. We had an overwhelmingly strong case for accepting the Committee's more drastic recommendation and we could defeat the Foreign Office and the Board of Trade, who, for the sake of exports, don't want to have a row with the countries concerned. This was a real chance to help the Government regain a little popularity with the agricultural industry and it had all been given away by the officials agreeing to the second-best proposal. I was told that it was too late to propose and that it had all been agreed. However I then said, 'I won't just send a protest, I will circulate a new document for the Cabinet Committee saying that in my view there is an insoluble contradiction between the interests of animal and human health and in this situation we ought to accept the drastic proposal of the Northumberland Committee.' I circulated this and within twenty-four hours the Ministry of Agriculture had reversed its position and agreed that, despite the certain risk to animal health, meat including the lymph glands should be imported from South America. That little worm Cledwyn Hughes had done a complete about-turn on his original paper.

At S.E.P. this morning I could in fact have won, because the case I had made was overwhelming and Willie Ross, who is a kind of agricultural Minister, admitted that they had been caught with their hair down and that

---

further outbreaks. Part I of the Report (Cmnd 3999) was published in April 1969 and Part II (Cmnd 4225) in December 1969.

we should really have gone for the extreme proposal, which would have given us kudos. However it was too late really to get the thing reversed so I didn't try very hard but merely made them all look damn fools. As you can read in the minutes, Harold concluded that the meeting only marginally agreed to accept the action recommended by the Minister of Agriculture, the Secretary of State for Scotland and the President of the Board of Trade. It was no good pressing too hard on this but we did insist on appallingly stiff conditions and the first time any suspicion arises there will be a total ban on meat from the Argentine. Once again this shows what a politician can do but it also shows how the official machine with its official committees not only reaches administrative conclusions but political conclusions as well.

At Question Time I dealt with a Statement on abortion and my campaign against the private nursing homes. Then we came to a fantastic incident, which indicates why it is that poor old Fred Peart is such a burden to the Chief Whip. A sub-committee of the Specialist Committee on Education, five M.P.s, Fred Willey and so on,[1] went down to Colchester to try to find out about student unrest.[2] They were thrown out by the students and I was amused to see that last Friday there had been attempts to ask the Speaker whether it had been a breach of privilege to treat M.P.s in this way. I would have thought that M.P.s who instead of sitting in the House of Commons choose to go down to universities and, without a by-your-leave, say 'we are bloody well going to sit here and cross-examine you all', must expect to have a fairly rough time. Today the Speaker gave his decision that there had been a *prima facie* breach of privilege. Fred Peart now had to move the motion that we should refer the matter to the Committee of Privileges. Quite right too. This is a very important principle. Committees sit outside the House quite often and they can travel anywhere. The Estimates used to wander round our overseas possessions inspecting what was going on. However we haven't had a case before where a Committee travels in Britain with no protection. In this case, inside a university the police couldn't protect it so it was submitting itself to contempt and ridicule. Should M.P.s go out into the country and purport to be Select Committees? It is an important and fascinating issue but to my amazement Fred Peart just moved the motion and then said that 'if there were indications that such a course was not generally welcomed I should be happy to seek leave to withdraw the motion.' The Opposition were immediately on their feet asking what the hell the Leader of the House was doing. It was his job to make a firm recommendation but poor old Fred wavered to and fro in the way that he does and had a terrible come-down.

[1] Labour M.P. for Sunderland 1945–50 and for Sunderland North since 1950. He was Minister of Land and Natural Resources 1964–7 and Minister of State at the M.H.L.G. 1967.

[2] The sub-committee of the Select Committee on Education and Science, investigating student problems, had been obliged to abandon their sitting at the University of Essex on April 24th, when they were confronted by a violent demonstration of militant students.

In the middle, however, I had to go out to a meeting on the pension problem. One of the continuing difficulties of our new scheme is what to do with the miserable Tory earnings-related scheme which they had spatchcocked into the flat-rate scheme. We now have a scheme of flat-rate contributions and flat-rate benefits, both with a graded element on top. We had decided to let the graded element fade away and the first day our new scheme started people would stop paying contributions for the Tory graded benefit and we would freeze whatever pension entitlement people had already earned. When I was launching our White Paper, the C.B.I., representing the employers inside the Tory scheme, sent a powerful letter to me saying that the people who had contracted into the Tory scheme felt it was unfair that they shouldn't share the advantage of post-award dynamism in our new scheme, and, like our contributors, their graded benefit should be increased in value according to increases in the cost of living. It was a perfectly reasonable demand, but this would in a sense let down people outside the Tory scheme because it would be changing its conditions after they had decided to contract out. At the very least we would have to allow them to contract back in again. The complaint of those inside the Tory scheme would then be that those outside had done far better over the last seven years because of the soaring rise in equities in which most of them had invested the money they would otherwise have spent on contributions. Today Crabbe and Bayley from the Life Offices, brilliant, cool, able, collected men, brought forward their own plan, saying that we could only remedy the injustice to those in the Tory scheme by increasing the flat-rate contribution of those who had hitherto contracted out.[1] They are coming next week with detailed plans but I suspect that though their argument is irrefutable it is politically impracticable because we cannot increase the contributions even further this time.

However, it is obvious to me that this is simply a balance of politics. If we can get both the C.B.I. and the T.U.C. wanting us to dynamize the benefits of both our own and private schemes and if they don't insist that this is unjust to those who have contracted out of the Tory scheme, we can probably bring it off. Will the Life Offices be able to stir up a tremendous row about our injustice if we help those in the Tory scheme? Will those in the Tory scheme stir up a row if we don't? What will the nationalized industries do, as most of them have their own private schemes and might by our action be compelled to dynamize them? It is an extremely interesting calculation, closely linked with the problems of our new scheme, because how we help existing pensioners will influence people's decisions whether to contract in or contract out. One of the unknown factors is how far the public is going to be interested in all this and how far they will understand what is going on. It is a thrilling thing to discuss and I greatly enjoy it.

[1] Reginald Crabbe, the Chairman of the National Pensions Joint Committee of the Life Offices Association and the Associated Scottish Life Offices, led the Life Offices' team in their consultations with the Government.

I went to dinner at the London Hospital, where I had been invited by some of the junior staff. It was a tremendous dinner party like a High Table, and I was just sitting down to a splendid evening with very good food and very good drink when I found myself dragged off to a three-line whip on the betterment levy. Meanwhile Harold has been wining and dining the Italian President and has still not found time to see Barbara and me.

Tuesday, April 29th

At long last Barbara and I were to see Harold at 9.30. I had already heard from Callaghan that I was to be made a member of the Northern Ireland Committee after my complaint, so Harold had met me on this, and now here we were. He started off straightaway by saying that he was going to let us have an inner Cabinet of seven and that he was thinking of sacking the Chief Whip. Barbara immediately said, 'Be careful. Who are you going to put in his place?' and Harold said, 'Well, it hasn't really got as far as that yet. I am only making overtures at present.' He played with Barbara in this way and pushed her off and then we discussed the committee of seven. I said, 'It all depends who is on it. Is Callaghan in or out?' 'What do you think?' he said, and Barbara and I both answered, 'If it is going to be a real group, an inner Cabinet of likeminded people fighting to win and fighting to build you up, Harold, then it is no good having Callaghan. This is an acid test of your intentions.' He made it quite clear that he agreed with us and that Callaghan should be excluded. We talked about this at length and tried very hard to put over to him that what is wrong with his leadership is his lack of contact with us, with the Left, and with the Parliamentary Party. But it was a stiff interview, with a man very much on the defensive, handing to us the main thing we had come to ask for quickly, before we could mention it. Once we had got from him an inner Cabinet with Callaghan out there wasn't much more to say. So we stopped at 10.30 and Harold and I went down to the Northern Ireland Committee.

There, as one always must at the first meeting of a Committee one has just joined, I went all through the papers. I found the Committee had already come to the conclusion that it was impossible to evade British responsibility if there was civil war or widespread rioting. Strictly speaking, the police in Ireland or the Government can ask for British troops to come in. This right to troops has been watered down recently and now it has been agreed with the Northern Ireland Government that such a request would have to be channelled through our Government. Nevertheless, if the request came it was made clear that it would be extremely difficult to say no, so preparations have been roughly worked out, I was told, perhaps to propose an all-party conference to fill in time and perhaps in the last resort to substitute direct rule, a kind of colonial rule, for the present Government, because, rather than having to support the Orangemen and put British troops in to shoot down civil rights protesters, we would take over the government ourselves. That was roughly the situation as it was explained to me this morning.

I had to rush to the Italian Embassy to see Saragat and Nenni,[1] who are here for an interminable presidential week of entertainment, jollification and formal meetings at which nothing is achieved. They asked me what I thought would happen now de Gaulle had gone and I had to say that even those of us who are opposed to the Common Market or aren't keen on entry must admit that to get in now is somewhat a point of honour for poor, battered Britain, who has been on the doorstep for six years. So even I want to see a successful entry but, considering the burden of the balance of trade, not too fast.

Back to the Ministry for hours and hours of sitting in the larger Ministerial Conference Room at a whole series of meetings. First of all I had a long meeting with the Joint Consultants Committee, a very high-grade committee of the eight leading men in the medical profession. They wanted to talk to me about the Green Paper but Godber had warned me that in his view the medical profession was going to explode about various things, in particular my reaction to Ely. So I passed him a message that I wanted to discuss this, and after quite an easy consultation about the Green Paper I said, 'Now we come to Ely,' and told them about the inspectorate. What interested me was that they had got a completely false impression. They thought I was going to have an inspectorate of civil servants who would look over the doctors' shoulders. 'No,' I said. 'They'll be drafted from the National Health Service and will be on short-term secondment to me. The whole idea is to have eyes and ears and let the Health Service people feel I really want to understand them.' The more I talked the more the J.C.C. felt they had been misbriefed. And by whom? Nobody except Godber and the Ministry. In the course of that hour and a half I had to overcome the impression which the Ministry had been sedulously creating and I think it went pretty well.

Next a briefing meeting with the Department on Regional Hospital Boards and then another meeting about post-Ely work, in the middle of which I was sent for by the Prime Minister. He wanted to tell me that he had just sacked John Silkin as Chief Whip and brought in Bob Mellish.[2] Bob was my old number two at Housing and I know him pretty well. He had been one of my worst enemies in the trade union movement and suddenly became a faithful, adoring lieutenant. We really liked each other. I think him a pretty good replacement for John, who has been getting idle and terribly two-faced and

[1] Pietro Nenni, Deputy Prime Minister and Chairman of the Italian Socialist Party. He and Giuseppe Saragat, both socialists, had for twelve years worked to unify the Italian Social Democratic and Socialist Parties, and in October 1966 they had succeeded. Nenni was to resign the party chairmanship in July 1969 when deep divisions between Left and Right reappeared.

[2] On May 29th Robert Mellish was appointed Chief Whip, replacing John Silkin, who took Mr Mellish's post as Minister of Public Building and Works. The Parliamentary Committee was replaced by an 'inner Cabinet' of seven senior Ministers, who were to plan and co-ordinate long-term policy.

ambiguous in his relationships, far too friendly to the Left, and far too much the Prime Minister's poodle. Mind you, to be fair to John, the liberal regime did work fairly well after an appalling beginning but I think it is time for him to go. It is impossible to run a liberal regime under very great difficulties, with the increasing unpopularity of the Government, the decreasing success of Harold Wilson, and an amiable nonentity as Leader of the House. Liberal whipping requires authoritative leadership and my disappearance and Harold's decline have made John's position so impossible that a change was necessary. I talked this over with Harold, who said, 'I know Barbara will be upset.'

Just as I got upstairs Judith came in, looking very grey and seeming terribly upset about Bob Mellish. Next was Barbara, furiously angry at what Harold had done, taking it as a personal insult. I took her out to dinner and she fumed. After all, he had talked to us for an hour this morning and given us the impression that he was just thinking about having a new Chief Whip and then, under her nose, he swept John Silkin away and put in Bob Mellish, a *bête noire* of Barbara's, without consulting her and in the middle of her own negotiations with John about the conduct of her Industrial Relations Bill. She said it was intolerable, she would never forgive Harold, she was going to destroy him and finally I advised her to write him a really stinking letter. I think she had every right to be angry. It is exactly this kind of conduct that makes Harold an intolerable, mean leader. When he does this he is a timid, awful little man who to avoid a scene lies and is evasive. So over dinner Barbara worked out the phrases for her letter and afterwards we went into Fred Peart's room to discuss the progress of the Bill with the new Chief Whip. She was fairly civil to him but it was a difficult evening we had there, trying to make sense of it all and to look forward to the future.

I went home and after midnight the Prime Minister rang me up. I have never in my life heard him so frightened. He had received Barbara's letter and wanted to read it aloud to me. 'No,' I said, 'it is a private letter to you but I tell you she is very upset. She isn't going to do what you think, though. She isn't going to resign. Don't try to speak to her tonight but arrange to see her early tomorrow and do for heaven's sake realize that you can't treat people in this way, Harold. But I assure you she isn't going to resign. You are all right.' He said, 'Thank you, Dick. At least I shall sleep tonight.' And that was Tuesday.

Wednesday, April 30th

First of all I had to see John Davies about the dynamizing of the new pensions scheme. The meeting went far better than I expected because he roughly agreed with my analysis and it seemed to me that he and the C.B.I. would be prepared to back the Government. They made it perfectly clear that, like the representatives of the occupational pensions schemes, they would support the dynamizing of the benefits. They also had some important statistics and when the Life Officers and the T.U.C. come back to see me next Monday it will be most interesting to try to weigh up the anomalies and the advantages and disadvantages of the decision.

Then we had the crucial meeting of the R.H.B. chairmen whom I had summoned for a formal confrontation. There were fifteen chairmen and sixteen members of the Department, plus myself and Serota in the middle of the table. A couple of them perhaps are strong, powerful men worth £6,000 a year, Desmond Bonham-Carter, for example, and Graham Rowlandson,[1] but the rest of them are fairly feeble creatures trying to do a bit of public service but really dominated by their officials. This became only too clear as the meeting went on. I got them to agree that I would write them a letter once again defining their responsibility for the management of the hospitals, something which many of them have devolved to the Hospital Management Committees and which Geoffrey Howe had exposed in the Ely Report. I got them to agree to my inspectorate and when I offered them one, too, I was amused to find that, no, they were content to see me having a National Advisory Service and they would rely on their present facilities, i.e. they didn't want to take responsibility. The one thing they rejected was Brian Abel-Smith's suggestion for a 1¼ per cent switch of expenditure from the rest of the service to the sub-normal hospitals. Here I did get into difficulties, but I finally got them to realize that there was a whole series of changes—food, carpets, furniture, toys for the children, clothing for patients, more community activity—that they could make simply without great cost. I put to them a long list of things we could actually do which would make an enormous difference to sub-normal hospitals.

Thursday, May 1st

The sacking of the Chief Whip and the creation of the inner Cabinet, which Harold had announced at his lobby conference yesterday, dominated everything. There were two Party meetings yesterday, one in the morning at which apparently Barbara got an ovation after a disastrous start by Gerald Gardiner who had given the legal aspect of the Industrial Relations Bill, and then another in the evening when the new Chief Whip orated to the Party and did very well. None of this got into the press today because there were no papers on May Day.

At O.P.D. we had the old problem of the supply of arms to the Israelis. For weeks the situation on the Suez Canal has been worsening.[2] The

[1] Sir (Stanley) Graham Rowlandson, Chairman of the Rowlandson Organization, Senior Partner of S. Graham Rowlandson Co., Chartered Accountants, and Chairman of the Finance and Industrial Trust Ltd, was Conservative Member for Enfield on the G.L.C. from 1964–73 and Chairman of the G.L.C. Finance Committee 1969–73. He was a member of the North-East Metropolitan R.H.B. from 1952 to 1974 and Chairman 1956–74, and was also Chairman of the Chairmen of the Regional Hospital Boards 1971–4. He was knighted in 1956.

[2] Neither the U.N. Special Representative, Dr Gunnar Jarring, nor the four major powers had been able to find a solution to the Arab–Israeli war. The Israeli Foreign Minister continued to reject proposals from intermediaries and to demand direct talks with

Egyptians have been firing enormous numbers of shells across the Canal in an effort to stimulate the Israelis into activity and the Israelis have now struck deep inside Egypt to get at power stations. Harold was not in the chair since he had gastro-enteritis (but I heard in fact this was a hangover from a party for the industrial correspondents last night, when he stayed up boozing with them until 3 or 4 a.m. They were all so exhausted that they all had gastro-enteritis this morning).[1] Whether that is true or not I don't know, but he was upstairs in bed looking at his papers while Michael Stewart kept O.P.D. going on below. Michael had produced a paper saying, with passive support from Denis Healey, that we should at least postpone our decision to supply the Israelis with Chieftain tanks in 1972/3.[2] Negotiations had started months ago and it was suggested that we should hold them up at least until September and send out a delaying communiqué. Michael was saying for the Foreign Office that otherwise we would suffer appalling losses if the Arabs discovered what we were doing. I don't know what Denis Healey really thinks; he was saying that this would shift the balance of power in the Middle East and that if the Israelis knew we were cancelling support for them the effect might be to start the war earlier. Fred Peart said we ought to supply the arms to Israel anyway and Tony Crosland for the Board of Trade said that we really must be sensible and not supply them. Barbara Castle wanted to be honest with the Israelis and Callaghan in rather a muddled way said the same thing. One of the most terrible things was that in Michael Stewart's initial statement he said he had succeeded in persuading the Americans that if we didn't supply Chieftains they wouldn't supply tanks either. This gave me my chance and I said, 'Look, this is outrageous. I will accept that if necessary we must always let the Israelis down and I will accept if necessary that we can't afford to supply them with tanks because of the desperate position we are in with the Arabs but, if so, shouldn't we openly tell the Israelis that although we are their friends we can't help them and that we leave them free to get arms elsewhere?' Funnily enough, therefore, I finished up with the pro-Arabs, but anyhow we ended with some kind of formula and went on to Cabinet, with Michael Stewart still in the chair.

---

the Arabs. Israel refused to withdraw from the occupied territories before a peace treaty had been secured and the Arabs refused to meet Israel until the occupying forces were withdrawn. On April 8th Jordan broke her unofficial truce in the Gulf of Aqaba, when guerillas launched a rocket attack on the port of Eilat, the armistice and cease-fire agreement collapsed, and a state of war now existed in the Suez Canal region.

[1] The Prime Minister's own account explains that he was suffering 'from a mild gastric complaint following a dubious fish course at one of the Italian state visit functions'. See *Wilson*, p. 646.

[2] In retaliation for an Arab attack on December 26th, 1968, on an El-Al aircraft at Athens airport, the Israelis had destroyed thirteen Middle East Airlines aircraft at Beirut airport. They had used French helicopters and on January 6th President de Gaulle had totally banned French arms supplies to Israel, even though the Israeli government had already paid for the Mirage jet aircraft it had ordered.

We had a thoroughly bad-tempered Cabinet. On Rhodesia Michael Stewart suggested that we ought to edge a little further forward and offer them some kind of assurances. This was opposed by Barbara, who weighed in to say fiercely, 'My God, why should we make any concession at all?' and Cabinet uneasily sided with her against Michael.

There was appalling bad temper too on the Private Member's Bill on Employers' Liability.[1] I had been dubious about this and so had Barbara, but it had been put forward by David Watkins with the full support of the T.U.C. and Gerald Gardiner had got us to agree to a sub-committee to look into it.[2] He didn't want to oppose the Bill because he said it wasn't the kind of thing a Labour Government should stop. It had got to Committee Stage and now we had to decide who should run it. I didn't wish to and Barbara had waved herself out of it because she was so busy on industrial relations. The Prime Minister had ruled that it should go to me but poor old Clifford Jarrett had pointed out very powerful reasons for saying no. Though it would no doubt remedy a minor evil, it would be enormously complicated to administer and enforcement would involve us getting up against a million small employers. It had gone to Legislation Committee and now it was back again after nine weeks' delay. It was decided that we should stop the Bill with blocking amendments. I pointed out this morning that this was intolerable because if we had allowed it to get to Second Reading without any objection we couldn't then spend our time blocking it in Committee. Cabinet just agreed with me and said that the decision should go to Home Affairs on Monday. I talked today to the Attorney General and the Lord Chancellor about it and insisted that another Department must take it on and fight it through. There is appalling confusion here and I was very angry with the Lord Chancellor, so angry that finally the Attorney General said, 'I can't go on seeing the Lord Chancellor insulted by the Social Secretary. The Law Officers have done nothing wrong. Why does he abuse us all the time?' I sympathize with the Attorney General, I sympathize with the Solicitor General, but I have no sympathy with Gerald Gardiner, whom I regard as a tight-lipped, hypocritical, bloody-minded Quaker, and I probably made this too clear and probably made an enemy for life this morning.

The next thing we had was the case of Gerald Brooke, a British student imprisoned in Russia, whom we have been trying to get out.[3] Then Michael Stewart's voice went boring on about France after General de Gaulle,[4] and

[1] The Employers' Liability (Compulsory Insurance) Act 1969 obliged employers to insure against injury and damage to their employees.

[2] David Watkins has been Labour M.P. for Consett since 1966.

[3] A London lecturer who had been arrested in Moscow on April 25th, 1965, held incommunicado for eleven days and finally brought to trial on July 22nd, charged with anti-Soviet agitation and propaganda. On July 25th he was sentenced to a year's imprisonment and four years' detention in a labour camp.

[4] When the General's resignation was announced, the President of the Senate, M. Alain Poher, assumed interim authority until the election of the successor to the Presidency of the Republic. There were seven candidates for the first ballot, to be held on June 1st,

about Northern Ireland.[1] It was a terrible morning but in one way it was good because no one could really think we would be better off with Michael Stewart as Prime Minister instead of Harold Wilson. After all this we reached the first item on the agenda, the old Left–Right issue of whether immigrants should bring with them to this country a certificate of entry obtained in their own country before they left. Callaghan had prepared his ground very well. He had gone to see everybody in the House of Commons and he proved that here we were doing something civilized, not anti-immigrant or racialist, that would simply be a matter of trying to tack some new paragraphs to the Immigration Appeals Bill now in the House of Lords. It went through Cabinet as easily as it had gone through the Committee.

This evening Jimmy Margach came to see me with an astonishing story of how all the Commons' lobbies were seething with revolt against Harold and with talk of a round-robin sent by 100 Labour back benchers, some for Callaghan, some for Healey, a few for Jenkins, a few for me, but that they were mainly shouting against Wilson.[2] So I was not surprised to have a message that I was urgently wanted by the Prime Minister at 10.15, along with Barbara. I was engaged to dine at George Weidenfeld's party for

---

including M. Poher himself, M. Georges Pompidou, the former Gaullist Prime Minister, M. Gaston Defferre, the socialist Mayor of Marseilles, and M. Alain Krivine, a conscript private second-class, representing the Trotskyist Ligue Communiste.

[1] Agitation from the Civil Rights Movement and terrorist attacks on public buildings and utilities worsened during April. To control the violence, variously attributed to the Irish Republican Army and to Protestant extremists, the military had on April 20th assumed responsibility for guarding vital installations. The Government continued their reformist policy, brought in legislation for the creation of a N.I. Parliamentary Commissioner, and on April 23rd accepted that, as the Civil Rights Movement demanded, there should be universal adult suffrage in local elections. On May 28th the Prime Minister, Terence O'Neill, resigned, to be succeeded by Major James (Robin) Chichester-Clark, the former Minister of Agriculture, who appointed a Cabinet that included three members who had previously been opposed to Captain O'Neill. Further reform measures were announced and Civil Rights agitation was suspended but sectarian tension increased. The Civil Rights programme was largely supported by Roman Catholics, who alleged that they were discriminated against in the allocation of housing and employment. The Protestants were not reassured as they saw the Government yielding to the Roman Catholics' demands and they feared that the way was being prepared for the transfer of Northern Ireland to the Irish Republic. Miss Bernadette Devlin's speeches made the Protestant fears all the more keen, as did the Dublin government's reassertion of demands for the ending of Partition.

[2] A number of Labour M.P.s had abstained in the vote on the clause to raise S.E.T., and in the vote on the budget resolution on April 21st the Government's majority had fallen to 28. The new Chief Whip's first act was to deal with four of the abstainers who had long records of indiscipline and, with the support of the Prime Minister, he announced at the P.L.P. meeting on April 30th, which had been called to ratify the suspension of the four, that he had decided to 'wipe the slate clean' and take no action to withdraw the party whip. Unfortunately, according to the Prime Minister, despite Mr Wilson's advice Mr Mellish also declared several times that failure to carry the I.R. Bill would lead to a dissolution. These remarks provoked the anger of the left wing and by the following day some M.P.s were proposing that 100 signatures be collected in support of a demand for a Party meeting to consider the leadership. By May 2nd the revolt had died down but the Party remained discontented and divided, above all over the Industrial Relations Bill. See *Wilson*, pp. 644–7.

Hubert Humphrey,[1] the ex-candidate for the American Presidency who is now seeking to sustain his life with the hope of making himself the candidate next time. (I don't know why anybody could conceivably want to be an American Presidential candidate; the thought is depressing in the extreme.) I went along to George's marvellous party, where I found Mary McCarthy on one side of me,[2] and on the other an exquisitely pretty and amusing Frenchwoman who is the third wife of Pierre Salinger.[3] I was having a splendid evening with them when 10 o'clock came and I had to leave.

It was a remarkable contrast with Tuesday morning. Then Harold had been his old, devious, bilateral self, keeping us where he wanted and at the same time facing us with the *fait accompli* of conceding the things we were about to ask for, but now, for the first time since I have known him, Harold was frightened and unhappy, unsure of himself, needing his friends. The great india-rubber, unbreakable, undepressable Prime Minister was crumpled in his chair. It was a touching evening for Barbara and me. We sat with him as old friends who wanted to help. Mind you, he had been spending the previous night boozing with the industrial correspondents, claiming that he had a stomach upset when he really had a hang over, but we saw at last that he was injured, broken, his confidence gone, unhappy, wanting help. Yes, he had agreed to the inner Cabinet last Tuesday, but reluctantly. Between Tuesday and Thursday something had happened to his self-esteem and the inflated gas balloon had been punctured. It became clear early on in the conversation that he had changed his mind about Callaghan's exclusion from the inner Cabinet and that he would be in after all. Harold tried to persuade himself that he had told us this, which was quite untrue because he had said the opposite. Anyhow, he had now seen Callaghan and told him that he was an essential member of the group. I don't think Harold is lying in these things and I don't think I blame him, except for once again changing his mind, twisting and turning and saying different things to different people. Barbara and I stood beside him and she said, 'My God, we want to help you, Harold. Why do you sit alone in No. 10 with Marcia and Gerald Kaufman and these minions? Why not be intimate and have things out with your friends?' We said, 'If you have to have Jim in the inner Cabinet, all right, but do also have your friends. We must be in and out of the house. For God's sake, realize that the inner Cabinet won't just meet once a week. It will be the seven people you call together for any crisis. You can't just call five one day, three another and six another, always

[1] In 1972 Hubert Humphrey lost the nomination as the Democratic candidate to Senator George McGovern from South Dakota.

[2] The writer and novelist. Her books include *The Stones of Florence* (London: Heinemann, 1959), *The Group* (London: Weidenfeld & Nicolson, 1963) and *Vietnam* (London: Penguin, 1968).

[3] In 1965 Nicole Gillmann had married Pierre Salinger, Press Secretary to John Kennedy 1959–63, appointed to serve as a U.S. Senator August 1964–January 1965. He has been Roving Editor at *L'Express* in Paris since 1973.

varying them, creating new committees to keep us divided. We all want to help you and we want to put you back.' I was saying this all the evening from 10.15 till midnight, with all the more feeling because I knew, after what Jimmy Margach had told me, what was going on in the lobbies and what was likely to be reported tomorrow.

Friday, May 2nd

Sure enough, every newspaper reported the anti-Wilson ferment in the Parliamentary Party. Names weren't mentioned but I got them later – Brian Walden, John Mackintosh, the old independents, all turning against Harold and saying the only hope was to get rid of the leader. There was one article which I read with some interest, a report from Peter Jenkins, the *Guardian* columnist. It partly came from me. I had lunch with him last week and he had been clever enough to get a little from me and some more from Roy, so that the whole picture was of Callaghan insisting that Harold couldn't afford to leave him out of his inner Cabinet. It was probably true that Callaghan had brazened his way through and that Harold had funked what I had begged him to do on Tuesday night on the telephone, to have Callaghan in, talk to him straight and tell him either to be loyal or to get out. But, as the press made only too clear, that hadn't happened.

After a meeting at the Department I had to rush to No. 10 for the Northern Ireland Committee. Cabinet had made it quite clear yesterday that, not unreasonably, they were determined to be in on our policy and not to be faced with a *fait accompli*, so the Committee went through the material once again and in twenty minutes we decided that we would hand the matter over to Cabinet to make up their own minds. I got back early to No. 70, where poor Janet looked up from the box to say, 'Oh my God, what a disaster. The Minister's back thirty-five minutes early.' 'What work have you got for me, what letters have I got to sign?' I asked. 'Come on, boys, hurry up now.' Of course it is the division between John Adam Street and Elephant and Castle that causes our difficulties and this was a day when they were in great confusion. They gave me a few things to do and then I thought since I had a few minutes to spare I would draft a press release for my speech this evening at Yardley. I had been lying in bed this morning thinking a little about what I might say, when suddenly it occurred to me that I could say something important on the challenge to Harold's leadership. By the time I had to leave for East London to study a group of hospitals I had a draft which I dictated very rapidly to Janet. I said Ron Matthews must meet me at the last hospital so we could discuss the draft in the car on the way back to Euston. I also rang up Percy Clark and said, 'Look, I haven't got a press release but I think it's worth telling the press that I am going to say something important tonight.' I didn't bother about it much, I just thought it was a sensible thing to do.

After looking at the great King George Hospital at Ilford I was taken on to Barking Hospital, where at lunchtime I was suddenly told that Judith wanted to talk to me. She said, 'I hear you are going to speak this evening. Have you got a brief? Have you got a press release?' I said, 'No, but you can go across the passage to 70 Whitehall and see what I have dictated.' She then said, 'I'll send you down my own speech.' So I began to realize that things were warming up a bit.

This afternoon, after my usual routine round of the hospitals, I took the 5.15 train to Birmingham and sat down to work on my speech, basing it on the little piece I had dictated, which didn't look too bad. Just as we were getting in to Birmingham, Brian Walden, the most brilliant of the young intellectuals, dashed into the carriage, sat himself down opposite and said, 'You must stop this nonsense. We must throw Harold out. You must take his place.' He had been followed by a *Daily Express* journalist and I said, 'For God's sake, don't talk like that, Brian, there are other people here.' 'I must talk to you,' he said. He was obviously neurotic and obsessed, thinking that I was the right man to be made Prime Minister and that Harold must go. I began to realize that Jimmy Margach was right in saying that there is a neurosis in the Parliamentary Party. I was also to realize that there was a neurosis in Birmingham. When I got to the new station concourse, there were the arc lights, I.T.V. and the B.B.C. waiting for me and two or three journalists asking what I was going to say at the meeting. Well, I had no advance release and I had enough gumption to fend them off. We walked round and round the concourse twice with the arc lights following us and our poor little car trying to edge itself towards us. I was forced to say a few words to the T.V. people and the *Daily Express*. Then we motored out along the Coventry road to Yardley, and up to the Good Companions hotel and as I got out there was the A.T.V. and the B.B.C. and the *Daily Express* again. I realized that if I gave them a story for the evening news the London papers would not be interested in it tomorrow, so I had to hold it until 9 o'clock.

I got inside and though there were very few people waiting, the hall slowly filled up. This was the annual dinner of the Yardley constituency Labour Party, the kind of annual dinner which I would have had at Coventry last week if Albert hadn't lost heart and cancelled it. It was very pleasant. I sat down to dinner with Ioan Evans the Welshman,[1] John Silkin's liberalizing friend, terribly battered and bruised at the loss of John, and afterwards the journalists were all brought in and there I was sitting on a dais with the lights switched on and the B.B.C. taking the whole of my speech. It is a great strain doing these things but I did it, and then, because I had done all this for the cameras, I had to stay on for two hours and go from table to table chatting with the comrades and making them feel that

[1] Labour and Co-operative M.P. for Birmingham, Yardley, 1964–70 and since 1974 for Aberdare. He was an Assistant Government Whip and a Government Whip 1968–70.

I was talking to them. I didn't get into my car until 11.30 and I was dumped in Coventry just before midnight.

Saturday, May 3rd

At the same time last night Judith was speaking and, though I didn't know it, Tony Greenwood. But the press this morning was dominated by Crossman, with the centre of the newspaper coverage the single paragraph which I had handed out. Funnily enough, my decision not to issue a press release but to say I was making an important speech and to make available half a dozen copies of the paragraph I had drafted turned out to be the ideal way of concentrating press attention. I woke early and anxiously switched on the radio, to find myself the lead story. I heard my own voice and was able to see that the start I had given had received the proper emphasis. I had said that we are all supporting Harold Wilson in getting the Industrial Relations Bill through and that we all want to do this while healing the rift between ourselves and the trade unions. It was all there, with my mockery of anybody who thought that Harold could be overthrown. I realized I had made a big impact and done quite a good job and without having told Harold or Judith I was going to do it. By the way, it just shows you how little politically minded the newspapers are. I had started my speech by mentioning Ioan Evans and speaking about the liberal regime which John Silkin and I had introduced, and I had added that I knew Bob Mellish very well, that he would carry on faithfully with the liberalizing regime in his own fashion and would not destroy the principle by which Labour M.P.s are treated as responsible people with a duty to make up their own minds. This statement was extremely significant in certain ways but the fact that it was said was not printed by a single newspaper.

All day I spent in Albert Rose's area at a conference with the field workers, psychiatric workers, children's officers, health visitors, child-guidance officers, doctors and headmasters, discussing Seebohm. Paul Odgers was there as well. I slipped off at lunchtime to see Dr Rudland,[1] a splendid, rugged, old-fashioned doctor with a lovely house and an acre and a half of garden right in the heart of Coventry, who gave me a glass of sherry and shared a bottle of claret with me before I tottered back home in the afternoon. All day Harold had been trying to telephone me.

Sunday, May 4th

I have been reflecting on the reports of the anti-Wilson campaign boiling up in the P.L.P. and talking to people in Coventry, and I think I now appreciate the reasons for it. The truth is that not only have the trade union leaders written the Government off as finished and as a mere prelude to a Tory Government but most of the members of the Parliamentary Party itself are

[1] Senior partner in a Coventry general practice. He was appointed Honorary Physician to the Queen in 1958.

just fighting to keep up their morale. Deep underneath they know they can't win next time. This is what has undermined confidence because they then ask why we should even try to have our own Industrial Relations Bill, when the Tories are bound to introduce one. So we have had the mutterings of revolution and the open demand that Wilson must go and now I have started the fight back. I began it with my speech on Friday evening and the climax will come with Harold's May Day speech this afternoon.

The P.M. got through to me this morning on the telephone to give me a tremendous round of congratulations on the timing, the drafting and the press relations of Friday evening's speech. There was a lot of luck in it but certainly it came off with a bang. It was the one thing Harold needed. I have done this more than once for him and he was pleased and fairly confident about his speech today. I have been very careful this week. I have given support to his efforts to get the Bill through but I haven't said a word about his quality as a leader. I haven't been a Wilson man, not at all, and I notice that the only journalist who has finally got it right is our friend Alan Watkins of the *New Statesman*. In his piece this week he says I am the middle man in the Cabinet and I am. There are Roy and Denis on the right, Fred Peart floating round, Barbara on my left. We are still, yes, left-of-centre Wilsonites, but after we have got the Bill through, Wilsonites prepared to go into the election under another leader. I think Roy and Denis have the same view. Then there is Callaghan who regards himself as the alternative and who for that reason, I think, is bound not to take over. Only one thing could go wrong on this and this is what Callaghan was hinting at in his speech at the Party meeting. He was formally supporting Harold but leaving things open. A hundred back-bench M.P.s could sign a round-robin demanding that Wilson must go and requisition a Party meeting to dethrone Harold, and if that were to happen and if there was an open demand in the Parliamentary Party for Harold's resignation, it would help Jim, and it is this which, under the new Chief Whip, Roy, Barbara, Denis and I will unite with Harold to defeat.

I discussed this with Roy this morning, when I rang up to brief him after his week with the I.M.F. in Washington. He couldn't remember whether he had been in favour of Jim's exclusion or inclusion in the inner Cabinet when he discussed it with the Prime Minister on the Friday before he left but I am absolutely clear that, after telling Barbara and me on Tuesday morning that Jim would be excluded, that same evening Harold told Callaghan he was going to be in. Well, we have got the inner group, something I have been struggling for for five years, and Roy told me this morning that we are going to meet on Tuesday and that it will be the inner Cabinet which Roy and Barbara and I chose.[1] As I said to him, what we have absolutely clearly established this week is that, come what may, we have

[1] Its members were, in addition to the Prime Minister, Michael Stewart, Roy Jenkins, Richard Crossman, Barbara Castle, Denis Healey and James Callaghan.

got to get this short Industrial Relations Bill through with the necessary concessions to avoid an irreversible split in the Labour Movement and to conciliate the Movement and bring it along with us. We must do all that and we must do it under Harold Wilson.

Equally, now we have got away from the individual non-leadership of Harold and have established collective leadership, we have changed the situation because if Harold completely fails to mend his ways and can't regain his magic and dynamism and the confidence of the Party, once the Bill is through the collective leadership might agree on his successor. But I don't think this is likely. Anyway what we have to do now is to reinflate Harold, give him confidence and launch the balloon once more.

Monday, May 5th

There was a splendid account of Harold's speech on the news last night. His phrase was, 'They say I'm going—well, I'm going on', and it had come off. As I travelled up in the train this morning I read the speech and saw that he has had an immense success and that this is a turn for the good. So there I was, excited about last weekend, looking forward to the Home Affairs Committee where we were dealing with that awful nuisance of the Employers' Liability Bill, and the battle we were having against my Department's taking it on, and with my mind full of the problem of dynamizing the graded element in the pension and this morning's negotiations with the T.U.C.

But when I got to the office I found waiting for me a Statement on teeth and spectacles. I knew this was a bit unpleasant. It had been postponed because of the Scottish local elections and then I had been too busy to deal with it, so it had come down to Prescote in my fourth red box this weekend. It was quite a trivial regularization to relate the charges for N.H.S. teeth and spectacles to the cost and I had corrected it last night and banged it in the box for the post office to collect at 9.30 p.m. when they send the boxes back to the office to be dealt with on Monday morning.

When I arrived I was mildly surprised to find this and I half realized it must be for today because I knew I had a few Questions and a Statement to deliver. I tidied it up a bit and forgot about it until lunch time, when I was talking to a B.B.C. correspondent at a little restaurant in Northumberland Avenue. He told me that the increased charges were banner headlines on the front page of the *Evening Standard* and I suddenly realized that I was going to be in trouble this afternoon. My God, the local elections! Tam, by the way, had gone off to Indonesia and hadn't been there to warn me and, because of a new procedure by which the Speaker puts up in the No Lobby at midday an announcement of any Statements which are going to be made, the lunchtime press was full of it. It was on the B.B.C. and the front page of the *Standard* and the *News*, and by 2.0 p.m. it was the news of the day.

By 3.30 the House was filled with people. There were a lot of Statements and then came my short Statement and my replies.[1] I did quite well, I was cool and controlled and sensible, but of course the Parliamentary Party didn't bother to listen to what I was saying. They hadn't realized that this was only a minor readjustment of the cost of teeth and spectacles; for them it was another breach of faith. By the time I got into the lobby at 6.30 for the first division on the Post Office Bill the wolves were howling and spitting round me. One can hardly blame them. They had been shattered by the row over Barbara's Bill, then they had Callaghan's sensation and the Prime Minister's come-back and now here was I, on the Monday before the local elections, bashing them with teeth and spectacles. I took the responsibility and said as they stood round me, 'It is my fault. I didn't realize until last night that the Statement was on today and the local elections weren't in my head at the time.' Perhaps I was unwise to say this but I did and within minutes they had all rushed out and were giving the press an account of this ghastly Crossman and his ghastly gaffe, and I, who for a few months had had quite a good reputation with them and had been talked about as a possible alternative to Harold, there I was a broken idol, smashed. Just a few hours after I had been dictating that complacent diary I was down at the bottom with the worst clanger, I suppose, in my political career since my *Mirror* article on the trade unions.[2]

I went through five divisions today, and every time I walked through the lobby I was spat at, shouted at, whispered at behind the scenes. Shortly after I got back into my room in came Bea Serota, shaken. She had agreed to go to a meeting of the Health Committee and had arrived to find twenty people howling and baying at her because of something she knew nothing about. It was a dreadful evening. I had to make up my mind what to do. Ironically, I was having dinner with John Silkin, demoted or promoted to the Department of Works, and I decided, I think quite rightly, to go on the air. So I went up to I.T.V. headquarters and did a sensible, level-headed interview, talking to people outside the Party and doing the best I could. I did realize that Fred Peart and Bob Mellish had been conspicuously absent this afternoon and that I was taking the whole blame for the mess I had made. The truth, as I have now discovered, is that this had gone through all our Private Offices, and Ron Matthews reckons that sixteen people knew that the Statement was coming up, in my Office, in Peart's, Mellish's and also the Prime Minister's Offices. I was to blame but, equally, so were others.

[1] Mr Crossman announced a 25 per cent increase in charges for dentures and spectacles provided by the National Health Service. £3½ million was to be raised by a modest increase in the charge to patients, some £1 extra for dentures and 5*s*. for spectacles (and the decision had been published in the P.E.S.C. White Paper), but it provoked indignation in the Labour Party, particularly on the eve of the local urban and borough elections.

[2] In an article in the *Daily Mirror* on July 5th, 1957, Crossman had said that only four trade union M.P.s were serious candidates for key posts in a future Labour Government.

Tuesday, May 6th

I spoke to the Prime Minister on the telephone and told him what had happened and that I had decided to say openly that it was entirely my fault. He agreed that I had done the right thing. Then I saw the newspapers and discovered that the back benchers had filled the press. Every headline was about the increase in the health charges. I went into S.E.P., which was busy discussing Tony Wedgwood Benn's effort to save Upper Clyde Shipbuilders and Jennie Lee's fight to stop the Arts Council budget being cut by £400,000, but in the course of it I went out to be interviewed by the B.B.C. I had been pressed to do this by Peter Brown and it wasn't nearly as good as last night's I.T.V. interview as I did a bit too much of being sorry and made it slightly worse.

Then I had to decide whether or not to go and speak at L.S.E. I decided I would and drove up Houghton Street to find hundreds of students massed outside, and television cameras. We drove round to the back and when I got myself into my meeting I found it full of T.V. cameras and journalists whom I had the sense to have thrown out. I did a talk on Labour in the affluent society and the contrast between the revolution of 1848 and that of 1968, and I think that in my own way I stilled the students. We had a good discussion and I got a little help from it. But I am still fretting. No doubt I was right to take the blame but perhaps I overdid it. I remember that one of the Labour back benchers said to me, 'You have lost us 500 seats in the local elections,' and I thought perhaps it would be better for the Labour Party if people think that it is because of me that the seats are lost on Thursday.

I went over to the Great Committee Room and stood at the back watching the memorial meeting for Sydney Silverman,[1] and then I went off to a dinner for Senator Humphrey at Phil Kaiser's house. It was a pleasant, civilized party but I rushed back to a three-line whip on the Finance Bill, annoyed and angry that people should be so beastly to me. I was in one sense pleased with myself for becoming the scapegoat. What I have said in this diary shows whether I accepted it or not – I didn't really and yet I did – but underneath it is churning inside me all the time.

Wednesday, May 7th

The big news was yesterday's Party meeting, which I had missed. It had been attended by very few people. Douglas Houghton had delivered an ultimatum warning the Cabinet that they shouldn't break with the T.U.C., speaking as Chairman of the Parliamentary Party, summing up the Party's point of view while the debate was still under way. It was headlined in every paper but whereas I got the blame on Monday for destroying our chances in the municipals Houghton got no blame at all.

We discussed this at Cabinet but the main subject was Northern Ireland

[1] Labour M.P. for Nelson and Colne from 1935 until his death in February 1968.

again. Poor incoherent, inarticulate landowner O'Neill, who had set himself the task of reforming the Ulster Unionist Party, couldn't make the impact and couldn't communicate enough to win convincingly in last February's election and last week Chichester-Clark,[1] another inarticulate upper-class landowner, finally took O'Neill's place. So the problem remains. It became clearer and clearer today that Cabinet wanted to know more about Harold's intentions in Northern Ireland. Barbara began to ask questions and the more we studied the paper giving the various so-called possibilities the more dubious we became. It was suggested to Cabinet that in the last resort we were constitutionally bound to let our troops be used to defend law and order in Northern Ireland and I asked whether it would be a good thing for us to have some political intelligence so that if we were faced with a civil war we should know what it was all about. Callaghan said, 'I don't think we really need that. After all I am seeing Chichester-Clark every day.' He resisted the whole idea, saying it was absurd, and that the Northern Ireland Government would dislike our behaving in this way, though it would be all right if we were to ask them for ideas. But I was suggesting that we need political intelligence such as we had during the war and that if we have to know about Russia and every other country in the world, we should at least spend some money finding out something about Northern Ireland. The Prime Minister supported Callaghan but Denis Healey came in on my side, saying, 'Frankly, Northern Ireland has completely different conditions from Britain and we shall be as blind men leading the blind if we have to go in there knowing nothing about the place.'

In the course of an hour of fighting, Callaghan said, 'I am working with a very small staff. I actually have only two men on Northern Ireland and we have nobody else dealing with it.' So there it is. After five years in which I and others have believed that we must have a basis of sound intelligence and sound information on which to base our policy, this is the way we prepare for the possibility that we might have to take over direct rule of Northern Ireland. As we went out of the room, Healey said to me, 'You have no idea what it was like before you came on to the Committee. The Prime Minister was always demanding active intervention early on, with this crazy desire to go out there and take things over, that we should side with the Roman Catholics and the Civil Rights Movement against the Government and the Royal Ulster Constabulary, though we know nothing at all about it.' One of the questions I had asked was whether we had any reliable information on the work of the R.U.C. Did we have any objective view as to how far they were oppressive to the Catholics? Of course, I gather they are oppressive but we haven't got any reliable picture of the degree of their

[1] James Chichester-Clark, Unionist, M.P. for South Derry in the Northern Ireland Parliament 1960–72, was Assistant Whip March 1963, Chief Whip 1963–7, Leader of the House 1966–7, Minister of Agriculture 1967–9 and Prime Minister 1969–71. In 1971 he became a life peer, taking the title of Lord Moyola.

oppression and I still don't know to this day how far I succeeded with that particular request.

This evening Brian Abel-Smith gave a little dinner at his house in Elizabeth Street for me, Bea Serota and Professor Jimmy Morris, who was one of Bea's colleagues on the Seebohm Committee. We had all got together to talk about the reorganization of the Health Service and they calmed and soothed me a bit. An astonishing fellow, Brian, with his house full of antique furniture, his modern portraits, somehow slipping out and in ten minutes producing a brilliant meal. It was a pleasure which I could enjoy even in my misery.

Thursday, May 8th

By this morning I had simmered down. The press stories continued and I knew talk was going on inside the Parliamentary Party but it was no good fretting any more. I must now concern myself with what Jim Callaghan and Douglas Houghton were up to. I rang Barbara and Roy and said to them, 'We have Cabinet this morning. What are you going to say with Callaghan there? What is our situation? Here we are with Douglas Houghton saying the whole Parliamentary Party is against us and that we can't possibly get the Bill through, openly threatening us on behalf of the Party and siding with Callaghan. What are we to do?' But neither of them had much of an answer. We agreed to try to keep the subject out of Cabinet and to talk to Harold before the Management Committee,[1] so I telephoned the Prime Minister and pleaded with him not to try to talk too much. We agreed that we four would meet at 3.30 directly after Prime Minister's Questions and, having done this, we would then face Callaghan at Management Committee.

However there wasn't much time for talk before O.P.D. at 9.30. We sat down to a discussion of the M.R.C.A.[2] I was amused when the case was made for spending £7 million on the first development work. This military plane would cost us hundreds of millions but everybody said it was O.K. until Roy Jenkins said, 'I suppose we have to have it but I suspect that when it comes to action it won't be here for about ten more years and by then our successors will be as sceptical and mystified as to how we made our decision this morning as we were about the TSR2.'[3] It wasn't much of a discussion but it was enough and at Cabinet afterwards it was O.K.'d in two minutes. I couldn't help remembering how in my Introduction to Bagehot I had described Attlee's method of railroading through the decision to develop the A-bomb by discussing it only in the Defence Committee and then reporting it to Cabinet. Well, this was a little better because it was talked about for two minutes before the major decision was taken.

[1] The new inner Cabinet.

[2] Multi-Role Combat Aircraft.

[3] A strike and reconnaissance aircraft whose development was begun in 1958 but scrapped in the autumn of 1965. See Vol. I.

The main thing at Cabinet was the Industrial Relations Bill. Although this morning Barbara and Roy and I had begged Harold to stay off the subject he couldn't resist talking about it and, before we knew it, he had made a long speech about the constitutional point raised by Houghton's intervention. This opened up a full-length discussion. On the other side we had Dick Marsh saying much the same as Callaghan, asking why on earth we were destroying the party by getting into a conflict with the whole trade union movement, and others saying that after all Douglas Houghton is speaking for the P.L.P. and, constitution or no constitution, a Government has to keep its majority in the House of Commons and the Chairman of the Party is entitled to make this point. Harold was arguing on the constitutional position but Callaghan was getting the better of the argument. He maintained that the Prime Minister was quite wrong and that it was unrealistic to talk of constitutionality. The issue was whether the Government could sustain its majority. I finally got irritated with Callaghan and said, 'But look, we are not facing the real issue, which is that Douglas Houghton has lined himself up with people who are trying to get rid of the Prime Minister. That is the meaning of his speech. He is prepared to see the Prime Minister go because he hopes to get another Prime Minister who will drop the Bill. As I tried to say last Friday at Yardley this is totally unrealistic and it would not be credible unless it was believed that there was somebody in the Cabinet who held the same view. I know and you all know that Roy Jenkins and Barbara Castle are as deeply committed as the Prime Minister and that there is no sense in suggesting that the Prime Minister could be got rid of. I detest these rats who are leaving our sinking ship to climb on to another sinking ship. We have got to sink or swim together.' At this point Callaghan said from the other side of the table, 'Not sink or swim, sink or sink,' and I said, 'Why can't you resign if you think like that? Get out, Jim, get out.' We had never had such a scene in Cabinet before (I was told later on that it was a phenomenally dramatic moment) and there was an awkward silence. Then Jim muttered, 'Of course, if my colleagues want me to resign I'm prepared to go if they insist on my going.' He had been punctured. He hadn't responded, he had crawled, and it was quite a moment. We didn't get much further with that this morning.

Then we got on to Rhodesia,[1] where Michael Stewart and the Foreign Office still wanted to apologize and make concessions and Barbara Castle powerfully exposed the futility of what was going on. I went out at this point to lunch with Pam Berry at Cowley Street, in the gay, lively company

[1] On May 21st, Mr Smith's Government published their proposals for a new constitution, which would break all ties with the Crown and establish a new Republic. In a broadcast on the previous day Mr Smith told the Rhodesian people that it was the British Government's 'intractable attitude' which had ended all possibility of a settlement. The new constitution, with its proposals for a voting system that would guarantee perpetual domination by the white population, completely contradicted the Six Principles.

of Tom Driberg, Aidan and Virginia Crawley and Perry Worsthorne.[1] I went back to the Prime Minister's Questions, which he did as well as ever. His stature has diminished in Cabinet and in the Parliamentary Party but it hasn't diminished in Question Time. There he was, bright, gay, agile and amusing and in a way as authoritative as ever.

Afterwards we four, Harold, Barbara, Roy and I, slipped out into his room where he had his glass of brandy and we all settled down round the table. Barbara said, 'The worst of it this morning was that your talk about the constitution enabled Jim Callaghan to suggest that we should postpone the Bill at least until after the Whitsun recess to give more time for discussion. I think we ought to do this now because, after all, if we don't at least listen to the Party and leave the Bill until after the Trade Union Congress,[2] how can we say that we have really been trying to reach agreement?' We rapidly agreed that we should make this proposition and that if we postponed the Bill until after Whitsun we should probably have to run into August. We should also have to have my pensions up-grading Bill before Whitsun. At 4 o'clock we had to break off because the others were due to come in. Harold, very characteristically, ordered the postponement of the Management Committee for a quarter of an hour and said to us, 'Slip out so that nobody notices you and come back as though we haven't met.' Although we had had our inner inner Cabinet, Harold's fear that others would see the three of us had been there and would think the worse of him made him contrive this little piece of deception. When we came back, he greeted us with 'Hallo, Barbara, how are you?' and 'Hallo, Dick, where have you been?', elaborately trying to pretend that we hadn't been with him five minutes before. In came the full Committee and we worked out the schedule, with Callaghan all meekness and mildness and collaboration.

I had to go off afterwards to a meeting on research priorities for the Ministry of Health and then for the rest of the evening we continued our discussions on dynamizing the graded element of the existing Tory pension scheme. When I saw the T.U.C. on Monday I had discovered that they would support this and indeed they also wanted us to force employers outside the scheme to dynamize their own schemes. We can't possibly do this and I had pointed out to them that there would be trouble. As a result of my warning, I had a message from Harold Collison that the five T.U.C. representatives would support us,[3] but they would have to report back to the T.U.C. Social Services group, who in turn would report to the T.U.C.

[1] Aidan Crawley, Labour M.P. for Buckingham 1945–51, was Parliamentary Under-Secretary of State for Air 1950–1. He was Conservative M.P. for West Derbyshire 1962–7, Chairman of London Weekend Television 1967–71 and its President 1971–3. His wife, Virginia Cowles, was a writer and journalist.

[2] The special Congress to be held in Croydon on June 5th.

[3] General Secretary of the National Union of Agricultural Workers 1953–69, Chairman, Social Insurance and Industrial Welfare Committee of the T.U.C. 1957–69 and Chairman, Supplementary Benefits Commission 1969–75. He became a life peer in 1964.

General Council, which would probably split. However I now have the C.B.I. and T.U.C. more or less on our side for dynamizing the present scheme and so our only implacable opponents are the Life Offices, the people I least want to quarrel with, the nicest people involved. After my muck-up on Monday I suppose I am losing confidence a bit because I am rather anxious about this. Still, it should be all right.

This evening I saw two back benchers. First of all, I gave dinner to my old P.P.S., Geoffrey Rhodes.[1] There he is, now a smooth man of the world. He has been spending the last two years as a member of the Council of Europe and has got on to the ancient buildings side and travelled all over the place. He is away from Parliament a good part of the time and he is slightly scornful and aloof about it and quite open about this soft option. He said, 'It's expanding my personality. My wife finds me much more interesting. This is a chance which I can't resist and I am no longer quite as dedicated to Parliament as I was.' I thought, 'That is exactly what has happened to so many of the '64 and '66 intake.'

After the 10 o'clock division I got hold of John Mackintosh, who admitted that he had been one of the main people who caused the sensation about the plot against Harold last week, by taking round his own private poll to see how many M.P.s would sign a round-robin demanding a special Party meeting for a secret ballot on a vote of confidence. This he put to me in all seriousness and I said, 'For heaven's sake, we have got to get this Bill through,' and John said, 'I don't oppose the Bill. I just want to get rid of Harold Wilson.' On this he is like Brian Walden and a good many others. I had to spend a couple of hours painfully explaining to him that Harold couldn't be got rid of because Roy, Barbara and I, and for that matter, Denis Healey, all think we have got to get the Bill through whatever happens and that the back benchers can't possibly get rid of Harold without disintegrating the Party. I said, 'After the Bill is through anything can happen. You could plead for a change of leadership in the winter, though it will be much too near the election, but until then it's unrealistic.' We argued it to and fro and I hope I made an impression.

Friday, May 9th

We had the local election results.[2] In Coventry last year we only lost one seat and had the best result in the country and now we are back in the rut like Birmingham. Eight out of ten of our councillors had been defeated. I rang up Albert Rose, who obviously felt that his Dick Crossman, with his teeth and spectacle increases, was to blame. He was utterly disheartened. I then had to run off to No. 10 for an eight-hour session of the N.E.C.

[1] Labour M.P. for East Newcastle from 1964 until his death, at the age of forty-six, in 1974. He was Crossman's P.P.S. for fifteen months, taking the place of Tam Dalyell. See Vol. II, p. 136.

[2] In the local authority elections, May 5th–10th, Labour lost 917 seats to the Conservatives and retained control of only 28 out of 342 borough councils in England and Wales.

Harold had managed to prove to himself that these election results were a considerable improvement on last year's, with less of a swing against us. I suppose nationally this is true, in the sense that fractionally fewer people abstained or fractionally fewer Tories voted, though it wasn't true in Coventry. We sat around in that great big room at No. 10, just like the old days on the Executive. We didn't fuse; though we were civil to each other we were utterly remote. The eight hours were as boring as usual. Roy Jenkins started with a good, powerful speech on the economic situation and then burbled along a bit and Joe Gormley rose to say what a muck-up I had made on health charges and how the Government must stop tearing the Party to pieces and climb down on the Bill. Denis Healey made a serious, pro-Government speech but the only dramatic remarks were from Jim Callaghan. We had all had a dressing-down from Harold at the previous Cabinet and we had all agreed that we must speak on this big issue with absolute collective responsibility – but not old Jim. He got up and gave us all a long lecture, saying that of course Cabinets have the right to be authoritative but they can't impose a Bill unless they are absolutely certain and have proof positive that it is necessary. He lectured us and he lectured them and his was the only speech which had no kind of applause whatsoever. After him Barbara replied, looking neat and trim despite her tiredness. She was immensely moving and everybody there cheered their redhead but it didn't make the faintest difference.

I went off for a hectic lunchtime sorting-out of my afternoon's brief and got very bad-tempered doing it. When I got back I started confidently enough by telling the Executive exactly what happened on Monday. I took full blame, partly because as Leader of the House I had created the machinery for ensuring that Statements should be submitted several days in advance to the Lord President's Office, the Chief Whip's Office, the Paymaster's Office, the Prime Minister's Office, as well as the Minister's own Office, and on this occasion the machinery hadn't worked. I said that of the Ministers concerned not one knew on Sunday night. Only the Prime Minister and I were aware of the Statement and by Monday morning it was too late to stop it. I hope that Bob Mellish felt slightly uncomfortable during this. Then I turned to the substance of the increased teeth and spectacle charges and said that I knew the Executive thought this was cheese-paring but, as Roy had explained, we had to keep public expenditure rigidly within our departmental maxima. I explained how at Cabinet Ted Short had come out badly over his education cuts and how we had felt that we ought to transfer something to him. I told them how I had made the effort to do some block budgeting and make transfer arrangements within the Social Services, so that Ted Short could give grants to twelve key comprehensive schools, and that the dental and spectacle charges were a contribution to the £4 million I had got for him. I had done it for his sake and caused all this commotion. I must say after I had finished Tony Wedgwood Benn came up to me and said, 'Once again, Dick, the compulsive communicator has revealed in deadly light exactly how Government works,' and that he wondered what the impression would be. I replied, 'Well, I'll do it again at the Party meeting on Wednesday.'

The whole of the afternoon was deadly dull and it was ended by George Brown making a very incoherent speech and then Harold reading his speech aloud. The Prime Minister had been writing away all through the afternoon. He writes all his speeches down and when he reads them aloud it's inconceivable how blurred and undistinguished and boring they are. To be frank, I fell asleep during it and only woke up with a start when a thunderstorm broke out towards the end.

Back in my office I found a frantic rush with people being brought over from John Adam Street with the draft of the uprating paper for Cabinet. I said, 'What the hell is this?' 'We have just had a message,' they said, 'from Burke Trend's office that the paper is to be taken at the Management Committee on Tuesday.' I said, 'It's not, it's at Cabinet on Thursday. What the hell do you mean?' I was furious. As I said to Ron Matthews, I had been sitting next to the Prime Minister all afternoon and if Burke Trend had changed his mind and got the agenda wrong for the Management Committee, why hadn't Harold told me? I could have checked all this with Burke and with the Prime Minister at any time this afternoon. I was too rough but, as the Office insisted that the Bill had to be ready for Tuesday, I had to go through it at tremendous speed, revising the paper on the whole complex of benefits and contributions. I rushed this because I was terribly anxious to get back to Vincent Square to see John Maud. Though I had been told that Maud was incommunicado he said that of course he would tell me everything I wanted and for half an hour we discussed in detail how the local government plans were working out.[1] I got a very clear picture of the structure he intended and became more and more doubtful about how on earth I was going to defend keeping an absolutely self-perpetuating oligarchy of R.H.B.s completely unintegrated with the community services of the local authorities.

[1] The Report of the Royal Commission on Local Government (Cmnd 4039) was published on June 11th. It proposed a two-tier structure for England and Wales, outside the G.L.C., with eight provincial councils responsible for economic and social planning and 61 area authorities, of which 58 would be responsible for all services. The three exceptions, Liverpool, Manchester and Birmingham, would have authority for transport, planning and redevelopment, while education, personal social services, health and housing would lie with subsidiary metropolitan authorities. As a result of the proposals, 124 county and borough councils and over 1,000 district councils would disappear. Larger authorities with more effective powers and responsibilities would, it was believed, be more efficient; democratic participation would be encouraged by the introduction of small councils at the neighbourhood level, with no defined powers but to which some local functions could be devolved and where local pressures might be made known.

In a Statement on the day of publication the Prime Minister announced that the Government accepted the recommendations in principle and would begin consultations with a view to implementing the proposals in 1970/1 after the General Election.

Then it was time to change quickly, because I was due to go to the first night of *Elektra* to hear Birgit Nilsson, the Swedish soprano. There we were with the Swedish Ambassador and his wife in the sixth row of the stalls, listening to a terrific performance with the orchestra conducted by Solti. After an exhilarating two hours we went back to the Swedish Embassy, where I sat next to the Ambassador and Solti and had a wonderful evening with them.

Sunday, May 11th

Yesterday morning I got the 9.15 train to Coventry where I was to address the A.E.U. Old Age Pensioners' Fellowship at the A.E.U. Hall in Corporation Street. I hadn't the face to ask Albert Rose to come and meet me with his car so I got a taxi in the pouring rain. I was rather dreading the meeting. After all, I had given the pensioners nothing in the White Paper and I had had the teeth and spectacles disaster. Sure enough, outside I found five or six journalists with microphones, all anxious to get in. I didn't want to stop them but fortunately the Fellowship did.

I set about explaining to about seventy or eighty of the old boys, looking tidy and neat in their best suits, exactly what the situation was. We had a splendid morning, they were sensible and sound and sober and they liked me. After that Anne and Virginia came in and as we came down the stairs there were all the journalists. The B.B.C. man shoved a microphone in my face and said, 'What did the pensioners have to say to your teeth and spectacles?' I was very surprised and said, 'Nothing at all. They never mentioned the subject.' Outside Parliament, I dare say, my schemozzle in the House isn't so bad. I have had very few letters, from seven or eight local parties perhaps, mostly in the South, and twenty or thirty letters from outside. May Cower rang up from Bath this evening to thank me for a birthday present and to ask Anne to tell me that four or five of her friends had said how nice it was to hear a politician honestly admitting his mistake and saying he had forgotten something. That was reassuring but the whole thing was pretty damaging all the same.

This morning's papers weren't too bad but I did notice an extremely malicious piece in Jimmy Margach's column saying that Roy hadn't wished to have these increased charges in his budget and had felt that an old Bevanite should be made to move his own increases. I felt riled by this and couldn't help ringing Roy up. Of course Roy said he hadn't had anything to do with it, and nor had he, but I suppose I revealed that I really minded and this weakened me. The diary hasn't been incoherent this week but it's obviously the diary of someone who has had a rough time and who has been shaken. My own feelings have been dominated by a sense of oppression about my own miserable situation, by my anxieties about myself and also about the crisis we are facing. It has shaken me out of my complacency, my feeling I was doing too well. It's true that in politics you carry along and then suddenly you go, or I do, down with a bump and a clatter to the bottom. It's good for one I suppose and I have certainly learnt a lot this week. I can't say it has done me much good in the party and it won't ever be forgotten there. Thank God I'm not on the Executive now, worrying about that. It has damaged me in Coventry but there it will be forgotten. Roy says it is a storm in a teacup. It isn't quite that but it doesn't matter to me because at sixty-one I am on the edge of retirement. I shan't survive this Government, and if I were defeated in Coventry East I could get down to work on my books. Chelly Halsey,[1] who came to see me this week about the Community Development Project, discussed the prospect of getting me in as a visitor at Nuffield. I was pleased at his excitement and I must say I am getting more and more interested in preparing for the time when I leave the Cabinet and politics and get down to writing about it in the way that I know that I can. I have been looking at horrible, difficult proofs of a book for Chatto & Windus and getting that feeling of surprise and amazement that I am able to do them.[2] I know I can get back into writing again, that I am fit and ready and more than ever looking forward to that time.

We have had Chris and Jennie Hall over this afternoon and it has been lovely. Everything is now growing green in the rain. This morning I had a visit from the engineer of the Oxford Water Board to tell me that Banbury is desperately short of water. He is deeply grateful to me for getting, as Minister of Housing, the final amalgamation of the Banbury water with the Oxford supply, as now they can pipe the extra fifteen miles to bring Banbury the water it needs.[3] I felt quite gratified. He was keen and respectful and excited to see me. I wanted, I suppose, a little restoration of my self-esteem.

Monday, May 12th

At S.E.P. we had a fascinating paper produced by Solly Zuckerman's officials, showing that £14½ million could be saved on defence research without any damage. My God, if they admit that £14½ million can be saved, what could the saving really be? Proposals for spending it had been put in by Education, Transport, even the Home Office, though for some extraordinary reason Solly had forgotten the Ministry of Health and Social Security, so I was able to make an effective intervention insisting that our present £3 million research programme should be rapidly expanded, with special attention to sub-normality. But the thing I shall really remember was Harold's comment. 'I am afraid,' he said, 'there is no political capital in this because nothing we decide will have any effect until years after the next Parliament gets going.' What an extraordinary remark. If we want to recover our reputation in the universities and get the intelligentsia on our

[1] Professorial Fellow at Nuffield College, Oxford, and Director of the Department of Social and Administrative Studies at the University of Oxford since 1962. He was Adviser to the Secretary of State for Education 1965–8.

[2] *Government and the Governed.*

[3] See Vol. I, pp. 350–1.

side, the fact that we have made a switch from military to civil research is the one thing to bring these people back to us. Yet here is Harold saying it has no political significance.

I had been invited weeks ago to lunch with the nationalized industries chairmen and today I found myself in a very solid first-floor private room at the Paddington Hotel with Julian Melchett in the chair, and with B.E.A., B.O.A.C., Gas and Electricity, but no Alf Robens. I decided to tell them all about the pension scheme and I warned them of the problem of what should be done with those who had contracted out of the Tory scheme and sent them all back to consider it.

I had been told that we were to see the Prime Minister this evening, and, sure enough, at 8.0 there were Barbara, Roy and I, the inner inner Cabinet, sitting with Harold drinking brandy and discussing Jim Callaghan's future.[1] We were all clear that he couldn't stay on. Was it that he couldn't stay on during the negotiations with the T.U.C. or that he couldn't stay at all? We didn't want him in and it was decided that Harold should tell him not to attend the Management Committee tomorrow. Harold promised to do so but Barbara bet me half a crown[2] that he wouldn't carry out his promise and I was extremely dubious myself.

Tuesday, May 13th

However, this morning Callaghan was sent for at 9.30 and told he couldn't attend the meeting at 10 o'clock. So there we were without him and we spent the first hour discussing how this should be handled in the press. We finally decided that no reason should be given and the No. 10 habit of simply giving the names of Ministers who attended Committees should be continued unchanged. No. 10 should simply say that the six of us had a meeting with Harold and leave it to the press to notice that Jim was not there.

We then settled down to a really frank discussion of how to handle the Industrial Relations Bill. By jove, it was valuable. At last people were talking freely. Barbara gave us a long, optimistic account of the changed atmosphere in the T.U.C.[3] This is perfectly all right but she sees things

[1] The remarks that the Home Secretary had made at the N.E.C./Cabinet meeting on Friday, May 9th, had leaked into the press and, as he appeared to be dissociating himself from the rest of the Cabinet on the issue of the I.R. Bill, the Prime Minister decided that Mr Callaghan should be excluded from future meetings of the Management Committee.

[2] 2*s*. 6*d*. (12½ new pence).

[3] On May 9th the Prime Minister and the First Secretary dined at No. 10 with Vic Feather, who reported that the T.U.C. was working steadily on its alternative proposals for new powers for the T.U.C., in part relating to the handling of inter-union disputes, and that he was about to submit a draft document to the T.U.C. Finance and General Purposes Committee. At a further meeting between Ministers and the T.U.C. on May 12th, the Prime Minister announced that the introduction of the I.R. Bill would be deferred from the original date of May 22nd until early June, after the T.U.C.'s special Congress. The Ministers learnt that the draft document had that morning been accepted by the T.U.C. Committee and that its proposals were far-reaching.

tremendously from her point of view and when she said that the T.U.C. leaders' attitude was far more conciliatory and they had moved a long way towards her, I just whispered, 'But you have moved a long way towards them. The smack of firm government is not so clear now.' But in the back of her mind and Roy's it is. They feel they must assert their strength and there is a certain brittleness in their attitude.

This morning they both revealed that on no account did they want us to postpone the Bill to the next session but to shove it through at almost any risk. Michael Stewart was rough with them but Denis Healey, Bob Mellish and I were much more willing to see the need for compromise. Bob Mellish, unlike John Silkin, came straight out and said, 'You couldn't shove it through. If you start the Bill as late as this and don't send it upstairs but take it on the Floor of the House, it must be carried on to the spill-over period in the autumn and you will be in great trouble.' Bob is a crude fellow but he came out as someone who means his word. Curiously, he and I found ourselves on the same side in asking Harold and Roy to face the fact that trying to fight this through on the Floor of the House and get it through by the end of July will mean days and days and days in Committee, at the same time as the Uprating Bill.[1] Still, the great fact about this meeting was that we were talking absolutely freely and naturally to each other and revealing our deepest thoughts.

There is a good deal of difference between Barbara and Roy on the one hand and Denis and me on the other, with the Prime Minister balancing between the two. We are now going to have this discussion regularly and we will meet again next Tuesday. There is no doubt that if Harold had held this kind of meeting from 1964 on many of our mistakes could have been avoided.

This evening I went to address the British Insurance Association at some place in the City. I found myself in a magnificent upper room with 150 professional life insurance men. I had no difficulty whatsoever in winning Crabbe of the Life Offices over to my side and it was quite a successful evening.

Wednesday, May 14th

The papers were absolutely dominated by the news of Callaghan's exclusion, and we got a fairly bad press for it with *The Times* saying that it was inefficient and that we couldn't really have an inner Cabinet without Jim. But the real reason for the bad press was the grave mistake Harold made in announcing the formation of the Management Committee as though it were a Cabinet Committee. It isn't a normal Cabinet Committee and this could have been presented in an invaluably useful way.

[1] The pension increases announced in the budget were to be partly financed by increased National Insurance contributions, put before the House in the National Insurance (No. 2) Bill, referred to by Crossman (and hereafter cited) as the Uprating Bill. The measure was introduced on June 10th, 1969, and received its Second Reading on June 17th.

My problem today, however, was how to handle the special Party meeting at which they were to hear about teeth and spectacles. I rang up Barbara and Harold and, though I don't often do this, I asked them if I should tell the truth and explain how we had done it to help Ted Short over a difficult crisis with his comprehensive schools programme. Both Barbara and Harold thought it was much better to tell the Party the truth about what had really happened. I went along to the meeting.

Barbara spoke first, in what I think was the sixth Party discussion on Industrial Relations, and at long last two or three people spoke in her favour. There was an excellent speech by Edwin Brooks, in whose constituency, I found later, the famous Girling strike had taken place,[1] and there was a remarkably good speech by old Arthur Woodburn.[2] Then Barbara got up and said a few words tremendously skilfully, creating an impression of hope and conciliation between herself and the T.U.C., making the Party feel that perhaps they were out of tune in being so savage and dogmatic. What a splendid operator! She did it magnificently.

Then it was my turn. I had a tremendous, high-minded harangue from Laurie Pavitt, as though I had introduced brand new prescription charges, and a great attack from Edith Summerskill, speaking for Shirley who was absent. She lashed me as clever, academic Crossman, psychological warfare Crossman, but rather funnily she got into a controversy with Norman Atkinson and suddenly rounded on him, saying in her dear, traditional, female sergeant-major way, 'Stand up, man. Stand up and say what you mean.' Within three minutes she lost the whole audience, leaving them feeling what a terrible woman she was. In the end I spoke as I had intended, explaining first that there was no principle of charges involved. I have been helped here by a Question John Dunwoody had asked on May 5th, which he now repeated. He had said that many people were anxious that my suggestion that there should be an automatic relationship between the level of charges and the cost of the services concerned seemed to be introducing a new principle into the question of N.H.S. charges. I repeated all the assurances he required and I also tried to explain how this fitted in with our new idea of block budgeting and how we had adjusted our own estimates to help Ted Short. This flabbergasted them and they received it in a slightly bewildered silence, so I thought perhaps I had managed to bring it off.

The other important meeting today was of PEP, our post-Ely policy advisory council. Peter Townsend, Dr O'Gorman, an excellent nurse, and Geoffrey Howe are keen and want to help. They are being flooded with paper and next week I shall get them to devote themselves wholly to working

[1] A recent unofficial strike had halted production among a large number of motor-car firms, which were dependent on Girling's for essential components. The strikers had refused to heed the warnings of Hugh Scanlon himself.

[2] Labour M.P. for Clackmannan and East Stirling 1939–70. He was Parliamentary Secretary at the Ministry of Supply 1945–7 and Secretary of State for Scotland 1947–50.

out how we shall spend the money on research into sub-normality. But, frankly, this effort to get a joint working party of outsiders and insiders is causing every kind of difficulty in the Ministry. One of the difficulties is that Miss Hedley and Sir George Godber don't disguise their feelings about Serota and myself. I thought I had squared the Joint Consultants' Committee, for instance, but apparently they have come back again insisting that either we should have a statutory inspectorate run by themselves or nothing at all. There is a tremendous opposition to this inside the Ministry but we are getting somewhere.

Thursday, May 15th

Before Cabinet we had O.P.D., to discuss the annual negotiations that have started on German payments to offset the cost of British troops in Germany. It was a curious paper, with a statement that from the presentational point of view it would be possible for us to claim that up to 80 per cent of the offset costs had been paid. Roy said, 'Of course, this is all bogus. We don't have anything like as much as that because what we count as payment is their purchasing from this country goods which they would buy anyway.' I asked why we should want to keep this statement for presentational purposes. Now we want to enter Europe we have obviously got to get used to the idea of having troops there with their families and not keeping them in barracks, at enormous cost, all round our coast. But there we were, it was obvious that we were starting annual negotiations which would end much as they always did and we should get roughly what we usually got.

Cabinet started with Roy. In all the papers, left, right and middle, people are talking about a letter of intent and the pressure the I.M.F. is putting on the British Government.[1] The disintegration of the Government and the palpable series of failures and crises has created more and more of a 1931 atmosphere and everything is being interpreted as a bankers' ramp. I don't think it's the I.M.F. which is really the difficulty, but our own internal economic situation. Here we are with the pound still tottering along the bottom owing to the continuous speculation about the revaluation of the Mark, with exports not going up satisfactorily and with a constant steady improvement in the standard of living, where people are becoming better off and thoroughly discontented. However I think there is some truth in

[1] Speculation continued against the franc and despite an announcement in Bonn on May 9th that the Mark would not be revalued, it was widely believed that after the German General Election in the autumn the government would be unable to resist the pressure to do so. Sterling suffered not only from these uncertainties but also from the instability of Britain's own fortunes. In February the visible trade deficit had risen steeply from £10 million in January to £64 million and it remained high, at £52 million in March and £59 million in April. The Chancellor of the Exchequer was preparing a Letter of Intent to be delivered to the I.M.F. on May 22nd, assessing Britain's economic trends and setting out the action the Government proposed for remedying her position. Labour M.P.s were, as always, worried that Mr Jenkins might have given to the international bankers undertakings that might increase unemployment or cut the level of public expenditure.

what is being said. Roy told us that he will bring the Letter of Intent to Cabinet next week and then publish it.

After this we turned to a long discussion of uprating pension contributions. I had asked for David Ennals to be present and he made an admirable, neat, concise speech. 'How well he does it,' said Roy, but the moment after he had done it everything blew up. All this had come as a complete surprise to me, which only shows how aloof and remote I am getting. In the Management Committee last week we decided that since Barbara's Bill was to be postponed until after the recess, mine should be brought forward and we should publish the uprating Bill possibly on the Wednesday or Thursday of the last week before Whitsun, with a Statement about it. I had assumed this would be so and actually told the Party that I was going to have the Bill and the Statement next week, something which made my colleagues furious. Eddie Shackleton, Tony Crosland and Roy Mason were shouting that there could be no question of Cabinet considering this paper since they had only had it last night and it contained lots of important things concerning the nationalized industries and the Civil Service union. Obviously they had been seething and had ganged up against me. My fiercest opponents were Dick Marsh and Roy Mason, the representatives of the nationalized industries, both of whom dislike and distrust me. Tony Crosland is angry because he is kept out of the Management Committee and, since we parted about the House of Lords, Eddie Shackleton has, I think, got rather hostile to me precisely because he was once so friendly.

It was a most unpleasant meeting and the main reason for the whole Cabinet's objections was revealed when Harold said, 'Oh, dear, what about the Chichester by-election?'[1] Then I knew that was it. I hadn't even known there was a Chichester by-election nor do I think we have the faintest chance of winning it. However, so great had been my boob about the municipal elections, that Cabinet simply wasn't prepared to have this announcement of an Uprating Bill and of increased pension contributions on Wednesday, the eve of poll, or Thursday, the day itself. After a lot of discussion, Harold, who conducted the meeting quite skilfully, finally said that the thing would have to be postponed. Then suddenly he saw a way out. This afternoon we were to have a debate on a vote of censure which the Tories had put down against me.[2] I had assumed that because I would be speaking on the Uprating Bill next week, David Ennals would handle this but Harold now proposed that I should go down to the House and make a speech this evening outlining the principles of the Uprating Bill, giving the full facts which Roy had not given in the budget speech. I should analyse the situation and explain that we were not going to put all the contributions on the flat-rate pension but

[1] Caused by the death in March of Walter Lewis, who had held the seat since 1958. Christopher Chataway was to retain the seat for the Conservatives with a majority of 26,087, on a 17 per cent swing from Labour.

[2] The motion deplored the fact that in the budget speech the Government had announced pensions increases but not the increase in contributions.

that we had to divide it between the flat rate and the graded element and that I should state the problem of dynamizing the pension. Then I should announce that the Bill would be published after the recess. Many of these difficulties stem from Roy's determination to give the good news, the 10*s*. increase in pensions, in his budget but to refuse to put in the teeth and spectacles charges and to make no more than a very short reference to the increase in contributions. Sometimes I wonder whether Roy's reputation is ever going to suffer—we don't have to worry about mine. There I was in Cabinet really in the dog-house. I was being disowned because I had fucked up the announcement of teeth and spectacles and because I had, as they thought, revealed too much to the Party meeting last night. They were taking this out on me but really they were angry about the Management Committee. It was a shattering experience.

I rushed from there to *The Times*, to a lovely flat at the top of the building, where in a cool, placid, academic atmosphere I met long-faced, bespectacled vice-cancellarial Rees-Mogg, my old friend Iverach McDonald, David Wood, bright and perky as ever, John Grant the Defence Correspondent, and young Michael Cudlipp,[1] the son of Percy. I had a good lively talk with them. First of all we discussed the value of memoirs and historical records and then they asked me a great deal about the social relations of the Cabinet. Were we more isolated from each other than Tory Cabinets? Did we have any cliques and groups dining together? I said no, Barbara and I have been friends for a long time but there isn't much community spirit within the Cabinet. I explained to them the whole issue I was going to deal with this afternoon and then back I went to the Department to prepare my speech.

I had very little time because first of all I had to go into the House and hear Harold and then I had to see a delegation from the Royal College of Nurses, full of anxieties about my advisory service. After that I saw a woman who had written me a very charming letter. She claimed to be a secretary in a sub-normal hospital near London who had grave things to tell me. I thought she would be off her head, but no, she had typed out for me a sober analysis of her hospital, which she thought had been one of the best but was now beginning to go sour. She was a splendid girl with a splendid memo and it cheered me no end. But still no speech. David Ennals had said he would try to bash out something with the Department but I only got an inadequate draft forty minutes before I had to go down to the House. tA 7 o'clock we had a vote on a censure motion on Housing,[2] and then straight-

[1] Iverach McDonald, former diplomatic correspondent and Foreign Editor of *The Times*, was the paper's Associate Editor 1967–73. Michael Cudlipp was Senior Deputy Editor of *The Times* 1967–73, Chief Editor of the London Broadcasting Company 1973–4 and Consultant on Public Relations to the N.I. Office 1974–5. He has been Director of Information at the National Enterprise Board since 1975. His father had been Editor of the *Daily Herald* and, later, Political Columnist on the *News Chronicle*.

[2] The Conservative motion deploring the Government's policies on mortgages and house-building was defeated by 266 votes to 217.

away we were on. Balneil got up and I had to answer him. I had written out two or three of the key passages and prepared the rest of my own speech just in note form. I think it was one of my best performances. I did a kind of mini-budget speech, thirty minutes long, laying out the Government's policy and explaining the nature of the crisis, with a competence and skill which I think was pretty praiseworthy. Still, when I got up there were only twenty people on the Tory side and perhaps ten or a dozen on ours and in the last hour there was nobody on the Labour side and eight on the Tory side for what was after all a Tory censure motion on the whole system of national insurance contributions.[1] True, many of them didn't know I was going to speak but it nevertheless shows the amazing lack of interest the Labour Party now has.

I walked home, where I found a very dishevelled man who said that he wanted a photograph. I said, 'Why?' He answered, 'I come from *The Times*.' I said, 'I don't believe you,' but he explained that he was very sorry but they had got him out of bed in his pyjamas because they wanted him to photograph me leaving my house. I knew in a second what they were up to. It was clear at lunchtime the *The Times* was highly critical of Roy and wanted to knife him in the back for having made me the fall guy. They were going to show Crossman leaving his house with his mini-budget. I said, 'Look, you can only take me entering my house.' It was a nice photograph in the end but it wasn't the one they had intended.

Friday, May 16th

I had an excellent press but by the afternoon both evening papers had huge headlines of Crossman in the dog-house and it was clear that my Cabinet colleagues had been actively going round and sedulously working up the story of Cabinet rebuking me and sending me back in disgrace. This was a pity because I had done extremely well on the Floor of the House and we had really prevented the Tories from exploiting the issue. The whole thing would have been excellent if Cabinet had only held its tongue.

I spent the morning trying to tidy up with Clifford Jarrett and David Ennals all the work on the Uprating Bill. The Management Committee's first decision to bring my Bill forward and postpone Barbara's till after Whitsun had meant that my paper couldn't be presented to the Social Services Committee, which was why it had come straight to Cabinet yesterday morning and infuriated all my colleagues. Now the Bill had been postponed the appalling rush was over and we would have time to prepare it for putting to Social Services Committee next Tuesday and for defending ourselves in Cabinet next Thursday. I found Clifford Jarrett a bit bewildered by all this and I realized that he hasn't been a great help to me this week. Whereas in Housing I always had the Dame driving, steering, believing at my side, I now have no Permanent Secretary to do these things. My Private Office is

[1] The censure motion was defeated by 273 votes to 218.

faithful and decent in its devotion but Ron Matthews has no great political intuition. Maybe the mistakes I make are partly due to that.

I went to lunch with Nicholas Davenport and then, after a whole series of minor meetings in the afternoon, I finally caught the 5.38 home. I began to feel terrible with a headache from being battered, so when I got back I plunged into the pool and felt a bit better. I suppose the whole thing had been a tremendous shock, with the Wednesday Party meeting and then on the Thursday my being bashed, doing extremely well in the evening and then bashed again in the press this morning. Yes, it has been a dispiriting time.

Sunday, May 18th

I was really tired when I got down here this weekend and, though I am now back where I was, it disgruntles one, shakes one inside a bit. Here was today's *Sunday Express* delighted to say that the National Executive Committee is going to rebuke me and, despite my having a word with Ivan Yates[1] and seeing Jimmy Margach, the *Observer* and the *Sunday Times* today still have this picture of Cabinet rebuking a senior Minister and sending back a paper for him to do his sums properly. I suspect it's Eddie Shackleton and Tony Crosland who have been busily telling the press all this. This morning when Harold Wilson rang up he asked me who I thought had leaked the whole of last Thursday's Cabinet and given this picture of Crossman. I have been made to look a fool and now I am feeling sorry for myself, which is a most dangerous thing for a politician. I was grateful that Harold didn't sympathize but just began to seek out the causes of the leak. I said to him that I felt fairly angry and he said, 'Fairly angry? I'm spitting with fury. It was outrageous of them to do this to you.' He was his old-fashioned, most loyal self.

I prefer this to Roy who also rang me up this morning and began to talk and talk round the subject, never bringing himself to allude to his unfairness to me. He was clearly trying to be friendly without apologizing and I was rather curt. I began to realize that if Harold is anxious about me, Roy is getting very uneasy lest he has strained my good humour and willingness to carry burdens a bit too far. Throughout this week, as *The Times* and the *Guardian* are discreetly beginning to say, I have been carrying the can for the Chancellor. Still, I have to remember that I have only had a fortnight of this. There are people who have had it week after week. Poor Gordon Walker was increasingly persecuted by the press, with increasingly vindictive comments. What I have had is nothing compared to what Harold or George Brown or Callaghan or Gordon Walker have had to put up with. It is therefore no good being sorry for myself and I have got to shake myself out of it. I have suffered extraordinarily little in these last five years. Perhaps

[1] Ivan Yates was Political Correspondent of the *Evening Standard* before he joined the *Observer* in 1960. He was the *Observer*'s Assistant Editor and Chief Leader Page Editor. He died in February 1975.

this seems the worst knock I have had because it has come when I was near the top of the tree.

The other thing I have to be careful about is my willingness to say I'm going to resign and get out. My life at Prescote here, the farm, my writing, and my children always keep me aware of the possibility of running away. This alternative does make me forget by-elections, does make my feelings about politics remote from ordinary party workers who are working and slaving for me. They, with their faithfulness and desire to see the party doing well, must often be shocked by my liking for the job, for being in Cabinet, and my simultaneous detachment. How much of the ideals and emotions of the party do I still share? I have been thinking about this since the dinner party we had on Saturday evening for David and Marilyn Butler and John Hodgkin, the Labour Party agent for Banbury, and his new wife. We had a gay and amusing evening and I told them a great many anecdotes and instructed them all in Cabinet government. I wasn't defeatist in any normal sense but when they drove off at midnight I couldn't help wondering what they had thought. I knew that David and Marilyn would think I was in good form and enjoying life despite the hopeless situation, but what about John Hodgkin? He is a quiet, extremely intelligent man, who was obviously buoying himself up and trying to believe in the victory of the party, but perhaps he felt, 'What has that fellow got for us, and why is he still in the party? He is a rich man, living in that magnificent house with his swimming bath and his wonderful new furniture. Hasn't he floated away from the party altogether? Isn't he just there as a professional politician. Is there only a vestigial remnant of former socialist fire in that man's belly?' No, I don't think so. I am detached because I am near the end but I am no more detached than Roy who is not near the end and who might lead the party, and I am no more detached than Tony Crosland, who seems to me not much nearer the party than I am. I suppose in certain ways, through the W.E.A. ideology, for example, or in length of time, I am much nearer than Roy and Tony, who don't seem to me to share either the emotions or the thinking of the Left. I do that intellectually but it is in my personality that I am getting more comfortable and more detached and that, I think, is what puts people off and makes the Parliamentary Party so angry. When they meet me I am frightening and argumentative, yet remote and disconcerting.

Well, we are entering a difficult week for me, but I ought to be able to get through it. If I can get through Monday without too much trouble the Government should get through till Thursday and then on Thursday we are off to Italy for our holiday. Barbara is tremendously keen to keep it secret that we are going on Charles Forte's yacht, so we are simply saying that we are going to a villa near Rome. The children are getting excited too. We have had tremendous thunderstorms today and after weeks of drought we now have rain but the corn is growing. It is a lovely night outside.

Monday, May 19th

I had my Question Time and in fact I handled all the seventy or eighty Questions with pretty good skill. Nevertheless it was a balls-up! I now see that part of the trouble is that for two months I have been short of a Parliamentary Secretary. Bea Serota is wonderful and awfully good in the Department but of course she can give me no help in the Commons and indeed she is a positive minus there because the Labour M.P.s are so jealous of her having the job. So with that and with Julian away I am the only person dealing with the whole Health side. True, David Ennals does lift a burden off my shoulders on Social Security, where he has been magnificent, absolutely first-rate – clever, shrewd, ambitious and competent. Despite this, there is no doubt that I made a great mistake in thinking I could carry the Health load alone. As my Private Office bluntly put it to me, I have been working too hard and was almost bound to have the fall I most certainly got. Paul Dean got up and said it was absolute folly to raise £3½ million more in health charges and then hand it over to the educational services.[1] I replied, 'It would be folly if it was done. But any Minister who attempted to do this would be forbidden to do it by his Permanent Secretary. Therefore I would advise the Hon. Gentleman not to believe in something it is said I did.' Then Shirley Summerskill got up, 'Would my Rt Hon. Friend bear in mind that he gives the impression of somebody whose left hand does not know what his other left hand is doing? Are we to take it as a precedent that the National Health Service now has so much money that it can afford to give it to another Government Department?' 'That', I answered, 'would be the wrong conclusion to draw from my answer to Question No. 33.' That was all I said, a glimpse of the obvious, and the only mistake I made was to say Permanent Secretary when I meant Permanent Secretary and Accounting Officer,[2] but there it was, I'd boobed again. I was in the middle of a typhoon of attack, egged on by the back benchers who immediately went out to feed the press.

All day after Questions I lay low. Fortunately this evening the Czech Embassy had invited me to see a travelling company doing a rather ingenious miming show with lights and shades, so I crept away and hid myself pretty thoroughly.

[1] Conservative M.P. for Somerset North since 1964. He was Parliamentary Under-Secretary of State at the D.H.S.S. 1970–4.

[2] The Permanent Secretary is the Accounting Officer for the Department and must show the Comptroller and Auditor-General's office and, if necessary, the Public Accounts Committee that funds have been spent on the programmes for which they were voted. At the end of Question Time, however, Stephen Hastings, Conservative M.P. for Mid-Bedfordshire, asked the Speaker for a Standing Order No. 9 debate to discuss Crossman's answer, which, he alleged, stated that Permanent Under-Secretaries could forbid Ministers to take certain courses of action. The Speaker refused the request. (*House of Commons Debates*, Vol. 784, cols 9–10.)

Tuesday, May 20th

Huge headlines in today's papers, Calamity Dick, Muck-up, Disaster. At Management Committee I was item number one. How was I to be rescued? Considering the fact that my colleagues quite like seeing people in the soup, they were not unfriendly and I got some support. They had to admit that they had urged me to explain the thing to the Party and to try to educate them in the language of priorities and they agreed it had all come unstuck. But I had got a phenomenally bad press, Dick who always drops clangers, Crossman the intellectual who is always wrong, and I knew I had plunged even further into unpopularity. A Question on me had been put down for this afternoon and I said I thought it was essential for Harold to answer it. He said that he couldn't deal with the matter, really, I suppose because he felt he couldn't manage an irate House of Commons. He said he would deal with it in the T.V. broadcast he was doing tonight and that he would also give a Written Answer, a combination which would cope with the topic. I must say I was extremely dubious about this and insisted that if it failed he should answer another Question on Thursday. This he agreed to do. But I had very little faith that I was going to get away with it.

Then we went on to the Industrial Relations Bill, where we had our first really frank discussion. I told Harold it wasn't good enough to say that the Government was going to do this and if the Party defeated us the Government would go down. It wasn't necessarily true, somebody else might be called upon to be Prime Minister, and that would give Callaghan his chance. Harold said, 'Brinkmanship is essential; we have to push it right up to the edge.' So we spelt out the five possibilities and they are all down absolutely clearly in the minutes. One: not to legislate in the current session. Two: to introduce a Bill containing penal clauses in relation to union disputes but omitting the conciliation pause and the fining of strikers. Three: to introduce a Bill containing the penal clauses about the conciliation pause but saying they would be deferred for a specified minimum period and could be further deferred as the T.U.C. proved itself capable of exercising its own authority. Four: to introduce in the current session a Bill to incorporate . . .[1] Four and Five, however, were agreed to be impracticable.

After a long discussion we agreed that as we couldn't really stop the Bill, the only two possibilities were either, two, to introduce a Bill without the conciliation pause or, three, to introduce a Bill with the pause but with power to postpone its coming into effect. Harold, Barbara and Roy all wanted to go for number three. The Chief Whip and I went for number two. Bob Mellish, who is a yapping terrier, at least speaks up and he is coming out in his true colours. He just said, 'You won't get anything except a Bill without the conciliation pause because, after all when the unions have approved the T.U.C.'s new policy you will find that the penal clauses will

[1] Crossman appears to have decided that the fourth and fifth possibilities did not deserve description.

seem to be a worse alternative and even on the merits of the case we wouldn't be able to persuade the Parliamentary Party to do it.' We argued this at length but, as the minutes show, at the end we decided the Government would face a choice between the second and third courses.

> On merits the third course may be judged preferable but the final decision must depend to some extent on the degree to which dissident elements in the P.L.P. were satisfied that the T.U.C. would acquiesce in the Bill in whatever form it was finally introduced. The discussion with the T.U.C. on the following day might clarify this point, particularly if they and their supporters in the P.L.P. realise that continuing intransigence might make it impossible for the Government to carry on. Meanwhile it was essential that there should be no overt indication that the Government were contemplating alternative courses of action or were prepared to compromise to any extent on their published proposals.

That was it. Michael Stewart, Denis Healey, Roy Jenkins, Barbara Castle and Fred Peart are all solid with Harold. I am not solid with Harold and neither is Bob Mellish.

On my way out to lunch at the German Embassy with Helmut Schmidt I heard that Douglas Houghton had just issued a statement to the press denouncing me for attacking him in the House yesterday.[1] I must say I found this absolutely outrageous. I had only said in answer to Paul Dean that I would advise the Hon. Gentleman not to believe in something it is said I did. Douglas Houghton said that in my answer I had refuted the account of the Parliamentary Party meeting which he had given to the press. Of course I was refuting not that but the false version given in a certain number of papers and given by Shirley Summerskill. However, the fat was in the fire and once more we had banner headlines, Crossman Disowned by Houghton. Houghton was also at the German Embassy, and I took him aside, and made it perfectly clear I hadn't been attacking him. I said, 'You really might have held your fire.' He saw Mellish and the Prime Minister alone later this afternoon and they must have taken violent action because by the end of the day he had withdrawn his remark.

This afternoon was the key meeting of the Social Services Committee on the National Superannuation Bill. I managed to hold the meeting to order and we got the whole of our dynamizing proposals through intact in two hours, quite an achievement. We then got on to the second item, what we should do about the Seebohm Committee's Report in the months before the decisions were taken on the Maud Report. Could we at the end of July

[1] Helmut Schmidt has been Vice-Chairman of the West German Social Democratic Party since 1968. He was Minister of Defence 1969–72, Minister of Finance and Economics 1972 and Minister of Finance 1972–4, and has been Chancellor of the Federal Republic of Germany since 1974.

make a Statement on Seebohm, as Callaghan and I wanted? George Thomson, the Chairman of the Committee dealing with Local Government Reform, said it was impossible to commit ourselves to anything in Seebohm until we had undertaken careful consultation about Maud. That knocked out any Statement in July and we could also say goodbye to any legislation for the next session. I had the further difficulty of having to point out that if we were to make a Statement on Seebohm it would have to include a Statement on the Green Paper on the *Future of the National Health Service* and that we would have to repudiate the tentative suggestions Maud was going to make for bringing health under local government control. Most of my colleagues, of course, weren't prepared to repudiate Maud's recommendation before they had seen it and I couldn't blame them. Callaghan and I were utterly defeated and again I had received another blow.

By the evening, my God, I was in an even lower state as I sat in my room to look at the Prime Minister's broadcast. In forty-five minutes' cross-examination by Robert McKenzie, Harold was at the top of his smooth, professional form. I admit I fell asleep during the middle bit about liquidity, but not before he had defended me very generously and satisfactorily. He knocked the whole thing on the head, describing it as a mere press stunt and following this up with the redrafted Written Answer which was to be in Hansard tonight. The attack on me was dead and I had to admit that he had kept his word. I thought, 'There's our Harold, at his best in this kind of thing.' In such practical matters he knows how to do what I am quite unable to do. He was extremely adroit. People thought he looked tired and worn out but I didn't. I suppose I see him too close. I thought he looked a very professional politician, a bit too professional. He's become rather like his caricatures, a round, complacent, 'statesmanlike' figure, but it was a terrific performance and it will put a bit of morale back into the Parliamentary Party.

Wednesday, May 21st

I had a slightly better press and suddenly I felt the typhoon had blown itself out, as indeed it had. So I'm O.K., provided I don't put my foot in it again, and provided I keep steady, don't overwork, keep my nerve and make sure that when Julian Snow comes back he takes his fair share so that I can relax and sit back a bit. Provided all these things happen, I shan't have done myself irreparable harm, though of course one result is that this has completely knocked out any idea of my being a substitute or alternative to Callaghan as Harold's successor. Michael Foot's idea has utterly gone. Even those who defend me will say, 'Dick has these odd lapses and this arrogance of manner and he has created this deep suspicion of himself.' It is a fact that all the old suspicion of me has now revived and, that being so, I am clean out. It's really an enormous relief. I am free. People accept it. Though there wasn't really any chance at the time, the Left had thought about it,

I am told, but they also knew it was impossible to persuade anybody else to have me.

The first thing I had this morning was an irate Peter Brown saying that I must cancel my holiday to stay and make a great speech this weekend. He had misjudged the effect of the Prime Minister's broadcast and he was completely wrong. The real fact is that I can't afford to say another damned thing because then I could be accused of having Crossman version three, version four, version five, and the press would find differences and inconsistencies whatever happened. The best thing for me is to put my head down, say nothing and get off for a fortnight.

I had a fairly full day, with a big meeting on the care of the elderly and on an eighteen-month campaign for domiciliary services. It was a difficult meeting but I think I was fairly tactful. I simply said I wanted to have seminars set up and so we got on with that. Next came lunch with Julian Snow, back from hospital. He is very lucky to be here at all. He has a slight limp but his stroke doesn't seem to have affected his mind which wasn't very good anyway. Next I went down to Fred Peart's room, dear old Fred, who let me down so terribly at the beginning of my fiasco on teeth and spectacles. He has been fairly friendly to me since. Barbara and I worked out with him the relationship between the Uprating Bill and the Industrial Relations Bill, and how to time the two of them. Bob Mellish came in late and in a fairly reasonable way we examined the problems of June and July and saw that we will be running well into August unless the Industrial Relations Bill can be got through reasonably fast. I think it will have to go upstairs. If it is on the Floor of the House with a guillotine we shall have terrible trouble, so we want to send it upstairs, guillotine it and take the Uprating Bill on the Floor.

Then to the Prices and Incomes Committee, where, thank God, Bea Serota came and we got the nurses' crisis out of the way. After that I escaped to the Hilton Hotel for dinner with the C.B.I. I was the only member of the Government there. On the one side was the Chairman, and on the other Ted Heath, who was making the big speech. I was pretty subdued and depressed by now but fortunately Denis Coe had arranged a meeting for me with members of the Social Services back-bench group, so I was able to slip out before Heath's speech and come back to the House. I found my room full, with about twelve of them, a good cross-section, and Douglas Houghton in the chair. David Ennals and I briefed them as fully as we possibly could on the presentation of the new contribution levels and we did a bit of fence mending on the pension increases. We had been terribly caught with our pants down by not seeing the Health group or briefing them at all on teeth and spectacles so I was glad that we did a decent job this evening. I am hoping we shall be able to handle things better after the recess when we come back to the P.L.P. to discuss the new National Insurance contributions.

Thursday, May 22nd

Today we were to go on holiday, though the children and Anne had been waiting and wondering whether we should be able to get away. Harold had insisted that Barbara should have her fortnight's holiday, although at Management Committee he had made it clear that talks would have to go on while she was away and I rather thought she might be summoned back. However here we were. I had already packed my stuff at Prescote last Sunday and today I just had a Cabinet in the morning and a Cabinet in the afternoon.

The first item, rather characteristically, was a report on the strike in the Stationery Office, which had been holding up publication of Government papers and might hold up the publication of the Maud Report. Then we came to Northern Ireland, where the great crisis has been suddenly relaxed as the result of the disappearance of O'Neill and the coming of the much tougher Chichester-Clark. He has ganged up with Brian Faulkner,[1] another reactionary. As often happens, the reactionary may be able to push through a progressive policy, so Northern Ireland seems to have disappeared into the background again. The next major problem was the reorganization of Upper Clyde Shipbuilders. It had started with George Brown taking over Fairfield's in his happier 1966 days and now they have been sucking in more and more government subsidies and the battle has developed between Jack Diamond and Tony Wedgwood Benn. The battle was barked out in Cabinet and Tony seemed to me to have the right of it. He has been doing a great job, going up there and batting for the Government, but still trying to prevent our having 10,000 unemployed.

Then we got on to the discussion about the I.R. Bill. The first part, about the non-controversial clauses, hardly mattered but after that we came to the crisis. For the first time the Management Committee were listening to the rest of the Cabinet. It was obvious that Tony Crosland was absolutely unregenerate and indeed he made it perfectly clear that he wanted to see the penal clauses postponed. Dick Marsh was also fairly certain that this wouldn't get through the P.L.P. and that it seemed to be insane to pick this quarrel. James Callaghan, of course, was biding his time. He begins to see, I think, a genuine possibility of becoming Prime Minister this summer, simply by waiting for Barbara, Harold and Roy to kill themselves. So he didn't play a particularly vigorous part and other people didn't declare themselves very much either. I didn't get a clear picture of George Thomson.

[1] Brian Faulkner was Unionist M.P. for East Down in the Parliament of Northern Ireland, 1949–73, Unionist Member for South Down in the Northern Ireland Assembly 1973–5 and Unionist Party of Northern Ireland Member for South Down in the Northern Ireland Constitutional Convention 1975. He was Government Chief Whip and Parliamentary Secretary at the Ministry of Finance 1956–9, Minister of Home Affairs 1959–63, Minister of Commerce 1963–9 and of Development 1969–71 and Prime Minister and Minister of Home Affairs 1971–2. He became a life peer in January 1977 but ten days after he joined the Lords he was killed in a riding accident.

Peter Shore sounded dubious, so did Cledwyn Hughes and Roy Mason. Shackleton, as he had told me beforehand, was highly dubious. Wedgy Benn and Tony Greenwood were careful. Altogether, it was a doubtful meeting and when he summed up the discussion the Prime Minister said that, 'The Cabinet would be invited to consider the proposed legislation afresh, and in detail, after the special Congress of the T.U.C. and in the light of the further discussions which would then follow between the General Council, the First Secretary and himself.' So we left it very open.

The other thing was a question I asked about Roy Jenkins's Letter of Intent, which I have no doubt whatever will be harmless. Roy has worked very hard with the I.M.F. and he has got a Letter which he is able to publish perfectly straightforwardly, with nothing difficult in it except an exclusion of import controls. Nevertheless, there is a growing feeling that we are in for a period of increased unemployment and deflation as a result of this Letter, unless we initiate a new policy like floating the pound. But we got nothing out of Cabinet this morning on that.

In the afternoon Cabinet at 4 o'clock we had to deal with the Uprating Bill and here I had an unexpected battle. I had got it through Social Services successfully where we had the officials and the people who knew about it but now people were attacking it because they have been left out of the discussions. I thought Barbara took things a good long way in leading the opposition. She and James Callaghan led an attack upon the whole principle of the White Paper and the whole National Insurance concept. They simply said it was outrageous to charge the workers the cost of these increased pensions and it ought to go on the employers' contributions. I must say I got pretty angry with Barbara for this. If it's put on the employers it is put on the cost of living. When I remember her attitude to putting one halfpenny on school milk! She couldn't possibly do it because of the cost of living and here she was proposing exactly that. Of course she doesn't really believe in the earnings-related pensions scheme and I had her whipping up emotion against the Bill, saying it was impossible and intolerable. Callaghan was asking why we couldn't put the increase on the Exchequer, or alternatively on the employers, and why it was that in his winding up speech on the budget Roy had committed us to this without consultation with Cabinet. It's a fair question and here Cabinet was reacting against the whole Industrial Relations Bill and the new Management Committee. We conceded to them on contributions and they chose a solution which keeps down the lowest level at the cost of higher rates at the top level. I didn't particularly mind that. Dynamizing I got through, at least in principle, and I was enormously grateful to Eddie Shackleton here, who stood by my side at the Social Services Committee and then at Cabinet. He fought loyally with me on this and if he had been against me the fat would have been in the fire. (He says he still wants to see me as P.M. when Harold goes.)

Then I was able to rush back to Vincent Square where Anne and the children were waiting and in appalling rush-hour traffic we got off to the airport. There were Ted and Barbara. We couldn't go to a V.I.P. lounge because, as Barbara had pointed out, there have been new rules and on a private trip like this we would now have had to pay £17 for the privilege. So, with no difficulty at all, we went through the airport and on to the plane.

Friday, May 23rd—Friday, June 6th

When we got to Rome last night there were two cars waiting for us and a very sleek Café Royal waiter, Gino, who had been specially flown out to look after us. Within twelve minutes we had been motored to a tiny little port and we were on board prowling round exploring this gorgeous vessel, with a splendid cabin in the front with a double bed for Barbara and Ted and for Anne and me a nice little room with a bed each and a four-bunk cabin for the two children. Perfect it was and it fitted us like a glove. We had this beautiful yacht and three seamen, Giovanni the captain, Renato and the cook, plus Gino. It sounds wonderful and for the first two or three days it is. You then discover that the boat is so valuable that unless there is absolutely no wind there is practically nowhere you can anchor and, even when the weather is perfect and you are anchored off-shore, there are very few ideal moorings for fear of the treacherous coast and the totally unpredictable winds. You can start with a fine morning and get within two hours a sirocco blowing and a grey, overcast sky, the colour drained out of it. The yacht was ridiculously expensive, a toy which cost Charles Forte a fortune. We had wonderful food, wonderful drink, every comfort laid on. But I think myself that an hotel and a car give you infinitely more mobility than a boat. Nevertheless it was tremendous fun to do it, as all the family agreed.

Off we sailed into the Mediterranean towards the island of Ponza, for four days' wandering round the remote islands of the archipelago, in lovely weather and exquisite water. On about the fourth day Barbara revealed her plans. She had told me on the first day that she had to fly back on Sunday, June 1st, to Chequers for secret talks with a few trade union leaders, so that we would have to be in Naples in time for her to catch the morning plane and she would be ready to come back on the Monday afternoon. Gradually over the next few days she revealed that she had warned Harold about not blackguarding people or threatening them with resignation. She said that she and Harold and Roy, who was slightly tied in with them, must be prepared to resign if the Bill was so emasculated that their position was undermined and that it was Harold's duty to tell people this bluntly. I warned her of the results because the moment it is known that they are prepared to resign and let somebody else be invited by the Queen to form a Labour Government with a majority of 100, it gives Crosland and Callaghan their chance. Crosland would take the Chancellorship if Roy goes. A Callaghan–Crosland Government would not be able to win the next election but it would be a government which could go to the next election with a united Labour Party, the trade unions and Transport House on our side. So I had to say, 'If you put the Parliamentary Party up against the choice of splitting with the T.U.C. or of losing you and Harold and Roy, I have no doubt that the majority would choose not to break with the T.U.C.' She had a couple of sleepless nights but I got it into her mind before she left.

The other thing which came out in the course of our conversation was that she had managed to persuade herself that the I.R. Bill is not the problem. The real difficulty is the Uprating Bill, this outrageous Bill, as she said at one point, that will break the Party and which we ought never to have allowed. She means by this, of course, not only the present Uprating Bill but the whole of our new pensions reform. This is partly a rationalization because she wants to put on to me the cause of our unpopularity. It's ironical that, as she knows, I have thought ever since last January that her whole strategy of going ahead and challenging the T.U.C. is insane, while she has thought ever since last January that the whole of the National Superannuation Scheme is insane, and here we were, with our families, together on a yacht for a fortnight, the two members of the Cabinet most deeply committed to two measures each of which is condemned by the other as fatal and catastrophic.

All week there was a tremendous fuss about how Barbara was to get back. She had been given an elaborate code, with the Prime Minister, for example, as Lion and herself as Peacock and me as Owl and members of the T.U.C. General Council as different animals, all tremendous fun, no doubt, for the Civil Service. They only forgot one thing, to make any contact with the consulate at Naples, through whom all communications had to come. So at the very last moment on Saturday, May 31st, she rang the vice-consul and he was there on Sunday morning to help her off the boat on to a little, slow, trundling special plane, which had been sent out by the R.A.F. to Naples.

Since the previous Tuesday we had been anchored off Ischia, a great island with a mountain nearly 1,000 feet high which Barbara and Ted and I climbed. God, it was rough scrambling on a terribly hot day. We bathed from the boat, anchored off all these lovely islands. They are intensively cultivated still, with plenty of vines, lemons and oranges. The men who man the Italian navy and merchant marine retire early to live there on their little lemon farms. All Sunday we went over to Baia, to see the magnificent Roman thermal baths and we had a wonderful time prowling through the cave of the Sibyl at Cumae. We saw Lake Avernus and all week I was reading Robert Graves's *I Claudius* and Norman Douglas's *South Wind*, two splendid books which I enormously enjoyed.[1]

On Monday we went to the Aquarium and saw a magnificent collection

[1] Lake Avernus was believed by the Ancients to be the entrance to the underworld.

of fishes and turtles and every kind of undersea growth from the Bay of Naples while we waited for Barbara. When she came back we visited an hotel at Castellammare di Stabia, the Roman town nearest to Vico Equense, and that evening we bathed off the hotel beach on the Sorrento peninsula. It was like a rocky Riviera, handsome but severe. As far as I could gather, Harold and Barbara's talks on Sunday were with Scanlon and Jack Jones, plus John Newton,[1] Chairman of the General Council this year, and Vic Feather. It seemed that nothing happened except to confirm everything her critics had warned her of. Scanlon and Jones were perfectly clear that they were not prepared to co-operate in any way with the Government and would do everything possible to wreck it if we went ahead with any penal clauses whatsoever. So they confirmed the hard line. According to her, they were still friendly and pleasant but that doesn't matter.[2] As I said to her, the point was that the Government had not been able to move them an inch. This meeting was just before the special T.U.C. Conference, where it was clear that the General Council would receive a far higher degree of support than anybody would have thought possible.

However, after the others had left, the Prime Minister and Barbara had had a word together. They decided to send Vic Feather a letter insisting on a tightening up of the T.U.C. General Council's position with regard to disciplining unofficial strikers. We then spent a lot of time drafting this letter and telephoning with our yachting code. The letter was to be sent before the Congress took place in an attempt to influence them. I thought it was impossible to make the T.U.C. consider this but it was what Harold and Barbara had already decided and virtually committed themselves to. The other thing we talked about was nerve. Barbara said to me that the greatest quality in politics is good nerves. I said, 'I'm not so sure, Barbara. I think it's good nerves and wisdom, because brinkmanship without any wisdom can bring you to catastrophe.' One of her troubles is that she thinks she has got to go right to the brink and then the T.U.C. will finally give way. Well, it is my considered opinion that over the last two months the T.U.C. has completely out-manoeuvred the Prime Minister and Barbara. The T.U.C. have made concessions at the right time and put themselves in the right with the Parliamentary Party, and they can almost dictate their terms. I don't think Barbara and Harold have any bargaining position now

[1] John Newton was General Secretary of the National Union of Tailors and Garment Workers until 1970.

[2] According to Mr Wilson's own account:

> they warned us against an excessive preoccupation with unofficial strikes. As power shifted more and more from the centre, they said, there would be more ferment at factory level. This would be exacerbated by the fact of the legislation, and would lead to greater and, they argued, irresistible pressure to turn local unofficial action into officially recognised disputes.

Hugh Scanlon also warned that any fines imposed would be met by sympathetic demonstrations. See *Wilson*, p. 654.

because, if they ask us to pass a Bill which means a complete break with the T.U.C. and also with Transport House, I doubt whether they have the P.L.P. behind them or even, in the last resort, the Cabinet.

On Tuesday we went to Herculaneum, fascinating in its detail and much better than Pompeii. By this time the weather had broken and it was cooler and by the time we got to Capri on Wednesday the weather was foul until the sun came out for a wonderful walk up to the Emperor Tiberius's palace at the Villa Iovis out on a headland. Just by making that walk I could believe every word of Tacitus's *Annals* and the description of what happened to Tiberius and what he did. Thursday, our last day, was deplorable, with hailstorms and showers and there wasn't really very much we could do. On Friday the young vice-consul looked after us, sending us in three cars in a fantastic hailstorm to the airport, where we were packed on to an Italian plane to Milan. There we had a three-hour wait before we got on to a new Trident and in an hour and a half we landed in London in beautiful sunny weather. This time I was able to go to the V.I.P. lounge because David Ennals wanted to see me and within minutes there was Barbara in one corner with her civil servants and I on the other side busy with David on the Uprating Bill. I went back with him to John Adam Street for a relaxed time with Clifford Jarrett and Miss Riddelsdell, sorting things out before I took the 5.35 back to Prescote, where I have been ever since.

We arrived home in the gorgeous June weather and at the front door I breathed the air laden with the scent of may. When it comes the English summer is far more beautiful than the Neapolitan summer but I am glad to have been there. See Naples and die; well, I could see an awful lot of things afterwards. It's a hard, cruel place, an area which rich men have used as their playground since 100 B.C. It's overpopulated, the rich are very rich, the poor are very poor and the weather is totally erratic. Nevertheless we all felt infinitely better. I had been worn out before the recess and it took me a week to recover. I am afraid I was difficult and abrasive during that time and easily annoyed and upset. I don't think I could really help it and now I certainly feel infinitely more ready for the fray.

Saturday, June 7th

I have had a little talk with Bob Mellish about the Uprating Bill. I have now discovered that we have got to have Callaghan's Bill on the Parliamentary Boundary Commission,[1] to deal with London and the ten or

[1] The House of Commons (Redistribution of Seats) Bill. By the terms of an all-party agreement of 1958 the Parliamentary Boundary Commission reported every fifteen years on the realignment of parliamentary constituency boundaries that demographic shifts had made necessary. According to the agreement the Home Secretary was required in 1969 to lay before both Houses Orders implementing the Commission's recommendations 'as soon as may be'. The Government feared that the changes might put at risk as many as thirty Labour seats and as early as May 1966 some Ministers had wondered how the most injurious of the Commission's recommendations might be postponed. Their solution was

twelve urgent constituencies so that we can avoid dealing with the rest. As this will have to be shoved in the business managers want to put the Uprating Bill upstairs. We talked about this and then discussed the Industrial Relations Bill. Bob takes entirely my view and thinks it's absolutely impractical. The T.U.C. Congress has now approved the General Council's policy by overwhelming majorities,[1] and in his view it would be impossible to get any sensible members of the centre or right of the Party, let alone of the left, to go to war against the T.U.C. and fight on the penal clauses and the conciliation pause, neither of which are very effective. Now the Tories have joined in and are pointing out the rag-bag mess of Barbara's Bill, which really seems only designed to save the reputations of Roy, Barbara and Harold. At tomorrow's Management Committee meeting I have no doubt that six of them will be saying that we must go ahead and I shall be the only one who will not because Bob Mellish has not been invited. However I shall be speaking for a sufficiently large minority of Cabinet and, I am sure, for a sufficiently large minority of the Parliamentary Party to make a guillotine on the I.R. Bill impossible, which really means to stop the Bill going through at all.

Sunday, June 8th

We are having the most perfect June weather here. I spent the morning with the Makepeaces and then at midday Charles and Mary came over and they all stayed to lunch.[2] I went off on the 4.40 for this evening's critical Management Committee meeting but I looked in first for a meal with Bea Serota and then went on to the Prime Minister at 8 o'clock. We had a three-hour discussion of the new tactic Harold wanted. He believed that the thing to do was to insist that if we were going to have no legislation on a conciliation pause with penalties the T.U.C. itself must write the same enforcements into its rules and take it upon itself to compel trade unions to intervene in unconstitutional strikes. Barbara and he were hoping for this and we talked for a long time about it. I must say I was dubious the whole way through because I know we are missing a great opportunity. Last Thursday the T.U.C.

---

to postpone for all but the most seriously anachronistic constituencies the introduction of new boundaries until the local government reforms recommended by the Maud Report had been implemented. See Vols I and II.

[1] The General Council's own proposals *Programme for Action*, published on May 19th, gave the Council new powers to intervene in strikes, with binding authority over the unions involved. Affiliated unions were to be obliged to notify the T.U.C. of any unofficial stoppage. Failure to accept a recommendation from the T.U.C. could lead to a union's suspension or disaffiliation. All the unions had accepted these proposals but as the Prime Minister had indicated to the T.U.C. representatives there was no 'follow through, no specific programme of action'. (*Wilson*, pp. 650–1.) At the Croydon Conference on June 5th there was an overwhelming vote against the Government's industrial relations proposals, including a vote of 8,252,000 to 359,000 against the principle of penal sanctions. Hugh Scanlon also suggested that if the Bill became law the unions would be prepared to consider industrial action against it.

[2] John Makepeace is a furniture designer and his wife, Ann, a craftsman in textiles. They lived near the Crossmans in Oxfordshire and designed some of the furniture at Prescote.

approved by an enormous majority a new programme of action far and above anything we thought possible not only six months or six years ago but six weeks ago. Barbara and Harold had achieved this by their tactic of going right up to the edge. I felt this was the moment for them to say to the trade unions, 'You've done very well and with this we can drop the short Bill and the whole idea of penal legislation for a year. We'll push the Bill back for a year and see how things get on.' But there was no question of that. The P.M. and Barbara took the view that although the trade unions were giving us sufficient T.U.C. sanction on inter-union disputes, their attitude on unconstitutional strikes was vague, and that as Jack Jones and Scanlon clearly didn't want to do anything else, we had to come back at them. The letter Barbara had drafted in Italy had not been sent but its substance had been published on the Friday morning after the Congress, confirming the specific pressure that was being put on the General Council to increase its authority to take disciplinary action in the case of unconstitutional strikes. Moreover, even before Barbara returned to Italy on June 2nd the D.E.P. had come back to the unions with a statement and the P.M. had followed it up with a statement in a speech yesterday. Today they were at it again, pushing further towards the brink. I also doubted whether the T.U.C. could go any further than they had at the Congress or that we could extract from them further concessions that would have to be confirmed at their annual Conference in September.

I was out of sympathy with Harold and Barbara, but at the Management Committee five of my colleagues were backing the Prime Minister. Peart and I had been impressed by the Chief Whip's warning but the others were not so firm and were anxious for a settlement. We were clearly outweighed this evening and the Prime Minister got what he wanted for his meeting with the trade unions first thing tomorrow morning. Management Committee gave him agreement for further negotiations.

Monday, June 9th

While the Prime Minister was seeing the T.U.C. this morning, I had to go to Social Services Committee to see if I could make a kind of comeback on my Uprating Bill. It wasn't too difficult because I only had to report to the Committee on dynamizing the graded pension and on the difficulties that had been encountered by the Ministry of Power with regard to the nationalized industries and by Eddie Shackleton with regard to the Civil Service. Only if these difficulties were insuperable would we be disallowed our package announcement for tomorrow. It was pretty obvious that nobody would dare to disallow it and I got the thing through.

We also had a meeting on the Maud Report. I had just had enough time to glance at it and get some idea that it was a disappointing document. The idea of the city region had been compromised and watered down to an almost indefensible structure and in certain ways Derek Senior's minority report,[1] though perhaps impracticable as an alternative, is a deadly criticism of the weakness of Maud. It is criticism on two points, the weakness of the actual units Maud has created and the hopeless sacrificing of the city regions and, secondly, the futility of Maud's provincial council and his ghostly local councils down below. I think this is pretty poor but the Prime Minister has got it into his head that we must be seen to be actively implementing Maud. This morning we met to approve a draft Statement which the Prime Minister wanted to make on the day after tomorrow. We were sitting under the chairmanship of George Thomson. (It is significant that a Scot has been put in as Chairman of a Committee dealing with the Royal Commission's Report on England but of course this is simply because he has nothing else to do and Harold had completely forgotten that he promised that Kenneth Robinson would be dealing with this Bill.) It was fascinating to see Harold's draft. I had seen the original officials' draft but this was very different, committing us to approve Maud in principle and, instead of saying that we can't legislate in this Parliament, leaving things open. Speed, speed first and foremost and with the speed the commitments.

It is clear that the Prime Minister's view is largely influenced by the issue of the Boundary Commission and that therefore he wants us to accept Maud immediately and get on with the job of reforming local government. I don't say that he doesn't also want to show that he is modernizing but certainly he needs this narrow party advantage. We had to water down the draft Harold put forward and say, 'This really won't do. We can't go as far as this and accept Maud overnight without considering it more carefully.' All this will go to Cabinet on Thursday.

At 2.30 Management Committee met again to consider what Harold had achieved with the trade unions this morning. It was quite clear that he had got nothing more than an agreement to negotiate further. Mellish was present and he strengthened my position a little as we considered the three possibilities. One: the T.U.C. rewriting their own rules. Two: strengthening our own legislation but removing the penal clauses, which is more or less what I thought we would get. Three: a cold storage Bill, i.e. penal clauses but not to be put into practice for at least a year, which I thought was out of the question anyway.[2] We really had to decide between one and two.

[1] A member of the *Manchester Guardian* editorial staff 1937–60. His Memorandum of Dissent, published as Vol. II of the Royal Commission's Report, recommended a predominantly two-tier system of 35 directly elected regional authorities and 148 directly elected district authorities (which would be responsible for the Health Service). This administrative structure would be complemented by directly elected common councils and 5 provincial councils, with members nominated by the regional authorities within their areas. Mr Senior proposed that the educational service should be transferred to central government but that local authorities should be responsible for all branches of the Health Service.

[2] This was a scheme for a Bill which would grant powers to the Government but not put them into immediate effect. Like Part IV of the Prices and Incomes Act, such powers could only be applied after Parliamentary approval had been given.

At 4 o'clock the three possibilities were presented to Cabinet. Nobody spoke out at all because the Prime Minister was merely asking to be permitted to put these ideas to the T.U.C. and try to get them through. Since all this was on the clear understanding that there would be no Cabinet commitment Harold didn't find it difficult. Cabinet was very piano. He worked hard to extract opinions from everyone but me, which was unusual but characteristic, since he knew what my opinion was. He tried to get Cabinet support but what he got was acquiescence without enthusiasm. Denis and Roy were stalwart, Michael gave unqualified support to a strong line and then there were Barbara and Harold but, apart from these, nobody else was for the strong line. I kept my mouth shut and nobody outside Management Committee spoke. It was all long and all boring.

Tuesday, June 10th

We had two interesting subjects at O.P.D. First of all, Malaya. Denis Healey had himself written the directives for the Canberra Conference of Australia, New Zealand, Singapore and Malaya on our withdrawal and on future policy. Everything is going perfectly smoothly, there is not the least shock at our withdrawal and it is all being taken for granted. What alarmed me when I read the papers was the elaborate preparations for a jungle warfare training school, which we were to virtually take over and run for ourselves, with our troops, ships and aeroplanes going out there every year. This seemed to me very like having a presence so I was delighted when Roy came right in before I could and pointed out that this was more than just a capability. It was one of those cases where something really important was said in committee and since Roy and I were saying it strongly it meant that Denis and the Prime Minister had to give assurances that we really are getting out and that this is just a practical way of giving us not merely a Malayan but a world capability. The assurances were given but there is a difference between a policy in which assurances are asked for and must be given and a policy where they need not.

The second item was the decision to give associated status to St Vincent. This was only amusing because in the discussion on Anguilla it had been resolved and minuted by the Committee that there should be no further concessions of associated status to any other island, pending reconsideration in the light of what had happened in Anguilla. Here we were coolly going ahead and we were told that this was a process which couldn't be stopped as Malcolm Shepherd, the Minister of State, had already made the promise. Barbara rather peevishly said, 'We were promised a report on why we based all our Anguilla policy on wrong information. Is there any reason to think we are not basing it on wrong information in St Vincent as well, where there is a very dicey situation about elections?' The Foreign Office got away with it though, and we shall go along on St Vincent. It will probably be all right because you can't have such a muck-up twice running but it was characteristic of how little the Foreign Office worries about pledges which have been given to the O.P.D.

This was followed by S.E.P. which was only interesting for its amiability. We settled down to discuss investment grants for ships built in foreign markets and then we got on to a delicious old-fashioned talk about the difficulty of finding industries to refer to the Monopolies Commission. The problem is that, what with the I.R.C. and other bodies being invented, we are in fact as a Government rather in favour of creating bigger and better mergers, with the whole notion of anti-monopoly legislation seen by interventionists like Peter Shore and Tony Wedgwood Benn as old-fashioned liberalism. But no, the Monopolies Commission was invented by Harold Wilson when he was President of the Board of Trade so we must find uses for it. There we were, meandering in this amicable way, and it reminded me how wonderfully soothing Whitehall is to the frayed nerves of the politician.

We are supposed to be drifting near the edge of disaster but at these meetings where we chat together we are borne along by the structure of Whitehall politics and Whitehall administration. It isn't of course only Whitehall. It's the black cars, the Departments, the standing in Parliament, buoying us up and insulating Ministers against shocks to an extraordinary degree. Every now and again the real world impinges on us but only when Whitehall and Westminster politics require it to do so. And this means that although we have ceased to be an effective Government or to have any authority we are quietly carrying on in this quiet atmosphere, feeling ourselves, as we did this morning, secure and relaxed.

Yesterday afternoon I had reported on the meeting of the Social Services Committee and all evening and the rest of this morning I worked away at my Statement, which I made fairly successfully in the House this afternoon. I dealt with the questions reasonably confidently but at one point I was so nervous that when John Pardoe[1] asked me a question I thought it came from my own back benches and turned my head to answer, showing a certain Crossman absentmindedness which amused the House. Then up to the lobby for the usual kind of peevish questioning. Nobody really wants to understand, only to show how much they know, but I didn't do too badly.

This evening for the second time, I don't know why, the Dutch Ambassador and his fox-hunting wife,[2] both aristocrats, gave a dinner in honour of Anne and me, and we found our fellow guests were Oliver and Lady Franks.[3] Oliver Franks took me aside and we had a wonderful talk. He is a funny

[1] Liberal M.P. for North Cornwall since 1966.

[2] Dr Jan Herman van Roijen, Netherlands Ambassador to the U.K. 1964–70.

[3] Oliver Franks (K.C.B. 1946) was a temporary civil servant at the Ministry of Supply 1939–46 and Permanent Secretary 1945–6. He was Provost of The Queen's College, Oxford, 1946–8, British Ambassador to Washington 1948–52, a Director of Lloyd's Bank Ltd 1953–1975 (Chairman 1954–62), a Director of Schroders, Chairman of the Committee of London Clearing Banks 1960–2 and Provost of Worcester College, Oxford, 1962–76. He became a life peer in 1962.

man. I always think he must be rather stuck-up and Establishment-minded, but he is sleek, young and vigorous at sixty-four, and gayer and more irresponsible than ever before. He is Head of a college and Chairman of a bank and we were discussing whether as Ambassador in Washington he had more power than any senior Minister. He said he thought he probably had. He negotiated NATO and any number of things for Eden and Macmillan.[1] He had a fascinating time out there and altogether has had a staggeringly successful Whitehall career and a great war career too. What most interested me tonight was that he said, 'We're heading for a 1931, I tell you that. With American lending rate going up to 8½ per cent, we are now probably in the most dangerous situation since 1929.[2] The Americans are ineluctably creating conditions to deal with their own trade deficit and the rest of the system might break down as thoroughly as it did in 1929–31. Of course,' he added quickly, 'we know more about it now. Nevertheless the crisis is as grave.' I added, 'Yes, it's a spiral history. We are moving to a point where we can look down on 1931 as a parallel position in a previous generation.' This struck me very much because it is roughly what Tommy and Nicky have been telling me. Appalling dangers are looming as a result of the Nixon Administration's common-sense policy of cutting back expenditure in order to deal with their trade deficit and, by making recovery more difficult for us, it may well be that this and not the Industrial Relations Bill will determine the fate of the Government.

Wednesday, June 11th

This morning I had to decide who should succeed Ron Matthews as my Private Secretary. He has had an appallingly difficult time trying to transform Kenneth Robinson's quiet backwater and the Private Office has been understaffed from the start in quantity and quality. Perhaps I made a mistake in making my darling Janet Newman into a full personal assistant, this beautiful creature who plays ping-pong for the Treasury. She and Ron have just about held their own. Then I had Michael Fogden brought in from Social Security, who in his bearing is an ideal Assistant Private Secretary but who hasn't enough imagination. The whole Office is terribly amateur and under strain and it has let me down pretty often. Well, Ron is now due for a move and I can either have as his successor an elegant, good-looking young man who looks like a young Westminster product, correct, able and

[1] Sir Anthony Eden (K.G. 1954) was Conservative M.P. for Warwick and Leamington 1923–57. He was Secretary of State for Foreign Affairs 1935–8, for Dominion Affairs 1939–40, for War 1940, for Foreign Affairs 1940–5 and was also Leader of the House of Commons 1942–5. He was Deputy Leader of the Opposition 1945–51, Foreign Secretary and Deputy Prime Minister 1951–April 1955 and Prime Minister from April 1955 until his resignation in January 1957. He was created 1st Earl of Avon in 1961. He died in 1977.

[2] On June 9th American banks raised their prime lending rate by 1 per cent to the unprecedentedly high level of 8½ per cent. President Nixon cut $7,500 million from his predecessor's budget for the fiscal year June 30th, 1969–June 30th, 1970, and planned further reductions to keep government spending within $192,000 million.

Foreign Officey, or a much more knock-about, lively individual, John Cashman.[1] I had been rather against him. However he came to see me this morning, and he's a tough nut, clever, not smooth and I think he will be more interesting and value for money. He'll get nearer to me and he'll get on with me better. I'm also getting on extremely well with Alan Marre. He's a nervy man, a Polish Jew who was brought over from Poland when a boy, I suppose. He's well-intentioned and I'm beginning to make some contact with him.

I got quite a good press this morning for my Statement yesterday and this was confirmed at the Party meeting. True, only twenty-eight people turned up but it was a success and I was almost embarrassed to hear all the main speeches saying how wonderful I was, with personal tributes, as if they were saying, 'We're sorry we treated you so roughly about teeth and spectacles before the recess. Now you are on a good wicket we like praising you if we possibly can.' People came up to me in the lobby and I remembered straightaway how before Whitsun I had been a lobby pariah. On Charles Forte's yacht Barbara had told me that it was the Uprating and the Superannuation Bills which were really going to split the Party. She was wrong about that. We have successfully put it over to the Party as a socialist policy.

This evening I went to a dinner at the Israeli Embassy for Golda Meir.[2] Fred Peart was there with Fred Mulley and Goronwy Roberts from the Foreign Office, Ted Short and myself.[3] Somehow the subject of Chieftain tanks came up. I have reported how O.P.D. has been discussing this problem for a good many months. The Israelis have been testing two Chieftains in the desert and, as Remez,[4] who sat next to me this evening, told me, George Brown had apparently given an explicit assurance that we wouldn't let the Israelis down, even though he had been warned about pressure from the Arabs. The Ministry of Defence had also shown itself quite enthusiastic about the sale, which wasn't in any case to take place until 1972 or 1973. It was only quite recently, in the last six months, that the Arabs began to twig that we were about to do this and they have been working up tremendous propaganda against the sale. Two months ago and again a few weeks ago Michael Stewart

[1] A civil servant since 1951, who had served as Kenneth Robinson's Private Secretary from 1962 to 1965. He was Crossman's Private Secretary in 1969 and since 1973 has been the Under-Secretary in charge of the Computers and Research Division at the D.H.S.S.

[2] On the death of the Israeli Prime Minister, Mr Levi Eshkol, in February 1969, the Deputy Prime Minister, Yigal Allon, had been appointed Acting Head of the Government but his rivalry with Moshe Dayan, Minister of Defence, led the Israeli Labour (Mapai) Party and the Cabinet to appoint as acting Head of State, until the General Election, Mrs Golda Meir, Israeli Minister of Labour 1949–56 and of Foreign Affairs 1956–66 and Secretary of the Mapai Party 1966–8. After the election on October 30th Mrs Meir, who was to remain Prime Minister until 1974, formed a Government of National Unity. Her visit to London in June was to attend a meeting of the Socialist International.

[3] Goronwy Roberts, Labour M.P. for Caernarvonshire 1945–50 and for Caernarvon 1950–February 1974, was Minister of State at the Welsh Office 1964–6, at the Department of Education and Science 1966–7, at the Foreign and Commonwealth Office 1967–9 and at the Board of Trade 1969–70. He became a life peer in 1974, taking the title of Lord Goronwy-Roberts, and has been a Minister of State for Foreign Affairs since 1974.

[4] Aharon Remez, Israeli Ambassador to London 1965–70.

gave us a most awe-inspiring picture of the appalling results of selling Chieftains to the Israelis and of how we might be in danger of losing our oil supplies and having our installations burnt down and so on. His recommendation had been to postpone any decision to the autumn and I had said I would rather tell the Israelis the honest truth and let them buy the tanks from somebody else. We were trying to get the best of both worlds, to placate the Arabs by postponing the decision and keep the Israelis tagging along.

This afternoon there had been a row about this in the House,[1] so I found myself in great difficulty at dinner, because I was spelling out to Golda the ambivalence of British policy and the fact that we were enormously aware of our Arab interests and the pressure they were exerting on us. Golda got more and more angry. I was of course doing this almost deliberately. I was not actually saying what I had said in Cabinet, that Albion was perfidious and that I recommended the Israelis to go and buy elsewhere, but I came pretty near it. I knew Fred Mulley and Goronwy Roberts would report back to the Foreign Office, so I simply gave an objective account, explaining that until we had our last soldier out of the Persian Gulf we had to be enormously sensitive to the Arabs and enormously aware of Arab public opinion. Therefore I must warn the Israelis that they must understand this. Mind you, they already know it perfectly well. What Golda and Remez tried to say was that there was no alternative source of tanks but I don't believe for a moment that the Russians could stop the Israelis getting their tanks in Eastern Europe, and in the last resort they could get them from America, though of course Britain is the most convenient manufacturer and I think they do actually prefer trading with us. Altogether the dinner was pretty vigorous.

Thursday, June 12th

I had in Dick Taverne, a very good and loyal friend of mine, who gave me the complete inside picture of Roy's mind and told me that the Chancellor is going to ask for a £400 million cutback in public expenditure this year in order to avoid sharp rises in taxation in next year's budget. I am sure that though Roy may ask for £400 million he will get only £200 million at most, of which half will come from Defence, but we are now all up against it. This was interesting news because this morning I had to have a formal meeting with Ted Short about the £10 million which he is supposed to raise by increasing fees for further education. This cut was in the 1968/9 P.E.S.C. exercise and he was told that if he didn't get it by raising fees he must do it some other way. I wasn't going to help him any more after the thanks I got in the teeth and spectacles episode. As Short had continued to delay and just wasn't paying up, Roy and Harold had asked me to try to deal with it. I asked Short along and pointed out that he should make these savings as part of a

[1] Reginald Paget, Labour M.P. for Northampton from 1945 until he became a life peer in 1974, had asked for a Standing Order No. 9 debate on the Government's proposal 'to sell to Libya Chieftain tanks which they have refused to sell to Israel'.

deal in which we all share. If it's all plonked on the table together there is to be much less damage to each of us individually. 'If', I said, 'the teeth and spectacles charges had been announced as one of a comprehensive set of measures rather than dished out as a minor and ridiculous charge to be judged on its own it would have been far more palatable to the Party.' After half an hour I got him to agree to write a letter telling the Prime Minister that rather than increasing further education fees it would be better to put 3*d.* on the price of school meals. I am glad that this little co-ordinating job has been done and the letter written.

Management Committee met again for half an hour for another report. The Prime Minister had worked out in even greater detail the exact changes he wants in the T.U.C. rules and he and Barbara are now firmly committed to this.[1] He came out with the view that if he could get the rules changed he would drop the penal clauses. I intervened at this point to say, 'That doesn't mean that if you don't get the change in the rules Cabinet is automatically committed to the penal clauses,' and, to my surprise, the moment I said this it was agreed, because I warned Harold that if he tried to commit us this afternoon to the penal clauses he would get a split Cabinet.

When Cabinet met Barbara and Harold played fair and left the question open, although they made it clear if the T.U.C. refused to agree they would expect strong support for a no-climb-down, no-surrender Bill. If T.U.C. policing is inadequate there must be Government policing as well. It was clear that the longer this conversation with the T.U.C. went on the more difficult it would be to bring the Parliamentary Party to support a Bill which would have to be forced through in defiance of the T.U.C. Once again we managed to get agreement because Cabinet was merely being asked to allow the P.M. to negotiate. We were given the three possibilities and told that Cabinet would only make up its mind on the Bill next Tuesday or Wednesday when we had heard the result of the negotiations.

The main item was the Boundary Commission. This has been a terribly dicey problem, because the recommendations of the Commission must be published and implemented and we have to announce our implementation

[1] Mr Wilson's own account describes the meeting he had with Mrs Castle and Mr Feather on June 10th, at which it became clear that amendments to Nos 11 and 12 of the T.U.C. Rules would remove the necessity for the controversial clauses in the Government's proposed legislation. At a meeting with the forty-one members of the T.U.C. General Council on the following day, June 11th, the Prime Minister's suggestion for a small negotiating body was accepted. A committee was appointed, consisting of Vic Feather, Sir Fred Hayday, Alfred Allen, Sydney Greene (General Secretary of the N.U.R. 1957–74, a life peer since 1974), Hugh Scanlon and Jack Jones. During this meeting, however, the Prime Minister told the T.U.C. that their proposed amendment to Rule No. 11 was too weak and the meeting was adjourned to the next day, June 12th. On the following day the Prime Minister again emphasized to the T.U.C. that, given an adequate alternative in changes to the T.U.C. Rules, the Government would be prepared to drop the 'penal clauses' in the I.R. Bill. If the T.U.C. refused to make appropriate changes, the Prime Minister had in mind 'a proposal...for legislation to prescribe "Model Rules", including rules to deal with disruptive action', as a condition for trade union registration. See *Wilson*, pp. 655–6.

this month, so that there is just enough time for the new parliamentary constituency boundaries to be drawn up before the next election. For ages we have intended to avoid this and I have often talked to the Prime Minister about it. It provides one explanation of our determination to implement the Maud Report on Local Government Reform. Harold and I always agreed that the real let-out on the Boundary Commission would be Maud, which would abolish counties and county boroughs and would justify our postponing the redrawing of the constituency boundaries. So I wasn't in the least surprised when Callaghan came forward today with his recommendation that this session only a few constituencies which were much too big could be split into two or three but that otherwise we should postpone things until after the implementation of Maud. The only difficulty is that Willie Ross, whose Wheatley Report is not due for another five or six months, is very anxious to implement the Boundary Commission's Report because it will save the Labour Party in Scotland, whereas we reckon that in England it will lose us fifteen to seventeen seats.

Of course everybody knows that politicians are politicians, but Home Secretaries have to be careful. Even if we are looking out for party advantage, we want to combine this with moral rectitude and, as you might expect, Jim has done this very nicely. He thought it would be awkward for him to recommend one thing for England when Ross wanted to recommend the opposite for Scotland, so fortunately George Thomson had a compromise ready. All Ross needed to do was to say that he was postponing consideration of his Boundary Commission Report until the publication of the Wheatley Report in the autumn. This would separate what we did in England from what the Scots did.

This evening there were a lot of divisions and I was going through the lobbies a good deal. The people I met were more and more baffled. The T.U.C. have turned the rule change down flat. Cledwyn Hughes, who is a little twister and turner, said to me, knowing I was one of the people who was critical, 'Is it possible? Can Harold really drive us into a conflict with the T.U.C.?' Tony Greenwood certainly felt that way, and, I would think, even Wedgy Benn. Harold and Barbara are now trying to find an alternative, which I know has got to be to strengthen the Bill without penal clauses, and this is virtually a come-down. I think we are going to have a great deal of bitterness, with Barbara and Harold believing Cabinet has let them down. There have been a great number of stories in the press about Callaghan, Roy Mason and Dick Marsh, Tony Crosland and me, as people who have been doubtful and critical. I haven't particularly been talking to the papers but I haven't disguised my view that we really must settle and that we can't afford a break with the T.U.C. now. We shouldn't go on with brinkmanship beyond this limit. Harold and Barbara think Cabinet should have given them absolute support so they could go right up to the brink and force the T.U.C. to climb down but I've always thought that the T.U.C., following Jones's and Scanlon's wishes, were not going to move from the position the Congress took on June 5th.

Friday, June 13th

I had a whole day in Coventry looking at hospitals. It was valuable but enormously hot and so exhausting that I hardly had the energy to go round a social security place in Birmingham, where I called before catching the 5.15 to Newcastle.

The train got in at 10.15, after wandering all round Yorkshire, and I had been in the same carriage all the time. When I arrived there had been a heavy rainstorm and it was thought that the weather was breaking up and would spoil the Northumbrian Miners' Picnic. I was met by old Holliday,[1] the President of the Northumberland Miners' Union, and a charming good-looking man of forty or so who turned out to be his Assistant Finance Secretary. They motored me out to a rather squalid hotel facing the sea at Tynemouth, where we discussed colliery closures for an hour and a half although I wanted to go to bed. I got the usual picture. There are now less than half the number of miners in Northumberland than there were ten years ago. The young men are leaving, the old men are taking their redundancy payments and getting out and the industry is demoralized.

Saturday, June 14th

I woke up early to a thick mist. I had once been to the Durham Miners' Gala but this was my first Northumbrian Miners' Picnic, which I had been told was a magnificent show, in certain ways physically much more attractive than the Gala, and so it proved to be. When I woke, I saw the outline of my speech pretty clearly. I had done a press release on the train to Coventry on Friday morning and had sent Janet back with it to the Private Office. It had been a press release on the Uprating Bill, but suddenly I had a new theme, the one I had used at Cambridge on the achievements of my sixty years with the Labour Party, the breaking-down of the privileged class society and the transformation of society to one of a prosperous majority with a poor minority, all this leading up to social security as a means to abolish poverty in the midst of plenty.

After a breakfast party for the senior social security officials in Newcastle, we motored up to Bedlington where the terriers come from, a tiny village where the picnic takes place. It's a dull village but wonderfully spacious, with an immense wide High Street that was already packed with people at 11.30 in the morning. The families had arrived at 9 o'clock from all the surrounding villages and the pubs were open. There were 60–70,000 people going down the hill from the village to a beautiful natural amphitheatre at the bottom, where an elegant little stage had been built. I made my speech to a crowd of, I

[1] Tom Holliday, long-serving President of the Northumberland Area of the N.U.M. He retired in April 1977.

suppose, about 10–15,000 around the rostrum and over 30,000 behind. It wasn't a great speech but it was competent and I held my own against a little heckling. I was followed by Shirley Williams, who was extremely adroit and was obviously going to make a good speech, but I had to leave. I am afraid it meant missing the miners' tea, but I had attended a big cold-meat lunch in the Co-op, with tea and hock served simultaneously, and had made a speech there, so I had really done enough. I had a marvellous sense of the wonderful spirit of the miners, although the way we have treated them has been ghastly. I have a horrible feeling that first Fred Lee and then Dick Marsh and Roy Mason, these working-class trade unionists, have with the bureaucrats in the Ministry proposed a rate of closure which is outrageously fast. I know it would cost us a bit to keep some of these pits going, but it is going to cost us appallingly dear if as a result the young men we need in the industry walk out and the old men are voluntarily retired. Nevertheless there it is. It was a marvellous day, but I was determined to catch the 4.15 train home to see my family. I caught it with minutes to spare and Anne met me and drove me home to the farm.

Sunday, June 15th

A splendid day, the twelfth day of the wonderful summer we've been having ever since we got back from Italy. Anne has been sunbathing every day and the children have been pouring in from the village to swim in the bath. This afternoon I was cutting weeds on my island and then we had a tremendous thunderstorm which cut off the electric light and the gramophone. Now the electricity is back and I have been dictating the past week's diary until after midnight.

Monday, June 16th

I was working at Alexander Fleming House this morning, when Barbara, looking very distressed, put her head into my room and said she'd had a terrible weekend. She asked me to come and see her, so at 6.30 I went along. I knew that one of the things she wanted to talk about was a very unpleasant piece which Alan Watkins published in his column last week, saying that I had remained uncorrupted by a fortnight with Barbara on Charles Forte's luxury yacht. The secret that he was our host had at last leaked out, though ever since Barbara said she wanted a veto on the story the whole of our family has been religiously careful not to speak about it. Alan Watkins has never even approached me on this and I have an uneasy feeling that he must have known it all along. It's fully possible that weeks before Barbara told us this should be a secret I mentioned to one or two people that we had this wonderful offer and were thinking of taking it. Perhaps, for example, in all innocence I told Paul Johnson that I was going but I now felt very uncomfortable because Barbara disliked it so much. However she is a sporting girl and agreed that we should give Charles Forte a John Piper watercolour as a tribute and I am going to give Barbara a pair of silver sauce-boats for her silver wedding celebration.

She said how miserable and unhappy she was and how she hadn't been sleeping over the weekend. I was pleased that she asked me to go to see her because I was aware that we were both terribly at loggerheads about the crisis over the Industrial Relations Bill. I found her with Bob Mellish and naturally he and I were on one side and she was on the other. We spelt out to her what the situation was, how we couldn't possibly get the Bill through the Party and that this would mean that if we didn't withdraw it in time the Party would reject it. She was saying how she had thought all this out clearly and she would have to resign. 'But that', I said, 'would be playing into Jim Callaghan's hands.' We went all through the argument together and then she said she was thinking of further proposals which would avoid putting penalties on the workers but she could only tell us a little before I had to rush off to Gluck's *Orfeo* at Covent Garden. I was in *The Times* box with Stanley Sadie. It's a marvellous opera but it was being done by Solti, who is a great Wagnerian conductor, not an eighteenth-century classical conductor, and I found the whole thing too romanticized for my liking. There was a terrible homosexual atmosphere about the settings, with men and women in indeterminate dresses. It was not an attractive production but nevertheless I saw the whole of it before rushing back for the 10 o'clock vote.[1]

By then the news was out that Douglas Houghton and the Liaison Committee had met and sent a powerful letter to Harold, warning him that the Party would not endorse any kind of penal sanctions. After the vote, I went upstairs for a drink with Tony Crosland. He and I saw completely eye to eye. Like everybody else, we had said that it would be inconceivable that we should be rushed into this Bill and that there must be a climb-down. But I warned Tony that we were still miles away from a compromise. 'Look,' I said, 'I don't think that is Barbara's mood and I don't think it is Harold's. In my view, they are intending to try the supreme brinkmanship of threatening to resign in the hope that first Cabinet and then the Party won't accept their resignations. But in the last resort the Party will accept them. I am sure they are playing for the highest possible stakes. They believe the Bill will have to be presented to the Party, they have it ready with the penalty clauses and they are going to force it through Cabinet this week and then hope to carry the Party with them. This is what we have to fight, for the danger is that they'll come unstuck and get defeated at the Party meeting or, if not defeated, the minority will be so large that it will be like Chamberlain in 1940.' Tony and I discussed this at length.

[1] The division was on a Conservative motion censuring the Government for refusing to accept the recommendations of the Science and Technology Committee, set out in their Report on Coastal Pollution. See Vol. II, p. 302. The motion was defeated by 280 votes to 232.

Tuesday, June 17th

We started with Management Committee at 10.30 and it really was most extraordinary. Immediately we got there Barbara Castle said she had thought up a new idea. We would drop the penalties on individual trade unionists which she had been fighting for for six months and instead have a new system of penalties imposed on trade unions as such, to be paid by the trade unions. This would remove the sense of individual victimization and she thought it would be infinitely more acceptable to the unions. It was something, she said, that she and Harold had thought up late last night.

I must say that when she described this Management Committee was bewildered. She had a short document but it contained nothing more than what she had said. Here was, no doubt, quite a bright idea but it was yet another improvisation. The history of this Bill has been a history of improvisation. The White Paper was very largely rewritten when some of us criticized it and no Bill or anything near it emerged from that. Since then we have had a series of improvised measures from the parliamentary draftsmen, trying desperately to keep up with the modifications flowing from Barbara and Harold. That's all right for negotiation but it's not all right for the drafting of legislation. In this case it wasn't any good for negotiation either because, as most of us instinctively felt this morning, in their present mood the trade unions are not going to agree to being fined for failing to order their members back to work from unofficial strikes. That is a non-starter and in trying to put it forward at the last moment Barbara would merely decrease confidence in herself and Harold.

The other thing we discussed was timing and whether the aim now was to get Cabinet committed to a Bill with penal clauses before Harold and Barbara met the T.U.C. tomorrow morning. I made it quite clear that I thought this most unwise. But Harold and Barbara were both obviously worried and it was clear that they hoped to be able to go to the General Council tomorrow and say, 'It is either/or; we have full Cabinet backing. We tell you we shall publish a Bill tonight and it will be in the papers on Thursday morning. The Bill with penalties is ready; it has been through Cabinet.' I am quite certain it was their plan to get Management Committee to agree to this but they were unable to do it.

Cabinet started at 11.15. We only had an hour and a quarter because Golda Meir was coming in for a talk before lunch. Barbara embarrassed us straightaway by saying she had a bright new idea and that she wanted to hand round a paper on it. I spoke early because I thought it essential and said, 'Before we do anything in detail about this idea, let's get clear what you are aiming at. Do you want to get Cabinet backing for a Bill with penalties in it before you go to see the General Council tomorrow? Because if you do I am against it.' Everbody heard my challenge and everybody quietly knew this was what the P.M. and Barbara were after, but Harold is a clever chairman and didn't take up my challenge. His friends in Cabinet tried to avoid this discussion, so most of the morning was spent talking about Barbara's new idea. It was a thoroughly bad and unfortunate thing to have put forward and the more she was made to talk about it the less convincing the proposition appeared, though she continued to say that she was convinced that the trade unions would prefer it. It was certainly clear that Harold had a timetable.* He was going to get this through Cabinet this morning and put it to the Trade Union group of the Party at 7 o'clock this evening, telling them why he couldn't accept the T.U.C.'s terms. Tomorrow afternoon he was going to present the Bill to Cabinet and announce the terms to a special Party meeting. He and Barbara had clearly made up their minds that now was the moment to force the issue and present the Bill as a further stage in their brinkmanship negotiations with the T.U.C.

This morning it became clear that the plan was coming unstuck. Harold was getting a bit rasped and he said, 'It's about time people pulled themselves together and faced their responsibilities.' Then came Peter Shore's intervention. Gripping himself, as members of the Cabinet do when they really have got to say something, Peter said, 'Right, if I am challenged, I will,' and he spelt out why in his view Harold had it all wrong. He said, 'The real thing wrong with Harold and Barbara is that they now say that an agreement under which we should be content with the advance registered at Congress, plus a declaration of intent, is a helter-skelter retreat. This is a complete misjudgment. So far from a retreat we have made an enormous advance and this would be to stabilize it.' Peter spoke with tremendous strength. Everybody in Cabinet agreed that it was the first time he had ever said anything which had a real effect. Somehow it summed up the real reason why Cabinet couldn't authorize Harold and Barbara to go ahead and threaten the T.U.C. with a Bill including penalties and it's got to be understood that this embittered Barbara all the more because Peter was the only member of the Cabinet who had been present at the Sunningdale Conference where, along with Tommy Balogh, Barbara and her civil servants had evolved the idea of *In Place of Strife* and devised the package that was put to us last autumn. Peter had been in on this deal from the start, even before Roy, and had fully sympathized with the whole thing. When he abandoned it this morning it was a tremendous blow for Barbara. I don't think there was any other speech that surprised me except for Gerald Gardiner, who said that there could be other penalties for the trade unions and he couldn't quite see why we should force this Bill through. Even he was not on Harold's side.

Throughout the morning Jim Callaghan behaved with an egregious smoothness and oiliness which was almost unbearable. He kept saying, 'Ah, but Prime Minister, we don't want to tire you too much, we want to enable you to save your resources,' and he significantly repeated, 'I believe that if the Prime Minister tries to force this through he will succeed.' I can't

* And I heard from a very good source that at the meeting of the Socialist International at Eastbourne yesterday Harold had let this be known through Gerald Kaufman.

help feeling that Jim has come to the conclusion that the best thing to do is to let Harold and Barbara destroy themselves and that he may profit by their destruction. It's the only explanation I can give because Jim was completely contradicting what Bob Mellish told us. It was interesting that no report was made of Douglas Houghton's letter. Management Committee had been told about it in close confidence but anyhow Douglas had given it straight to the press. It had a tremendous impact but today Harold tried to keep it from Cabinet and it was never shown, never discussed, as though the episode had never actually happened. Although Harold refused to read the letter out, Bob Mellish was as firm and solid as ever. Each time I called on him from my end, saying, 'Couldn't we just hear the Chief Whip again?' Bob said, 'I tell you, I'm sorry, but you can't get this Bill through the House of Commons.' This view was naturally opposed by Barbara and Harold, who both said that they were convinced that with guts the Cabinet could, but it was very disturbing that Callaghan also denied it and said he believed we would be able to scrape the Bill through. It was an odious combination of Harold's enemies supporting him and his friends opposing him.

At 12.30 we got off to the lunch with Golda Meir. Poor Michael Stewart was in a terrible fix because at the last moment Reggie Paget had got his Standing Order No. 9 debate and this had put the fat in the fire. We can't refuse to sell Chieftains to Israel without showing that our 'neutrality' favours the Arabs. Michael Stewart and Harold sat close to Golda and their problem was made the more acute by her presence in London, her lunch with us today, and the fact that she is speaking at the Socialist International tomorrow. I must remember that this is the kind of thing which embarrasses the Prime Minister. Although he was primarily concerned with industrial relations today, he also had hanging over him this awkward question of the Israelis and the Chieftain tanks. (The debate went on from 3.45 to 6.35 but it came to nothing and Reggie Paget's motion was withdrawn. Michael Stewart didn't give anything away and he certainly didn't say formally that there were not going to be any sales to Israel. Nevertheless I just throw this in because I suspect that the whole Paget incident made the situation more difficult.) I was feeling frightfully upset by what was going on and, I don't know why, I lashed out at lunch and told Wilson I couldn't understand why the Israelis regarded Britain as a good source for the purchase of tanks. Wouldn't they be far wiser to realize our perfidious nature and the Arab pressure on us in the Persian Gulf and the whole of the Middle East? Sitting opposite were Marcus Sieff and Harold Lever, cheering me on,[1] and I realized that real friends of Israel like ourselves are appalled by the duplicity of the Foreign Office and the simplicity of people like Michael Stewart and George Brown, who make all kinds of promises to the Israelis and then let them down. But the Israelis are very sensible people,

[1] Sir Marcus Sieff (Kt 1971) was Vice-Chairman of Marks & Spencer Ltd 1965–71, Deputy-Chairman 1971–2 and since 1972 has been Chairman. He was Chairman of the Export Committee for Israel 1965–8.

who ought to be able to judge us as we are, so one must add that we shouldn't be too sorry for them if they are disappointed.

At 5.30 Cabinet started again, the most devastating Cabinet meeting I have attended. This evening Harold found people committing themselves in detail for the first time.[1] It had been a bad meeting in the morning and it was bad now. I said again, 'Look, the real issue we have to discuss is whether Cabinet should be committed today to a Bill with legal penalties and, if so, what are the penalties? Should we commit ourselves to this today before Harold and Barbara return to negotiate with the T.U.C. tomorrow morning and should they be empowered to tell the T.U.C. that either they should actually change their rules or we shall publish the Bill?' On this everybody cast their vote and gave their opinion and, apart from Cledwyn Hughes and George Thomas, everyone overwhelmingly turned Harold down. Person after person said no. Tony Wedgwood Benn said in his thoughtful way, 'We are in advance of the times. We only started talking about trade union legislation a year ago, and it is too early to talk about a statutory obligation when we haven't yet had a process of education,' so he turned it down. The Foreign Secretary was away on the front bench dealing with tanks for Libya, so Harold's only real supporter was absent. Roy Jenkins sat there aloof and detached, saying a few words but never committing himself, never helping Barbara.

It became clear that Harold's self-confidence, complacency, bounce and good temper were all breaking down. At one point he said, 'Well, you're all giving this up because it's unpopular. You're committed by Cabinet's decision on the White Paper. Cabinet has given the go-ahead on the short Bill. Everyone here is committed by that and you are abandoning your Cabinet commitments because they are unpopular. You're soft, you're cowardly, you're lily-livered. If you do that, why shouldn't I?' he said. 'Why shouldn't I suggest abandoning the National Insurance Bill, with its increase in contributions, or the teeth and spectacles changes? If you abandon yours, I abandon mine.' He repeated this theme of how cowardly we were and how we couldn't stick it and he finally said, 'I won't negotiate on your terms. If you order me to go back to the T.U.C. and say I'm to accept a declaration of intent I refuse to do it, because a declaration would not be worth the paper it is written on. I insist on getting the change of rules or on standing for the penal clauses. You can't deny me this.' He was a little man, for the first time dragged down on our level. It was painful because in a sense he was sabotaged and utterly nonplussed.

After all these disavowals Harold said, 'What is the Cabinet decision? What do you want me to do?' Jim Callaghan said, 'I could easily frame a decision if you wish: that we wish you to seek a settlement on the basis of a firm declaration of intent.' The moment Jim said this Harold scented danger and shied off, realizing that this would have bound him. He is very much aware of the force of Cabinet decisions. 'No, I won't accept that,' he said.

[1] See *Wilson*, pp. 656–7.

'Barbara and I must not be tied down. We must be free to negotiate as we wish and I warn you I shall certainly say what Barbara and I will do about the penal legislation if we don't get our way. Without a weapon to threaten them with we should be completely impotent.' (One of the themes which he and Barbara had used throughout the afternoon had been that unless, with the Cabinet behind them, they had an effective threat, the T.U.C. wouldn't give anything away.) The meeting ended with no Cabinet decision and with the Prime Minister summing up how he and Barbara would tomorrow morning seek to negotiate but with no Cabinet backing and no decision whatsoever.

So it was a victory for those of us who had said the one thing we were not going to give Harold today was the right to a Bill with penalties. We had won at the cost of the most searing, awful, bloody row I have ever had with Harold. It's very difficult to have a row with him. At one point I had said, 'Don't be mean, Harold. Don't attribute motives to us. Of course we are not lily-livered cowards, we just disagree with you. We think you are wrecking and destroying the movement. Do, for heaven's sake, see that your critics have the same principles as you have. They care about the party.' These were the kind of arguments we had all afternoon.

The meeting became more and more awkward because at 7 o'clock the Prime Minister was due to address the Trade Union group. He said, 'I've got half my speech written here, the half which says why I must insist on the rule change and why I can't accept a declaration of intent. I suppose all that is out of date.' We had to say, 'Yes, we're afraid you won't be able to deliver it.' 'What am I to say to these people?' By this time it was ten to seven. 'What shall I say to them?' and somebody suggested, 'Give the history of the thing for thirty-five to forty minutes. You can space things out.' He said, 'You mean you are asking me to be dull?' and everybody gave rather an embarrassed laugh and said 'Yes'. So there it was, a terrible exhibition in which the P.M. was rasped, irritated and thoroughly demoralized, really shouting I won't, I can't, you can't do this to me, terribly painful because he expressed a loathing, a spite and a resentment which is quite outside his usual character. Although I didn't see it, both Fred Peart and Roy Jenkins said afterwards that three large double brandies were handed to him out of the cupboard during the last half-hour. I have never seen the P.M. driven to drink in the course of an evening. And all the while beside him sat Roy. In the morning he had intervened at one point, saying, 'Aren't you leaving Barbara Castle in rather a difficult negotiating position? Shouldn't we just remember that?' but this afternoon he didn't say anything. He is letting Harold down. As Peter Shore said, Roy's failure was perhaps the most dramatic feature of all this.

While Harold went to talk to the Trade Union group I gave dinner to Clifford Jarrett and Brian to discuss uprating and pension policy. Today had been my big afternoon on the Second Reading of the Uprating Bill and thank heavens I had said David Ennals should do it, because, as it turned out, the Cabinet meeting prevented me from even sitting beside him. However I got there for a short time at 7.0 and we sat on the front bench together. I decided to wind up myself.

As Brian and Clifford and I were sitting talking in the Strangers' Dining Room the results of the Trade Union group meeting came through and it was clear that Harold had put up a good show. He had talked for about forty-five minutes, giving absolutely nothing away, and then he had answered questions for another hour. Charlie Pannell said that the only interesting question was his own, when he asked who was responsible for the statement from the D.E.P. which came within an hour of the end of the special Congress, saying that the declaration of intent was no good and tearing it up. Was it really Barbara Castle's officials who did it while she was away or had she telephoned from her luxury yacht? Harold had replied, 'I take personal responsibility for this.' Apart from that, I don't think the Party gained any information but the meeting completely confirmed what Bob Mellish had said, for there was not a single person in the group who said a word in favour of the Prime Minister. At the end Jimmy Robertson,[1] a most weak and amiable character, had to say, 'Well, Prime Minister, you have no support from any individual in the Trade Union group.' This was a formidable thing for a Labour Prime Minister to hear, especially after his own Cabinet had completely disavowed him. Harold is now up against it.

After dinner I went in to wind up the Uprating debate. I was in quite mellow form and put the House into fits of laughter with a gay, amusing speech. As we came out, Boyd-Carpenter said to me, 'If I may say so, that was brilliant. One of the best speeches I have heard you make.' Well, why did I make such a bright, brilliant speech about dynamizing pensions? I think it was sheer reaction against the general darkness. Once again there were only twenty or thirty people in the House but the debate had been very mild from our point of view because we had no attacking speech from our side behind us and the Tories weren't able to criticize either. It was a success. I had referred to it in Cabinet earlier, when Harold had spoken of attacking unpopular policies such as the increase of national insurance contributions, and I'd said, 'Well, Prime Minister, at least I can say this. That issue will go through tonight after a full debate, without a division. This I have managed to achieve, which is more than you can say for your Industrial Relations Bill.' And so it was and after it I retired to bed.

Wednesday, June 18th

Ironically, I woke up this morning to read in the papers that the National Opinion Poll showed that the Tory lead had been cut to seventeen points, the lowest for months, mainly because the public thought we were tougher than the Tories in dealing with the trade unions. I was busy in the office at first but I heard the news that a Cabinet was fixed for midday, so I had to abandon an engagement to speak to the Hospital Management Committees' annual

[1] Labour M.P. for Paisley 1961–76 and Scottish Labour M.P. since 1976.

conference at Weston-super-Mare and let Alan Marre read the speech I had been preparing for some weeks.

At 11.30 I went across to see the Chancellor. I have had more time with Roy during the course of today and seen him at closer quarters and in a more interesting situation than ever before. I asked him about his remark at Cabinet yesterday morning about the difficulties of Barbara's position. 'Did you really want to give her anything?' He said, 'No, I was just filling in time at a rather awkward moment by saying something which sounded good.' How often does Roy reveal himself quite as clearly as that? He revealed himself as a man who consciously felt nothing except what was to his own advantage.

Now, you have to remember that this morning we had no idea what would happen. Harold and Barbara had talked in the wildest way about insisting on a Bill with penalties and Cabinet hadn't yet voted them down. That would have to be done this afternoon. This morning Roy started by saying, 'You appreciate that, though I agree with you that we can't have the Bill with penalty clauses, I am bound to vote with Harold and Barbara if the issue comes up. I expect we shall be voted down but that is that.' I said, 'But if you do that, Roy, if you vote with Harold and Barbara, you are doomed. You will be bound to resign with them when resignation comes.' I explained what I had been saying to Barbara on the boat about how we would sort this out and how my mind was clear, and I said, 'If we have to vote on the Bill and defeat Harold at Cabinet, this is the real issue. Probably we won't defeat him despite the 19 to 3. He might well win by a majority of one or two but if he wins with a majority of that size it won't make any difference if the Trade Union group is solid against and the Party votes him down. The crisis is upon us. I can assure you that, if he and Barbara resign, you will have to resign with them and Callaghan will come in your place. Do you really want to do this?' I urged him to make up his mind that he couldn't possibly vote with them and that, on the contrary, if this were put to us it would be his duty to get the meeting stopped as quickly as possible and say we must reflect on it overnight and then report back. We should say we couldn't take a decision on the Bill until tomorrow morning. We must have a delay, during which, as a last resort, Roy should go to Harold and throw his weight in, telling Harold that if he went on with this Roy would vote against him.

Roy said to me, 'You do appreciate, don't you, that I have kept my word to Barbara, though I really believe in the policy less and less. I have felt it my duty to keep my word to her rather than to Harold.' I said, 'Yes, but there come times when you have to decide on the future of the party and when you have to realize that if there is a possibility that Harold might go somebody has to take his place. You and I have to see that the party goes on running and that the machinery is put in motion for replacing the P.M.' So we spent a little time discussing the constitution of the party, how the Party meeting should be called and whether Roy could go to the Palace direct. All this we discussed and we made it quite clear that Roy would stand against Callaghan in the event of Callaghan's making a bid for the leadership.

Then I went through from No. 11 to No. 12 and had a long talk with the Chief Whip. He told me that yesterday evening he had been summoned very late to No. 10, where he found Harold pretty tiddly, and they had discussed the future far into the night. Harold had described to Bob the contempt he had for his colleagues, how they had betrayed him, how he would challenge them and fight the Bill through, and how, when the crisis was over, he would get rid of the lily-livered people and have a different kind of Cabinet, how Callaghan would have to go and that Jenkins was a coward. Bob said Harold didn't call me a coward because I had been fairly consistent on all this but that he had talked in this wild way as though he was prepared to see the break-up of the party as the price for getting his way. I found Bob pretty solid and both he and I, as Harold's close friends, agreed that if Harold and Barbara were to end the day like this we would have to have the vote postponed until tomorrow morning and try to get them defeated, to prevent Cabinet putting forward this Bill with penalties. It must be postponed until after the Party meeting at 7.0 tonight. I won't rehearse all the other chats and chivver we had waiting for the meeting at midday.

All day, however, Cabinet was postponed by half-hours and forty minutes, and finally, after hanging about all morning, and filling in the afternoon with a conference about heart transplantations, I strolled across to No. 10. Half of us didn't really believe Cabinet was on at last but there we were, with the whole General Council upstairs negotiating in the dining room. The door to the Cabinet Room was open so instead of standing outside as we usually do we filtered in one by one, Tony Greenwood, Judith, myself, Roy, and we all sat down rather sheepishly. In came Jim Callaghan and said, 'There is a settlement. I got it by telephone a few minutes ago.'

I was quite certain this was correct because I had heard it from the press half an hour before and, indeed, the longer the delay the more confident I had been that an agreement would be reached. Bob had been telling me how violent Harold was this afternoon and how he was talking about refusing to climb down but there was one very big difference. Last night he had been talking about resigning, refusing to be our negotiator, but he had obviously reflected during the night that this was not sound policy. Harold had said to Bob, 'I'm not going to resign. They won't chase me out, I'm going to stay,' and the moment I heard this I knew that he would settle. He was prepared to threaten to resign as long as he thought there was no chance of his resignation being accepted, but when he realized that Cabinet was solid against him he decided he must stay and settle. That, the view of the Cabinet combined with the view of the Trade Union group, is what forced Harold to go into the negotiations with the T.U.C. determined to get agreement and to survive as Prime Minister, knowing his bluff had been called in advance. He had to leave Barbara in the lurch to save his own muttons and his own Prime

Ministership. I have no doubt that this is the motive which drove him and of course there is nothing like the prospect of certain death to concentrate energy. This afternoon he had concentrated his energies on getting the best possible agreement.

In Mr Wilson's account of his meetings with the General Council of the T.U.C. on June 18th, he describes how he outlined, in the morning session, three possibilities: legislation on the lines the Government had proposed; legislation omitting the penal clauses but 'involving the statutory imposition of effective clauses in [*the unions'*] *rule-books', to deal with indiscipline, with the sanction that unions failing to do so would lose the protection accorded to them by the 1906 Act; or a decision by the T.U.C. 'to alter their procedures on the lines we have suggested'. He told the T.U.C. that the second course had been considered and rejected. The General Council then proposed that the Prime Minister and Mrs Castle should meet the negotiating committee to discuss amendments to Rule 11. This group was firmly opposed to an actual rule change which, Hugh Scanlon pointed out, would be opposed by the National Executive of the A.E.U., bringing with it a defeat for the other procedural changes agreed at the Croydon Congress. Instead, the group proposed that the T.U.C. should make 'a solemn and binding' undertaking to scrutinize the Government's proposals, an undertaking that would, after Congressional endorsement, eventually become a 'rule of Congress'. During the lunch-time interval, Mr Wilson, Mrs Castle and her officials considered the proposal and the Prime Minister and Mrs Castle decided to draft, with the Attorney General's help, an immediate statement to be accepted by the General Council as a binding undertaking. Meanwhile Cabinet, which had been postponed several times, was called for 4 p.m. In the afternoon the Prime Minister and Mrs Castle saw first Vic Feather at 2.15 and the General Council at 2.25. The General Council were left to consider the draft undertaking, while Cabinet waited, and eventually at 5 o'clock Vic Feather was able to assure the Prime Minister and Mrs Castle that the General Council was unanimous, that the draft had been accepted without amendments and that in the report to Congress the names of all the members of the Council would be appended to it. At 5.15 Mr Wilson and Mrs Castle delivered the report to the Cabinet.*[1]

I shall try to find out from Victor Feather and the others how much the T.U.C. knew of the real predicament. They certainly knew of Douglas Houghton's position and they certainly got a picture from Jim Callaghan but I don't think they knew how desperately weak Harold's position was in Cabinet by last night. They certainly knew that if Cabinet got into conflict with the Parliamentary Party it might well be defeated and this, I think, was the key issue which really moved the T.U.C. So I don't believe myself that Victor Feather and his colleagues were tremendously struck when Harold

[1] See *Wilson*, pp. 657–61.

threatened that if he didn't get his way he would impose a Bill with penalties. I don't believe they thought he had the power to do so. We can't know this but maybe I will find out in conversation later on.

So there we sat about waiting, until Harold finally came in, very abrasive, very tough, very furious with Cabinet. Despite all the difficulties of negotiating from the worst possible position, he told us, we have a settlement and Barbara chimed in, 'Yes, and despite this morning's disastrous press we managed to get a settlement.' There it was, a solemn declaration, not a declaration of intent but an agreement by the General Council of its attitude, including what we had asked them to include. Well, they had been moved to go a little way. The one surprise was that when I said, 'I take it you have left open what you have in the big Bill?' Barbara replied, 'Oh, no. We have excluded the penal sanctions from the big Bill as well.' I don't quite know why but they had just chucked them all away.

Then we had a series of little odious speeches, with George Thomas congratulating the Prime Minister and Jim Callaghan soft-soaping and saying that despite all the difficulties we now had a chance of re-election and he would like to say that all his energies would be on the side of the Prime Minister. People were saying that we shouldn't leave too soon, or it would be supposed that Cabinet had no serious doubts, so we spun it out for a quarter of an hour until Harold went out again and then came back with the announcement. He and Barbara once more had the congratulations of the Cabinet and we were ready for the 7 o'clock meeting with the Parliamentary Party.

This was perfectly straightforward. Barbara came in looking white and drawn and sat down beside Harold. When he arrived there had been a moderate cheer, but no one stood up and there was no standing ovation after he had read his typed-out speech. The press, no doubt on Douglas Houghton's instructions, all reported that he got a hero's welcome. I don't think that's true. I think the Party was relieved and that they heard the speech with somewhat cynical disdain. They had got the climb-down they wanted but you don't greatly admire a leader who climbs down, even when it is you who have ordered him to do so. My God, we are out of the wood, we are not tearing ourselves to pieces and at the last moment we have got him off the hook but there is no enthusiasm. I had dinner with Michael Foot and we discussed it in detail. I really love talking to him, he is one of the people I can talk to freely. What a day it has been. Somehow throughout the day I had been confident that this would happen, because I judged that after Cabinet yesterday Harold Wilson would decide to hold his position, to fight for his life and rebuke us. It will not be over this crisis but later on that trouble will come.

Thursday, June 19th

No Cabinet today. David Watt rang me up this morning and I discussed the whole situation with him and so clarified my mind that I decided to write a long letter to Harold. I had all kinds of business in Alexander Fleming House which interrupted me but I finally got a minute written and put it on the file. I tried to sum up what I think and the key fact is not that Harold is a cautious, devious man, but a reckless, impulsive creature, and that we have had six months of unnecessary, misjudged, unsuccessful cliffhanging. Once again he has rushed into a thing, come unstuck and got out.

I dictated the letter and got it into my box for tonight, and then I gave David Astor lunch at the Garrick. He simply wanted to ask me to write for the *Observer* after I had ceased to be a Minister, even if I was writing books for the *Sunday Times*,[1] and I said I could certainly do so. At 3.30 I went down to the House to hear the Prime Minister answering Questions as tactfully and brightly as ever. At the end he made his Statement and dealt with the Tory reaction.[2] Heath very cleverly asked just one question, 'What will happen should unofficial strikers ignore the trade union leaders, and go on striking?' It really did nonplus Harold, who had expected something more ferocious about surrender, and he was flushed and flummoxed. You could feel that he wasn't standing as firmly on his feet and he never quite recovered. Fortunately for us, the back-bench Tories behaved so ridiculously, giggling and shouting and showing such utter disrespect for the trade unions, that they really played into our hands. On our side there was naturally somewhat embarrassed enthusiasm and on the other an utterly illiterate, vulgar anti-trade union reaction. Mind you, the Tories had thought that we were going to tear ourselves to pieces in their presence and they were naturally peeved at being denied the sight of us committing *hara-kiri*. On the whole I thought the afternoon went as well as could be expected.

I had arranged to go to Glyndebourne with Anne and Peter and Jeanne Lederer,[3] but I had to stay behind for a three-line whip on Quintin Hogg's motion asking Jim Callaghan and Willie Ross to implement the recommendations of the English and Scottish Parliamentary Boundary Commissions.[4] Jim hadn't been there for Question Time and when I came in for the 7 o'clock vote I sat down beside him and asked him why. He said, 'No, I pulled out. I didn't want to be there to spoil Harold's fun.' 'Did anyone do any damage this afternoon?' I asked. Jim had announced that we were just going to deal with Greater London and the five very worst constituencies, those with

[1] In November 1966 Crossman signed a contract with the publisher Hamish Hamilton and the *Sunday Times* for two books to be written after he left office. The *Diaries* that he eventually prepared were to be published jointly by Hamish Hamilton and Jonathan Cape and serialized in the *Sunday Times*. See Vol. II, p. 309.

[2] The Prime Minister announced that the T.U.C. General Council had unanimously agreed to a solemn and binding undertaking, setting out the lines on which they would intervene in serious unconstitutional stoppages. The Government would not proceed this session with the interim I.R. Bill and consultations about the legislation to be introduced next session would continue with the T.U.C., the C.B.I. and other organizations concerned.

[3] Peter Lederer worked with Costains Ltd, the building firm, and Crossman had brought him to the Ministry of Housing and Local Government as an adviser. His wife, Jeanne, was a friend of Mrs Crossman.

[4] The Conservatives' motion was defeated by 270 votes to 219.

electorates of over 90,000 and 100,000 and leave the rest till afterwards, which the Tories called gerrymandering. 'Yes,' he said. 'Boyd-Carpenter did the dirt on me and was very effective.' So Jim's not even convinced about this either. After the vote I gave Patricia Llewelyn-Davies dinner. We were too tired to talk about industrial relations, so we discussed children and I talked in a depressed way about absentee fatherhood.

Friday, June 20th

The main news is that the C.B.I. have come out in the most withering way. They have been to see Barbara and Harold and have gone away saying that the two of them have no idea of what to put into their new big Bill. This is probably true. Barbara and Harold have been so busy making peace with the T.U.C. and discarding penal sanctions even in the big Bill that it is clear that the C.B.I. will begin to wonder whether we haven't sold out altogether. Barbara has attacked back, I think unwisely, and accused them of insulting the trade unions but all this is natural reaction.

I got into the train and found that by mistake I had slipped into my briefcase the text of my letter to the Prime Minister, so it would have to be sent back to London in a sealed envelope in time for him to get it in his weekend box. I therefore had a chance to withdraw and I wondered if I should send it after all. Anne had said, 'It sounds like a headmaster addressing a pupil', and I had said, 'Not exactly, it's like a senior housemaster addressing an unsuccessful headmaster'. I thought no, this was the most deplorable, catastrophic exhibition between a Cabinet and a Prime Minister and we shouldn't just let things slide. We have now got to get Cabinet right and the Management Committee right and get Harold to be a more sensible Prime Minister. Though I could have withdrawn my letter, I thought, what have I got to lose or to gain? I am sixty now, a senior member of the Cabinet and if I can't do this, who can? This is my function in life, to try to have things said to Harold which no one else will say and this, which I could never say to him, he will have to read, and I will have it for the record. It doesn't read too badly and on the whole I think it is right to send it.

I was going to Cheltenham for a meeting with the Town Clerks' Annual Conference. In the morning Dame Evelyn Sharp was speaking on the Maud Commission and in the afternoon I was coming in on 'The Town Clerk and Politics'.[1] I was able to lunch with her and I found that she was very scornful of Derek Senior's Minority Report. I don't agree with her and I think it's extremely well written but she was pretty convincing. She said there was no question that the Health Service could possibly be taken over by local authorities, mainly because of finance. She didn't want to force that kind of

[1] Dame Evelyn Sharp (D.B.E. 1948) was Permanent Secretary at the Ministry of Housing and Local Government from 1955 until her retirement in 1966. She was a member of the Independent Broadcasting Authority 1966–73 and since 1973 has been Chairman of the London Quadrant Housing Trust. She became a life peer in 1966.

thing. She obviously feels that now the Government should accept the broad outline of Maud and her speech was extremely interesting. I think I must try to get her to come and talk to me again before I finally make up my mind on N.H.S. reform. My own speech was fairly bright. I had asked the Ministry of Housing for a brief but had got nothing from them about the relation of the town clerk to party machines and party loyalty, so I went back to my own Ministry to get something better. I was able to formulate the difference between the loyalty or the integrity of a Permanent Secretary towards the Minister and the ethics and loyalty of a town clerk towards the majority leader and the majority party. It was an interesting meeting and then Anne came over to drive me home in time for a swim in the bath.

Sunday, June 22nd

I spent yesterday at a conference for handicapped children, which was greatly encouraging because I began to feel that my campaign for the sub-normal is really bringing results. Here in the Midlands they know what the Minister has done. I enjoyed being there and feeling that I had started a campaign which could be carried out.

This morning's press was far too detailed, naming Ministers and giving their views, but fortunately it didn't give a full impression of what actually happened in Cabinet and there was no account of Harold with the brandy or of the actual words or phrases which passed, just an accurate calculation of what each person said. I don't know why but this is the one kind of leak we get from our Cabinet. I don't happen to give these details; I try instead to get the press to come to the right conclusions about Cabinet. As I said to David Watt, 'You must estimate how successful this decision is. It is not a catastrophe because, even seen in the medium term, we have positively shifted the trade unions more than ever before and got a bit extra out of a reckless piece of brinkmanship. Seen in perspective it is something which will probably be remembered as an achievement by the Labour Government.' These are the things which I try to talk to the press about but of course they love sensation and as sensation equals people that was what today's stories described. I am sure we are going to have a bleeding row with Harold again about leaks and naming people and I fear it will deflect his attention from the really serious matter of getting Cabinet right.

Let me put down one other thought. Harold may think he can get Cabinet right by reconstruction and it is just conceivable that because I have been unpopular and in view of what I have written to him he may want to drop me. If he does I shan't be too sorry. He can't get rid of Callaghan who has been proved right in the end, I don't see how he possibly could. I am the one inside person who has been a far more serious opponent than anybody else, the one formidable counter-force in the Cabinet. I am weak, though, because Harold can get rid of me on the ground of failure or dodderiness or clanger-iness, all the things which the press have attributed to me, and I would think he could get rid of me without a trace. There wouldn't be any great commotion outside and he could afford to do it. This is something which may well weigh in his mind. But I am ready for it now, ready to start writing and thinking. I hate my severance from my family. I don't think it's likely but it is a possibility and we shall see.

Monday, June 23rd

I was terribly busy with a series of routine interviews and talks in my room at the House of Commons when in rushed Tam to say that George Clark, number two Political Correspondent at *The Times*, must see me. I said I would give him two minutes. In he came and said, 'I've got a hot tip that you are going to drop teeth and spectacles. It's all round the lobby. Have you any comment to make?' I said, 'But my dear George, my only comment is that I haven't had time even to consider it. Last week was a busy week. The question of the timing of the Order is simply a matter for the Chief Whip, the Lord President and myself and that is that.' I didn't think very much more about it but I hoped I had scotched the rumour.

Tuesday, June 24th

We often blame the press for being the cause of our troubles and sometimes they are. This morning down rushed Tam to tell me that the first item on the B.B.C. was that teeth and spectacles charges are now being deferred indefinitely and in *The Times* the great lead front-page story was headlined 'Charges for Glasses and Teeth Deferred'. If you looked very carefully at George Clark's story you would see that it doesn't actually say this but *The Times* now is prepared to go further than its writers are encouraged to go and *The Times* itself surmises and hardens up the story, so already it was firm news that we were having second thoughts and changing our minds. All day the press were ringing up to ask if the story were true and saying that we must give them some news. I was in some difficulty and thought I'd better have a word with Harold. I didn't want to commit the Management Committee to tabling the Order for the increases because it *was* just conceivable that we would have the Order postponed and decide on a different policy. But telling the literal truth that the timing had not yet been considered wasn't good enough to scotch the story, which went on and on, with the underlying theme of the shuffles and uncertainties about teeth and spectacles. Tam has been around the back benches and I have had a word with Reg Paget, Douglas Houghton and Stanley Orme,[1] who warned me once again of the phenomenal emotion this damned thing has raised. The Party has a fixation on it and from outside a dozen or fifteen letters a week are still coming from secretaries of constituency parties, all pleading for a return to a free Health Service. I have been thinking about this, because luckily on Thursday evening

[1] Labour M.P. for Salford West since 1964, Minister of State in the Northern Ireland Office 1974–6 and Minister for Social Security since 1976.

I have to give the Herbert Morrison Memorial Lecture to the G.L.C. and months ago I chose the subject of paying for the Health Services. Brian Abel-Smith and the officials in both parts of the Department have been pouring information into me about the way in which the services are paid for and what the real choices are between taxation, social service contributions, charges and the enlargement of the private sector. I have also put it down for discussion at Management Committee next week.

At O.P.D. we had a tiny problem of the Black Power Conference in Bermuda. Should we have two frigates and some troops there to prevent disturbance? This kind of thing must now be cleared through the Committee, not that there is any disagreement between Defence and Foreign Affairs, but because they just want the secret Cabinet clearance. It made me realize how totally ineffective O.P.D. is. All this side of the work is run by the Prime Minister and his little inner group. At the Committee Harold said that he wanted to see me tonight and that I should go along at 9 o'clock, and immediately after the Committee Barbara asked me to go up to her room at the Ministry of Labour. She has spent hundreds of pounds on the most lovely decorations, new wallpaper, new furniture, new carpets and curtains, and there she displayed for me the watercolour with which we are to thank Charles Forte. It is a splendid John Piper. It is strange – Barbara couldn't be pallier with me now and she is still enjoying the thoughts of the holiday. She doesn't resent at all what has happened between us and she is still close to me. We are an amazing pair in the sense that we manage to keep our personal relations clear despite strong disapproval of each other's tactics and methods. Indeed, while criticizing each other quite a lot behind our backs, we still remain good friends, partly because Ted is such a splendid person, but also because Barbara is a real Girl Guider and that is what she will always remain – unfortunately.

After a meeting in the Department on post-Ely policy and a quick interview for Thames T.V. on why we were delaying the implementation of the Seebohm Report, I had dinner with Brian Abel-Smith and Tommy Balogh until at 9 o'clock I had to break off to walk across to No 10. There was Harold in his study, which is dominated by a big photograph of Attlee. He sat on the sofa a long way off on the other side of the fire and we got down to two enormous drinks and really chatted. He started quite simply, 'I got your minute. I thought out a reply and dictated it and as it has been typed out I may as well read it to you because it's going to be in my memoirs, not in yours. You can have your letter to me and I will have my letter to you.' (This is what actually happened.) He read aloud very fast a long, detailed reply, perfectly friendly, accepting that I had been consistent throughout, even in supporting him on the short-term Bill when I wanted the crisis overcome, and then he defended himself on my main charge of cliquiness on the ground that he couldn't trust the Management Committee with Callaghan in it. Out of this defence it clearly emerged that Harold was saying that he must have a Cabinet of cliques because there are always members he distrusts.

We got down to a long two-hour discussion of our colleagues. Harold has ruled out Jim Callaghan, who has been in cahoots with the T.U.C. throughout, who is playing double and is only concerned with getting the leadership. But Harold's wrath was now concentrated on two other people, Tony Crosland and Dick Marsh, who I believe he thinks are the chief sources of the leaks. He is probably right, these two do chat maliciously with the press and, while at Cabinet Dick Marsh always asserts his innocence, Tony Crosland is silent. The fact remains, however, that we will always have leaks from our Cabinet because Harold is the leakiest of them all. We talked this evening about the Sunday press and, when I said I thought Tony Howard was very much better than anybody else in the *Sunday Times*, Harold said, 'Yes, I did brief him and I briefed Margach. I put Gerald Kaufman on to put them straight.' Harold sees nothing at all improper in doing this, while he bitterly blames Crosland and Marsh for doing the same against him. I have no doubt that Tony and Dick have very different motives. Tony has never forgiven Harold for making Roy Chancellor and has never lost hope that if Roy goes he will be Chancellor in his place. His best chance would be the breaking up of this Government and Callaghan's taking over. Though this sounds a terribly remote possibility I can't help thinking that it has been at the back of Tony's mind during the course of the last six months, when he has switched from demanding stronger anti-trade union measures to being 100 per cent pro-Callaghan. Harold is right, Tony and Jim do see a lot of each other and I know it because my room in the House is on the same landing as theirs. They are in cahoots with Douglas Houghton, the Chairman of the Party, and it has been their triangle which has really endangered Harold in this crisis.

What else did he say about our people? He almost ran down the list. Yes, poor Peter Shore—he's out, not that he wasn't out before. He's admitted to be a failure. Harold said, 'I over-promoted him, he's no good.' He was short and sharp on him. On the other hand, Mason, in contrast to Peter Shore and Dick Marsh, is a solid success in Harold's view and so is Tony Wedgwood Benn, who also turned against Harold on that famous Tuesday. He is recognized as having really done his job and Harold said, 'Though he talks nonsense outside Mintech., when he's on the job he talks sense.' We discussed Roy at great length and his particular relationships with Harold and agreed that he sat on the fence. I said, 'You can't blame him because he and I both sat on the fence, Harold, on that Wednesday morning when we didn't know whether you and Barbara were going to bring back an agreement.' We agreed that Roy had remained canny and aloof and had looked after himself and mustn't be expected to expand but that, provided you accept his limits, he is a man of integrity and loyalty. It became clearer to me that Harold is steeling himself to try to get rid of a Cabinet which makes life intolerable and creates an atmosphere of no confidence in the Government. If he is really not going to have everything done by hole-and-corner methods in special little cliques of Ministers, he must have an inner Cabinet he can trust. His final conclusion on all this was, 'You know, you and Barbara and I ought to see even more of each other.' So the Management Committee is in a sense too big for him and now he's driven back to talking about his three old friends. At least he says that to me. One can never be sure with Harold that in talking to others he won't talk very differently. But his relationship with me was as good as ever and there was no discussion of my failings or my difficulties, which were all left to one side, except for the assumption that we would have to find some solution to the teeth and spectacles problem. There it was, a real old-fashioned gossip, a long discussion of scandal and success and failures and how the P.M. was looking forward to the reconstitution of the Cabinet. There was no great argument about winning the election but a great deal of discussion about unifying the Party and getting the leadership right.

Wednesday, June 25th

At last I saw John Davies and Norman from the C.B.I. about their reactions to our superannuation scheme.[1] We had rather feared that they were going to demand, for instance, two levels of contracting out and that they would insist on removing several essential features from the plan. But they couldn't have been easier or more accommodating and lively. The fact is the C.B.I. approves the scheme and I think they appreciate what I did in arranging a 50/50 basis for the employer/employee contributions. This reminds me that last night Harold explained at great length the new ideas he had for getting out of our difficulties about increasing taxation next year. This was to increase the employer's national insurance contribution in preparation for getting into Europe.[2] There is something in this as an electoral gimmick and device but it is going to complicate my relations with the C.B.I.

After the meeting Alan Marre stayed behind. As a result of endless prodding by Ron Matthews, he is beginning to learn how to behave as a Permanent Secretary, that he should regularly drop in, for instance, and clear four or five minor things with me instead of writing long submissions. At last the Department are beginning to learn how to work with me but they still find it difficult not to have a Minister who works to their routine but who demands a much more rapid pace. They say the trouble is that I write all my memos at night and deliver them in the morning and that it puts the Department under great strain. They are used to having a Minister who spends a good many hours of his departmental day reading his papers and writing notes.

In the afternoon I chaired another meeting of our post-Ely policy advisory group. We had got on to the whole question of how, far, far away, outside the Department, right down in a ward in a hospital, we could get the ward

[1] Sir Arthur Norman (K.B.E. 1969), Chairman since 1964 and Chief Executive since 1972 of the De La Rue Company, was President of the C.B.I. 1968–70.

[2] In most E.E.C. countries the employer's social security contribution is higher than the employee's contribution so that there was plausible political justification for the Prime Minister's suggestion that to increase the employer's contribution would be a useful alternative to increasing income tax.

orderlies to understand our directives and to be prepared to communicate with the Secretary of State up in the stratosphere in the Elephant and Castle. We had a really constructive discussion.

By this time the Tories had suddenly decided that next Tuesday, the day of the investiture of the Prince of Wales,[1] they would put down a vote of censure against me over the muddle about teeth and spectacles. They are already trying to force the pace, so I went in to see Peart and Mellish to try to sort this out.

Thursday, June 26th

I woke up to discover that the job I did last night had got me an extraordinarily prominent press. I had been to the dinner at the formal opening of the Family Planning Association's annual conference, and I had said virtually nothing except for making an informal remark about family planning. However, because I had been the first Minister ever to attend and had spoken with great warmth and feeling and because it was on family planning and sex, I had got an enormous press, and a good press too.

Another front-page story, in *The Times*, gave apparently verbatim something which the Chief Whip and Harold had said to each other on Tuesday, the Chief Whip's line against the Prime Minister and the anger Harold had felt against Bob for prejudging issues and how the Chief was in a strong position. God knows who put it in the paper. I strongly suspect it came from Bob himself or perhaps from Peart or someone near the Chief. Anyhow a blank denial was issued and for the moment relations between Mellish and Harold are patched up.There is no doubt that Bob Mellish is a far more important, independent character than the P.M.'s poodle John Silkin was.

This did not make any easier the discussion on leaks with which we began Cabinet. Tony Wedgwood Benn asked if we couldn't stop the leaks by giving more positive information on what the Government was doing and Harold said, 'I am not going to put on the leaks procedure. I have decided what to do.' This virtually meant a reconstruction, to exclude the disloyal elements in the Cabinet. After this Harold was able to announce that the excellent Joe Haines has at last replaced Trevor Lloyd-Hughes. Trevor has been promoted to become the head of the Government Advisory Services (which, when I was made Lord President, I begged him to do and he refused), the official in charge of the co-ordination of government publicity. So Judith Hart, the Paymaster, will now have a chance of getting this right. When I asked Judith about it she said, 'Oh, we have spent hours, the P.M., Burke Trend and I, writing minutes to each other on the precise relationship of Trevor Lloyd-Hughes to me and Trevor Lloyd-Hughes to No. 10 and where he will sit. It has taken hours and hours of negotiation and I don't know how well it will actually work.'

[1] See below, p. 543 and n.

The other big thing at Cabinet was Gerald Brooke,[1] where it is clear that we are in fact selling out for the sake of good relations with Russia, because we hope to play a part in the American–Russian rapprochement which Nixon is announcing this week.[2] It's a blatant piece of appeasement and it was put out by Stewart in his most dry, unconvincing way. Roy and I were against it but the rest of those mealy-mouthed people sat there uncertain. We were told that the Foreign Secretary was so far committed he couldn't go back. I am sure it will give us a thoroughly bad image and I am also sure it's wrong to let them exchange an innocent hostage for two valuable spies, but there it is. Cabinet was asked for a view but it was too late to reverse the action.

Immediately after this we went on to S.E.P. and the interminable saga of help for Cumberland. The Leyland proposal has now broken down and there has been a new suggestion of a bus factory for the National Bus Corporation. Leyland made it clear that they would like to put this project in a Development Area although other sites would suit them far better, so that if we insisted they should go to Cumberland we should pay through the nose, £28,000 a job. Roy and I again stood out, saying this was intolerable and that at least the decision should be deferred until next Monday's P.E.S.C., when we will have Roy's demand for further enormous cuts in public expenditure. The Prime Minister is emotionally committed to this but I think it is impossible to keep Whitehaven, one of our two constituencies in West Cumberland,[3] and in fact a few thousand people from Cumberland should move South where there is work. To go on trying to bring work there is fantastically expensive but Harold won't entertain anything different. This kind of intervention is exactly what he likes and what we can't afford. I walked out half-way through because this is useless.

I delivered the Herbert Morrison Memorial Lecture, off the record, to a rather good selection of 140 G.L.C. people at Caxton Hall. It was far too long, some seventy minutes, followed by thirty-five minutes of discussion,

[1] Agreement had been reached with the Russian Government to exchange Gerald Brooke, the British lecturer arrested and accused of distributing anti-Soviet literature while on a visit to Moscow in 1965, for Helen and Paul Kroger, two senior Soviet agents who were serving a twenty-year prison sentence for their part in the Portland spy-ring case of 1961.

Although the British Government also secured the release of two other Englishmen imprisoned in Russia for drug smuggling and obtained exit visas for four Russian citizens who wished to marry Britons, it was generally felt that the Government was submitting to blackmail and that the exchange was very much to the benefit of the Russians. However, Brooke's health was reportedly deteriorating and there seemed little alternative.

[2] On April 14th the Russian and American governments had opened talks in Vienna on the peaceful uses of atomic energy but these were at a technical level and hardly represented the thawing of relations for which President Nixon hoped. By the autumn, however, both governments simultaneously ratified the Nuclear Non-Proliferation Treaty and in November the long-delayed Strategic Arms Limitation talks opened in Helsinki.

[3] Joseph Symonds's majority at Whitehaven was 8,791 at the 1966 General Election and Labour retained the seat in the 1970 Election. Workington had given Fred Peart a majority of 10,505 in 1966 but Labour were eventually to lose this traditionally safe seat in a by-election in 1976.

but I couldn't really cut it. I wanted to get this philosophy clear and Brian has slaved over it with me in the last two days. I had seen in perspective the difficulty of N.H.S. charges but I also know that the present system of exemptions, where people simply write their names on the back of a prescription, is open to scandalous abuse. There are very good administrative reasons why we shouldn't have charges and good public opinion reasons why we should. The public rather like the charges because they feel they actually get value for money if they are paying something. It's not public objection but fanatical Labour Party objection that we face and I am going to propose to the Management Committee next week that they should consider the possibility that in the big Superannuation Bill next session we should increase the N.H.S. contribution by a large enough sum to make charges unnecessary. It would only take roughly ½ per cent extra, at most, to get rid of them and it may really be easier for the party if we carry on with the teeth and spectacles Order in July on the clear understanding that in the big Bill we will take steps to get rid of charges altogether. By now the Tories, after a row with the Chief Whip, have dropped their proposal for a censure debate next week and they will just have an anodyne debate on the finances of the Health Service, avoiding a vote on the day of the investiture.

Anne came up for the lecture and afterwards we drove straight off to Prescote. On the way we heard that we had lost Ladywood to the Liberals.[1] Oh God, losing that cast-iron Labour seat, Victor Yates's seat. But only 51 per cent voted and, as we all expected, the Liberals won on the local issue of rates. That is the brutal fact, so it honestly hasn't mattered. It was a sensational by-election but the Tories came out badly and, unlike Orpington, the Liberal increase is not a symbol of things to come.[2]

Sunday, June 29th

Yesterday I opened a health centre at Daventry and I took tremendous trouble with the press release and an excellent speech on the state of health centres and the importance of getting doctors into groups. Nothing in the press this morning. I had enormous coverage for family planning where I said nothing but not a line when I said something that really mattered.

Monday, June 30th

Last Wednesday Roy had a great triumph in the House with his speech on

[1] Victor Yates, who had held the seat since 1945, had died on January 19th. The seat was won by Wallace Lawler, a Liberal, who had a majority of 2,713 over Mrs Doris Fisher, the Labour candidate.

[2] On March 14th, 1962, there was a by-election at Orpington, caused by the appointment as a county court judge of Mr Donald Sumner, Q.C., who in the 1959 General Election had held the seat for the Conservatives with a majority of 14,760. In the by-election Eric Lubbock took the seat for the Liberals, with a majority of 7,855. The Labour candidate came bottom of the poll and forfeited his deposit.

the Letter of Intent approved by the I.M.F. He had made an almost optimistic speech saying everything was going a great deal better than people hoped.[1] He largely got consent from our people and the Left voted with him but his Cabinet colleagues know that this week he is going to come to us, as happens every July, to ask yet again for massive further cuts in public expenditure. This year it will be all the more remarkable because of his optimistic speech and this year he will tell us that there is a crisis not because things are going badly, but because they are going well and we must cut back consumer demand. He will really be saying that we must maintain the degree of deflation, accept a fairly high level of unemployment and even sacrifice growth for the sake of the balance of payments.

A secondary aggravation has been the sensational revelation that the Board of Trade have been miscalculating the size of the export trade and month by month for some years now have underestimated by quite a considerable percentage what we have actually been exporting.[2] So when we thought we were deeply in the red we were really quite often somewhere in the black. All this made considerable difference to Roy's colleagues and in Management Committee this morning Barbara and I sat down really sceptical. Mind you, Tommy Balogh has been priming me, and Peter Shore and Barbara too, in our scepticism. Tommy is an intrepid man, who believes that we should have import controls, possibly import quotas and control of the export of capital. He thinks this is the right line and the only way to maintain relatively high employment. He and his number two, Andrew Graham,[3] who is still in No. 10, wrote a most powerful piece which Tommy circulated to us and which I have no doubt was seen by Treasury officials.

At Management Committee Harold said, 'I hear that somebody has been briefing at least three Cabinet Ministers,' and he looked, not very severely, at Barbara and me. I suppose he suspected that Tommy had briefed Tony Wedgwood Benn, Peter and Judith as well. The discussion was interesting because, as I said before, this was Barbara's first effort, now the compact with Roy has broken, to put up a real fight for an alternative radical policy.

[1] The visible trade deficit had fallen to £14 million in May and although it doubled to £28 million in June the Chancellor forecast a levelling-off in the growth of imports, a rise in exports and in investment by private industry and a fall in unemployment. There had also been a significant improvement in 'invisible earnings' from insurance, banking, investment and other services. The Chancellor declared that he expected to realize his target of a £300 million balance of payments surplus for 1969/70.

[2] The Government's statisticians had discovered that, every month since 1964, exports had been under-estimated by 2–3 per cent, some £10–15 million, as a result of a simplification of documentary procedures. The balance of payments itself was not hurt in real terms since the earnings continued to be credited but the error had affected the monthly trade figures used by the Treasury to forecast economic trends and by observers to judge the position of sterling. The discovery was announced on June 24th, the eve of the debate on the Letter of Intent. The Government vote was 292 and the Opposition's 243.

[3] Economic Assistant at the Cabinet Office September 1966–June 1968, while Thomas Balogh was at No. 10, and Economic Adviser at the Cabinet Office June 1968–July 1969. He has been Tutorial Fellow in Economics at Balliol College, Oxford, since 1969.

She wants to see us turn sharply away from what she regards as Roy's deflationary policy, and this is what Tommy had pledged her to.

My difficulty was that I had been briefed by Thomas too and I thought his argument was pretty powerful but from the start I felt that it was too late and I had told him that we couldn't get off the tramlines now. When we had our earlier discussion on the Letter of Intent,[1] I had pointed out that there was a specific limitation on import controls and Roy said, 'As long as we take a loan from the I.M.F. we can't impose import controls,' and that had been made perfectly clear to all the Cabinet. So this morning it didn't seem to me that if things are going well, as apparently they now are, it was suddenly possible to rely on import controls. It's only if they are going badly that you can do it. Roy made it clear right from the start that if the situation declined, if we had a run on the pound or a disastrous run of trade figures for exports, we might be driven to a siege economy, with import controls and more severe restrictions on the export of capital than at present but, as he rightly said, you can't change to that when you have just signed a Letter of Intent and your economy is responding reasonably well to the recipe of the I.M.F. doctors. I thought this morning that it was an equal contest between Barbara and Roy. Denis Healey was, as always on these occasions, solidly on the side of Roy. Michael Stewart was saying, 'On other occasions I might like it but...', and Fred Peart came straight out and said he accepted Roy's position. This discussion is to continue at another Management Committee on Wednesday afternoon.

I lunched with the Chairman of the Essex Regional Hospital Board and then had a meeting with the Board itself about South Ockendon. After our working party had visited and reported on the hospital we came to the conclusion that the idea of putting new buildings there is wrong and that we must break it up into smaller units. We proposed to improve staff morale by taking 200 people out of Ockendon and putting them in other hospitals, while stimulating the local authorities to take their share in this and prepare long-term plans for smaller buildings. The Department and the Regional Hospital Board disagreed and I had to be fierce but in the end I gave way. I got round it by saying, 'If you think you can build new buildings as cheaply and more quickly than we can upgrade old ones, you can do that for two of them, but you can't put up four new buildings instead of upgrading two.'

Jack Mendelson came to see me about teeth and spectacles. He wanted to explain that we ought to concede to the Party and not lay the Order at all. I began to argue, saying, 'Have you ever considered the case? Teeth and spectacles aren't like prescription charges.' He replied, 'Don't worry about the details. I know it's not rational. This is a traumatic party reaction but I'm going to vote with the party on this. You have upset them by timing it wrong, now you must accept it.' It is infuriating to have an intellectual like Jack Mendelson saying he's not going to reason with you, that he's not even

[1] See above, p. 502.

going to attack the Order for itself but simply as a kind of traumatic test case of the relationship between the party and the Government. This is important because, although other people won't say this, they will do it. The real difficulty is that people have committed themselves, on the moral issue, to signing Laurie Pavitt's resolution (rather like Biafra which continues to be an issue of principle) and now they find it difficult to uncommit themselves.

Tuesday, July 1st

I rang up the Prime Minister early this morning, just before he went off to the investiture, and read aloud to him a passage I had been working on since 6 a.m., a statement about my attitude to N.H.S. charges, describing them as something temporary which had been forced on us as a lesser evil during devaluation but expressing my wish that they would disappear when the conditions that produced them disappeared. Harold accepted it. It took me the whole morning to persuade the Department to send a copy of this very brief couple of paragraphs round to Roy.

Meanwhile I was waiting in my room in the Commons, because at 10.30 the first meeting of the Uprating Bill Committee was being held in Committee Room 11. We had not been sure whether I should be a member of this Committee at all but I had thought that there might possibly be a policy issue on which I would want to speak and (with the exception of the Finance Bill) if you are not on a Committee you can't speak. I had therefore, rather reluctantly, agreed to put my name down and I had to be present at the first meeting. David Ennals was taking charge of the proceedings. As Tam had to go to Scotland the Committee was short of people and we only had a majority of two, so I found myself sitting there from 10.30 to 11.30, going back and forth down the passage to my room to be available on the phone. Each time I came in and out I was booed as frivolous and flighty but back in my room I was sitting doing absolutely nothing while I waited for the typed pages of my speech to come over from Alexander Fleming House and for word to come from Roy.

Eventually Roy rang me and said my two paragraphs were terrible and that this statement would be disastrous. 'You will take the headlines from the investiture. You can't do this, Dick.' So I said, 'What would you do, Roy?' 'I wouldn't make any personal statement. I would try to play it cool, play it soft, say it unemphatically. Why not just say that you sympathize with your predecessor and you very much take his view? I remember Harold once saying this, once you have said you agree with your predecessor and support all he said, they don't listen to anything else you say.' I took Roy's advice as I didn't want a row with him and, though I had got Harold's agreement, I scrapped the draft and put in a reference to Kenneth Robinson, just saying that I now more and more felt with him. I wrote a very careful piece about charges and then went straight on to my new ideas about contributions.

Sure enough, when we came to the debate at 3.30 it worked like magic. The

Opposition had asked me to speak directly after Maurice Macmillan, who was feeble and conscientious and very nice about me and the work I was doing for the sub-normal. He asked endless questions but he had nothing positive to say. Then I made what was really quite a big, constructive speech to fifteen or twenty people. This was a sweltry summer afternoon, the day of the investiture, when the Tories had decided to have instead of a vote of censure a mere adjournment debate, and a delicious sense of lassitude had descended on the House. I got away with it on charges. Behind me people listened and didn't object too much. True, Laurie Pavitt, who had just before promised his loyal support, made a routine speech 100 per cent against me but he is that kind of man. However, we got fairly loyal backing from our side with quite a decent wind-up at 7.0 by Julian Snow and Roy came in to listen.[1]

At 8 o'clock I went up for a little gossip with Barbara and Peter Shore. We discussed what had happened at the Management Committee on Monday and what would happen in Cabinet on Thursday. Peter appeared to be cautiously in alliance with Barbara but unhappily and somewhat ineffectively. It was pleasant together and Barbara and I found ourselves talking freely and naturally and not quarrelling any more. We were trying to bring Peter along but we were also uneasily aware that he is unlikely to remain in the Cabinet all that long.

Meanwhile the investiture was going on.[2] The press has been building this up for days, and thank God I am not Lord President of the Council any more, concerned with all the flummery. It was the working-class members of the Cabinet who took part, Jim Callaghan and George Thomas, Harold Wilson, Michael Stewart and Fred Peart, and the Chief Whip would have been there if he had been free. They could adore it and share in it but Barbara, Roy, Tony Crosland and I, the middle-class, are out of it. We were thanking god that we were not there and I must admit that I didn't bother to put on the television and neither did my family. I think we are out of touch, old-fashioned radicals who dislike the mumbo jumbo of royalty, who are bored with it and don't want to take part.

Wednesday, July 2nd

In the afternoon I met the T.U.C. representatives, to hear their considered view on our National Superannuation White Paper. It was a nice, easy meeting, as it always is with Harold Collison and the rest of them, and I couldn't help reflecting on how well our consultations with the T.U.C. and the C.B.I,

[1] The motion on National Health Service (Financing) was withdrawn and there was no division. For Crossman's major speech on the various methods of financing the Health Service by taxes, rates and contributions or charges, see *House of Commons Debates*, Vol. 786, cols 253–66.

[2] The investiture as Prince of Wales of the Queen's eldest son, Prince Charles, took place at Caernarvon. Extremist members of the Welsh Nationalist Movement had threatened to disrupt the proceedings and security arrangements were strict. There were only one or two small hostile incidents and the ceremony, which was seen on television by several hundred million people, was generally accounted a success.

have gone. Heaven knows, they might naturally suspect me as a lumbering, dangerous intellectual but in fact my relations with both of them are solid. That is because I have genuinely consulted them and cared about doing it and because the job we have done together is far more thorough than, for instance, Barbara's White Paper. It's very rare for any scheme to be put up by this Government which isn't thought to be a half-baked intervention by a lot of amateurs.

At 4 o'clock I rushed over to No. 10 for the continuation of Management Committee. The only issue was the one I raised. Granted the economic tramlines and that we must continue roughly as we are, is the Chancellor right to say that in order to achieve a good budget next year with no increases in taxation we must accept yet another savage cutback in our plans to expand the social services? We all accept that this year's £160 million overspending has to be cut back. The question is whether we should cut £240 million beyond that, making a total of £400 million. A solid portion, some £160 million, would come from defence and savings in the investment plans of the nationalized industries, but the rest would have to be found from the civil programme. Is that necessary? Is it right that we should at all costs avoid higher taxation and put the whole burden on public sector expenditure? Roy's only defence is that he needs a cut in demand and, frankly, you cut demand more effectively by raising purchase tax or by other direct imports than you do by cutting public expenditure.

I raised this issue and then Barbara had her go, with a frontal attack on the tactical question of how large the cut in demand should be, whether it should be by public expenditure cuts or by actually cutting demand, and how far we still ought to rely on a prices and incomes policy. I must say I then pointed out that I didn't feel quite as shocked as Roy had been when he spoke of Reggie Maudling's gamble before the 1964 election.[1] I would like to see something of a gamble. I know we couldn't repeat the Maudling policy but we might be able to take certain risks and we should also face the fact that cuts in public expenditure were much less effective and more painful than cuts in demand and might produce devastating effects. We have already been wringing a lot of water out of that flannel, running big programmes on small, worn shoestrings. If we went on doing this and, to avoid detection, simultaneously maintaining the size of the programme, we really could come unstuck.

The discussion was on the whole friendly and good-tempered. At the end Roy said severely, 'It's no good. It's not true that the Social Services Ministers

[1] In the budget of April 1963 Reginald Maudling, then Chancellor of the Exchequer, had given £169 million in tax relief for 1963/4, of which over two-thirds had been in personal income tax, mainly at the bottom of the scale. Firms in areas of high unemployment were allowed to write off the costs of their capital equipment for tax purposes, and were also encouraged by a 30 per cent investment allowance. Mr Maudling's 1964 budget took only £100 million out off the economy, in taxes on tobacco, beer and spirits, but although in the summer months share prices continued to rise and the unemployment figures to fall the production index was stationary and the trade gap continued to widen.

can't get economies if they really want to. The fact is that they don't really want economies; psychologically they are spending Ministers.' He had to be reminded that we had already loyally carried out the economies he had asked for. We had been given a four-year programme and told that in 1969/70 there could be 3 per cent growth, so we had planned for that. It wasn't fair to say that we were not economical. We had kept within the margins that were given us. 'You have changed your mind,' we said, 'and cut us further and further each month.' By the end of the afternoon, Barbara and I had secured one major success. We persuaded Roy not to circulate his paper but to discuss this orally, 'on the basis of the medium-term prospects and the various economic documents', but without his specific project of a 2½–3 per cent cut, which we didn't want to see in the newspapers. Roy agreed to that and admitted that he must direct himself to the Cabinet more tactfully and not present us with this kind of unconditional ultimatum.

Harold asked Barbara and me to stay behind for a minute or two. I was surprised because we really had no time but he sat down with us and said, 'What do you think about a smaller Cabinet? Don't you think it is essential that I should have a reconstruction?' I said, 'Yes. We now have a contradiction in terms. We can't function as a Cabinet because you don't trust Callaghan, Crosland and Marsh. When you select your Cabinet in future the first requisite should be that you trust its members. Otherwise you not only behave badly to the three you distrust but you also upset all your friends by your hole-and-corner methods of consultation.' Harold talked as though he was determined to remove Callaghan, Marsh and Crosland from the Cabinet. He is infuriated by Crosland and I must say that Tony's behaviour at the Board of Trade has been more than usually irritating. He has been inefficient but nonchalant and cavalier, just not seeming to mind. He seems thoroughly browned off, sick at not being Chancellor, sickened by the Chancellor's policy and, having failed to become Chancellor, he now seems to have got into that peevish frame of mind which I believe is one of the bases of leaks. I find I am inclined to talk when I feel frustrated, left out, when I don't know things. This is ironical because then I start talking, feeling 'I haven't been consulted about this, therefore I am entitled to talk to the press about it because my guess is as good as anybody else's.' This is my view of Crosland's psychology. Marsh is a bit different. He is brash, promoted far beyond his merits. He is not corruptible but Melchett and people can get at him easily and so can the press. His leaking is more like Gunter's used to be.

Harold added that he must deal with some other failures. He mentioned Peter Shore again and said how disappointing Judith had been. I said, 'You know, she would have done better to have stayed as Minister of Social Security outside the Cabinet,' and it looks as if this might be Harold's plan. Then he said, 'I shall cover this up by another big piece of departmental reconstruction,' and he hinted that Mintech. and the Board of Trade are to be fused under Tony Wedgwood Benn to make it seem that people are being not excluded but just pushed away. The great unknown is whether Barbara will stay in her present Ministry or whether she would go to the Home Office instead of Jim. I believe this would be the right thing since what's happening now indicates pretty clearly that she has completely lost control. One of the effects of dropping her short-term Bill has been a rash of unofficial strikes – dock strikes, Leyland strikes, G.P.O. and National Health Service threats. So it is possible that she might be moved and I think she should be. But the inner group remains clear enough. The P.M. feels at home with Barbara and me, he talks to us freely and says, 'At any rate, even if we disagree, Dick, you and I, you never quarrel or do the dirty on me as other people do.' Roy of course is perfectly in but he is not psychologically or personally in with us. He still remains aloof, the Chancellor in No. 11, biding his time, calculating, with his own friends, his own society.

I finally got to Judith's room, and there was the N.E.C./Cabinet Consultative Committee having a little meal. There was some rather nice food and the atmosphere was pleasant. They are producing various think-pieces, including one on industrial relations, one on social services and one on poverty, discussion papers out of which will be boiled one policy paper to be presented at Conference. I looked with the greatest interest to this evening's paper on economics, which they were submitting to Roy. There was only one serious point, a mild paragraph in which they referred to the possibility of devaluing the sterling rate of exchange. It couldn't have been more watery but Roy had this out with them. Here one sees the difficulty. They had obviously felt under great pressure to show their independence by putting forward a cautious and considered view. Heaven knows, I think Terry Pitt had tried hard to make this into something harmless that the Government could take, but Governments can't take it and I had every sympathy with Roy, who rightly said that it would be interpreted as something he had permitted and from which conclusions could be drawn. Yet I also felt Harry Nicholas and the Executive were saying to themselves, 'If we can't mention it we are mere stooges.'

Nevertheless the really striking feature of the evening was the new relationship between the Party and the Cabinet which has been achieved by the climb-down on industrial relations. No wonder the Tories are furious at being denied the pleasure of watching us destroy ourselves because, though I think we will have lost heavily among the women of the country and in the short-run discredited ourselves with the public by apparently selling out to the trade unions and letting them get out of control, inside the Party there is no doubt whatever that we have a new belief that we can now get on together and fight the election. That feeling is there but it has come too late, accompanied by the feeling that we can't win.

Thursday, July 3rd

We had worked properly together at Management Committee and carefully thought out Roy's presentation to Cabinet this morning. Still, nobody's views were in any way inhibited. We disagreed in Cabinet in much the same way as in the Management Committee and Barbara and I were again the two chief disagreers. Once more Barbara projected her alternative policy and really got no support at all. I don't think anybody saw it as a serious possibility and Roy quietly demolished her, pointing out quite rightly that it was a policy which could only follow disaster and which would in no way obviate the need for the cuts in public expenditure or demand which he required. Barbara only got a little support from Tony Crosland, who once again wondered what had made our prediction of 3 per cent growth unjustified, what the imbalance in the economy really was and whether we had to accept the level of unemployment that the cuts required. He put this in his usual detached economist's way, exerting quite a powerful influence, but Roy had solid support from Denis Healey, Michael Stewart, Fred Peart and Gerald Gardiner. This time the Prime Minister was absolutely solid with Roy. They are obviously lined up on this policy and that's always so. Ever since I can remember the Prime Minister and his Chancellor have always come into a Cabinet meeting, even into Management Committee, fully prepared in advance. The only people who were dubious were Judith Hart and Peter Shore. Peter was muted this time. I think they both know they are in the doldrums and are anxious not to cause any more trouble.

I, of course, did not put in full Cabinet the suggestion that we should take risks like Reggie Maudling and gamble a bit but I did put the simple thought that it was much more difficult than Roy seemed to imagine to impose these cuts undetected and just squeeze 2½ per cent out of the Ministries with no changes of policy. I said that it was frankly impossible. We couldn't make cuts without declarations and in particular we couldn't impose their half of the cuts on the local authorities without a squeal.

We had some success, a great defensive victory. Roy didn't get Cabinet to agree to his cuts, only to agree to his having bilateral talks with Ministers, so that at next week's Cabinet he can present his cuts and we can then see whether they would be more painful than the increases in taxation which are the alternative. That's where we have got to this year on the July public expenditure crisis and we will see what happens next week.

The Prime Minister was very terse this morning, once again telling people that he was going to handle the leaks and disloyalty in his own way and I have a feeling he may be steeling himself to it. By the way, he told Barbara and me that he wasn't going to think of doing it for three or four weeks, 'not until Douglas Houghton's out of the way'. Obviously the role the Chairman of the Party has played in the Industrial Relations dispute and the influence he has in the Party are of tremendous importance to the Prime Minister. They are to me too and I am taking the greatest care to ensure that Douglas Houghton will be on my side when I come to my own minor little trouble on teeth and spectacles.

In the course of the afternoon I had two people to see me about this. One was the fanatical Laurie Pavitt, decent, boring, virtuous, ineffective, vain and unprepared to listen to reason. I had a quiet talk with him and said, 'Look, Laurie, you are working yourself up about the increased charges. You know these are not like prescription charges, indeed you know it so well that, though you led the Party into the lobby against prescription charges last year, when the Order in Council for increasing dentistry fees came up you withdrew the Prayer after a little discussion.[1] Surely you can't see this as an issue of principle and surely this shows that when we followed the increase in dentistry charges by putting up the charge for dentures we were right?' 'Ah,' he said, 'but perhaps I was wrong that time. It must be an issue of principle.' I said, 'What issue? If you think it is that one shouldn't pay for illness while one is ill but while one is well, could I point out to you that we pay for spectacles while we are well. That is a service and the same is largely true of teeth. Anyway we have had a charge for twenty-five years without complaint.' It made no difference and, later on, when I tried Frank Hooley, one of these Christians, a nice, decent man, I got absolutely nowhere with him either.[2] They all like the speech I made in the debate and are pleased and proud but they aren't going to think rationally, however high a priority it is to get rid of charges and whatever the value of each charge on its merits.

This evening I had to go to Edmonton to talk to the local party G.M.C. on the National Superannuation White Paper. I was busy talking to Tam and hadn't prepared myself carefully enough. I gave a little offhand talk and got a rough reply and I realized that you must never underrate or neglect a local party. You have to give it your full attention and interest to carry it along.

Peter Smithson got me back from Edmonton in about fifteen minutes in time to hear Barbara Castle wind up the Tory motion of censure on the dropping of her Bill.[3] Harold had told me earlier today that he was going to make one of his old-fashioned speeches and he hoped they would enjoy it. I gathered that for twenty minutes he had made a real knockabout attack on Heath, it had gone down well with our side and Harold had enjoyed it enormously. I arrived just as Barbara was getting up to boos and cheers and for the first seven minutes she was on her feet she only got out half a dozen sentences. I was sitting right at the end below the Speaker's chair and I saw her trembling as she got up, nervous, tense and tiny and somehow pathetic. If you are little and can only just see over the top of the dispatch box, if you have a high-pitched woman's voice and if you are trying to still the post-prandial, alcoholic clouds of noise you are at a terrible disadvantage, especially if you are a bit schoolmistressy and try to hector and lecture them at the same time. Barbara did her best and the angrier she got the more effective she got. A bit of a break came when the news was brought in that one of her strikes had been settled, though this seemed a bit too obvious for the Tories, but the

[1] On May 30th, 1968.

[2] Labour M.P. for Sheffield, Heeley, 1966–70 and since 1974.

[3] The Conservative motion was defeated by 301 votes to 242.

House was ferocious and violent and she got through very little. I began to wonder whether it wasn't time for her to move to the Home Office.

Friday, July 4th

The papers were full of fantastic stories about abortion. It had started at Aberdeen at the annual conference of the B.M.A., where doctors had got up and begun to complain about the working of the Act. Suddenly there came a sensational story that 40,000 Danish women were going to be imported to have their abortions done in London. The stories are as phoney as they could possibly be and are a great discredit to the British press but I had to think what to do about them and to think hard because the 'World At One' wanted me to speak on it this afternoon. I called in the officials and Peter Brown and said I simply wanted to go on the air to cool things off and remind people of the facts I gave in my Written Answer last Monday. I had wanted to make a Statement at the end of Questions but Bob Mellish had gone to the Prime Minister beforehand and Harold had rung me up before Management Committee to ask me not to press this now because they all thought I shouldn't get too closely associated with the row over the Abortion Act. I had to let it go and just gave a Written Answer, which showed that foreign women took up only 7 per cent of our total abortions and 17½ per cent of our private enterprise abortions. I told the officials I wanted to repeat this today but Peter Brown said, 'I don't want you mixed up with this because the figures aren't reliable,' and John Pater said,[1] 'They certainly aren't reliable. We have grave suspicions that the notifications of abortion don't include all the abortions done in the clinics.' 'What the hell,' I said. 'You people came to me only a fortnight ago and virtually forced me to give all these nursing homes another year of licences by telling me that they had satisfactorily fulfilled our conditions, including their registration methods.' I was wild with anger, rude, violent and unpleasant, because I thought they had done me down. I think it has been absolutely infuriating.

Here is an area, of course, where Ministers have great difficulty. Godber and the doctors get information which they say they are not entitled to give me because of confidentiality and clinical freedom. I only get rumours and then I have Peter and the lawyers saying we shouldn't do anything, shouldn't upset anybody, that this is a perfectly responsible business and that we ought to let these people run it. But Bea and I are uneasy because we hate this private sector. I think it's outrageous that our Abortion Act should be sullied and smirched by the activities of these money-making commercial doctors, and I ferociously believe that if they refuse to let me discipline them, they should discipline themselves through the G.M.C. However the Department were probably right to insist that I shouldn't go on to the 'World At One' but I am preparing now for Questions next Monday and I have lined up

[1] Director of Establishments and Organization at the D.H.S.S. 1969–5 and Under-Secretary from 1967 until his retirement in 1973.

Renee Short so that I can get this out of the way well before the teeth and spectacles censure debate at 7 o'clock.[1]

Sunday, July 6th

All I did yesterday was to go over to Coventry for the B.M.A.'s annual cocktail party. A few Coventry doctors came up to me but most of them just looked at me. I don't think they were openly hostile but just too reserved to admit that they knew I was the Secretary of State. We had quite a pleasant time and then I went off for a long talk with Peter Lister and Betty Healey about Council rates and Council tactics. There is less bitterness in our relations now, and they are no longer saying, 'You have destroyed our power of winning elections and our chances of getting into Parliament'. They are resigned to defeat in the next election and find it easier to be kind and gentle, but in a terribly defeatist way.

This morning we went over to see Jennie and Chris Hall. It had only been spotting with rain here but it was raining steadily up there on the Chilterns. Now it's 7 o'clock and I shall go and have a bathe and then read to the children before supper. After that I shall have to get down to preparing for the censure debate tomorrow.

Monday, July 7th

Today was very much a Health day because I was first in Questions. Fortunately Renee Short asked Question No. 3 on foreign women seeking abortions and I was able to report that though I had sent letters to seven nursing homes asking for information about this I had received only one reply. My answer was brief and quite unsensational but, as you can imagine, every paper seized on it. The journalists were all up in the gallery and the moment I had dealt with Question No. 3 they all walked out, abandoning the other 100 Questions. That shows the degree to which the press has become obsessed by abortion during this past week...It's an ideal story, with just a little salaciousness. It's medical and mysterious and slightly dirty and there has been this marvellous rumour about the 40,000 Danish women. Everything is believed and everything is printed and so my answer pretty well blanketed this evening's censure debate. After Questions I was glad to give a quick press interview, conscious that there would be less space in the newspapers for the censure debate.

After a little debate on Clydeside, teeth and spectacles started at 7 o'clock. I had finally decided to grant David Ennals's own request that he should follow Balneil at the beginning. David is a most effective speaker, who would slam back at Balneil, and then we would get Douglas Houghton and Laurie Pavitt to come in on my side before I wound up with a short speech before the vote at 10 p.m. Balneil gave what we expected, synthetic indignation on the

[1] Mrs Renee Short has been Labour M.P. for Wolverhampton North-East since 1964 and a member of the N.E.C. since 1970.

alleged delay and muddle, and David came back with a long and quite irrelevant passage about the achievements of the Health Service, to the delight of our people and the fury of the press and the Tories.

Right at the end Macmillan made a feeble kind of speech and at 9.40 I got up with a full House behind me, not so full on the other side. People strolled in after dinner for the vote but it was like the tough, ferocious, post-prandial House Barbara had last Thursday. I had a half-hearted House and I am sure that part of the reason was because most of the Tories thought this was a damn silly debate, and that I would get the better of it. This was not the way to handle me. There had been a three-and-a-half-hour censure debate on our delays in introducing the Uprating Bill, now we were to have three and a half hours on our muddle and confusion in introducing the charges which the Tories themselves approved. I had decided not to have anything much written out but I had insisted that Peter Brown should get out all the press cuttings, so I could do a speech entirely on the non-event of my having decided to defer the Order, all illustrated from the press.

When I got up it had been a miserable and tedious little debate and it was clear that the Tories didn't believe in it themselves so I let myself give a highly hilarious performance. I was arrogant, self-confident, enjoying myself. My side looked pleased and the front bench on the other side more and more tight and tense; even the Tories behind them were laughing. I was infinitely easier in my mind, I knew I had atoned for the mess about the local elections and had given our people gaiety, hitting power and self-confidence. They knew they had a Minister who would really fight and could dominate the House of Commons. As someone said to Tam, 'The thing we really don't forgive him for is dallying with his House of Lords reform. He fell in love with his confounded agreed measure but otherwise we think he's a first-rate Minister.' I went to bed a pretty happy man, knowing that things were much easier.[1]

Tuesday, July 8th

I missed Prices and Incomes Committee because at 7.45 I found myself in a train on my way to Sheffield. Oddly enough I was deputizing for David Ennals, who had agreed some time ago to address the annual conference of the Maternity and Child Care Services but had to stay behind for the last sitting of the Committee Stage of the Uprating Bill. Since he has been running the Bill, it was better for me to go in his place. I made a little speech about the importance of the voluntary services and among other things I was able to insert a bit about family planning and abortion, which of course got all the press. The Sheffield Labour people were in tremendous form. They were giving a little lunch, ostensibly to discuss maternity and child care but actually to celebrate with me the winning back of their majority this year. Morale was splendid and it showed what can be done and what Labour people can be like. The mayor rather impressed me when he said, 'I was out all last Sunday. We

[1] The motion of censure was defeated by 290 votes to 244.

have started the canvassing for municipals next April.' That is the way things get done. I was also very impressed with what I saw of the social and medical services there. Once again, however, my press conference, television and radio interviews were only about abortion. It's all the journalists want.

Back to the Department for meetings and then I went to a dinner for Kay Graham, the tremendously powerful owner of *Newsweek* and the *Washington Post*. It was given by Pam Berry, whom I haven't seen for ages. There was Arthur Schlesinger, as quiet and servile as ever, with the woman he hopes to have as his new wife. There were Isaiah and Lady Berlin and Anne and me.[1] Pam is marvellous at getting parties together but it was largely ruined for me by the Seats Bill,[2] because this was the night on which we were trying to take the Committee Stage on the Floor, to demonstrate the determination of the Tories to filibuster so that we could use the guillotine tomorrow night.[3] I had to go back to the House several times to vote and then at 10 o'clock there were great rows on the adjournment motion, with order papers being thrown about. I really can't stand these contrived, synthetic scenes so I went home with Anne.

Wednesday, July 9th

A nice full day which I will go through just to give a characteristic account of my life as a Secretary of State with a huge Department and a good many other responsibilities. I had to get to the office at 9.30 to see Peter Brown and fix up a mass of details about abortion and also about a fluoridation press conference we were having this afternoon. At 10 o'clock in came Marre (Clifford Jarrett was ill) with a whole mass of departmental things to deal with. We finished at 10.30 and then I had a meeting with Dick Bourton,[4] Brian Abel-Smith, Marre and Douglas Overend to discuss the presentation

[1] Sir Isaiah Berlin, a fellow of All Souls' College, Oxford, 1932–8, 1950–66 and since 1975, and of New College, Oxford, 1938–50, was Chichele Professor of Social and Political Theory in the University of Oxford 1957–67 and Professor of Humanities at the City University of New York 1966–71. He was President of Wolfson College, Oxford, 1966–75, and since 1974 he has been President of the British Academy. He was knighted in 1957 and in 1971 received the Order of Merit.

[2] On July 2nd the Home Secretary had asked for a Second Reading for the House of Commons (Redistribution of Seats) (No. 2) Bill, of which Clauses 2 and 3 sought to allow the Government to implement the Boundary Commission's recommendations for Greater London and the four constituencies with electorates of over 90,000 and one of over 100,000. Clause 1 of the Bill sought, first, to relieve the Home Secretary of his duty to lay the other Orders before Parliament; secondly, to defer the submission of further reports by the Parliamentary Boundary Commission for ten years; and, thirdly, to re-activate a Commission and lay Orders as soon as the reorganization of local government had been implemented. The Second Reading was approved by 298 votes to 246.

[3] On July 8th the House was not adjourned until midnight, and on July 9th the guillotine motion was approved by 291 votes to 246. The Committee on the Bill was to report it to the House on or before July 14th.

[4] Cyril Bourton, Under-Secretary for Finance and Accountant-General at the D.H.S.S. 1967–74 and since 1974 Deputy Secretary (Finance) and Accountant-General for Health and Personal Services.

we were making to the Chancellor this morning.[1] We looked at three alternative schemes; two had broken down and the third requires £22 million in cuts from us, which is really £39 million, because it also requires us to accept that we don't get the £17 million extra this year which we need for implementing the Todd and the Seebohm Reports. We know pretty well what the Chancellor is likely to ask for. However, we agreed that the first thing I should point out is that I don't accept the necessity of anything like this degree of cuts. I should retain my position that there are possible alternative revenue methods, one of which could be increased employers' contributions to the Health Service but I should not mention that this time and merely deal with Roy's proposals.

We got to No. 11 at 11.15 (the Chancellor is very precise in these things) and sat around not in his little Private Office, but in the dining room. I started by telling him a little about Health Service charges and what I intended to do. Then we turned to the £22 million and I got the point across that it was £22 million plus £17 million. Roy said he was very disappointed that we couldn't make any positive proposals for squeezing hospital revenue. I then explained, 'It has been squeezed dry and building new hospitals doesn't allow us to make economies. We are closing down the little hospitals but the cost of running these vast new ones is an enormous expense.' 'In that case,' he said, 'can we have a halt?' He had already asked us for a building halt for three or six months and I had got all the figures out for him. I showed him that if he wanted to save the £39 million he would have to have a one-year halt in all starts for hospital building. That would just about do it. That would save £18 million and halting them for three months would save £9 million. The three months could be done without great economic damage but we would have to announce it. The six months would start to be seriously damaging and would produce all sorts of anomalies, like building a hospital with no nurses' hostel. We put this to him and said that we would consider the possibility of a three-month delay and we would add to that another £9 million which we hoped to get by a new charge. I then outlined Brian's idea that we would institute a new levy of all the accident patients. It would be a collective responsibility rather like the redundancy levy. Roy jumped at this, so we got those two, and then he pressed me to get a little more out of local authority capital expenditure and I said I would look at that. We went over it all again and he said how disappointed he was and how generous he was being to Health and Social Security. He wasn't being generous to Social Security, he knew there was a contract there that he couldn't go back on, but he re-emphasized that others were taking their cuts and I said, 'Well, we shall have to wait and see. If, for instance, we are to have a three-month standstill on new hospital building, we will want to know how it relates to other forms of building, shall we say, to schools. We can measure these things when we see them in relation to each other.'

[1] Douglas Overend has been Assistant Under-Secretary of State at the D.H.S.S. since 1968.

Right at the end Roy said, 'If you want your £17 million for Todd and Seebohm reckoned in, I'll agree to do it if you will have a six-month rather than a three-month delay.' He tried to play a very tough game, saying how generous he was and how he must insist and talking all the time. I kept saying, 'I have come to hear what you want and because I don't accept the need for these cuts I can only tell you what priorities I can give you if you win in Cabinet.' We have done that today fairly clearly.*

That was over by midday and I was able to rush down the passage to Cabinet Room A, where I was taking the chair in the Social Services Committee at an important meeting on Seebohm. Here, to my amazement, we had two papers, one from Kenneth Robinson and George Thomson and the other from Jim Callaghan and me. The first suggested that the Seebohm reorganization should be mandatory on roughly two-thirds of the local authorities, London and such authorities as would not be very much affected by Maud, while roughly one-third would be omitted. Our paper urged that we should make the Seebohm reorganization cover the whole front, mainly because the London authorities would otherwise pick up all the best staff and leave the one-third unreformed in the most miserable position. Frankly, the trouble is that Seebohm has been overtaken by Maud and is a damned nuisance in the sense that it is reporting on a small segment of the internal structure of local government at the same time as Maud wants to reconstruct the whole thing. Jim and I have two powerful points, the first being whether we could really defend ordering 100 authorities to reorganize themselves when they are going to be wound up within three years. My view is that we should have to get our way across the whole front but make the concession that the authorities could ask for and without too much difficulty obtain permission not to carry out the reorganization if they had good reason. This was an advance on a front which is departmentally important to me and where Jim and I are completely together. One of the oddest things now is the extraordinarily intimate relation which has grown up between the Home Office and my Department. It derives entirely from my assurance to Jim early on that I had no desire to take over the Children's Department and that as long as he was Home Secretary I was not even going to ask for this. We had then made an alliance to push Seebohm through and I had explained to him

* Two days later, by the way, a note of the meeting arrived, full of inaccuracies. They had even got the date wrong. I had said we would have to make an announcement even for a three-month delay. Roy's note said there would be no announcement. The Treasury said that at the end I had made offers but I had of course made no offers at all. The document is well worth looking at and Dick Bourton sent a really devastating reply. It just shows how inaccurate is a Treasury record of a conversation and this is largely because the Treasury can always bully Departments to accept their version of everything. Departments are too scared to dare to challenge the Treasury version, so the Treasury is curiously full of ill faith. They go back on their word quite cheerfully. This year, for instance, having asked us to keep within 3 per cent, they then coolly say that we must now have another series of cuts. They don't really understand why people get so angry. I think the real reason for the mistakes is that they know so little about the subjects under discussion that they can't avoid making howlers.

that I couldn't do this unless I could give assurances to doctors that the Health Service would be kept outside local government.

It was quite clear that Jim and I prevailed on preference. We were supported by a phalanx of Ministers including Judith Hart and Ted Short, against Kenneth Robinson and poor George Thomson, who is now in charge of the Maud Commission and is also a Scot who knows nothing about it. However, all this, which was complicated enough, got further complicated when, quite rightly, George Thomson and others began to point out that we were in some danger of inconsistency. We were told that it would seem we were anticipating Maud by carrying out Seebohm and people might ask why we could not anticipate Maud and carry out the recommendations of the Boundary Commission. This was put to Jim Callaghan, who brushed it aside. It wasn't for me to say that it was a powerful point but I would have thought it was. And yet at today's meeting we got on excellently together. If the Home Secretary and I can work together it carries our own senior men along with us. Morrell is on excellent terms with Odgers.

After discussing pensions over lunch with I.C.I., I had my press conference on fluoridation and then a long meeting with the insurance section of the C.B.I., with whom I had a perfectly friendly expert conversation on the rights and wrongs of dynamism. Upstairs in the House Micky Barnes was waiting to see me about a hospital in his constituency that is right in the path of a proposed motorway. He hadn't been able to get a straight answer from Tony Greenwood and I was able to brief him fully off the record. It is extraordinary how often one can satisfy a back-bench M.P. by simply telling him the truth about what is likely to happen. This is the kind of problem where one M.P. can't find out from three Ministries, Transport, Housing and Health, what is actually going on.

I also had to see the Chief Whip and the Leader of the House about Laurie Pavitt's Early Day Motion on Health Service Charges. On Monday an official delegation, led by Harry Nicholas, had come to talk to me about this and I had patiently tried to explain my intentions. Then yesterday I had an interview with six or seven people including Laurie Pavitt, Shirley Summerskill and John Dunwoody, and I think I got them to realize that I had some new thoughts which I was going to try to clear with Cabinet. They promised me that if they put down their Early Day Motion, which they have duly done, they would individually listen to me and consider the issue before making up their minds. Laurie Pavitt is a bit of a trickster and shyster because, having put down a Motion without telling the Chief Whip, he has now circularized 138 people urging them to vote against me. There were undoubtedly only 30 names on the Motion when it went down but, I don't know, Laurie Pavitt may think that circularizing is a necessary formality. However the thing has not gone like wildfire at all, there has been a great movement inside the Party, led by Douglas Houghton, to get it over with a vote of 40 to 50 if we can, and with Douglas and the Chief on my side I am going to have a much better time than Barbara, where both of them were against her and Harold. Well, Bob Mellish and Fred Peart couldn't have been more helpful today. We decided that the way to play it would be for Douglas Houghton to have a rallying Party meeting next Wednesday morning, urging everybody to get together at the end of the session and not to quarrel or down the Government. We would then break off the Finance Bill at 10 a.m. and put on the Early Day Motion. This was to be put to Cabinet tomorrow.

Meanwhile there was a queue outside my room, because Bourton, Alan Marre, Brian, David Ennals and Bea were all waiting for the report on the meeting with the Chancellor this morning. We considered Roy's proposal to reckon in our £17 million in exchange for a six-month delay on new hospital starts, and we all agreed to turn it down. This was partly because we know we have £45 million of hidden reserves, which Dick Bourton hadn't told the Treasury about, and, also because, frankly, a six-month delay would be a major disaster. The Chancellor seems totally unaware that two years ago we said we had introduced prescription charges to save the hospital building programme. If we are now going to knock it back by six months it would put us in an appalling fix. We agreed that we had done reasonably well on my other replies. We finished in time for me to see Richard Faulkner,[1] a very pleasant member of the staff of Transport House, who is now moving to the Construction Industry Training Board and, while we were talking, in came David Marquand and Tommy Balogh for a drink. Then I went downstairs for a delightful dinner with David Marquand and David Owen, two of the youngest and brightest of our back-bench M.P.s, and a wide, amusing discussion that made me feel more in contact with these younger people. And that concluded Wednesday.

Thursday, July 10th

I had to be in my office at 9.30 to see Ted Short. This is the kind of thing which wastes time. Ted Short has two excrescences on his Department, the Youth and Sport Section run by Denis Howell and the Culture Section run by Jennie Lee. Whereas Ted has to pay attention to Jennie because she is in with the Prime Minister, Denis Howell is unpopular with the P.M. because he is an old member of the C.D.S., a big-mouthed typical Birmingham Labour Party fellow. He and his working party had produced a pretty flatulent report on a draft White Paper on the reorganization of the Government Youth Service and it had come to the Social Services Committee for approval. The Ministers there had all been briefed by their Departments on some ten or eleven of his forty vague recommendations and at last I had said it should go to a working party for a report before publication and before we finally decided what the Government's attitude would be. I hadn't thought much more about it until I had heard that great difficulties were being made by Ted

[1] Labour candidate for Devizes in 1970 and in February 1974, and for Monmouth in October 1974.

Short, who was insisting that the official working party should be chaired by someone from D.E.S. The Cabinet Office insisted it should be chaired either by a Cabinet Office official or by my Paul Odgers, who is not attached to any Department but who is a co-ordinator attached to me in my co-ordinating capacity.

I had to spend twenty-five minutes explaining this to poor Ted Short and suddenly he realized that it wasn't ignominious for him to accept Odgers, especially since Paul was an ex-Ministry of Education man who would be sympathetic and helpful. Many hours had been spent behind the scenes by officials trying to persuade D.E.S. to see reason and half an hour had been spent by me. Ted and I had a quiet talk and he explained the pressure that had been put on him by the Chancellor. Short had first of all come up with big cuts in the minor works programme for schools, which is a disaster because it means that all the local village schools and all the extra classrooms have to be cut back. Then he had been pressed to find more on higher education and simply couldn't, so he had been obliged to propose a charge for school transport, a charge even for borrowing books from school libraries, and then he had been told that this wasn't enough. D.E.S. clearly finds it more difficult to resist the Chancellor than we do. Short was violent but defeatist. What could he do? However we went round to Cabinet together, both of us convinced that the major confrontation with the Chancellor was to come this morning.

The first item in Cabinet was procedure and Bob and Fred put to Cabinet our proposal for dealing with Laurie Pavitt's Early Day Motion on Health charges. Roy pointed out that it might be difficult for them to break off the Finance Bill at 10.0 and then resume because it is a Bill which has no time-limit and he added that anyhow there was a possibility of an all-night sitting on Wednesday and it wouldn't suit him to have my motion on that day. So we were driven to having it on the following Monday, July 21st. This is the day the American moon men will be landing and I think that the back benchers' minds will be otherwise engaged. We are going to insert it at 10 p.m. before the Lords' amendments to the Post Office Bill. That is also convenient because it enables me to go to Cabinet next Thursday with a Paper on charges and a draft draft-statement, which I must try to get the Chancellor to agree beforehand.

After this long discussion about the timing, I gave a short account of the difficulty and the sort of statement I needed to make and how I must announce that prescription charges are purely temporary. I knew Roy was against me but it was down in the minutes. I got it duly recorded that I would like to have a statement of this kind, which means that the Prime Minister wanted to record it, and wanted me to be helped in this particular way. This was the first advance and I am looking forward with fair equanimity to next week's Cabinet. I may lose my battle with Roy about cuts but I should avoid a battle with him on charges if I can come with an agreed solution. I don't think it will be impossible and it will be a great help to the Government because we shall have got the issue of the charges in a form with which we can go into an election.

Next we had a whole series of items from the Foreign Secretary and then we came to the constitution. By now the Tories and the press have succeeded in turning into a potentially major constitutional issue what you might, at worst, have called a slight case of the Government's being a judge in its own cause. They are saying that the deliberate delaying of the Boundary Commission's recommendations is an effort by a decrepit Labour Government to change the rules to suit its own purposes. This is partly unfair; we do have a case for postponement. The Boundary Commission's present terms of reference are very precise. They have to frame the boundaries of our parliamentary constituencies so that they are in line not just with local government boundaries, but with the structure of the county boroughs, which are thought of as areas which like to have their own M.P. As Maud has recommended the abolition of the county and county borough, there is basically a good and sensible case for saying that it would be absurd to re-draw all the constituency boundaries now and then do it all over again in four years' time. But the case hasn't been very well put and it has been marred by the fact that we have agreed to change certain boundaries of over-large constituencies which can easily be split into two.

This qualification is being looked at very carefully and we are asked why, if we say we will do London and ten or twelve over-large constituencies, we haven't included Huyton and Coventry, for instance, where the Prime Minister and I have our constituencies? Why is it that we have said 90,000 was the lowest limit for a change, which completely excludes both these? To this extent there has been minor gerrymandering but the Tories' case is that we are simply disregarding the Boundary Commission and just bloody well cheating to try to cling to power.

We had an interesting discussion, in the course of which the Prime Minister suddenly said, 'It looks now as if we might have been wiser to have told the Boundary Commission two or three years ago that we weren't going to implement their recommendations and told them to stop work.' Well, I was Lord President then and this thing must have been considered on and off for four or five years, as I suspect this diary shows. When Roy Jenkins was Home Secretary he was very sanctimonious and difficult about the issue and the advantage of the change from Roy to Jim is that Callaghan is a much more adaptable and realistic politician. The Prime Minister and I had always said that we couldn't possibly let the recommendations be implemented. True, we said it against the advice of Transport House, where Sara Barker said that party organizers were anxious to have the modernized boundaries, partly because they couldn't get efficient London Labour Parties when the constituency and borough boundaries had no relation to each other. Strangely then, though the Tories are talking about gerrymandering, the machine, if by that one means Transport House, has not been against implementation and has given fairly consistent advice that it would prove no great loss to us and a great convenience in areas like London. The opponents have been, I am afraid, largely Harold Wilson and me, so why didn't we announce it earlier? Because Harold wouldn't. He preferred fencing with Heath, who has constantly tried to press him at Question Time on implementation. Harold wouldn't come clean. I think we are now paying a heavy price for Harold's lack of candour and continual tactical manoeuvring. He doesn't look ahead and always postpones a row until what turns out later to be a very unfavourable moment.

We are moving into a difficult situation because if the Lords turn down our Seats Bill we may well have to defeat all the Orders the Boundary Commission recommends, some thirty or forty of which are greatly to our advantage. The proposal now is that we pass the Orders on London and the five over-large constituencies but defeat every other Order.[1] Another issue is the future of the Lords. If Heath and his advisers feel this is a good issue to fight on and to drive the final nail in the Labour Government's coffin, the Lords will throw the Bill out and then our people will be happy enough to abolish the Lords altogether.[2] We will have the whole issue of a short Abolition Bill all over again. It would be a gesture but one which the Labour Party would like.

I am sure most people in the country are still indifferent to this interesting constitutional crisis. Most people think it's just the two parties shouting at each other on some narrow party issue which the public is too superior to understand but I have an uneasy feeling that if the thing goes on it will turn sour. We shall not be able to say the Lords have no right to interfere and people will say that marginally the Tories are right, that the awful Labour Party not only dragged out the life of this Parliament but that they are even trying to cheat on the issue which will determine their fate in the next election.

[1] If Parliament refused to pass the Government's Bill postponing the laying of Orders to redistribute parliamentary seats, an alternative tactic would be for the Home Secretary to lay the Orders, as he was statutorily required to do, but to ensure that the Whips instructed the Government's own back benchers to vote against them.

[2] The Seats Bill was not covered by the mandate convention, by which Conservative peers customarily acknowledged that legislation which was part of the Government's electoral programme was entitled to a Second Reading and, given the dubious nature of the Seats Bill, the probable distaste of peers of all parties for the device and the fact that this seemed an ideal issue on which the Lords could stand as the guarantors of constitutional rectitude, it seemed likely that the Lords would throw the measure out. Parliament was by now nearing the end of its five-year term and at the very latest a General Election had to be called in April 1971. In theory this would give the Government, if necessary, sufficient time under the provisions of the 1947 Parliament Act to pass legislation rejected by the Lords, for on paper they needed only two successive sessions (1969/70 and 1970/1), with one year as the period of delay from Second Reading in the Commons, in which to pass a rejected Bill. But, in effect, the Administration had really run out of time by summer 1969. Using the Parliament Act to secure the Seats Bill would be expensive in terms of time and prestige and would inhibit the Prime Minister's freedom to choose the date of the General Election; the necessary drafting would have to be done extremely quickly; and the inevitable controversy not only about the Bill itself, but also on matters of definition and procedure, would give the Opposition as thorough an opportunity for exploitation as they had enjoyed on the Parliament (No. 2) Bill.

In Cabinet nobody challenged the decision to proceed with Callaghan's Bill, so he and Shackleton and the Lord Chancellor all discussed at length what would happen if the Lords turned it down and whether there could be a short Abolition Bill. At least Harold agreed that it should be the old Parliamentary Reform Committee chaired by Gerald Gardiner, with me on it, which should consider the possibility of the reform of the Lords and the abolition of their powers. Meanwhile the smaller group, the Prime Minister, Callaghan, the Foreign Secretary, no doubt, and the Minister without Portfolio, would go on with the Seats Bill, which they clearly felt was beginning to come to pieces in their hands.

Then we came to the main item on the agenda, Civil Service pay. As I was in Sheffield last week, I missed the Prices and Incomes Cabinet Committee that considered the issue of higher Civil Service pay and had decided that the Plowden Committee's Report recommending a huge increase should be accepted,[1] but only on condition that ultimately we pulled ourselves together and took a decision to refer to the N.B.P.I. all pay increases including those for higher civil servants and doctors. Once the Committee had decided this it was extremely difficult to get it reversed. Barbara had swung the Chancellor and the Committee to her view. She doesn't believe in comparability as a basis for deciding the legitimacy of wage and salary claims and she hated first the Kindersley Report and now the Plowden Report being pushed through. I suppose all that's left to her is to say that Aubrey Jones and his N.B.P.I. must be built up as a substitute for our statutory prices and incomes policy. Eddie Shackleton had rung up yesterday evening and again this morning to say how serious the situation was and that Barbara was once again forging ahead. As he said, if we overturn the Plowden and Kindersley machinery there would be an unholy row and I would lose any hope of getting the doctors to collaborate on the N.H.S. Green Paper.

This morning it wasn't difficult to defeat Barbara on her first point, because the majority of the Prices and Incomes Committee had recommended that Plowden should be implemented, although it should be the last acceptable implementation. What was important today was how much should be written into the Statement about what happened next. Last time we discussed Kindersley we had talked about eventually reviewing the machinery. Now Barbara wants us to write in a Government decision that in due course we would hand over these reviews to the N.B.P.I. I was fighting a defensive action on behalf of the doctors and Eddie on behalf of the higher civil servants. Both of us accepted something of the principle that to get a single integrated procedure would be a good thing but we also faced, perhaps more than Barbara, the need to accept comparability, because there is no other test.

[1] The Ninth Report of the Committee on Higher Civil Service Pay, chaired by Lord Plowden, recommended that salaries of Permanent Secretaries should be increased from £8,600 to £14,000 per annum, of Deputy Secretaries from £6,300 to £9,000, and of Under-Secretaries from £5,500 to £6,750. The increases were to be implemented in stages, beginning on July 1st, 1969.

I did fairly well, though I had once again to be *advocatus diaboli*, because the doctors are regarded as devils by Barbara who, like civil servants, she says, embarrass her in dealing with wage earners, just as Fred Peart says they embarrass him in his dealings with M.P.s. There was a long battle and I managed several times to interrupt the Prime Minister's summing-up to say, 'We must get it clear that we haven't decided on a particular device and above all that it won't be handed over to the present N.B.P.I. but to a restructured N.B.P.I. That is what we must get because that is less offensive to the doctors.' I felt fairly satisfied with this and the Prime Minister said that the draft of the Written Answer which would be given tomorrow must be along these lines. I felt, though, that I had been inadequately briefed by the Department which should have woken up earlier to the crisis which was threatening it.

I rushed off for a very nice lunch with Lilo Milchsack and we had a long talk about Weimar Germany.[1] Then it was time for me to see Jim Callaghan about the future of our two Departments after Seebohm. If we manage to implement the Seebohm recommendations the Children's Service will become part of the new local personal services and we had to decide to which Whitehall Department the local authorities should be responsible. Our Department had thought this out, and we had given Jim a paper saying that at official level there must be joint Home Office/D.H.S.S. responsibility and at the top level we could either answer Questions as we liked or the senior Minister would have to answer. Today Jim came along with Philip Allen to discuss the paper and the Whitehall implications and to my amazement he simply said, 'Since you are the senior Cabinet Minister you will answer all the Questions.' He gave it all away, partly of course because I didn't fight for it. The funny thing is that I think I was wise not to fight because my merged Department is in a terrible mess. It isn't yet merged and it's not ready to absorb anything else, whereas the Home Office Children's Department is extremely competent and well organized. I don't want to take them over until I am ready to assimilate them. So my political prudence was also administrative wisdom. Paul Odgers was staggered that I had got so much out of Callaghan, who doesn't naturally give things away.

This afternoon we had the debate on Nigeria.[2] It was to be a great issue but it petered out, as these things often do, and though I went back to vote it was only because Michael Foot and I had gone out to dinner with Connie Bessie.[3] We had a splendid old-time gossip. There is nobody who makes me enjoy life so much and who makes me talk more freely than Michael. When we went back to the House for the 10 o'clock vote I had already been told that the Prime Minister wanted to see me urgently afterwards. This was, I knew,

[1] Lilo Milchsack, the initiator of the Deutsche-Englische Gesellschaft e.V. (the Königswinter conferences), and its Honorary Secretary since its foundation in 1949, was awarded a D.C.M.G. in 1972 for her services to Anglo-German understanding.

[2] In the division the Conservatives abstained and Labour and Liberal M.P.s voted 162 to 44 against Sir Alec Douglas Home's adjournment motion.

[3] The former wife of Crossman's American publisher.

about the draft Written Answer on the Plowden Report, which Shackleton had sent across. I had said I couldn't accept the draft in that form and that I must see the Prime Minister about it because it didn't carry out the directive of the Cabinet. I hadn't of course seen the minutes but I had to say this. I was so excited at the excellence of our dinner and our talk that I forgot all about the appointment until, a quarter of an hour after the vote, I ran into the policeman at the back of the Speaker's chair, who said, 'The Prime Minister is in there waiting for you.' I ran across to No. 10 – no Harold. I borrowed a car to rush back to the House, put my head in and there he was sitting at the table in his room with Gerald Kaufman and Arnold Goodman. So I waited outside for about twenty minutes, until out came Harold and said, 'Sorry to keep you waiting.' He got rid of them, sat down and asked, 'What is the trouble?' 'Look,' I said, 'I can't accept that we have decided in advance to hand this over to Aubrey Jones,' and he replied, 'Well, surely you don't think I'm a great friend of Aubrey Jones after the story in the *Telegraph* today?' (There had been an exclusive story, obviously given by Aubrey Jones, that Harold had given him two more years at the N.B.P.I. at a vast salary.) I said, 'It's not about that, it's simply the whole of our good relations with the doctors.' 'After all,' Harold said, 'you have to accept the decision we took to integrate all the various salary-fixing organizations. In principle we've decided to do it.' 'Yes,' I said, 'but not to the same N.B.P.I., to a reconstituted, restructured one.' 'Yes,' he said, 'that was in my summing-up and you insisted on it's being in the minutes. All right, there must be an amendment and we must have a meeting tomorrow at 9.30.' 'In No. 10?' He replied, 'No, I won't be there, it won't be my meeting. You must have it with Barbara, Eddie Shackleton and the Treasury.' I knew how angry my colleagues would be at being summoned unexpectedly on a Friday morning and that I wouldn't be able to attend Home Affairs Committee. However, I thought that was that and went home to bed.

Friday, July 11th

Ron Matthews rang me up at 7.15 this morning and we discovered how extraordinary the Prime Minister's performance actually was. He had in fact cancelled my appointment yesterday, and it was by sheer misunderstanding that I went to see him last night. He didn't have the face to turn me away and, having got me into his room, he had made a major concession that included this morning's 9.30 meeting. This indicates the kind of person Harold is. If you are with him he doesn't want to have a row. Barbara, of course, was furious and, sure enough, when I went in this morning there she was sitting alone in Conference Room A looking very bad-tempered. A bit later Eddie came in but nobody turned up from the Treasury because Dick Taverne thought the Home Affairs Committee more important. Barbara was really angry. 'You are a great bully,' she said. 'You can't get your way on this, it's in the minutes. You are always getting your way.' She is often like this. It sounds mean but obviously this was to some extent a compensation for her defeat on the Industrial Relations Bill. If she wasn't able to get the sanctions she wanted on the unions she was at least going to build up the prices and incomes policy through N.B.P.I. and, by knocking out comparability, help the working class. I resisted as far as I could but we couldn't have much further discussion because the P.M. had submitted his amendment and once a P.M.'s amendment is submitted Ministers fall into line. It was just jammed in and it didn't fit particularly well, but I got a sentence put in to say that for the time being there would have to be rethinking about the nature of the review bodies.[1] Then I hurried over to the House to the Home Affairs Committee where they were discussing the de-rating of factory farms and a paper on flooding and sluices.

After a quick meeting in my room it was time to set out for Poole with Peter Smithson. I had asked Alan Marre to come with me because I particularly wanted his help with the Cabinet paper and the draft statement on N.H.S. charges. I was going down to the opening of a brand-new hospital by the Queen and the Duke of Edinburgh and I had been extremely surprised to find that Alan wanted to go. I was also amazed to hear that five members of the Department had intended to take the day off, though three of them gave up when they knew I was going. When I looked at the programme in bed this morning as far as I could see all I had to do was stand there when the Queen arrived, and I wasn't even to introduce the Chairman of the R.H.B., Mr Templeman,[2] because the Lord Lieutenant of Dorset was doing it.[3] I tried to get out of it but the Department said no – my name was on the list and I must go.

We set off on an absolutely perfect day for a wonderful journey through Winchester, past St Catherine's Hill and the water meadows, and through the strawberry-growing areas and the New Forest, down to this awful suburb of Bournemouth, with the lovely Poole harbour, the sea and the sun beyond. I think Alan was nervous but we had an excellent long discussion about charges and plotted out the paper. We managed to have a relaxed conversation on every kind of departmental topic, which I think he appreciated. He said afterwards, 'It's the only chance I ever get of a three-hour talk with you,' and it made me realize he does feel a tremendous strain. He worked for nine months under Barbara Castle at the Ministry of Labour before coming to me and I asked him how Barbara compared. Of course he is extremely

[1] The Written Answer said:

More generally, the Government have decided that the arrangements for determining pay in the public sector in its widest sense should be more closely co-ordinated...The revised arrangements will envisage giving the N.B.P.I. a more central role, and consideration will also have to be given to what changes to the N.B.P.I. are necessary in order to enable it to carry out this new role. There will be full consultation with all those concerned before any change is made. *House of Commons Debates*, Vol. 786, cols. 320–2.

[2] Philip Templeman, Mayor of Bournemouth 1956–7, Alderman 1961 and Leader of the Council from 1968, was Chairman of the Wessex Regional Hospital Board from its formation in 1959 until his death in 1972.

[3] Colonel J. W. Weld, O.B.E.

tactful and diplomatic, but he said, 'You have one thing in common, astonishing vitality and limitless energy, and you work the Department mercilessly. She gets extraordinary support from her Department, despite the fact that she makes her civil servants keep late hours and that she demands a hell of a lot. They like her, and they realize that the whole status of the Department has changed from the time of Ray Gunter, who left the running of things to the officials.'

I asked him about the work and he said, 'There is one big difference. Hers is a very small Department. True, she has had a whole series of crises to deal with, strikes and so on, but apart from that she doesn't have the mass of work you have on all social security and all aspects of health.' It's worth remembering that Barbara didn't have this even at Transport. I have a much wider area to deal with, many more decisions in my boxes, many more letters to write, many more administrative decisions to take. 'The other thing,' he added, 'is that she can be very emotional and sometimes when things go wrong she is nearly in tears, but the civil servants don't mind that, they feel with her. In that way she is very different from you. You take things much more toughly and you swallow things much more. She is more explosive temperamentally.' I said, 'What about her mind?' He said, 'Ah, she takes a thing away, thinks about it and when she has made up her mind she keeps to it.' I felt he was saying that, as I am aware, I am not nearly so inclined to commit myself and never think again. Maybe it's better to be a politician who gets a set view and fights to keep it, as Barbara does. Alan said, 'For instance take the small I.R. Bill. The Department never liked it and, frankly, they would have dropped it months before she did, but she held on to the whole idea of industrial relations legislation of the kind she wanted long after the Department had abandoned hope. In that way she is very different from you.' I found this an interesting conversation.

When we got to Poole we had about half an hour to wait. There were a lot of people lining the streets, on a hot, sunny day with a little breeze blowing over the harbour, exquisitely beautiful, and there was this huge wonderfully-appointed, luxurious hospital, with Mr Templeman, who had inherited a firm of monumental sculptors, people who do gravestones, but has devoted his life to voluntary work. I asked what I was to do but it was quite clear that my main job was to keep out of the way. He was to take the Queen and the Duke of Edinburgh round the hospital and I was to drag along in a crowd behind. Well, I could hardly complain. It was clear it was Mr Templeman's day, he had been twelve years at this job and he was partly responsible for the new hospital. The Queen came through the doorway and shook my hand, looking rather embarrassed. She didn't say anything, I didn't say anything and then he took her over. I played absolutely fair and kept in the background and when we went round the hospital I let them go ahead and didn't interfere, the only result being that there was nobody to tell Prince Philip or the Lord Lieutenant anything about the hospital. Of course when royalty goes round the hospital is all dolled up and everyone is agog and you can't really see anything. It was no good my trying to talk to people because if they had seen or spoken to the Queen or Philip they had touched the holy garment and were so ecstatic that they had no time for a Secretary of State and if the royal visitors hadn't spoken to them they were so disappointed that I was no good as a consolation prize. I did think it was a bit undignified to have the Secretary of State there and keep him so totally in the background, but effacing myself during the ceremony was a small price to pay for the Chairman's loyal service and goodwill. Still, when we had finished going round there were eleven minutes left for tea and at least they put me at a table opposite the Queen, so I was able to make up with a little bit of civil conversation. I hadn't wanted her to think that I was standing aloof and I hoped she'd realize I was being tactful. When they had all gone Templeman asked me up to his room for a gin and tonic. He felt marvellously relieved and I am sure it has cemented between us a firm relationship which I shall need. Anyhow John Revans is his Senior Medical Officer and I didn't want to quarrel with him.

Off again at 5.30 and we had a most wonderful drive through Wimborne to Salisbury, right across the downs until, up on top, the land suddenly opens and you see Jude the Obscure's view, miles across the Vale of the White Horse to Oxford, Banbury and Coventry, exquisite vistas of green, pale blue and aquamarine stretching out before you. We got back to Prescote at 8.30. What a drive and what a country!

Saturday, July 12th

This morning I listened to the 'News From Westminster' and I was surprised to hear no mention of the Uprating Bill, which yesterday had its Report Stage and Third Reading. Yes, two or three other minor Bills were mentioned but had mine dropped out? I got a copy of *The Times* and found it had gone through formally, with no discussion at all. Here was this Bill for raising £360 million in increased contributions, going through its Committee Stage in two sittings fewer than we agreed with the Tories and going through so automatically that it was not mentioned on the B.B.C. This shows you the difference there is between the budget and other methods of raising money, and how important it is not to underestimate the difference in the way people view contributions and taxes. Despite all the fuss and bother two months ago, the Tories hadn't delayed it. This is one of the main points I'm going to make to the Chancellor in my argument that he needn't cut public expenditure and that, if he must cut demand, he should do it by making skilled use of contributions.

The Plowden decision came out this morning too but all the emphasis was on the salary increases for higher civil servants and, as there was also further news of the constitutional crisis, the other part of the Written Answer simply hasn't been noticed. Nevertheless I'm glad I got my sentence included. I think it will help me when in due course there comes a blazing row, with the doctors asking if they are going to lose their autonomous review body and be simply pushed under Aubrey Jones along with the armed forces and everybody else.

Sunday, July 13th

We are having a splendid summer now and we have had another splendid weekend, this time with my niece Gay, her nice husband David and his younger brother Tim. They stayed last night with their new daughter Kate, just four months old, and we had a most enjoyable dinner party for them with Harry and Mary Judge and Oscar and Margaret Hahn.[1] There we were, two generations of friends, sitting round our great golden dining table drinking Beaujolais Blanc, of which I had bought a dozen bottles, and afterwards in the drawing room with our wonderful chairs, and then enjoying a midnight bathe. It was a lovely evening and life is enormously well worth living. It's true that we are living in a highly privileged fashion now. To be fair, though, there has been not a levelling down but a levelling up of society and science and technology have made it possible and not expensive for masses of people to have good clothes, cosmetics, foreign travel, television and all the consumer durables which are a substitute for the labour of millions.

I have been thinking, sitting back here at Prescote, that the abolition of privilege means not destroying privilege but allowing everybody to share in it. Of course that changes the nature of the privilege but it does make sense. It makes me realize how futile a lot of the press criticism and present running down of Britain is, for we are a highly civilized and gentle country. We are a bit slack in business methods but if you are going to be as nice to each other as we are, with such a civilized social security system, for example, you are going to have a bit of slackness. You won't have all the drive and thrust and selfishness and battering of German business, and the crude, vulgar, narrow, bourgeois efficiency of certain French business. It will be more genial, kinder, more easy-going, and yet we tell ourselves what a hopeless society we are. Of course in this weather it's impossible to look at things quite as ruthlessly and depressingly as one does on a bad winter day. The British summer is the best in the world and this must have been about the sixteenth or seventeenth day of real sunshine. That's a far higher average than we usually get and the crops, the grass and potatoes here are being transformed. I have described our beautiful drive to Poole and back on Friday and things are lovely here too. Prescote is a base from which to like things, especially as our children are growing up well and are in every way very satisfactory.

The weather, and the investiture, have no doubt won the Government some votes and the poll this week shows the Tory lead has slumped from 27 per cent to under 20 per cent.[2] I also think people are slightly more satisfied about our

[1] Oscar and Margaret Hahn were friends and neighbours of the Crossmans.

[2] Crossman was optimistic. The Gallup Poll showed a rise in the Conservative lead from 13 per cent in June to 20 per cent in July, the National Opinion Poll a fall from 16·7 per cent to 15·9 per cent and the O.R.C. poll a fall from 21 to 19 per cent.

economic situation and when unemployment is not so high the whole atmosphere is easier.[1] The improvement may well be temporary but it's there. However there are factors against us. These confounded unofficial strikes continue, with the T.U.C. palpably unable to curb them and of course there are the two other issues, the constitutional crisis about Parliamentary seats and the internal crisis, about which hardly anything has appeared in the press, of Roy Jenkins's demand that in preparation for next year, election year, we should plan our Government spending cuts now. I have been hardening up against the Chancellor this week and if it came out that the Government was planning major cuts there would indeed be a great sense of crisis and we might be put back another twenty points. I must also add that part of the reason for the improvement in the poll is a strange sense that this Government is coming to an end. I doubt if anybody now, including Harold, really believes we are going to win the next election. In the Parliamentary Party, the constituencies, in the country, we all know that our period is over. I personally feel very much that five years in government as a top Cabinet Minister is long enough for anybody. I am not browned off but I am certainly not as alert as I was. I drive hard at the Ministry, I have gained by experience but, heavens alive, the excitement of the first eighteen months isn't there any more and I have ploughed into the Cabinet Minister's routine. This is where I think there is a lot to commend the British system, where five or six years is a Government's normal life and it has to struggle hard and be very lucky to have a second term. I think this is what the British people feel and why, though there may be a slight swing against the Tories, it's not in any expectation of another Labour Government after the next election.

Monday, July 14th

I had been invited to go down to Wilton Park this morning, which would have meant coming up to London last night, but I decided to stay here, partly because I so passionately resent losing any moment at Prescote, and also because I wanted to have this morning in the office to prepare the paper on N.H.S. charges, so that I could show it to Roy before it went to Cabinet. I sent David Ennals to Sussex instead and he really enjoyed it.

He is not a mysterious man and in certain ways he is terribly straightforward, but his standards and behaviour fascinate and impress me. He is extraordinarily efficient and willing. He simply does what I ask him and he adores being a Minister. He is a first-rate Minister of State, with great ability but there is some quality that he lacks. It's not that he has no political principles. He has violent feelings, he likes writing to the Prime Minister to protest against incomes policies, he likes making speeches and getting publicity. I don't know what the unattractive thing in him is. Is it that he is cold? No, more that he is metallic, almost not flesh and blood, but I am enormously impressed by him.

[1] In June unemployment had fallen below 500,000 for the first time in twenty-three months.

My first job was to see Alan Marre, with whom I am finally having a great success. It's very characteristic of our Ministry that he went in on Saturday to write this draft paper himself. He wrote it all out in longhand and when I got in this morning it wasn't ready, because it had been divided up into three portions for the pool of secretaries to deal with. Alan hadn't been prepared to bring a secretary in on a Saturday afternoon to do the work. That is very sweet but it is also incompetent and it largely defeated the whole point of my coming in this morning.

This evening I had Thomas to dinner. Harold and Roy don't want him back in circulation so he's wandering around at a loose end. He can't cut away from Whitehall and sit down to write the book he ought to write, so there he is along the passage in the Lords, doing a bit of broadcasting but virtually useless to me because I know roughly what his line is and without a complete knowledge of all the papers he can't advise me. But I'd rather like to have him back. I have a different but parallel problem with Nicky Kaldor, whom I tried to get as Thomas's replacement. Nicky has a much better reputation in Whitehall and, on the whole, he is liked in the Treasury and the Inland Revenue. He is not thought of as a malicious Whitehall-manoeuvring politician, constantly fermenting ideas and launching attacks. Nicky doesn't bother about Whitehall, he really likes tax law, knows his friends and he is frightfully adroit and ingenious about taxes and contributions and all that kind of thing. I can use him along with Brian Abel-Smith but I can't lever him out of the Treasury. They would let him go but they won't let him come across to me because Roy thinks S.E.T. damaged our image and is ashamed of Nicky as an adviser. There we come down to it. Roy and Harold feel embarrassed by Buda and Pest, the two Hungarians. They don't want the Government associated with Tommy and Nicky, who are in a way martyrs of the malicious gossip of the press.

Tuesday, July 15th

I got up weary and fagged out because I stayed up last night for the Report Stage of the Seats Bill. We had the guillotine vote at 3 a.m. so that the Third Reading could resume at 10 a.m. today, before the vote at 1 p.m. I had to stay until 2.30 a.m. Tam is awfully good and has persuaded Bob Mellish to let me off most nights so that, at my age, I could do my work next morning, but last night I stayed on and tried to sleep a bit upstairs. That always makes you feel terrible. When I got home at 3.15 it was too hot and late to go to sleep, so I started work at 6.30.

This morning I had my talk with Roy, who had let it be known that he had received my draft Cabinet paper and draft Statement and didn't like them at all. I went over to see him and it was clear that he didn't want any Statement made. He said exactly the same as before, 'Don't blow this up into a sensation or start the issue over again.' I said, 'I'm afraid we can't do that, Roy, and I think the best thing is not to give an agreed paper but for me to put my paper in and for you to put in your parallel draft of what you think I should say.' 'That is embarrassing,' he said, 'because people don't write each other's speeches.' I said, 'If you don't want to, all right, but I think it would be easier for Cabinet if they saw what you thought I could say to these back benchers and compared it with what I thought I could say.' We were perfectly friendly with each other but we didn't get any further.

After that I gave lunch to Laurie Pavitt, something I should have done years ago. He has spent his life in the Health Service and he is very concerned with deaf-aids. He is a nice, self-important man, terribly upset at not having had a job, and fanatical on the subject of N.H.S. charges. We sat at a little table for two at the entrance to the Members' dining room, where Ernie Bevin used to sit. I gave him a jolly good bottle of the white wine he likes and we discussed things. He didn't want to talk about teeth and spectacles, just to feel that he was being brought in. There is no doubt that I have neglected this sort of thing and I am mending my fences now, and seeing the people, Douglas Houghton and so on, who really matter here.

After lunch I had a fascinating seminar on hospital revenue. Dick Bourton had put up an absolutely first-rate paper on how the hospital budgets are fixed. A terrific lot of money goes into the teaching hospitals, most of which are in the South, and this shifts the balance even more in favour of the London hospitals, with great unfairness to Sheffield, Newcastle and Birmingham, which are really greatly under-financed. The trouble is that the historic costs are gigantic, with about 85 per cent already committed, and I should be very surprised if we can get even 5 per cent reallocated in any one year, especially a year of appalling constriction such as this. Nevertheless, it was a really good discussion.

After this across to 70 Whitehall for a session with the B.M.A. on the Green Paper and Seebohm. They were as tough as they could be in demanding that the Health Service should take over all the local authority welfare services, something which is totally impossible, since in fact there is a strong demand for things to be the other way about. Their arguments were put to me at great length as we sat in Committee Room D on the ground floor. It's normally a loathsome place but as there was an open window and it was a hot day the dark, subterranean room was cool and we had a very good discussion.

I was just finishing with them when Tam came in to say that the vote on St John Stevas's Ten-Minute Rule Bill was being taken.[1] This was designed

[1] The proposal was defeated by 210 votes to 199. Norman St John Stevas, Conservative M.P. for Chelmsford since October 1964, was Parliamentary Under-Secretary of State at the Department of Education and Science 1972–3 and Minister of State for the Arts at the same Department 1973–4. An author, barrister and journalist, he has edited the writings of Walter Bagehot, published under the titles *The Literary Works*, Vols I and II (London: Economist Newspaper Ltd, 1966), *The Historical Works*, Vols III and IV (London: Economist Newspaper Ltd, 1968) and *The Political Works*, Vols V–VIII (London: Economist Newspaper Ltd, 1974).

to introduce an amendment to the Abortion Act stipulating that permission for an operation should be given by two consultants rather than just two qualified doctors. The Department had told me that this requirement would be an appalling clog on the service and would probably introduce into the Health Service some of the difficulties which are now concentrated in the private sector. However I was inclined to think in the first instance that it was a pity the amendment was defeated. They lost by only eleven votes, largely because the number of people there was far greater than ever discussed the Abortion Bill itself. When the legislation was left to back benchers there were never more than majorities of 80 or 90 for any of the clauses, but here were 409 people voting. Why? Because they were all waiting for a three-line whip on the Finance Bill this afternoon. This shows you something about the House of Commons. Give the private Member the right to decide for himself and perhaps 250 people attend, but for a mass House decision you must fix an artificial three-line whip so that, being present, they find themselves voting.

I had to break off at 5 o'clock to rush back to the Prime Minister's room for a meeting on Northern Ireland. There had been commotions, on St Patrick's Day, it may have been.[1] Anyway, on one of those days, rioting had broken out and the question was whether we should permit the R.U.C. to be equipped not only with tear gas but with the most modern kind of gas which they had asked for.[2] Callaghan had said that we would never use such gas on a crowd in Britain and asked whether it would be in order to forbid it to them. I thought we should let them have it. They have a totally different situation out there, with far greater risks and, indeed, using the gas might remove or reduce the need for British troops. Our discussion was all very amicable. Although this is another of those areas which the Prime Minister keeps in a separate section, I had expressed dissatisfaction at being excluded and, Callaghan, who wanted to be friendly, had put me on, but nobody could quite remember why I was there.

After this I had a meeting of the special working party on National Superannuation, which Douglas Houghton had asked me to set up. He had sent us eighteen questions in writing, to which we had given extremely detailed, careful answers. The Department had done a first-rate job and I went along with David Ennals and John Atkinson.[3] There were only eight people there, just over half the working party, and the discussion was almost entirely monopolized by a couple of people who have always detested our scheme. That is our National Superannuation working party, as unconstructive as the Parliamentary Group which also asks for full consultations.

[1] The rioting took place on July 12th, the anniversary of the Battle of the Boyne. St Patrick's day is March 17th.

[2] C.S. gas (o-chlorobenzylidine malononitrile) was patented in 1946, as a smoke, generated by pyrotechnics. It was held to be significantly more effective and less toxic than the short-term incapacitant 'tear gas' (C.N. gas, chloroacetophenone) used hitherto. A formal inquiry into the Medical and Toxicological Aspects of C.S. was held in 1971 (Cmnd 4775).

[3] Under-Secretary at the D.H.S.S. 1966–73 and Deputy Secretary since 1973.

Wednesday, July 16th

There was a similar lack of enthusiasm for the P.L.P. meeting this morning, when Douglas Houghton was to give his big address demanding loyalty to help me to reduce the vote against us on the Early Day Motion on teeth and spectacles. The trouble was that only ten or eleven people were in the room when we arrived and there were never more than the same old thirty who always turn up, mostly from the Left, with a few reliable people of ours. The speech got into the press and was quite sensible but that was all. I got a report from Tam but didn't go to the meeting as I was spending nearly six hours with the Regional Hospital Board chairmen, who were to report to me on what they had managed to do about switching reserves to the psychiatric and geriatric sectors. It didn't add up to much. Only one Board had managed to switch a substantial amount and this was because they said they had put aside £500,000 for increased costs after devaluation and found they hadn't really needed it. The provincial Boards from north of the Trent raised their eyebrows at how much a London Board had in reserve and my own Birmingham Board countered by saying they couldn't find a penny. By and large, the important point was not what they had to announce but from our side to give the impression that they must do something about this themselves. We continued the seminar after lunch and wound up with my proposal for a conference on sub-normality, in a Cambridge college perhaps. I pointed out the importance of communication. Maybe they went away thinking that I wasn't very effective but nevertheless it seemed to be fairly O.K.

Directly I had finished this I had to go across to a Cabinet Meeting at 4.0. The first item was Lancashire textiles. Lancashire is of course the county where, among others, Barbara Castle, Tony Greenwood and Harold Wilson are keenly engaged. It is a tremendously political place and Lancashire textiles is political too. Tony Crosland, our extremely Southern-minded President of the Board of Trade, had put up a proposal to help Lancashire by accepting a suggestion that we should substitute textile tariffs for quotas.[1] It was a bit queer because here was Barbara Castle fearlessly opposing him, not on behalf of Lancashire but of the under-developed territories, places like Hong Kong and India. The issue was really beyond me. In Cabinet one just doesn't fuss about this kind of thing, at least I don't, so I listened to Tony and Barbara. The Prime Minister said that he in Huyton is not concerned with textiles but, heaven knows, he is concerned with the textile unions. I heard Roy weigh in with the judicious remark that he was much in favour of the scheme provided that we didn't commit ourselves to aid to India and I found

[1] On July 22nd the President of the Board of Trade announced that the Government was prepared to consider an application by the Textile Council for an increase in the depreciation allowances for textile machinery. On March 25th, 1970, Harold Lever, Paymaster-General, announced that the Inland Revenue had agreed that the normal allowance for machinery used in the cotton and allied textiles industries, and worked for three shifts, should be increased to 25 per cent, the maximum possible under existing legislation.

myself supporting him. All this took a very long time and we will have to come back to it again.

The second big item was my report from the Social Services Committee on our action on the Seebohm Report. We had already had long discussions in Social Services, with the division of opinion between the Minister of Housing, Kenneth Robinson, and the Minister without Portfolio, poor George Thomson, the Scot in charge of the Maud Commission, and on the other side myself and the Home Secretary. We had come up with a statement and I had found myself becoming an obstacle because I couldn't agree on an announcement promising to implement Seebohm or a mini-Seebohm unless I could include in it something like an assurance to the doctors that they would not be taken over by the local authorities. This was all the more necessary now that the Maud Report seemed to favour local take-over.

I have put all this down in my diary at some length because I want to remind myself of what a complicated subject this is. It is the sort of matter where those in Cabinet who are not directly concerned are inevitably inclined to avert their eyes and say, 'For God's sake, we can't deal with it.' That was how we divided in Cabinet today, one lot interested in the Lancashire textiles and another lot mainly interested in this, with the Prime Minister and the Chancellor interested, as they must be, in everything. I got, as we wanted, agreement that before the end of the session I could make the statement I had recommended to Cabinet, and an agreement that we should postpone the controversial question of what kind of legislation we should have. It was decided that in July we should simply declare that, after consultation with the local authorities and the doctors, we intend to announce our policy in the autumn and prepare legislation for after Christmas, and that there would be a similar statement about the future of the Health Service to placate the doctors.

Then George Thomson raised the point about the inconsistency between our rushing ahead with this, despite everybody's objections, without waiting for Maud, and our saying that in the case of the boundaries we must wait for Maud. Callaghan kept on saying, 'Oh, I can explain that,' but I felt he couldn't and that he doesn't appreciate what a row there will be. So after Cabinet I got together with George Thomson, Callaghan and the Prime Minister and we all agreed that, in view of the new situation created by the boundary crisis, we should not make the statement on Seebohm before the end of the month. There will be a great outcry from social service workers in papers like *New Society* and terrible disappointment among the progressive forces but if I make the statement at the end of August or the beginning of September that will be good enough. This was a very important decision.

I just had time to get in the car and drive to Islington to answer questions on Health and National Insurance from the G.M.C. of the Islington Labour Party. It was another sweltering day and I answered questions and complaints from fifty or sixty people gathered in a very hot room. I was able to lambast them and show the enormous amount we had done on the Health side and that we were making a great change in Social Security, but nevertheless as I climbed into the car, sweating like a pig, to get back for the 10 o'clock vote, I said to Peter Smithson, 'It's no good, the Labour Party is just an anti-Government Party. It likes complaining. It is embarrassed by having us in Government and it won't have us there for very long.'

Thursday, July 17th

The big story in the morning papers was Hugh Cudlipp's announcement that next January the *Sun* would be wound up, and Bob Maxwell's announcement that he is determined to take it over and have it printed on the *Evening Standard* presses.[1] His idea is to turn it into a *Daily Worker* bought by the élite, with very little advertising, and he thinks that with half a million circulation and a rather higher price he can keep it going. Maxwell is a strange, roguish man and I can't really believe that he is going to make this thing a success. Nevertheless the blow is tremendous. Here is the death of yet another London paper and our own people are shaken. Ted Castle will be particularly disappointed because until the last moment he was hoping that the I.P.C. could be persuaded to prolong the *Sun*.

The first item at Cabinet was a most interesting incident with the Postmaster-General, Mr John Stonehouse. I must say, for all my suspicions about Stonehouse, at the same time he has an extraordinary way with him. What was he up to this week? There has come out what will be a famous report by Charles Hill threatening to close down B.B.C. orchestras and God knows what because the Corporation hasn't enough money to pay its way.[2] Charles Hill proposes to make drastic economies of a deplorable character, particularly in radio, where the Third Programme is virtually to disappear. There is also a contradictory proposal that there should be an extension of television

[1] At the beginning of the year Robert Maxwell, the Labour M.P. for Buckingham and owner of the Pergamon Press publishing company, had made an unsuccessful bid to take over the *News of the World*, which, with its stories of sex and sin, had achieved the world's largest Sunday circulation. The newspaper was acquired by Rupert Murdoch, an Australian newspaper proprietor, who was also to purchase the *Sun*. The International Publishing Corporation had been making an annual loss of some £1 million on this popular newspaper of the broad left, one of the group of *Mirror* papers for which Crossman had formerly written.

[2] *Broadcasting in the Seventies* set out a plan for 'streamed radio', providing an all-'pop' music service on Radio One, an all-light music service on Radio Two, a large classical music service with reduced hours of talks and drama on Radio Three and an all-talk service on Radio Four. The local radio service was to be expanded by the establishment of forty new stations, while the B.B.C.'s regional stations were to have their non-networked output cut. The Report caused considerable disquiet within the B.B.C., where there was already some resentment that, since Sir Hugh Carleton Greene's departure, many fewer controversial and innovatory programmes had appeared and current affairs and political programmes had been less challenging. The possibility that certain B.B.C. regional orchestras might have to be disbanded also led to protest from the Musicians' Union, as well as from the general public. The greatest outcry, however, was against the proposal to scrap the old Third Programme, which provoked the establishment of a campaign for better broadcasting.

hours, for which I.T.V. is pressing for the simple reason that the more hours they get the more money they make, whereas the more hours the B.B.C. gets the more work it has to do with the same amount of money from the licence fees. Absolutely characteristically, the newspapers were full of how Stonehouse was going to react to the report and the issue of hours, finances, the future of local radio stations, and so on. He has been busy committing the Government, as everybody does to some extent. I have certainly made my share of Statements which I hoped would gradually let the Government into a position where they had to back me, but Stonehouse does this in a very extreme fashion and he has had the unwisdom to do it when he is a mere Postmaster-General, so there has been a tremendous outcry. Fred Peart, who with Mellish is cursing Stonehouse, told me that yesterday the Broadcasting Committee had agreed to recommend an increase of 10*s*. in the licence fee and possibly an extension of hours.[1]

The question of timing the announcement came up in today's Cabinet discussion of forthcoming business because the Tories have been clever enough to put down a request for a Supply Day next week on B.B.C. finances. Stonehouse was brought in and said he wanted to make a Statement on the Committee's decision. Cabinet blew up; they weren't going to have it. Tony Crosland led the way and I supported him. So did Tony Wedgwood Benn and everybody agreed that Cabinet must have time to consider this, because we have only had the B.B.C. report for a week and we don't have to rush into print.

Then it became clear that Stonehouse had been to the Prime Minister and half got Harold to agree that he should be allowed to make the Statement. I watched, and this is the striking thing, Harold didn't smack Stonehouse down or punish him. Indeed, right at the end Stonehouse said, 'Wouldn't it be a good thing at least if we gave both sides of the case and explained the choices?' 'God forbid,' I said. 'If you do that you will explain it in such a way that one choice will prevail. There must be a frank Statement that the Cabinet refuses to be rushed.' I knew this was embarrassing for Stonehouse because he had already committed himself. I wouldn't put it past him to persuade the Prime Minister to allow him to say something definite and I shall be very surprised if he doesn't squeeze something past Harold.* No one can understand why Harold lets people twist him round their little finger in this way, even when, as in Stonehouse's case, he doesn't like them.

Yesterday afternoon's Cabinet had got rid of the other items before the big Cabinet this morning, so now we turned to public expenditure. At the beginning some of us, Crosland and I, Barbara and Judith, all very carefully said that there wasn't any question yet of our having to agree that £350 or

[1] In 1969 the licence fee was £6 p.a. for a radio and a black-and-white television set, £11 p.a. for a radio and a colour television set.

* Sure enough, the next day four or five papers carried inspired stories about the Statement Stonehouse was due to make.

£400 million should be found by cuts. This was only one possibility; others were to find it by reducing investment grants or increasing taxation. Cabinet was merely going to listen to what the Chancellor put before it. This the Chancellor didn't like but he and the Prime Minister had to take it. Most of the morning was spent in the really unsensational story of the fix Roy had done with Denis Healey. Denis has a great margin with his £2,000 million and he made a tremendous speech about how once again he would have to cut but, after all, his job is to cut defence and if he can get it down further and faster presumably he ought to like it. He never admits that cuts are very different for those of us whose aim is to expand the social services. However, this morning we had them one after the other, the non-controversial Ministers, Defence, the nationalized Industries, the Transport people. For some reason Dick Marsh can once again be squeezed successfully and there was Barbara Castle being very virtuous and saying that she was contributing half a million by building two fewer new training centres this year. Then we got to Education, where Ted Short offered a 20 per cent cut in the minor works programme, starting with the provision of new classrooms in primary schools, particularly denominational schools, an enormous cut in the most sensitive and damaging area, with another 3*d.* on school meals, £5 million on charging people for school transport and small cuts for the universities. This package is dynamite. It could certainly not be implemented quietly because the school meals increase would need one announcement and the transport charges would require legislation. Only the cuts in the minor works programme can be made without announcement and they on the whole are the most damaging and disastrous thing of all. At this point we had to break off.

In the meantime I must refer to the Prime Minister's Questions this afternoon, because I think they were one of the most brilliant parliamentary occasions I have ever attended. We shall never understand Harold's hold on the Parliamentary Labour Party until we understand this. If you look at today's Hansard you will see his elegant answer to Sydney Bidwell on the announcement of the resignation of John Davies from the C.B.I.[1] Then the P.M. switched to rather a delicate Question about the nationalization of the pharmaceutical industry and then to another on nuclear weapons. On health he just put things in their place, on nuclear weapons he was serious and gave nothing away. Eldon Griffiths asked a snide Question on whether the Prime Minister had received representations on parliamentary boundaries from residents of Huyton.[2] Harold waited, making little interludes, and then said with tremendous effect, 'The total number of communications about the Government's Bill which I have received in both my capacity as Prime

[1] Sydney Bidwell was Labour M.P. for Southall 1966–74 and has been M.P. for Ealing, Southall, since 1974.

[2] Conservative M.P. for Bury St Edmunds since May 1964. He was Parliamentary Secretary at the M.H.L.G. June–October 1970, Parliamentary Under-Secretary of State at the D.O.E. and Minister for Sport 1970–4.

Minister and as constituency M.P. from constituents – the total number – is not one, Sir. With regard to the number received from the whole of Britain, the answer is about twenty.'[1] Then he rebuked Geoffrey Rippon and scored off our friend Jeremy Thorpe.[2]

It was the most deft and brilliant exhibition of parliamentary lightweight boxing. Harold prepares it all carefully in advance, working on all these quips and quiddities and interesting facts. As he sat down he said, 'That was fun.' But I had expected them to be really sticky Questions and I thought he got away with murder. So brilliant was it that I listened on after 3.30 and forgot for the moment that I was due to take the chair at the Green Paper consultation with the local authorities. My God, I got to the great ministerial conference room seven minutes late, to find all my colleagues sitting round the table.

It was like old times in the Ministry of Housing. There were the C.C.A., the A.M.C., the London boroughs, the G.L.C., the U.D.C.s and R.D.C.s and on our side myself, the Home Secretary, the Paymaster-General, my own Bea Serota and a whole lot of officials. Now this was a delicate subject because we had to tell them that without waiting for Maud we wanted to implement Seebohm and make an early decision on the future of the Health Service. First of all, we very quietly got each of them to commit themselves on Seebohm and, surprisingly, they all expressed an eagerness to have part of it implemented. I moved on and said, 'Well in that case we shall have to have a round of discussions now. We want to be able to announce this in October and at the same time I must also make an announcement about the future of the Health Service.' The fat was in the fire and I was suddenly in trouble. Every one of them was saying that they couldn't possibly have this, that one of the most important parts of Maud was the idea of extending local government control to the Health Service and that they couldn't possibly agree. I think myself that though they will protest they will agree but in a way I was relieved that we had decided not to put out the statement about Seebohm next week.

I had to rush back to Alexander Fleming House for a party for the Israeli Minister of Health. It was a flop. You can't get people over there and if they do come they won't stay. I arrived at 6.0 but at 6.15 I had to leave for the resumed Cabinet at 6.30.

Now we had to deal with the really controversial parts of the public expenditure cuts, that is to say, education and health. It became clear that

[1] *House of Commons Debates*, Vol. 787, col. 881.

[2] Geoffrey Rippon was Conservative M.P. for Norwich South 1955–64 and since 1966 has been M.P. for Hexham. He was Parliamentary Secretary at the Ministry of Aviation 1959–61, Joint Parliamentary Secretary at the M.H.L.G. October 1961–July 1962, Minister of Public Building and Works 1962–4, Minister of Technology 1970, Chancellor of the Duchy of Lancaster 1970–2 and Secretary of State for the Environment 1972–4. Jeremy Thorpe, Liberal M.P. for North Devon since October 1959, was Leader of the Liberal Party from 1967 until May 1976.

Cabinet was not going to tolerate the education cuts. All this was complicated by Barbara's complaint that the decision to raise school meals by 3*d.*, instead of getting another £10 million by increasing the fees for further education, had not gone to Cabinet and that she couldn't possibly agree to it. This is a nice question. It was pointed out that since this was only a substitute device preferred by the Minister concerned, it wasn't something that would usually go to Cabinet. When it had come to me in Social Services I had advised Short not to take it to S.E.P. but to go straight to the Prime Minister and the Chancellor, so we had agreed it a bit hanky-panky and Barbara was now out for blood because she thought that raising the price of school meals would hit the lower-paid worker. There was something in what she said but I didn't know how we were going to get out of it. There was a long and ardent discussion with much the same line-up. Tony Crosland, of course, as an ex-Education Minister, was for having no cuts and virtually everybody else supported Ted Short, saying that this was impossible and we ought to raise taxation.

So we got through that very well and then came Health. Here the Chancellor started by saying what his cuts were in my case and then handing over to me. I again made a mistake because I explained how I really needed £17 million extra but I was willing to absorb this revenue cut. Apart from that I would introduce a new charge on insurance companies to cover the cost of the hospitalization of accident cases, which I said would raise £9 million. The Minister of Transport was a bit surprised and said that was the first he'd heard of it, and it's true, but still I got it across as something bright and new which we could do. Then I turned to the hospital building programme and said if it was insisted I should have a cut I could postpone new starts for three months and save £9 million but I would have to announce it. There were great cries of 'Oh, nonsense, here is Dick deceiving us. He doesn't have to announce it. He can do it by slippage.' That's all right for me because I shall go back to Cabinet and say, 'Right, if I don't announce it, it will only be £5 million instead of £9 million,' so I shall get away with another £4 million. I didn't do too well on this, because as I am a big spending Minister with £6,500 million, and as there are cuts in Social Security, Cabinet was certain that some small amount could be taken out of the hospital building programme without being noticed. Of course it can, but whether it is to be £9 million is a different matter. That is about as far as we got. We are going to have a discussion again next Thursday to put the whole thing together and then we shall measure the advisability of accepting all these things. My suspicion is that Roy will be well over a £100 million short and that he should remain so. We shouldn't let him try to extract any more.

After that we turned to the last item on the agenda, N.H.S. charges. Cabinet already knew that Roy and I had come to no agreement because in front of them there was a very reasonable paper from me (which had been largely written by Alan Marre) and a peremptory note from Roy just saying that the whole matter is a great mistake and that we shouldn't blow up the issue. But the situation had been entirely changed for me yesterday evening because at long last they had found the text of a letter the Prime Minister had sent to Laurie Pavitt. Curiously enough, ever since the fiasco on teeth and spectacles I have been asking for a Statement which I thought had been made by the Minister of Health saying that we didn't regard charges as a permanent part of our policy and that in due course we would return to a free service. I had been told that there was no such Statement and the Ministry had absolutely no record of one. However, Laurie Pavitt did mention in his speech on July 1st a letter he had received from the Prime Minister,[1] and with this clue we searched for it in my departmental files, but Kenneth Robinson had left no such paper behind. Then the Prime Minister was asked and it was found, not in his public but in his personal file. The letter had been written by Marcia Williams and it was therefore in her private file. I suppose it had also been in Kenneth Robinson's private file, which is why I never saw it and why it had never been available. The text of what the Prime Minister offered was a great deal more precise than the draft I offered from only a vague memory and, as the Department had said, with no authority.

So this morning, in a rather genial way, I said, 'Things are a bit different now.' I explained that I wasn't going to press too hard for the text of my actual draft Statement, which the Chancellor objected to, because I had now found a letter which had been mislaid. Well, Cabinet couldn't conceive how it had been mislaid, and I don't think half of them understand it yet. I said, 'It was mislaid and then it was found in the Prime Minister's Private Office.' Harold said, 'It was a letter which was co-ordinated by you as Lord President, and you will find the text in the Lord President's Office.' That may be true, I haven't asked Fred, but there was a roar of laughter, 'Good old Dick, losing documents again and messing things up.' Then I said, 'However it was, we have now found the letter.' I had taken the precaution of ringing Harold up at breakfast-time today and giving him the text. I asked if he had any recollection of this and he said, 'Yes, I think I have some memory of it. I think I was shown it at the time but I do hope you won't blow it up and remind people of it too vividly.' I did read it aloud and I must say people looked a bit silly. I suspected that Roy and his friends might even refuse me leave to say anything specific at all about prescription charges or our attitude to them but after this he didn't try very hard. Somehow the whole Cabinet relaxed and found it farcical and funny – the lost letter, the confusion between the P.M.'s Private Office and Marcia's and mine, the fact that I had accused the Prime Minister of suppressing the letter and that he accused me of having co-ordinated it. It all became a great frivolity and I was left with quite a good minute,

[1] Mr Pavitt quoted the letter as saying, 'It would be wrong for you to assume that these charges, reluctantly introduced to meet a serious economic situation, carried the implication of a permanent change in the Government's policy or of its approach to Health Service financing.' See *House of Commons Debates*, Vol. 786, col. 291.

enabling me to make my reply on the basis of the letter which Laurie Pavitt had never published.

By then Cabinet had gone on a long time. I gave Nicky Kaldor dinner afterwards, before I went to the reception at Lancaster House for the Finnish President. I never saw him, or the Foreign Secretary, but I ran into Heinz Koeppler and then I met two people from Nuneaton. 'Ah,' they said to me, 'we are just ordinary comrades. Somebody slipped and asked us to come and we wondered what we were doing here. Isn't this just the kind of party the Tories hold?' 'Well, yes,' I said. 'I should say that 98 per cent of the guests would be here whatever Party was in power. This is an Establishment party, it's true. Nevertheless you and I are part of the 2 per cent who come and go, so let us be grateful for it and have a drink together.' The weather was enormously hot but it was quite enjoyable and at 11.45 I got out. I quite enjoy these receptions when I get there but as far as I can see I can manage without them perfectly well.

Friday, July 18th

I went into my office to prepare a speech for a great Regional Labour Party conference at Stoke tomorrow, and to open the St Thomas's Hospital computer centre, which handles the accounts and payrolls of 600 hospitals. It is a smart little building, with elegant furniture, decorations, carpets and girls, inside a ghastly public assistance hospital in Lambeth. It was formidable. Here were, it seemed to me, hundreds of light-suited dark men, with little tabs with names on their pockets, all looking like, not members of Rotary clubs exactly, but like senior bank officials. These were the computer men. I had taken a great deal of trouble with my speech and had written and rewritten it but as I read it aloud it sounded terrible. Yet I believe it was a very good speech. It is something new to me, to find that in this kind of work whether it is heart transplants or computers you are dealing with subjects you can't get right unless you are prepared to use a script and you have to believe in a script and read it vividly and convincingly, with a few insertions. I am only gradually getting used to this. I think today's speech was all right because as I went out I heard somebody say, 'That was a first-rate speech. How did he know so much about us?' I knew not a darned thing!

Saturday, July 19th

Anne drove me up to Kidsgrove, a ghastly drive right across through Warwick and then through back lanes to Coleshill and on to the A5, until at last we got on to the motorway. We roared up, getting there only twenty minutes late to find dear Harold Davies waiting to take us into Kidsgrove. The last time I was there was, I think, in 1938. It was an area of chronic unemployment and I remember going on several Sunday mornings to give extension lectures to unemployed miners. That was difficult and you were really tested and had to find out whether as a university person you could get the right touch – and the unemployed weren't the easiest to talk to. Today the Club, the only thing which was like the old days, was still the Club, still sordid and dirty and, although it has been jazzed up a bit, our meal was still simple and proletarian. But the gathering of the clans in the clubroom, with their glasses of beer in front of them, was not the kind of school I was used to. We had a good conference but the young Miners' Union Secretaries and the young candidate at Newcastle said, 'Your pension scheme is no bloody good.' Most of them were saying it was all too difficult and intellectual and that once again the party was going too fast and too far. It was a spirited meeting and I learnt a lot. The gap between the Government and the rank and file is real because the rank and file are now bewildered and beaten. They are good, willing, loyal, decent people but they have lost faith in this Government and are utterly dejected. Every new thing, therefore, is suspect. Why do we have to have pensions on top of everything else? On the way home we got off the motorway one exit early, and found it was possible to motor slantwise, parallel to the A5. This was a splendid discovery and it shows how much you have to know about short cuts when you are dealing with motorways.

Sunday, July 20th

I suppose one has to admit that the whole of this week has been increasingly dominated by the moon, the only British news being that John Freeman refused to attend the launching.[1] I suppose he felt it was too undignified. We members of the Government have been delighted to have the limelight taken off us by lovely weather and the astronauts. I have been reflecting on this. On Friday night we stayed up with our colour television in the drawing room and there we had a whole two-hour programme on, what was it called, 'The Violent Universe'. It was a wonderful title and a wonderful programme, just showing us that the universe only consists of vast amounts of gas blowing off, infinity in a really profound sense. Millions of light years away, however far you go, there is only more gas blowing off. It was a universe of violence, of eruption and explosion, and we were shown that sooner or later it is inevitable that life on this planet will be wiped out when a star explodes and the gas swoops across and sweeps us up.

Afterwards Anne and I discussed the meaning of this. We don't often argue about things but it was a hot stuffy night and we lay on the bed without blankets and I said, 'Well, the Hoyle Big Bang theory and the other theories are all equally futile because they are postulations about the whole of the universe and the one thing to get clear is that there is no comprehensive

[1] On July 16th Apollo 11 was launched with a crew of three and at 03.56 B.S.T. on July 21st Neil Armstrong, the Commander, stepped from the lunar landing vehicle on to the moon's surface, watched on television by some 600 million people. He was joined by a second astronaut and before they rejoined the orbiting Apollo the two men collected samples and fulfilled various scientific tasks. The space craft returned safely to earth, splashing down in the Pacific on July 24th.

theory for us to grasp.[1] Things are further away and more meaningless than ever and it becomes even more meaningless to think of a God who conceived all this purposely. One can look at life on this planet and imagine that nothing but a mind could have planned how everything has come about, but when we understand that life here is an accident, what comfort does it give us? I don't think it makes any difference really.' I know that before I was twenty-five I had formulated a philosophy of life which explained to me why questions of religion, immortality and metaphysics were literally meaningless and, having got that clear in my mind, I have always applied this theory to what I call semi-metaphysical explanations of scientific data such as you hear in these great debates. If there hadn't been the Big Bang versus the Continuous Creation debate to discuss, the programme would have gone on and on describing – what? Well, it described the vast human ingenuity and expense devoted to picking up with inordinate skill fascinating tiny fragments of knowledge in order to understand more about something where in a sense more is meaningless, because when you have an infinite universe a tiny piece of knowledge about it is simultaneously infinitely worthless and infinitely valuable. There it is.

It made me feel that the astronauts were even more insignificant, not in terms of human endeavour because it is a fact that if a human being can by modern technology put men on to the moon, take them off again with a scoop of moon dust and bring them back to earth, it is the beginning of a new age of exploration, because in time they will no doubt get to another planet. But the trouble is that the distance they move will be infinitely small compared to the distance they have not moved. Whether you move that far or this far, whether you remain tied to a village or expand to Saturn, the experience is in terms of infinity equally small or equally large, and that gives me my real philosophy. It means that you can either go to the moon or you can stay at Prescote. The test is the intensity of experience, the vitality of your life, the genuineness of your affection for your family. These are things you can achieve as human beings whatever your range although there is something in human beings which drives us on to inquire and conquer and organize. Indeed, these are the motives of my life. Why do I spend my time organizing, having this political life, instead of merely sitting at Prescote? They are the same drives and neither is superior to the other.

Meanwhile, as I say, the astronauts have taken the heat off the politicians for a bit, but our constitutional crisis has continued in the closest secrecy. Harold is conducting it, as usual, with a tiny *ad hoc* group of Ministers. I know who they are because the other day I was waiting outside when they came rushing out, Eddie Shackleton, Gerald Gardiner, Fred Peart, Jim

[1] Professor Fred Hoyle was Research Professor at the University of Manchester and Visiting Professor of Astrophysics at the California Institute of Technology. He was Professor of Astronomy at the Royal Institution of Great Britain 1969–77. As well as scientific books and articles, he has written several novels.

Callaghan and the Attorney-General. This is the small ministerial group which has been working out our tactics for dealing with the Lords, when tomorrow they move their amendment to the Seats Bill.[1] On Tuesday morning we shall have a Cabinet meeting and, just like any other Cabinet of this kind, we shall be asked to ratify what is virtually a *fait accompli*. This is what has happened to us on almost every other important issue, except possibly entry into Europe. All one can say is that the Prime Minister has returned to his old technique. Not only did this issue not go to the Management Committee, it didn't even go to the P.L. Committee, as we were told it would. The preparation of some short Bill or motion to abolish the Lords is part of what this small inner group is doing and Harold has rather assertively put the issue in these terms and Cabinet hasn't challenged him.

The Management Committee hasn't really worked because it didn't suit Harold and he used it in the most abrupt and inopportune way, always having a meeting just before Cabinet, so they knew we were pre-deciding an issue. Since one of the main functions of the Management Committee was to consult without Callaghan and he is now back in the middle of the constitutional crisis, it is now out of date. And as Jim couldn't conceivably be dropped from the Government now, either before or after the summer recess, I think Harold's old ideas, which he discussed with Barbara and me and Roy, are also out of date. When I talked to Fred Peart and Bob Mellish the other day they had both been approached about a big reshuffle and like me they had both been told that Callaghan might go and that Harold was certainly considering the high jump for Judith Hart, Peter Shore and Dick Marsh, and possibly for Tony Crosland. I agreed with Fred and Bob that the big change was not dropping Callaghan. Barbara has also found that this decision is out and I think it has all been postponed. Harold has pushed aside his idea of having the reshuffle shortly after Parliament breaks up for the recess and Douglas Houghton is away, and the announcement of Roy Hattersley as Gerry Reynolds's replacement has confirmed that there is no immediate reshuffle in the offing.[2]

Meanwhile the Prime Minister continues to be obsessed by leaks. I have

[1] The Lords had prudently given the Seats Bill a Second Reading on July 17th, although peers from all sides of the House had condemned the measure as a disreputable Parliamentary procedure. Carefully refraining from 'answering a trick with a trick', the Opposition front bench decided not to propose a wrecking amendment to the Bill at Committee Stage but to adopt a more moderate device. Amendment No. 1, tabled in the names of the Conservative and Liberal leaders and two highly regarded cross-benchers, in effect gave the Home Secretary another three months to table the Orders, absolving him until the end of the current parliamentary session. The amendment was carried decisively by 270 votes to 96. Of the Government supporters, 93 took the Labour whip and 16 held ministerial office. The amended Bill was then returned to the Commons.

[2] Gerry Reynolds, Labour M.P. for North Islington from 1958 until his death on June 7th, 1969, had been Parliamentary Under-Secretary (Army) at the Ministry of Defence 1964–5, Minister of Defence (Army) 1965–7 and Minister of Defence (Administration) 1967–9. He was succeeded by Roy Hattersley in the last of these offices on July 15th.

often said and I am going to say that Harold in fact regards the leak as some inner piece of information, appearing in the papers, which doesn't suit his own plans. Everything which Harold says to the press is briefing, everything which he asks me to do is briefing, but the habit of counter-briefing which grew up when he was dominating the press with press conferences twice a week, pouring information into them, is thoroughly demoralizing. People brief against each other, letting malicious stories out about who does what. There is a difference between these malicious and damaging announcements and the things I do, which are all designed to put the Government in a decent light. There are three or four people I talk to regularly, Jimmy Margach of the *Sunday Times*, David Watt of the *Financial Times*, Alan Watkins of the *New Statesman*, and occasionally Ian Aitken of the *Guardian* rings me up. I do a certain amount of steering and No. 10 does a great deal, with Gerald Kaufman and Marcia both used extensively for this purpose. Then there is Roy Jenkins and his boon companion John Harris, who is a kind of American character, a real 'kitchen cabinet' in one. He steers Roy a great deal and represents him to the press. Barbara is convinced she doesn't do any briefing and she certainly doesn't use Ted in any way at all but she has always had an extremely good press office that is perfectly capable of steering people and she talks extraordinarily freely, though she is never systematically malicious about her colleagues. In fact almost every Minister does a certain amount, every Minister is approached and airs his views. Is this Cabinet worse than other Cabinets? Whitehall says that it is not. I rather think that it is, but what is certainly worse is the Prime Minister's obsession about it, his constant rebukes to Cabinet and the fact that Cabinet is not in the least impressed. However he organizes his Cabinet, however many people he sacks, there will always be this uncertainty between us and there is born out of this the readiness of Ministers to say more than they ought when they are cross-examined by the press.

I have just sent the boxes back and now I have finished dictating this very verbose diary. Tomorrow I am off at 8.0 a.m. to Leeds to make a speech and then back by the Pullman to prepare for the speech on teeth and spectacles. I don't want to cause a sensation and I certainly don't want to compete with the moon men who are landing tomorrow evening. We want to let the moon dominate, not teeth and spectacles.

Monday, July 21st

This morning Patrick and I came down at 6.30 and sat in the kitchen with the television set, and there we saw the astronauts' feet appear as they jumped out on the moon. For the first time, I think, I was slightly impressed, not by the fact that they got out and picked up rocks but by the incredible achievement that all over the world the muttering of these two men 250,000 million miles away could be heard. It was an impressive telecommunications feat, which is why Kennedy decided to do it. Though the adventure would have no great scientific value it would help America to regain its self-confidence, reputation and superiority.

However this morning my main concern was not the moon men but the press reports of Roy's speech. On Saturday evening at Abingdon he had made an important speech on the general philosophy of the Labour Government, saying this is not 'the permissive society', it is the civilized society. He defended all we have been doing in the last five years as a great act of civilized progress in our whole attitude to social, abortion, homosexual law and divorce reform. I must say this is nothing to do with the Government because these matters have been much more the concern of private Members, but it was a thoughtful, creative speech, which Roy made extremely well. John Harris did a good job and Roy got a whole page of the *Sunday Mirror* and an excellent display in the *Sunday Times* and *Sunday Express*. It was the first ministerial speech for a long time that has been more than a departmental brief.

I left Prescote at 8.15 and at 10.15 we were off the motorway and on the road to Leeds where I had agreed to address some association of workers in geriatrics. Fortunately I got there half an hour early because I had to make the speech at 11.30 and leave at 12.05 in order to get the train back to London for some Ministry business before the debate on teeth and spectacles. I gave them a fifteen- to twenty-minute speech and then fifteen minutes' questions, scrapping my written text and doing it *ad lib*. It worked very well and I got a much better press as a result. Then I hurled down, with a police car ahead of me, to Leeds Central station and got on to the train, where Patrick Benner was waiting to travel down with me and discuss teeth and spectacles on the way.[1]

This debate has been hanging over me for weeks. Although I had managed to persuade Cabinet to let me make a Statement which would seem sensible to the Party and would make it clear that prescription charges were only temporary, I had only succeeded at the cost of accepting the Statement in the Prime Minister's letter to Laurie Pavitt. Since then I have been having more and more second thoughts about this, and wondering why, if the letter was all that good, Laurie Pavitt had never used it in the debate on prescription charges on May 30th. Nor had Kenneth Robinson and this morning I rang up Kenneth and asked him about this. He said, 'Laurie didn't use it and I would never dream of using it except to defend myself against him because I didn't want to raise the whole issue. If I had quoted it they would have said to me "When are charges going to be abolished?" and that would not have pleased the Treasury.' I said, 'I'm not out to please the Treasury. I'm out to get a Statement which makes sense.' But I felt that Kenneth also thought it wasn't all that good just saying we imposed prescription charges against our will and we would abolish them when priorities allowed.

[1] Under-Secretary at the D.H.S.S. 1968–72 and Deputy Secretary at the Cabinet Office since 1972.

However that was all I had to say so on the way down from Leeds and over lunch on the train, Benner and I worked the speech out and I gave him precise instructions. When I got in I had a series of meetings and meanwhile Benner drafted a perfectly decent speech, which I worked on from 8.0 p.m. till 10.0, so that I had a written script of some twelve pages, about twenty minutes' worth, before the time came to go down to hear the debate. It was going fairly mildly, with Maurice Macmillan and Balneil and perhaps five Tories on the other side, and about sixty to seventy people on our side, but I began to feel uneasily that it wasn't too good. We started at 10.01 with Laurie Pavitt himself, who was relatively mild, and then after an hour I was on.

The moment I began I knew that I was going to have terrible trouble, because the benches were filling up. Certainly Tom Driberg, Lena Jeger and Will Griffiths had had quite a lot to drink and they were out to down me.[1] I soon realized that what I said didn't matter in the faintest degree. Jim Callaghan had said, 'Dick, for once be dull. Stick to your brief and read it aloud,' and Roy Jenkins had said, 'Don't let off steam, don't set it going again with an exciting speech, just play it down,' so I suppose for the first time in my parliamentary life I didn't try to be interesting. Never before have I thanked God for a script. I put my head down and read through it, slowly enough to fill in between 11.10 and 11.30, the time for the vote. When they shouted 'Take your glasses off,' as a joke, I took my glasses off. There couldn't have been a more humiliating performance. I just thought I had to get through it and I had no heart in it. If they had listened to the speech they might have thought there was some concession there but they didn't want to. This was the final demonstration of the Left. They had won on Lords' reform, they had won on Industrial Relations, and they were going down fighting in the last protest before we went off for the recess.[2] It was odious, painful, humiliating. It wasn't greatly agonizing but I came out numb. I went upstairs and, thank God, Michael Foot had had the decency to suggest that he wanted Connie Bessie to spend her last evening with me. He brought Jill and Connie up to my room and we drank and talked about nothings and they kept me going until I went home at midnight.

Tuesday, July 22nd

I woke up at 3.0 full of panic about the morning papers, so at 3.15 I got out my boxes and worked until 5.45 to steady my nerves. Then I had a little bit more sleep until at 7.45 I was eating breakfast with Tam and seeing that I was

[1] Mrs Lena Jeger, Labour M.P. for Holborn and St Pancras November 1953–September 1959 and 1964–74 and for Camden, Holborn and St Pancras South since 1974. She has been a member of the N.E.C. since 1968. William Griffiths, Labour M.P. for Manchester, Moss Side, 1945–50 and for Manchester, Exchange, from 1950 until his death in 1973, was P.P.S. to the Minister of Health 1950–January 1951 and to the Minister of Labour January–April 1951.

[2] The Prayer to annul the Order for increased charges was defeated by 199 votes to 59.

not in the press. The moon men safely off the moon was one story and the Lords' overwhelming rejection of the Seats Bill was the other. Still, these things hit you. I know I am tremendously insensitive to physical pain but I am more sensitive to this sort of pain and I minded this terribly. I minded the indignity and also the fact that I had done everything out of gear to make the thing worse. It has been one of the most unsatisfactory incidents in my whole political career, the most unsatisfactory I suppose since my clanger about the trade unions in the *Daily Mirror*.[1] I realize that once over soon forgiven but it was a horrible and unpleasant situation.

At Cabinet we had a number of interesting items. We started with a report by Michael Stewart on the opportunities for entering the Common Market, with Harold Wilson following him up. There were little counter-attacking questions, particularly from Fred Peart. Was it really the right time now for us to try to go in? Wasn't it even more difficult in terms of agricultural policy or in terms of the balance of payments? Harold said, 'No, we mustn't have a change of stance or go back on it or re-examine it again but we oughtn't to be over eager.' I suppose I felt that was right but I also couldn't help feeling that in this, as in so many other issues, Cabinet no longer minds. We are all too tired, too absorbed in our own interests to feel any great collective responsibility.

I may say that but in fact the next item proved the opposite, for this was M.P.s' salaries and there was tremendous strength of feeling.[2] Three or four weeks ago, when we had decided to accept the Prices and Incomes Board's recommendation about higher civil servants, Cabinet all firmly agreed that there could be no question of increasing Members' salaries before the election. I am sure this is right. The electorate would never forgive us. Nevertheless, here was Fred Peart bringing forward a number of proposals from the Services Committee for some functional things which were perfectly all right but also proposals that whether Members had secretaries or not they should be paid an allowance of £1,000 a year. I made a rapid calculation that, if you add £1,000 to the present £3,500, in the course of the last five years an M.P. would have done far better than an old-age pensioner. I put this very strongly and Barbara supported me but it was striking how many people said, 'Oh, nonsense!' Bob Mellish, who is usually sane, said, 'We can't have all this talk. Members really must be considered and we can't deny them their allowance. Let's just give them their £1,000 and not ask any questions.' Here he was strongly supported by a number of other members. It was an awkward

[1] See p. 476 and n. above.

[2] In 1964 M.P.s' salaries had been raised from £1,750 to £3,250 a year, of which £1,250 could be claimed against tax as an appropriate amount to cover necessary parliamentary expenses. From October 1969 Members were able to claim a secretarial allowance of £500 a year, payable quarterly in respect of secretarial expenses actually incurred. There was no salary increase, however, until December 1971, when the Review Body on Top Salaries, formed in May 1971, recommended that M.P.s should receive, together with certain other allowances, annual salaries of £4,500.

division. I am wealthy; how can I deny the increase to others? Harold was really on their side too, having been persuaded that this was necessary, I suppose, to keep his position in the Party. I think Michael Stewart and Willie Ross were also on the side of the Members, while Dick Marsh, on the other hand, saw the dangers. It was one of those occasions when the Cabinet really was divided and Barbara and I only won because we were solidly with Roy.

Then we came to the Ombudsman, another of Harold Wilson's things. He is now moving into the stage where he sees everything in terms of elections and popularization and he wanted to make a Statement saying we were going to extend the Ombudsman's jurisdiction. Tony Greenwood, who has been away with a kind of allergy for weeks and weeks, put it to the P.M. that it could be extended to cover local government. I had been warning Harold for some weeks that he couldn't extend it to the Health Service and that I must reserve my position. But it didn't prevent him from pushing and shoving, saying he wanted to have this Statement this afternoon. Although there was good strong opposition, he got his way in the end because it was part of his preparations for the election.[1]

Then there came an item from me on the short-term social security benefits White Paper, which was whisked through in a few minutes. The last item was on whether the Concorde test route should be over the North Sea or whether it should be a west coast route over Scotland and Wales and the poor old Scots and Welsh had to concede the overwhelming technical case for the latter. This brought up the doubts and worries we all still have about Concorde. It was a pretty full Cabinet but we were all really looking forward to Thursday's Cabinet on expenditure, and polishing everything else off first.

This afternoon George Thomson's Committee on Local Government met to consider the Maud Report for the first time and for Ministers to give their departmental reactions. You might have thought that this would be an important meeting but unfortunately the local government issues all got submerged by the Boundary Commission. However it was clear enough from what was being said that, though there was overwhelming recognition by the Committee that we had got to accept Maud in general and the basic unitary structure of the top authorities, his chapters on local and provincial councils were disappointing and couldn't be accepted. A vast amount of work would have to be done on this and it was really outrageous of Harold to require the local authorities to finalize their views on Maud by the end of October. There

[1] The Prime Minister announced that the Government had accepted in principle that an ombudsman system should be established for investigating complaints of maladministration by local government. It would be separate from the Parliamentary Commissioner system and independent reports would be considered by the appropriate local authority. He repeated the Secretary of State for Social Services' announcement to the House of May 19th that, though there was a substantial case for a Health Commissioner, this office should not be confused with the new Hospital Advisory Service which was being established. The Prime Minister added that further consultation was necessary to see how far the new Service would meet the problem and how a procedure to deal with complaints would fit in to the proposals now being worked out for the future administrative structure of the N.H.S.

is a kind of quiet conflict going on between two entirely different timetables, Callaghan's and mine, dealing with Seebohm and the Green Paper aspects of Maud, and the Prime Minister's driving and shoving the idea of getting a White Paper out in January. In this kind of conflict one side can be fairly sure of winning because it is backed by Whitehall.

I moved from this to a meeting of the Home Publicity Committee and then on to the annual cocktail party for the County Councils Association. Finally, after a long day, back to give dinner to Bea Serota and Brian so we could go through all our current business and see how much work we shall have to do in the first fortnight of August.

Wednesday, July 23rd

I was interested to see the press on John Stonehouse's debate yesterday on *Broadcasting in the Seventies*. He is a resourceful man and he had virtually committed the B.B.C. to an increase in the licence fee but otherwise he had fairly well kept to his rule.[1] He got a good press for it. He is an astonishing fellow, this Stonehouse, tall and handsome-looking, with his dark eyes and his little whiskers on each side, sleek, with that slight stutter, slight unsureness of himself, and yet firm and courageous. Roy really can't abide him and I think he is profoundly untrustworthy.

This morning I had a whole number of characters to see me. The first was Lord Douglas,[2] aged seventy-nine, who used to be Chuter Ede's P.P.S.,[3] and whom Attlee had, to everyone's astonishment, made Governor of Malta, where I had last seen him in 1946. He is a passionate leader of the anti-fluoridation squad and a passionate believer in composting. He told me how in Malta he had saved the vegetables in the Governor's garden by using proper natural compost. We didn't get very far. He believes that fluoridation is the medication of water and that you can't add extra medicine merely because you want to improve teeth. There he was sitting opposite me, looking like one of those birdy creatures with a high laugh, a typical 1920s progressive, hale and hearty and bright as ever, and really curiously enough not caring, so committed, so thoughtless and in a way so happy.

My next visitor was Dan Smith,[4] the big boss of the North-East, whom I

[1] 'I do not want to make any announcement this afternoon, but the House should bear in mind that our licence fee is one of the cheapest in the world for a service that is among the best in the world' (*House of Commons Debates*, Vol. 787, col. 1536).

[2] Francis Douglas, Labour M.P. for Battersea North 1940–6. He was P.P.S. to the Parliamentary Secretary of the Board of Education 1940–5 and to the Home Secretary 1945–6, and Governor-General of Malta 1946–9. In 1950 he became a baron, taking the title of Douglas of Barloch.

[3] James Chuter Ede, Labour M.P. for Mitcham March–November 1923 and for South Shields 1929–31 and 1935–64, was Parliamentary Secretary at the Ministry of Education 1940–5, Home Secretary 1945–51 and Leader of the House of Commons March–October 1951. He became a life peer in 1964. He died in 1965.

[4] T. Dan Smith, company director, Councillor and Chairman of the Finance Committee of Newcastle-upon-Tyne City Council, was Chairman of the Northern Economic Planning Council 1965–70 and of the Peterlee & Aycliffe Development Corporation 1968–70. In 1971

put on the Maud Commission and who, I gather, has done a good job of work there. He had come to see me about the news that I was going to go ahead with the Regional Hospital Board's plan for building a new hospital in Geoffrey Rhodes's constituency at Newcastle. The plan would split the new building between two main sites, the campus of the university, where there are two hospitals to be fused, and another site some distance away. It had taken the Department a long time to sort this out as I had come under some pressure from Henry Miller,[1] Vice-Chancellor of the university, for a 3,000-bed campus hospital, which I thought was a case of elephantiasis. I was going ahead on a rather smaller basis because I was concerned with the patients. Dan Smith was as red-faced and bright as ever, full of his concept that the hospitals must help in the export trade and must provide a base for Newcastle's industry. I was able to say, 'Well, a hospital on the campus will but having the district hospital a few miles away can't totally upset that.' I had time to take a look at him while he was there – he is a great talker. I doubt really whether he added much to the Commission's Report. As I took him in my car on the way back to Whitehall I asked, 'Why on earth did you ever allow that fantastic solution of Northumberland being a separate unit?' and he said, 'Well, I came to the conclusion that one had to compromise on all secondary issues.' I doubt whether he was much good to me.

This afternoon we had a most interesting meeting of the Immigration Committee under Callaghan. First we had a report on the urban programme and the £25 million which was to be concentrated in the areas of greatest social need. This is absolutely first-rate. It all arose out of a speech which Harold made a year or so ago at Birmingham,[2] promising special arrangements there. He said it without knowing exactly what he meant but he has made good sense of it since. It is a good example of a political initiative of Harold's working out really well. It isn't costing too much and we are getting kudos for it. The next item was the one I was concerned about. This was the Registrar-General's request that he should now publish further detailed figures based on the last Census calculation, projecting to 1981 the number of new Commonwealth immigrants coming into the country. Now, the other day I went to the Registrar-General's office at Somerset House. It is a curious office. He is a mild, willowy creature, but obstinate, and evidently no friend of mine. He is responsible to me and for some time he has been worrying me on this, saying that he must be allowed to publish these figures. Last time he tried I let Nicky have a look at them and he took one look and said, 'There are some fascists in that office. These figures would do incredible harm because they could confirm Powell's accusation that we are

---

he was acquitted of a charge of offering a bribe to the Chairman of Wandsworth Borough Council; in 1974 he was found guilty of corruption charges and sentenced to six years' imprisonment.

[1] Professor of Neurology at the University of Newcastle-upon-Tyne 1964–8, Dean of Medicine 1966–8 and Vice-Chancellor from 1968 until his death in 1976.

[2] See pp. 40 and n., 46–7.

flooding the country with immigrants. They assume that immigrant fertility remains constant and that you can draw a linear projection of the figures, whereas most people agree that, even with the first ten or twelve years of immigrants entering the country, their fertility diminishes. As they become integrated into the community and become better off, they have fewer children, so the growth of the immigrant population tends to decline proportionately.' He added, 'You want a logarithmic projection, not a linear projection.'

Since then the Race Relations Board has published a great report with figures that have a logarithmic progression up to 1986. The Registrar-General thinks these are too optimistic and he now wants his linear projection to 1981, which could easily be projected forward by Powell to 1986 and would show a colossal figure. Here Nicky Kaldor was invaluable. Only he would have taken the trouble to brief me with the full details, the projections, the calculations and the arguments and only he could have discovered that there was a big difference between the R.R.B. figures and the Registrar's figures. The R.R.B. only had genuine new Commonwealth citizens, whereas the Registrar-General included Cypriots, Maltese and Gibraltarians, who are Mediterranean people, all put in to swell the number of immigrants. I brought this along, thinking I was the only person to have noticed, but no, David Ennals was alive to it, Merlyn Rees and George Thomson. This is a good little Committee and my fellow-Ministers were uneasily aware of the situation and anxious to help. There was a good spirit and I was given the instructions I wanted, to take back to the Registrar-General.

After a series of meetings in 21a in the House of Commons, it was time for Anne to pick me up and we went off with Tam to a play. There had been rave reviews of Brecht's *The Resistible Rise of Arturo Ui,* with a stunning performance by Leonard Rossiter. It is a very simple play, a history of Hitler's coming to power, done in terms of the Chicago gangsters of the 1920s and '30s, and the story of Al Capone capturing the little suburb of Cicero. The chief gangster was Hitler, his assistant gangsters represent Göring and Goebbels, and there you have them all. It sounds very heavy but it turned out to be the most brilliant piece of political drama I have seen. Anne didn't like it and said it was ham but she was wrong about that. It was full of subtleties and surprises, more Dickensian, more Shakespearean in that way, with tremendous panache and political passion. We ran into the Danish Ambassador and his wife but the theatre was mostly full of young people, boys and girls in their new get-up, all come to venerate Brecht. I had a feeling they must find it very boring. Afterwards we walked down to a little Greek restaurant in St Martin's Lane and went on arguing about it.

Thursday, July 24th

Today we were to have the revelation of the secret plans about the Seats Bill. As I described last week, Harold has not been able to put this to Management

Committee because Callaghan is not a member, so it has been dealt with by a special functional committee of Callaghan, the Lord Chancellor, the Attorney General, the Chief Whip and the Leader of the House. Roy, Barbara and I were excluded. Theoretically, we had been holding the House of Commons in suspense about the date of the adjournment for the recess and maintaining that we were prepared to go on until next week in order to force the Seats Bill through. By this evening, though, everybody knew that we were going to rise tomorrow afternoon and therefore the great secret must be that we were just going to postpone the thing to the overspill in October and play it out. What brought this murky story to a head was the vote in the House of Lords on Monday night, when only one independent peer voted with the Government. All the Tory peers rejected the Bill and the only people to vote for the Government were the strict Labour peers, up to Thomas Balogh, so in this sense the Lords have made a demonstration. Eddie Shackleton and I have been having to restrain ourselves during these past weeks, and there has been no reference in Cabinet to the lack of foresight in dropping the Parliament (No. 2) Bill, to the fact that if we had got that Bill through and reformed the Lords, the rump peers would have been gnashing their teeth but in their last three months of power could have done nothing at all. We had warned the Government that one of the major arguments for reform was to prevent the Lords from acting inopportunely in our last period of office and now they have acted inopportunely and extremely skilfully. They have embarrassed the Government and no one dares to speak about it.

Spread on the front page of the *Telegraph* this morning was a full-length story of what we are going to do, so the great secret degenerated. I don't blame Harold too much for this leak because Cabinet has been leaky on this, since none of us particularly wanted to be thought to be immersed in this murky issue, which has gradually become more and more unsuccessful. I expect the story came from Bob Mellish, who isn't very skilful at keeping things to himself. This morning I had a word with Barbara and learnt that she didn't know about it. Neither did Roy and nor did I. There it was, the move was out.

We sat in the Commons from 10.0 to 10.30, chatting away while we waited for the vote on the adjournment debates on the Consolidated Fund Bill, after which Peart was to make the great announcement of Cabinet's decision to adjourn the House tomorrow.[1] When it became clear that the Government was not going to be pressed to a vote, we sat down for a Cabinet in Harold's room. He explained his new strategy on the Seats Bill and told us there was something else to be done. An ingenious amendment was to be tabled, proposing that the Home Secretary should be indemnified for the present, but that by March 1972 either a Boundary Commission should be reactivated or the 1969 recommendations implemented. Well, this goes half-way to meet the Lords but it still limits the implementation for the next General Election.

[1] Parliament adjourned for the summer recess until October 13th.

I didn't think this was terribly important but it was interesting that this had all been thought out by the little inner group as a device for placating the Lords and making us look a bit more respectable, with no consideration for the progress of local government reform. I leaned round the back of Willie Ross and said to George Thomson, 'Have they consulted you?' and he said, 'As a matter of fact I went to see Callaghan and the Prime Minister yesterday after the meeting of our Local Government Committee, when you instructed me to tell them our timetable. I worked out a timetable and put it to the Prime Minister and it was then that I found the amendment being cooked up.' This is entirely typical of Harold Wilson's methods of conducting government. He gets himself into great difficulty with the Boundary Commission and in order to justify the postponement of that he refers to the Maud Report. In order to make that justification stick he then begins to shape a timetable for Maud, which is designed not on the merits of getting local government reforms that are acceptable to the local authorities and public opinion but solely to suit his argument that he is genuinely postponing alteration of the boundaries. So he begins to upset everybody in local government and suddenly gives an order that they should have ready by the autumn all their answers on reform, which is quite ridiculous. Here is Harold careering along with proposals for a much faster treatment of local government simply in terms of his tactics on the Boundary Commission. All his thinking is tactical. He is always dealing with the immediate situation and finding methods of getting out of a particular difficulty which involve implicit strategic decisions on a related problem, so that we commit ourselves without knowing it on another problem, which brings its own tactical difficulties and then, in order to escape these, we commit ourselves on something else. So we move sideways like a crab.

This came out with the greatest clarity from our discussion round that table. It was all so ridiculous, too, because Cabinet hasn't had a single paper on local government reform or the progress of the timetable. We are busy working it out in our Committee and it goes to Cabinet after the recess but suddenly these things had to be argued out. There is also a great danger that we are going to take a snap decision on a short Bill to curb the powers of the Lords. I have been steadily pressing in Cabinet for a paper on the actual proposals for the Lords and now I find that secretly the Lord Chancellor has been instructed to prepare a detailed Bill. (I know this Bill, it was prepared last year when I was away in Cyprus.) This is the snap Powers Bill which Harold has always had available and which would make him a popular man in the Party. Again, he is not concerned with the merits of the case because on the merits he knows perfectly well that I am right. Although he is convinced in his own interests of Prime Ministerial patronage and the working of the Lords that our proposal is excellent, he is now lurching into another strategic decision about Lords' reform.

All this went on and on, until we finally managed to persuade Harold that now the crisis on the Floor of the House was over we could move across to No. 10. One of the things one really does learn is the effect on Cabinet of having to meet in the Prime Minister's room at the House of Commons, rather than the Cabinet room at No. 10. The Prime Minister's room, like the Ministerial Conference Room on the floor below, is said to be secure enough for meetings, although God knows what the difference really is, but it is so crowded that we can scarcely get round the table and some people have to sit on sofas and at little extra tables. The atmosphere is always bad-tempered. There is something slightly more relaxed about the Cabinet room, which is bigger. The table is longer, the room is higher and it gives more room to breathe and argue, relax and talk to each other as human beings.

This was the Cabinet for the great discussion of the cuts and it became clear that on Education Roy was going to have great difficulty, because item after item was challenged. It also became clear that the increases for school meals, transport, etc., would require a public statement and that there would be a major crisis in the Party. More and more people were saying that if we really had to raise an extra £10 or £15 million it would be better to do it by taxation than by this. However we didn't get very far before we broke off and I went along to 70 Whitehall for the second of my informal drinks with medical journalists.

The House this afternoon was distracted, rushing through its business, getting through endless Lords' amendments and into the difficult bits of the Seats Bill. Meanwhile at 5.30 we started Cabinet again, once more in Harold's room in the Commons. All this morning we had heard announcements about offers from Treasury Ministers and the nationalized industries – how much Roy Mason would offer, the reduction in gas and electricity investment, how much would be cut off the railways. This afternoon we turned back to the public sector and I was the part of the public sector where we had halted on the previous occasion. Instead of doing what he usually did, this time Roy turned to me and I began to explain the situation as I saw it. Within a matter of minutes there was a furious confrontation between us. I explained in answer to a challenge that in order to get the £9 million from hospital building cuts, I would have to make a Statement next week. I could confirm this because only £12 million of the building programme was under my control and the rest was under the control of the R.H.B.s, with a firm arrangement that in the course of this programme they could go straight ahead within the cost limits allowed. I would now have to instruct them to hold back artificially, so the story must come out.

I said Cabinet must be quite clear that there would either have to be an announcement about this, or I could only cut it back to £5 million and, before we knew it, we were in the middle of a terrible row. I had already said I would no longer ask for the £17 million and that I would try to contain that requirement by cutting my revenue expenditure, but this was regarded by Roy not as a give-away but as proof that I had that amount of fat to take off. We got very heated and finally I simply said, 'If the Treasury insists, someone else can carry out the announcement of the suspension of the hospital building programme. It's absolutely crazy. I can only do it if it's part of a general announcement of a general cut and therefore it is all a question of publication and the package we present.' Unfortunately, in the course of all this argument I also said that Roy's officials had bullied my officials into consent, but as a matter of fact this was completely untrue. We had known Roy was going to ask for £23 million and we had gone to see him about it and showed him the choice between a six-month cut or a three-month cut and said that in either case we would have to have publicity.

It was perhaps the roughest row we have had but I have not forgiven him for his last budget, when he took from me all the nice things, the benefits, and, by refusing to announce the increased contributions for teeth and spectacles, caused endless trouble in the summer. I am not going to let him do it this time, now that he has already started preparing for a splendid budget next year, with reductions in taxation at the cost of making us cut back our programmes. Not bloody likely! From the start I had been determined to defeat him on this and bring Cabinet round to saying that rather than have cuts in Health and Education we would have increased taxation.

After this stormy meeting, with Harold trying to make peace and divisions interrupting us, the Prime Minister said, 'We must have some starred items. We shall have to put together all the items which are doubtful and look at them again next week and, then, when we come to our general decision, we can see whether we wish to do the job by increased taxation or by cuts in expenditure or by a different mixture of both.' I got my £9 million hospital capital building cut included in the starred items, so I have fended off the immediate danger. It's only £4 million I'm touting for now, to cut it down from £9 to £5 million. My other proposal, to introduce a levy on motor-car insurance companies to pay for the cost of accidents, has gone pretty well on the official level. We could get £10 million from this. It was only attacked by Dick Marsh and I was able to explain the principles behind it. I came out of that Cabinet meeting enormously elated, I must admit.

Then I had drinks with Tommy Balogh and Richard and Pat Llewelyn-Davies and we had an immense, very expensive dinner. I was really celebrating the release of energy. After a bloody awful time I had got a little of my own back by asserting myself in Cabinet in a fairly decisive way and I had shown Roy where he could get off. I had been given solid support by Tony Crosland, which doesn't help me much since Roy regards him as an enemy, and I was also helped by all the social service people. Callaghan had been silent and judicious, but I had Ted Short, the Welsh and Scottish Secretaries, and even George Thomson. Yes, Roy was really pretty well isolated now, along with the standard supporters of Government policy, Michael Stewart and Denis Healey. This evening I could retire feeling that I had achieved something and I am looking forward almost with relish to next week's meeting.

Saturday, July 26th

Today was Barbara's silver wedding. She asked us to lunch weeks ago and we had got her two little silver sauce-boats. We dumped the children at Stokenchurch with Venice and Christopher and got to Barbara's at 12.15, just as the Prime Minister's car arrived and his detective was being hauled out to have a drink. Throughout yesterday's Prices and Incomes Committee Barbara had been muttering about how she desperately wanted to get things over quickly and go home to prepare. She told me there were seventy-five people coming and that she didn't know what they would do if it rained. The clouds were mounting a bit but Barbara had the last hours of sunshine and in her beautiful garden, sloping down the hill in the Chilterns, seventy-five people was a mere nothing. We were soon split up into sects at various tables thirty and forty feet apart. We had given up drinking champagne and had collected our food and gone back to the tables with the hired chairs. There was the Prime Minister, very tubby in a yellow shirt, blue trousers and pale blue shoes. I was tubby too, as Phil Zec and several others noticed.[1] This is because Harold and I had to wear our shirts inside our trousers, I suppose, and if you do that you expose your elderly corporation. Who else was there? Judith and Tony Hart, Curly Mallalieu and his wife and daughter, but no one else from the Cabinet, no Roy Jenkins, no Dick Marsh, no Ted Short, none of those kind of people. Jenny Lee was there of course, Harold and Diane Lever, and Mia Connor, Cassandra's widow, with her son Robert, now a charming Oxford undergraduate, the Stonor family and Phil and Hannah Kaiser.

It was a pleasant kind of party. A lot of champagne was drunk and we ate salmon and turkey and strawberries. It wasn't all that elderly because there were quite a lot of young people in fancy dress. Barbara and Ted had stuck up on the hedge enormous blown-up photographs of what they looked like on their wedding day and it was under the shadow of these that, instead of speeches, we had calypsos written by Robert Connor and sung by a friend. The Prime Minister's deck chair collapsed under him just before Barbara and Ted were to make their little replies and he was given the job of planting a cox's orange pippin in memory of the day. He chatted with us about his appearance on David Frost's programme, which was recorded a fortnight ago and finally put on the air last night. Most of the people at the party hadn't thought much of this and felt it was somehow degrading but I suspect it was an extremely successful piece of public relations, of the sort which works very well with the British. Harold was shown in his study, almost entertaining Frost and Mary, chatting about his life at school and his being in the boy scouts. As we left I said to Anne, 'Has there ever been a British Prime Minister who seemed so unimportant, so insignificant – physically and as a personality? Certainly not in modern times.' Harold seems just what you might

[1] The former *Daily Mirror* cartoonist.

call a routine Oxford intellectual Labour politician and it struck me more than ever before this afternoon.

We drove back to tea with Venice and Christopher at Cherry Cottage, where they live in a pool of tranquillity. They are a lovely family with a lovely house, and I remembered, thank God, that it was Venice's birthday and took her two little china pots for her dressing table.

We left at 6.0 and before we got home the rain began to come down. This evening we switched on the television and there was the Kennedy story.[1] If one had asked for a second-rate detective novel with this plot, any author would have shied. It really does reveal the difference between America and Britain. An American senator can plead guilty and then go on television the same night to beg his state for a plebiscite in his favour. If that kind of thing happened to a British politician there would have to be an inquest to establish the cause of death. An inquest is impartial and is nothing to do with guilt but there would be a long cross-examination and the fact is that so far Kennedy has been able to avoid this.[2] Young Kennedy and the two friends he went back to for help all felt that Kennedys can't be treated as normal people. Normal people call the police and go to neighbours near by for help. Kennedys don't do that, they must be special. Kennedys must be saved for the good of the state. The whole clan can meet together and decide how to present him on television to save him for the future. These are my impressions of a kind of law where an inquest is not required, and the kind of society where Kennedys are so special that they can try to get away with it. It is a staggering story and has certainly excited me far more than the moon men.

Monday, July 28th

Every paper had a statement that Harold wasn't going to have a reshuffle. I wasn't surprised because it is clear that he has dropped his ideas for the time being. He had told us at Management Committee that we were all too

[1] Senator Edward Kennedy, younger brother of John and Robert Kennedy, and himself a senator from Massachusetts and Assistant Democratic Leader in the Senate, had been involved in a mysterious accident on the night of July 19th. His car had plunged from a bridge on Chappaquiddick Island, off the Massachusetts coast, and Miss Mary Jo Kopechne, a twenty-eight-year-old secretary, had drowned in eight feet of water. Some ten hours later Senator Kennedy told the police about the accident, his attempts to summon help and to rescue his companion. On July 21st he was charged with the misdemeanour of leaving the scene of the incident and, after pleading guilty at a court hearing on July 25th, he was given a two-month suspended sentence. In a television appearance that evening he confessed to panic, confusion and doubt but denied allegations of drunken driving and immoral behaviour. It seemed that there was now little possibility of his being a presidential candidate in 1972.

[2] Massachusetts law does not provide for an automatic inquest. The medical cause of death is determined by a doctor's certificate, unless the district attorney chooses to order an autopsy. (In this case the body had been moved to Pennsylvania and buried and the local court refused to require its disinterment and return to Massachusetts.) The district attorney may request the court to hold an inquest if he believes there is a question as to the legal cause of death and such an inquest was in fact held, in December 1969, after some manoeuvring as to whether it should be closed to the public and the press, Senator Kennedy was cleared of blame, though rumours about his conduct persisted.

overwrought and needed a good month's holiday before we took our decisions. What does this mean? Well, he may have dropped his great plan for a Ministry of Industry, which I think Barbara, or perhaps Tony Wedgwood Benn, was to run, because most of the ideas he ventilated to Barbara and me are being repudiated in the press. Today's other big news was of the steel strike at Port Talbot.[1] This will be something of a major catastrophe because they make the country's whole supply of sheet steel for the car industry. Barbara is more and more worried about it but it has not been worrying me. Let's be honest. I insulate myself against the news of industrial unrest, it is not in my Department, I don't care enough about it really and this new mood is my weakness now.

My first job was the new weekly meeting I have established at Peter Brown's urging. He says I did this at the Ministry of Housing but I can't remember it. This meeting is not only with the Permanent Secretary and his Deputies but with their Under-Secretaries as well, to discuss forward ideas and get initial reactions. I decided to have an experiment with it this morning and gathered together fourteen or fifteen people at 70 Whitehall. After a lot of discussion we agreed the best time to meet was over a sandwich every Monday morning between 1 p.m. and 2 p.m.

I then slipped into Downing Street by the Privy Council entrance and Mike Fogden and I strolled up in time for Management Committee at 10.0. There was only one item, Barbara Castle's paper on the future of the Industrial Relations Bill. Barbara was saying that she wanted sanctions relating to the registration of trade unions and other things and that, through Vic Feather, the T.U.C. had said that no kind of sanctions could now be allowed and had banned the lot. So she told us that if she couldn't have the essential sanctions and Government authority behind her, there would be items which she couldn't put into her big Bill and she wondered if instead she should have only a minor Bill, dealing with the rights of individual trade unionists as distinct from trade unions, or whether she should have no Bill at all. She certainly was putting in the possibility of no Bill at all because a Bill which was nothing but pro-trade union would be hopelessly unbalanced.

All the rumours in the press have been that Barbara is to be moved from her present job because she has failed so lamentably and, with her there, we can't get on with the T.U.C. This is pretty good nonsense; I don't think her presence there prevents us getting on with the T.U.C. at all. Though she has failed they accept her as a distinguished, pleasant person and they know that she is now demonstrably no great danger to them. Nevertheless I wondered

[1] At the Port Talbot steel works, the largest in Britain, 1,300 blast furnace men had gone out on strike against the advice of their leaders on June 26th, in support of a wage increase of £1 a week for lower-paid workers there. By the end of July the works were at a complete standstill and the men refused to be persuaded to return to work either by their own union or by Vic Feather. On August 7th Barbara Castle appointed a Court of Inquiry, which found in favour of the men's claim and severely criticized both the union and the management. When the strike ended on August 24th 25,000 tons of steel had been lost, at a cost to the company of £6 million. Moreover the T.U.C.'s solemn and binding undertaking had clearly failed its first test of intervention in an unofficial strike.

how far this morning's discussion would confirm all this talk. Well, though it didn't confirm it, it rendered it possible. If she is going to have a Bill of secondary importance, if, for instance, it is not going to include our social security clauses about payment of supplementary benefit and unemployment benefit to strikers, because such clauses are now regarded by Barbara as too pro-trade union, if all that is to go and the Bill is wholly different, maybe she will lose interest in her job. We discussed the case pretty well on its merits and decided that we couldn't drop the Bill altogether, though everybody agreed with her that maybe the best she could do was to have legislation about the rights of individual trade unionists.

By now it was time for O.P.D. and a fascinating proposal from Michael Stewart that at the U.N. this September we should have a British initiative for a draft peace treaty between Israel and her neighbours. His argument was that the Americans are trying very hard in talking to Israel, and the Russians to the Arabs and the Egyptians, but the bilateral conversations weren't getting anywhere and the hope is that a British move might get somewhere. Michael produced his draft treaty and, my God, it required Israel to go back to the 1966 frontiers, it resurrected the whole of the United Nations control of the Gaza Strip and the Gulf of Aqaba, and of course it left open the question of the Syrian border, because the Syrians were not going to be approached in this initiative. It was only going to be negotiated with the Egyptians, the Jordanians and the Lebanese.

To me, thinking of the atmosphere in Israel, it was plain ridiculous to suppose that after winning the war they would permit the reimposition of that ghastly superstructure of United Nations control, armistice commissions and armistice frontiers. It horrified me that Michael should put this forward and yet regard himself as impartial. I realized how totally he had been taken over, body and soul, by the Foreign Office. It was bad of me, but I couldn't help blowing my top and I was as vulgar and one-sided and prejudiced as Fred Peart, who is also pro-Israeli. The Prime Minister heard the noise and took up the point about Jerusalem changing its status from being part of Israel to becoming international, pointing out that this would be unfortunate. He tried to mediate between Michael and the rest of us and said that anyway this ought to go to Cabinet because there is no chance of it being simply taken from O.P.D. There wasn't much of a fuss but the main argument was fascinating. 'What good would it do,' I asked, 'for us to be known to be putting something forward which will infuriate every Jew and at the same time seem not to be wholly reliable to the others?' Michael Stewart said, 'We can't give up hope of peace. If the Americans and the Russians fail we must be ready to play our part,' and I suppose he sincerely believes it.

More meetings, one with Kenneth Berrill about teaching hospitals and then a long-delayed meeting with the local government section of the Ministry about domiciliary home helps where I got licked, because there was no money. Back to my room for a meeting with Clifford Jarrett, Miss Riddelsdell and

David Ennals, because suddenly I had been told over the weekend that a crisis about parliamentary draftsmen meant that the Superannuation Bill might not be ready for our November Second Reading. I was furious that I hadn't been warned in time and I thought maybe David was wrong. We had a talk and I was asked to write an urgent letter to the Lord President to see if we can get an extra parliamentary draftsman. I sent the letter off and I shall have a little drink with Fred Peart and hope this little crisis can be relieved for the time being. There was just time for a delegation from a pro-family planning society and then a meeting on the Minister's powers and the Minister's role in the Health Service.

Finally Alan Marre stayed behind with Bea Serota this evening to discuss the first fifty or sixty names of applicants for the job of Director of the Advisory Service.[1] Quite a distinguished collection of people had applied and we tried to reduce the numbers to a short list of fifteen. We have at last managed to decide on what is called 'the board' for making this appointment. The Ministry were pressing me to have endless members of the Department but I said, 'No. After all, this is my personal appointment,' and finally I agreed to have the C.M.O., Alan Marre and Serota, with Miss Skellern and John Revans as the two assessors. It took quite a struggle to protect myself against the Department.

Tuesday, July 29th

This was the day for the big Cabinet to which I had been looking forward so much last week and which, somehow, in retrospect I didn't enjoy. The morning session took from 10.0 till 1.0. First there was a statement by Harold and the Chancellor on what the situation was. Roy said he had asked for £400 million and that if he managed to get everything, including the starred items, he would have £304 million. If he didn't get the starred items he would have only £292 million, far less than he needed, because he wanted to have a neutral budget in which he would be able to prevent more working-class people coming under income tax. We went into the details of the problem and he carefully reserved the disputed education items and my item, the extra £4 million. To my surprise he said he must have the £4 million from Health because he had to have something flexible for new claims for extra money. There were four claims: for the Land Commission, which was a technical P.E.S.C. claim, not really an increase; two claims from the Board of Trade, for the retention of the National Film Finance Corporation and for a national consultancy organization;[2] and then one from the Lord Chancellor who wanted rather more money for legal aid. All these would add

[1] The inspectorate which Crossman had established after the Ely scandal.

[2] The 1966 Films Act had prolonged until the end of 1970 the life of the N.F.F.C., which had been set up in 1949 to lend money to prospective producers of British films. At the same time other legislation providing for a screen quota for British films and a levy on exhibitors' takings had been extended until October 1970. In May 1970 a new Act was passed to continue support for the British film industry until 1980.

up to about £10 million and the Chancellor said it was for this he needed my £4 million. Now it is my impression, for what it is worth, that this very morning Roy and the Prime Minister had talked it over and knew they couldn't get the £4 million out of me, so I think they had pretty well agreed to drop that demand and concede most of the demands for minor extra things and that the whole day was a slightly put-up job. Anyhow the morning passed mainly in this detailed argument until lunch-time, when, as we got up, Roy said, 'What do you want, Dick? Are you going to have a big battle in this afternoon's discussion?' I said, 'I just want to stop you making a fool of yourself with the £4 million.'

We came back at 3.30 and went on to 5.30 and all the time I was very carefully holding my breath and saying, 'Let all the claims be made and then let us ask the basic question of whether we have got the priorities right and whether the Chancellor is right to say it is more important to have a neutral budget than it is to keep our public expenditure programme going.' But when it came to it I made a speech. Willie Ross told me I spoke for so long that I nearly lost it. I don't think that is true but I don't think I did myself any good. I said it was absolutely demented to be squabbling about £4 million from the Ministry out of a £17,000 million total. We had already had prescription charges and teeth and spectacles, and now the Chancellor wanted an announcement that we were cutting the hospital building programme as well, all for the sake of £4 million. I said I couldn't take it, it was just nonsense, I just wouldn't pay it. I was in a tizzy, I was too worked up and of course I didn't realize at the time that I made a bad impression. The backing I got was striking. Judith Hart supported me and Tony Crosland and everybody else looked awkward. Barbara never said a word and none of them wanted to take part in this gladiatorial fight between Roy and myself. Well, I won. Finally Roy gave in and the Prime Minister summed up. You won't find the summing up in the Cabinet minutes, but, let's be clear, the defeat took place. Roy didn't get his drastic cuts in either Health or Education. On Education he got the minor works, half a million off the school building programme, and 3*d.* on school milk, but he lost on school transport.

My own Department certainly hadn't expected me to win on this. Dick Bourton sent me his warmest congratulations afterwards but somehow I didn't enjoy it. We'd discussed it for six hours and I had perhaps been overwrought. I had in a sense shouted and abused my position too much, that's my own feeling. I thought, what the hell shall I do? It was a sweltering evening. Ben Whitaker was giving a party so I made Peter Smithson motor me up to Hampstead, where Ben has a magnificent house with a huge great garden behind. I walked into the main room and there was Roy. 'Ha,' he said, 'we have said enough to each other today,' and I felt the same and turned to the bar. After three or four hours I went home.

Wednesday, July 30th

Another Cabinet and Harold started by saying, 'Well once again we have full reports and details from the usual two, the *Guardian* and the *Financial Times*.' Tony Crosland said, 'I have read the reports. There is nothing in them, mere guesswork. All they know is that there was a P.E.S.C. meeting and that people have been discussing their budgets with the Chancellor. There is nothing here to prove there has been any kind of leak.' Dick Marsh chipped in too, saying it was absurd, and of course it is absurd, and yet Harold was convinced that the press had been given real information. I watched him as he thought, 'Now I've got Crosland and Marsh.' He is determined to regard them as leaky and probably, in some way, to demote them but today there was no evidence whatsoever on which to base the belief.

One item that was raised was Gerald Brooke. Last week he had appeared on television and said he had not merely distributed literature in Russia but had also brought in with him codes to pass on to the opposition. The Foreign Secretary was asked whether this didn't somehow make a difference and whether we ought not to have known about this. Michael Stewart said, 'We don't know anything much about it, only what he said on television. We'll talk to him later.' I said, 'When you had him on the plane for four hours on the way back, with Foreign Office people with him, wouldn't it have been possible to defuse him by questioning him and getting something out of him?' 'Oh, no,' said Michael Stewart, 'we couldn't have done that. It's a free country. We couldn't arrange that.' I said, 'In any other country in the West, if you brought back a man of this sort you would have found out about him.' Michael answered, quite rightly, 'But think how suspicious it would have been if we had treated him as a British agent when he really wasn't one.' So it was clear that nothing had been done by the Foreign Office. Brooke had gone home, been interviewed by journalists and gone on T.V. without any kind of discussion with the F.O. What lunacy, yet I couldn't resist saying, 'Well, God was on our side, because by not saying anything to him it certainly made things look far better for us. When it was announced he had taken in these codes, the country thought it was a fair swap with the Krogers after all. We got something out of it through luck that we didn't deserve.' Maybe it wasn't a wise thing to say, the kind of thing I do in the Cabinet, but I did make a complete fool of Michael Stewart. We all knew that this was Foreign Office incompetence reaching new bounds.

The other important item was Northern Ireland. We were warned by Callaghan that we were coming up to a tremendous demonstration on August 12th by the so-called Apprentices of Derry, and there might be major catastrophes.[1] Cabinet was asked to give clearance for the Royal Ulster Constabulary to have the C.S. gas, so that British troops would not have to

[1] The annual Apprentice Boys' March was a Protestant demonstration celebrating the relief of Derry on August 12th, 1689, after a 105-day siege by James II's Roman Catholic soldiery.

intervene. All the thoughts which I had expressed quite freely at the special sub-committee were voiced here by Bob Mellish, who is now playing a leading part in all our discussions, giving a kind of brutal, simple point of view. He boomed in and said, 'But, if we do this, won't British troops be engaged anyway and won't it be a bloody scandal and won't our own people be against it, and won't we find ourselves with British troops fighting on the side of the Ulster reactionaries?'

After Cabinet I took Fred Peart back to my room for a drink and straightaway he offered me the parliamentary draftsman to help with our Superannuation Bill. He told me he was afraid of losing his job. He had been reading in the papers that the idea was that he should be dropped and I knew what he was saying. I think he probably ought to be dropped but there he was talking to me and showing his anxiety about it.

After this yet another Cabinet, this time on the B.B.C., where John Stonehouse has already publicly committed himself to an increase in the licence fee and an extension of hours. This time we decided to have no increase in the licence fee and no extension of hours but to develop our local radio stations. We would simply postpone the increase in the licence fee until 1971, after the election. Wilson was saying that we would demand that the B.B.C. should do everything but we wouldn't give them the means to do it, and that was carried. It was a terrible decision, and shows how tired we were, but at all our Cabinet meetings it is becoming clearer that from now on nothing will be decided except in terms of electoral advantage.

Next there was a meeting of the P.L. Committee, where we were shown the draft short Bill to take away the powers of the Lords. It was a silly Bill, which the Lord Chancellor had been ordered to prepare for the Prime Minister. Anyhow, it was clear that with the Parliament Act working as it does it wouldn't pay to have a short Bill, so we were back where we were – the same Committee which had been consulting on the House of Lords, with once again none of us entitled to say what fools we were to drop the Parliament Bill in favour of the Industrial Relations Bill and then to drop the Industrial Relations Bill. This is a Cabinet which has failed in its two major reforms. For the first time Parliament has stopped us in our tracks and we are unable to carry on. The main result is that in future we are not going to do anything which might damage us.

After that I went down to Chelsea Cloisters to see a Mrs Huie who is one of eighty respiratory polio victims. She can't breathe without a machine which goes punk, punk behind her chair, but she lives at home, with a woman to look after her night and day. It brought home the whole issue with a bump. I had to feed her dry Martini and listen to her case. She is right. It saves money to have her in her own house rather than in a hospital, where special nursing would cost probably £200–£300 a week. She is spending her capital and she ought to be given a disability pension and more money. I knew very well that we couldn't possibly concede this principle, because it wouldn't only be her, but 50,000 other people demanding exactly the same thing. From there I went on to a restaurant in Chelsea where Eddie Shackleton gave me a meal. God knows why he did it, just to keep in with me, I suspect. I didn't really get anything out of the evening but it was a pleasant kind of public relations exercise from Eddie.

Thursday, July 31st

Our first meeting was on Prices and Incomes future policy and I really began to wonder about Barbara. She was asking for major decisions, first the decision on comparability, which she didn't dare to force here. She said any public announcement would have to be postponed but she wanted a general view on the new powers of the Prices and Incomes Board. Somehow it was all stale and unprofitable because now Aubrey Jones has announced that he will be retiring next year, I suspect, to the I.P.C., to succeed Hugh Cudlipp.[1] So here is Barbara's own policy coming to pieces in her hands. We turned to her draft of the future prices and incomes policy, where she wanted the decision that, in future, the Minister of Agriculture, Fisheries and Food and the President of the Board of Trade should give up regulation of prices and hand it over to her and the N.B.P.I. Here she got another major defeat. If I had those defeats I would feel thoroughly disgruntled and unhappy. Her aims have now sensationally collapsed and, though I may feel tired and disjointed, she must feel infinitely more disillusioned.

On from there to Downing Street and another meeting of the Management Committee, where we had a general discussion about the future, the plans for the election and for organizing ourselves at Transport House. After some pressure Harold agreed that when we came back from our holidays we would have a Chequers meeting of the Management Committee on September 5th, when we could get down to actually planning the election. It was clear now that the election campaign committee, announced in the press as a Transport House Committee, must be merely formal, with Management Committee as the effective body behind the scenes. We will see how that goes.

Then we sat on for something like a Cabinet S.E.P. First we dealt with winter closures and how much we should spend in the Development Areas in the winter to try to reduce the rate of unemployment. The final item was the proposal to close down at long last the Central Wales Railway line which has in winter only 100 people travelling on its ninety miles, 200 in summer and only 6 regular passengers. This is a parody of a railway and there is an overwhelming case for permanent closure next January, because otherwise we will have to pay a £300,000 subsidy. Dick Marsh moved this proposal and the Chancellor supported him. I barged in and said, 'Look, if you are going to start playing politics with this, you mustn't do it,' but they did. Roy half-heartedly stood out, I stood out with Dick Marsh, but round the table the

[1] Aubrey Jones was named as the Chairman-Designate of I.P.C. in 1968/9 but he changed his mind and stayed at the N.B.P.I. until the Conservatives came to power in 1970.

others were in favour of the £300,000 subsidy, because three seats were in danger in central Wales. It wasn't just the rest of them because Michael Stewart also voted against closure for political reasons and I realized what kind of mood we have got into. Here we are in the run-up to the election and this was the third time we had overwhelming evidence that from now on this Cabinet is to be dominated simply and solely by the thought of losing votes. They will take no decision which will be unpopular with the Labour Party, the House of Commons or the electorate. It took the pleasure out of my victory in Cabinet on Tuesday because it was only formal; they had all known that electorally the Chancellor couldn't cut the hospital building programme.

I took Peter Shore out to lunch at the Garrick, poor Peter, the man who two years ago was created Economic Secretary when the Prime Minister was going to take over the running of the economy through the D.E.A.[1] Endless newspapers have been saying Peter is for the high jump, Harold has been saying it to me and to others, and Peter asked me anxiously about his future. What could I say, except that Harold was against him and I couldn't guess the outcome?

That was Thursday. S.E.P. was the final meeting and Harold sort of said goodbye. I told him I wanted to see him next week for an informal talk about a new Chairman for the Supplementary Benefits Commission and, as he is very sensitive on these matters, I had sent him a minute on the two names I wanted to put forward, Harold Collison and Reg Goodwin.[2] Harold simply said, 'I agree with either of those names if you can get them,' which was a way of avoiding seeing me next week. I knew quite well that he didn't want to see me again before he went on holiday. I don't blame him, knowing what mood I have been in, and how difficult and bloody-minded I have been but it was interesting, compared with two years ago, that he didn't want to see me again before he went away. So he is going to go to Mildenhall tomorrow to see Nixon.[3] The P.M. is as exhausted as we are, he is not having his shuffle, he is off and it's much better that I shouldn't see him till I get back.

Sunday, August 3rd

Instead of feeling exhilarated at the thought that I am going on holiday I am thoroughly jaded and exhausted, but it has been one of the toughest weeks I have had. I spent Friday touring hospitals near Horsham, visits that gave me a lot to think about.

Meanwhile this is the end of a week dominated in the public eye by Nixon's

[1] On August 29th, 1967, Peter Shore had become Secretary of State for Economic Affairs, with the Prime Minister taking ultimate command of the D.E.A. and modernization plans for industry.

[2] Reginald Goodwin, Leader of the Labour Party on the G.L.C. 1967–73 and Leader of the Council 1973–6, has been Deputy Chairman of Basildon Development Corporation since 1970. He was knighted in 1968.

[3] On his way back to the U.S.A. from his Asian and Roumanian tour, President Nixon's aircraft touched down at the U.S.A.F. base at Mildenhall in Suffolk.

tremendous Roumanian reception and by the ghastly Port Talbot steel strike and, for us, an endless wind-up Cabinet and the end of a session in which Cabinet has been stopped in its tracks and suddenly reversed. It is just a Cabinet preparing for an election, jettisoning proposal after proposal and judging everything simply in terms of votes.

Monday, August 4th

This was my first week of trying to give the Department their marching orders for the recess, after the end of my first session with them. This morning we had a meeting about the transfer of staff from John Adam Street to the Elephant and Castle. It is a sad thing but at last we are moving in the top level, David Ennals, the Deputy Secretaries and the Under-Secretaries, Miss Riddelsdell, Atkinson and Swift.[1] We have already created on the fifth floor the News and Press Office under Peter Brown and this is now fully integrated. They all find that, whereas it was possible to walk in about quarter of an hour from John Adam Street to Whitehall, it is about half an hour's journey by public transport from Elephant and Castle and psychologically it's miles away. Mind you, now that Parliament isn't sitting I spend more time in my room on the seventh floor and as it has been lovely weather I have really quite enjoyed having my conferences up in the air, looking out over London. It is quite a nice ivory tower but desperately remote and inconvenient.

My second meeting was on the Green Paper. I have never had a more intractable problem, because everybody believes in the integration of the hospital and G.P. service with the government health services but both sides assume they can integrate wholly their way. Wherever we draw the line will be arbitrary and detested by both sides and anyway we shall be leaving unresolved the major problem that on one side of the line the services are financed by the ratepayer and on the other side by the taxpayer. I have been frantically bashing round to find a way of avoiding this frontier and now my mind is fixed on the idea of a joint board, like the Metropolitan Water Board or the Gas Board used to be. We might have a joint board, appointed from both a Regional Health Authority and the local authorities. The whole of this afternoon I fought with the Department in an obstinate way and made them go through it again, poor things.

They had their own elaborate plan they wanted to put but I wasn't going to listen to it because I said the joint board was all I wanted to hear about.

After another meeting to sort through our short list for the Director of the advisory service, Bea Serota, Julian Snow and I jointly gave a kind of end-of-term party for the staff. It seemed to be going well when I had to leave to take the children to see *Much Ado About Nothing* at the Aldwych. It is a silly story and I had forgotten how appallingly difficult the language is and how full of Elizabethan quips and clevernesses. Beatrice and Benedick speak stunning

[1] Reginald Swift, Under-Secretary at the Ministry of National Insurance 1962–8 and at the D.H.S.S. since 1968.

complications and frankly I don't think I understood much of it. I am an awful dozer in my old age and when I got back home and started looking at the text I was amazed how little I had actually heard compared to Anne. It was also amazing how the children, aged nine and eleven, think the theatre a good thing whether or not they really like the play, because they do get some sense of acting and of excitement.

Tuesday, August 5th

Abortion goes on being a trouble and Bea Serota and I become more and more worried because we know perfectly well that in the eight private enterprise nursing homes all the regulations are probably being violated, yet it is nobody's business and the Department does not want to take action. This morning I said again that the police must be brought in to investigate. I knew as I said it that when the officials put it to the Home Office nothing will happen because there is an astonishing, pertinacious refusal by the Department to spy on private enterprise nursing homes. Civil servants don't want to get mixed up in it. Unfortunately Pater, that little Andrew Aguecheek of a fellow, is in charge, and he is enjoying proving that nothing can be done. He drove me nearly frantic. However, we are now going to press ahead on two fronts, first to see whether I can't somehow strengthen the G.M.C., and give them a backbone and guts. The G.M.C. is disgusting. I can't interfere with the doctors because of clinical freedom and the G.M.C. does all the policing and discipline but they say there are only two crimes for doctors, advertising and sleeping with other people's wives. Things like peddling drugs or doing illegal abortions are not regarded as crimes unless the doctors are caught by the police. Forcing the G.M.C. to be an effective policing authority will be one line of approach, the other being to blow up the nursing homes by getting the police to prove that they are evading the law. That is what we decided this morning.

This afternoon we took the children to a fantastic adventure film, *Where Eagles Dare*, about a raid during the war on an S.S. fortress in Bavaria, full of blood and thunder and adventure. They also went to the Science Museum and the Planetarium, and they visited Harrods, so I think they enjoyed their trip to London. This evening Brian gave dinner at his house to a really good lot of people. There were Serota, John Revans, Professor Morris and Jim Sharpe,[1] who did the research for the Maud Commission. Brian gave us a splendid dinner of delicious cold salmon—a marvellous cook is Brian—and afterwards we went all over the joint board question again. We didn't get very far as everybody came to the conclusion that the only form of joint board which would be practicable and acceptable to the local authority was one the doctors wouldn't accept, and the only one acceptable to the doctors

[1] L. J. Sharpe, Lecturer at London School of Economics 1962–5, has been Fellow and University Lecturer at Nuffield College, Oxford, since 1965. He was Director of Intelligence and Assistant Commissioner to the Royal Commission on Local Government 1966–9.

wouldn't be a joint board. Maybe my idea is falling through. Brian goes on holiday today, leaving behind a last will and testament indicating that I must try to do the best I can with powerful regional executives and, down below at the district level, the maximum popular participation. What I hate is that this is dressing the thing up to look like local participation with in fact the decisions still being taken at the top.

Wednesday, August 6th

I had a whole day in the Birmingham area. As Anne and I drove up I should think an inch of rain must suddenly have deluged from the sky and we found the whole of the sides of the road filled with stationary cars with their headlights on because people wouldn't drive through the rain. How extraordinary the English are, to give up so easily and sit and wait it out.

We got there at 10.0 so I had time for a pretty good look at two hospitals, Chelmsley, which is an old workhouse near Chelmsley Wood, and Coleshill, a great big Victorian hall built for the Digby family. I had been told these were the two worst places in the area and that the small Birmingham group had a first-rate Chairman and Secretary in Kirk and Elliott.[1] Kirk is a rough, tough, ruthless businessman, and Elliott an extremely efficient and imaginative secretary. They are a fine pair, who took over only three or four months ago and were horrified by what they found. Elliott had taken the trouble to come up specially from his holiday in Cornwall, to spend the whole day with me and Kirk and the eternal gang from the Board. We had the R.H.B. Secretary, Mr Adams, the SAMO Dr Gordon,[2] and the Bishop of Lichfield,[3] who was there on behalf of the Chairman. Chelmsley was terrible, in ghastly 100-year-old, two-storey buildings, with open stone stairways and bleak lavatory architecture. It was terribly overcrowded. Across a field was a modern ward, but for sixty children when it should have had ten to fifteen at the most, as a harassed nurse told me. The situation is absolutely defeatist; there was no privacy. It was a terrible, terrible place.

Coleshill had a much nicer atmosphere. It was magnificently spacious, with beautiful gardens, but again appallingly overcrowded. Still, the cases there aren't nearly so difficult and the overcrowding is compensated for by a wonderful lively doctor, really forward-looking and helpful. After I had visited them both I had long television interviews, because there had been a great sensation about my visit, which was all mixed up with a great row on the Birmingham Regional Hospital Board, where two of our Labour women had gone to the press with reports of what was going on. So I made some very strong remarks on television. This is my crusade and I am going to win it now.

[1] The Chairman of the East Birmingham Hospital Management Committee was B. C. Kirk. J. R. Elliott was the Secretary.

[2] Dr C. W. Gordon, SAMO of the Birmingham R.H.B.

[3] The Rt Reverend Arthur Stretton Reeve, Bishop of Lichfield 1953–74.

In the afternoon I went to the headquarters of the group, which was in the East Birmingham hospital some distance away, and there we discussed the problem with the Regional Hospital Board. We didn't come to any conclusion, but for two hours I pressed on rations, on personal possessions, on dealing with overcrowding, and I knew I was winning.

In the evening we went to a psychiatric hospital in the southern corner of Birmingham, nearly out in the country beyond King's Norton. It was obviously a grander place, and I know it costs £18 a patient per week as against the £11 of the places I had just been seeing, but here was the same thing all over again. There were some enormously expensive research units trying experiments in behaviourist psychology, which apparently is a mixture of drugs and shocks and cross-examination, but I didn't feel the hospital itself was really much better. It was also inordinately expensive because most of the people there weren't acutely ill patients, just elderly people dying away. After that I had two hours at a huge do for the voluntary workers for the whole of East Birmingham. They were given a jolly good cold supper and dance, and until 9.30 I tried to answer their questions. It wasn't until 11.0 p.m. that we got back to Prescote. It was a long and tiring day, but creative, because I knew I had really succeeded in making an impact.

Thursday, August 7th

My interviews got into all the press today and I had a lot of headlines. In the Ministry too this kind of smash by the Minister has its effect so they began to get a move-on. As a result I was able to call a special meeting and push through the plan I have discussed with Richard Llewelyn-Davies and his partner John Weeks for a critical assessment by an outside working party of architects, a nurse and a doctor who will go round looking at new buildings, at how much they cost and what return we get for the money. We must see what we have actually been doing in the last five years and assess this before we build any more. We are going to concentrate in the first place on subnormal hospitals and crash programmes for dealing with overcrowding and understaffing and that is now all set in hand.

I then had three meetings, the first on epilepsy, then an hour with the Sheffield Regional Hospital Board, who had come to complain that they just couldn't manage on the money they were getting, and after that a meeting of our own people on the capital investment programme. Very little can be done here, because 85 per cent is really committed for the next ten years. We are going to have another working party to review the district hospitals we have put up and see whether they are value for money. All this needs to be investigated quickly.

After that I gave a lunch party at the Garrick for Harry Nicholas, now the remarkably efficient though very bureaucratic Secretary in Transport House. We were discussing with a young man from the T.G.W.U. the problem I have been worrying about for so long, unemployment benefit paid during a strike.

It isn't paid to strikers but is supplementary benefit only for their children. This definition is absolutely vital and we had promised the trade unions that we would make big concessions on unemployment benefit. But suddenly Barbara had said that she wasn't inclined to make this concession now, because she couldn't have a 100 per cent pro-trade union Bill. This will be jolly embarrassing for us because we promised the concessions publicly and discussed them in detail with the P.L.P.

However at lunch today the man from the T.&G. made an extraordinary remark. He said, 'What we would like to do is hand the whole thing over to D.E.P. officials. If they were giving the decision as to whether we should get unemployment benefit, we should do far better.' He said this because he believed that the National Insurance Commissioners, to whom under our system the appeal goes, are D.H.S.S. agents, mere stooges, and that the unions would do better with the honest D.E.P. officials. The implications of this are amazing because the one thing which is clear is that if we were to transfer this to D.E.P., when the Tories came to power they would be able to order the officials to pay out unemployment benefit as they saw fit, whereas the Insurance Commissioners are completely independent of the Government. I think by the end of the lunch we had completely persuaded the T.&G. how wrong they were but again it emphasized for me the abiding problem of the remoteness of Labour Government from the Labour Movement. We ought to have had this meeting before.

After lunch we had a most fascinating meeting on the statistics of the coloured population. I had been told that there was a fascist nest in the Registrar-General's Office and I didn't believe a word of it but, after an hour of sitting with the staff, I became convinced that there was a real ideological pattern to the behaviour of this Office. We almost came to open warfare when I bluntly told them that they could not publish figures designed to disprove the Race Relations Board's figures. Neither was I prepared to have them publish figures which they knew were likely to be far too high, even if they put a footnote saying that they were far too high. I said, 'We must have the figures projected to 1986 and it must be a logarithmic not a linear projection.' The meeting got sharper and sharper as we finally discovered that we were nearly nakedly fighting, I to prevent them from running statistical propaganda, and they to get in past me. Thrilling, that.

It was a very hot evening and Ron Matthews gave a nice little farewell party. I said a few words, he said a few words and he was given a little present by the Office. I think he was deeply pleased and that he will look back on his time with me as tremendously exciting. He is a man of tremendous moral character and decency, who has been lovely to work with, patient, tenacious and faithful. He hasn't got the intellectual grasp to work with me, as John Cashman certainly has, and he found me rough and difficult and far too active, but he has had a fascinating time running the office of a senior Cabinet Minister. Oh dear, I have no doubt that sleek John Cashman, neat, tidy, complacent, clever, will run the Office well, but I already miss this splendid, sterling man.

Friday, August 8th

I remembered this morning that Harold was off to the Scillies, so I rang him up to say goodbye and that I was sorry I hadn't sent him across some notes for a speech on social services he is going to give at the T.U.C. Conference.[1] I found he had already gone on the 12.45 p.m. train. I don't think it matters and though I felt it would have been pleasant and nice to have talked to him, I must now try to do the work for him, because I feel that my position has begun to decline. Yesterday it was announced from No. 10 that Harold has selected the three members of the Cabinet to work with him on the Campaign Committee, Wedgwood Benn, Bob Mellish and Denis Healey. It's true that I am on the Management Committee, which Harold says will in effect have the real strategic control, but nevertheless he has not chosen me. I grant that if he had taken me and not Judith Hart it would have been terribly hard on her but I think he wants to keep her out of the new Cabinet. True, he wants to give a young image, and Denis and Tony Benn are younger people who are going to be in his next Cabinet, whereas I know deep down I am not. It is a mark that he thinks I am getting on, a senior member of the Cabinet who doesn't mind too much because I have no future. All that has an impact on Harold's estimate of me and I think he sees me as an old friend who is becoming a bit of a ruddy nuisance.

Saturday, August 9th

Albert Rose had suggested that some thirty people from Coventry should come over and discuss policy with me. There had been some disagreement and Betty Healey wanted another bus load, so suddenly eighty people were about to turn up. This knocked out any idea of a policy discussion in the house but fortunately we got the village hall for tea, and when they arrived in the afternoon they just had time for a little bit of a bathe and a trip round the farm on three trailers before we got back into the hall just as the rain started. There we were, endless anti, anti, anti. Your pensions are no good, your Health Service is no good, everything is no good, and I went to bed extremely depressed.

Sunday, August 10th

A wonderful blazing day today after yesterday's torrential rain, which has started our kale, potatoes and grass growing again. Pritchett is pretty pleased with himself now, he feels that the crops are coming on well, and altogether things are moving on the farm. We have had Charity James down from Williamscote with Mr Edwards, a strange businessman who has taken over

[1] The Trades Union Congress was held at Portsmouth from September 1st to September 5th.

the job of running the Cropredy Fair next year, when we are going to have a two-day celebration of the three-hundredth anniversary of the Battle of Cropredy Bridge. We were working out this afternoon how to get Lord Saye and Sele,[1] whose ancestor was a Parliamentarian, and Lord Northampton,[2] whose ancestor was a Royalist, to come to the Fair and I had fun planning it with Mr Edwards, lying by the pool where everything looks so beautiful.

But I am feeling more than usually depressed this week. I suppose it was really because of the Coventry people yesterday and, to be truthful, I must add that the *Evening Standard* poll showed the popularity rating of Harold Wilson going down, Barbara's rating hardly affected and, as the Minister far below everybody else, me. I would have said at one time that this was entirely due to teeth and specs and the imbecility which I was said to have displayed but of course it's not only that. I'm also unpopular for the pensions plan and part of my gloom now is that the general mood is so anti-taxation, anti-contributions, anti-Government, that what could have been accepted fairly willingly as a burden which ought to be borne is now going to be resented, and I think the Tories will be able to make the most formidable propaganda against us.

There has also been a great change in the public's view of the rest of the Government. A poll the other day showed there is a feeling that Wilson has been let down by his Cabinet. I should say that for the first time in two years the Tories are succeeding in spreading an impression that we are just incompetent, which means that each individual must be incompetent too. I suppose Barbara stands out as a real character and, though she has totally failed, after all what she failed at was something the public wanted her to do and she is thought to have fought valiantly for it. Callaghan is probably thought to be a pretty good Home Secretary, Roy Jenkins retains a certain respect as Chancellor, but certainly I don't. I think I am doing a phenomenally good job behind the scenes inside the Ministry but after teeth and spectacles and the increase in national insurance contributions my rating is going down.

In fact all the departmental side has been going splendidly this last week, though I must admit the general situation has been gloomy in the extreme, the whole week dominated by the steel strike and, finally, on Friday evening, the news of the successful devaluation of the franc, in staggering contrast to our own failure in November 1967.[3] M. Pompidou pulled this off in the middle of the holiday season, on a Friday, without consulting anybody. No panic, not a single speculative loss, and they bring off a 12½ per cent cut. The British Government, well, the less said the better. I suppose everybody must

[1] Nathaniel Fiennes, 21st Baron Saye and Sele.

[2] William Bingham Compton, 6th Marquess of Northampton.

[3] Georges Pompidou, who had won a clear victory in the Presidential election in June, had decided in mid-July to devalue the franc but he did not announce the devaluation until August 8th. The franc's value was reduced by 11·11 per cent (one-ninth) but, since each unit of foreign currency now cost one-eighth more in terms of francs, the size of the devaluation was generally referred to as being 12½ per cent.

feel this. There was Harold just getting an hour with the President of the U.S.A., going off to the Scillies, with the franc being devalued next day, Roy Jenkins being in France and nobody knowing about it. Britain was impotent and excluded.

Another extraordinary thing is the remoteness of the Government on Europe. Here we are trying to get inside again. Con O'Neill has been brought back into the Foreign Office,[1] for about the fourth time, to head the desk dealing with entry into the Common Market in the last year of the Labour Government. It is interesting that there is obviously a public mood of complete scepticism about entering Europe and the public recognize that economically it would be disastrous, because our food prices would go up and the balance of payments deficit would be another £300–£400 million every year. We would have to have another devaluation and there would be no economic advantage at all. The reasons are all said to be political, and what are they? That we have no future anywhere outside, which means that the politicians can't think of anything to do. I myself am less and less convinced that going in will do us any good. If we go in we shall be a backwater inside Europe, whereas if we stay out we shall have a reasonable chance of becoming an island off the coast of Europe with its own character, linked with Europe in defence, but with its own vitality and pace of life. Yet as a Government we are committed to trying to enter Europe and we have Harold, Michael Stewart and George Brown, with the whole Foreign Office and Whitehall behind them, fanatically anxious to get in. Why? Frankly, I don't know, except that they feel there is no greatness outside. They want a kind of bogus greatness which we have lost and they don't share the philosophy of the ordinary person who thinks we can perfectly well survive outside. The Government is also remote from the back benchers and I think the anti-Common Market agitation which the Tribune Group has started this week will have great strength at Conference,[2] because people will resent what, unless it is a counsel of desperation, is the real nonsense of trying to get in now.

Tuesday, August 12th

Yesterday I had to go down to Frimley to see the area where they are to close seven local hospitals and build a brand-new one on our standardized model. I found, as one might expect, that the local authorities are bewildered and frightened by the prospect of closures and I think they were relieved to talk to the Minister.

[1] Sir Con O'Neill (K.C.M.G. 1962) was Ambassador to the European Communities in Brussels 1963–5, Deputy Under-Secretary of State at the Foreign Office 1965–8, a Director of Hill, Samuel & Co. Ltd 1968–9 and Deputy Under-Secretary of State at the Foreign and Commonwealth Office and Leader at the official level of the British Delegation to negotiate entry to the E.E.C. 1969–72. He was Chairman of the Intervention Board for Agricultural Produce 1972–4 and Director of the Britain in Europe Campaign 1974–5.

[2] The Labour Party Conference was held in Brighton from September 29th to October 3rd.

Meanwhile John Cashman had taken over and today I had him in for a private talk with Bea Serota about the difficulties of our Private Office. One essential change is that within twenty-four hours I must have the notes of the meetings which go on in my room and hers. 'Oh,' he said, 'you can't do that. I'm afraid they take several days to prepare.' It then emerged that these notes, which have been getting worse and worse, are composed and circulated for comment to the divisions in the Department before they come to me. I said, 'That won't do at all. These are decision notes and we need to know who was at the meeting, the decisions taken and the action required, with, in each case, the note marked for the civil servant who has to get on with things.' He resisted but finally conceded and now, because he is efficient, there will come in the red box at the end of each day a note of the six or seven meetings that have taken place. It will make an immense difference. There is no doubt that the Department is impressed by the fact that I have stayed behind in August. We have worked solidly for very long hours each day in a determined effort to resolve departmental doubts and give the directives which civil servants really like to receive from Ministers. I have been grappling with the capital investment programme for hospital building in the fourteen regions and with the revenue programme too, laying down the principles of allocation, and we have had the exhilarating indication that the Department has given itself over to the priority I am affording to sub-normal hospitals. We are going to dock all regions of some £50,000 capital expenditure, and we have found another £3 million for the problem of sub-normality. I have also been struggling ahead with the difficult problem of the reconstruction of the Health Service. I loathe these self-perpetuating oligarchies of R.H.B.s, but I can't yet see any substitute for them. I keep turning everything down and asking for further suggestions which, like my idea of joint boards, are then found to be dead ends.

On the Social Security side David Ennals and I are moving ahead on the details of the Superannuation Bill, while tidying up on bits and pieces of Barbara's Bill. There are all the decisions to take on the mass of things about the payment of unemployment benefit to strikers and the payment of income tax rebates. I have finally got another parliamentary draftsman, so we can get on in time to give the Superannuation Bill its Second Reading immediately after the Queen's Speech. Then I have one other intractable problem on this side, the payment of unemployment benefit for occupational pensioners. Cars line up outside the labour exchanges at Worthing or Southport because the people who have just retired on their Civil Service pensions, even a Permanent Secretary at £3,000 a year, are for six months able to draw a tax-free, earnings-related benefit, while they are, so they say, trying to become the Secretary of the local Golf Club or something of the sort. Titmuss, who is on the National Insurance Advisory Committee, agrees that we really must stop this abuse because unemployment benefit is for the genuinely unemployed, and he has proposed a tapering means test, but Collison, who is also on the

N.I.A.C., says we can't penalize these people who are entitled to this because they have already paid their contributions. Now I have had another report telling me that the Committee can't be made to change its mind so the Department will have to take a decision. We are now going to try to estimate the impact on pensioners of changing this confounded thing in election year and I rather fancy I know the answer.

Wednesday, August 13th

Harold Collison came to see me because I had decided to ask him to be the new Chairman of the Supplementary Benefits Commission. He is a great big, tall, gangling man, a real slow working-class chap with a lovely face and a very pleasant wife, one of the few people I like meeting at the great turn-outs for foreign dignitaries at Lancaster House. I have known him for twenty years now because for nearly seventeen years he has been Chairman of the T.U.C. Social Services Sub-Committee, and we have always got on extremely well. This job is three days a week at £5,000 a year but I thought that he would turn it down because he loves the International Labour Organization and goes to Geneva every year for five or six weeks.[1] However he is seriously considering it and it was a real pleasure to offer it to him, an occasion when patronage was enjoyable.

The other people I saw today were Alma and Ellis Birk. Alma is now being quite a successful Chairman of our Health Education Council. She is a dashing, vigorous woman, who drives us frantic by being such a bore on the telephone, but she is dynamic and a publicist and gets things done. This evening Anne and I went out to Hanover Terrace for dinner alone with her and Ellis at their magnificent house with pediments and statues, with a great plaque outside saying 'H.G. Wells lived here' and inside a plaque saying 'Ellis Birk lives here', a nice joke. Ellis is over six feet tall, the chief legal adviser first to the *Daily Mirror* and now to I.P.C., a man who went through it all with Hugh Cudlipp when the Board got rid of Cecil King. Ellis is a powerful figure, I think, in that group. He claims to be a keen socialist and likes having a chat with me about the incompetence and inadequacy of the Government. He has a withering contempt for Michael Stewart and Harold Wilson, a considerable respect for Callaghan and me, and we had a really lively evening together. It was nice of them to do this for us. I think it is true to say that for politicians good food, good drink and good political gossip is the best thing in the world. In that sense we are like actors, who only want to eat and drink and talk about their profession.

Thursday, August 14th

I had a delegation from the B.M.A. It is huge and each delegation always seems to be different from the last. This one was on a long, detailed problem

[1] He was a member of the Governing Body of the I.L.O. 1960–9.

about the valuation of G.P.s' surgeries and their premises. It is staggering that the Minister has to listen to such details, which should really go to some official. This made me late for a long-delayed meeting with Barbara Wootton.[1] She is a brilliant, hard-headed, immensely able, difficult, pugnacious, eccentric woman, an economist at the L.S.E., whose second husband was a taxi-driver. Square spectacles, clean complexion, fair hair, a good eater, a good drinker, a good talker, she is a real old-fashioned member of the eugenic society, so to speak. Bea Serota is an old friend of hers and she had come to talk to us about the drug problem. She got into trouble with Callaghan for recommending that, oh, what's it called, not heroin but one of the other drugs, should be categorized as a harmless drug, although many people regard it as leading to heroin addiction. Callaghan slapped her and her Committee down and there was a row about it all. I think Callaghan was quite right but she held out against it and now she hates Callaghan for his rudeness.

We had a chat about the whole thing. She would have liked to see the Department take over the whole drugs thing and asked why on earth we had left the Home Secretary in charge of policing the distribution of dangerous drugs when we are responsible for both the prevention and curing of addiction. I said I thought logically she was right. Afterwards I took the trouble to look this up and after two refusals the Department finally agreed to show me the interchange of letters on this between Callaghan and my predecessor. It was pathetic. On the advice of the Department and with the support of Scotland, Kenneth Robinson had written a feeble letter asking for the whole thing to be unified in his Department. When Callaghan gave a lordly No, Kenneth had said, 'I didn't really mean it,' and that was that. It was too late now to do anything, as I later told Barbara Wootton, but we wanted her to help us with research on drug addiction. Anyhow, in half an hour we managed to make her forgive me for being late.

I went back into my room for a fascinating meeting with the Treasury and Jack Diamond on abatement, which is the great subject of the terms for partial contracting-out from National Superannuation. Last night I had had a long, detailed meeting with the Government Actuary, Sir Herbert Tetley, and his staff and our expert Ministry staff, preparing for this confrontation. We didn't know which side Sir Herbert was on but the Ministry suspected he was against us. At that meeting we had a staggering letter from the Treasury, who

[1] Barbara Wootton was Principal of Morley College for Working Men and Women 1926–7, Director of Studies for Tutorial Classes at the University of London 1927–44, and Professor of Social Studies 1948–52, Nuffield Research Fellow at Bedford College, University of London, 1952–7 and a Governor of the B.B.C. 1950–6. She became a life peer in 1958. She was Chairman of the Sub-Committee of the Government's Advisory Committee on Drug Dependence, which had published on January 7th, 1969, a controversial Report on the drug cannabis. The Report argued that taking cannabis had an effect of roughly the same magnitude as alcohol and recommended a reduction in legal penalties for its possession, and new legislation distinguishing between this and 'hard drugs' such as heroin. On January 23rd the Home Secretary announced the rejection of the Report, saying that otherwise it might appear that the Government did not take a serious view of drug-taking.

seemed completely oblivious of the effect of a real break with the private pension interests. The letter blithely said that they couldn't conceive how the credit of the Government could in any way be improved by any settlement which was particularly favourable to the Life Offices. I know that if the occupational pensioners were to denounce me as deliberately trying to make contracting-out break down, there really would be a crisis of confidence, with millions of workers being persuaded that their pensions were in danger, and indeed there would also be great difficulty in the City. However, it was quite clear that the Treasury were relying on the fact that the Government Actuary had already advised a certain line and said we shouldn't go beyond 1:1·25 as the ratio between a certain level of contribution and the level of benefit which goes logically with it. Sir Herbert is a tall, simple man with enormous pale blue eyes, and a complete candour and honesty of face, and at last night's meeting I put my difficulties to him and found to my great relief that he agreed that the Treasury were being very narrow-minded and completely failing to see one part of the problem. They were looking at it solely from the point of view of the contributions to the Exchequer and not of the effect on the economy.[1] So I knew that Sir Herbert was on our side, and I asked him to attend today's meeting.

Jack Diamond started off in a very lordly way. He had come to tell us the amount the Treasury would permit. I said perhaps we could make one or two points and that there were other things to consider, for instance the Government's credit which could be endangered by our proposing a solution which the insurance interests in the City thought was a sabotaging solution, rather than one devised in the spirit of my claim of partnership between the public and the private sectors. Jack Diamond said, 'Would you like to ask Sir Herbert Tetley?' Sir Herbert was extremely quiet but he said that of course he appreciated the Treasury's desire for savings and he knew that when one channel was blocked savings would go into another and the funds which had been saved by the pensions schemes would go somewhere else. Nevertheless there was quality in saving as well as quantity and he thought the Treasury would realize that pension funds were very different from building societies. Building societies handled short-term money going in and out; pensions

[1] Contributors to approved occupational pension schemes were to be allowed partial contracting-out of the National Superannuation Scheme. They would pay lower contributions to the state scheme but their benefits would be lower and the terms of this 'abatement' were expressed as a ratio between levels of benefit and levels of contribution. The Department of Health and Social Security was anxious to give generous terms so that the existing private occupational pension schemes would not campaign against the state scheme but the Treasury wished the terms to be stiff because they had in mind the effect on government revenue. The Treasury argued, on the other hand, that to offer reasonably generous terms would encourage the growth of private pensions schemes, permitting more saving and more investment without higher taxes. The Government Actuary suggested that individuals who were dissuaded from paying contributions to private pensions schemes would put money into building societies instead and since these funds, unlike pension funds, do not stay in the capital market during the remainder of the contributors' working lives, they would be less useful intermediaries for financing investment in manufacturing industry.

funds were solid, traditional things which kept money and they therefore had a particular quality of saving which the Treasury should distinguish. He thought the Treasury ought to realize that if we fixed a level of abatement which closed down many pension schemes or which was regarded as a blow to the pension interests it would have an adverse effect. I looked at Jack Diamond and his Treasury man, Jordan Moss, and young Mr Wiggins,[1] a typical young Oxford intellectual waving his arms, with black hair and a white face. They were all flabbergasted at Sir Herbert's advising them to let the Minister go beyond the limit he himself, as Government Actuary, had set. I knew that it was wisest to break off at this point and I have agreed to meet again next week to see if we can get any further.

This afternoon I had a very interesting talk to Mr Lewis,[2] the Chairman of the Birmingham Hospital Board, who has just got back from America. He came to see me about the crisis at Chelmsley and Coleshill, and about the mess caused by his two Labour ladies who have been breaching the confidence of the Committee and behaving in a fairly irrational way. I think that this was out of sheer desperation at the bloody-mindedness of the Tories on the Committee but I had a terrible time tidying up the Committee and getting my two Labour ladies into line without making them feel I have let them down, and keeping Mr Lewis quiet. I have a knighthood up my sleeve for him for the New Year's Honours in January and I was able to talk to him about the whole sub-normality crisis. It was a thoroughly satisfactory meeting.

Then I came to a fantastically interesting meeting on research and development. On the way back from Frimley in the car on Monday with Peter Brown and little tough Goodman the architect, I had vaguely heard that a great project was going on at Worcester and Sheffield. The Worcester project was designed to empty one great big hospital by putting most of the people in it into local hospitals and some patients from psychiatric wards into two new district hospitals. The experiment at Sheffield was to build eight or nine hostels in the town, sub-centres that would make it unnecessary to build a huge new sub-normal hospital. This is quite a good concept and feasibility plans are being tested in these two areas. All these ideas about 'main stream', as it is called, are forging ahead and I had asked why I didn't see them. They had said, 'Oh, they won't send them on to you,' so I demanded a meeting.

Today there came a retinue of people, Mottishead, sitting in front of me blinking through his glasses like a small old owl, Dick Cohen and Dr Baker, Peter Brown and Goodman and, as usual, Miss Hedley.[3] The officials were

[1] A. J. Wiggins was a Principal in H.M. Treasury.

[2] John Lewis was Chairman of Davenports C.B. and Brewery (Holdings) Ltd 1952–74 and of Midland Caledonian Investment Trust Ltd 1951–73. He was Chairman of the Birmingham Regional Hospital Board 1963–70 and was knighted in 1970.

[3] Richard Cohen was Deputy Chief Medical Officer at the Medical Research Council 1957–62, and at the D.H.S.S. 1962–73, Chief Statistician, D.H.S.S. 1972–3. Alec Baker, Senior Principal Medical Officer at the Department of Health 1968, was Director of the N.H.S. Hospital Advisory Service 1969–73. He has been Consultant Psychiatrist to the North Gloucestershire Clinical Area since 1973.

all looking at me rather uncomfortably and they presented me with a complete survey of research and analysis, saying how far this project had been successfully pushed forward. I fairly soon led the discussion round to the issue of 'main stream' and asked what these enormous new projects were about and why I hadn't heard of them.

I still to this day don't know how much Miss Hedley, Mottishead and Dick Cohen really knew about the schemes. Very little, I fancy. Certainly Godber and Alan Marre had never bothered to tell me about them. This is a great puzzle. I think it is really because the driving force of the Department is at the Assistant Secretary level. Dr Baker is higher up but he, Goodman and Wilkins[1] are the people who really drive ahead. The brass hats up above are extremely obtuse. Things are done and the upper levels are committed to them and take them over in due course and get the credit. I have nothing against this Worcester and Sheffield scheme, which is very exciting, a marvellous idea that's well worth working out in a feasibility study. But we can't be committed to it as a long-term policy without fitting it in to PEP. I have been working on this for six months now, yet it had not occurred to anybody that the 'main stream' studies had any relevance to the other work we were doing on sub-normality. I have got all the papers and next week I shall have all this pulled together. I don't think there is any ill-will at the bottom level. Goodman, Baker and certainly Wilkins are thoroughly friendly to me and want all the help they can get but they are tremendously ambitious men who think they know what is right and who want to get ahead with their plans. They are completely inexperienced in Whitehall politics and they don't care much about old buffers at the top but just shove their way through. That is how it looked to me.

Jim Callaghan had come up from his farm in the country to spend the day in the Home Office and I decided to ring him up to see if we could have a chat. All last week we had the trouble in Ulster hanging over us. There was more rioting, this time in Belfast and, as everybody dreaded, during the Apprentice Boys' March in Londonderry.[2] We had discussed it in Cabinet and Callaghan made it clear that troops would only be used in the last resort and that if they were used we couldn't be responsible without becoming responsible for the country, but of course I thought we were bluffing. I thought that if a crisis did come and the troops went in we wouldn't throw Chichester-Clark

[1] Dr Rodney Wilkins was a Principal Medical Officer at the D.H.S.S.

[2] Serious fights had broken out between Protestants and Catholics, rioting in Londonderry on August 12th. Police had eventually lost control and were driven out of the Bogside, the Catholic area of the city. On August 13th the police used C.S. gas for the first time in the U.K., to dispel Roman Catholic rioters but, in all, 109 people were injured. On August 14th the Northern Ireland Parliament was recalled for an emergency sitting and Mr Wilson returned from the Scillies to discuss with Mr Callaghan the Northern Ireland Government's request for military support for the police. That evening 300 British troops entered the Bogside and barricaded it with barbed wire against Protestant rioters and on August 15th troops also moved in to Catholic areas in Belfast, where there had been shooting and petrol-bomb throwing.

out and we would find ourselves supporting the Orangemen in Northern Ireland. Late this evening Callaghan came through to me and said he was busy at the Home Office but he had to eat somewhere, so I suggested that we should have dinner together.

At about 9.30 he came to Prunier and we sat in the same corner where I lunched with David Watt on Tuesday. Jim told me he had been down to Cornwall today to see Harold and they had thought carefully about the situation. It was obvious that the troops would have to go in because the Royal Ulster Constabulary were too exhausted to move. We would start in Londonderry but he had got various alternative plans. He was working out in the Ministry either a partial or a total take-over, which would all have to be presented to Cabinet. It seemed to me perfectly sensible and what we need here is something sensible and unimaginative. Imagination is a dangerous thing in Ireland and what we need is common sense and caution. The only place where I can see the need for imagination is in devising the peace-keeping force.[1] Should it be more than just British? Instead of letting this thing drag on for ever, should we consider going to the United Nations? I don't think we can do this without setting a hopelessly dangerous precedent. I don't think we could admit that the United Nations has the right to intervene in an internal affair but Barbara Castle might have this temptation, and so might I. Otherwise I think we shall find that Cabinet will agree to a constitutional experiment fairly easily.

Jim was big and burly and happy. 'By God,' he said, 'it is enjoyable being a Minister. It's much more fun being Home Secretary than Chancellor. This is what I like doing, taking decisions, and I had to take the decision to put the troops in while I was in the plane on the way back from Cornwall.' So by this evening British troops were patrolling the streets of Londonderry.

Friday, August 15th

I spent the whole day with the interviewing committee looking at candidates for the Director of my Hospital Advisory Service. We had a short list of six or seven but there was nobody strong enough to stand out and we shall have to have another go next week. I had an enormously enjoyable time and excellent company in my fellow interviewers, whom I got to know a great deal better. We had a feeling of comradeship and at the same time saw something of the variety of personality one meets within the Health Service. After that I was able to catch my train down to Banbury, where Richard

[1] On August 13th Mr Lynch, Premier of the Irish Republic, declared that the presence of British troops in the North was unacceptable to his Government and called for the intervention of a United Nations peacekeeping force. When the Foreign Minister, Dr Patrick Hillery, arrived unexpectedly at the Foreign and Commonwealth Office on August 15th he was reminded that the Northern Irish troubles were an internal affair of the United Kingdom, of no concern to the Republic or the United Nations.

Hartree was over from Canada again.[1] We gave him dinner before he and his mother drove off to Cambridge.

Sunday, August 17th

By yesterday morning British troops were also patrolling the streets of Belfast. Northern Ireland has driven the steel strike to the bottom of the front pages and even the French devaluation has been almost forgotten. Yesterday I had a message from my secretary saying that a Cabinet has been called for Tuesday afternoon. It is fortunate that I have not had to break off my holiday and that next week I will still be finishing my stint in the Ministry. Indeed, I think Barbara and I are the only two who are still here, together with Jim who has not been far away and has been in and out of the Home Office. Cabinet must now discuss the constitutional consequences of the involvement of British troops. I don't think we can get them out of Northern Ireland at all easily now they have gone into Belfast as well and I think we are bound to take over the responsibility for part of the government to try to see the reforms through. I fear that once the Catholics and Protestants get used to our presence they will hate us more than they hate each other. This is something we have all dreaded and looked away from but which has always been recognized as the inevitable consequence of letting the rioting get out of the control of the Ulster police. A year ago it was the Russian invasion of Czechoslovakia that dominated my life and now we have got this but, unlike Czechoslovakia, no sense of tragedy or principle is involved. It is so dirty, mucky, untidy; it really is street rioting, with boys and girls chucking beastly petrol bombs at each other and potting each other with old guns. It is the most messy kind of civil war one has ever seen and it doesn't give a sense of stirring, epic tragedy but is just awful and depressing. Nevertheless, from the point of view of the Government it has its advantages. It has deflected attention from our own deficiencies and the mess of the pound. We have now got into something which we can hardly mismanage. The Tories are with us on this, Maudling has been strongly supporting us and Ted Heath will find it very difficult to disagree with anything Jim does. I am not going to predict what will happen on Tuesday but I don't myself see any issue on which Cabinet is likely to be deeply divided.

While Jim and I were sitting discussing Ireland on Thursday and the enjoyment of being departmental Ministers, I saw a parallel between the two of us. We both love handling a Department, taking decisions the Department looks to us to take and to some extent also imposing our own policies. I think I am more interested in new policies and Jim is more interested in the drama of decision-taking. He hasn't a good policy mind but he is terribly good at public opinion and at wisely playing the role of the link between the public and Whitehall. Denis Healey, Barbara, Jim and I are good departmental

[1] Richard Hartree and his wife Ann were neighbours and good friends of the Crossmans. He worked for the aluminium company Alcan.

Ministers, really natural Cabinet Ministers, miserable without a department. It's very doubtful, on the other hand, that Harold ever was a natural Cabinet Minister. He was a bad one at the Board of Trade and of course as Prime Minister he has no department at all, and he likes putting out his hand on to everything else. Roy Jenkins, whom I was discussing today with Phil Kaiser, who was here with Hannah for the weekend, is interested only in being a success as Chancellor and that is what makes him so terribly limited. Phil knows us all very well and he agreed that Roy doesn't really like his department. He doesn't work there and the Treasury go crazy because they see so little of him. Other people say he is run by the Treasury knights but really he is just not interested in convertibility and the international liquidity crisis or in pensions. He is interested only in his personal success.

We have had a wonderful weekend with the Kaisers and there is quite a gay party out on the terrace. I shall go out and bathe and talk to our guests in the cool of the evening before we give them supper and they drive off to London.

Monday, August 18th–Saturday, August 23rd

I am not going to worry too much about the winding-up week in my Ministry. We have been pretty successful in ploughing through all the policy issues with civil servants. My main discovery this month, with a combination of fury and ironic humour, has been 'main stream', on which I have had a second meeting. They were all as nervous as hell and I said, 'I back the whole thing but I am going to turn what you do from a mere memorandum into a White Paper, a tremendous Ministry policy.' They are enormously excited. On the other front, we have got no further on the appalling question of the Green Paper on the reorganization of the N.H.S. and its relationship to Maud. Almost the last thing I did before I left for my holiday was to give dinner to Paul Odgers, my amusing pink-faced, white-haired former philosophy pupil at New College. I have discovered he is one of the shrewdest operators in Whitehall, a real Whitehall warrior, and he has been trying to work out the new version of the Green Paper on Health Service reconstruction. We agreed that even if I did evolve any satisfactory solution it would be vetoed by the Treasury, so we didn't get very far. I have also spent a day and a half studying hospitals.

The only thing I need really record has been the big Cabinet meeting on Tuesday afternoon, where the main subject was Northern Ireland. There had been the sudden decision last week to put in the troops and now we had to evolve the policy to be presented to Chichester-Clark, who was coming over to talk to the P.M. and Callaghan. Harold and Jim had really committed the Cabinet to putting the troops in and once they were there they couldn't be taken out again, so we had to ratify what had been done. I think it is fair to say that Callaghan wanted to put very strong pressure on Chichester-Clark and to extract from him an agreement that we should take complete control of the police force, that we should wind up the 'B' Specials, change the command and get ahead with the reforms, and that we should do all this without taking over, but with Chichester-Clark as our agent, and if he wouldn't agree we should have to be prepared to take on direct rule.

On the morning of August 18th the Prime Minister, who had returned to Downing Street the previous evening, discussed the crisis with the Home Secretary and his advisers. After the Cabinet meeting in the afternoon, Mr Wilson and Mr Callaghan saw Major Chichester-Clark at 5 o'clock. The Northern Ireland Prime Minister reported on the emergency discussions he had held with his Minister for Home Affairs and with General Sir Ian Freeland, the General Officer Commanding in Northern Ireland, and his staff. Agreement was reached on the 'Downing Street Declaration' (Cmnd 4154), which announced that the Army would take over control of Northern Ireland, General Freeland would be answerable to the Secretary of State for Defence and not only the Army but the police must also be seen to be politically neutral. Accordingly there must be disarmament of the 'B' Specials, the part-time reserve security forces in Northern Ireland (an almost wholly Protestant body, much hated by the Catholics), and an inquiry must be held into the R.U.C. and changes made in its leadership.

Mr Oliver Wright, a Foreign Office official who had been a Private Secretary at No. 10 from 1964 to 1966 and Ambassador to Denmark since then, was to be attached to the N.I. Premier's Office as the British Government's representative, with direct access to Mr Wilson, and the right of the Home Secretary to advise and intervene in N.I. affairs was accepted. The Declaration affirmed the right of all N.I. citizens to 'the same equality of treatment and freedom from discrimination as obtains in the rest of the United Kingdom, irrespective of political views or religion'.

The only difference was between the Home Secretary, the civil authority, on the one side and the Minister of Defence on the other. Healey, representing the military, was rather more cagey and said on no account must we risk having to take over, so we must only push Chichester-Clark as far as he wanted to go. If there was any real danger of his giving up and our having to take over we would have failed. This is true in a sense, because a take-over would put the British soldiers under pressure from the Republicans and the Catholics. Callaghan and Healey both reminded us that our whole interest was to work through the Protestant Government. The Protestants are the majority and we can't afford to alienate them as well as the Catholics and find ourselves ruling Northern Ireland directly as a colony. We have also to be on the side of the Catholic minority and try to help and protect them against their persecutors.

There wasn't any tremendous disagreement. It was one of those Cabinets where Harold takes great trouble to make sure each Minister is consulted, going round the table for opinions from each. Nor do I believe there was much difficulty in deciding what to do. It was a case where in a sense our mind was made up by events. It wasn't so much deciding what policy to have as being able to excuse it and for the execution of this kind of policy the combination of Callaghan and Harold is quite good. Whatever his other deficiencies, Harold is a very competent tactical negotiator in the short run. So we gave him full power to negotiate with Chichester-Clark and to press him as far as he possibly could but it was certainly made perfectly clear that if Chichester-Clark jibbed at the transfer of power from the police to our military force, Cabinet was to resume later tonight, because the House of Commons would have to be recalled to pass legislation for direct rule. It wasn't a very exciting meeting because, as I say, it was the formal Cabinet acceptance of a *fait accompli*. We went on for three hours because we were questioning and investigating and testing, so afterwards there was only a break of about forty minutes before Harold and Jim sat down for their six-hour conference with Chichester-Clark.

Harold has always fancied himself as a negotiator and he thinks that this is all you need to be if you are Foreign Secretary. However in this case, because Northern Ireland isn't a foreign country but part of Britain with the same language, I had confidence that he and Jim would handle it fairly well, and this happened. Chichester-Clark gave them practically everything they wanted, indeed rather more in certain ways, because a complete take-over by the military had not been what we expected. We had expected the nomination of a new Head of the R.U.C. but, no, the military were to take over as well, and the 'B' Specials to be withdrawn, and towards the end of the discussion Chichester-Clark and Harold went on the ten o'clock news programme to announce the agreement. There was some uncertainty, though, and during the next two or three days there was a good deal in the Tory press about Harold's having cocked it up again, making an announcement on '24 Hours' which didn't square with what Chichester-Clark was actually intending to do in Northern Ireland. But it came out right for us, because these were merely the contortions of the Northern Ireland Government, who didn't like to admit how far they had surrendered. In fact what Harold said was true, we had made a take-over, British troops were in Belfast and Londonderry and the British Commander in Chief was in charge of the Northern Irish police. All this went on between the Tuesday and Saturday, by which time I had slackened off and had left for my holiday.

Saturday, August 23rd–Tuesday, September 2nd

Our holiday only lasted ten or twelve days, but it was nicely divided. We started off on Saturday 23rd to drive to Edinburgh, where we stayed with the Dalyells, and saw *Richard II* and heard *Rigoletto* and not a particularly interesting symphony concert. We also took the children to see the Torchlight

Tattoo, all part of the Edinburgh Festival. We had a lot of wonderful excursions into the hills, in bright and breezy cold weather, but the children loved staying in the castle, most of which the Dalyells gave the National Trust in 1936, and climbing the battlements and over the roof. Then we had two days on the Roman Wall. I had mugged this up and with some difficulty got a collection of books about it. The House of Commons library had none and I finally discovered them in the library in the Ministry of Health. I soon found that there hadn't been a rip-roaring Wild West city stretching along behind the wall. On the contrary, it had been a sort of customs barrier, hated by everybody round about because it cut a naturally linked community into two, artificially separating the life of the north and south. The wall wasn't manned, as I had thought, by legions but by auxiliaries, and they were only commanded by Roman citizens. We walked along it with the children and it was tremendously interesting. We also had four days in the Lakes at a wonderful, very friendly hotel with lovely big rooms and excellent food. Sunday we spent with Anne's cousin Michael Haslett and his wife Isabel. Arthur Haslett was at Winchester with me, a mathematician and a scientist, who ended up as Science Correspondent of *The Times*. He was a dear old thing with a great bony face and wavy grey hair, and Michael is a quieter version of his father. He is a passionate walker, who with his wife and their two little boys of eight and four had climbed mountain after mountain with great mountaineering boots. Oh dear, how we fat, lumpy Crossmans toiled up the hill on a tiny climb while they strode ahead. Actually we were so inspired by them that we did have some really good walks on our last two days, Monday and Tuesday.

Then we had to come home because I had a Cabinet on Thursday and the children's school was starting as well. We motored down through the mountains on a lovely translucent day and got home after roaring down the M6. I walked out over the farm and there was the last combine coming in. They had just finished the harvest, which has been magnificent this year, making up for last. Pritchett's only difficulty is that the men, who up till now have been willing to work all out through the harvest, are beginning to jib and say they won't work every day for twelve hours and they won't work at weekends. I don't blame them, they are just like the hospital workers. So that was our family holiday. The children felt that they had really had three separate holidays and it was a great success. The only difficulty was that I had trouble with my left leg. This is the leg which always goes wrong ever since it had a clot and I nearly had to have it off. At Whitsun I had just scratched it slightly but the ulcer had never properly healed and when I got back this time it was very unpleasant. I have begun to get anxious because it is now swollen and bad.

Wednesday, September 3rd

I hadn't even seen the papers although we had a wireless with us and kept in touch. The ten days had been completely overshadowed by Jim Callaghan's visit to Ireland, which had followed the agreement with Chichester-Clark, and was a sensational success.[1] He had gone, he had seen, he had conquered. He had got the confidence of the Protestants, the confidence of the Catholics, and he had dominated the news on the radio for three days. Frankly, it is the only successful diplomatic episode in these five years of a Labour Government, a one-man success.

The other story is that Bob Maxwell has had to give up his bid for the *Sun* and Rupert Murdoch, the owner of the *News of the World* is now bidding for it. I must also mention that the polls have been moving pretty steadily in favour of the Labour Party.[2] Once again the summer months, with Parliament in recess, have been good for Labour, good for Government, good for people in power.

Thursday, September 4th

I had to begin work again and I must admit I was deeply depressed as I crawled up to London by the 8.38. The children were much less melancholy about going back to school. Five years has been enough for me. The first thing at the Ministry was a big conference on abatement. One of the last things I did before going on holiday was to have my second meeting with Jack Diamond and we came near to an agreement with the Treasury on the terms we ought to get. For 1 per cent pension abatement rate the Treasury wanted 1·25 contribution and I wanted 1·3. I had said it must be either one of these but the following morning I suddenly got cold feet. I rang up Miss Riddelsdell and said, 'Look, we shall have to have an agreed official paper drawing up the terms objectively and stating what the situation is, but I must retain flexibility of manoeuvre. I mustn't just say I am content to go for 1·3, but we should have a tactical paper as well, rather like a farm price review. On no account should we accept that we must be content with 1·25 or even 1·3. We must reserve the possibility of going further because we might have to pay a little more danegeld to get agreement.'

While we were in the Lakes a red box arrived on the Saturday, but this wasn't much good because I had frantic difficulty in getting a key posted up, which only arrived on our last day, the Tuesday. When I opened the box I found that Miss Riddelsdell had done exactly what I told her not to do and had written a paper firmly committing me to 1·3. I telephoned her and she said, 'Oh, I am so sorry. It is a real misunderstanding, I must apologize.' A few years ago I would have been furiously saying that these bloody civil servants deliberately deceive the Minister but I don't say that any more. I

[1] On August 27th Mr Callaghan had arrived in Belfast for three days of discussion with Ministers and representatives of all interested groups. The communiqué issued at the end of the visit, published as a White Paper (Cmnd 4158), reaffirmed in detail the principles of the Downing Street Declaration.

[2] The Gallup Poll showed a Conservative lead over Labour of 20 per cent in July and 11 per cent in August, the National Opinion Poll a lead of 15·9 per cent in July and 15·5 in August and the O.R.C. poll a lead in June of 19 per cent, dropping to 18 per cent in August.

simply know Miss Riddelsdell assumed that I, being intelligent, would want what she wanted, and therefore she heard me say what she wanted me to say and misunderstood me.

When I got in this morning the paper was perfectly adequate and corrected in the way I wanted. There was David Ennals back from his holiday in Cornwall. He had also seen the first draft and entirely agreed with me. This morning's meeting was really an O.K.'ing of our tactics and of the paper to be circulated. Our job now is to try to get Roy Jenkins to accept it next week. However the pressures from the occupational pensions schemes and the representations of the T.U.C. are now becoming formidable. During the recess NALGO has denounced our proposals and the T.U.C. had duly denounced them as well, so we really are in the soup.

After a series of other meetings I had lunch with dear Bea Serota, who is worn out. I calmed her down and she is off now for three weeks' holiday on a slow boat to Israel and back. I love Bea but she has absolutely no sense of proportion between big and small and feels everything with an equal intensity. She knows a lot about children and about politics in one sense. She hasn't got as much confidence as I have, so she really is a lieutenant, whereas David Ennals is always perfectly prepared to take my place at any moment. That is the difference between them.

At 3.0 this afternoon we had Cabinet, I don't quite know why. There was a longish piece at the beginning on foreign affairs, and Michael Stewart explained to us the take-over in Libya, where a revolutionary committee has thrown out the seventy-nine-year-old king. Apparently we need to recognize the new regime because of the vast interest we have in oil and in the arms contracts.[1] Then Callaghan described what was happening in Northern Ireland. I was fascinated to see what Harold would do after Callaghan's magnificent success, which had given credit to the whole Government. Would he praise Jim? He has praised many people, including Barbara, but, no, on this occasion he nearly got himself to do it but mostly he was describing what he and Callaghan had done together, taking it as a joint responsibility. Harold is not in that sense a generous or a relenting man. The line was cool and collected and Jim was cool and collected too. Peace had not been made between them. Jim knew he had done well but also he knew that Harold wasn't going to thank him for it.

The only other item on the agenda was equal pay.[2] We had already discussed this at Management Committee before the recess and agreed what line

[1] On September 1st a small group of army officers seized power, deposed King Idris, who was allowed to settle in Egypt, and proclaimed the Libyan Arab Republic. The Revolutionary Council, led by the twenty-seven-year-old Captain Muamnar Qadafi, appointed as Prime Minister a Palestine-born Arab, Mohammed al-Maghrabi, and pledged full support for the Palestine Arab struggle against Israel. Britain and the United States were asked to evacuate their bases and Britain agreed to withdraw from Tobruk and El-Adem by 1970 and, in December, to end a contract to supply a £120 million air defence system.

[2] The Equal Pay (No. 2) Bill had its Second Reading on February 9th, 1970; it received the Royal Assent on May 29th, 1970, just before the General Election.

to take. Cabinet was duly persuaded to support Barbara's Bill for equal pay for men and women, to be introduced early in the session. There was some difference in Cabinet. Some thought that equal pay was like the national superannuation scheme, a vital part of our policy that as socialists we needed to implement, but not popular with the general public. Others, like Barbara, thought it would be enormously popular. I think she is probably right. Roy warned us of the cost. He is a curious man. He resisted it knowing he would be defeated and took his defeat with a good grace. Unlike Dick Marsh, Tony Crosland and, I think, George Thomson, who were all against it and said there was no point in doing it, Roy said it was obviously right but dangerous, and that Barbara should be careful to go slow in her negotiations with the T.U.C. But she got exactly what she wanted.

Cabinet took three hours, so I was an hour late for our second round of examinations to select the Director of the Hospital Advisory Service. We had retained two candidates for a second go, but one was not really big enough for the job and the other was too smooth, so at the end it was obvious what would happen. I took John Revans aside and offered him the job. I am in some difficulty as to whether he will be able to accept but I had known from the beginning that he was the man I should actually have to get. Godber said to me at the end of this meeting, 'I knew you wouldn't get it by advertisement. You have to advertise and have a board first and then do it by invitation.' After this I was as tired as hell but Alan Marre took me to the Athenaeum and we had a delightful dinner together. He is really beginning to warm to me and I to him. He is not a strong man and all his instincts are different from mine, but I find this useful and I find him useful as well.

Friday, September 5th

At the end of July the Management Committee had decided to have a whole day at Chequers. Here today were Harold, Roy, myself, Fred Peart, Barbara, Michael Stewart, Bob Mellish, now regularly there, but not Denis Healey, who was on holiday recovering from a hernia operation. It was another lovely September morning and I decided to motor down with Roy. His great Austin Princess drew up outside 9 Vincent Square at 8.55 and we were off punctually at 9.0. On the way down Roy was careful. He said to me, 'Do you appreciate my view of Tommy Balogh? He is one of my oldest friends, I was his first pupil at Oxford and I have always liked him. I don't know him very well and it's striking that he has never offered me any advice at all. Sometimes when we've met he has tried to angle me to talk about central issues of politics and I have always avoided it. Do you think he likes or dislikes me?' I said, 'Well, I think he thinks you have rebuffed him,' and Roy said, 'Oh, well, perhaps I have.' He was interesting about Callaghan, too, saying, 'You know there is nobody in politics I can remember and no case I can think of in history where a man combined such a powerful political personality with so little intelligence.' I was a bit taken aback because I think Jim

Callaghan is a wonderful political personality, easily the most accomplished politician in the Labour Party, and I think he is quite able as well. I said, 'He works hard.' 'Ah,' said Roy, 'yes, he is very conscientious with his briefs. I don't work nearly as hard as he does,' and I thought, 'My God you don't.' We talked a lot about the Cabinet reshuffle and exchanged notes. 'After Harold asked you and Barbara your advice,' said Roy, 'I asked Harold about it and he told me his intentions for Callaghan, Tony Crosland and Dick Marsh, which I was strongly against, and his intentions for Tony Greenwood, Judith Hart and Peter Shore, which I strongly approved.' We discussed the new industrial Ministry to some extent and the possibility of Harold Lever being promoted, finding that we had roughly the same story on that but that neither of us had heard anything at all recently.

When we got to Chequers we settled down not in the big room as usual, but in comfortable armchairs in the long lounge which stretches right across the side of the house. The Prime Minister began by saying how much the situation had improved, how much the polls were turning in our favour, and how Heath had a record bad result, so bad they couldn't publish it. I was interested because of course a major factor of political life since the beginning of the week has been the disastrous reaction of the T.U.C. to the Prime Minister's speech at the T.U.C. Conference. On Monday he had gone down to Portsmouth to make his oration, a stolid, dull speech with a lecturing tone to it, 'There can be no backsliding etc., etc.' and making too much of the agreement between himself and Victor Feather.[1] He obviously displayed an offensive, unsuccessful attitude which had been followed by the rejection of any kind of sanctions for a voluntary prices and incomes policy. Day after day the whole Congress had been anti-Government, snubbing, crushing, but Harold didn't seem unduly depressed. He recalled that last year they had had an even worse Conference and the Labour Party had an even better one as a result. Anyway, in his view the situation was improving economically and in terms of public opinion.

Bob Mellish, direct and narrow-minded, was asked to open the discussion and he simply said that the things that worried people were the cost of living, mortgages and unemployment, and these were the three things which we ought to consider. Roy Jenkins then came in with a very interesting statement that the balance of payments had improved enormously this year, and that we were going to have a good third quarter too, but accompanied by a very dicey situation for the pound.[2] Ever since the French devaluation and the publica-

[1] For the 'strong meat', that he did not expect to be received with enthusiasm, see *Wilson*, pp. 699–701. The Congress not only declared that the Government should not renew the powers in Part II of the Prices and Incomes Act, allowing them to delay wages settlements, but also passed by 4,652,000 votes to 4,207,000 a resolution demanding repeal of the entire Act, including price controls.

[2] The current balance for July–September 1969 showed a deficit of only £7 million. There was a £40 million surplus on visible trade for the month of August, but June and July had shown deficits of £24 million and £37 million respectively.

tion of our latest trade figures the pound had been doing extremely badly. He then made a statement about the N.E.C. document on economic strategy, which includes a demand for a wealth tax and a whole series of other new taxes. What a disaster, he said, that this should give the impression that we have old-fashioned ideas of restriction and heavy taxation, when it is really taxation that is our difficulty. I must say Roy is right. Barbara and I rubbed in what Bob Mellish had said about mortgages and said that this was only one aspect of people's feeling that they are overtaxed. Roy lectured us, saying that we have gone beyond the limits of taxation, and it is true. One of the things which came out, I think, in this conference at Chequers was our agreement that we must get a neutral budget, one which does not actually increase people's tax burden. This means that we must get another £130 million to help with the personal tax allowances, because, if you don't do this, as the pound falls more people are brought into the tax system. 'But,' said Roy, 'though we need a neutral budget we are very far from getting one and we can't risk any kind of repetition of what Maudling did in 1964.[1] He may or may not have been right but he had some flexibility of manoeuvre and we have not. We are deeply in debt and, anyway, it would not be credible if we were suddenly to start a pre-election boom now, and it would end in a catastrophe like the November catastrophe of 1968 because people would see through it. No trickery between now and the election.' He was strongly supported by Barbara, who said it was quite true, we had to take as it is the economic situation we have and even the amount of unemployment. We can't have any stunts but we must simply go for the balance of payments because any other policy would be seen through and would fail. There are no gimmicks we can use.

These were really answers to my questions as to whether there weren't risks we could take, though having said this Barbara did add that there were a number of things we ought consciously to do. Compassion and courage, that was the phrase she felt was right. Harold had tried to illustrate this in his speech at Portsmouth and we must all try to do the same, but with the theme that we are a compassionate and courageous Government. I supported this very strongly, giving the example of Ely, and saying how I hoped that out of my campaign on sub-normality I might be able to get something corresponding to what she was hoping to get from equal pay.

Then Michael Stewart talked about the Common Market and how it was now likely that the French would lift their veto and that we might be invited to start negotiations. In that case he would want to make a positive statement in favour. Fred Peart doesn't add much to the conversation but he barged in and said we couldn't possibly do this, it would upset everybody. It is quite true that anti-Common Market feeling is now very strong in the country but Barbara and I both made it quite clear that we knew we couldn't possibly go back on our decision to seek admission. Both of us pointed out, though,

[1] See above, p. 544 and n.

that the question was of what posture we should adopt. We must seek admission but at the same time defend ourselves and consider the terms. Do we accept the Common Agricultural Policy without question? Do we sacrifice the sugar agreement and New Zealand? Barbara went so far as to say that she thought we couldn't afford to give too much away in the period of negotiation, but we couldn't afford to stall because if it went on next summer and we were forced to have an election this might be dangerous. Here we came to the interesting question of timing because Harold had assumed at the beginning of the meeting that we would be having an autumn election. Barbara strongly argued that there might be a great risk in holding out beyond May until the autumn and we might well lose by it. Autumn is always a difficult period economically and in terms of the pound. If the difficulties of the Common Market might be added to this, we ought to be thinking of a spring or early summer election. Then Harold said, 'Even if it meant losing your Industrial Relations Bill?' and Barbara answered, 'Well, if we have started on it, that is all that matters.' I found this very interesting.

We sat there from 10.30 until at 1.0 we broke for lunch. After lunch, to my surprise, Harold gave a full account of his new reshuffle, practically the same as he had told Barbara and me before. He wants to cut down the size of the Cabinet but he doesn't think he is going to get down to fifteen or sixteen as he thought earlier. He is going to make a most drastic change of junior Ministers, for example Jim MacColl at Housing and Joe Slater at the Post Office are both over sixty and have to go.[1] He then said that Callaghan had done well for himself and the party on Northern Ireland, he had played the game and it was time we brought him back into the Management Committee, but of course only if assurances were given that he wouldn't play hanky-panky with prices and incomes in the trade unions again. Harold is clearly implacable on this and thinks that he and Bob Mellish know the real story of the treacherous deals which were being done by Callaghan and Houghton with the T.U.C. General Council. Harold doesn't want that repeated in prices and incomes next year, though of course it is not likely to happen again now we have abandoned the policy and are only going to reactivate the Bill by an affirmative order. So Callaghan is not only to stay but to be brought back into the Management Committee. As for George Brown, he gave a press conference this week in his constituency, saying he had fully recovered and was back in politics, and it has been surmised that he is to return to the Government. It's true that Harold talked to him in July and also much more recently and George made it clear that he wanted to come back but only with the full status of Deputy Leader. Today Harold said, looking at Michael Stewart, that this was out of the question, so he wouldn't have George back now but that he might later on, just before the election, as a kind of mark of unity. The P.M. also made it clear that Tony Greenwood would be leaving the

[1] Joseph Slater was Labour M.P. for Sedgefield from 1950 until he became a life peer in 1970. He was Assistant Postmaster-General 1964–9.

Ministry of Housing and that he was going on with his plans for a new Ministry of Industry. He added that I would be taking over the Children's Department from the Home Office and said, 'I am not sure, Dick, whether in your case we merged the right two departments.'

The other big thing was that Roy put forward his need for cuts in the 1970/1 programme, something I had discussed at length with Dick Bourton and the department. We had to decide whether to put forward a genuine bid of, say, £10–15 million in total because £350 million cuts would be demanded, or whether to put forward a formal £5 million offer. It was lucky that we only put forward the formal £5 million because Roy read aloud what he was requiring from the departments and this was all he was asking from Health and Social Security. Some £90 million would come out of Defence again and the rest is small beer. He is not seeking much and he asked us to back him in his demands for 1970/1.

We had a long discussion of Barbara's Industrial Relations Bill and her new proposal for an Industrial Commission which will wrap up in one single institution the Monopolies Commission and the Prices and Incomes Board. Then I reported on my problems of abatement. The general atmosphere was amiable. The Prime Minister is not now pretending that we are certain to win the election and he even talks as though there might be an interval before the next Labour Government. He is much more detached and relaxed, better able to face reality. But what was hair-raising was his description of the deplorable relations between the Party and the National Executive. The first thing the N.E.C. Campaign Committee had done was to fix a meeting on August 12th when neither he nor Callaghan nor Stewart could be there, then, at that meeting, they had decided on an advertising campaign costing £100,000 with the slogan 'Labour has Life and Soul', or some such nonsense, which has been launched without consultation with the P.M. He is now hoping that we can have everything done not by the Executive and Harry Nicholas, but by the real campaign committee of Denis Healey and Bob Mellish, and that this will make a difference in our relations with the Party.

We sat there for two hours until 4.0 in the afternoon, It was easy going, it wasn't very profound, but I suppose that we each got a picture of the others' philosophy, and it was clear today that there is now no chance of a run-up to the election with a different policy, with a planned expansion, planned risk-taking. We are simply going to plough ahead on the present policy with no unexpected changes. As Roy quite rightly says, if we do anything else we shall risk another November, and looking back it was that sudden hitch last year, the sudden imposition of the regulator, that was the fatal thing. The Government can't take any risk which might lead to another crisis. The one thing that was clear to the five of us was that we were regarded by Harold as his big lot, he is content with us and with Callaghan as well, and we are going to be the powers which run this party until Parliament ends.

Monday, September 8th

The morning started a bit dismally and I was anxious about the news that British troops in Ulster had used C.S. gas. When I got to the office one of my first assignments was to see Les Huckfield,[1] a bearded young man of twenty-seven, who found himself in one of the safest seats in the country. He looks rather like a kind of D. H. Lawrence–Jesus Christ type, and I didn't like him much at the beginning, but now I have seen a good deal of him I must admit that he is a really vigorous M.P. He is battling for the George Eliot Hospital at Nuneaton and he wanted to have precise assurances about when it was going to be built. Unfortunately, no attempt has really been made to put over the fact that the enormous, monstrous new palace at Walsgrave in my constituency has to cater for the whole catchment area and that to justify the expense all the acute cases have to be transferred there, leaving only secondary activities at Rugby and Nuneaton. Les Huckfield was simply saying that he could never get his people to see the Coventry hospital as theirs and, even if they did, they couldn't get there because there is no transport. This is a typical problem and it perfectly illustrates the difficulty I shall have to try to settle tomorrow with the R.H.B. chairmen.

After this came the meeting I had been looking forward to with some trepidation, the confrontation between the Secretary of State for Social Services and the Chancellor of the Exchequer about the terms of abatement. I took Miss Riddelsdell with me and he had two officials with him. It went, as it often does between Roy and me, relatively easily. In the rewritten paper I had put in a paragraph indicating that we might have to go for 1·4, in case I might have to accept 1·3 as a compromise. Roy reacted by first of all fighting for his own figure, 1·25, and, then, when I said we must go a bit further, he said, 'Even if I did let you go to 1·3, it would really be a jumping-off point for 1·4.' 'Supposing I abandoned 1·4 as well?' I said. 'That would be quite different,' said he, so I knew I had got 1·3 safe. That was really all there was to the whole interview, apart from courtesies. Roy said, 'This is really a difficult case. We had to spend two hours on this paper.' Two hours wouldn't be enough to make anybody really understand it and indeed he didn't. Why should he? This is one of the most difficult, complicated and irritating subjects there is.

So after half an hour we went out of the room with exactly what we wanted, a firm commitment that we should start the negotiations at 1·25, that I could go as far as 1·3 and that I was to go to the Cabinet with that. My paper would go to Cabinet unchanged but I gave a kind of assurance that I wouldn't press very hard either for going to 1·4. I went out of the room and Miss Riddelsdell said, 'Well, Secretary of State,' in rather a breathless way, 'it certainly worked, didn't it? I couldn't believe it when you asked me to write the paper that way. We couldn't write in 1·4 with any conviction but it worked.' She

[1] Labour M.P. for Nuneaton since March 1967 and Parliamentary Under-Secretary of State at the Department of Industry since April 1976.

had a naughty glint in her eye, as if to say 'To think that the Chancellor of the Exchequer could fall for such a simple device as that.' It only indicates what political negotiation is and that the papers put up between Ministers are political in a sense that civil servants, particularly, I think, the civil servants in Social Security, find it hard to understand. I don't think it would be true to say that all civil servants are like this, that nobody ever battles in a calculated way, but she was excited by this naughtiness and pleased that her Secretary of State had been so successful.

Tuesday, September 9th

All the morning I had my big meeting with the R.H.B. chairmen to discuss closure procedure. I won a complete victory for my proposal that the Regional Boards and the local authorities should work together in discussing closure policies, the siting of new regional hospitals and alternative uses for the smaller hospitals, something which fits into my idea of an integrated service. On this occasion I could see that the Hospital Boards liked the whole new approach and, above all, liked it because the Minister was giving a strong personal lead and backing them to the full. They have got a kind of permissive independence and now what they want is a much stronger central policy, because they prefer to work as my agents than as semi-independent satraps. It was a very satisfactory meeting from my point of view.

After lunch I had an equally exciting meeting. Ages ago I had discovered that the County Councils, the Municipal Corporations Association and the doctors had been having secret talks together on the Green Paper, and I had suggested at the cocktail party of the C.C.A. that they might come informally to discuss it with me. We sat down together in my room, Dr Stevenson with Dr Gibson, and another man from the Medical Office of Health, Jim Swaffield from the A.M.C. and Arthur Hetherington from the C.C.A.[1] 'I want you to tell me,' I said, 'how far you have got with any kind of agreement between the local authorities and the doctors on the Green Paper and in particular on the thorny issue of the future of the Health Service.' After half an hour or so it was clear that their talks had been based on the assumption that the Health Service would be independent but that local authorities must insist on a large slice of participation at district and at regional level. They hadn't of course decided on where to draw the line and the value of this to me was to find that, though I had been assuming that we must announce the right frontier between the local authorities and the independent Health Service, this wouldn't be necessary. What we have to do is to announce, first, that the Health Service will not be coming under the local authorities and, secondly, that in the reorganized Health Service the local authorities will have a large

[1] The Secretary of the B.M.A., Derek Stevenson. Sir Ronald Gibson (Kt 1975) was Chairman of the Council of the B.M.A. 1966–71. Sir James Swaffield (Kt 1976) was Secretary of the Association of Municipal Corporations 1962–72 and has been Director-General and Clerk to the G.L.C. since 1972. Arthur Hetherington, Secretary of the C.C.A. 1964–74, has been Secretary of the Association of County Councils since 1974.

number of representatives not selected by me, as the Department wants, but nominated by themselves as their own representatives alongside others nominated by the doctoring and the teaching professions.

Our whole discussion centred on the terribly complicated issue of the Seebohm Committee, which had brought out its Report at the right time just when I ceased to be Leader of the House and became co-ordinator of Social Services. Our great predicament arises because the Maud Report, due last October, was only published this June and to make anything of Seebohm we shall have legislation next session. Otherwise Medical Officers of Health will retain their power to take over integrated services, which will mean the death of Seebohm's essential principle that personal social services should also be brought together under a single Director of equal importance to the Director of Education and the Treasurer. On the other hand, I can't agree to legislate on Seebohm without a simultaneous declaration of the independence of the Health Service, which will be pre-judging an essential part of the Maud Report, which the local authorities don't want. There is the circle. Today's conversation allowed me to make Swaffield and Hetherington understand my position. It only shows how useful it is to set up informal private talks. They all said, 'Why didn't we talk to each other sooner? Why didn't we talk to the Minister in this way?' and went out of the room in good heart, as I also did after this very unusual meeting which actually came off.

Wednesday, September 10th

It was amusing to see in all the papers a statement that George Brown is not going to be a member of the Government. This occurred because yesterday morning Walter Terry of the *Mail* had announced that George was coming back.[1] No. 10 had obviously issued a denial within twenty-four hours, which I suppose is a tribute to Walter Terry as a journalist and to the importance of George and also showed me that the P.M.'s briefing at Chequers was correct and George was out. Harold hasn't changed his mind.

The first thing I did this morning was to go down to the hospital in London to visit the ward containing the women with respiratory polio. The discussion was all about their rights, and how they needed vehicles and accommodation, and they all said they would like the hospital to recognize the need for domiciliary services. Even if they had all this equipment at home it would save the hospital a bed and the vast cost of keeping them. They also said they would like to have an income tax concession like the £100 for business expenses that the blind get. It was an excellent meeting. They were staggering people. There are only twenty or thirty of them in the whole country and they asked me to treat them as a separate class. It was stimulating to see them and I learnt a great deal about the problems of the constant attendance allowance.

I lunched with Nicholas Davenport at the Athenaeum, as we do every

[1] Walter Terry was Political Editor of the *Daily Mail* from 1965 to 1973 and of the *Daily Express* from 1973 to 1975, when he joined the political staff of the *Sun*.

three or four weeks. We discussed the lunch he had previously had with Crabbe of the Life Offices, when Crabbe told him confidentially that they would have been content with a 1:1·25 abatement ratio. This is the one which the Government Actuary thinks is fair. I could hardly believe it because I had got 1·3 out of Roy and thank God I did because I am quite sure that, even if the Life Offices think 1·25 is fair enough, they won't be able to say so and what I have got is the very minimum. There will be the hell of a row about even this. However it was very nice to have Nicholas as a contact with Crabbe. He really has been invaluable to me and I feel extremely grateful.

I had to rush back to chair a Social Services Committee where we got them to approve our attitude on preservation of pension rights. The great news was that Eddie Shackleton would be able to make the announcement that the civil servants would voluntarily introduce complete transferability, introduce the new scheme and set an example to employers. Then we turned to the abatement paper. After seeing Roy I was aware that I would have to keep my word and go for the relationship of 1:1·3 and that I wouldn't be allowed to go to any higher ratio or the alternative of 1·2 benefit abatement and 1·5 contribution abatement unless there was very great pressure from my colleagues. There seemed to be a chance that all the people concerned with pensions schemes would be asking for much better terms. These would be the Minister of Transport because of the railways, the Minister of Power because of all those industries, coal, electricity, steel and gas with huge superannuation schemes and, above all, local government. There should have been a big lobby. Roy had said to me yesterday, 'My trouble is that nobody who knows anything about it goes to Cabinet and the whole Committee will be on your side.' He was really afraid of a ganging up which would force on him a more generous offer than I had tried to get. However at this meeting none of them bothered about it. Dick Marsh failed to turn up, Roy Mason was somewhere in Europe and had left Freeson, his Parliamentary Secretary, poor old Jim MacColl spoke for Housing, so there was no effective representation at all, and the discussion was flat. Everybody supported my 1:1·3.

After that it was time to be one of the hosts in the beautiful Painted Chamber of the Whitehall Banqueting Hall at the Government reception for 600 demographers, part of a huge conference for thousands of statisticians. I have always avoided this job of shaking hands at the door on behalf of the Government and given it to the Minister of State. However Bea Serota is on holiday and I found myself having to learn how to get the line moving and yet be nice to people as I stood and shook hands for forty-five minutes. I found my leg aching and swollen as a result. At last I was able to depart to give Tommy Balogh dinner at the Garrick.

Thursday, September 11th

The *Daily Mail* had the news that the National Opinion Poll showed a slight swing against Labour in the first week of September, thanks, no doubt, to the T.U.C.[1] I don't regard this too seriously because the swing towards us has been going on and the Gallup Poll shows a marked improvement. I have a feeling that by the time of the Conference we ought to have the Tory majority down to 10 per cent, if N.O.P. is right that it is still 18 per cent now.

There were only about fifteen people at Cabinet this morning, a reasonable number. Barbara and Peter Shore were up in the North-West on important visits and Denis Healey was away somewhere. Harold lectured us first on visits, saying we were making double the number that the Tory Government had made and this was very bad. I must say it's obvious that Labour Ministers do systematically use their positions to get free holidays and jaunts abroad and they all go to Yugoslavia, America or Canada on the flimsiest of excuses.

Then we had Michael Stewart on Nigeria, where at last there was a chance of a truce after pressure had been put on at the Conference of the O.A.U.[2] But these were minor points before we came to Callaghan on Northern Ireland. It has been a bad week, when we have had the use of tear gas by the British troops and then an extraordinary broadcast by Chichester-Clark, suddenly abandoning his neutrality and his retiringness and laying down the line that the troops must take over. By today all this had taken place, the peace line had been announced, the troops had persuaded the people to pull down the barricades and had taken over and the Catholic parts of Ulster had been turned into isolated areas, rather like, I suppose, the Turkish enclaves in Cyprus. It was interesting to hear from Callaghan, who had not been warned about Chichester-Clark's dramatic announcement until two hours beforehand, or consulted. I found Jim very sensible. He said life was very bleak, the prospect very bleak and he saw no hope of a solution. He had anticipated that the honeymoon wouldn't last very long and it hadn't. The British troops were tired and were no longer popular and the terrible thing was that the only solutions would take years, if they could ever work at all.

He was most alarmed by the Catholic and Protestant radio broadcasts whipping people up and there was no doubt that the demonstration that had caused all the trouble had been started by a secret radio station calling on the Protestants to demonstrate at a certain point. Jim said, 'I wanted to jam these stations but I found to my amazement that there was some B.B.C. objection.' Harold said, 'Well, we'll have that knocked aside.' This is interesting because it shows you how a great political principle can be jeopardized the moment it is inconvenient to Britain. I suppose it is true to say that during the war and for many years after the principle was that jamming was a fascist, communist or totalitarian action, which no decent democratic country would take. Every British Government was proud of the fact that we would never

[1] According to the N.O.P. the Conservative lead had risen from 15·5 per cent in August to 18·8 per cent in September. The Gallup Poll showed that the Conservative lead had dropped from 11 per cent to 8·5 per cent.

[2] In September the heads of state met in Addis Ababa for the Conference of the Organization of African Unity but there was little progress towards the settlement of the Nigerian civil war.

jam radio stations, that we believed people should be allowed a free radio service and allowed to state the uncensored truth or even falsehood. But the moment we have a problem, as in Northern Ireland, Harold, Jim and the rest of Cabinet say, 'What is all this nonsense of the B.B.C. being so choosy and intellectual?' and out goes a civil liberty straightaway. Apart from that I found Callaghan once again shrewd and sensible, keeping himself in charge of the situation, restraining Harold and not letting him poke his nose in too far.

Finally Roy announced that there had been a wonderful balance of payments surplus in August and that things were really beginning to go our way.*

During the course of the chat about this Harold said, 'Perhaps you oughtn't to spend too long on this since I know that every one of you is eagerly looking forward to the treat of the next subject on the agenda.' This was abatement and there was a roar of laughter. 'Yes,' said Harold, 'it is a thing we can all enjoy because we have all studied it.' I knew then that it was a terrible subject which people were anxious to avoid because they couldn't understand it. I had been wondering about this during the earlier discussion on Nigeria and I decided that the only thing to do was to modify my notes at the last moment and give them a real little lecture. So, for the first time, I instructed Cabinet on the nature of occupational pensions schemes, the history of the Labour Party's superannuation scheme, why we had to introduce contracting-out and I led them up to the two narrow issues. When I had finished there was a spontaneous round of Hear Hears. Afterwards Callaghan, I think it was, said that Harold had said, 'By Jove, what an expositor that chap is.' When I had finished, Roy said, 'Well, I prefer the Secretary of State in his expository rather than his argumentative mood.' They were enormously impressed. For a blinding moment they thought they understood abatement and contracting-out and I think for a moment they did. After that there wasn't much discussion. Roy put his case for 1·25 and nothing more, and there wasn't, as I thought there might be, a great demand for enlarging the whole scheme and having it not 1:1·25 but 1·2:1·5. I was tempted, but I didn't get much support except from Dick Marsh, who has really studied this for himself. He saw the danger of the bleeding row we were likely to have, which would deflect millions of votes, but he wasn't greatly supported, and even Kenneth Robinson was as meek and mild as ever. So in the absence of Barbara and Denis Healey, the Chancellor and I got what we had agreed on and I was able to go back to the Department and say we had got just what we wanted, the 1·3 and no more. As the result of a great deal of work beforehand,

* Of course, as I knew would happen, by the next day Harold had rushed into a speech capitalizing on the facts. No man has been more ingenuous or more determined to rush into statements when there is no point in making them. What is the use of doing this when it may go wrong on you and you will be accused of being super-optimistic again? But he is a bouncing boy, and can't resist it.

it was a successful Cabinet but this will cause me a great deal of trouble in the future.

Harold had asked me to stay behind after Cabinet and now he said, 'Oh, it was only because I thought you were going to America next week and I was going to tell you about the Cabinet changes.[1] You will get two new Parliamentary Secretaries, all right? We will discuss it later.' I shall write to him next week about it. When I got back to 70 Whitehall I busied myself over lunch preparing a draft press release for a meeting tomorrow. For ages I have been due to spend a whole day studying the mental health services in Coventry and there has now been added to this a lecture for NALGO, who have asked me to dinner. This will possibly be of national interest because NALGO has not only issued a press statement denouncing the whole Government pensions scheme but also a printed pamphlet warning its members that accepting the Government scheme means dismantling all public schemes. The amazing thing is that the General Secretary, a very nice man called Walter Anderson,[2] was one of the four members of the T.U.C. General Council who had been in on the informal consultations with us and of eleven meetings he had taken part in six, including those on abatement, and had at no point suggested that he was out of sympathy with the whole thing. He had discreetly absented himself from the T.U.C. Conference where the wholly hostile debate had taken place with the local government officers leading the way, talking the most appalling balderdash and making the wildest assertions about what was going to happen as a result of our scheme. I knew I would have to make a complete answer to them and thought it was a good chance for a press release too.

Friday, September 12th

At 2.0 in the morning my stomach evacuated totally and absolutely, and by 8.0 a.m. the diarrhoea was still continuing. I took the usual tablets and went off to Coventry in the car about 9.45, nervous as to whether I could possibly get through a whole day of inspecting all the services provided for the mentally handicapped, from the very young to the very old. I was to go to lunch with the Lord Mayor and then to dinner with NALGO and after that to a huge hall holding about 1,000 people in Lanchester College. By God, I was warned, NALGO have got it in for you, they are going to tear you limb from limb. There is a mass meeting and they will be booing and jeering.

We started off in my own constituency, where a magnificent building costing £200,000 has been built up at Wyken and then to an old knock-about civil defence hutment about half a mile away. I asked the woman in charge what the real loss was to her compared to the wonderful building I had just seen, and she said, 'Our lavatories aren't as good and we need a separate

[1] On October 5th.

[2] General Secretary of NALGO 1957–73 and a member of the T.U.C. General Council 1965–73.

room for the medical officer.' That wouldn't cost us much. Is it really necessary, I wondered, to go in for the staggering expense of new buildings, instead of adapting old buildings and saving ourselves some cash. After lunch with the Lord Mayor I had an excellent discussion with Dr Clayton, Medical Officer of Health since 1947,[1] a tall, wambly Irishman, kind and gentle, and his number two, an excellent, vigorous, alert doctor. After an hour and a half's discussion I was motored down to Long Itchington to see a British Legion old people's home. It was splendidly done, spacious and beautiful with a lovely water garden but it didn't take me ten minutes to learn that the old people were bored stiff. I don't blame them. I could not have found a duller bit of country and they were used to cities and just wanted to be given the chance to get back to Birmingham or London and sit in the pub with their friends. It teaches you a lesson.

Now it was time to get back to Coventry and I was already half an hour late. I found Mike Fogden had come down specially by train and we were taken to a private room where I just had half an hour to prepare my speech. We were given an absolutely first-rate dinner in an atmosphere of ferocious hostility. They had brought down three members of the London executive and kept on talking about overflow meetings and how terrible it was going to be. Over dinner I began to thaw the ice and weaken the confidence of my neighbours in the righteousness of their cause and when we went across to the big hall there were only 750 people there and no question of an overflow. Still, I found myself in a most frigid atmosphere and the beginning of my speech was greeted with hisses. I knew it was no good coming to the important part till I had got them used to me, so I made a very long speech for an hour, quite deliberately playing myself in slowly. There were a great many interruptions and my speech was hardly applauded, just courteously received. Then the Treasurer of NALGO got up to ask a series of telling questions. This really was outrageous and I was determined to beat and batter that audience into understanding. When I'd finished I knew that unfortunately in Coventry they were saying, 'Whenever we get Dick down he can always prove himself in the right.' But they were not nearly as confident as they had been and I was hopeful that I would get a big press. Anne had come across for the dinner, and she motored me and Mike Fogden back to Prescote at 10.30. A very long day it had been but a solid day of achievement, in spite of my appalling stomach collapse.

Saturday, September 13th

I got hardly any London press for my speech yesterday but I suspect it was my own fault because I had a press conference at lunchtime and released the fact that I had given a £20,000 experimental unit to the Coleshill Hospital to relieve their overcrowding. I had given an interview to the B.B.C. and explained how I got the money and, newspapers being what they are, they

[1] Dr Thomas M. Clayton. He retired in 1972.

excused themselves by saying that they couldn't have a second story about the Secretary of State on the same day. Although *The Times* had given enormous prominence to the NALGO attack they gave no prominence to my reply. The B.B.C. gave quite a good account on the 8 o'clock news this morning but I think the press reports have been very thin. However I should have something in the *Coventry Evening Telegraph*, and I think it was a success and certainly a try-out of a reply to the unions. I shall now have to get used to this because we are going to have a tremendous battering before we are through. Over the next few weeks I shall have to begin negotiations. Cabinet have asked me to play it very slow because they don't want a row at the Labour Party Conference or to give the Tories a row at theirs.[1]

This morning I went to Oxford to see about my leg. Last Saturday I found it was swelling more and more and that the ulcer on the ankle wouldn't heal, so I went over to see Dr Long.[2] He told me I was much too heavy and must take off a stone and he also said that I must go and see Mr Tibbs, the best surgeon for varicose veins. He had fixed an appointment with Tibbs for 9.30 this morning. I was going privately because it takes you ten weeks to get an appointment with him on the National Health Service and Long only just managed this one. We drove into the magnificent forecourt of his surgery next door to the Acland Nursing Home and Anne dropped me while she took Mike Fogden on to the station. I was taken straight in to this trim, keen, business-like technological man, good-looking, terribly nervy and excitable, aged perhaps forty to forty-five. 'Was it safe to leave the car outside?' He didn't on any account want to let the press know I was here. As for coming privately, I did appreciate that Aneurin Bevan had two things done by private practitioners and hadn't wanted it to be a secret. So I had to explain to him all about private practice, all about myself, and he gradually got more interested. He looked at my leg and confirmed Long's view that I was much too fat and then he said that I would have to wear surgical stockings, which I should have been using for the last six months. I asked him about swimming and he said that was all right but that I must keep my feet up and not ever stand about. He thought an operation would be a bit risky, but that he would keep me going for the present and see how I was after three months. He adored discussing the Health Service, he was all of a tither and quiver of excitement at having the Secretary of State there. Then he sent me to a little shop in the Broad to get my surgical stockings. We were served by an old man who lives in Banbury and I said I had been to see the famous Mr Tibbs. He replied, 'Oh, these surgeons come and go but they know nothing about support stockings. I have to tell you that he has ordered the wrong thing. I will give you the right ones.'

From there we went down the High to the Oxford Gallery where we deposited the portrait of my dear old great-great-uncle Robert Howard, the

[1] The Conservative Party Conference was held at Brighton from October 8th to 11th.
[2] John Long, Crossman's family doctor.

9 In February 1969, just three months after his election as President of the United States, Richard Nixon visits Prime Minister Wilson at No. 10 Downing Street. Britain's Foreign Secretary Michael Stewart is on the left and the American Secretary of State William Rogers is on the right.

10 A grim Harold Wilson sits between Acting General Secretary of the Trades Union Congress, Vic Feather, and the Secretary of State for Employment and Productivity, Barbara Castle, at the press conference in June 1969 at which they announce the eleventh-hour deal between the unions and the government that resulted in withdrawal of the controversial Industrial Relations Bill.

11 Richard Crossman walks through the crowd at the entrance to Downing Street on his way to the special meeting, recalling Ministers from holiday, on August 19, 1969, to discuss with the Northern Ireland Prime Minister, Major Chichester Clark, the worsening situation in the province.

12 August 27, 1969. The Home Secretary, James Callaghan, visits Belfast to talk to the people and get a first-hand view of the violence that is dividing the Catholic and Protestant communities in Northern Ireland.

father of Luke. I had shot an arrow through the eye of the portrait at the tender age of eight at Aunt Florence's Christmas party. We are having it repaired and properly framed and then this lovely portrait will hang in the hall here. It was a terrible afternoon but we went to the gymkhana at Great Bourton where there was a Coke stall run by Virginia and her pals from the village school, who took not the faintest interest in the activities of the horses. Back to my thirty-four length bathe, in lovely water, and then a peaceful evening in the drawing room in my pyjamas and a smoking jacket which Anne has bought for me, settling down with the record player.

Sunday, September 14th

John Makepeace has been over to try to design a footstool which will be an extension of my orange velvet chair. The furniture is looking more and more wonderful and we are very happy with it. We had to put the electric fire on last night after dinner because the weather has broken and now the skies are grey and falling in on us, but it's not cold yet and the grass is still growing thick and green. We have had a good harvest but the summer is over. I am sipping my tea as I sit in the study here and all day I have been putting off this diary. Anne is playing the Rasumovsky Quartets in the drawing room, half-asleep, Virginia is in the kitchen looking at the 'Golden Bullet'[1] programme on I.T.V. and Patrick and Peter Pritchett are, I suspect, down in the barn burrowing in the caverns of the hay.

I have been preparing last week's diary, going through the press cuttings, and I notice that John Cashman and I really have introduced a remarkably improved system. At the end of each day I am given a succinct account of each meeting I have attended, which will be useful for the diary as well as an invaluable means of progress-chasing. Instead of trying to run a progress meeting with my two P.U.S.s, I have a progress meeting with myself each evening and each weekend, going through the red box and throwing in the notes on the action points required. I suppose other people have always done it but I only thought of it some months ago. It has been a good non-parliamentary week. My God, what a difference it makes when Parliament isn't sitting and one can really get down to work as a Minister. There was terrible pressure in July but now we are settling down. One can really run the Department and have time to read the telegrams and to be a Cabinet Minister as well.

Today, for example, I was going through the telegrams on the Common Market, and I found that, through Con O'Neill, we were complaining bitterly to the German Ambassador about any delay there might possibly be in inviting to us to resume negotiations. I have been waiting for this moment and now I can write a minute to Harold on the whole issue of the Common Market. I walked along with Fred Peart to the Lord President's room this week and he said he was terribly worried about the attitude to the Common

[1] The 'Golden Shot' programme.

21

Market which had been revealed by Michael Stewart at the Chequers talks. That weekend I also felt that we were being dragged into this almost automatically and that another round of negotiations will almost certainly end in a snub, because I am sure the French will prevent us getting in. It is already clear from the telegrams that they are insisting that the Common Agricultural Policy must be absolutely fixed before we are allowed to enter, which means fixed in a way satisfactory to the French and expensive to ourselves.

Another thing which has been happening here has been the staggering swing in public opinion. According to the public opinion polls, clear majorities in both parties are now opposed to our entry. This is completely different from two years or even a year ago, and, curiously, the trend has been accentuated since General de Gaulle resigned. I suppose people now feel it is necessary to make up their minds and public opinion is now educated in a way it wasn't before about the choice before us, the fact that the price of food will go up, that it will cost something like £600 million on the balance of payments, that it will certainly mean a second devaluation and that it is by no means certain that our industry will do all that well. Economically we will pay an appallingly heavy price for what we are told is a great political advantage or, rather, we are told there is no future for us outside. You know I have never been very sympathetic to this; I am a Little Englander at heart, and am therefore greatly cheered. I shall write to Harold this week to tell him that I wonder whether it is wise for Michael Stewart to rush into this, or let it be thought in Europe that we are uncritically urging the resumption of negotiations. 'Shouldn't you adopt,' I shall say, 'a posture of willingness to negotiate, but also defining where we stand?' This is the point I put at Chequers.

Last Monday morning I went up in the train with Neil Marten, who I noticed had been quoted as making a weekend speech supporting Enoch Powell, who, with his nose for a popular cause, had now turned against the Common Market. Neil told me of the pressure which is now being put on Heath to be careful. Heath realizes he can't push too far ahead and in speeches this week both he and Maudling have begun to talk about reassessment of the terms. Certainly opposition is growing in the Tory Party. In our party the Common Market split will be worse than that on the Industrial Relations Bill if the pace is forced too strongly. My own view is that we ought now to work out our terms soberly and objectively, on agriculture, the sugar interests, Australia and New Zealand, on the balance of payments and the assistance the E.E.C. will give us there. I must make an effort to force the issue, as Fred Peart asked me to do last week. I found myself very much in agreement with Neil when he observed that much the same kind of struggle is going on in the Shadow Cabinet. It may even be true that with the two parties virtually indistinguishable and the issues becoming more and more obscure with less and less confidence in either party, a decision by Wilson to say 'I must have a mandate for negotiations and that is why I am coming to the country now,' might not be a bad issue on which to stand against the Tories. They are committed to the Common Market, to agricultural levies and increased food prices, and we could put them in a terrible predicament. This is my view and Fred's view. I know that Harold and Michael are personally deeply against this, they would think it is politicking, opportunism, departing from principle, they and George Brown, who has just written two more dedicated Common Market articles as though nothing had happened. The real marketeers are Harold, Michael Stewart and George Brown. I noticed at Chequers that Roy was pretty discreet. He finds the whole Common Market approach extremely dangerous from his point of view of safeguarding the pound and he will stay neutral on this as on industrial relations. On the whole I think he would come down on the side of caution. Barbara sides with Fred Peart and me and I would guess that Denis Healey would as well. I told Fred that when Denis gets back I would get hold of him because if we can get him as a partner we will really have an overwhelmingly strong position inside Cabinet.

Monday, September 15th

I started this morning with Reg Crabbe, Bayley and Lyon from the Life Offices. I had prepared a sort of verbatim speech to them at the beginning and it is clear that I have their support for 1 per cent benefit abatement, but they are asking 1·5 contribution in return. The nationalized industries and the Local Government Association want much higher levels of contribution abatement, altogether more like 1·4 or 1·5. There is no doubt that with 1·4 I could get virtual agreement but of course that I am not permitted by the Cabinet to go beyond 1·3. I have been thinking about this and how I might conceivably get a little beyond 1·3, perhaps in return for an important concession. The Life Offices have come up with one proposal, a very technical thing, that I might introduce into this discussion my formula for post-award dynamism, that is to say, the formula would be cost-of-living increase plus what the nation can afford, moving towards wages dynamism. That formula might allow one to be more generous on the contribution terms. Anyhow, thank God I didn't go abroad this autumn, as it is clear that I may well have to meet all these people three or four times.

I had a horrible office lunch of particularly disgusting sandwiches and in the evening I desperately began to feel as though I had been poisoned. I was at a dinner with the Royal College of Gynaecology, in one of these slap-up buildings that Royal Colleges have, and there I was surrounded by Sir John Peel,[1] and nine other men (not a single woman). After the meat course I suddenly felt as if my inside was going to collapse and I felt a white sweat. My host took me out to the lavatory and I sat there with my head between my hands just feeling ill. Back I went to the sitting room, and it was difficult, sitting there feeling desperately ill, fussed about by ten leading gynaecologists with nobody knowing quite what to do with me. I got back to the lavatory

[1] Consulting Obstetric Physician and Gynaecological Surgeon at King's College Hospital since 1969. He was Surgeon-Gynaecologist to Her Majesty the Queen 1961–73.

and in ten seconds had emptied everything in my body. This is one of the curious effects of my operation and unbelievably I felt a little better. George Godber tottered me home and I lay on my bed for an hour and a half. Godber was spending the night in the Elephant and Castle and he rang me at 11.30 to tell me that I should be off to catch my train. I got into the train at 1.0 a.m., lay on my bunk and slept like a log. At 6.30 I woke up and got myself to an hotel in Plymouth, furious to find that our local man there hadn't booked a room and it was all full. During the course of the day I was to recover from this appalling mishap and I really had no choice about going down to Cornwall. One can't cancel a tour in that way.

Tuesday, September 16th

I am doing two days in Devon and Cornwall this week, two days next week in Wessex, the third week in Sheffield and Leeds. I needn't go into detail about these tours. They are run, as usual, as a combination of showing me off to help the morale of the hospitals and to enable me to meet people and I have insisted on dinners and lunches with local authorities to discuss the Green Paper.

I had heard that the Plymouth branch of NALGO wanted to send a delegation to me and I had agreed to see them before lunch today. When I arrived I heard there was going to be a mass demonstration and as I slipped into the famous new Town Hall, sure enough, 500–600 people were outside, booming and yelling, with placards and cars, policemen and firemen. Into a little room came three very senior civil servants who rapidly handed me a petition and tried to get out. I said, 'No thank you. I am glad to see you here. Come and sit down and let us discuss your claims.' I have never seen people more embarrassed and sheepish. I showed them what nonsense they were up to and finally said, 'Would you please go out now and pacify your people?' They went out and stood on the front door step but the demonstration went on for forty minutes or so. I refused to go out to the demonstration but walked upstairs for a good press conference and television interviews, where I explained all about it.

On to a small lunch party with the Plymouth County Borough, who are friendly to me because of course I was very friendly to them as Minister of Housing and gave them Plymstock, a vital extension of their boundaries.[1] There is a Conservative majority there now but I had an easy time. This evening I had dinner in my hotel in Plymouth with the Chairman and Secretary of the South-Western Region.[2] I talked to them about waiting lists and learnt a great deal about private practice.

Wednesday, September 17th

I went round with John Dunwoody, the local M.P. and a doctor himself.

[1] See Vol. I.
[2] R. J. English and W. H. White.

We did a good deal of visiting and I saw the good relationship between the county council, the M.O.H. and the doctors, and the limited number of people who work for the Health Service in Cornwall. I lunched at the big hospital in Truro and asked two or three consultants there about private practice. I found them vague. Cornwall is a funny place. The one who sat opposite me said he didn't have any private practice because there virtually wasn't any in Cornwall. 'Don't get the impression', he said, 'that there are vast numbers of Cornishmen who are willing to pay. They are too mean and they insist on getting treatment on the Health Service.' I am sure that is also true in Devonshire to some extent. We looked at the central assessment centre in Redruth and some local authority places and in the evening I met Kim Foster, the old boy of whom I saw a great deal when I was Minister of Housing and used to go down to Polzeath with the family. He gave a splendid dinner for me and we had an excellent discussion together before I got into the train feeling pretty pleased at surviving after my poisoning on Monday.

On the way back I went through my stuff and saw the minutes of the Cabinet which took place yesterday. I realized how rarely I miss a Cabinet meeting. I had sent David Ennals to represent me when the item on the abatement conversations came up and the Chancellor had obviously been right on top of him, trying to pretend that we had to have further consultations before I got my approval. David had done jolly well for me, though. In the public expenditure discussions Cabinet had broadly agreed to Management Committee's suggestions, so this slipped through very quietly. I think there was also a discussion on Ireland, but altogether I missed very little.

Thursday, September 18th

I crept in at 7.0 a.m. to find Anne waiting for me. She had come up to London for the memorial service for her cousin Arthur Haslett, who had died suddenly on the top of a mountain in the Lake District. At the office I was mystified to see that I was booked for 'Cabinet photograph, Transport House', because the Cabinet photograph is taken in the garden of No. 10 and we had it a few months ago. A garbled message from my Private Office said I was wanted with the Lord Chancellor and one or two others and I thought it must be some election thing.

I was desperately keen to get to the meeting of the Local Government Committee at 10.30 and here was the photograph at the same time, with the Prime Minister insisting on my presence. So I got there at 10.20. Being early was no help; there was the photographer in No. 3 Committee Room in Transport House, trying to set it up as a mock Cabinet room with a curved table, and I learnt that a special selection of people had been summoned by the P.M., some ten or twelve of us, for a photograph of us working with him. He would have liked it in the Cabinet room itself but that would have been too difficult to arrange. As Fred Peart and Roy Mason came in, it suddenly struck me that if Harold needed a Cabinet photograph taken now, he could only have certain members because of the forthcoming reshuffle. It came out that Harold wanted the photograph for the first number of the *Daily Mirror* colour supplement, which appears in a fortnight, and he had very secretly got together a group of Ministers without revealing it to the rest, so it was of some interest to see who was there. On the far side of the table was Tony Wedgwood Benn, next to him Barbara and Roy, and on our side of Harold there were Fred Peart, myself, Roy Mason and Gerald Gardiner, an extraordinary lot. People I knew to be in London who weren't included were Peter Shore and Judith Hart. Tony Greenwood was in America so it was open about him and we were ostentatiously told that Michael Stewart couldn't come.

There was a great deal of joking and when Harold came in I said, 'We have come to the conclusion that we are the ten to whom you are saying goodbye before your St Bartholomew's Day massacre, before you do a Macmillan on us.'[1] Harold looked very sheepish. He has great delight in playing about with reshuffles, and he didn't deny for one moment what it was all about. We had endless photographs taken, first one side, then the other, with Harold in the front. At one point we said, 'Turn round to us for a change,' because it was a horseshoe table and he was supposed to be in the middle but he had got inside the horseshoe and was being photographed first with our side and then with the other. He turned round suddenly and said, 'No, that is my wrong profile, I must only turn the other way.'

I rushed out to the Local Government Committee, chaired as usual by George Thomson. I was nearly three-quarters of an hour late and George said to me afterwards, 'We all thought we were going to get away with it. Everything was agreed until you came in and were difficult.' That is true. They had had first of all the Wheatley Report on Scotland,[2] and then the paper from the Secretary of State for Wales demanding a Bill to carry his local government reforms through in this session of this Parliament. The Wheatley paper is a very good report recommending a two-tier system, contradicting the one tier of Maud, but the Welsh paper, I reckon, proposes five tiers. It has the Secretary of State for Wales, the Welsh Council, Welsh counties and county boroughs, with, underneath these, U.D.C.s and R.D.C.s and then parishes. It is a ridiculous proposal, making concessions to everybody, and little Thomas was saying, 'I want the Parliamentary draftsmen to get on with it. We must get it through because I have promised it.'

This was one of my failures from the start. Jim Griffiths persuaded Cabinet that, instead of having a Royal Commission for England and Wales, we should have one for Scotland and one for England and the continuation of

[1] On July 13th, 1962, in Harold Macmillan's 'Night of the Long Knives', as it came to be called, the Prime Minister dismissed seven out of his twenty-one Cabinet colleagues, giving most of them only a few hours' notice.

[2] The Wheatley Committee published its report on local government reform in Scotland (Cmnd 4150) on September 25th. It recommended the replacement of 450 existing authorities by seven regional and 37 district authorities.

the 1967 consultations on Wales, and it ended in this disaster. At least I was able to insist this morning that nothing could be done without Cabinet consultations and that anyway we can't possibly agree to a Bill this session before the White Papers on England and Scotland have been considered, and probably published. I managed to keep that going and also to get an understanding that we needed a paper on the Wheatley Commission's proposals for a two-tier solution, which seem to me very superior to Maud.

After that I had lunch at Political and Economic Planning, where, in the old days before the war, when Max Nicholson was Secretary,[1] I did a tremendous lot of work and lunching. They used to be in Queen Anne's Gate, and are now in classy buildings in Belgravia. I found myself having an interesting chat. They have a new secretariat, nice, able people, and we discussed the future and what things we really wanted. Suddenly I had an idea and said, 'One of the things we don't know about is private practice. Could you do an analysis? We would pay you for it. Everything is shrouded in darkness because private practitioners don't like telling the Ministry things and we don't want to interfere. P.E.P. is the right institution to do it.'[2]

I dined with Clifford Jarrett, who wanted to discuss his future. On December 10th this year he will be sixty, with the right to retire on full pension. He is keen to do so and, as he said, he could then get another secondary job but if he waited until he was sixty-two or sixty-three it would be more difficult. I thought very hard and made it perfectly clear that he couldn't possibly get out and leave me with just Alan Marre and Miss Riddelsdell because on the Social Security side I need somebody to lean on. In the course of the evening we suddenly thought of Bruce Fraser, the man I refused to have when I was at Housing.[3] I found him impossible then but he had been having a difficult time of great personal unhappiness. He has now completely recovered and is wasted as Comptroller and Auditor-General. I have also learnt, since I have been at my new job, what a marvellous Permanent Secretary he was, how he founded the research and development side and had really been most vigorous and creative. I suddenly thought, 'Why shouldn't

[1] Max Nicholson, Secretary of the Office of Lord President of the Council 1945–52, a member of the Advisory Council on Scientific Policy 1948–64 and Director-General of the Nature Conservancy 1952–66, was Convenor of the Conservation Section of the International Biological Programme 1963–74. He was General Secretary of P.E.P. from March 1935 until 1940. On this occasion Crossman lunched with John Pinder, the former International Director of the Economist Intelligence Unit, who became Director of P.E.P. in 1964, and Richard Davies, who had worked with the British Institute of Management and the Industrial Welfare Society before joining P.E.P. in 1962.

[2] The study was published as *Opting out of the NHS: A Review of the Private Sector of Medical Care* (London: P.E.P., 1971).

[3] Sir Bruce Fraser (K.C.B. 1961) joined the Scottish Office in 1933 and transferred to the Treasury in 1936. He was Third Secretary 1956–60, Deputy Secretary at the Ministry of Aviation January–April 1960, Permanent Secretary at the Ministry of Health 1960–4, Joint Permanent Under-Secretary of State at the Department of Education and Science 1964–5, Permanent Secretary at the Ministry of Land and Natural Resources 1965–6 and Comptroller and Auditor-General 1966–71. See Vol. I.

he come back for his last four years with us?' Nobody could take offence and Alan Marre couldn't mind working under him. Otherwise I said I hoped Clifford would stay on, at least until I was finished. He said we mustn't rule out a Labour victory, almost as though he was outside the Ministry, and it was clear from our talk that he is pretty sympathetic to me. He is an old Admiralty man, but very complacent, and very much wanting to look after his own interests in his old age. Well, why shouldn't he feather his own nest as far as he can?

I went on to a party given by Julian Melchett and Sonia, his elegant wife. I spent a long time talking to the wife of the French Ambassador,[1] Madame de Courcel, a beautiful girl, much younger than Courcel, who sat with me and John Foster. We managed to spend forty-five minutes with her discussing Gaullism and why Britain should join the Common Market, with her making up to me and asking me to come to lunch. I spent the rest of the time with Mrs Annenberg, who is rather dull and just chatted to me about what it is like to be the American Ambassador's wife here in Britain. I managed to make it up at last with her husband for my disastrous rudeness on the occasion when he came to pay a call on me at the Commons and I kept him waiting outside my door for ten minutes like an old lobby boy.[2] He shook my hand and said, 'I'll never forget it.' That was my evening in this distinguished company.

Friday, September 19th

I had the last of my pensions consultations, this time with the C.B.I. They were helpful on the whole and then I managed to tidy up a lot of things before catching the 5.45 down to Prescote. This week we have had Sue Bardsley, my sister Bridget's daughter, and her husband Michael Nunn, who is a nice young publisher. She works in the children's department in Barnet and I was able to learn a great deal about the attitude of an active officer in the field. She doesn't really know about the Green Paper or all the things I have to do because at her level people seem to work together perfectly happily. She is concerned about practical things, like looking after the children, and doesn't have to fuss about who is local authority and who is government. She reminds me that at the field level things are working pretty well in a good borough like hers.

Sunday, September 21st

I shan't do lengthy reflections after the diffuseness of last week, but this has been one of those good weeks in politics, good in the sense that the position of the Labour Party has improved a great deal. Last Thursday we published the

[1] Baron Geoffrey de Courcel, Ambassador to London 1962–72 and Secretary-General of the Ministry of Foreign Affairs, France, since 1973.

[2] Walter Annenberg, the newspaper proprietor and publisher, was U.S. Ambassador to London 1969–74.

best trade figures we have ever had and the Gallup Poll on Wednesday showed the Tory lead had dropped to $8\frac{1}{2}$ per cent.[1] We always have this annual improvement when Parliament isn't sitting and it has been a decent summer, with at long last a sense that the economic situation is improving. The newspapers are now full of discussions about the possibility of Labour winning the next election, or at least giving the Tories a run for their money, and Heath's unpopularity and the Tories' failure to cash in on our failures have improved our own optimistic tendencies a great deal. Meanwhile, though the Northern Ireland crisis is black in one sense, it has got a great deal better, partly because we have hung on. The British Army is gradually persuading people to take the barricades down, the take-over has been absorbed, and we have done all this without the Chichester-Clark Government either breaking with us or being broken by their own supporters. On the whole, despite Callaghan's pessimism, one can say that what has actually been happening out there has not been too bad.

Monday, September 22nd

Janet Newman has gone to Ibiza for a fortnight's holiday. I have had no real personal assistant, so I realize how invaluable Janet has been. But it also means I haven't got the records of the week so I can't remember at all what I did on Monday morning. Oh, I know, I had the Life Offices in to see me and we had a long discussion.

Early in the evening I was driven down to Wessex for the beginning of my two-day tour. I spent the night at Southampton in order to meet Kushlick,[2] a South African doctor who has been doing a study of sub-normality in the Wessex region, getting a register together to assess the extent of the problem. He had slides and demonstrated his figures and statistics. It was exciting though very characteristically the Department told me that I could read his report but there was nothing to be gained from meeting him. I found him one of the best people I have met and I shall telephone him tomorrow morning and ask him to come to a conference we are having on the study by the 'main stream' working party. Forty or fifty people will be there, a mixture of academics and people who work in sub-normal hospitals.

There we were, drinking red wine with Dr Revans, a tall, splendid, ex-Army type, tough and difficult. He has turned down the job of Director of the Advisory Service and I wonder why. I think it is partly that he really feels Wessex can't do without him, and he is right. It is the smallest region, he is the

[1] There was a £28 million surplus in the visible trade balance for September and seasonally adjusted figures showed an overall surplus of £214 million for the third quarter of 1969, compared with a £72 million surplus (revised figures) for the second quarter.

[2] Dr Albert Kushlick, a South African who emigrated to England in 1956, was Assistant Lecturer and then Lecturer in the Department of Social and Preventive Medicine, University of Manchester 1960–3 and Director of Research into Subnormality at the Wessex R.H.B. 1963–71. Since 1971 he has been Director of the Health Care Evaluation Research Team at the Wessex Regional Health Authority. He is a member of the External Scientific Staff of the Medical Research Council.

Chairman of the SAMOS, a tremendous, outstanding driving force in the service, and we have already taken him half-time from Wessex just when they are building a new medical school and in the last four years of his career. It's difficult, we can't really take him altogether, and I have decided that I will go back to the Department to see if I can get Dr Baker.

Tuesday, September 23rd

My first day was at Southampton. Hampshire is a county of lush parkland and here at Tatchby was a beautiful magnificent park with great playing fields where you could have a county cricket match and, because the Chairman of the Hospital Management Committee, an ordinary G.P., is a keen cricketer and because the dim medical superintendent you always find is a keen hockey player, sport is one of their major means of therapy. It's fantastic how people create a hospital in their own image and here in this lovely place I saw what a splendid thing sport could be for the sub-normal. There was a marvellous gym for physical training and a rumpus room where the difficult children could knock about. The school had wonderful equipment, no staff shortage whatsoever, but the staff had a military or a naval look to them, or perhaps even the warden of a hospital look. I went into a very nice new ward with sixty beds in it. 'Oh, yes,' the man said to me, 'we can manage sixty beds.' I said, 'Wouldn't you like to have thirty, with everyone giving all their time to nursing?' 'No,' he said, 'I think sixty is all right,' and I saw him eyeing the blankets. His military test of the cleanness of the ward was whether the blankets were folded in the right way and there was one of those poor sub-normal chaps measuring the sides of the beds to get the space between them accurate. It was just like a military kit inspection, a reactionary hospital being run in an old-fashioned, totally disciplined way. Still, it was genuine and I certainly learnt something good from it.

I had the usual interviews and this again was interesting. I.T.V. were asking me about abuse because the *Spectator* has published a very sensational article attacking the Supplementary Benefits Commission for tolerating too much abuse and before I left we had a serious discussion about this in the office. David is very anxious to talk about this in public but I am reluctant until we have something to talk about. We have agreed that we would hope that the Supplementary Benefits Commission would ask for an enlargement of their executive staff so they could do their job and their visiting properly. I gave a pretty interesting interview to I.T.V., saying that I don't want a huge army of snoopers but more trained people doing the job. If the initial investigations aren't properly carried out, you will get abuse. I.T.V. were prepared to extract news and information but then I saw the B.B.C., whose young men just wanted to go on and on about some scandal about a child in a Wiltshire hospital. This is very characteristic. The B.B.C. is not independent, but an upright, staid institution that has to demonstrate its independence by being bloody-minded and asking awkward questions.

After lunch at Southampton town hall with the Mayor,[1] I continued the tour with a lovely drive through the New Forest to Hurn, where I looked at a social security reception centre, a vestige of the old days of tramps and public assistance. Then we went on to the social security offices in Bournemouth for an extremely interesting talk with an alert, dapper young man, whose previous post turned out to have been head of the London investigation office. He wanted more investigators and thought we should clean up the question of abuse.

You can see why the *Spectator* didn't find it difficult to get an article on this. There is a great deal of feeling that Peggy Herbison's entitlement campaign has made us soft and floppy and also that, although it brought vastly more people into the scheme, we haven't increased the staff sufficiently to deal with them. After that I went to a lovely hotel and up to my magnificent suite on the eighth floor. There I was, in a splendid sitting room with windows on both sides, one looking out to Studland where we once took the children for a summer holiday, the other facing the Needles, brilliant in the sun, and I thought, 'My God, the bay of Naples.' The bay here with the Needles on the one side and the sun on the other is a great deal nobler than anything I saw in Naples. I took my clothes off and after a quick bath I sat there in my dressing gown just looking at this lovely sight. Then I went downstairs, for a dinner to talk about the Green Paper and the sort of discussion I wanted to take place.

Wednesday, September 24th

We started by driving to Weymouth to see the local hospital. It was the usual routine but the local authority school for handicapped children really stood out. They were giving these children some kind of intellectual discipline and bringing them out. It was a school with artistic vision, where in each room they were doing something creative. On I went to talk to a little group of M.P.s in Weymouth and then down to the front, behind that magnificent statue of George III, to the Gloucester Hotel. I sat opposite their elegant young County Clerk, who put me through it again on the subject of local authority control of the Health Service.

After lunch we drove across to Dorchester to a slap-up psychiatric hospital, a real hospital where the doctors cared about doctoring, the consultants thought they could do something with their patients, a place where there was a sense of medical hope and medical technique, with nurses responding to good, vigorous doctors and a good, vigorous Chairman of the H.M.C. I got into the car to drive straight home to Anne. I got back in under three hours, right into Westminster, for a quiet dinner together before Cabinet tomorrow.

Thursday, September 25th

A tremendously cheerful atmosphere at Cabinet, transformed, and in the

[1] Mrs H. K. Johnson.

course of the general discussion people were soon talking about the new situation. Actually there was a run on the pound this week because of the imminent German elections and a scare about the revaluation of the Deutsche Mark,[1] but nevertheless people are feeling confident again. In politics emotions swing in the most extraordinary way. All that talk around the Cabinet table – if Roy had been there I am sure he would have discouraged it. It reminded me of that pre-devaluation autumn when Callaghan and Harold made such tremendously optimistic speeches at Conference and when I went into Harold's room and he said 'The smell of success is in the air.' That was in the weeks when the pound was draining away and we were going to devalue with nothing left in the till, so I am pretty canny about these changes in mood and the way people deceive themselves and I didn't take the new atmosphere too seriously. It is true, though, that things are better and that the balance of payments is generally good this year, or was. It is also true that the pound could be upset in a few days' time if there should be deadlock in the German election results.

We started with a discussion of the Party Conference, how it was going to be handled and what was to be done about the new policy document which was being launched,[2] and then we turned to the spill-over, the fortnight of this parliamentary session before the Queen's speech and the new session. We discussed the order of items and how to get this confounded Seats Bill, which the Lords refuse to accept. Callaghan also wants to have an Irish debate on the first day and get that over, so all this was argued out at some length, deeply influenced by the prospect of five key by-elections at the end of October.[3] Everybody was concerned that nothing should happen during the next five weeks because if the by-elections go badly we will be right back in the soup. I am uneasily aware that I shall be announcing my abatement formula, which may produce a howl of dismay, not only from NALGO but also from the other unions. I mentioned that this might come on in the spill-over and it was suggested that we should postpone it until the Queen's Speech. Then we discussed the death penalty, because, under the present Act, sometime or other we either have to stop the death penalty altogether by an Order in Council or bring it back when the Act lapses. Do we want to force

[1] The West German Federal elections were held on September 28th and for the first time since the Federal Republic was founded the C.D.U. were pushed into opposition, and an S.P.D./F.D.P. coalition was quickly formed. The question of the parity of the Mark had been one of great difficulty for the previous 'big coalition' Government but the new Government decided on October 24th to revalue at midnight on October 26/27th. The Mark was revalued upwards by 9·3 per cent from the point of view of German exports and 8·5 for imports.

[2] The N.E.C. document, *Agenda for a Generation.*

[3] On October 30th by-elections were to be held in five Labour seats: at Glasgow Gorbals, caused by the death of Alice Cullen on May 31st; at Lincoln North, caused by the death of Gerry Reynolds on June 7th; at Paddington North, where Ben Parkin had died on June 3rd; at Newcastle-under-Lyme, Stephen Swingler's constituency; and at Swindon, where Francis Noel-Baker had resigned.

abolition through this autumn or should it be postponed until after the by-elections?

At this point the Foreign Secretary gave his usual dry, boring report, and mentioned the Common Market. Barbara, Fred Peart and I were saying, 'For heaven's sake, why do we assume that negotiations should be resumed as soon as possible, why assume that we want another snub when there is really no conceivable chance of our getting in?' Michael Stewart, who has called back into the Foreign Office Con O'Neill, the arch-evangelist of European entry, brushed my point aside. Denis Healey also said, 'No. The other members of the Six will be powerful enough to stop the French.' I didn't know if it was right or not but I did raise the issue and succeeded in having an hour's discussion, insisting that what mattered was that we shouldn't be seen to have no alternative. A number of other people put this, Fred Peart and Barbara among them, and Harold was good about the posture we should adopt and the tone we should use. The P.M.'s point is that we are now in a much stronger economic position and the balance of payments strong enough for us to see an alternative outside the Common Market, as, after all, we have for the last two years been going it alone with conspicuous success. Therefore, says Harold, we can stiffen our position, and this is going to be the kind of line he will take at Conference. I wanted to make sure that the Cabinet discussion predetermined the attitude of the Government before Conference next week, so that whatever George Brown might say in introducing the subject, Harold will be tied tightly in his reply. It was a success and by the end of our discussion it was evident that whatever Michael Stewart says at the meeting organized by Geoffrey de Freitas of the pro-Common Marketeers,[1] when the P.M. comes to make the declaration in the hall, he will be careful to make it clear that we shan't go in on any terms and that Cabinet is going to review the situation since our last effort, examine the economic cost of entry and publish the results. Harold committed himself to all this.

You may think these things are unimportant but they are not: this is where Cabinet matters. Though such a discussion may not say anything particular, if one gets it at the right time it does give a Cabinet directive of which a Prime Minister must take scrupulous account. Once it is noted and put down it is important. Even though in this case the civil servants weakened it in the summary and didn't give it quite the strength I would have liked, I knew that Harold had noted it. I also knew this because I had sent him a minute suggesting this line and warning him of the strength of people's feelings.

I saw no sign whatever of any prospect of Michael Stewart's retiring from the Foreign Office and being replaced by Denis Healey. There has been a lot of talk about this but the rumours are wishful thinking. It looks as though

[1] Sir Geoffrey de Freitas (KCMG 1961), Labour M.P. for Central Nottingham 1945–50, for Lincoln 1950–61 and for Kettering since 1964. He has been Vice-President of the European Parliament since 1975 and was Chairman of the Labour Committee for Europe 1965–72.

Harold is as tied to Michael Stewart as he is to me and, although some people would like to see me out and Barbara in my place, and the Superannuation Bill dropped, it is not practical politics for Harold. I think Michael is fixed in the Foreign Office, I am pretty well fixed in Social Services, and Fred Peart and Barbara seem to have fixed themselves in their present jobs. The only move Michael could make, in order to let Denis into the F.O., would be to take over as Leader of the House, but if Harold were about to do this it would have been extraordinarily dishonest of him to have behaved as he did in Cabinet this morning.

Then we came to the main item of the agenda, which was Barbara's. Her main proposal was for a Bill to establish an Industrial Commission, which would wrap up into a single organization the present Prices and Incomes Board and the Monopolies Commission, a political notion which as far as I could see had been cooked up between her and Harold. She had already tried this out at the Prices and Incomes Committee and got nowhere at all, because the sponsoring Ministers, Wedgy Benn, Roy Mason and Dick Marsh, didn't see any point in the change. She wanted to give the prices and incomes policy a new direction and interest and this was a non-balanced policy, with all the emphasis on prices and none on wages. Although Roy's promise in the budget means that she has to pass the Order in Council renewing Part II, she admitted that this would be purely symbolic. We would have no effective Government powers there and as it is clear that the prices and incomes policy is in fact in ruins, here was an Industrial Commission to put in its place.

She didn't have much luck in Cabinet either. She even got Jack Diamond, who was representing Roy, saying that for once he couldn't follow her arguments because they seemed to be fuzzy. There was outright opposition from people like Dick Marsh and Roy Mason and more tactful opposition from Wedgy Benn and me. We both said we liked the idea of the Commission but it must not be the main instrument of Government intervention and we mustn't just invent new machinery for the sake of it. The real attack was launched by Tony Crosland, who started by saying, 'I don't often say this but I have thought about this possibly more than any other member of the Cabinet. I have thought about it for a full twelve months and I just don't think Barbara's solution is right. She might have to have fusions but she should have two organizations, one dealing with the efficiency of industry in the broad sense and the other dealing with salaries and prices. She shouldn't try to roll these up into one.' He spoke with fervour. Harold was obviously trying to save something from the rocks though he couldn't possibly say Cabinet agreed to it. He and Barbara were trying to force this through, not like the Industrial Relations Bill by evading the Cabinet, but by pleading with us to let them have a Bill in principle and then consider the details. By and large, the P.M. tried to sum up in favour of the Bill in principle, and as we went out of the room Dick Marsh said to me, 'Mark my words, he is going to get that Bill through.' I don't think this can be done and I shall have to raise it and possibly write a paper opposing Barbara. I can see the beginning of a row.

It's interesting how Harold and Barbara work together. Their minds are very similar and they both think in terms of tactical solutions to get themselves out of difficulties. These are ambitious, but half thought-out, and this was a significant and characteristic joint Wilson–Castle gambit. Everybody there knew it and what was sad was that people with less brains than Barbara would just have gone to Harold and said, 'After my Bill has been jettisoned I can't stay in this job. Why don't you move me somewhere else?' Barbara will fight on and as far as I can see she is fighting with a new line on equal pay on one side and an Industrial Commission Bill on the other, which she hopes will establish her forward-looking reputation as a person who makes historic changes.

I rushed back to 70 Whitehall for lunch and over a plate of cold meat Brian and I redrafted the Herbert Morrison Memorial Lecture on how to pay for the social services. It has gone the round of all the Departments and it is interesting to see how little the text has been changed by the Treasury, or the Ministries of Education and Housing, all having their go. Then I saw Godber, whom I had suddenly called over because I had to deal with the crisis of the Director of the Advisory Service. Godber said, 'Dr Baker is really valuable in the Department and I can't spare him for the Advisory Service.' We got into deadlock and then we thought that perhaps we could get a possible third candidate and I said, 'You have to find me an alternative, my dear C.M.O.' I shall have to put the heat on Godber but at least he has given me leave to see Baker next week and to try to persuade him.

I had to get back to No. 10 for a meeting of O.P.D. and I found them discussing the question of whether Wasp helicopters should be exported to South Africa. We were back in the terrible row we had about arms sales to South Africa,[1] with the formation all over again of the group who wanted to sell arms and the group who didn't. Harold didn't want to sell arms. Fortunately I came in twenty-five minutes late and too late to vote. They were tied 50/50 and the Wasps will go to Cabinet for discussion. Finally we had a fascinating item from Fred Mulley, who is always in trouble with the Minister of Defence. Fred is the Minister for Disarmament and he brought up a fantastic proposal for banning C.S. gas. This gas is used for suppressing civil disturbances but it is banned as a weapon of war. Fred had discovered that in 1930 Hugh Dalton had made a speech on behalf of Arthur Henderson,[2] saying that C.S. gas

[1] See Vol. II.

[2] Arthur Henderson was Labour M.P. for Barnard Castle 1903–18, for Widnes 1919–22, for Newcastle East 1923, for Burnley 1924–31 and for Clay Cross 1933–5. He was Secretary of the Labour Party 1911–34, its Treasurer 1930–5, Leader of the Labour Party in the Commons 1908–10 and 1914–17. He was a member of the War Cabinet from 1916 until he resigned in 1917. He returned to Government as Home Secretary in 1924 and was Foreign Secretary 1929–31 and Leader of the Labour Opposition 1931–2. He died in 1935.

should be banned in war, and Fred said we couldn't go back on this because Philip Noel-Baker would remember and denounce us.[1] When the issue comes up at the U.N. we must therefore lead the way and say that whatever anybody else does we will ban it voluntarily. Fred wanted us to do this to sustain the position of the Labour Government of 1930, a strange argument that Healey just lambasted as unnecessary nonsense. We should try to avoid a declaration because, after all, this gas could be useful to us and the Americans will certainly refuse to ban it because they use it in Vietnam, where they find it is a much more humane way of clearing people out than blowing them up or shooting them. Mulley said there was a danger of escalation, and if you once use this kind of gas you might use other kinds and so move into higher and worse biological warfare. This is where I am sometimes useful and I was able to say, 'Look at Ulster. We have got troops out there in great difficulty and they have to use this gas to suppress civil disturbance. Are you really saying that we should announce in the U.N. that we are not prepared ever to see it used in war? What will we say when people ask why we are using it in Ulster? Are we to say this is peace not war? Surely, if we have just denounced it they will say this is hypocrisy?' So the Committee here rejected the proposal.

I was already half an hour late and had to rush back to Elephant and Castle. Bea Serota is just back from her holiday in Israel, but with the temperature and cold which you often get afterwards, so I had to take the chair at PEP. I was able to start them on the discussion of the membership and organization of the conference and we tied it all up just in time for me to catch the 6 o'clock train to Newcastle.

Friday, September 26th

When Ministers of Housing have a big planning decision to take they are perfectly used to going out studying the thing on the spot, although one has to be careful about not having new evidence. At Housing I did a great deal of this up and down the country but I was the first Minister, I think I am correct in saying, to do it at Health. Newcastle had asked me to intervene in a three- or four-year-old dispute between the R.H.B. and the Board of Governors of the hospital on one side and the University Vice-Chancellor and the Hospital Management Committee on the other.[2] The R.H.B. were in favour of a new hospital being built in two parts, a 2,000-bed complex in the present Royal Victoria Hospital on the university site and a 1,000-bed complex two and a half miles away at Freeman Road. The other protagonists were saying this was lunatic since they had discovered a site adjacent to the Royal Victoria

[1] Labour M.P. for Coventry 1929–31, for Derby 1936–50 and for Derby South 1950–70. The posts he held included those of Secretary of State for Air 1946–7, Secretary of State for Commonwealth Relations 1947–50 and Minister of Fuel and Power 1950–1. He was Henderson's P.P.S. 1929–31. He won the Nobel Peace Prize in 1959. He became a life peer in 1977.

[2] See above, p. 589.

site on a piece of open town land, next door to the new hostels of the university, and they proposed scrapping the plan for Freeman Road and putting the 1,000-bed hospital next to the present one, with just a road tunnel between them. It was an enormously attractive vision but the R.H.B. and the Board of Governors had said they couldn't make such a change at the last moment. They had been working on this for five or six years and the Freeman Road plans were completed. The row had got so fierce that finally Henry Miller, the Vice-Chancellor, Dan Smith and the City Council had all written to ask me to intervene. This was unusual and I had been strongly advised not to interfere by the officials but I had replied that of course I would go up, spend a day listening to all sides and adjudicate.

Last night I travelled up by train with David Somerville from the hospital section, a funny little architect called Nicholson, my John Cashman and Henry Yellowlees.[1] I had spent the first hour before dinner reading the brief, which was just a series of arguments for the Regional Hospital Board's case. I had said I would come up as an impartial investigator and think things out for myself, so I had to say to my officials, 'You have got to go up in a very different state of mind. You must not be committed; you are experts. This brief must not be left about because if it seems that I have been briefed with the R.H.B. line, all the suspicions about the Department will be confirmed.' We arrived at 10.0 p.m. and were taken to the Station Hotel, where I found myself in an appallingly noisy little room, on the second floor, which wasn't even large enough for my officials to come in to check things over.

It was a cloudy, wet morning, most of which I spent going round the sites. I had insisted that our Ministry architect should wake up the university architect last night. He had apparently made a feasibility study of the new central site for Henry Miller. A charming young man turned up, got together with my architect and we walked all over the ground. I then went to the Royal Victoria and saw their site and to the General Hospital. What seemed crazy to me was that all these plans wanted to scrap the General Hospital, a very dreary place littered over a twenty-three-acre site, where four or five first-rate new buildings and an ultra-modern Institute of Urology had been added to an 1840 public assistance institution. The long-term proposal was to get rid of this site and everything on it and concentrate everything in the two new hospitals, the Royal Victoria complex and Freeman Road. This sounded the most extraordinary solution and I had no doubt that the doctors and the staff of the General Hospital disliked the feeling that they were going to be run down. It was true that they were angry but they admitted straightaway that everything on their site would have to go in the long run. It wasn't that, though, that really mattered to them but the fact that it seemed absurd that if their excellent buildings were to go it was for the sake of building a hospital two and a half miles away, with some of their own specialities. Now

[1] David Somerville has been an Assistant Under-Secretary of State at the D.H.S.S. since 1968.

Richardson,[1] the leading doctor, who was on Henry Miller's side, was himself a cardio-thoracic surgeon and it was the putting of the cardio-thoracic unit on the Freeman Road site which had really made him blow his top. He said that this unit must be on the central site because it had to link up with all sorts of other expertise and couldn't be separated off and put in a district hospital site a mile away. So it was clear that if he could move the cardio-thoracic unit to the centre it would eliminate some of his ferocity.

The only people I hadn't seen were the City Council and the new Council Leader. Why was it that the city had suddenly come round? They had taken no active view, but their Planning Committee, Arthur Grey, the leader of the Tory Group, and his deputy, the Town Clerk and the chief planner were all convinced supporters of the central site. I never quite got to the bottom of this. I think they wanted the Freeman Road land for housing and that their planner was convinced that the university was the right place, and they were also friends of Richardson, so they had come in with a bang on the Vice-Chancellor's side.

So I then saw people separately, for a total of forty minutes' cross-examination, making each of them tell his story. The R.H.B., the Board of Governors, the City Council and then Henry Miller and his group, and in the middle I gave a lunch party at a beautiful new hotel, where I saw the M.P.s, one Tory and one Labour,[2] and Dan Smith and we had a free discussion there as well.

Then I had the hearing, sitting at a table at the end with these people grouped at tables facing me. The Department had wanted to have it round a great big table, but I said no, it was not a round-table discussion but an adjudication. During the morning I had fortunately told Somerville and Yellowlees to prepare a list of all the points that were agreed by all parties and then a list of the items in dispute, in the order in which I was to cross-examine them. They prepared an admirable paper and I was able to handle the meeting in just this way. I started by reading aloud the six points on which I found agreement. There were to be only two hospitals, either one in the centre and one in Freeman Road, or both in the centre, that was the alternative. Yes, there was agreement on that. It was agreed that the 2,000-bed complex was the minimum required for the university. I started off with these points and said, 'Please, I don't want anybody to say anything unless they disagree.'

When I had read the six points I said, 'Well, there's a basis for agreement,' and then boiled and boiled the thing down and found that everybody agreed that if we could start afresh we would at least try the new site. If there was mining subsidence underneath it wouldn't do but if it were found to be suit-

[1] G. O. Richardson, a consultant surgeon at the General Hospital.

[2] Sir Robert Elliott (Kt 1974), Conservative M.P. for Newcastle-upon-Tyne North since March 1957, and Robert Brown, Labour M.P. for Newcastle-upon-Tyne West since 1966. (Edward Short, the Minister of Education, represented Newcastle-upon-Tyne Central and Geoffrey Rhodes, Crossman's former P.P.S., Newcastle-upon-Tyne East.)

able and the Freemen would provide it for the city, although that would require a Private Member's Bill and mean a year's delay, it would be the better place. The only issue was whether it would be so much better that it would be worth the delay. Could one estimate that? The R.H.B. and the planners said it would take seven years to replan. There was a great deal of incredulity and I said, 'Let's have that settled by an independent arbitrator.' I saw that my own people, who were committed to the R.H.B., were terrified by my proposal for an independent arbitrator, but I wasn't afraid because I knew that the estimate couldn't be less than three years and that was too long to wait. I knew that Freeman Road was in fact the site and by the end I think they all did too.

I then turned to the cardio-thoracic unit and said, 'Here's something. I can't see the case for having that on Freeman Road. Couldn't you rethink the university site and have it there?' So they are going to see if they can fit it in. All this took from 9.30 in the morning till 6.0 at night and I knew that I had achieved something of a triumph. One of them said, 'It was worth coming up here just to be taken for a ride by that Secretary of State.'

I then gave them a tremendous dinner. They were all tottering to their feet and the Conservative Leader of the Council kept on saying, 'I can say this, I've never heard anything like it. Whatever else the Secretary of State recommends, I shall give him my support.' I think they all knew what I was going to recommend, that they should continue with the Freeman Road plan and that the cardio-thoracic unit should be moved, which would placate Dr Richardson of the General Hospital. At 10.43 I got on to the train, where I fell sound asleep until I got out on Saturday morning and came down here. Newcastle really was a great day, tremendous, invigorating, exciting, just the kind of thing I can do. I have shown them that a Minister does not just sit in London and sign papers, he comes to the spot and sees for himself. I think, too, that our staff have seen the appalling image they have, because everybody agreed when we discussed delay that three months in every year could be attributed to the Department's asking questions and holding things up. The officials have learnt a great deal and I think they were impressed by me and by what the Minister can do by making a personal impact.

Saturday, September 27th

I got to Prescote by the first train and found five boxes waiting, which I began to plough through until Joseph and Celia Gimpel came over for lunch in their little white car.[1] This afternoon Anne started house-hunting with them round the North Oxfordshire villages while I settled down to complete my work. I then went over to the island for two hours' hard digging, to try to let some grass grow through. I have decided to grow lilies of the valley by the river, with bluebells and primulas, not much else, except possibly some

[1] London friends of the Crossmans.

irises in a bit of sun down by the water. Anne wants me to work in the garden with her but I somehow have my island on my own and it is the place where I like to go away and sweat it out before coming back and plunging into the bath. There are ground frosts at night now and the bath costs quite a lot to heat up but I like my delicious bathe.

In the evening Harry and Mary Judge came over, Harry in wonderful form, young, vigorous and alert, and we had a really pleasant time. All this is my own normal weekend while Conference is meeting down at Brighton. But not me. This is the third year I have not been there and it is a jolly good thing, in view of the unpopularity and the fuss about N.H.S. charges last July. Ever since I resigned from the Executive I have felt I didn't want to return to Conference and hang around, a senior Minister with nothing to do, not allowed to speak. It's true that if I pushed hard, I suppose, I might have got myself asked to speak on any other year but this but this time I should be an embarrassment on the platform and I am best away, safe at Prescote.

Sunday, September 28th

We have had a wonderful weekend and the weather is warmer with a west wind streaming in. Today, on a brilliant, chilly September morning, I did my thirty-six lengths and then had a Sunday quietly at work while Anne got ready for another lunch party with Charles and Mary Woodhouse, my sister from Oxford. It is marvellous being away from Conference. I remember how in the old days one turned up on the Thursday and on Friday the Executive held its normal meeting. Then on Saturday one went to the meetings where they were working out the, what were they called, the combined resolutions for the debates.[1] Sunday was for ploughing through the resolutions, discussing them in Conference and having the excitement with the press. I used to be absorbed by it, of course, but frightened, scared about the N.E.C. elections, and really I hated it. I felt strangely apart this morning because I had to ring up Harold, who wanted to insert a passage in his speech about handicapped children and had asked for a draft. I rang through to No. 10 and got a direct line to Brighton. I chatted with him about the speech and asked him how Conference was going. He said there had been a row with George Brown attacking him in the meeting. George was out of control and Harold, I am sure, was glad he hasn't got him back in the Cabinet. Harold seems confident and quiet and, of course, entirely absorbed in it all. Last year he insisted I should go down but this year he hasn't. He expects me to go but I shan't. I have filled my life with visits to Leeds on Tuesday and Sheffield on Wednesday and I have a two-day conference on sub-normality next Friday and Saturday. I think I have probably done this deliberately, to make it clear to myself that I really don't mind not being there. In a way I don't, as I have said, and there is something deeper to this than my feeling that I would cause great embarrassment down there. The

[1] It was called 'compositing'.

decision not to stand again for the Executive was a decision to withdraw, whether I liked it or not, a decision which people like Barbara couldn't conceivably make because they are 100 per cent politicians. By not being on the Executive, not attending their monthly meetings or Conference, I remain a senior Minister who is known to be able but elderly and not in the leadership stakes. I have accepted this and it is deeply connected with my alternative life as a writer, and the way I have set myself to do this diary to make my reflections on being a Minister part of my life as a Minister. This is something which is unusual and I don't think it has been done for a very long time.

Curiously enough, there came this week a minor sensation when Jeremy Bray announced his resignation from the Government because Harold refused to allow him to publish his book on decision-taking.[1] He came to ask for my sympathy months ago and I had said, 'Don't be a damned fool, Jeremy. Of course you can't publish a book on how Government works while you are in Government. You have either got to be in or get out and write.' How on earth did this young Methodist lay preacher from Middlesbrough, an I.C.I. computer man, ever have time to write this book? He has not been a success as a Minister and in every way he has been awkward, cussed and very conceited, and has shown no administrative drive or capacity. The fact that he has written this formidable 100,000-word book full of technical discussion on the improvement of planning and decision-taking is proof that he wasn't much good at taking decisions. The book is a substitute for action. At least I haven't done that. Nobody says I am not vigorous and dynamic in my Department.

But do I really want to get out and write my book? Various people asked me this once or twice last week. What are my real intentions? If we lose the next election it is simple. I can retire. I shall stand for Coventry East, I shall be elected and if Labour lose I shall offer my resignation, get a life peerage and start my book. That is clear in my mind. But if we win? Shall I really then ask Harold to retire me from the Cabinet or will he retire me anyway? I must say I hope that won't happen. I know now that if we win again I shall want to go on with the job because, looking back, I really have learned how to be a departmental Minister and a Cabinet Minister and how to blend the two. Inside the Department I am doing it enormously better now. On the other hand, in these last five years I have got a great deal older physically. I am sixty-one and I feel sixty-one, in a way that I certainly didn't feel sixty. This is why I have become worried about my leg in the last few weeks. I am trying to reshape my life and say, 'Right, no spirits, ruthless dieting'. I have tried to keep this up through all these dinners and lunches I must have on my tours and I am succeeding. We are having a new appliance designed

[1] Jeremy Bray, Labour M.P. for Middlesbrough West 1962–70 and for Motherwell and Wishaw since October 1974, was Parliamentary Secretary, the Minister of Power 1966–7 and Joint Parliamentary Secretary at MinTech. 1967–9. His book was called *Decision in Government* (London: Gollancz, 1970).

at King's College, an aluminium stand I can carry round with me to the office and the Cabinet room so that I can keep my leg up. I am feeling infinitely better than I was and all this has made me aware of how I revel in this life of ministerial decisions, an opportunity that came right at the end of my career, when I never thought it would.

Monday, September 29th

First I had an amusing little meeting with Des Wilson, the chap who runs Shelter, the organization for homeless people. He has recently published a very annoying pamphlet saying that we define homelessness in the heartless sense of simply covering the people who are technically living in Part III accommodation because they have been thrown out of their homes. He says that the really homeless are people who live in filthy slums and so these should be counted in. Kenneth Robinson said rather pedantically that this was a misuse of terms and I had little sympathy with him because I knew we shouldn't gain from it. So I got Des Wilson today and said, 'Look, I will take your definition but in that case you should look after my 8,000 children in sub-normal hospitals. They are homeless in your sense of the word.'

After Des I had three Birmingham people to see me about a terrible row caused by the Labour members of the R.H.B. taking confidential reports to the press even before they had been put to the Board. I had said the simplest thing was to have decent standing orders under which people had to obey the rules but then I thought I had better see these ladies and warn them. Before I could do so the storm had broken because poor Lewis, the Chairman, had written his new standing orders and plunked them down on the table, so that the Board simply appeared to be trying to suppress information. I had to have a quiet talk with the women and ask them to be sensible. They said, 'It's an impossible situation,' so I think I shall now have to go and investigate in Birmingham as I did in Newcastle.

We had the Bessies, Mike and Cornelia, down here this evening. I still think it's a terrible thing for Mike to leave Connie and take on this tough, professional hostess. It was a beautiful evening again but they wouldn't bathe because it was too cold for them. However we had the usual good dinner before they go back to London tomorrow.

Tuesday, September 30th–Wednesday, October 1st

I had Peter Smithson down here last night. He is a marvellous fellow, absolutely devoted. He buys everything for me, goes everywhere, he will mend our house for us, he is the biggest handyman in the world as well as being the biggest butler-footman. He is everything to me. This morning he drove me up to Leeds in an hour and fifty minutes, averaging 100 m.p.h. on the motorway. I am not going to spend a lot of time on the two days in Leeds and Sheffield. They were nicely balanced. Once again I was seeing acute hospitals, sub-normal hospitals and psychiatric hospitals, and I had my fair share of local authority health and welfare services and social security offices, where I discussed abuse and how to handle it with the men on the spot. I had two splendid dinners, one at Harrogate where the R.H.B. offices are, and one at the Towers Hospital at Leicester. On Wednesday night we drove back in an hour and a half from Leicester to London, again an average of 100 m.p.h.

Meanwhile, at Conference Harold had been back at the peak of his form, brilliant, gay, on top and overpowering Heath. On Tuesday he made a sensational speech in which he absolutely dominated Conference.[1] The only mess occurred when Barbara spoke on behalf of the Executive and laid down a Ministry policy in contradiction to Executive policy. I suspect she wasn't wholly to blame but her mistake rumbled all the way through the Conference. When I got back this evening I decided I couldn't hold out any more. There was too much talk and too many rumours about my absence and I didn't want a lot of stuff in the Sunday papers. Peter Brown had invited me to dine at the Caprice with him tomorrow night and I begged him to let us go down to Brighton together instead.

Thursday, October 2nd

This morning I saw three major delegations, the Life Offices, the nationalized industries and the C.B.I., all on the pensions scheme, to wring the last drop of interest out of abatement. We shall have a bleeding row because the Department is going to say that the terms should be 1:1·3 and they are going to say 1:1·5, which is a fairly big difference. They will then exploit this politically in a basic attack on the scheme and on the Government for letting them down. But we have gone through every conceivable detail and I think our logical position is impregnable. Then I had the B.M.A. to see me about Barbara's Industrial Commission, at least, this was the ostensible reason. They were actually coming as the result of the Statement in July,[2] that there was going to be a new Government look at the Prices and Incomes Board, with a view to giving it a more central role in the whole prices and incomes policy. This had alerted the doctors and they had come in full force, anxious about their sacred Kindersley Commission and how it must not be defiled. This has produced a major crisis for me because in fact Barbara is proposing that her Industrial Commission should mop up Plowden and Kindersley and bring everybody under one organization. If she does introduce this Bill all my collaboration with the doctors will be destroyed.

After that Peter Brown and I took the train to Brighton. He is a funny man, you know, with his dyed hair, but he is the best information officer there is and on the fifth floor at Alexander Fleming House he is building up a pretty good organization. He is devoted to me and works extremely hard and when I had said to him, 'Come down,' he obliged. I found that he had never

[1] See *Wilson*, pp. 703–7.
[2] See pp. 560., 562–3 and n, 565–6.

been to a Labour Party Conference in his life because departmental information officers mustn't.[1] The first person we found when we got into the train was Tony Greenwood, who said, 'What are you doing here? You will be in trouble for coming.' When we arrived we took a taxi to the Grand Hotel and went into the bar, where we met the Chief Whip. 'Where have you been?' he asked, and we had a drink and a chat. Then we met Paul and Marigold Johnson and everybody was saying, 'Why haven't you been here? Strange rumours have been going around.' I suddenly discovered that the rumours are that I am somehow going to be dropped from the Cabinet at the end of the week. Harold had let it out quite plainly that there would be a reshuffle, so there was all this talk. I wondered what to do because, a few minutes later, Kenneth Harris of the *Observer* came and asked me to dine with him and Barbara and Ted in the Starlight Room at the Metropole. I had refused Pam Berry, so I couldn't really join him and anyway I thought I ought to do my few hours in the Grand, so Peter and I went down and sat at a little table. There, facing me across the room, was Harold with his private family. He strolled over and said, 'Ah, you're not coming to Conference these days? Have you been having a quiet time in the office?' I said, 'No, out on tour studying the sub-normality hospitals, but I thought I would come down and put in an appearance.' We had a pleasant, friendly chat. I knew that everything had been fixed and laid on for me by him and I had nothing to fear and I thought I had just registered with him. Then we went up to the B.B.C. room where I saw him doing an interview and discussing his reshuffle and the Common Market and the position we were adopting. He was ebullient, on top of the world and I have never seen him so confident and happy. He is a man on the crest of the wave, by jove. Back we went on the 11 o'clock train after a longish day. I have had a very tiring three days and the rest of the week is going to be pretty tough too.

Friday, October 3rd–Saturday, October 4th

We had forty to fifty people for the Conference on Sub-normality, which lasted two solid days, from 3 o'clock on Friday afternoon till 11 o'clock that night, and from 9.15 today until 5 o'clock, session after session. I took the chair the whole time and it was pretty successful. I think the main thing, as Brian says, was that they had this contact with their Minister. They know they are working with a human being at the top of the Department and that he isn't just being briefed and doing what the Department says but really knows about things himself and is on top of the show. Also, we were working away at a policy. We had the draft of the 'main stream' report, which is abstract, vague and, by the standards of the conference, nothing drastic but we have caught it in the nick of time. Next we shall have a nurses' conference and continue to work at our policy, so that it will be ready, I hope, in January

[1] As a civil servant, Peter Brown found himself in an embarrassing dilemma, which the Prime Minister seems to have recognized.

or February. It will be a five-year programme for dealing with sub-normality and it took many, many hours yesterday and today.

Meanwhile I have had quite a problem about this fellow Dr Baker. He is a little dark man with glasses, a purist actually. He has been running a big sub-normality hospital and he is also our leading man on psychiatry, whom George Godber has got into the Ministry. I am going for him as my Director and though he obviously wants to come he doesn't want to upset the C.M.O. Now he has talked to Godber, who has merely written me a minute saying he would be a serious loss to the Department. I must now bring in Clifford Jarrett and work out how to lever Baker away from the C.M.O., because I can't break with Godber. He is a very powerful man in the Department and people never like acting against his wishes. He is away half the time around the world, advising the World Health Organization, in America, lecturing. He is remote, out of touch now, I think, except with the lord high panjandra and the physicians in the Royal Colleges in London. He knows all the top people but nothing about ordinary life, yet on the other hand he is radical and left-wing. I don't want to quarrel with him. I shall be seeing him next week, when he and I are giving a dinner in the Athenaeum to Lord Cohen of Birkenhead, the head of the General Medical Council, and we shall have more to say to each other then.

Sunday, October 5th

The Prime Minister announced that the Ministry of Technology was to assume the responsibilities for Industry that had previously belonged to the Board of Trade, the D.E.A. and the Ministry of Power. Harold Lever became Paymaster-General and Anthony Wedgwood Benn's principal Minister at MinTech. The Ministry of Power was abolished and Roy Mason, who had been its Minister, replaced Anthony Crosland, former President of the Board of Trade, as a Minister assisting Anthony Wedgwood Benn. The D.E.A. was also abolished and Peter Shore became Minister without Portfolio. Eric Varley became a Minister of State at MinTech.

Anthony Crosland became Secretary of State at the new Department of Local Government and Regional Planning, assisted by Anthony Greenwood, who continued as Minister of Housing and Local Government, Fred Mulley, who replaced Richard Marsh as Minister of Transport, and Tom Urwin, now Minister of State for regional affairs. Kenneth Robinson, formerly Minister for Planning and Land, left the Government, together with Richard Marsh and Fred Lee,[1] who, as Chancellor of the Duchy of Lancaster, had dealt with regional questions for D.E.A.

George Thomson took over as Chancellor of the Duchy of Lancaster, with

[1] Frederick Lee, Labour M.P. for Manchester Hulme 1945–50 and for Newton 1950–February 1974, was Parliamentary Secretary in the Ministry of Labour and National Service 1950–1, Minister of Power 1964–6, Secretary of State for the Colonies 1966–7 and Chancellor of the Duchy of Lancaster 1967–9. He became a life peer in 1974, taking the title of Lord Lee of Newton.

responsibility for E.E.C. negotiations. Judith Hart became Minister for Overseas Development and Reginald Prentice was invited to become a Minister of State for Industry but resigned after two days and was replaced by Charles Delacourt-Smith.[1]

I got home late last night and we spent a lot of the day preparing for the bathing gala this afternoon. Six boys turned up for Patrick's birthday and I organized a game of water polo. It was a delightful party on a wonderful cloudless day. I am feeling much better now. The truth, I always find, is that in the long recess I can just about hold the Department down but with Parliament as well it is terribly difficult for me to keep the same good-tempered, continuous, sensible control. I have got through my long recess and the week after next Parliament will resume, possibly until next July and then after the holidays we will almost certainly have the election.

In the evening came the news of this famous reshuffle which had been dominating Brighton. I rang Barbara this morning, who said she knew nothing and had no contact with Harold about it even though she sat in Conference with him. What do we see when we compare it with Harold's great talk of July and early August of removing Callaghan, Marsh and Crosland? Callaghan is exactly where he was, stronger than ever as a result of Ireland. Crosland is promoted to the gigantic job of running Housing and Transport, with Tony Greenwood under him. The only man who is clean out is Dick Marsh. Harold has kept his word there. Benn has been promoted, as he thought he would be, to run the big industrial Department with several people under him. Benn and Crosland are now super-Ministers of industry and planning, the same level as Barbara and me. Judith is out of Cabinet and into the Overseas Department and Peter Shore is in Cabinet without a job, but I suppose he will be the Prime Minister's aide, as well as doing public relations. Kenneth Robinson, who has done a faithful job, is finally thrown out. This is a most extraordinary thing to do while leaving that wet Tony Greenwood at Housing. George Thomson is back in European affairs. I thought Tony Crosland would go to Europe but he is being put in charge of local government, which he knows nothing about. These are ups and downs and the shuffle is a great deal less drastic than Harold intended. He has got his two ministerial groupings as we expected, but he has made very many fewer changes. There is no move for Healey or for me, of course, and Barbara and Roy are unchanged. Harold Lever has been promoted into Trade because Roy won't have an expert of that kind with him in the Treasury, more's the pity. These are my first impressions. The shuffle leaves the seven people at the top unchanged, it gives Benn a big leg-up and, to everyone's surprise, Crosland too. Peter Shore is left in the Cabinet quite undeservedly and

[1] Charles Delacourt-Smith was Labour M.P. for Colchester 1945–50 and General Secretary of the Post Office Engineering Union 1953–72. He became a life peer in 1967 and was Minister of State at MinTech. 1969–70. He died in 1972.

Judith is out, I think rightly. Tony Greenwood and Roy Mason are out, I think rightly.* There it is. We are left with two fewer people in Cabinet.

Monday, October 6th

I went up to London and had only just time to go to the office before I was off to Eastbourne to address the Public Health Inspectors. I went down with John Cashman in brilliant sunshine, addressed a couple of thousand people, had lunch and then came straight back. Directly I got to Victoria I was whirled to St James's Square to a secret meeting with Barbara which we had arranged on the telephone yesterday. My office had told her office that if she and I didn't reach agreement I would be circulating a Cabinet paper advising against having only the Industrial Relations Bill this session and suggesting a White Paper. I got there a bit early, went into her room, and there she was with Denis Barnes and Alex Jarratt,[1] a grey-haired, distinguished gentleman, like a handsome American. She gave me a drink and we sat down together to discuss her Industrial Commission and my insistence that the doctors must be excluded. It was an interesting meeting because she put her case and then I put mine and then I said, 'I am sorry but the very announcement of the intention to have a Bill will force me to define to the doctors where we stand. There is no half-way house here. Either they must be completely out or we bring them right in and say their salaries will be dealt with by the new Industrial Commission, along with higher civil servants and everybody else, in which case there will be hell to pay and I can say goodbye to a revised Health Service.' She was resistant at first but then Jarratt and Denis came to my assistance and said, 'Frankly, whatever happens, no Government will dare to discipline the doctors.' They accepted my view that we had done extremely well under Kindersley, which had got the doctors to accept limits on their salary increases and the principles of the prices and incomes policy in a way that no Industrial Commission could have done. We have nothing to complain of in the Kindersley Committee except that it is not tidy and the doctors seem to be in a privileged position. We finally reached firm agreement. Barbara gave me a secret understanding that, provided I didn't press for special favours for the doctors and that I was easy with her when the thing came before the Management Committee and the Cabinet, she would give me a tacit understanding that when it came to the drafting of the Bill the doctors' position would not be affected in any way. Jarratt has put this in writing so I have got her tied up tight. She has bought me off but the price

* I made one mistake. I thought Roy Mason was out of the Cabinet but in fact he is in the Cabinet and actually promoted, I think. He is President of the Board of Trade, which is now really a Ministry for exports.

[1] Alex Jarratt, an Under-Secretary at the Ministry of Power 1963–7, was seconded as Secretary to the National Board for Prices and Incomes 1965–8. He was a Deputy Secretary in 1967 and then Deputy Under-Secretary of State at the Department of Employment and Productivity 1968–70 and Deputy Secretary at the Ministry of Agriculture 1970. In 1970 he joined the International Publishing Corporation as Managing Director, becoming the Chairman and Chief Executive of Reed International in 1974.

is a very high one and one for which I am bound to stay quiet because all I want is to keep the doctors out. I'm not in any way against her having the Bill.

Tuesday, October 7th

I reflected on our talk and wondered how often such secret understandings are arrived at between members of the Cabinet. There we were, me with my Permanent Secretary and her with her two officials, reaching a secret agreement. I took care to indicate to Burke today that Barbara and I had reached this understanding because he is in the centre of things and it is very important that he should realize what has happened. I didn't of course tell any politician about it but it was probably the most important thing I shall do this week.

After a morning visit to the Southwark reception centre and my weekly luncheon meeting in the Department, we had a Cabinet at 3 o'clock. The first item was Ireland and when we had all settled down Callaghan put forward his next package.[1] He wanted to go over there and, after two days, with Chichester-Clark's permission, suddenly substitute the Commissioner of the Metropolitan Police as head of the R.U.C. He also wanted to announce drastic changes, including the establishment of a National Housing Board that would remove responsibility for housing allocations from the local authorities. I said, 'My God, that is a mouthful for Chichester-Clark to swallow,' but Callaghan looked confident. I think it may come off and if it does Callaghan will have been a superb success.

Then we had a very delicate discussion about Welsh local government, where we are in an awkward position because Tony Crosland has only just taken over, and this first issue is very important. George Thomas, who is an adept leader, has been pushing and cajoling for years for the Welsh to have their own reform Bill and we had a battle. Their White Paper provides no radical revision, they are retaining their county boroughs and, if they have that measure passed this session, there is a poor chance of our getting the English county barons to abdicate on behalf of the new unitary authorities. Tony Crosland came out fairly clearly on the side of Greenwood and me, so on the first round we won that point.

Meanwhile there had been all the excitement about the London dustmen, who had gone on strike to force a wage demand on a local authority who

[1] The Report of an inquiry into the Royal Ulster Constabulary, led by Lord Hunt (Leader of the British Everest Expedition 1952–3, Chairman of the Parole Board for England and Wales 1967–74 and since 1974 President of the National Association of Probation Officers), recommended on October 3rd that the 'B' Specials be disbanded, and that the R.U.C. should become an unarmed civilian force with a new volunteer force, the Ulster Defence Regiment, being created and put under Regular Army control. In the new parliamentary session legislation was passed to give effect to this proposal and meanwhile the Inspector-General of the R.U.C. retired, being succeeded by Colonel Sir Arthur Young (Kt 1965), Commissioner of the City of London Police 1950–71, seconded as Chief Constable R.U.C. from 1969 to 1970.

hadn't been very good about productivity deals.[1] They have already been out for a week, it's hot weather and it was being said that there was the possibility of disease. George Godber had assured me there was no danger now, this being the autumn and, although accumulating refuse is a horrible public health nuisance, it's not a public health risk in the modern world. We no longer have the kind of diseases, like bubonic plague, which were spread by flies and rats, and the flies are mostly dead at this time of year. I was just pushing off at the end of Cabinet to deal with some press releases when I was told to come back because Harold wanted me to discuss this. The Government didn't want to interfere in the strike and Barbara thought we ought to wait until Thursday when the unions met at York. I was able to say that there was no danger to health till Thursday and I would put this out to the press through Godber.

Later today I asked Harold about the reshuffle at the lower level. 'When can I discuss it?' I asked, and he said, 'Discuss it now for a minute or two,' so I gave him my views in three minutes. He said, 'Of course Ministers have been sending me endless lists telling me how they want their own people moved and whom they want. I am amazed at the number of requests I have had for so-and-so. I have had everybody wanting Reg Freeson, for example.' Well, other Ministers may write to him, I don't. I think I do better by keeping my preferences in store and at the last moment being obliging to him.

Wednesday, October 8th

I had been going to Wilton Park but I simply couldn't miss a Management Committee on the Industrial Relations Bill, so for the second time I had to cancel it and upset Heinz. It was fortunate in a way because this morning we also had a very interesting O.P.D. on the Arabs and the Jews, when Michael Stewart put forward a paper on a bridging policy. As nothing had been achieved by many months of American conversations with the Jews and Russian conversations with the Arabs, Michael proposed that we and the French should put in our middle-of-the-road policies. The famous British middle-of-the-road policy is a requirement that the Jews should go back to the 1948 frontiers, that the good old Gaza strip should be in United Nations hands and so on. It was a fantastically pro-Arab policy and I said how ridiculous it was. It would neither satisfy the Jews nor get anything from the Arabs because it still proposed that Jerusalem should stay partly in Jewish hands. 'We are in a terribly weak position out there,' I said, 'and, in my opinion, until we have got out of our obligations in the Persian Gulf we had better stay quiet and not expose ourselves by putting policies forward.' Roy strongly supported me and so did Fred Peart but Harold backed the Foreign

[1] On September 23rd refuse workers at Hackney began a strike in support of a pay claim. The strike spread to other areas of the country, involving other manual workers employed by local authorities, and by the time the dispute was resolved on November 18th a total of 17,400 workers had been involved.

Office, as he always does. All I achieved was that no British plan should be published, it should only be an *aide-mémoire* for Lord Caradon when it came to discussions with the Americans,[1] the French and the Russians. I don't believe they will stop there for a moment but at least I got something conceded.

We had a first-rate meeting of the Management Committee, just six of us because Denis Healey and the Chief Whip were away, and this is the right number. Harold has always said that we must have Callaghan back, which would make a total of nine, but he is now wondering if we should add the other two super-Ministers, Tony Wedgwood Benn and Tony Crosland, making it eleven, in which case we already represent half the Cabinet. This is a real problem for Harold. I think he will probably enlarge it but if he does it will become a public meeting. I can see now that the size of these committees is all-important. If you can get down to fewer than seven important Ministers, something like a natural conversation takes place between fellow-politicians who are not just pontificating from briefs, on points and postures relating to their job. The whole point of a committee of this kind is to loosen one from one's job.

We discussed absolutely frankly the problems of Barbara's new Industrial Relations Bill and the Industrial Commission. Over the last week or two she has switched from saying she wants a small limited Bill to saying she is going to have a big Bill, even though this has the disadvantage of being wholly pro-trade union. All it has omitted from *In Place of Strife* are her three sanctions proposals, so the trade unions get everything they want. I accept her view that she can't afford to go without any Industrial Relations Bill and that it must please the trade unions and keep to the terms by having no sanctions. It may look like a sell-out but there is no choice, because if we were to put sanctions into it our own party would accuse us of breaking faith with the unions and their undertaking. We argued this out at length and, on the whole, I backed her, but of course I had my secret arrangement.

Thursday, October 9th

First at Cabinet we had Wasp helicopter exports to South Africa. At O.P.D. there had been a division, with Denis Healey, Tony Crosland, Eddie Shackleton and Roy all wanting to sell Wasps only on a replacement basis, but Harold had not liked this and had brought it back to Cabinet. He collected opinion all round the table and we had a clear majority saying we can't sell arms to South Africa, resurrecting the whole atmosphere of December 1967. I was pretty cowardly and, when I was asked my opinion, I said, 'I hear from John Diamond and Roy Jenkins that not to sell them will cause a disastrous political commotion and from Barbara Castle that if we do it will cause a disastrous political commotion, so I would like to hear

[1] Sir Hugh Foot (K.C.M.G. 1951), U.K. Representative at the United Nations 1964–70. In 1964 he had been made a life peer, taking the title of Lord Caradon.

from the Chief Whip which is true.' The Chief said, 'To sell them will cause a disaster in the Party.' I am not sure he was right but Harold got his way and prevailed against the sane rational views of Denis Healey and the others.

Then we had an interminable talk about Barbara's two Bills. She droned on and on and on at inordinate length, just thinking aloud and reading every clause of the Bill. Oh dear, what a bore! Everybody agreed that it was an untidy and incoherent Bill and she didn't know what she meant. The opposition, led by Tony Crosland, had all the best of the argument, yet it was felt Barbara would have to have the Bill as a substitute for the prices and incomes policy, to cover up the vacancy of it all. I know very well that if I had been tough and pushed hard I could have made it very difficult for Harold to interpret the Cabinet view as anything but an opposition to legislation this session but I kept my word. She rambled on until after 1 o'clock. In a way it was lucky for me because Cabinet had no time to hear my report on the abatement negotiations, so I slipped the scheme through. I must say I was pleased when Peart said, 'You said more in ten minutes than she said in forty.' I got an agreement and that was that.

Before Cabinet I had had a frantic message that Tony Crosland wanted to lunch with me. I took him to lunch. (I don't know why he doesn't take me, perhaps because he doesn't have a club.)[1] So off we went to the Athenaeum where I gave him grouse and claret and he told me the following story, which rather confirmed something Roy told me. I had guessed that making Tony an overlord at Transport and Housing wasn't what Harold originally intended and it is certainly true that he was only offered this job about ten days ago, just before he made a voyage to Tokyo as President of the Board of Trade. He was offered it in vague outline and he came back on the day of the reshuffle to find that it had all been done in his absence. This shows he wasn't part of the original plan for this Ministry, which, I would like to bet, was that Healey should be moved into this world, and I think Roy has some evidence that Denis was offered this and turned it down. My suspicion is that, at the time when Harold was violently anti-Crosland, he intended to put Denis here and try to transfer Crosland from the cut-down Board of Trade to the job of Minister for Europe at the Foreign Office. Over lunch we discussed his role in his new super-Ministry or non super-Ministry. He has taken over the D.E.A.'s regional planning, but not the parts of the Board of Trade which deal with regional planning and industrial development certificates. I remember from being Minister of Housing that Douglas Jay's power to bitch up my housing plans was gigantic, because he could control the I.D.C.s and the permission for industry to move, and the chap who runs that controls the speed of development of the new towns. All this has gone to Tony Wedgwood Benn, and is still to be industry-dominated, so in this battle for power Benn already has powers far greater than Crosland. Benn's

[1] His entry in *Who's Who* gave his club as Grimsby Labour.

Ministry of Technology has also swallowed the whole Ministry of Power and a large section of the Board of Trade, whereas there has been no change in the relationship of Transport and Housing, the two very different Ministries under Crosland.

The poor man is in the position of an overlord but he won't run the Ministry, because, even more depressing for him, it has been publicly announced that the integration of his Department will take low priority, and his job now is to conduct negotiations for the Maud reforms and to deal with pollution. Although Harold has created this Department of Local Government and Regional Planning, he has left the two Permanent Secretaries at the Ministry level, one at Transport[1] and Matthew Stevenson at Housing, and Tony with apparently no one at all. Tony said, looking rather shamefaced, 'Ten days ago I got the impression that I was going to get Matthew Stevenson, but now I come back to find that the Permanent Secretaries are to remain at Ministry level.' 'Well,' I said, 'you'd be crazy to let that happen. You must go back to Harold and fight your battle. Stevenson is a powerful man and, let me tell you, if you fail to get him you will be alone in the stratosphere.' I couldn't help remembering exactly what happened to me when I was Lord President and gave up the Leadership of the House for a general co-ordinating job in the Social Services, and the promise of a merged Ministry in due course, with in the meantime the two Ministers staying and my having supervisory powers. As we all remember and you will see, my God, if you look at my diary,[2] I found that my supervisory powers were completely ineffective. Even though the Civil Service knew that I was not only overlord but taking over a merged Ministry in a matter of months, they began to suspect the thing wasn't coming off and I had to press the P.M. to make announcements all the time in order to get any authority at all. In Tony Crosland's case it is known that there will be no merger before the election and in my view this is a disaster for him.

Moreover, he knows absolutely nothing about local government and has no interest in the job. I remember how, long ago, when I was trying to reorganize the General Grant,[3] I went to him and said, 'Surely as Minister of Education you want to keep a specific education grant, don't you?' and he said, 'Oh, I couldn't care less about rates, I don't know how you can bother about such things.' He is a macro-economist, interested in the budget, a natural Chancellor, in fact a disappointed Chancellor, and I think he will probably remain a disappointed Chancellor all his life, unless of course Roy becomes Prime Minister. Tony will have no influence on economics from his new position and he has been shoved into a terribly specialized field in which he has no interest and in which another super-Minister, the Minister for

[1] Sir David Serpell (K.C.B. 1968) was Permanent Secretary at the Ministry of Transport 1968–70 and subsequently Permanent Secretary at the Department of the Environment until 1972. Since 1973 he has been Chairman of the Nature Conservancy Council.

[2] See above, April 22nd–November 1st, 1968.

[3] See Vol. I, pp. 82–3.

13 Harold Wilson with his Political Secretary, Marcia Williams, and Joe Haines, who became his Press Secretary in January 1969.

14 Towards the end of 1969 Richard Crossman and Barbara Castle go to the Prime Minister to implore him to confide with his friends in the Cabinet rather than with his personal staff in what became known as the 'Kitchen Cabinet'.

15 Harold Lever, Paymaster General (left), with Tony Benn, Minister of Technology and Power, in conference. October 1969.

16 In April 1970, Roy Jenkins, Chancellor of the Exchequer, knows that he will have to take unpopular measures in his Budget to bolster the ailing economy and thereby risk seeing the Tories come to power later in the year.

Social Security, is an expert. He's got me with him but he's got this awful thing of taking over only a matter of days before we have to take major decisions on local government. If I am at all successful, he and I will work together against the official view and the Treasury view, so I may well gain by having him there. But the problem in the foreground is to make the Statement about Seebohm and the N.H.S. by the end of this month and to finish the first round of consultations on hand with the local authorities, all with a brand-new Minister who knows absolutely nothing about it.

I had to get back for a meeting of the Social Services Committee at 2.30. For the first time I was presenting the outline of how we would reconstruct the N.H.S. with regions and districts, each of them with indirect election. We could have one element nominated by myself, one nominated by the local authorities and one by the professions. Bea Serota put it forward and the moment she finished there was a tremendous indictment by Dick Taverne and Eddie Shackleton, saying this was totally incompatible with the principle of accountability. Their recommendation was that at the regional level line managers should be put in who would be responsible to the Government for the spending of money. Poor Dick Taverne said, 'Like a new town corporation,' and that gave me my chance. I looked at Jim MacColl, who was over on the other side, and said, 'How do they work?' He said, 'Not very well. New town corporations don't get on at all with the local authorities.' You won't find a word about this in the minutes but I was really able to lay the thing on the ground and to say that there was no evidence that our Regional Hospital Boards, which are at the moment all directly accountable to me and to the Treasury, are better controlled in their expenditure than, say, local authority education. On all the evidence we have got a much better control of expenditure in local government than in the R.H.B.s. Secondly, how could we possibly take over an area of local government services and subject it to line managers and how would people tolerate this, especially if we let them know that new town corporations had disastrous relations with the local authorities?

Everyone supported me, because they knew from practical experience that there was no conceivable chance of getting what the Treasury wanted and, anyway, it wouldn't work. I must say Eddie Shackleton said, 'From what I have heard from the Social Services Secretary I have changed my mind and I ask Dick Taverne if he would like to go back to the Treasury and think it out, because it must come to Cabinet.' This was an interesting meeting, because I had been warned by the Department that if I put this idea of joint appointments forward the Treasury would organize an official opposition and there is no doubt that the official committee had obviously opposed the Green Paper policy, on the Treasury's ground that with 100 per cent Government financing there must be 100 per cent Government appointments and no kind of democracy. I have got to fight and win this and I am lucky to have Tony Crosland brought in. It was a jolly good try-out today.

I had a meeting of PEP and then for three hours I slaved away on the White Paper. It was a long and tiring day and I left the office at about 9.30 feeling worn-out, went down to Lockets for a quiet meal and then trotted home.

Friday, October 10th

A marvellously sunny day today and I was grateful to be able to spend it going down to Folkestone to address the Executive Council Services' Annual Conference. There were the pharmacists, opticians, G.P.s and the dentists, three or four hundred of them in a very stuffy hall. I had asked the Vice-Chairman if they would like questions and he said, 'Oh, no, there are no questions here.' 'Are you sure?' 'Oh, we don't do that.' Fortunately when I got there I asked the Secretary if I could shorten my speech and have questions. 'We haven't had that,' he said, 'since Aneurin Bevan,' so I knocked my speech around, jazzed up the script I had been given, and then had twenty minutes of questions and a standing ovation. Answering frankly off the cuff is the door to communication with them. After that there was a little lunch with the Labour Mayor of Folkestone,[1] who is surrounded by Tories, before I went back in the train to tidy things up at the office before getting the 5.30 home to Prescote.

Saturday, October 11th

I spent the whole day motoring up to Blackburn with Anne. We had lunch at Nelson and Colne, where we want to win the by-election. There is an astonishing difference in the party now, and it seems cheerful and in good heart. From there on to Blackburn where in the town hall I talked to four or five hundred delegates for fifty minutes and then had an hour of questions. At Folkestone yesterday I had another NALGO delegation, but this time there was much less protest. On the way up the M6 I managed to get all my work done in three and a half hours – two big boxes of it. On the way back at about 8.30, just as we got to Coventry, there was a terrible noise in the car. We didn't know what had happened but the engine had become very hot and we drew up at a garage. Heavens, no mechanic, but the attendant rang up a friend of his and a nice young man came round with his wife. He looked at the car and said, 'Your fan belt's gone,' so while we went and had a drink he tried to find a new one, but without success. Eventually he and his wife motored us all the way back to Prescote. It was his birthday evening and that was his birthday treat. Charming people, a lovely wife, and they had just had their first child. Wayward, interesting people, and I felt very warmed.

Sunday, October 12th

Jock and Phyllis Campbell and Tommy Balogh came over to lunch today and Tommy and I discussed Roy's position. There is no doubt that, whether

[1] C. A. Ellender.

Harold intended it or not, one of the major effects of this shuffle is completely to reaffirm the dominance of the Treasury and of the Chancellor. The elimination of D.E.A. has taken away what Harold described as creative tension, at the time of George Brown and Callaghan,[1] and the removal of Tony Crosland from the Board of Trade and its transformation into a mere foreign trade organization under Roy Mason has removed a second post which was traditionally held by an economist who could stand up to the Chancellor.

A third but not insignificant factor is the character of Wedgwood Benn. Here is this inordinately large Ministry of Industry headed by Wedgy Benn, an intellectually negligible whizz-kid who simply can't stand up to Roy at all and won't have the staff or the time to deal with economics. Of course it may be said that Tony Benn has been strengthened by giving him as his intellectual adviser Harold Lever but that is really moving Harold away from things he understands, like liquidity, international affairs and currency, into industry, of which he knows very little. I know from that long talk which I had with Roy on the way down to Chequers that he doesn't really trust Harold and has been wanting to get rid of him. Nicholas Davenport and I know this perfectly well. Harold Lever has been moved out of the Treasury because Roy is jealous of his expertise and the Treasury were glad to get rid of what they felt to be a dangerous, awkward customer. So in a sense this also enormously strengthens Roy, though at the cost of denying him powerful advice.

A final advantage to the Treasury is the continuation of the D.E.P. under Barbara and the extension of its power. We all know that when Barbara was put into D.E.P. or, rather, when D.E.P. was created out of the traditional Ministry of Labour because Roy refused to have her at the counterbalancing post at D.E.A., she tried to build up the department constructively and keep in with Roy. She accepted his economic policy and he accepted her industrial relations and prices and incomes policy. Now her prices and incomes policy and Industrial Relations Bill have collapsed, she has nothing except to try to conceal the disaster and to build up some substitute to bolster her position. This really means that again it is the man with a clear-cut Ministry who has his position strengthened. I must say Tommy Balogh didn't deny this and, as he has himself said, it doesn't matter so much, our economic policy is now set on the rails. Either it succeeds or it fails but it can't be changed now. I said, 'Yes, I knew that six months before you did, Thomas, and that is why I refused to have you very near me and bother my mind too much about economic affairs and prognoses; no influence can be exerted there.'

This is the last reshuffle we will have and it is obvious that there will be nothing but minor changes between now and the election. We have had two Cabinets this week and we've begun to settle down. My first impression,

[1] In 1964, when the D.E.A. was created as a counter-force to the Treasury.

although it doesn't really agree with Roy's, is that it is a better Cabinet. Roy said our Tuesday discussion was awful but that wasn't really what I was thinking of. I suppose I am thinking more of the inner nine, whose pecking order remains unchanged after five years – the P.M., Stewart, Jenkins, Gardiner, Crossman, Callaghan, Healey, Peart.[1] This is the established core of the Cabinet and I think it is fair to say that we have all learned a hell of a lot as Ministers and we are a good, competent, hard core. Even the press has been obliged to admit this. More important, Harold has had to admit it by leaving those nine unchanged. It is obvious when you sit there that we are the ones who, in a sense, matter. Certainly Peter Shore talks a great deal, Tony Benn no doubt will talk a little more, and Crosland does his fair share, but nevertheless it is true to say that here is the weight of the Cabinet. Yes, including Peart. He counts. He says what ordinary people are thinking, he and Mellish are the men who represent *l'homme moyen* or *l'homme moyen socialiste*. So that is the first point, stability at the top. I suppose the one change Harold might possibly have made would have been to include George Brown but he made it very easy for Harold by making it clear that he would only come back if he could be No. 2, which we nine would not automatically accept. So fortunately for us and fortunately for the party and the Cabinet that schizophrene George Brown, that Jekyll and Hyde, is out. He is useful at Conference and at publicity and maybe he will come back right at the end but he is out for the time being and a good thing too.

Then we have the two new super-Ministries. It is interesting that the newspapers all refer back to the Ministry of Defence as Harold's model for these and not much is said about the two other super-Ministries, the F.C.O. and the D.H.S.S., rightly I suppose, because we have hardly played ourselves in yet. Now we add the Ministry of Industry and the Department of Local Government and Planning but there is an enormous difference between them. It looks as though Harold has taken a great deal of care and trouble in the planning of what he really cares about, Benn's new Ministry of Industry, Harold's first love. Instead of creative friction between the two economic Ministries, D.E.A. and the Treasury, Harold's design was to wind up D.E.A. and the Ministry of Power and create a Ministry of Industry as the big counter-balance to the Treasury. Here he really has created a new position of immense political influence. Whoever runs this group has got under him practically the whole of British industry and raw materials, including the Ministry of Power with electricity production and distribution, gas, steel, coal mines and all the power of the nationalized industries. He is the sponsoring Minister for virtually all raw material production in the country. Part of this operation was, as I have said, to destroy the Board of Trade and cut it down to an overseas trade Ministry, replacing it by this

[1] In Crossman's original dictated transcript Lord Gardiner is mentioned twice and the diarist seems uncertain about the placing of Crosland.

great new complex clustered around Technology. But it is no counter-balance to the Treasury, especially when it is headed by Wedgy Benn.

Having created that Ministry Harold then came to the second area, that of Housing and Planning, and the taking of the other bit of D.E.A. Here he was going to give Healey the chance but he turned it down, so Crosland was offered it only ten days ago. I am sure that both Roy and I have spoken to Harold more than once and warned him against getting rid of Crosland but in Harold's first July anger Tony was going to go, as well as Callaghan, Dick Marsh, Judith, Peter and Tony Greenwood. This brings me to my third comment, Harold's use of the axe. I needn't repeat all those talks he had with Barbara and me, with me alone, Roy alone, the Chief Whip alone and Fred Peart alone. We have all compared notes since. There is no doubt he was going to wield his big axe and aim at cutting Cabinet down to seventeen or eighteen, by removing those six and shifting the Ministries about a bit. Frankly, it was idiotic ever to dream of getting rid of Callaghan and this was knocked on the head first of all by the key position Callaghan had on the bloody Boundary Commission Bill and then, of course, the enormous positive strength he gained by his handling of Ulster. Clearly he couldn't possibly go.

Crosland? Well, he has not proved himself a good Minister, he is too dilettante, too much of an intellectual. But somehow he is such an able man that it would be impossible for Harold to get rid of him, especially from a Cabinet which hasn't got an outstanding amount of merit in it. I was against his being got rid of and so was Roy. I was strongly in favour of sacking Shore, Hart and Greenwood and I thought Marsh should go, although here I know Roy thinks Marsh an able man and was strongly against it. What actually happened was that Callaghan, Crosland and Shore stayed, Hart and Greenwood were demoted and the only people to be sacked were Dick Marsh and poor Kenneth Robinson. Quite naturally, Marsh got on to his high horse and has got himself into the press for four days as the poor injured bright young man of the Cabinet thrown out, because his expulsion sticks out like a sore thumb. If Greenwood and Shore, two of the P.M.'s poodles, had gone as well as Marsh, Harold would have been thought to have done a sensible thing. The P.M. got the worst of all worlds by being thought vindictive to Marsh and soft to his old pals. The retention of Greenwood as Minister of Housing and the expulsion of Kenneth is an outrage. I rang up Kenneth and he told me, 'Yes, it is true, Harold explained to me that he expected Greenwood to resign when he was demoted but as he didn't I had to go.' What a confession from a Prime Minister to an outgoing colleague. Poor Kenneth, he was bitter. 'Well,' he said, 'I am fifty-eight. It's a sad end. I thought at least I would be allowed to soldier on in the job I had loyally accepted, but no.' I said, 'I think it is a complete outrage.'

Marsh has had a run for his money, but Shore, why was he saved at the last moment? God alone knows. Roy, Barbara and I all thought he was to leave the Cabinet along with Judith but no one knows what final sentimental feeling, presumably, held Harold to keeping him. Then, at the tag end, we have the resignation of Reg Prentice, who had been moved from Overseas Trade to make room for Judith Hart, into the new big Ministry of Trade under MinTech. I checked on this when I was talking to Harold about my own junior Ministers. It is perfectly true that Prentice agreed perfectly amicably to move to his new Ministry, and two days later he suddenly changed his mind, simply because he couldn't face leaving O.D.M., about which he made a very critical speech at Conference, which perhaps he expected to be thanked for.[1] What an idiot. When he was offered the change he had only to say, 'If you move me I will resign in protest,' and undoubtedly he would have held his Ministry. In a way this proves that he is a bad Minister because a man who can't make the critical decision at the right time and only comes to the right conclusion two days late is the kind of man who is not really capable of being in a Government. I miss him and as he was a trade unionist an important part of our image has been lost but this is entirely his own fault and Harold cannot be blamed.

The last point, I suppose, is to ask myself what I think Harold should have done. Perhaps I shouldn't do this but I am just reminding myself. First, he should have moved Barbara. The catastrophe of her failure is accentuated by her staying at D.E.P. because there she has to try to make good her damaged reputation. I am not saying it isn't a virtue that she has the courage to stay and fight it out but we are already seeing the disaster of her remaining there in the Bills we are having to produce, the Equal Pay Bill, the Industrial Commission Bill, and we see it also from the trade unions. Fred Peart and I were chatting about Victor Feather this week, and Fred said, 'The trade union people now loathe the sight of Barbara because before she sits down she lectures them with one of her emotional tirades.' I have no doubt that her relations with the unions are disastrous. It is true, though very unlikely, that a woman could conceivably succeed with them, but when she has blatantly failed a woman is at an appalling disadvantage. I think Harold should have given her the big industrial job rather than Tony Benn and that the Ministry of Labour should then have gone to a trade unionist like Roy Mason. The second move he clearly should have made was to have put Denis Healey into the Foreign Office, given Stewart Peart's place as Leader of the House and let Peart drop out. Everybody both inside and outside the Government really knows that Michael Stewart is a complete nonentity. He is a man with a brilliant capacity for parliamentary debate but departmentally he's an utterly hopeless stooge. Denis Healey has waited for five years yet he is still sitting there at Defence. I am told by Roy, and I think it is true, that Denis turned down all the offers Harold made to move him either to the new Industry

[1] Mr Prentice feared that his transfer from O.D.M. signified that there was to be a Treasury cut in the aid and development programme and to draw attention to this he resigned from his new office. See *Wilson*, p. 712.

Ministry or the Housing job. He only wants the Foreign Office. It is the one job he could really do and Harold should have given it to him. The third thing he should have done was to have made a real job of Tony Crosland's new department and given him a basis by merging the two Ministries. Lastly, not only Judith Hart but Peter Shore should have been pushed out of the Cabinet, and Greenwood should have been sacked along with Dick Marsh. That, as I have explained, would have made the Marsh sacking seem less vindictive, and then Harold could have spared Kenneth Robinson for a decent job.

There is the Cabinet as I see it today and this evening we have just heard the announcement of the junior appointments, completely overshadowed, however, by the eruption of more violence in Belfast. I have been lucky in my own appointments. I fought hard and without much trouble got John Dunwoody (I now have all three of the family – Norah Phillips, her daughter Gwyneth,[1] who is Mrs Dunwoody, and Gwyneth's husband). John will make an enormous difference because he will fill the House of Commons gap and he is a really vigorous man, who can take over Questions and letters from M.P.s and relations with the G.P.s. And Brian O'Malley? When I was offered him I learnt that he was sour at not becoming a Minister of State and Harold doubted if he would come. I had the sense to say I would think it over and I rang the Prime Minister the following morning, last Wednesday, and said, 'Tell O'Malley I specially asked for him and that I particularly want him. We may win him over.' Sure enough, Harold did say this and O'Malley rang me on Friday evening. Although he said he was sour he was obviously gratified. He is a bit of a gamble. I knew him quite well when I was Leader of the House and I got on with him. He is a man full of ideas, with quite a good mind, although illiterate. I think he is a jazz band leader, he is in the Musicians' Union, but he is highly intelligent and infinitely superior to Norman Pentland.

In a reshuffle of the lower levels of the Government the Prime Minister announced on October 12th that ten Ministers had resigned. Lord Stonham was replaced as Minister of State at the Home Office by Shirley Williams and her place at D.E.S. was taken by Gerald Fowler, who had been at MinTech. Bill Mallalieu left Technology. The other eight were Parliamentary Secretaries who were replaced by younger men and women. Dick Taverne succeeded Harold Lever as Financial Secretary to the Treasury and his place as Minister of State at the Treasury was taken by William Rodgers. Goronwy Roberts moved from the Foreign Office to replace William Rodgers at the Board of Trade. Edmund Dell became Minister of State at D.E.P., taking up the office that had been left vacant when Roy Hattersley had moved to Defence in July. The two new Parliamentary Under-Secretaries at the Department of Health and Social

[1] Mrs Gwyneth Dunwoody, Labour M.P. for Exeter 1966–70, and for Crewe since 1974 was Parliamentary Secretary at the Board of Trade 1967–70. Her marriage to Dr John Dunwoody was dissolved in 1975.

Security were Brian O'Malley, formerly Deputy Chief Whip, and John Dunwoody. Julian Snow resigned, to become a life peer in 1970, and Norman Pentland moved to the Ministry of Posts.

Who got sacked? Lord Stonham, a bloody-minded, ambitious junior Minister at the Home Office, who has been driving everybody in the House of Lords nearly frantic. Poor old Curly Mallalieu has gone from MinTech. A very odd bunch have got a leg up, including that awful little Gerry Fowler.[1] Charles Delacourt-Smith is a thoroughly good man who now goes into Wedgwood Benn's new Department and replaces Stonham on the Lords' front bench. Then we get, I suppose quite legitimately, Dick Taverne taking our friend Harold Lever's place as Financial Secretary and in another piece of careerism Bill Rodgers comes up from the Board of Trade to replace Taverne.[2] God knows why. Bill doesn't seem to me to show any particular intellectual excitement. Practically all the outstanding people, headed by David Marquand, have once again been left out. My God, it is expensive to be able, under a Labour Government.

Tomorrow Parliament reassembles and we will sit from now until the end of July, except for a very short recess. Do I want it? No, no Minister does. By the way, I should add in an interesting talk I had with Jock Campbell. He said to me, 'We would rather like to have you as editor of the *New Statesman*. We have told Paul Johnson, who wants to go. Could you take his place?' I said, 'No, I can't possibly do that because I am going to go right on till the election and then I shall be bound to fight it.' It's true that during the past week I have been thinking that I may want to go on but I will be sixty-two, and if I go on for another five years... So I quickly made up my mind, because both Patrick and Virginia desperately want me a little more at home, and I thought, 'Well, that's it, the editorship of the *Statesman*. Let us see if we can get a compact to agree that immediately after the election I will take over.' It's apparently what Jock Campbell and the Board of Directors want. Isn't it ironical? I couldn't get it when I wanted it,[3] and now, after I have had this wonderful time as Minister, I am retiring to be the editor of the *New Statesman*. Shall I be too old? Yes, I'll have it for a few years and then a younger man will have to replace me but, by God, I can do something for the paper. It is an exciting thought for today.

[1] Gerald Fowler, Labour M.P. for The Wrekin 1966–70 and since 1974, was Joint Parliamentary Secretary at the Ministry of Technology 1967–9, Minister of State at the Department of Education and Science October 1969–June 1970, March–October 1974 and January–September 1976 and Minister of State at the Privy Council Office 1974–6.

[2] William Rodgers, Labour M.P. for Stockton-on-Tees 1962–74 and since 1974 for Teesside, was Minister of State at the Board of Trade 1968–9 and at the Treasury 1969–70. From 1974–6 he was Minister of State for Defence and since 1976 he has been Secretary of State for Transport.

[3] In 1958 Kingsley Martin told Crossman that John Freeman was to be appointed Deputy Editor and in 1961 Freeman succeeded to the editorship.

Monday, October 13th

I got up to London and there was Curly Mallalieu on the platform. Month after month, year after year, he has been at Defence, the Board of Trade, MinTech. doing a decent job. I remember him as a brilliant scrum half at Oxford, whom I used to watch playing for the university, and I next saw him as a brilliant *Tribune* commentator who combined that with sports writing. He was a great friend of Nye and was rewarded for that, because in due course Harold gave him his job. He has been worthy, uninspired, and in this shuffle he finally had to go. I gave him a lift in my car because he can't use his official car now he is out. We discussed it all and he seemed in great form. He said, 'Of course I need some money now,' so I said, 'What do you want to do?' 'Ah,' he said, 'Hovercraft.' I have the feeling that he has been preparing the ground and will get a fairly decent directorship. Is that corrupt? No, it isn't. It is the British way of life. When I consider all the rest of the reshuffle it seems only moderately good because, on the whole, Harold hasn't satisfied the back benchers. Here is Mr Varley, now a Minister of State, thank you, along with Tom Urwin, two of the most incompetent people but for different reasons, Urwin because he is stupid and Varley because he is young and inexperienced. Most astounding of all is Gerry Fowler, whom I remember as that little nitwit who was a tutor at Hertford College, Oxford, and candidate for Banbury in 1964, before he moved to The Wrekin. First of all he was given a Parliamentary Secretaryship at MinTech., although he is an ancient historian, and he has now been promoted even further. When you think that John Mackintosh and David Marquand, the two ablest men, are without a job, you realize that sheer intellect isn't greatly respected in the Labour Party, least of all by Harold Wilson.

Then, in a nauseating disrespect for departmental work, Shirley Williams has been ripped out of Education, where she has been doing an absolutely first-rate job and providing some sense of permanence and durability, and popped back into the Home Office in order to balance Catholic Shirley against Protestant Jim. She has been an outstanding Education Minister and she ought to be allowed to run her course. But Harold has never allowed anything to run its course in education; he sees it all in terms of politics. This is typical. He has never had a feeling about departmental responsibility and his ministerial shuffles are all political shuffles. Perhaps that is because he himself was no good as a departmental Minister when he was President of the Board of Trade.

However I have no complaint. I had asked for Kenneth Marks and Denis Coe,[1] two absolutely solid centre people, who each in his own way overwhelmingly deserved a leg-up. I have actually got John Dunwoody and Brian O'Malley, and they will be very satisfactory, though O'Malley had to be

[1] Kenneth Marks, Labour M.P. for Gorton since November 1967, was P.P.S. to Anthony Crosland 1969–70, to Roy Hattersley 1974–5 and to Harold Wilson 1975–6. He was an Opposition Whip 1971–2.

given a job after being thrown out as Deputy Chief Whip because Bob Mellish didn't like him and this doesn't help the public relations in the party. In a way, it's a kind of parallel case with Ben Whitaker, who is a great dilettante, a left-wing barrister, who is almost certainly not going to be an M.P. after the next election. Why give him a job instead of one of twenty or thirty solid members of the centre of the Party?[1] I think Harold is going to find a lot of people are discontented and browned off by this last reshuffle. He should have started rewarding youth and talent and energy three years ago and because of this and his curious perversity of mind in choosing the Fowlers and the Whitakers, he does save up for himself the devil of a lot of trouble.

In the office I had my final conversation on abatement with the T.U.C. I was rather alarmed because after the last meeting there had been a T.U.C. Congress and a change in the composition of the Social Services Committee but there was dear old Harold Collison, now Head of the S.B.C., to bring them in and introduce me to them. To my amazement they were sturdily standing by the T.U.C. principles, saying the abatement terms shouldn't be too generous, although there were certain anxieties from the Firemen and from NALGO. There was Mr Anderson, the NALGO fellow, sitting beside Harold Collison, talking as coyly and coolly with me as anything, saying how reasonable I was and how understanding. I suppose this was partly because I had acceded to Harold Collison's request and written NALGO a letter excusing him for all his misbehaviour. So I had won the day and the good support of this committee.

After that I saw the C.M.O., and then Brian O'Malley and John Dunwoody came for a working lunch to settle in with us. I don't know what impression they are getting but I think we have got a good pair there. I have been getting Bea Serota to arrange the precise slab of work we shall give John Dunwoody and, what is more difficult, trying to get David Ennals to give a proper share to Brian. David is sharp as a needle, able, driving, ambitious, loyal, but he is determined to get on. He always does what he is told in the end but he won't be generous to his subordinates.

Today was the return of Parliament and there was a big debate on the Northern Ireland situation, with both Hogg and Callaghan making tremendous speeches, completely in accord with each other, showing Parliament at its best, rather as a Council of State. It was a most exciting, dignified debate in a critical situation but I was far away, struggling with the Battersea Labour Party at a packed meeting in a small room. There was the usual bad temper and snarling. They were narking about the pension plan and I didn't bother to go back to the House after I had finished.

Tuesday, October 14th

Cabinet started with Jim Callaghan. He is an astonishing phenomenon. As

[1] He became a Parliamentary Secretary at the Ministry of Overseas Development.

Home Secretary he has carried, I should think, 40 per cent of the main burden of the legislation of the last twelve months and he is now carrying it again. Yesterday he was the main speaker on Ulster and today he was to be the main speaker on the Seats Bill and our attempt to defeat the Tories' effort to force redistribution on us before the next election. Jim is going to triumph on this. He has managed to engineer a situation where the Tories are given the choice of either getting what they partly want, which is to have redistribution in London at least, before the election, or of accepting total defeat, and they are accepting total defeat rather than have any compromise.[1] We have therefore done the job of actually making it impossible to redistribute the constituencies before this election. Certainly we have had to concede a redistribution before the next election but this has been a great achievement and it has come out right because of the skilled work between Callaghan and Wilson. What are their relations now? They work closely on this kind of thing. This week Harold almost got himself to praise Callaghan for his achievements in Ulster. Almost. Harold brought himself to the point and said, 'Once again he has come back with success.' He didn't say how wonderful he had been but nevertheless they are getting on well together.

The next item was the poor old dustmen. I went back to London yesterday a bit worried about how I should defend myself because after a press conference last Tuesday, when I had said there was no danger of an epidemic, everybody had been telling me what a relief it was to have a Minister who seemed to be honest and thinking for himself, but now the weather has become terribly hot, 80° in the shade, with a great many flies, and people have been saying I was complacent. Extremely funny, except that I had articles in the *Sunday Telegraph* and the *Sunday Times* describing me as an idiot for saying that the dirt wasn't actually a menace to health. Well the strike is collapsing because at York two of the unions accepted the settlement and the T.&G. are giving in.[2]

The main thing was the Queen's Speech and on the whole it is clear that we have got an electioneering speech. Things are being packed in that we can't possibly carry through even if we run into next October. Harold goes on talking as though we are running till next autumn, but if we did, and then had a September or October election, everything which was overspilled from next July might fall by the way. I am pretty sure that the election will be earlier than that, and I think that if it is at all possible Harold will have it in May. I am a bit concerned to get the Superannuation Bill published and put on the Statute Book in time.

Cabinet was fairly quick, so I was able to catch Harold for ten minutes to

[1] On October 14th the Home Secretary ensured that the Commons rejected the Lords' amendment giving him another three months to lay the Orders. The Commons passed a Government amendment proposing that by March 1972 either a Boundary Commission should be reactivated or the 1969 recommendations laid before Parliament and the Bill was returned to the Lords for passage.

[2] The dispute was finally settled on November 18th.

clear up two things I wanted to ask him about. The first was the Herbert Morrison Memorial Lecture, which I had sent him three weeks ago and which he had at last read. 'First-rate,' he said. 'Very exciting. I agree to publication, provided you clear it with Roy and Tony Greenwood.' So I have got that behind me. Then I said, 'What about the Godkin Lectures at Harvard?'[1] 'Ah, yes,' he said, 'subject?' 'Well, I think I am bound to do Presidential and Prime Ministerial Government – Bagehot revisited,' and he said, 'You'll show me the text?' I said, 'There won't be a text, I'll *ad lib* it and I'll arrange that no television or radio will be present.' Harold said, 'And publication? You can time it for after the election?' 'Yes, that has been arranged.' He looked relieved and when he asked, 'You can time it for after the election?' it was almost as if he said, 'You can time it for when you have retired from the Government?' It is just possible that Harold is expecting me to go. After all I shall be nearly sixty-three next autumn and he will have a great group of sixty-three-year-olds, Gerald Gardiner, who will obviously go, but also Michael Stewart and myself. He will want both of us out so he might be positively relieved if I go. However there it is, the die is cast, I have made the decision to go to the *Statesman* and sooner or later I shall have to tell Harold. After this little conversation I have a feeling he may well be prepared for it.

I lunched at the Ritz with Peregrine Worsthorne whom I hadn't seen for many months. He is a friend of Pam Berry's, rather like St John Stevas in some ways, but stronger and more elegant, a strange creature with melting grey-blue eyes and elegant clothes. I read the *Sunday Telegraph* largely to see what he is saying because he writes so well. He is personally identified, he speaks out and is provocative and most readable, and this is what I want to make the *New Statesman* if I get the chance to edit it. I love going to the Ritz. There is space between the tables and, though the food is not very good, the drink is splendid and there's a wonderful ritzy air. It's not particularly expensive either, I believe. We had a lovely informal chat. I suppose I am helpful to them. I didn't really tell him anything, just chit-chat, before I ran back to take the chair for the final stage of the negotiation between the Ministry and the Pharmaceutical Society on a voluntary compact about the price of drugs. On the whole I managed to get them round and I got far more in an hour than the Department thought possible, so the voluntary thing was signed. I had been brought in to this at the twenty-first meeting, which I suppose is what Ministers are for.

Anne and I gave John and Gwyneth Dunwoody dinner. Gwyneth was brought up in our village and went to the Banbury School, so there was a great deal of common ground between us. I am going to have Brian O'Malley, this strange, tall, gawky man with the small head and bespectacled brown

[1] Crossman had been invited by the President and Fellows of Harvard College to give the annual Godkin Lectures in April 1970. They were eventually published as *Inside View* (London: Cape, 1972).

eyes, to dinner at the Athenaeum, so I am getting on with running my Ministers in.

Wednesday, October 15th

Today we had a press conference with a select number of medical journalists to launch Dr Alex Baker as my first Director of the Advisory Service. This little man, with round, black eyes and heavy black eyebrows, said to me the other day, 'I know I give the impression of being ineffective. Maybe I am not quite as ineffective as I look.' I think that is about it. He is rather innocent and very ingenuous but determined, and as utterly on my side as I am on his in our whole attitude to the sub-normal and the Advisory Service, and against the C.M.O.'s wish he has taken on this job. Last night I found in my box the draft of a press release, an astonishing document produced by Miss Hedley and Alan Marre, against the advice of Peter Brown, refusing to mention that the Service arose out of the whole Ely Hospital scandal and my promise then, and giving no account of what Dr Baker was going to do or of the independence of his inspectorate. This morning I got Baker in to rewrite it. At 1 o'clock we had the press conference and, considering everything, it was pretty good, even though the press invented the title of double agent or troubleshooter.

I went on to No. 10 for a big O.P.D. on Chieftains for Israel. We had said we would make a final decision in the autumn and once again the Foreign Office wanted not to send them. I knew this would be so. It is perfectly true that after the leaks about this the Arabs have worked up a campaign and the F.O. have had telegrams from all their embassies saying that they would be burnt down and asking if the women and children could be sent home. Since last April we signed a £180 million contract to sell Chieftains to Libya only on the supposition that the tanks were also going to Israel, we now have a murderous situation. It was a tremendous debate. Michael Stewart is passionately keen that, if the new Russian tank is to be given to the Egyptians, these should be given to Israel but he felt that in that case we would be escalating war in the Middle East. Denis Healey reluctantly supported him and Roy Jenkins and the Board of Trade supported him from a very different point of view. Roy Mason is fanatically in favour of as much trade as possible and of our unloading £500 million-worth of the most modern kind of armaments on these poor Arabs, which is perfectly safe because they are not fit to use any of them. It was the most ignominious and terrible example of a real old-fashioned Foreign Office policy, combined with a cynical merchant of death arms sales policy. A number of us, including Wedgy Benn and me, said, 'It is probably true that we can't sell them to Israel but what we can't do is to ban them there and at the same time send out six new Chieftains for their triumphal procession this year. Moreover, if you ban them from Israel on the ground that by sending them out you would be escalating, how are you not escalating by sending them to Libya?' The

Prime Minister, who wanted to sell them, was totally on our side in this and we were so deadlocked that we decided to meet again on Thursday morning before Cabinet.

Thursday, October 16th

In the early morning we continued the O.P.D. and by now the Foreign Office and the Ministry of Defence had got together and found an excuse for a month's delay. Yesterday they had said it was impossible to delay any further because the Israeli General was coming to Britain and he couldn't be put off again. Now they found that nobody really knew what was going on in Libya since the fall of King Idris and we didn't even know if this vast quantity of tanks and the air defence system was really wanted by the new government.[1] They might be able to get something much cheaper from the French. I agreed with the month's delay and that was where we left it.

Then we turned to Cabinet and Roy presented his P.E.S.C. exercise for 1971/2. He had shown much greater skill than last time by fixing it all up with each of us separately, and we were all in agreement with him. After that came Judith, who had put in a long paper saying she must have extra increments in 1971/2 for overseas aid. She was supporting the paper Prentice had put in before his resignation, and making it clear that if she was to stay she must get a lot more as well. Judith is not a clever girl. She didn't handle people well and she bullied and chivvied and although she had seen the Chancellor yesterday and he had given her £18 million extra, she was now asking for a firm commitment for £33 million by 1975. She was supported by the aid lobby, by Barbara who looked hysterical and tired, and whipped us up into a fury. She gave an emotional speech and the rest of us sat silent, because I wasn't going to move an inch and let her get away with more for overseas aid than I got for sub-normal hospitals. However Roy stood firm and, despite the tricksiness of Harold, who is an aid man, Judith was held down and Cabinet stood pretty firm.

We had gone on a good long time so no proper time was left to consider my abatement White Paper. I have great luck, because National Superannuation always comes at the end of Cabinet, they don't understand it and they never have time to discuss it. I got general approval of our attitude, so that is finished until the actual White Paper is published the week after the Queen's Speech. After Cabinet Roy said to me, 'Barbara looks ill; I am worried about her. Is she all right really?' I said, 'I'm not sure she is. I think Barbara's physical health depends on her mental and spiritual health. She has had a terrible down and she is fighting it by sticking on at this Ministry. These next twelve months will be hell for her. I wish to God she had moved,' and Roy agreed with me.

[1] At the end of December Britain and Libya cancelled the contract for an air defence system, worth an estimated £120 million, and in January 1970 the Libyans signed contracts with the French for the supply of over 100 Mirage jets, with delivery to begin in 1971. The future of other British contracts to Libya remained in doubt.

It was a beautiful day in this wonderful week of St Martin's Summer, hot weather with cool mist in the evening, and down I went by train to Canterbury University. Some charming boys motored me up in a little car to the top of a hill, where you look down on the cathedral from the gigantic new university, very different from modernistic, industrialized Warwick. Canterbury is consciously humanist, consciously based on languages and history, and not full of celebrities, just quietly and studiously a kind of superior Keele. As I said to the students, 'These are the kind of buildings Tennyson would have had for the Knights of the Grail.' It couldn't have been a nicer Labour Club and 300 people turned up for a meeting.

Then I got on to the train for Dover, where I was expecting another quiet meeting, to find 200–300 people there. It was rough and dirty. I think there were twelve young men who had been trained as naval officers at some school in Dover and twenty NALGO people. Perhaps I was tired and I got it wrong but I never felt right with them, and, though David Ennals had a quiet time, I had constant interruptions and interference. We got on to the train at 10 o'clock and I intended to talk to David about abuse in social security. I found out only this week that next Monday he has got himself on a 'Panorama' performance on the welfare state and an eight-minute interview on abuse had been booked up and agreed before I had even heard of it. But we couldn't talk because David had got up at 4 o'clock this morning to go down a coal mine and now he fell asleep. As we came up in this terrible stopping train, taking two hours and twenty minutes, I worried more and more about this particular problem. I know David wants to do a lot more about it and that Titmuss and the other members of the S.B.C. know this and are very reluctant to be ordered about. I also know the mood of the public and I have got to try to stand by the principles of entitlement and humanity, yet I must show that we are going to stop real abuse by wastrels and drunkards. I suspect there are a lot of real abuses going on because of the rather pedantic interpretation of the doctrine of entitlement and because the civil servants aren't using their discretion wisely. However I have taken my courage in both hands and asked Harold if we can have this subject at Management Committee next Tuesday, along with my other controversial issue of the constitution of my new Regional Health Boards. This way we will deal with abuse several weeks in advance. I am preparing the way for this and also preparing for the time when Titmuss and Brian, Jarrett and I sit down with Harold Collison, when he has run himself in, and talk together on how to handle it.

Friday, October 17th

This morning I rang David at 7.0 a.m. (he says he is always up at 6.30 and he was up by 7.0) and talked to him for half an hour about the 'Panorama' programme. I told him how careful he must be not to upset Titmuss and Collison and I gave him various constructive ideas, which I think he took quite well. He is the kind of driving and energetic man who does all he can to get publicity for himself, although if I catch him in time, he always does what he is told in the end.

I went to another hospital this morning, Alec Baker's, at St Mary Abbot, and then I gave lunch to poor old Julian Snow. I had tried to get him when he went to the Prime Minister last week but first he was having his medical examination in hospital, then he was too proud and then he was disappearing to his constituency. I finally rang him on Tuesday and said, 'Julian, are you trying to avoid me?' 'Oh, no, I wasn't told by anybody you wanted to see me,' so I got him to lunch. Half the time Bob Maxwell was coming and interrupting us, but nevertheless we managed to have a chat about the future. Julian always behaves like a gentleman, with not a suggestion of grievance, but I know very well that he feels hurt, and I may have reduced it by 20 per cent. Another blazing hot afternoon and I was off on the train to Birmingham. I found Roy on the same train, so we tried to sit together, the net result being that of the two whole compartments hired for us one was unoccupied. We did manage to discuss Barbara and Tony Crosland. It is clear now that Tony didn't really want to move at all, and nor did Shirley Williams. We also discussed Callaghan and went round the Cabinet. Roy was discreet but quite full of anecdotes, not particularly interesting anecdotes, but they added to the sense that we were looking after each other. He and Jennifer have asked Anne and me to lunch on Monday at No. 11, the first time, by the way, that we have been asked since he became Chancellor.

I got off at Coventry and went on to Warwick University. What a difference between Canterbury, comparatively cultured and frightfully nice, thoughtful, old-fashioned socialists, bred from a middle-class, public school or grammar school atmosphere, and here, in the modern world of modern students, intellectually more tough, more at a loose end. However another 300 turned up to hear me on the social services, and listened with extraordinary civility and patience. Then I went round for an excellent meal with Jolly Jack and Doris Butterworth before going home in the fog to Prescote.

Sunday, October 19th

The swimming bath closed this weekend and, by jove, I missed it, so I spent three hours desperately tearing up nettle roots on my island and cleaning it up to make it a grassy glade. Patrick and I cut down our first great pine tree successfully, although we smashed a saw in the process, and today we went over to Nettlebed to lunch with the Campbells and I read *Hornblower* to the children on the way. I think I have got them converted to C. S. Forester, who is far better than Captain Maryatt. We discussed it over lunch with Jock and charming Phyllis and the seven children they have between them from their two families. They live in a great big comfortable Edwardian house with a big garden and the Baloghs are at the far end in a cottage. Jock had brought over Paul Johnson from Iver, where he lives in state with Marigold and their three children, and also Jeremy Potter,[1] the Manager of the *New Statesman*, and after lunch we had a conference. I was able to say that I had been thinking things over and had made up my mind that whether we won or lost the next election I wanted to give up politics, not so much for the *New Statesman*, but mainly so that I could have a life of my own and really see the family. I had also thought very carefully about my books and my contract with Hamish Hamilton for two books in five years.[2] The book they really want can best be done at the beginning, if for the first two or three years an archivist works away at it, and this is what we decided to do. It was a business-like conference. Jock obviously felt it was essential that I should take Paul's place. He said I was ten times as good as anybody they could get from the younger generation and I said, 'Well, yes. In five years I could groom my young successor.' We discussed why you couldn't get a young man now. The difficulty is that when Kingsley took it on as a young man the *Statesman* had, what, a circulation of 18–20,000 and was a small thing. Now it has a circulation of 85,000 and it's a prosperous business, which can in a sense afford to lose circulation, provided it maintains its prestige. Anyhow we firmed it up and they are going to get the Board to send me a letter. I am beginning to wonder whether I shan't have a different view of Parliament now I know that this is my last year and I shall be out for good at the end of the session. Parliament is back and, as you see, I have hardly been there. It has been a quiet beginning and my real test comes tomorrow, when I am No. 2 in Questions.

Monday, October 20th

I went up in thick fog. It had kept Tam in Edinburgh, so he wasn't going to be here for my Question Time, the time when I most want my P.P.S. David Ennals and I took a lot of trouble this morning because we thought we were going to have a Question on abuse and we discussed it at the weekly ministerial lunch. I found we had to be upstairs where we couldn't have drinks, in a miserable room, because there were so many people there. It always strikes me how many people from the Ministry like to be at a meeting even when they say nothing. Only four people, the P.U.S., myself, David Ennals and Crocker really discussed this.[3] Question Time was perfectly simple and straightforward. I made quite a decent reply on abuse although it got no press and as Hansard hasn't been printed for some days there was no full report of what we had said. We were back in form and Brian O'Malley and John Dunwoody were blooded by being asked to answer fairly easy questions.

After that I went down to the big Ministerial Committee Room for the

[1] Jeremy Potter was Managing Director of the *New Statesman*, in charge of all non-editorial matters. He left the paper in 1969 and became Managing Director of I.T.V. Publications.

[2] See p. 530 n. above.

[3] Anthony Crocker, an Under-Secretary at the D.H.S.S. He was responsible for the division looking after the Supplementary Benefits Commission.

long-awaited visit of the local authorities to discuss Seebohm. This was the meeting which started in July and had been postponed until today. I had Callaghan on my left, with his officials, and on my right Serota. The Ministry of Local Government brought their officials and so did Transport, Scotland, Wales, and whole retinue. Opposite us were the C.C.A., the A.M.C., the London boroughs, the G.L.C., the Port Authorities and then the U.D.C.s and the R.D.C.s. It's amazing how all these people like sitting there silent, wasting time.

It was very routine. I had been carefully briefed by Paul Odgers, a really first-rate assistant who has turned out absolutely trumps. There he was giving me in the right order the four right questions so they could be punctiliously answered by each delegation. It was very boring and it became clearer and clearer that they weren't going to say anything until they heard from me about the future of the National Health Service. But right at the end (and very characteristically this is not recorded in the minutes) Hetherington of the C.C.A. said, 'We have been talking again to the B.M.A. and it has been quite helpful. Why should we always talk about this scheme being either inside or outside local government? Why shouldn't you help us to evolve a mixed scheme?' He said it right across the table to me. I have been thinking about this during the summer as I have travelled around the country and I was able to reply that this was something very helpful which I would consider. He had given me precisely the lead I wanted. It is also clear from a meeting I had with Tony Crosland this morning, in preparation for the afternoon, that he is going to be sensible and constructive so I was satisfied with that.

Tuesday, October 21st

I was rung in the morning by Tommy Balogh. Had I heard about what was going on in Cabinet? I knew there was a Cabinet and I knew it was about so-called commercial policy, so I guessed it was about import deposits and pretended to know a bit. Tommy asked me to ring Harold Lever, so I got on to him and within two minutes he had coughed up the whole thing. Yes, there was a proposal to extend import deposits for one more year but reduced from 50 to 40 per cent, and to maintain at £50 a head the limit on the travel allowance for holidays abroad.[1] There had been a great many suggestions in the press that Roy was to make concessions on these two, especially from the *Financial Times*. (This happens regularly before one of Roy's announcements. I don't think he and John Harris manage it very well.) Tommy had been saying it was crazy to make any concession and I thought these doubts were pretty sensible. True, we have had two or three months' good trade figures

[1] The restrictions had been introduced on November 22nd, 1968 (see pp. 269–71). The Chancellor announced on October 21st, 1969, that the import deposit scheme was to continue for a further twelve months from December 5th but the rate of deposit was to be reduced from 50 to 40 per cent. The travel allowance, of £50 foreign currency and £14 in sterling for each traveller for a twelve-month travel year, was to continue.

but now is not the moment to do this. I gathered from Harold Lever that he was in some difficulty and that Barbara had been stirring things up. Sure enough, I was to learn from Barbara herself, after Cabinet, that she had been invited to a small meeting of the Ministers who deal with secret economic decisions, where she had been told that they intended first to reduce the import deposits to 40 per cent and then to phase them out as quickly as possible and that they were equally anxious to get rid of the travel allowance. Roy wanted to do this by agreement with the three other members of this small meeting. Barbara had blown up and said this was intolerable and that it was not the right time to make these concessions. There had been a battle because Harold Lever had on the whole wanted to have a concession on the travel allowance. The main thing Barbara achieved was that this should be referred to Cabinet and hence the sudden call for this morning.

At Cabinet things were unusually interesting. Roy put his case and then Barbara opposed it at phenomenal length, while Harold Lever, who had promised Barbara some support, remained embarrassingly silent. Barbara said she didn't think we ought to cut the import deposits and she certainly didn't think we ought to remove the travel allowance. Roy was in some danger of losing, although he had the Prime Minister and Harold Lever on his side, because Barbara was swaying a whole number of people to feel that Roy was making concessions to city opinion too early. I came in on Roy's side. I thought that actually the important thing was, as Harold Lever had taught me, that import deposits were being continued for another year and to do that without even a token reduction would really have upset EFTA. Continuing at 40 per cent seemed reasonable and since we were doing nothing about the family holiday allowance I thought it was satisfactory. I added that I thought the import deposit reduction ought to be put forward with no indication that we were going to phase them out and no suggestion that we would give concessions on the travel allowances in the near future. We should save these up for nearer the election and not throw them away now. On the whole I got Roy through. Afterwards Barbara was very upset. She said, 'Why didn't you talk to me?' I said, 'Well, you didn't talk to me.' She had talked to Thomas and we have now agreed that next Wednesday we are going to try and have a left-wing dinner together, where we can discuss the situation.

Immediately after Cabinet we got on to Management Committee, where I had asked to have the National Health Service. As Crosland and I had agreed, I wanted to change the reference to Seebohm in the Queen's Speech from 'legislation' to 'proposals'. I had agreed, under pressure from Callaghan, to put a reference to Seebohm in the Speech but only provided that it is all carefully spelt out in the Prime Minister's speech that the Seebohm legislation cannot be worked out until the Government has made its latest decisions about the structure of local government, towards the turn of the year. That way I can allay the alarm of the local authorities and the doctors. My request caused great alarm and despondency. The Prime Minister didn't like changing the Queen's Speech at this late date, Callaghan thought I was double-crossing him and it was all discussed at length. We cleared it up but only after a nasty sort of scratching row between Callaghan and me.

Then I got on to my main theme which was that I wanted to ask Cabinet for an agreed temporary solution for the Health Service, neither in nor out of local government. I would like a substantial block, perhaps even more than half, of the members of the Regional Health Executive to be local government professional representatives. Roy then made his usual titular stand. 'No,' he said. It couldn't be more than half, it could only be 49 per cent, and there he would stand firm. Well, for me to get 49 per cent when the Treasury had asked for none and had asked that they should all be government-appointed managers was all that I wanted, and I left knowing that I had got the backing of my ten colleagues on the negotiations which I shall now have to start with the local authorities and the doctors. For a change Management Committee was extremely useful. Even Barbara was helpful.

When I had finished my afternoon meetings in the Department, I popped off to the Athenaeum with Anne to give Bea Serota and her husband Stanley, the soil engineer, dinner in the Ladies' Annexe. I used to think it was terrible when it was first opened some ten years ago but now, measured by the standards of most London restaurants, it is tolerable. We had grouse and excellent claret, preceded by a decent course of potted shrimps, and something afterwards. It was an extremely pleasant dinner and an amusing evening, although it cost me nearly £9 for the four of us.

Wednesday, October 22nd

For ages I had promised Dame Kathleen that I would go and see the nursing officers, so off I went to one of those long dreary conference rooms in the Ministry, where some twenty earnest-looking women were seated. When I asked who had joined the Department from the N.H.S. they all put up their hands and I realized that all of them were paid more to work for us and that we had skimmed the cream of the matrons. I asked, 'All right, what do you do? Does your stuff get through to me?' There was a boom of 'No, no, no. We report and nothing happens.' I wasn't clear even by the end what on earth they do and why we have them all here. When I asked Godber and Alan Marre they smiled and said they wondered too. I am not sure we are justified in keeping them as well as an Advisory Service. Nevertheless I got quite a lot out of talking to them and a good reaction to the news that this morning at the annual conference of the Royal College of Nurses at Harrogate some leading matron had said the morale of the nursing profession was worse than at any time in its history. I asked what that meant. Did it mean really that their morale was low, or that they were in high spirits but militant against us? Well, they couldn't quite sort the difference out but they all agreed that the standard of nursing in hospitals was going down because nurses felt that we had no appreciation of their status. This is something which I have been feeling for weeks but now I had this evidence and I didn't forget it in the course of the day.

Back in my room I had David Ennals to see me about a sensational leak. I had been told that he was giving an off-the-record briefing to the *Daily Telegraph* Health Correspondent, and suddenly there appeared a series of firm announcements that the Government had decided to deal toughly with scroungers, with headlines saying that we were going to stop the abuse of unemployment benefit by retired senior civil servants. All these ideas had been listed as decisions we had already taken. It couldn't have been more damaging because I was already uneasily aware that Richard Titmuss and the members of the S.B.C. were becoming anxious about David forcing the pace, and he and I announcing without consultation decisions which they would have to carry out. However Peter Brown had been with David Ennals and assured me that not a word of this had been said to the actual correspondent, who had just twisted it and announced as decisions what David had told him we were only thinking about. 'Right,' I said, 'that is fine as long as you produce a total denial.' This news angle is awkward though, because this is coming up at Management Committee next week.

I rushed off to Baker Street to lunch with Marcus Sieff, where we discussed the speech I am due to give at the seventy-fifth birthday dinner for Meyer Weisgal.[1] Somehow I have got to find the time to prepare a memorable speech for the lovers of Meyer by next Tuesday evening. Then I returned to the Elephant and Castle for a fascinating meeting about a concrete proposal from the chemists, who have said they are prepared to market the contraceptive pill if it is obtainable from the Health Service with a doctor's prescription. Frankly, I didn't know the pill was not on the Health Service and that unless people get it through the Family Planning Association or through the local authority we make them pay for it. Apparently people usually have to pay a considerable sum themselves. I learnt at this meeting that only 1·2 million out of 12 million married women are on the pill so far, though many use other contraptions and appliances. I had been told by Bea Serota that the Department were wholly opposed to the pill being free on prescription, so I asked why not. Bavin looked across and said, 'It will cost too much, at least £5 million a year.'[2] I said, 'Only £5 million? Here is something which would really help the nation. If we can do this for £5 million, how can anybody doubt that the pill should be free?' All around the table I had blank opposition from the Department. I don't know whether it was only the cost or a moral feeling as well but I finally told them to go back to the pharmaceutical industry and say we wouldn't turn down their proposition as the

[1] President of the Weizmann Institute of Science, Israel, 1966–70.

[2] Alfred Bavin was an Under-Secretary at the D.H.S.S. 1960–8 and a Deputy Secretary 1968–73.

Department had recommended, but I couldn't agree unless they were prepared to come forward with positive proposals for cutting the cost. We shall see what happens. Since then I have been asking what the objection is, and everybody is staggered that if we could put the pill on prescription for £5 million the Department should turn it down.

This evening I went to a party at Claridge's given by the American Ambassador and his wife, where I found very few Americans and most of the members of the Government standing around drinking champagne. After that to the Little French Club just behind Prunier, where Thomas Balogh talked to me about the *New Statesman*. It was he who had suggested to Jock Campbell that there was a chance of my agreeing to join them and now I was telling him that I was agreeable. Thomas sees a good deal of Harold, with whom he had discussed my future and I chatted pretty freely.

Thursday, October 23rd

I had terrible cold feet during the night and early this morning I rang Thomas to ask him for God's sake not to repeat to Harold what I told him because the first person to tell the Prime Minister I should be leaving after the next election, win or lose, must be me.

Cabinet met at 10.15 and we confirmed the tactic which we agreed last week for getting rid of the boundaries issue.[1] We agreed to have all the Orders put to the Commons and the trick would be to put them but not approve them, so that in one go we would negate the lot. Callaghan and Wilson have won. We have not been discredited because the ordinary public are convinced that both the Government and the Tories are concerned with boundaries for our own self-interest. Apparently our line has won, we have defeated the Lords and the Tories and killed the redistribution, so we shall be fighting the next election on the present boundaries.

The next thing was abatement and we agreed that we should have my Statement on the Tuesday at the end of the two-day debate on the Queen's speech.[2] Harold thought that this would be the day on which the Tory motion of censure would be moved and if we put the Statement on at 3.30 that day, it would take the edge off and divert the attention of the press. It was a characteristic Harold device which I had never even thought of, but there we are, and if we have it next Tuesday no doubt the debate will come

[1] The House of Lords had rejected the Commons' amendment and, under the terms of the 1947 Parliament Act, the Seats Bill was delayed for a year, which obliged the Home Secretary to lay the Orders. Mr Callaghan then adopted the ingenious device of laying the Orders before Parliament for affirmative resolution and requesting Labour M.P.s to follow the advice of the Whips to vote against him. When the Conservatives returned to office in June 1970 they announced their intention of proceeding with the implementation of the Boundary Commission's recommendations as soon as possible and the Orders were laid in October 1970.

[2] The Statement was eventually made on Wednesday, November 5th. The traditional Conservative amendment censuring the Government was made on November 4th. It was rejected by 303 votes to 241.

a week later. The Foreign Secretary had his usual boring routine but this time reporting on something quite important, that Willy Brandt has become the Chancellor of West Germany.[1] We expected Kiesinger to win as he had been making a come-back towards the end, but, no, although the Christian Democrats were the biggest party, the Social Democrats plus the Free Democratic Party have now been able to form a coalition to keep the C.D.U. out. The Social Democrats have twelve members in the Cabinet including Helmut Schmidt and a number of people I know, and I expect they will be more anxious and more positive in trying to bring Britain into the Common Market, something I don't particularly want.

Then we had Barbara, who had to admit that the whole industrial field is in complete anarchy, with strikes in the motor-car industry, the whole of the coal mines on strike,[2] including the prosperous fields, and now this madness affecting the nurses, who are steaming up at their conference at Harrogate. We find this unrest and disarray everywhere in the public service, firemen, dustmen, local government officers. Barbara reported that everything was out of control. Heavens alive, here we are, we have taken it upon ourselves in the Queen's Speech to reactivate Part II of the prices and incomes policy and we know it is going to be completely meaningless. Barbara says quite openly that the policy is in ruins.

Only two people really asked anything. I asked if it were not true that this was a kind of conscious reaction against prices and incomes, and I have no doubt that to some extent I am right because, as somebody else said, when Stafford Cripps gave up the two-year wage freeze in the first Labour Government it was followed by a staggering period of industrial unrest. Take down the dam and water flows through all the pasture, and I am sure this is true today. Barbara is trying to stop the water like Queen Canute, and it is dismal. I was able to use the opportunity, however, for something I had picked up from my meeting with the nurses yesterday. I warned people that we needed a new deal for the nurses, and I got a surprising amount of response from the Prime Minister and others. So I can go back to Dame Kathleen, this funny old thing with her golden hair and her blue eyes and her pink and white cheeks, this typical ex-matron with her collection of matrons, and say, 'Get on with it. We will get you a new deal; the P.M. is now in your favour.'

[1] After the federal elections on September 28th, and the subsequent formation of the S.P.D./F.D.P. coalition, the new Bundestag elected Willy Brandt as its Chancellor on October 21st. Dr Gustav Heinemann was President and Helmut Schmidt, previously the parliamentary leader of the S.P.D., became Minister of Defence.

[2] On October 13th an unofficial stoppage began over a demand for a forty-hour week, inclusive of meal breaks, for surface workers. It began in Yorkshire and spread until 121,000 miners were involved. After three days of discussions between miners' leaders and Vic Feather, on October 24th normal working gradually resumed, but 979,000 days had been lost in what was the largest single stoppage in the coal-mining industry since 1944. A month's stoppages had begun at Vauxhall in September, at Standard Triumph International from late August to November, and labour relations in the motor-car industry were generally troubled. Firemen had threatened to strike on Guy Fawkes Night, November 5th, but their claim was settled and a strike avoided.

After that the Cabinet polished off the problem of Welsh self-government. George Thomas got cold feet and had to climb down and agree to postpone the Bill this session to give time to reconsider the impact of the Maud Commission on Cardiff and Swansea. This was partly because Callaghan said he thought that leaving county boroughs in Cardiff and Swansea would be indefensible if they were going to be abolished in England and that the notion of the city region should be considered. George Thomas finally came to his senses. I had been very puzzled because he has kept on telling me that I must go to his constituency annual dinner, I must see him here, I must see him there. He works away but when he couldn't get round us he conceded.

Back to 70 Whitehall for a little press conference about the Newcastle hospital decision. I had redrafted the whole decision letter and, against Peter Brown's advice, I said it should be released and that there should be a press conference in London. I signed the letters last night and saw the press today so the kind of decision which I perhaps gave once a fortnight as Minister of Housing has been given in this Ministry for the first time.

Friday, October 24th

All day yesterday I had been trying to prepare a speech for the opening of Greenwich Hospital, the first hospital we have ever built as a Ministry. It is extremely expensive, for instance, it is the only hospital where they are testing air conditioning at a cost of £3 a week per patient, but it is full of interest, with lots of experimental methods of communication and everything else. I got the speech clear early this morning and then saw Paul Odgers, who is having to clear with all the Ministers concerned the reference to the Seebohm Report in the Prime Minister's speech. I can't tell you how much time and trouble he had to go to to get Callaghan's agreement. I said to Odgers, 'Come along with me,' and we went down the little staircase outside No. 70, through the Privy Council Office, out into Downing Street and through the front door of No. 10. Callaghan was sitting waiting for O.P.D. and I said, 'This passage is all right,' and he said, 'Oh, no it isn't. I have seen that draft and I am not content with it.' He is such a suspicious man and has been watching and waiting to see me try to double-cross him. Still, Odgers didn't tell me how but we got the passage we wanted in the Queen's Speech.

At O.P.D. we had two fantastic items. The first was the hijacking of planes and what the British were going to do about it at Heathrow, and the second was even more James Bondish and ridiculous – no, not Bondish, novelettish. This was what to do about the Falkland Islands, where a thirty-nine-year-old American was thinking of collaborating with a British company to spend millions on a potential oil strike, apparently based on some geologist's vague talk fifty years ago. Indeed, you might well ask why on earth we don't welcome someone who is willing to spend his money testing for oil at the Falkland Islands; it's not much worse than Alaska. The chiefs of staff at the meeting are usually silent but one, an admiral, said, 'Yes, it's further off but it's far easier to get at all through the year.' There was an elaborate paper from Michael Stewart saying that if the Argentinians suspected an oil strike they might land an army and then where would we be if they tried to take over the islands and the oil. Frankly, no one knows if there is any oil there or not and, as I said, this may be an undergraduate idea but the striking fact was that the Foreign Office said the only thing to do was to conceal the suggestion and prevent any testing.

Jim Callaghan and I often have the same idea and he came out with exactly what I was thinking. He said, 'I don't see why we shouldn't make this the basis of consultation with the Argentinians. Why don't we talk to them about this? We could say, "There is this American who wants to spend his own money looking for oil and if this spreads further into your territorial waters we should have joint control of the tests".' Of course this was too simple. We were told that the Foreign Office had thought of it but it was too dangerous because we might still provoke the Argentinians into landing an army. In the end we universally settled for a suggestion of George Thomson's. 'We don't want to go into this in the year before the election,' said he. 'Let us play for time during this year.' With his brilliant words ringing in my ears I rushed out back to my car, read through my speech and got down to Greenwich.

There were Dick Marsh and his wife and all the local worthies standing about and we did our tour. Mind, you, the tour was timed for forty-five minutes and all the press were there and I began to have some impression of how ghastly royal tours must be. You can't look at anything or speak to anybody because you are being pushed round. Off we went to lunch, cold meat, salad and rosé, and then I delivered my speech to an unreflective audience.

After a big press conference with lots of good, shrewd questions and doctors there to answer them, I was up and away to Thames to record a piece for Eamonn Andrews's programme on different aspects of the Health Service. It all went with a tremendous bang, perhaps too big a bang. I found myself elated by that speech at the hospital and here I was speechifying to the four journalists who were cross-examining me, and afterwards sitting drinking with them because I had just missed the 5.35. My God, it was suddenly 5.50 and Peter and I had to get the 6.15 from Paddington. The whole of the Strand and Park Lane was blocked, right up to Marble Arch. Peter dashed through and in Bayswater we suddenly found the whole of one street blocked, so up he went, driving on the other side of the road, straight past the two lines of traffic, the green light went, we turned left and were in Paddington with a minute or two to spare. We drove right down to the bottom thinking my train was at Platform 10 or 12. It wasn't, it was Platform 13, right at the back. We ran, we galloped, and the train wasn't even in. When it arrived I tottered into it and got back to Prescote at 7.30.

Sunday, October 26th

Albert Rose came over last night from Coventry but there's nothing happening on that front. He is a little less depressed but my constituency is totally inactive and Albert makes no proposals for any meetings, not even surgeries. I think it doesn't matter. Winnie Lakin has been selected as my agent again and the party will go through the manoeuvres of fighting the election but as the fight doesn't really take place there I am not concerned. My God, though, I might be concerned if I had less than an 18,000 majority.

It's been another beautiful weekend and I have managed to get two or three hours each afternoon on the island, apart from going to Banbury with Patrick to *The Longest Day* which David Ennals had taken his children to see and which I thought was going to be a tremendous, masterly film, but was in fact a kind of entertainment spun out to interminable length. I have been thinking more and more about the life I shall be leaving when I stop being a Minister. Will my new life take as much time and energy? No, I shall be finished by Thursday lunchtime and above all I shan't have these red boxes following me down.

An interesting thing this week is that Edward Boyle has retired from politics. I suppose one of his troubles was that he started too brightly and then he had his dramatic resignation over Suez.[1] He has found Opposition more and more trying, with the Tories going further and further to the right, and it has been especially difficult for him that they are anti comprehensive schools. He found, I have no doubt, that he wouldn't be Minister of Education in a Tory Government and now he has been offered the Vice-Chancellorship of Leeds. I would say he is possibly working for a peerage and then perhaps a Ministry, though I think he is probably out for good. Nineteen years is long enough in politics for a man who started that young, which only shows you ought to start a bit later. There's a good article on him in the *Spectator*, by the way, by Peregrine Worsthorne, pointing out that Boyle's real mistake was not to recognize that the strength of the Tory party is its vulgarity, the part he most disliked. He was in fact a real Tory intellectual and now he has been replaced by Mrs Thatcher.[2] She is rather a pal of mine, I got on very well with her when she was at Pensions and she is one of the few Tories I greet in the lobby. She is tough, able and competent, and, unlike Boyle, she will be a kind of professional Opposition Spokesman.

The other thing was the death of Emrys Hughes,[3] the son-in-law of Keir Hardie,[4] and M.P. for Ayrshire. I used to know him quite well. He was a

[1] Edward Boyle resigned over Suez in November 1956. He was first elected to Parliament in 1950, at the age of twenty-seven, as Conservative M.P. for Birmingham, Handsworth.

[2] Mrs Margaret Thatcher was Conservative M.P. for Finchley 1959–74 and since 1974 for Barnet, Finchley. She was Joint Parliamentary Secretary at the Ministry of Pensions and National Insurance October 1961–4, Secretary of State for Education and Science 1970–4 and since 1975 has been Leader of the Conservative Party and of the Opposition.

[3] Labour M.P. for South Ayrshire from 1946 until his death in October 1969. He was Editor of *Forward* 1931–46.

[4] James Keir Hardie, Labour M.P. for South West Ham 1892–5 and for Merthyr Tydfil

fellow journalist, editor of *Forward*, and I remember when I was a young Bevanite going up to some Keir Hardie anniversary and making a speech for Emrys in the rain. We felt a certain link with each other and I watched him running down, in a sense running to seed, as he became a kind of professional funny man, a little bit like the way Jimmy Maxton went.[1] They were both great stock figures. As often happens, one tends to parody oneself and play one's own caricature.

Monday, October 27th

My first departmental meeting was on social security. The Government Actuary had sent his latest figures for the proposed contribution which employers should pay to cover the National Health Service and social insurance parts of our scheme. We knew that our figure of 6¾ per cent, as the employer's total contribution in 1972, was too small but we had always known this might be the case and our January and July White Papers had indicated quite clearly that we might have to add something, not on the pension side but to the 2 per cent covering short-term benefits. Indeed, the July White Paper on short-term benefits gave the actual figure and said we would have to raise the percentage from 2 to 2·2.[2]

As David Ennals wasn't there this morning I was asked what we should do about this. I said that we had always kept the N.H.S. contribution as a flexible reserve and that we should try out on the Treasury a new idea, that only 0·3 per cent should be for the Health Service instead of the 0·5 per cent we had reckoned on. That way we wouldn't have to increase the total contribution by 0·2 per cent. The Ministry were aghast and said, 'What do you really mean?' and I said, 'We kept it flexible, let's try it out on them.' 'But what will the Treasury think?' they said. I replied, 'I don't know but if they don't like it they needn't like it,' so we decided to try this out.

The next meeting I had was with the people concerned with nurses. We had already as a Department decided on a committee on nurses' pay and now we have got both the Management Committee showing great interest in a new deal for nurses and Cabinet sanction for it. I said to them today, 'Now is your chance. You nurses tell me twelve things we ought to be doing, twelve areas where they have failed to get through to me. Give me a nurses' charter, a manifesto, so that we don't only make a concession on salaries.' I see the difficulty. We are due to raise salaries next April, so we can't put anything forward now which would somehow undermine that, but there

from 1900 until his death in 1915, was the founder of *Labour Leader* and the Chairman of the Independent Labour Party.

[1] Chairman of the Independent Labour Party 1926–31 and 1934–9. He was Labour M.P. for Glasgow, Bridgeton from 1922 until his death in 1946.

[2] The White Paper had an appendix written by the Government Actuary proposing that the employer's contribution should be the equivalent of 6¾ per cent of earnings for each employee. This rate would cover superannuation, the N.H.S. contribution, the social insurance contribution and the redundancy fund.

are other things we can do between now and then. We have to make them feel we really care about them, while facing the fact that for the next few months we can do little about wages. All the departmental people sat round the table numb and glum while the nursing staff were told that if they had really been denied their right of access to the Minister they had their chance today.

The third thing was our Prices and Incomes Further Policy Committee, with Roy Jenkins in the chair, and Barbara Castle once again putting forward her new version of incomes policy and demanding her Industrial Commission. We all knew that if we reactivated Part II of the Prices and Incomes Act it wouldn't really mean anything. The car workers and the firemen, who have threatened a strike on November 5th, will in the meantime be getting 10, 15, 20 per cent increases, the whole of the incomes policy is completely out of control, but we have to go on pretending that the Government can control wages and pretending that the Industrial Commission would become an adequate substitute for the policy. For most of the afternoon we sat solemnly under Roy's chairmanship and none of us was going to object because we all thought the prices and incomes policy was ruined anyway and didn't mind what Harold did to try to pick up the pieces.

Then it was time to go to No. 10 for the little party which Harold gives before the Queen's Speech, for all the Ministers. I shot upstairs and looked in just for a moment, long enough to see Patricia Llewelyn-Davies and a few others, and John Mackintosh who was moving and Joyce Butler who was seconding the Queen's Speech. Harold was going to read it aloud as usual and discuss it with us but though I would have liked to stay for this particular one I had to motor off to Hatfield.

I was off in Douglas Garnett's car to a meeting that I thought was going to be a bloody waste of time. I found some 200 people, every seat taken, more chairs being brought in, and a very keen, enthusiastic Labour Party on its toes, enjoying itself. I think I maybe spoilt it a bit by talking too long and we had rather short questions afterwards but everyone agreed it was a wonderful meeting. Then Doug Garnett motored me back down the A1 and just before Apex Corner we looked for somewhere to eat. We stopped off at a pub where there was a snack bar, admirably staffed by a young Polish waiter. The proprietor came up and told us he was a friend of Ted and Barbara Castle and Mia and Bill Connor, and that he'd had them all there and had been to the silver wedding party.

Tuesday, October 28th

Today was the State Opening of Parliament and also Patrick and Virginia's half-term. They came up to London last night and had a terrible time because the Ford Executive packed it in on the motorway and they had to get a hired car at a garage. It produced a real family tiff because they all want a smaller car, a Capri, much cheaper and very good. I want another Executive because it gives me plenty of room in front but Anne wants something lighter to drive. However they got up last night and here they were for the State Opening. Anne and Virginia had decided to stand outside near the Norman Porch, where they could see the Queen arriving, but Patrick didn't, so he and I walked back across St James's Park for a haircut with Mr Large. Then we strolled back to watch the crowds forming and see the crown jewels being carried along in their special coach with the lights on them, the best bit of the show.

Patrick had had a sudden bright idea yesterday and asked why we couldn't have a little party at No. 70 Whitehall, just at the corner of Downing Street and Whitehall, for all the children of the Private Office. Heavens alive, we thought of it on Monday and by this morning we had Ralph Cox with his wife, his boy and three girls, Michael Fogden with his wife and three children, John Cashman, who is a bachelor, and Peter Smithson with his wife and his four boys. When we strolled in there were all the children playing about. The grown-ups hadn't all met each other before, we had a pleasant morning sitting around and Anne and Virginia came in halfway through. Peter Smithson's wife was certainly the smartest there, very elegant, and undoubtedly Michael Fogden's wife is the nicest of them all and the least tidy, with three delicious children. There was Cox's slim, retiring, good-looking wife with a boy of fifteen and one girl of thirteen. I took them through and showed them the Cabinet Office and got them through to No. 10 and showed them everything there. I hope they found it worth while. At 12.30 the Crossman family went off to the Farmers' Club for lunch after a very nice morning.

Meanwhile the Queen's Speech was delivered and in the afternoon there was the debate, with Harold making his speech, Heath's reply and then the knockabout starting. We were back in election year. Harold apparently made a very dull speech and Heath a lively one. The surprise was that Harold gave the House a completely different picture of our prices and incomes policy. He said we were going to reactivate Part II only as a bridging measure until the establishment of the Industrial Commission.[1] Yesterday we had no vestige of a suggestion that he was going to do this and I still don't know at what point he agreed with Barbara to make this concession. These are things Prime Ministers can do and none of us will object, as we can't do anything about it.

However, my own worries were for the speech I had to make at Meyer Weisgal's seventy-fifth birthday dinner. He is the head of the Weizmann Institute at Rehovot, a man to whom I feel enormously grateful. It was a worry because all British Jews of any distinction who care about Zionism and about Meyer were going to be at the Dorchester tonight. What the hell should I say, I who for five years have been out of contact with Israel, who

[1] The Prime Minister's exact words are to be found in *House of Commons Debates*, Vol. 790, col. 42.

am somehow rusty on the whole thing? Finally I got from Marcus Sieff a book on Meyer and today I took two or three hours off to try to think what I could say. It was a terrific gathering. Anne and I got there a little late and went straight through from the reception lobby into a bar at the back of the ballroom so that no one knew we had arrived and we could get a drink before the reception committee came to meet us. Then we were planked down at table. I had pulled myself together and made a speech which was touching because it centred on Weizmann,[1] with the theme of what he had done for me and what he had done for Meyer and how we had both been changed by him and had our best qualities brought out. It was true that Weizmann allowed to very few people the liberties he allowed to Meyer and me, so at least I was able to say that. And Anne was able to say afterwards, 'Well, you weren't talking about Harold Wilson were you? You were talking about a leader you really admired.' It came off and it showed I could make a speech honestly based on my own life, on profound feelings and attitudes, and, looking back over my life, it is true that what I did between 1945 and 1948 for Israel and Palestine has fixed itself as the time which stirred my emotions most of all, and when I was possibly at my best.

Wednesday, October 29th

The papers are full of the by-elections and the latest polls indicate that we might possibly lose Swindon and Newcastle-under-Lyme. The euphoric sense that we are bound to win has been suddenly shattered and people are terribly anxious because the polls are telling us that there is really a chance for the Tories.

This morning we were back again on the terrible issue of Barbara's Bill. We have a special, very small and select Committee to deal with this, on which I have to sit because of the trouble she got by excluding me from it last time. Barbara is in charge here because she is to have her way on the Bill but there is another Committee chaired by Roy which is dealing with future prices and incomes policy. During the course of the day it became clear to me that these Committees overlap to an astonishing degree and that it is no good having one Committee on the Bill creating the new Industrial Commission and another dealing with future prices and incomes legislation because the first is the second, the new institution is the substitute for the old policy.

We painstakingly went through the Bill and it was quite clear that this Commission was to have all the powers of the Monopolies Commission, but applied to almost every subject. In the case of the Monopolies Commission, if a monopoly is demonstrated, considerable powers to act are given to the Government, and Barbara is now proposing that we should have the same powers to use against a company which can be proved to

[1] Chaim Weizmann, President of the World Zionist Organization 1920–31 and 1935–46, was first President of the State of Israel from 1949 until his death in 1952.

have abused fair competition. This is an entirely different scale of intervention in private industry and we found ourselves in tremendous difficulties. Once again we had the feeling that Harold and Barbara had fixed all this up behind the scenes and now we were supposed to concede.

All this came into the open later in the day when Roy took the chair at Prices and Incomes Committee. There was a downright row because Roy thought that this segment of Barbara's paper on the Bill would be taken by this Committee and she thought it would be agreed by us in the other Committee. Roy said he would put all this to the Prime Minister but I haven't yet seen the result because I have looked through the minutes and can't find any of this there. The row was only ended by Roy saying he would try to get a Prime Ministerial decision on the overlapping of the Committees.

Then I had another very difficult committee, Home Publicity. We had been asked to deal with the publicity connected with abatement. This was the Statement which Harold had wanted me to make next Tuesday at 3.30 in order to take the publicity off the Leader of the Opposition on the wind-up of the Queen's Speech debate. However I had finally got the P.M. to see that this would be a terrible mistake because if I am going to make a ministerial broadcast next Monday, we don't want another big thing the day after. So it was moved to the Wednesday, and Home Publicity was now dealing with this enormously complicated matter.

The other theme was how to deal with the subject of Civil Service pensions. Thank God Eddie Shackleton was there. He made it clear that the Civil Service, the Treasury, the Inland Revenue and the new Civil Service Department had not thought at all about the problem of over-pensioning which could arise as a result of my Bill. My Bill says that in addition to occupational pensions we shall introduce a good, earnings-related state pension, and when people get the two together they will often be getting 80 per cent or 90 per cent on retirement, and sometimes 110 per cent or possibly 120 per cent. It was obvious that the Treasury would have to modify its rule that you shouldn't get more than 66⅔ per cent of your former earnings and all this should have been considered months ago, when we were drafting the White Paper. The Treasury should have come forward and said that this would have the most serious consequences for them but it hadn't been said and it hadn't been pressed on the Treasury by Mildred Riddelsdell or Clifford Jarrett, because they didn't concern themselves with occupational pensions and were only busy with the state pension. The Departments had simply behaved with exactly the same attitude as a private firm or the trustees of a private pension fund, saying, 'We will wait and see until after the terms of abatement are settled.' I had been a bit puzzled for a long time as to why the NALGO people were able to work up these government officials against us, why they were able to make them think they were going to lose the lump sum they receive on retirement and why the policemen and firemen were saying they weren't sure they would get their pensions at fifty and that the whole age of retirement might be changed. All this had seemed to me insane. At this meeting I realized for the first time that with the Treasury and the C.S.D. in this mood, all these things might be true. In the last four years they had never considered this but left it until now on the assumption that after our Bill over-pensioning would be defined in the same way as before. People would be forbidden, broadly speaking, to get more than 66⅔ per cent and therefore when we introduced a good state pension it would indeed be at the cost of the private or occupational pension. This has now been driven home to me. However we are going to win all right, simply because nobody dares to tell the firemen or the policemen that this is all a theory of the Treasury and the C.S.D. My God, we had a terrible time dealing with it.

We were all settling down to a discussion when in came Dick Taverne, terribly tense with a tight face, saying, 'I am terribly sorry, there is an issue I have to raise which may involve the postponement of the whole Statement.' It came out that as he and the Treasury now felt that 6¾ per cent employer's contribution was inadequate we would have to put a new figure into our publicity. 'That', I said, 'is ridiculous. This is something we can discuss privately with the Treasury. Figures can be changed and anyway we are covered on all this because we are merely popularizing the White Paper, where we have made it clear that the figure might have to be increased when we come to the Bill. We cannot see how the Treasury is responsible for the publicity for the White Paper because this has already been put to Cabinet and passed.' But Dick Taverne insisted that our figures had been put forward as firm.

Immediately afterwards I went home and said to all our civil servants, 'What is this? Why is the Treasury taking this line?' I was assured that they had gone to the Treasury officials, who didn't seem to object, and my officials were quite sure that we were in the clear on the abatement figures for the White Paper because we had certainly made it obvious that we might have to alter them upwards. It disturbed me, though, because it had upset the whole meeting.

This afternoon I saw Sir Herbert Tetley, the Government Actuary, and persuaded him to appear with me at the press conference next Wednesday. I wasn't sure if he would but he had no doubt at all that he would come along to give evidence on our behalf. He is a lovely man with fair hair and large blue eyes, and in the course of these discussions he has somehow become my solid ally. After that, while the debate on the Queen's Speech was taking place, I had arranged to see the Health group at 4 o'clock. I wasn't going to let them feel I had neglected them on the Green Paper and they had put on the whip that I would be at the meeting.[1] I turned up in Room 13 to find Shirley Williams with two other people. Every single

[1] The whip is, theoretically, a notice of the week's business, but the term is generally used to refer to the requests and instructions M.P.s receive to attend and vote.

member of the group knew about the meeting. It looked a bit silly, and we had to break up. That is the extent of the activity of the Labour Members who want to talk about the Green Paper, on an afternoon when there is nothing of any great interest on in the House. In fact that, of course, was the trouble. As there was no vote this evening, no Labour Members were there and even with our restored morale this particular Party defect hasn't changed at all. It was a bit depressing.

Barbara had at last agreed that we should have a series of regular meetings on future policy and said she would have the first one tonight at her flat, which is somewhere out in Highgate. She got Tommy Balogh and Peter Shore to go and she wanted me to bring Brian. I had forgotten how to get there, so it was terribly difficult to find. The trouble about the meeting was that she only wanted to discuss negative income tax. On Harold's instructions, I had sent around the text of my Herbert Morrison lecture before it was published by the Fabian Society and begged Ministers to clear it within a week. Barbara had fastened on the section on negative income tax, because she hates the contributory system and she thinks this is a solution I shouldn't rule out. She spent the whole time arguing about this with me and Brian, so that Tommy and Peter Shore were a bit bored and we didn't get anywhere with anything else. She thought it was useful but at 10 o'clock I went home with Tommy Balogh, who was a bit depressed.

Thursday, October 30th

It was the day of the by-elections and everybody was rather tense. The first thing was S.E.P., the first meeting of this central strategic and economic committee for a good long time. It doesn't do any economic strategy now, that is left to a much smaller group of Harold, Roy and Barbara. I'm not on that and don't even know the members but S.E.P. is a largish committee and as usual most of the Cabinet seemed to be there. A civil aviation White Paper was being presented and an important modification of S.E.T. but I wasn't interested in those because I was waiting for the third item, the motorists' levy to cover the costs of accidents. After Roy had bought the idea, Cabinet had agreed provided it was regarded as workable. I had the greatest difficulty in getting anybody to consider it workable and the more it was examined the more resistance there had been from the Ministry of Transport, who said we would have a bleeding row with all the motoring organizations, and also from the Treasury, which regarded the levy as merely another form of tax and therefore no real, genuine saving.

I had got it through my own Social Services Committee only by saying that if we didn't get our £9 million this way, we would have to cut the hospital building programme, which would give us even worse publicity. Nevertheless, the new Minister of Transport, Fred Mulley, had reserved his position, so I took it to S.E.P. Here it got even worse treatment, more and more people objected, and the only way I made the thing acceptable at all was by saying that otherwise the £9 million would have to be raised by the cut in hospital building and it's now too late to do that without bringing the whole of this year's programme to a stop. It shows you how completely this awful P.E.S.C. dominates proceedings and decisions. There it was and I was told to put a paper to Cabinet along with Mulley.

Immediately afterwards came Cabinet and a very extraordinary thing happened. The Prime Minister started with a longish talk about the political situation and the by-elections, in which he showed that he had suddenly lost his nerve. The euphoria had gone, he was scared stiff by the latest polls and said we might well have to face the loss of all five. If we did Cabinet should stick together and show the same reaction and he advised us all how to handle it. I have never heard him in that mood before. Up, and then right down. He was deeply depressed, trying to hold us for the catastrophe which was coming. To be honest, I have always been uneasy about these by-elections and his euphoria. He also went on to say that in this new situation we must hit back at Heath. He was deeply upset by Ted Heath's personal attacks on him and the thing we must do now is (and these were the words he used), 'Kick Ted in the groin; we must be rough with him.' I must say that at this point Tony Wedgwood Benn coolly and quietly said, 'This is a great mistake. It won't do you or us any good. If you kick Ted Heath in the groin you will build him up. You have done so very well over the summer because you have been attacked by the Tories and you have come through it. Why should we give Heath the advantage of treating him as a leader when they are really a leaderless party?' Person after person put this argument and Harold began to modify his tactics. He said, 'I don't want you to attack Ted Heath, only his policies.' Then I said, 'That would be a disaster. The biggest thing in the summer has been your recovery, Prime Minister, from a desperate position. Why should we harm that by reversing our attitude just when it is most successful?' I added, 'Of course you might say that, apart from attacking Heath, we ought to praise you more. Well, frankly, we all talk a lot about you.' At this point the whole Cabinet was convulsed with laughter. They were laughing because they thought this meant that they gossiped about him outside and to the press. It didn't upset Harold or me too much but it did reveal to me that Cabinet think I am a great, compulsive communicator about Harold Wilson and that I had caught myself out. Anyhow, there it was. We all told Harold that to take this line would be a terrible revelation and he stopped at that point. The rest of Cabinet was entirely about Barbara's I.R. Bill, which we had to go through again, discussing each clause in detail. She is now an interminable proser and I couldn't listen to it twice.

I was due to go to Bristol this evening for a dinner with the Regional Hospital Board at which we would discuss the Green Paper, and then spend a whole Friday going round a sub-normal hospital and on various other engagements, but I had suddenly been told that we were to have a Management Committee tomorrow morning, so I thought at first I would have to cancel the whole visit. Then I thought no, if I could go down this evening to the dinner, which had been arranged weeks before, I could come back on the early morning train on Friday, have the Management Committee while John Dunwoody filled in for me, and then catch a train back for the rest of the afternoon's performance in the South-West. This is what I actually did.

On the way down with Janet and an official from Social Security, I dictated the text of the five minutes I have for the ministerial broadcast on the new pension increases and contributions and on abuse. This was Harold's idea, although I warned him that if I did this the Tories would demand the right to reply. First he had agreed, then he had changed his mind and now I was being told to do an objective broadcast that didn't require a reply. Anyhow I sweated away with Janet and as we drew into Bristol I had just about got a rough draft ready.

The dinner was O.K. except for some rather drunken general practitioners who got up and spoilt it. We were warned that the press were all waiting outside because the result of the first by-election was out. As I left they told me we had won North Paddington and I thought, 'My God, we must have won everything else.'[1] I went back to the Grand Hotel and lay watching television from my bed from 11 p.m. to 1 a.m. I saw that we had scraped home at North Islington and at Newcastle-under-Lyme and that we had quite a good result in the Gorbals, but there was a recount at Swindon and I ruled that out.

Friday, October 31st

I woke up at 5.0 and began to worry, and suddenly I began to think about the awfulness of having a special Bill to raise £10 million by a levy on the motorist.[2] I thought, 'My God, this is almost as bad as charges on teeth and spectacles. It is terrible. I must think of something better.' Then I remembered that in my Herbert Morrison lecture and in my speech last July I had talked about a National Health Service levy on employers and it suddenly occurred to me that, instead of waiting for the introduction of the new scheme in 1972, we should for the intervening period have a special scheme for an employers' levy, which would get us out of our difficulty.

[1] At Paddington North Arthur Latham held the seat for Labour with a 517 majority, on a swing to the Conservatives of 11·4 per cent. At Islington North Michael O'Halloran held the seat for Labour with a 1,534 majority, on a 9·2 per cent swing to the Conservatives. At Newcastle-under-Lyme John Golding kept the seat for Labour with a 1,042 majority, on a 10·7 per cent swing to the Conservatives. At Glasgow, Gorbals, Francis McElhone held the seat for Labour but there was a Conservative swing of 7·8 per cent and the majority of 9,940 in 1966 was cut to 4,163. At Swindon the seat was won by a Conservative, Christopher Ward, who had a majority of 478 votes. The swing to the Conservatives was 12·8 per cent.

[2] See pp. 577 and 594. Proposals to revive this scheme were made in 1976, but in 1977 they were abandoned as impracticable.

I rang Mike Fogden, who was in Bristol with me, and told him, and then I rang the office and said I must see Dick Bourton and Douglas Overend as soon as I arrived in London. At 7.20 I caught the train and in the breakfast car I saw a man whose newspaper had a big headline saying that the Tories had won Swindon. He could see I was looking across and said, 'Do you want my paper?' 'No, no, no,' I said but he sent it over to me and then I saw my photograph on the front page as the man who came to dinner the night before. I said, 'Remarkable. I am glad I am proved to have been in Bristol last night.' He hadn't worried about the by-election, he was a businessman from Bristol and he had just worried about my face.

When I got to Paddington I found to my surprise that one of the junior members of the Private Office was there with an urgent paper from Douglas Overend. He had been approached at 8 o'clock last night by the Treasury, who were still terribly worried about abatement, and the Chancellor was going to raise the issue of the 6¾ per cent employer's contribution at Management Committee this morning. Thank God I had come back. There was a long paper saying that the Treasury thought that if I got the 6¾ per cent printed in the White Paper I would get away with it and this would mean a lot of extra money on public expenditure. It also said that the Treasury were thinking that so far from reducing the N.H.S. contribution, it ought to be increased in order to avoid pressure on taxation. This long paper played completely into my hands. 'This is lucky,' I said, 'because I want to raise this very issue for quite different reasons.'

I felt I must be fair to Roy, so I rang him up and began to explain what I was thinking of and that really there was no danger whatsoever because we had covered ourselves on the 6¾ per cent in the White Paper. It wasn't a fixed sum at all. He said, 'But I thought you wanted to reduce it.' I suddenly realized that when on the Monday I had told my people to tell the Treasury I wanted to reduce the employer's contribution to the National Health Service from 0·5 per cent to 0·3 per cent, this 0·2 per cent reduction in contributions would require a 90 per cent increase in the revenue raised for the Health Service from taxation. It explained why Roy and the Public Expenditure Section of the Treasury had seen red. They thought I was up to some ghastly scheme and Roy had got into a panic and decided that he must handle it. He was rough with me and he suddenly said, 'Now I have to go and see the Prime Minister,' and slammed down the telephone. This was at 9.50 and as our meeting was at 10.15 I thought it showed he was rushing off to try to get the P.M. on his side.

When I arrived at Management Committee I found that for some extraordinary reason Burke had rearranged the cards and I wasn't sitting in my usual place next to the Chancellor but opposite the P.M. and Roy, whom I saw worrying and fussing as we went through a whole series of items. The meeting started with Harold saying, 'We all got pretty nervous about the by-elections,' and he was very candid about it. He said, 'It got worse and worse throughout the day yesterday and it was even worse in the evening when Transport House said we were certain to lose Paddington and Islington North.' However we were all jolly relieved and agreed that this was about the best result we could have had because it would neither discourage the Party nor make people over-optimistic.

The main item on the agenda was supposed to be Tony Crosland on local government but, as soon as he got his chance, Roy said he must raise an issue. He said he was worried about the White Paper and the 6¾ per cent and I realized that he hadn't been properly briefed and didn't know I had already covered myself, that the White Paper had been passed by Cabinet, that the 6¾ per cent was said to be a tentative figure which might have to be varied and probably put up, and that I had gone further than this in my July White Paper, when I had actually mentioned the extra 0·2 per cent making 6·95 per cent, just what Roy was asking for. He was very nonplussed when I showed him this and said, 'But Social Services Secretary, you were asking to have it reduced.' Harold turned sweetly to me and said, 'I am sure Dick never suggested it should be transferred to public expenditure.' Of course this is exactly what I had suggested but only informally, through officials, and I hadn't put myself on the record for it, so I could cheerfully reply, 'No, no, it is perfectly O.K.' I was then able to launch into my own idea and say, 'Look, what I am really thinking of now, and why can't we decide it this morning, is that we must transfer that £9 million to the employers' contribution.' Barbara, who is fanatically in favour of this, was unfortunately away but I explained it all and Harold finally said that I was to put in a paper next Tuesday.

I rushed back to 70 Whitehall, where Douglas Overend and Dick Bourton were waiting, and instructed them on what kind of paper to write. I think I have got a reasonable chance of getting rid of my confounded motor-car taxation and getting spatchcocked in at the last moment my and Harold's favourite idea of a National Health Service contribution paid solely by employers. Mind you, what Roy did was pretty odd. I had been trying to see him all last week but he wouldn't see me and when I had asked him at Cabinet whether he wanted to take this at Management he said no, he was perfectly content to fix a meeting next Tuesday to discuss it. Suddenly all this had been bulldozed in while I was in Bristol and if I hadn't come back to London the whole thing might have been disastrous for me.

I caught the train at 12.45 and lunched on the way back to Bristol. There I went over a real, old-fashioned sub-normal hospital and then on to an I.T.O.[1] I didn't know what to expect and I found it fascinating. This was a great big empty factory with a hostel that looked like a perfectly ordinary, rather dingy private hotel, but in fact there were living there twenty psychiatric patients from the hospital, under the guidance of one nurse and her husband. It was explained to me that this company had not only a sheltered workshop

[1] Industrial Therapy Office.

but was training people to go out to work in ordinary factories and they had already sent out the first sixty or seventy. They are running this half-way house with no subsidy and no funds and I was enormously stirred by it.

I was then driven down to Weston-super-Mare where we found in the street the usual NALGO demonstration, which had been waiting for me for two hours. I got out to a great burst of cheers and boos as the large Rolls-Royce drew up. Five or six demonstrators came to talk to me and they were as amenable as ever. Then I went into a tiny room upstairs for a pleasant good-humoured chat with 100 Labour Party people, in this hopeless Tory seat. I motored on to Bath after what I must admit have been a long two days.

Saturday, November 1st

I was staying with Anne's aunt, May Cowper, in her lovely flat in Cavendish Crescent and in the middle of the night my stomach collapsed. I think it may partly have been the chill I got going out in the cold after the heat of the Labour Party room, or it may have been sheer exhaustion, but I could hardly move this morning. However I took Anne and May out to lunch and we drove over the Cotswolds, in beautiful sunny weather. We stopped at Malmesbury to see the wonderful abbey, of which only the Norman nave remains and a porch with real Romanesque sculpture. I thought of Vézelay,[1] the marvellous village on a hilltop in France, and all my past poured out to me. I walked inside and there was the verger and a marriage going on. At that point a man bustled in and said, 'Hallo, Mr Crossman, you will remember me from Dauntsey.' He was the parson we had met when we went to see the church and house at Dauntsey where Ann Stradling was married to John Danvers in the fifteenth century and the Danvers fortunes were settled.[2] What a miraculous coincidence. On from there to Fairford to see the glass and then to Stanton Harcourt, before we got to Rhodes House, where I was due to go to a funny thing called the All Souls' Group. They had pressed me very hard, saying they had a distinguished group of people who wanted to discuss the Health Service. I said I wouldn't attend myself but that I would try to get Bea Serota or one of my people instead. None of them could manage it so I found myself there this afternoon, when I should really have gone home for a good rest.

I turned up at 5 o'clock, and there were thirty or forty people, with a fire, which was very nice. There was Bill Williams,[3] John Maud, Theo Cooper, Derek Morrell, Revans from Wessex, and a number of people, mostly distinguished in Whitehall or education, to discuss the Health Service. I think it was quite a useful discussion and I had a pleasant time.

[1] Vézelay, in the Department of the Yonne, has a Norman abbey, founded in A.D. 864.
[2] G. C. W. Wallis, Rector of Brinkworth with Dauntsey since 1961.
[3] Sir Edgar Williams (Kt 1973), Warden of Rhodes House and Secretary to the Rhodes Trust since 1951.

When dinner was over, I was standing in the gents and who should come in but Harold Wilson. He had come up for the degree-giving to see his son Robin, the one who is a mathematical genius. Harold was looking ten years younger, his hair rather untidy, all that pontifical statesmanship off him, nice and fresh just as I knew him before, and I thought, 'How different he is when he's not the P.M. but just the father of that boy.'

Sunday, November 2nd

I have really recovered now and I spent some of the day reading the discussions of the by-elections in the Sunday papers. We had an average swing of 10 per cent against us, after all the euphoria that was worked up by the polls of a 4 per cent swing, but it has been a tonic for us to have scraped home in four seats out of five. This has had a pretty good effect. It has given the Tories a sense that they have a good chance of winning a general election, even though Ted Heath isn't proving much of an attraction as a leader, and they have given us a feeling that we have made some sort of comeback from the ultimate disasters of three or six months ago but that we have a long way to go before we have a chance of winning next time. We have to remember that all this has taken place in a week with really disastrous strikes going on all over the country but nevertheless we held what were relatively safe seats with disgracefully low majorities.

I am fascinated by the article in the *Sunday Times* on the background to the Islington North by-election.[1] This story has appeared at the same time as Nigel Fisher and Edward Boyle have both been subject to the pressure of the party machines.[2] Nigel Fisher is one of the left-wing Tories on Rhodesia and capital punishment and the threat has been made that he won't be re-nominated for Surbiton. Edward Boyle has retired as Conservative Member for Handsworth because he is left-wing. People are becoming very sensitive to this now, it is stimulating and I think a lot may come of it.

Well, that's the end of the week. I am trying to stoke as much as I can into this diary which, I realize, isn't really a diary but a kind of Acts of the Apostles—acts not thoughts, because I don't really have enough accounts of people and conversations. Nevertheless I still think it has value, more value than ever now I have decided not to stay on in Government. On this, one final little anecdote. When we were sitting in Cabinet, Jim Callaghan suddenly whispered to me, 'Have you decided yet whether to stand next time?' 'What do you mean?' I said. 'The election after next?' 'No,' he said, 'the next election.' 'Of course I'm standing,' I said. 'Why do you think I'm not?' That was the end of that conversation. It must have made a deep impact because last night I had a staggering nightmare and I woke up and

[1] See *Sunday Times*, Nov. 2nd, 1968.

[2] Nigel Fisher, Conservative M.P. for Hitchin 1950–5, Surbiton 1955–74 and since 1974 for Kingston-upon-Thames, was Parliamentary Under-Secretary of State for the Colonies, July 1962–October 1963 and for Commonwealth Relations and the Colonies 1963–4. He was knighted in 1974.

told Anne about it. I thought it had been revealed that I was not standing in the election and that consequently I had ruined myself in Coventry. Today I signed the *New Statesman* documents. I am standing but I shan't be a Member of Parliament for long after that, or, rather, a Member of the House of Commons. I shall try to get a peerage and I shall now have to consider when to tell Harold my decision.

Monday, November 3rd

Over the weekend I got Douglas Overend and Dick Bourton to prepare a paper for Management Committee tomorrow. Roy got it from us this evening and I was warned by my spies, Overend and Bourton, that he was raving mad, the Treasury was furious with our paper and the Chancellor said he wasn't going to go to the meeting of the Management Committee because they simply wouldn't discuss it.

Now it so happened that Roy enjoyed a great triumph today. There had been the first Opposition amendment to the Queen's Speech concerned with the so-called cooking of the books, an accusation that Roy and the President of the Board of Trade had been rigging our export figures. This insane suggestion had been made first by Anthony Barber, and the Tories were trounced to smithereens by the Chancellor of the Exchequer. So Roy was warmed and excited and then no doubt furious when he received the paper which he had to study in preparation for tomorrow morning. However I didn't take all this too seriously. The thing was on the agenda of the Management Committee, the Prime Minister expected it, I had been told to bring it back there and not even the Chancellor can say no to that.

I was occupied with a series of meetings, beginning with Alan Marre on honours for nurses. We also had an important meeting of the Social Services Committee on Green Papers. This was to discuss our proposal for having 51 per cent of the new Health Boards nominated by me and 49 per cent by local authorities and professional groups. Shirley Williams was very good, even Dick Taverne was sensible and the whole thing went through easily, although they said they wanted to have the Boards as small as possible and that they were scared of having too many doctors. But this was helpful to me because I don't want too many either. Once again I noticed the amazing amateurishness of the Treasury. Dick Taverne had been briefed to say he thought that sometimes the Hospital Board Secretary or the Chief Medical Officer should be appointed, to emphasize the managerial status of the Board. The Treasury has got managerial status on the brain and I had to say, 'But, look, you must be clear about this. The Boards are the managing directors and the manager really must not be mixed up with the directors.' But you will find this all the way through the Treasury now. They are completely cock-a-hoop, lords of Whitehall, and because they are overworked and always changing their jobs they come to meetings unbriefed and phenomenally ignorant about the realities of life.

Today we were also first for P.Q.s. We had a meeting with our own politicians at 12.30 in my room, followed by the weekly lunch with the officials, and then down we went at 2.30. There was no kind of difficulty and afterwards I had to rush off immediately to the B.B.C. to make my ministerial broadcast. This is the first week of November and the pension is going up by 10*s*. and contributions by 7*s*. at the top and 1*s*. at the bottom. I had taken an hour preparing this ministerial five minutes and had worked very hard at the script because I didn't at all want to give an opening to the Tories. I was amused when Willie Whitelaw said to me later, 'We were all looking at the first of the new kind of ministerial broadcasts but I am afraid you didn't give us a chink in your armour, you were so strictly objective.' I think it was reasonably successful but it made me late for the Committee on Barbara's Industrial Bill.

She is now absolutely schizophrenic in her attitude to the trade unions. She wants to appease them and she seems to have not only abandoned prices and incomes but thrown them away with a smash, like Moses throwing the tablets of the law on the ground. Yet she also realizes that the unions are becoming more and more unpopular and, as the wave of unofficial strikes continues to mount, the case for action is becoming stronger. Every time I look at the press the first six items are unofficial strikes. The coalfield strike is over, but the car industry is still in complete disorder and now we have a strike at the Stationery Office and from day to day we never know whether our Hansards are coming out or our Bills being printed. Barbara is saying she should have tough reserve measures against the unions. I also have a problem because in the National Superannuation Bill I have to deal with the problem of the payment of supplementary benefit either to strikers or their families, the awkward fact of income tax repayments, and the whole question of who is denied unemployment benefit or supplementary benefit in the case of strikes, unofficial and official. So here we had Barbara sitting at her work at the end of the table in the great Ministerial Conference Room, struggling along with a Bill which is a gimmick. She and Harold have cooked up this merger, nobody quite knows what the powers are going to be and I think, if we don't look out, this Bill will be another appalling frost.

After that I rushed off to Cork Street, to Terry Frost's private view.[1] He is one of these modern painters, a charmer, and I had an hour surrounded by modern artists before I slipped back to the House, but I didn't hear or see anything of the debate because I was busy in my room preparing for the row at Management Committee tomorrow.

Tuesday, November 4th

At 11 o'clock we had Management Committee and a brief discussion in quite a breezy way of the situation in Islington North. We have known for

[1] Reader, and since 1977 professor, in Fine Art at the University of Reading, and a neighbour of the Crossmans in the country.

a very long time that this local party has been corrupt and the *New Statesman* and *Tribune* have actually agitated against this scandal. The party has been frozen off by Transport House and it's a wholly good thing that this should have come into the open. We were not very anxious about it and laughed at the idea that you could get rid of corruption by having primary elections,[1] a suggestion some papers have launched. Heaven knows, there is much more corruption in America and if you have a primary you still have the same problem, of choosing the small group who fix the candidate. However, it so happens that life is a bit easier for us, because the O'Halloran thing has been accompanied by the scandal in Surbiton. Nigel Fisher has been triumphantly elected to the executive of the Monday Club, the reactionary group who were supposed to be trying to get rid of him.

Then we came to my confrontation with Roy who, as he had threatened, had come virtually unbriefed. The Prime Minister started quite tactfully by asking whether we had reached agreement on the White Paper, which had of course been cleared, provided my figures were hypothetical. Harold then steered us on to the rest and Roy made no effort whatsoever to stop the discussion. I put my proposals forward and then Roy said, 'It is intolerable that I should be asked at such short notice to make a snap decision. It's an outrageous way to treat a Chancellor. First I have this hare-brained scheme of Dick's for a motorists' levy, now I have an equally hare-brained scheme shoved on to me. I won't have it.' The Prime Minister said quietly, 'Look, there is no question of any decision this morning. The Management Committee doesn't take decisions; it's a place where people are allowed to air views and try them out on their colleagues. Therefore Dick is entitled to try out his new proposals, so I suggest, my dear Roy, that we have it discussed.'

Roy had to remain silent and Tony Crosland weighed in: 'Well, whatever mess-up Dick has made it's a good thing, because for fifteen years I have been rooting for increasing the employers' contribution and here at last is a chance of doing so.' He was supported very strongly by Barbara and then Roy came in again and said it was outrageous, a major change of policy which couldn't be considered in a week or a fortnight. It would take him many months to make up his mind and it must be seen in connection with his budget. Here was Dick asking to go to the employers and, if it was a 1 per cent employer's contribution, proposing to raise £100 million a year or more. I said I didn't want to force the issue. The Chancellor had forced it last Friday. I wanted to leave plenty of time and I was perfectly prepared to write 6¾ per cent into the Bill or even 6·95 per cent if Cabinet decided it but it couldn't happen without a Cabinet decision. I was reasonableness itself and when I am reasonableness itself I am at my most maddening.

[1] Elections at local and state level, where voters, usually registered, choose their nominee for the national elections and, in most cases, pledge their delegates to vote for him at the national nominating convention.

I also pointed out that this was a little harsh of Roy. Since he had described the motorists' levy as a mare's nest and dismissed that proposal of mine, surely it was right of me to seek a more sensible and less bogus way of raising the £9 million he needed, and it was clear enough that I didn't want to raise it by cuts in the hospital programme. The P.M. intervened very quickly and supported me, so Roy was corralled. In the course of two hours everybody present agreed that the best thing to look at was an increase in employers' contributions. There was nothing intrinsically against it. Nobody could deny my suggestion that we should have a short Bill, quite near the budget if Roy wished, to increase the employers' contribution. We could increase it by whatever Roy liked, by 2*s*. only to raise £50 millions if he preferred. It was a terrible day for Roy because he had staked everything on defeating me and he ended up by having a meeting where, though nothing was decided, it was clear that the motor levy was out and that in due course he would have to accept the new proposal. He had started off tense and querulous and it suddenly occurred to me how feminine, petulant, unwise and hysterical he is. He committed himself in a shrill voice to the intolerable misconduct of the Social Services Secretary. I had outwitted him, bullied and I had also blustered, but I meant every word and I hadn't been bluffing. My threat of resignation had won. From now on the Treasury and Roy will be determined to have their own back on me. As he put it, 'I'm not going to be sold a second pup at a later meeting.' I said, 'Frankly, Roy, if the first one had no teeth, the second one is much better. When I sell pups the series improves.'

However we were to have a second confrontation. By great luck I had fixed a meeting with Roy in his room to discuss three items: first my proposal that he should avoid committing himself to a firm statement that there was no prospect of ever removing the anomaly by which if you pay contributions to a private occupational pension scheme, you get a tax concession, whereas you don't if you are going to pay into our new state-run earnings-related scheme; then the problem of over-pensioning; and, thirdly, the contribution point we had discussed this morning in Management.

So at 4 o'clock we went into that big room, rather like visiting Mussolini, and there we sat at the long table with Roy in the middle, flanked by his five Treasury advisers, and I with Mildred Riddelsdell, Douglas Overend, David Ennals and John Atkinson. Immediately Roy was on his high horse again but by the end of the interview it became clear that at least it wasn't certain that he and his Treasury people were right and that there was in fact another side to the case of the tax concession.

On the second question, the problem of over-pensioning, I am afraid that under our prodding Roy was driven to make a quick ruling. He said he proposed to announce that the tax concession of 66⅔ per cent should remain for everybody who contracted out but that if they stayed in the scheme the top limit for private pensions should be 50 per cent, which would be not only for private schemes but for all occupational pensions schemes.* This would automatically cut back to 50 per cent those of them which were now 66⅔ per cent and for me it was the bloody limit. Again I was able to show how impossible it was and Roy was once more plunging about like a delicate, highly bred horse, angry, indignant and frustrated by this Social Services Secretary and his staff. The Treasury staff were hopeless compared to my competent people. We know our side, they don't know theirs.

Then we got on to the third point, the employers' contribution. I was told very clearly by Roy that nothing had been decided yet. 'No,' I said, 'but I think it would be unwise to do much more work on the motor tax scheme. It seems to me that is out for good and therefore we must start working fairly soon to see what should be done about this alternative.' After a bit of fencing I left. But I hope I can get over this row. It's a bad thing if I have a searing, personal row with Roy for long and this couldn't have been more personal. On both occasions he'd humiliated himself utterly, first before his political colleagues and then before his own staff and mine. He is enormously sensitive and must feel this desperately.

I then went back to the House and ran into Heath walking along the passage. For once we got into conversation and I said, 'Back at school. I always feel one can manage the Department nicely until Parliament starts.' 'Yes,' he said. 'Why on earth haven't you taken the opportunity to relieve yourself of that problem?' 'What do you mean?' I said. 'Why haven't you arranged to have Ministers outside the House of Commons?' I really was surprised. Ministers outside? 'Oh, no,' I said, 'I don't want that at all. I find it a strain but I wouldn't lose my position in the Commons for anything.' Heath pursed his lips and I suddenly realized he had let out something he really meant. He would like an American presidential system with Ministers outside the House and suddenly he had let his guard down and said something true about himself. He won't say anything to me again for five or six months, I know that very well.

This evening Anne and I gave dinner to my stepchildren, Gilbert and Dorothy Baker, at the Garrick. Here they were, Gil with a beard and Dorothy looking tremendously sleek in a beautiful long black dress, because with mini skirts we now have maxi gowns as well. We had a splendid evening together. Later on, after the vote, I went up to Tony Crosland's room for a quick drink and asked him what he thought of the Committee this morning. He said, 'Frankly, Roy is like that. He is not an economist, he doesn't work terribly hard, but you must give him time.' I also asked Jim Callaghan, who had of course supported me in this, and Jim said, 'I didn't like your motor-car levy in July, I wanted you to raise more money from the employers' contributions, but I am sorry for the Chancellor in the present situation.

* If a private pension scheme gives more than 66⅔ per cent of final salary, it isn't eligible for tax concession. That is the top limit which was laid down, first in the Civil Service and then extended to the outside world.

It's unbearable, the Chancellor is bound to react like that. Nevertheless he will come round if you give him time.' So this week I am giving him time.

Wednesday, November 5th

An astonishing item in the press. I had heard the Prime Minister saying to Peter Shore after Questions yesterday, 'I didn't get to the question about you. I must see it goes into the press,' and now I see Harold has made Peter Deputy Leader of the House of Commons. I greatly disapproved when he made John Silkin Deputy Leader under John's pressure,[1] but he was Chief Whip and Chiefs sometimes want a little encouragement. Harold has now insulted Bob Mellish by not making him Deputy Leader and by giving it to Peter Shore, who is Minister without Portfolio, one of the most catastrophic failures in the House of Commons and no good at the dispatch box. Sometimes Harold has an unerring ability to do what jars. It is in these minor appointments that he shows his amazing taste. I am not saying that this is wrong, only that his taste and mine are different. This afternoon I looked in on the Chief Whip and Fred Peart next door and said, 'I suppose your advice was taken before the Deputy Leader was appointed?' Bob Mellish leered at me, 'The fact is that our Leader is a funny little man, but not so funny.' Harold's action must have caused appalling feeling with Mellish and Peart.

Ironically, Roy has made one surrender. For months and months since I took this job I have been trying to get Nicky appointed as my economic adviser but Roy, having dropped him, has kept him in reserve. A few weeks ago I finally got Clifford Jarrett to write formally to Sir Douglas Allen, who replied, 'The Chancellor isn't using Kaldor but might want to use him some time, so we don't think there should be any change.' Then I wrote a really hot letter to Roy, saying how unfair and dog-in-the-manger this was, and today I got a very short reply saying he had realized he was wrong and he was releasing Nicky. It was a kind of tiny *amende honorable*.

The main thing today was the final launching of the abatement White Paper.[2] Peter Brown and David Ennals had done endless preparation, with a special lobby brief and a special press release for everybody including the M.P.s, and we had worked away at various visual demonstrations. The other secret was that we had a big meeting for city editors this morning from 12.0 to 1.0 and then (this was a last-moment inspiration I had) John Beavan and Alan Fairclough who had helped us on the popular version came to lunch with me from 1.0 to 2.0. At 2.30 I had the B.B.C.—yes, I actually did my whole press conference with them before I delivered the Statement in the House, which was grossly improper—then the Statement at 3.30 and right over to the Festival Hall for a general press conference, to

[1] See above, p. 25 and n.

[2] The White Paper (Cmnd 4195), on the terms for partial contracting-out from the national superannuation scheme, was published on November 5th.

which all the technical press, the trade union press and the voluntary societies to do with pensions had been invited. About 130 people turned up. After that I went up to I.T.N. off Tottenham Court Road for an interview with Midlands Commercial Television. There was a gap in which I went to the annual get-together of the Midwives' Board at W. S. Gilbert's house in Kensington, where for two hours I discussed midwifery and gynaecology, and then I came back to I.T.N. for the 10 o'clock news programme. Quite a day. It all went fairly easily but the biggest success was to include the city editors and people like Nicholas Davenport and to brief them early, before the Statement. It was also very important, by the way, to have the *Daily Mirror* there. The questions in the House were very quiet and Balneil simply made a long propaganda speech, so I had quite a lot of help from our side and got through it with incredible ease.

Thursday, November 6th

We didn't have a bad press. The T.V. broadcasts were undoubtedly useful and we had columns and columns of visual aid in the papers today, all properly used. This is partly because it is a difficult subject and it was as good a show as we had put on in January.

Cabinet. Suddenly Vietnam was mentioned, and the Lord Chancellor woke up and said, 'I don't often speak but I have strong views on this. It is what I care about more than anything else. How can we possibly have a Statement from the Foreign Secretary this week approving of Mr Nixon's statement?'[1] I was a bit surprised because Nixon had made a statement saying he was trying to get out of Vietnam. Someone said so and Gerald Gardiner then said, 'The last time, we had a statement approving American bombing. Why can't we dissociate ourselves from those Americans?' He spoke like an innocent, young left-winger, with an amazing ignorance, and he hadn't actually read Nixon's statement. On the whole we had only picked out for praise the decision to withdraw but it was difficult to blame the Foreign Secretary for this.

Then we had the E.E.C. We had all recently received letters, one from Michael Stewart suggesting that all junior Ministers should now join the organization for stimulating the creation of the Common Market, some all-party organization we have allowed ourselves to get into, and then we had the Prime Minister writing to tell us all to be enthusiastic about the Foreign Secretary's policy and not to be obsessed by the terms of entry.

[1] Little progress had been made in the Paris talks but President Nixon was determined to reduce the strength of American forces in Vietnam. On November 4th he announced in a television broadcast that he had written to Ho Chi Minh, the North Vietnamese leader, suggesting that the time had come to negotiate a peaceful settlement, but that in a reply received three days before Ho Chi Minh's death on September 3rd this initiative had been rejected. Meanwhile the planned withdrawal of troops continued. The President had stated that 35,000 troops would return home between mid-September and mid-December and military activity was reduced. Nevertheless Americans at home continued to demonstrate and protest against the war.

I said I couldn't really see the point of these letters and I thought we had got our posture right. 'Yes,' said Harold, 'look at my Statement.' 'Yes,' I said, 'look at your Statement.[1] But why, then, these letters telling us to show enthusiasm?' Michael Stewart very unwisely said, 'The fact is that we have to make all the pro-speeches and we would like more Ministers to join in.' 'Would you really like Fred Peart or me to join in?' I said. 'We will if you like but I shall take the proper posture the Prime Minister recommends, which is that we haven't changed our view that we should enter if the conditions are right because we are now strong enough to ensure they are right.' There wasn't much discussion. The P.M. looked a bit peeved and his face puckered. He doesn't like being treated in this way by me and he knew that in this discussion Cabinet was registering a check on him and Michael Stewart, who are still hell bent on getting the negotiations going as fast as they possibly can. The one thing which struck me was that when it was suggested that the negotiations couldn't get going until the New Year or even later, he added, 'Anyway, we can ensure that the election comes first before anything gets embarrassing.' I think myself he must be working to have a spring election if he possibly can.

After that we had a long discussion about a Bill for creating the Ulster Defence Regiment as a substitute for the 'B' Specials. If we really can get rid of these bloody 'B' Specials and organize a regiment under the British Army it will be a tremendous achievement and will really produce a change in the Ulster power structure. During this discussion I couldn't help reflecting on what an amazingly good job this Labour Government has done in Northern Ireland. It took over in an impossibly difficult situation and with Jim Callaghan in the lead we handled it with the greatest skill. We have always acted through their own people, first O'Neill and then Chichester-Clark, and made them do the jobs and, while just retaining Protestant support, we've made the necessary consensus with the Catholics. I think this success is very largely due to the combination of Callaghan and Harold. They may have been a disastrous combination when Callaghan was Chancellor but in this particular situation it is very powerful.

This afternoon I had to make a speech to 1,600 parish councillors. I did a formal thing about the Health Service but I included some amusing and lively comments on Maud which made them all laugh. Not a word of it has been reported, as far as I know, in the press. The fact is that journalists are not now equipped to take down an unusual speech of this kind. You can be fairly sure that your remarks won't be reported, even if you are a senior Minister like myself, who is regarded as being capable of making clangers and whom journalists ought to watch.

Friday, November 7th

I had in Douglas Overend and Bourton and they are preparing the draft

[1] See Vol. II, pp. 337–40.

paper before I see Roy next Monday evening. I must do my best to get what's necessary without humiliating him any more. It's been a tough moment although I had the P.M. solidly on my side and I knew it. It has completely confirmed my view that Roy is really a literary man, an indolent man, who is solely concerned with his image, where he is superb. Enormous, inordinate trouble is taken over his speeches. Every time he appears on television, every time he makes a speech in the House of Commons, even when he answers a Question, everything is beautifully prepared, and his whole concern, year by year, is his budget speech. This is what infuriated him, that I was pre-empting and forcing decisions. The only trouble was that he got it all wrong. This is no great issue of principle, simply that he refuses to be treated in this way. He was petulant, thwarted, frustrated, and he had a tremendous setback.

After a meeting of appalling boredom at the Central Council for Post-graduate Medical Education, I took the train to Cambridge, where Quintin Hogg was to debate against me. He tottered into the train looking jolly ill after two days of living on kaolin. We were doing a most difficult motion, prepared by that charming Hugh Anderson, who is now President and is said to be dying of leukaemia.[1] He had talked over the motion carefully with me and Quintin; and it was 'That this House is determined to explode the myth of the classless society,' difficult, but suitable for the Union and for intellectuals. On the way down, Quintin told me something about his problems. I thought, 'My God, what a difference between his life and mine. There he is, at the age of sixty-one, sweating his guts out to earn his living as a Q.C., tied into politics for another five years if they win the election and, even if they don't, he can't get out. How lucky I am compared to him.'

The debate was as nice as ever. Quintin made a very able and competent speech despite his stomach upset but I out-trumped him with a dangerous speech which might have got me into serious trouble if it had been reported. The emphasis was what might be called fascist, on the fact that myth is the more powerful thing in politics. I had a most effective piece saying that what was wrong with Heath was that he had nothing of Disraeli's quality, nothing charismatic or legendary, he was just a professional politician put in because he was the next best thing to Harold Wilson, who for his part did have some mythical capacity to him. How much better it would have been, I said, for the Tories to have relied on Alec Douglas Home, who has the whole myth and tradition of the aristocracy behind him. The whole Union cheered this and I had a standing ovation afterwards. I was driven home by a Ministry car and got back at 2 a.m. for my two days at Prescote.

Sunday, November 9th

I did something yesterday I've never done before. I felt so bloody tired that I decided to let Brian O'Malley, who was terribly keen to do it, take on an

[1] Hugh Anderson died of leukaemia in August 1970.

engagement I had at Slough. I did it partly because I've been to Slough twice recently and was sick of the idea of going again and it has given me two days to rest and recover at home. We have had sunshine and rain and now this brilliant classical autumn has gone we are in winter with gales blowing. I have had long digs on my island in the howling wind, very cold.

This morning when I saw the Sunday papers I knew my launching on Wednesday had gone pretty well. I had a whole page of the *Observer*'s business section purporting to be a very friendly interview with me, simply because the *Observer* chap had been there at the 12 o'clock show. There was a not unfriendly account in the *Sunday Times* and only the *Sunday Telegraph* was anti-Government. The weeklies have not done us so well but the subject is pretty unintelligible. It was not too bad and I am reasonably satisfied.

Monday, November 10th

My first meeting was with Barbara, whom I had originally agreed to see not at Elephant and Castle but at 70 Whitehall. Then last Friday a message came to ask if I would mind coming to her. I am senior to her in the pecking order and if I were a stickler she ought to come to me. I knew she wanted to be at her office early to consult her officials but I had nothing against it so I drove straight from Paddington to St James's Square. We opened the door and there she was, with her officials. I was in the wrong room.

We had to discuss several problems, the first that eighteen months ago the Attorney General had suddenly ruled that the practice of disregarding up to £4 of a striker's income for tax purposes is illegal. Ever since last July we have been waiting for a Bill to legalize this and put it right. We have also had a long-standing complaint about men who, though they are not on strike themselves, are put out of work by some other strike and denied their supplementary benefit. The Donovan Commission had recommended that this should be changed and another clause of my Bill deals with this.

There are several other awkward things that worry us, including the question of occupational pensioners receiving unemployment benefit for six months free of tax, over which the National Insurance Advisory Council is split, with Titmuss on one side and Harold Collison on the other. David and I had worked out what we thought was a reasonable package to deal with these and other anomalies and it seemed to us that we couldn't go back on the income tax refund, though in principle it's indefensible. On the last point I had convinced myself that unemployment benefit is not to help a man who retires from work but to help men when they are thrown out of a job.

So in I came, and before I knew it Barbara had launched into a long speech, whose interest was that it revealed the terrible state of mind that she is in now. In this schizophrenic mood she was saying that on no account could we do anything that would upset the unions. She then went through everything in principle and it took two hours. I was severely reprimanded for interrupting all the time and told I was prejudiced and that I must be quiet but it was clear that she wasn't speaking for her officials. Once again I found her running ahead. Her officials and ours had talked together and agreed on the package we were putting forward. Barbara had only really discussed it with them this morning and hadn't evolved a policy. After two hours we went away with exactly what we wanted and it is to go to Management Committee on Tuesday and Cabinet on Thursday.

Another important meeting was with the Chancellor of the Exchequer. I had received a message on Friday that he wanted to see me today with a very small number of officials and that he could only manage 5.30. I had arranged to go to a lecture at the L.S.E. on German propaganda and its effect on German morale but along I went to his room with Mildred Riddelsdell, Bourton and Douglas Overend. Roy had on his side of the table a man from the public revenue side and a man from the pensions side, no one else. We had provided him, at very short notice, with a paper drafted over the weekend, just putting forward our proposals intact, keeping the employee's total at 6¾ per cent and raising the employer's contribution to 7 per cent by means of increasing the employer's N.H.S. contribution, the most ingenious idea which I had aired last week. Here we had worked out in detail the figure to write into the paper. My officials had wisely put in that the immediate short Bill could be at a time Roy wanted with the figures he wanted. We went through it all and it was comic because he kept on trying to add up and check all the figures but getting them wrong. We were obviously far better briefed and Mildred Riddelsdell stood out as superior in intellectual content and mastery of the subject. As we went out, Dick Bourton, who had carefully kept silent, said, 'We are three-quarters of the way home.'

We got this meeting over so quickly that I was able to rush off to L.S.E. and hear the last part of the lecture, which was very good on the Goebbels psychology and mystique. Afterwards I found myself sitting down to the first of a whole series of official dinners I am having this week.

Tuesday, November 11th

At Management Committee we spent a lot of our time discussing the fantastic strike in H.M.S.O., which is delaying the publication of Hansard by two or three days and making it very difficult to get the Order Papers printed. Constitutionally we have to publish things in the *London Gazette*, which isn't coming out, and it's very difficult to find ways of getting civil servants to take part in printing it, because the Civil Service unions might refuse to blackleg. We took extraordinary trouble over this because the Government is impotent and terrified of the parliamentary advantage it might give the Tories, just before the Christmas recess. No doubt that fellow

Dick Briginshaw,[1] the head of SOGAT, has been egging the H.M.S.O. printers on to put this stranglehold on the Government.

However the big item today was the incident of Philip's broadcast.[2] I had missed this but on Sunday night Prince Philip appeared on a recorded television interview in America, making astonishing remarks about how hard up the Queen was, how they were going into the red and how they might have to sell Buckingham Palace. It had caused a major sensation. The Prime Minister had let it be known that he would make a Statement this afternoon. I don't think myself that this was any deep-laid plot by Philip to put pressure on the Government to increase the Queen's screw but simply a sheer piece of exhibitionism, showing off how good he was on T.V. We discussed it at length and here you see the real point of Management Committee. We couldn't have considered it in this way at Cabinet. First the Prime Minister told us about his text. He had it all ready and made it quite clear that it was his Statement and we couldn't try to redraft it. It was very adroit and revealed a whole mass of facts of which, though a member of the Cabinet, I had no notion. It revealed that discussions had been going on even before we took over and since then the Prime Minister and the Chancellor of the Exchequer had been making elaborate arrangements for other ways to carry more and more of the Queen's expenses. Despite the fact that the royal grant had been kept at the level fixed in 1952 she wasn't in the red and wasn't due to go into the red until next year. Some of her expenses had been transferred to various departments, for example the Ministry of Works was carrying the cost of the royal castles and all her royal tours abroad and expeditions in this country were being paid. A perfectly respectable story of what had been going on had very discreetly been put in the Statement.

We all agreed the Statement and began to discuss the situation when Barbara suddenly blew up and said what I had been feeling: 'I must say

[1] Richard Briginshaw, General Secretary of the National Society of Operative Printers, Graphical and Media Personnel (as SOGAT became) 1951–75. He became a life peer in 1974.

[2] During an interview on American television on November 9th Prince Philip had been asked about the state of the royal finances and he had replied, perhaps with deliberate exaggeration, that the Royal Family would 'go into the red next year' because the Queen's civil list allowance, voted annually by Parliament, was 'based on costs of eighteen years ago' and was insufficient. Prince Philip's remarks annoyed those who felt that the matter should first have been raised at home, horrified those who believed that the Government had been neglecting the Queen's difficulties and embarrassed the Government, which was not only struggling to devise new prices and incomes legislation before the present Act expired on December 31st but was also preparing for a General Election.

In a Statement on November 11th the Prime Minister explained that for some time Government and Palace officials had been discussing the civil list, that the figure had been put at £475,000 p.a. in 1952 in order to produce an annual surplus of £70,000 to accrue against later deficit and that the accounts had remained in surplus until 1961, after which there had been increasing deficit. It was estimated that the reserve would be exhausted by 1970. The Prime Minister proposed the appointment of a Select Committee to review the Queen's income and stated that in the meantime arrangements had been made to cover any deficit from 'funds available to the Queen' from other sources.

this is absolutely outrageous. We agree with your Statement, Prime Minister, but I think we should make some political capital out of this. Now that Prince Philip has put all this before the public, complaining about the Government as though we are being unfair to them, at least let's have a Select Committee to look into the private fortune of the Queen.' This is something I've thought about for many, many years. The Queen pays no estate or death duties, the monarchy hasn't paid any since these taxes were invented and it has made her by far the richest person in the country. Not only has the family accumulated pictures and riches, but their estates and actual investments must have accumulated and they are inordinately wealthy. Harold himself said, 'Most rich men feel that part of the job of a rich man is in spending a good part of his wealth for charitable and public purposes. It takes royalty to assume that all their private income is to be kept to themselves and accumulated and that they are not obliged to spend any of it on seeing them through their public life.' It was a fair point but Barbara, radical, determined to have a go, brought it out very clearly.

Barbara, Roy (which is striking) and I are republicans, we don't like the royal position, we don't like going to Court or feel comfortable there, and we know the Queen isn't comfortable with us. Fred Peart, on the other hand, was appalled. Not only did he think it was politically unwise to have any radical taint to what we do but he naturally adores being Lord President and gets on with the Queen just like George Brown and Callaghan do. Callaghan said, 'I am a loyalist. I wouldn't like to see the royal family hurt and I think Philip is a very fine fellow.' By God, Jim made a speech of such banality and appalling conventionalism, attacking the sentiments of middle-class intellectuals. He really is putting himself forward as the spokesman of the conservative working man, and his new role is growing on him. Harold also had apparently no sense of indignation with Edinburgh,[1] no anxiety to take the opportunity to get death duties applied to royalty or all the other things we naturally wanted to do. He is a steady loyalist and, roughly speaking, it is true that it is the professional classes who in this sense are radical and the working-class socialists who are by and large staunchly monarchist. The nearer the Queen they get the more the working-class members of the Cabinet love her and she loves them. Fred Peart and Harold adore public dinners and most of my working-class colleagues and their wives think of this as part of the perks of office. It's only Barbara, Roy, Michael Stewart and I who intensely dislike these occasions. Last Monday was the City Guildhall dinner when the Prime Minister makes a speech and I asked Roy if he'd gone. 'No,' he said, 'I never go to the Guildhall,' and it's true that if he is going to have a private social life he doesn't want to dine in public. We discussed this for an hour and a half and afterwards Roy said to me, 'Come and have a drink.'

We went through to No. 11, where he took me into the downstairs study

[1] Prince Philip.

and said, 'I want to talk to you about your Bill.' He just gave in and then he asked for a clear understanding that he would be able to decide on the timing of the short Bill and the amount of the increased contribution when it came nearer to his budget. 'Of course,' I said. 'That's all right.' It was a slightly awkward interview because of the scenes he has made but I realize I am pretty awkward sometimes and on this occasion I had been both awkward and ingenious. Roy gave me a very charming smile, the smile of a boy who wanted to be friends, and I knew we had managed to efface the row. I was terribly anxious to efface it so, provided I didn't talk about a climb down, it was all right, it was over, and I had cleared that particular row with the Chancellor and won a total victory for what I wanted, scrapped the motorists' levy and introduced an increase in the employers' contributions. I shall have a row with the employers but in terms of Cabinet strength it's something which Dick Bourton and the officials thought we couldn't possibly achieve.

In the afternoon I went down in good time to sit next to Harold and hear his Statement. He had just had a very rowdy Question Time, scoring off the Opposition in his most brilliant party pugnacious way. He revels in the battledore and shuttlecock of parliamentary politics and he lives for it. Thank God the Statement was long and detailed, because while he was making it the mood of the House changed sufficiently for Harold to handle Heath. We had known this morning that Heath and Maudling and the Tories had decided to make a political issue out of this and to insist that a Select Committee be appointed immediately because of the desperate situation which Philip had revealed. Harold was able to say that there was no new situation, that it was all perfectly in hand, and he was able cautiously to reveal that he himself had already agreed to the Select Committee being appointed for the next Parliament. It was superb and it knocked out the Opposition. If Harold had mishandled it we should now be in a long unpopular row in which we should lose votes by seeming to be mean to royalty. He got over the fact that we hadn't been mean, that basically there was no case for having an immediate Select Committee that would bind a future Parliament and, above all, he got over the fact that Heath and Maudling were playing party politics with the monarchy and the constitution, while he was putting country and Queen first.

It was by far the best parliamentary performance I have ever seen, because Harold was speaking without the snide, anti-Heath, knockabout party polemic which he loves to indulge in. At all costs he wanted to show restraint, reticence, real statesmanship, very like the way Baldwin with his instinct and closeness to the people handled the abdication crisis of 1936.[1] Why? Because Harold cares passionately about the Queen and the monarchy. It was astonishingly different from his normal performance and I thought,

[1] When Baldwin advised Edward VIII that he must abdicate if he wished to marry Mrs Wallis Simpson.

'Oh God, Harold, if only you could behave like this on other issues and not always feel that everything is a matter of making party capital.'

Wednesday, November 12th

Harold was actually praised by the *Daily Telegraph* for being statesmanlike. I rang him up this morning to tell him how marvellous he had been and I could hear him purring at the other end. The only thing I didn't say was that he ought to put this on a bit more often but he can't, he doesn't feel it. I didn't say to him he was like Baldwin but before I had got the thought through my head he was saying to me on the phone, 'Yes, I don't like to say so but I am really looking back to what Baldwin did in the abdication.' So I could have said this to him without being insulting.

I got up at 6.30 to work at my red boxes and this was lucky. I was puzzled because this morning I had a meeting I had been asking for for ages to make the big decisions about how to spend the £3 million we had allocated for my sub-normal hospital campaign, but I looked through the propositions which were being put to me and the Department showed that £3 million is quite ineffective in the short run. The minimum I would require would be £30 or £40 million, and therefore little could be done. Of course it couldn't, because they had spread the money over half the adult hospital population, whereas I wanted to look after only the sub-normal patients. This morning I gathered round me at 70 Whitehall all the hospital divisions. 'There's some mistake,' I said. 'We want to put it all on the sub-normal.' 'Oh no,' I was told by Miss Hedley, that tall, pre-Raphaelite, severe schoolmistress, who had been working away for the last four months on this. 'But surely you know,' I said, 'that our campaign is about sub-normality. We had a two-day conference on sub-normality, we're having a White Paper prepared.' 'Oh, but Minister,' they said, 'you will remember that the minute we had last April dealt with long-stay, which of course covers geriatric and psychiatric as well as sub-normal patients.' I said, 'The minute may have dealt with long-stay but you know quite well what I'm out for. We've got to figure this out in terms of concentrating it all on sub-normals and it had better be quick.' Suddenly Dick Bourton, our solid, fair-haired, sensible, literal-minded man, told me from the other end of the table that he needed the figures by lunchtime today because he had to write them into the estimates. I was furious. Once again they were giving me a decision to make in an hour and a half. It was quite a tough meeting. I insisted on the switch and on the concentration on the sub-normal hospitals, so we had to try to work out a new formula. I had to think desperately and I said, 'Well, we'll just give it per patient. Simply give the money to the regions according to the number of patients they have.' I fought and fought and I got £1,350,000 for food and extra kitchen staff and more for chiropodists for the old people, for personal clothing and to start on getting some accommodation for the nurses. We worked it out in the nick of time because this week we have to take it to the PEP Committee. I was wild about the lack of communication in the Department. Why should the hospital division do this to me? They knew perfectly well what I wanted, why should they frustrate me?

At 11 a.m. I had a Party meeting on pensions and when I got there there were seven people in the room, but about forty or fifty turned up in the end, quite a good turnout. David made an absolutely first-rate presentation at the beginning and after the usual questions I wound up. I think it was good public relations and I should add that, despite all the hoo-ha about the abatement White Paper, the Opposition haven't asked for a debate next week, which is good from our point of view. They see this isn't an area in which an attack will be successful and during this last week we've been gaining ground with the press. I think it's encouraging, although I am well aware that there are a good many people, like Jim Callaghan and Barbara in Cabinet, who are going round saying what a bloody nuisance Dick Crossman's unpopular pension scheme is. But we have a good team with David and Brian O'Malley, who is developing into a first-rate assistant. We ought to be able to do the Committee Stage excellently and I think we shall gain in the next six months but we are certainly starting with profound suspicion.

Today Bea Serota did something very useful. She gave a lunch in the House of Lords to Alex Baker, the new Director of our Advisory Service, who is just settling in to his job, and to Mrs Robb, who wrote *Sans Everything*, the book that made a searing attack on the long-stay hospitals.[1] Mrs Robb has always been a terrible danger to us, because Kenneth Robinson mishandled her and instead of treating *Sans Everything* sensibly Kenneth set up committees of investigation into her charges and then published a White Paper as a non-controversial document to answer her, which it didn't. This left a very dirty impression and since then she has become a kind of clearing house for all complaints about cruelty and torture in hospitals. I knew we had to defuse this bomb. The setting up of the Advisory Service and the Ely Report have helped but this lunch was pretty important because it got her to meet Alex Baker and me again. She was gratified and then she spent the whole day in the Lords hearing Bea and Patricia Llewelyn-Davies speak in the debate on mental health.

In the Commons we were having the end of the debate on gerrymandering. Callaghan had tabled all the Orders implementing the Boundary Commission's Report and asked our back benchers to vote them down. Six of our people were conscientiously abstaining, including the bearded, socialistic, vaguely revolutionary Peter Jackson.[2] He is a very sweet man, anti-

[1] See above, p. 134.

[2] Labour M.P. for High Peak 1966–70, Lecturer in Sociology at the University of Hull 1964–6 and Fellow 1970–2. Since 1974 he has been the Senior Planning Officer of South Yorkshire County Council.

foxhunting, pro-abortion, all the good causes, and he's utterly disillusioned with life and with the Labour Party. I lunched with him one day this week, only because there was no other table with anybody sitting at it, but by the time the room had filled up they were all eyeing him and wondering what we were doing together. We were discussing his attitude to the Abortion Act and gerrymandering, and here he was today making a great speech, saying that his conscience would be smirched by being dragged down to this level. I had tried to explain the history of this to him, and the arguments for deferring the Boundary Commission's recommendations until we had the Maud Report. Today, owing to the extremely efficient work of Callaghan, the vote was carried decisively by big majorities and we shall be fighting the election on the old boundaries.[1]

Thursday, November 13th

At Cabinet we had an interesting discussion on the question of televising the proceedings of Parliament. Bob Sheldon has been lucky in the ballot and is proposing to move again my motion for a television experiment, the one that had previously been rejected by a single vote.[2] After the experiment in the House of Lords inertia set in. Fred Peart is against both radio and television broadcasting of proceedings and he wanted to be able to intervene in the debate and show a neutral attitude. Discussion revealed that some of Cabinet who had not spoken on this subject last time had strengthened their views and the Prime Minister is now convinced of the importance of getting television accounts of Parliament. Maybe he thought how much he missed last Tuesday by not having his magnificent performance televised, because, though he did wonderfully and the whole public would have been impressed, there was no real account of his achievement in the newspapers, apart from the *Daily Telegraph*. I think Barbara, Roy and a number of others are quite keen on television now but the antis are as strong as ever, headed by Peart and Callaghan. Once again, curiously, intellectuals are lined up against the working-class. Anyway the situation is totally different now, so that when Fred Peart said, 'We had a Cabinet decision and we must carry it out,' we could say, 'No. The Cabinet decision was for the experiment which has already been done in the Lords. We have no Cabinet policy on this.' We finally decided that the front bench should not vote but everybody else should be allowed a free vote. What I think will happen is that there will only be about seventy or eighty people in the House and that closure will not be obtained. It will only be a little discussion.

Then we had Fred Peart again on M.P.s' allowances. Fred and the Chief Whip are concerned with the morale of our own back benchers and simply say we have to give them something. At a previous Cabinet meeting we had resisted an increase in salary but had been driven reluctantly to agree that

[1] The Orders were defeated by majorities of 303 and 302 votes to 250.

[2] On November 24th, 1966. See Vol. II, p. 136.

something had to be done about secretarial assistance. So Fred was able to rely on a Cabinet decision (this is always a sore point) and Harold pushed at this all the time, saying it was now only a question of how much and how it should be given. Fred's proposal was to allocate £750 a year to each M.P. as an additional secretarial grant, and he had agreed with John Diamond, the Chief Secretary, that in order to get this each must sign a pledge that he was really going to use it for a secretary and he must give the name of the secretary to the income tax authorities.

By jove, we got into confusion. We always get very excited in Cabinet about this type of thing. Barbara was terribly aware of the damage it would do. I think she is right, although Fred Peart and the Services Committee and Selwyn Lloyd himself are in favour of a grant of perhaps £500, £750, even £1,000 for secretarial assistance.[1] I've no doubt it will be very unpopular with the public, just at the end of the incomes policy. Coming immediately after Prince Philip it shows that everybody is rooting for cash now including M.P.s, and when M.P.s want cash and get it they are the most unpopular of all. Barbara is right and, as Chancellor, Roy felt the same.

Fred made his proposal for £750 and then Harold Lever, who is a new member of the Cabinet and hasn't spoken yet, weighed in and said, 'This is just a gimmick, a way of giving an increase of salary without saying you're giving it. If you are going to do that give them a decent amount, £1,000.' Barbara said, 'No, only £500. More than that and the gimmick will be obvious.' Then I said, perhaps wrongly, 'Look, frankly, all they will have to do is give a name. If they haven't got a secretary they must give their wife's name.' Oh, what an uproar in Cabinet. That would be an absolute scandal but I said, 'A lot of us do it already. My wife *is* my secretary,' and Anne is, ever since Jennie gave up she has been doing all my constituency work. Ironically, it's true that all the better-off people who can already afford to have secretaries will be able to pay more of their secretary's salary and it will also pay them from the tax point of view. All those who actually have wives who are genuine secretaries will also gain by it and the rest, the poorer people, will have to pretend their wives are secretaries even though they are not. Cabinet was tremendously confused.

Harold finally said he would call for names and he went round for support for £500 or for £750. He said it was a tie but Roy, who always puts the names down too, said Harold had counted wrong and we voted again. There was chaos. It was eight for £500 and seven for £750. It was nearly 1 o'clock and Fred Peart said he just couldn't sell this to the House. Then both Harold Lever and I said, 'The worst thing of all in this proposal is that the M.P.s

[1] Selwyn Lloyd, Conservative M.P. for Wirral 1945–70 and, after his election as Speaker, M.P. for Wirral 1970–6, was Minister of State at the Foreign Office 1951–4, Minister of Supply 1954–5, Minister of Defence April–December 1955, Secretary of State for Foreign Affairs 1955–60, Chancellor of the Exchequer 1960–2, Lord Privy Seal and Leader of the House of Commons 1963–4 and Speaker 1970–6. In 1976 he became a life peer, taking the title of Lord Selwyn-Lloyd.

should have to sign a guarantee that this would be used for their secretaries and give the names. Why insist on this for secretarial expenses when you don't do it about any others? If you do you will be palpably showing that we are doing something shifty and underhand.' Of course we were right. Eddie Shackleton was on our side as well and said the proper thing would be simply to add on whatever amount we choose to the present £1,250 of the salary that is tax-free for expenses and make the whole thing tax-free.

So great was the confusion, however, that Harold said we should consider this again at the next Cabinet.

As I was going out I ran into Harold, who said, 'Oh, God, of course I should have cast my vote.' 'Which way?' I asked. 'You know, Dick, I would have gone for £750.' (I knew this quite well because last night Fred Peart pressed me to support him and I had in fact supported him partly because of this promise. It's difficult for a wealthy person like me not to support the maximum for my colleagues.) There was Harold who, characteristically, had not given his vote or revealed himself. He is terribly canny as P.M., he never wants to commit himself unless he has to, and when he must he does it with great reluctance. So we ended in some disarray.

Friday, November 14th

Alan Marre came in great distress this morning with a pile of documents about the misinterpretation of my wishes on the long-stay hospital paper we dealt with last Wednesday. He said, 'How could we know? We knew of course you'd been making statements but we really can't judge from press cuttings.' 'Well,' I said, 'Miss Hedley could have come into my room in the last five months, she could have walked in.' John Cashman said, 'You know, you are very busy and your timetable is very full.' 'I'm not,' I said, 'if someone wants to see me. There is something wrong in this Department.' Alan and I had quite a fuss about this because it brought to a head a terrible feeling. Bea Serota and I do spend a good deal of our time complaining to each other about the Department and how frustrating they are, but I think there is something to be said on their side, and as John Cashman said, though they can walk into my room, my busyness makes it a great deal more difficult to try to book an interview with me. Nevertheless, there is something in my saying they don't hear what they don't want to hear and that they try to get a departmental view against mine. On the other hand, though, Alan is right in saying they don't consciously try to do me down. We argued all this out but by ill-luck I then found that Bea Serota was going to discuss the Department with him immediately afterwards. She was to have another go at him and I realized I was depressing and disheartening the poor chap.

Another great dinner in London tonight. I had already had the College of Pathology on Wednesday and now I was at the College of G.P.s in their own beautiful house in Kensington, the house that Joseph Kennedy bought from Pierpont Morgan when he was American Ambassador in the 1930s.[1] It was an enormous dinner, such a big meal that they had a sorbet in the middle before the meat, a real Victorian thing. I couldn't get through it all. I had deliberately asked to make a speech and I preached my doctrine of the new, integrated Health Service, before I got into the car to motor down to Prescote, arriving at 2.0 in the morning.

Sunday, November 16th

Another dinner last night, with the Leamington Medical Society, all the doctors, consultants and M.O.H.s of the Warwick, Leamington and Coventry area, in the old Masonic Hall at Warwick. Back at 1 o'clock in the morning. Dear, dear, so many dinners. As a result I am afraid my weight has gone up slightly. However I had my two hours digging on the island this afternoon and otherwise I have had an easy weekend. Today we went to see our neighbours, the Curles, at Appletree House in Northamptonshire. Mr Curle is the Ambassador to Liberia.[2] He has a wife and daughters who ride round on horseback when they are here and for years we've intended to visit them. He's conventional and nice with one more job ahead of him before he retires. Over drinks we discussed the Duncan Report,[3] an astonishing Report which I missed at O.P.D. last week when I was at the Party meeting. I asked John Curle what he thought and he said, 'It's all absolute nonsense, the opposite of the truth. The Report recommends that we should concentrate our main diplomatic activity in the area of main commercial interest in Western Europe and the North Atlantic area but that, of course, is an area where trade goes on by itself, without ambassadors helping. We need ambassadors for the peripheral areas where we haven't got direct interests.' Then he added something which I myself would have said, 'Look at Israel and what she did in Africa. She hadn't a single friend there and now she has got half Africa on her side because she worked hard with people with whom there was no direct commercial interest.'

In a way it's tremendously characteristic of the age we live in that an expert group of Foreign Office officials had to come out with this astonishing Report, suggesting that now we are a second-class power we should give up being interested in political Intelligence and the kind of role we played before and just use our embassies to improve our trade balance. No doubt when they were given their terms of reference the trade balance was very bad but

[1] Joseph P. Kennedy, businessman and banker, and father of John, Robert and Edward Kennedy, was U.S. Ambassador to London 1937–41. John Pierpont Morgan (1867–1943) was an American industrialist of immense wealth and power.

[2] Sir John Curle (KCVO 1975) was Ambassador to Liberia 1967–70 and Guinea 1968–70, and to the Philippines 1970–2. He was Vice-Marshal of the Diplomatic Corps from 1972 until his retirement in 1975.

[3] In August 1968 a Committee on Overseas Representation had been appointed, under the chairmanship of Sir Val Duncan, Chairman and Chief Executive of the Rio Tinto Zinc Corporation Ltd. Their Report, Cmnd 4107, was published in June 1969.

it's better now. Nevertheless I was pleased when Curle said this, because I couldn't have agreed more.

I was worried at leaving Alan Marre in such a terribly upset state on Friday so this morning I rang him up at home. I said I was sorry if first I and then Bea Serota had given him too big a basinful of complaints. We talked about it for a good half-hour and it emerged that Bea is very unpopular in the Department and this is one of the causes of the trouble. I had also been warned about this by John Cashman. The Department thought well of her at the beginning, but now they would rather go direct to me because they say they never get any decision from her. There is something in this, she is a marvellous lieutenant, a very sympathetic, intelligent woman who cares about the subject, but somehow she lacks decisiveness. However Alan was glad I rang him up and we decided that he and I and Clifford Jarrett should have dinner together to celebrate the anniversary of the merging of the Departments. We will try then, I dare say, to sort things out.

Talking of Clifford Jarrett, my Permanent Secretary, that big, bluff fellow, with his blue eyes, his uncomplicated exterior and his extraordinary competence, I now have a problem with him too. I have received a top secret letter from him, all covered up in envelopes, saying that when he retires he wants to be given leave to accept a job he has been offered as President of the Corporation of Society of Pension Consultants. He says, 'the billet will become vacant in the autumn of 1970, which would fit in with my personal plans for next year.' He has got a letter from William Armstrong, the Head of the new Civil Service Department, saying that if I concur it would technically be perfectly respectable. Well, here we are in the middle of a battle royal with the whole of the private pension interests, including the pension consultants, and he has been talking with them about this forthcoming job. I am sure there is nothing dishonest about it, and, as he explained to me, he just wants this job to earn enough to visit his daughter in America each autumn. Nevertheless if they have been approaching him while he is still in the Department, from their point of view they are buying in his expertise. The Superannuation Bill will be passed by the autumn of next year but in the following three years all the important decisions will be taken about its application and he will be there to look after their interests. Is that improper for a civil servant? Strictly speaking, no, but it seems to me that if my top civil servant has without my knowledge been talking to the pension consultants about a job with them, in any other country that would be thought to be an improper relationship.

I have to think what to say to William Armstrong and what to say to Clifford Jarrett. I suppose the truth is that Jarrett is psychologically detached now, he is fifty-nine, on the edge of retirement, and concerned only with his life afterwards. If he stays on until next autumn and suits my convenience —the time by the way, when I myself have privately decided to give up— I personally have no cause for complaint. Still, it does produce a perfect example of the difficulty of the proprieties one should have about a civil servant retiring early in order to join a private enterprise which will enormously value his services in its struggle to do better against the government.

Monday, November 17th

Up in the train as usual with Spencer Summers,[1] Lola Hahn and Neil Marten, in my reserved compartment. There they are protecting me from being eyed with hatred because I am surrounded by empty seats. I saw in my *Times*, 'Sandwiches for Benn, says David Wood.' David Wood may be a superficial writer but he is sometimes very bright and very perceptive. This column had a nice story describing how Benn had asked Harold Lever to come to the weekly ministerial lunch with sandwiches, and Harold said he would bring his little hamper from Fortnum & Mason.

When I got up to London my first job was to get ready all the publicity arrangements for the Bill. We are doing a new second edition of the popular version of the pension plan and we also had to run together the three White Papers, the January one, the July one on short-term benefits and the November White Paper on abatement. Doing this is a little risky and we had hoped to get Opposition support. I saw Willie Whitelaw behind the Speaker's chair and he said there would be no difficulty at all, and even Balneil agreed, but now the Tories are all changing their minds again. Fortunately this is entirely a Government responsibility and it's too late to go back on it. We've alerted them and though they've threatened to attack us if we use the popular version for party propaganda, we have made it absolutely all right by not writing the actual figures from the Bill.

My only big committee was Tony Crosland's Local Government,[2] to deal with the Maud recommendations, the biggest administration-shattering proposals put forward in the last five years. We now have a timetable of trying to get out by the end of January the first White Paper on structure. The Committee has clearly been briefed by the civil servants only to deal with departmental interests, and there aren't any real departmental interests here except for Local Government and the narrow ones of the Treasury. Even I am only concerned to get a structure which helps the Health Service reorganization. It's staggering how little serious discussion there has been of the basic principles.

This morning Mr Crosland most skilfully steered us through the subjects he had selected in a six-page paper. We resolved each question with a simple yes or no, and in an hour he had got just what he wanted. He was able to

[1] Conservative M.P. for Northampton 1945–50 and for Aylesbury 1950–70. He was knighted in 1956.

[2] He had taken over the chairmanship when George Thomson assumed responsibility for E.E.C. negotiations, on October 6th

write in the structure of the White Paper, which was basically to take Maud with minimum alteration.[1]

The only remaining issue was the problem of the local councils. If you have the proposed large unitary authorities wrapping within themselves four or five present local authorities, what happens below? Maud had dealt with this by recommending that the present existing councils – the county boroughs, the urban and rural district councils – should all disappear except for neighbourhood councils, which should exist and elect members but be limited to dealing with amenities. From the start I had thought this was barmy but Crosland tried to push it through, and say he would basically accept this unworkable proposal, with the addition perhaps of some area committees such as the C.C.A. provided at present. Nobody had a brief which enabled them to challenge him, so I did and found myself committed to writing a paper. It will be the only paper apart from Tony Crosland's formal one.

So much for there being any serious discussion of a major reform. It just shows you that once a Royal Commission has reported on modern institutions, and once a Minister has been given charge, the timetable fixed and Whitehall alerted to get it through, serious discussion ceases altogether. At least it did in this case.

Outside Cabinet Committee Room A I met Harold Lever and we went into a little empty room beside Burke Trend's offices, and, standing by the table, we chatted about life and how he was doing in his new Department. 'Of course,' he said, 'I see much more of Roy than I did in my last few months at the Treasury. Then I was cut off altogether, out of favour, because I had made a couple of speeches that the Treasury disapproved of. Now as number two at MinTech. I am in a position where Roy must consult and discuss things.' We went through it and there was no doubt that Harold was got rid of because the Treasury didn't like a man who really knew about national finance. He went into great detail about the three or four occasions, twice in Washington and twice in London, when he had saved Roy from monumental mistakes which the Treasury were going to make, like putting up the bank rate by 2 per cent at one crucial moment, and by signing the I.M.F. letter with far tougher conditions than were really necessary. Harold Lever said the Treasury was all right under William Armstrong but when Douglas Allen arrived, an old professional civil servant, it meant that Civil Service jealousy got going. The row they made about his speeches, the tales they told Roy out of school upset Harold Lever and made his ulcer bleed and finally, to get rid of him, he was promoted up and out.

[1] The Maud Commission had proposed that all of England, outside London, should be divided into 8 provinces, 58 unitary authorities and 3 metropolitan areas (Merseyside, with Liverpool as the centre; West Midlands, the area around Birmingham; and, around Manchester, 'Selnec'—i.e. S.E. Lancashire and N.E. and Central Cheshire). Within the metropolitan areas would be 20 metropolitan districts. In the Government's White Paper (Cmnd 4276), published on February 4th, 1970, the 8 provinces were abandoned and 2 more metropolitan areas, South Hampshire and the West Riding of Yorkshire, added.

The actual business we were discussing was pensions and the difficulty about the Treasury definition of over-pensioning. They allow 66⅔ per cent of final salary as the upper limit for a tax concession and I was explaining to Harold Lever that the Treasury were now proposing that our new scheme should only allow 50 per cent as the top limit for the pensions which were contracted out. Could I send the papers to him? After all, he deals with all the nationalized industries, which have a major pension interest, and so I hope I can bring him in as an ally if I run into any difficulty with Roy and the Treasury on this particular score.

At 6.30 this evening we expected the vote on the three-line whip on the Import Deposits Bill but the debate continued until 10.0, so I couldn't go out to an official dinner.[1] I wasn't terribly sorry. I sat and dined with Alex Lyon and Judith Hart, and after dinner Judith came to my room and told me her closest secret.[2] As Minister for Overseas Development she has discovered an appalling situation. It has always been assumed that when the present Chairman of the Overseas Development Corporation retires next February, Jock Campbell will replace him. It had suddenly been revealed to her that at Conference Reg Prentice had agreed that Tony Greenwood should be the new Chairman, as a price for resigning from office next February. Jock Campbell had just been told and had observed, 'It's not for me to say it but there will be a scandal about this.' What could Judith do? I told her to see Barbara, who is a friend of Harold's and an ex-O.D. Minister, and who could talk to Tommy Balogh as well. This is very characteristic of Harold. He says he must look after his friends but for me it is the date that is much more significant. Why did he want to get Tony Greenwood out of politics in February? Because he wants a by-election then and thinks Rossendale an ideal test for the chances of a spring election. I am convinced that this is Harold's main motive for tying this neat package together, to look after a friend and serve his electoral interests at the same time.

Tuesday, November 18th

Today the papers published the announcement that the Secretary of State for Education was going to put up school meal charges by 3*d*.[3] It had been announced in the House of Commons yesterday. By God, Ted Short got away with it more easily than the last announcement I had on a Monday.[4] Mind you, this wasn't just four days before the local elections and there had been the most convenient leak yesterday morning to soften the effect. I also think that on the whole, people have learnt their lesson about rowing with Ministers and Short has handled M.P.s far more skilfully than I but, still, it gave me a jar to remember the old days.

[1] The Customs (Import Deposits) Bill was given a Second Reading by 297 votes to 220.

[2] Alex Lyon has been Labour M.P. for York since 1966. He was Minister of State at the Home Office 1974–6.

[3] The school meal charge was to rise from 1*s*. 6*d*. to 1*s*. 9*d*. on April 1st, 1970.

[4] See above, pp. 475–6.

Our weekly meeting of Management Committee was mainly notable for an extraordinary discussion of timetables for the last ten days before Christmas. Politicians adore discussing timetables and they will spend ages rearranging parliamentary business. Harold plays with timetables in an extraordinary way, to fit in with by-elections or to fit in with embarrassing Heath, who wants to get away to his yacht for the last week of the session. After that Barbara asked a question of the Home Secretary about his Order in Council this evening on the Gaming regulations.[1] Where were the new gaming clubs to be and was the decision to locate them in certain districts and ban them in others to be final? Jim said yes, it was all fixed up. 'What about Blackburn?' she said. 'They have just got this splendid new town centre with a smart restaurant, a band and dancing and what they want is a little bit of gaming as well. That would really make it. This is what we could do to revive the North.' It's interesting, we can't revive the North without having a casino as well but I thought there was something in what she said, funnily enough. Callaghan had to say, 'This may be true but we now have fifteen hundred gambling clubs and thousands of these damned betting shops and it is really becoming an addiction that I don't think we ought to encourage any more.' But Barbara, infatuated with her own constituency, was all for gambling in Blackburn.*

For the second week running I lunched in the House of Lords with Bea Serota. There was the best grilled sole, excellent white wine and most interesting company, top trade union leaders, top doctors, bishops, ex-civil servants, the leaders of science and culture generally. It is undoubtedly the best club in London. It's a fascinating place and I must admit that I like it more and more and the Commons less and less. We were lunching with our Chief Nurse, Dame Kathleen Raven, back from her fortnight's holiday in Malta, and discussing how to deal with an enormously expensive claim the nurses have just submitted. It's quite clear that we shall have to give them far more than the Chancellor thinks possible.

This evening the two Permanent Secretaries, Alan Marre and Clifford Jarrett, very kindly organized our celebration dinner at the United Services Club. My God, what a place. The worst possible food I have ever had, a totally unripe avocado pear and an overcooked chop, but of course a decent claret with it. We started far too early and I was horrified at the thought that we would have to go on chatting until I went back to the 10 o'clock division, but then Ifor Evans came in with George Godber and we had some pleasant chat to fill in time.[2] I completely occupied myself in talking to

* The Order in Council went through quietly this evening and some suggestion was made that the list of towns might be extended.

[1] A Prayer against the Gaming Clubs (Licensing) Regulations 1969 was defeated by 206 votes to 145.

[2] Ifor Evans was Principal of Queen Mary College, London, 1946–51, Vice-Chairman of the Arts Council 1946–51 and Provost of University College, London, 1951–66. He became a life peer in 1967, as Lord Evans of Hungershall.

these two, because I have suddenly turned against Clifford Jarrett. I always was a bit ambivalent as to whether he was a very good sort or just a stuffy civil servant with a free and easy manner, but now I can't forgive him for the consultations he has been having about his prospects of a job with a body with which I am in contest. I can't help remembering all the time that he has done this, and all without feeling that there is anything wrong. David and Bea Serota also think it outrageous and I am going to see William Armstrong next week to tell him how I feel. I shall be very interested to see what happens.

Wednesday, November 19th

I lunched with Aharon Remez and his wife at an extraordinary place in Hamilton Terrace, just behind Apsley House, a sort of gamblers' and millionaires' club, where we had very poor food at very great expense. We had a serious talk about arms sales to Israel and I advised them not to rely on us. What interested me was the response. The Ambassador's wife, an upright, able woman, was shocked that I could stay in the Cabinet. I explained that I had done what I could to put pressure on Cabinet not to lead the Israelis up the garden path or leave them in the lurch but to warn them in advance that we are a bad ally. She said, 'Do you like it that when Golda Meir arrived in London last time and we went to receive her at first she wouldn't get out of the plane, and she said, "I don't want to set foot in a country where there is a Labour Government whose name is synonymous with treachery"? She agreed with you, Dick.' 'Well,' I said, 'I think she does. Her analysis and mine are the same. The only thing is you think I oughtn't to be in a Labour Cabinet.' I thought about this afterwards and realized that one does settle down to assume that one accepts a whole area of policy even while believing it to be totally wrong. I think I do in this case because I am not at all sure what I would have done as Foreign Secretary. Would I not have sold all those arms to the Arabs? Would I have deliberately taken the Israeli side and jeopardized our relations with the Arabs and seen our embassies burnt down? No, I would have tried to get out of the Persian Gulf and would have placated and appeased during this period. The difference is that I would have carried out this policy without trying to pretend we could really do anything for the Israelis meanwhile.

I went back to a meeting with Swaffield and Hetherington on their reaction to our draft N.H.S. Green Paper. Like the B.M.A., they simply said it was unacceptable but for the very different reason that the local authority participation was far less than they had expected. I asked them to put forward their own proposals and Hetherington suggested that alongside the biennial discussions about the allocation of the rate support grant there should be discussions about the total money allocated to the National Health Service and its division among the regions. If the whole thing were looked at in a biennial review the local authorities would be able to see that

24

the Health Service really was being considered alongside the other services. They wanted a 40 per cent share in the representation. I found the whole thing extremely stimulating and they were giving us far more constructive ideas than I can get from the Department. The idea that we can from inside produce sensible ideas for the integrated N.H.S. is absolute nonsense. Thank God, I am having the sense, even at this last moment, to have consultations with the B.M.A., the C.C.A. and A.M.C. to get some original, creative ideas which add up. It's desperately late but better late then never.

Then came an interesting meeting. Months and months ago I had got some of the people dealing with prescription charges to write a paper saying what they thought about the way the system was working. Suddenly I found that a meeting had been staged today with Alan Marre and every kind of important person present. It was said to be about a reply to a letter from John Diamond asking us to check the increase in the cost of drugs but I soon found out that it was really because Mr Marre thought he might be in trouble himself. He was going to be cross-examined by the Commons' Estimates Committee, who wanted to know why on earth it was that, when he did his sample test on the working of the prescription charge and half the people didn't answer our letters, we didn't follow it up and investigate. What answer was he to make? I said, 'I'm not going to have my Department run in order to provide, at great expense and trouble, answers for the Estimates Committee.' It was fascinating. Here they were fussing again. I had found Somerville fussing on the hospital side, deflecting half his work into preparing for the Estimates Committee, and now here was Alan Marre trying to get us to change our policies and have investigations and prosecutions about prescription charges. A few months ago they assured me it was going miraculously well, with no sign of serious abuse, but now they were going to go into all this because the Department and the Permanent Secretary found themselves about to be embarrassed. These matters count for a tremendous lot in the mind of the Civil Service. I managed to persuade them not to be so silly and told them I would give a perfect answer, which is to say that we are now a merged Department and we know where the serious abuse is. We aren't going to take investigators off social security and put them on to an area where there is no evidence of serious abuse. I think I have satisfied him but I only caught it in the nick of time. It's quite clear that if I hadn't been there David Ennals and Bea Serota would have allowed the thing to go through.

Thursday, November 20th

At Cabinet the next item after foreign policy was Barbara's incomes policy. On Tuesday at the Prices and Incomes Forward Policy Committee, a rather high-grade committee chaired by the Chancellor of the Exchequer, we had all been asked to express an opinion on whether we should have Barbara's proposal that in the new White Paper on Prices and Incomes, where we drop all Government sanctions, we should allow a range of increases from 2½ per cent to 5 per cent or whether we should have, as we do at present, a norm of 3½ per cent. Barbara had wanted a range not a norm but the Chancellor had said he wanted to stay at 3½ per cent and he was strongly supported by Roy Mason, who said that this was the only sensible thing because the 3½ per cent was all we could afford. Everything beyond that is inflationary because productivity isn't going up. Barbara said it would look ludicrous to have a 3½ per cent norm when everybody's claims were going up to 5, 6, 12 per cent. Harold Lever and I had taken rather the same view. What we put forward doesn't influence wage claims or the people who are actually negotiating them. It probably does influence the I.M.F. to some extent and gives a signal of Government policy but the issue is which signal is the more effective. My God, it is abstract. What trouble we have got into with the creation of this abracadabra of norms and principles, all of them as though the Government can influence this. Now we admit that the whole thing has broken down and, if it is voluntary, the Government can only make noises of exhortation.

Today we came back to this again and I thought Roy put it fairly and got a striking number of people supporting him. He wanted realism and the only realism was to admit that, although everybody will be above 3½ per cent, it is all we can afford. I told him the disadvantage of his case was that the gap between what we can afford and what people are actually taking will demonstrate the rapid rate of inflation and he will be forced to have a deflationary budget. That was my argument against a norm. However I must admit that when I see the figures, the raging inflationary claims that are now being conceded and the new ones that are being put forward, it looks to me as though Roy will urge that we go to the country before the next budget, because he won't want to impose a savagely deflationary budget and he'll say, 'Better to lose the election honourably before the budget than to have the mess afterwards.' This is perhaps the only conclusion I can draw from this morning's Cabinet discussion.

Finally came M.P.s' pay again. We had taken the decision for £500 and now the issue was whether this should be paid only on written guarantee or as part of the normal expenses. Harold Lever and I were able to prevail by saying, 'For God's sake, no special guarantee. Just raise the expenses part of an M.P.'s salary from £1,250 to £1,750 and apply it to the Lords as well. It will be profoundly unpopular with the general public but if that is the deal...' Then Fred Peart made another great effort for an increase of £750. He said Jack Diamond had lied about Selwyn Lloyd, who had shown himself willing to go up to the higher sum, whereupon Jack Diamond said, 'You fixed him after the event.' Barbara looked across and said, 'But we don't say that to each other, Jack.' And we don't. One of the most extraordinary things about our Cabinet is how polite we are, how genteel, how very rarely we say what we really mean to each other, leaving the unpleasant truths unsaid, because we don't wrangle and fight. I suppose I am one of the very few people who blurts out. Everyone else is too refined, letting things go wrong rather than speak the truth. The P.M. finally asked, 'Does anybody want to change his vote?' Silence. 'Right,' he said, 'The Cabinet voted last time, I must take the vote unchanged.' So £500 it was.

This evening I had to catch a train to Birmingham, where I had to go into the R.H.B.'s terrible rows about confidentiality and public relations which had publicly rent the Board.

Friday, November 21st

I went down in the train with Miss Hedley, Peter Brown, Mike Fogden and John Cashman, who got off at Birmingham while I went on alone to Wolverhampton. Mr Stuart, the Department's Principal Regional Officer on the Health side, and I dined with Mr Lewis and his two men, Adams the Secretary and Gordon the C.M.O. I had a long go with them and spilt the beans: 'I must say in your presence, Mr Adams, that since you have taken over they don't think you believe in public relations. I am afraid it's unfair on you but they think you are a tin-pot dictator. You must have a man who reports directly to the Chairman and to me. There must be a professional public relations officer, not one of your officials.' I watched to see how the Chairman and Secretary took all this. We went on till midnight.

I was still anxious about the Chairman when we got to the meeting this morning but it was easier than I hoped, because the Labour people, who had so grossly misbehaved over confidentiality, gave in and agreed that the standing orders were perfectly all right and must be observed. They concentrated quite rightly on the complaints about public relations and the refusal to circulate the minutes and we got a tremendous lot of changes in structure. Minutes will in future have to go out to all members, delegated powers to committees will be revised, a new public relations policy instituted. We achieved all this and then I announced it at a big press conference and the Birmingham press sent up a howl of incredulity. 'We don't believe a word of it. We like you all right but as long as Adams is there we shan't get a damned thing out of him. Adams is wrong, Adams.' Poor Mr Lewis sat beside me, hearing from the press what was wrong with his Secretary. Mr Lewis and I both did little television interviews. I supported the Board in full and described what was going on. I said they were underprivileged and were right to complain, because compared with London they were not getting their fair share of cash. It was a thoroughly good day for me. Once again my personal intervention had come off reasonably well. It was nearly as successful as Newcastle and I was driven back home early enough to dictate my Cabinet paper on local government for next week and to go and dig a bit on my island.

Saturday, November 22nd

The only thing in the news today was the American astronauts' second landing on the moon. The lack of interest in astonishing.[1] I had always thought it would be an anti-climax but in this case the rapidity of the fall-off is phenomenal. I think it's got something to do with the fact that the action itself is not intrinsically interesting. Once it has been shown that they can land accurately with absolute precision and walk about in their space suits, there is very little they can do which is interesting and relevant, so the only real excitement is whether they get killed or not. I hope that people will now begin to consider whether it is worth investing these vast sums in the technology of space travel. Is it really justifiable to divert them from other more helpful scientific activities? As I've said before in this diary, no doubt the real justification is simply the easing off of the cold war between America and Russia. When their energy goes into space flights instead of wholly into nuclear weapons and when ambitions can be satisfied in this way, I suppose the motivation for world war is slightly reduced. I say 'slightly' because nobody knows what the effect of this is on the Chinese.

What we do know is that this week the Americans and Russians have started the Helsinki talks and we shall see whether the cooling-off of the cold war really will bring about any firm agreements.[2] Here I have no views and no way of knowing one way or the other. My own mild interest is because my book has come out and in the last chapter I very boldly describe the future in terms of a gradual cooling-off of the cold war into indifference but not positive mutual understanding.[3] I still hold very strongly that that's what will happen.

Meanwhile there is a sensational story about atrocities in Vietnam,[4] which will strengthen the anti-war forces in America. Within a few months of Nixon's inauguration, America has a President who has apparently seen through himself and a people who have already seen through him. They have a dangerously unstable government, with vast galvanic forces underneath, the Left demanding an end to imperialism and a return to isolationism,

[1] Apollo 12, with a three-man crew, had been launched from Cape Kennedy on November 14th and on November 19th Commander Conrad and Lieutenant-Commander Bean landed on the moon. The space craft returned to earth successfully on November 24th.

[2] In October the U.S.S.R. had at last announced their agreement to holding Strategic Arms Limitation Talks with the United States and the preliminary discussions opened in Helsinki on November 17th. On November 24th Russia and the United States simultaneously ratified the Nuclear Nonproliferation Treaty at ceremonies in Washington and Moscow.

[3] *Government and the Governed* (London: Chatto).

[4] On November 13th the U.S. Army announced that as a result of an official inquiry Lieutenant William Calley had been charged with the murder of at least 109 Vietnamese civilians during a 'search and destroy' mission in the hamlet of My Lai, part of a Viet Cong stronghold code-named 'Pinkville' by the American military. On November 24th Lieutenant Calley was tried by court martial and found guilty of the charges. The conduct of twenty-five other soldiers and former soldiers was also to be investigated. The public in America and throughout the world were shocked by the incident and by newspaper and television accounts of what had taken place.

the Right demanding violence against the blacks. It's a dangerous situation and I suspect the situation in Russia and China is unstable too. I can't believe that the nonentities who are running Russia will be there for ever and will be able to hold down all the energy and talent and in China there is obviously a tremendous struggle going on for the succession to Mao Tse-Tung.[1] Interesting. I read in one of the F.O. papers from China that their universities have been closed down for four or five years. If this kind of convulsion is going on there it makes us seem relatively stable.

Another exquisitely beautiful sunny afternoon. I was expected to go to the Coventry bazaar today. When I first went to Coventry in 1937 this was the great annual event and the whole of the Coventry baths were taken over, stocked by competing wards, each with a magnificent display. It used to raise hundreds of pounds. Now it has dwindled and they were going to have one in Coundon Road and open it at 11.0 a.m. Anne was asked to go but, as she put it, they must have been desperate to have asked her. Just as we were starting out, with the children, Anne said, 'I'm not sure they are expecting you.' We looked at the correspondence and she had actually written to tell them I probably couldn't come. As we set off I suddenly said, 'I've just got too much work to do,' because I had looked at the load of work. We are first in Questions on Monday, I have to clear two boxes to send up to Glasgow tomorrow morning, three boxes were down last night, and I have a speech tonight. If I was to have any time off for a walk this afternoon, I oughtn't to spend three hours going to Coventry, yet if I didn't go to the bazaar, what chance would I have of being a father to my children? At least I could have read aloud to them in the car. I am now terribly cut off and every weekend when I come back I am more and more aware of how they are growing up and away from me. I worry increasingly about it. But no, I got out of the car and went back home and worked all morning, so that this afternoon I had my walk with Anne, up through the spinnies and the Fisherman's Cottage, chatting round the farm.

Monday, November 24th

On Saturday evening I had to go to the Commons for a meeting of the Colchester Medical Society before I caught the sleeper up to Scotland to arrive on Sunday morning.

Yesterday I had to address a big T.U.C. rally of 1,600 delegates in the town hall, and then drive out to some remote place for a meeting with the Federation of Lanarkshire Labour Parties. By then I was feeling iller and iller, before I got back into my sleeper on Sunday night to go down to London for a full week's work. I was beginning to realize this was too much but I couldn't stay in bed today because we were first in Questions. Even worse, my Private Office had arranged that after S.E.P. I should

[1] Chairman Mao Tse-Tung was born in December 1893. He died in the autumn of 1976. As Mr Crossman anticipated, his death was followed by internal struggles in China.

lunch at the *Financial Times* at 1.15. They have a magnificent dining room, facing the finest view of St Paul's. I sat next to Robbins, with Drogheda opposite, and a nice gang of young men round me,[1] but before we could really settle down to a proper argument I had to be back in the House for Question Time.

Then I had a long and difficult meeting with Titmuss and Collison about supplementary benefits. David Ennals has been pressing for a big statement on abuse because he wants to show that we are grappling with it and believes this is something which public opinion demands of us. I have been uneasily aware that when the Superannuation Bill comes we shall be making important concessions to strikers, so I am prepared to write in two amendments which make it a reasonable package but, frankly, the only way we can persuade the ordinary public to believe we are dealing with abuse is if Collison and Titmuss tighten up on young, work-shy people. We are already pretty tough to single men, we cut off benefit and send them back to seek work after four weeks, but we fail to apply the same toughness to married couples, even married couples without children. I tested Collison and Titmuss on this today and I soon became aware that they and the whole Commission had been alienated by David and felt that they weren't going to give an inch to this politician. Titmuss doesn't think, for example, that the four-week pressure on the single man is right. I asked him, 'If we put this pressure on a single man, why not on a married couple with no children?' 'Because the man with a wife has extra responsibilities.' 'But,' I said, 'the wife can be work-shy too. They may have been work-shy while living separately; why shouldn't they be work-shy when they are married? There are 10,000 of them, you know.' This conversation raised mutiny and resistance all round the table and I realized we were not going to get very far by pushing the S.B.C. They were not prepared to concede anything to the anti-scrounger campaign.

I had to finish because I had promised the Labour Party Health Service group a meeting on hospital closures. When I got there at 6.0 there were three people, but I was feeling pretty tired by now so I broke off and let Jim Wellbeloved drive me home for a quick meal with his wife, son and daughter.[2] He is a plumber by trade and became the agent for Norman Dodds,[3] who was perhaps one of the most constituency-minded M.P.s, the friend of all the gypsies. When Norman died it was felt that his trusty machine man should take over. Jim did and got a very good majority. As

[1] The 11th Earl of Drogheda. He was Managing Director of *Financial Times* Ltd 1945–70 and its Chairman 1971–5 and Chairman of the Newspaper Publishers' Association 1968–70 and of the Royal Opera House, Covent Garden 1958–74.

[2] Labour M.P. for Erith and Crayford November 1965–74 and for Bexley, Erith and Crayford since 1974. He was an Opposition Whip 1972–4. Since 1976 he has been a Parliamentary Under-Secretary of State (R.A.F.) at the Ministry of Defence.

[3] He entered Parliament in 1945 and sat for Erith and Crayford from 1955 until his death in August 1965. See Vol. I.

we drove down together we talked about the House of Commons. He had been one of my bitterest opponents when I introduced the liberalized regime and I remember arguing with him for three hours during an all-night sitting trying to explain it. Now he told me how shocked and disillusioned he had been by his first six months in the House, by the hard-boiled, cynical attitude of all the back benchers. He had gradually settled down and was now more content. I asked him about the liberal regime and it looks as if he, like Bob Mellish, has really accepted it. After supper we got to the school hall where there were sixty or seventy people, just enough to make a respectable meeting. I made another speech on pensions and got home feeling more and more tired.

Tuesday, November 25th

Cabinet and we dealt with Ulster once again. We have now passed the Act setting up the Ulster Defence Regiment, against tremendous opposition from our left wing.[1] Bernadette Devlin has been saying we are setting up 'B' Specials in another guise and surrendering to right-wing reactionaries. The Labour Left kept the House up all night on this issue. I think myself it has been an extremely successful operation and that the Ulster Regiment is totally different. It's entirely under the control of British officers. I think it really is a cover under which Chichester-Clark can maintain his subordination to us.

The main contest this morning was between the Minister of Defence and the Chancellor. Denis had a long elaborate argument to show why, even after the withdrawals from east of Suez, we would have one or two expensive years. He said that other nations were now moving ahead and were using a higher percentage of their G.N.P. for defence than we were. We would be falling behind our allies. (That statement brought forth cheers from me.) I am not sorry to say he didn't stand a chance. The Defence Minister is now in a hopeless position and what he was saying was that he would have to have a fifth Defence Review if he didn't write in an increase in one of these two years. He was told that these figures in the White Paper were just as notional for defence as for anybody else's programme. They didn't absolutely mean a cut but there couldn't be a White Paper publishing an increase in defence expenditure as the net result of final withdrawal from east of Suez. I don't know how far Denis put this on as an exhibition piece. I suspect it was done in order to carry the chiefs of staff by showing how hard he fought for them before giving way.

My main worry today was a meeting with NALGO at the Central Hall, Westminster. The hall was packed with 2,000 delegates and if we put a foot wrong they would be demonstrating. I knew this was one of the most important speeches of my life as a departmental Minister and I had already

[1] The Bill was given its Second Reading on November 19th and on December 1st it was taken through its remaining stages and passed.

done a great deal of work on it. NALGO were circulating a pamphlet on transferability of pensions dealing with the eight so-called fallacies in my scheme and I had got the office to prepare for me frightfully carefully eight exposures of the NALGO arguments, so I had a pretty good presentation ready in my head. I arrived punctually at 7 o'clock and went in through the back to the platform. True, the hall was full and there were virtually no cheers as I came in. After a few words of introduction by the General Secretary of NALGO, I was off on fifty-five minutes of a severe talk about the nature of the scheme, the place of transferability and the fallacies. I got them laughing a good deal at the beginning and cajoled them along with what people regarded as a pretty good performance. Then for one and a half hours I answered the questions which streamed in. Thank God they came in written form so I had a moment to glance at them each time.

After that I had to go to St Ermin's Hotel to have dinner with the NALGO Executive. At least I had the sense not to go to the American Ambassador's afterwards, because by now I knew I really had got 'flu, and I gave instructions to my Ministry that I would stay at Vincent Square tomorrow. Fortunately Anne was coming up and would be able to look after me.

Wednesday, November 26th—Thursday, November 27th

For the last two days I have mainly stayed at home, trying to combine doing work with 'flu, in a not very satisfactory way. I didn't go to the Elephant and Castle but I have had some very good meetings, one on the hospital building capital development programme and one on local government capital investment. Sir William Armstrong also came to Vincent Square to discuss my letter about Clifford Jarrett's retirement. I told him my feelings and said, 'I don't think he ought to do this. It's a terrible thing and if he is to be allowed to do it I want him to get out as soon as possible. I really don't want to have him as my Permanent Secretary if he is negotiating with the enemy about crossing the line as soon as he leaves the Department.' William Armstrong was very shaken and upset and said that no doubt he ought to have thought of this himself. He talked a great deal about it and went off. I shall wait to see what he says.

I also saw Swaffield and Hetherington, who were enormously excited, with Hetherington saying he hoped within ten days to bring me a paper agreed with the B.M.A. I was a bit sceptical and I could see Swaffield looking sceptical too but I welcomed the news. I have certainly been greatly helped by their suggestions. They want local authorities to have a financial stake in the Health Service and to see the Health Service grant considered alongside the rate support grant. I see movement here and I realize that at least one thing I've learnt is that we have to give up the idea of my having 51 per cent nomination by Regional Health Authorities and 49 per cent by the local government authorities. With 51 per cent I am demanding too much and I can't get enough representation from the local authorities and the professions. I have to concede, say, 60–65 per cent local authority and only, say, 20–30 per cent of my own. If I do that I may be able to carry them along but I am getting more and more gloomy, because I haven't had a single constructive idea out of the Department and there is no one to write it. Finally, however, this very evening Alan Marre said he had found a young man who could possibly get down to writing something for me. I think, though, I shall get Brian to come down next week to work with me for a day and think out the whole problem.

I managed to go to Cabinet on Thursday. Once again Michael Stewart and Harold Wilson are in trouble on Nigeria.[1] Half-way through I couldn't help saying to Roy, 'The truth is, you know, that Harold and Michael are deeply, morally convinced that the Federal Government is fighting a righteous war. They really believe in maintaining the unity of Nigeria and that if this is not done tribalism will recur. The only mistake they are making is not to give their side every encouragement to win fast, because they also believe that the Federalists, being good people, must somehow hold back and make concessions all the time to prevent the starvation which is their most powerful weapon against the rebels.' Colonel Ojukwu, the rebel leader, is not at all a virtuous man and he is quite ruthlessly permitted to exploit and complain about the starvation he perpetuates. He could end the starvation perfectly easily if he allowed daylight flights of food into his territory, but then the food planes would no longer fly at night and cover for the arms planes. He is cleverly persuading the world of the wickedness of the Federal Government in trying to starve him out when in fact he is getting the arms at the cost of starving his people. I see danger here in the fact that the will to victory of Colonel Ojukwu of the Ibo is far stronger than the will to victory of Harold Wilson's friends. It overwhelmingly reminded me of the Israeli determination, compared with the Arabs! I made this point and said, 'For heaven's sake, don't make the mistake we made elsewhere of getting ourselves on the wrong side. When you are in on the birth of a nation that is born by separatism, by civil war, it's no good saying that you must maintain the unity and the fabric of the state. You must recognize the existence of the new nation and that however many treaties it breaks, however much it tears apart the administrative structure, it is going to do this in defiance, as the Israelis did it in defiance of the United Nations.' Harold replied, 'The analogy isn't with Israel but with the American Civil War. General Gowon is seeking to do exactly what Lincoln did, to prevent a separatism which will destroy the state.' 'Yes,' I said, 'but no armies could have been more ruthless than Lincoln's armies in the will to victory and their determination to exterminate the enemy. Why are you weakening the will of your Abraham Lincoln?' Perhaps Denis Healey partially understood

[1] Both the Federalists and the Biafran authorities continued to obstruct relief flights to Biafra and in December the emergency worsened after a reduction in the number of air-lifts and a new advance into rebel food-growing areas by Federal troops.

the argument but Barbara was totally opposed, saying, 'We must relieve the starvation.' Half the Cabinet want to do anything possible to stop the starvation and it is true that in the country as a whole there is no strong feeling on the side of the Federalists, because we just don't like being held responsible for cruelty and inhumanity. Michael and Harold are quite unable to make the British people accept the significance of the moral principle they both stand for, the federal, the unitary principle, rather than the appeal to humanity. That's the difficulty they find themselves in.

By the end of today I was getting weary and I know very well I will have to go to bed when I get back to Prescote but I still have half a day's work to do tomorrow.

Friday, November 28th

I rushed off this morning feeling very, very seedy to Home Affairs Committee and then I had to go over to the Elephant and Castle for a one-day conference of eighty nurses on sub-normal hospitals. I gave them an introduction and tottered out to a press conference we were giving at 70 Whitehall on my Fabian pamphlet. At long last the Herbert Morrison Lecture is to be published and a number of press people had been collected for a drink and a discussion before they write their Sunday pieces. I don't know how successful the thing was. Nora Beloff and Auberon Waugh were there. This pamphlet, however, has been round seven government Departments and has been approved by Sir George Godber and everybody else, so I'm not too worried about it, however sensational the treatment in the weekend press may be.

This was the last thing I did before staggering to the train. I noticed Harry Judge on the platform and he got into the carriage with me, obviously very worried at how ill I was looking. Directly I got home I was put to bed and Dr Long came to see me and felt my chest all over. He said it was in a terrible state and that I had congestion of the lungs and must stay absolutely quiet. I was dosed with antibiotics and just sank below the surface.

Monday, December 1st

I have never had this kind of bronchitic 'flu before. It makes you feel as if your lungs have been staved in, your ribs broken, and you feel twisted and miserable and unhappy. Of course you feel worse because the antibiotics are going into you at the same time. The Fabian pamphlet, however, has had a tremendous impact. The most substantial publicity came from the *Sunday Telegraph*, who had assumed that I was launching a bitter attack on private medicine. They dug out my reference to BUPA and my argument that it would be no solution to our N.H.S. financial problem to increase the number of people in BUPA.[1] I had also mentioned queue-jumping and

[1] The British United Provident Association was the main private health insurance organization. One of the arguments of opponents of such private schemes was that they permitted private patients to jump the queue for treatment in illness.

this was treated very sensationally in the *Sunday Express*. Nora Beloff had given the pamphlet a good write-up in the *Observer*, so it has certainly had a very good send-off.

One of the immediate consequences of my being away is that every advantage is being taken to knock my poor old National Superannuation Bill on the head and I had a furious row about this on the telephone with Fred Peart this morning. I was feeling pretty ill when he rang up to tell me that the debate on the Abatement White Paper has suddenly been postponed. This makes it impossible to have a debate on the Bill before Christmas and we shall get into Committee only at the end of January. It is really a minor disaster and if there is any chance of a spring election it will be a major disaster. I blew my top to Fred and told him what I thought of him, that they were double-crossing bastards to do this to me, and incompetent. But underneath I knew the Department felt they were being rushed and wanted more time and Departments get their way on this kind of thing. Secretly nobody really minds it being put back, because we may save a week in Committee by having a better drafted Bill.

Wednesday, December 3rd

David Ennals came down to report on everything and told me that, sure enough, in my absence Legislation Committee had postponed the Bill. We shall have publication in the last week before the Christmas recess, when I shall probably be fit enough to make the Statement in the House. It's not a disaster but somehow it's humiliating and it all piles on to me while I'm ill.

Thursday, December 4th

David made a thoroughly competent speech on the National Superannuation White Paper on partial contracting-out. We had prepared it together yesterday and there was no great harm at my not being in the House. Having made a tremendous fuss, the Tories had very little to say and we have come out of it with no loss or damage at all.

Sunday, December 7th

I am beginning to feel better but I am still pretty weak and I don't want to get back to work too fast. I am going to take the whole of this week off to convalesce. I rang up Harold and Barbara this morning to tell them what the situation was on nurses' pay. We have had a series of teachers' strikes building up all over the country and I hear the N.U.T. are asking for an annual increase of £125 and we are offering them £75, Ted Short having been refused the £85 he wanted to try.[1] We have announced that there is

[1] On November 11th the National Union of Teachers and the National Union of Schoolmasters began a series of half-day strikes and on December 1st they extended this to fourteen-day withdrawals from selected schools, threatening to spread the strike still further in January if their claims for increased salaries were not met.

to be a nurses' award at the end of March and we are supposed to be making our first offer to the Whitley Council next week. It's clear we can't start negotiating there without an initial idea of where we stand with the teachers, because we are trying to get staff nurses' pay roughly linked to the pay of the non-graduate teacher. I am making a great bid to postpone discussion of the nurses until something has been fixed about the teachers next week and here again my absence may be convenient. I arranged with Harold and Barbara that Bea Serota could go to the Cabinet where Barbara's White Paper is under discussion and where we want to get a paragraph drafted to give us a free hand with the nurses. I hope to God it's all right. I don't think anything disastrous has happened there.

One small good thing in the balance. After six months of struggle it has been agreed that I should issue a letter to all R.H.B. chairmen and to all the teaching hospitals recommending them to introduce family planning advice in hospitals. George Godber was a tremendous problem on this, holding back on it, saying it was terribly difficult and that there would be major trouble. Eventually when Bea Serota saw the President of the Royal College of Obstetricians and Gynaecologists, she found that he was urging us to do more.[1] The fact is that George has been unduly sensitive. He regards family planning and the pill and all these things as not pukkah doctoring of the sort the Ministry deals with. We have had the same kind of attitude to vasectomy. I saw no reason whatsoever to resist the Simon Trust's proposal that we ought to make it known that sterilization was available on the Health Service for men who wanted it. If people know the consequences but prefer sterilization and want to have it after they have had three or four children, provided it is done with advice from a doctor it should be done. But again there has been resistance from the Department.

Finally, something connected with my own Fabian pamphlet, the problem of the inquiry into private practice which I discussed weeks ago with P.E.P.[2] The Department has been back-pedalling, resisting in every possible way. I finally rang George Godber and said, 'What's it all about?' He gradually came round to say, 'Actually I doubt if an inquiry would be any good or whether the profession would really co-operate. They are resistant to any inclination to ask questions about this.' I said, 'I'm not concerned with the co-operation of the profession. What I am concerned about is that an absolutely objective organization should collect what information is available and publish it. Surely we can't resist this?' Well, he did resist. It's going to be driven through, I think, but on this kind of thing I do find the Department extremely difficult.

Meanwhile I have been rather surprised by the tremendous impact of the

[1] Sir Norman Jeffcoate, Professor of Obstetrics and Gynaecology at the University of Liverpool 1945–72 and now Professor Emeritus. A Fellow of the Royal College of Obstetrics and Gynaecology, he was the College's President 1969–72. He has been Vice-President of the Family Planning Association since 1962. He was knighted in 1970.

[2] See above, p. 647 and n.

Fabian pamphlet although the publicity has centred on BUPA and the allegation that I am attacking private medicine. This has been taken up more and more widely and means that a large number of people who didn't read the pamphlet have assumed it was true. I have been warned that the C.M.O. is in grave alarm, because Sir John Richardson has written to me in high dudgeon,[1] saying that I am imperilling all the negotiations about consultants' pay by launching an attack of this kind. I refuse to give way and I have simply written him a letter giving him a let-out, saying that I am sure once he has seen the pamphlet he will see I made no such allegations and I am so glad he hasn't jumped to this conclusion. But there's no doubt it has been jumped to and it's been taken up by the Tories, who have put down a half-day debate for next Wednesday. It's quite a good thing that I'm not going to be there and that George Thomas will deal with it along with John Dunwoody.[2]

Turning to the outside world, the big thing apart from Nigeria is the Pinkville massacre and the admission that American soldiers shot down women and children in a Vietnamese village. American reaction against the war is boiling up into isolationism and we shall hate facing the full consequences of American withdrawal. I don't know how they are going to get out of their crisis now without a major disaster, because they've convinced themselves that they are fighting an unjust war in a way I can't believe we ever did. On the Boer War we were divided but at least half the nation thought it was right. I don't believe any Americans now think they are right. What concerns us about this is our Government's attitude.[3] Harold and Michael have consciously believed that it was our duty to support the Americans if we were to be brought into the peace negotiations. Now the war won't be ended in this kind of way. Now they are losing, from Harold's point of view we are losing as well. It's astounding how reactionary we have managed to be in our American policy.

The by-elections at Wellingborough and at Louth on December 4th show the extreme remoteness of a spring election.[4] The results were not too bad

[1] Physician at St Thomas's Hospital, London, since 1949 and at King Edward VII's Hospital for Officers since 1964. He has been President of the General Medical Council since 1973 and was President of the B.M.A. 1970–1 and Chairman of the Joint Consultants' Committee 1967–72. He was knighted in 1960 and in 1963 he became a baronet. In 1973 he became President of the General Medical Council.

[2] In the debate on December 10th on a Conservative motion 'welcoming the development of schemes for private health insurance', the Government amendment, that 'these cannot provide an adequate alternative to existing methods of financing a comprehensive Health Service', was carried by 296 votes to 225.

[3] Left-wing Labour M.P.s, in particular, had led the growing hostility to the Government's support for American policy in Vietnam and the My Lai massacre had stirred their anger. Over 150 Labour M.P.s signed a motion condemning the U.S. action and they were to express their repugnance during the Foreign Affairs debate on December 8th.

[4] In the by-election at Wellingborough caused by the death on August 8th of Harry Howarth, Labour M.P. since 1964, Peter Fry took the seat for the Conservatives with a majority of 6,049, on a 9·7 per cent swing from Labour. At Louth, in the by-election

but not too good either. I am sure one of the reasons for the lack of improvement in our situation is the uncontrolled wage inflation. While increases of 10, 20, 30, 40 per cent are being demanded in the public sector, Barbara is putting forward the reactivation of Part II for a few months until her Industrial Commission Bill gets through and this itself will be palpably a gimmick. I am more and more unhappy about what she and Harold are doing, because it is so obvious that they are trying to conceal the failure of their policy, seeing it only from their point of view.

Apart from that the economic situation gets steadily better. Roy Jenkins sits there, quietly telling himself his policy is working, he has the credit for it and it's coming right now. If the wage inflation really gets out of control we might have to have an unpopular budget, but Nicky Kaldor, who is now, thank God, my official economic adviser, tells me there isn't really a great risk of this. He says we've a reasonable chance of getting through all right and he thinks the economic situation looks good. Visible exports are good, our balance of trade really is a plus balance and we are piling up an enormous budget surplus, which Roy feels he will be able to use. So that side is not too bad but with all this going on this week I am glad I'm not there.

Monday, December 8th

A beautiful day and I am sitting downstairs for the first time. Paul Odgers is coming to stay the night. I am beginning to feel really better but I am still pretty weak.

Tuesday, December 9th – Wednesday, December 17th

A huge vacuum of illness, of being up in the bedroom and then crawling downstairs, going for a walk and getting tired and trying again, always being told by the doctors, 'Don't hurry this time. You've had a nasty knock.' I suppose I really did, with double pneumonia in both lungs. For the four or five days while I was still up I was really nastily ill and it's taking me a long time to recover. On December 10th I had my X-ray, which showed I still had some pneumonia at the bottom of both lungs. Though I had of course decided not to go to London at all that week, I hadn't decided to absent myself from the critical divisions, on December 16th and 17th,[1] in the last

---

caused by the death of Sir Cyril Osborne on August 31st, Jeffrey Archer held the seat for the Conservatives, with a majority of 10,727, on a 14·3 per cent swing.

[1] In December 1964 the House of Commons had decided, in a free vote on the Murder (Abolition of the Death Penalty) Bill, introduced by Sydney Silverman, to do away with capital punishment for murder. A clause added by Lord Brooke of Cumnor provided that the Act should expire on July 31st, 1970, unless Parliament otherwise determined by a Resolution of both Houses.

On December 15th, 1969, Quintin Hogg introduced a motion deploring the Government's action in asking Parliament to reach a conclusion on the continuance of the Act 'at an unnecessarily early stage' and declining 'to come to a decision … until after the publication of all available and relevant statistics covering the full year 1969'. The motion was defeated

week of Parliament, but after the X-ray it was clear that I would have to give an instruction that I would be out of action until January 1st. This was the first time Peter Brown had allowed people to know I was really ill. In the newspapers my name was still being associated with most of the Department's troubles and nobody had known I was away until they were suddenly told I was recovering from pneumonia. It eased my difficulties a bit when people realized that I wasn't fit and about but it also meant that they didn't bother to write to me because by then I was recovering.

I haven't done this diary now for a long time and, playing back what I recorded on December 7th, it strikes me how close I still was to politics as well as to the Department, although I was weak and ill. Now, while I recuperate I am less interested in Cabinet, the Commons and all that world, but nevertheless during the whole of this time I have kept pretty tight control of the Department.

On the afternoon of December 10th Peter Smithson brought Peter Brown down to lunch and we talked at length about Clifford Jarrett. Peter was extremely useful because he straightaway advised me to forbid Clifford to take the job and to ask him to stay on at least while I remained a Minister. That Wednesday was also the day of the half-day debate on private practice, which the Tories took out of their own time.[1] George Thomas introduced the amendment for the Government and John Dunwoody wound up admirably. There was no trouble about that and in fact my absence was really a great convenience, because only my presence could have made any kind of bitterness or scene. As it was, we managed to get out of it without any backsliding from what I had written in the Herbert Morrison Lecture and without further antagonizing the private sector. That evening there was a long discussion on '24 Hours' between the Secretary of BUPA and Derek Stark-Murray, the Chairman of the Socialist Medical Association, but this really finished the subject of my so-called attack on private practice, at least as a Parliamentary affair.

On the 11th, the Thursday, I summoned the Department to Prescote for a mass meeting. Brian had already come down earlier in the week for a long talk and had shaken me by his dislike for the structure of the draft Green Paper. He had gone back with the understanding that he should work out a new paper to put to Alan Marre and now we were assembled, ten members of the Department in the drawing room here. We found it was a splendid room for a policy meeting, with an excellent atmosphere, because one can't be rude to one's host.

---

by 303 votes to 241. On December 16th the Commons voted in favour of retaining the provisions of the Act. On December 17th the Commons approved, by 289 to 261, the Prices and Incomes Act 1966 (Continuation of Part II) Order 1969.

[1] The motion, moved by Maurice Macmillan, welcomed the development of schemes for private health insurance. George Thomas moved an amendment recognizing 'that these cannot provide an adequate alternative to existing methods of financing a comprehensive Health Service' and this was passed by 296 votes to 225.

I think if I hadn't been ill I wouldn't have had anything like the time to spend on this. Of course I now realize our tremendous loss in not setting up a Royal Commission on the Health Service as we did on local government. This would have been first-rate because no one really knows how the Health Service is run. All the doctors, nurses and administrators I have talked to know their bit but no one has a complete picture of the tripartite Health Service, with the local authority services, the G.P.s, the hospitals, the medical colleges in London and the teaching hospitals. Kenneth Robinson's first Green Paper was just an abstract document cooked up in the Ministry without any outside consultation. I have been through elaborate consultations and my first reaction, as we remember, was to say that the single Area Boards were terribly remote and that we should have a two-tier system. That had been broadly agreed but then six months afterwards the Maud Report came out, knocking two-tier on the head as hard as it possibly could. I thought for a long time and decided the only thing was to have, as the equivalent of the Maud unitary authority, seventy or eighty second-tier bodies, with, above them, a top tier of sixteen regions. While I was lying in bed ill, Brian had come down to warn me that everybody thought this scheme was terrible. They felt our two-tier system wasn't getting near to the grass roots. It was as far away as ever, because our second tiers were very much the same kind of Area Board which Kenneth had outlined in his original Green Paper. That day Brian and I had a tremendous go for three or four hours. He went back and wrote a magnificent paper, and then today he brought down the Ministry to discuss my proposal for knocking out the regional tier altogether. We worked from 3.30 till 7.0 and there was tremendous opposition to this major change. I wanted to eliminate the regional tier, then have our Area Boards and under them our District Committees. The District Committees would report directly to the Area Board and to the Ministry, with no intermediate body except for regional consortia for specific purposes. After four hours' discussion we came to the conclusion, not that I was right, as we couldn't knock the region out altogether, but that we ought to put all the power in the Area Board and to make our Districts parallel to the Maud Districts. They wouldn't have the same frontiers but they would have parallel and equal administrative devolution. Having got that we would then just have the Regional Council for specific functional purposes, particularly postgraduate education and specialist activities, and for specific services like ambulances and the supply of blood, etc. Out of this had come an extraordinary convergence of opinion and we had managed to work out something we could put to the doctors.

The ten who had come down, including Liz Shore as Godber's number two, were tremendously excited and over supper in the hall we realized we had got something down here, in my house with me as host, which couldn't possibly have been done in the Ministry.

On December 13th I had to go to Oxford to see Mr Tibbs about my varicose veins. I kept the appointment and after a very satisfactory interview I took my first little walk down the Giler and lunched at Balliol with Tommy and his new girlfriend Catherine.[1] On Sunday, 14th, a lovely afternoon, I tried a walk to Upper Prescote and back across the fields with Anne and found it was just a bit more than I could manage. On Monday it was my birthday. That day we were down for Questions, and the day before I had been right through the list, found that a lot of the answers were very inadequate and sent up my suggestions, prepared much more carefully than I usually do, on how they should be handled by John Dunwoody and David Ennals. By then Brian O'Malley had 'flu too, but though there were only the two of them to manage they did extremely well and I had no complaints. Meanwhile I was having a delicious birthday tea, with a beautiful cake made by Virginia, and for the first time for years I was able to enjoy a weekday birthday with the children. There I sat and blew the candles out and Anne gave me a wonderful walking stick, and Venice, who always remembers, gave me a Chiltern Society tie. Altogether it was a thoroughly enjoyable birthday. That was the evening, too, of the first vote on hanging.

On Tuesday, 16th, Atkinson came down from the Department. He is quiet, studious, detached, and by far the best of my civil servants in either Ministry. He and Miss Riddelsdell are really outstanding and able people, of deep personal integrity. He briefed me on the vital issue of the next new pension scheme, which the civil servants, the local government officials and the nationalized industries will all have to put forward to fit in with the Government scheme. This is a crucial issue, because if these people find their new schemes unsatisfactory there will be a hell of a row. As a matter of fact, this won't happen, because the schemes are going to be satisfactory, although they may well not involve contracting-out but simply take over a large amount of the Government scheme, with rather less of their own. This evening the P.M. at last rang me up about Clifford Jarrett's decision and I shall get Clifford down to see me later this week.

On December 17th I had visits from Janet and Tam and I did a new introduction to *New Fabian Essays*,[2] which I have been putting off and off. Tam had to rush back to vote on Prices and Incomes that night. In the afternoon David Ennals made the long-delayed Statement on the publication of our Pensions Bill.[3] He had intended to come down to see me again on the Wednesday but he got 'flu. The Second Reading will be on January 19th and we will go to Committee straightaway. We shall have lost a month but nevertheless the Department tell me they have improved the Bill enormously, so we will save as many days in Committee as we have lost by the postponement.

[1] Catherine Storr, whom he married in 1970.
[2] Edited by Richard Crossman (London: Dent, 1970).
[3] The Statement was on the National Superannuation Bill, which was to implement the proposals published in the three White Papers, two of which had already been debated in the House.

Thursday, December 18th
I got excellent news. I had written to John Mackintosh, to ask whether he would help me with the Godkin Lectures which I am to deliver at Harvard in March. Tam had strongly advised me against this but I thought it would be all right and that I would offer John the Harvard fee. Sure enough, he seemed glad to help and rang me today to say he was going to think over his ideas and put them up to me. This is an enormous relief because it means we can get a text properly prepared for the P.M. to see. This evening I had Clifford Jarrett down for the night and for our awkward interview. When I last discussed this on the telephone with William Armstrong, he had said I should talk to Clifford. 'No,' I said, 'I won't. I think the best thing is for him to go as soon as possible and for Mildred Riddelsdell to take his place. Clifford and I both think she is the right person, so I hope we can do it quite easily and smoothly.' 'Well,' said Sir William, 'I shall have to consult some of my friends.' I rang him on December 7th and he said, 'We have consulted. Miss Riddelsdell is good at policy but she couldn't manage the Ministry. You will have to have somebody from outside like my number two, Mr Rogers,[1] or possibly Barbara's Permanent Secretary, Denis Barnes.' 'But,' I said, 'Clifford and I think she is the right person. We can't be far wrong.' However I let Sir William talk to Clifford to find out how things stood. I really am amazed that Clifford's intentions should be regarded as sensible and proper but I have never thought for a moment that he is doing it out of wickedness. It is just thick-skinned naïveté, because he doesn't understand how things will look to the outside world or to a person like myself, nor does he seem to appreciate how difficult I shall find it to work with him. The fact is that I am now hardly aware I've got a Permanent Secretary. Clifford is simply biding his time for retirement and I can never forget how he said to me at our famous anniversary dinner, 'If I had been asked my opinion when I was offered this job at D.H.S.S. I would have said it was a thoroughly bad business. The merger doesn't really make any sense and that's still my view.' He's not a man to encourage one.

When the Prime Minister telephoned me on Tuesday, December 16th, he said he had had a long talk with William Armstrong. Harold entirely agreed with me that Clifford's intentions were wrong but he also agreed with Armstrong that, according to the precedent set in the last three or four years, if we refused Clifford this we would have to change all the rules and protocols on the retirement of Permanent Secretaries. So William then had to get down to the job of seeing Clifford and telling him that although there were plenty of precedents for what he wanted to do, the Prime Minister had decided that the precedents are wrong and the rules must be changed. One

[1] Sir Philip Rogers (K.C.B. 1970), Deputy Secretary of the Cabinet 1964–7, Third Secretary at H.M. Treasury 1967–8, Deputy Secretary at the C.S.D. 1968–9 and Second Permanent Secretary 1969–70. He was Permanent Secretary at the D.H.S.S. 1970–5 and has been Chairman of Outward Bound Trust since 1976.

of my big achievements has been saying no and forcing the Prime Minister into action in this particular case, and I am looking forward with the greatest interest to seeing how the rules will be altered. But, as you can imagine, I was not looking forward to my talk with Clifford this evening.

Fortunately we had a lot of other things to discuss. John Cashman is to be moved and in his place I am going to have Robin Wendt, the assistant to Lewin, that pertinacious Russian Jew who is really the brains and foster-nurse of the whole pensions scheme. Wendt is a tremendously bright little squirrel, a vivid, able, clever man, whom I am absolutely certain will suit me a great deal better than John Cashman. Simultaneously I shall be moving Ralph Cox, the good-looking chap with side-whiskers and a nice wife and children at a comprehensive school. Cox is one of those curious characters, a person who looks very collected but who has learnt nothing in six months. He is as thick-skinned as Jarrett, whereas Mike Fogden is just that little bit better than Cox and first-rate at dealing with me personally. He is absolutely perfect as a Private Secretary. I hope things will work better after these changes.

Clifford and I got down to discussing his own personal life. He told me how injured and sore he felt at the whole thing. 'After all,' he said, 'I didn't care about the job; I didn't take it at all seriously. I just wanted enough money to visit my daughter in Seattle every year.' 'Well,' I said, 'I wouldn't have minded if you had gone in for a large salary. Selling yourself for so little seemed to me a bit cheap.' 'I'm not selling myself,' he said. 'I just wanted to get a little bit more and this seemed to be the easiest way of earning it. I never gave a thought to the work itself or felt any particular interest in it. I just knew that as I had been the head of the state insurance scheme I could be useful to them.' I must say I absolutely believe that this was his attitude. I asked him, 'You know me pretty well by now. Didn't you think I might be upset by your talking to these people behind my back?' He said it had never occurred to him that I might mind. He is a big, bluff, red-faced man with pale blue eyes, who is in a way incredibly obtuse, but who has a marvellous sense of detail. I am sure he is level-headed in running the Department, he knows every detail of the Pensions Plan but, by jove, if a senior Permanent Secretary has to be a politician, good at handling politicians and understanding politics, Jarrett has absolutely no such quality. Frankly, as head of the merged Department he has been a complete flop and he hasn't really tried to assert himself there at all.

At first he wanted to clear out straightaway but I gradually persuaded him to stay on and I think he will remain until July. Meanwhile William Armstrong has told me whom I am likely to get instead. In his view there are two possibilities, Rogers, the number two in the Cabinet Secretariat, a very clever and able young man, or Denis Barnes, who might be ready to move across to me in July. My idea of having two P.U.S.s, Mildred Riddelsdell and Alan Marre, is, I now think, quite impossible, and it would also be to confess our failure to merge the Departments properly. So the plan is now that Clifford will stay on as P.U.S. 1 until next July, really until the election, when I will get either Rogers or Denis Barnes. I rather think I shall have Rogers, but I haven't yet talked to Barbara about it.

There was Clifford sitting in front of the fire arguing the issue out with me like a bear with a sore head. He's been unwell recently, with an allergy and 'flu, and he is feeling the wear. I am glad we had it all out and I think we reached a kind of understanding. The only other complication is that the other night, when we were talking on the telephone, Alan Marre said, 'You'll find me on the list of knights in the New Year's Honours List.'[1] (It's a very odd fact that honours for Secretaries and Deputy Secretaries are not discussed with the Minister concerned but are entirely a matter for the Prime Minister and William Armstrong.) In giving Marre a knighthood I had a feeling that they were clearly tipping him to be the P.U.S. 1 of the merged Department but I am now told that in due course all P.U.S. 2s automatically get a knighthood. Alan Marre has got it reasonably early and is terribly pleased but he is obviously hoping to become the P.U.S. 1 and it will be a blow for him when he doesn't. He is an absolutely charming man with a lovely wife, he is brilliant on paper, subtle and full of political sagacity. He and Paul Odgers are about on a level, though Paul is much shrewder and I would rather have Paul any day as the head of a Department because he can assert himself and has a kind of authority.

Friday, December 19th

George Godber and Dr Hunter,[2] the Vice-Chancellor of Birmingham University, were due to come down early this morning, but George's Rover broke down at Watford and they finally arrived just in time for lunch. For the third day running I took people to lunch at the Red Lion. It is a little pub which now has an enterprising host and hostess, who give an absolutely first-rate lunch. It's very simple, with quite good wine and splendid food. I think it is characteristic of what's happening now all over the country. They have ten or twelve people coming in for lunch every day and it is full up on Saturday evenings.

Godber and Hunter had come down to discuss my new ideas about hospitals and that went very well.

Sunday, December 21st

I was strong enough to go across to Pam Berry at Oving and there as the guest of honour was Arthur Schlesinger. I hardly talked to him but I did

[1] He became a K.C.B. in 1970.

[2] Robert Hunter, Dean of the Faculty of Medicine at the University of St Andrews 1958–62, Professor of Materia Medica, Pharmacology and Therapeutics at the University of St Andrews 1948–67 and at the University of Dundee 1967–8, was Late Consultant Physician to Dundee General Hospitals and Director of Postgraduate Medical Education there. He has been Vice-Chancellor and Principal of the University of Birmingham since 1968.

talk a lot to Michael and Pam. Perhaps I talked too much because I came back feeling profoundly depressed, thinking, 'Oh dear, this is the first impact of political life.' It made me shiver and I realized what an effort it's going to be to pull myself round and into action again.

Monday, December 22nd

Another of my mass meetings here, with all the doctors, the B.M.A. Joint Consultants Committee and people from the Department. From 2.45 in the afternoon till 10 o'clock at night we were discussing the Green Paper. After the meeting on December 11th, ten officials had gone back and worked at this and today five of them came down to go through things with me.

We worked from 2.45 till 4 o'clock, and then the doctors arrived. It was jolly nice – they came from all over the place, two from Cambridge, the C.M.O. from Bedford, the Chairman of the G.P.s from Winchester, two from Gloucester, three from London, a tremendous gathering. From 4.30 till 7.0 we worked to sell it to them. They were tremendously suspicious at first but then they divided and the senior consultants began to see how important the scheme was. For the teaching hospitals and the vice-chancellors the new proposition is pretty good. It's also pretty good for the G.P.s, because they are involved at district and area level and they don't care about the regional level at all. The people who hate the watering down and destruction of the regions are N.H.S. administrators, the R.H.B.s, and, in addition, what you might call the provincial consultants, who will be scared of being squeezed out from their present key positions. However, we worked all this out very satisfactorily and Alan Marre is now clearing the draft for the B.M.A. to consider on the 31st. I have an elaborate timetable, so that on January 2nd I shall put up our revised structure to a Social Services Committee. It's pretty drastically revised because not only have I this new concept of the Area Board but it's also composed one-third/one-third/one-third, challenging the Treasury's sacrosanct principle of 50 per cent government appointment.

I suspect we shall have a tremendous time putting all this over at Social Services before it goes to Cabinet. If I get all this through I shall really have a plan which I think is tolerable. It's ingenious and difficult but it makes sense and we couldn't have got it except by these seminars I have had down here, first with the Department and then with the doctors. The doctors loved it, and, as one of them said to me, 'When we come to see you in the Ministry you send us a bit of paper which is a kind of ultimatum and when we turn up in your room we are on one side of the table and you are on the other. We know we only have an hour, so how can we have any rational discussion? But in this relaxed atmosphere we have taken as long as we needed. This is real consultation.' If I have achieved anything with the doctors it is to have made them feel that this time the consultations were real and now I hope to God I can bring it off and get the public to accept these very drastic changes.

Tuesday, December 23rd

All this time the other problem has been nurses' pay, where Bea Serota has been awfully good. She went to Cabinet, worked away at it and, though the P.M. refused to intervene, yesterday she had a key meeting with Barbara and secretly showed her the proposal. Now our officials have gone to Barbara's and we think that they now see the impracticability of their own proposals. We are hoping that for the two lower ranks, student and staff nurses, D.E.P. will have to accept our proposals and, if we can get these as part of our first offer, we shan't be so desperate for the other part. We've got to make an offer which isn't derisory but that means it will go beyond 4½ per cent and break through Barbara's prices and incomes policy. I think we can only get away with this by saying that nurses are low-paid workers and that we must now give them completely new standing and a new pay structure. I have also persuaded Asa Briggs to undertake a special investigation of this.[1]

I had Brian and Ian Dewsbury down today with the revised draft of the first half of the Green Paper and we slogged it out before it went back to Alan Marre.[2] This morning I shopped in Banbury to buy Anne's Christmas present, a rocking chair I fortunately found, and pots of flowers for Brenda, Mrs Hopkins and Jackie upstairs, so everything is ready.

Thursday, December 25th

While Anne went round with the presents last night I listened to the carol service from King's College, Cambridge, sitting in front of the fire with my leg up on my gout stool. One of the most wonderful things is that May Cowper found in a shop in Bath, as my combined birthday and Christmas present from Anne, this exquisitely made mahogany contraption, which folds up into a neat little footstool and expands to any height you like. £55 it cost. Curiously enough John Makepeace tried to design a modern gout stool and, though he didn't dare to make as complicated a contraption as this, he was going to charge £80 for a much heavier, cruder thing. So there is Christmas. Patrick has had 'flu for the last five days, so poor Anne has us both on her hands and a terrible cold herself, but she has carried on heroically.

I have been reflecting on this long period of illness. I have certainly kept control over the Department and, indeed, Alan Marre apparently remarked at the Ministry's Christmas party that in many ways I was more trouble when I was kept at home. I have had time to read and make minutes on everything and master all the departmental paper work, exerting a more detailed and continuous grip than when I am up and about with Cabinet and

[1] Professor of Modern History at the University of Leeds 1955–61 and the University of Sussex 1961–76. He was Dean of the School of Social Studies at the University of Sussex 1961–5, Pro Vice-Chancellor 1961–7 and Vice-Chancellor 1967–76. In 1976 he became Provost of Worcester College, Oxford, and a life peer. The Report of the Committee on Nursing (Cmnd 5115) was published in 1972.

[2] Ian Dewsbury, an Assistant Principal at the D.H.S.S., and later a Principal, worked in the division concerned with mental health.

Parliament and public meetings. This last few weeks I've been running the Department more as I run it in the recess and, in addition, psychologically I've kept right out of the Cabinet team and certainly out of the Parliamentary Party. Day after day I resisted getting down to the diary because I didn't want to face the vacuum that entered my political life, not immediately I became ill, but while I was convalescing. Meanwhile it has been an historic week in the House of Commons, beginning with our decision on capital punishment. Cabinet had discussed for hours and hours *ad nauseam* the timing, detail and tactics, and we decided to have both the Lords and Commons vote on this in the same week. The Tories then took umbrage and on Monday, December 15th, they had a vote of censure on us for rushing the issue. We had the Commons vote on Tuesday and undoubtedly the Lords vote on Thursday was influenced by the decision in the Commons and the fact that the Leader of the Opposition voted with us for abolition.[1] Once again Callaghan conducted things very well.

The other thing was Prices and Incomes. On Wednesday we had the debate after tremendous to-ing and fro-ing and Party meetings. At least we wisely got Douglas Houghton on our side, though I don't think the Chief Whip was much with us. Again it was very respectable. We had, I think, only 28 abstentions and a majority of 28, so that was out of the way, and the Government had cleared up these two difficulties in the last week before the recess. Nevertheless the Gallup Poll still shows us tagging away ten points behind, despite the phenomenal improvement in the balance of payments, which has been continuing all winter. We really are piling up a surplus but it's not having much effect on ordinary people at home. Though they admit that the Government has done well, we haven't begun to win back enthusiasm or confidence but on this I shall have something more to say in the next day or two.

As for my colleagues, I've kept in touch with the Prime Minister only because of the problem of Clifford Jarrett. On Christmas Eve Roy Jenkins rang me up from his home in the country to see how I was doing and really to establish relations with me. He'd had very bad 'flu with a touch of pneumonia but had been forced to go back to make the winding-up speech on Prices and Incomes. Apart from these two, the only person who has made any contact with me is James Callaghan, who wrote me a letter in longhand, saying he hoped I would get well and that Cabinet was very different without me. Very characteristically he didn't say whether it was better or worse. I don't say he is two-faced, only that his feelings about me are ambiguous, but he does genuinely feel for me as a person. Otherwise I've had no contact with Cabinet. My effort to get hold of Tony Crosland failed and I spoke just for a moment to George Thomas to brief him about his speech in the debate on

[1] In June 1956 a Death Penalty (Abolition) Bill passed by the House of Commons had been rejected by the Lords. In 1969 the Lords debated capital punishment on two days, Wednesday, December 17th, and Thursday, 18th, and Lord Dilhorne's amendment to retain only until July 31st, 1973, the present Murder (Abolition of the Death Penalty) Act was rejected, by 220 voting Not Content to 174 voting Content.

private practice. Barbara has not rung me up though I know she saw Bea Serota last Monday. I think Barbara's real trouble is that for the last ten days she has been so desperately busy with her own problems and her own frantic Prices and Incomes debate. She is very much aware that I am not on her side here, so I can't blame her for not making contact but I think I shall ring her up this weekend.

But it's a funny Cabinet isn't it, with each of us so inhumanly detached one from the other, where one member can disappear with nobody noticing? This is what George Brown and Ray Gunter felt when they walked out. They went, other people took their place, and that was that. One's colleagues are colleagues and no more. Harold Wilson too, hasn't otherwise been too desperately sorry to see me away. He urged me not to come back. He knew I wasn't keen on Barbara's Prices and Incomes, he didn't want me about and, anyway, from his point of view I'm not too successful a Minister now.

This brings me to something else, my unpopularity in these last few months. Take the Herbert Morrison lecture, which I took tremendous trouble to clear with all my colleagues and with Godber too. There was this great attack on me in the Sunday newspapers and in the half-day debate the Tories fixed. The debate fizzled out but it did me considerable damage.

Once again I was thought to have made an unnecessary blob. Harold was shown the script and thought it excellent and he doesn't really blame me for not noticing the trouble it would cause. However I have no doubt that he felt embarrassed. He and Mary are both members of BUPA. I wasn't, as a matter of fact, terribly worried about the newspapers. I had completely forgotten when I did the Fabian lecture and when I passed the script that Anne had insured herself and the children with BUPA and that we regularly pay the annual subscription. It's true that we have never used the insurance. Patrick had his tonsils out in the ordinary way through the N.H.S. and when Anne had her little operation she paid for the operation privately and never got around to claiming from BUPA. Nevertheless it would have been embarrassing if it had come out that I had attacked BUPA while at the same time my wife and children were insured with them. That would have been the end for me because I would have looked ridiculous. It didn't happen however. In the first week when I was very ill the *Express* was down here nosing round all the members of my own Dr Long's group practice. They went all round the hospital but they couldn't find anyone there who remembered me. Still, I am worried and edgy about the whole of this private practice story.

All this has also had a deplorable effect outside. Sir John Richardson wrote me a letter saying that the whole prospect of getting a decent relationship with the consultants had been imperilled by what they regard as an outrageous attack from the Secretary of State. Of course I haven't made an attack. I had merely said that private insurance was no substitute for taxation and was an inadequate way of paying for the N.H.S. Nevertheless it was interpreted as an attack and the phrase 'queue-jumping' was certainly disturbing.

Sir John was terribly upset and when they all came down last Monday I got him to stay behind to talk the thing over. He said how embarrassing it was and asked whether we could help him at all, at least by ensuring that where there was a real need for private beds we shouldn't stop hospitals from providing them.

I said, 'Surely we have had to cut back the number of private beds by some 60 per cent in the last five years simply because they are not fully used?' 'Yes,' he said, 'but the difference is that in some parts of the country like Bournemouth or London you need a lot of them and in others like Doncaster you need none at all. Couldn't we at least allow enough of them in new hospitals to satisfy private demand?' I said, 'Yes, of course we could, if there is a genuine case and if they are fully used.' Maybe we shall get some good out of this but nevertheless it's shaken my self-confidence a great deal and I suppose this illness, combined with the ridiculous incident of the Herbert Morrison Lecture, has worried me more than I have worried about anything since teeth and spectacles. It has made me realize that I am right out as a member of the Government, unpopular with the local parties, detested by them. It's not uncharacteristic that, in one of those endless assessments of the 1960s that all the Sunday papers are printing, I appear with full marks as the most tactless Minister of the year. Tactless, Anne Scott-James has said,[1] first because of the announcement of the cost of teeth and spectacles three weeks after the budget (which only shows you how memories fail. She knew I had done something tactless but it wasn't the fact that it was three weeks after the budget but four days before the municipal elections) and then I showed my tactlessness once again by plunging into an attack on private practice. I have also had complaints from the Slough and the Greenwich parties about my misbehaviour in cancelling engagements. These have been brought to my attention by Bob Mellish. In all these ways I am failing now. This is serious. I'm failing, of course, because I wanted to. I gave up being on the Executive and in giving up—this is the interesting thing—you cease to try as much as you did before. In that sense I am on the way out, I know it. I am on the way out and I have made these arrangements to take over at the *New Statesman* directly after the next election.

But here I am having terrible second thoughts. In looking at the *New Statesman* and at the kind of writing which is fashionable now and at the modish way of dealing with things, I am square, absolutely out-of-date. Can I possibly be the editor at the age of sixty-three, with this illness behind me, with my decline? Am I in my decline? Well, I am sure that if I put that question to anybody in the Ministry they would be knocked backwards, because they would say, 'You kill yourself with overwork but you are doing two or three times as much as the others, Minister. You are enormously

[1] Women's Adviser to Beaverbrook Newspapers 1959–60 and columnist on the *Daily Mail* 1960–8, she has been a freelance journalist since 1968. In 1967 she married the cartoonist Osbert Lancaster, who was knighted in 1974.

energetic and vital.' I know that to be true, yet on the other hand in the last twelve months I've been feeling in my bones my old age coming on me. Is it just that I am ageing or is it perhaps the strain of the fifth year of being a Minister? Or is it the strain of seeing one's children growing up and getting to an age when they feel you are old? Whatever it is, this illness has shaken me up a great deal, detached me even more from my colleagues but left me passionately keen on running the Department. Heavens alive, though, I am even keener on getting out.

I was discussing this last Monday, while we were giving the doctors supper in the hall. I found myself sitting next to Richardson and one of the other big consultants, and I made some of these remarks about how divided I was between keeping on my work at the Ministry or getting out to write and see my family. They looked at each other and said, 'We've heard a politician say that before.' 'Who?' 'Ah,' said Richardson, 'Macmillan.' I had quite forgotten that he is now Macmillan's doctor. They said they'd heard him use those actual words about getting out and writing books, about how after a time the strain comes and you feel divided. 'This is not true of many people, not many have your choice of profession.' That interested me a good deal.

Wednesday, December 31st

This Christmas and New Year there have been a whole series of television programmes looking back not only at 1969 but at the whole decade. I saw one which had the President of the Oxford Union,[1] a young Tory, handsome, good-looking, waving his delicate fingers about as he sat on a dais and put questions – this is the strange thing – to Michael Foot, Elizabeth Longford, Iain Macleod and Alf Friendly.[2] The idea was to see the 1960s through the eyes of a child of the decade, someone who had grown up in the age of television. This young man had no ideas or ideals. He just shared the general disillusionment and all his illustrations of the decade were public occasions in the newsreels, Vietnam, the murder of Jack Kennedy, the murder of Robert Kennedy, of Martin Luther King,[3] everything that obviously illustrated the 1960s as a period of degeneration, decline, disappointment, lack of hope, deflation. This young man didn't stand for anything. Michael struggled with him from his elderly position, Elizabeth, in her own Catholic style, stood for something, and even Iain Macleod did but it was an extraordinarily depressing programme. Not only were they being cross-examined by this young pup, but they fawned on him, all saying, 'It's you that matters, your ideals, your beliefs.'

[1] Gyles Brandreth of New College.

[2] Alfred Friendly, until 1966 Managing Editor of the *Washington Post*, came to London in that year as a roving correspondent. His main subject was the Middle East and he was awarded a Pulitzer for his coverage of the Six-Day War. He retired in 1971 but continued to live in London until April 1976.

[3] Dr Martin Luther King was the pastor of the Baptist Church of Alabama, U.S.A., from 1954 until his murder in 1968. In 1964 he was awarded the Nobel Peace Prize for his work for the National Association for the Advancement of Coloured Peoples.

Next day I saw another strange programme, which Arthur Schlesinger mentioned when we were over at Pam's last week. There was Jimmy Savile, one of the radio disc-jockeys, with long, golden hair down his neck, questioning a whole series of people. He had Arthur on violence in America, Enoch Powell denouncing the decline of Britain's faith in herself, Yehudi Menuhin, the violinist, denouncing the decade in which pollution had gained control, and Malcolm Muggeridge ending up with a fanatical proto-Christian appeal for reconversion and the total repudiation of the things of this world.[1] That was depressing too. Neither of these programmes brought out any of the positive achievements of the 1960s. After all, in this country, certainly, enormous advances were made in the standard of living. The majority of people became car owners, they got washing machines, central heating and, as for pollution, even here I read the other day that they have improved the Thames so much that a few fish now exist in it again. It is astonishing to see how television media have created this simpliste opinion that things are either all good or all bad and are clearly all bad.

Last night Patrick and I stayed up at 10.30 to see another programme where they were choosing the man of the decade. Alistair Cooke put forward the case of our friend John Kennedy, with the theme that we have never recovered from the shock of his death.[2] Then there was a ridiculous scene with Mary McCarthy, whom I last remember meeting at George Weidenfeld's dinner party, lecturing us that Ho Chi Minh was the man of the decade, the man who is against technology, the man who speaks for the small people and for participation against the wickedness of the modern world. It was absolute nonsense. Then there was a curious piece with Desmond Morris,[3] the fellow who has made a tremendous success with a couple of bestsellers about sex and the human race. He had John Lennon as the man of the decade.[4] Well, some days ago I saw on '24 Hours' an extraordinary interview with John Lennon, who is now a kind of Jesus Christ figure. Here he was again and, do you know, he was the only person who said that it hadn't been a bad decade, that we'd made enormous advances and that a lot of people were happier than ever before. In their own way he and the Beatles were saying, 'We disown the whole Establishment not out of utter depression and pessimism, but because we are confident of the future and that we can take over and create a world of peace and amity.'

[1] Malcolm Muggeridge, a journalist, broadcaster and author, was Assistant Editor of the *Calcutta Statesman* 1934–5, a member of the editorial staff of the *Evening Standard* 1935–6, the *Daily Telegraph* Washington Correspondent 1946–7 and Deputy Editor 1950–2, and Editor of *Punch* 1953–7.

[2] Alistair Cooke, journalist and broadcaster, has been Commentator on American Affairs for the B.B.C. since 1938 and is author of the B.B.C.'s weekly 'Letter From America'. He was given an honorary knighthood in 1973.

[3] Curator of Mammals at the Zoological Society of London 1959–67, a painter and author of, among other books, *The Naked Ape* (London: Cape, 1967) and *The Human Zoo* (London: Cape, 1969).

[4] One of the Beatles (see p. 773n). His wife was Yoko Ono.

In his strange fashion, looking through those spectacles, with his beard and his odd Japanese wife, he was, I must admit, the only person in all these programmes with a gospel, a hope and a belief. Of course, as Alistair Cooke himself said in his 'Letter From America' the other day, an American might say the 1960s were a decade of disaster, of loss of faith, but it does seem ridiculous for England to be feeling like this. Compared to America we have had virtually no trouble in our universities. We have a tiny race problem, which we are perfectly capable of managing, and we have handled a whole number of things fairly well.

Nevertheless the mood is anti-political, anti-Establishment, anti-structure, and I admit our Labour Government hasn't broken through the problem of the inequality of power or of social inequality. This, the distinctive feature of Labour thinking, binding together Left and Right of the party, has not been put into practice. In the last five years we haven't attacked such inequalities, and it has made people see us as an Establishment party, as I think we are. Looking at my own self now, I know I must also be even more of an Establishment person than the rest of them, because of living at Prescote. I suppose in that sense I have become integrated and have lost any revolutionary fervour I possessed, though in some ways I don't think I ever possessed much. However I can't help thinking that the television picture of the 1960s is staggeringly simplistic, Americanized and stuntized. The basic difficulty is probably the gap between the generations and the American and British failure of confidence. I believe it's all curable and I think it's conceivable that this coming year, if Roy does well and we are doing better in the balance of payments, the Government may recover. It's got so little to fight against on the other side and it really may get another term of office, though I'm pretty sure I don't want to take part in it myself.

Another strange thing, looking back on this year, is that only one person, Ronnie Butt, has mentioned the staggering reassertion of parliamentary strength. Parliament rejected two major Government proposals, the reform of the House of Lords and the Industrial Relations Bill. In each case there were totally different methods and reasons, but I would say that 1969 showed the revival of Parliament. Simultaneously M.P.s are saying how futile it is and more and more of them show their discontent. You have the odd fact that, even when Parliament as a whole does reject parliamentary form and the Parliamentary Labour Party revolts against the Government, it doesn't restore respect for Parliament but merely produces less respect for the Government.

As a Government we have had these tremendous rebukes all this year. I remember that while I was lying ill Michael Foot rang me up, just before the P.L.P. meeting on prices and incomes, to ask if I could persuade Harold not to threaten us with a General Election. 'No,' I said, 'I can't. If the P.L.P. were to vote the Government down on this interim four-month prices and incomes measure, the reactivation of Part II until Barbara's Industrial Relations Bill gets through, I don't see how the Government's position could be restored.

It would be an appalling blow to the Government and, even if we were to carry a vote of confidence, I'm not sure we should survive.' Michael said, 'We are used to surviving blows of that sort.' I suddenly realized something and said, 'Look, it's true that in July the Parliamentary Party was threatening not to give the Government a majority on the Industrial Relations Bill but the vital fact was that by an overwhelming majority Cabinet had declared itself against Harold if he went on with it. As a result of that declaration, Harold and Barbara rushed to the T.U.C. and made their agreement there, which got them out of having to go to Parliament at all.' It did seem to me extraordinarily interesting that Michael hadn't realized the difference. I think the crucial thing was that last July one or two of us made it clear that in the last resort, if Harold and Barbara went on and then resigned because they had been rejected by the P.L.P., we would support Callaghan as P.M. The significant moment was when Roy tipped off the fence and made that clear to the Prime Minister. Then Harold and Barbara knew that there would be an alternative P.M. Though Callaghan might last only three or four months, the Queen would have been bound to send for him if it had been clear that he could form a Labour Government and at that point he knew he could. This was the critical thing which made them come to heel and abandon the Industrial Relations Bill.

This time was different. Barbara and Harold had a united Cabinet behind them and Callaghan hadn't moved hand or foot. There was no threat of a *coup d'état* inside the Cabinet, so there was no crisis in Cabinet and it was no longer true that a Government defeat in Parliament would be fatal. If the Cabinet had been defeated there would have been no alternative to Harold and he would have gone to the country. Would he? I don't know. Anyway it worked, because with the help of Douglas Houghton and a number of loyalists the threat was driven off.

As you see, I have been thinking a great deal in the last ten days about Parliament, about the critical points and decisions, about presidential and prime ministerial government, because I have been re-reading John Mackintosh's book and preparing myself for the Godkin Lectures next March. In terms of Parliament I see this as a tremendously important year, one that will be in its own way historic, with a history in which I shall have played some minor part. Another thing is the economic recovery. By bringing the damned industrial relations crisis to a head in June and July, we have enabled the Government to take full advantage of the steady improvement in the balance of payments. Some people have been disappointed that we have only, say, lost half our unpopularity, that we are ten instead of twenty points behind in the Gallup Poll. I am not really surprised because, though the public is pleased to see us winning, they don't get any direct benefit. Prices are rising, there is the same storm of wage demands, the same industrial disorder and, although the Government is getting some credit for the economic recovery, it's slow to operate. I am not in the least depressed about this and I don't think real recovery will start until next summer. We ought to get rather better results in the municipal elections and, if all goes right, move ahead from there. Indeed it may all go right now and, provided the new West German regime maintains its present attitude and provided the Americans don't go mad, there is now a reasonable chance of Roy getting the kind of budget he wants. The staggering fact is that though Harold has made appalling mistakes, with the total humiliation of June and July, over the summer he has entirely recovered his personal position. Of course it's a lonelier position and out of this has come Roy's strength. Roy has betted on this one thing, the balance of payments, keeping himself absolutely apart. It's one way to succeed in politics and I think his standing has been rising all the time but I wouldn't say it gives him a strong position in Cabinet. People there have seen that he is a narrow man, who has only succeeded by being so.

Poor Barbara is the opposite. Having completely failed and totally broken down in July, she is now coming forward with this terribly phoney interim package, which we are having to push through. There again you see why people succeed in politics. She is determined to keep her image and she has. She is still regarded as a fine, determined woman, remarkable in her own way. I wouldn't say she's successful but she has proved that you can retain strength not merely in circumstances of lack of success but in failure. Then there is Jim Callaghan, the only member of the Cabinet who wrote me a nice letter when I was ill. Look at him. He started the year by leading almost public opposition to prices and incomes and to the Industrial Relations Bill, he flouted the Prime Minister last November and December and right into January he was building himself up against Barbara. He did it on the Executive, he was disloyal in every possible way and behaved really abominably. What was he trying to do? I don't know but he was doing it and refusing to resign. It shows again how important it is not to resign. I would have done so but, no, he thought he would be impotent outside and that he must stay in the Cabinet and survive the humiliation of eventually buckling under as he did. He survived the P.M.'s hatred and the P.M.'s belief that at the end of July he was going to get rid of him. Then suddenly there was the Boundary Commission and on top of that came Ulster. There Jim made his name, not, strangely enough, through success because we aren't succeeding in Ulster and in the long-term it looks very black. Nevertheless he has handled these two things with superb political acumen and he has continued to develop the picture of himself as the bluff Home Secretary. Altogether he has had a tremendously interesting and exciting year, in which he has been fighting for his political future.

My trouble is that I am not fighting for my political future and I begin to see now that if you don't you slip back. It's curious, you don't stay still in politics. If you haven't got a future you haven't got much of a present and perhaps that's the conclusion I finally draw at the end of 1969.

Here I am feeling like a schoolboy going back after the holidays. I have lost my nerve and am waking up at 5 o'clock with morning panic. Somehow I've no confidence in myself. Of course a lot of this is natural depression after having 'flu and being away and I mustn't be too distressed by it. Nevertheless it's disheartening and in these next three or four days as I feel my way back to work I shall have to see how I get on with my colleagues, and whether this is just 'flu or something deeper.

I went up to London really for only one major thing, the meeting of the Prices and Incomes Committee on the problem of the teachers and nurses. Barbara had insisted on having this today because she wanted an uninterrupted New Year's Day and I suspect that Roy had insisted as well because at the end of the week he is off to San Francisco, New York and Washington. I got to London at 2 o'clock and was driven across to the Ministry, where Bea Serota met me and we went off to Cabinet Committee Room A together, a few minutes early. Fred Peart came in, Fred Mulley, Reg Freeson and Ted Short, not a particularly outstanding collection of Ministers. We sat around until at three or four minutes after 3 o'clock Barbara and Roy came in together. I knew they had been chatting things over and I began to feel rather gloomy. The nurses were put on No. 1 and the teachers No. 2. This was a test case and I had decided, because I had been ill, to let Bea Serota plead for us. Mind you, we had worked for weeks on this brief and I had given instructions that we should argue that the nurses were *sui generis* and that we insisted on conceding their full demands. When Bea Serota had discussed this with Barbara just before Christmas we had suggested that the wage demand should be phased over two whole years, not one, and that we could try three ways of phasing it, (a), (b) and (c). Barbara had taken this away and we had now been told by D.E.P. that (a) was untenable, (b) was possible and (c) the one they would like to accept.

So today Bea put forward our document, a fine presentation of our case rewritten by Brian and approved by me. The key point in the discussion came when Barbara said, 'The whole issue is whether we can treat the nurses as unique. If we have to treat the question of nurses' and teachers' pay as the beginning of a second wave of public service demands, that's one thing, but if we can say the nurses should get what is demanded by D.H.S.S. and we can concede it without relating it to the teachers, that is quite different.' Roy took this up very quickly from the chair. He insisted on getting each person to answer and we got some immediate support from Scotland and Wales, who had in fact backed our original claim. As a former teacher, Fred Peart was obliged to say that we ought to link together the nurses' and teachers' claims and Denis Howell supported him. I was convinced that this was quite sensible and I thought the point where comparability should come in was at staff nurse level. We were asking for £1,000 per annum for the staff nurses and we had always argued that their salaries should stand somewhere near those of the non-graduate primary school teacher. When I put this forward I was immediately and very forcibly attacked by those who argued that no comparability was possible. However, Shirley Williams supported the unique claim of the nurses and even Eddie Shackleton said they were a special case. As we went round the table it became clear that everything depended on the Secretary of State for Education.

Of course he said he couldn't accept that the nurses' claim was special; it was linked with his teachers' claim. 'Couldn't we', I said, 'have a roughly comparable position for the staff nurse and the non-graduate teacher? Our demand for the nurses is comparable to a demand for £100 per annum increase for the teachers who are at that middle level.' No, this was no bloody good for Ted Short, the teachers wouldn't dream of anything less than £120 increase, £100 was absolutely hopeless.

So our whole attention switched to the teachers and whether or not they should be forced to arbitration if they didn't take our initial offer of £85. Ted Short was against this. He argued that their refusal would make them able to veto compulsory arbitration and that in that case the whole thing should be referred to the Prices and Incomes Board. This got very short shrift because we don't go to the P.I.B. for a decision we ought to make ourselves.

Roy then revealed his hand. He said he could see no good reason for conceding anything like the nurses' full claim of 26 per cent, even if it were spread over two years. 'Why not 18 per cent or 16 per cent?' he asked. He then made a very ominous point: 'An award of 26 per cent would cost £80 million, equal to 3*d.* (or was it 6*d.*?) on income tax. If we were to give this to the nurses there would be that much less for tax concessions in this year's budget.' I must say this didn't go down too well. Eirene White said, 'People might feel that rather than have a tax concession they should be willing to concede the nurses' claim.' It was clear that Barbara's question had very shrewdly forced the issue and that most people felt the nurses' claim had much stronger public support and social justice than the teachers' claim. After all, the nurses are 15 per cent behind while the teachers have been forcing their way up year by year and have put in their new claim before the time limit after the last one has elapsed. Even people like Fred Peart and Denis Howell admitted that if there was to be linkage it should be in the way which would give the nurses more of their claim than the teachers. I watched with great interest but Ted Short refused to have any connection between the two and, in a sense, he fought against a settlement. He said that the teachers were insisting on £130, they would only take £120, and he repeated that the £100 link I was suggesting was no bloody good. He wanted nothing of that sort.

The thing went to and fro and it became clear that, thanks to Ted Short's negative attitude, the Committee was prepared to give the nurses the substance of their claim, divided over two years but not according to the allocation of plan (a) or even plan (b), but the worst possible plan, (c). However, I knew very well, that, even though we wouldn't get all we wanted in the first year, this would be a sufficiently good start for our negotiations. A decision had to be taken today because we've got the first meeting of the Whitley

Council on Tuesday, January 15th. There is no Cabinet at all next week and I shall be in Salcombe. Roy will be away in America and he can't get back on Monday, January 14th, for a Cabinet before we start our negotiations. This timetabling factor determined the issue and we finally decided that the Committee unanimously agreed that we should concede the substance of the nurses' claim, divided and phased according to solution (c). The Department has been allowed to have this as its objective in the negotiations, so the only question now is whether I shall be able to come back and say, 'With phasing according to (c) I can't get agreement and I want (b) instead'. However Roy insisted that I should not only forgo certain concessions on hours and special payments but also that I should agree to start the negotiations at a lower level, with plan (c) as the ultimate best we could offer.

I was pretty excited as I left the meeting. This afternoon I saw Alan Marre and Bavin, who could hardly believe it was true. As we celebrated over our sherry, I said, 'Well, we sometimes get the impossible,' and Bavin, who has always been defensive towards me and in a way fairly hopeless, said, 'With you as Secretary of State I shall never exclude the impossible.' As he and Alan sat there on the sofa in this dreary steel-grey room at the top of the tower with the sun shining in, I realized that to some extent I had perhaps got them to believe that I had achieved something which Kenneth Robinson couldn't possibly have done.

Anne had brought the children up in time for lunch and then Peter Smithson very kindly asked them to tea with his children at his house in South London. This evening he brought them back with his two eldest boys and off we all went up the Tottenham Court Road to the Dominion Theatre to see the film *Battle of Britain*. We thought it would be too gory for Virginia and Anne and they stayed behind. It was tremendously bloody and I wondered what Patrick and the boys would feel. They were excited by it and a little uneasy about the burns but of course they didn't really recognize its horror. On reflection it was a film that impressed me. We drove back down St Martin's Lane and into Trafalgar Square, where the crowds were gathering for New Year's Eve, ready to throw themselves into the fountains. Down Whitehall we went and got ourselves home and the children to bed. We completely forgot that this New Year's Eve was the end of a decade, so we quietly read ourselves to sleep and into 1970.

1970

Thursday, January 1st

The first thing this morning was the New Year's Honours List, with Alan Marre to be congratulated on his knighthood, the Chief Nurse on her D.B.E. and John Lewis, the Chairman of the Birmingham Hospital Board, on his knighthood. It is a not uncharacteristic, deeply Establishment, Harold Wilson list. He has failed to give Nicholas Davenport a life peerage but there are one or two things I like, including a life peerage for John Beavan, the chief political adviser of the *Daily Mirror*, though this has forced him to resign his job straightaway. Most remarkable of all is the knighthood for Walter Adams, the head of L.S.E. Well, sometimes Harold is right in these things and sometimes he is wrong. Looking back I think he was right to give the Beatles their M.B.E.s.[1] How respectable they seem now, how useful, how neat their hair-cuts and their dark blue suits, compared to the hippies of five years later. But whether he is right to side gratuitously with Walter Adams, who has been at the centre of the L.S.E. troubles, I don't know. It is very typical of Harold.

Today was really a fill-in for me before tomorrow's meeting of the Social Services Committee and in preparation for this I saw Dick Taverne this afternoon. I was aware that the Treasury would object to my new notion of democratic representation on the Area Health Boards but I want to have one-third local authority members, one-third professional doctors and nurses and so on, and one-third appointed by me. I had convinced myself that if I compensated for this by vastly increased central control through regional offices the Treasury would have nothing to fear and I went through my scheme with Dick and did my best. Tony Crosland has been away the whole week and I'm not really afraid of Shirley Williams because I know I will have no trouble with the Home Office. However I should have consulted Eddie Shackleton and the Civil Service Department and I am afraid they might be troublesome tomorrow morning.

This evening Tommy Balogh and Catherine came to us for drinks at Vincent Square and then I took them out to Overton's, just opposite Victoria Station, the restaurant which Dickens used to go to after a rough Channel crossing. It's still one of the best restaurants in London, with tiny old waiters, excellent fish, some good carafe burgundy and, according to the Baloghs, quite good veal as well. It was an excellent evening.

Friday, January 2nd

Today was the meeting of Social Services Committee at which we were to consider our revised Green Paper, putting forward our new one-tier system with its subordinate district committees and our proposals for our one-third/one-third/one-third composition. I had taken great trouble with this paper.

[1] In the 1960s four young Liverpool musicians, George Harrison, John Lennon, Paul McCartney and Ringo Starr, formed a group called the Beatles. They were immensely successful and their music sold so well abroad, as well as in Britain, that in June 1965 they were awarded the M.B.E. for services to export.

A draft had gone out to the officials last Monday and then we redrafted it once more and circulated it to Ministers on Tuesday night. Even this is too late because the officials often want to chew papers over before they go to Ministers, who therefore don't get them from the Department until thirty-six hours later. I was very worried about this meeting because I was aware that I had turned the last paper topsy-turvy and was giving the Committee quite new proposals, something they were bound to object to. Sure enough, there was a great deal of complaint. To start with, I was unpopular because I had forced people to turn up in the vacation and in fact it was mostly number twos or number threes who came. Tony Crosland hadn't bothered to turn up and Jim Callaghan was away with 'flu. I was in the chair and Bea Serota came to speak for me again. With her help I handled it fairly skilfully. The main problem was that Eddie Shackleton was deeply injured because I hadn't had time to talk to him separately and therefore he had to object in every possible way. By and large, though, I had a good deal of support from Shirley Williams and from Reg Freeson, representing the Ministry of Housing, and even from Denis Howell. Against me I only really had the Treasury and the C.S.D. but they are the most powerful Departments. However they were open to suggestions and certainly the Treasury had been softened by my talk to Taverne.

We tottered out of the meeting and I quickly went to my room at 70 Whitehall where David Ennals was having a meeting of friendly journalists and the Transport House people, on the popularization of the pensions plan. They were all discussing why the scheme couldn't be popularized and why something that is meant as a number one propaganda weapon of the Labour Government is such a flop. Perhaps I said the wrong thing but I pointed out that a proposal which has higher contributions and which upsets millions of people in occupational pension schemes is a very good and powerful thing in which we must believe but it can never be very popular. 'It's something which we must take credit for while confessing that it is unpopular but ... ' Having got this far, I realized that I seemed to these young people old-fashioned and out of date and that David Ennals was suffering by having me there, so I slipped out quietly.

This afternoon I had a meeting of all the Social Security people to discuss how to handle the National Superannuation Bill. At first I thought 'Monday 19th is the day we resume after the recess. Nobody will be there at 3.30 when the Second Reading starts but with a three-line whip and a vote at 10.0 p.m. the obvious thing is for me to wind up.' Then I decided that this was basically wrong because I ought to move the Second Reading of my own Bill, so, reluctantly, I shall let David wind up. The terrible danger is that the debate will be *Hamlet* without the Prince of Denmark. We then discussed what should be in the Second Reading speech, where we have another difficulty, because what do I say in fifty minutes when moving something that has taken me seventeen years of work?

Curiously, we followed this with an extraordinary discussion about an interesting technical problem which has arisen, whether Ministers and M.P.s should be allowed to be contributors in the normal sense. You can't be a contributor to the pensions scheme unless you have an employer and, while you can say that the Crown employs the Minister, nobody employs the M.P. Eddie Shackleton had written a good minute saying that he thought Ministers should be treated as employed persons, who should therefore contribute to the scheme and earn benefits, but M.P.s shouldn't. On the whole, I had accepted this view but now I found myself being furiously opposed by Brian O'Malley and David Ennals, who were saying, 'Surely you must give M.P.s the benefit of the doubt? You ought to help your friends, who, after all, come in and out of Parliament, and are not secure.' So I agreed that we would first consult the Chief Whip and then the Opposition Chief Whip because this is a nice problem. The Tories would not like to be regarded as salaried employees, but as self-employed, while on the other hand nothing would suit many Members better than a fully transferable pension scheme.

I can see that Monday is going to be difficult because nobody will be there that afternoon. I am going to ring Tam and ask him to organize the back-bench speeches and give me a bit of a cheer and I am writing letters to Douglas Houghton and Peggy Herbison, and also to Woodrow Wyatt, who has been good on pensions. In any case it's going to be difficult to get anything like a successful Second Reading. The pension plan is foundering now and I'm not very energetic or enthusiastic about it. After seventeen years I must admit I've lost my élan.

This evening Gilbert and Dorothy Baker and their children came with us and our children to supper at Helga Connolly's and then we all went on to the Royal Court Theatre just round the corner. They were doing *The Three Musketeers* as a kind of knockabout pantomime and it was an enormously pleasant evening, which all the children greatly enjoyed. Afterwards, as Paul Odgers has been insisting I should, I got down to reading the Cabinet Committee paper recommending the line of the Bill implementing Seebohm. I suddenly realized a terrible incompatibility. I had just dealt with Brian's draft of the Green Paper on the Health Service, in which we had said that the definition of the frontier between local government and the N.H.S. must be left open for further discussion. Here was Odgers saying that in this Bill, setting up a social services division with its own boss inside each local authority, the frontiers must be clearly defined. Well, how can we both make an absolute division and have a Green Paper saying it's all open to discussion? I decided to sleep on it.

Saturday, January 3rd

This morning I realized that this is a case where one keeps things in separate compartments. The Seebohm discussions are in Bea Serota's compartment and in the other is the N.H.S. Green Paper, where I have done most of the work. It's also a question of layers of time. Months ago, when we last thought about Seebohm, I wasn't sure I would be able to get an independent Health Service outside local government but now the major decision has been taken and the N.H.S. Green Paper agreed, inasmuch as we are putting forward suggestions on how to organize an independent Health Service. Now we must decide on the frontier between local government and the Health Service. I realized we'd got the Green Paper all wrong. Paul, Alan Marre and Bea Serota hadn't noticed this. Oh dear, yesterday I had been bullying Bea about this, Bea who has been wonderful to me in every way, working like a navvy, giving me books, getting me seats at the opera. She has done wonders for me and she and David have treated me beautifully. Yesterday she was so tired she could hardly stand up, so this morning I felt really miserable and I rang her to tell her I thought I had got a compromise which would get round our difficulties. I hope to God I have. I am pretty sure we can draft both the N.H.S. Green Paper and the Seebohm Committee Bill in the right form and that when I get back after my week's holiday we can get it all right.

Today was nice, a whole day with the children. At the V. & A. this morning we saw a special exhibition of drawings of Winnie the Pooh. The children and Anne were brought up on this, something I was too old for, and they liked seeing the actual drawings and the actual toys, the teddy bear, the kangaroo and the donkey, about whom A. A. Milne had written, and which Ernest Shepard had drawn. It was the first time I had ever been to the V. & A. I had remembered reading in Elizabeth Longford's first volume of her life of Wellington a footnote about the curious musical box that had been found in India in the form of a servant of the East India Company being mauled by a tiger.[1] Music plays from its innards while the tiger bites the man. We found it in the V. & A. and, though we weren't able to have it played for us, I was able to tell Elizabeth about it when we got to our next stop at the House of Commons. Here were Peggy and Douglas Jay, a dignitary of the party, for the marriage of Catherine, one of their twin daughters. There were Elizabeth and Frank Longford sitting behind us, the crypt humming with conversation and Patrick and Virginia looking forward to the eats in the Harcourt Room afterwards.

It was a nice afternoon and at 5 o'clock I shot off to do an interview for tomorrow's 'World This Weekend'. They wanted to talk to me about my return to public life after my illness and I thought it was worth taking the risk. Maybe I shouldn't have done it but I've got what Jennie Lee calls compulsive communication. I can't help talking freely and I think one gains by it. After a couple of glasses of champagne with Anthony Howard and Andrew Boyle,[2] I did the broadcast and then came back to Vincent

[1] *Wellington: Years of the Sword* (London: Weidenfeld & Nicolson, 1969).

[2] Andrew Boyle, a journalist and author, joined the B.B.C. in 1947. With William Hardcastle, he launched the radio current affairs programmes 'The World At One' in 1965 and 'The World This Weekend' and 'P.M'. in 1967. In 1976 he became Head of News and Current Affairs in Scotland.

Square to pick up the children and take them out to the Coliseum for Gilbert and Sullivan's *Patience*. It was delicious and, though it's a difficult opera for children of ten and twelve, the rhythm, the words, the charm of the music and the gaiety of it all made them enjoy it greatly. We had bought the records and played them at home, so by recognizing what they already knew they enjoyed it all the more.

Monday, January 5th – Sunday, January 11th

A splendid week at Salcombe. It's a comfortable hotel and perfect for us because there are very few people there in winter. The little town was shut up and we had a week to ourselves without the children, telephoning back every other day, strolling out, sleeping in the afternoon if we felt like it, nobody there to speak to, fortunately for us. The boxes came down and I kept control of the office. I re-did the final draft of the Cabinet paper on the Green Paper by telephone and I helped Bea Serota through some awkward moments, though David Ennals didn't bother to ring me up from the Social Security side. I also read the enormously long page proofs of the third volume of Asa Briggs's history of the B.B.C., *The War of Words*.[1] It was fascinating reading because it was the history of what I did during the war, but seen through the eyes of the B.B.C. Asa Briggs had only been given access to B.B.C. documents and records and he hadn't heard any evidence from either P.W.E. or the other government services.[2] It was fascinating and when he comes to lunch I shall be able to go through it with him. Altogether we had a splendid time.

Monday, January 12th

One of the controversial items at this morning's S.E.P. was the future of the Beagle Aircraft Manufacturing Company, which we took over when it was almost bankrupt. We put in £6 million, but we have now decided to wind it up and put it in the hands of the receivers. Even though the Government had bought the Company, if it is bankrupt we are not legally bound to pay its debts but the argument today was whether we were morally bound, or, to put it another way, whether it would pay the Government to default.

The argument went to and fro with Tony Benn and Harold Lever both strongly arguing that we were morally bound and ought in fact to pay the debts in full, say so and get some kudos for it. The Treasury ferociously said this was ridiculous and that, if we did this, all the other companies in which we had intervened, Short Bros and the Clydeside shipyards, would put us under the same obligation. Then, to my surprise, the Prime Minister suddenly

[1] *History of Broadcasting in the United Kingdom: I: The Birth of Broadcasting* (London: Oxford University Press, 1961); *II: The Golden Age of Wireless* (London: Oxford University Press, 1965); *III: The War of Words* (London: Oxford University Press, 1970).

[2] Political Warfare Executive, the wartime propaganda organization with which Crossman had served.

said, 'Look, I don't want to see us paying out money for Beagle. Think what use would be made of this in the election campaign.'

This shook me a bit so I immediately took up the point and managed to defeat Harold by saying that in electoral terms we must keep the good name of the Government. If we believe in intervention in private industry, we must take the consequences and pay up when we are bound to do so. I quote this only to indicate how the prospect of an election does actually impact on Government. It affects every matter on Harold's mind now. It also hurries up certain parts of our legislation, pensions, the nationalization of the ports and the production of the White Paper on the reform of local government and the reform of the Health Service, because we think we shall take credit for obtaining these things. But we shall undoubtedly slow down others, like Barbara's Industrial Relations Bill, or even her Industrial Commission. What is changed is the pace at which measures move. I am not sure if in an election year this Government isn't rather better.

This afternoon I had the key meeting of the Social Services Committee to put to them the revised version of my Cabinet paper on the Green Paper on the reform of the Health Service. It went very much as I expected, with support all round except from Dick Taverne and Eddie Shackleton. The Committee accepted everything in my paper, apart from the proposal that the new Health Service boards should be one-third local government members, one-third professionals and one-third my appointments. It was essential the Treasury said, that I should retain majority control, as though this was needed to provide me with a satisfactory financial control! But this is the kind of issue you can't discuss with the Treasury or C.S.D. because they never get outside Whitehall, and they judge the R.H.B.s in an extraordinary way, as if their members are remote from the realities of local government. I may still have a tussle at Tuesday's Cabinet when I try to get this very original and unusual composition accepted.

After this Jock Campbell came to see me. I had asked him to let me know whether he would be interested in joining one of the Regional Hospital Boards, with perhaps a chairmanship, and I found he was. He told me he had just written to Harold to say he had been deeply hurt to hear that remarks were being made behind his back about the appointment of Tony Greenwood to the chairmanship of the C.D.C. instead of him. Jock had had a letter in reply saying the whole thing was a misunderstanding and wasn't necessarily firm yet. I am quite sure Harold is keeping his options open and that he will be prepared to upset Jock in order to have a by-election at Rossendale in February or March, if that turns out to be essential. Tommy told me the other day that Harold might possibly offer Jock the chairmanship of the P.I.B. when Aubrey Jones goes but I am almost certain that Jock would be wise enough to refuse.

Tuesday, January 13th

At Cabinet we had a good deal of discussion about Nigeria.[1] On January 8th the so-called Biafran nation suddenly caved in, Colonel Ojukwu had fled and the war was over, so we had backed the winning side and the wisdom and foresight of Harold Wilson and Michael Stewart was proved. France and Portugal, who had been supporting Biafra, are now banned from giving any help, and the Catholic Church is out of it, with only the British and Russians, the two Governments who steadily supported the Federalists, in with them. To do Michael Stewart credit, he and Harold had been deeply and intellectually convinced that it was in the interests of Africa as well as of Nigeria that the Federal Government should win against tribalism.

Then we got on to the subject of the gas workers. At yesterday's S.E.P. we learnt that Sir Henry Jones,[2] the Chairman of the Gas Council, had talked about the possibility of his having to concede far more (I think an extra 3*d.*) on the gas workers' claim and, though we were clear that we could hardly risk a strike, we had sent back a message saying that this was quite impossible and that Sir Henry would have to stand firm. Today the issue came up again and Harold Lever, as number two at MinTech., said he had just received a message from Sir Henry saying that, though he would try to resist, he now felt there was no choice but to concede, and that he was going to do so this morning. Harold added that this would have to be paid for by taking £50 million out of the consumers' pockets through a price increase of roughly 6*d.* a week. Poor old Barbara! This is a great blow to her in the present avalanche of claims but out of this long discussion came the suggestion that while it was no good our trying to order Sir Henry Jones not to do this, we still had control over prices. Why shouldn't we tell him that he would not be allowed to raise his price even if he made the concessions? He must pay for them out of savings, out of income and by slowing down capital investment. A great deal of doubt and scepticism was expressed about this but Harold and Barbara were very keen and fought hard for it. It was one of the very few Cabinets where I have heard a real discussion and seen it issue in a sensible new line of action. I was talking to Burke afterwards and we agreed that it's very, very rarely that Cabinets take new decisions which are unlike anything anybody had thought of beforehand or that any Department had briefed their Ministers to say. It's very rare and when it is done it is usually very unfortunate and misguided but in this case there was a remarkably intelligent discussion and a remarkably good result.

The remainder of Cabinet was devoted to Tony Crosland's local government items. This was the first big issue where I had to confront him in his new super-Ministry position and, to my surprise, I managed to carry Cabinet

[1] On January 12th Federal forces had captured the rebel capital, Owerri, and Colonel Ojukwu had sought asylum in the Ivory Coast. The British Government promised to contribute £5 million for relief work.

[2] Sir Henry Jones (Kt 1956), Deputy Chairman of the Gas Council 1952–60 and Chairman 1960–71.

with me. I defeated him on his desire to make two more metropolitan areas, one in central Lancashire and another in Nottingham. He disagreed with me when I tried to get the Seebohm paper through but after twenty minutes I defeated him on his wish to allow the local authorities to select which areas should implement Seebohm. I got it settled that implementation should be mandatory on all local authorities and that it should be for us to make what exceptions we thought suitable. That was a great relief because it meant that during my absence I hadn't lost my hold on Cabinet. It was nice that they listened to what I had to say and it was nice, too, that they cheered my return.

Wednesday, January 14th

For the whole of Management Committee this morning, some two and a half hours, we solemnly discussed electoral strategy. Everybody assumes that we will go to the country in October and I was fascinated to see how much Roy Jenkins wants to be the Chancellor who puts the balance of payments right, gets a £500 million surplus and keeps it. There should be no ugly rush to accept the avalanche of wage claims and then go to the country before their effects have worked out. Roy's theme is, 'We ought to keep the economy sound'. He was strongly supported by Barbara and there was no real opposition. Frankly, I don't see any chance of allowing an avalanche of wage claims which will make us popular and then fitting in an election before prices begin to rise. I don't think we can. This time is very different from 1966. We have a vast body of debt which we would like to reduce, and prices are already beginning to rise. It's clear that we shall only be able to go to the country on a policy of sanity, steady recovery and moderation. There will be no extremes, no dazzling ideas and all we can hope to say is, 'Well, we got the balance of payments right and we're on a sensible course'. We shall have, as one or two commentators are saying already, a deeply conservative policy. Our theme will be, 'Vote against the radical innovations of Heath and Powell, vote for Wilson and keep things going along as they are at present.'

Harold very carefully said that there might before the autumn come an opportunity for the election. I added that we should have a policy of gradually rebuilding confidence and that, judging by the West Midlands, we need many months to get back the votes we have lost. The whole trade union movement is still against us. I said I thought the crucial thing was to win the local elections, to settle with the schoolteachers and the nurses and pretty soon to get a better housing policy. We also need to increase supplementary benefit. Harold agreed with me that these are the kind of concrete things we require.

Immediately afterwards I caught the midday train to Coventry for a meeting of the Coventry N.U.T. The executive met me and took me to a room in the Leofric, where we mostly discussed the tactics of their strike. I very much doubt whether these are paying or whether they are justified. Both sides have handled this extremely badly. I think that, through Ted Short, the Government should have offered, say, £80 instead of the £50 they did offer and I am sure the teachers should not have gone in for strike action on this scale. I think that in the end we shall have to settle round about the £100 I suggested and which Ted Short said was far too low. Then we went down to look at schools and for the meeting with the N.U.T. Only 100 of them out of the 2,000 teachers in Coventry were there but they were all amenable and easy to talk to. It's well worth asking oneself why it is that the NALGO people are so wild and agitated, demonstrating *en masse* about the new pension plan. The N.U.T. has just as vital an interest in this but they are unconcerned. It only shows the enormous importance of the union leadership. If, as NALGO did, they issue a pamphlet they can stir up the rank and file.

Thursday, January 15th

I dropped in to see the Prime Minister for a minute or two this morning and I was able to congratulate him on his Nigerian success. We talked a bit about electoral prospects and for the first time Harold seems to realize that we may have an honourable defeat. I didn't mention my own future but simply said that I was old and he said, 'Yes, but you are old with young children.'

Then we came to Cabinet, which was dominated by Barbara's Industrial Commission Bill and her running argument with Tony Crosland about the whole wisdom of what she is doing. The battle goes on between the interventionists – Barbara, Tony Benn and Peter Shore – on the one side, and the more cautious people who prefer to rely on fiscal policies – Roy Jenkins and Tony Crosland – on the other, with most of us briefed by our Departments to side with the Treasury. This is a genuine, old-fashioned, Left–Right controversy between interventionists of the Balogh–Bevan school and fiscal socialists of the Gaitskell–Jenkins–Crosland school, the first issue I have seen which really brings out an old-fashioned Bevanite row. What strikes me most of all is how much trouble poor Barbara is in because she is so half-baked and so ill prepared, bringing up to Cabinet things where she has to say, 'I haven't got the final draft quite ready yet but I'm having a press conference next Thursday so I must have this rushed through.' The more she does this, the more irritated Cabinet becomes. Of course I have to stay completely out of the discussions because I have made my fix with her about doctors' pay. She has given me a written understanding that they won't be brought into her scheme and I've made it clear that in return I won't make difficulties for her in getting the principle of her Bill through Parliament. But this morning, as the discussion went on, my position became more and more awkward because gradually everybody else, even the judges, were being brought under the scheme. We went on for two hours with this until at 12.35 we reached my major issue, Health Service reform.

I said I didn't quite know what to do. 'I only really want two decisions this morning, Prime Minister, first, a Cabinet decision that the Health Service should be outside local government and on the exact frontier which will divide local government from the Health Service and, secondly, I would also like a decision that the Health Service will be reorganized in area authorities, which will have the same boundaries as the local government unitary authorities and report direct to me.' This was the essence of my scheme and all I did was to get it through and leave till next Tuesday the dispute I have with the Treasury over composition. All this was agreed and most of Cabinet thought, 'My God, we've had two hours of brawling between Barbara and Tony Crosland but, with Dick knowing his mind, he's got this through in twenty-five minutes.' Afterwards Harold ran into me and said, 'In twelve minutes you got the biggest change in the Health Service for twenty years and you did it because you prepared it well.' It is also clear to me now how important a factor it is in a Cabinet struggle to have the Cabinet Secretariat on your side. The reason is very simple. The Cabinet Secretariat briefs the P.M. on these things. They brief him on Barbara and on me and, if you get Burke on your side by doing your homework, being conscientious in committee and getting a good reputation in Whitehall, the P.M.'s brief is favourable. I am rather pleased to find my reputation is good on this particularly difficult work on the reconstruction of the Health Service. It gives me an enormous advantage in the battle for power.

Friday, January 16th

For most of the day I slaved away at my speech for the Second Reading of the National Superannuation Bill. Yesterday afternoon Peter Brown, whom I haven't seen for a long time, came into the office and asked me, straightaway, how the speech was going. I told him I was having to sweat it out from a vast brief. 'Oh,' said Peter, 'forget about all that. Do it impromptu. You have it at your fingertips and you can do it off the cuff. You must pick up all these details and then in a broad sweep make people enthusiastic about it.' I felt he was right, so I have been trying to reorganize the huge brief prepared by the Department to make it far more punchy, simple – rhetorical, if you like. It's a bit of a gamble but I'm fairly pleased with it and I think, under Peter Brown's influence, it may be a great deal more successful than it would otherwise have been.

Sunday, January 18th

Yesterday Robin Wendt came over with his wife and little daughter. He is keen and able and has already established himself well in the Private Office. We worked on my speech for a couple of hours and he's taken it back to have it typed out.

The main news this week, apart from Nigeria, has been the Prime Minister's Swansea speech last Saturday.[1] The whole of last Monday's 'Panorama' programme followed it up with a cross-examination and everybody, including

[1] Mr Wilson spoke of Britain's economic recovery and of the Labour Government's social achievements. See *Wilson*, pp. 741–4.

Anne, agrees that though pretty awful questions were asked of Harold he did extremely well. The speech was a tremendous sloshing thing proving that we'd done all the right things and that he'd been right all along, leaving out for the most part things like the prices and incomes policy. It was a directive, a line showing the kind of leadership he will give, just about what one would expect but a little bit more so. But it was effective because a better, nobler speech would not have captured the moment. For our purpose Harold is the ideal political leader and there he is, bounced back to the top of his form. Yesterday I heard on the wireless a report of a speech Heath made in reply on Friday night. Heath had said that the Prime Minister had started the election a week ago and that he should now go to the country quickly, because the people couldn't last the terrible strain of another eighteen months of electioneering. I have no doubt that a long period of electioneering is undesirable but Heath couldn't be more wrong in saying that an electioneering Government takes no decisions. I think the proper way to put it is that different decisions are taken and that decisions which are thought to be favourable are hurried up. I have already reported in this diary our ridiculous decision four or five months ago to keep the Central Wales railway going at a cost of £300,000 a year.[1] A more recent example is the decision on nurses' pay, where our response was, partly at least, due to the proximity of the election. Then we had the Beagle aircraft decision at S.E.P. last Monday. It's perfectly true that as we sit here we judge everything by the election, and this means that we are much more sensitive to public opinion than we were two or three years ago, when Harold knew he had lots of time before him. We're trying to mend our fences before the coming of the campaign.

Monday, January 19th

At S.E.P. we had Roy's paper on the 1970/2 economic assessment, which was to be presented to NEDO. Frankly I had been so busy preparing my speech for the afternoon's debate that I had hardly glanced at it. Roy moved this as though it was a self-evident paper with which he wasn't very satisfied but there it was, very satisfactory, and the whole survey seemed all right. This was a case, though, where the man without a Ministry could be of decisive importance. Suddenly Peter Shore popped in and said, 'Look, if you put this in as it stands, you are including the prediction that our economy will only grow at 2·9 per cent a year, the lowest estimate we've ever heard. On this assumption, unemployment will stay at between 500,000 and 750,000, which assumes practically no prospect of success for our regional policies.' Barbara followed Peter and then everybody began to plough in. The Prime Minister said the paper had to be amended because 2·9 was too low, the assessment must be raised and the regional side looked at. Roy had to beat a hasty retreat and, simply because Peter Shore had used his position as Minister without Portfolio to master the paper, the whole thing had to be with-

[1] See above, pp. 603–4.

drawn. I congratulated Peter afterwards because he really had made a difference.

My preoccupation, though, was my big Bill. Robin Wendt came over this morning and we got the speech finished, so that all I had to do was to go across to the Elephant and Castle to find the pages being worked up and add a final paragraph or two. The afternoon began with Harold's Statement on our relief efforts in Nigeria. I assumed that he would steal most of my thunder because there was tremendous excitement. Harold handled himself with dignity and self-control and though his Statement was inordinately long, he didn't try to get too much credit out of it. Then came the debate. I had deliberately made my speech popular and partisan, challenging the Tories to oppose us and arousing our own people. It was fifty-five minutes long and I think in electioneering terms and in its intelligibility it was an able speech. I was right back at the top of my form, fully recovered, capable, rallying the Party not only to me but to the scheme.

I was followed by Balneil, who, to my amazement, quite unexpectedly came out with the outline of the Tory alternative. They have got off the fence and this is enormously important. The rest of the debate went perfectly all right for us. Houghton made a helpful speech with a characteristically unhelpful end to it and David Ennals made a rather dull but perfectly capable winding-up speech. It was a good team and at the end, on a three-line whip, we had a very good vote. There were two votes, one on a Conservative reasoned amendment and one on a motion clean against giving the Bill a Second Reading.[1]

Afterwards I checked with Balneil that the Tories intend the Bill to go on the Statute Book. That's quite clear, as they need the earnings-related contributions, but they're going to try to amend it. They're not simply opposing the Bill but opposing all the essential parts of the benefit scale, but their variant is one which will be extremely easy for us to score off and it's taken away a great deal of their manoeuvring power against us. I am greatly relieved that they have done this.

Tuesday, January 20th

The press was mean to Harold this morning. He is very unpopular and in some of the papers I actually got as much coverage as he did, mainly because our Bill is so unpopular, I suppose, that they want to play it up. However the press admitted I had made a competent speech and they gave it prominence.

This morning was the Cabinet I had been waiting for. I had got through the first half of the Health Service reconstruction with flying colours and licked the Treasury and the Civil Service Department in the arrangements for funding the new N.H.S. Today I came back with my formula for having

[1] The Conservatives' amendment was defeated by 307 votes to 236 and the Bill was given a Second Reading by 304 votes to 244.

one-third/one-third/one-third composition, a pretty original and heretical proposal, which produced a basic attack from the Treasury, C.S.D. and the Inland Revenue, the government powers-that-be. However the attack was not waged very effectively. I had already persuaded Eddie Shackleton not to rely on his departmental brief but to say that my approach was the only realistic one if we want to keep the Health Service outside local government yet encourage local government to collaborate. Roy, to whom I hadn't spoken, simply sat there and let John Diamond complete the Treasury case. Barbara was very keen, the others supported me, and above all I had the Prime Minister on my side. I hadn't talked to Harold, but Burke and the Cabinet Office had, and the P.M. and No. 10 had come to the conclusion that I had done a good job and that the Committee had worked this out, so I was given full support. I sailed through without a single change in the whole scheme, except for a little tiff with Education on play-groups.

I gave dinner to John Mackintosh, who has now provided the outline for the Godkin Lectures. He is an enormously industrious man, terribly keen, I think, to get the £1,000 fee. We worked through the draft and though it's very clear that he knows what he wants I shall have to do a lot of work on it and I'm going to find it difficult.

Wednesday, January 21st

This afternoon I had a funny thing. Nahum Goldmann,[1] that dazzlingly good-looking man from America, one of the cleverest Jewish politicians, head of the Zionist Federation, blew in to tell me he had picked up the information that the Russians, who are getting very impatient, will intervene in the Middle East if the Israelis go on behaving as they are doing. I don't know how much truth there is in this but the story is important because it shows how hostile American Jews are becoming to the policies now being carried out by the Jews in Israel. I am really rather pro-Israel these days because, on the whole, I think they have no choice. They've won the war and must hold to their victory, which means that they can't make peace even if they want to. I don't see any prospect of the Four Powers producing agreed peace terms and, if that is so and if the present state of near-war continues, it is quite likely that the Russians will intervene. I said, 'Well, from the Jewish point of view it could be worse. In such a case they will have to draw back to their frontiers. They might want the Russians there to get them out and stop the present difficult situation drooling along.'

Thursday, January 22nd

A wind-up Cabinet, getting all the timing of the White Papers done. I managed to arrange that, provided I clear the details of my N.H.S. scheme at a Social Services Committee on Wednesday 28th to which, if they feel strongly about it, all Cabinet Ministers may go and make their points, Cabinet

[1] Dr Nahum Goldmann, President of the World Jewish Congress since 1951.

approval should be formal. This is because next week the Prime Minister is away in Ottawa and Washington so the normal Cabinet can't take place.[1] There are also printing difficulties and this means I won't have to go through it page by page in Cabinet as Tony Crosland will have to with his local government paper. Of course this kind of clearance and concession is only possible if the Cabinet Office and, above all, Burke are on your side.

I lunched with Alf Robens,[2] to whom I read the riot act because Guy's is always overspending and, more important, we discussed the new Green Paper. After that I had a visit from Dr Baker. It is good to report that my inspectorate is really going far faster than I thought possible. He has been building up two teams and before he's finished he is going to have four of them. He's now finishing his first visitation to all sub-normal hospitals. It looks as though I have turned the corner. I've had luck and I've got a certain intuition about backing this man.

Friday, January 23rd

Earlier this week we had the usual O.P.D., when we ploughed through the Defence White Paper page by page. As usual I knocked out the more violent justification for NATO's piling up the strength of the anti-Russian forces in Europe. This is regularly put in and taken out every year. That meeting enabled us to take the White Paper formally to Cabinet and this morning we had a special O.P.D. before Harold goes to Washington. Here was Michael Stewart with a paper asking for authority to put forward this British plan for four-power talks on the Middle East. Some months ago we turned down his draft plan on the grounds that it was unnecessary and would only cause trouble. Now he was coming back, saying, 'I myself am going over with the P.M. to talk to Nixon and as Foreign Secretary I must go to the U.N. I must have a plan, otherwise what can Caradon do, and how can we defend our position as a member of the four-power talks if there's a French, an American and a Russian plan but no British plan?'

When I had read his paper carefully in bed this morning I had spotted one major difference between the British and the American plan, a tremendously anti-Israeli point about refugee policy. The French and the Americans both proposed that the Arab refugees should be given the choice between compensation and returning to their homes in Israel. Michael Stewart proposed to offer them both return to their homes and compensation, an absolutely crazy proposal. The Prime Minister had also noticed a difference in the proposals for phasing the order of any agreements which were reached, but I didn't see as much importance in this as he did.

Michael Stewart made his proposal and when the Prime Minister replied

[1] From January 26th to 29th the Prime Minister visited Canada and America for talks with M. Trudeau, President Nixon and U Thant. See *Wilson*, pp. 750–6.

[2] He was Chairman of the Board of Governors of Guy's Hospital 1951–74 and since 1974 has been Chairman of Guy's Hospital Medical and Dental School.

it was immediately clear that there was an open conflict between the two of them which O.P.D. would have to resolve. Michael wanted the plan and the P.M. didn't, because it would be unpopular with the Jews and lose us the Jewish vote. 'Here we are,' said Harold, 'moving one-third of the way towards the Arab position from the American position. It will cause us great trouble. Why should we do it?' Then I made my point about the refugees, whose significance I don't think anybody else had noticed, and Michael Stewart immediately agreed with me that if he was allowed his British plan he would drop this refugee proposal, even though, I think, it was the only original point he had. Denis Healey came in and said, 'What's the point of having a British plan. Non-visibility is what we need now. A British view only makes us unpopular in the very year when we are trying to get out of the Persian Gulf.' I agreed with every word he said. The trouble of course stems from George Brown's success two years ago in getting through the British resolution establishing four-power talks and since we are a member of these there is a strong feeling that we must make ourselves seen and heard in some way or other. Apparently the best way to do this is to put forward a plan close to that of the Americans but rather more pro-Arab, which will curry a little favour with our Arab friends, just as the French plan did. The French are now having a tremendous pro-Arab drive. They have undercut us with the new regime in Libya, where they are selling Mirage fighters and armaments, taking over everything from under our noses. Michael Stewart clearly wants to counter the French success but today he wasn't going to admit it.

However, apart from George Thomson, our number two at the F.O., Michael was the only person in favour of a British plan. Denis Healey, the Prime Minister and Fred Peart knocked him down and even Eddie Shackleton had little to say for it, while Barbara had nothing. That was that. The interesting lesson of this is that we only get foreign policy discussed in O.P.D. or Cabinet when there is disagreement between Harold and the Foreign Secretary. As long as those two get on we don't have serious Cabinet control. I think the difference between them this morning was very largely caused by the fact that we are in election year, with Harold once again seeing the danger of our losing the Jewish vote and saying so quite openly in the discussion. It was not, as it would have been a year ago, Crossman who called Caradon pro-Arab, but the P.M.

Sunday, January 25th

I had a terribly muddy walk yesterday and today. We really are in the grey, cloudy period of the year, the time when, unless you love the country and Prescote, you don't find it very attractive. I have been with Denis Pritchett, going over all our plans for a new spinney down by the Broadmoor, the repairs to the roof along by the side of the wall and the clearing out of the moat. Each week I am more aware that I'm slipping back, reducing my ambition, and that I am now one of the old 'uns in Cabinet. I have a great power over the others now and I don't think my intellectual domination has ever been greater than in the last three weeks or so. However I have really no future to look forward to. I must admit I've been depressed by the press on my Bill. The Sunday papers don't mention it and the weeklies are so anti-us that our plan is regarded as a dud, unintelligible and basically unpopular. We are seen as having muffed it and I get the blame for this.

The recovery that some people forecast last autumn hasn't happened. We are ten to eleven points behind the Tories and I suppose the effect of the trade balance has been almost cancelled out by the avalanche of wage claims and the feeling that things are now out of control. Here at Banbury we have had the teachers on strike for a fortnight, with Patrick at home, and they are now planning another prolonged series of indefinite strikes. We've got everyone pushing and shoving ahead, with sensational demands for higher wages, we had bad unemployment figures this month and, though this is the time of year when they tend to go up, it doesn't do us any good.[1]

I think, as everybody is saying, that this knocks out a chance of an early election, either before or after the budget, unless it's in a situation like 1951 where we give up trying and go to the country because we see things will get worse later on. I suppose there is one other thing that, as a party, we have to admit – the new enthusiasm, courage and drive of Ted Heath, who rather gallantly went out to Australia and won the first prize in the great Sydney–Hobart yacht race. He's back again with his cup and, now, this week he showed real courage in standing up to an even more provocative racial speech by Enoch Powell.[2] Ted dismissed him as inhuman and made it clear that he'll have nothing to do with Powell. I would say Heath has reached his nadir and is now back on the way up. As for Harold, he has consolidated his position as Leader of the Party in the Commons and the Cabinet and this evening he is off to America to see Nixon in his traditional way. But I don't see much room for the expansion of confidence in Harold's leadership, and Ted Heath will be able to catch us up till the end.

[1] In January 2·4 per cent of the total work-force was unemployed but the visible trade balance continued to improve, with a surplus of £20 million recorded for November 1969, £5 million for December and £38 million for January 1970. On January 1st the Chancellor of the Exchequer announced that the £50 annual limit on foreign currency for overseas travel was to be raised to a nominal ceiling of £300 for holiday travel and £40 per day for business travel.

[2] In a speech on January 17th Mr Powell demanded that the facts of Britain's growing coloured immigrant population should be debated by the Conservatives '... in the open as a party without prevarication or excuse'. He argued that the Government's financial assistance to areas with a high immigrant population should be devoted instead to a repatriation programme. In a B.B.C. interview the following day Mr Heath called the speech an example of 'man's inhumanity to man which is absolutely intolerable in a Christian democratic society'.

Monday, January 26th

This evening I gave dinner to Chris Price.[1] I like him. He's a brawny, highly intelligent teacher, one of our better people. At his suggestion I had already gone to Les Huckfield, our M.P. for Nuneaton, and asked him whether he would consider being a member of the Birmingham R.H.B. Our old friend Sir John Lewis, the Chairman, was terribly upset but I think Les will turn out to be good. I doubt, though, whether I can combine this, as Christopher Price wants, with the replacement of the Bishop of Lichfield. I might at least try to get him changed from being Vice-Chairman, but whom should I put in his place? We talked about this at length while the House discussed Nigeria.

Yesterday evening Hugh Fraser had got a Standing Order No. 9 debate for today,[2] the very day when the Tories published their agricultural policy and Joe Godber was trying to launch it in an opposition debate.[3] Three hours of his time was taken by the Nigeria debate, to the fury of the Tory front bench. On the other hand I think the anxiety in the House about Nigeria justified using S.O. 9, which I still think is one of our best reforms.

Tuesday, January 27th

I had to get in early at 9.30 for Legislation Committee, the first item being equal pay.[4] I had received a series of letters from Barbara trying to get the Equal Pay Bill to cover pensions and we were absolutely clear that we didn't want this. The Bill concerns pay and wages, not benefits, our side of things. I thought at first I had persuaded her but she is inveterate and this very morning I got an urgent letter saying she hoped I would at least agree to putting in at Committee Stage a new clause giving her the power to deal with pensions. I wasn't prepared to do this, so along I went, but she hadn't bothered to turn up and sent poor Harold Walker instead. I asked him about pensions. 'Oh no,' he said, 'there is no question of that. We've given up all idea of dealing with pensions and Clause 6 in particular repudiates it.' 'But,' I said, 'I think your First Secretary doesn't have that view any more.' 'Well,' he said, 'I can tell you without doubt and the officials here both say so.' There

[1] Labour M.P. for Birmingham, Perry Barr 1966–70 and since February 1974 for Lewisham West. He was Editor of *New Education* 1967–8 and Education Correspondent of the *New Statesman* 1969–74.

[2] Conservative M.P. for the Stone division of Staffordshire 1945–50 and for Stafford and Stone since 1950. He was Parliamentary Under-Secretary of State and Financial Secretary at the War Office 1958–60, Parliamentary Under-Secretary of State for the Colonies 1960–2 and Secretary of State for Air 1962–4.

[3] Conservative M.P. for Grantham since 1951. He was Assistant Government Whip 1955–7, Joint Parliamentary Secretary at the Ministry of Agriculture, Fisheries and Food 1957–60, Parliamentary Under-Secretary of State at the Foreign Office 1960–1, Minister of State at the Foreign Office 1961–3, Secretary of State for War June–October 1963, Minister of Labour 1963–4, Minister of State at the F.C.O. 1970–2 and Minister of Agriculture, Fisheries and Food 1972–4.

[4] The Equal Pay Bill was introduced on January 28th. It proposed that equal pay for men and women should be introduced gradually, becoming universal by the end of 1975.

were many other areas where people were asking about uncertain points. This Equal Pay Bill is another of the bills Barbara is shoving through without any consideration for her colleagues and without turning up at the Committees. It infuriates us. On the other hand I am devoted to her, she is still sprightly and, despite the disastrous things which are happening in the prices and incomes field, she stays on at the D.E.P., fighting for her position and for recovery.

I went back afterwards to Fred Peart's room with the Chief Whip, to discuss with Eddie Shackleton the interesting question of whether M.P.s and Ministers should be allowed to contribute to full membership of the National Superannuation scheme, with the state paying their employer's contribution. We found ourselves, however, discussing Barbara and the way she is battering things through, coolly staying away from Committees. I don't think there will be any question now of pensions being in Barbara's Bill and I shan't really have to bother to talk to her about it. She has lost it by failure to attend. Indeed, it's one of the striking differences that, after five or six years, our senior Ministers tend to come to Committees less and less and send their juniors along instead. This makes the Committees more and more of a waste of time because there is less and less serious discussion.

Back in the Ministry I had a meeting on the tactics of the nursing negotiations. It's strange to look back at how optimistic and excited we were three weeks ago, when we got through Prices and Incomes what we regarded as a generous offer. It's fair to say we did warn the Committee that they were taking the least attractive phasing of the total claim. We wanted them to give the total in the first year with a two-year interval before the next award but, at Barbara and Roy's insistence, the Committee spaced it out and took away a lot of the attraction. Still, it was a good offer. We were agreed today that though the unions aren't so bad, the ladies of the Royal College of Nursing are working themselves up like the teachers and the doctors to demanding the total in one year or nothing. There has been no real negotiation. What are we to do? We have practically nothing else to give away. We decided to stay put and possibly to see the Chancellor. The truth is that the atmosphere in which we launched the nurses' claim three or four weeks ago was not unfavourable but now, in the new grabbing emotional climate, even the nurses are out of control.

I had a queer lunch with a girl called Muriel Bowen, the *Sunday Times* Local Government Correspondent. I wonder if she is the daughter of the other Elizabeth Bowen,[1] because she comes from a castle in Waterford and a hunting and fishing family. There we were at the Dorchester and I've almost decided to give the *Sunday Times* the scoop next Sunday of what is likely to

[1] Muriel Bowen, Local Government Correspondent of the *Sunday Times*, was the daughter of a second cousin of Elizabeth Bowen, the novelist. She was born and brought up in a castle in Co. Waterford, and had ridden with 138 packs of hounds in five continents, but her family were not serious fishermen.

be in the Green Paper on the Health Service. Miss Bowen is a funny, screwed-up woman, who eats a lot, drinks nothing, looks after me and somehow gets on with me, and we found ourselves discussing what my colleagues think of me as a person who runs a 500-acre farm and what her editor, Harold Thingummyjig,[1] thinks of her as a woman of privilege.

I had a trying time this afternoon with the Child Poverty Action Group, who have published a manifesto attacking the Government for making the poor poorer than ever before. At 10 o'clock I did a B.B.C. television piece on it, a gritty little programme with Peter Townsend. He used to be so young and handsome and debonair and now he is a grey, dreary man who kept us arguing about unemployment benefit far too long. I think it did me a great deal of harm. I managed as usual to give away too much but I think I did the programme fairly well in a defensive way. We are in trouble here because the attack is on our most sensitive point, our humanity. We ourselves are uncomfortable about the record Peter Townsend and his friends in the Child Poverty Group are attacking. In one way we are terribly bureaucratic. There was another Tory Private Member's Bill on Friday, seeking to grant the full national insurance pension to the over-eighties who are excluded from the 1948 Bill.[2] It would have cost us practically nothing because half of these people are on supplementary benefit already, but, no, we won't do it because of the sanctity of the contributory principle and this kind of attitude looks meaner and meaner.

Wednesday, January 28th

John Silkin, the Minister of Works, came over to tour the Department, because the officials, especially the staff side, have been pressing me to try to get the whole place double-glazed to keep out the ghastly draughts going through the building and the appalling noise from the motorway on one side and the Underground on the other. I took the liberty of going into one or two of the rooms and talking very freely to the people there. It was clear that the amount of noise and draughts had been oversold but what is really wrong is the beastliness of this absolutely characterless and formless building. The government is building a new place in Horseferry Road but we've no chance of getting in there or out of here. Indeed, we are moving all the Social Security people out of John Adam Street into this ghastly place, of which only our block is double-glazed and air-conditioned. But, as we went round and I breezily asked what people thought, they didn't by any means give a unanimous view. I can see Silkin going away and saying, 'Not on your life shall you automatically have universal double-glazing. We will do it selectively in the areas which are important.' I am pretty sure he is right about that and the air-conditioning, but, as I said, the people who come here

[1] Harold Evans.
[2] See above, pp. 359, 360.

want some special treatment and, as we are paying an incredibly low rent for the building, about one-fifth of what we pay on the other side of the river, we should be able to do some special thing to heal their woes while they are here. It was nice taking him round.

The only big thing today was a meeting of the Social Services Committee to deal with the Green Paper. Paul Odgers has been extremely spry so we have got this through the processes of Cabinet government in record time and, unlike Barbara who bulldozes her way through, we have in fact fulfilled our Committee obligations. The last device which Paul invented was to circulate our document as a Cabinet Paper last Monday, telling members of Cabinet that if they wished to comment or amend it they should come this afternoon, so that the corrected version can be submitted to Cabinet on Tuesday next week. This is to try to ensure that Cabinet members will be put in the wrong if they try to raise points next Tuesday. The reason for all this of course is the timetable. The local government Paper is coming out next Wednesday and ours a week later. A fortnight's gap would be extremely damaging, since you've got to see the two of them together. Seebohm, too, will appear the day after ours, so the thing had been circulated with a less perfect draft, going out to the officials last Thursday or Friday, and to Cabinet the day before yesterday for today. One of the difficulties about the machine is that even though you circulate papers on Monday for members of the Cabinet, they may well not get them until Tuesday evening and this is an enormous, full-length Green Paper. They only had one evening to look at it but it was the best we could do.

I was in the chair, Bea Serota was there for us and round about were a collection of relatively minor people. Neither Tony Crosland, the most important person from our point of view, nor Tony Greenwood bothered to turn up. They both sent Denis Howell, who had been given one hour's notice that he was to read the paper and came protesting and foaming. We had expected to have Jim Callaghan from the Home Office, or Shirley Williams, but three weeks before she had booked a day inside Holloway jail and didn't want to miss it, so Merlyn Rees came instead, much less formidable. Peter Shore wasn't there, nor Roy Jenkins, but there was Dick Taverne, who is highly competent and had brought with him a mass of important amendments.

We started with a detailed item about the Seebohm Report and then we got on to Ted Short's sudden, last-minute claim for Education to have responsibility for play-groups for the under-fives. He'd put this right at the end of the meeting on January 20th and Cabinet had been vaguely sympathetic. I thought we'd reached agreement with him that this should be a Social Services responsibility, but with Educational consultation. Once again, however (Short always does this), at this actual Committee he said no, he wanted to have legislation to put play-groups under his own control. I had put his item last on the agenda but I really had to bulldoze him by saying,

'You can't do this. It's either got to go under the doctors or under the Social Services,' and with an aggrieved look he had to agree.

The other big issue concerned Dick Taverne's four or five amendments on behalf of the Treasury, all emphasizing the need for central government to exert continuous, detailed control. I had to accept them. I had received an ominous letter from Roy, saying that he had seen my determination to get the Green Paper through and he would decide whether or not he had to act at next Tuesday's Cabinet after seeing what happened today. I knew that if I didn't broadly take the Treasury opinion I was done for but I did get out of him one vital thing, his agreement that the new Health Authorities would not be described as agents of the central government. Nevertheless I am pretty sure that both the doctors and the local authorities will be infuriated. After all, we are trying to emphasize that this should be an area of local participation. We ploughed through the thing page by page and I got it through in one and a half hours.

This evening Solly Zuckerman and I dined at Brooks's to discuss a lecture he is doing on Cabinet budgeting in the Health Service. Burke Trend had wanted me to look at it and I wasn't very satisfied. The club was almost empty and we sat in a corner and drank plenty of white wine with our oysters and then claret and masses of ancient port. It was an old-fashioned slap-up dinner and I tried to get him to discuss with me the differences he saw between the conduct of Harold Macmillan or Alec Douglas Home or Harold Wilson. Solly is an extraordinary creature, an old Whitehall warrior who has become a professional Whitehall politician, Chief Scientific Adviser to successive Prime Ministers, but he is elusive and I didn't manage to extract any clear picture from him. It wasn't only that the drink was too good. Perhaps these chaps don't see Cabinets enough. All I learnt was Solly's conviction that the Healey regime has been a disaster, maintaining the brass hats in power. This judgment reflects the fact that Solly and Healey have quarrelled. In all the battles Solly has nearly always been on the side of people like Mulley and the F.O. advisers. I didn't get very much out of it but we had an enjoyable evening.

Thursday, January 29th

This morning was chiefly notable for the start of the Standing Committee on the National Superannuation Bill. I was able to attend because, as Harold is still flying back from America, there was no Cabinet. All the newspapers have carried stories about the Tories fighting our Bill line by line but there were in fact no more than the normal number of amendments. I sat there in that great Room 9, horribly crowded, because I had insisted on a Committee of thirty members. I have to be away a great deal and we don't want just to have a majority of one or two. Against me are Balneil and Paul Dean and we have a strong number of people on our side. Our only nuisance is Tom

Price,[1] aged, I should think, nearly seventy. He hates my guts, he is against our Bill and is going to be confoundedly difficult. When I saw his name on the list I insisted he should be taken off and David Ennals went down to the Whips. I was finally told that we couldn't take his name off because he had been promised membership of the Standing Committee in a deal to persuade him to do some business the Whips wanted and if his name were removed he would stand up in the House and object, delaying the proceedings. This is characteristic of the Whips' relationships. They like to run the Committees, to nominate the people and have the whole thing in their hands and they much resent Ministers interfering. So we had to carry J. T. Price, though we changed two other names. I did get as our Whip Walter Harrison,[2] a good friend, who was being kept by the Chancellor for his Finance Bill, and I also got Brian O'Malley. It's a jolly good team. We got quite a lot of business done but, though we couldn't possibly complain of any delay or filibustering, we calculated that if we go on at this rational pace, it will take 250 hours of Committee time to complete the Bill. Sooner or later we shall have to have three days a week of open-ended sessions and almost certainly a guillotine at the end.

After half an hour I slipped out to S.E.P., which in the absence of the P.M., was under Roy's chairmanship. Here was the old hoary problem of the British Museum Library, as item No. 1. When I left the Ministry of Housing they were still consulting the trustees and considering the possibility of withholding planning permission for the proposal to rebuild the Library in Bloomsbury Square. Then, in one of his biggest boobs, Patrick Gordon Walker suddenly announced a proposal to change the location of the new Library to a site in Covent Garden, doing this without consulting the trustees. There was a terrible row and we had to set up the Dainton Committee.[3] Today we had Ted Short, rather a similar type to Gordon Walker, with a proposal to end the connection between the Museum and the Library altogether. I had heard from Eddie Shackleton how dubious this all was and how we were in for another row, yet it looked perfectly O.K. on paper. Short said that this had of course been discussed with the trustees, who were absolutely agreed on the principle, and that there was nothing wrong with the proposal at all. Eddie and I were not convinced. I said, 'Are you sure?

[1] Labour M.P. for Westhoughton from June 1951 until his death in February 1973. He was an Opposition Whip 1953–64 and a Council member of the Association of Superannuation and Pension Funds 1937–68. He was born in October 1902.

[2] Labour M.P. for Wakefield since 1964, Assistant Government Whip 1966–8, a Lord Commissioner of the Treasury 1968–70, Deputy Chief Opposition Whip 1970–4 and Deputy Chief Government Whip since 1974.

[3] Sir Frederick Dainton (Kt 1971), Vice-Chancellor of the University of Nottingham 1965–73 and Dr Lee's Professor of Chemistry at the University of Oxford 1970–3, was Chairman of the National Libraries Committee 1968–9. He was also Chairman of the Advisory Committee on Scientific and Technical Information 1966–70, of the Committee on the Swing Away from Science 1968, of the Advisory Board for Research Councils 1972–3 and a member of the Central Advisory Council for Science and Technology 1967–70. Since 1973 he has been Chairman of the University Grants Committee.

Have you agreed that the Library should be separate? Does it mean, for instance, that the Reading Room, which is part of the Museum building, will be separated from the new central Library, or will that part of the Museum be divorced from the British Museum?' 'Well,' said Short, 'these are all details. I have discussed the principles. It can't be held up in this way.' The more he talked, the more the conviction grew round the table that he was not telling the truth and that the trustees had not been adequately consulted. Finally (this shows you how these things happen) Roy ruled that Short must submit to us a detailed paper giving the exact, concise history of what has happened till now and what has been discussed with the trustees. Short was caught and held. This is partly because his colleagues know our Ted now, that he is an untrustworthy character. He will put something down on paper, agree it with you, and then come to the meeting to try and get a bit more.

The other matter was of great importance, a paper on the age of retirement for civil servants. For some months now Eddie Shackleton has apparently been convinced that it is his duty, as head of the Civil Service Department, to urge us to take the opportunity of the new National Superannuation Bill to rethink Civil Service pensions and postpone the age of retirement from sixty to sixty-five for all but, perhaps, Permanent Secretaries. Eddie hadn't for a moment denied that all the Civil Service unions would object or that to associate this change with our Bill would be unfortunate. I had put this to him very strongly and so had David Ennals but Eddie insisted he must push the paper forward and he did so today. Ironically (or is it?), it was clear that the paper didn't stand the ghost of a chance. Everybody saw the difficulties and we were particularly conscious of the danger of the proposal because we had already given assurances that there was no reason for people to believe that they would be worse off as a result of our Bill. After half an hour Eddie said, 'Whichever way it goes, we should have a decision,' and the net result was a categoric assertion that we have no intention of postponing the age of retirement. If the paper had never been put forward we wouldn't have got this assurance because, if I had asked for it, I might easily have failed against the C.S.D. and the Treasury. The defeat of Eddie's proposal secured this for us and I suspect that this is what he intended all along.

I had lunch with Peter Shore in the Members' dining room. It had seemed to me that he wouldn't recover from the last Cabinet reshuffle and that he would be so despised he wouldn't count. Well, that's not true. He is now Minister without Portfolio, one of the two people who have no special job apart from reading Cabinet papers and working hard at them. He does do this and he is making his mark. I have recorded how he trounced the Chancellor last week on the deplorable memorandum from NEDO. Peter does speak extremely well and he has got his second and third wind. Whether he is liked or not I don't know, but he is respected now. Of course his other difficulty was that he was a disaster in the House. He is one of those tall, gangling men with a lah-di-dah voice and at the beginning he had a very bad front-bench manner. He was an encumbrance and became more and more unpopular with our people but even in the House he has gradually got through and people have become used to him. This shows that if you really are able and are determined to struggle you can survive the most appalling mistakes and come out at the end.

I had wanted to go to the *Valkyrie*, the first night of the English production at the Coliseum, with Reginald Goodall as conductor. The maddening thing was that tonight, when I thought I was going to be absolutely free, we had another Standing Order No. 9, this time on the scandal of the slump in the housing figures.[1] It looks as though we are going to have only 360,000, a disaster, instead of 400,000. This in itself is interesting because it shows what a difference people can make. If I had stayed as Minister of Housing and dug myself in, the Chancellor couldn't possibly have cut the houses back below 400,000. Substituting Tony Greenwood for me in that Ministry has led to the collapse of the housing programme, just as substituting me for Kenneth Robinson in Health has meant that the hospital building programme has been sustained when otherwise it was bound to be cut. Now, of course, Roy and Barbara, the two people who said housing should suffer, are appalled at the result. Going back on this pledge is a serious political blow to the Government. Harold doesn't like it and it's now far too late to get a single house added to the programme before the election.

Tony Greenwood started the reply on the vote of censure and Tony Crosland wound up. I looked in at the beginning and was surprised to see that the Tory benches were only half full for the first and second speeches. Of course it doesn't much matter what happens in the House of Commons now. This is something which will matter outside. After the 7 o'clock vote I could at last go to the opera. It was a most exciting, invigorating performance. I sat in the stalls with Jack Donaldson and Lord Drogheda and his wife, tremendously enjoying it, and afterwards we slipped off to the little Beoty's restaurant where everybody knew us. It was a warm lovely evening with drenching rain and I felt exhilarated.

Friday, January 30th

After a big meeting on hospital building programmes, I went down to Coventry to talk about pensions to the Rolls-Royce shop stewards. I didn't expect anyone to turn up but it was an absolutely first-rate lunchtime meeting, with 130 or so there. I explained the scheme for twenty minutes and then they asked me questions. Talk about the scheme being incomprehensible! People can understand it perfectly well if they want, and this audience did. Good God, I suddenly realized, this is a good meeting of shop stewards because I'm not having to quarrel with them about prices and incomes policy. The price we paid for that policy was that we were always at loggerheads. This

[1] A Government amendment to the motion deploring the fact that the number of houses completed in 1969 fell by 46,922 to 366,793 was passed by 273 votes to 244.

time we weren't. They wanted my help, I wanted theirs and it was a stirring hour and a half.

From there I drove out with Peter Lister to look at a clinic in a little village called Baddesley Ensor and then we drove back to Coventry, where Bill Wilson, Maurice Edelman and I were to meet the Federation of Council House Tenants. The meeting was difficult, much easier for them than for me, but it went quite well. We drove it into the tenants' heads that the Council is Tory and that the Tories should be blamed for their problems. There we were, the three of us together on the same platform for the first time since the 1966 election. I haven't really seen Maurice since we read and enjoyed his latest novel,[1] but George Hodgkinson had rung me up to tell me that Maurice had asked him to be his agent in the next election. The fact is that Maurice has no party at all in Coventry North and his asking the help of poor old George, who is well over seventy, shows how desperate he must be. Bill Wilson is not nearly so desperate. He's an efficient, expert man, a solicitor running a very good firm, with plenty of money. He's a good M.P. as well, with first-rate ability, but an unattractive man, tough and hard, without charm. Of the three of us I, as a senior Minister, am now respected to some extent but I am tarnished by the failures of the Government.

Anne picked me up and we went off to an hotel in Meriden, a little village in the centre of Britain, where the psychics gather every year on midsummer eve. The Coventry social security offices were holding their dinner and dance there and we all had a pleasant time. I didn't have to make any speeches but I did have quite an interesting talk with them, the young men saying to me, 'I don't know how you can expect us to join your scheme because after all we are paid too little at the start.' They were quiet and decent about it. There were the girls all dolled up to the nines and the boys, too, with their long hair and whiskers, a tremendous standard of appearance. I watched all the boys and girls dancing and it gave me quite an idea of the modern affluent society.

Sunday, February 1st

Harold is back from America. Nothing went wrong and he only appeared to hit the news when it was revealed that five minutes before his conference at the British Embassy in Washington he had slipped on the marble floor, cut his lip and bruised himself, but he carried on as though nothing had happened. I wasn't in the House on Thursday when he came back and I didn't see him, though I was told he got up and down with a little difficulty. Obviously he managed the journey with his usual confidence and competence but there can't be said to have been any real life in it. In fact it's been another week in which we've got no lift, in which the intolerable wage situation has continued and the demands for everything anyone can get have become steadily worse.

The Warwickshire N.F.U. came over to see me this morning, six of them

[1] *All On a Summer's Night* (London: Hamish Hamilton, 1969).

including the new chairman, Henry Plumb.[1] The farmers have now caught the infection of violent protest. They have been blocking the streets at Stratford and next weekend they are threatening to block the streets of Banbury. Jim Callaghan was pushed and jostled in Haverfordwest and had cakes thrown at him. Poor old Jim! He is the only other person in Cabinet besides myself who has a farm and understands the farmers' point of view. Certainly they and the teachers have said to themselves, 'If other people, dustmen and Ford workers, can get their way by striking, we mustn't be inhibited or smug but we must blackmail and browbeat too.' I told the N.F.U. that I doubt whether the teachers will get their way in this fashion. It's very nice for Conservative councils not to have to pay their teachers, nice to have weeks of strikes that reduce the rates and, as for the farmers, I doubt whether actually inconveniencing people will get them support. Those of us in Cabinet who want to give the farmers something realize that they are trying to force our hands and that whatever we do they won't be grateful, so this time we will probably be really tough.

All this side of the Government's work is still dreary in the extreme and meanwhile we have Heath and the Tories getting down to business. This weekend they are holding a very well-advertised conference to prepare their election address.[2] They are building up their own and public confidence, not only in their determination to win, but in their ability to do so. All that's going very well for them now though, mind you, January and February are always very bad months for Governments.

Last night we had David and Marilyn Butler over to dinner, along with Anthony Booth and his wife.[3] David Butler was more careful than ever to maintain his neutral position and, for once, he didn't bully me or try to get information out of me in any way.

So here I am plunging through the winter. It's been an awful two days of squally bitter cold weather, with the river constantly rising and water soaking in, but Prescote is lovelier than ever. This morning one of the farmers asked why I ever go to London when I've got this lovely place. I can't see any good reason why, except that I quite like this job. Yet Prescote grows on me all the time.

Monday, February 2nd

I started with a little consultation with Bea and Barbara, who had been upset by the news of an N.B.P.I. proposal for a gigantic increase in Forces' pay

[1] Sir Henry Plumb (Kt 1973) was Deputy President of the N.F.U. 1966–9 and has been its President since 1970, and President of the Comité des Organisations Professionels Agricoles de la C.E.E. (COPA) since 1975.

[2] The weekend conference of senior Conservatives and their advisers was held at the Selsdon Park Hotel in Croydon. The Opposition's election strategy included the reaffirmation of their determination to reduce the level of direct taxation, reform trade union law, restrict immigration and give priority to the enforcement of law and order.

[3] Anthony Booth, the candidate for Banbury, was a director of a small leather-processing firm near Witney.

and Denis Healey's threat last Friday that these rises are agreed and that the computer is already operating on that assumption. He is determined to bulldoze this through but, frankly, if we announce an increase in Forces' pay, we will have no chance whatsoever of getting any agreement with the nurses or the teachers and we will find ourselves either surrendering totally or having large-scale teachers' strikes and possibly even a nurses' strike. Barbara, rather to my surprise, was extremely anxious to reach a settlement with the nurses. The difficulty is that as First Secretary she apparently can't allow the unprecedented things the unions want, either a break clause allowing them to start negotiations before the end of two years or, even better, to get the period shortened, to, say, twenty months. However she did suggest the possibility of proposing arbitration on the second point and she is anxious to try very hard.

After that Barbara and I went into No. 10 for Management Committee and another meeting devoted to tactics. The minutes say it was devoted to strategy but, heavens alive, we were not discussing strategic considerations but what could be done in the shortest term, between now and next October, to improve the situation. The Prime Minister started by referring to the Tories' Selsdon Conference as a great success. I have seldom heard Harold admit a success to the other side but he said this had depressed him and that they had pulled off a successful publicity stunt. He was also anxious about the build-up of Heath and we were asked to discuss how we could counter this. Were Ministers prepared to go into action to destroy the other side? Harold always asks this when the critical point comes and implies that only he does it.

The trouble about these meetings of Management Committee is that, though having eight or nine of us makes it the right size and we don't leak because we know and trust each other, nevertheless there isn't what I call a real argument. Partly as a result of Harold's leadership, people don't let themselves go nor do they disagree. We make little speeches to each other round the table and all the morning consists of is a five- or six-minute speech from each individual, with a few questions at the end of each one and the P.M. noting the points. That's one way of conducting a meeting but it's not really a way to raise the difficult and awkward issues. I've noticed this as one of the characteristics of Harold Wilson's Cabinet, particularly since the disappearance of George Brown and the end of the open rows we used to have between him and Callaghan. We are almost too mealy-mouthed. Only on quite secondary or departmental issues have we disagreed and the underlying potential clashes are not allowed to come to the surface. Harold would detest that and, indeed, even in a private talk with him he discourages any of us from raising basic issues. As a result there are very few really tense moments of real conflict and the underlying tensions are only hinted at.

Look at this morning. Here were Barbara and Roy disagreeing on a basic point. Towards the end of the morning Roy was saying, 'Frankly, we know we don't like the word consolidation but as a Government we are bound to have a conservative policy and to say, "You will be safer with us and you will find the Tories more frightening".' (One of the conclusions we had come to was that the only way to keep the Tories out was to say we were a lesser evil.) Barbara, though, felt passionately that this would be to sacrifice the whole of her left-wing tradition and that she must stand for new radical ideas and so must the party. Neither of them really brought this out into the open. Roy says we stand for a civilized society; we certainly stand for a civilized Cabinet, one which pulls its punches, which makes little speeches in succession but which doesn't really have it out across the table. So today each person listed the points they felt we ought to consider but we did all this only a few weeks ago and there wasn't very much more to be said.

All right, what can be done? Housing is putting to a special committee on Friday a paper about minor methods of improving housing credit and the possibility of special subsidies, but all that is going to be virtually ineffective if we are considering having an election in or before next autumn. I was able to show that if we were to complete the National Superannuation Bill a few minor things could come into action the moment it got the royal assent, like the constant attendance allowance and the widows' pension, and in our uprating of supplementary benefit we could introduce a differential higher rate at the age of eighty. But all these things are secondary and very few and far between. We really have to depend entirely on Roy's budget and on the economic policy upon which that itself depends. The net conclusion of the meeting was that, judged by the suggestions we made, there is damned little which can in fact be done and although it's true that formulations of policy are useful, in due course we only marginally affect our vote by discrediting the Tories. I think the margin can be very important, but our first job is to win votes back.

I spent most of the rest of the day briefing the B.M.A., Hetherington and Swaffield on the contents of the Green Paper and especially on what it says about the Health Service. I have now got my Department thoroughly used to the idea they found so extraordinary, that the Minister does talk with great freedom and trusts the people he consults. In fact I have told all the people I have consulted what to expect, not so much in detail but fairly clearly in outline, and not a peep of a leak have I had from any of them. The only informed story was in yesterday's *Sunday Times*. It was written by Muriel Bowen, the strange Irish girl who came to see me, to whom with Peter Brown's help I had given a carefully controlled story, just a kind of hors d'oeuvre, an original *soupçon*. She has been very careful not to go a yard beyond what I wished and as she got it from me I know where the information came from. Nobody else has behaved improperly at all. This, I admit, is partly because I have been briefing them on what isn't really exciting news.

I think a more controversial and exciting fact is that we have decided to disregard Maud and keep the Health Service out of local government, so there may be a bit more interest in my announcement that I'm implementing the Seebohm recommendations but, even so, I think we've got to face it that people aren't terribly interested in what we are promising to do after this coming election. Our 1966 technique of pouring out White Papers for this Bill and that Bill, which worked such magic, is not going to work again this time unless we can get some degree of confidence in our chances of winning. Only if people believe in us will the press and radio, which are what really matter, treat things like my White Papers seriously.

At 7.30 I had Stark-Murray and John Dunwoody in for a drink and we sat in my room with Tam and watched the new, confident Heath on 'Panorama'. I found him extremely unconvincing. He was jumping down the throats of the two people who were examining him, being rude and domineering, interrupting them. I don't think he made a particularly attractive impression but I suppose from the point of view of proving that he was on top of his form, even this appearance was a good follow-up to the Selsdon Conference.

Tuesday, February 3rd

When I woke up this morning a very disconcerting thing had happened. It was 4 a.m. and I felt perfectly well but I couldn't remember anything that had happened after watching Heath on 'Panorama', which went on until about 8.30. I couldn't remember going to dinner or what I had said. I did vaguely remember meeting Tam, who had my overcoat in his arms, and walking home together. I did notice that his speech was a bit incoherent, as mine was, and I remembered getting my papers out and getting into bed. Otherwise, from half-way through Heath to half-way home I had a complete cut-out. The last time this odd thing happened was at the Brighton Conference in 1957, just when Patrick was about to be born and I was going to make my reply to the debate on national superannuation. On that occasion I had a tremendous success within three hours at the Conference.[1] Anyway here I was feeling perfectly fine and ready for this morning's crucial Cabinet on the Green Paper.

This was extremely dicey. As I've explained I had circulated my final draft as a Cabinet paper addressed to all my colleagues, with a covering note telling them to attend the meeting of the Social Services Committee with any objections they might have. Since then, Harold had sent me one or two minor amendments. Today, before I knew it, Barbara was saying, 'I am so sorry but there are one or two alterations I am bound to make and I know Dick will appreciate that I have been very busy.' Tony Crosland had amendments, too, and there was tremendous pressure on me, so I said, 'But both of you could have come to Wednesday's meeting and made the amendments there. Are these points which were put to me there but which I haven't adopted?' No, they weren't. One of Barbara's amendments was that I had

[1] It also happened on one occasion while Crossman was Minister of Housing. See Vol. I.

called the Government 'they' and not 'it' and Harold rather amusingly said, 'Dick's right about this.' The rule (I don't know why we keep it) is that in a White Paper we traditionally refer to the British Government as 'they' and to a foreign Government as 'it'. I slipped out of this and then Barbara said, 'You must give me these other amendments. They are very important.' I had to depend on Harold's support and if he'd given her the chance she'd have made a hell of a fuss. As it was, I had a look at her amendments as we left Cabinet and they were all points which her own man had put in on Wednesday and which had been incorporated. Barbara had been looking at the wrong draft. It's awfully characteristic of her. Tony Crosland wasn't nearly so insistent. I was able to whisper in his ear and he said he didn't really mind. Harold was absolutely on my side. He was magnificent and said, 'The White Paper will be held up. You've had your chance. Unless the Minister has actually failed to interpret what was said on your behalf at the meeting on Wednesday, you won't be allowed to include any more amendments.' All this was only possible with the help of Burke Trend and the Cabinet Office and after half an hour I was able to go out of Cabinet to telephone the office and say that I had got the damn thing through. By then the presses were actually running.

I went across to the Committee on National Superannuation for the debate on the married woman's option and this took all morning until lunch-time. Now, just as I had sat down at the start of Cabinet, Roy had asked me if I was free for lunch. Curiously, I was free but for a rather discreditable reason. I had arranged to lunch with Arthur Gavshon,[1] whom I last lunched with a fortnight ago. He had been asking me about the British refusal to condemn C.S. gas, and the trouble we were getting into at the U.N. I didn't have to tell him very much, because he knew the whole story and was telling me how vilely Cabinet was behaving. I had tried to explain why the Cabinet was in the right and he had said, 'This is the kind of story which must be published. It will teach you a lesson. It's impossible that the British Cabinet should behave in this way.' I said, 'I'm afraid I'm quite convinced that if it is published it will show that Denis Healey is right, not Michael Stewart, because it would clearly be hypocritical for us to make speeches in the U.N. opposing these gases and then to use them in Northern Ireland.' Arthur told me that he had got this whole story beforehand but now Tam had seen in the *Daily Express* a sensational story by Chapman Pincher and I knew this must have come from Arthur.[2] I don't think I can deny that by arguing that we were right I had given a little more for his piece and I knew straightaway that there would be trouble. So I had cancelled our lunch today and, now, when Roy leant across and asked me to join him, I said I could.

[1] Associated Press's Foreign and Diplomatic Correspondent in London.

[2] Chapman Pincher was Defence, Science and Medical Editor of the *Daily Express* 1946–73. Since 1973 he has been the Assistant Editor of the *Daily Express* and Chief Defence Correspondent for Beaverbrook Newspapers.

However, it went completely out of my head. I gave a drink to Tom Price, the old boy who is on our National Superannuation Committee and who needs to be humoured, and then I went downstairs and lunched with John Golding, the new Member for Newcastle-under-Lyme, whom I also wanted to see.[1] Towards the end of lunch I suddenly got a message and remembered about Roy. 'Well,' said Roy on the telephone, 'I can't really believe you did it on purpose. I waited until 1.55. It was a good lunch and you missed it.' It's a great pity because I could have had my pre-budget talk with him today. However I suppose it's also fair to say that he must have been stood down by somebody and I must have been a last-minute fill-in. But there it was, I had forgotten.

After P.M.'s Questions this afternoon I went off with Harold, in order to talk over Gavshon and the leak. During the course of the morning I'd reflected on this and came to the conclusion that whoever leaked must have known about a meeting on the previous Friday after Harold's return from Washington, when he had discussed this with Denis Healey and Michael Stewart. I had not known of this meeting, and moreover, Arthur's story had been all about U Thant and his objections, something I also knew nothing about, so the main source was quite clearly somebody right inside.

I went upstairs where our dear friend Bea was waiting, eager to get me crumpets for tea. I sent for Janet Newman and there we sat in the House of Lords over the nicest afternoon tea, square crumpets and home-made cakes. But my particular job this afternoon was to see Sir John Lewis. A tremendous lot of work has been done and we have found two or three quite good people to put on the Midlands R.H.B. to reduce the average age and get solid socialists who aren't just talkers and viragos, like some of those whom we already have and who have been bullying poor John. However I had suddenly realized that we must represent the northern part of the area, Nuneaton and Rugby, and, after a fortnight's thought, Les Huckfield had said he was prepared to take it on. This means he won't be able to get any more publicity for attacking the Board. I had also talked to Bill Price,[2] who said he couldn't do it because Rugby is a marginal seat and he can't forfeit the votes he gets by being anti-Board – a cynical view of an M.P.'s job! Today I had to sell to the Chairman my suggestion of Huckfield, plus two other solid left-wingers. Curiously, Sir John just said 'Yes'. I would have had terrible trouble with some people but he said, 'I've got to do it,' and capsized.

Then we had our annual dinner for the R.H.B. chairmen, at the Foreign Office place at Carlton Gardens, in a delicious room, with good food and drink. This year the chairmen have all got to know me personally and I have

[1] Labour M.P. for Newcastle-under-Lyme since October 1969. He was Opposition Whip July 1970–4 and a Whip February–October 1974. Since 1976 he has been Parliamentary Under-Secretary of State at the Department of Employment.

[2] William Price, a staff journalist on the *Coventry Evening Telegraph* 1959–62 and on the *Birmingham Post and Mail* 1962–6, has been Labour M.P. for Rugby since 1966. He has been Parliamentary Secretary at the Privy Council Office since October 1974.

got to know them and a great deal about their regions. Each one wanted to come up and talk to me afterwards and there was an amazing lack of personal ill-will towards me over the new scheme. I made a little speech and then Stephen Lycett Green replied.[1] I had said that the only perk I ever gave them was this dinner and he said, 'In thirteen years of Tory rule I never even got a cup of coffee or a glass of sherry.' Then he described life with me and how difficult it was, just as I had described how difficult I was. It was a very successful evening personally. No doubt my attempt to communicate with them directly has paid hands down and without it there would have been a blow-up such as I can't imagine. It was most exciting and enjoyable, interrupted by votes first at 7.0 p.m. and then at 10.0 p.m. with a final vote at 11.30 before I tottered home.[2]

Wednesday, February 4th

I spent the whole morning with the R.H.B. chairmen, who I knew were in tremendous dudgeon because an annihilating paper had been submitted to me, not actually by the chairmen but by their SAMOs, Treasurers and Secretaries. It quarrelled with the new policy of winding up the R.H.B.s as such and handing the chief power over to the Regional Health Authorities, an attack that is perfectly understandable because all the officials feel a threat to their position and the whole R.H.B. structure. What had pleased them about the idea of a two-tier structure, which I had been talking about before I got ill, was that everything would remain the same and they believed that they would be the power in the land, running the integrated Health Authorities with their old self-perpetuating oligarchies. When I came back at Christmas the whole thing had suddenly been changed and they found that the R.H.B. is to be relaced by a much weaker regional council and the main power planted in the Health Authorities. Anyhow, here were the chairmen suffering terribly under pressure from their officials, to whom most of them were prepared to give the benefit of the doubt. But I said, 'Look, we had a lovely dinner last night. Now say what you think,' and it was said. I then spelt out my view and I realized that they understood the politics of it and that we were holding our own. I also frankly explained that I had been careful to leave the question of the exact power of the regional council open for discussion, and that I knew that many of the consultants would be on their side and would really think all this out. The Green Paper was a consultative document. But in fact

[1] Sir Stephen Lycett Green (he succeeded to his father's baronetcy in 1941) was Chairman of the King's Lynn Hospital Management Committee 1948–59, Chairman of the Association of Hospital Management Committees, 1956–8 and Chairman of the East Anglian R.H.B. 1959–74.

[2] The Conservative motion, deploring the fact that there had now been the longest continuous period of high unemployment since the war, was defeated in a vote at 7.0 p.m. by 309 to 246. At 10.0 p.m. the motion, deploring the Government's failure to ensure the provision of necessary supplies of smokeless fuel, was defeated by 305 votes to 247. At 11.30 p.m. a Prayer against the order for the continuation of the incomes policy was defeated by 213 votes to 169.

it's true that the old idea will never be put back, Humpty Dumpty will never sit on that wall again.

I had John Mackintosh to lunch at a corner table in the Members' dining room and we went through the draft of the Godkin Lectures. I told him the shape I wanted the first and second lecture to have. He is first-rate and somehow we devised the form in which he should write them. That is a great relief. After lunch I talked to a deputation from the College of Nurses. When I saw them before I had been worried as to what they had meant by saying that morale is low in the Health Service. Were they misusing words or is it really low? I put this to them again and today someone did give me an answer. She said, 'I think morale is low because a Sister goes into her ward, looks down it, sees that the nursing is extremely bad and knows she can do nothing about it.' I thought this was a very good description. Undoubtedly there is a combination of strains, especially the strain of a new technology, of changing techniques and of doctors setting nurses in the acute hospitals more and more difficult tasks as the job becomes more complex. Moreover, a nurse who twenty years ago would have a ward of thirty, some of whom were convalescent, now has nothing but really ill people. Equally as we remove from long-stay hospitals more and more children and people who can live in the community, we shall fill the hospitals with serious cases and there will be none of the mixture of easy and serious nursing which enabled a nurse to relax a little and enjoy her job. All this is terribly important. Then there is the question of money and status, and the feeling among student nurses that they want to be real students and not mere skivvies. There's also the recruitment problem. The kind of middle-class people who used to go into nursing now go instead for university and technical colleges and diplomas because that has higher status. It was a fascinating meeting and I enjoyed it a great deal.

Then Anne and I gave a drink to Lilo Milchsack, who came in looking dazzling, in a white dress, black stockings and shoes and a red scarf, beautifully got up. Anne looked fresh and exquisite, too, in her lovely salmony red suit, and Lilo said, 'How beautiful you look,' and Anne does. Very satisfactory. I think Lilo one of the smartest women and there she was, really admiring Anne, and, as I could see, envying Anne's appearance for her age. It was really pleasant for me. After that we gave dinner to my nephew Stafford and his fiancée, a doctor who trained at the Middlesex and is now an expert at University College. She is tiny, young, vivid and perfectly prepared to give up being a doctor in order to go abroad with Stafford, who wants to find a job in Paris, Stockholm or India. Well, it makes you realize the expense of training women doctors.

Thursday, February 5th

Yesterday Tony Crosland made his Statement on the Local Government White Paper and gave a press conference. I think it's been a tremendous flop, partly no doubt because it's a dull White Paper, not particularly well-written, interesting or original. But, more important, it has been written off as almost valueless because it only refers to events which will take place in 1971/2 at the earliest, when we shan't be in power. The lack of press interest is linked with the fact that, as a party, we have now been dispensed with. I am afraid this may affect my own Green Paper when it is published next Wednesday.

At our second Cabinet we had a very interesting problem about abortion. In Legislation Committee yesterday we had dealt with a Tory Private Member's Bill on abortion that is down for Friday next week. It simply consists of introducing into the present Abortion Act a single amendment to make it illegal to perform an abortion without there being a proper consultant gynaecologist present. When the Abortion Bill was going through, one of the last votes in the Lords was to reject this particular proposal, which I think had been put in by the professional gynaecologists. It had been turned down on the grounds that it was a wrecking amendment, which wouldn't reduce the misuse of the Act but would undoubtedly slow up the number of cases which could be dealt with. Anyway, yesterday I was able to argue that, whether the amendment was right or wrong, the Act has been in operation for less than two years and I didn't want it changed. I said that I merely wanted this Private Members' Bill to be talked out in the usual way. When this was raised at Cabinet today, the Chief Whip immediately said it was not so easy. It couldn't be talked out and there would have to be a free vote. I said, 'A free vote? But, look, I am administering the Abortion Act, and as Minister I say to you that I want the considered view of the Government to be that the Act should not be amended now but should continue to run. Therefore I would like the payroll vote of Ministers to be instructed to vote for me because to have the Government view defeated on a free vote would be intolerable.' 'Ah,' said the Chief Whip, 'You can't do that,' and Harold also said, 'You can't order Ministers to vote for abortion. Anyway, you certainly can't put the Whips on because if that were known there would be a tremendous fuss.'

This raised a most interesting constitutional issue, which Jim Callaghan was quick enough to see. 'There you are,' he said. 'I was against the Government allowing the passage of these Private Members' Bills on controversial and important matters.' We've legislated for the improvement of the law on homosexuals, on divorce, on abortion, all of which have been Private Members' Bills, passed with a lot of time and help from the Government. The Government remains technically neutral, so that the consciences of people like George Thomas and Willie Ross and, in the case of abortion, Shirley Williams, can be squared. We have got away with changes which were long overdue and which no Cabinet would ever make before because these matters of conscience would cause a Government split. When I was Lord President I evolved this technique, arguing that these were issues which the House ought to decide and, whichever way it went, that the Government should accept the Commons' decision. The difficulty arises because a Government which in a sense has no party authority for passing a Bill must administer the legislation and defy those who want to tamper with it. I think I was quite right to claim that constitutionally I ought to get Government backing but it was also politically clear, as the Chief Whip and Barbara said, that it would have to be on a free vote which we would have to win. It will be extremely difficult to run the Health Service when part of it can be chopped this way and that by a free vote, and that's something I certainly didn't think of when I was Leader of the House.

Having got ourselves out of the abortion problem, the Prime Minister was then extremely anxious to give Government time for, or indeed to take over as a Government measure, the Deer Hunting and Hare Coursing Bill. He thinks this is an election winner and that hundreds and thousands of people who read the *Daily Mirror* love this idea. You know, it's queer. Deer hunting probably is very unpopular but hare coursing is a very proletarian sport and people in the North enjoy it. I simply said that, looked at purely from the point of view of votes, I didn't believe we should jump into this without a much more careful analysis of the minority who would oppose us. Minorities are valuable people and on the whole those who are opposed to you are more likely to vote than those who support you. That was that. Then we came to Sunday opening of public houses in Wales, which everybody knows the public overwhelmingly wants. But George Thomas got his way and we dropped Sunday opening, because it would upset the Welsh Baptist minority. On this Harold and the Chief Whip are in entire agreement, whereas in the hare-coursing case Harold's whole inclination was to disregard the minority. I think he is simply unaware of the inconsistencies.

The last item was Harold's report on Washington. Roy leant across afterwards and said, 'You know, it's extraordinary how every word of Harold's reports of his foreign visits increases one's incredulity.' Roy is right. The Prime Minister started by saying this was by far the most successful visit he had ever paid to Washington. He added, 'You see, the President obviously feels the inferior intellectual capacity of the men surrounding him and he was impressed by the quality of the British Prime Minister and the Foreign Secretary. This is what gave warmth to our reception.' Here is a fantastic degree of complacency in Harold Wilson, a feeling that the Americans must really admire him and think how good he and Michael are. It was piled on and on. I asked him only one question, about Israel and the Arabs. Apparently our British plan was squashed by the Americans, who didn't want a British plan more pro-Arab than their own, so Michael Stewart and the F.O. had lost on that one.

This evening we had an interesting meeting of the Immigration Committee under the Home Secretary, all about the Asians in East Africa. They are still British subjects, with the right to come over here, and Callaghan had given a pledge that he would never keep out anybody who really was without a home. Trouble is piling up now, and the issue is whether we should give them 1,500 extra entry certificates or find some way of wangling it so that we can use the present total of vouchers for this purpose. It's a highly technical argument. There is great tension here. Callaghan had against him Foley from the Foreign Office and others of the liberal lobby.[1] I had been surprised when David Ennals asked to be on the Committee but I thought he wanted to be on as a liberal and now he turned out to be a Callaghan man, so obviously Callaghan had asked for him. Jim had been fighting the Foreign Office and he spoke right out, saying, 'What I resent is that whenever this issue comes up I always read an article about it in *The Times*.' In *The Times* this very morning there had apparently been an article giving the precise line that Maurice Foley was going to plead this afternoon. This is the oldest trick in the world but it very often works. Callaghan has had bad luck because he is having great difficulty with the Drugs Bill, where he is trying to get a different mixture of legislation, with heavier penalties for trafficking and lighter penalties for mere possession, and this has been interpreted by the newspapers as seeking concessions for pot smokers. Now the F.O. is on to him, but Jim had David and me on his side and he won for himself a fortnight to try to move the voucher system round a bit, so that we can let some East Africans in without having to announce a new policy.

Last of all, I had dinner with Tommy Balogh at the Little French Club. He's as happy as he used to be and now he's with his Catherine he doesn't really mind losing No. 10.

Friday, February 6th

I found myself on one of my visits, this time to Bury St Edmunds to discuss a best-buy hospital. There were *seven* people, all those doctors and administrators, with me on the 9.30 from Liverpool Street. Some of us had breakfast and I sucked the doctors' minds and talked to the nurse, as we travelled down on the most beautiful, brilliantly frosty February morning. It was so dry that I could even walk over the frozen mud on the site where the new hospital is being built. I had a marvellous morning and a marvellous time at lunch, discussing how to build a district hospital, with the community services planned round it. Despite their difficulties with the County Council they really are doing what the Green Paper is trying to create for the future. The whole atmosphere here is fascinating. The County Council is run by a nice elderly colonel who believes in a community service and is himself running

[1] Maurice Foley was Labour M.P. for West Bromwich 1963–73. He was Joint Parliamentary Under-Secretary of State at the D.E.A. 1964–6, Parliamentary Under-Secretary at the Home Office 1966–7, for the Navy at the Ministry of Defence 1967–8 and at the Foreign Office 1968–70. Since 1973 he has been Deputy Director-General of the Directorate-General for Development and Co-operation at the Commission of the European Communities.

an executive council of G.P.s. Here in remote Bury St Edmunds people are together making the Health Service work.

In the afternoon we went out to a magnificent new social security building, with the Executive Council offices on top. I opened the building and got into the car tired, as I tend to get since my 'flu and pneumonia. We had a wonderful drive back through the East Anglian sunset and got home at 7.30.

Meanwhile another meeting of Prices and Incomes Committee took place today, where Barbara managed to persuade Roy to give us the go-ahead for minor concessions on nurses' pay in the second year. At the same time we are to offer them arbitration in the second year because people on a two-year contract now fear that they will be leapfrogged by others.

Sunday, February 8th

Another week, and from the electoral point of view, still no progress at all. Since Heath came back from Australia with his new self-confidence, the papers have been cracking him up, saying the tide has turned and that the Tory opposition is now in a winning mood. This threat was clinched last weekend by the public relations exercise at Selsdon Park. Suddenly Ted is described as a winner. I don't think he has changed much but I think it is what the newspapers were waiting for. Heath's new standing has come just at the right moment. I dare say what was said behind the scenes at Selsdon Park wasn't very important but I think it was of great importance to the Tories, to Heath's image and their image in the country. Now Harold has come out with a tremendous political speech against Heath and the Tories. He spoke on Friday, rumbustious, old-fashioned party propaganda which should arouse our own people, but which I suspect is very unwise unless he really has got an early election on his hands. But there it is, as we saw at Management Committee last Monday, this is Harold's mood. He has to hit back and we must all join in.

Mind you, I think Harold really is alarmed by the Tories' threat that they will make law and order one of their biggest themes. Harold didn't mention race at Monday's meeting but I thought much more frightening the Tory promise to put Commonwealth immigrants on a level with Germans and Frenchmen and, indeed, as Enoch Powell has said, the Southern Irish too. Harold is also worried that the Tories will attack us for failing to be compassionate. It's true that if the press and the Opposition work hard enough the Government can seem to lack compassion and this is even more credible when our own friends like the Child Poverty Action Group mercilessly attack us, as they have done in this week's *New Statesman*. All we have done on pensions and benefits and national superannuation is dismissed as utterly hopeless and, once we are denounced by our own side, the Tory stuff, odious as it is, becomes effective. These threats have seriously alarmed Harold.

Monday, February 9th

All morning I was helping to launch the Green Paper. We had three versions of an absolutely first-rate press release that Peter Brown had gone over very carefully. He had already got the I.T.N. and the B.B.C. lined up for news interviews and today I saw a whole list of people for specific interviews, Ann Shearer of the *Guardian*, Alan Fairclough of the *Mirror*, Anne Lapping of *New Society*, and the Editor of the *Lancet*.[1] Our presentation can make an enormous difference and we want to launch the scheme as the biggest proposal for the Health Service since 1948.

My other preoccupation today was Questions, where we were first again. John Dunwoody is shaping up wonderfully well. Poor David Ennals, that ambitious man, had only a few replies to make on Social Security. He is now immersed in the Committee Stage of the Bill, where there's a great puzzle. We know we ought to guillotine it and yet Paul Dean, our Tory opposite number, has promised to let us have it by Whitsun. Tories don't usually fail to keep their promises, so, though the Bill is inordinately long and it looks absolutely impossible to finish without a timetable, we should have it by then. Nevertheless David is, wisely I think, playing the promise along. Now why in the present circumstances should the Tories give us the Bill? Mainly, I think, because they know they need it themselves, because unless earnings-related contributions are enforced by 1972, they can't finance any pensions. Secondly, I suspect that, though they are vaguely talking about a Tory alternative, they want to leave this open so that if they win the election some legislation will exist and they will have plenty of time to decide how to amend it.

My whole team is up to scratch now. Bea Serota, who has been having appalling trouble with bronchitis, is a loyal lieutenant, quiet and efficient in the office. John Dunwoody is good, and Brian O'Malley, this strange young man from the Musicians' Union, is keen as mustard on the scheme and makes speeches everywhere, working away on the Committee. We have every reason to be pleased and Question Time is easy for us, because we are on top. Mind you, we also have very weak opponents, Robin Balneil, a gilded young man, not really interested, and young Maurice Macmillan, who is interested but totally incompetent. We wish to God we had bigger figures against us, Keith Joseph, say, or Quintin Hogg, to make us more newsy.

Tuesday, February 10th

At S.E.P. one item really interested me. The merger had been announced between I.P.C., which runs the *Daily Mirror* and all those magazines, and the Reed Group of paper manufacturers. When Cecil King was sacked in that famous *coup d'état*, Hugh Cudlipp found that running I.P.C. wasn't exactly his kind of show, so he very sensibly agreed to a merger with the associated Company, Reed, to strengthen the management of the business. The question

[1] Dr Ian Douglas-Wilson was Editor of the *Lancet* 1965–76.

was whether this should be submitted to the Monopolies Commission? This morning Barbara said it should be submitted, whereupon, before anybody else could speak, Harold launched into a great attack, saying this was political suicide. The *Daily Mirror* was the only paper likely to be loyal to us in the election and we must be political people, not mere runners of Departments. Surely it was clear that we should not refer this case and alienate the *Daily Mirror*. The merger was perfectly sensible. Roy strongly supported Harold, and then little Wedgy Benn said he was sort of on Barbara's side, but in view of Harold's remarks, not too enthusiastically. There wasn't a single supporter for a reference. Normally Barbara is a tremendous fighter, but she just sat there and didn't even reply. She seemed to have felt it her duty just to put the matter forward. Did she feel it was a departmental brief she ought to carry out, had she not adequately prepared it, had she come just with the brief and then seen how stupid it was when she got there, or had this anything to do with Ted Castle, who was an employee of I.P.C. when he worked on the *Sun*? Now that the *Sun* has been bought by Rupert Murdoch and has become a tabloid Ted has lost his job. Is there some grievance there? We all noticed this. Fred Peart threw a note across the table to me saying, 'Why on earth did she do it?' None of us knows and it was a puzzle.

The other item was Wedgy Benn's proposal for an Order in Council to regulate the West Coast route which had finally been agreed for the Concorde test flight. The President of the Board of Trade said, 'At the same time we ought to announce a ban on flying the Concorde over Britain.' It's almost inconceivable that Roy Mason should have wanted this or that anybody else in Cabinet should have supported him, but a number did. It would hardly have been sensible to announce the test flights and at the same time the banning of overland flights for this aeroplane on which we are spending hundreds of millions. Fortunately sanity prevailed. I was away at the time, but I gather that we decided to announce the test flights and postpone the announcement of the ban or its consideration.

The other item I should note for today was the publication of the White Paper assessing the economic costs of entry to the Common Market.[1] Cabinet had looked at this two weeks ago. It was an appallingly complicated, boring economic paper, which of course really proved that you can't work out the economic consequences, not even in agriculture, except within the widest possible margins. Why had this paper been produced? Well, because this was a promise we apparently made at Conference. I don't quite know

[1] The White Paper, *Britain and the European Communities: an Economic Assessment* (Cmnd 4289), estimated the cost to the visible trade balance in goods other than food at between £125 and £275 million p.a. during the transitional period, with the cost of food rising by between 18 and 26 per cent p.a., though the overall cost of living would rise by no more than 4 to 5 per cent. Paragraph 101 pointed out that the total effect could not be assessed by an arithmetical exercise of adding up favourable and unfavourable estimates in all fields, such as agriculture, community finance, trade and industry, capital and invisibles. It was stated that a conjunction of all the most favourable factors might run to £100 million and of all the most unfavourable to £1,100 million.

how we got ourselves into making it but now we were in great difficulty, because this gives the anti-Common Marketeers a tremendous fillip and a great deal of ammunition for their campaign. The papers are full of the idea that Harold Wilson may be backtracking. Is he planning, as I have often wanted him to do, to reverse his stand and fight the election on the ground that it will cost too much to go in? I've watched him very carefully and I don't think this is so. I think he and Michael Stewart are still fanatically convinced of the need to go in and of the statesmanship required to appreciate this. As on Nigeria, Harold will go for things which lose you votes and which are unpopular, because he thinks them right. In this case he clearly thinks it's right to do everything possible to get us into Europe. On the other hand, he's protecting his flank with this White Paper. He will say, 'I was truthful. I gave the costs.' I think he is also allowing the anti-Marketeers to hang themselves by being so extreme. They will now say, 'We told you so.' He thinks negotiations will start in July, and by then, whatever happens, he will have got himself a position where the Common Market isn't a losing issue for us, where Ted Heath will be suspected of wanting to go in at a higher price, and where we shall be making it quite clear that we are not prepared to pay the price and are using our newly recovered economic strength to insist on reasonable terms when the negotiations start. I think Harold is playing this fair but I shall watch with great interest what happens on that particular front.

At midday today I gave a press reception in a beautiful suite of rooms in old Admiralty House, with plenty to drink. I talked for twenty minutes and then we had questions until 1.30, all in preparation for the Statement tomorrow. Then, from 7.30 till 10.30, I sweated away trying to get a speech together for the debate on mental hospitals tomorrow evening. This adjournment debate has just been thrown in and makes the day really busy. Last week I had a meeting of all the people concerned and asked for a big dossier on mental health. It had all been put together and yesterday I asked Dr Wilkins if he would come down with me tonight so we could spend the evening together and deal with the speech. Well, a great draft had come up today but Wilkins had handed it over to a poor little hardworking assistant, who had done the whole thing because Dr Wilkins was too busy meeting a number of people on the 'main stream' project. This shows you what the doctors in the Department are like. When an administrator has a job to do for the Secretary of State, he puts everything else aside and does it as the first priority. But not a doctor. They feel totally aloof and I increasingly find that their part of the Department runs on its own and doesn't like even to feel that it is being ordered about by the Secretary of State.

Wednesday, February 11th

Management Committee again and a continuation of our discussions on strategy, for which we have now decided to have a Saturday at Chequers.

But this morning we began an extraordinary discussion. Harold started with a half-hour lecture, giving us the whole history of his relations with the B.B.C. and the battle he has been waging. Yes, he has had his success in bringing in Hill as Chairman and in replacing Hugh Greene with Charles Curran, whom I thought, when I met him at the Kaisers, a mere nincompoop, a cypher. According to Harold, down below in the Features Department under John Grist there is implacable enmity to the Government. I think there is some evidence for this. At any rate Harold talked at inordinate length about the score between Heath and himself, saying that the number of times they had appeared on television stood at four to two. First of all, Harold said, Heath had been given an unprecedented television opportunity to attack the Queen's Speech and then, after the Selsdon Park statement of the Tory programme (yes, he was still concerned with that), Heath was given appearances all over the place. Harold was going to reply to this and get back the one-one relationship. He didn't want too much of a war with the B.B.C. but he wanted to tell us this, and tell us he did. On the one hand he is obsessed with leaks from the Department and on the other with B.B.C. unfairness, so we had very little time to discuss anything else this morning.

The only suggestion I could make was that we ought to concentrate on the news and on ministerial appearances in news bulletins. I pointed out that on regional visits, if one works hard there are always two interviews, one on the B.B.C. and one on I.T.V., and they often go out both on the regional programmes and on the national programmes. This is the way Ministers can get a two-minute appearance and it may be of more help to the Government than a forty-five-minute 'Panorama' programme of the sort Harold loves. But he was as self-centred as he has ever been and as much concerned with the personal struggle between him and Heath which will decide the next election.

I'm not sure things will change. I think from the Tory point of view Heath will improve, and Harold will no longer be useful to us as a one-man show. We are no longer a Wilson Government. What is really important to us is that we have, for instance, a Home Secretary in Callaghan, so that when the Tories take law and order as one of their themes, Jim's image will probably be steadying. What we must develop is a much more routine image, with Jim as part of the team, with Roy Jenkins as our superb Chancellor. We might even have to build me up a little bit as a decent, elderly, good, wise person running Health and Social Security. Then Barbara is still popular, but of course she is in a disastrous position of failure now. Will Wedgy Benn contribute anything to the image? Yes, he is a younger person we can bring out. Denis Healey? So far, no. He's a good Defence Minister but he doesn't put himself across as anything much more. I think we shall have to put over this collective image, and this is one thing Harold may have to learn.

I not only had meetings all the morning but at lunchtime I made a big speech to the Industrial Society, some 500–600 pensions consultants and industrial experts, and here launched my first major attack on the Tories. I warned them that our Bill was a practicable scheme, which had been developed in consultation with pensions experts in private industry, and it was a lesser evil than the Tory alternative. They were flabbergasted at this first major attack. I think I've now found the line of assault, and I feel much more confident now on the pensions side.

I got down to the House to make my Statement at 3.30.[1] I had taken the trouble to give Shirley Summerskill an early look at the Green Paper and she asked the first question. The House was exceptionally friendly and the whole thing clicked, which made a tremendous difference. On our side people were warmly congratulating me and even the Tories were pleasant. It had gone like a bomb, no, not like a bomb, quietly, and I was really pleased.

But we also had Prices and Incomes Committee this afternoon, to discuss the huge N.B.P.I. Report on service pay, all this against the background of the Ford workers' threat of a strike for an increase of more than £5 a day. The Report wanted a 20 per cent increase for the military, with professionals being paid as professionals, young flight-lieutenants getting £2,500 a year for instance, and additional payments for disturbance and wandering abroad. Frightfully expensive! We had to consider both this and an enormous claim from the Post Office, with the usual problem of leaks through John Stonehouse. Then we had the teachers, who are still deadlocked and are stepping up their strike activities all over the country.

There is an avalanche of public claims. When we talked about a 3–5 per cent norm in the Prices and Incomes Paper a few weeks ago, some of us had said this was quite unrealistic and that it was bound to go to 11 or 12 per cent. Now it's going to 18–20 per cent and we sat and discussed it all the afternoon.

Last week we had an absolute deadlock with the nurses, who wouldn't take our award. Negotiations resume next Tuesday and I now had to get a new concession to offer, so I had to discuss this today, even though it wasn't on the agenda and also get it on the agenda for tomorrow's Cabinet. Here again it is important to be a really senior Minister. A junior Minister couldn't have got this discussed at P.I. today and certainly no non-Cabinet Minister would have got it on tomorrow's agenda.

Meanwhile I had to make my speech in the mental health debate. I plodded along, putting together something like a speech, and at 7 o'clock I left Prices and Incomes. Balneil started with a very moderate speech and then I made mine, much too long, forty-nine minutes even with a quarter cut out of

[1] In his Statement on the future structure of the National Health Service, the Secretary of State explained that it would not be administered by local government. There would be an administrative boundary between the Health Service and the public health and personal social services, which would continue to be run by local authorities. Health authorities would be responsible for those services where the primary skill needed was that of the health professions, while local authorities would be responsible where the primary skill was social care or support. The number of areas of the new Health Authorities would in general match those unitary authorities and metropolitan districts outside London proposed in the Maud Report and there would be special arrangements for London.

the text. It was a speech that came from the bottom of my heart and it was about something I knew from A to Z. I got very nearly a standing ovation. Afterwards everybody congratulated me and of the thirty or forty people who were there almost all of them had some special reason for knowing about mental handicap or psychiatric illness. Fascinating, and it was a very successful debate at the end of a pretty exciting day. The only annoying thing was that my three big speeches today, the lunch-time one on pensions, the Green Paper statement at 3.30 and this one at 10 o'clock, cancelled each other out in the press. Nevertheless, today's debate has been a really successful launching of our policy for the mentally handicapped.

Thursday, February 12th

Today saw the publication of the Seebohm Bill implementing the Report, so the week is still full of Health Service news. Cabinet was most extraordinary. It started with Roy warning us that there might have to be July measures or an autumn budget if the situation got out of control. If all four of these public service claims were met in full he would have to warn us solemnly that all the work and achievements of the past year would be undone, and he must therefore advise Cabinet to halt all the Services' claims, the Post Office, the nurses', and not to give way to the teachers. Roy said it in a very stirring and moving way and after this high-minded speech the Prime Minister intervened, time after time emphasizing the political aspect. 'I can be as statesmanlike as any of you,' he said, 'but really we must look at politics now. What about having the Services' claim phased in three stages, so as to get most of it after October? Let's think in the context of an October election. If we lose the Tories have the problem and if we win at least we'll have a new Parliament behind us.'

Next each of us specifically stated our claims and then there was a general discussion. It pretty soon became clear that I should get something for the nurses. I asked for 20 per cent and I shall get it in one year or in eighteen months. It was also clear that Denis Healey had so bored P.I. yesterday, so bored the Cabinet today, that he wasn't going to get all he wanted. The Post Office was bound to get their claim because John Stonehouse knows how to leak and how to present a *fait accompli* to the Cabinet. As for the teachers, Ted Short is such a bloody stupid, awkward cove and as a teacher himself knows too much about it that he is going to have to drag out a prolonged strike, which he doesn't seem to be able to settle. We went on and on. Fred Peart said we had to listen very carefully to the Chancellor but Roy had few other supporters until George Thomson came out in support of the Establishment. Finally Harold Lever said, 'This makes no sense because, from what the Chancellor says, we can't with the best will in the world halt the wage demands now we have destroyed the whole of the prices and incomes policy. We've got to face the fact that Roy's demanding the impossible. We must give these wage claims and anyway they won't do us a great deal of harm.

The difference between what Roy is allowing and what the Ministries have in mind is so small in terms of the total national economy that it can't really make any difference. No world banker is going to undermine the pound because of 3 or 4½ per cent on a particular public service wage claim.' That was pretty powerful and then Peter Shore came in from his independent standpoint. It was clear that no one felt Roy was doing anything more than making a gesture and it was embarrassing to see on the one side the Chancellor being high-minded and on the other the Prime Minister playing politics.

Then I made one of my mistakes. I felt fairly safe because the nurses were, as Barbara had said, *sui generis* and I thought I would get somewhere near what I wanted. I thought the whole thing was over and I was sick of Cabinet so I slipped out to tell Bea Serota and the others that we were all right and had our nurses' claim in our pocket. This was a great mistake because one should never leave a Cabinet meeting before the summing up. I found later that after I left Willie Ross had said that we were asking too much for the English nurses and we ought to give them a bit less than 20 per cent. I discovered that the Cabinet minutes said we had reached agreement that the exact amount which the nurses should be allowed to have should now be fixed by a conference between Roy, Barbara and myself, and that if we didn't agree it could come back to Cabinet. Just imagine! The nurses' negotiations start at 12 o'clock next Tuesday morning and Cabinet meets at 10.0, so what was put down in the minutes is clearly quite unrealistic. I must now ring up Barbara and Roy and go to see Roy, and I hope I can get what I want, though I've been told by Barbara that Roy will ask for 19 instead of 20 per cent.

This illustrates my basic criticism of the whole of this prices and incomes policy and the idea that you can run the delicate operation of wage negotiations either by the P.I. Committee or, even worse, by the Cabinet. After all, I had given the P.I. Committee three choices, they settled on (c) and (c) has failed. Now I want (a) and Roy wants to cut us down somewhere below (b), but this haggling absolutely defeats the whole object, because time after time the Minister says, 'I can get so much,' the Committee or Cabinet says, 'No, you must try for so much,' you do and fail, so you come back and say, 'May I try my original plan?' but by then the original has somehow been undermined and you can't even get that. In the end you have to settle for even more. I see now it's no good, you can't do it this way, and nurses' pay is a perfect example of how it happens.

This evening I found myself at the Bow Group, the Fabian Society of the Conservatives, to talk to them about the N.H.S. They had asked me four months ago and, by extraordinary luck, here I was speaking the day after the Green Paper had been published. They asked me to dine at the Cavalry Club, a magnificent place in Piccadilly, where I found standing at the bar elegant young men who then took me upstairs for an excellent dinner. Out after that to the Royal Commonwealth Association, where I found they had gathered about 160 intelligent, prosperous, upper-class men and women. I gave them a racy account of what we are doing and enormously enjoyed myself. I discovered I was the first Labour Minister they had ever asked to the Bow Group. I explained why we couldn't put the Health Service under local government because I couldn't just destroy the compact Nye Bevan had made in 1948 to give the consultants the key position. I was fairly confident because no journalists were there, and as Bow Group meetings are off the record nothing can be printed. But in a way I felt uneasy at the fact that I didn't feel wholly out of place in that company, having that kind of discussion.

Friday, February 13th

I was to catch a 9.30 train to Southampton for one of these formal D.H.S.S. expeditions, so after a little quick work in the Ministry I got on the train to find this time not five or six of the Department but only Peter Brown and the Inspector of Anatomy, Dr Dooley, a queer, remote, eccentric creature, and Robin, my Private Secretary. At Southampton 1,000 people had come from all over Hampshire to a huge ten-pin bowling rink, where I made my speech explaining the Green Paper before laying the foundation stone for a new teaching hospital. Actually the stone was in front of me on the dais and had to be carried out afterwards to the site two and a half miles away but the ceremony was a success, and what warmed me with satisfaction was that a really interesting Green Paper was being sold to the public.

I was a little puzzled when the SAMO said to me, 'I shall be on the train to Reading with you,' and after all the speeches were made and I had received a delegation, we got on the train and, sure enough, John Revans was there. He said, 'Look, the moment I saw your report I knew that you had made a political decision that the boundaries of the Health Authorities should be conterminous with the boundaries of the new local government unitary authorities and the new secondary authorities of the metropolitan areas. I'm telling the others that we must accept this decision and make what we can of it. I've come to discuss how it can be done.' All the way to Reading Revans discussed with me practical ways to get regional councils of the right kind to work under my new set up. 'Look,' I said, 'shall we set up a working party?' 'Yes,' he said, 'if you'll take the chair.' By the time I got to Reading I had clear in my mind how we can transform the vague structural ideas of the Green Paper into a real flesh-and-blood structure which actually makes sense. I owe that to Revans. The rest of the SAMOs have said, 'We can't have our R.H.B. system destroyed,' but he has said, 'Right, let's find out how to make the new system work,' and I have every hope we shall actually be able to do so. I said to Revans, 'What are you doing at Reading?' and he replied, 'I'm going back now.' He had just come all that way because he wanted to talk to me.

When I got home there was a great parcel with twelve beautiful cut glasses, instead of the confounded commemorative pestle and mortar I might have expected. I gather from Anne that Southampton had rung her up and discussed how to give me this very nice present.

Saturday, February 14th

It's been a beautiful week apart from blizzards and three or four inches of snow on Thursday. A lovely, shiny, brilliant week, freezing all the time, with heavy frost at night. I had a wonderful walk by myself this afternoon and this evening we had the farm dinner, which we should have had before Christmas, when I was ill. Last year we had it in the pub but some of them got drunk and began to attack Mr P. in the most undignified way. I said that this year we'd have it at home, so we brought in a trestle table from the village hall, and Anne and Brenda (her old nurse) had the whole job of preparing a meal for sixteen people. 'Now,' I said, 'we'll avoid trouble this time by having the serious business before dinner.' First I told them about the farm and then Mr P. followed up by telling them how we had distributed the profits and what their bonus would be. It all went very well but the evening got longer and longer and they stayed on and bickered with him about the whole routine in the cowshed. Then Mr P. began to needle me about the farm price review.

Now it so happened that this afternoon I had time to read the paper on the farm price review and it also happened that one evening last week Cledwyn Hughes had slipped in from his room in the Commons, which is next door to mine, and explained how he and the Chancellor had reached a deal. They had got together last October, without any outside consultation, their officials had met and a sensible agreement had been made so that for the first time this year's farm price review is an intelligible, clear-cut paper, working out the real questions and giving the answers. So this evening I knew the total amount which the Government is prepared to concede to the farmers, and when Mr P. went on provoking me, saying, 'What is your personal opinion of what we shall get?' I finally said, 'Oh, you are ignorant if you think I'm going to answer that kind of question.' By then it was nearly midnight and Mr P. walked out with his wife. I'm sure there will be trouble because I insulted him before his men. I feel miserable about it and I shall immediately write him a little letter of apology. There it is, one of those things that happen with him.

Sunday, February 15th

In the middle of the farm dinner last night, Jennifer Jenkins rang up to ask the whole family to lunch today and I jumped to the conclusion that Roy wanted to talk to me privately and that he was reissuing the invitation I forgot the other day. Off we went on a brilliant morning and as we sped along I read *Our Mutual Friend* aloud. We had a very good lunch with Roy and Jennifer and Edward, his youngest son, who is at a London grammar school, and afterwards, as we all sat together in the sitting room, I waited and waited, thinking there would be a moment when Jennifer would say to Anne, 'Let's go out with the children for a walk.' But there wasn't.

Then Roy suddenly said, 'Well now, Dick, are you standing at the next election?' 'Yes,' I said. This was awkward because of course I have made my agreement with Jock Campbell for the *New Statesman*, but my reply came quite naturally. Next Roy asked me what I thought the chances were and I found he didn't want to talk to me about the budget as I had expected, or to brief me secretly, but just to chat about my ideas for the future and the reasons why I was standing. I found myself saying, 'You and I, Roy, are the only two who have an alternative career outside politics.' But he wasn't telling me anything, only trying always to find out what my view was of a summer or an autumn date, of our chances, of what we should do after the election. I made it clear that I didn't think there was much chance of winning and that it will depend entirely on what he can do in the budget, where I don't see much room for manoeuvre. But if we don't win I shan't have any great enthusiasm for political life afterwards. I didn't really tell Roy more than that. Then we discussed Harold and the other people in the Cabinet and agreed that Michael Stewart should retire this time and that Tony Crosland is neither an Establishment figure nor like me a really independent figure, but a man with no future outside politics who yet makes himself awkward in politics. We agreed that Peter Shore has his uses now.

During this conversation I thought, 'Why have I motored over? It's been a lovely drive and a lovely lunch but why has Roy brought me here?' When I got home I rang Nicky Kaldor, partly because I want to get him and Tommy over to hear their expert opinion on the economic prospects for the next six, nine and twelve months, but also to tell him a little about this conversation with Roy. Nicky said, 'I've been seeing Roy this week and I know Tommy is seeing him next week. There's something queer about this. It's unsettling. I think Roy feels that if he stays on he wants the leadership of the party.' An hour later Nicky rang me up again. 'Roy was trying you out. He wants to know whether you'd be there to support him.' I wonder if that is right. I've asked Nicky to come tomorrow evening and explain things further. This may all be imagination but I think there is something in it. It was very odd today. We had lunch and the family sat about. It was very boring for the children and out of it nothing came except chat about my prospects in the election. I suppose the real answer is that Roy is now making up his mind about his budget. He can be cautious and conventional and keep his reputation as Chancellor, making an election defeat absolutely certain and keeping himself in a position to seize the leadership afterwards, or he can conceivably take the other risk and have a more expansionist budget, which could give us a chance of election victory but could also ruin his reputation if it went wrong. I wonder. I hope I didn't say anything which would influence him one way or the other.

I have now arranged with Anne that next Wednesday evening we will have a dinner at Vincent Square with Peter Shore, Wedgy Benn, Barbara and possibly Harold Lever. The trouble is that we may be too late because Management Committee is meeting on Tuesday. Every day counts now. Nevertheless the view we take and the pressure we make might be quite important because I know how susceptible Roy is, and how decisions hang in the balance and in their critical moments are influenced by the pressures which come up at the time. It's been an interesting week.

By the way, when I got back home on Friday, I found that Jennie Hall had sent me down an enormous transcription of diary. It happened to cover the crucial period from June to July '66, that period just after the '66 election when we threw everything away in four months, when I was one of those, along with Barbara and Roy, who wanted a floating pound and we were defeated by the coalition of Harold and Jim and George Brown went out in bravado.

Today at lunch Roy was saying, 'It was July '66, that's when we should have had the floating pound, that's when Callaghan and Harold defeated us. I used to like Callaghan and to get on with him. Of course, one is bound to have a bad relationship between the Chancellor and his successor and now I can't stand him. I can't help it. I know he is devious and intriguing, all the things Harold is accused of being but which Jim really is. But one can't help liking talking to him, although one knows how tricky he is and how totally responsible he and Harold were for the disasters of 1966.' Now, when he says that, is Roy thinking that this time he himself might with Harold be responsible for the disaster of 1970? Will his budget be disastrous, not in the sense that it is too easy but that it is too tough and determines our election defeat? These are the issues which seem to me to be coming up now, issues which will be decided in the next two or three weeks.

Monday, February 16th

Our negotiations with the nurses began today and the most awkward thing was a leak which was splashed all over the *Daily Mail* and the *Sketch* on Saturday morning, and has now spread to the other papers. It was an extraordinarily detailed story showing an understanding of something that I think Bea and I had not fully understood, that though we had been permitted to offer 24 per cent, split into 15 per cent the first year and 9 per cent the second, we had actually made an offer of only 22 per cent. Where did the leak come from? I don't think for a moment it was from our office because it certainly didn't come from John Dunwoody or Bea Serota, least of all from me. I was in Southampton all Friday. The trouble is that there are just too many Parliamentary Secretaries at the meeting of Prices and Incomes, six or seven of them. Harold suspects Denis Howell and I think this is probably right. I suspect David Ennals just a little bit and I think this is right too. However it was a confounded nuisance and made all our negotiations very difficult.

Mrs Cameron, the Chairman of the management side of the Whitley Council, was white with anger. Bea had to placate them all and explain that the leak was as embarrassing to us as it was to them.

I had to talk to Barbara and Roy about this before Cabinet tomorrow. I was anxious because though the Cabinet minutes were fairly satisfactory they quite clearly obliged me to choose between time or money, between 20 per cent in one year or 24 per cent spread over two years, which came to very nearly the same thing. Though I had this choice I had already heard rumours in the Department that Roy would try to whittle it down and, sure enough, when I went into the Treasury he said, 'I don't think you ought to go for the 20 per cent, it's very embarrassing. It will put the nurses well above the Forces and we don't want to see the 20 per cent barrier broken in one year.' 'Well,' I said, 'would you rather have us doing a year and a half?' No, that was not on. Then Roy suggested that we offer the nurses 18 per cent rather than 20 for the first year and 4 per cent for the second year. I finally said, 'Look here, the negotiations are tomorrow and anyway I'm not doing them, it's the Whitley Council.' Barbara said, 'Yes, you can't change the offer. It would be back-seat driving.' They were quite reasonable so I got a note made of what they wanted and said I would certainly start by putting the initial offer as a two-year proposal, then reduce it to eighteen months, and do everything to avoid the 20 per cent in one year, but I was sure that 20 per cent in one year is what the staff side really want.

This was really the Chancellor of the Exchequer's day, as he pointed out at 5 o'clock when I saw him for the third time in twenty-four hours. By some extraordinary accident we had another appointment to discuss tax concessions in relation to pensions. Roy got what he wanted. I couldn't remove the unforgivable anomaly that whereas in the case of private pensions contributions are free of tax, this is not true of state pensions. I got him at least to admit that this was a mess and to agree that he would announce that it would be reconsidered in the general review four years from now. Then he asked all the others to clear off and told me he just wanted to say he had received my letter setting out Brian Abel-Smith's proposals for reducing income tax in the most beneficial way for the largest number of people and to ask me if I would tell Brian that this was the ninth scheme he had received. He wasn't going to use it but he promised me that it had been seriously considered.

This evening Nicky came round to Vincent Square and we talked. He was very well-informed. He had been to see Roy last week to put to him a most ingenious plan for a massive income tax reduction for people below average wages, the cost to be carried by S.E.T. increases or increases in the employer's contribution. Nicky had seen Roy and the Inland Revenue and the Treasury and he described Roy's extraordinary coyness. Then he had lunched alone with Jennifer, Roy's wife, during the week and they had discussed Roy's future. In Nicky's view, the real difficulty was whether Roy wanted to win the election or not. Did Roy feel he wanted to take the risk of making the massive tax reductions which would be necessary to win the election or did he feel that he should be the Iron Chancellor and do the only correct thing, which couldn't possibly win, but with the hope that if we lost he might take Harold's place? Nicky had got out of these talks with Roy and Jennifer, as far as I could see, without committing himself to any firm opinion.

Tuesday, February 17th

At 9.30 we were to have Management to discuss Barbara's papers on Prices and Incomes and something on decimals but at 9.15 we were suddenly told that the meeting had been cancelled and I gathered that Barbara had a heavy cold and wanted to stay at home for the day. The moment I heard of the postponement I drove straight to the Elephant and Castle to get in an extra hour's work. I was able to see George Godber about abortion clinics, Alan Marre on the timetable of the Green Paper schedules and my own staff. As Callaghan said, when we eventually met at 11 o'clock, having an extra hour is a wonderful thing, which is an interesting comment on the life of a Cabinet Minister.

At Cabinet the only real thing we had to discuss was decimals. A minor campaign has been worked up in the *Financial Times* and other papers for saving the sixpence.[1] Mind you, what we are doing is pretty awful because against the advice of the experts Callaghan has gone for a decimal system where £1 remained the equivalent of twenty old shillings rather than ten. There is absolutely no doubt that this is the wrong decision and it has been complicated by the fact that we have got rid of the half-crown and the sixpence, which means for instance that the G.L.C. has coolly announced that the lowest bus or tube fare will in future be a shilling, five new pence. This has caused consternation. Roy said he would try to do something about this, although of course the coin-machine people insist that they don't want new machines to be used for old sixpences. Roy said on the whole he had got a decent Statement for Bill Rodgers, saying that we would allow the sixpence to go on for a certain length of time, letting it run until we finally made up our minds.

Then there was a tortuous, difficult issue about the transfer of London

[1] Decimal currency was to be introduced in February 1971 and although the public had, with some qualms, accepted the replacement of the 10*s*. note by a hexagonal 50 n.p. piece and of the traditional 1*s*. and florin by 5 n.p. and 10 n.p. pieces, there was considerable unhappiness at the threatened disappearance of the sixpence. The Decimal Currency Board maintained that to retain the sixpenny piece (the equivalent of 2½ n.p.) would complicate the new arrangements. The Commons debated the subject on February 19th and, after strong parliamentary pressure from both sides of the House, Mr Jenkins eventually announced that he had asked the Board to report again on whether it might be desirable to retain the sixpence as legal tender, at least for a transitional period. The Board unanimously advised the Chancellor to abandon the sixpence but Mr Jenkins stated on April 20th that the Government had decided to retain the coin for at least two years after decimalization day.

County Council houses to the boroughs, but I went off to the negotiations with the Whitley Council. The leak had been a confounded nuisance and made the negotiations very difficult. We started late and all that happened was that the management side religiously put the offers in the order which we had suggested and there was no interest in anything until we got to the 20 per cent, which was clinched. There was some doubt at the beginning whether the 20 per cent, which is an average, wouldn't be postponed while the staff side took a week to consider it. Thank God, we've avoided that. By 4 o'clock I was able to walk down from 21a[1] to Harold's room to tell him we'd got the nurses in our pocket. I went in and there he was sitting at his place in the middle of the table with at the end of the table, about fifteen yards from him, his sister, the headmistress of a primary school in Cornwall.[2] They were sitting a long way away from each other, discussing things, I suppose. I barged in, gave the news and went out, leaving this odd pair together.

All through Monday and Tuesday I have had a problem with B.B.C. television. They had arranged to have a one-hour documentary programme about nurses last night and then at 8 o'clock tonight the 'Man Alive' programme was to do forty or fifty minutes more. I was told they had already invited Clive Jenkins, Jack Dash, Patricia Veale and a lot of militants, with some fourteen or fifteen nurses, and I had been asked to join in the mêlée.[3] If I wouldn't do it they said they'd ask Balneil. I was a bit doubtful myself and at the time they asked me I didn't know whether we would have an agreement in our pocket or not. However I took a gamble and said that whatever happened I would go on, because if we hadn't had an agreement and there was a terrible schemozzle there would have been a fracas anyway, and I couldn't have sent Bea Serota to face that. So I went down at 6.0 this evening and spent from 6.0 to 9.0 doing the filming. First I was shown last night's programme, quite a decent, straight, colour documentary on the life of a nurse, and hardly had it finished when I was taken downstairs to a big studio where across a circular floor, there was a kind of Greek theatre with some fifty or sixty people massed in rows one behind the other, including a lot of nurses and a lot of soloists from all the militant organizations. 'Man Alive' is said to be quite a tough B.B.C. programme, which enjoys being really sensational and hounding people, and I was supposed to be the man alive. Fortunately, however, by the time I arrived the agreement had been announced and the nurses were therefore faced with a *fait accompli*. Their own leaders and negotiators had agreed the terms with me. It wasn't too bad because they all

[1] Crossman's room in the House of Commons.

[2] Miss Marjorie Wilson.

[3] Clive Jenkins, General Secretary of the Association of Supervisory Staffs, Executives and Technicians (ASSET) 1961–8, was Joint General Secretary of the Association of Scientific, Technical and Managerial Staffs (A.S.T.M.S.) 1968–70 and since 1970 has been General Secretary. He has been a member of the T.U.C. General Council since 1974. Jack Dash, a communist and a T.G.W.U. shop steward, was an unofficial leader of the dockets.

fell to quarrelling among themselves. I thought Clive Jenkins discredited himself and I gaped open-mouthed when he said, 'My God, those doctors, they don't know how to negotiate salaries.' I must say the idea that the doctors haven't done well for themselves without Clive Jenkins's help has a sort of irony about it. It was lucky, I did well, and as I came out at 9.0 with a lot of hysterical nurses foaming round me, I was relieved.

Wednesday, February 18th

The result of my being successful is that there was nothing much in the press this morning, apart from a few stories, 'Nurses' Settlement Arrived At.' Nobody said it was too big and nobody really accused us of being lavish. The award was just assumed to be sensible and therefore it received no prominence whatsoever. I must admit to a tremendous relief, though. All Saturday, Sunday, Monday and Tuesday I had been fussing about this and on Monday night I didn't sleep very well.

We had a meeting of O.P.D. to discuss pensions for civil servants serving overseas but it was only interesting for what Burke Trend said to me as we walked away together afterwards. He said, 'We spent a whole hour on this in the official committee (he thinks an hour a very long time to discuss it) and we couldn't agree, so I'm not very surprised that you couldn't.'

In the evening Anne and I gave our dinner at Vincent Square. We haven't dined there for a long time but we got the house warmed up and Anne brought up the food and wine, and I brought over the gin and the sherry from my store in the Ministry. Peter Shore was there, Wedgy Benn, Barbara and Tommy Balogh, and we managed to give them all an extremely good time. Again, the whole discussion wasn't really about policy but about Roy, and this was right, because never has the Government been so wholly dependent upon one person as we are upon him. I don't myself believe that Harold has an undue influence on Roy. Harold has hardly any influence and Roy can do what he bloody well likes *vis-à-vis* the P.M., as we saw last week when Harold made that deplorable exhibition of himself in our discussion on prices and incomes. He played politics quite openly, playing into Roy's hands, and Roy had said, 'Let us be dignified and clean and decent.' Roy has an absolute choice between being a stern, severe Chancellor who doesn't do much or of having a smashing budget which really gives us a chance of victory. I think it is true that his choice will largely depend on his calculation of what will happen after the election and that this explains why on Sunday he asked me about my intentions and thoughts after the election. I suppose it is also true that when I showed I was unlikely to go on in Opposition he lost interest because I guess that he was thinking to himself whether he could talk to me about his own chances afterwards. Now it's true that after a defeat the chances of a change of leadership are somewhat greater and Roy clearly feels that he has some chance of becoming leader. I also think he feels that if the election is a success, the whole thing will continue in the same way with Harold and Jim at the top and Roy as number three. Then he might join me in writing books. I believe that is what is in his mind.

The result of my talk with Nicky and my talks with Barbara and Peter and Tommy tonight were all the same. We decided that we had to persuade Roy that his future depends on a really good budget, that a high-minded, Iron Chancellor's budget would ruin his chances of the leadership of the party. This I think to be true. In one sense Roy is in such a weak position with the party, so remote from it, that there would be a tremendous revulsion against him if he produced a budget which couldn't win the election. Barbara and I will no doubt speak to him and try to have a dinner for him next week or the week after and we shall have to see where he stands. But there is very little doubt, and we all seem to share the same view, that he is uncertain. Nicky feels that Roy hasn't yet revealed his intentions to the Treasury nor to the Inland Revenue, and that Jennifer is anxious about him and would like him to be all out for the party and for a victory this time. I think the rest of us all feel the same about this strange, inscrutable young man, this extraordinary mixture of ingenuousness, feminine petulance and iron determination.

Thursday, February 19th

I'm still rather mystified about what happened after our discussion on decimals last Tuesday, because this morning the *Daily Mail* had an exclusive story that Cabinet had changed its mind and decided to save the sixpence. I don't really know very much about this because I had only been half attending but apparently we weren't firmly committed to saving the sixpence or even committed to saying it would run for two or three years, only to considering the possibility of consulting the Decimal Currency Board. The Tories had put down for this afternoon a half-day debate in protest,[1] and the unfortunate Bill Rodgers was now faced with an inaccurate leak which went much further than he was entitled to go. He ballsed up the whole thing in the House and there was a terrible mess and a terrible row in the P.L.P. meeting. I think this row will stumble on and the leak will be examined with great ferocity. We have had a series of extraordinary leaks in the last ten days, including those on nurses' pay and the Post Office.

In Cabinet we had the farm price review. At last Sunday's lunch Roy had confirmed Cledwyn Hughes's story to me, and said that after twenty years agriculture had for the first time come clean to the Treasury, worked the whole thing out and educated Roy in the facts of life. He had said, 'This is the only good thing Peter Shore has ever done. He's the Chairman of the Agricultural Committee and he was insisting on having an official committee which would work to him. They were so angry with this that Agriculture and the Treasury had come together.' Poor old Peter Shore had been faced with

[1] The motion, regretting the system of decimalization of the currency to which the Government had committed the country, was defeated by 284 votes to 240.

a *fait accompli*, an unheard-of thing, and there was nothing for his Committee to do except to give unanimous support to the deal. When we came down to it this morning there was really nothing to discuss and I was able to go across to the Standing Committee on my Bill.

I found that Tam had paired me, but I thought I'd better spend the morning there. After an hour I walked out again feeling that I was doing no good, because as I was paired I couldn't even vote. David Ennals and Brian O'Malley are perfectly happy without me, happier in fact, because they like to get the credit and they want to run the Committee themselves. On the other hand, I don't feel quite happy about never being there. Balneil had absented himself too and it is a nice question how far a senior Cabinet Minister should or should not be present at the Standing Committee of a major Bill of this kind. Instead I struggled away at a speech I have to deliver tomorrow morning to the National Association on Mental Health and then at lunch-time I went along to the House of Lords to see Alma Birk, the Chairman of my Health Education Committee. She is a tremendous chatterbox, but she is serious-minded and a great girl for birth control and modern progressive methods of education, and we went through all our schemes together.

I had to go back punctually at 2.30 because I was told that the two Permanent Secretaries were coming to see me. I had been very much impressed by what John Revans had told me on the way back from Southampton and had spoken to the Department about the idea of a working party with myself in the chair. This morning I received a minute from Alan Marre saying he wondered whether I was wise to be in the chair, and whether it shouldn't be the C.M.O., with the Secretary of State held in reserve. 'Come and see me,' I said, and into 21a there came rather sheepishly Clifford Jarrett, Alan Marre, the C.M.O., all the top brass, to plead with me that it was unwise for the Secretary of State to do this, that it would be dangerous and would upset people outside if they were excluded from the working party. I spent twenty minutes explaining that this wasn't a working party in their sense of the word, but a brains trust, and that I couldn't work without bringing in people from outside. I had already had this in PEP, and you could call this PEP Mark II if you like, an informal think-tank, not a formal departmental working party. I suppose I got them to agree but then they immediately started filling it up with people I have never heard of. I have had to refuse to sign their letters now because if it's going to be the kind of brains trust I want it must be of like-minded people, who can work with me easily and familiarly. It is strange how deeply suspicious civil servants are of people being brought in from outside and of having a mixture of civil servants and outsiders to think out new policies.

After that we went downstairs to a fascinating meeting on our figures for the PESC exercise. We had already been instructed to send in our figures for 1971/2, '72/3, '73/4 and '74/5, and our anticipations of the amount of money which the Health Service requires for the next three years, because '71/2 is pretty well fixed. I had taken a good look at the papers in the early morning. (The time I spend between 6.30 and 8.30 in the morning is vital now. If I am in good form and wake up in time it enormously improves my contribution to all these meetings.) I was able to say, 'Look, gentlemen, for the last two years we have written in purely formal figures here but it is now time we put in serious figures, because I can tell you the Health Service is on a shoe-string. We shall have to have major increases in '72/3, '73/4, '74/5, and we really must insist on these if the Health Service is not to break down.' This is the kind of thing a Minister can decide. If I hadn't said this they would have filled in an estimate a little bit higher than the Treasury's figure and we would have been tightly held within the PESC straitjacket and committed to staying there. Now I have forced them to put in writing a much higher figure, which I shall be O.K.'ing early next week, and then, to justify these figures, a policy paper will go straight to S.E.P. It will explain that while one can constrict National Health Service expenditure for two or three years, as we are doing now, after that one has either got to cut the service back in vital particulars or let it go ahead. Even if we are going to have the Health Service running on the same principles as we have now, we shall have to get a larger part of the national product and a larger share of the budget. This is an issue which I shall have to fight for. Dick Bourton, Alan Marre, Bea Serota, John Dunwoody and Nicky Kaldor and Brian Abel-Smith would have liked to have warned me about this but none of them had brought the matter up. It was I who had to do it and that is what a Minister is for.

I then had a long and rather desultory delegation from the National Association for Mental Health, and then a visit from Maurice Hackett,[1] who came in to tell me how to win the election. His idea was to see that all old age pensioners got half their fares paid on all public transport however far they went. It was a marvellous idea and he was full of it. I think it would be a winner but it would also be rather expensive. After this I went out to the Garrick to give Dom Mintoff dinner.[2] I am arranging to borrow his house in Malta for the family at Whitsun and he filled me in with Maltese politics. When we left at 10.0 there was Peter Smithson waiting outside with my car and three sinister-looking characters waiting to collect Dom. Dom is a little party boss, powerful, shrewd, intensely intellectual, the son of a cook in the docks. He is part of the Malta mafia and so are they and I enormously enjoyed going out for an evening with him.

[1] Sir Maurice Hackett (Kt 1970) was Chairman of the N.W. Metropolitan R.H.B. 1965–1974.

[2] Dom Mintoff, Leader of the Maltese Labour Party since 1949, was Prime Minister and Minister of Finance 1955–8 and Leader of the Opposition 1962–71. Since 1971 he has been Prime Minister and Minister of Foreign Affairs. Crossman had been a member of the Malta Round Table Conference in 1955 and he and Mintoff were old friends.

Friday, February 20th

I had an important meeting in the morning with the Registrar-General. We have always had a worry with this fellow. For some reason the Registrar-General is never a trained statistician but a sort of squashy humanist from the Ministry of Health, who is perhaps good at Latin verse. The person who really runs the thing is a tough, ruthless lady, whom we must check all the time because these two are hell-bent on providing Powell with the statistics he really wants. We had only just stopped them doing this four months ago. Now they were producing the new draft of their projections of immigrant figures. I must say we had got a lot of our own way. True, they had described one of the lines, the one which showed the greatest number of coloured children, as the most realistic projection, but that was easily taken out. Nicky, Brian and David Ennals were all there and we got the officials tight in our procrustean bed, so that was a useful job.

After that I saw Dr Baker, who now clocks in once a fortnight and ticks off the things for which he wants my approval. He is an extremely efficient man and he had just come back after his first visit to a hospital. He introduced his team and I was able to thank them. This is probably one of the most exciting and successful things I have done. But my main job today was to lunch first in the House of Commons with the Executive Committee of the National Association for Mental Health and then to address their conference. I had a tremendous struggle getting my speech into line and lunch was frightful, rowing with the Executive Committee all the way through on everything under the sun. But I made my speech and answered questions and wound up what they obviously thought was a very good conference, before I caught my train to Rugby.

Here I was to give my usual address to the boys at Rugby School. On my first visit President Kennedy was murdered, on the second George Brown resigned, but this time, so far as I know, nothing disastrous happened. We had a new headmaster,[1] a curious young man about thirty-seven or thirty-eight, very quiet, very thoughtful, almost a parody of a high-minded public school boy, with a high-minded Roedean wife and four children. I had never seen the headmaster's study before. It is Thomas Arnold's study and looks out over the rugby football field. It was fascinating. We had drinks and a very good dinner and then I did my turn with the boys, describing what it is like to be a Minister. Afterwards we settled down and I found myself talking mainly to a very keen young man who teaches economics to the fifth form and has just got himself made the Labour candidate for Warwick and Leamington.[2] He was full of the story of Warwick University, where the students have been holding a sit-in in the Registry, and have broken open the files and found that Jack Butterworth has been corresponding with industrialists in Coventry and in America, discussing his staff and his undergraduates in a

[1] James S. Woodhouse, Headmaster of Rugby School since 1967.

[2] J. T. Watkinson.

most undesirable way.[1] I am in two minds about this. I deeply feel that no one can run a university or a Ministry if private files are broken open and people are allowed to see confidential letters. On the other hand I have also felt for a long time that Jack Butterworth would kowtow to industrialists with no kind of scruples about academic independence because he wants them to give money to the University. A lot of his staff rather suspected him of this and in the political climate there is at Warwick the discovery of these letters seemed to clinch this suspicion. Yet the manner of their discovery makes life absolutely impossible.

Saturday, February 21st

I drove back from Rugby last night with Anne, and got off again this morning at 9.15 to drive to Birmingham for an all-day T.U.C. conference on pensions. There was a good gathering of delegates, perhaps a couple of hundred, and I was able to deal with their questions before I drove home after lunch. Everybody felt a bit sore at my going off and leaving the Chairman to fend for himself, with my Regional Manager to long-stop for him on questions, but I have a streaming cold and I insisted on having some time off. I think that at my age I have to be careful about these things.

Sunday, February 22nd

It's strange that whereas my rating in the Gallup Poll last August was −14, I have now crept up to −6, and if things go on like this I shouldn't be surprised to get into a plus position by April.[2] I think we are doing rather better in the Department and I am doing better than I ever did as Leader of the House, but not as well as I did as Minister of Housing and Local Government. The poll is generally more encouraging. Though it was advertised in the *Daily Telegraph* as showing a Tory lead, the really striking fact is that during this very trying period of the year their lead has not increased. I thought it was quite good that we have held the figure there and I also thought that it was a sign of strength that we were almost able to disregard the Tuesday trade figures.[3] Not only climatically is this a trying time of year for the Government but it also happens that the trade unions are appallingly

[1] The demonstrations at Warwick spread to Oxford and then to other universities, where students raided university offices in a search for files on the political activities of students. On February 27th the university vice-chancellors met representatives from the National Union of Students, led by their President, Mr Jack Straw. As a result of the meeting the Chairman of the Committee of Vice-Chancellors and Principals, the Vice-Chancellor of Durham University, Sir Derman Christopherson, announced that in future details of a student's academic record would be open to the individual concerned. He added that in his own mind he was quite certain that no university kept files on the political or religious affiliations of students.

[2] In February 1970 the N.O.P. showed a 10·5 per cent lead for the Conservatives, compared with 6·7 per cent in January, the Gallup poll showed that the Tory lead had fallen to 5·5 per cent, from 6 per cent in January, and the O.R.C. poll showed a fall to 12 per cent from the 15 per cent Tory lead in January.

[3] A £7 million deficit in the balance of payments was recorded in February.

out of control. The Ford strike is finally off after a series of crises that have dominated the week. We had competition between Jack Jones and Scanlon of the two big unions, the T.G.W.U. and the A.E.U., and then the confusion caused by a factory at Swansea which voted by a small majority to stay out, when the two big factories voted to go back. We had Reg Birch playing his Maoist-Communist role on the Executive,[1] and it was altogether wholly characteristic of the kind of chaos that we have in the trade union movement.

Meanwhile the teachers go on embedding themselves deeper and deeper in their strike and every proposal which Ted Short puts forward for placating them fails, as every time we warn him it will. There is now a serious threat that they will stop the O-level examinations. The odd fact is that we all almost wrote off Tuesday's trade figures, although they were good, because we are now so anxious about wage inflation.

The other big political story this week has been Europe. The White Paper was brought out with a bump, giving the most appallingly powerful figures to the anti-Europeans. Yesterday evening Harold made a big speech to a Labour Party rally,[2] a very balanced, skilful performance. I spent a lot of last week with Arthur Gavshon and David Watt telling them that Harold just wouldn't play double about Europe and that he still wanted to go in, but I also added that he would take full advantage of the situation. He certainly did so yesterday, demonstrating that whereas we were willing to go in only if the price was not too high, the Tories were prepared to pay the price whether we went in or not. This is one of his favourite phrases and he brought it out again today in a long interview after the 1 o'clock news. Heaven knows why he suddenly decided to do this. I suspect he wants to back-pedal on Europe.

In fact the only news he gave at lunchtime was that he wouldn't go to see the South African cricketers play this summer.[3] In a way this shows you the

[1] Reg Birch, a member of the A.U.E.W. Executive Committee, was originally a communist but became the founder of the British Maoist Party.

[2] At Camden town hall in London. See *Wilson*, pp. 761–4.

[3] Opponents of apartheid, led by a young South African, Mr Peter Hain, had been demonstrating against the South African Springbok rugger team, as part of a campaign to stop the forthcoming visit of the South African cricket team, who were to play in the Test Matches. The cricket authority, the M.C.C., declared that politics should be kept out of sport, that a more effective way of ending apartheid was to encourage contact with South Africa and that the British Government had a duty to preserve the right of citizens to enjoy their private pleasures. However on February 12th the M.C.C. announced that the South African tour was to be cut from twenty-eight to twelve matches, to be played on closely guarded pitches. The Conservative legal spokesman, Sir Peter Rawlinson, stated that the Government was acknowledging the licence to riot.

Later in the spring it became clear that if the South African visit took place other Afro-Asian countries would withdraw from the Commonwealth Games, to be held in Edinburgh in July, and on April 30th the P.M. appealed to the Cricket Council to think again. On May 21st the Home Secretary met leading officials of the Council and, explaining the Government's anxieties about the future of the Commonwealth Games and the possible threat to public order that the tour might provoke, he formally requested them to cancel it. Mr Quintin Hogg, for the Conservative Party, described Mr Callaghan's intervention as 'a classic illustration of the inability of this Government to preserve freedom . . . or to maintain law and order'.

danger of T.V. and radio appearances. Harold went on the air to deal with Europe but he was asked a direct question about the cricket tour and now he has committed himself to the line that while we agree with the demonstrators that the tour shouldn't take place, we agree with the supporters of law and order that we must enable anyone who wishes to see it. I think myself that this is too subtle. It's not the position Jim Callaghan would adopt. Once again Harold showed that when he is challenged on a simple moral principle he stands by it.

Nicky Kaldor rang me this weekend and has added a little more. He is a tremendously pertinacious lobbyer is our Nicky and he had been to see Jim Callaghan, who told him that Harold was now wondering whether he shouldn't in the course of the summer retire Michael Stewart and put Denis in the Foreign Secretary's job. That would keep Roy's nose to the grindstone and remove the only slot he could possibly escape to. I found this an interesting comment of Jim's because it is so unconvincing. After all, if you do that to Roy it means that he can do what he bloody well likes to you. It is much more likely that Harold would allow Roy to believe that if he produced a really good budget he could be promoted to the Foreign Office. That would seem to me more likely and that Harold is leaving this job open in the summer so that he can give it either to Roy or Denis, neither of whom he likes or trusts but both of whom I'm sure want it, although both must be very clearly aware that it is very unlikely that the job will remain in Labour hands after the election. I rang Roy this morning to ask him to dine on Tuesday with Barbara and me, but I rather stupidly forgot that this was the first day of the Common Market debate,[1] and he is absolutely 100 per cent engaged. Soon enough, though, we are both going to have to talk to him.

Monday, February 23rd

At Management Committee, just like last week, we had to listen to Harold discussing the B.B.C. This time he was talking about the row which has been riproaring through the correspondence columns of *The Times* about the restructuring of B.B.C. radio. They are scrapping the Third Programme and various regional things and introducing a series of vertically stratified programmes for music and for the spoken word instead of mixed programmes designed to blend music and drama and the rest. Ian Trethowan has been doing all this and it has produced a tremendous crisis with Hugh Greene, now a governor, coming barging in, rebuking the B.B.C. people for their disloyalty in writing to *The Times*.[2] Usually nobody worries about radio but here was Harold full of his anti-B.B.C. feeling and wondering if we should

[1] The debate to take note of the White Paper on Britain and the European Communities (Cmnd 4289) took place on February 24th and 25th.

[2] Ian Trethowan, Editor of Independent Television News 1958–63, joined the B.B.C. in 1963 as a commentator on political and current affairs. He was Managing Director of B.B.C. Radio 1969–75 and of B.B.C. T.V. 1975–7, Political Commentator for the *Economist* 1953–8, 1965–7 and for *The Times* 1967–8; he has been Director-General of the B.B.C. since 1977.

intervene. God forbid. Nevertheless it is interesting that we should have discussed it. Then we came to the issue of the eighteen-year-olds who can now vote in the forthcoming election. We have to consider how we can get at those who have bothered to have their names put down on the register. Barbara told us, as we politicians often do, what had happened to her in Blackburn when last weekend she went around three secondary-school sixth forms to tell them about the significance of the lowering of the voting age. Very moving it was and she said we should all do the same. Then Jim Callaghan said he'd done this in Cardiff and Fred Peart in Cumberland, and it turned out that they were describing what everybody had been doing for years, except me.

At our weekly departmental lunchtime meeting I raised the whole problem of D.E.P. Over the weekend I had discovered a document from a working party of D.E.P. and D.H.S.S. officials unanimously recommending that, when D.E.P. becomes a pure management and employment Ministry, D.H.S.S. should take over from them the distribution of unemployment benefit. The announcement was to be made now, although the actual transfer would take place only after we had completed our own reorganization after the introduction of earnings-related contributions. When I read this I was furious but I now know how to do these things, so I explained how this unanimous report had been put in without telling me and that I gathered there had also been a meeting at the Permanent Secretary level. Clifford Jarrett sat looking very uncomfortable. I just threw it into the lunch and it made quite a spicy addition.

This evening I had a delayed meeting in 21a with Michael Foot, Eric Heffer, Stanley Orme and Jack Mendelson, the four leading left wingers, who had asked to see me to discuss election strategy. I gave them plenty to drink and they found it a relief to talk to me. I told them very frankly that Roy had the power either to have an election-winning budget or not and that everything depended on how we spread our favours and how much tax he was prepared to raise.* I was very tickled when at one point Eric Heffer said, 'I think you ought to face the fact that what matters this year is winning the election and nothing else.' I said, 'There speaks a fellow-member of the Cabinet.' They found this tremendously funny and roared with laughter. They had never thought that they might be asking me to say something which, heaven knows, my fellow Cabinet colleagues are inclined to say anyway. It was an amiable meeting but not much more than that.

Tuesday, February 24th

The first thing this morning was a meeting of the officials, Somerville and Bourton and the rest of them, on the PESC exercise. There had been all the excitement over the '72/3, '73/4 figures last week and, after a tremendously

* I told them everything I had been thinking about on this subject and sure enough it's now coming out in articles in the press on the anxieties of back benchers.

hardworking weekend, they were coming back with new figures to show what the Health Service really needs. I heard from Brian that Harry Salter had said, 'I have had to spend the whole weekend on the figures, but it is worth it. We've now got a Secretary of State who really knows his job and gets work out of us.' It's true that I sometimes forget how much work I cause these officials but it's also true that the best of them are excited when they are given a real job to do and of course Salter and Bourton know very well that this is the kind of lead the Department should take. We should go back to PESC, back to the Chancellor, and say, 'We're sorry, you can run us on a shoestring for three or four years but after a time we must warn you that it is impossible to operate the Health Service in this way.'

This afternoon I found Mildred Riddelsdell and Clifford Jarrett waiting to talk to me with Swift and Atkinson on the subject of the extraordinary joint official paper on the future of D.E.P. and D.H.S.S. We had a tremendous row and it became very clear how badly the Department had behaved. This was not just a recommendation from an inter-departmental committee because the matter had also gone to a meeting at the very top between Denis Thingammyjig[1] and Clifford Jarrett. This ridiculous proposal had been supported without their speaking to me or, as I now discovered, to David Ennals. Why had Jarrett and Mildred Riddelsdell done this? Out of sheer decency, I suppose. It was clear that the First Secretary was determined to get this and once she and her officials were committed, our officials on the departmental committee, who weren't concerned with the merits of the case, had to say, 'Well, of course, if they are bloody-minded and if they turn their Ministry into one concerned only with management and employment exchanges and not social service, we must protect the unemployed by taking this over, though of course we can't do it for eight or nine years.' It had been a typical official compromise. D.E.P. officials had won on the principle that they were going to make their Ministry what they wanted it to be and drop the dole image, while our officials had won on the principle that even though they accepted the responsibility they couldn't take it on for some years. The combination of the two compromises is plain ridiculous. We spent two hours on this, cancelling meeting after meeting. I raved at them because I was angry that they could do this to me. Only a year ago they had told me they were at all costs determined to prevent it and I had said I could play it out by setting up a working party. Then suddenly things changed in Whitehall and my people, including my Permanent Secretary, had gone along with the change. The more I thought about it the odder Jarrett's performance was and when I discovered he hadn't even mentioned it to Marre on the Health side, I realized once again that I still have two Departments carrying on as though they are independent Ministries.

Before I went out with Anne this evening I had to go to the Policy Coordinating Committee of the Labour Party. This is the Committee which

[1] Denis Barnes.

used to meet under Judith Hart and now meets under Peter Shore. I had missed the last two or three meetings, so I thought I ought to go in for an hour. Peter's room is rather like Judith's, on the ground floor of the Cabinet Office, and there were sitting round Harry Nicholas, Terry Pitt, Willie Simpson, Walter Thingammyjig,[1] the chap from USDAW, Michael Stewart, Denis Healey, Peter Shore and I. This session was on foreign and defence policy and we discussed C.S. gas. The leak is still rumbling on and causing difficulties and I thought we really would have trouble with Transport House, but no, one can never tell. Denis Healey, rather unconvincingly explained his position at some length, rather bluntly and rudely. Suddenly Willie Simpson said, 'In the war this was my job. We were constantly being put into a closed lab and being made to take off our respirators for tests with this gas. I can tell you this C.S. gas doesn't hurt anybody, it's a jolly good thing.' Harry Nicholas, too, had tested for gas in the war and he understood that it wasn't a wicked or painful thing but an infinitely better method to use than bullets. Why should we be against it? Then Michael Stewart said, 'I needn't say in this closed company that I was against the majority on this. I was for banning it and I was overruled but it is not that important and we oughtn't to go on making a fuss about it.' So they turned to the Common Market and other affairs and at that point I slipped out.

I had a snack with Anne and we went off to see Marlowe's *Edward II*. I thought the production was pretty good and it struck me how much simpler his language is than Shakespeare's. The other striking fact was that every seat in the theatre was taken for a really very stodgy Elizabethan chronicle play. One wonders what brings people to it, except of course the fact that this is apparently the most brilliant young actor of all time.[2]

Wednesday, February 25th

For three hours this afternoon we had the National Health Service Labour Conference in the Grand Committee Room in Westminster Hall, a ghastly room. There were gathered together the three or four Labour chairmen of R.H.B.s, people like Peggy Jay and Clarissa Kaldor, and Patricia Llewelyn-Davies and Audrey Callaghan, who are chairmen of Hospital Management Committees or Boards of Governors, and prominent people from the local authorities, although I must add that appointees from the hospital side were in a majority. It was a Conference to try out the Green Paper and I started by talking about it for forty minutes. It was very striking that, apart from the small professional pressure group for handing things over to local government, the meeting was not against our proposals. This is not unimportant because in all this the party has been our great problem. They have been committed to democratizing the Health Service by handing it over to local government and we have had many Conference resolutions

[1] Walter Padley.
[2] Ian McKellen.

on this but we're not doing it, even though there is an overwhelming case for doing it now, if ever, when new local government structures are being set up. So this was a tremendously testing moment and it came off. Mind you, it was relatively easy because all the people I had appointed, like Peggy Jay, were on my side. Bea Serota and John Dunwoody and I sat there at the top with an excellent Chairman in Willie Simpson and it was an enormous relief.

After that I went upstairs to 21a for a fascinating meeting on pocket money for people in long-stay psychiatric hospitals. During the half-day debate which the Opposition had staged Robin Maxwell-Hyslop,[1] an odious M.P. who represents part of Devonshire, had raised for about the third time the question of pocket money and I had found there was no adequate answer. In rather a facetious way, meaning to be funny, I had said, 'I've got no answer out of the gentlemen in the box but I promise I will give one in reasonable time.' This reference to the box had been noticed in 'Albany', the gossip column in the *Sunday Telegraph*, and there was a very unpleasant piece saying I had insulted my officials in the box. However it had a miraculous effect because, after waiting for six months, a paper was at last provided revealing the facts. These were as follows. Everybody in hospital who has no other means is allowed to have so much pocket money per week, provided by the S.B.C., but in mentally handicapped hospitals it has been the practice not to involve the S.B.C. at all, because the patients are supposed to be incapable of dealing with pocket money.

It has been entirely a matter for the doctors in the hospital and the money has been drawn not from the S.B.C. but, if you can believe it, out of the provisions money. It was only too clear from what the officials told me that the doctors have used this as a method of disciplining the patients. Some months ago, after pressure from me, approaches were made to the S.B.C., especially Harold Collison and Titmuss, to consider the matter and they had decided not to exert their rights in these hospitals. They had looked into it and seen there was an established understanding that this was no longer a matter of rights for the patient, because the doctor could always say that the patient didn't understand money and the S.B.C. didn't want to be muddled up in that. I spotted this. I have just cleared up the question of inadequate provisions for the mentally handicapped and now we have discovered this second scandal. The vast majority of the patients in these hospitals are perfectly capable of understanding money. They go down either to the hospital shop or walk out to the shop in the village to buy things and we find that any pocket money is taken out of their provisions money. It is quite clear that I shall have to put this to the chairmen and try to get it changed, bit by bit.

I was supposed to be spending the rest of the evening preparing a speech for the introduction of the Seebohm Bill tomorrow afternoon but when I

[1] Conservative M.P. for Tiverton since 1960.

got to my room at 70 Whitehall I found an official from the Home Office, Paul Odgers and John Pater with a long and virtuous official draft on the kind of speech they thought I ought to deliver. After an hour's talk with them trying to get it straight, I left these three officials to do it for me while I went across to the House at 9 o'clock to listen to the final part of the Common Market debate. Harold wound up and he was as boring as ever until he got on to his own old theme of dear food. Last Saturday he had made a tremendous attack on Heath, saying the Labour Party would be prepared to pay the price of dear food only if we got compensating advantages from the Common Market, whereas the Tories were committed to pay the price before they ever went near the Common Market, because they have already announced they are going to wind up our present system of agricultural deficiency payments. This was a good point and he whipped it out again in the last ten minutes. There he was putting it over and enjoying himself enormously.

Thursday, February 26th

Harold scored all the headlines this morning. Poor Roy had apparently made an absolutely first-rate speech, elegant, alpha-plus as an ardent European, but it got very little notice because Harold had come bashing in. It's true that Roy had done his positive best to upset Harold by saying rather primly that he was in favour of entry and wasn't qualifying this in any way. He couldn't have been more different in tone from Harold and I have no doubt that this was deliberate. There is growing tension between them. I have by the way rung up Harold as well as Barbara on the affair of the D.E.P.-D.H.S.S. official fix. I had told Barbara that this couldn't be done and she was polite because she knew she couldn't get it through without my help. Harold immediately saw the departmental proprieties of the matter and said it would have to go to William Armstrong at the C.S.D., so I am now getting the thing in order.

At Cabinet we had Barbara on the settlement of the Ford strike, and whether we should refer it to the Prices and Incomes Board. How mad that would be! But she wasn't pressing very hard and she dropped the matter and turned to a speech Donald Stokes had made, attacking the madness of the motor-car industry and saying it wasn't all management's fault. She wanted to rebuke him for it. Barbara's arguments are getting worse and worse and on this occasion she was at her most futile.

Then we had an extremely interesting item, Callaghan on drugs. At Home Affairs Committee he had put up a proposal to have drugs reclassified into three sorts, hard drugs, drugs of secondary danger, such as purple hearts and cannabis, and drugs of tertiary danger.[1] We had agreed on this and that we

[1] The Misuse of Drugs Bill, published on March 11th, discriminated between hard and soft drugs and, for the first time in British law, between dug trafficking and possession. The Bill divided drugs into three categories. Class A covered injectable amphetamines and

should reduce the penalties for possession of drugs in the second class but enormously increase the penalties for trafficking. There was then an absolutely outrageous press leak saying that Callaghan had been overruled and that the Government was going to go soft on drugs and make major concessions on cannabis. This was very awkward because it wasn't quite true. Nevertheless Callaghan was coming back to Cabinet to say that, partly in view of the leak and partly in view of public opinion, he now proposed to have no reduction at all in any penalties on cannabis. This was unusual. One usually only brings things to Cabinet where there is a disagreement at a Cabinet Committee but he was asking for the advice of his colleagues on whether the Home Affairs proposal was right or whether he shouldn't go back to very heavy penalties.

As we discussed this it became absolutely clear that the issue was really whether we should kowtow to public opinion or not. It was fascinating to see that at this point we had for the first time a sociological vote, that is to say, every member of the Cabinet who had been at university voted one way and everyone else voted the other. Michael Stewart happened to go out but I checked him on the front bench later and there was no doubt he would have voted with the university people for maintaining a discrimination, reducing the penalty for possession and increasing it on trafficking. Gerald Gardiner, Barbara, Denis, Tony Crosland, Roy, Dick Crossman, Wedgwood Benn, Peter Shore, Shackleton, Diamond and Harold Lever, we were all progressives. The antis, all saying public opinion was too strong for us, were Willie Ross, Ted Short, Roy Mason, James Callaghan, Fred Peart, George Thomson, Cledwyn Hughes and George Thomas, and also Harold Wilson, who was on the side of Peart and Callaghan. But they were outvoted and Harold gave the clear majority to us. Having lost this battle, however, Callaghan whipped in with another suggestion and we did in fact give him the major concession that we would make the maximum penalty for cannabis offences not the three years originally proposed but five. The discussion was particularly fascinating because no one really doubted the rightness of the tripartite classification of drugs, the reduction of the penalties for possession and the creation of a new crime of trafficking. Nobody denied this, they simply said that the public wouldn't understand it and that we now couldn't afford to alienate people on this issue.

This afternoon, after Harold's Questions and the Business Statement, we

hallucinogens, such as L.S.D., and these were subjected to the same controls as heroin, opium, morphine, pethadine and other narcotics recommended for the strictest control by the United Nations Convention on Narcotic Drugs 1961. Class B contained, in addition to cannabis and cannabis resin, six narcotics, such as codeine and five stimulants such as benzedrine, dexedrine and drinamyl (purple hearts). Class C covered nine named amphetamine-like drugs, which were considered to be less dangerous. The maximum penalty for possessing Class C drugs was two years and an unlimited fine, although trafficking in these could incur a five-year sentence. Possession of Class A and Class B drugs could incur a maximum of seven and five years' imprisonment, but trafficking and smuggling offences in drugs of these two categories could attract a maximum penalty of fourteen years' imprisonment and an unlimited fine.

got to the Seebohm debate.[1] My officials had worked away and made as good a speech as they could but, though I had interlarded it with comments and additions to give it a little vitality, it was a mistake to get them to write it. I shall never do it again because it was a flop. I didn't make this a big occasion, a declaration of the tremendous change we were introducing and how the personal service would help millions of people. I just treated it as a machinery Bill, speaking in that officialese which civil servants love. I suppose there were ten or twenty people behind me and after my speech never more than one or two on the Labour benches, with perhaps ten or twelve Tories during the whole of the afternoon. It drooled along, flat and boring. Shirley Williams wound up admirably but there was no interest because people knew that there would be no vote.

Friday, February 27th

I spent most of the day visiting the Maudsley psychiatric hospital and the Royal Bethlem, called Bedlam for short, which is linked with it. The two hospitals are some seven or eight miles apart, so I spent the morning at one and then motored across for lunch and the afternoon at the other. But it was an unsatisfactory day because there wasn't really anything to see. All you could do was chat to the nurses and to the patients, who were quite chattable to. I got back from there for half an hour's discussion at Elephant and Castle with Clifford Jarrett and Alan Marre about this question of D.E.P. Now the thing is going to William Armstrong, I could tick off the officials.

Then I went off to Welwyn Garden City for a soirée of the federation of Hertfordshire Labour Parties. Douglas Garnett met me at the station and we went to a huge great dance hall. It gradually filled up and I gave them a pep talk. There is no doubt that the party's mood is definitely better now, but again I still found nobody who thought we had a chance of winning. Everybody feels it all depends on the budget.

Sunday, March 1st

Douglas Garnett motored me down through Hatfield on Friday and stayed overnight until early on Saturday morning. I talked to Harold on the telephone about Roy. All last week Barbara and I were trying to get Roy to see us this weekend, and he still hasn't given us a time. I don't know, I've got an inhibition about ringing him up and haven't done so, but I have fixed that Barbara and I should see Harold next week. From our telephone conversation I learnt that Harold has been extremely worried because Roy has been feeding the *Evening Standard* and the *Financial Times* with stories about how he is going to be the Iron Chancellor, doing enough but not too much, and how he has alternative careers if we lose the election. The P.M. was extremely alarmed by the posture Roy was adopting. Harold said, 'Remember

[1] On the Second Reading of the Local Authority Social Service Bill.

his attitude at that meeting of S.E.P. and how he turned down the suggestion that he might do a Maudling.' I talked to Nicky Kaldor too, as we have all been constantly talking to each other, because of course Roy is omnipotent now. Harold can only pressure him. I believe the only sensible thing to do is for Harold to say to Roy, 'Look, if you give me the right budget I will make you Foreign Secretary.' Would this be practicable? I shall certainly put it to Harold when Barbara and I see him next week because the whole future of the Government depends on Roy. The Chancellor is inscrutable and remote. He knows very well what everybody is thinking but he is in two minds. He is certainly under pressure from the Treasury this way and that way but so far he has avoided any possible decision.

I discussed all this with Bob Mellish who came down yesterday evening to the Banbury Labour Party dinner. Anne and I went along and brought him home afterwards. He had made, in his racy way, a long forty-minute speech full of funny stories, but the only interesting thing he told me concerned the leak about decimal currency last week. Bob had been anxious to take the matter up and he had become more and more puzzled about it. He had wondered whether it hadn't come from the No. 10 morning prayers meeting which is attended by the Chancellor, the Foreign Secretary, the Lord President, the Chief Whip and the Prime Minister. Bob had said to Harold, 'Surely, this has something to do with Walter Terry?' and the Prime Minister just evaded it, so it was quite clear that Harold knew the leak had come from Marcia talking to Walter Terry. That interested me. Bob also talked a great deal to Anne and gave her a picture of me as a ferocious man who didn't want the Ministry of Housing, who was miserable, rude and violent, and yet, on the whole, over a period of months got to be some good.

Bob stayed on until this morning when Henry Plumb, the new President of the N.F.U., rang up from his farm at Coleshill in Warwickshire to ask if he could come over to see me. He came with David Darbishire from Wormleighton and he really wanted advice.[1] The farm price review negotiations are starting next week and I warned him that the Chancellor and the Minister of Agriculture had come to a firm understanding and that the farmers were being offered a much more solidly based, considered package than usual. They shouldn't think that they could alter it too much. Henry said that they had been given an assurance that the review would be open to negotiation but I know the package is final. However I advised him that if they wanted to exert pressure the best thing to do was to require very little that would be a burden on public expenditure because the Treasury would much prefer to help the farmers at the expense of the housewife and the cost of living.

[1] David Darbishire, who farmed 550 acres of mixed sheep and corn at Manor Farm, Wormleighton, Warwickshire, joined the National Farmers' Union in 1938 and was County Branch Chairman for Warwickshire in 1953. From 1968 to 1971 he was Chairman of the Union's Economics and Taxation Committee, and since 1971 has been a vice-president. He became a member of the Metrication Board in 1969.

Monday, March 2nd

At 10 o'clock I went along to No. 10 for one of these famous miscellaneous Cabinet Committees, No. 264 on Housing Finance. Neither Peter Shore nor I had been at the first meeting, where they had decided against any idea of an improved housing subsidy for public sector housing, and this morning we both found ourselves discussing whether we should lend £100 million to the building societies for mortgages for pre-1939 houses, whether we should give a £250 subsidy to council house dwellers if they would leave their council house and buy another and whether there was anything else we could do for local authority housing. I said, 'Clearly what you could do now is to let up on the controls which are canalizing all houses into the sixty or seventy top priority authorities.' Harold agreed this would be sensible, and so did Roy and everybody else, but then, rather embarrassed, Greenwood and Crosland said, 'But all that was given up last year. The whole priority system has collapsed. People are now so discouraged from building that we are getting anybody to build any house they can.' That shows you how hopeless housing is, as a result of Harold's leaving Tony Greenwood there for three years.

After this I went along to my own room in the Cabinet Office where we were having an informal meeting for selected medical and political correspondents, about my Statement on nursing this afternoon.[1] These informal talks are extremely successful. We had twenty or thirty people there to discuss dentistry and the nurses, and it went very well. Then I did an interview for I.T.N., had an office lunch and at 3.30 made my Statement, which was warmly received from all sides of the House. The fact is that you can't fail on nurses and there were plenty of questions.*

This evening I had a crucial meeting with the First Secretary in her room next door to mine. We had drinks with Denis Barnes and my own Clifford Jarrett and discussed the whole D.E.P.-D.H.S.S. difficulty. Denis Barnes had done a brilliant operation in selling this to the official committee and to the Permanent Secretaries' meeting. He had also torn the youth employment scheme from Ted Short's officials, so both Ted Short and I had had the experi-

* One amusing thing happened. I announced that tomorrow we would start an immense recruiting campaign with £200,000 of advertising. It was immediately discovered by the *Daily Express* that the girl who was photographed as the ideal nurse wasn't a nurse at all but an artist's model. This might have been disastrous but, on the contrary, old Peter Brown, who really is an operator, turned it into a great success by challenging the press to find us the right nurse. All the papers were full of photographs and cartoons of bright-eyed hospital nurses and out of it we got immense publicity and a good send-off for our recruitment campaign.

[1] Mr Crossman announced that though he was glad the agreement had been reached in the Whitley Council for higher pay for all nurses in the N.H.S., there were other urgent problems for the profession. An independent committee would be set up under the chairmanship of Professor Asa Briggs to review the role of the nurse and the midwife in the hospital and the community and the education and training required for that role, so that the best use could be made of the available manpower to meet present needs and the needs of an integrated Health Service.

ence of our Permanent Secretaries doing something behind our backs, something that doesn't happen very often. Barbara kept on wheedling, saying, 'You always get your own way in everything else, you are a great old steam-roller, but you must give me this one.' I kept on resisting until she suddenly got steely and tough and said, 'Well in that case I must just carry on.' I said, 'That's fine, but I am sick of this thing. What infuriates me is this conspiracy of Permanent Secretaries. That's what I resent.' I stalked out of the room. I was white with anger, furious with Barbara, furious with Clifford. It was 7.50 and I had to go home to Vincent Square and change before taking the chair at the first dinner ever given for the chairmen of the teaching hospitals. I arrived late, when they had already gone in to dinner, and I slumped down in my chair between Lord Todd and Lady Compton, the wife of the Parliamentary Commissioner. In half an hour Lord Todd had somehow soothed me with his mellifluous, self-centred professional conversation and I was back in the hospital world, far away from departmental bother, and I found it quite a pleasant evening after all.

Tuesday, March 3rd

I had a free morning, so I made one of my rare appearances at the Pension Bill Committee, where we were dealing with a clause for changing the rule under which a man can receive unemployment benefit when there is a strike at his works. This was one of the clauses we were doing for Barbara Castle. Up until now, if you were the same grade and class as those who were striking and if of course you belonged to the same trade union and were therefore in a way financing the strike, you were not entitled to receive benefit, even if you were not actually participating in the strike, only affected by it. Peggy Herbison had especially asked for this to be referred to Donovan and they had unanimously said it was socially unjust. We had written into the Bill and Barbara had announced at the Party Conference that this rule should go and I rather expected tremendous Tory opposition to this much more generous treatment of the striker, especially as we are now in the middle of a high-strike period. However, there was extraordinary caution. Half the Tories weren't there, and the only argument was not on the substance of the clause but on the timing. Was it right to do it, they asked, until we had seen the whole of Barbara's Industrial Relations Bill package? I found no great difficulty in putting my case and I just sat there for the morning and did my job on it.

Wednesday, March 4th

Another heavy fall of snow. At 9.30 I had a meeting on new hospitals for the mentally handicapped, after that a short Management Committee to prepare for our discussion at Chequers next Saturday and then the Party meeting to discuss the election and election strategy. I found Jim Callaghan addressing them, Harry Nicholas and fifty people who had bothered to turn up out of the whole 350. The lifelessness of the Parliamentary Party is something to be experienced. There is no enthusiasm here and little belief in our victory.

I slipped out at noon and went across to see how the monthly meeting of the R.H.B. chairmen was going. I was just in time to tell them about the latest scandal and I told each chairman to make a report on the pocket money situation and deliver it in two months' time. Off from there to the Garrick, where at last I was having a long-postponed lunch with Jamie Hamilton.[1] Upstairs in the bar we found Geoffrey Cox and Peter Ustinov.[2] We had a gay party with dry Martinis being quaffed and then down I went with Jamie for a splendid lunch over a bottle of claret, before the Prices and Incomes Committee.

Now last week the Committee had overruled a wage claim the hospital pharmacists had put in. Our advisers on the Whitley Council had told me that the pharmacists would walk out to better jobs in retail pharmacy unless they got a response to their demand for 25 per cent, but I had been forbidden to offer even 15 and told to offer 10 per cent. The pharmacists had received this with ridicule and today I was going to ask for 15 per cent with powers to go up to 18 per cent, knowing that this would settle it. However, as P.I. was at 3 o'clock and at 3.30 I had to meet a deputation about a hospital closure, I thought it was wiser to hand this item over to John Dunwoody, and at Management Committee this morning I had told Roy that John knew all about it and would be at P.I. I came out of the meeting with the deputation to hear that once again Barbara and Roy had turned the pharmacists down. Everybody else there had seen the case and said, 'Don't be so ridiculous. Surely the Whitley Council know better. You can't frustrate them a second time.' No, Barbara and Roy thought they knew better, on the very afternoon when they were giving 22½ per cent to a lot of thugs in SOGAT. I was furious. Without these hospital pharmacists we can't get the drugs mixed and it will cost a vast sum to buy them all from outside. I tried to ring Roy but he was at a committee and then off to a cocktail party and a dinner. As he is the Chairman of P.I. I knew that without his leave I couldn't take it to Cabinet. However I then rang up Burke and No. 10 and made a tremendous fuss. I was told it couldn't be an item on the Cabinet agenda and I would have to put it as a point of order, so that is what I have arranged to do.

Thursday, March 5th

It was quite amusing to find that Cabinet had a vast agenda of wage claims to be considered. First Ted Short had dramatically settled the teachers' strike by intervening and suddenly clinching it. They had asked for £135, they

[1] Hamish (Jamie) Hamilton, Managing Director of Hamish Hamilton Ltd, Publishers, 1931–72, and Chairman since 1931.

[2] Geoffrey Cox was Editor and Chief Executive of I.T.N. 1956–8, Deputy Chairman of Yorkshire Television 1968–71 and Chairman of Tyne Tees Television 1971–4. He was knighted in 1966. Peter Ustinov, the actor, is also a dramatist and a film director.

had been offered £75, then £85 and now they were settling at £120, though of course it wasn't only £120 but £120 now and new restructuring on January 1st next year. Two terrific victories for the teachers and a disaster for us. If we were going to offer this why hadn't we done so last January and why hadn't we decided on a common policy for teachers and nurses as I had wanted? Poor Short had said six months ago that he would need to go well above £100 and he had been disregarded. The teachers had held out for five months in a terribly damaging strike and now we had surrendered. People hinted at this but nobody really pointed it out. Cabinet was too decent.

Then after discussing a number of other minor strikes, I came in on a point of procedure. I said, 'I must ask what I am to do and I want to warn Cabinet that if the pharmacists walk out I am faced with the possible collapse of the Health Service in Birmingham and Liverpool.' Harold said this was a point of order but he asked why the papers weren't here. I said, 'I wasn't allowed to put a paper round.' Then Roy said, 'You see, the fact is that this was carried by a majority of the P.I. and, as Mr John Dunwoody did not reserve the Secretary of State's position, he is not entitled to bring this up at Cabinet.' This shows you how important procedure is. Because Dunwoody had not used the single sentence, 'I reserve the Secretary of State's position', I was not entitled to circulate a paper or to bring up the matter again today.

Harold had to be rigorous because Roy was insisting on this point but I went on arguing it procedurally and in the course of my argument I managed to explain to Cabinet how dangerous the case was and how I resented the interference and the inflexibility being imposed upon me. The Home Secretary looked up and said, 'I think, you know, the Secretary of State for Social Services is doing pretty well in failing to bring this matter up so vociferously for the last thirty-five minutes.' But I made my point and it was minuted successfully.

Off to dinner at the Écu de France with old John Silkin, for a nice quite old-time dinner. We sat at the table where years ago he had told me that the Prime Minister was going to make me Lord President with him as Chief Whip. Now John is Minister of Works, still fat, comfortable, lazy, pleasant, able but not vigorous, and he solemnly told me that after we had won the next election he would resign from politics because he couldn't go on with these secondary jobs. He went on telling me how we trusted each other and how wonderful we were together. I think we were quite a good pair but, looking back, I think it was fortunate I got rid of myself when I did because the men who actually introduce liberal reforms are not the men to carry them out. It was ideal to put in to execute our reforms someone like Bob Mellish, a rough, tough, hatchet henchman, because though he still hews to our line, no one thinks he is being liberal.

Friday, March 6th

As I predicted, our offer to the pharmacists has been turned down and we have got to go back to P.I. At the same time I shall go to the Prime Minister and present the case to him because under Barbara and Roy the whole P.I. exercise is an extremely expensive farce. They are always preventing unfortunate people who are trying to negotiate a settlement from making a reasonable offer and making us pay a great deal more afterwards.

I rang the Prime Minister to talk about Jimmy Margach, who came into my room on Thursday and said, 'I hear you are going to have a Chequers meeting this weekend.' I was really flabbergasted because I didn't at all want to be responsible for a so-called leak, knowing what Harold felt, so I replied, 'Oh, I don't know anything about that,' and tried to put Jimmy off, adding that anyway I thought it most unlikely that we would have it with the Chancellor so busy just before the budget. But Harold said this morning, 'It's all going to be official,' and I realized that No. 10 had already been telling the press that they could expect a Chequers meeting. All the papers are speculating, speculation which is being fed pretty steadily by John Harris on Roy's behalf and no doubt by a number of others.

I had also to tell the Prime Minister about my conversation with Roy last night. For the whole week my Private Office and Roy's have been fencing with each other about a meeting which Roy had promised would take place between him on the one side and Barbara and me on the other to discuss the budget. I finally fixed that Roy should come to dinner at Vincent Square next week but I also arranged to see him before then to talk about national insurance contributions. So after last night's vote on Defence,[1] while the House was still putting on a disgusting display of shouting and booing, we had our talk. Roy was cool and charming as he sat there in his evening dress. He said, 'If you want a big increase, it will have to be paid not only by employers but also by employees.' I said, 'No, no. We are going into Europe. This is the employer's contribution.' He said, 'Surely there has to be parity?' and I said, 'No, not on the National Health side.' I then realized he didn't really understand what I was talking about because he wasn't briefed on contributions.

I have mentioned it again today and no doubt we shall discuss it again when Barbara and I see him next Wednesday but I don't think he knows enough about the contributory system. Indeed, he mystified me even more last night by looking up and saying, 'Can you promise me you won't have to have an increase in pensions and national insurance this winter?' 'Of course not,' I said, 'they are biennial. This is the year for supplementary benefits,' and Roy said, 'But I thought you might have to have national insurance this winter.' This bewildered me. One finds him with such gaps in his knowledge and they are so difficult to deal with. At this point the division bell rang again. Though Roy didn't want to continue the conversation I had already

[1] An amendment to the motion approving the Statement on Defence 1970, contained in Cmnd 4290, was defeated by 289 votes to 231. On the main question, the motion approving the Command Paper, the vote was 251 in favour and 230 against.

got a great deal of information – that he wasn't considering using contributions, that he didn't even know and therefore hadn't considered the possibility of deliberately paying for the Health Service out of the employers' contributions and that he was alarmed about pension increases. The Treasury had put some absolutely inane fears into him. We went back into the Chamber where the House was still braying, with James Wellbeloved on his feet accusing the Tories of being drunk.[1] Denis had deliberately provoked people and in the second vote on our White Paper thirty-eight of our side, including George Brown, managed to abstain. The Chief Whip blew his top and made it twice as bad and so the week ended pretty badly for us. I went away feeling sure that when we got to Chequers we would get very little change out of Roy.

Sunday, March 8th

Ages ago we had decided to have a meeting of the Management Committee at Chequers and during the past week we had fixed a good many of the subjects to be discussed, and we had also considered whether we could afford to make it a Management Committee or whether it should be a private meeting. By making it a Management Committee in the morning with Burke Trend attending and a private meeting in the afternoon, we were able to come in our own official cars and,* incidentally, to announce that we had met. Harold wanted the meeting to be a close secret at first but he thought it a good thing that the facts should be published eventually. This is ironical when we remember what happened with Jimmy Margach.[2]

For once I took a full note of the meeting and I intended to put down here what actually happened, but, and this is a funny thing, when I opened my box I found I had got Barbara's notes of the Management Committee and not my own, so I shall have to remember the morning's discussion as well as I can. First we dealt quite shortly with immigration and the problem of the figures. Then we went on from that to law and order, starting with the whole problem of how to handle university uproar. By and large Callaghan took the traditional view, saying, 'Naturally I must always permit people to demonstrate even if I disagree with them.' Barbara and I tended not to say this. 'I can't take quite such a simple line as that,' I said. 'I remember how the Weimar Republic went down and I think we are entitled to say we can't possibly give people the right to destroy democracy. As long as the enemies of democracy are weak we can let them demonstrate. The moment they become strong we must be resolute and attack them. It's true that in Britain

* This matters to me because I can't drive and if I can't use my official car Anne has to ferry me about.

[1] After the debate Mr Wellbeloved complained that he had been unable to hear the closing words because of 'the organized attempt by the Conservative Opposition to stifle free speech'. He asserted that 'Hon. Members on this side of the House were sick and tired of the drunken behaviour of Hon. Members . . .' After a further half an hour of altercation Mr Wellbeloved withdrew his remark.

[2] See p. 844.

they have been weak up till now but it's rather different in universities, where the opponents are strong relative to the strength of the university. We believe that vice-chancellors should have been much tougher in winkling out the ring-leaders and dealing with them.' There was disagreement here, with some people saying we would have made martyrs of the student revolutionaries, but Barbara and I replied, 'We're not talking about our doing it or the police doing it. We are talking about encouraging vice-chancellors to do it.' Everybody agreed that we shouldn't in any way meddle in the universities or take responsibility for them.

Then we came to the Springboks, where there is no doubt whatsoever that the demonstrators have terribly damaged their own anti-apartheid cause. They have strengthened racialism and turned sportsmen against them, and there will be more trouble when the South African cricket team comes in the summer. We have to oppose both the disruption of sport and apartheid and this double role is extremely difficult. Our policy of banning arms sales to South Africa is also very unpopular in the country and, in my view, we have in this respect been a puritanical, prim Government.

The next thing was a paper I had prepared listing social priorities, the goodies we could actually produce. Number one was more money for legal aid, which Gerald Gardiner wanted, and another raising of supplementary benefit next autumn, not by the minimum 5*s.* but by 6*s.*, 7*s.*, or 8*s.* We went through them all, Ted Short's increase of nursery classes, the introduction of the constant attendance allowance before the rest of the National Superannuation Bill in 1973 and increased widows' pensions. Roy was quite firm in saying that the only thing we needed this winter was a 5*s.* cost of living increase in supplementary benefit and no more. He was prepared to consider the possibility of helping the over-seventy-fives or the over-eighties but he thought that was all we could afford. That is really as far as we got in the morning and then, after a very good lunch and a lot to drink, we settled down to a solid session from 2.30 till 5 o'clock.

The Prime Minister started by going round the table asking everyone for their views of the date of the election. Here are my notes of what was said. Harold said one of the problems was the World Cup.[1] If it wasn't for that, he would favour the end of June, and was now trying to find out at what time of day the match was played, because he felt this was a determining factor. Denis Healey was then asked his opinion and in a nutshell he firmly declared for the autumn unless we could manage the end of June. Fred Peart pointed out that we have never had a June election, and he thought we wanted late September or early October. Wedgy Benn said that with a reasonable budget he would go for early June.

I said I had no desire for early June because I thought we wouldn't have got public opinion or our own Party woken up by then. I wanted early

[1] The World Cup soccer matches were to be held in Mexico in June. Britain, as the 1966 winner, held the Cup but was to be defeated by West Germany by three goals to two.

October. So did Crosland but since the Tories had a 7 per cent lead he would wait beyond that. Peter Shore said he wanted the earliest possible date and he emphasized that the Opposition were unprepared. Mellish said that he thought there was a very strong case for October but if there was a chance in June he would consider it. Jenkins said he thought we ought to have organizational planning for a June possibility and policy planning for October. Stewart said that, if it was an irrevocable decision, October, but if there was clear evidence of a big swing in public opinion he considered we should have it earlier. He said waiting for spring 1971 was a counsel of desperation.

Callaghan said we should have the election as soon as we felt we could win, subject to the World Cup, and that if the Tories' lead was 3 per cent or less the date should be June. Barbara made the point that saying we should have it when we could win didn't carry us very much further; the question really was whether we should have it when we had put most money into most people's pockets. That, if we could fix it, would be the best time to win.

Then we were back to Harold. He said he had tried hard to work this out in January 1966 and at that time he had discussed an Easter date. Now autumn 1970 is the obvious date but that meant the Tories would pile up their propaganda and be ready for us and, again, the World Cup was crucial. The longer we go on, he said, the greater is the danger of our balance of payments being undermined. The Tories are well organized and from early June until September there would be a closed period in which they could do anything they liked, even causing a run on the pound. There could be strikes, endless hazards, he said, and clearly his mind was moving to June. Healey then said that the message should go out from this meeting that we are planning for a long haul. The optimum is either mid-June or early October. The risk of June is the World Cup, the risk of October is rising prices. The trouble is that no announcement made after June will do us any good. For instance, the knowledge of an increase in supplementary benefit in October is better announced in June, Harold added, 'In June the evenings are light right up to the close of the poll.' That was the end of that little discussion and it revealed quite clearly that Harold is anxious for an early election and he intends to have one.

He then took the second question, going round the table the opposite way. (We were sitting in fairly comfortable chairs by the fireplace in the middle of the long room.) The P.M. said, 'What are the issues which you people think should dominate our campaign?' 'Well,' said Barbara, 'we are prisoners of our own economic commitment but we shouldn't really talk about the balance of payments. We must have something humane, like a 10*s.* increase in the supplementary benefit with a good budget. But, frankly, we have to liberate ourselves from our economic commitment which interests nobody.' Jim, who was sitting next to her, said that this was all very well but we had won the balance of payments battle, as we deserved to win it, and we've got some credit for it. We are half-way through our tremendous change and this should be our theme, solvency, which appeals to the middle class, the Government has won and deserves to win. We should point up the choice between us and the Tories. Then he emphasized that we need time, time, and we need trade union secretaries to work up the anti-Tory campaign. He could tell us, as Treasurer of the Party, that they are terribly slow in reacting to our appeal. On the whole his theme was one of a continuing slow progress and a display of steady, continuous competence. Michael Stewart said that elections are always fought on economics and the standard of living and the theme should be that though the standard of living has risen we need a new term of office to complete the job. Jenkins said he wouldn't speak, so Bob came next and he said, 'Let's think of the Tory themes. They will talk about our failures, for instance the land commission, mortgages, interest charges. We must do something for the trade unions, they must feel the need for a Labour Government and we must work up their feelings of fear of the Tories.' Shore's main point was to stress achievements, the economic turn-round, achievements in the social field, the adjustment of our historic role overseas. And what next? We must do some hard thinking about that. We haven't really got a 'what next?' but we should stress the regional programme.

I then said that, were we really to face it, the one thing which matters in the polls is not people's voting intentions but their expectation of recovery and they are still overwhelmingly expecting a Tory victory. To get off the ground we need to regain our own people's confidence that we are going to win. I thought we could do this in two ways, by proving our competence as a Government, not by compassion or concessions, but by presenting ourselves as a team led by Harold, compared with Heath's alternative. We were doing quite well on this but we needed the summer and autumn to bring it off. Secondly, we needed a budget that would really get us off the ground. I described the Nicky Kaldor budget, plus supplementary benefits far in advance of the usual 5*s*. cost-of-living increase. With this we might regain the working-class vote and make them fear the Tory alternative.

Finally I stressed the need for people to participate in the community. In the morning session we had discussed criminals and drug-addicts and even lay-abouts. These were all people who had repudiated society and society seemed to repudiate them. I thought an enormously important theme was that of ordinary people in voluntary effort. Harold intervened and said, 'We must believe that we are winning, not we shall win if we do something or other.' This was the opposite of my point that we could only encourage expectations of winning if we did certain things.

Harold, with Wedgy's strong support, said, 'No, we must believe we are winning now. This is the essential message. It is this which disturbs the Tories. They didn't like it when we were in Opposition. We must make Heath believe we are winning.' There was something in this argument and I agreed. Wedgy said, 'The electorate must fear them and like us and for liking us there are good foreign policy themes, Rhodesia, Biafra, entry into Europe, even getting out of Vietnam. We must make people feel confidence in themselves with things like the budget and comprehensive schools. We must make them feel they are a responsible society and, for a lift on our own side, the great thing we want is healthy reflation. Not a flash but a sense that the economy is growing, and without upsetting the international bankers Roy must see that it grows fast.'

Peart went on again about the will to win. He keenly resented my reference to a working-class budget. I had said, 'Even if it means that the budget hits the top people, the car workers, the £30 to £40 a week workers, I can't help that. We must have a budget which overwhelmingly helps the vast majority of people whose wages are average and under and, with the money Roy has, we can only do that by being very egalitarian, very distributive and not helping the middle classes at all.' This to Peart was terrible nonsense. We must not talk about the working class but about people as a whole. Denis Healey said that the whole of my working-class budget concept was unreal. In any working man's club, you learn that people want a budget that relieves them of bother. What matters is our competence. The budget must be seen to be the direct result of Wilson's premiership and of this Labour Government. Our advantage is that we have been in for six years, the electorate are used to us and we have succeeded. Denis only feared that we would stumble this year, which was why he wanted the election as soon as possible. He then got on to talking about a budget which really reduced the cost of living for the housewife. That was the line-up. I've left out Tony Crosland because I didn't make notes while he was speaking but he and I both put forward the Nicky Kaldor budget, all the money to be spent not on reducing the standard rate of tax, but on tax concessions designed to help the average and lower-paid worker.

To my surprise Michael Stewart backed me strongly. Callaghan sided with Healey and Peart, though Mellish came out with his usual stuff: 'Roy, don't be a Stafford Cripps.' After that, he too supported me and so did Peter Shore, who also said he wanted to help the average person and below, along with having an expansionist economy that would reduce unemployment. After all this Harold said, 'The message is frightfully important. We should rattle the Tories by saying we are going to win. Their 14 per cent lead has dropped to 7 per cent despite the Selsdon Conference and we must drive Heath into the hysteria with which he always responds to our provocation. The polls show that the Tory lead is smaller than the numbers of don't knows and the don't knows tell us nothing about our expectation of victory.' It was quite clear that, in Harold's view, things are going fairly well.

Then it came to Roy, who had held back. I kept a fairly good note of what he said. First, in reply to Barbara, indeed to nobody else, he said we shouldn't underrate our balance of payments success. 'My time of greatest depression,' he said, 'was in May last year. I felt we were not going to hold on and that we'd have to float the pound, with terrible deflationary measures, but this week we shall be announcing the best annual balance of payments figures since the Labour Government of 1950.'[1]

The second point he made was that if our test was competence, as Denis Healey and I had both said, we must keep our balance of payments healthy. The positive balance was achieved in 1969 by a most unusual inflow of £200 million private capital, and there was no reason to feel that this was very stable. Our balance of payments could deteriorate all over again in 1970 if last year's private capital began to flow out again. We don't want to rely on hot money as we are doing now. Again, lower interest rates require a healthy balance of payments and we must have a budget which allows this.

Thirdly, he said that last week's N.I.E.S.R. forecast advising us to have an easy, generous budget was entirely wrong, as it nearly always has been. 'It underestimates the rate of consumption,' he said. 'It puts it at 2 per cent but I think it is 3½ per cent, which gives me very little room for manoeuvre.' Having made these three points he replied to Tony Crosland and me, knowing we had seen Nicky Kaldor's paper and therefore knew of a specific scheme. 'Now,' said Roy, 'first of all to those who were saying we could now add an extra £200 million of income tax concessions by putting up S.E.T., I would point out that the demand effect of S.E.T. is about half. In order to be able to give £100 million concession we would have to do £140 million of S.E.T. increase.' The demand effect of employers' contributions, something which I pressed him on, is even worse, so only £50 million of tax concessions would be earned by £100 million of that. Then Roy said that Nicky's scheme was impracticable, because it hit terribly hard at the top-level chap. The man who earned more money or more overtime got nothing in return and it has a terrible disincentive effect. I won't go into great detail but what interested me was his specific repudiation of Nicky's scheme. Old Nicky had not only been to see Roy but also Tony Crosland and me, and he had also seen John Allen,[2] who worked with Harold in the 1964 campaign, got the sack and is now back in Transport House. Nicky had told Allen, Allen of course had told Harold, and Harold had told Roy, that Nicky was blabbing to people in Transport House, so there was an anti-Nicky mood.

There were numerous interruptions at this point. Healey jumped in saying, 'Nicky Kaldor, that fellow is a revolutionary. He caused revolutions in British Guiana, he is a hopeless man with no political sense at all.' A tremendous anti-Kaldor line was taken by the opponents of major income tax concessions. Then Roy made his fifth point, saying there was no room for

[1] The estimated balance of payments for 1969, published on March 9th, 1970, showed a surplus of £366 million on current account, compared with a deficit of £322 million for 1967 and £309 million for 1968.

[2] Son of Sydney Scholefield Allen, the Labour M.P. for Crewe from 1945 until his death in March 1974, John Allen had been an Adviser to the Labour Party in Opposition and worked as a Political Adviser in the Cabinet Office October 1964–May 1965.

national redistribution this year, i.e. no room for a wealth tax. It was impracticable anyway and despite the agitation of the N.E.C. it wasn't suitable for this year's budget. These were Roy's only main points but they were absolutely specific and he was showing very clearly that he wasn't going to risk the kind of budget Tony Crosland and I wanted. He would prefer a cautious budget which helped him with the balance of payments. At this point Harold summed up and he was extremely careful to repeat Roy's point. He said, 'If you are going to have the kind of budget which Tony Crosland and Dick want, you'd better have the election pretty quick after it in June, because after that kind of budget it's too risky to wait long.' Harold was saying that to wait for the autumn would be dangerous. If you choose a low-risk budget you can modify the situation as you go. You can make further concessions, e.g. on mortgage payments, or you can even decide to have more generous supplementary benefit, but once you have chosen a high-risk budget you have to go to the country soon because you might come unstuck. Jenkins then said, 'One must go for at least a £250 million balance of payments surplus.' This was in reply to Callaghan who suggested £125 million.

From this summary of the main points of our discussion, it is quite clear how the Cabinet lined up. Tony Crosland, Peter Shore, Barbara and I all wanted a high-risk budget combined with an autumn election. We all thought this would be the launching rocket to get us off the ground so that we could pull the party with us and spend the summer coasting to victory. On the other hand Harold seemed to imagine that by June we had a chance of getting the party into a victory mood. We shall know this pretty well by May, after the local elections, and I should say that if those are reasonably successful Harold will go to the country at the end of June. However I would like to bet that they won't go reasonably well and I think we shall find ourselves hanging on until the autumn, with what is called a low-risk budget, i.e. an unexciting, undramatic budget which doesn't help much.

On the whole I came away from this meeting fairly depressed. Roy was exactly as I expected, conventional, rigid, narrow, low-risk, balance-of-payments conscious, not, I believe, expecting to win in this way but saying there is no other way that leaves intact all that economic policy has gained. It was quite clear he had swung Harold to his side and that Callaghan and Healey were also with him. Healey was extremely assertive throughout, in a sense intellectually vulgar, tough, hearty and reactionary. Barbara was as always talkative and lengthy and really rather ineffective because she didn't get her points out clearly. I suppose Tony Crosland and I were the two who put our philosophy perfectly clearly, in a way too clearly, because it was disliked and repudiated not only by Roy, Denis and Harold but also by the working-class people, Fred Peart in particular. As for Bob Mellish, he was in such a muddle that I suppose he could be said to be on my side on that particular issue. Of course we had Michael Stewart on our side as well and

Peter Shore. Yes, it was the socialist intellectuals who were on one side and on the other … no, I won't classify them. I have just given their names.

I drove back through the snow to Prescote, depressed at two things, I suppose. One is my colleagues' blindness to the fact that they are staring defeat in the face unless they can basically change the situation. They think they have a good chance of victory if they don't stumble and fail. This is such a difference of outlook that I can feel very little sympathy with them. I am also depressed because I see no chance of getting the budget which I have been trying for and this is just another nail in the coffin of the Labour Government. The Government is going to get knocked on the head next October because neither Roy nor Harold is prepared to take the steps that are necessary now however risky they may be. Perhaps they wouldn't be a success, perhaps the budget can't do it but I know very well that a budget of the dimensions Roy and Harold are planning can't succeed. It certainly can't succeed in June and if we carry on until October we shan't get any real pull at our own people.

Nicky rang up this evening and asked me to send his plan on to Harold. I said, 'It's no good. They rejected it.' The poor man was desperately distressed and I really didn't know what to tell him because it was so hopeless.

Monday, March 9th

Though I haven't very much inspiration for the diary I must say the week started with something novel and I suppose it did in a way illustrate the problems of politics. This was the row about my reserved compartment. The Commuters' Association, people mostly from Princes Risborough and High Wycombe, have for some time resented the fact that I have a compartment reserved for me on the Monday morning train to London. The train is full at that time and people who get in at Bicester or Risborough or High Wycombe, put their nose in and see me with Neil Marten or maybe Lola Hahn or even just me alone occupying a whole compartment, are understandably angry. I can see why they resent this. When I first became a Minister I resented it too and for a long time travelled in the restaurant car instead, until some security person reported to Burke Trend that I had been seen reading papers with my red box open.[1] This was thought improper and I was ordered back into my compartment. Then the railway company refused to reserve the compartment unless I paid for all the seats and for a time Sir Godfrey Agnew was compelled to buy all six for me. The company relaxed again and for the last six or twelve months the compartment has been reserved from Birmingham as a favour from the railway. I buy one seat and they give me the rest. The Commuters' Association have now made another complaint and the week before last they got a piece on my bloody-mindedness in the William Hickey page of the *Daily Express*. Sure enough, when I travelled down last weekend I was photographed even though I had no

[1] See Vol. I.

reserved compartment and it was obvious that they would be working up for a big show this morning. My colleagues had all seen this in the papers and at Chequers I asked Roy what he does when he comes up from Didcot. He said, 'I don't reserve a compartment. To avoid a row I always have just a reserved seat in the restaurant car.' I thought to myself that this was what I would do, so this morning I decided that the 'Reserved' sticker should be taken off my compartment window and I would sit in the restaurant car.

When I got to Banbury the stationmaster said, 'We have half a dozen journalists and half a dozen photographers all waiting on the bridge. They are going to have a tremendous time with you this morning.' The train was twenty minutes late so I sat in his office reading the paper until he said, 'Come through the luggage lift.' I slipped through on to the platform and got into the restaurant car, which was enormously full. I sat down in the second class at a table for four and started breakfast. All through breakfast I was watched by two, three or four photographers and, sitting at the table in front of me, by another man who turned out to be an *Evening News* correspondent. You sit for an hour and a half being photographed all the way through your breakfast and you will realize how maddening it can be. I had already had Thursday, Friday, Saturday and Sunday's newspapers and now there would be a great deal of material for tomorrow's papers as well. However I was struck by the fact that when I got off the train three of the passengers came up and said they were sorry for the intolerable misbehaviour of the press.

Meanwhile there in the reserved compartment was Neil Marten explaining how all this came about. Of course it's all right for Roy, who comes up on a fast train which doesn't stop between Didcot and London, but mine is a commuter train, and commuter psychology resents the empty seats in a compartment full of me. It only shows you how a stunt can be worked up because there is no doubt that Cabinet Ministers are entitled to have a reserved compartment. When the Conservatives are in power no one objects. But there's the rub. I am a Labour Minister who is against queue-jumping in the National Health Service and they say, 'Why should a Labour Minister who is against privilege have this privilege?' That is really what blew it up. I have been persecuted for a week, and, well, one has to get used to taking this kind of persecution. Nevertheless I was very, very irritated by it, and I must admit it gave me pleasure to sit in the restaurant car and defeat the journalists.

Tuesday, March 10th

At 11 o'clock I had S.E.P. I was still frightfully angry with Barbara, and with my Permanent Secretary for having fixed up behind my back the unanimous agreement that D.H.S.S. should take over the job of paying unemployment benefit and Ted Short was equally angry that she had taken over his Youth Employment Service. This morning I was puzzled to hear Harold going on and on about the British Museum, where we had got some sort of understanding about the new library building, but he let it run for an hour and a half before he popped off suddenly for a little job at the Guildhall. Then I knew he was getting away from a row between Barbara and me and leaving it to Roy. The row took place. I put in a short and not very fierce paper, just saying that though Barbara had arguments on her side we must be careful that the unemployed didn't feel they were getting a raw deal and that the T.U.C. didn't feel that the worker was being sacrificed to management. The main objection came from Ted Short, who was backed strongly by Tony Crosland. Ted said that, after all, we were saying we believed more jobs should be given to local government, but when it came to the point here we were taking them away.

Barbara got very angry and I didn't have to say very much because the net result was that the meeting gradually turned against her. She has become very unpopular now with her colleagues, having imposed upon us a great deal, and now she pushed her hand too hard. Roy finally adjudicated that she should be allowed to put forward a consultative document but that there should be no question of the Government announcing its decision, least of all on timing, on either the transfer to me of unemployment benefit or the transfer to her of the Youth Employment Agency. In Harold's absence we had an easy victory.

I was first in Questions today and after the usual lunch with my own people at 70 Whitehall I for once became a little firmer than usual with the House. I definitely declared that I thought it was inevitable that we should consider legislation on fluoridation, something which was highly controversial, and I also made a strong statement on the value of the Abortion Act and of the 20,000 illegitimate babies who would have been born had it not been for the Act, and all the social consequences there would have been. I managed to put this across with a bang. It was valuable by the way, because it meant that all the stories and photographs about me and my reserved compartment had to take second place.

Bea Serota was opening the Lords' debate on the Green Paper, so I went along the passage to sit on the steps of the Throne and hear her make the opening speech and from there I had to go straight into the Prices and Incomes Committee to discuss the hospital pharmacists again. This is the third time we have gone back to P.I., and I said I wanted to settle and that I knew I could do so for just under 20 per cent. It was the usual P.I. Poor old Tony Crosland had been told there wouldn't be a quorum unless he was there and then there were the Secretaries of State for Wales and Scotland, Edmund Dell, the number two at D.E.P., Barbara, Roy and me. Roy and Barbara decided that 20 per cent was too much and they both said that it was terrible that we should concede to the pharmacists the same award that we had given the nurses. If we did the whole dam would break. But the dam broke months ago and we have no prices and incomes policy. Moreover, the pharmacists have nothing to do with the nurses and nor was mine a claim that they should have the same. The difficulty is that neither Barbara nor Roy knows anything about all this and they just want to keep down the wage increases if they possibly can. I pleaded and finally I got permission for 18 per cent. I said, 'In that case I go to Cabinet. I must get a settlement this week, otherwise I really will have a walk-out.' I had a frightful row and although I had on my side Tony Crosland and George Thomas, that twister, formally with me but half backing out, Edmund Dell said he had to go for 18 per cent. 'All right,' I said, 'I'll take 18 per cent.' But when I went back and saw our people I said, 'Go up to 18½, because I must settle.'* Roy and Barbara were delighted. They thought they had defeated me and I realized I am unpopular with them because I am too big for them. They thought I was getting more than my share and so they held me in my place.

After that John Mackintosh came in to see me. I am having great trouble with him over the Godkin Lectures because he is an obstinate man with his own views and the second draft of the first lecture wasn't much good. I still doubt whether I shall get much of a draft before I fly off to America in three weeks' time.

Wednesday, March 11th

I am having some trouble with John Mackintosh because today I was urgently rung up by David Watt to say that an account had just been published of a lecture John had given to some learned society in Manchester. In this lecture he had given a sensational story about what happened last summer on the Industrial Relations Bill and how the P.M. had been forced to settle with the T.U.C. because Roy and I had gone to Harold and threatened to support Callaghan as P.M. This really was extremely embarrassing because Mackintosh said he had got it from an unimpeachable source, which could only have been me or Roy or Harold or somebody round him, and frankly he had got it from me. I had told John the story last week and explained that on the whole the crucial fact had been that Harold and Barbara's plan to threaten to resign had been defeated when Roy and I made it clear that if they resigned we would stay. That is true. What isn't true is that Roy and I went to Harold and gave an ultimatum. This shows the extreme difficulty of getting people to understand what goes on in Government. John Mackintosh has written a book on Cabinet Government, he is an experienced man, yet even he simplified and vulgarized what I told him. I suppose he actually drew the conclusion that Roy and I must literally have gone to Harold and presented him with a joint *démarche*, but it was much more subtle than that. I must check with my diary. It's still all on tape and I don't remember what really happened. Anyhow John had jumped to conclusions, made a simple, effective story out of it and so distorted it. In a way this made things easier for me because I was immediately able to deny

* Actually we settled next day.

the story, just as Roy denied it, but it was an embarrassment to me because I suppose I was suspected. I was very puzzled that John had given it to the press, but I now gather that he didn't know that the lecture would be reported. When he comes back from the South Ayrshire by-election I shall have to discover what actually happened. He isn't such a fool as to think that it could be published without being denied. Still, it has left a slightly awkward taste in my mouth.

I gave evidence to the Select Committee on Science and Technology who were asking a whole series of questions about birth control, pensions, population policy in general, and how far the Government were planning pensions policy in relation to projections of population figures. The cross-examination became extremely interesting, because yesterday's papers were full not only of the Registrar-General's quarterly figures (which we had discussed at Chequers last weekend) but they also reported a sensational attack by Enoch Powell. He had issued a Statement saying that the Government would have to revise all its calculations about the numbers of immigrants in the country on the basis of the fertility figures of immigrants who are already here. Yesterday I spent a lot of time being briefed by the experts and also by the Registrar-General on the particular population figures, because this morning's appearance gave me the chance I thought I wanted to comment quickly on all this and smack Powell down. It was perfectly easy because Powell had come to the wrong conclusions. The fertility figures would not mean a major amendment of the Government projections and indeed I had all the projections ready for publication in June. I answered questions for two hours and though it was tiring, I think I did it pretty well. This is an extremely interesting example of the problems of Ministries. We had deliberately let the Registrar-General publish his figures together with a press release, but the story was unsensational because the figures were unsensational. Indeed our whole point was that there wasn't anything remarkable in the fertility figures, so the papers found nothing interesting about our story and then, immediately Powell made it sensational, they headlined it.

Barbara, Roy and I were going to meet this evening for dinner at Vincent Square, but Roy told me that after Chequers he didn't want another Cabinet discussion and I had to agree. So I just got Ted and Barbara to come along and we had a very nice evening, never getting near the bone, never getting controversial, just having a plain political gossip. How well we do this in our Government and how much better it would be if we had more social life of this kind. We all enjoyed ourselves and our evening was all the better because we weren't on edge, fighting and trying to extract victories from each other.

Thursday, March 12th

At Cabinet we were back to Harold's desire to give support to the Private Member's Bill abolishing deer hunting and hare coursing, which he still thinks will really help us at the General Election. Fred Peart and I had both said we wondered whether in an election year it was wise to commit ourselves to something which made so many enemies, particularly since they were people who could organize money to campaign against us. Harold is very obstinate when he wants to get his way and he had a Cabinet decision on his side, so we discussed it again, trying to decide whether the measure should be a Private Member's Bill for which we would find time or whether it should be taken over by the Government. Jim Callaghan, Fred Peart and I said, 'If you are going to do it at all, do it as a Government measure,' and we got our way.

The other fascinating issue was teachers' salaries. Ted Short had intervened in the Burnham negotiations and settled with what he had told the Chancellor was a maximum of £42 million concession this year, the equivalent of conceding £120 out of their claim for £130 annual increase. It had come out in the N.U.T. press release that this was not a maximum but a minimum. Short was away from Cabinet today and Barbara reported the item. Short will be summoned to explain things. I am longing to hear what happened, because there is no doubt that to settle the strike he said different things to different people. I am not in the least surprised. He seems to me to be a twister who is always trying to squeeze through and get a bit more than he deserves. Now he's got himself into trouble. In five years I have never seen a Minister so caught as being personally responsible. It only shows you the danger of Ministers intervening directly in industrial negotiations. I don't think we have heard the last of this particular difficulty.

Finally we had the farm price review. I described the fix between the Treasury and the Minister of Agriculture and a first-rate fix it is, much better than usual. Roy really understood things and a very good offer has been made. At Cabinet we agreed that we should put 2*d.* on the price of milk. There is also to be a special grant for a brucellosis eradication scheme. It is a good sound review, which will help the farmers to earn a bit of money.

This evening I took myself off on a train to Harrogate for dinner with a small number of people from the R.H.B. Laycock, the Chairman, came with his great Rolls-Royce at the station.[1] He's a very big businessman, smooth and amiable, but only a figurehead. Dr Driver,[2] the powerful SAMO, and his Secretary were there and we argued everything out about the Green Paper once more. I learned an enormous lot from it.

Friday, March 13th

I had a whole day studying hospitals in the York area, the usual business of going round re-moralizing, and then an evening meeting on pensions for

[1] Sir Leslie Laycock (Kt 1974), Chairman of the Leeds Regional Hospital Board 1963–73.

[2] Dr Albert Driver was Deputy SAMO, Liverpool Regional Hospital Board 1952–9 and SAMO, Leeds Regional Hospital Board 1959–74.

the York Labour Party. Nearly 200 people turned up. They were in tremendous form, full of excitement and exhilaration at the news from Bridgwater, where in the first by-election since the voting age was lowered to eighteen, there had been a swing against us of only 8·6 per cent,[1] the lowest for the last three years. I think that over the country as a whole recovery is beginning, and if Roy has even a moderately good budget we might move forward.

Saturday, March 14th

I spent the morning going round the conservation area of York, one of the four historic towns which, when I was Minister of Housing, we chose for a special survey. York hadn't in the least wanted to take part in the scheme and I had had to bludgeon them into taking Esher,[2] to whom they had behaved abominably, never entertaining him once during the two years he worked there. Now that his report is out they are taking all the credit they possibly can. The scheme has worked marvellously and we wandered round seeing these extraordinary places within the old city walls. About half of it is the worst kind of mess, odd mixtures of little factories, stores, warehouses, tumbledown houses, shops, miserable areas, but nothing can be done because if you clean up these properties people will want compensation. I also went to the Minister, and saw how they are pumping £2 million worth of cement into the foundations, which after 600 years are beginning to crumble.

Then I had an excellent time with Alex Lyon, the very sober, Nonconformist M.P., a pawky, solid non-drinker, with a university background of solemn respectability. If anybody can hold York he will.

From there I was motored to Sheffield, where it so happened that the semi-finals of the League Cup were being played on one football ground and on the other Sheffield United were at home. There were no NALGO demonstrations here, and I think we are doing better and better, with pensions once more becoming an asset. I had good, sensible discussions and we got off early in order to leave before the football crowd. Anne met me on the motorway and we got back here in an hour and a half in good time to see the children.

Sunday, March 15th

I had one jolly good day off here and this evening I've been reading *Our Mutual Friend* to the children. Frankly I don't feel any inspiration to reflect on this week. I have, however, rung the Prime Minister about a piece in the

[1] In the by-election caused by the death on November 1st, 1969, of Sir Gerald Wills, Tom King held the seat for the Conservatives with a majority of 10,915 votes, a swing from Labour to the Conservatives of 8·6 per cent. The Conservative majority increased from 2,986 at the 1966 General Election.

[2] Lionel Brett, 4th Viscount Esher, the architect and planner. He was Vice-President of the R.I.B.A. 1958–9, 1962–3 and 1964–5 and President, 1965–7 and has been Rector and Vice-Provost of the Royal College of Art since 1971.

Sunday Times today, where they have called my Department palpably negligent for not properly elucidating the population figures and for permitting Powell to make his charges. Powell took the headlines and the Registrar-General's figures were completely suppressed, but we couldn't tell the press to make a big sensation of the fact that our figures were unsensational. The sensation arose when Powell said they were after all sensational and, though I replied to him the following day, the man who comes in second gets a very poor reception and we got blamed. I thought the P.M. would be angry about this and I asked him whether he would like me to put out the projections this week rather than waiting till June. Characteristically he said, 'No. I don't want to drag out the argument between you and the *Sunday Times*. I don't want you to react to Powell again. Keep quiet.' He is very good about this sort of thing, he wasn't upset about the *Sunday Times*, and didn't blame me at all, at least I don't think he did. He saw that we were caught and that it is wickedly unfair for newspapers to complain that we aren't spoon-feeding them with an elaborate interpretation of the figures but are simply letting things speak for themselves.

Monday, March 16th

I have now settled down to the restaurant car and I went up to London, where I found myself talking to Brian Abel-Smith about the problem of Mrs Barbara Robb. Bea Serota and I have placated her, we have had lunch together and have even told her about our new Hospital Advisory Service, but to my annoyance we have now received a letter from two nurses in one of the hospitals she has been attacking. They are terribly upset because I said, in a purely extempore speech in the debate on mental illness, that I was cross with Mrs Robb for making allegations about this particular hospital. Oh, dear! Are we going to open all the old sores and have her attacking us all over again? I have written a long and careful letter to the two nurses, explaining that whereas in the case of Ely I wanted an annihilating report in order to reveal a scandal, I did not want such a report in order to show up a small incident of cruelty in a hospital that is otherwise a place of tremendous reputation and initiative. I took trouble over this letter because I want them to understand and I have also sent a copy to Barbara Robb.

After that we had a most important meeting to discuss how to handle the first reports of the Hospital Advisory Service and how all its suggestions are to be channelled. There I was sitting down with the usual lot, Alan Marre and Miss Hedley, all busy proposing that Dr Baker's suggestions should be selected from the report and sent to the Regional Hospital Boards for their written comments. I said, 'To and fro the paper will go and the only effect will be to snow us under with new paper.' I stopped that and said that if there is anything in the reports worth discussing, there must be a direct face-to-face confrontation, a discussion between the Department at the top and the R.H.B. chairman and the SAMOS. I think I have saved us from a minor bureaucratic disaster there.

This evening I went off to the Israeli Embassy for a dinner in honour of Shimon Peres,[1] a Young Turk who for some time was Ben-Gurion's number two, and then, I think, his Minister of Defence.[2] Now he is a member of Moshe Dayan's party. Last time I saw him was at Rehovot, when we were in Meyer Weisgal's house, and somehow a tremendous debate blew up between Peres and me. Twenty or thirty people were standing round listening to him saying that Israel should have an atom bomb. I was saying no. He was callow, rough and unskilled and I annihilated him but nevertheless his was the voice of the future. His line is now the Israeli Government's line and the whole country is hawkish, committed, if you like, to an Armageddon, to being crusaders and being wiped out. It is terribly depressing. They are committed to a warlike posture and every action they take burns another bridge and prevents an effective peacemaking policy. The only difference as far as I am concerned is that I now accept that the Israelis whom I love are like that and I no longer find I have to fight against it. How can I? So I came to the dinner tonight to say it was too late for peace and that funnily enough I back them more loyally now that, because they have destroyed it, there is no alternative to backing them.

Tuesday, March 17th

The first thing we had was a meeting of the P.M.'s Housing MISC. This device of setting up hundreds of MISCs simply to deal with specific jobs, instead of sending awkward subjects to the standard Cabinet Committee, is one of the strange features of Harold's method of running things. I am not on many of these committees now because I am out of favour and too busy to be one of the Cabinet members who are put on them to add weight but I do see how important they are for helping the Prime Minister to get his way. In the standing committees every important issue is appraised by a group of Ministers who have been carefully balanced for the purpose and there is a rule that what is agreed there doesn't go to Cabinet but now everything of real importance is pushed outside the normal channels and through special committees, specially packed, so the situation is very different and the Prime Minister can exert far more influence. Harold has circulated a very interesting

[1] Shimon Peres was the Israeli Deputy Minister of Defence December 1959–May 1965, Co-founder of the Rafi (Israel Labour List) Party on leaving the Mapai Party in 1965, Secretary-General of Rafi 1965–8 and, after the foundation of the Israel Labour Party by the merger of Mapai, Achdut Ha'avoda and Rafi in January 1968, Deputy Secretary-General of the Party. He was Minister without Portfolio, in charge of Administered Areas and Refugee Rehabilitation December 1969–70, Minister of Transportation and Communications 1970–4, Minister of Information March–June 1974 and Minister of Defence 1974–7.

[2] David Ben-Gurion, one of the founders of the Israel Mapai Party, was its leader from 1930 to 1964. He was Prime Minister of Israel and Minister of Defence 1949–53 and 1955–1963. He died in December 1973.

personal minute on Cabinet Committee procedure, M 23/70.[1] I will set down an extract from it:

> ... it is clearly understood that Cabinet Committees operate by a devolution of authority from the Cabinet itself, and their procedure therefore follows the Cabinet's own procedure, particularly in the sense that it is the chairman's responsibility at the end of a discussion to specify clearly the decision which has been reached, and that he does so, not by counting heads, but by establishing the general consensus of view around the table. [That is interesting.] Nothing in these arrangements derogates or should be allowed to derogate from the right of any Minister to dissent from the final decision of a Committee, or to reserve his position to say that he wishes to appeal to the Cabinet. This is the basic right of all Ministers, and it must be maintained. Nevertheless like all rights it can be abused, and the abuse will weaken both the right itself and the whole system, which exists to preserve it. If the Cabinet system is to function effectively, appeals to Cabinet must clearly be infrequent. Chairmen of Committees must clearly be free to exercise their discretion in deciding whether to advise me to allow them. It goes without saying that they must not be made lightly, still less for reasons of mere obstructiveness, and if they are made they must carry with them the full authority of the Minister concerned, and must be supported by very compelling arguments. It is for these reasons that I decided some time ago that I would not entertain appeals to the Cabinet except after consultation with the chairman of the Committee concerned.

The whole note is very interesting and if you had standing committees with permanent members who worked as a team, as a microcosm of the Cabinet, it would be satisfactory. But if half the awkward decisions are shoved outside into these special MISCs, Harold can get his way and in my view Cabinet Government can be frustrated.

Today's MISC was meeting for the final discussion on our interim housing policy. I don't know what Tony Greenwood thought he was about, because it is an absolutely futile policy, just building a few more houses and giving more 100 per cent mortgages. Tony Crosland and Tony Greenwood had put up a series of feeble suggestions, which wouldn't get a single extra house built before the election. I still don't understand how Harold could have consciously allowed the cut in the housing programme.[2] About six months ago he suddenly discovered how catastrophic the figures were, yet that knowledge was there all the time and he wouldn't alert himself to it. Now a feeble answer is to be made in the House tomorrow.

[1] Compare Harold Wilson, *The Governance of Britain* (London: Weidenfeld & Nicolson and Michael Joseph, 1976), pp. 64–6.

[2] Housing completions were running at 365,000 p.a. rather than the 500,000 promised by the Government at the time of the 1966 election.

After P.M.'s Questions I went upstairs to see a little deputation. Harry Nicholas and Terry Pitt, terribly embarrassed, had come to ask me about the Transport House pension scheme. Their question, when they managed to get it out, was whether I would be politically embarrassed if they contracted out. I said, 'Of course not. It's an actuarial calculation. We don't believe it's disloyal to contract out.' They looked extremely relieved. Then in came Mr Minney[1] to ask me about Puffin Asquith.[2] All I could remember was that Puffin, the son of Margot Asquith and the Prime Minister, was senior prefect at Winchester in my first year, a fellow with curly, golden hair and bright blue eyes and a shrill, rather feminine voice. I described the life in Second Chamber downstairs and the little desks at which we sat. There was I, a small boy of twelve, hungry because of the miserable food we got in college in those days, with no butter and once a week astonishing fish, so foul you couldn't possibly eat it.

This was the post-war period when College was split into athletes and aesthetes. I was in the aesthete side and the aesthete prefects protected their juniors. I did in fact play games enormously keenly and did all the things which were expected of a boy, but I also loved the Chamber Shrogguses. (The Shakespeare Society was called Shroggus and the senior prefects went to read with the headmaster. The Chamber Shroggus was on Saturday evening when we went upstairs and, sitting on our beds, read and acted highbrow modern plays. I remember at the age of twelve or thirteen being introduced to all the Chekhov stuff and Maeterlinck and Flecker.) We small boys played the parts of girls. I don't think there was any homosexuality. There was in College, but though Puffin was epicene and in some ways very feminine and solicitous, I think he was neutral. I don't think he made love to one but I was very insensitive at that time and didn't know what was going on. I told Mr Minney how one day when I fell downstairs with a can of water and thought I was going to be beaten, Puffin rushed out and was very solicitous about whether I had been hurt. I also told him how Margot Asquith and Puffin's sister Elizabeth came to tea and what a splendid spread we had, and how we cooked the muffins and produced the cakes, and sat there waiting for them to finish tea because when we had washed up we could stuff ourselves on what was left over.

I had quite a cultural day, because after Mr Minney I went out with Anne to see *Women In Love*, the film of the D. H. Lawrence novel. The film keeps

[1] Rubeigh Minney, Editor of the *Strand Magazine* 1941–2. He was also a novelist, biographer and playwright. *Puffin Asquith* was published in 1973 (London: Frewin).

[2] Herbert Asquith was Liberal M.P. for East Fife 1886–1918 and for Paisley 1920–4, Home Secretary 1892–5, Chancellor of the Exchequer 1905–8, Prime Minister and Leader of the Liberal Party 1908–16, Secretary for War 1914. He formed a Coalition Government in 1915 but resigned as Prime Minister and became Leader of the Opposition in 1916. He was created the First Earl of Oxford and Asquith in 1925, and in the following year he resigned the leadership of the Liberal Party. He died in 1928. Anthony (Puffin) Asquith was the second and younger child (and the only son) of Asquith's second marriage. He was a film director.

extremely close to the book and it's amazing, extremely beautiful, with lovely colour and not in the least obscene, because it is seriously describing the relationships between these four people. I thought it was one of the best things I had seen in ages. When I mentioned to David Ennals that I had seen it, he said, 'Oh yes, I think it is wonderful,' and suddenly I learned that David and his wife genuinely like D. H. Lawrence, the first thing about them which I find we share.

Wednesday, March 18th

I don't think there was a single item at S.E.P. that interested me. We had a long piece at the beginning about the British Museum Library and an important item about export levies, with the Chancellor and the President of the Board of Trade discussing long-term policies, but by and large it was a dull, dreary meeting, ending with a great argument about how the merger of Courtaulds and Viyella should be conducted. I have now become a purely social services Minister, simply opting out of all industrial and commercial policy and also out of the whole economic field, because after devaluation nothing can be done. We are set upon the appointed tramlines and we can't get off them or change them very much. My withdrawal also indicates how specialized Harold allows his Cabinet to be and how little interest we take in each other's work.

The one thing of minor interest was that John Stonehouse came in for a complicated item about the B.B.C. licence fee. I happened to sit next to him on the front bench this afternoon, so I asked him about this and also about something else. I had noticed that he had suddenly been able to announce that the commercial T.V. companies, who had been asking for a reduction in the advertising levy, had been given a very generous deal which hadn't been brought before S.E.P.[1] The deal was fixed between the Chancellor and Stonehouse. There is no doubt that this Chancellor is in a very powerful position. Just as in January he announced the abolition of the foreign travel allowance without asking anybody, so in the same way he fixed this T.V. levy although there is some £6–7 million in it.

I had to go to another of these formal dinners, this time with 300 or 400 anaesthetists, all in tails and decorations. This is one of the Secretary of State's chores. I don't think I do them too badly but I don't blame Anne for avoiding them. She tends to find herself seated between two doctors with no interest in her and these really are the stuffiest occasions you can imagine. They don't want a serious speech from me but something light and easy. I'm not at all bad with the doctors now but I endure these dinners with boredom and resentment.

[1] On March 16th Mr Stonehouse announced that the levy would be reduced and that the four small regional I.T.V. companies would be totally exempt. The estimated yield to the Exchequer would be cut from £29 million to £23 million p.a.

Thursday, March 19th

The papers are full of the farm price review which Cledwyn Hughes announced to the House yesterday.[1] It's a very considerable success and I think the farmers will find it rather difficult to make a row because everybody knows the Government has treated them fairly. It's a great feather in the cap of Roy Jenkins and Cledwyn Hughes but I doubt whether there are any votes in it, especially as much of the award is at the expense of the housewife.

This morning we had another MISC, this time the special committee on Ireland. Callaghan gave us a little report on the political and the economic situation in Northern Ireland and a little report on their relations with Eire. As I listened I thought about our amazing success. There have been ups and downs and this Easter there will be nervousness about rioting, but by and large the presence of the Army and the stripping of the R.U.C.'s powers have all gone amazingly well. Chichester-Clark has been much more successful than his predecessor and he is now pulling off the job of trying to create there not merely Protestant and Catholic politics but sensible, conservative, Northern Ireland politics, while we are trying to create a Labour Party.

On the economic side there is real difficulty, because Northern Ireland has a high unemployment rate and, though we are putting a lot of money into housing, one of the basic areas of discrimination, we can't do too much or give too many R.E.P.s, for example, for political reasons. Fred Peart's region in Cumberland, just across the water, won't like it at all if they think Ireland and Stormont are getting more than their share. All this is very delicate and, after all, politically we gain absolutely nothing. They elect only Conservative M.P.s and, in an election year, with terrible unemployment in Wales and on the North and East coasts, you can see the difficulty in overdoing help to Ireland. Yet we must do something if only because this is one of our few successes.

I raised the issue of emigration and said, 'Surely if you feel you ought to do a great deal more for Northern Ireland, shouldn't you encourage emigration? I know very well you don't want the skilled workers and the Protestants to leave but shouldn't you stimulate the emigration of Catholics, whether to England or Australia or anywhere else? It would be much cheaper than promoting policies to create new industries in the region.' The Cabinet minutes are interesting. You will find that this proposal is dismissed as impractical, but at the time I was promised that this suggestion would be explored and that Callaghan would look at it. I suppose the Cabinet Office checked with the Home Office. They don't want the possibility of losing skilled labour to England. I should think that is almost certainly it.

At Cabinet we dealt with a lot of bits and pieces, inlcuding Harold's

[1] The Government were to increase commodity prices on beef, pig-meat, wheat, barley, milk, sheep and potatoes. The guaranteed price of eggs was to be reduced. Lime and fertilizer subsidies were to be raised and there was to be an annual grant of some £5 million for an incentive scheme to eradicate brucellosis. A further £20 million was to be added to the agricultural capital grant scheme. In all the award totalled some £85 million.

17 With his wife and two children, Patrick and Virginia, at Prescote, May 1970.

18 & 19 Fellow commuters complained about the Secretary of State reserving a whole first class compartment of the train between Paddington and Banbury while many had to stand. Crossman himself has the 'reserved' notice withdrawn and uses the crowded restaurant car in the morning. March 1970.

favourite proposal on hare coursing. We had finally decided that the Government should take over the Bill but without the provisions on deer hunting, because we had discovered that the Bill proposed that even the shooting of deer should be illegal. This would be intolerable because deer do so much damage to crops that their numbers must be kept down. However it is now a mere anti-hare coursing Bill and Harold has got his way.

We then had a report on Rhodesia, where Michael Stewart has had one of his rare successes. He and Harold have persuaded the Americans to agree to come into line and close down their consulate.[1] I haven't mentioned Rhodesia for ages because it has been taken completely out of general Cabinet control. Though I don't know who is on the Rhodesia Committee, I don't think it includes anybody who disagrees with Harold. Roughly speaking, he is getting off the hook by carrying out my recommended policy of gradually becoming decommitted and letting the thing fade out.

Then we had Heathrow airport, where for a fortnight a firemen's dispute had led to an absolute nightmare. There has been endless trouble with the whole of the ground staff getting out of hand and Heathrow having to close down every night. I gather that after days and days of negotiation they have agreed on terms of reference for a Committee of Inquiry and poor Barbara is slaving away at this. She is as vigorous, as elegant and as nice as ever but she is just catastrophic for our relations with the trade unions.

Ted Short was the other Minister in trouble. We had a long statement from him about the extraordinary discrepancy between the N.U.T. press release and the Chancellor's view that £42 million was all that was available. Short said that the press release was put out totally irresponsibly and that the N.U.T. is committed and can't go back on it. However the two key N.U.T. officials have agreed that £42 million is not a maximum but the actual figure agreed and this makes an enormous difference. We shall have to see what happens when all this is explained at the N.U.T. conference. I'm not sure there won't be a bleeding row.

This evening I had a meeting of my brains trust, together with some

[1] On March 2nd the Smith regime declared Rhodesia an independent republic, with Mr Clifford Dupont (a member of Mr Smith's Cabinet who became unofficial Governor of the illegal regime on the declaration of unilateral independence in 1965) as Acting President. After the UDI, thirteen nations had retained diplomatic missions in Rhodesia, though they were accredited to the British Crown and to the Governor (Sir Humphrey Gibbs, Governor of Rhodesia 1959–69) and the rebel regime hoped that these countries would recognize the republic's *de facto* independence. The U.S. Government was divided on the issue, as Mr Smith's Government had influential support from Southern Senators and important American business interests while the State Department was anxious about Black African opinion. On March 3rd the British Government asked for an emergency meeting of the United Nations Security Council to discuss the issue. On March 9th the United States announced the closure of its consulate in Salisbury and all the remaining nations except for Portugal and South Africa followed her example. On March 18th a resolution was passed in the United Nations requesting member states to refrain from recognizing the illegal regime.

SAMOS and county clerks, to discuss Regional Health Councils. I am beginning to see the light here and half-way through the meeting we suddenly thought that we could have the Health Authorities nominating some of the members of Regional Councils, which would therefore partly represent the lower levels and not just the Minister's nominees. I believe we have now got very near the appropriate formula.

Brian and I went out to dinner and I told him (the first person I have told) about my intention to go to the *Statesman.* He was sharp and clear-headed and thought it was crazy. He said, 'You can either go on in government or you can retire and write a book but to go out of government and waste your energies on all that ephemeral journalism makes no sense at all.' He may be right. Making that promise to Jock Campbell may have been an idiotic mistake. My top secret intention is becoming more and more difficult now that there is some chance of the Government's winning the election because if we won it would be very odd for me to resign to go to the *Statesman*, unless I simply did it on grounds of age. And in that case to go to the *Statesman* would be just as odd. No, I think I am in rather a fix, because I have promised to do it. Paul Johnson has stayed on specifically to give me time and it would be a terrible thing to pull out now. Yet I feel unhappy about it. I also feel unhappy because as I read the weeklies I feel less and less sympathy with the *Statesman.* I actually prefer the *Spectator* now and, although I am told its style is hopeless, to me it seems readable. I am bored by the weeklies, bored by the Sunday papers, and in fact I now seem to be bored by most things – that is another worry.

Friday, March 20th

It was a good morning, with a 5½ per cent opinion poll, and then the South Ayrshire by-election result, the best result we have had since the General Election.[1] It has come at a critical moment and will steady everything in Scotland. Indeed, judging by Harold's attitude at Chequers, it may tip him into having an early election in June or July. Tam took a leading part in the by-election, organizing teams of canvassers, and obviously he cared about this more than anything else. I suppose I feel frustrated because I don't really care. Though I see things we can usefully do, I don't terribly want us to win the election and, if we do win, I don't think we will do particularly well. I am irritated with myself and in my relationship with Tam and I am also uneasy in my relationship with other members of the Party and of the Cabinet.

This morning I was thoroughly bad-tempered, partly after my dinner with Brian and also because I had seen the draft of my Green Paper speech, which the Department had prepared after careful directions from me. It is absolutely

[1] In the by-election, caused by the death in October 1969 of Emrys Hughes, James Sillars, an official of the Scottish T.U.C., retained the seat for Labour. He had a majority of 10,886 and there was a swing of 2·9 per cent to the Conservatives. In December 1975 Mr Sillars announced that he was forming a separate Scottish Labour Party.

ghastly. On top of all this, at one of my departmental meetings I was presented with another wage claim, this time for an average of 24 per cent for seven or eight grades of N.H.S. ancillary staff. That is pretty formidable and I discussed with Bavin and Bea Serota how to knock it round. 'Don't have a percentage at all,' I said, 'let's just try the trick of giving a bundle of wages claims saying this is the best we can do on each of them and that they are not to be averaged.' This is what we did with the pharmacists and we shall see if we can get away with it without another row with Roy.

The other thing I did was to send off my monumental paper on the needs of the Health Service in 1972/3. I sent it only to Harold and, with a tactful covering letter, to Roy. Roy sent a very nice reply, saying he appreciated this and telling me that claims are pouring in from other Ministers. The sting is in the tail. Roy wants me to concede figures which enable him to go ahead this year. I shall have to fight him on this but it's interesting that, though I have obviously prepared my case more thoroughly, I am not the only Minister concerned. Before the summer is out we shall have had some tremendously interesting discussions.

Sunday, March 22nd

Somehow I have felt bored, bad-tempered and frustrated all the week, partly no doubt because the Private Office has been racked by 'flu. Janet Newman and Robin are away and poor Bea Serota is hit by it as well. But it isn't only that. I don't know what it is about this present period. I have even felt angry all week with darling Tam, who cooks my breakfast for me. We had a tremendous row about the South Ayrshire by-election because he wanted to be away for a whole week to help his friend Jim Sillars. The by-election has been an immense success, but nevertheless I personally despair. And then I have had this curious and unpleasant problem with John Mackintosh. After my denial of the story that appeared in his Manchester lecture, the poor man came along in a terrible tail-spin to see me, and he has also written a grovelling letter of apology.[1] I found out that he had been addressing the Manchester Statistical Society just as his wife was about to have a baby and he was all het-up about her. Nevertheless it was a very odd episode and doesn't really explain why he wanted to append this footnote to a learned statistical study of the Industrial Relations Bill. Whether he intended it to be published God only knows, but it has upset me and the more so because of our work together on the Godkin Lectures. We have been through the third draft of the first one and I shall have something I can show to Harold, even though they are not yet in my own style and I must modify them a great deal before actually delivering them at Harvard.

Last week I lunched with Anthony Howard, who knows that John Mackintosh is doing this for me, and it is embarrassing that we are linked in this way. Neither Harold nor Roy has spoken to me about the Manchester

[1] See pp. 855–6.

story. We whispered or muttered something to each other about it on Thursday morning and since then there has been a total silence, on their part I should think of frank puzzlement, but somehow the combination of Tam's attitude, the fact that I took no interest in the by-election, the Mackintosh story bubbling along all week, and the particularly boring meetings of S.E.P. and of Cabinet have made it an unhappy week for me. Another thing I must note is that the whole business of recording events in this diary is now becoming a chore and a bore to me. I suppose I have recorded several million words and I am beginning to wonder if I should go on. I am sure it will be interesting for people to read later on and I suppose I am just stale. I hope to God that it isn't too obviously something dictated by somebody who is bored by the life he describes.

The local police telephoned me yesterday to warn me that on Monday morning the farmers were going to cause trouble at the station. Well, they won't find me on the train because it so happens that I have come up to London tonight to prepare my speech on the Green Paper. I brought sandwiches up with me and ate them on the train and at 8.30 I went round to No. 70 where Janet Newman was waiting for me, recovered from her second bout of 'flu, with young Peter Harbourne,[1] who is amiable and nice, but so far not very efficient. (He is the chap with whom I replaced Ralph Cox.) Then there was Brian to do the main work and for three hours we slogged away and knocked off a revised version. It's totally uninspiring work to draft these written speeches, which then have to be shaped so that they say everything and upset nobody. I was bored stiff, and I am afraid Brian was too, but we finished in time to have it all typed up and ready by lunchtime tomorrow.

Monday, March 23rd

We started Management Committee with the Official Secrets Act. The editor of the *Sunday Telegraph* and one of his correspondents was being accused of violating the Act because he had published a document giving a sensational estimate of the strength of the Biafran Army. Ironically, it was published on the day the Army collapsed and as a result the *Sunday Telegraph* looked extraordinarily silly but nevertheless appalling ill-will has been caused by the fact that this was a secret document that came from our military attaché.[2] I

[1] Peter Harbourne was a Principal at the D.H.S.S. He became an Assistant Secretary and later moved to the Foreign Office.

[2] The *Sunday Telegraph* had published an appraisal of the Nigerian civil war, allegedly prepared by the British Government's representative in the British High Commission in Lagos, and on March 17th the Attorney General had served summonses, issued under the Official Secrets Act, on Mr Brian Roberts, the newspaper's Editor, Mr Jonathan Aitken, a journalist and prospective Conservative candidate for Thirsk and Malton (and, since February 1974, Conservative M.P. for Thanet East), and Colonel Cairns, the British representative on the international team of observers which the United Nations had sent to Nigeria. An account of the case is set out in Mr Aitken's book *Officially Secret* (London: Weidenfeld & Nicolson, 1971).

suppose there was a very strong case for saying that people who purloin documents and pass them on to a paper should be punished but there are some puzzling aspects to this case. Hugh Fraser has said he had a copy of the document but he hasn't been prosecuted. This I imagine is because he wasn't bribed, which seems to be the crux of the matter. I felt very strongly that there couldn't be a worse time for us to have a row with the press like the one on D-notices, but the P.M., exactly as one would expect, said that he left all these things to the Attorney General. It is quite clear that our Prime Minister's passionate spiritual and emotional commitment to our relations with the Nigerian Government makes him willing to do almost anything to help them and he sees this whole case in that light. I see it in the context of our relations with the press in an election year. Harold said, 'Of course, for all we know there may not be a verdict of guilty,' and I said, 'Well, that would be a good thing for us all.' 'Why?' asked Barbara Castle. 'Surely,' I said, 'you understand that what we most want is to get this case over with the minimum of fuss and without laying charges against the press.' But my view wasn't shared by the others, who were all deeply anti-press.

Then we had a general discussion of the effects of the by-election. The Prime Minister was indignant at the way the press was describing him as preparing to snatch a victory in June. Nobody could have been more cool, more detached, or less ready to jump to conclusions after the South Ayrshire result, but Harold was clearly optimistic. We were all asked for our views, and Barbara said that in Blackburn things weren't quite as good as Harold might think. Callaghan declared that at his annual general meeting there had been a bigger turnout than ever before. I described the complaints and apathy I had encountered at the Coventry East annual constituency dinner last week but, broadly speaking, Barbara and I were the only two who were doubtful. Each man had his little story of enthusiasm. Roy said he never finds Birmingham quite as depressing as I find Coventry, but I remember Jennifer's remark when we visited them the other day. She said, 'You haven't canvassed there for twenty-four years.' Most people were optimistic, feeling the tide had turned, particularly Bob Mellish, who reported on the mood in London as we prepare for the G.L.C. elections in the first week of April. I don't think we can possibly make a sensational recovery there.

After that we came to the only major item on the agenda, the small goodies in social services. It was clear that we were going to sacrifice all the other possibilities like legal aid and nursery classes in favour of a supplementary benefit increase of more than the necessary 5*s.* cost-of-living increase. I went for 8*s.* or, if I couldn't get that, 7*s.*, and 1*s.* on the long-term allowance for people aged sixty-five and over and those who have been on supplementary benefit for more than two years. There was immediate general agreement that supplementary benefit was the single most important thing, particularly as it became clear that the Chancellor was not prepared to increase family allowances. When I asked for my 8*s*. the Chancellor showed great reluctance and said that we could only do that if everything else were abandoned, so we agreed to 7*s*. Now we have to be extremely careful at Management Committee, where we are taking decisions that affect other colleagues. The minutes of this item are dangerously firm. This is one of the real difficulties of a Management Committee or a Cabinet. Colleagues who are affected by a decision taken in their absence naturally feel sore and upset and in this case it was likely that Ted Short and the Lord Chancellor would each in his own way see red, if they were to feel that the inner group had turned down their seriously considered proposals. Let me remind myself who was there—Harold Wilson, Michael Stewart, Dick Crossman, Jim Callaghan, Fred Peart, Roy Jenkins, Barbara Castle, Denis Healey, Tony Crosland and Tony Wedgwood Benn. That is the full Inner Cabinet, and Peter Shore, Bob Mellish and Burke Trend were there as well. It is a powerful group but nevertheless you see how dangerous the situation can be. We had to state that no decision had been taken and no decision would be taken until after the budget, although the decision had of course been taken, if only because Roy had to know for his final thoughts on the budget how much he should allocate to the supplementary benefit increase. He had to have an early decision, even though officially we couldn't take one. This is the kind of difficulty you get into when you have an Inner Cabinet or indeed when you have to devise a budget in secret and take account of certain expenditures. Anyway I got my 7*s*.

After that I had to rush to 70 Whitehall for an important meeting on abortion. Weeks and weeks ago the C.M.O. and I had given instructions that the Department should revise and tighten up the conditions under which we would issue licences to private nursing homes. We had gone through this in great detail and characteristically there came up at midday today a most miserable draft letter, without a copy of last year's draft letter attached to it, simply saying, 'Dear Sir, I am instructed to say that your licence has been granted but the Secretary of State feels that ... or is anxious about this ... ' The Department takes a wholly *laissez-faire* view of this problem. For instance I discovered this morning that since the initial inspection the nursing homes have been visited at most once in twelve months and I have had to give instructions for a team to be sent to make regular inspections. I then said that we must break this relicensing operation into two stages. A letter must be sent out to tell people that before I issue a licence I must have assurances (a), (b), (c), (d), including the key assurance that whenever my officers were to visit a nursing home a nurse would be available to show them records and let them see whatever they wished. Instead of saying, 'I give you the licence but I warn you ... ' we must say, 'I won't give you the licence until I get your written assurances'. This is a real example of departmental foot-dragging, if not sabotage, but Bea and I have struggled and we have at last got our way.

The rest of the day was devoted to the Green Paper debate.[1] I began soon after 3.30 and found myself getting through at tremendous speed. When I am speaking I am too tense to look at the clock and, after cutting out much of the speech to keep myself under fifty-two minutes, I finished in half an hour. I had read it much too fast to have any real effect but it made no difference.

Tuesday, March 24th

I got all the coverage I could possibly want and the record in Hansard was correct. I am afraid that from the departmental point of view the most successful method of speechmaking is in fact to write the thing the night before and simply read it all aloud. As I walked into S.E.P. this morning there was Miss Bernadette Devlin looking very cold sitting outside No. 10 on the pavement. She was wrapped in blankets, waiting to be photographed with us as we went in. I remember the day of her maiden speech, when she was fawned on by everyone, while I felt almost physical nausea at the hardness of what she had to say and at her kind of personality. I think my view of her is rather more widely shared now and it seemed a very characteristic stunt for her to protest against the death of someone in Londonderry by sitting outside No. 10 all night, having hot coffee brought out to her occasionally, and trying to put the P.M. in the wrong.

Our first task was to decide what was to be done about her. The Prime Minister didn't want to do anything but I had a bright idea and suggested that Harold should ask her to come to see him in the House at 3.30 this afternoon. She agreed and he was able to make a reference to her in the course of his replies to Questions at 3.15 and then to say nothing to her when she arrived. Her little stunt didn't come off.

After an office lunch and an office meeting, I had a rapid talk with Dick Bourton and Alan Marre about PESC and the Chancellor's reply to my paper. They told me a little more about it and explained that four other Ministries, including Education and Defence, had also put in very high bids, although

[1] The Secretary of State reminded the House that the central proposal of the Green Paper on *The Future Structure of the N.H.S.*, was to replace the tripartite structure of the hospital service, the executive councils and the local authority health service by a fully integrated Health Service operating through about ninety Area Health Authorities, which would, in general, correspond to the Maud unitary authorities and the metropolitan districts. He announced that in the interval since the publication of the first Green Paper, the Government had decided to give the new Health Authorities a composition of one-third local authority nominees, one-third nominees from the Health Service professions and one-third appointed by the Minister, who would also appoint the Chairman.

The Secretary of State had also decided to ask the new authorities to divide their areas into Districts, each normally centred on a district hospital and each managed by a district committee composed of members of the Area Board and an equal number of local representatives. He also stated that there were certain functions which might be more satisfactorily performed by a further tier, a separate Regional Council, above the Area Health Authorities. Planning of consultancy appointments, the development of specialist services, responsibility for postgraduate education and research and, a new suggestion, for the hospital building programme, would be appropriate functions for such regional bodies.

nobody was thought to have put in such a reasoned paper as ours. We finally decided that our draft reply must concede certain figures to the Chancellor.

This evening we had a meeting of the Policy Co-ordinating Committee of the Labour Party, the show which has been set up to put the National Executive and the Cabinet on better terms with each other and to discuss problems informally over a sandwich and a drink. The meeting had been moved from Judith Hart's room to Peter Shore's room on the ground floor of 70 Whitehall. As I got into my car in Palace Yard, Michael Stewart's car stole out in front of me and then George Brown edged in from behind. I came third and all three cars went 100 yards to 70 Whitehall.

The meeting had all been carefully planned so that Judith would first explain about overseas aid before we went on to our difficulties in housing and then to a motion on Cabinet consultation with the N.E.C. but, before we knew it, George Brown sat down and took over the meeting, saying, 'I am Joint Chairman here with you, Peter. What are the issues on the agenda? I've got to change the order because I'm going to have an answer specifically on housing. This is something the Home Policy Committee requires of me.' 'Look,' said the poor Transport House officials, 'it's been agreed that we should deal with overseas aid first, because Judith Hart has to go away at 7.30.' 'I will have the agenda arranged the way I want it,' said George and, after shouting for forty minutes, he finally had his own way and for an hour we discussed a singularly inane proposition about more credit for building societies.

Before Judith left she started a discussion on Africa and finally we got to Joe Gormley's motion on co-ordination between Cabinet Committees and the N.E.C. Then, typically, George's mood changed. Hyde went out and Jekyll came in and as we moved towards 9 o'clock he became breezy, talented, full of creative proposals, stopping any remarks that could cause a row. There couldn't have been a greater difference between the bleary, rude, caddish man at the beginning, exploiting his colleagues' good nature, and the helpful, creative man of an hour later. It was an object lesson in George Brownery, indicating why people are always ready to give him a second chance and why, on the other hand, those who have been around him longest hope in a way he won't ever get his second chance. I pray God there won't ever be another Labour Government with George Brown in it because despite all his talents he will break it up.

I spent the rest of the evening until 12.30 reading happily through the text John Mackintosh has produced for the three Godkin Lectures. I suppose he's worked pretty hard and his drafts are just good enough to send to the P.M. I knocked out quite a lot which clearly derived from Mackintosh, including a discussion on how to overthrow a P.M. by a *coup d'état*, which shows the kind of crazy, reckless fellow John is at the moment.

Wednesday, March 25th

I woke at 6.0 to do two boxes and to prepare my speech for the Institute of Hospital Administrators, who were having a whole day's conference on the Green Paper. This took me until 9 o'clock, and at 9.20 we arrived at Dean's Yard, the back entrance to Church House, Westminster, where I went straight on to the stage. Some 700 people were in the hall and I was told that 300 had been turned away. It was a very wide audience, including representatives from all areas of the service, local authorities, Regional Hospital Boards, Hospital Management Committees and staff organizations. I did the exact opposite to Monday, a spontaneous speech carefully based on notes. Alan Marre said it was the best speech he had ever heard and although it covered almost exactly the same ground as Monday's this time it was an enormous success. The audience started lukewarm, almost hostile, but I brought them along and won them over. At 10.45 I went off for a short meeting with Paul Odgers at 70 Whitehall and then into O.P.D. at No. 10.

This was a very important meeting. First the Foreign Secretary patiently came back with the F.O. policy, asking once more that we should be able to put the British point of view on the Arab–Israeli situation. His paper quite clearly stated that our failure to do so has been very expensive for us and is possibly endangering our interests in the Middle East but the Prime Minister blandly stopped the discussion. He said that he and the President had talked this over and there could be no question of the British putting forward any different point of view. We must not move towards the Arab position. The Prime Minister and the Foreign Secretary do not see eye-to-eye. In this election year at least the P.M. is resolutely opposed to any policy of appeasing the Arabs. Harold's attitude made it easy for me to point out that at any rate we couldn't possibly approve of the Foreign Secretary's paper, which implied that it was wrong to take this neutral position, keep our heads down and not have any positive stance. Denis Healey and I passionately believe that at the moment there is nothing to be gained by having any British policy at all in the Middle East. The Prime Minister has been converted to our position purely by his election anxiety and his wish to get on well with Nixon.

Then we turned to arms sales to Libya, where we had the same kind of difficulty. Now that there is a new government in Libya, British troops have all been withdrawn and we are merely trying to sell arms in competition with the French, who outbid us in every way. Again we discussed the problem of what the Libyans are going to get, Centurion rather than Chieftain tanks probably, and again we were threatened with the F.O. line that if the Libyans didn't get the Chieftains we might have a very dangerous situation in the Middle East. Again the F.O. line is unchanged and again the Prime Minister is opposed to Michael.

This evening I went home to change for dinner at the Society of Apothecaries, where I was Sir John Richardson's guest. I thought Apothecaries meant pharmacists but in fact this is an old city company that dates from the time of Pepys and can still award degrees. They have a marvellous Hall in a beautiful little square just by Blackfriars Station. The room was magnificent with lovely portraits but the food was pretty awful (I gather the chef was away). About 150 people sat down to an immense dinner with lots of drink. These old buffers were all in decorations and full evening dress, all except me, the Secretary of State. I was just in my dinner jacket. I won't wear full evening dress and don't possess it. There they were, the well-fed, over-fed, elderly leaders of the medical profession and their friends. I was in some trouble as to what I should say but I talked to them in an airy way about what it feels like to be a Minister, describing how enjoyable the job is and how one's value as a fresh eye only lasts for the first two or three years. Then I gave them a few professional criticisms. I gather it went down quite well and that Sir John, who is a stiff old thing, was proud of his guest. I left at 10.30 and got home at 11.0, so I had been working for seventeen hours today and feeling pretty well on it. I said to myself afterwards, 'Is this just a false impression?' I really think that seventeen hours would have been an easy day when I was Minister of Housing but Tam tells me this is not so and that I am certainly not working any less hard than I was then. He thinks I am imagining things.

Thursday, March 26th

End of term today, with the adjournment debate in the House and the Prime Minister answering Questions at 11.45, so that Cabinet at 10.0 was in the P.M.'s room in the Commons. What did we do at that Cabinet? I had heard on the wireless this morning and noticed in the papers that Peter Shore had been addressing the Manchester Junior Chamber of Commerce and had made a remarkable speech on the Common Market.[1] He had been very much more critical, saying that there were formidable disadvantages to entry and that this was something which couldn't be decided by the politicians. The people must also make their decision and we mustn't go in unless it really paid us to do so. This is exactly what I felt and feel, an attitude which I think is shared by the vast majority of the people. The anti-feelings have been growing steadily for the last six months and something like two-thirds of the people in this country are against going in, though, like me, they are quite prepared to have a go and see whether the terms are tolerable or not. But Peter's speech was certainly a great deal more anti-Common Market than anything which had been said by a Government spokesman before and every newspaper had jumped to the conclusion that Peter Shore, the co-ordinator of home publicity and the P.M.'s ex-P.P.S., was speaking as the P.M.'s *alter ego*.

At Cabinet the Foreign Secretary went through a whole series of items in his usual boring voice, and then he suddenly said, 'There is one more thing

[1] Mr Shore had made a speech in Manchester on March 25th in which he said that Britain's decision to join the E.E.C. should not be left only to politicians but should be a matter for public debate.

I have to refer to, the Minister Without Portfolio's speech. This completely upsets the balance, Prime Minister, and I must insist that the balance is restored, because otherwise I shall not be able to explain this speech to Europe.' Harold said, 'I knew nothing about the speech. I see the papers say I did, but I had absolutely no notion it was being delivered and I have already made that perfectly clear.' Michael Stewart tried again to get the balance redressed. Peter Shore then said he saw nothing wrong with the speech, which he had made very carefully. He was offering his own point of view, whatever other people might think, and it was in accord with our policy. Then the P.M. said the speech hadn't given the whole balanced policy, only one aspect of it, and we had all told each other all the time that we must be careful to get the balance right, and in particular that we were making a real and serious bid for entry. It was that point which hadn't come out clearly in the speech. I don't know whether I helped at all, but I then said, 'Tell me, was this extempore? Were you reported straight or was there a press release?' Peter said, 'It was a press release. I only just had time to give it to Transport House. I didn't have time to show it to the Foreign Secretary.'

That really did take my breath away. To release it to the press without any previous consultation with the P.M. or the Foreign Secretary was an act of total recklessness and, curiously, I had absolutely assumed that such a thing could not have occurred. I had asked Roy if he thought Peter had talked to the P.M. Roy said, 'No, I don't think he did. I don't think the P.M. would go back on his agreement to that extent.' But Roy has a very poor opinion of Peter and he simply said, 'It shows again what a hopeless fellow he is.' To me it showed how impossible it is to interpret politics and be sure you are right. When I heard about the speech I would have said that Peter couldn't have made it without prior consultation of some sort. Of course I haven't yet had time to see Peter and find out whether, in his view, there was no prior consultation, or whether (with some encouragement) he was flying a balloon. What I do know is that the evidence so far is that he did it on his own and that the P.M. was able to show complete ignorance of the press release. Yet into battle in the House the Prime Minister had to go.

Within a few minutes the P.M. was on the front bench answering a Question into which all this was dragged in. He didn't disown Peter in any way but merely said he supported him loyally, though the speech should be seen as giving a single viewpoint. Harold also took care to make Peter give a press release for tomorrow morning's papers, saying that this was entirely his own personal view. The P.M. dissociated himself to that extent but he showed himself loyal to a friend, even though the friend had made his life extraordinarily difficult. So this afternoon there was Harold performing away, Heath and he, hammer and tongs at each other, accusing each other of being double-crossers and ratters, enjoying themselves no end, neither doing his own side much good.

That is the end of the diary for the week. Parliament has risen, I can go and work on my island in this cold, clear weather and see a bit of the children as well. I shall be in London for a couple of days next week but Parliament won't be sitting and then I'm off to America on April 6th.

Tuesday, March 31st

Anne and the children and I motored up to London. We had a very grand supper at the Criterion and then Virginia had chosen for us quite a pleasant Canadian film about a boy living on his own on the side of a mountain. It was pretty and well acted but it didn't seem very realistic to me or to have even the verisimilitude of the Swiss Family Robinson.

Wednesday, April 1st

It's a quiet week because Harold doesn't come back from the Scillies until tomorrow and there's no Cabinet but I had a day of work, beginning with an awkward interview with John Lewis, who has decided to retire from the chairmanship of the Birmingham R.H.B. We tentatively discussed his successor. Sir John favours another member of the Board, a quiet person who is perfectly O.K. but, like John, a local businessman and completely what is called non-political. I wanted one of our appointees, a Labour man. We decided to think it over and then we went downstairs to the monthly meeting of the R.H.B. chairmen. When I started holding these the Department thought I was barmy but they have now become a considerable institution and indeed I thought it a good sign that the officials had insisted I should break my holiday and come up to London for this one.

It was a long and arduous morning. First I had to discuss the allocation of revenue among the fourteen Boards and our new formula for reducing the disparity between well-off places, London and the Home Counties, and poorer places like Newcastle, Manchester and Birmingham. The amount of uncommitted money we were talking about is only some £5 or £6 million out of a £90 million total but, even so, there was a tremendous struggle to maintain the *status quo*. When we came to discuss the Green Paper there was a kind of *démarche*. Stephen Lycett Green, an amiable, rather courageous man, said his colleagues wished him to ask me whether I would object to the chairmen preparing and publishing a document stating their collective view. 'That', I replied, 'would be a very dramatic step to take. Your views are pretty well-known already because the Opposition spokesmen in both the Commons and the Lords have had access to your SAMO's report, and to your preliminary paper. I suppose this document would be a denunciation of the Green Paper and the Secretary of State. There's no doubt about your views but perhaps you want to make a collective demonstration against me?' There was a great deal of quivering and they said, 'Not at all. We just want to protest against the decision to have nothing but an advisory Regional Council.' So I told them, 'There has been no such decision. As you know I have a weekly meeting of a brains trust, which is working out exactly what the Regional Council should do and what executive powers it should have.' The chairmen all looked embarrassed and I knew that there was going to be formidable resistance to the scheme not only from these people, the chairmen and the hospital consultants, but also from their officers, especially the SAMOS, the Board secretaries and treasurers, key men in the present Regional Hospital organization. They all hate the bureaucracy at the centre and they will see this as an attempt by the Department to take over. They like our permissive attitude to the R.H.B.s and their system of self-perpetuating nomination. I mustn't be surprised at their opposition but what I must do is to produce a reasonable compromise, a Regional Council with some teeth in it. I think I can rely on winning just four or five of the chairmen over and by dividing them I can make the opposition harmless. At least I realized the politics of it this morning.

Thursday, April 2nd

Patrick and I went for a hair-cut, our first since January. Children can wear their hair long so Patrick hadn't looked unduly untidy but mine was getting a bit straggly and, as a result of leaving it all this time, Mr Large was at last able to redesign my hair as he's wanted to do for years. It's cut differently, longer at the back with rather more on top. Even hair-cuts are politically significant – there's been a whole revolution in men's appearance. They can now have their hair designed in a way which five years ago would have been thought kinky or unnatural. I think there's everything to be said for more exciting clothes and hair-dos. I would have gained enormously by this as a young boy but I was repressed. We enjoyed our expedition this morning.

My first job was to see Peter Brown's deputy, Ian Gillis, to discuss a very difficult problem about the pill. Some months ago the Committee on Drugs had come to the very awkward decision that three or four contraceptive pills with a high oestrogen content were demonstrably rather more liable to clause clotting and coronary thrombosis. The Committee was preparing to issue this Report cautiously and soberly but it got into the hands of Chapman Pincher and was presented by the *Daily Express* in a most sensational fashion. There were discussions on the B.B.C. and all those doctors who are fanatically opposed to the pill were able to campaign, with the disastrous result that several hundred thousand women suddenly stopped taking the pill and in January, February and March the number of abortions soared. The Committee had promised to prepare a second and judicious Report, finally and carefully announcing their view about the pill and the safeguards. This is now ready and the C.M.O. had decided that the Editor of the *British Medical Journal* should be given exclusive rights to publish it, because that is the only way to reach the doctors.[1] The Editor of the *B.M.J.*, of course, insists on choosing his own week of publication and he refuses to be interfered with in any way. This has worried the C.M.O., who says that he really

[1] The Editor of the *British Medical Journal* from 1966 until 1975 was Dr Martin Ware.

must write a letter to warn the doctors that the Report is coming. At this point Peter Brown reminded the Department about the women who were actually using the pill. 'Oh,' said the officials, 'the daily press will get a copy of the *B.M.J.* the day before publication and they can print what they like.' Peter said it was essential to brief the press beforehand, so that the newspapers would have a proper statement on the morning when the *B.M.J.* is published. We have had great trouble co-ordinating all this, because the C.M.O. has the strange idea that the Editor of the *B.M.J.* must be allowed his tantrums, which means that we are deciding on our timing solely at his dictation. But it's a good example of Godber's total concern with the doctors. He was apparently much less concerned with the effect on the women. I have to keep both in mind.

My next meeting was on contracting-out and employee consultations. A few weeks ago I had used the occasion of the meeting with the T.U.C. to insist to the Department that the Bill must have a stronger clause requiring employers to consult their employees, even though our only sanction would be that employees could denounce their employers for not doing so. We have now found that Barbara's Industrial Relations Bill is also going to cover this, with clauses laying down that employers must provide information necessary for negotiations, some of which could be about pension negotiations and fringe benefits. I had thought at one point that we could transfer the whole thing to Barbara's Bill, leaving all the consultations to her, but it has become clear that her Bill isn't going to become law before the election, whereas if we can possibly make it, my Bill will be launched before the end of July. At today's meeting we wrote all this into the Bill. I often ask myself why the Department is so profoundly reluctant to act in these matters. I think it is because they don't like declaratory legislation. The Home Office, for example, was much opposed to the Race Relations Bill, which has been extremely successful. I am sure that in my Bill this clause will be effective, even though we cannot police it adequately. I think that, as we move forward, the Pensions Bill is steadily becoming less unpopular but I won't say more than that.

I lunched at the Athenaeum with Nicholas Davenport, who has just been out to South Africa with Olga. They were intoxicated by the beauty and excitement of it, excusing their visit by saying that they went to strengthen the liberal opposition. I had great fun ribbing Nicholas about this, saying that he was really conniving but, to be candid, I don't share Barbara and Harold's fanatically hostile attitude towards South Africa and Spain. I think it's perfectly true that the liberal element there is more discouraged by our total apartheid than it would be if we had closer contacts with these countries. I am quite sure it hasn't really paid us to have this hypocritical policy of cutting off arms sales to South Africa while keeping a major export/import trade with them. So I rather share Nicholas's view though I still teased him about it.

Now that the children have gone home, I spent the evening working away at the Godkin Lectures, with a break at 7 o'clock for a quiet little dinner at the Athenaeum. Over Easter I have been worrying a great deal about these three lectures and the longish draft I sent to Harold. I am waiting for his reaction but though he was back from the Scillies today he hasn't rung me. I want to know whether I should stay in London tomorrow or perhaps go down to Chequers on Saturday, but there's been no word, and he's obviously not terribly keen to see me.

Friday, April 3rd

Yesterday the Prime Minister received the Annual Report of the Kindersley Committee, which makes an astonishing across-the-board demand for a 30 per cent increase for all doctors and dentists, far more than the B.M.A. asked for, and based, the Kindersley people say, on the comparison between doctors and their opposite numbers in the outside world, i.e. accountants, university dons and senior civil servants. This has come at a most awkward time. I rang Roy and Barbara to warn them about it and to ask them not to blow their tops but to leave it for me to deal with. I told them that while I am away in America the Department will be working on this submission to me and looking at the Kindersley Committee's recommendations to see if they are justifiable. We shall almost certainly propose that the award should be phased. It will be extremely difficult to repudiate the agreement at this stage, though Barbara will of course want to mop up the whole Kindersley machinery into the single review body she is seeking. But I doubt whether she will be able to do that in an election year.

I also rang Harold about this and then I asked him whether he had read the Godkin Lectures. He said he hadn't read them last night as he had hoped to do, which slightly bewildered me, but he simply added, 'It will probably be all right. Burke has read them and he has one or two points and there are one or two points from Douglas Allen at the Treasury.' Then he rang off, leaving me feeling just a little disconcerted because it didn't appear that he would want to see me.

I spent the day looking over a big hospital in Sutton and then I crossed into Surrey to see the County Council's magnificent new ambulance centre in Gil's constituency at Carshalton. There I had a splendid tea with the civil servants and I was enjoying it all a great deal when suddenly a message came from my Private Office to say that the Prime Minister wanted to ring me this evening. I was also told that Michael Halls had died. Four years ago he had replaced Derek Mitchell,[1] who was a clever man, an intriguer, pretty anti-us, who also quarrelled with Marcia. The Prime Minister had come to

[1] Sir Derek Mitchell (K.C.B. 1974) was Principal Private Secretary to the Prime Minister 1964–6, Deputy Under-Secretary of State at the D.E.A. 1966–7, Deputy Secretary at the Ministry of Agriculture, Fisheries and Food 1967–9, Economic Minister and Head of the U.K. Treasury and Supply Delegation, Washington, 1969–72. From 1972–7 he was Second Permanent Secretary (Overseas Finance) at H.M. Treasury.

dislike Mitchell and in place of this clever, cold, able, ambitious young man there came as Harold's Private Secretary Michael Halls, a kind, rather silly Territorial officer from exactly the same *petit bourgeois* milieu as Harold, with very much the same cultural values. Tommy Balogh found Michael Halls unbearable and I found him a dim reactionary, but he suited Harold and, unlike Tommy, Burke or I, worked his way into Harold's life. He really joined the inner group, along with Marcia, Joseph Stone,[1] Harold's doctor, and Gerald Kaufman. Michael Halls was only fifty-four and he had just come back from a week's holiday, when he suddenly had a coronary and died in hospital on Wednesday night. Yesterday Harold had been given the news, just before I rang him, and that is why he talked to me in that rather stand-offish way.

The P.M. rang me up at Gilbert's this evening, where I was having supper before speaking at his political meeting. We talked a little about Michael Halls and then Harold said he had now had time to look at the Godkin Lectures and there were one or two points he was very concerned about, particularly the reference to Cabinet minutes. He would like to see me tomorrow morning at 9.30. I said, 'For heaven's sake, I want to get down to Prescote. Can't you make it 9.15?' He said that would suit him and I went off to Gil's meeting.

Saturday, April 4th

At 9.15 I went in to the P.M., who looked rather white and puffy, as he does when he is tired. I said something about Michael Halls but Harold only talked a little about Mrs Halls being upset and then we got down to work on the lectures.[2] I made some notes.[3] On the first page there was a story about the contrast between a day in the life of President Johnson, absolutely driven in his work because he is Chief Executive, and a day in the life of the British Prime Minister, who, as many of them have said, can relax because he hasn't got a Department. Harold didn't like this at all. 'Did I really say all this? I think Marcia may once have said it in your presence.' 'No,' I replied, 'you said it in a T.V. broadcast and I took it from there. You don't like this?' 'No,' Harold said, 'I don't think you ought to give that impression about me because in fact this is a full-time job. I can tell you this, I have never read a book in No. 10. At Chequers I've read a book but, unlike Sir Alec Douglas Home, who used to go downstairs to the big room and read novels, I don't. I've got to cover everything. Take this morning's news, the Post Office charges.[4] I feel personally guilty because I have allowed the Tories a second

[1] Sir Joseph Stone (Kt 1970), a general practitioner in Hampstead. He became a life peer in 1976.

[2] These were the drafts which John Mackintosh had made. The lectures Crossman actually delivered at Harvard are published as *Inside View* (London: Cape, 1972).

[3] Mr Wilson gives his own account of the discussion in *The Governance of Britain*, p. 56.

[4] On March 23rd Mr Stonehouse had told the House of Commons that the Post Office was considering increased telephone charges and, during the recess, he announced that

bite of the cherry. The Postmaster-General announces it just before the recess and we get a bad effect on the G.L.C. elections. Now he gives the full details and the story is told for the second time. The third time will be when the Tories move a vote of censure. I ought to have seen to this. This is the kind of area, you understand, that I have to keep check of. That is the job of the British Prime Minister. He is on the go the whole time, covering everything. And then, you know, there is the strain of leading a team.' I said, 'Yes, of course, and with Ministers working away on their own I suppose keeping control is a great difficulty.' 'Yes,' he said, 'I must keep complete coverage of the Government.' But I never feel he does keep complete coverage of the Government, though I suppose the answer might be that he gives me a free hand. Still, it was an interesting point.

The next point that upset him was that I said that unlike the American President, the Prime Minister was relieved of a great deal of official ceremonial by the Queen and Prince Philip. Harold said that this would be a most unhappy way of putting it. 'I hope you won't say that. After all, let's be clear about it. Macmillan was an idle man, who just didn't work as Prime Minister, and Douglas Home was idle. I am not an idle man, I have never worked harder than I do here.' Then he said he thoroughly approved of my contrast between the Prime Minister's attitude to Cabinet and the President's view of them as mere agents. He added, 'I was amazed at that story about your leaving out of your introduction to Bagehot that paragraph about Russia.' This had been a paragraph saying that the British P.M. had more power to sack people than the Russian P.M., and the publishers had advised me to take it out. Harold said, 'I didn't know publishers did that.' I said, 'They had a good reader who suggested that this was incredible. Of course the day on which the proofs went to the printers Macmillan sacked more than half his Cabinet, proving my point.' The P.M. said, 'No Russian Prime Minister can sack anybody. It's almost impossible. I don't know how anyone would ever think he could.' I just note this here as an interesting sidelight.[1]

But Harold was mainly concerned with the section about Cabinet minutes. This had been written not by John but by me and I had made the point that, because the P.M. alone approves the minutes after they have been drafted by the Cabinet Secretariat and because he is able to have the minutes written as he wants, the record of Cabinet discussion and decision can be slanted and this greatly strengthens the P.M.'s hand. I absolutely meant what I said and Harold said it was completely untrue. He said that very occasionally he might have seen the minutes, or very, very occasionally Burke might have

---

there would be a rise of 20 per cent in charges, an 18 per cent increase in the connection charge, 25 per cent in domestic rentals and 50 per cent in business rentals. Mr Stonehouse had refused to be drawn on the question of increased postal charges but it was rumoured that the Post Office intended to raise to 7*d.* the charge for first-class letters and to 6*d.* the charge for second-class mail. A Conservative motion of censure, debated on April 21st, was defeated by 286 votes to 327.

[1] See *Inside View*, p. 47.

consulted him before they were written, but rarely has he been consulted before they are issued and very rarely does he bother to read them afterwards. This is interesting. I have spent six years with Harold in his Cabinet and, having often talked to Burke, I am deeply convinced that the P.M. does approve the minutes, but no, according to Harold this is not so.

The other point was that I had said that Burke was Harold's grand vizier, and the Cabinet Secretariat his praetorian guard. Harold said, 'You know, Burke isn't all that close to me. He is such an Establishment figure and the Cabinet Secretariat is very much an independent force, standing on its own. I don't think you should describe it in this way.' But I *do* think Burke has been Harold's grand vizier, and in the first two years they were very close. I suspect that Harold has never trusted him quite so much since the D-notice mess, for which Burke was responsible, and that they have grown much more distant. Nevertheless I think that although Harold doesn't feel Burke is very close to him, Burke feels his first loyalty is to the Prime Minister and to strengthening his position, a loyalty which he doesn't feel to other Ministers. Harold was also critical of my observation that the way to the top of the Civil Service is via the Cabinet Secretariat. He thought this wasn't true at all and he said that the mark of the coming man was to spend some time as a Treasury official, although that isn't as true now as it used to be. In another passage about the Prime Minister's control over the Civil Service I pointed to his power to veto, at least, the appointment of every Permanent Secretary and Deputy Secretary. 'Yes,' Harold said, 'that is true but I have set up a new arrangement so that the names are discussed by a panel before they come to me. This has reduced my personal power,' and he then told me the history of this. The other thing he particularly wanted me to emphasize was the importance of the confrontation between the P.M. and the Leader of the Opposition at Question Time on Tuesdays and Thursdays. This is perfectly true and it's really quite a modern phenomenon. Until 1961 the P.M. took on Tuesdays and Thursdays Questions after Number 35, and Question Time was often finished before we could reach this point. Putting them on at 3.15, whatever the other business, has made P.M.'s Question Time an institution and we have a twice-weekly confrontation whenever Parliament is sitting. In this sense Parliament is still a better forum for a confrontation between the party leaders than anything the Americans have.

These were Harold's main points and he was obviously concerned, as he often is, that he shouldn't be quoted out of context and anxious, in case it upset us in the election, that the Labour Party shouldn't be described as having totalitarian discipline. But Harold was free-and-easy and his relations with me were apparently absolutely spontaneous. We seemed to behave naturally towards each other but of course we now keep a certain distance. He knows me very well, I know him very well, neither of us says everything to the other, nor says what he thinks of the other and frankly I wonder if he wants me to stay on after the election. Does he think that it would be a convenient moment for me to retire? I have no idea and maybe when I come back from America I will ask him.

Sunday, April 5th

The main feature of last week was Northern Ireland, where, as Harold feared, trouble has blown up again.[1] It has confirmed all his warnings of how tender the structure is and how the goodwill towards the British would evaporate. The violence and bomb throwing now seem to be organized and to take place in both Catholic and Protestant areas. It's an ugly position locally but it does not damage us politically, because in the last six months Callaghan has been so successful and because the Tories are in no position to do any better. Meanwhile the other important news has been of the continuing wage inflation, with strikes in the motor-car industry and demands for huge increases, including the claims of my own Kindersley Committee. This has been combined with glowing news about a possible budget surplus and about the gold reserves.[2] Here we are, one of the strongest currencies in Europe, sucking money into the City of London and piling up our reserves.

Meanwhile I was off to America. Apart from holidays, it is only the second time I have been abroad as a Minister. There was my brief visit to Stockholm to study the Swedish pensions system, but, as Harold has emphasized to me, this American expedition is a private visit, privately arranged. We had already had an amusing contretemps last Thursday, when the Private Office told me they were having great difficulty in getting me an American visa. The American Consul-General in London was saying he couldn't give me an earnings visa, which I needed because I was getting a fee from Harvard. 'In that case,' I said, 'I won't take a fee.' But the Office told me it was too late because I had signed a form which said I was receiving a fee, 'and after all,' said Robin Wendt, 'you are.' So the Consul-General was within his rights. Robin Wendt had to ring up Harvard and Harvard had to

[1] On April 1st there had been fresh rioting in Belfast and on April 3rd 500 troops were flown to the city to reinforce the 6,000 who were already there. Although the troops were armed, hitherto they had relied on other ways of dealing with rioters but now the G.O.C., General Sir Ian Freeland, warned that the troops would use firearms and that anyone using or making a petrol bomb was liable to ten years' imprisonment. He also stated, 'Anyone throwing a petrol bomb after a warning is liable to be shot dead.' In a later statement the General seemed to suggest that British troops might be withdrawn altogether, a remark that caused concern in Ulster and among M.P.s at Westminster. In a Commons Statement on April 7th the Home Secretary reassured the House that there was no immediate question of withdrawal, stating that British troops would remain in Northern Ireland as long as it was decided by Her Majesty's Government that they should remain there and that would be for as long as it was necessary for them to do the work for which they were there. A worrying aspect of the latest outbreak of rioting was that Ulster's Roman Catholic minority, which had at first welcomed the arrival of British troops, seemed to be losing confidence in the impartiality of the Army and in particular that of the Scottish regiments.

[2] The 1969/70 financial year, ending on April 5th, had shown a record revenue surplus of £2,444 million and figures published on April 2nd showed that after short-term debt payments, unofficially estimated at £100 million, and a £16 million net repayment to the I.M.F., the gold and dollar reserves had increased by £28 million to £1,129 million.

ring the State Department and pay a 25 guinea charge for the privilege of having me over and paying me $3,000 for the Godkin Lectures. Of course this has always been a delicate question. We looked it up in the Cabinet Office directive to Ministers to see whether I was entitled to take the fee. Well, I am doubtful myself but as this was a private visit to give an academic lecture in a distinguished series and, as I confirmed when I got there, no other politician who has done this has ever refused a fee, I decided to accept it. In any case most of it is going to John Mackintosh. Actually, as John guessed and as I knew, I shan't read aloud the texts he's prepared. They aren't quite right for me despite all the changes I have made and anyway the only real purpose of the draft was to give Harold something to criticize. Very sensibly the Harvard authorities have written to ask me not to lecture from a script because they much prefer the Oxford style, so this is what I shall do.

Saturday, April 11th[1]

During the flight home I slept for two and a half hours and when I woke up I saw England and Wales with a brilliant covering of white snow on the Black Mountains. We swooped down on London Airport at 9.30 in the morning and there I found Robin Wendt, who had motored over to give me all the news. I felt very pleased to see him. It was sunny at Heathrow but as I drove through the Chilterns it began to cloud over. I stopped at Watlington to see Jennie, who had been wonderfully kind. She and Gil and Jessica had been out into the woods and had collected for me a box full of bluebells in their own earth for my island. I was back at Prescote by 12.30 and, while I was getting myself shaved Anne told me that the swimming bath had been cleaned and was heating up, so tomorrow I shall be able to dive in for my first bathe of the year.

My only contact with Britain during my Sabbatical week in Cambridge, Mass., was on Thursday last, when I was rung early in the morning by the Consul, who had received a telegram from the Prime Minister. I thought, 'Oh, my God, what is this?' The message simply said that there was a sensational story in that morning's *Daily Mail*, in which Walter Terry had asserted that Harold Wilson and George Brown had planned to intervene in the Israeli Six-Day War, but by the second day Harold had become less keen on the plan and it was dropped. This was a strange story and I know how it had come about. Just before I left London, the *New Statesman* had asked me to review Patrick Gordon Walker's book,[2] and I had noticed that the fictitious meeting he had described was remarkably like one of the Cabinets where we discussed the closing of the Strait of Tiran and the British role.[3]

[1] From Monday, April 6th, to Friday, April 10th, Crossman was delivering the Godkin Lectures at Harvard.

[2] *The Cabinet* (London: Cape, 1970; rev. edn 1972). The description of the imaginary Cabinet meeting appears on pp. 153–67 of the revised edition and the author indicates that it is partly based on three debates held in Mr Wilson's Cabinet in May 1967.

[3] See Vol. II, pp. 356–9.

Walter Terry had apparently deduced from this passage that it revealed a secret. I was very amused because I had discussed Gordon Walker's book with Harold, who told me that the text had been cleared by Burke Trend, so this very passage had in fact been approved by the Secretary to the Cabinet. Harold had now specially telegraphed to tell me not to give any public or private interviews about this and that further directives would follow. When the airmail edition of *The Times* arrived, there on the front page was a formal denial from No. 10, giving maximum attention to the story. I gather that next Monday there is to be a debate on the Middle East, so no doubt this will come up again. Ha, ha! It is true that I had discussed Patrick's book at Harvard and there was always, I suppose, a danger that I could be cross-examined on it, but it was amusing that all Harold could think of was to stop me talking about the story.

Sunday, April 12th

Yesterday afternoon I did a little bit of clearing and weeding on my island and planted the bluebells. I went down to see Virginia's hut, which is to be put up at the far end of the island, and I felt I was back at home, knowing that if ever I cease to be a Minister there is a wonderful life waiting for me here. I can really indulge myself in academic lecturing and writing, without the constant anxiety that an unfortunate phrase will put me in the wrong. What fun it will be to sit and write and see more of my family.

London was all right, thirty-five seats to sixty-five, about what we expected and just enough to prevent the whole thing from being a disastrous failure.[1] Nothing else has happened and the only other news is of preparations for the budget. I have read the Cabinet minutes but nothing much is going on there. They've been working on Barbara's Bill and I gather that last week, without any fuss, we got inserted into my Bill the retrospective preservation of pension rights. I haven't been much missed of course, though Tam has rung up to find out how I am. But it's a good thing to get a bit detached, if in due course you are going to detach yourself. Here I was off in this life of my own and I've come through it.

Monday, April 13th

Traditional Cabinet meeting on the day before the budget. There is no agenda so there are no red boxes and Harold always says, 'I don't want any notes taken and if they are taken I don't want them taken out of the room.' We sat very quiet and listened to Roy describing his budget. I would call this a spineless Cabinet but it is an election year when none of us want to break things up, so perhaps that's why there wasn't any real discussion. Jim Callaghan was the only man honest enough to say, right at the end of the meeting, that the budget was an anti-climax but he also rather touchingly

[1] The Conservatives made a net gain of 55 seats in the English and Welsh counties and in the Greater London Council elections they retained control, with 65 seats to Labour's 35. Labour gained control of the Inner London Education Authority.

added that he was deeply impressed by Roy's mastery of the international monetary situation, which is really the basis of the budget. Of course, after two and a half years Roy's got the job in hand, just as each one of us has learnt the rigmarole and mastered the ideology and arguments of his Ministry. Roy has got this at his fingertips and he can talk the Treasury language to us. His budget was exactly what I had predicted. Instead of the £400 million income tax remission which Nicky Kaldor had planned, Roy had limited it to half that amount, which meant that he didn't have to offset another £200 million by raising money from an S.E.T. increase or an increase in employers' N.I. contributions. This is the correct, prim and proper thing to do and it is also positively socialist, because the remission only applies to people with incomes between £16 and £19 a week.

I went back to the office for my discussion with Bea Serota, John Dunwoody, David Ennals and Brian O'Malley about our P.Q.s this afternoon and afterwards we had the office lunch. Perhaps the sandwiches were slightly better this time. We discussed Bavin's first report on his researches into the Kindersley recommendations. Bavin is a man of very strong, powerful convictions. When I first came to the Department he was running into retirement but now he has got a new lease of life. He is clever and, on the whole, the best man in the Department. He and Alan Marre both write good minutes but whereas Alan is a purely non-political, charming, sweet man, with a darling wife, Alfred Bavin is a man of some kind of principle.

Then we had George Godber for our talk about the pill. On Thursday week I shall specially brief the medical correspondents and I am sending letters to Charlie Hill at the B.B.C. and Bert Bowden at I.T.V. George is writing to the doctors and we are doing our best to avoid another disaster with this.

Then it was time for Questions. There are only thirty or forty people there on a Monday so it's always an easy day to be first in Questions, because it just teeters along. Once again only the abortion Questions aroused any feeling. I answered quite good-temperedly but I know for certain that tomorrow's press will concentrate on this. Tony Crosland, Secretary of State for Pollution, Crossman, Secretary of State for Abortion – that is more or less the impression the general public gets.

Tuesday, April 14th

It was not so much budget day as Apollo day. Tam came down to breakfast and said, 'There has been some bust-up on Apollo 13.'[1] This flight has gone wrong from the beginning and it has only aroused people's interest as things have started going wrong.

This morning I drove up to St James's Square to see Barbara. We had to

[1] The Apollo 13 space craft was to have been launched on March 12th but the flight had been postponed for a month. On the second day of the journey to the moon there was an explosion on board and plans for a moon landing were abandoned. Emergency arrangements were made and three days later the space craft splashed down in the Pacific and its crew of three returned safely to earth. No other manned space flights were made during 1970.

talk about another batch of wage claims, including one from the hospital laundry managers, a very militant group. These claims are mostly consequential on the nurses' award and I wanted Barbara's authority to go above the 15 per cent to which the P.I. Committee had limited me. I explained that, if I could go to at least 15½ for the first offer, it would enable me to do some restructuring for the laundry men but I might possibly want to go to 18 per cent. She consented to this with a good grace. Then I turned to the Kindersley Committee and it was clear that Barbara was going to urge us to accept the recommendations and phase the award but to take this opportunity to put the consideration of doctors' and dentists' salaries under a central commission, just as we are doing with judges' salaries. I must admit that there are very powerful arguments for this, though I know I shall have a hell of a row with the doctors and that my Department is against it.

I went round the corner into Mayfair, where Ronnie Grierson had asked me to lunch to meet Arnold Weinstock,[1] the biggest man in mergers, who has, for example, built a vast concern out of English Electric. Ronnie Grierson, who used to be the chairman of the I.R.C., has now become a member of G.E.C. and is a kind of lieutenant to Weinstock. It was a very gay lunch. I was given plenty to drink and excellent food while this adventurer Weinstock stimulated me to give a lecture on pensions and teach him life's realities. He claimed that he had an old stick as his pensions expert and that he himself knew nothing about the subject. I am curious to know what Ronnie Grierson thought of it all. He had brought along this donnish member of the Cabinet, who was performing like an intellectual sea-lion, balancing balls on his nose in the presence of Weinstock, who was performing too. I suppose I ought to have been slightly ashamed.

I rushed back to the House just in time to squeeze myself on to the front bench at the end by the Speaker's chair. I must admit I fell asleep during Roy's budget speech, which was pretty heavy going, especially the international part.[2] Before we came to any of the goodies I had to slip away to catch the 5.15 to Swansea, where I was to lecture on the voluntary services. It was a drenching wet night at Swansea and we were met by Sir Goronwy Daniel,[3] who used to be George Thomas's Permanent Secretary at the Welsh

[1] Sir Arnold Weinstock (Kt 1970), Managing Director of Radio and Allied Holdings Ltd 1954–63, Director of the General Electric Co. 1961 and Managing Director of G.E.C. Ltd since 1963. He was Director of Rolls-Royce (1971) Ltd 1971–3.

[2] The Chancellor hoped to avoid new pressure on the pound and a fresh burst of inflation by making only limited fiscal concessions, although there was a budget surplus of over £220 million. The concessions on personal taxation were held at £175 million in a full year and they were designed to help the lowest-paid by increasing the personal allowance and thus relieving some 2 million people from income tax. There were no changes in direct taxes on cigarettes, petrol and alcohol. The Chancellor abolished the ceiling on bank loans to the private sector and reduced from 40 to 30 per cent the rate of the import deposit levy. Mr Jenkins hoped that these measures, together with a reduction in bank rate from 7½ to 7 per cent, would stimulate industrial investment and export.

[3] Sir Goronwy Daniel (K.C.V.O. 1969), Permanent Under-Secretary at the Welsh Office 1964–9 and since 1969 Principal of Aberystwyth University College.

Office, and is now Vice-Chancellor of Aberystwyth University. He is a kind of caricature of a Welsh senior civil servant, tall and black and subfusc, with his neck clicking over a butterfly collar and a prim and bogus religious method of address. He was also a nightmare to drive with, especially on a wet night in Swansea. When we got to the huge, wonderful university campus, I was forced to go down to the International Night, so I left my staff preparing notes on the speech and off I went. It was the usual business. We heard a Negro intoning his national songs in a curious monotone and then we had a man from Aberdeen singing in Welsh. I was introduced to people from twenty-eight nations and I realized that this conference is a tremendous social welfare racket.

Wednesday, April 15th

I woke at 6.0 and fixed up the lecture, basing it on the theme of the role of the voluntary organizations. At 9.30 I spoke. It was a success and then, after their various working groups had delivered reports and we'd had a rather dim lunch, I got back on to the train and worked on my review of Gordon Walker's book.

Directly I got back to 70 Whitehall I dictated the review and then I went home to Vincent Square to take Anne out for her birthday dinner. Peter Smithson and the other girl driver came in to have a birthday drink and then Anne tried on a dress I had brought back from America. It is a lovely colour and it seems to be a fair success. Anyway it is quite possible. Then off we went to Prunier, where Madame Prunier and the whole staff were waiting to receive us. She offered us a bottle of champagne and we had a wonderful celebratory evening.

Thursday, April 16th

I had to go out early to see David Ennals, who was concerned about a speech he is to deliver to the Child Poverty Action Group's annual conference this coming Sunday. I still feel unhappy about the way I fell into a bitter argument with Peter Townsend, when he came to represent the C.P.A.G. a few weeks ago. In this respect Roy's budget is a relief to me because it does give some money to the lowest possible income groups, and to this extent we should have spiked the guns of the C.P.A.G. and of Peter Townsend and his friends. David had brought me a long, intricate defensive speech and we struggled over it with Brian before I went to Management Committee at 10.30.

This is turning out to be very useful. As Patrick Gordon Walker quite rightly says in his book, the Prime Minister has to have a very large Inner Cabinet because at least eight people are too important to be left out and he has less freedom in choosing his Inner Cabinet than his main Cabinet. The problem with the Parliamentary Committee was that it both limited the Prime Minister's freedom and infuriated those non-members who found that decisions were being taken in their absence. But the Management Committee meets merely as an informal discussion group, exactly as it should. Though we leave firm decisions to the Cabinet, the initial discussion brings us into line with each other or else reveals differences, so that at Cabinet itself it is much easier to get a decision.

This morning I had to report to Kindersley and see that we didn't take the recommendations to the P.I. Committee, which would leak, but to a special MISC headed by Barbara. I also had to clear the raising of the supplementary benefit increase, which I had set for S.E.P. next Tuesday. These two items were dealt with in fifteen minutes. Otherwise we discussed, as we always do, the local election results and the prospects before us and we talked about decimalization and the future of the sixpence, and whether we should write a series of pre-election articles for *The Times*.

Immediately afterwards we had Cabinet and the first reactions to Gordon Walker's book, which was published this morning. Last week while I was away Cabinet had discussed the fantastic story about Suez and this morning members of Cabinet were asked not to permit the meaning of Gordon Walker's reference to be elicited from them. Harold was as fussy as ever but he was unable to do anything about the book, and he didn't mention that I had agreed to review it.

We then came to a most interesting item, a Top Secret paper from the Home Secretary on the case of Colonel Ojukwu, the former head of the Biafran rebel regime, who had been overthrown by General Gowon and had fled to the Ivory Coast, a French colony. It seemed likely that Ojukwu would seek refuge here and, as that would create a real breach between the British and Nigerian Governments, Harold had decided when we first discussed this before Easter that there must be full Cabinet backing to stop him. Our friend Callaghan was his usual uncertain self, behaving on this rather as he has done on drugs. He almost asked Cabinet to prevent him from doing as the P.M. and the Foreign Secretary wanted and he said that he couldn't do anything unless Ojukwu actually got here, though a watch would be kept at Customs and if Ojukwu were spotted he would be shipped back on the next plane. When Jim had made his case, I said, 'Look, last time we discussed this I asked what precedents there were and I was told that nobody knew. Since this paper does not mention any precedents, I assume that none exist. So we are proposing that the Home Secretary should take an unprecedented action that is a departure from the long tradition that there is a right of asylum in this country. Liberty is very unpopular. It is an unpleasant, difficult thing, but let us at least be clear about what we are doing.' The Solicitor General confirmed that banning Ojukwu would be an unprecedented action and Callaghan leant across and said, 'Are you opposing it?' I said, 'Well, you must know your business, you and the P.M.,' and that was that. The thing went through and the minutes didn't even have a reference to my remarks. Afterwards, as we were getting up, Callaghan said to me, 'Of course, if you had opposed that I would have gone along with you,' and Roy said, 'Yes, if you had opposed it I would have supported you as well.' It was a shock. What had happened to me? Why hadn't I opposed Harold and Michael Stewart and split the Cabinet? I knew the Home Office proposal was wrong and I believe I could have carried the majority with me. I suspect that it was because I have lost the spirit, the dynamic, for taking such a stand. Am I a member of Cabinet at all? Or am I just sitting there watching? Years ago I would have done it, but now I am a senior member and carry more weight I don't act. It shook me a good deal.

But I didn't have much time to reflect on this because I had to go to the lunch for the National Federation of Professional Workers, who were having their golden jubilee conference. These people have supported our pension scheme and I was able to thank them for it.

This afternoon I was sitting next to the P.M. listening to his Questions, when Roy sat himself down beside me and said, 'I've got a joke to tell you.' I said, 'For heaven's sake, not at the moment, I'm trying to listen to Harold.' After Harold's reply, Roy turned to me and said, 'This is my funny story. You will remember that you sent me Brian Abel-Smith's proposal for the budget. I had already got the same recommendations from the Treasury but I just wanted to tell you that though the idea didn't come from him, I carried out his proposals and I know that I did.' I rang up Brian, who seemed pleased with the story. I said, 'I hope you think his budget was good enough.'

My biggest meeting this afternoon was our weekly session of the brains trust, where we had an absolutely first-rate discussion on the role of the district authority. Would it just be advisory, in what sense could it be executive, and what should be its exact functions? By jove, it was stimulating and it proved how valuable outsiders can be to a Ministry. The truth is that you can only have very few whole-time outsiders. I have managed to fit in Brian and Nicky, but they are the only two who are permanently attached to the Department. The best method is to have these working parties. The outsiders are enormously excited and they will come from anywhere in England to sit for half an hour once a week and work with you. They are gratified to be asked and the people inside learn a lot from them.

I gave Nicky a slap-up dinner at the Garrick. He's a man who is always preoccupied by a single idea at a time, and he'd only one thing to say to me. A fortnight ago he had published in the *New Statesman* an article saying that the E.E.C. agricultural policy is hopelessly reactionary and terribly expensive and that from every point of view, that of the members and of the world, the E.E.C. is a hopeless organization, and there is no reason whatsoever for us to join it. It was a most expert article and very powerful. Nicky said this evening, 'Now that you have failed in your budget, which will neither win nor lose you any votes, you have to get another election-winning instrument. What you must do this summer is to choose your time and then say, as a Government, "Unless the E.E.C. changes the Common Agricultural Policy we won't go in." You, Dick, you alone, could put this forward to Cabinet with any chance of success.' This made me recollect what happened at Cabinet this morning. If I were to choose my time and insist on doing as Nicky suggests, I think Harold, Michael and Roy would find it difficult to refuse me and I would have people like Barbara and Fred Peart supporting me and, I suspect, Ted Short and Peter Shore as well. But I had to say, 'Nicky, I don't want to do this. I don't want to split the Cabinet. I have done that once before when I fought Harold, Barbara and Roy on industrial relations. I don't want to fight Roy, Harold and Michael on this. I am too old, too divided and anyway I don't want Labour to win the election. I want to be out writing my book.' He said, 'This is discreditable.' I said, 'Yes, it's only half my attitude.' I went away disturbed and uneasy about myself and my role in Cabinet, and I am still brooding. Would it be all right, should I do it? I had better hurry up because there isn't very much time.

Friday, April 17th

Public attention is completely dominated by Apollo 13, which is to land tonight. I laughed when I read in the morning papers that President Nixon had postponed a televised address on Vietnam so that he and the American people could devote themselves to Apollo but I was even more amused to learn later on that Harold had cancelled a meeting at Darlington so that he could watch the touch-down this evening. But here am I addressing a business meeting of Coventry social workers tonight. The great difference is, I suppose, that if it were a public meeting no one would come.

The other big news this morning was the victory of the Reverend Paisley and his subaltern in the Ulster by-elections, two ultra-reactionary Protestants defeating official Unionist candidates. It has forced on our attention the more important fact that the Chichester-Clark Government, which has been trying a moderate reformist policy, is not carrying with it a majority of Northern Irish Protestants.

This morning I dictated a letter to Nahum Goldmann, who wanted to see Nasser and try to negotiate peace terms but was refused leave by the Israeli Government.[1] He has sent me a translation of five articles he has written for *Ha'aretz*, *The Times* of Israel, and I wrote to tell him that they are first-rate. I hadn't very much else to do today and I was working on my review when I was suddenly told that a member of Nixon's Cabinet, a Professor Moynihan from Harvard,[2] was passing through London and wanted to lunch with me. I sat about with my Private Secretary until Moynihan turned up, a gangling

[1] Gamal Abdel Nasser was President of the Republic of Egypt 1956–8 and of the United Arab Republic from 1958 until his death in 1970. He was Prime Minister of Egypt 1967–70.

[2] Daniel Patrick Moynihan was Professor of Education and Urban Politics at the University of Harvard 1966–73 and Professor of Government 1972–6. He was Counsellor to the President and Assistant for Urban Affairs 1969–70, Consultant to the President 1971–3, U.S. Ambassador to India 1973–5 and U.S. Permanent Representative to the United Nations 1975–6. In November 1976 he was elected junior Senator for New York State.

Irishman, tall and red-faced, who looks as if he'd been a good drinker in his time. We gave him whisky and then we took him downstairs and gave him Moselle followed by brandy. He was enormously nice. He remembered my providing him with a drink when whisky was short in London twenty years ago and he said he had been sorry to miss my lectures at Harvard. He told me that he'd just had a thrilling telegram saying that the House of Representatives had accepted his plan for a national minimum income of $1,500. This much resembles the 'income guarantee' that Douglas Houghton sold to the National Executive when he was Chancellor of the Duchy of Lancaster, but which we had failed to implement. Moynihan also had an extraordinary story of how 6,000 members of Harvard University had stood in Harvard Square baying and smashing about and battling with the police, in an anti-Vietnam protest meeting yesterday.[1]

Sunday, April 19th

Beautiful days, sunny and brilliant with rolling white clouds. At last the grass is beginning to grow. It is cold but the bath is warm. This morning David Ennals rang up to tell me that late last night he had done an interview for 'The World This Weekend' and to apologize for not asking my leave. I turned the radio on but I couldn't make the broadcast out. It was no interview but a fairly hopeless row between David and Peter Townsend, unintelligible to ordinary people. I don't think I need to worry because although David always sloshes to and fro and has a terribly defensive and guilty way of arguing, Peter Townsend was even worse and he didn't sound in the least compassionate about the very poor. His argument was donnish and pedantic. I was a bit relieved to find that David hadn't done any better or worse than I would have done and at least the interview was related to the budget, seen from my narrow point of view. The budget has been a national non-event, in which nobody was really helped, yet even Mr Pritchett was impressed by the fact that here was a Chancellor who hadn't gone electioneering and that what little has been given away had gone to the very poorest. I think that in this sense the budget has probably been a positive event for the Government, so I mustn't underrate it.

Monday, April 20th

As I was waiting outside the door before Management Committee, Roy came

[1] Although the number of American combat troops in Vietnam was being steadily reduced, protests continued against the war. In April American forces also moved into Cambodia where Prince Sihanouk had been overthrown in March by Communist opponents of the regime. President Nixon promised the American nation that the American advance would be limited and that the troops would withdraw by the beginning of July, once communist forces were expelled from their sanctuaries and their military supplies destroyed. The withdrawal was completed by June 29th, the same day on which the American Senate voted to deny funds for an American military operation in Cambodia. Though in one sense this action was too late, it did signify that the Congress was determined to curb the President's freedom of manoeuvre in foreign policy and it represented the first major victory for congressional opponents of the war.

up and said, 'By the way, I wanted to mention that I shall be raising the issue of the Kindersley Report.' I noticed that he had a long speech written out and I realized that he was going to cause trouble. After the first item, he started trying to make a great speech but I was able to stop him, saying, 'Look, this is ridiculous. Most people here haven't seen the Report. The Chancellor is away next week, so if he is anxious about this, let us postpone consideration of the Report, even though it's a bit of a nuisance, because it will mean that we can't deal with it before the B.M.A. meet on May 8th.' This nonplussed Roy, who had been determined to do me down by having it all discussed in detail today and having it knocked out in one. But even if you are Chancellor you can't do that.

Our main discussion was about the legislation programme and whether we should plan for a normal new session after the summer recess or whether we should carry over the existing session until the election in spring 1971, assuming we weren't going to the country this September. All the arguments suggested that it would be impossible to start a new short session in the autumn and that we should run the present session through until March, giving us time to complete Barbara's Bill and various other things. However, the more we discussed it the more obvious it was that we no longer have that option. Only a devaluation threat or some ghastly disaster could force us to carry on. We really have only one date for the election and that is October 10th. It is either that or bringing it forward to June but, as Bob Mellish has discovered, June is clearly impossible because no Member feels he is ready and nobody is going to consider that possibility until we have seen the results of the municipal elections. Who is going to tell me that we will have such a triumphant result in May that we can have a snap election? No, we realized today that autumn is the only time.

Towards the end of the meeting I raised the problem of the Common Market. Nicky had rung me on Saturday night to make me read his *New Statesman* article, and he had convinced me that I must do something. I managed to say, 'Look, let us discuss the programming of our Common Market attitudes. Would the P.M. tell me something about this? Are we planning to open negotiations or not?' Of course I have been reading the telegrams but the fact that I asked this shows how little I know about these things and how departmentalized we are. It emerged that in July we are to have what Harold described as 'a Victorian family portrait'. He said, 'That is what Willy Brandt has called it, a family portrait, with all the members of the E.E.C. and all the applicants coming to record their official positions.' I said, 'Marvellous. It would suit us very well to have that in July. But, in that case, Prime Minister, you must appreciate that we are hoping you will be able to use it for electoral purposes because, after all, the only thing wrong with Peter Shore's speech was that Peter Shore said it.[1] If you had said it, from your central position, it would have been O.K. What I am expecting of you

[1] See pp. 874 and n., 875, above.

is that in July you will be able to make a speech about food prices and the cost of entry and of the C.A.P., and you could suggest that Britain isn't going to join. With that you would win the election. As we have given up the idea of an election-winning budget, we are left with the E.E.C., where Heath is suspect. We are depending upon you to do it.'

We discussed this for thirty-five minutes and, although Harold continued to say we couldn't discuss the Common Market without Michael Stewart (the Foreign Secretary is in Turkey at the moment), we were obviously doing so. There was not even a denial from Roy, who might have said that appearing to manoeuvre in this way would be very dangerous, and that we shouldn't exploit the Common Market in the election. Denis and Fred Peart also sat silent, merely smiling. Barbara and I made it clear that in the summer we would expect the P.M. to make our negotiating posture an election-winning issue. We reached a general agreement that Michael Stewart had been wrong to urge members of the Cabinet to do their share of speaking on the Common Market and that only the inner three should do so. The minority would express their view by remaining silent and any speaking I were to do would be misunderstood. Harold and Michael are ardent Common Marketeers now, more I would say than Roy who, as Chancellor, sees the real difficulties and is certainly prepared to postpone if demanding higher terms would win us the election. The other ardent marketeers are Tony Crosland and Denis Healey, who certainly wasn't before but now, I think, feels that he has to be in favour of entry if he is ever going to become Foreign Secretary. As for the rest of Cabinet, Barbara and I are willing to try but not on terms that are too high, Fred Peart is firmly opposed, Bob Mellish is a sort of Marketeer and George Thomson is infatuated because he is at the F.O. Nobody else is very enthusiastic one way or the other.

Afterwards as Burke was using his key to get the two of us into the Privy Council offices, I said to him, 'We had better not have any of that in the minutes.' He said, 'No, I agree with you. It was a useful discussion but not one we will mention.' Sure enough, no minute of this discussion is to be found.

Tuesday, April 21st

At the beginning of S.E.P. Harold called attention to a front-page story in the *Daily Express* that accused him of ordering Permanent Secretaries to refuse any policy advice the Shadow Cabinet might ask for. There wasn't a word of truth in the story, which obviously came from the Shadow Cabinet, but it did stimulate a lengthy discussion on the prevailing practice and we found that when we'd been approached most of us had almost automatically conceded to the Opposition front bench. When Maurice Macmillan had asked me whether he could be briefed on the Green Paper by Alan Marre and the Department, I had said of course he could. On the other hand, when Jim Callaghan had discovered that four of his relatively junior policemen were being asked to lunch to meet Heath, he had, on the advice of his officials, said this would be improper. Harold paid great attention to this discussion and, indeed, he left the Committee and went away for two hours to prepare a Statement to scotch what he thought was a damaging plot organized by the Opposition.

When Harold left, Roy took over what became an extremely boring meeting. First of all we celebrated the fact that Willie Ross has today served longer as Secretary of State for Scotland than any of his predecessors. He and Denis Healey are the only men who have held the same job from 1964 to 1970. There has been constant pressure to move Willie but he has stuck it out, and he has also stuck out the period when it was modish to concede to Scottish nationalism. In his own dour, bitter way he has been right, as we saw when the Scottish Nationalists were defeated at South Ayrshire. Willie is always grousing, he is always depressing and hopelessly narrow-minded and parochial, but if you are going to have in the Cabinet somebody for Scotland and for Wales, I suppose you can say that they have got to be like that by nature.

The last item was decimalization, where we have overridden Bill Fiske's Decimalization Board.[1] Roy is to make a statement that the sixpence is to be preserved for at least a year or two. We have conceded to public pressure, something we would only do in an election year.

At 2.45 this afternoon William Armstrong came across to 21a, to discuss the future of the Department. It is now clear that our friend Clifford Jarrett wants to get out in July and I was able to say, 'If he goes, I would like to have Denis Barnes, whom you offered me, and if I can't have him I'll take Philip Rogers.' I went on to say that since I last talked to Armstrong Alan Marre had come on very well and if we could find a really good, vigorous Deputy from outside, who could start changing things in the Department, I wouldn't mind having Alan as Jarrett's replacement. Armstrong had obviously been apprised by Jarrett of how terrible the Health side was, and how good Social Security was, and he saw my point and said he would have another look, adding however that Barbara wouldn't release Denis Barnes, and I would have to be content with Rogers. I don't feel terribly committed, because I shall be going anyway, though I didn't tell Armstrong that. Anyhow I have made this gesture on Alan Marre's behalf and at least I got out of Armstrong the assurance that if I have to replace Jarrett with someone from outside, Alan might well replace Sir Edmund Compton as Parliamentary Commissioner. That would be an advance.

Wednesday, April 22nd

I spent the whole day in a special conference on the Green Paper, with the

[1] Sir William Fiske (Kt 1965) had been a member of the L.C.C. 1946–65 and Leader of the G.L.C. 1964–7. He was Chairman of the L.C.C. Housing Committee 1955–60. From 1966 to 1971 he was Chairman of the Decimal Currency Board and he was made a life peer in 1967. He died in January 1975.

chairmen, SAMOs and secretaries of all the R.H.B.s. I took the chair and conducted the meeting like a seminar. During the morning we allowed them to have their way and after lunch I made my concessions. I told them I had already conceded that there should be a Regional Executive Council with executive powers on the subject of the appointment and payment of all higher medical staff, with complete control of all education, undergraduate and postgraduate teaching, ambulance and blood-donor services and, I added, hospital building above the level of £150,000. This really means all hospital building, because a lesser sum only allows you to do minor extensions and I threw this in after a long and important meeting yesterday, where it had become clear that the Department's only alternative to doing hospital building through the Regional Authorities was to create a new regional organization, which would be impossible. This was useful because giving the chairmen building as well would, I thought, win them over. Sure enough, after they had been able to blow off steam and after I had made them at last understand the reasons for our proposals, we managed with these concessions to break the chairmen's resistance. But it's important to notice that I committed the Department without their knowing. It was only yesterday that we had discussed hospital building, we hadn't yet had the minutes and my brief for today gave no indication of this concession.

For the first time since Easter I had a free evening in the House and I had got Tam to organize rather formally fifteen-, twenty- and thirty-minute interviews with back benchers in my room. The results of this month's Harris and Gallup polls have now appeared and everybody I talked to overwhelmingly wanted an October election.[1] Not only people from the Midlands like Chris Price, but Michael Foot, for instance, felt that jumping into June would be a disaster.

Thursday, April 23rd

I rang the P.M. this morning because I was worried about my review of Gordon Walker's book. I had sent a draft across to No. 10 on Monday, explaining that it had to go to press on Friday, and I had mentioned it to Burke at Management Committee and at S.E.P. Burke had said yes, he knew about it, he was quite impressed and he would get it into the P.M.'s box. But Harold had been away at Oban addressing the Scottish T.U.C. and today he told me hadn't had time to look at my draft. I said, 'Well, I am off to Winchester tonight. Could you possibly read it in the course of the afternoon?' It was difficult to talk to him about it when his whole mind was obviously full of his success with the Scottish T.U.C. and the improvement in the polls, and he probably felt that Dick needn't and shouldn't be messing about

[1] The Harris Poll, published in the *Daily Express*, had shown a 7 per cent Conservative lead in March 1970 but by April Labour were leading by 2 per cent. The Gallup Poll in the *Telegraph* indicated that the Conservative lead over Labour had dropped from 5½ per cent in March to 3½ per cent in April.

20 & 21 The General Election of June 1970 brought an end to the Labour Government. Crossman, after campaigning with his wife in Coventry East, the constituency he has represented for 25 years, learns that he has held his seat with a reduced majority.

22 His Party defeated at the polls after six years in government, Harold Wilson makes way at No. 10 for the incoming Tory Prime Minister, the musical Edward Heath. While Mr Heath has his piano delivered at the front door, workmen carry out Mr Wilson's harmonium by the rear.

23 As editor of the *New Statesman*, November 1970.

with a ridiculous little thing like this. However he was pleasant and he promised to read my article.

At the beginning of Cabinet Harold again spent a great deal of time on the question of what help the Opposition should be entitled to have. It was clear that a number of us had given the Opposition some access, although as Harold made clear, only on matters of machinery. For instance, I had allowed the officials to discuss not the policy of Health Service reform, but Health Service reconstruction and its consequences. We all automatically understand that an Opposition which might take over must be allowed to discuss the machinery of government, just as George Brown was permitted to do on the whole question of the establishment of a Department of Economic Affairs.

Harold now ruled that we must make the following distinction: the Opposition must be permitted to discuss the machinery of government with our civil servants but, if they want to discuss a matter of policy and brief themselves for the speeches they are going to deliver aginst us in the Commons or the country, they must not go to the civil servants but must see us. The Common Market is a very good example. If the Conservatives were to demand, as apparently some of them are doing, that they should be allowed to find out from the Foreign Office what our negotiating position is or what sticking-point we are proposing, we could not permit it. It is true that we must allow a simple, straight, effective switch-over after an election and it is important that an Opposition should be briefed in an appropriate way but there should be nothing beyond that.

It was interesting to discover how little we had asked for help before 1964. True, one was entitled to be briefed by Foreign Office officials when one went abroad but that was a well-established practice, and our Defence people also had a little briefing, mainly by the chiefs of staff and by the Ministers rather than the officials concerned. But as a Shadow Government we had not really expected contact with officials and certainly I didn't expect it. Harold himself admitted that his chance only came on the last day of the 1963/4 parliamentary session, when he was able to talk to the key officials. Today Harold was extremely careful to lay down the line. He had made his Statement denying the *Daily Express* story and each of us had been asked to send him a note of what contacts our officials had actually made.

The next item was Summer Time. Originally, purely as a gesture towards European entry, we had abandoned Greenwich Mean Time and Roy had introduced a measure for permanent Summer Time.[1] We'd agreed to try a three-year experiment but Harold now almost asked Cabinet whether we should drop it and whether there had been any public proposal for doing so. Willie Ross, who had passionately opposed B.S.T., now said we ought to wait until the end of the three years. Jim Callaghan and I agreed, so the P.M. didn't have his way and we will run it for a third year. This shows a certain

[1] See pp. 259 and n., 278, above.

self-confidence among the Cabinet and that we do not always consider so-called pre-election prospects. No doubt this is partly due to Roy's success with the budget.

During this week it has become evident, partly from all these post-budget polls, that not having an election budget might have been electorally the cleverest thing to do. It is clear that Roy's posture has paid off. He is honest Roy, Aristides the Just. One should keep to one's adjectives. One of my difficulties is that I am a bit chameleon-like. I tend to have too many different ideas and this confuses the electorate. But Roy succeeds in keeping a single adjective and in this case too he thought that, though British Summer Time may have been a mistake, having taken the decision we should play it out for the full three years.

This afternoon I was having a highly technical meeting of Coventry shop stewards when Robin Wendt came down to the House to say that the Prime Minister urgently wanted to see me. I rushed up and found him sitting in his room (I rarely go there now) and I saw he had in front of him my review, with another long piece of paper attached to it. Harold said, 'Now this is quite a thing. It seems to me that first of all we have Gordon Walker on *The Cabinet* and then Macleod's review of Gordon Walker, then Crossman on Macleod and now Burke Trend on Crossman.' He threw across a five-page review of my article from Burke Trend's office. It was the most extraordinary stuff, a kind of public school, prim, pious critique of Crossman as an easy-going person who didn't appreciate the meaning of collective responsibility. It was a picture of the non-loyal member of the team, who is using his position in an improper way, and about whom nothing can be done.

Among this there was a proper criticism saying that I had mentioned three times that members of the Cabinet had got away with writing books violating the Official Secrets Act. Harold said this was highly embarrassing not only because this week such a prosecution is going on,[1] but also because Ministers can't be prosecuted in this way. He said, 'For God's sake, can't you get the Official Secrets Act out and substitute "collective responsibility"?' I said, 'Of course I can't. It doesn't fit.' But to my amazement I found it did. I had learnt something staggeringly important. Burke and Harold admit that the Official Secrets Act, which is really the only threat against a Cabinet Minister, doesn't operate. No one can be prosecuted under it, so there is therefore no sanction against a Cabinet Minister at all. He must be allowed to have access to the documents, he writes what he likes and then it is a matter of whether the Secretary of the Cabinet and the Prime Minister of the day can manage to persuade him to leave out things they think improper. In fact it is a question of whether sufficient sense of collective responsibility is instilled into you to ensure that, after you leave office, you will in your book-writing still feel enough of a member of the team, a part of the Cabinet system, to behave properly. That is all they rely on. It may sound obvious

[1] See below, p. 913 and n.

now I have said it but I certainly hadn't known it before. I had thought the ultimate sanction was the threat of prosecution.

It made me realize that Burke can be two-faced. He has never indicated in any possible way that he disapproves of me but I now know that he does. He actively distrusts me, mainly because I am not a reliable member of the team and when I get the chance I am liable to write a book which will say more than should be said and which he therefore won't approve. Burke knows this and I now think it is quite right that I should do it.

These were some of the points which came out in the course of our discussion. Harold said, 'I don't know. I stand somewhere half-way between you and Burke Trend. I don't hold all that Burke holds but I do think you are wrong about the Official Secrets Act. Couldn't we get that bit right?' Then he went right through my review and made a number of drafting suggestions, introducing far more clever propaganda into it than I wanted. I took very careful notes of each point. Towards the end I said, 'Look, Harold, what about my future after the election?' He said, 'What do you mean?' I said, 'You'll be making changes. I assume that Michael Stewart will be retiring.' 'Oh,' he said, 'not retiring, I think, but he has certainly got to have a change.' I said, 'What about me? Do you think that at sixty-two I am ready to retire from the Cabinet?' He said, 'I have never thought of such a thing,' and he obviously hadn't. I remarked, 'Well in that case you'll want me to stay at my present job but with enlarged powers?' 'That's it,' he said, and I realized that he couldn't conceive that I should want to retire. Harold's main anxiety was that I wanted to be Foreign Secretary and was competing for promotion. There are only three jobs I could get. I could become Minister of Defence, not that this is much promotion, Chancellor or Foreign Secretary, and obviously Harold heaved a sigh of relief that I wanted to stay where I was and have my powers extended. Now I didn't say I didn't and I didn't tell him anything about my own intentions.

We sat side-by-side at the table in his room in the House of Commons and chatted about the election and what was going on on the front bench, about Burke Trend and Roy and his budget and his success. An anodyne chat it was but I had learnt something of Harold's thoughts about my future. It doesn't make life any easier, because the more I think about this the more I realize that after six years I've had enough. In a curious way this conversation with Harold has confirmed it. I know where I am. Now I know I can go on if I want to, I know I don't want to. Writing this review has taken me a stage further towards resigning and going back to journalism and my books. Perhaps the most amusing thing was that when Harold talked about his own book-writing he said, 'When I retire I shall be the youngest retired Prime Minister for 100 years and I shall have time for plenty of writing. I have got my plans clear. The first part will be my three- or four-volume memoirs and the big job will be the twenty-volume memoirs I shall leave for posterity.' I remember his saying something of this sort at least once before. One improves one's remarks by trying them out and he now said it with such complacency that it seemed to have been rounded and finished.

The inner group of the Wessex R.H.B. had invited me to Winchester and, though I had asked them not to put on a dinner because I had a three-line whip and couldn't leave before 7.30, they had laid on an excellent cold buffet. They had brought along half a dozen other people, including the Lord Lieutenant,[1] an old general who runs the Isle of Wight, and we had a long off-the-record discussion of the Green Paper. I found that I have made a terrible mess. Their case shows why the R.H.B.s are against my scheme, because to have something parallel to the new unitary local government authorities, this new compact, original, creative region must be torn to pieces. It is a devastating blow to them and I learnt a tremendous lot about their difficulties.

Friday, April 24th

We all stayed at the Wessex Hotel and this morning I looked over the Close and the cathedral before going to see the N.F.U. for half an hour. Then we drove right across the Hampshire downs to Basingstoke, where I had last been as Minister of Housing and where I now saw a ghastly lot of buildings rather like military cantonments slashing the chalky hillside. Amongst all these a new general hospital is being built in the forty-acre grounds of the Park Prewett psychiatric hospital, which I spent the morning visiting. It is unusual and I thought it was quite good. Morale was high and everything is being reformed with tremendous gusto and drive by a wonderful new Chief Nursing Officer. We had an excellent lunch in the hospital before we went off at 2 o'clock to lay the foundation stone.

After visiting another hospital in Basingstoke and seeing a group of local G.P.s, I got the 6.15 train home, and once again John Revans and Miss Gundry travelled up with me as far as Oxford. He is an enormously ambitious man, very pukkah, able and full of drive, precisely the kind of man who would travel up to Oxford with the Minister and then travel back again. Into my suitcase he put a splendid and beautiful cut-glass decanter to go with the glasses they gave me at the last hospital opening at Southampton.

I got back at 8.0 dead-tired after a long day and a very exhausting week. At lunch Miss Gundry had said, 'We are getting to know you quite well and we think you look a bit tired today.' I said, 'It's Friday and I want to get home,' and she answered, 'Well, we will get you home in good time.' She didn't know I was going to have an exhausting Saturday as well.

[1] Alexander Baring, Lord Ashburton (K.G. 1969, K.C.V.O. 1961), succeeded his father as the 6th Baron in 1938. He was Chairman of the Hampshire and Isle of Wight Police Authority 1961–71 and Lord Lieutenant and Custos Rotulorum of Hampshire and the Isle of Wight 1960–73. He has been High Steward of Winchester since 1967 and was Receiver-General to the Duchy of Cornwall 1967–74.

Saturday, April 25th

This morning I had to be off again, up to Nuneaton, where Les Huckfield had asked me to visit the George Eliot Hospital, about which there have been tremendous rows. Bill Price in Rugby and Les Huckfield in Nuneaton have been bashing about, attacking the Walsgrave Hospital in Coventry. Each of them wanted his own district hospital and now each has one. The Nuneaton hospital is an old workhouse, a ghastly public assistance building, with a chilly, awful atmosphere, but eventually we are to give them a new £6 million hospital and all I could do was to look at the present place and see what was wrong with it. Before lunch I had a press conference. These have their usefulness, because if I go out and do one of these jobs and then have a press conference, I take decisions, whereas if I sit in Elephant and Castle the office always defeats me. So I made the announcement about plans for the casualty and accident wards and on the timing for the new hospital, and I got the whole thing tidied up in one.

I drove back to the centre of Coventry for a borough party conference on pensions. Although the meeting had been advertised in the papers the day before, there had clearly been a terrible response and there was a lot of pretty bloody-minded opposition from the old age pensioners. I went on to a social which Betty Healey was running. It was a kind of test case. By Friday evening everybody had been talking about the fact that the polls were showing Labour ahead of the Tories, with a chance of winning the election, and I wanted to know if Coventry was responding to the new mood. Much the same thirty or forty people turned up. We did have a new enthusiasm and excitement. We drank sherry and had a few minutes of speeches and the forty people contributed £7, of which by the way I gave £1, which was thought very lavish. On the whole you could say there was a glimmer of hope there. It is true though that because of the badness of Coventry I am inclined to be more October- than June-minded.

Sunday, April 26th

I didn't get home till 9.30 last night, so I've had a quiet Sunday. I've had a real day off doing the diary, working on the island, where Virginia is now sleeping in her new hut, and bathing in the pool on a cold, cold day. The poor farmers! We have not only given them a fairly tough farm price review but we have given them an even worse spring.

Monday, April 27th

Roy is still away, so this morning we had a more practical Management Committee and hardly discussed electoral prospects. We talked about whether we should refer to the P.I.B. the Ford and Vauxhall wage awards, as Barbara insists. In theory she has quite a strong argument. She said, 'If we have a prices and incomes policy we must occasionally refer something to do with wages and what better than the 18 per cent Ford settlement and the Vauxhall settlement? Refer them together. Anyway we've long wanted our friend Aubrey to take a look at the motor-car industry.' The moment she said it everybody was up in arms. Tony Benn, just back from ten days in America, said, 'I can't possibly upset Ford's and Vauxhall. I sponsor them, there is no case. We didn't protest against the settlement in any way and last year Vauxhall actually lost money.' I must say it was very difficult. Harold chipped in pretty quickly, saying he could see no point in the reference and that it would upset our relationships. Poor Barbara had lost and she only said, 'If in a few weeks' time you want to refer the Kindersley award to the P.I.B. I hope you'll remember this. You can't refer the doctors' pay and refuse to refer anything from the industrial front. Just bear that in mind.' That remark was recorded in the minutes.

The other item, unemployment in the North, was also Barbara's. Things are particularly bad in the North-East, where pits have been closed too rapidly, and we discussed what should be done. We all agreed that emergency winter works are futile and I think that we should work on a public sector expenditure programme, out of which I hope to get an early start on some hospital building. If we are to have any chance of doing well up there in the election something of the sort must be launched this summer.

After this businesslike meeting I went straight to my room, where I found Bea Serota engaged with that old villain Alf Robens, on the awkward subject of the drug-addiction centre at Guy's Hospital. They had put an £80,000 building in Bermondsey without seeking full co-operation from the local councillors and as a result there have been mass demonstrations by tough Bermondsey dockers against bringing lousy drug-addicts into their neighbourhood. Bea had gone down to see things for herself and she said, 'Frankly, Guy's have made such a muck-up of their public relations that they must be persuaded to put the centre somewhere else and use the new building for other purposes.' At this meeting we were discussing how to do it. Alf is a curious character, clever and shifty, by nature a real tycoon, immensely vital and energetic, but a man of considerable charm and of a craftiness which makes me thank God he decided to go into business and leave the leadership of the Labour Party to Harold Wilson.

Tuesday, April 28th

Walter Harrison had told me that he needed my vote at the National Superannuation Committee. As this diary shows, I've only attended twice and I've left the whole Committee Stage to David Ennals and Brian O'Malley, who have been carrying on splendidly, running faster and faster. Indeed the only problem now is on the Tory side, because they have somehow to spin things out until Whitsun so that the outside world doesn't conclude that there has been no real fight over the Bill. They have given up and one sign of this is that Paul Dean and Tim Fortescue have taken over the leadership from young, gilded Balneil and that has made things even easier.[1]

However, Walter Harrison was very worried about today's proceedings but, as it turned out, my attendance held everything up, because the Tories all seized the chance to show their political power to challenge and debate with the Secretary of State. We took the whole morning over a discussion that would otherwise have taken twenty minutes. Afterwards Harrison told me, 'That very often happens. Senior Ministers make it too political and we don't like them to come. It's easier for us to have the number twos and to get into a quiet routine, just plugging along and reading the briefs.'

This makes you realize the inanity of the whole Standing Committee procedure. It is utterly futile to have this method of taking a Bill to pieces in order to improve it and moreover it's utterly debilitating. The Government back benchers waste their time in Standing Committee, where they are hardly allowed to speak because that would prolong the business and anything they say may provoke another Tory speech. The Opposition arguments are amateur and bogus, because half the time they don't really understand the details of the clauses they are discussing. I think they should be given access to the Government briefs. From time to time dramatic Second Reading debates are staged and the Bill rolls along, getting through without any critical dissection. It is this kind of thing that brings Parliament into disrepute and our modern back benchers find it quite intolerable. Today they were quite glad and amused to see me there but they realized that as soon as I became interesting and lively progress was slowed down, so the sooner I was got out of the way and the back benchers could go on writing their letters the better for all concerned.

I took Muriel Bowen to lunch and she gave me a fascinating briefing on what is going to happen in the borough elections next Thursday. It is dangerously likely that, unless we do extremely well, we shall actually lose places like Stoke-on-Trent and Sheffield, where this year there are aldermanic elections. I think that across the country the swing to Labour will be 2, 3 or 4 per cent, rather than the 6, 7 or 8 per cent we got in Central London a fortnight ago. We need the inner cadres to do the knocking-up and get out the votes and they aren't sufficiently active or woken up. I don't think we are going to get enough swing to justify a June election.

After dinner with Tommy Balogh and Catherine we came back to the House to see the exciting part of the televised Cup Final reply. John Mackintosh came in and began to talk very freely. There was a good deal of whisky about but I drank bitter lemon and watched them. John first attacked Tommy for being the worst kind of adviser and then he turned on me. He said, 'Where are the good left-wing Ministers who really stand by their principles? People like Roy Jenkins see that their right-wing young men get their chance, but

[1] Trevor Fortescue was Conservative M.P. for Liverpool, Garston, 1966–February 1974. He was Assistant Government Whip 1970–1 and Whip 1971–3 and has been Secretary-General of the Food and Drink Industries Council since 1973.

what do you do? You appoint John Dunwoody and Bea Serota and Brian O'Malley, not the brains like David Marquand.' (He didn't add himself.) I was interested, and in a way it's true. I tried to appoint David Marquand at least once, but I've never tried to appoint John and I wouldn't dream of doing so. Intellectuals, the exciting people, aren't necessarily the best Parliamentary Secretaries or the best Ministers.

Wednesday, April 29th

At Management Committee we talked about electoral prospects. Burke and his staff were absent and Harold gave us a special warning that the meeting was secret.* He started by saying, 'This is your meeting and I'm not going to say anything, I'm leaving it to you.' Then he spoke, and I timed him, for twenty-five minutes. These days Harold is becoming more and more verbose and he talks more and more prosily as his personality sinks further and further into his image. His face is getting greyer and he becomes more a part of his suit. He began, of course, by saying that one had to consider all the practical possibilities and at inordinate length he discussed the timing of the South African cricket tour, the timing of the Wakes Weeks, the timing of the Coventry shut-down week, not forgetting the World Cup at the end of June. All this had been worked out to show there was really only one election date, the third week of June, unless we were to look forward to October. He then talked about the pros and cons. Wage inflation is continuing and in the country there is a wild sense of unreality, far worse than in 1966, when we got in before things busted and wage inflation won us the election. This time people fear that boom will be followed by bust and we may as well get in first.

Roy, who had only just returned from a week's holiday after the budget, said early on that he wanted to wait a week before giving his considered judgment. Last night Thomas had primed me to ask at all costs about America and Roy replied that up till now he had not thought that this could really affect our prospects. After all the Americans have their own mid-term elections in November and the administration will do everything it can to prevent a crash. However, as Denis, Barbara and I pointed out, the world is full of doubt and uncertainty. The American stock market has just had its worst two days for very many years and the news from Cambodia is alarming.[1] During the summer a crisis of confidence might sweep across the Atlantic. Things are also getting steadily worse in the Middle East, where there has been increasingly direct intervention by the Russians.[2] Having an

* Next day Harold felt entitled to say he had not discussed election prospects with the Cabinet or with any of his ministerial colleagues, though he had in fact spent two hours doing so.

[1] Throughout 1970 unemployment rose steadily in America and by May the Dow Jones index of industrial averages sank to 631, the lowest point for eight years.

[2] During April there had been reports that the U.S.S.R. were giving massive assistance to Egypt in the construction of a new defence system, with SAM-2 and SAM-3 ground-to-air missiles.

election in June reduces the risk that we may be knocked sideways by some world crisis or by a crash created by external forces.

Denis, Barbara and I put these points, but Roy was judicious. It was clear from our discussion that Harold himself is enormously tempted by the idea of a June election. He seemed to feel that though we might be able to stay ahead of the Tories during the summer, the danger would be that a sag of morale would cause us to slip back again. Harold was supported by Bob Mellish, who said that when he took the straw poll of M.P.s it was 2:1 for October, but since then there has been a change in the Parliamentary Party and everybody was now telling him, 'The P.M. knows things we don't know. Trust the P.M. If he wants to go in June, we are ready to go then.' Fred Peart and, to my surprise, Michael Stewart, both favoured June and only Barbara and I were firmly for October.

Let me make a note for the record. In the spring of 1966 Harold was deciding election dates absolutely on his own, perhaps consulting a small circle of Marcia, Gerald, Peter, Tommy and me, but virtually no one else. Now he sits around with nine of his colleagues at Management Committee perfectly prepared, apparently, to see this as a matter for consultation, first with us and then with the N.E.C. on the 18th (when I shall be in Malta). As Gordon Walker says in his book, all this formalization indicates a weakening of the P.M.'s position. Harold really has got an Inner Cabinet round him and now we would all question his right to decide the election date by himself. As P.M. he has grown in stature in the last ten years and he's back on top of his form and his popularity. When electioneering he is in his element. Yet his Cabinet colleagues who used to be unknown and inexperienced have now won themselves some position in the party, in Parliament and in the public eye, and the balance of power is very different from what it was.

We stopped punctually at midday so we could all go to St Margaret's Church, next door to Westminster Abbey, for the Memorial Service for Michael Halls. There was a tremendous turnout. The Permanent Secretaries were there, Territorial Associations, at least half the Cabinet and many back-bench M.P.s. It was the works of a memorial service, with the usual hymns and the usual lesson, read by one of Halls's Civil Service colleagues. The P.M. got up to give the address and it was a total failure. It was exactly like the obituary notice signed H.W. in *The Times*, a totally anonymous routine recitation of a career, with the routine commendations like an official publication. When we reached the part where Harold said, 'And now I come to what is, alas, the apex of his career ... ' I waited. Surely, I thought, we shall have the point at last, but no, even this was described in the customary journalism of the higher Civil Service. Afterwards, as we came out, I said to Tommy, 'You see, in the presence of Burke Trend Harold couldn't say the one appropriate thing about Michael Halls.' Tommy said, 'That he was loyal. Michael Halls was loyal to the Prime Minister rather than to the Civil

Service.' I said, 'That's quite right. Halls's predecessor, Derek Mitchell, was sent away for talking to Burke out of court, being one of the boys and helping to surround Harold. Halls went in with Harold and was completely his man. He was also naturally attuned to Harold, with the same inhibitions, the same limitations of taste. Harold doesn't really like literature or art, the theatre or the opera. He prefers golf and the telly and the Cup Final and if he hadn't been a civil servant in the war he would have been a Territorial. They are both of the educated petty bourgeoisie, men of the same scale. Michael Halls was a small civil servant and even if Harold is a successful Prime Minister he is a small politician, because a Prime Minister doesn't have to run a Department or be a big man.'

Losing Michael Halls is an appalling blow for Harold. He has replaced him with Sandy Isserlis, a strange Jewish character, whom I got to know in the Ministry of Housing. He was in Planning, but I discovered that his real interest in life is a great history of the Jews under the Roman Empire. He is an inward-looking, persecuted, difficult, learned man. I came across him again when he was with Judith Hart and when I reminded Harold of this the P.M. rather peevishly said, 'Oh, he was only there for a few days.' Now what brought Isserlis into No. 10? What makes Harold feel that they'll share the same outlook? Perhaps they belong to the same social class, but their background is very different. I suspect there was some contact through Gerald Kaufman, or possibly through Marcia, because it's now only through this tiny group that Harold extends his little inner circle when he does extend it. A most astonishing choice.

This evening Nicky Kaldor came to dinner with me. By this time the whole House of Commons was brimming with rumours that tomorrow's opinion poll would show a 2 per cent lead. The moment has arrived when one can sense a great lift of desire for a June election. I tried to get from Nicky an objective estimate of what the situation was likely to be in October but the economists can't be sure. There has never been a time when things have been so unpredictable because America is totally unpredictable, particularly after Nixon's vast gamble in Cambodia. We should have a clearer picture before the summer is out.

Thursday, April 30th

I woke up early and went downstairs to put on the 7 o'clock news, because I was so anxious about the N.O.P. I was dreading the 2 per cent Labour lead that might create the deadly atmosphere in which a June election would become inevitable but it was 2 per cent down, just enough to deflate us.

I started the morning by discussing the Kindersley Report with Bea Serota, Alan Marre and the C.M.O. The Department has done a lot of work and the C.M.O. has already told me he accepts the recommendations but it's a ludicrous Report and it's impossible for the Government to accept the statement that we must reassess doctors' incomes on a basis of comparability with other professions, right back over the last ten years. I can't help thinking, as Alan Marre suggested, that this may have some political content and that the Kindersley people at least don't mind presenting a Labour Government with a very awkward problem. However here we were soberly discussing the award. The C.M.O. said that whatever happened, even if we were to refer the matter to the P.I.B., there must be an immediate payment on account of at least half of the 30 per cent, with the understanding that the rest would be paid later, whatever other arrangements the P.I.B. recommended. Alan Marre thought even this was going too far. He said there would be the hell of a row and that he preferred the notion of accepting the award and trying to phase it. I have been thinking very hard and trying to discover whether there is any other way in which I can accommodate the Chancellor. From what he said to me this week it's clear that Roy is going to ask for the outright rejection of this Report. Well, that can't be done. Whether it's rejected or referred there have to be a whole host of consultations with Kindersley but the Chancellor was obviously in the mood for rejection and today's meeting was really held in order to prepare our people. I've got the Department, including the C.M.O., to recognize that the Report is unacceptable but that we have got to find some way of avoiding a complete breach with the medical profession.

Then we had Cabinet and the first news of Cambodia.[1] Nixon has thrown away the only American consensus he had achieved of those who want to get out of Vietnam. If he doesn't manage to force a peace on the enemy, as he has committed himself to do, he may have a sensational crisis in America. This new war has split the nation. All the universities are up in arms against Nixon and practically every idealist will oppose this attempt to reassert the power of the American generals. Cabinet showed absolutely no reaction. Only Peter Shore asked for Government repudiation of the American action and he was icily refused. It was all so correct. We were told that we must wait and see. There was a profound F.O./No. 10 reluctance to break our supine relationship with America, which has really achieved nothing for us. I suppose it was for the sake of our negotiating position, because we and the Russians are Joint Chairmen of the Laos–Cambodia Armistice Committee, but, heavens, we've paid a price for not intervening actively and I shall be interested to see how Cabinet handles this.

Then we turned to the problem of the test matches. At the beginning of the year we had demonstrations against the Springboks rugby team and now we have the visit of the South African cricket team. They are to play some

[1] On April 20th the President had revealed that during the next twelve months a further 150,000 American troops would be withdrawn from Vietnam, bringing the authorized number of troops down to 284,000 by the spring of 1971, compared with 549,500 in January 1969. Mr Nixon called upon Hanoi to agree to a political settlement but there was no constructive reply from the North Vietnamese. The President had also announced that the American advance into Cambodia had been specifically limited to nineteen miles and that all United States troops would be withdrawn by the beginning of July.

twelve matches, some at Lord's and some at Edgbaston, and there is already a major threat of demonstrations at the grounds. Harold and Jim Callaghan are taking enormous time and trouble over this because, if the tour takes place, black countries of Africa may refuse to come to this summer's Commonwealth Games. Jim goes on making preparations, getting out his policemen at £11 per man per day. It will cost each county £1,200 a day to have sufficient men to guard the grounds, quite apart from the men in the neighbouring streets, who will of course be our responsibility. By and large I think Harold and Jim have handled this issue extremely adroitly in a way that is simultaneously liberal, fair-minded and pro-sport. I am told that a new organization has been formed to stop the tour, with Edward Boyle and Reg Prentice as very good Vice-Presidents. It seems that the Tories are beginning to disagree on this. Cricket has become an important pre-election issue.

Friday, May 1st

The news about Cambodia has got worse and I rang up No. 10 this morning to ask Harold for a Government repudiation of the American invasion. It was too early for him, so I left a message and I haven't yet heard what happened. No doubt other people have been bringing pressure on him. Meanwhile I had to catch the 8.15 to Birmingham for a whole day of visiting hospitals for the mentally handicapped. I was at it for fifteen hours and when Anne motored me home I was pretty worn out.

Sunday, May 3rd

If I were a normal M.P. I would be out marching in a May Day celebration but I just refused to go. I've had my boxes out, done my diary and prepared a big speech on poverty for the Cambridge Union tomorrow and I'm glad I haven't had the rush of a procession as well. But it shows that I am not really committed to the party and, though I didn't realize it at the time, that my resignation from the N.E.C. was the beginning of my opting out. My review has come out in the *New Statesman* and it looks all right. Anne suggested an important change at the end to make sure I wasn't appearing in any way to run down a Cabinet Minister's right to keep a diary. There it is in print, another little sign that I am on the way out.

Another curious little thing happened last week. I was sitting in the Members' dining room when a girl came up and handed me a letter. I saw it was for Tony Crosland and I said, 'No, I'm abortion, not pollution.' This story got into the *Guardian* Miscellany column and it's been kicked all round. It's not the remark of a man who is on the up, who is in; it's that of a person who's detached, who doesn't mind making fun of himself or saying things which would in normal circumstances do him damage.

One reason why I am reflecting on all this is because the whole of last week has been another test of my intentions. On Wednesday Bob Mellish was running round saying it was now understood that the N.O.P. would show us two points ahead and to some extent Wednesday's Management Committee took place on that assumption. The fact that we were actually two points behind took the edge off the June boom. We were almost being lifted into a compulsory June election and I had felt not only a sense that it would be June, but June because we were bound to win. It made me consider the immediate future and to my surprise it showed me that I could look forward to it.

Monday, May 4th

We have learnt that American troops are going into Cambodia on three fronts and this crisis now dominates our thinking. How should the British Government react? Barbara, Roy and I had come to Management Committee this morning convinced that we must have it out but there was Harold saying that in Michael Stewart's absence we couldn't discuss it. However we managed to talk about it for forty minutes by discussing the urgent question of our reaction to Michael Foot's request for an S.O.9 debate this afternoon. We knew that the Speaker would agree to a debate and so we considered whether, instead of being forced to have an S.O.9, it wouldn't be better for the Government to take time from our own business for a debate tomorrow. In that case, though, we wouldn't be able to guarantee that the Cambodia discussion would stop at 7 o'clock and give time for the Finance Bill. We finally decided to let Michael Foot move his motion and that when he had done so the entire front bench should rise along with the back benchers to indicate our desire for a debate.

Considering this technical point allowed us to have quite a discussion, enough to show that every member of the Management Committee thought the Americans had made a grave error. Barbara and I were obviously concerned. Healey said that though we couldn't come out as anti-American, they had clearly made a terrible mistake. So did Fred Peart and, though he is staunchly pro-American, Jim Callaghan. Roy cautiously sided with Barbara and me and Peter Shore supported us. Bob Mellish particularly warned us that if we continued to take the line about our being Co-Chairmen of the Armistice Committee along with the Russians, we would have a revolt against us tonight. Michael Foot would move the adjournment of the House and the Party would split. Could we not avoid this?

Then we turned to a general discussion of the political situation. This time Roy said he would formulate his position, which was that he couldn't see very much risk in carrying on until the end of October and that the home front would be all right because, as Barbara had pointed out, Jack Jones and Hugh Scanlon were clearly going to keep their boys from striking during this period. On the whole, therefore, Roy was clearly in favour of waiting until October but the Prime Minister was still itching to have an early election, terribly anxious lest over the summer recess the band-wagon promoted by our success in the polls and the G.L.C. elections might fade away. On Harold's side were Fred Peart and Bob Mellish, the gut socialists, and Jim Callaghan, rather doubtful but on the whole agreeing. Barbara and I were for the time being firmly against the earlier date. Barbara said, 'You must have hard facts on the side of June, not mere hunches, mere hopes, mere polls. We haven't got any hard facts yet.' I added, 'Yes, there may have been an improvement in the G.L.C. and the inner areas of London, but so far we have no evidence from the two key areas, Lancashire and the Midlands. That's where we've got to look for a majority. That's why we mustn't jump to any conclusions.' So again we walked round it and it was obvious that the Prime Minister was wanting the election, just the opposite of 1966, when he had to be dragged into it. This time he was having to be dragged back.

Tuesday, May 5th

At Cabinet we were concerned with Cambodia, and Michael Stewart started by outlining the speech he wished to make to the House this afternoon. It was a dry, detached defence of the Americans, theoretically right in certain ways but in a form which would antagonize the whole of the Left and also the whole liberal opposition among the British public. The Prime Minister immediately came in without waiting for anyone else. He said, 'That isn't good enough. Somehow we must avoid this position of total neutrality and move to the position of a friend who is warning and advising an ally.' Harold outlined this in twenty minutes, warming up Michael's remarks and adding a sop to our own back benchers. Then the fat was in the fire. Barbara broke out and said this was totally impossible. A completely new situation had arisen, the Americans had now apparently abandoned the whole of their plans to withdraw from South-East Asia and Nixon was in the hands of his generals. I spoke with passion too. All this stirs me from the bottom of my heart and I said, 'It's no good. We put pressure on Johnson to stop the bombing of the North, supported him in the withdrawal policy and we have supported Nixon. Since it seems that Nixon is abandoning this policy, we must say to him, "If this marks your abandonment of the policy of withdrawal or, even worse, if you still intend to keep to the policy but are becoming so deeply involved that you can't withdraw this summer, we have reached the parting of the ways." ' I said the test of Michael Stewart's speech was whether he could say that the Americans' action might have been a dangerous and tragic miscalculation and for this I was sternly rebuked by Jim Callaghan, who was staunchly for the Americans.

It went round the table and there was an interesting line-up. Roy Jenkins was sitting there making notes and he threw across to me one that said, 'Here is the spectrum of the Party as I see it.' The spectrum ranged from Harold Lever on the extremest pro-American right, saying this was a tactical manoeuvre for getting out and that we must stand by them. Along with him were Michael Stewart, George Thomson, Roy Mason and Shackleton. On our side were Barbara and me, Peter Shore and Tony Wedgwood Benn. Tony put in an admirable contribution, saying that it wasn't the content of the speech that mattered but the style and that we must show sympathy with the liberal forces in America. If we were going to bring youth to our side we mustn't seem to be supporting age against youth.

We also had, rather surprisingly, Ted Short and Cledwyn Hughes, Fred Peart in a sort of way, and Bob Mellish, not because the last two felt very strongly, but because they knew the Parliamentary Party required it. Roy was trying to get the best of both worlds, as he often does now. He and Harold were very unsatisfactory but they knew the Cabinet was split and they were trying to hold it together. Denis Healey stayed woodenly in the middle, trying to ease the situation but basically siding with Michael Stewart. Harold finally summed up. Cabinet minutes are fairly truthful here, though they don't express the strength of the support for the switch Barbara and I wanted. Michael Stewart was told that his speech wasn't good enough and that he must take a position of detachment, so that he could still play his role as Co-Chairman. We all hoped that something had been achieved, though I didn't have much confidence that anything we had said had made the faintest impact on the Foreign Secretary.

Towards the end of Cabinet Harold had said, 'I think I shall have to wind up this afternoon.' (The Chief Whip had mentioned that the P.M. might have to do it.) I jumped in and said, 'Certainly,' because we all thought, 'My God, if Michael's going to be like this, we mustn't have the final speech made by George Thomson who would be worse, but by the Prime Minister, who might improve things a little.'

I had to go out to a meeting with the local authorities but I came back in time to hear the Prime Minister make a tremendously valiant effort. But of course he was tied in by Michael, whom he couldn't repudiate. Harold went as far as he possibly could to put the issue in a more reasonable frame and, indeed, I should think he held ten or twenty votes at the end. Harold is a brilliant tactician and his speech was sufficiently different from Michael's to split the Tories, a lot of whom had wanted to go into our lobby but now refused to do so and in many cases abstained. The debate ended in a terrible schemozzle. There were 68 votes against, of which 59 were Labour and if Harold hadn't split the Tories successfully, we would have heard nothing but a tale of Labour splits. As it was, appalling damage had been done and the Party was furious. I was white with anger. I told the Chief Whip how impossible it was and we fumed together. When I went upstairs there was Brian O'Malley looking green, saying that as a junior Minister he hadn't approved of Michael's speech. I said, 'My God, *you* didn't approve. Do you think I did? What have you been up to?' 'Oh,' he said, 'I'm so relieved.' He stayed for a drink with me and Barbara came in with Ted and we stormed. For once I told Tam, 'You can go and talk to Ian Aitken this evening and tell him that we are enraged.'

Wednesday, May 6th

Though Tam couldn't find Ian Aitken, I think he must have talked to Barbara and Ted because today the *Guardian* had a very good story. Everybody knew that the Cabinet had been split. I think this is a case where you are entitled to give what Gordon Walker calls 'an unattributable leak'. You may believe that the doctrine of collective responsibility imposes silence when Cabinet Ministers carry out Cabinet agreements but if you think a Cabinet Minister has violated an agreement you feel liberated from the pledge. That's what had happened in this instance, so nobody could be blamed for today's leaks.

After the monthly meeting with the R.H.B. chairmen, I went out to the B.B.C. for lunch with Charles Hill and Curran, the new Director-General, with whom I wanted to discuss medical programmes. We talked about last winter's alarmist programme on the pill and the results of the sudden panic rumour that it was unsafe. All this indicates the power that a broadcast by one man can have. I gave Charles Hill some other examples, telling him, 'Medical programmes have a tremendous attraction anyway, you needn't jazz them up to make them popular. The most effective programmes are the quietest and, for God's sake, if we can't even get the medical side right, how can we hope to get the political side right?' He quickly agreed. Time after time we came back to the problem of bias and whether I thought the B.B.C. was biased against the Government. I said I didn't but that I thought great trouble was caused by the instructions that staff were given. I reminded him of the time when the supposedly impartial Chairman of my round-table discussion on trivialization popped in an absolutely unexpected question at the end and joined in the attack.[1] I also emphasized the difference between B.B.C. and I.T.N. interviewers. The I.T.N. people just come to get your news and to get you to put it over objectively in your own way. The B.B.C. come to argue with you, to keep something in reserve and then pounce on you, and this makes you wary of them and produces a worse broadcast. When they asked about 'The World At One' I said, 'The P.M. is a fanatical supporter of that programme now that you have given him a decent interview,' and we laughed a good deal. 'Well,' said Charles Hill, 'you've always had a good time.' 'Yes,' I said, 'but you and I are radio men. We've been on the air time after time putting over the Government case, and,' I added, 'that is the third thing wrong with the B.B.C., their ruthless cutting of interviews. You give them twelve minutes and you find only two minutes are broadcast and that has been unfairly edited.' They both agreed that this must be changed.

I rushed back to a big confrontation with Roy and Barbara on the Kindersley Report. The Department had worked extremely hard and I had a possible basis for agreement with my colleagues. I think the doctors will stay quiet for 20 per cent if they can get it, backdated to April 1st, and that the rest of the award should be referred to the P.I.B. I knew that Roy wanted 15 per

[1] See above, p. 238.

cent, so I thought I might be able to get 20. It was a small meeting. Eddie Shackleton was there, rather on my side, but Willie Ross, who as Minister in charge of Health for Scotland should have been on my side, was entirely concerned with some negotiations on teachers' salaries. We sparred around and we've agreed to meet again next week. Roy stuck firmly to 15 per cent, I was firm on 20 per cent, but the reference to the P.I.B. is now inevitable and will cause a tremendous row. Everything will depend on whether the storm comes before or after the election.

Thursday, May 7th

The big news this morning was that poor old Will Owen had been acquitted.[1] He had been accused of violating the Official Secrets Act by receiving some £2,500 from a Czech diplomat for services rendered, presumably for providing secret information from the Estimates Committee. The case has been going on for the last ten days and it was clear to me that there was absolutely no evidence whatsoever that any information had ever passed. It would be nice to think that Will had been clever enough to do this and then report to M.I.5, but no, he is a stupid, vain old thing, and it was a humiliating trial. How idiotic these Czech Embassy people are and how easily they waste their money on bogus information.

I was going to have a hair-cut at 9 o'clock but I waited at Vincent Square until 9.10, when one of the girls telephoned to say that Peter Smithson had been held up by some accident that had caused a two-mile queue. It made me realize how utterly I rely on him. He must be the most intrepid, skilful and vigorous driver in London. He is absolutely reliable, always turning up on time, and I am going to miss him when I cease to be a Minister.

To O.P.D. and then to Cabinet. The interesting question was whether there would be a row after the Stewart performance and whether people would denounce Barbara and me for leaking. But there was no word from the other side and nothing from our side either, because I had talked to the Chief, who had said, 'Please God, no. Harold doesn't want a row now. We've got local elections. Don't spoil the good work. What does it matter?' So there was absolutely no post mortem. Instead we had a whole series of interesting items, including the South African cricketers again.

After lunch with Nicholas Davenport at the Athenaeum, I had to catch a train to Birmingham to make a speech to the Institute of Hospital Engineers. When we got back to the hotel afterwards, somebody came in to say that there had been a swing to the Left.[2] I went up to my room and lay on my bed watching the municipal election results come out between midnight and 1.0 a.m. In Coventry we won six seats and a clear majority of votes, in

[1] Labour M.P. for Morpeth 1954–70.

[2] In the borough elections in England and Wales Labour made a net gain of 443 seats, at the expense of the Conservatives who made a net loss of 327, the Liberals who lost 24 seats and the Independents who won 67. In Scotland Labour gained 57 seats, the Scottish Nationalists lost 23 and the Conservatives 4.

Birmingham twelve seats. I knew this would clinch the election date in Harold's mind and that, now he has the facts that Barbara and I told him he needed, he would have a go in June.

Friday, May 8th

I spent the day with Nottingham City Council, looking at a junior training centre and returning to a great lunch in the vast, palatial Edwardian town hall. I was sitting beside an enormous, boring Mayor, who told me that he was the agent for the Liberal candidate at Oxford at the time of the famous Lindsay–Hogg by-election in 1938.[1] It had been he who had told the Liberal candidate to offer to stand down if Labour would stand down, never thinking that we would accept, and they were staggered when we did withdraw and they were compelled to do so too. This man had become a tremendously solid Tory and was now finishing his last seven days as Mayor. There was Nottingham enjoying itself, over excellent food and drink, but, God, it was heavy going.

I went off to put up plaques at a couple of health centres and then I drove on to Coventry to address the annual dinner of the College of Midwives, with Doris Butterworth, Jolly Jack's wife, who is their President, in the chair. On the way I looked in on Albert Rose and we went through the newspapers together. He was very excited. There had been an astonishing transformation in East Coventry. What is striking is not that the Tory vote has gone down (in fact in some wards it has actually gone up) but that our vote has doubled and trebled. Despite the heavy rain, despite the fact that people couldn't vote after 8.30, Labour supporters turned out, and with better weather we would have had a bigger vote and an even bigger majority. Albert told me that he had so many cars on polling day that he couldn't use them all, that all the fair-weather friends who had disappeared in the bad period were returning and that we have got the party back.

Why? As I drove home on Friday night, weary after another fourteen-hour day, I wondered about this amazing change. I have no doubt that it is basically explained by the abandonment of the prices and incomes policy and the fact that wages are rising faster than prices, exactly the same as in March 1966. The second factor is undoubtedly that people are impressed by the polls, and the G.L.C. election result. Thirdly, of course, there is the contrast between Harold Wilson and Edward Heath, especially after the Tories came out with Selsdon Man and their alternative 'law and order' policy. Instead of this being good for the Tories it did them harm and from that moment Heath began to fall back in popularity. We have moved a long way back towards Prime Ministerial elections and Harold, whom a few months ago I described as just one amongst his colleagues, is now right ahead, far ahead of anybody

[1] A. D. Lindsay, Master of Balliol, was the candidate of a Popular Front of Labour, Liberal and Conservative critics of Chamberlain. Quintin Hogg was the successful Conservative candidate. The Lord Mayor of Nottingham was W. G. E. Dyer, C.B.E.

else, dominating the television every day. What a remarkable man. And there is Edward Heath dry and retired, away in Europe all last week making speeches, trying to give the impression that he won't go into the Common Market if the cost is too high. A bit late in the day for that. He timed his absence miraculously badly. The Tories are now in total disarray after our unexpected success. But it's not so much a change, more the simple fact that abstentionists are beginning to come back and Labour voters have returned to Labour. I don't think there is much more to it than that.

Sunday, May 10th

Yesterday I was able to have some time off. I had to do a lot of work in the morning but in the afternoon I de-nettled my island and talked things over with Mr Pritchett. Today I rang Barbara to find out what she thought about the results but as it turned out our entire conversation was, as usual, about working together at Management Committee and so on. There I was saying yes and how this was fine, when I know I'm not going to be there after the election. Barbara was more cautious than me but she is beginning to think there is something to be said for an early election. Another big factor last week was the threat of a national newspaper strike after trouble at the *Daily Mirror*. Vic Feather made a superhuman effort and by Thursday he managed to avert it, which shows that at least he is serious about the T.U.C.'s pledge to take responsibility for stopping wild-cat strikes. Vic Feather has been a tower of strength and he is bringing the whole trade union movement back to our side. It is most important that he and Scanlon and the rest of them are now rooting for us. On this vital issue the Tories have played into our hands. They are now firmly committed to their policy of disciplining the unions, bringing them under the law and making them liable for civil damages, while we are off the hook because we have abandoned the prices and incomes policy and because the Industrial Relations Bill which Barbara has published is pro-trade union. This is one of the reasons for the long-delayed Labour recovery in Coventry and Birmingham, where all the paid organizers of the T.G.W. and A.E.F. are at last on our side. The men who didn't turn up at my constituency dinner will now be collecting the money and organizing the shop stewards on our behalf. This is where Vic Feather plays such an enormously important role. He is far more vigorous and far less neutral than George Woodcock, far more solidly pro-Labour and pro-Government.

I also rang Roy, who is beginning to think that we ought to work on the June assumption. Anyway we all know that Harold wants it and there are now few reasons for holding him back. But I really wanted to get Roy's support for making the supplementary benefit increase 8*s*. instead of 7*s*. As he very quickly pointed out, if we have the election before October, we can make do with a 7*s*. increase and rush the order along with the Finance Bill in the few days when Parliament comes back after Whitsun.

Well, that is it. We are on the way and I should like to bet that we shall just be able to get our fortnight's holiday in nicely. By Whitsun we shall have decided on an early election and I shall then have the job of telling Harold my intentions. He has no notion of my plans and when I rang him tonight we were back in the old days, discussing how to fix the programme together. He is interested and I think excited to know that after being one of the chief opponents of June I have now more or less come round to his view. He is obviously anxious to get my information and, above all, to work with me. I don't know what he is going to say when he hears my news. Of course there is some advantage in it for Harold, because he will be able to use my place for somebody else and my big job will perhaps go to Barbara. It is useful to have a vacancy at Social Services if there is to be a shuffling at the top and anyway in a Cabinet no one is missed for long. Politicians are ambitious people who like seeing each other but don't miss their colleagues. Do I miss George Brown? Perhaps I do, because he was an interesting element. I suppose one or two of them will miss my toughness and the fact that I could speak up to Harold, but by and large I shan't be missed. I think they will cheer when they learn that I am to be Editor of the *New Statesman* but that is another matter.

Monday, May 11th

As I went up in the train I reflected on all the inconvenience that an early election would cause me. I had already made it only too clear to Management Committee that I should be the person who loses a major Bill, which would then take another six months to put on the Statute Book. It's sad for me because I shan't be there to carry it through or to deal with my other two big projects, the White Paper on the reform of the National Health Service and the preparation of a White Paper on mental handicap. All these will be left half done for my successor to finish. I have privately asked Tam, Brian and Tommy whether it wouldn't be possible for me to stay on for a year or even six months to see the Superannuation Bill through, but to prepare the two White Papers and the draft legislation would, of course, require a three- or four-year stint. I tend to think that I can't go back into the Cabinet and then get out and in any case I am beginning to feel ready to move. Moreover, I have promised Jock Campbell that I will be ready to take over at the *Statesman*. We haven't spoken to each other yet about the election date but that I suppose is the next thing I ought to do.

I am greatly encouraged by my talk with Tam, who is no fool in these matters. He sees the enormous advantage of my moving to the *Statesman* and making it a platform for constructive criticism. If we win this election we shall have a Government with no strategy at all and virtually no policy. There will be a lot of work in progress at N.H.S. and in local government reform but the basic problems of the economy and of prices and incomes have not been solved and the position will be much the same as in 1966. We shall be repeating the pattern of wage inflation followed by damping down because that is how the British public likes it. I think it is true that as Editor of the *New Statesman* and a back-bench M.P. I could exert more influence and perhaps be more useful than slogging it out in the Ministry.

It was the beginning of a routine week, with the Department first in P.Q.s this afternoon. This evening there was an Israeli Independence Day party and I thought it was my duty to turn up because I remain fanatically pro-Israel, but there was a huge crowd and I found myself totally isolated. As Nahum Goldmann says, we are old men now, completely out of tune with modern Israel, which is moving beyond us to the holocaust and disaster. They are now crusaders hoist on their own machinery of destruction and the whole Middle East issue is one of appalling danger. I stood about for an hour feeling so depressed that I dropped out and went to a film at the Curzon. It was one of those extraordinary new permissive films about two American couples, mostly taking pot and going to bed together. I suppose that to be able to show such things marks a revolution in production and this film happened to have very realistic dialogue. It gave one an impression of the life of rich young Americans, so it had a kind of fascination for me.

Meanwhile the House was discussing the Report Stage and Third Reading of the Seebohm Bill, but I just went home. Shirley Williams and John Dunwoody had put it through in Committee and in normal circumstances I should have been there. John had gone off to a speaking engagement but when I had said I would sit on the front bench, I had been told that Eirene White would be there for Wales and they didn't really want me. So when I got home at about 9.30 I simply went to bed and started reading. Tam rang through to tell me that divisions were going on and I asked if I should come. 'No,' he said, 'you're properly paired, so you can't vote.' I thought, 'Hell, I ought to be there. I am the Minister in charge of this Bill; but, still, Callaghan is staying away so I'll stay away too.'

Tuesday, May 12th

This morning I discovered to my amusement that Jim Callaghan had in fact gone along last night, quietly putting his oar in and seeing to his public relations. Marginally, I suppose, the fact that the Home Secretary was there while the Secretary of State for Social Services was not has strengthened Jim's position in the struggle for the Children's Department. No doubt I stayed away partly because I know I'm on the way out. It's interesting to see the degree of detachment that has come into my behaviour.

Legislation Committee was very brief, so I had a free moment and asked Odgers to come up. He brought me a report on the standardized means test, a project on which the officials have been working for nearly two years. They have decided that, although supplementary benefit can't be included because it has local variations, six or seven of the other central government means tests for benefits can be brought together as a single formula. The officials had worked out the actual questionnaire that we would need. It's the beginning of the negative income tax. Paul asked whether I thought the report should be submitted to the local authorities and I said, 'No. I think that in this rather half-baked form the report is too modest. They would just discourage us. Instead we ought to take it back to the Social Services Committee and get Ministers to appreciate its importance. We must show them that with appropriate legislation we could extend it to cover more than the six or seven existing tests. For instance we could alter the conditions on which people are entitled to rate rebates or the means test for free school meals.' 'Oh,' Paul said, 'if we have legislation we can include three or four more.' This was a very important discussion and out of it we may get a new Bill. That's something the civil servant doesn't think of, even a man as skilled and resourceful as Paul.

At 12.15 I was to see the Chancellor about supplementary benefit. I had raised this at the weekly departmental lunch yesterday and I had been told that what the Chancellor was inclined to want and what the Prime Minister possibly thought was that we could have an immediate 7*s.* increase if the election was early. However there was no doubt that by October the full 8*s.* increase must be implemented, because my own officials had discovered that the secret Treasury calculation, on which the budget had been based, now forecast an increase in the cost of living that would take off not the original amount of 5*s.* from the value of supplementary benefit but, now, the equivalent of 6*s.* Management Committee had decided to uprate supplementary benefit by 2*s.* more than the increase in the cost of living would demand so this new fact meant that we now needed an 8*s.* rise. I had spelt this out in a paper which I proposed to put to Cabinet and I had asked to have this item on Thursday's Cabinet agenda. I then got a message that the Prime Minister didn't want to take it at Cabinet but would like the Chancellor and me to consider it together. So this morning I went along to the Treasury and walked up the two flights of stairs, where John Harris was waiting for me. We discussed the election a little. There wasn't much to say, though I indicated that in my view an early election is now inevitable, whether we like it or not. Then I went in to Roy, who said, 'The Prime Minister is not very keen on this and I don't want the 8*s.* increase either if I can possibly avoid it.' I explained the case, saying, 'It's all very well, but we have to think about the people, not merely about electioneering. Either they need the 8*s.* or they don't and if they really need it we ought to give it to them.' Roy said, 'Well, what date? Will you give me November 1st?' I replied, 'I'll think about that if you'll give me twenty-four hours,' and out I went.

Wednesday, May 13th

I began to think that Roy might be diddling me and I grew more and more worried. I had asked for twenty-four hours' delay before I made my decision, but I suddenly remembered that if it was to go on the Cabinet agenda I had to give twenty-four hours' notice. So I rang Harold to tell him I was anxious and he asked, 'Can't you settle it with Roy?' 'Yes,' I said, 'but I want to be quite clear that if I can't it will be on the agenda.' 'Yes,' said Harold. 'Anyway, it will either be reported to Cabinet as unanimous or you will have to have a Cabinet decision.' I thought that was all right and I went off to S.E.P. As we were starting, I sent a note across to Roy saying that I had spoken to Harold, who was expecting either an agreed report from us, or that I would put forward my 8*s*. for Cabinet to discuss.

After S.E.P. I rushed off to Kettners restaurant, where I had been asked by Anthony Shrimsley[1] to meet Rupert Murdoch, the new proprietor of the *Sun* and the *News of the World*, and the Editor of the *Daily Mirror*, Larry Lamb. I found Murdoch a mild, interesting man, not very well-informed and not apparently a ruthless tycoon. He is very unlike our friend Cudlipp, who has had such a disastrous short life as an I.P.C. tycoon and has had to go back to journalism. The *Mirror* is for the first time being challenged by a rival paper of the same type and the *Sun* is pushing in with some success. We had a most interesting discussion about how the *Mirror* had become a part of the Establishment, and how the *Sun* must acquire the bump of irreverence. I talked to them at length about the role of the *Mirror* in the old days and tried to get Murdoch to see that, if the *Sun* is to compete with the *Mirror*, the best thing he can do is to criticize the Labour Government as much as he likes. I said they must be as irreverent and as radical as the old *Mirror*, which means that in the forthcoming election they should come out in favour of keeping Harold Wilson, so that later on they could attack him for being too conservative. I looked at my watch. By God, it was already 2.35 and at 2.30 I was supposed to be taking the chair at Social Services Committee.

Peter shot me down Whitehall and I slipped in twenty minutes late. It makes me realize that on the whole Cabinet has made me much more punctual than I used to be. Our meetings do start absolutely on time, chairmen are always there and there is no sympathy for other members who are late. I found that Barbara had taken the chair and they were still discussing the first item. They just took it for granted that I was late and nobody said a damned thing before or afterwards. I suppose I am an old crusty thing and they were afraid to say anything in front of me. They just carried on talking about a new clause Barbara wanted to put into her Equal Pay Bill when it is read to the Lords this afternoon. It would give her powers to provide equal pensions and my Department had furiously opposed this idea. Today I persuaded her to drop it. She could say that the Government were determined to deal with this by legislation, before equal pay becomes effective five years from now. The compromise satisfied everyone and it pleased her a good deal.

By this time I had received a message to say that the Chancellor wanted me to telephone him. I was too canny for that, so I went down to his room. Roy looked a bit surprised but I sat down and said, 'Well?' He said, 'Harold isn't very keen on this. What about the date? Will you take November 1st?'

[1] Anthony Shrimsley was the Political Editor of the *Sun*.

I said, 'Yes, if the election is early, as it will be, but I can't be definite. If the election is in October it will have to be changed back.' So we clinched it in three minutes. Roy had quietly given me the 8*s.* I needed. I had already seen Clifford Jarrett about printing and drafting the regulations and I shall announce it on Friday morning, the last day before we break up for the Whitsun recess.[1] It will certainly be taken as an election portent.

Thursday, May 14th

Management at 9.30. Harold said, 'We needn't, of course, decide anything yet,' and then he made a twenty-minute speech. The most interesting point was that he had got Roy's certificate that it would be just as safe to have the election in October as in June. Nevertheless Roy had decided that in the circumstances June was right. 'Basically,' Harold said, 'I really decided this a month ago.' That is right. He made up his mind a month ago, he wanted June and waited for the facts to come his way. Perhaps we could have dragged him back but events have been on his side. Harold has got his way and he has done so by being an election Prime Minister, creating the atmosphere and the news, working up the fever, making postponement impossible. We then discussed whether we shouldn't announce the date after today's Cabinet. Many papers were expecting this but Harold wanted to wait until next Monday. We heard some of the detailed mechanics – how Harold had warned the Queen before she went off on her New Zealand trip and how all the arrangements had now been made for him to talk to her on Monday.[2] It became clear that the Prime Minister didn't want the announcement before next Sunday's joint Cabinet–N.E.C. meeting at No. 10. If an announcement were made they would sit down to write the manifesto, which Harold wants to do himself with Peter Shore. He intends to leave the N.E.C. in suspense, which means the meeting will be a sheer waste of time. Thank God I won't be there.

It was quite easy-going. I wanted to know about timing and whether one could go away on holiday. Harold said that if necessary he wanted us all to come back. Judith, who would be touring by car, would have to clock in by telephone every day. I said, 'Well, I shall be in Malta.' There was a bit of surprise and then Harold said, 'I excuse the halt, the lame, the blind and the old.' I said, 'I qualify in all four categories,' and there was a hearty laugh. It is interesting that Harold is allowing me some time off and it is more evidence that he may not be utterly surprised when I bring him my news. But I don't know.

[1] On Friday, May 15th, the Secretary of State announced that from November 1st, 1970, the rate of supplementary benefit would be increased by 8*s.* a week for a single person and 13*s.* a week for a married couple. The benefits would accordingly rise to £5 4*s.* and £8 10*s.* a week, respectively.

[2] The Queen, the Duke of Edinburgh, Princess Anne and Prince Charles visited New Zealand and Australia from March 30th to May 3rd, to take part in the Cook bicentenary celebrations.

Meanwhile Cabinet was waiting outside and after forty-five minutes in they came. They were just told that there was still no decision but that it was most important to say there had been no discussion. Then we arranged the business for the first week in June but all this will fall to the ground, because in fact Parliament will be brought back a week early, on the Tuesday after the Whitsun bank holiday, and after three days it will be prorogued, so that we can go right into the campaign. The election will be on June 18th, the date Harold has always wanted. Barbara was eagerly saying she must get her Equal Pay Bill through but I told her, 'That doesn't matter, we can have it again. What matters is to get the Seebohm Bill through, because that has an appointed day and delaying it would hold up the whole of local government reform.' Old Barbie always tries to get everything for herself. Then we were told there was to be another inquiry into the B.B.C.[1] I asked why colleagues weren't consulted and Harold said some colleagues were. Here is another instance of a major decision being privately taken by Harold and a few others.

By this time the newspapers were blazoning the results of the polls. The Tories were six points down in Gallup and 3·5 in N.O.P. and it was obvious that everybody knew we were going to have an early election.

I returned to the Department for a press conference on my letter to the R.H.B.s about recruitment of nursing staff, and then I spent the entire afternoon having hours of discussion about the N.H.S. Green Paper, working through it as fast as we could. I said to my officials, 'Don't imagine that when the election comes I shan't be here. I've arranged with the Prime Minister that I shall campaign in East Anglia near London and on a good many mornings I shall be available. I intend to concentrate on N.H.S. reform and on the White Paper on mental handicap.' They all looked at me a little bleakly. I don't know what they were hoping. They are now beginning to think we shall be returned and, though they don't know whether I shall be back, they rather expect it.

This evening I had a long dinner with Brian and from 8 until 11.30 we discussed his future. He has been my closest personal friend and without him I could have done very little in the past two years. He knows that I am getting out and he now sees that there is a case for my going. Should he stay on? I said, 'If I could see to it that Barbara took my place, it would be worth your while to stay. She is good with research people. If it's Denis, I wouldn't stay.' After a splendid dinner at a little restaurant just by Brian's house I came back home.

[1] The Prime Minister announced that a Committee to inquire into the future of broadcasting was to be set up, with Lord Annan as Chairman. After their election victory the Conservatives announced that no Committee would sit but when Labour returned to power in 1974 Lord Annan was once more asked to undertake the inquiry and a Committee was appointed.

Friday, May 15th

At 9.30 we had a short meeting of Management, where Roy and I raised the matter of the Kindersley Report. We pointed out that we should decide whether to publish it or just suppress it and announce that we would decide on doctors' pay after the election. After a working lunch with the P.U.S.s and the Ministers, I went off to Heathrow to catch the 5 o'clock plane to Malta.

The Foreign Office had sent me a message yesterday to say that they had heard I was staying with Dom Mintoff and I replied that I wasn't staying with him but that he had been kind enough to get accommodation for me and my family. Still, I am afraid there will be a bit of a row because we are in the middle of a Maltese crisis. I couldn't care less, because after the election I'm not going to be about.

Saturday, May 16th–Monday, May 25th

I flew off to Malta, knowing that there was some surprise that I was really going. The day before I left I had rung Harold to say, 'If you want me to stay, please tell me now, because I have to cancel within twenty-four hours.' As he had said no and left the matter there, he couldn't officially complain, yet I was very much aware that he thought I ought to have stayed behind, particularly since we have the joint Cabinet–N.E.C. meeting tomorrow and all next week Peter Shore and the others will be drafting the manifesto. But I had made up my mind that I wouldn't hang about unless Harold specifically demanded that I should stay and admitted that I was one of the inner group he needed for planning the campaign. So I just popped off, on the understanding that I could be contacted in Malta, but that I shouldn't be contacted unless it was necessary.

A pool car took us down to the airport and we got there just at the right time for the plane but, blow me, if there wasn't a strike of the luggage carriers. The whole of the departure area was still and quiet and nobody was moving. I ran into Harold Lever and his wife, both trying to get to Manchester, and much more amusing, into Jack Jones, Secretary of the Transport and General Workers, and his wife, both of whom had been on their way to Dublin, but who had been called off the plane because of the strike. It lasted for forty-five minutes, and we hung about and shuffled our luggage, until at last we set off about an hour late.

We arrived at 10.0 p.m. in pitch darkness, and among the people who'd come to meet us was the Naval Attaché, Steve Forrest,[1] who handed me a top-secret missive from the High Commissioner. This is Duncan Watson, an enormously solid, sensible, kindly reactionary, who had arrived in Malta only three weeks ago.[2] In his letter he welcomed me to the island but he

[1] Rear-Admiral Sir Ronald Stephen Forrest (K.C.V.O. 1975).

[2] Sir Duncan Watson (K.C.M.G. 1967), Political Adviser to the C.-in-C., Far East, 1967–70, High Commissioner in Malta 1970–2, Deputy Under-Secretary of State at the F.C.O. 1972–4.

said he wanted to warn me that my visit was going to cause a great flurry and I might not be able to get the quiet I needed. He asked me to accept his apologies for not coming to the airport and causing a sensation, to take the greatest care and to make an official courtesy visit to the Prime Minister on Friday. So I told Steve Forrest this was all right and off we went through the night to pursue our way to Dom's villa.

At the airport, Jack Jones had said, 'Oh, yes, Dom has a little beach cottage. He has offered it to us twice.' I thought, 'Oh, dear, a little beach cottage,' but when we got there we found an enormous, roomy old farmhouse, with a great spacious downstairs sitting room with windows all round, two big bedrooms downstairs and one upstairs, and lavatories and bathrooms on both levels, all splendid and easy and comfy, with room for us all. It was here we spent our very nice fortnight. The wind blew and kept the weather fairly cool and we only browned very gradually in the wind and didn't roast or blister. The sea was much colder than the bath at home but, once you plunged in, after the first twenty seconds or so you could stay perfectly happily without getting cold. There were wonderful limestone lagoons and rocks to jump from and sun on, and practically no sea urchins. It was tremendously exhilarating.

This end of Malta is not sandy but our children were just the right age for it. There are some flowers and a little greenery at this time of year but nevertheless it's a dusty place, terribly untidy and ramshackle. I could see the hopelessness of the island, of which about half is now deserted. The rest is naval and R.A.F. bases, wonderful expensive buildings, half-vacated by the British, with the dry docks now handed over to some kind of company which is already losing £2 or £3 million a year. Yet the standard of living has risen enormously in the last fifteen years and there is much less unemployment than anybody expected. Amazing. Malta has been pirouetting along on a tightrope, rather like us in fact.

What did I learn? First of all that the island is nothing like as good for tourism as Crete or Cyprus. It is a lovely island, especially the old town of Mdina and the magnificent cliffs in the middle area. This gives it shape but its colour is monotonous and it is appallingly overpopulated. Dom's dream is that it should be a kind of Switzerland in the Mediterranean, a tiny independent entrepôt area with a special British relationship, a defence treaty as well as a lot of aid. I told him this was no go and that the last thing we wanted was to sign treaties committing us to the defence of bits and pieces scattered all over the world, like the Falkland Islands, Fiji, Mauritius, Brunei. Malta is valuable either to NATO or to no one. In the Mediterranean we are now simply and solely a NATO power, with no other special interests, no staging post in the Far East, and in two or three years' time, no staging post to the Persian Gulf either. Dom and I argued about this for ten hours or so. He wasn't just going to see Malta handed over as a subject nation to NATO.

Nobody tried to exploit my visit at all and none of the excitement about my presence being a nuisance materialized. We lived quietly in Mintoff's house and no newspaper mentioned my visit. On Friday I had a pleasant seventy-five-minute talk with Borg Olivier, who was very cagey, and whom I found very close to Dom on foreign policy. We got into a long argument about whether they could afford to build a £2 million hospital for about 2,500 people on the island of Gozo, an absolute nonsense. I began to appreciate Dom's observation that, under their present Government, the Maltese are probably wasting the money we are giving them.

After seeing Borg Olivier I was having lunch with the High Commissioner when an enormous telegram from No. 10 was brought in, the text of a letter from the doctors, bitterly protesting that they didn't want the Kindersley settlement postponed. There was also a draft reply from Harold, briefly telling them he had decided that the matter ought to be dealt with after the election and that unless they wanted to press him he saw no purpose in seeing them. I thought this reply very unwise, so I firmly suggested that he omit the phrase about there being no purpose in seeing them. I decided not to think any more about this until I returned to England.

Tuesday, May 26th

I flew back today, leaving the family behind for the rest of their second week. During the flight I got down to the job of writing my election address. Albert had found my 1964 and 1966 addresses and I found it wrote itself. It was a beautiful day and I looked down at Ponza, where we were last year in Charles Forte's yacht, at Genoa, Mont Blanc and then Lake Geneva. When we landed England was beautifully sunny and I learnt that there hadn't been a drop of rain since we left. Nothing very much had happened while I was away except for the ridiculous sensation that Bobby Moore, the Captain of the England football team, had been charged with stealing a £600 bracelet from a Colombian shop just before the World Cup championship in Mexico.[1]

Robin Wendt was not at the airport because he had to look after his daughter while his wife was giving birth to their second child. But there were Janet Newman, Mike Fogden and Peter Smithson, my dear, darling Private Office, and before I knew it I was in the car and they were bringing me up to date. The main news was that the P.M. wanted to see me about the doctors. It was rumoured that he had changed his mind and that he now felt it was necessary to publish the Kindersley Report, which would mean trouble for me.

Before going round to the Elephant and Castle I called in at Transport House, because the Private Office had made a mistake and thought that a joint meeting of the N.E.C. and the Cabinet was taking place there this morning. I looked through the door and there only seemed to be about twelve people in the room. Tony Wedgwood Benn said, 'Hallo, Dick, what are you doing here?' and I told him that I thought there was a joint meeting

[1] He was cleared of the charge.

to draft the manifesto. 'No, no,' he said, 'this is a drafting Committee but do come in. We have just reached your bit on social services.' A curious coincidence. I sat down and read it, tidying it up as much as I could. I realized that poor old Peter Shore must have had a very tough time trying to draft this without me. But in fact my presence wouldn't have made the faintest difference, because they had been given a ruling that the Chancellor must not be committed to any extra expenditure. As there is nothing we can do which doesn't cost money, the only pledge is the thoroughly bad one to reform the House of Lords. So all they could do was write the manifesto shortly or at length and I don't think I had missed a great deal.

I went up to the Elephant and Castle to sort things out before going over to the Athenaeum for a quick lunch by myself and to prepare for this afternoon's departmental meeting on the final draft of the Social Services Committee on mental handicap, the preliminary to the White Paper. But after lunch I learnt that the meeting had been scrubbed and that I was to see Harold straightaway about the doctors. A letter had just been received from the B.M.A. with a sensational press release saying they were so angry and fed up that, unless we published the Report by the end of the week, the B.M.A. action committee would advise the Council to advise the profession to take the first steps of protest, i.e. to break off all contact with the Government and stop signing sickness benefit certificates. Pretty hot stuff; with no warning, Stevenson and Gibson were blowing the thing up into a sensation.

This letter was handed to me the moment I walked into Harold's room. He was about to tell me that postponing Kindersley was no good. The doctors' indignation was mounting and we had to publish. I said, 'But if you publish after seven weeks' delay, it will look much worse. People will want to know why we couldn't make up our minds and meanwhile the doctors will use the Report to put pressure on every parliamentary candidate. I see no advantage in publishing, Harold.' 'Well,' he said, 'I assure you that we have to give way now. You don't understand the opinion that is building up in the country.' I replied, 'We certainly can't publish at the very moment when they are threatening strike action. This has given us a great chance. I have already summoned the doctors to see me at 5.30 and I suggest that we simply reply that I am not prepared to surrender to strike action. We can certainly say that, though you and I were considering publication last week, there is no question of our doing so in the face of this threat.' 'Yes,' Harold said, 'that's right. Draft a statement on those lines and we will have Management Committee at 4.30.'

So I brought a draft statement into Management Committee but nobody seemed to like it very much. Indeed, Harold once more made it clear that he thought it a great mistake not to publish, despite the fact that last time this had been brought up at Management he had capsized within four minutes and agreed not to publish. Barbara also thought we ought to publish and to publish our decision as well. Roy immediately supported her and I realized that, if we had to publish, it was certainly a lesser evil to publish the Report and the decision together and that to do this in an election atmosphere would not be such a bad thing, because the doctors' demand for 30 per cent across the board and their outrage at getting only 15 per cent would seem extremely greedy. I also saw that if we published now I could perhaps get 15 per cent flat-rate payment on account, plus the full amount for the junior doctors, so I straightaway switched to support Barbara and Roy. This discussion went on until 5.20 and I was due to see the doctors at 5.30. I said, 'I must tell them that the Prime Minister and I will agree to see them this week.' Harold said, 'All right, I'll see them but not tomorrow or Wednesday because that would spoil the press for the manifesto. If I see them on Thursday it will get into the Friday press.' We agreed to see them on Thursday morning in No. 10. I also made it clear that if we were going to have this during the election we would have to give the junior doctors the full claim. With Barbara's help I got it without a hitch, the full 30 per cent for junior doctors, that is, £6 million extra on the claim and for the others an initial holding payment of 15 per cent. That is to be the offer, with the remainder of the Kindersley Report to be referred to the P.I.B. I had come out with a much more attractive package than we had originally and this must now be worked out by the Department.

I must say I felt a bit sulky about the whole thing, and at these sudden changes, and I was angry with Harold. It's characteristic, of course, and as I told him, 'The fact is you and I never really change our minds. Even if we are persuaded to do so, we try and hark back to our original idea.' I now know this characteristic of Harold's and it is what he had been doing on this occasion. But he had been defeated and, instead of returning to his original position, he had agreed to something new which was much more sensible, much riskier and much more unpleasant. There will be a bleeding row during the election instead of afterwards, but I don't think we'll lose electorally.

Five minutes late, I walked in to see the doctors, having decided to have a long row with them. I made a bitter complaint and said, 'How can I be your sponsor and look after you if, without a word of warning to me, you slap down this ultimatum, the threat of a strike within twenty-four hours if we don't publish within twenty-four hours? You know that is physically impossible.' They said, 'We had no choice. The whole profession is outraged, you were away on holiday and we didn't know you were back.' I said, 'If you didn't know I was back why did you write me a letter this morning to say that you were waiting by the telephone?' Of course it was a lie that they didn't know I'd returned. I soon discovered that Stevenson and Gibson were scared stiff. The whole profession was suddenly boiling for a tremendous row and they had been caught floating on the foam. I upbraided them and said, 'How can I possibly represent you in Cabinet if without any warning you do this to me?' They said, 'You don't understand. You may feel personally resentful, but we feel damnably angry at what you have done to us. You have destroyed the goodwill we have built up over the last two years and the atmosphere is worse than ever. The whole profession will never forgive you. There is a suspicion you are repeating the trick you played on us in 1966.' 'Look,' I said, 'this is over and done with. You want to see the P.M. Well, I'll arrange for you to see him on Thursday at 9.45 a.m.,' and that was all fixed.

The minutes of this meeting (I have them here) show that the only decision was to meet the P.M. on Thursday at 9.45. I already knew that the earliest we could publish was Thursday week, so what I had to do was to persuade Harold to say to the doctors, 'Right, if you insist we will concede. We think it's a mistake but on June 4th you can have your publication of your Kindersley Report and the Secretary of State will give you a decision.'

Then I had to go to the lobby and explain what was going on. I didn't tell the press we'd already decided to give way but I said that the Prime Minister and I would listen to the doctors' request on Thursday and I made it pretty clear that provided they were to stop this nonsense about a strike we would concede.

Albert and Winnie were terribly anxious about the election address, so this evening they came up to London and we dictated it to Janet Newman and all four of us had dinner together. It was a very pleasant evening at the end of a pretty busy day, my first day back.

Wednesday, May 27th

Apart from making all the arrangements for Harold's meeting with the doctors tomorrow, we also had to work on the decision itself because of course nothing had been done on this. Meanwhile I had a lot of long departmental meetings, which went on until 2.30, when I had to make a Statement on doctors' pay. It was fairly easy. The Tories tried to make some capital out of it and they seem to think that we ought to have given the doctors everything. They will be in some difficulty when they see what the Report recommends, and I did all right on that.

All day there had been a meeting of the N.E.C., not with the Cabinet this time because they had managed to dispense with us. They had started at 9.30 and gone on for six hours trying to draft the manifesto.* This evening the P.M. was giving a party at No. 10 for the sixty to seventy M.P.s who are retiring, but, strangely, Harold wasn't to be seen. I turned up about ten minutes late, but as I couldn't find anyone I really cared about and I felt curiously out of things, I slipped into Harold's study. There was Marcia, whom I hadn't seen for ages and ages, and Gerald Kaufman. I had a little chat with them, not really like old times because I'm now very much out of

* At the end of the week I gathered from an account in the *Sunday Times* that they slogged and slogged away throughout the day, fighting out the issues. The wealth tax was knocked out by Roy Jenkins, the references to Cambodia were knocked out and the whole thing was anodyne. I wasn't sorry to be absent.

the inner circle. Not only am I personally and socially out of this but I am also absolutely excluded from the group whose advice Harold is taking during the election campaign. He has got Callaghan back and William Camp,[1] a very able young professional public relations man, who has taken Gerald Kaufman's place. Tommy Balogh is back to help to write Harold's speeches and Peter Shore is there, but Barbara and I are excluded. We are, in a sense, no longer part of the personal entourage but regarded as powers in our own right.

I gave Thomas dinner and afterwards Jock Campbell came to see me in 21a, to talk about the *New Statesman*. A terrible thing had happened yesterday, when it was announced that Tony Greenwood would be leaving the House for the chairmanship of the Commonwealth Development Corporation, the job which Reg Prentice and Judith Hart had promised Jock. According to Patricia Llewelyn-Davies, Tony hadn't asked for this but it had been almost forced upon him in a deal last October, with a peerage and £10,000 a year. It was separation money for a man to whom Harold had offered the Secretaryship of the Party but had failed to deliver. Jock was furiously angry but that was that. We discussed the *Statesman* and agreed that I should join them on July 1st. If we won the election it should be announced immediately; if we didn't we would perhaps wait ten days or so, because if Harold were still Prime Minister there would have to be an exchange of letters. I knew I must talk to Harold soon, before the election, but Tommy Balogh was very much against this, saying that Harold is so nervy just now that it would upset him. It was marvellous to talk to Jock and to feel inspired and excited, and to know that we would get on together. I must also admit that it was marvellous to feel that Jock is going to take a certain vengeance for the vile things which Harold has done to him, a vengeance of which Harold still has no idea.

Thursday, May 28th

The first thing was the meeting with the B.M.A. at No. 10. I got there a minute or two early and went in the back way to join Harold. Then they all came in – Dr Gibson, Dr Cameron, Dr Stevenson with his assistant secretary, and two dentists. They were on the far side of the table, facing Harold and me. The P.M. did practically all the talking and started by being very strong to them, as he had promised, and rather offensive about their threats of industrial action. Then he said, 'Let's put a veil over the past,' and announced that we had conceded publication next week. That was the soonest they could have it, both in terms of printing the document and of getting our decisions ready.

[1] Public Relations Adviser to the Gas Council 1963–7, Director of Information Services at the British Steel Corporation 1967–71, Special Adviser to the Milling and Baking Industries since 1972, to British Leyland Motor Corporation 1975 and to British Rail 1977. He was unpaid Adviser to the Prime Minister in the 1970 General Election.

I should add that ever since I had got back from Malta it had been pretty clear to me that the doctors had seen the advantage in having publication without a Government decision, because Kindersley would then become an election issue, and, whoever won, the next Government would be virtually compelled to implement the recommendations. Though the doctors still didn't know what was in the Report they knew that it would be to their advantage to delay the decision, so I am sure that they were nonplussed by Harold's announcement. I also think they had been nonplussed by my warning that they would do better to wait for a decision taken dispassionately and by the end of this morning's meeting I think they had begun to suspect that maybe they had miscalculated. The meeting was tough and there were a great many speeches. They kept saying, 'It's impossible, you must publish this weekend or the whole thing will blow up. Our relations with the Government have been put back ten years.' They made the wildest claims but we insisted that they could only have the Report in a week's time.

Then they demanded that we must guarantee that the Government decision would be nothing less than the whole recommendation. Harold and I said that it was absurd to ask this. A Government doesn't say these things, doesn't automatically grant everything a Report recommends. We hadn't finished considering it yet and we couldn't possibly give such an assurance. They said, 'Without it the whole profession will be in chaos.' As a matter of fact, all these predictions were quite wrong because the B.M.A. which was in session today, agreed to wait for a week and the junior doctors and everybody else agreed, although there were mutterings that if the decision wasn't satisfactory they would proceed with strike action.

As soon as the meeting was over, we had Cabinet. It consisted of bits and pieces, foreign policy from Michael Stewart, the usual interminable list of industrial disputes from Barbara and parliamentary business from Bob Mellish. So the last Cabinet of the session petered out mildly and ineffectively and Harold wished us good luck. I went straight along the passage to No. 70 Whitehall to talk to the medical journalists for forty-five minutes. The C.M.O., by the way, hasn't turned up at all in the past two days to give us any advice. Alan Marre was standing behind me terrified but he admitted afterwards that he had never heard such a brilliantly conducted press conference. I indicated that we had taken a strong line and that the doctors were playing with fire. I said they were being utterly irresponsible and that it was outrageous to threaten industrial action only because they were getting the Report a week later than they wished. All this was put over to the press with some success and I greatly enjoyed doing it.

After being interviewed by the B.B.C. and I.T.V., I went down to the House for another Statement and then to the Department to work on the announcement of our decision. The Department is petrified because we have now done the one thing they thought we couldn't do and gone in for a tremendous row with the doctors. It is a strange Department and I got no help from them at all. Bea and I had to think of everything ourselves. It was left to me to realize that if we are making a payment on account we must arrange to have it paid within a matter of weeks. This means we must guarantee them 15 per cent of last year's salary and make a real effort to make the adjustment by the time they receive next month's salary, because if the payments were held up the B.M.A. would say, quite rightly, that we were denying the junior doctors and G.P.s the hard cash they really need. All this, together with the question of whether we should commit ourselves to the P.I.B. reference, were things I had to raise myself. Bavin was in a cold sweat and a tizzy, Alan Marre was confident but very distant, the C.M.O. was absent and Bea and I struggled to get the work done.

After that I took Bea out to dinner. Poor woman, her departure for her holiday in Yugoslavia had been delayed for a week and then she only had from Friday to Tuesday before she had to fly home for this crisis. She is a conscientious, lovely person, a marvellous lieutenant, though I must admit she's an ineffective administrator who can't chair a meeting and get decisions taken. Then we went back to my room to watch Harold in the first round of the television election on a programme called 'Your Questions Answered', questions sent in by some 18,000 people. Jeremy Thorpe had appeared on Tuesday, yesterday was Heath and today we had Harold. He was confronted by a series of corking questions, practically every one about a broken promise, a broken pledge. He did it as well as any human being could and I thought he was magnificent. I was afraid that it would damage us in the polls but it is essential that we bring into the open what people are thinking. It's necessary that Harold should answer these doubts. He's learning, because on housing, instead of trying to make excuses, he said, 'I bitterly regret that we had to give up the housing programme when devaluation meant that we had to cut back our costs.' He is certainly far better at this than before.

Then I went home and listened to the same programme on the radio, where of course it's much better without the distraction of the face.

Friday, May 29th

All day yesterday I had been asking to see Harold. I had tried before I went to Malta but he hadn't got time. I tried to see him yesterday and I finally got a message to say that he wondered what it was I wanted because he was very busy. I thought that wasn't good enough, so I rang him up this morning. First I congratulated him on his broadcast and then we discussed the doctors and the press on that, and eventually I said, 'You know I've been wanting to see you,' and he replied, 'Well, yes, it is a bit difficult today. I am preparing a speech for this evening.' I said, 'I'm not wasting your time, it's about my future intentions. You see, I have decided not to stay on as a minister in the next Government. I shan't be far away. I'm not just going to write books and I want to discuss my intentions with you.' Oh, well, he was very anxious to talk about that. He managed to completely conceal his reaction and just said, 'Yes, we must discuss it.' I added, 'You see, I wasn't just wasting your time, it does seem to be important and I don't think it's fair to go on with my plans without telling you. Incidentally, the other thing I wanted to mention is about Barbara. I would like you to know that she is the person who should take my place.' 'Yes,' he said, 'she is rather down a crevice now.' I said, 'My God, she is and if I go there is a space for her. I can't think of anybody who could replace me and do the job as well as she could. She couldn't do the pensions side as well as I have done but she would be fine on the hospital service. She would give D.H.S.S. panache and drive and imagination and it is big enough for her.' Harold liked that idea and he said, 'Of course she ought to have moved in the last shuffle. I offered it to her.'

I think I have planted the idea in his heart and I am giving Barbara a real opportunity, that is, always assuming that we win the election. Now I am going to see Harold, who must be beginning to wonder what on earth it is that I am doing.

At 10 o'clock we had Social Services Committee at which I just wanted to get authority for the officials to go ahead on the multiple means test during the four weeks of the campaign. In walked Peter Shore, who sat down and said this was most unsuitable. He could not conceive why we had meetings of this kind called just at this time, most inopportune, most improper, and moreover, the papers should be marked 'restricted' or 'confidential'. I was glad to see that everybody round the table told him not to be so silly. Of course the officials must do something and the Committee was only being asked to give them a directive to go on working. 'I think it is wholly proper', said Dick Taverne, 'that we should get on.' But Peter was upset. I suppose he feels that while the inner group are deeply committed and deeply involved in drafting the manifesto, we are not taking things seriously.

I walked across to the House to see the prorogation. During the past three days we have been winding up a whole mass of business, getting all the Bills through with the agreement of the Opposition, including Barbara's Equal Pay Bill. But my Superannuation Bill and the Ports Bill have fallen by the way and will have to start all over again. There had been a series of Statements, most of them to hand out goodies, the Minister of Transport on roads, David Ennals on the constant attendance allowance, Tony Crosland with a White Paper on pollution, a stream of the things a Government will always do before an election. A few people on our own side had been cheering rather lustily and morale was quite high, but it is a dying House of Commons. There I was today, sitting on the front bench for positively the last time. Then we walked across to the Lords and it was quite impressive to hear the prorogation speech listing the measures we had achieved in this last session. By then I had really had enough, so I didn't go back to the Commons to shake hands with the Speaker but slipped off down the passage to give lunch to Alma Birk.

After lunch I went back to the Department for an excellent meeting on the mental handicap paper. I went through it making my amendments, every one of which the officials accepted. They have got used to it now. Then it was time to go down to Heathrow with Peter to pick up Anne and the children. The flight from Malta was half an hour late and we had a twenty-five-minute wait for the luggage but at last we got into the car to drive back to Prescote.

Saturday, May 30th

A lovely day. In the morning the *Coventry Evening Telegraph* people came over and took a lot of photographs for the election and the Health Correspondent asked me endless questions, terribly pleased to have some time with the Secretary of State. We were told of their new arrangements for covering the election, with very little reporting of speeches. But they didn't tell me what I later learnt from Albert Rose, that Maurice Edelman had arranged that he and his opponent will each publish a daily article. I don't mind, but Bill Wilson is furious and it is a bad start to the campaign. The candidates are not going to have a joint kick-off meeting as we usually do and I gather that there is not even to be an eve-of-poll meeting. Still, in summer indoor meetings aren't well attended. I have decided to do processions round the place, with meetings outside the pubs, and I shall do my usual week's campaigning in the constituency and a week in East Anglia with Doug Garnett, as well as working in the Department.

This afternoon we had the adoption meeting. There were very few people there, only thirty or forty, but they were given very little notice. The atmosphere was pleasant and in my speech I tried to stress the importance of ideas, saying that if we won we must have a free, independent, socialist policy of equality. This was intended to warn them of my news, because I knew they would be surprised and disconcerted about my move to the *Statesman*. So that was that, and tomorrow I shall have plenty of time on my island, pruning it back and cutting it up, and lovely bathing before I go to London in the evening.

Monday, June 1st

I caught the 9.30 train to Norwich for my first day of election touring. There I did a television programme with Peter Rawlinson and Mr Banks, who I think is the research organizer for the Liberal Party.[1] We were up against fourteen East Anglian journalists and it was striking that they didn't ask us a

[1] Sir Peter Rawlinson (Kt 1962) was called to the bar in 1946 and became a Q.C. in 1959. He was Conservative M.P. for Surrey 1955–74 and since 1974 has been Conservative M.P. for Epsom and Ewell. He was Solicitor General July 1962–October 1964, Attorney General 1970–4 and Attorney General for Northern Ireland 1972–4. Desmond Banks, a life assurance broker and unsuccessful Liberal candidate in 1950, 1955 and 1959, was President of the Liberal Party 1968–9 and Chairman of the Research Committee 1966. He has been President of the Liberal European Action Group since 1971 and Vice-Chairman of the Liberal Party Standing Committee since 1973. He became a life peer in 1974.

single question on the cost of living, on wages, leadership, pensions or the law. It was a pleasant, flat programme, which did not do the faintest harm, and I found Peter Rawlinson a very nice and obliging person. Douglas Garnett picked me up and drove me to the University of Norwich, which made itself notorious a few weeks ago, when the students had booed Roy Jenkins out of the hall. Oh, God, what a change of climate. There were thirty-five amiable students, the heckling was good-tempered and they really wanted to help the Labour Government. This is all due to Hugh Anderson's organization, Students for a Labour Victory, a remarkable achievement.

We drove on to an open-air meeting at Thetford and afterwards to Cambridge to open the campaign there. Then we went to Letchworth, at the far end of Shirley Williams's constituency, where I found her giving a portentously good election address to just over 200 people in the school hall. I got back to King's Cross at 11.14 and took myself home by taxi, because I can't use my big black car or Peter Smithson for electoral business.

Tuesday, June 2nd

I had a very plain Ministry day. Apart from Roy who is doing a little bit at the Treasury, I don't know of any other Minister who is doing so much work. Indeed, my impression is that the Government, including the Prime Minister, has virtually ceased functioning. The most important event today was a meeting of the big MISC chaired by Roy. With most of the Ministers and the Prime Minister away, we couldn't have a Cabinet and we couldn't have a Prices and Incomes Committee because that wasn't quite right, so Harold had nominated to a MISC those people who wanted to take decisions on Cabinet's behalf. On doctors' pay the Committee finally decided to give me full backing on almost everything I wanted. The one concession I made was that instead of four weeks it should be six weeks before the reference was made to the Prices and Incomes Board, which seemed to me quite a sensible change. After the MISC I was able to see all my officials and give them their marching orders. The whole Ministry is in an absolute tizzy because they hate the idea of confronting the doctors. It's pathetic.

I caught a train to Dover by the Chatham–Rochester line. Poor old David Ennals is anxious about his future. All these people in the South-East feel very strongly that they would have done far better in an autumn election. David doesn't disguise his feelings, though he is very honourable about all this. As a matter of fact we had a splendid audience of over 200 people in Dover town hall, where we arrived just in time to hear Marjorie Proops of the *Daily Mirror* making her contribution.[1]

I made my points about pensions and talked about David, we answered questions, and then a very odd little thing occurred. We were rushed to the

[1] Mrs Marjorie Proops, journalist and broadcaster, wrote for the *Daily Mirror* 1939–45 and for the *Daily Herald* 1945–54. Since 1954, she has again written for the *Daily Mirror*.

station and I had just got into the carriage for London, Victoria, when David came rushing up and said, 'I have got a shorter way for you, via Ashford. Change your train.' So we changed our platform and our train, along with Alma Birk who had spoken at the beginning of the meeting, and David's wife. Blow me, at Ashford we were turned out again and told to get into a bus. So we did, and we were driven through the countryside for twenty-five minutes or so until we were deposited at a very remote local station called Pluckley, where we were told that the London train would pick us up. It was about 10 o'clock by now and we realized that Dover had been wrongly informed. There had been a derailment and we were doomed to sit at Pluckley for ever. To cut a long story short, Alma and I telephoned to hire a car, which arrived precisely the same moment as a stopping train for all twenty-two stations to London. Our taxi got us home in just over an hour and Alma dropped me at Vincent Square. The interesting aspect of this little incident is how little attention was paid to ordinary passengers at Pluckley station. Nobody took the faintest notice of us. There must have been fifteen or sixteen people on that damned local station and all the railway staff were just too uninterested, simply saying, 'It's not our fault, we don't know what has happened.' I had a terrible feeling that the traditional kindliness to passengers or to people who are suffering has absolutely evaporated. They were just being defensive, explaining themselves away and leaving us to pay £10 or £11 for our taxi to London.

Wednesday, June 3rd

Another mixed day. After a meeting with the Permanent Secretary, I went straight to No. 70 for my last meeting with the R.H.B. chairmen. We were discussing capital grant allocations, because they won't agree to the new system of redistribution between the South-East, the Midlands and the North. Our second item was trust funds, where I was insisting that hospitals should be entitled (a) to solicit and (b) to use for themselves any money they get. I got this fairly quickly and, right at the end, I said, 'Gentlemen, the election is now on. Whatever happens I want to thank you, because the most important things I achieved in my two years here were firstly the setting-up of the Hospital Advisory Service and, secondly, the monthly meetings with you, through which we have established an entirely different relationship between the R.H.B.s and the department.' One of them said, 'Is that a swan song?' and, though I laughed and said no, of course it was.

There was just time for Mike Fogden and me to catch a train to Margate, where I was to address the Hospital Management Committees' conference. After lunch I made my speech from a decent, rather dull brief, and when I sat down after forty-five minutes I found I hadn't turned over page 1 and had done the whole thing *ad lib*.

Back to Chatham, where Ann Kerr, the Member, had insisted that I make a speech for her. I was met at the station and driven to a restaurant where we sat drinking until Ann Kerr arrived with the famous Dr Spock,[1] the American child-rearing expert, and his wife, who had met Mrs Kerr at an anti-Vietnam war demonstration in Chicago, where she had been kicked and gassed by the police. After dining together we went off to the town hall in Chatham, which Ann Kerr has probably lost by her bloody-mindedness and blowsiness and her violently anti-American pacificism. The hall was only half-full and I don't know what happened to Dr Spock, because I had to motor back to London for a meeting to complete the press release on my decision to refer the doctors' pay award. Peter drove down with Brian and we worked on the Statement all the way back to London. We arrived at 9.30 and sat down for a couple of hours with Clifford Jarrett, Bavin, Marre and ten others, slogging our way through until we got it into some kind of order for tomorrow.

Thursday, June 4th

My first job was to see Lord Kindersley himself. He turned out to be a genteel, faded man of some seventy years old, with a kind of club-foot. It turned out that his review body consisted of completely reactionary economists and vice-chancellors, whom we hadn't bothered to change, and from his attitude after he had read our report it was clear that he was against me. I told him not to resign. I said, because I had persuaded Harold this morning to agree to it, 'The Prime Minister would like to see you as soon as possible, you and your members, so for heaven's sake don't do anything drastic without seeing him.' But I was uneasily aware that Kindersley wasn't all that amenable.

Meanwhile I had received a vigorous message from the ten B.M.A. delegates, who had arrived at 9 o'clock in order to have time to study the Kindersley Report, which they had received last night with our accompanying statement. They were waiting in Alex Baker's room along the corridor and their message said that unless they could come along pretty soon they would leave. It was only 10.25 and we had asked them for 10.30. I thought this was a bad sign. However I went downstairs to Cabinet Room A and they were brought in. Gibson, a nice fellow, the doctor from Winchester, started by saying, 'I don't know why we should stay here at all, let's go out,' but he was restrained by one of the G.P.s and a consultant. I presented them with the Report, and they couldn't have been more hostile or violent. All last night, while we were preparing the papers, and the day before, we had been discussing what the B.M.A. were likely to do. The C.M.O. had said that on balance there was just a chance that they might, not accept, but acquiesce in the Report, but I had never thought there was much chance of that. On the other hand, I didn't expect them to be quite so ferocious.

The meeting took about an hour. They said they were utterly opposed to

[1] Dr Benjamin Spock, Professor of Child Development at Western Reserve University, U.S.A., 1955–67. He is the author of *Baby and Child Care* (London: Bodley Head, 1955) and *Bringing Up Children in a Difficult Time* (London: Bodley Head, 1974).

us tooth-and-nail, that they were not prepared to collaborate in any way, that they were going to meet the B.M.A. Council on Saturday and there was little doubt of the advice they would give. We just had time to go round to Admiralty House for the press conference. No drinks now. There was one serious question, and then in a very undramatic way I presented to the press the generosity of the deal and all its ingenuities. I said that it was worth £55 million as against the £87 million of the Kindersley recommendations, that it was money on account and that the cheques would go out on July 1st, backdated to April 1st. I told them that we were not rejecting the Report, only submitting it for a second opinion. I did the best I could but I was well aware that it was relatively easy to present my case to the press in a way that I couldn't to the doctors. From there I went straight to Eaton Place for lunch with Jock Campbell and Paul Johnson, to work out the exact plan for the transfer of the *New Statesman* editorship. Paul seemed anxious to leave the paper as fast as he could. He wanted me to take over a week before the end of June and he wished us to spell out the fact that he had postponed his resignation from last October. It was all perfectly all right and my only difficulty is that I still haven't told the P.M.

Back at the Elephant and Castle I had another go at the N.H.S. Green Paper but meanwhile I was full of doubts about Lord Kindersley. So I rang him up again and said, 'If necessary I want you to talk to me this evening. You will have seen your people by then and before they make up their minds I would at least like a chance to tell them the Government's position.' He said, 'Don't worry about that. I shall see them and then at 8.30 I'm going off to dinner.' I went home to Vincent Square, exhausted after my enormously long night yesterday. I thought I'd rest for a bit but in came Nicky Kaldor and Tommy Balogh, so I gave them dinner at the Athenaeum. Then I rushed off to Thames T.V. for a programme with half a dozen new young voters. It was more of a shouting match, in which they were saying they wanted participation and that they didn't believe in the system. Peter Rawlinson was there again and I think we made quite a decent impression. I stayed on and talked to them for half an hour before tottering home to bed. But when I got back I found a message that the P.A. wanted me to ring.[1] They told me that they had secret information which they couldn't give me, but under pressure they disclosed that the Kindersley review body had resigned *en bloc*. Now, as I have said, I had talked to Lord Kindersley this morning and again this afternoon and now at 11.0 p.m. I learnt that his Committee had carefully arranged their block resignations for midnight for publication in the morning press. It was a put-up job and they must have decided to resign the moment they met this evening.

Friday, June 5th

I had to decide what to say in reaction to the announcement of the review

[1] Press Association.

body's resignations, but first of all I went to a meeting of the *Statesman*'s Board. We made the arrangements and they told me that I ought to be out of the House in a matter of days. I explained that I couldn't possibly do this because it would depend on my constituency and the size of my majority, and anyway I hadn't talked to Harold about it. We had a long argument about the communiqué but it was all perfectly amicable.

I got out in time to rush back to the Elephant and Castle to talk to Clifford Jarrett about the payment of sickness benefit in the event of a doctors' strike and to have one more go on the Green Paper. Then I did 'The World At One' and rapidly dictated my reaction to the resignation before I was off in the car to Buxton, where I was to address the Personnel Management Society's annual conference, taking Barbara's place. It was perfect summer weather and we had the most beautiful drive through the Peak District until we came to a vast hotel, where I got into a bath and thought about a speech on equal pay, something I know nothing about. There were endless excitements just before the Conference dinner, with the B.B.C. saying they wanted me to go down to Stockport later on to answer questions from Robin Day in London on the storm of indignation which the doctors had aroused. So I ate the dinner, made my little speech fairly satisfactorily and then drove off with Peter to Stockport, where we found an enormous empty hall with broadcasting facilities. I had to look at a tiny little television set and though I couldn't see Robin Day and Reg Maudling I heard them through a damned thing in my ear. I found that the questions were not about doctors' pay but entirely about the economic situation and I discovered that something I had said in my secret talk with the doctors had caused great alarm and despondency. They had apparently rushed out and complained that I had said the reason why we couldn't accept Kindersley in full was because the instability of the economy had put the nation in peril. This has been one of the great Tory lines, which fitted the doctors' line, and I had to spend my time denying it. We finished at about 11.0 and sped down the M1 at over 100 miles an hour to Coventry and home, where Peter Smithson and Mike Fogden went to bed. Little do they know it's the last time they will be working with me.

Saturday, June 6th

I left them bathing with the children while Anne and I went off to Coventry for the formalities of my nomination. Well, I say formalities but I found there had been a hitch, because we had used an out-of-date form, without the eighteen-year-old voters, so it was a dud. It was partly Albert's fault because he should have burnt these forms, but when it had been presented to the Town Clerk's department last Thursday, they had passed it, so everybody was to blame. It was a ridiculous situation, because the Town Clerk was away playing tennis or something and there was no lawyer present. The whole place was totally disorganized. I said, 'This is obviously invalid, but there is fortunately time to draw up a new form which Winnie Lakin can submit on Monday, the last day.'

We went back to Prescote for lunch to find that Mike Fogden and Peter Smithson were still there, because a great red box had arrived from Clifford Jarrett with a paper insisting that there must be a meeting of Ministers on Monday to deal with the problems that a doctors' strike will cause. Clifford is putting forward drastic and very offensive proposals to deal with the doctors and I was very angry. Yesterday we had quite a tiff on the telephone, when I had said, 'Look, Tuesday is perfectly O.K. for Ministers, it's the first day Roy Jenkins can come. The officials should meet on Monday and we'll meet the day after unless you absolutely insist.' I found that he did absolutely insist and Burke had supported him, so all my engagements had to be changed and I had to try to redraft the paper very rapidly, with secretaries and typists being brought in to the Department so that it could be circulated to Ministers in time.

Sunday, June 7th

Harold rang me from Edinburgh where he is on his rounds. He was worried first of all by a headline report in the *Medical News Tribune*, an independent medical newspaper, that I had said in an interview that N.H.S. funds should be given a £350 million annual boost by cutting investment grants and agricultural deficiency payments. This had upset Cledwyn Hughes. Harold also said that the whole of the front page of the *Sunday Express* was covered with the bombshell that, in a secret conference, I had admitted the parlous plight of the economy. Would I also deal with this? I rang Peter Brown, but he was deeply unwilling to touch it at all, saying that this was an election issue. I said it was entirely a departmental affair arising out of the Minister's and the Department's presentation of the case to the B.M.A. but I know that they have all got cold feet in the office. Fortunately for me the *Daily Express* Birmingham Correspondent came over today and I gave him a careful statement. I also talked to the *Sketch*, and said a few words to one or two other correspondents and I.T.N., so as far as I can see I have dealt with this quite respectably.

Then we drove off to Coventry to a delicious ceremony, the opening of a flower garden round the vicarage of St Chad's in Wood End, the dreariest part of Bell Green, a ghastly place where the vicars replace themselves every two or three years. This vicar and his wife are good people, who have built a garden to try to teach the public the beauty of flowers.[1] The Bishop of Coventry was there, with me as the Rt Honourable, and they prayed for me in the church. The Bishop preached a sermon and we sang hymns. We bought an enormous fuchsia, three foot high, and as we put it into the car I told the Bishop of the future I had chosen for myself, that I had decided to stop being a king and become a prophet instead.

[1] The Reverend and Mrs Roy Boole had been at St Chad's since 1965.

When we got back to Prescote there were more endless telephone calls about the doctors. The B.M.A. had met and decided on a partial strike but fortunately for us the junior hospital doctors' breakaway union had come out on our side, and so had the Medical Practitioners' Union. We have at least succeeded in splitting them that much.

So here we are at the end of the first week of my last election campaign. Apart from doctors' pay, the only other sensation has been Tony Wedgwood Benn. He made a sensational speech, not attacking Enoch Powell but asserting that Heath was really a cover for Powell, who was the real power in the Tory Party. Tony made some very wild remarks about Belsen and Dachau, delivering himself into Tory hands, so that Heath was able to demand that Harold should repudiate such extremism. Harold went as near repudiation as anybody could and, ever since, the Tories have been mounting an attack on Wedgwood Benn. So now we have two extremes, with Powell and Benn somehow cancelling each other out.

I talked to Harold on the telephone about this, and he said, 'As a matter of fact, the Campaign Committee had decided they wouldn't play up Enoch Powell and now Benn has gone completely against the directive.' Harold was furious. Still, I don't think it's been disastrous, just as I don't think the tremendous row which is now building up between the Government and the doctors is in any way disastrous for us. Indeed, the Tories may well have discredited themselves by automatically jumping on the doctors' bandwagon within a few hours of the publication of the Kindersley Report and announcing that every penny of the £85 million award should be paid.

I suppose my main impression of this campaign is that it has been masterminded by Harold and this new fellow William Camp. The P.M. has evolved a new technique of being televised and photographed with party workers and this has brilliantly contrasted him with Heath. Harold is the easy-going, nice fellow, while Heath is making boring, serious speeches. Harold has got the bit between his teeth and he is fighting the election in his own individual style. He has dispensed with practically all policy and there is no party manifesto because there are no serious commitments at all. In that sense we are fighting a Stanley Baldwin, 'Trust my Harold', election, or a 'Doctors' Mandate' election, call it what you like.[1] The Tories are fighting a scare election, simply and solely on the threat of rising prices, of a wage freeze and the imminent breakdown of the economy. Their theme is, 'If you put Labour in there will be another crisis,' and to make it effective they have been searching out ministerial statements which indicate that we think there will be a wage freeze after the election.

A tremendous stunt is now being worked up to say that I admitted to the

[1] Stanley Baldwin, Unionist M.P. for Bewdley, Worcestershire, 1908–37, was Financial Secretary to the Treasury 1917–21, President of the Board of Trade 1921–2, Chancellor of the Exchequer 1922–3, Prime Minister 1923–4, 1924–9 and 1935–7, Lord Privy Seal 1932–3 and Lord President of the Council 1931–5. He became the first Earl Baldwin of Bewdley in 1937. He died in December 1947.

doctors that the country was in grave economic peril, whereas what I really said was that the consequences of accepting such huge awards might be to set off a wage inflation and to bring the country into economic peril. All this shows is that the only thing left to the Tories is for them to say that if we trust Wilson we will once again have an economic crisis. If they can't put that over, I think we are bound to win, and the polls have been slowly moving our way. Perhaps the most important fact is that throughout this period the weather has been absolutely perfect, fairly hot, with cloudless skies but freshened by a slight breeze. Perfect electioneering weather, perfect complacency weather, weather which suits Harold Wilson's propaganda of 'Trust Harold; we have got through; Britain is strong; Britain has got over her problems'.

Monday, June 8th

I spent the morning in London on sickness benefit instruction and on the whole presentation of the doctors' and dentists' award. The difficulty is that once again the Department is in two absolutely separate halves. The old Health Department is concerned with the relation with the doctors while Social Security is concerned with, in the short term, prevention of abuse during the period when doctors refuse to sign sickness certificates, and the long-term need to prevent the doctors from getting into the habit of abstention. Last week I had rowed for a long time with Clifford Jarrett, who had been insisting that we should report all the doctors to the Executive Council and that patients should go to their doctors each time and repeatedly ask for their certificates, instead of taking one refusal as a definite statement. I had smoothed all this out, simply saying, 'I want the minimum of fuss between now and the election. That is that.'

This morning we were supposed to have the ministerial meeting on which Burke and Jarrett had insisted. I had rung up Harold, who had countermanded the order and told Burke it was quite absurd because the Chancellor must be in the chair and Roy couldn't come today. Anyhow, what was the rush? So I now found the officials a bit cowed by their defeat. Jarrett was looking at me with a blunt, blue-eyed, curious friendly hostility and there was Miss Riddelsdell, a terribly noble and nice woman, who on this issue was being noble on behalf of the Department. Altogether it was a difficult, hostile atmosphere.

I spent the rest of the morning dictating my last memorandum, a long report on my impressions of Malta and of Dom Mintoff. I sent a copy to Harold and I shall also send it to Michael, Jim and Denis Healey. It is quite lively and it will be there for the record. This afternoon I.T.N. demanded that I do something for their news programme on the economic peril remark. 'Oh,' I said, 'that old story. I wouldn't have thought people would want to hear any more about that.' But I discovered that I.T.N. had a guilty conscience because they felt they had been giving too much attention to the doctors and too little to me. This news item would restore their balance. So I looked in on the way to Euston and in an excellent three-minute interview I corrected the record again. Mind you, this business goes on and on. I suppose it's done me a certain amount of harm but at least this evening I was able to say that Dr Stevenson was spending more time on Conservative propaganda than he was on the good of the B.M.A.

Let me get the story absolutely straight. As I was describing to the doctors the possible repercussions of clamping an £85 million claim into the economy, I had said it was a perilous situation. Three or four minutes later one of the doctors had said, 'You said we are in economic peril.' I had said, 'No, I didn't. I told you that the impact it would produce would be a perilous situation.' 'No,' he had answered, 'I heard you say the other.' Then, and this was probably a mistake, I had said, 'If you heard that I withdraw it and substitute what I have told you, because that is the real reason.' They had gone off and immediately talked to the Tories.

This evening I did two Black Country towns, Halesowen and Oldbury, and then motored over to Smethwick, where I found a big school hall full of television cameras and lights, and Andrew Faulds,[1] that ape of a bearded actor, performing. Racialism has been extremely violent in this area but there were many more questions about doctors and nurses and secondary schools. There is no doubt that stopping immigration, which was one of Callaghan's great achievements, has done an enormous lot for us and that in places like Smethwick the racial undertow, which was enormously strong in 1964, is now even weaker than in 1966. It was interesting to watch Andrew Faulds, who is a great actor and therefore a superb candidate. He is a real vulgarian and in the House of Commons a shouter, but here he has to behave properly and stay sober. He couldn't have been more modest, responsible and competent. I was terribly sad to learn that because of Smethwick's romantic history,[2] all the students are streaming in to help Andrew, while at Halesowen poor John Horner,[3] who is really up against it, has no assistance at all.

Tuesday, June 9th

For the second day running the engine broke down but I got to London in time for MISC 267, only to find that Roy had been delayed as well. While we were waiting Peter Shore asked me, 'What is all this for? There's nothing difficult here.' So I explained that at the last MISC we had been specially instructed to call Ministers together to confirm our decision on what to do about sickness certificates. 'Anyway, my dear Peter,' I said, 'it is only because things are going right that you are not worried.' Everyone at today's meeting seemed to have found that in the constituencies there was now very little

[1] Labour M.P. for Smethwick 1966–74 and since 1974 for Warley East.

[2] Patrick Gordon Walker had been defeated at Smethwick in 1964 and Alderman Peter Griffiths, the Conservative candidate, had been elected with considerable support from constituents hostile to coloured immigration. The Conservatives lost the seat in 1966.

[3] Labour M.P. for Oldbury and Halesowen 1964–70.

sympathy with the doctors. Although the announcement of the review body's resignation and their declaration of war had given them a good send-off last Thursday, by the weekend it appeared that they had over-played their hand. When Roy arrived we had a short discussion of this but we then turned to this morning's news that the B.M.A. had sent out instructions to their members, with a broadsheet for each doctor to put up in his surgery, stating that he withheld his support from the N.H.S. until the Kindersley claim was paid in full. This was a downright declaration of war. Oddly, *The Times* had also published a letter from Ronald Gibson, the B.M.A. Chairman, pleading for the Prime Minister to intervene and stop the dispute. During the weekend I had been worrying about this very point because Harold had seemed rather inclined to see the doctors, while it was quite obvious to me that this would be tactically unwise. However I put the point to the Committee (it is always useful to do this) and Roy took the very strong view that the doctors should be allowed to stew in their own juice during the election campaign and, anyway, they couldn't simultaneously break their contracts with the Health Service and call on the Prime Minister to invite them to a conference.

Everybody agreed that this was an unreasonable demand. I decided to go through into No. 10 to see if I could catch Harold, who at that time in the morning is holding his press conference. In he came and I described the situation and the Committee's recommendation that I should state at the press conference that, if the doctors would write to us suggesting negotiations we would certainly consider it, but that there could be no question of the Prime Minister initiating negotiations while they behaved in this way. I got that rapidly agreed with Harold. Then he asked me how I thought the campaign was going and I said, 'If we don't put some substance into it we'll be in trouble. We ought to have a confrontation on defence, on the Common Market, on social security or pensions.' He said, 'Oh well, it has been arranged between the parties that confrontations are undesirable.' I replied, 'I wouldn't mind confronting Balneil or anybody else,' and Harold said, 'I'll tell you what. You tell Doreen Stainforth[1] that you are prepared to do this on social security. That's a good idea.' It emerged that the parties had refused confrontation and in consequence we have had not news but a mass of election gossip and just a few bits of speeches from Harold. This election campaign has had fewer speeches and less substance and has been more personalized than any previous one. I think that running the campaign on these lines is terribly dangerous. We attract frivolous, superficial support which a shock could blow away. However as a result of this conversation, Macleod and I are to discuss social services on '24 Hours' on June 15th. This is just after the Prime Minister's final broadcast, when people will probably be tired of listening.

As soon as I'd fixed this with the Prime Minister I had to go off to Admiralty House for the big press conference. I was cross-examined for forty-

[1] The Labour Party Broadcasting Officer at Transport House.

five minutes and I very carefully spelt out our attitude to the letter in *The Times* and to talks. Then I lunched at the Epicure with Alan Watkins, whom I briefed in great detail on the background to the doctors' crisis. I didn't, of course, tell him that in less than a week he would know that I am to be his new Editor. I wonder what he will think of that.

Wednesday, June 10th

My last day of real work as a Cabinet Minister. I spent it talking about post-graduate teaching work in hospitals, dealing with the case of a day nursery at Redhill and at two final important meetings. The first was on the Health Service Green Paper and the basic concept of the relationship between the Department and the regional area and district authorities. I preached and preached to the office how necessary it was to have genuine devolution from the Department and how this should be written into the Act. I found that all their opposition was nonsense.

My last meeting, just in time, was to deal with Brian's White Paper on mental handicap. I think we have almost got the draft into its final form and my successor will be able to publish it as soon as he or she likes. There was just time for lunch at 2 o'clock before I caught the train to Watford, where Doug Garnett had arranged five meetings.

Thursday, June 11th

At lunchtime yesterday I said goodbye to the staff and today I dealt with my last red box. This morning we went off to the headquarters of the Coventry Borough Labour Party at Coundon Road and the next few days will be full of constituency meetings.

Friday, June 12th

Today I had to dash to Oxford to make a speech at a joint election meeting of the University Labour Club and the Oxford Labour Party. Days ago, Brian and his assistant David Piachaud[1] had proposed that I should make this a serious policy speech about the future of social security. David came down last night and we'd worked away, trying to give an account of what we had done and what we planned to do and to outline our philosophy of caring for the underprivileged members of a modern society. Unfortunately the text was only mentioned in the local press because for the last three days there has been a newspaper strike. It was also disappointing that neither I.T.N. nor anyone from radio turned up this evening. The poor audience had first to listen to the Chairman, who also talked on social security, then to Evan Luard[2]

[1] David Piachaud, Lecturer in Social Administration at the London School of Economics, has been a member of the Prime Minister's Policy Unit in No. 10 since 1974.

[2] Evan Luard, Labour M.P. for Oxford 1966–70 and since October 1974, has been a Fellow of St Antony's College, Oxford, since 1957. He was a member of H.M. Foreign Service from 1950 until his resignation in 1956. He was Parliamentary Under-Secretary of State at the F.C.O. 1969–70 and since 1976 he has held the same office.

and then me, but I got a great ovation for the speech. A couple of eggs were thrown and that was that. As we drove back to Prescote the battery suddenly failed again but as we were trying to push the car to the side of the road someone drew up behind us. It was the Halls, the fellow who works at the brewery, with his wife and son, and thank God, they drove us home. What a merciful deliverance.

Sunday, June 14th

Yesterday afternoon we had Patrick's school fête. I might add that on Wednesday he made his speech in the school mock election and, as he is an independent boy, I had left it to him. That morning I got him up at 6.30 and after a short bathe we went out on to the terrace and rehearsed his speech. I found that he had worked out a perfectly sensible speech, describing why we were having the election, what we were promising to do and why the Tories wouldn't fulfil their promises. The only difficulty was to persuade him not to talk as though he had a potato in his mouth. I'm glad to say that he appeared to do fairly well and at least the other two candidates didn't do any better, so he hadn't disgraced himself or us. Yesterday his father was opening the fête arranged by the Parent–Teacher Association, an arrangement that had been made long before the announcement of the date of the election. There was a great judo demonstration organized by Miss Atkins and in the boiling sun I went round the school. While we were all having tea someone said what a wonderful M.P. Neil Marten was, whereupon the Headmaster, a rather grim, withdrawn man, said, 'It might be time for a change.' What did he mean? Do we have here a Labour supporter we never dreamed of? I don't know. Anyway it will be interesting to see how the children vote in the mock election next week.

Today I took a complete rest. There are just four days to go and so far it has been one of the easiest campaigns I've known. I think I can best sum up the mood by saying that it most reminds me of the 1959 election, the 'You never had it so good' election, when the Tory Government had no real programme. This time we are in a very similar situation, though of course the real resemblance is not between Wilson now and Macmillan then but between Gaitskell then and Heath now. Heath is nicer-looking than Gaitskell was, but they both have that lock-jaw effect, that remoteness and glazed eye. In Hugh it was beginning to rub off as he learnt a bit about being less detached and intellectually superior (and became as a result somewhat dogmatic), but Ted Heath hasn't learnt even after four years. He is still a waxwork, stiff and tense, and, poor man, during this campaign he has been subjected to a most merciless press.

As in 1959, the Opposition are fighting a fine weather mood and a sense of complacency, yet I have to record that we can't say the electorate has never had it so good. Macmillan could point to five years of economic expansion and a tremendous rise in living standards, five years of Tory easy-going. We have given them three years of hell and high taxes. They've seen the failure of devaluation and felt the soaring cost of living. Yet Harold Wilson is running the election in this Macmillan-like way and he has suddenly found that the mood is on our side and that people are good-humouredly willing to accept another six years of Labour Government.

I think this is a result of most unusual circumstances, in which three separate factors have converged. The first, quite simply, was the end of the prices and incomes policy, following on the dropping of the Industrial Relations Bill and our decision to rely on the T.U.C.'s voluntary effort. This has allowed the official trade unions to be friendly with us again and it has permitted Jack Jones and Hugh Scanlon to feel it was time to end the animosity which was wrecking local parties. The abandonment of the policy brought about the second factor, that for some months now wages have been rising faster than prices. Everybody knows, of course, that prices will catch up within the next twelve months but at this particular moment, as in the spring of '66, the British elector feels good and, though he knows this won't last long, it changes his attitude to the Government. The third thing which actually crystallized the feeling of lift and the sudden transformation of our chances was the Tories' announcement of their carefully contrived exercise at Selsdon Park. It came as a shock to have this tough, strong picture of Selsdon Man leading a virile, capitalist, anti-trade union revival, and suddenly people thought, 'My God, if that is the alternative, there is something to be said for dear old Harold now that he has learnt his lesson.' I think this is what has given us such an easy election. The country isn't in the mood for Cassandra prophesying doom nor does the electorate want, or have any confidence in the effectiveness of, Heath's reconstructed, reactionary Toryism of free enterprise and anti-trade unionism.

Into all this Enoch Powell has suddenly instilled a tremendous sense of crisis with his theme of the secret enemy, the traitor upon high, who has been falsifying the immigration figures.[1] He now sounds a real fanatic, even on the wireless, and I have no doubt that he is an incipient fascist leader. This is the oldest fascist trick of all, to work up the threat of a conspiracy within, which must be exterminated for the sake of democracy. Powell's nearest parallel is Senator Joseph McCarthy and I think that the most sensible course for the Tories would be to denounce him immediately and to expel him from the party.[2] Nevertheless he may have rallied the Tories' chances and in the last days of the campaign injected just that note which could cause some of our supporters to abstain. The British public don't

[1] Mr Powell had stated that Government officials had deliberately falsified immigration statistics. He alleged that 'the people of this country have been misled cruelly and persistently, until one begins to wonder if the Foreign Office was the only Department of State into which enemies of this country had been infiltrated'.

[2] In the 1950s Senator McCarthy alleged that a large number of Americans were Communists and fellow-travellers and denounced them before the then Un-American Activities Committee.

deeply care about this election and, if Powell manages to crystallize their feelings or help them to decide whether to vote or not, it could make a gigantic difference. My own feeling is that there could be variations of 6, 7, 8 per cent depending on the day and the mood, whether the electorate are hot or whether they are cold.

Monday, June 15th

Today's trade figures show us £31 million in the red and this evening, watching a dusky television set while I waited for my own show, I saw Iain Macleod spiriting disaster out of Aladdin's cave. Then I watched Harold addressing a huge meeting in Hammersmith and making jokes about half the deficit being due to the purchase of jumbo jets. That sums up the campaign, but still Harold was more effective than spooky Macleod. It is now clear that the only thing which the Tories have to hang on to is the rise in the cost of living and its effect on the pensioner and the housewife. I am not sure whether there will be a large Labour abstention or how many pensioners and housewives will switch to the Tories but it won't win them the election.

Tuesday, June 16th

A routine electioneering day and I also heard from the Ministry about the doctors' protest. Some 75 per cent of the G.P.s are refusing to sign sickness certificates, far more than the Ministry expected, but far fewer than the doctors had hoped. There's also an enormous regional difference. The South-West has many fewer doctors on strike, whereas Scotland has nine out of ten. I would say that among the profession the mood is hardening against the government and some urgent fence-mending will be necessary. One advantage of my going is that it gives a good excuse for fixing up the relationship between my successor and the doctors.

Last night Anne and I discussed my resignation and whether people would think that Harold had thrown me out. I shall make it clear that I made my arrangements with the *New Statesman* several months ago but it will still suit a number of people to say caustically that I am getting old, that I'm a clanger-maker who will be no great loss and that the *New Statesman* has taken on an addled, old politician. I don't think I shall get a good press for this move, though other people will describe it as a threat to Harold and say that under new management the *Statesman* might provide the critical leadership the Left now lacks. I don't know. When the news is announced next weekend the reaction may be a mixture of all this.

Wednesday, June 17th

Nora Beloff is coming to talk to me today about the new mood and I shall have to be careful not to reveal my true situation. I suppose I'm bound to feel in a sombre mood because, yes, I'm unsure of this job at the *Statesman*, unsure of staying on as the Member for Coventry East and I'm feeling a little elderly and, above all, that I've been pushed aside. By jove, I am relieved that I took my decision before the campaign started because I'm now very much an ex-leading member of the Party along with Michael Stewart and Fred Peart. I'm not among the dynamic people like Jim, Roy and Denis, those whom Harold has marked out as his colleagues. As for Barbara she is in an awkward situation.

My other thought is that I was wrong about Enoch Powell's intentions. He hasn't come out with a tremendous speech in favour of loyally voting for Heath and the Tories as the lesser evil. On the contrary, Powell has said that he has been abominably treated by his colleagues and he has crawled back to Wolverhampton in self-pity to lick his wounds. I think it is just possible that this will have alienated a great many people who would have liked to have voted for a stronger policy on race. Powell may have overtipped the bounds.

One of the polls is now predicting a 2 per cent swing to Labour, another an 8 per cent swing. My final view will come tomorrow but today my opinion is that in Coventry East we shall not get out all the women, especially the young women, that we shall lose some Catholics on the abortion issue and that we shall have some new votes from the Indians. I think that this time we shall get a pretty solid vote from the men and that is very useful.

Nora Beloff arrived in Coventry at about 10.45. She had come to talk to me about the *Observer* piece on Labour's third term, for which she had already seen Harold in Manchester and Liverpool. He told her that he wouldn't be doing his Cabinet-making on the Friday after polling day in time for the Sunday papers and I'm not surprised. I think that, if we win, the present Government will carry on during the weekend, so that we shall still be Ministers on Monday morning. The changes will take place on Monday or Tuesday. In the morning Nora came round with me to the Standard works to see my factory-gate meeting, and then we lunched at the Bridge restaurant with Anne, Bill Wilson, Winnie Lakin and the new Secretary of the party. Nora heard how people were dropping the *Observer* because they didn't like it and she learnt something of the way in which feeling in Coventry East has changed from the sullenness at the time of the constituency dinner to the band-wagon that began to roll faster and faster. I think that is largely because of the polls and I am a little worried about the way in which this competition has been worked up.

In the afternoon we had a real hard go round Upper Stoke and then we did another round of meeting the people, with eight or nine helpers going along both sides of the street while I rushed from side to side shaking people's hands. This technique has now become immensely popular and Harold has done a great deal of it. Yesterday even poor old Maurice Edelman, who up till now had merely been loudspeakering, finally got out of his car for the first time in three weeks and actually walked the streets.

It suddenly began to rain as we went off to the eve-of-poll meetings in Rugby and Leamington. It is a pity that we didn't have one in Coventry. In

Rugby the party was tremendously stirred and excited, and fairhaired, brilliant lively Bill Price had a packed meeting. The hall at Leamington was fairly decently filled, and after the speech of the candidate, the young Rugby schoolmaster,[1] I made a rousing farewell speech and answered questions. Then at about 11 o'clock we came home in the drenching rain and I did the filter on the swimming bath.

Thursday, June 18th

A perfect day, warm and sunny with not a drop of rain. We began our formal journey round the polling stations, ninety-eight of them in the whole constituency. I suppose we went to about seventy or seventy-five, more than I have ever done before, because there was really nothing else to do. Winnie Lakin went tootling ahead, her little car covered with posters, with Anne and I driving slowly behind. So the day went on in an absolutely inane routine of driving to the polling stations, getting out, looking inside, saying how do you do to the polling clerks and asking how much had been polled. The candidate has the right, I don't quite know why, to go in and talk to the returning officers and ask them for the number of votes that have actually been cast. I took notes all the way round, so I felt able to form an opinion and from 6.30 onwards it was obvious that something was going very badly wrong. The poll was only just over 50, 52, 55 per cent, even in our safest, biggest wards, and by 9 o'clock it was only 60 per cent. I was sure that I had found in microcosm what we were going to discover in macrocosm.

In the evening Winnie Lakin, Albert, Anne and I all went to the Craven Arms Hotel in the centre of the town for a rather solemn, good meal, and in the middle of it a young man, someone who was doing a technical training course at the Lanchester Polytechnic, came up and insisted on standing us a most inappropriate bottle of champagne in which to drink our health. Then we went over to the Police Hall for the count and stood about until the ballot boxes arrived at about half-past ten. The count took three and a half hours, an appallingly slow process, but it wasn't long before we began to suspect that things were not going well. Albert became terribly nervous and told me that the boxes were showing 50/50 Labour and Tory. We very soon discovered that we were getting 3,000 votes to 2,000, 4,000 to 2,000, not at all the proportion we expected. At a count you are supposed to be cut off from the outside world but somebody had brought in a little transistor radio and we heard the first result from Guildford, a swing of 5·3 per cent to the Tories.

Then came the news that Enoch Powell had increased his majority, with an 8 per cent swing in Wolverhampton, and a 9 per cent swing against Renee Short in the other part of the town. Within an hour I knew we had comfortably lost the election. There were of course redeeming features. By 1.0 a.m. we'd learnt that Bill Price had retained Rugby with an increased majority, Bill Wilson was back with a somewhat reduced majority in Coventry South and

[1] J. T. Watkinson did not take Warwick from the Conservatives.

there was a rumour that we ourselves were probably going to have less than a 10,000 majority. Finally, after an interminable time, at 2.10 a.m. we had our result and our 12,000 majority. What I had learnt between 7.0 p.m. and 9.0 p.m. reflected not only our own polling stations but the whole town.

Afterwards we all went off to watch television. The end wasn't quite as bad as the beginning. They'd talked about a Tory majority of 100, but the figure fell to 45 and then to 39.[1] Suddenly it was 4.30 a.m. and Anne and I motored home in the cool, delicious dawn of an exquisite June morning.

Friday, June 19th

We got to bed at 5.0 a.m., and woke in time to send the children to school at 8.0. Then I was off to London on the 9.30 train and on the way I reflected on the results. Yes, despite the unanimous prognostications of the press, in the last three days of the campaign Heath's warnings had begun to count, particularly his final warning on the trade figures and on the threat of further devaluation. It was rather like the 1964 campaign, only more so. Harold's comfy, complacent, good-humoured mixing with the crowds hadn't been able to sustain itself for more than a fortnight and by the end of the second week the voice of doom, the endless repetitive reminders of rising prices, broken promises, unfavourable trade figures, all took their toll. Mind you, it wasn't a very big toll. In a 4·7 per cent swing, the biggest swing since 1965, there must have been some switching from Labour to Tory but I think most of it was the result of Labour abstentions.

As the day passed I gradually began to learn the full extent of the news. Despite all the talk, outside Wolverhampton itself there had been very little sign of Powellism. Peter Lister had been comfortably defeated at Meriden and, as I feared, John Horner had been thrown out at Halesowen. At Banbury Neil Marten's majority had gone up. Eric Lubbock, the Liberal, was at last defeated at Orpington, Jennie Lee had been knocked out of her 10,000 majority at Cannock and Jack Diamond was defeated at Gloucester. Sadly, poor old David Ennals was beaten by well over 1,000 at Dover and the two Dunwoodys lost, one at Exeter and one at Falmouth. On the other hand, strangely enough, David Owen scraped through and held his tiny marginal part of Plymouth, alongside Joan Vickers.[2] So it was a definite Tory victory, a clear majority of some forty to forty-three seats, with very few sensational failures. Everybody was taken aback because the polls had nursed the illusion that Labour was going to win and now Heath had won after all.

At No. 70 I had to talk to Paul Odgers about his future and quickly to see Nora Beloff and Jimmy Margach to warn them and brief them about

[1] The Conservatives gained 74 seats and lost 6, Labour gained 10 and lost 70, the Liberals lost 7. The final figures were: Conservatives 330 seats; Labour 287; Liberals 6; Scottish Nationalists 1; Welsh Nationalists 0; Independent Labour 1; Protestant Unionist 1; Unity Party 2; Republican Labour 1.

[2] Dame Joan Vickers (D.B.E. 1964) was Conservative M.P. for Plymouth, Devonport, 1955–February 1974. In 1974 she became a life peer.

the *New Statesman*. I had a hurried lunch with the boys in the office, before I went across to Alexander Fleming House, where I found poor Janet Newman really unnerved and utterly broken. She couldn't stand not working for me. It was very touching and very painful. I made my formal farewells to the C.M.O., Clifford Jarrett and Alan Marre, and told them there wasn't really any need to fuss, because I had already decided to get out. Alan Marre was very nonplussed. He said, 'That was a very well-kept secret,' and I replied, 'Well, my dear Alan, there are some secrets that I can keep if I wish to.' They hadn't really anything to report. They were ready for the alternative Government to take over and, though they were polite, they knew that by Monday I would be gone. I said they could show my successor, whoever it was, all my thinking on the N.H.S. White Paper and I told them that as the White Paper on mental handicap was not political I hoped that it would be printed and published fairly soon. I said what little I could and then I had to get ready for a meeting of the Management Committee.

At 4.0 I was driven up to Downing Street in a pool car, because Peter Smithson is away on holiday in the South of France, confidently expecting to come back and drive me again. I found a great crowd shouting 'Out, out,' with a few bystanders who were sympathetic and in a political way quite friendly. Then I was inside. There was poor Tony Wedgwood Benn looking white and drawn, appalled by the result, and Michael Stewart, who'd lost his voice from so much public-speaking. Roy breezed in, Harold arrived and we drifted into the Cabinet room for the last time. Barbara told me later that she wasn't asked to this meeting but in fact they couldn't find her. Denis Healey came in a little late and there we were, a smallish gathering without Fred Peart, Bob Mellish or Tony Crosland. We chatted about the election and the future. Harold said that when the Queen's Speech was presented we must make only formal opposition. We must give the Tories a honeymoon period but maybe within two years we should find an opportunity for attack. Then I think it was Roy who said, 'We might have some meetings, because the party's morale will need bolstering a bit,' and somebody else added, 'They ought to be private meetings.' I observed, 'If they're private, you'll be having inquests about the election,' and Michael Stewart said, 'We can't afford to have any inquests about the election; it would be terrible to disagree.' Denis Healey put in, 'I hope that in public we can all say the same thing. I've been doing a bit of morale-building on I.T.N.,' and I thought to myself, 'You may hope there will be no inquest, but there will be, because the party will indeed be asking how it was that we were forced into June, how it was that we were given the illusion that we were winning and how it was that we were let down. There will indeed be a reaction and the *New Statesman* will have something to contribute.' But I didn't mention the *Statesman*, although just before the meeting I had rung Harold to say that I would have to make my decision and see the *Statesman* today.

It was a desultory meeting, pleasant and friendly, and Harold was cool, collected and apparently self-possessed. At one point, while I was getting myself some iced water from the decanter at the end of the room, I looked out and saw thirty or forty packing cases. I said, 'What is that?' Harold said, 'Those are our files.' I asked, 'Is that your twelve-volume book?' and he said, 'No, they include my constituency files as well. We ought to be out of No. 10 today and we're still packing. By the way, I shall be living near you. We have taken 14 Vincent Square for three months while Mary is househunting. She wants to live in the centre of London rather than going back to Hampstead.'

We discussed where we should meet in future and arranged that Management Committee should meet again, because until the Shadow Cabinet is elected we remain in control. Harold will then appoint those whom he wishes to lead the new Opposition. He said he thought that Bob Mellish should continue as Chief Whip and it was also agreed that we hoped Harold himself would be automatically re-elected to the leadership but that there should be a re-election for the Deputy Leader. In the presence of both Callaghan and Roy, we were all far too discreet to ask whether this would be a contested election. I would have thought that since Callaghan is Treasurer of the party, it would be tactful to let Roy be Deputy Leader to allow him to be a member of the Executive, but it won't happen like that and I think the two of them will probably fight it out in the Parliamentary Party.

Throughout the discussion I was thinking of my forthcoming meeting with Jock Campbell, Paul Johnson and the three members of the *N.S.* staff who had been invited. I got to Vincent Square just after five to find them all waiting, among a vast number of bottles, because all my surplus drink had been brought across in red boxes from Alexander Fleming House and unloaded on the floor. So we settled down to our first *New Statesman* meeting. We decided that the press release should be issued at 6.0 p.m. tomorrow, and that I would brief the Sunday press, spelling out that the whole thing had been fixed well before I knew that the party had lost and that Paul Johnson was unwell and wanted to resign. Paul and Jock then drifted off leaving me with Tom Baistow,[1] the Assistant Editor, Anthony Thwaite,[2] the Literary Editor, and a fellow from management, and we sat quietly over a drink and chatted about the future of the paper. It was all natural and spontaneous and I tried to create the feeling that I was coming home to the *Statesman* and that they were going to have an editor who belonged to their traditions.

Saturday, June 20th

The weather has remained perfect and I was able to have a splendid early-morning bathe before doing a lot more telephoning. Barbara rang up full of excitement about my news and we arranged that the inner group should

[1] Tom Baistow, a former Foreign Editor on the *News Chronicle*, became Deputy Editor of the *New Statesman* in 1965.

[2] The poet Anthony Thwaite was Literary Editor of the *Listener* 1962–5, Assistant Professor of English at the University of Libya 1965–7 and Literary Editor of the *New Statesman* 1968–72. He has been Co-Editor of *Encounter* since 1973.

meet with Harold at her house next Tuesday, in preparation for Management Committee the following day. She was delighted about the *Statesman* and when I told Wedgwood Benn and Peter Shore yesterday they were also really excited and thought it was obviously a good thing. So I think that among the leadership there's going to be a much better response than I had expected.

Anne and I drove off to lunch with Nicholas and Olga at Hinton, where we found Peter Jay and his wife Margaret,[1] and an extremely intelligent young man called Skidelsky,[2] who wrote an interesting book about the 1931 Labour Government, and Augusta Hope, whom he is going to marry. It was a most beautiful day and from the terrace we looked over the stripling Thames and from the front of the house across to White Horse Hill and at the great trees with their different shades of green and the lush lawn. It was wonderful and, do you know, I was relaxed because I had no red boxes. This morning I had no work to do. I could do just what I liked; I could read, I could think—the burden had fallen off my shoulders like Christian in *Pilgrim's Progress*, and I was released.

My God, I am lucky. I am the only member of the Government who has stepped, not out of the frying pan into the fire, but out of one job I wanted into another job I wanted. I shall miss Peter Smithson and the car but I shan't miss the Private Office because I shall have my own Private Office at the *Statesman*. I shan't miss the newspapers the Ministry provided for me: they will come. A great deal of what I liked about being a Minister, the conveniences, the facilities and the spoon-feeding, will be there for me in Great Turnstile as well. I shall go in for the first time on Thursday morning and I am beginning to feel at home already, to know that I can manage the job. What luck it is for me to be able to do this, to have the job I want which will give me time to relax with Anne and the children, with this lovely house as well, and this lovely life in the country. What incredible good fortune I have compared to other people.

As we were driving back from Hinton we listened to the 6 o'clock news on the car radio, with the announcement of my appointment as the second item. I soon got squeezed out, because at 7 o'clock the Tory Cabinet was announced and we learnt that Keith Joseph is to take my place at Social Services. There couldn't be a better choice. He is a civilized, cultivated man, who is certainly intelligent enough, if he can take the strain. The other appointments were obvious, with no surprises: Iain Macleod at the Treasury, Alec Douglas Home

[1] Peter Jay, the son of Douglas and Peggy Jay, had been an Assistant Principal 1961–4, Private Secretary to the Joint Permanent Secretary 1964 and a Principal 1964–7 at H.M. Treasury. From 1967–77 he was Economic Editor of *The Times* and from 1969–77 Associate Editor of *The Times* Business News. In 1977 he became Ambassador to the U.S.A. His wife, Margaret, is the daughter of James Callaghan.

[2] Robert Skidelsky, Visiting Professor of History at Johns Hopkins University School of Advanced Studies 1970–6, and since May 1976 Head of the Department of History and Philosophy, Polytechnic of North London. The book to which Crossman refers was *Politicians and the Slump* (London: Macmillan, 1967).

as Foreign Secretary, Maudling, yes, a little surprising, as Home Secretary, and Quintin Hogg as Lord Chancellor. It was all pretty sensible.

Though this pushed me aside, I nevertheless had a whole string of journalists ringing up about the significance of my decision and I fed them stuff and will talk to 'The World This Weekend' tomorrow. The *New Statesman* itself has published a jolly good write-up and as I am the only piece of Labour news there will be decent coverage in tomorrow's press. On the whole, I think I can now say that the news will be welcomed and I can feel reasonably satisfied. People will see me as a round peg fitting into a round hole and they will think I really am capable of doing this.

Monday, June 22nd

My last day with an official car. I arrived at Paddington at 11 o'clock to find a woman driver waiting for me. Oh dear, what a problem. Poor Peter Smithson, my wonderful driver, was still away in the South of France, and now I am out and Keith Joseph has come in, so the driver this morning was Molly, whom I took over from Keith Joseph in '64. She is seventh in the seniority list of drivers and Peter is nineteenth, and Molly has been allocated to Keith Joseph again. How well I remember her stories about how she used to mother him. What will poor Peter be doing? He used to tell me that he always liked driving for the Government because he could choose his own master but I hope he will be able to, because it looks to me as if he might find himself unallocated and put back into the pool.

We tidied up at Vincent Square and then went round to No. 70 for a party Bea and I were giving for the Ministry. We had some fifty guests, whom we welcomed in relays, Social Security first and Health second. We had all the typists, all the Private Office, then the P.U.S.s, the Deputies and Under-Secretaries, a good many people who came to say goodbye. There were no speeches of any kind and it was a gay, pleasant party. It was over by 1.30 and then I took Ron Matthews, Mike, Janet and Tam out to the Ladies' Annexe of the Athenaeum for a last lunch together.

After that I went back to Vincent Square to change before we drove to the Palace. Barbara went in just before me and then it was my turn. I made my farewell to the Queen and told her that I was sorry I wouldn't be there to receive her when she opens the new Walsgrave hospital in Coventry but that she would understand how embarrassing it would be if I were present. She thanked me a little bit and it was perfectly decent and formal. I asked her whether she minded elections. She said, 'Yes, it means knowing a lot of new people.' I suppose that's it. She doesn't make all that difference between Labour and Conservative and, for her, all this simply means that, just when she has begun to know us, she has to meet another terrible lot of politicians.

[illegible]

Thinking things over, I [illegible] a whole team of journalists [illegible] about the [illegible] and will [illegible]. The World This Weekend [illegible] on the subject of Labour [illegible] think I can now say that the [illegible] will be welcomed and I can feel reasonably satisfied. People will see me as a [illegible] and they will [illegible]. I really am capable of [illegible].

Monday, [illegible]

My last day with an official car. I arrived at Paddington at 11 o'clock to find a woman driver waiting for me [illegible]. Poor Peter [illegible], my wonderful driver, was still away in the South of France; and now I am out and Keith Joseph has come in, so the driver [illegible] this morning. Molly, whom I took over from Keith Joseph in '74, [illegible] is eleventh in the [illegible] list of drivers and Peter is [illegible] and Molly has been allocated to Keith Joseph again. However I remember the stories about how she used to mother him. What will poor Peter be doing? He used to tell me that he always liked driving for the Government because he could choose his own master, but I hope he will [illegible] because it looks to me as if he might find himself [illegible] and put back into the pool.

We tidied up at Vincent Square and then went round to No. 70 for a party Ted and I were giving for the Ministry. We had [illegible], whom we welcomed in relays: Social Security first and Health second. We had all the typists, all the Private Office, [illegible] the Deputies and Under-Secretaries, [illegible] many people who came to say goodbye. There were no speeches of any kind and [illegible] my pleasant party. It was over by 1.30 and then I took Ron Matthews, Mike, Janet and Jack out to the Ladies' Annexe of the Athenaeum for a last lunch together.

After that I went back to Vincent Square to change before I drove to the Palace. Barbara went in just before me and then it was my turn. I made my farewell to the Queen and told her that I was sorry I wouldn't be there to receive her when she opened the new [illegible] hospital in Coventry but that she would understand [illegible] and it would be [illegible] if I were present. She thanked me a little [illegible] and it was perfectly decent and formal. I asked her whether she minded elections. She said, 'Yes, it means knowing a lot of new people. I suppose that's [illegible].' She doesn't make all that difference between Labour and Conservatives and, after all, this only means that, just when she has begun to know us, she has to meet another terrible lot of politicians.

Members of the Cabinet 1968–70

When Volume III of the Diaries opens, April 22nd, 1968

Prime Minister	Harold Wilson
First Secretary of State and Secretary of State for Employment and Productivity	Barbara Castle
Lord President of the Council	Richard Crossman
Lord Chancellor	Gerald Gardiner
Lord Privy Seal	Fred Peart
Chancellor of the Exchequer	Roy Jenkins
Foreign Secretary	Michael Stewart
Home Secretary	James Callaghan
Department of Economic Affairs	Peter Shore
Agriculture, Fisheries and Food	Cledwyn Hughes
Commonwealth Relations Office	George Thomson
Defence	Denis Healey
Education and Science	Edward Short
Housing and Local Government	Anthony Greenwood
Paymaster-General	Edward Shackleton
Power	Ray Gunter
Scottish Office	William Ross
Technology	Anthony Wedgwood Benn
Board of Trade	Anthony Crosland
Transport	Richard Marsh
Welsh Office	George Thomas

Changes on July 1st, 1968

Ray Gunter resigns and Roy Mason succeeds him as Minister of Power.

Changes on October 17th and 18th, 1968

The Commonwealth Relations Office was merged with the Foreign Office. George Thomson became Minister Without Portfolio. Fred Peart became Lord President of the Council and Edward Shackleton became Lord Privy Seal.

Changes on November 1st, 1968

The Department of Health and Social Security was created and Richard Crossman became its Secretary of State. John Diamond, Chief Secretary to the Treasury, became a member of the Cabinet. Judith Hart became Paymaster-General.

Changes on October 6th, 1969

The Department of Economic Affairs was abolished and Peter Shore became Minister without Portfolio. George Thomson became Chancellor of the Duchy of Lancaster, with a seat in the Cabinet. The Ministry of Power was abolished and Roy Mason moved to the Board of Trade. Richard Marsh resigned from the Ministry of Transport and his place was taken by Fred Mulley, but the office no longer gave a seat in the Cabinet. The Cabinet post of Secretary of State for Local Government and Regional Planning was created and given to Anthony Crosland. The Minister of Housing and Local Government, Anthony Greenwood, no longer had a seat in the Cabinet. Judith Hart became Minister for Overseas Development and left the Cabinet. Her place as Paymaster-General was taken by Harold Lever.

Biographical Notes

ABEL-SMITH, Brian. Professor of Social Administration at the London School of Economics since 1965. He was a member of the South-West Metropolitan Regional Hospital Board 1956–63, Chairman of the Chelsea and Kensington Hospital Management Committee 1961–2, a Governor of St Thomas's Hospital, London, 1957–68 and of the Maudsley Hospital and the Institute of Psychiatry 1963–7. He served as Senior Adviser to the Secretary of State for Health and Social Security from 1968 to 1970 and was reappointed in 1974.

ARMSTRONG, William. Sir William Armstrong (K.C.B. 1963) was Joint Permanent Secretary at H.M. Treasury 1962–8 and Permanent Secretary at the Civil Service Department and Official Head of the Home Civil Service from 1968 until his retirement in 1974. In 1975 he became a life peer, taking the title of Lord Armstrong of Sanderstead. Since 1975 he has been Chairman of the Midland Bank.

BALNEIL, Robert. Lord Balneil, heir to the 28th Earl of Crawford and 11th of Balcarres, was Conservative M.P. for Hertford 1955–74 and for Hatfield February–September 1974. He was P.P.S. to the Financial Secretary of the Treasury 1955–7 and to the Minister of Housing and Local Government 1957–60, Minister of State for Defence 1970–2 and Minister of State for Foreign and Commonwealth Affairs 1972–4. He was Chairman of the National Association for Mental Health 1963–70. In 1974 he became a life peer. In 1975 he succeeded his father as the Earl of Crawford and Balcarres.

BALOGH, Thomas. A Fellow of Balliol College, Oxford, 1945–73 (now an Emeritus Fellow), he was Reader in Economics at Oxford University 1960–73 and from 1973–6 was Leverhulme Fellow there. From 1964 to 1967 he acted as Economic Adviser to the Cabinet and, in 1968, as the Prime Minister's own consultant. On leaving No. 10 in 1968 he became a life peer and from 1974 to 1976 he served as Minister of State at the Department of Energy. In 1976 he became Deputy Chairman of the British National Oil Corporation.

BENN, Anthony Wedgwood. Labour M.P. for Bristol South-East 1950–60 and since August 1963, after a successful battle to disclaim the title inherited from his father, Viscount Stansgate. He was Postmaster-General 1964–6 and Minister of Technology from 1966 until Labour's defeat in 1970. In 1974 he became Secretary of State for Industry and in 1975 Secretary of State for Energy.

BROWN, George. Labour M.P. for Belper 1945–70; in 1970 he became a life peer, taking the title of Lord George-Brown. He served as P.P.S. to the Minister of Labour and National Service 1945–7 and in 1947 to the Chancellor of the Exchequer, and was Parliamentary Secretary at the Ministry of Agriculture and Fisheries 1947–51 and Minister of Works from April to October 1951. In 1963 he was an unsuccessful candidate for the leadership of the Labour Party. In 1964 he became First Secretary of State at the newly created D.E.A. and in 1966 Foreign Secretary. He remained Deputy Leader of the Labour Party after his resignation in 1968 until 1970 and his elevation to the Upper House. He resigned his membership of the Labour Party in 1976.

BROWN, Peter. He joined the civil service in 1946 and served in the Information Divisions of the Ministries of Housing, Local Government and Planning, becoming Chief Press and Information Officer at the Ministry of Housing and Local Government in 1958. Since 1968 he has been Director of Information at the Department of Health and Social Security and Adviser to the Secretary of State.

CALLAGHAN, James. Labour M.P. for South Cardiff 1945–50 and for South-East Cardiff since 1950. A member of the Labour Party N.E.C. since 1957, from 1967–76 he was Treasurer of the Party. From 1955 to 1964 he was consultant to the Police Federation. In the post-war Labour Government he was Parliamentary Secretary at the Ministry of Transport 1947–50 and at the Admiralty 1950–51. In 1964 he became Chancellor of the Exchequer and in 1967 Home Secretary, holding that office until 1970. In 1974 he became Foreign Secretary, succeeding Harold Wilson as Prime Minister in April 1976.

CARRINGTON, Peter. Lord Carrington succeeded to his father's title in 1938 and held various offices in post-war Conservative Governments. He was U.K. High Commissioner in Australia 1956–9, First Lord of the Admiralty 1959–63 and Leader of the House of Lords 1963–4. He was Opposition Leader in the Lords 1964–70, Secretary of State for Defence 1970–74 and Secretary of State for Energy 1974. From 1972 to 1974 he was Chairman of the Conservative Party Organization and since 1974 he has been Opposition Leader in the Lords.

CASTLE, Mrs Barbara. Labour M.P. for Blackburn since 1945 and a member of the Labour Party N.E.C. since 1950. In 1964 she became Minister of Overseas Development, and in 1965 Minister of Transport, an office she held until 1968, when she became First Secretary of State at the newly created Department of Employment and Productivity, holding that office until Labour's defeat in 1970. From 1974 to 1976 she was Secretary of State for Social Services.

COX, Ralph. Entered the Ministry of Health in 1949. After working in the fields of finance, training and statistics, he served as an Assistant Private Secretary to Mr Crossman from March 1969 until January 1970. He is now a Principal in the D.H.S.S.

CROSLAND, Anthony. Labour M.P. for South Gloucestershire 1950–5 and for Grimsby from 1959 until his death in February 1977. He was Minister of State for Economic Affairs 1964–5, Secretary of State for Education and Science 1965–7, President of the Board of Trade 1967–9 and Secretary of State for Local Government and Regional Planning from 1969 until 1970. In 1974 he became Secretary of State for the Environment and in 1976 Foreign Secretary. He was the author of a number of books on the theory of socialism, notably *The Future of Socialism* (London: Cape, 1956) and *Socialism Now* (London: Cape, 1974). His wife, Susan Barnes, a journalist and author, gives her picture of Crossman in *Behind the Image: Profiles* (London: Cape, 1974).

CROSSMAN, Mrs Anne. Richard Crossman's third wife, Anne McDougall, whom he married in 1954. Their son, Patrick, was born in 1957 and died in 1975 and their daughter, Virginia, was born in 1959.

CROSSMAN, Richard Howard Stafford. Labour M.P. for Coventry East from 1945 until his death in 1974. He was Fellow and Tutor at New College, Oxford, from 1930 to 1937, Assistant Editor of the *New Statesman and Nation* 1938–55, Lecturer for the Oxford University Delegacy for Extra-Mural Studies and the Workers' Education Association 1938–40 and Leader of the Labour Group on Oxford City Council 1934–40. He served as Deputy Director of Psychological Warfare at A.F.H.Q., Algiers, 1943, and as Assistant Chief of the Psychological Warfare Division of SHAEF 1944–5. He was a member of the Anglo-American Palestine Commission in 1946 and of the Malta Round Table Conference in 1955 and was a member of the National Executive Committee of the Labour Party from 1952 until 1967. From 1964 to 1966 he was Minister of Housing and Local Government, from 1966 to 1968 Lord President of the Council and Leader of the House of Commons and from 1968 to 1970 Secretary of State at the Department of Health and Social Security. He returned to the *New Statesman* as Editor in 1970, remaining there until 1972. He died in April 1974.

DALYELL, Tam. Labour M.P. for West Lothian since 1962. He was a lodger in Crossman's London house and one of the diarist's closest and most loyal friends, serving as his P.P.S. from 1964 to 1970 with only one short interval. He was a member of the House of Commons Public Accounts Committee 1962–6 and of the Select Committee on Science and Technology 1967–9. Since 1975 he has been a Member of the European Parliament.

DAVENPORT, Nicholas. A civil servant during the war, he went into the City and worked with J. M. Keynes, becoming Deputy Chairman of the Mutual Life Assurance Society in 1960. Since 1923 he has also acted as Financial Correspondent of the *Nation* and then of the *New Statesman*, writing the City column from 1930 to 1953, when he became the *Spectator*'s weekly Financial Correspondent. He served on the National Investment Council from 1946 until its abolition in October 1947 and, briefly, on the National Film Finance Corporation established by Harold Wilson. His wife, Olga, was a ballet dancer and actress and is a professional painter.

DIAMOND, John. Labour M.P. for Manchester, Blackley, 1945–51 and for Gloucester from 1957 to 1970, when he became a life peer. He was Chief Secretary for the Treasury from 1964 until 1970. Since 1974 he has been Chairman of the Royal Commission on the Distribution of Income and Wealth.

DOWLER, David. A Principal at the Ministry of Aviation, he was seconded to the Home Office 1964–5, Private Secretary to the Minister of Aviation 1966, Assistant Secretary and Private Secretary to the Home Secretary 1967–8, and Private Secretary to the Chancellor of the Exchequer 1969–70. He returned to the Home Office as an Assistant Under-Secretary in 1970 and died shortly thereafter.

DUNWOODY, Dr John. Labour M.P. for Falmouth and Camborne 1966–70, he was Parliamentary Under-Secretary at the D.H.S.S. 1969–70. Since 1974 he has been Vice-Chairman of the Kensington, Chelsea and Westminster Area Health Authority.

ENNALS, David. Labour M.P. for Dover 1964–70 and since 1974 for Norwich North. He was P.P.S. to the Minister for Overseas Development in 1964 and to the Minister of Transport in 1966, Parliamentary Under-Secretary of State (Army) 1966–7 and at the Home Office 1967–8, and Minister of State at the Department of Health and Social Security from 1968 to 1970. From 1970 to 1973 he was Campaign Director for the National Association of Mental Health. From 1974 to 1976 he was Minister of State at the Foreign and Commonwealth Office and in April 1976 he became Secretary of State for Health and Social Services.

FOGDEN, Michael. Joined the Ministry of Pensions and National Insurance in 1955. After working in regional and local offices of the Department, a computer centre and Headquarters, he became Private Secretary to Mr Charles Loughlin, M.P. From November 1968 to November 1970 he was an Assistant Private Secretary to Mr Crossman and then to Sir Keith Joseph. He is now an Assistant Secretary in D.H.S.S.

FOOT, Michael. Labour M.P. for Plymouth, Devonport, 1945–55 and since November 1960 for Ebbw Vale. A member of the Tribune group, he was editor of *Tribune* 1948–52 and 1955–60. He was Political Columnist on the *Daily Herald* 1944–64. In 1974 he became Secretary of State for Employment and in 1976 Lord President of the Council and Leader of the House of Commons. He is the author of the biography *Aneurin Bevan* (Vol. 1, 1897–1945, London: MacGibbon & Kee, 1962; Vol. 2, 1945–60, London: Davis-Poynter, 1973).

FRANCE, Arnold. Sir Arnold France (K.C.B. 1965) was Permanent Secretary at the Ministry of Health 1964–8 and Chairman of the Board of the Inland Revenue from 1968 until his retirement in 1973. Since 1973 he has been Chairman of the Central Board of Finance of the Church of England.

GARDINER, Gerald. Lord Gardiner was called to the Bar in 1925 and took silk in 1948. He was an L.C.C. Alderman 1961–3 and a member of the Lord Chancellor's Law Reform Committee 1952–63. In 1963 he became a life peer and, from 1964 to 1970, served as Lord Chancellor. Since 1973 he has been Chancellor of the Open University.

GODBER, George. Sir George Godber (K.C.B. 1962) joined the Ministry of Health as a Medical Officer in 1939. From 1950 to 1960 he was Deputy Chief Medical Officer at the Ministry of Health and from 1960 until his retirement in 1973 he served as Chief Medical Officer at the Department of Health and Social Security, the Department of Education and Science and the Home Office. Since 1977 he has been Chairman of the Health Education Council.

GOODMAN, Arnold. Lord Goodman, who became a life peer in 1965, is the senior partner of Goodman, Derrick & Co., Solicitors, and since 1967 has been Chairman of the *Observer* Trust. He was Chairman of the Arts Council of Great Britain 1965–72 and of the Newspaper Publishers' Association 1970–5. Since 1972 he has been a director of the Royal Opera House, Covent Garden, and President of the Theatres Advisory Council, and, since 1973, Chairman of the Housing Corporation and of the National Building Agency. In August 1976 he became Master of University College, Oxford.

GORDON WALKER, Patrick. Labour M.P. for Smethwick 1945–64 and for Leyton from 1966 to 1974, when he became a life peer, taking the title of Lord Gordon-Walker. He had been Herbert Morrison's P.P.S. in 1946, and had served as Parliamentary Under-Secretary of State at the Commonwealth Relations Office 1947–50 and as Secretary of State 1950–1. In October 1964 he became Foreign Secretary but was obliged to relinquish that office in January 1965, when he failed to win a by-election at Leyton. In 1967 he became Minister without Portfolio and from 1967 to 1968 he served as Secretary of State for Education and Science. Since 1975 he has been a Member of the European Parliament.

GREENWOOD, Anthony. Labour M.P. for Heywood and Radcliffe 1946–50 and for Rossendale from 1950 until he became a life peer in 1970. He was a member of the Labour Party N.E.C. 1954–70. He was Secretary of State for Colonial Affairs 1964–5, Minister for Overseas Development 1965–6 and, succeeding Crossman, Minister of Housing and Local Government 1966–70. Since 1970 he has been a member of the Commonwealth Development Corporation and since 1972 Chairman of the Local Government Staff Commission.

GUNTER, Ray. Labour M.P. for Essex South-East 1945–50, for Doncaster 1950–1 and for Southwark 1959–72. He was a member of the N.E.C.

1955–66. In 1964 he became Minister of Labour and in 1968 Minister of Power but resigned after only two months in that office. He died in 1977.

HALL, Mrs Jennie. As Crossman's indispensable personal secretary who had worked with him since 1962, she joined his Private Office at the Ministry of Housing and Local Government in 1964 and stayed there until 1966. She worked in the Private Office of Harold Wilson from 1973 to 1974. Her husband, Christopher Hall, a journalist, had joined the Ministry of Overseas Development in 1965 as Public Relations Adviser to Barbara Castle, moving from there to the Ministry of Transport as Chief Information Officer. In 1969 he became Secretary General of the Ramblers' Association and in 1973 Director of the Council for the Protection of Rural England.

HARRIS, John. Former Research Officer for the Labour Party and secretary to Hugh Gaitskell, he was the Party's Press Officer 1962–4 and after Labour's election victory he became an official adviser to Michael Stewart and Roy Jenkins. In 1974 he became a life peer, taking the title of Lord Harris of Greenwich, and since 1974 he was been a Minister of State at the Home Office.

HART, Mrs Judith. Labour M.P. for Lanark since 1959 and a member of the N.E.C. since 1969. She was Joint Parliamentary Under-Secretary of State for Scotland 1964–6, Minister of State at the Commonwealth Office 1966–7 and Minister of Social Security 1967–8. She became a Cabinet Minister in 1968, as Paymaster-General, and from 1969 to 1970 she was Minister of Overseas Development, a post which she took once more after Labour's return to office in 1974. She resigned in 1975, but was reappointed in February 1977.

HEALEY, Denis. Labour M.P. for South-East Leeds 1952–5 and for Leeds East since 1955. From 1945 until 1952 he was Secretary of the International Department of the Labour Party. He was Secretary of State for Defence 1964–70 and has been Chancellor of the Exchequer since 1974.

HEATH, Edward. Conservative M.P. for Bexley 1950–74 and for Bexley, Sidcup, since 1974. From February 1951 to October 1959 he served in the Whips' Office, becoming Government Chief Whip in December 1955. He was Minister of Labour 1959–60 and Lord Privy Seal, with Foreign Office responsibilities, which included the direction of the British attempt to join the E.E.C., 1960–3 and was Secretary of State for Industry, Trade and Regional Development 1963–4. Elected Leader of the Conservative Party in 1965, he led the Opposition until 1970, when he became Prime Minister. From 1974 to 1975 he served as Leader of the Opposition until, in 1975, the Conservatives elected a new Leader and he returned to the back benches.

HOGG, Quintin. Conservative M.P. for Oxford City 1938–50, when he succeeded to his father's viscountcy. He was Joint Parliamentary Under-Secretary for Air in 1945, First Lord of the Admiralty 1956–7 and Minister of Education in 1957. From 1960 to 1963 he was Leader of the Opposition in the House of Lords and held various offices, including that of Secretary of State for Education and Science April–October 1964. From September 1957 to October 1959 he was Chairman of the Conservative Party Organization. In 1963 he disclaimed his peerage and stood, unsuccessfully, as a candidate for the leadership of his party. He was elected M.P. for St Marylebone and represented that constituency from 1963 until 1970, when he became a life peer, taking the title of Hailsham of St Marylebone, and Lord Chancellor. When the Conservatives lost office in 1974 he returned to the Bar.

HOUGHTON, Douglas. Labour M.P. for Sowerby from 1949 to 1974. An L.C.C. Alderman from 1947 to 1949, he became widely known as a broadcaster on the B.B.C.'s 'Can I Help You?' programme 1941–64. He was Chairman of the Public Accounts Committee from 1963 to 1964, when he became Chancellor of the Duchy of Lancaster, moving in 1966 to become Minister without Portfolio, with special oversight of social security matters. In 1967 he left the Cabinet and replaced Emanuel Shinwell as Chairman of the Parliamentary Labour Party, a post he held until the General Election of June 1970. He served in the same capacity from November 1970 until 1974, when he became a life peer.

HUGHES, Cledwyn. Labour M.P. for Anglesey since 1951. He was Minister of State for Commonwealth Relations 1964–6, Secretary of State for Wales 1966–8 and Minister of Agriculture, Fisheries and Food 1968–70. Since 1974 he has been Chairman of the Parliamentary Labour Party.

JARRETT, Clifford. Sir Clifford Jarrett (K.B.E. 1956) was Permanent Secretary at the Admiralty 1961–4 and Permanent Under-Secretary at the Ministry of Pensions and National Insurance (later the Ministry of Social Security and, subsequently, the Department of Health and Social Security) from 1964 until his retirement in 1970. Since 1971 he has been Chairman of the Tobacco Research Council and of the Dover Harbour Board.

JELLICOE, George. Lord Jellicoe succeeded to his father's earldom in 1935 and from 1947 to 1961 served in the Foreign Office. He was a Lord-in-Waiting from 1961 to 1962 and Joint Parliamentary Secretary at the Ministry of Housing and Local Government. From 1962 to 1963 he was Minister of State at the Home Office, from 1963 to 1964 First Lord of the Admiralty and from April to October 1964 Minister of Defence for the Royal Navy. In 1967 he became Deputy Leader of the Opposition in the House of Lords and from 1968 to 1970 he also served as Chairman of the British Advisory Committee on Oil Pollution of the Sea. On the Conservatives' return to office in 1970, he became Lord Privy Seal and Minister with responsibility for the Civil Service Department. He held this office, together with the Leadership of the House of Lords, until his resignation in 1973. Since then he has been a director of S. G. Warburg & Co.

JENKINS, Roy. Labour M.P. for Central Southwark 1948–50 and for Birmingham, Stechford, 1950–76. He was Minister of Aviation 1964–5,

Home Secretary 1965–7, Chancellor of the Exchequer 1967–70 and Deputy Leader of the Labour Party 1970–2. In 1974 he became Home Secretary, resigning in 1976 to become President of the Commission of the E.E.C. An author and journalist, his biographies include *Sir Charles Dilke* (London: Collins, 1958) and *Asquith* (London: Collins, 1964).

JONES, Elwyn. Labour M.P. for West Ham 1945–74 and a former Recorder of Cardiff 1960–4, and of Kingston-on-Thames 1968–71. He was Attorney General 1964–70 and, on the return of the Labour Government in 1974, became a life peer and, as Lord Elwyn-Jones, Lord Chancellor.

JOSEPH, Keith. Sir Keith Joseph, Conservative M.P. for Leeds North-East since February 1956, succeeded to his father's baronetcy in 1944. He was P.P.S. to the Parliamentary Under-Secretary of State at the Commonwealth Relations Office 1957–9, Parliamentary Secretary at the Ministry of Housing and Local Government 1959–61, Minister of State at the Board of Trade 1961–2 and Minister of Housing and Local Government and for Welsh Affairs 1962–4. In 1970 he became Secretary of State for Social Services, holding that office until the Conservatives' defeat in 1974. Since 1974 he has been Chairman of the Management Committee of the Centre for Policy Studies Ltd.

KALDOR, Nicholas. A Fellow of King's College, Cambridge, since 1949, Reader in Economics at the University of Cambridge 1964–5 and Professor of Economics 1966–75. He has been Economic Adviser to many foreign governments and was Special Adviser to the Chancellor of the Exchequer from 1964 to 1968 and from 1974 to 1976. He became a life peer in 1974.

KING, Horace. Dr King was Labour M.P. for Southampton, Test, 1950–5 and for Southampton, Itchen, from 1955 to 1965, when he was elected Speaker. From 1965 to 1970 he served as M.P. for Southampton, Itchen, and as Speaker of the House of Commons. In 1971 he became a life peer, taking the title of Lord Maybray-King, and since that date he has acted as a Deputy Speaker of the House of Lords.

LEVER, Harold. Labour M.P. for Manchester, Exchange, 1945–50, for Manchester, Cheetham, 1950–74 and, since 1974, for Manchester Central. He was Parliamentary Under-Secretary at the Department of Economic Affairs in 1967, Financial Secretary to the Treasury 1967–9 and Paymaster-General 1969–70. He was Chairman of the Public Accounts Committee from 1970 to 1973 and since 1974 he has been Chancellor of the Duchy of Lancaster.

LONGFORD, Frank. The prospective Labour candidate for Oxford City in 1938, he was created Baron Pakenham in 1945. He was a Parliamentary Under-Secretary of State at the War Office 1946–7, Chancellor of the Duchy of Lancaster 1947–8, Minister of Civil Aviation 1948–51 and First Lord of the Admiralty May–October 1951. In 1964 he became Lord Privy Seal, in 1965 Secretary of State for the Colonies and in 1966 Lord Privy Seal once more, an office he held until 1968. From 1964 to 1968 he was

Leader of the House of Lords. On the death of his brother in 1961 he succeeded to the earldom of Longford, as the 7th Earl.

MARRE, Alan. Sir Alan Marre (K.C.B. 1970) was a Deputy Secretary at the Ministry of Health 1964–6 and at the Ministry of Labour (later the D.E.P.) 1966–8. He was Second Permanent Under-Secretary of State at the D.H.S.S. from 1968 until 1971, when he became Parliamentary Commissioner for Administration, an office he held until 1976. From 1973 to 1976 he was also Health Service Commissioner for England, Wales and Scotland.

MARSH, Richard. Labour M.P. for Greenwich 1959–71. He was Parliamentary Secretary at the Ministry of Labour 1964–5 and at the Ministry of Technology 1965–6, Minister of Power 1966–8 and Minister of Transport from 1968 until his resignation in 1969. From 1971 to 1976 he was Chairman of the British Railways Board. He was knighted in 1976. He succeeded Lord Goodman as Chairman of the Newspaper Publishers' Association.

MASON, Roy. Labour M.P. for Barnsley since March 1953. He was Minister of State (Shipping) at the Board of Trade 1964–7, Minister of Defence (Equipment) 1967–April 1968, Postmaster-General April–June 1968, Minister of Power 1968–9 and President of the Board of Trade from 1969 to 1970. From 1974 to 1976 he was Secretary of State for Defence and in 1976 he became Secretary of State for Northern Ireland.

MATTHEWS, Ronald. Entered the Ministry of Health in 1939. He worked in Divisions concerned with local government, N.H.S. personnel, audit, teaching hospitals and departmental establishments, before becoming Private Secretary to the Minister of Health, Kenneth Robinson, in 1967. He was Private Secretary to Richard Crossman 1968–9. He is now a Deputy Secretary in the Department of Health and Social Security.

MULLEY, Frederick. Labour M.P. for Sheffield, Park, since 1950. He was Minister of State for the Army 1964–5, Minister of Aviation 1965–7, Joint Minister of State at the Foreign and Commonwealth Office and Minister for Disarmament 1967–9 and Minister of Transport 1969–70. In 1974 he again became Minister of Transport, moving to the post of Secretary of State at the D.E.S. in 1975 and to that of Secretary of State for Defence in 1976.

NEWMAN, Janet. Miss Janet Gates, who became Mrs Newman, was Crossman's invaluable private secretary. She joined him at the Ministry of Housing and Local Government and stayed with him throughout his years in Cabinet, later moving with him to the *New Statesman* when he became Editor of that journal in 1970.

ODGERS, Paul. An Under-Secretary at the Ministry of Education 1958–67 and in the Office of the First Secretary of State 1967–8. He joined Crossman in 1968 and moved with him in that year from the Lord President's Office to the D.H.S.S. In 1970 he went to the Cabinet Office and from 1971 to 1975 he was a Deputy Secretary at the D.E.S.

O'MALLEY, Brian. Labour M.P. for Rotherham from March 1963 until his death in 1976. He was an Assistant Government Whip 1964–6, Deputy Chief Government Whip 1967–9 and a Parliamentary Under-Secretary of State at the D.H.S.S. 1969–70. In 1974 he became Minister of State at the D.H.S.S.

OWEN, David. Dr David Owen, Labour M.P. for Plymouth, Sutton, 1966–74 and for Plymouth, Devonport, since 1974. He was P.P.S. to the Minister of Defence (Administration) 1967 and Parliamentary Under-Secretary of State for Defence (Royal Navy) 1968–70. In 1974 he became, first, Parliamentary Under-Secretary of State, and then Minister of State at the D.H.S.S. and in 1976 he moved to the Foreign and Commonwealth Office as a Minister of State. On Anthony Crosland's sudden death in 1977, Dr Owen succeeded him as Foreign Secretary.

PEART, Frederick. Labour M.P. for Workington from 1945 to 1976, when he became a life peer. A schoolmaster, he had been P.P.S. to the Minister of Agriculture in the postwar Labour Cabinets and from 1964 to 1968 was himself Minister of Agriculture. He was Leader of the House of Commons and Lord President of the Council 1968–70, and Minister of Agriculture 1974–6, when he became Leader of the House of Lords.

POWELL, Enoch. Conservative M.P. for Wolverhampton South-West 1950–February 1974 and since October 1974 United Ulster Unionist Coalition M.P. for South Down. He was Parliamentary Secretary at the Ministry of Housing and Local Government 1955–7, Financial Secretary to the Treasury 1957–8 and Minister of Health 1960–3.

RIDDELSDELL, Mildred. Dame Mildred Riddelsdell (D.C.B. 1972) was Secretary to the National Incomes Commission 1962–5, Under-Secretary at the Ministry of Pensions and National Insurance 1965 and at the Ministry of Social Security 1966. She was a Deputy Secretary at the D.H.S.S. 1966–71 and Permanent Secretary 1971–3. Since 1974 she has been Chairman of the Civil Service Retirement Fellowship.

ROBINSON, Kenneth. Labour M.P. for St Pancras North 1949–70. He was an Assistant Whip 1950–1, an Opposition Whip 1951–4, Minister of Health 1964–8 and Minister for Planning and Land at the Ministry of Housing and Local Government 1968–9. On leaving Parliament he joined the British Steel Corporation. He was Chairman of the London Transport Executive from 1975 to 1977, when he became Chairman of the Arts Council of Great Britain.

ROSS, William. Labour M.P. for the Kilmarnock division of Ayr since 1946. He was Secretary of State for Scotland from 1964 to 1970 and from 1974 to 1976.

SEROTA, Beatrice. A member of Hampstead Borough Council 1945–9, of the L.C.C., for Brixton, 1954–65 and Chairman of the Children's Committee 1958–65, and G.L.C. member for Lambeth 1964–7, when she became a life peer. She was a Baroness-in-Waiting 1968–9 and Minister of State for Health at the D.H.S.S. 1969–70. She was a member of the Community

Relations Commission 1970–76 and since 1975 has been a member of the B.B.C. Complaints Commission. Since 1974 she has been Chairman of the Commission for Local Administration.

SHACKLETON, Edward. Lord Shackleton, the son of the polar explorer and an explorer himself, was Labour M.P. for Preston 1946–50 and for Preston South 1950–5. In 1958 he became a life peer and in 1964 Minister of Defence for the R.A.F. He was Minister without Portfolio and Deputy Leader of the House of Lords 1967–8, Lord Privy Seal January–April 1968, Paymaster-General April–October 1968 and Leader of the House of Lords and Minister in charge of the Civil Service Department April 1968–70. He was Leader of the Opposition in the House of Lords 1970–4. Since 1975 he has been Deputy Chairman of the Rio Tinto Zinc Corporation.

SHORE, Peter. Labour M.P. for Stepney 1964–74 and for Tower Hamlets, Stepney and Poplar since 1974. He was Head of the Research Department of the Labour Party from 1959 until 1964 and was influential in Party councils. He was P.P.S. to the Prime Minister 1965–6, Joint Parliamentary Secretary at the Ministry of Technology 1966–7 and at the Department of Economic Affairs 1967, Secretary of State for Economic Affairs 1967–9, Minister without Portfolio 1969–70 and, in 1969, Deputy Leader of the House of Commons. In 1974 he became Secretary of State for Trade and in 1976 Secretary of State for the Environment.

SHORT, Edward. Labour M.P. for Newcastle-upon-Tyne Central from 1951 to 1976, when he became a life peer, taking the title of Lord Glenamara. He served in the Opposition Whips' Office 1955–64 and was Government Chief Whip 1964–6, Postmaster-General 1966–8 and Secretary of State for Education and Science 1968–70. From 1972 to 1976 he was Deputy Leader of the Labour Party and from 1974–1976 Lord President of the Council and Leader of the House of Commons. In 1977 he became Chairman of Cable and Wireless Ltd.

SILKIN, John. Labour M.P. for Deptford July 1963–74 and since 1974 for Lewisham, Deptford. He was a Government Whip 1964–6, Deputy Chief Whip April–July 1966, Chief Whip 1966–9 and Deputy Leader of the House of Commons 1968–9. From 1969 to 1970 he was Minister of Public Building and Works. In 1974 he became Minister for Planning and Local Government at the Department of the Environment and in 1976 Minister of Agriculture, Fisheries and Food.

SNOW, Julian. Labour M.P. for Portsmouth Central 1945–50 and for Lichfield and Tamworth from 1950 until 1970, when he became a life peer, taking the title of Lord Burntwood. He served as a Whip 1945–50, as Parliamentary Secretary at the Ministry of Aviation 1966–7 and at the Ministry of Health 1967–8. He was a Parliamentary Under-Secretary of State at the D.H.S.S. from 1968 until 1969.

STEWART, Michael. Labour M.P. for Fulham East 1945–55, for Fulham 1955–74 and for Hammersmith, Fulham, since 1974. He held various offices in postwar Labour Governments, and was Shadow Minister of Housing while Labour was in Opposition. He was Secretary of State for Education and Science 1964–5, Foreign Secretary 1965–6, First Secretary at the D.E.A. 1966–7. He returned to the Foreign Secretaryship in 1968 and held that office until the 1970 General Election. Since 1975 he has been a Member of the European Parliament.

STONEHOUSE, John. Labour and Co-operative M.P. for Wednesbury 1957–74 and for Walsall North 1974–6. He was Director of the London Co-operative Society Ltd 1956–62 and its President 1962–4. He was Parliamentary Secretary at the Ministry of Aviation 1964–6, Parliamentary Under-Secretary of State for the Colonies 1966–7, Minister of Aviation 1967 and Minister of State at the Ministry of Technology 1967–8. He became Postmaster-General in 1968 and Minister of Posts and Telecommunications in 1969. In December 1974 he disappeared, mysteriously, while swimming off the coast of Miami Beach, Florida, and was found in Australia. On his reappearance in 1975 he returned to the House of Commons, but in 1976 resigned the Labour whip and joined the English Nationalist Party. In August 1976 he was found guilty at the Central Criminal Court of eighteen out of nineteen charges involving theft and false pretences and he was sentenced to seven years' imprisonment.

SWINGLER, Stephen. Labour M.P. for Stafford 1945–50 and for Newcastle-under-Lyme from 1951 until his death in February 1969. He was Joint Parliamentary Secretary at the Ministry of Transport 1964–7 and Minister of Transport 1967–8. From 1968 to early 1969 he was one of Crossman's Ministers of State at the D.H.S.S.

THOMAS, George. Labour M.P. for Central Cardiff 1945–50, for West Cardiff 1950–76 and since 1976 M.P. for West Cardiff and Speaker of the House of Commons. He was Joint Parliamentary Under-Secretary of State at the Home Office 1964–6, Minister of State at the Welsh Office 1966–7 and at the Commonwealth Office 1967–8. From 1968 to 1970 he was Secretary of State for Wales and from 1974 to 1976 Chairman of Ways and Means and Deputy Speaker of the House of Commons.

THOMSON, George. Labour M.P. for Dundee East 1952–72. He was a Minister of State at the Foreign Office 1964–6, Chancellor of the Duchy of Lancaster 1966–7, Joint Minister of State at the Foreign Office 1967 and Secretary of State for the Commonwealth Office 1967–8. He was Minister without Portfolio 1968–9 and Chancellor of the Duchy of Lancaster, with special responsibility for negotiations with the E.E.C., 1969–70. After the 1970 General Election he acted as Shadow Minister of Defence until in 1973 he accepted Edward Heath's offer of appointment as one of Britain's two Commissioners to the E.E.C. He served as Commissioner with special responsibility for regional policy until 1977. In 1977 he became a life peer, taking the title of Thomson of Monifieth.

TITMUSS, Richard. Professor of Social Administration at the London

School of Economics from 1950 until his death in 1973, and the author of numerous books and articles, including *Income Distribution and Social Change* (London: Allen & Unwin, 1962) and *The Gift Relationship* (London: Allen & Unwin, 1970). He was Deputy Chairman of the Supplementary Benefits Commission 1968–73.

TREND, Burke. Sir Burke Trend (K.C.B. 1962) joined the Civil Service in 1936 and spent the greater part of his career in the Treasury, becoming Second Secretary in 1960. He was Deputy Secretary of the Cabinet 1956–9 and Secretary of the Cabinet from 1963 until his retirement in 1973. In 1974 he became a life peer. Since 1973 he has been Rector of Lincoln College, Oxford.

WARD, Frederick. An Assistant Secretary at the Ministry of Housing who became Crossman's Private Secretary in 1966. He remained in the Office of the Leader of the House when Fred Peart succeeded Crossman in April 1968 and later that year he returned to the Department of the Environment as an Under-Secretary.

WARREN, Freddie. Private Secretary to successive Chief Whips since 1961 and, as such, indispensable adviser on the niceties of procedural arrangement and legislative timetabling. He was knighted in 1976.

WEIDENFELD, George. Sir George Weidenfeld (Kt 1969), a publisher, has been Chairman of Weidenfeld & Nicolson Ltd since 1948 and of associated companies. He was a famous host. He became a life peer in 1976.

WENDT, Robin. He entered the Ministry of Pensions and National Insurance as an Assistant Principal in 1962. He was appointed Principal Private Secretary to Mr Crossman in December 1969 and remained in the Private Office, subsequently as Private Secretary to Sir Keith Joseph, until May 1972. He is now Deputy Secretary of Cheshire County Council.

WHITELAW, William. Conservative M.P. for Penrith and the Border since 1955. He was P.P.S. to the Chancellor of the Exchequer 1957–8 and served in the Whips' Office 1959–62 and as Parliamentary Secretary at the Ministry of Labour 1962–4. He was Opposition Chief Whip 1964–70, Lord President of the Council and Leader of the House of Commons 1970–2 and Secretary of State for Northern Ireland 1972–3. In 1974 he was made a Companion of Honour for his services in Northern Ireland. From 1973 to 1974 he was Secretary of State for Employment, and in February 1975 he was an unsuccessful candidate for the leadership of the Conservative Party. Since 1975 he has been Deputy Leader of the Opposition.

WIGG, George. Labour M.P. for Dudley 1945–67. He was Shinwell's P.P.S. in the postwar Labour Government and an Opposition Whip 1951–4. He became Paymaster-General in 1964, holding that office until he became a life peer in 1967. From 1967 to 1972 he was Chairman of the Horserace Betting Levy Board. His account of the 1964–70 Labour Government is to be found in *George Wigg* (London: Michael Joseph, 1972).

WILLIAMS, David. A member of the Colonial Service, he spent twenty years in Nigeria before moving to the Home Civil Service in 1961 as a Principal in the Ministry of Health. After serving in the Privy Council Office in 1968 as Principal Private Secretary to the Lord President, he was promoted to Assistant Secretary and went to the D.H.S.S. in November 1968. He was Chairman of the study group which in 1971–2 worked out the detailed arrangements for N.H.S. reorganization. In 1973 he became responsible for liaison with health authorities in the North of England.

WILLIAMS, Mrs Marcia. Mrs Williams worked for Morgan Phillips, the General Secretary of the Labour Party, at Transport House from 1955 to 1956, when she became Harold Wilson's secretary. She continued to serve him when he became Leader of the Labour Party in 1963 and, after the 1964 General Election, she worked at No. 10 as his personal and political secretary, an experience she has described in *Inside No. 10* (London: Weidenfeld & Nicolson, 1972). In Opposition, from 1970 to 1974, and, after the 1974 General Election, in Government, she remained one of Harold Wilson's closest advisers. In 1974 she became a life peer, taking the title of Baroness Falkender.

WILLIAMS, Mrs Shirley. Labour M.P. for Hitchin 1964–74 and for Hertford and Stevenage since 1974. She was P.P.S. to the Minister of Health 1964–6 and Parliamentary Secretary at the Ministry of Labour 1966–7, Minister of State at the Department of Education and Science 1967–9 and at the Home Office 1969–70. She was Opposition spokesman on Social Services 1970–1 and on Home Affairs from 1971 to 1974, when, on Labour's return to office, she became Secretary of State for Prices and Consumer Protection. In 1976 she was given the additional office of Paymaster-General, and in April 1976 she moved to the Department of Education and Science as Secretary of State.

WILSON, Harold. Labour M.P. for Ormskirk 1945–50 and for Huyton since 1950. He joined the Civil Service in 1943 as an economist and statistician. From 1945 to 1947 he was Parliamentary Secretary to the Ministry of Works, from March to October 1947 Secretary for Overseas Trade and from October 1947 until his resignation in April 1951 President of the Board of Trade. From 1959 to 1963 he was Chairman of the Public Accounts Committee. He was Chairman of the N.E.C. of the Labour Party 1961–2 and in 1963 he succeeded Hugh Gaitskell as Leader of the Party. When Labour won the 1964 General Election he became Prime Minister and First Lord of the Treasury; after 1970 he continued to lead the party in Opposition, becoming Prime Minister once more in February 1974. He held that office until his resignation and return to the back benches, as Sir Harold Wilson, in April 1976. He published *The Labour Government 1964–70, A Personal Record* (London: Michael Joseph and Weidenfeld & Nicolson, 1971) and *The Governance of Britain* (London: Michael Joseph and Weidenfeld & Nicolson, 1976).

Abbreviations Used in the Text

The following abbreviations occur in the text:

A.E.U.	Amalgamated Engineering Union
A.F.H.Q.	Allied Forces Headquarters
A.M.C.	Association of Municipal Corporations
ASLEF	Associated Society of Locomotive Engineers and Firemen
ASSET	Association of Supervisory Staffs, Executives and Technicians
A.S.T.M.S.	Association of Scientific, Technical and Management Staffs
A.U.E.F.W.	Amalgamated Union of Engineering and Foundry Workers
A.U.E.W.	Amalgamated Union of Engineering Workers
B.B.C.	British Broadcasting Corporation
B.E.A.	British European Airways
B.M.A.	British Medical Association
B.M.J.	*British Medical Journal*
B.O.A.C.	British Overseas Airways Corporation
B.S.T.	British Standard Time
BUPA	British United Provident Association
C.A.P.	Common Agricultural Policy
C.B.I.	Confederation of British Industry
C.C.A.	County Councils Association
C.D.C.	Commonwealth Development Corporation
C.D.S.	Campaign for Democratic Socialism
C.D.U.	Christliche Demokratische Union
C.E.E.	Communauté Économique Européenne
C.M.O.	Chief Medical Officer
C.O.P.A.	Comité des Organisations Professionels Agricoles de la C.É.E.
C.P.A.	Commonwealth Parliamentary Association
C.P.A.G.	Child Poverty Action Group
C.R.O.	Commonwealth Relations Office
C.S.D.	Civil Service Department

D.E.A.	Department of Economic Affairs
D.E.P.	Department of Employment and Productivity
D.E.S.	Department of Education and Science
D.H.S.S.	Department of Health and Social Security
D.O.E.	Department of the Environment
E.E.C.	European Economic Community
EFTA	European Free Trade Area
ELDO	European Launcher Development Organization
EOKA	Ethniki Organosis Kyprion Agoniston (National Organization of Cypriot Combatants)
ESRO	European Space Research Organization
F.C.O.	Foreign and Commonwealth Office
F.D.P.	Frei Demokratische Partei
F.O.	Foreign Office
G.L.C.	Greater London Council
G.M.C.	General Management Committee; General Medical Council
G.N.P.	Gross National Product
G.P.	General Practitioner
G.P.O.	General Post Office
H.M.	His/Her Majesty's
H.M.C.	Hospital Management Committee
H.M.S.O.	Her Majesty's Stationery Office
I.C.I.	Imperial Chemical Industries
I.C.S.	Indian Civil Service
I.D.C.	Industrial Development Certificate
I.M.F.	International Monetary Fund
I.P.C.	International Publishing Corporation
I.P.U.	Inter-Parliamentary Union
I.R.	Industrial Relations
I.R.C.	Industrial Reorganization Corporation
I.T.A.	Independent Television Authority
I.T.N.	Independent Television News
I.T.V.	Independent Television
J.C.C.	Joint Consultants Committee
K.B.E.	Knight Commander of the British Empire
K.C.B.	Knight Commander of the Bath
K.C.M.G.	Knight Commander of St Michael and St George
K.C.V.O.	Knight Commander of the Royal Victorian Order
Kt	Knight
L.C.C.	London County Council
L.S.E.	London School of Economics and Political Science
M.B.E.	Member of the Order of the British Empire
M.D.	Doctor of Medicine

M.H.L.G.	Ministry of Housing and Local Government
MinTech.	Ministry of Technology
MISC	Miscellaneous (Committee)
M.O.H.	Medical Officer of Health
M.P.	Member of Parliament
M.R.A.	Moral Re-Armament
M.R.C.A.	Multi-Role Combat Aircraft
NALGO	National Association of Local Government Officers
NATO	North Atlantic Treaty Organization
N.B.P.I. (and N.P.B.I.)	National Board for Prices and Incomes
N.C.B.	National Coal Board
N.E.C.	National Executive Committee
NEDO	National Economic Development Office
N.F.F.C.	National Film Finance Corporation
N.F.U.	National Farmers Union
N.H.S.	National Health Service
N.I.	Northern Ireland
N.I.A.C.	National Insurance Advisory Committee
N.I.E.S.R.	National Institute for Economic and Social Research
N.O.P.	National Opinion Poll
N.U.A.W.	National Union of Agricultural Workers
N.U.M.	National Union of Mineworkers
N.U.R.	National Union of Railwaymen
N.U.T.	National Union of Teachers
O.A.U.	Organization of African Unity
O.D.	Overseas Development Committee
O.D.M.	Ministry of Overseas Development
O.P.D.	Defence and Overseas Policy Committee
O.R.C.	Opinion Research Centre
P.C.C.	Policy Co-ordinating Committee
P.E.P.	Political and Economic Planning
PEP	'Post-Ely Policy'
PESC	Public Expenditure Survey Committee
P. and I.	Prices and Incomes
P.I.	Prices and Incomes Committee
P.I.B.	Prices and Incomes Board
P.L.	Parliamentary Reform: Lords
P.L.P.	Parliamentary Labour Party
P.M.	Prime Minister
P.P.S.	Parliamentary Private Secretary
P.Q.	Parliamentary Question
P.U.S.	Permanent Under-Secretary
P.W.E.	Psychological Warfare Executive

Q.C.	Queen's Counsel
R. and D.	Research and Development
R.A.F.	Royal Air Force
R.D.C.	Rural District Council
R.E.P.	Regional Employment Premium
R.H.B.	Regional Hospital Board
R.N.	Royal Navy
R.R.B.	Race Relations Board
R.U.C.	Royal Ulster Constabulary
SAMO	Senior Administrative Medical Officer
S.B.C.	Supplementary Benefits Commission
S.D.S.	Sozialistischer Deutschen Studentenbund
S.E.P.	Steering Committee on Economic Policy
S.E.T.	Selective Employment Tax
SHAEF	Supreme Headquarters Allied Expeditionary Forces
S.N.P.	Scottish National Party
S.O.	Standing Order
SOGAT	Society of Graphical and Allied Trades
S.P.D.	Sozialdemokratische Partei Deutschlands
T. and G.	Transport and General Workers Union
T.G.W.U.	Transport and General Workers Union
T.U.C.	Trade Union Congress
U.D.C.	Urban District Council
U.D.I.	Unilateral Declaration of Independence
U.D.R.	Union des Démocrates pour la Vme République
U.N.	United Nations
U.S./U.S.A.	United States of America
USDAW	Union of Shop, Distributive and Allied Workers
U.K.	United Kingdom
U.S.S.R.	Union of Soviet Socialist Republics
V.A.T.	Value Added Tax

Index

32